Canadian Anthology

Third edition, revised and enlarged

Selected and edited by

Carl F. Klinck
University of Western Ontario

Reginald E. Watters
The Royal Military College of Canada

Gage Educational Publishing Limited Toronto

ISBN   7715—1146—9

Contents

The eighteenth century

The pre-Confederation period

The new nation

The twentieth century

v

viii

Selected Criticism

Preface to the third edition, revised and enlarged

Canadian Anthology *was originally published in 1955, when courses in our national literature were few and far between. The editors, however, were themselves teaching university courses in the subject, and urgently needed a volume of readings in prose and verse to put in their students' hands. No such anthology was then available. There were no Canadian paperback series, and no journals exclusively devoted to Canadian literary studies. Today, Canada's literary scene has been completely transformed. Several anthologies have recently appeared, several paperback series are flourishing, and books and periodical articles on Canadian literature stream forth incessantly.*

In revising and up-dating this third edition, the editors of Canadian Anthology *have been excited and delighted by this surging vitality. Our knowledge of the earlier writers has been deepened by nearly two decades' experience in teaching them, and the multitude of new writers who have emerged since our first edition, or even since our second edition (in 1966), has been a welcome challenge. The central purpose of* Canadian Anthology *has, we believe, been successfully tested by time: to offer substantial samplings of work in both prose and poetry by Canada's principal authors, and to reveal, where possible, some of the literary development of those authors by including representative early as well as later work. Our twofold intention has been to display excellence and to reveal individual development.*

In order to present these principal authors in proper perspective, and to reveal the general growth and scope of Canadian literature in English, we have chosen to present the selections in natural chronological order, and to include, as well as the major authors, a generous gathering of material by lesser writers whose significance derives from their historical position, representative utterance, uncommon sensibility, or promise of future development. We have felt constrained to avoid extremes of either traditionalism or avant-gardism, *while recognizing the validity of interest both in the roots of our literary traditions and in the new tendrils searching for a future direction.*

Whenever equally valuable alternatives were available, we have avoided using excerpts from long works such as novels or from familiar and comparatively accessible books. Our intention throughout has been, not to substitute a part for a whole, but to supplement the known and stimulate exploration. To this end we have added exceptionally full bibliographies, in the hope that the reader may thereby be encouraged to pursue further his special interests in those authors whose work most appeals to him.

To reproduce as exactly as possible each author's original book text was, of course, the editors' ambition. However, a few authors elected to make some verbal revisions in their work before its re-publication here, and a certain measure of uniformity was thought desirable in the spelling and punctuation of material that had originally been published sometimes by British, sometimes by American, and sometimes by Canadian firms. Finally, certain archaisms of punctuation and spelling were removed from some selections of early date in order to enhance the readability of the material. The date following each selection is that of its first appearance in book form, unless of course the only previous publication of the material has been in periodicals.

C.F.K.

R.E.W.

The eighteenth century

[A BALLAD OF COLONIZATION]

In May 1749, Lord Cornwallis had arrived in Nova Scotia with a company of 2,500 settlers for the new town of Halifax. In England, in February 1750, The Gentleman's Magazine published the following verses, to be sung to the tune of "King John and the Abbot of Canterbury."

NOVA SCOTIA: A NEW BALLAD

anonymous

Let's away to *New Scotland,* where Plenty sits queen
O'er as happy a country as ever was seen;
And blesses her subjects, both little and great,
With each a good house, and a pretty estate.
    Derry down, [down, down, derry down].

There's wood, and there's water, there's wild fowl and tame;
In the forest good ven'son, good fish in the stream,
Good grass for our cattle, good land for our plough
Good wheat to be reap'd, and good barley to mow.
    Derry down, etc.

No landlords are there the poor tenants to teaze,
No lawyers to bully, nor stewards to seize:
But each honest fellow's a landlord, and dares
To spend on himself the whole fruit of his cares.
    Derry down, etc.

They've no duties on candles, no taxes on malt,
Nor do they, as we do, pay sauce for their salt:
But all is as free as in those times of old,
When poets assure us the age was of gold.
    Derry down, etc.

—1750

FRANCES BROOKE

(1724-1789)

Mrs. Frances Brooke has earned her place in Canadian literature by being the first novelist to live and write in Canada, indeed in North America. She was born in Lincolnshire, the daughter of the Reverend William Moore. Little is known of her early life, but by 1755 she was established in London and editing a weekly periodical entitled The Old Maid, *under the pseudonym of Mary Singleton, Spinster. This venture came to an end in the summer of 1756 when she married the Reverend John Brooke; but her literary activities survived and even multiplied. She published a volume of poems in the year of her marriage, and followed it with a translation of a French romance in 1760. Early in 1763 her husband was appointed chaplain of the British garrison at Quebec. Mrs. Brooke remained in England after his departure to finish her first novel,* The History of Lady Julia Mandeville, *and to see it through the press. By October of 1763, however, she was with her husband in Quebec. In November of the following year she sailed for England, but subsequently she returned to Quebec; Attorney General Francis Maseres writes of his meeting her there within a few days of his arrival in September 1766. It is perhaps not unreasonable to surmise that she remained with her husband in Quebec until the summer of 1768, when the* Quebec Gazette *reported that the Reverend Mr. Brooke was offering household furnishings for sale by auction preparatory to leaving for England. He continued to draw army pay as chaplain of Quebec until 1788, but there is no evidence that the Brookes ever returned to Canada.*

In 1769 The History of Emily Montague *was published in four volumes by T. Dodsley in London; it was reprinted in 1777 and 1784, and translated into French. In 1770 Mrs. Brooke published another four-volume novel,* The Memoirs of the Marquis de St. Forlaix, *also later translated into French. But whether or not both these novels were written in Canada — or only one — or only notes and letters — is perhaps impossible to prove. Subsequently, Mrs. Brooke published various other works of fiction and drama before her death in January 1789 — three days after the death of her husband.*

FROM *The History of Emily Montague*

LETTER XLIX

To Miss Rivers, *Clarges Street,* [London].   Silleri, Jan. 1.

It is with difficulty I breathe, my dear; the cold is so amazingly intense as almost totally to stop respiration. I have business, the business of pleasure, at Quebec; but have not courage to stir from the stove.

We have had five days, the severity of which none of the natives remember to have ever seen equalled: 'tis said, the cold is beyond all the thermometers here, though intended for the climate.

The strongest wine freezes in a room which has a stove in it; even brandy is thickened to the consistency of oil: the largest wood fire, in a wide chimney, does not throw out its heat a quarter of a yard.

I must venture to Quebec tomorrow, or have company at home: amusements are here necessary to life; we must be jovial, or the blood will freeze in our veins.

I no longer wonder the elegant arts are unknown here; the rigor of the climate suspends the very powers of the understanding; what then must become of those of the imagination? Those who expect to see

"A new Athens rising near the pole,"

will find themselves extremely disappointed. Genius will never mount high, where the faculties of the mind are benumbed half the year.

'Tis sufficient employment for the most lively spirit here to contrive how to preserve an existence, of which there are moments that one is hardly conscious: the cold really sometimes brings on a sort of stupefaction.

We had a million of beaux here yesterday, notwithstanding the severe cold: 'tis the Canadian custom, calculated I suppose for the climate, to visit all the ladies on New Year's Day, who sit dressed in form to be kissed: I assure you, however, our kisses could not warm them; but we were obliged, to our eternal disgrace, to call in raspberry brandy as an auxiliary.

You would have died to see the men; they look just like so many bears in their open carrioles, all wrapped in furs from head to foot; you see nothing of the human form appear, but the tip of a nose.

They have entire coats of beaver skin exactly like Friday's in Robinson Crusoe, and casques on their heads like the old knights errant in romance; you never saw such tremendous figures; but without this kind of clothing it would be impossible to stir out at present.

The ladies are equally covered up, tho' in a less unbecoming style; they have long cloth cloaks with loose hoods, like those worn by the market-women in the north of England. I have one in scarlet, the hood lined with sable, the prettiest ever seen here, in which I assure you I look amazingly handsome; the men think so, and call me the *little red riding-hood;* a name which becomes me as well as the hood.

The Canadian ladies wear these cloaks in India silk in summer, which, fluttering in the wind, look really graceful on a fine woman.

Besides our riding-hoods, when we go out, we have a large buffalo's skin under our feet, which turns up, and wraps round us almost to our shoulders; so that, upon the whole, we are pretty well guarded from the weather as well as the men.

Our covered carrioles too have not only canvas windows (we dare not have glass, because we often overturn), but cloth curtains to draw all round us; the extreme swiftness of these carriages also, which dart along like lightning, helps to keep one warm, by promoting the circulation of the blood.

I pity the Fitz*; no tiger was ever so hard-hearted as I am this weather: the little god has taken his flight, like the swallows. I say nothing, but cruelty is no virtue in Canada; at least at this season.

I suppose Pygmalion's statue was some frozen Canadian gentlewoman, and a sudden warm day thawed her. I love to expound ancient fables, and I think no exposition can be more natural than this.

Would you know what makes me chatter so this morning? Papa has made me take some excellent *liqueur;* 'tis the mode here; all the Canadian ladies take a little, which makes them so *coquet* and *agréable.* Certainly brandy makes a woman talk like an angel. Adieu!

Yours,

A. Fermor.

---

*Captain J. Fitzgerald, suitor to Arabella Fermor, and subsequently her husband.

To Miss Rivers, *Clarges Street,* [London].   Silleri, Feb. 25.

Those who have heard no more of a Canadian winter than what regards the intenseness of its cold, must suppose it a very joyless season: 'tis, I assure you, quite otherwise; there are indeed some days here of the severity of which those who were never out of England can form no conception; but those days seldom exceed a dozen in a whole winter; nor do they come in succession, but at inter-mediate periods, as the winds set in from the North-West; which, coming some hundred leagues, from frozen lakes and rivers, over woods and mountains covered with snow, would be insupportable, were it not for the furs with which the country abounds, in such variety and plenty as to be within the reach of all its inhabitants.

Thus defended, the British belles set the winter of Canada at defiance; and the season of which you seem to entertain such terrible ideas, is that of the utmost cheerfulness and festivity.

But what particularly pleases me is, there is no place where women are of such importance: not one of the sex, who has the least share of attractions, is without a levee of beaux interceding for the honor of attending her on some party, of which every day produces three or four.

I am just returned from one of the most agreeable jaunts imagination can paint, to the island of Orleans, by the falls of Montmorenci; the latter is almost nine miles distant, across the great basin of Quebec; but as we are obliged to reach it in winter by the waving line, our direct road being intercepted by the inequalities of the ice, it is now perhaps a third more. You will possibly suppose a ride of this kind must want one of the greatest essentials to entertainment, that of variety, and imagine it only one dull whirl over an unvaried plain of snow: on the contrary, my dear, we pass hills and mountains of ice in the trifling space of these few miles. The basin of Quebec is formed by the conflux of the rivers St. Charles and Montmorenci with the great river St. Lawrence, the rapidity of whose flood-tide, as these rivers are gradually seized by the frost, breaks up the ice, and drives it back in heaps, till it forms ridges of transparent rock to an height that is astonish-ing, and of a strength which bids defiance to the utmost rage of the most furiously rushing tide.

This circumstance makes this little journey more pleasing than you can possibly conceive: the serene blue sky above, the dazzling brightness of the sun, and the colors from the refraction of its rays on the transparent part of these ridges of ice, the winding course these oblige you to make, the sudden disappearing of a train of fifteen or twenty carrioles, as these ridges intervene, which again discover themselves on your rising to the top of the frozen mount, the tremendous appear-ance both of the ascent and descent, which however are not attended with the least danger; all together give a grandeur and variety to the scene, which almost rise to enchantment.

Your dull foggy climate affords nothing that can give you the least idea of our frost pieces in Canada; nor can you form any notion of our amusements, of the agreeableness of a covered carriole, with a sprightly fellow, rendered more sprightly by the keen air and romantic scene about him; to say nothing of the fair lady at his side.

Even an overturning has nothing alarming in it; you are laid gently down on a soft bed of snow, without the least danger of any kind; and an accident of this sort only gives a pretty fellow occasion to vary the style of his civilities, and show a greater degree of attention.

But it is almost time to come to Montmorenci; to avoid, however, fatiguing you or myself, I shall refer the rest of our tour to another letter, which will probably accompany this: my meaning is, that two moderate letters are vastly better than one long one; in which sentiment I know you agree with

Yours,

A. Fermor.

— 1769

JONATHAN ODELL

(1737-1818)

Jonathan Odell, born in Newark, New Jersey, was graduated from the University of New Jersey (now Princeton University) before taking up the study of medicine. He became a surgeon in the British Army and served in the West Indies, but resigned his commission in order to go to England, where he entered holy orders. He was ordained in the Church of England in 1767 and appointed rector of St. Mary's Church in Burlington, New Jersey, where he served with distinction as both minister and physician until the outbreak of the Revolution. Although he recognized some of the colonial claims as legitimate, Odell was vehemently opposed to armed insurrection. He was driven from his home and parish and eventually succeeded in finding refuge with the British garrison in New York, where he became chaplain of a loyal Pennsylvania regiment. His writings soon established his reputation as the most scathing and implacable of all the Tory satirists.

In 1783 he went to England, but in the following year he took up a grant of land in New Brunswick, where he was reunited with his wife and family after an enforced separation of over seven years. He was appointed provincial secretary and clerk of the executive council, and was one of the founders of the University of New Brunswick. He died in Fredericton.

Although he continued to write verse to the end of his life, the bulk of his poetry was composed and published during his years in New York. The American Times, a small book of forty pages, was published in London under the pseudonym "Camillo Querno." Odell's authorship of it has been questioned, but it is still almost universally attributed to him.

SONG

For a fishing party near Burlington, on the Delaware, in 1776

How sweet is the season, the sky how serene;
On Delaware's banks how delightful the
   scene;
The Prince of the Rivers, his waves all asleep,
In silence majestic glides on to the Deep.

Away from the noise of the Fife and the Drum,
And all the rude din of Bellona we come;
And a plentiful store of good humor we bring
To season our feast in the shade of Cold
   Spring.

A truce then to all whig and tory debate;
True lovers of Freedom, contention we hate:
For the Demon of discord in vain tries his art
To possess or inflame a true *Protestant* heart.

True Protestant friends to fair Liberty's cause,
To decorum, good order, religion and laws,
From avarice, jealousy, perfidy, free;
We wish all the world were as happy as we.

We have wants, we confess, but are free from
   the care
Of those that abound, yet have nothing to
   spare:
Serene as the sky, as the river serene,
We are happy to want envy, malice, and spleen.

While thousands around us, misled by a few,
The Phantoms of pride and ambition pursue,
With pity their fatal delusion we see;
And wish all the world were as happy as we!

—1776

A BIRTHDAY SONG

*Composed at New York, in honor of the anniversary
of the King's birthday, June 4, 1777*

Time was when America hallow'd the morn
On which the lov'd monarch of Britain was born,
Hallow'd the day, and joyfully chanted
      God save the King!
Then flourish'd the blessings of freedom and peace,
And plenty flow'd in with a yearly increase.
Proud of our lot we chanted merrily
      Glory and joy crown the King!

With envy beheld by the nations around,
We rapidly grew, nor was anything found
Able to check our growth while we chanted
      God save the King!
O blest beyond measure, had honor and truth
Still nurs'd in our hearts what they planted in youth!
Loyalty still had chanted merrily
      Glory and joy crown the King!

But see! how rebellion has lifted her head!
How honor and truth are with loyalty fled!
Few are there now who join us in chanting
      God save the King!

And see! how deluded the multitude fly
To arm in a cause that is built on a lye!
Yet are we proud to chant thus merrily
    Glory and joy crown the King!

Though faction by falsehood awhile may prevail,
And loyalty suffers a captive in jail,
Britain is rous'd, rebellion is falling:
    God save the King!
The captive shall soon be releas'd from his chain;
And conquest restore us to Britain again,
Ever to join in chanting merrily
    Glory and joy crown the King!

                    —1777

FROM *The American Times*

[On the Continental Congress]

Here Anarchy before the gaping crowd
Proclaims the people's majesty aloud;
There Folly runs with eagerness about,
And prompts the cheated populace to shout;
Here paper-dollars meagre Famine holds,
There votes of Congress Tyranny unfolds;
With doctrines strange in matter and in dress,
Here sounds the pulpit, and there groans the
    press;
Confusion blows her trump — and far and wide
The noise is heard — the plough is laid aside;
The awl, the needle, and the shuttle drops;
Tools change to swords, and camps succeed
    to shops;
The doctor's glister-pipe, the lawyer's quill,
Transformed to guns, retain their power to
    kill;
From garrets, cellars, rushing through the
    street,
The new-born statesmen in committees meet;
Legions of senators infest the land,
And mushroom generals thick as mushrooms
    stand. . . .

Yet though the frantic populace applaud,
'Tis Satire's part to stigmatize the fraud.
Exult, ye jugglers, in your lucky tricks,
Yet on your fame the lasting brand we'll fix.
Cheat male and female, poison age and youth,

Still we'll pursue you with the goad of truth.
Whilst in mid-heaven shines forth the golden
    flame,
Hancock and Adams shall be words of shame;
Whilst silver beams the face of night adorn,
Cooper of Boston shall be held in scorn. . . .

[On George Washington]

Strike up, hell's music! roar, infernal drums!
Discharge the cannon! Lo, the warrior comes!
He comes, not tame as on Ohio's banks
But rampant at the head of ragged ranks.
Hunger and itch are with him — Gates and
    Wayne!
And all the lice of Egypt in his train.
Sure these are Falstaff's soldiers, poor and
    bare,
Or else the rotten reg'ments of Rag-Fair. . . .

Wilt thou, great chief of Freedom's lawless
    sons,
Great captain of the western Goths and Huns,
Wilt thou for once permit a private man
To parley with thee, and thy conduct scan?
At Reason's bar has Catiline been heard:
At Reason's bar e'en Cromwell has appeared. . . .

Hear thy indictment, Washington, at large;
Attend and listen to the solemn charge:

Thou hast supported an atrocious cause
Against thy king, thy country, and the laws;
Committed perjury, encouraged lies,
Forced conscience, broken the most sacred ties;
Myriads of wives and fathers at thy hand
Their slaughtered husbands, slaughtered sons,
    demand;
That pastures hear no more the lowing kine,
That towns are desolate, all — all is thine;
The frequent sacrilege that pained my sight,
The blasphemies my pen abhors to write,
Innumerable crimes on thee must fall —
For thou maintainest, thou defendest all. . . .

What could, when half-way up the hill to fame,
Induce thee to go back, and link with shame?
Was it ambition, vanity, or spite
That prompted thee with Congress to unite;
Or did all three within thy bosom roll,
"Thou heart of hero with a traitor's soul"?
Go, wretched author of thy country's grief,
Patron of villainy, of villains chief;
Seek with thy cursed crew the central gloom,
Ere Truth's avenging sword begin thy doom,
Or sudden vengeance of celestial dart
Precipitate thee with augmented smart.

[*On the proliferation of rebellion*]

When civil madness first from man to man
In these devoted climes like wildfire ran,
There were who gave the moderating hint,
In conversation some, and some in print;
Wisely they spake — and what was their
    reward? —
The tar, the rail, the prison, and the cord!

Ev'n now there are, who bright in Reason's
    dress
Watch the polluted Continental press;
Confront the lies that Congress sends abroad,
Expose the sophistry, detect the fraud. . . .

But Error may not with such ease be quelled —
She rallies fresh her force, though oft repelled;
Cut, hacked, and mangled, she denies to yield,
And straight returns with vigor to the field.
Champions of Truth, our efforts are in vain;
Fast as we slay, the foe revives again.
Vainly the enchanted castle we surprise,
New monsters hiss, and new enchantments
    rise. . . .

Was Samuel Adams to become a ghost,
Another Adams would assume his post;
Was bustling Hancock numbered with the dead,
Another full as wise might raise his head.
What if the sands of Laurens now were run,
How should we miss him — has he not a son?
Or what if Washington should close his scene,
Could none succeed him? — Is there not a
    Greene?
Knave after knave as easy we could join,
As new emissions of the paper coin.
When it became the high United States
To send their envoys to Versailles' proud
    gates,
Were not three ministers produced at once? —
Delicious group, fanatic, deist, dunce!
And what if Lee, and what if Silas fell,
Or what if Franklin should go down to hell,
Why should we grieve? — the land, 'tis
    understood,
Can furnish hundreds equally as good.

—*1780*

JOSEPH STANSBURY

(1740-1809)

Joseph Stansbury was born in England and settled in Philadelphia in 1767. There his vivacity and conviviality won him many friends. Yet he was forced to flee the city in 1778, reportedly because he sang "God Save the King" in his home. With the British garrison in New York his rousing songs again won him popularity. By the war's end, he was willing to let bygones be bygones, and burned his papers and verses. He was not forgiven, however, and he was ordered to leave the country. For about two years he struggled to adapt himself to life in Nova Scotia, where he had received a grant of land. His longing for the more gracious life he had previously known led him to return to Philadelphia, but he was warned to leave the city. At last, in 1793, he and his family were permitted to settle in New York. There he lived out the rest of his life, apparently without venturing again into print.

LORDS OF THE MAIN

When Faction, in league with the treacherous Gaul,
   Began to look big, and paraded in state,
A meeting was held at Credulity Hall,*
   And Echo proclaimed their ally good and great.
      By sea and by land
      Such wonders are planned —
No less than the bold British lion to chain!
      Well hove! says Jack Lanyard,
      French, Congo,† and Spaniard.
Have at you — remember, we're Lords of the Main!
Lords of the Main, ay, Lords of the Main;
The Tars of Old England are Lords of the Main.

Though party-contention awhile may perplex,
   And lenity hold us in doubtful suspense,
If perfidy rouse, or ingratitude vex
   In defiance of hell we'll chastise the offence.
      When danger alarms,
      'Tis then that in arms
United we rush on the foe with disdain;
      And when the storm rages,
      It only presages
Fresh triumphs to Britons, as Lords of the Main!
Lords of the Main — ay, Lords of the Main —
Let Thunder proclaim it, we're Lords of the Main!

Then, Britons, strike home — make sure of your blow:
   The chase is in view; never mind a lee shore.
With vengeance o'ertake the confederate foe:
   'Tis now we may rival our heroes of yore!
      Brave Anson, and Drake,
      Hawke, Russell, and Blake,

*Independence Hall, Philadelphia.
†The Continental Congress.

With ardor like yours, we defy France and Spain!
    Combining with treason,
    They're deaf to all reason;
Once more let them feel we are Lords of the Main.
Lords of the Main — ay, Lords of the Main —
The first-born of Neptune are Lords of the Main!

Nor are we alone in the noble career;
   The Soldier partakes of the generous flame
To glory he marches, to glory we steer;
    Between us we share the rich harvest of fame.
     Recorded on high,
     Their names never die.
Of heroes by sea and by land what a train.
    To the king, then, God bless him!
    The world shall confess him
The Lord of those men who are Lords of the Main!
Lords of the Main — ay, Lords of the Main —
The Tars of Old England, are Lords of the Main.

— Rivington's Royal Gazette, February 16, 1780

GOD SAVE THE KING

Time was, in defence of his King and the Right,
We applauded brave Washington foremost in fight:
On the banks of Ohio he shouted lustily
    God save the King!
Disappointed ambition his feet has misled;
Corrupted his heart and perverted his head:
Loyal no longer, no more he cries faithfully
    Glory and Joy crown the King!

With Envy inflam'd 'tis in Britain the same;
Where leaders, despairing of virtuous fame,
Have push'd from their seats those whose watchword was constantly
    God save the King!
The helm of the State they have clutched in their grasp
When American Treason is at its last gasp:
When Firmness and Loyalty soon should sing valiantly
    Glory and Joy crown the King!

But Britain, with Glory and Conquest in view,
When nothing was wanted, but just to pursue —
To yield — while her Heroes chanted triumphantly
    God save the King!
With curses consign to the Furies his Name,
Whose Counsels thus cover'd his Country with shame!

Loyalists still will chant, tho' heavily,
    Glory and Joy crown the King!

Tho' ruin'd so deeply no Angel can save:
The Empire dismember'd: our King made a Slave:
Still loving, revering, we shout forth honestly
    God save the King!
Tho' fated to Banishment, Poverty, Death,
Our Hearts are unalter'd, and with our last breath
Loyal to George, we'll pray most fervently
    Glory and Joy crown the King!

                — 1783

TO CORDELIA

Believe me, Love, this vagrant life
  O'er Nova Scotia's wilds to roam,
While far from children, friends, or wife,
  Or place that I can call a home
Delights not me; — another way
My treasures, pleasures, wishes lay..

In piercing, wet, and wintry skies,
  Where man would seem in vain to toil,
I see, where'er I turn my eyes,
  Luxuriant pasture, trees, and soil.
Uncharm'd I see: — another way
My fondest hopes and wishes lay.

Oh could I through the future see
  Enough to form a settled plan,
To feed my infant train and thee
  And fill the rank and style of man:
I'd cheerful be the livelong day;
Since all my wishes point that way.

But when I see a sordid shed
  Of birchen bark, procured with care,
Design'd to shield the aged head
  Which British mercy placed there —
'Tis too, too much: I cannot stay,
But turn with streaming eyes away.

Oh! how your heart would bleed to view
  Six pretty prattlers like your own,
Expos'd to every wind that blew;
  Condemn'd in such a hut to moan.
Could this be borne, Cordelia, say?
Contented in your cottage stay.

'Tis true, that in this climate rude,
  The mind resolv'd may happy be;
And may, with toil and solitude,
  Live independent and be free.
So the lone hermit yields to slow decay:
Unfriended lives — unheeded glides away.

If so far humbled that no pride remains,
  But moot indifference which way flows the stream;
Resign'd to penury, its cares and pains;
  And hope has left you like a painted dream;
Then here, Cordelia, bend your pensive way,
And close the evening of Life's wretched day.

                — 1784(?)

The pre-Confederation period

ADAM HOOD BURWELL

(1790-1849)

Adam Burwell was born into a Loyalist family near Fort Erie, Welland County. Along with his brother Mahlon, the surveyor, he moved to the settlement on Lake Erie (near St. Thomas) dominated by Colonel Thomas Talbot, who became Adam's patron while the young man was preparing himself for the Anglican ministry. Using the pseudonym "Erieus," Burwell published at least two poems in newspapers between 1816 and 1820; the dedication to "Talbot Road" is dated "28th May, 1818," but the poem was not printed until 1820. He also contributed about twenty poems to two Montreal journals, The Scribbler *and* The Canadian Review. *After his death in 1849 three long religious poems appeared in* The Literary Garland.

FROM TALBOT ROAD

Now, first of all, on Talbot Road, began
The settlement, one solitary man;
An arduous task — unaided and alone,
The place a wilderness, and scarcely known;
But he, unmindful of surrounding toils,
Mock'd fortune's every frown — but caught her
    smiles —
He pierc'd the woods, his devious way he found,
And on the banks of Kettle Creek sat down.
Then bow'd the forest to his frequent stroke; —
There from his hearth ascended hallowed smoke;
Angels look'd down, propitious from above,
And o'er his labors breath'd celestial love: —
"Go on and prosper, for thine eyes shall see
The steps of thousands, soon to follow thee;
Go on and prosper, for the fostering hand
Of heaven, shall plant this highly favor'd
    land."
  Now fame's loud, brazen trump began to
    sound,
The tidings flew thro' all the countries round . . .
From far and near, all flock'd the truth to
    know,
But found their expectations quite below
What now their eyes beheld. "O blissful land,"
They cried, "sure nature has with lavish hand

Scatter'd her sweets — how rich these vallies
    lie,
How soft the purling streams meander by!
How lofty, towering, these deep forests rise,
These pines, majestic, intercept the skies!
What stately columns, that, aspiring run
To heaven's blue arch, and hide the noon-day
    sun!
Sure, Liberty must call this favorite soil
Her own, and o'er the whole benignly smile;
How fitted to fair freedom's chosen race!
How might the goddess here her sons embrace!
Then why should it neglected, waste remain?
No — here's an offer — we'll return again; —
We will return again, and fetch our sons,
Our goods, our cattle, wives, and little ones.
Here long and happy days are kept in store,
And plenty teems — What can we look for
    more?" . . .

  Now, ceaseless, crowd the emigrants along,
And moving families the country throng;
The fertile banks of Otter Creek, some take;
Some Talbot Road, and some prefer the lake;
While others claim'd a midway space between,
And all produced an animating scene.

15

Meantime the woodman's axe, with ardor
plied,
Tumbles the tow'ring pines from side to side;
Fells the huge elms, and, with tremendous crash,
Brings down the steadfast oak, and lofty ash;
Which, pil'd, and interpil'd, present around,
A heap of chaos on th' encumber'd ground.
Not more, should Boreas from his windy hall,
Arm'd with fell ire, his blust'ring forces call,
And send them, howling, o'er the sylvan plain,
While headlong fly the rifted trees amain.
In heaps on heaps the shivered timbers lie,
A scene of terror to the astonish'd eye.
So crackling, crashing, thund'ring, plunging
down,
The stateliest forest trees o'erspread the
ground;
So roar'd, from day to day, their constant
stroke,
So evening clos'd and so the morning broke.
    Then rose the cabin rude, of humblest form,
To shield from rain, and guard against the
storm;
Logs pil'd on logs, 'till closing overhead —
With ample sheets of bark of elms o'erspread,
And rough-hewn planks, to make a homely floor,
A paper window, and a blanket door.
Such dwellings, first, the hardy settlers
made —
What could they more ? — necessity forbade.
'Twas well — each one a full conviction felt
That fairer prospects waited where he dwelt;
That plenty soon would crown his honest toil,
And providence upon his labors smile,
And freedom keep her mild, protecting hand
Extended kindly, o'er so fair a land,
From her ethereal watchtower in the sky,
And guard his dearest rights with jealous eye.
How dear a thought is this to all who feel
The blood of Britons in their bosoms swell,
That whereso'er they be, fair freedom warms
Their glowing veins, and strings their manly
arms;
Asserts their rights, their dignity maintains
Inviolate from tyrants and their chains;
That laws, no offspring of a despot's will,
Laws equal, just, into their minds instil
A conscious rectitude, n'er to be found

Where grim oppression walks his jealous
round . . . .

    Now, Autumn's glowing suns with scorching
ray,
Dried the fall'n timber, as exposed it lay,
Fit for the office of consuming fire,
Which soon shall execute the sentence dire.
The Woodman issues with a flaming brand,
Pluck'd from the hearth, brisk blazing in his
hand;
Amongst the leafy brushwood fast he plies,
When lo! a hundred brilliant spires arise,
Columns of flame, and denser smoke that
shrouds
The mid-day sun, and mingles with the clouds.
Wide wasting conflagration spreads around,
And quickly bares the bosom of the ground.
Herculean labors next demand the arm
Well nerv'd (such labors must begin the farm)
To pile the pond'rous logs, and clean the soil,
Which is perform'd not but with hardest toil . . . .

    Now, through the shades of the autumnal
night,
The flaming log-heaps cast a glaring light
In contrast deep — the clouds, of sable hue,
Spread their dense mantle o'er the ethereal
blue;
Above is pitchy blackness — all below
Wide flashing fires — Around, far other show —
Majestic trees, whose yet unfaded bloom,
In pale reflection, gives a sylvan gloom —
A dubious maze, which leads th' uncertain
sight
To the drear confines of eternal night,
As it might seem: — While midst the raging
fires,
That upward shoot a thousand forky spires,
Th' assiduous laborer plies his ready hands
To trim the heaps, and fire th' extinguish'd
brands.
This task completed, homeward then he goes,
'Tis supper hour, and time to take repose;
But e'er he sleeps, when the repast is o'er,
Behold him seated by the cabin door
To take the long accustom'd evening smoke,
With wife and sons, and at the fire heaps
look;

And talk of days gone by, and times to come,
And scenes of pleasure at the new-found home.
New schemes for future happiness he tells,
And with complacence on each prospect dwells;
And portions out, for the ensuing year,

A barn to build, or some new land to clear;
Or plants an orchard on the sunny hills,
And with judicious hand a garden fills;
Rich waving harvests reaps from off the fields,
And all the golden treasures Ceres yields....

— 1820

THOMAS McCULLOCH

(1776-1843)

Thomas McCulloch was born in Scotland, and studied both Arts and Medicine at Glasgow University. He became a minister of the Presbyterian Church in 1799. In 1803 he emigrated to Nova Scotia where, as well as becoming pastor of the Presbyterian Church at Pictou, he soon established a small school which eventually grew into Pictou Academy (founded 1816), the first non-sectarian college in Nova Scotia. There he taught logic, moral philosophy, science, Hebrew, and theology, as well as serving as president of the institution. He was also responsible for originating advanced Presbyterian theological training in Nova Scotia. In 1838 he became the first principal of Dalhousie College in Halifax.

The Letters of Mephibosheth Stepsure *appeared in the* Halifax Acadian Recorder, *beginning in December 1821. During his lifetime, McCulloch was unsuccessful in his attempts to arrange publication of the* Letters *in book form; eventually, in 1862, the collection appeared in Halifax. Besides* The Stepsure Letters, *now available in paperback, McCulloch wrote numerous articles on educational and political subjects for the newspapers. His books include several works of theological controversy and two novellas,* William and Melville, *published in one volume at Edinburgh in 1826. In the Bible, Mephibosheth was the lame son of King Saul's son, Jonathan (see* II Samuel, *chs. 9, 19, 21).*

FROM *The Letters of Mephibosheth Stepsure*

LETTER 6.

Gentlemen: Since I wrote you last, nothing of consequence has happened among us, except that Mr. Catchem has been appointed sheriff. For the comfort of our town, it was really necessary that the office should be immediately filled. Our parson looks after the souls of his flocks; but they have bodies too; and I do assure you, that, in these times, the most of people's bodies cost them more trouble than their souls; so that such a man as the sheriff, who kindly takes care of them, is both very useful and has a great deal to do. As far as I can see, Mr. Holdfast will not be missed. Mr. Catchem has got a large house; and he has already been going a good deal about, expressly for the purpose of inquiring who are uncomfortable at home.

As soon as the new sheriff undertook the office, he proceeded to take charge of the farm of my neighbor Fairface; and, as he had several others upon his hands, and could not manage them all, he thought it better to sell the farm, and apply the price for my neighbor's benefit. The most of us imagined Mr. Fairface to be very well to do. Neither he, nor his family, it is true, were ever great workers. But they owned a fine farm, kept a very genteel house, and drove the best chaise in town: and you may depend upon it the chaises in our town are neither few nor shabby. It would appear, however, that my neighbor Fairface is one of those, who, as Saunders Scantocreesh says, cannot walk upon their feet like other sober folks; but trust in chariots and in horses, and go down to Egypt for help, and at last get themselves drowned in the Red Sea; for so he calls Mr. Ledger's large book with the colored lines, in which he records those events that the rest of the town are most apt to forget.

Thinking that the farm might suit my son Abner, I resolved to attend the sale; and knowing that my neighbor Saunders wanted it for his son Jack, I called in at his house upon the way, and took him along with me. When we arrived at the farm, riders and chaises and sleighs were turning in from every part of the town. Not that my townsmen in general had any design of buying; for, in talking together before the sale commenced, they all agreed that money was money now, and nowhere to be got; but having nothing to do at home, they rode over to see how the farm would go, and who would get it.

The farm is really fine property, and, a few years ago, would have given fifteen hundred pounds; but, though the sheriff did ample justice to the sale, it was at last knocked down to my neighbor Scantocreesh for four hundred and ninety. When the sale was over, our townsfolk began to joke Saunders about living with the sheriff; and Mr. Catchem, too, asked him pretty sharply about his mode of payment. Saunders replied, that, before he could pay him he must try to find out where all the money had been going to in these bad times; and pulling out the leg of an old stocking, tied at both ends, he told out of it as many doubloons as satisfied the sheriff, and made all the jokers marvel. After tying up the remainder, he told us that he had been turning up his fields and found it there. He, therefore, advised us all to do the same thing; and, perhaps, we might be as fortunate; but, withal to follow his plan, and not do like the Chester folks, who once dug for money, but got so deep at last, that they arrived in the other world; and falling in with the devil, were glad to get away with the loss of all their tools.

When we were about to separate, Ehud Slush, one of our townsmen, arrived, evidently at the expense of a good deal of kicking and spurring. Ehud's mare is old; and withal, not very well-fed. Besides, when he alighted, he told us that he had been out at his fox traps; and, having found Parson Howl's dog in one of them, he had been detained a little; so that he could not get forward to the sale. For his part he had no intention to bid; for there was no money in the country, and it was a strange thing where it could be all gone to.

Our townsman Slush is sometimes in Halifax with his furs; perhaps you may have seen him. He is a squab little man, with large prominent eyes, and lips unusually thick; which, according to the fashion of the world, because they are near neighbors, keep as far apart from each other as possible. I am inclined to think that the human face divine of Ehud Slush is so fashioned from the nature of his employment; for hunters must always look sharp, and everybody knows that the mouth administers great help, when the eyes are in earnest. But some of the neighbors affirm that it is in consequence of his intimacy with a bear, which scraped acquaintance with him one day in the woods, and shook hands so often that he could scarcely get away.

About twelve years ago, Slush was a good-natured young fellow. In due time, according to the practice of our town, he married and settled upon a lot of good land, and really had the prospect of being very comfortable. He had never, indeed, been guilty of hard work; but, now, he had got a wife in addition to his mare; and working or starving were his only alternatives. Ehud boldly chose the first, sharpened his axe, and determined that no son of the forest should resist its strokes.

When he began to cut down, he observed a great many fox tracks; and it naturally occurred to him that he had a trap in the house, and might as well set it as not. The trap, accordingly, was baited and set; and next morning he owned a black fox. The fox was brought home in triumph, and skinned, and dried, and carried to market, and sold; and Ehud put sixteen dollars into his pocket. Such an easy way of getting rich was not to be overlooked. In imagination he was already an extensive dealer in the skins of black foxes; and as a commencement of the business, he carried home with him traps to the amount of sixteen dollars. But no man is lucky forever. Though the traps were carefully managed and regularly visited, nothing sable came near them; except the little brother of Mr. Gosling's black wench, who happened to be strolling in the woods and got himself caught. And in the spring, Slush owned the skins of three red foxes and of as many martens. Hunters, however, as well as fishers, are a persevering generation; and hence, with a variety of luck he has ever since continued to lie in wait for foxes.

Good farming or indeed farming at all, in such a case, would be contrary to nature; for, in every country, fox hunters are the avowed enemies of everything in the shape of crop or enclosure. Besides, though Slush had been disposed to farm, it was out of his power. The man who sets a number of traps, has a great deal to do. In addition to visiting them, he must look after bait, and hence, when Ehud was not in the woods, he was wandering about the town in search of dead animals, tripes, and other garbage in the way of his profession. In stating his toils, I cannot say much about the amount of his gain. I am inclined to think that it is not very great; for his house and family are always in wretchedness and rags. Still they contrive to keep life in. In going about for bait, he gets an occasional belly full among the neighbors; which, like all hunting folks, he contrives to make sufficient for a long time to come. Mrs. Slush, too, is a very industrious woman in her own way; so that between making occasionally a little soft soap with the help of the bait, doing dirty jobs for the neighbors, and getting now and then a rabbit, they make out to live. Even in this way, however, they have not been able to get on without contracting a great many small debts; which have made Slush wonder fully as much about the security of cash, as about the security of foxes. Indeed, necessity has rendered the former a subject of daily admiration; for he rarely meets any of the neighbors without being reminded that they are very needful of money.

Ehud had come to the sale without much consideration. It had entirely escaped him, that, when money is scarce, men and beasts are very much alike: upon the least alarm, some run like foxes; and others are as familiar and crusty as bears. He was, therefore, in the middle of a scrape before he was aware. He had scarcely alighted from the old mare, when my cousin Harrow began to inquire how he liked the potatoes which he had sold him last year; and Slush had just wondered where all the cash had gone to; but here the conversation was interrupted by Mr. Catchem, who bid Slush come along with him and he would show him.

I hope, however, that Ehud's ill luck will deter nobody from setting traps. The country needs labor, and catching foxes is a laborious trade. They also are destructive animals; and, in a particular manner, ruinous to geese. Besides, in these days, catching plenty of black foxes is a lucrative employment; and it would be a pity if civilized people should let the Indians get them all. Everybody, therefore, should catch black foxes; and, I am sure, if we were all running about with dead pigs and pieces of horses, we would be a more industrious people than we are. For my own part, I wish the trade encouraged; and, therefore, give notice to all fox catchers, that by and by, when they want potatoes, or begin to wonder about the scarcity of cash, my cousin Harrow has the first for sale; and Mr. Catchem will tell them about the last.

— 1822

LEVI ADAMS

(? -1832)

The Charivari: or Canadian Poetics: A Tale, After the Manner of Beppo *was published in Montreal in 1824. The attribution of authorship to Levi Adams, whose name appears on the title-page of* Jean Baptiste: A Poetic Olio, in II Cantos *(Montreal, 1825), is based upon internal evidence examined by Carl F. Klinck in an article in* The Dalhousie Review *(July 1960). Little is known about Adams except a few facts related by Henry J. Morgan in* Bibliotheca Canadensis *(1867). Adams was born in Lower Canada, was admitted as an advocate in 1827, and died at Montreal on July 21, 1832. The wedding described in this extract was followed by a "charivari," a noisy serenade on old pots, kettles, and the like, provided by neighbors, according to an old French custom, at the door of a newly married and bedded pair, especially if the groom were older than the bride, or if both had been married before.*

FROM *The Charivari*

The wedding party met, and there were seated
    Annette's papa, and ma', her sister, brother,
The first was bred a surgeon, but he treated
    Cases of physic too, or any other
Which added to his practice, and had cheated
    (As it was said) Death of some later pother
In being before-hand with him, and ending
His patient's pains — which is one way of mending,

Altho' not the most pleasant. Then his son,
    His father's counterpart, was smiling Billy
Who, also, in the practice had begun
    And look'd a very Bolus, — rather silly
But quite good-natur'd, and more fond of fun
    Than physic, — whilst, the sister like a lily
All white appear'd, — and Ma', whose orange gown
For twenty years, at least, had grac'd the town.

Then came Baptisto's friend, — an honest chap
    To act his father upon this occasion, —
Which in reality, (as by mishap
    Report made known,) his kind consideration,
Had done to others; Nature's is a lap
    The softest, and the sweetest in creation,
And Love, without a chain, has charms, they say,
Beyond the zest of law's more fetter'd sway.

And there was Dib's, the merchant, and his spouse,
    And daughter too, a schoolmate of the bride.
His trade was wholesale, and the wealthiest house
    Upon this side, the vast Atlantic's tide.
And then a great North-Wester, Sammy Grouse —
    Alias term'd "Buffalo," — who terrified
His hearers with the wonderful relations
Of all he'd seen amongst the Indian Nations.

He'd talk to you, of beaver, and of bear,
    Till your hair bristled as upon their backs,
And how he liv'd for days upon such fare
    As bark, stew'd down, till you believ'd the acts;
And of grass soup; next, — and he would make you stare —
    Of wrestling with a buffalo; and facts
I scarcely dare, in seriousness, here mention,
For fear you'd think they were my own invention.

Then of the savage tribes, and of the squaws,
    Lord, how he'd prate with intellectual chatter:
The Crees, the Castors, and the Chicasaws,
    And hundred other ones. But of the latter
(The squaws, I mean) where Love has no curs'd laws
    To make a jurisprudence of the matter,
His praises grew ecstatic, in their service, —
Nor wonder, when you know, Sam was no Dervise.

"For in those cold-clad regions, where the weather
    Runs down to fifty below zero's point,
"Why," Sam would say, "to keep the soul together
    With frame, and rheumatism from each joint,

Requir'd some substance like a bed of feather
    To cause the radical heat, so to anoint
The body over with its perspiration,
To keep its vigor, in due preservation."

Then, of the party too, came lawyer Shark —
    Who lik'd no law, so well as a good dinner, —
And laugh'd at *Sam,* who spoke of eating bark,
    Saying, "Indeed? — you must have got much thinner."
And yet the lawyer could make trite remark
    And had prevented many a flagrant sinner
(By quibble, quirk, and eloquential hum)
Making his "exit," like a pendulum.

But before all arriv'd, now he and Sam,
    Got into argument on those sad matters
Which, in the North, occurr'd. This said, "I am
    Most positive, that Selkirk sham'd 'the Rotters,' "
At which odd sound, Sam answer'd with a "damn"
    And said aside, "Lord, how the jackdaw chatters,"
Whilst Shark talk'd on, saying "I can assure ye
You were all wrong, *de facto et de jure.*"

At length, a loud rap, whilst they held this farce on,
    Caus'd a slight silence in this wordy two,
When, with his book and register, the parson
    Enter'd, and made their oratory clue
All canvass up, for Sam's mind soon to arson
    Had been enflam'd, so high his feelings grew,
Whilst Shark an insult courted — on the itch
For a lawsuit — knowing that Sam was rich.

They were all met now; but I fain must mention
    Beau Beamish, and two sisters, but the elder
Said a bad cold prevented her intention
    Of being there. The fact is, what withheld her
Was the dislike of finding her declension
    Into the list of old maids, when age quell'd her
Bright dreams of Hope, and therefore direly hated
To go where she saw others elevated

Beyond her rank of Miss; for at the age
    Of forty, and beyond, when younger Misses
Who were not born when she first trod the stage
    Of life, at dances, dinners, routs, (for this is
The *entrée* of a belle's first pilgrimage
    To Love's young shrine) had long received the blisses
Which marriage showers — no wonder, that the bile
Arose, to jaundice o'er her looks, and smile.

Then, there was aunty Margaret — lac'd and capp'd
    With a rich satin, which had been in vogue
About the time when first the Fronde enwrapt
    All France in it, from Lyons to La Hogue.
Not to forget gay Captain Casey, strapp'd
    From head to heel in gold, who spoke the brogue
In all its elegance, and as to cousins
And their connexions, they came by the dozens.

You know what sort of thing a wedding is;
    Therefore I need not occupy your leisure
In recapitulating every kiss
    Relations gave each other, — when the pleasure
Of seeing two united in one bliss
    Was consummated by the priest (a measure
Which must be done) and the affair was over,
And wife and husband transform'd from the lover.

They feasted, frolick'd now; all sorts of funning
    Went on with spirit — dancing for the young,
Cards for the old (who had giv'n over running)
    Were the convivial sports, whilst raillery's tongue
Jok'd the new pair, and Casey, fond of punning
    When he could get a listener among
Those who surrounded, set his wits to fret,
And said Baptiste had got in *a net*.

                                        — *1824*

OLIVER GOLDSMITH

(1794-1861)

Oliver Goldsmith, a grandnephew and namesake of the famous British author of The Deserted Village *(1770), was born on July 6, 1794, in St. Andrews, New Brunswick. His father was a British Army officer who had served during the Revolutionary War. In 1810 the Canadian Oliver Goldsmith joined the Commissariat branch of the Army at Halifax. In 1833 he was transferred to Saint John, New Brunswick, and in 1844 to Hong Kong. Later he served in Newfoundland and Corfu. He died in Liverpool, England, on June 23, 1861.* The Rising Village *was first published in London in 1825; a second edition, including a number of other poems, appeared in Saint John, New Brunswick, in 1834. The extracts below are from the second edition, which incorporates the revisions made by Goldsmith subsequent to the initial publication.*

What noble courage must their hearts have fired,
How great the ardor which their souls inspired,
Who, leaving far behind their native plain,
Have sought a home beyond the western main;
And braved the terrors of the stormy seas,
In search of wealth, of freedom, and of ease!
Oh! none can tell but they who sadly share
The bosom's anguish, and its wild despair,
What dire distress awaits the hardy bands,
That venture first on bleak and desert lands.
How great the pain, the danger, and the toil,
Which mark the first rude culture of the soil.
When, looking round, the lonely settler sees
His home amid a wilderness of trees:
How sinks his heart in those deep solitudes,
Where not a voice upon his ear intrudes;
Where solemn silence all the waste pervades,
Heightening the horror of its gloomy shades;
Save where the sturdy woodman's strokes
        resound,
That strew the fallen forest on the ground.
See! from their heights the lofty pines descend,
And crackling, down their pond'rous lengths
        extend.
Soon from their boughs the curling flames arise,
Mount into air, and redden all the skies;
And, where the forest late its foliage spread,
The golden corn triumphant waves its head. . . .

The arts of culture now extend their sway,
And many a charm of rural life display.
Where once the pine upreared its lofty head,
The settlers' humble cottages are spread;
Where the broad firs once sheltered from the
        storm,
By slow degrees a neighborhood they form;
And as it[s] bounds, each circling year, increase
In social life, prosperity, and peace,
New prospects rise, new objects too appear,
To add more comfort to its lowly sphere.
Where some rude sign or post the spot betrays,
The tavern now its useful front displays . . . .

The wand'ring Pedlar, who undaunted traced
His lonely footsteps o'er the silent waste;
Who traversed once the cold and snow-clad
        plain,

Reckless of danger, trouble, or of pain,
To find a market for his little wares,
The source of all his hopes, and all his cares,
Establish'd here, his settled home maintains,
And soon a merchant's higher title gains.

Around his store, on spacious shelves array'd,
Behold his great and various stock in trade.
Here, nails and blankets, side by side, are seen,
There, horses' collars and a large tureen;
Buttons and tumblers, codhooks, spoons, and
        knives,
Shawls for young damsels, flannels for old wives;
Woolcards and stockings, hats for men and boys,
Mill-saws and fenders, silks, and children's toys;
All useful things and joined with many more,
Compose the well-assorted country store.

The half-bred Doctor next here settles down,
And hopes the village soon will prove a town.
No rival here disputes his doubtful skill,
He cures, by chance, or ends each human ill;
By turns he physics, or his patient bleeds,
Uncertain in what case each best succeeds.
And if, from friends untimely snatched away,
Some beauty fall a victim to decay;
If some fine youth, his parents' fond delight,
Be early hurried to the shades of night;
Death bears the blame, 'tis his envenom'd
        dart
That strikes the suffering mortal to the heart.

Beneath the shelter of a log-built shed
The country school-house next erects its head
No "man severe," with learning's bright
        display,
Here leads the op'ning blossoms into day;
No master here, in ev'ry art refin'd,
Through fields of science guides the aspiring
        mind;
But some poor wanderer of the human race,
Unequal to the task, supplies his place,
Whose greatest source of knowledge or of skill
Consists in reading, or in writing ill;
Whose efforts can no higher merit claim
Than spreading Dilworth's great scholastic
        fame.

No modest youths surround his awful chair,
His frowns to deprecate or smiles to share,
But all the terrors of his lawful sway,
The proud despise, the fearless disobey;
The rugged urchins spurn at all control,
Which cramps the movements of the free-born
    soul,
Till, in their own conceit so wise they've grown,
They think their knowledge far exceeds his own.

   As thus the village each successive year
Presents new prospects and extends its sphere,
While all around its smiling charms expand,
And rural beauties decorate the land . . . .

   Happy Acadia! though around thy shore
Is heard the stormy wind's terrific roar;
Though round thee Winter binds his icy chain,
And his rude tempests sweep along thy plain,
Still Summer comes, and decorates thy land
With fruits and flowers from her luxuriant hand;
Still Autumn's gifts repay the laborer's toil
With richest products from thy fertile soil;
With bounteous store his varied wants supply,
And scarce the plants of other suns deny.
How pleasing, and how glowing with delight
Are now thy budding hopes! How sweetly bright

They rise to view! How full of joy appear
The expectations of each future year! . . .

   These are thy blessings, Scotia, and for these
For wealth, for freedom, happiness and ease,
Thy grateful thanks to Britain's care are due;
Her power protects, her smiles past hopes renew;
Her valor guards thee, and her counsels guide;
Then may thy parent ever be thy pride! . . .

   Then, blest Acadia! ever may thy name,
Like hers, be graven on the rolls of fame;
May all thy sons, like hers, be brave and free,
Possessors of her laws and liberty;
Heirs of her splendor, science, pow'r, and skill,
And through succeeding years her children still.
And as the sun, with gentle dawning ray,
From night's dull bosom wakes, and leads the
    day,
His course majestic keeps, till in the height
He glows one blaze of pure exhaustless light;
So may thy years increase, thy glories rise,
To be the wonder of the Western skies;
And bliss and peace encircle all thy shore,
Till empires rise and sink, on earth, no more.

       *   *   *

— 1825, 1834

CATHARINE PARR TRAILL

(1802-1899)

   Mrs. Catharine Parr (Strickland) Traill was born in England into the Strickland family, which became well known in Canada because of Susanna Strickland (Mrs. Moodie) and in England because of Agnes Strickland, a noted author of historical works. Mrs. Traill and her husband emigrated to Canada with Lieutenant and Mrs. Moodie in 1832 and settled near Rice Lake in Eastern Ontario. Here Catharine Parr Trail wrote The Backwoods of Canada *(London, 1836) "being letters from the wife of an emigrant officer, illustrative of the domestic economy of British America." This book, published twelve years before her sister Susanna's* Roughing It in the Bush, *was very popular and was frequently reprinted. A very long extract from it appeared in N. P. Willis'* Canadian Scenery Illustrated *(1842) along with the W. H. Bartlett prints. Mrs. Traill continued to write books and articles for* The Literary Garland

and other Canadian and English periodicals. Some of her books, notably Canadian Crusoes *(1852), are still read by children. When she was over ninety years of age, her* Pearls and Pebbles; or, Notes of an Old Naturalist *(1895) was published with a useful biographical sketch by Mary Agnes Fitzgibbon, an appropriate tribute to Mrs. Traill and her life-long devotion to the flowers, birds, and all the other forms of natural life around her.*

FROM *The Backwoods of Canada*

[A "MATTER-OF-FACT COUNTRY"]

Though the Canadian winter has its disadvantages, it also has its charms. After a day or two of heavy snow the sky brightens, and the air becomes exquisitely clear and free from vapor; the smoke ascends in tall spiral columns: seen against the saffron-tinted sky of an evening, or early of a clear morning, when the hoar-frost sparkles on the trees, the effect is singularly beautiful.

I enjoy a walk in the woods of a bright winter day, when not a cloud, or the faint shadow of a cloud, obscures the soft azure of the heavens above; when but for the silver covering of the earth I might look upwards to the cloudless sky and say, "It is June, sweet June." The evergreens, as the pines, cedars, hemlock, and balsam firs, are bending their pendant branches, loaded with snow, which the least motion scatters in a mimic shower around, but so light and dry is it that it is shaken off without the slightest inconvenience.

The tops of the stumps look quite pretty, with their turbans of snow; a blackened pine-stump, with its white cap and mantle, will often startle you into the belief that someone is approaching you thus fancifully attired. As to ghosts or spirits they appear totally banished from Canada. This is too matter-of-fact country for such supernaturals to visit. Here there are no historical associations, no legendary tales of those that came before us. Fancy would starve for lack of marvellous food to keep her alive in the backwoods. We have neither fay nor fairy, ghost nor bogle, satyr nor wood-nymph; our very forests disdain to shelter dryad or hama-dryad. No naiad haunts the rushy margin of our lakes, or hallows with her presence our forest rills. No Druid claims our oaks; and instead of poring with mysterious awe among our curious limestone rocks, that are often singularly grouped together, we refer them to the geologist to exercise his skill in accounting for their appearance: instead of investing them with the solemn characters of ancient temples or heathen altars, we look upon them with the curious eye of natural philosophy alone.

Even the Irish and Highlanders of the humblest class seem to lay aside their ancient superstitions on becoming denizens of the woods of Canada. I heard a friend exclaim, when speaking of the want of interest this country possessed, "It is the most unpoetical of all lands; there is no scope for imagination; here all is new — the very soil seems newly formed; there is no hoary ancient grandeur in these woods; no recollections of former deeds connected with the country. The only beings in which I take any interest are the Indians, and they want the warlike character and intelligence that I had pictured to myself they would possess."

This was the lamentation of a poet. Now, the class of people to whom this country is so admirably adapted are formed of the unlettered and industrious laborers and artisans. They feel no regret that the land they labor on has not been celebrated by the pen of the historian or the lay of the poet. The earth yields her increase to them as freely as if it had been enriched by the blood of heroes. They would not spare the ancient oak from feelings of veneration, nor look upon it with regard for anything but its use as timber. They have no time, even if they possessed the taste, to gaze abroad on the beauties of Nature, but their ignorance is bliss.

After all, these are imaginary evils, and can hardly be considered just causes for dislike to the country. They would excite little sympathy among everyday men and women, though doubtless they would have their weight with the more refined and intellectual members of society, who naturally would regret that taste, learning, and genius should be thrown out of its proper sphere.

For myself, though I can easily enter into the feelings of the poet and the enthusiastic lover of the wild and the wonderful of historic lore, I can yet make myself very happy and contented in this country. If its volume of history is yet a blank, that of Nature is open, and eloquently marked by the finger of God; and from its pages I can extract a thousand sources of amusement and interest whenever I take my walks in the forest or by the borders of the lakes.

[A SLEIGH RIDE]

I left the dear children all soundly sleeping and accompanied my sister Susan home in the ox-sleigh; we made a merry party comfortably nested in our rude vehicle, with a bed of clean straw, and a nice blanket over it, with pillows to lean against; well wrapped up in our Scotch plaids, we defied the cold and chatted merrily away, not a whit less happy than if we had been rolling along in a carriage with a splendid pair of bays, instead of crawling along at a funeral pace, in the rudest of all vehicles with the most ungraceful of all steeds; our canopy, the snow-laden branches of pine, hemlock, and cedar, the dark forest around us, and our lamps the pale stars and watery moon struggling through "wrack and mist" and silver-tinged snow-clouds. Here then were we breaking the deep silence of the deep woods with the hum of cheerful voices and the wild mirth that bursts from the light-hearted children. No other sound was there except the heavy tread of the oxen and the lumbering sound of the sleigh as it jolted over the fallen sticks and logs that lay beneath the snow.

Nothing can surpass the loveliness of the woods after a snowstorm has loaded every bough and sprig with its feathery deposit. The face of the ground, so rough and tangled with a mass of uptorn trees, broken boughs, and timbers in every stage of decay, seems by the touch of some powerful magician's wand to have changed its character. Unrivalled purity, softness, and brilliancy, has taken the place of confusion and vegetable corruption. It is one of the greatest treats this country affords me, to journey through the thick woods after a heavy snowfall — whether it be by the brilliant light of the noonday sun in the cloudless azure sky, giving a brightness to every glittering particle that clothes the trees or surface of the ground, or hangs in heavy masses on the evergreens, converting their fan-

shaped boughs into foliage of feathery whiteness and most fantastic forms — or
by the light of a full moon and frosty stars looking down through the snowy tops
of the forest trees — sometimes shining through a veil of haze, which the frost
converts into a sparkling rime that encases every spray and twig with crystals.
The silent fall of the lighter particles of snow, which the gentlest motion of the
air shakes down, is the only motion the still scene affords — with the merry jingle
of our sleighbells.

— 1836

STANDISH O'GRADY

(fl. 1793-1841)

Standish O'Grady, the author of The Emigrant, A Poem, *printed for the author
in Montreal in 1842, was a graduate of Trinity College, Dublin, who embarked at
Waterford, Ireland, for the voyage to Quebec on April 3, 1836. Little is known
about him except what may be gleaned from his long discursive poem, the appended
notes that reveal an alert and colorful personality, and a few additional lyrics. He
settled near Sorel in Lower Canada, but wished that he had gone to Upper Canada.
"A Canadian stud horse with one miserable cow," he wrote, "were the only remnants
of my stock which survived the winter." In* Old Lamps Aglow *Lawrence M. Lande
reports that O'Grady returned to Ireland and that Standish James O'Grady (1846-
1928), the noted Anglo-Irish author of at least two dozen books, was a direct descendant. The younger O'Grady was given the title of "the Father of the Literary
Revival in Ireland."*

FROM *The Emigrant*

Bleak, barren spot, ah! why should I forsake
A fertile land to thread thy worthless brake?
Labor alone thy sterile land surveys,
Breathes the dull round, or prematurely pays
An hard won pittance, through distress and
    toil,
Still doomed again to lavish on thy soil;
O, land! that's slothful, miserable spot,
Ungracious sandbank! May it be my lot
Remote to dwell 'mong happier kind abodes,
And leave to grasshoppers a land of toads!
  Thou barren waste; unprofitable strand,
Where hemlocks brood on unproductive land,
Whose frozen air on one bleak winter's night
Can metamorphose *dark brown hares to white!*

Whose *roads* are *rivers,* o'er your fountains
See icebergs form your shining mountains,
And drifted snow, from arctic regions,
Gives sure employment to Canadians;
Here roads n'er known for many a summer,
Are now passt o'er by each new-comer,
All wrought one night, nor made of stone or
    gravel,
Complete withal and next day fit to travel,
Here forests crowd, unprofitable lumber,
O'er fruitless lands indefinite as number;
Where birds scarce light, and with the north
    winds veer
On wings of wind, and quickly disappear,
Here the rough Bear subsists his winter year,

And licks his paw and finds *no better fare;*
Here fishes swarm, now by reaction,
Congealed as ice seem petrifaction:
Till hottest ray with multiplying power
Dissolves and grants one genial shower.
  In winter here, where all alike contrive,
And still withal few animals survive,
Till summer's heat, so potent and so quick,
Enough to make the *Crocodile grow sick;*
With vile mosquitoes, lord deliver us,
Whose stings could *blister a Rhinoceros.*
If on the living insects are thus fed,

How ill must fare the worms when we are dead!
Each pest conspires, — how idle is precaution,
We're eat by these or perish by exhaustion!
One month we hear birds, shrill and loud and
    harsh,
The plaintive bittern sounding from the marsh;
The next we see the fleet-winged swallow,
The duck, the woodcock, and the ice-birds
    follow;
Then comes, drear clime, the lakes all stagnant
    grow,
And the wild wilderness is rapt in snow.

— 1842

[TWO BALLADS OF THE WAR OF 1812]

These ballads are presented in the versions found in Canada's Story in Song *(Toronto, Gage, 1960) edited by Edith Fowke. Of the dating of "Come All You Bold Canadians" Mrs. Fowke writes: "The Niagara Historical Society published a version of this song in 1928 as 'Lines by Private Flumerfilt, one of the York Volunteers, after their arrival at Little York from Detroit, 1812.' The Ontario Historical Society also has a copy written in 1824 by a man who learned it from his grandfather, who was in the Detroit Expedition."*

For "The Battle of Queenston Heights" the date of composition could not be earlier than 1824, since the phrase "monumental rock" presumably refers to the first Brock memorial, constructed in that year but destroyed in 1840. The phrase would be quite unsuitable for the present 185-foot shaft, erected in 1854.

COME ALL YOU BOLD CANADIANS

anonymous

Come all you bold Canadians, I'd have you lend an ear
Concerning a fine ditty that would make your courage cheer,
Concerning an engagement that we had at Sandwich town,
The courage of those Yankee boys so lately we pulled down.

There was a bold commander, brave General Brock by name,
Took shipping at Niagara and down to York he came,
He says, "My gallant heroes, if you'll come along with me,
We'll fight those proud Yankees in the west of Canaday!"

'Twas thus that we replied: "Along with you we'll go,
Our knapsacks we will shoulder without any more ado.

Our knapsacks we will shoulder and forward we will steer;
We'll fight those proud Yankees without either dread or fear."

We travelled all that night and a part of the next day,
With a determination to show them British play.
We travelled all that night and a part of the next day,
With a determination to conquer or to die.

Our commander sent a flag to them and unto them did say:
"Deliver up your garrison or we'll fire on you this day!"
But they would not surrender, and chose to stand their ground,
We opened up our great guns and gave them fire a round.

Their commander sent a flag to us, for quarter he did call.
"Oh, hold your guns, brave British boys, for fear you slay us all.
Our town you have at your command, our garrison likewise."
They brought their guns and grounded them right down before our eyes.

And now we are all home again, each man is safe and sound.
May the memory of this conquest all through the Province sound!
Success unto our volunteers who did their rights maintain,
And to our bold commander, brave General Brock by name!

— 1812(?)

THE BATTLE OF QUEENSTON HEIGHTS

anonymous

Upon the Heights of Queenston one dark October day,
Invading foes were marshalled in battle's dread array.
Brave Brock looked up the rugged steep and planned a bold attack;
"No foreign flag shall float," said he, "above the Union Jack."

His loyal-hearted soldiers were ready every one,
Their foes were thrice their number, but duty must be done.
They started up the fire-swept hill with loud resounding cheers,
While Brock's inspiring voice rang out: "Push on, York Volunteers!"

But soon a fatal bullet pierced through his manly breast,
And loving friends to help him around the hero pressed;
"Push on," he said. "Do not mind me!" — and ere the set of sun
Canadians held the rugged steep, the victory was won.

Each true Canadian soldier laments the death of Brock;
His country told its sorrow in monumental rock;
And if a foe should e'er invade our land in future years,
His dying words will guide us still: "Push on, brave Volunteers!"

— 1824(?)

MAJOR JOHN RICHARDSON

(1796-1852)

John Richardson was born at Queenston, on the Niagara frontier, the eldest son of a surgeon in the Queen's Rangers and grandson of Colonel John Askin, a wealthy merchant of pioneer Detroit. He spent his boyhood at Amherstburg on the Canadian border, facing the Indian lands of the West where Pontiac had made history, and where Tecumseh, Barclay, and Brock would fight their battles in the War of 1812-1814. As a young soldier he saw border romance unfold before his eyes, especially when he was captured by the Americans at Moraviantown, where Tecumseh was killed. Both the tales he heard about Pontiac and his own military experiences were to provide literary material for his later use.

Released from captivity at the end of the war, he sailed for England and commenced a career of garrison life abroad, in Barbados, London, Paris, and Spain. His first novel, Ecarté, was published in England in 1829, and recorded the gay life of British officers — probably the author's own gay life — in Paris. His historical romance, Wacousta (1832), was published in the year Scott died and during the height of Cooper's success. It introduced readers to a new-world borderland between the British and Indians at Detroit and Michilimackinac.

In 1838 Richardson came to Canada to report for the London Times on the political troubles which had flared into rebellion. An account of his travels and observations in his homeland grew into a book entitled Eight Years in Canada (1847). Meanwhile, two extracts from a work later to be entitled The Canadian Brothers, a continuation of Wacousta, appeared in March and April, 1839, in The Literary Garland. In this work the realism of Ecarté and of his historical narratives had toned down the melodrama of Wacousta. Many other writings of these years were printed in Richardson's own literary weekly, The New Era, or Canadian Chronicle, published at Brockville from 1840 to 1842. During 1845-1846 he lived in St. Catharines, serving as Superintendent of Police on the Welland Canal.

In his last years Richardson lived in New York, where, from 1850 to 1852, he re-issued cheap editions or revisions of Ecarté, Wacousta, and The Canadian Brothers (the last of these under the new title of Matilda Montgomerie). He also published several new works. His death occurred in May 1852, but his burial place is unknown.

◆

FROM *War of 1812*

The only loss sustained by Tecumseh was one man killed, and that by almost the last shot fired, in their confusion, by the enemy. This individual was a young Chief named Logan, who often acted as an interpreter, and who, from partially understanding the English language, and being in frequent communication with them, was nearly as great a favorite with the Officers and men of the Right Division, as he was with his own people. At the close of the action, Logan's dead body was brought in, and placed in a long, low, log building which the Indians chiefly used as a council room. Here the recently engaged warriors now assembled, taking their seats in a circle, with an air of great solemnity, and in profound silence. Up to that moment one prisoner only of the American detachment had fallen into their hands. This poor fellow had been wounded, although not in such a way as to disable him from walking, and he was made to take his seat in the circle. Added to the twenty-four warriors selected by Tecumseh, was the eldest son of Colonel Elliott, the Superintendent of Indian affairs, a very fine young man who was afterwards killed (and scalped I believe) and who, dressed as an Indian throughout the day, now took his station as one of the war-party, among his late companions in arms. It chanced that the prisoner was placed next to him. After having been seated some little time in this manner, Mr. Elliott, observing the blood to flow from some part of his neighbor's body, involuntarily exclaimed — "Good God, you are wounded." The sound of an English voice operated like magic upon the unhappy man, and his look of despair was in an instant changed for one of hope. "Oh Sir," he eagerly exclaimed, "if you have the power to save me do so." Mr. Elliott, who related the whole of the above circumstances to us later, stated that he had never experienced such moments of mental agony as he felt during this short appeal. Bitterly repenting the indiscretion which had been the means of exciting an expectation, which he well knew he had not the slightest power to realize, he was compelled to reply somewhat harshly that he had no more voice there than the prisoner himself, which indeed was the fact. The American said no more; he bent his head upon his chest, and remained silent. Soon afterwards a bowl with food was placed before him, evidently with a view (as the result proved) of diverting his attention. Of this he slightly partook or seemed to partake. While occupied in this manner, a young warrior, obeying a signal from one of the elders, rose from his seat, and coming round and behind the prisoner, struck him one blow with his tomahawk on the uncovered head, and he ceased to live. Not a yell, not a sound beside that of the crashing tomahawk was heard, not a muscle of an Indian face was moved. The young warrior, replacing his weapon, walked deliberately back, and resumed his seat in the circle. The whole party remained a few minutes longer seated, and then rose to their feet, and silently withdrew — leaving to those who had not been of the war-party, to dispose of the body of the victim. Tecumseh was not present at this scene.

Nor was this the only melancholy sacrifice offered to the manes of the lamented and unconscious Logan. On the very morning after this occurrence, as the Officers sat grouped together on the grass, literally imbedded in letters, the contents of the mail from Detroit, which had been captured by the Indians, and which were now being opened for the purpose of ascertaining the intended movements of the enemy, the wild and peculiar yell of several warriors announced that another captive was being brought in. We immediately rose and advanced toward the low, log building already described, when we beheld several Indians approaching it, preceded by a prisoner whom they had secured by a long leathern thong, made fast to another which confined his hands. He was a finely-proportioned young man, and the air of dejection which clouded his brow gradually gave way to a more cheerful expression, when, on approaching the encampment, he perceived those from whom he expected protection. Several of the men advanced to meet and converse with him, and the poor fellow had apparently banished all feeling of apprehension for his future fate, when an aged aunt of the deceased issued from her tent, and stole cautiously behind him. Even at the moment when the mind of the prisoner was lulled into confidence, and without any previous admonition, the heartless woman drew a tomahawk from beneath her mantle, and buried its point in the skull of her victim. Stunned but not felled by the wound, the unhappy man — his whole countenance expressing horror and despair — grasped at the first soldier near him for support; but the blow was repeated so suddenly, and with such violence, that he soon fell panting and convulsive to the earth. Fortunately he was not suffered to linger in his agony. The Indians around instantly despatched and scalped him, stripping the body of its clothes, and committing violations on his person in which the cruel aunt of Logan bore a principal share. The indignation of the men was excessive; but any attempt to interfere, could they even have foreseen the occurrence in time to render interference effectual, would not only have cost them several lives, but produced the most alarming consequences to our cause. Their displeasure was, however, expressed by their murmurs, and the atrocity of the act became the theme of conversation throughout the camp. At the moment of its perpetration, I had myself approached within a few paces of the group, and became an unwilling spectator of the whole transaction. The wild expression of the sufferer's eye: the supplicating look which spoke through the very distortion of his features, and the agony which seemed to creep throughout his every limb, were altogether indescribable.

In these two several sacrifices of human life, the motives for action, it will be seen, were wholly different. In the first case the Indians simply followed up a custom which had prevailed among them for ages, and indeed, if proof were required of this fact, it is at once to be found in the absence of all ferocity, or excitement, or disposition to insult the prisoner who had already been doomed to death. The very fact of their having placed food before him, with the manifest object of absorbing his attention, and quieting his mind at the very moment of infliction of the death blow, was an evidence of mercy — not mercy, it is true, as understood by the Christian — but still mercy — the mercy of the child of nature, whom the stern habits of his forefathers have taught the lesson of sanguinary retribution, yet who, in the midst of its accomplishment, seeks to spare all unnecessary pang to its victim.

The features of the second tragedy bore no resemblance to those which characterized the first. *There,* it was literally a religious immolation to the ashes of the deceased, whose spirit, it was presumed, could not rest in quietness, unless an enemy had been offered up as a propitiatory sacrifice. *Here,* it was a piece of wanton revenge, and perpetrated under circumstances of peculiar atrocity. Not a sound of triumph escaped from the band of warriors met to avenge the death of their recently fallen friend and comrade, although they might have been supposed to have been inflamed and excited by the action in which each had borne so prominent a part, in the early part of the day — not a look of levity derogated from the solemnity of their purpose. On the contrary, loud shouts and yells, and menacing looks and gestures, accompanied the actions of those, who, taking their tone from the cruel relative of Logan, scalped and otherwise mutilated the body of the second prisoner.

The demeanor of the first party was that of a Christian tribunal, which sits in solemn judgment upon a criminal, and beholds, without emotion, the carrying into effect of its sentence by the executioner. The bearing of the second was that of a Christian mob, to whose infuriated passions a loose has been given, and who, once excited by the sight of blood, know not where to set a bound to the innate and aroused cruelty of their nature.

— 1842

THOMAS CHANDLER HALIBURTON

(1796-1865)

Haliburton was born at Windsor, Nova Scotia, on December 17, 1796, the only child of Tory and Loyalist parents. He was graduated from King's College in Windsor in 1815, and after a short sojourn in England commenced the practice of law in Annapolis Royal. As representative of·this constituency, he was elected to the Legislative Assembly of Nova Scotia in 1826; three years later he was elevated to the bench, as a judge of the Court of Common Pleas in succession to his father; in 1841 he became a judge of the Supreme Court of Nova Scotia. During his later years he spent much time in England, moving there permanently in 1856. The same year a wealthy widow became his second wife. In 1858 he received an honorary degree from Oxford University, and the following year won election to the British House of Commons.

Haliburton's first publications were geographical and historical accounts of his native province. Then in 1835 the first of the Sam Slick papers began appearing in Joseph Howe's The Novascotian. *They proved immediately popular, and soon earned their author an international reputation. His various books ran through many editions, in both the United States and England; some of them were translated into several European languages.*

THE CLOCKMAKER

I had heard of Yankee clock pedlars, tin pedlars, and Bible pedlars, especially of him who sold Polyglot Bibles *(all in English)* to the amount of sixteen thousand pounds. The house of every substantial farmer had three substantial ornaments, a wooden clock, a tin reflector, and a Polyglot Bible. How is it that an American can sell his wares, at whatever prices he pleases, where a blue-nose would fail to make a sale at all? I will inquire of the Clockmaker the secret of his success.

"What a pity it is, Mr. *Slick*" (for such was his name) — "what a pity it is," said I, "that you, who are so successful in teaching these people the value of *clocks,* could not also teach them the value of *time.*" "I guess," said he, "they have got that ring to grow on their horns yet, which every four-year-old has in our country. We reckon hours and minutes to be dollars and cents. They do nothin' in these parts but eat, drink, smoke, sleep, ride about, lounge at taverns, make speeches at temperance meetings, and talk about '*House of Assembly.*' If a man don't hoe his corn, and he don't get a crop, he says it is all owin' to the bank; and if he runs into debt, and is sued, why, he says lawyers are a cuss to the country. They are a most idle set of folks, I tell *you*." "But how is it," said I, "that you manage to sell such an immense number of clocks (which certainly cannot be called necessary articles) among a people with whom there seems to be so great a scarcity of money?"

Mr. Slick paused, as if considering the propriety of answering the question, and looking me in the face, said in a confidential tone: "Why, I don't care if I do tell you, for the market is glutted, and I shall quit this circuit. It is done by a knowledge of *soft sawder* and *human natur'*. But here is Deacon Flint's," said he; "I have but one clock left, and I guess I will sell it to him."

At the gate of a most comfortable-looking farmhouse stood Deacon Flint, a respectable old man, who had understood the value of time better than most of his neighbors, if one might judge from the appearance of everything about him. After the usual salutation, an invitation to "alight" was accepted by Mr. Slick, who said he wished to take leave of Mrs. Flint before he left Colchester.

We had hardly entered the house before the Clockmaker pointed to the view from the window, and addressing himself to me, said: "If I was to tell them in Connecticut there was such a farm as this away down east here in Nova Scotia, they wouldn't believe me — why, there ain't such a location in all New England. The Deacon has a hundred acres of dyke." "Seventy," said the Deacon, "only seventy." "Well, seventy; but then there is your fine deep bottom; why, I could run a ramrod into it." "Interval, we call it," said the Deacon, who, though evidently pleased at this eulogium, seemed to wish the experiment of the ramrod to be tried in the right place. "Well, interval, if you please (though Professor Eleazer Cumstick, in his work on Ohio, calls them bottoms), is just as good as dyke. Then there is that water privilege, worth 3,000 or 4,000 dollars, twice as good as what Governor Cass paid 15,000 dollars for. I wonder, Deacon, you don't put up a carding machine on it; the same works would carry a turning lathe, a shingle machine, a circular saw, grind bark, and — " "Too old," said the Deacon, "too old for all those speculations." "Old," repeated the Clockmaker, "not you. Why, you are worth half-a-dozen of the young men we see nowadays; you are young enough to have —" Here he said something in a lower tone of voice, which I did not distinctly hear; but whatever it was, the Deacon was pleased. He smiled, and said he did not think of such things now.

"But your beasts, dear me, your beasts must be put in and have a feed;" saying which, he went out to order them to be taken to the stable.

As the old gentleman closed the door after him, Mr. Slick drew near to me, and said in an undertone: "Now that is what I call '*soft sawder*.' An Englishman would pass that man as a sheep passes a hog in a pastur', without looking at him; or," said he, looking rather archly, "if he was mounted on a pretty smart horse, I guess he'd trot away, *if he could*. Now I find —" Here his lecture on *soft sawder* was cut short by the entrance of Mrs. Flint. "Jist come to say good-bye, Mrs. Flint." "What, have you sold all your clocks?" "Yes, and very low, too, for money is scarce, and I wished to close the concarn; no, I am wrong in saying all, for I have jist one left. Neighbor Steel's wife asked to have the refusal of it, but I guess I won't sell it; I had but two of them, this one and the feller of it that I sold Governor Lincoln. General Green, the Secretary of State for Maine, said he'd give me 50 dollars for this here one — it has composition wheels and patent axles; it is a beautiful article — a real first chop — no mistake, genuine superfine, but I guess

35

I'll take it back; and besides, Squire Hawk might think it kinder hard that I didn't give him the offer." "Dear me," said Mrs. Flint, "I should like to see it; where is it?" "It is in a chist of mine over the way, at Tom Tape's store. I guess he can ship it on to Eastport." "That's a good man," said Mrs. Flint; "jist let's look at it."

Mr. Slick, willing to oblige, yielded to these entreaties, and soon produced the clock — a gaudy, highly-varnished, trumpery-looking affair. He placed it on the chimneypiece, where its beauties were pointed out and duly appreciated by Mrs. Flint, whose admiration was about ending in a proposal, when Mr. Flint returned from giving his directions about the care of the horses. The Deacon praised the clock; he, too, thought it a handsome one; but the Deacon was a prudent man. He had a watch; he was sorry, but he had no occasion for a clock. "I guess you're in the wrong furrow this time, Deacon; it ain't for sale," said Mr. Slick; "and if it was, I reckon neighbor Steel's wife would have it, for she gives me no peace about it." Mrs. Flint said that Mr. Steel had enough to do, poor man, to pay his interest, without buying clocks for his wife. "It's no concarn of mine," said Mr. Slick, "so long as he pays me what he has to do; but I guess I don't want to sell it, and besides, it comes too high; that clock can't be made at Rhode Island under 40 dollars. Why, it ain't possible," said the Clockmaker, in apparent surprise, looking at his watch; "why, as I'm alive, it is 4 o'clock, and if I haven't been two blessed hours here! How on airth shall I reach River Philip tonight? I'll tell you what, Mrs. Flint; I'll leave the clock in your care till I return on my way to the States. I'll set it a-goin', and put it to the right time."

As soon as this operation was performed, he delivered the key to the Deacon with a sort of serio-comic injunction to wind up the clock every Saturday night, which Mrs. Flint said she would take care should be done, and promised to remind her husband of it, in case he should chance to forget it.

"That," said the Clockmaker, as soon as we were mounted — "that I call *human natur'!* Now that clock is sold for 40 dollars; it cost me jist 6 dollars and 50 cents. Mrs. Flint will never let Mrs. Steel have the refusal, nor will the Deacon larn, until I call for the clock, that, having once indulged in the use of a superfluity, how difficult it is to give it up. We can do without any article of luxury we never had, but, when once obtained, it isn't in *human natur'* to surrender it voluntarily. Of fifteen thousand sold by myself and partners in this Province, twelve thousand were left in this manner, and only ten clocks were ever returned; when we called for them, they invariably bought them. We trust to *soft sawder* to get them into the house, and to *human natur'* that they never come out of it."

— *The Clockmaker, First Series, 1836*

THE ROAD TO A WOMAN'S HEART

As we approached the inn at Amherst, the Clockmaker grew uneasy. "It's pretty well on in the evenin', I guess," said he, "and Marm Pugwash is as onsartin in her temper as a mornin' in April; it's all sunshine or all clouds with her, and if she's in one of her tantrums, she'll stretch out her neck and hiss like a goose with a flock of goslin's. I wonder what on earth Pugwash was a-thinkin' on when he signed articles of partnership with that 'are woman; she's not a bad-lookin' piece of furniture, neither, and it's a proper pity sich a clever woman should carry such a stiff upper lip — she reminds me of our old minister Joshua Hopewell's apple-trees.

"The old minister had an orchard of most partikilar good fruit, for he was a great hand at buddin', graftin', and what not, and the orchard (it was on the south side of the house) stretched right up to the road. Well, there were some trees hung over the fence; I never see'd such bearers, the apples hung in ropes, for all the world like strings of onions, and the fruit was beautiful. Nobody touched the minister's apples, and when other folks lost their'n from the boys, his'n always hung there like bait to a hook, but there never was so much as a nibble at 'em. So I said to him one day: 'Minister,' said I, 'how on airth do you manage to keep your fruit that's so exposed, when no one else can't do it nohow?' 'Why,' says he, 'they are dreadful pretty fruit, an't they?' 'I guess,' said I, 'there an't the like on 'em in all Connecticut.' 'Well,' says he, 'I'll tell you the secret, but you needn't let on to no one about it. That 'are row next the fence I grafted in myself. I took great pains to get the right kind, I sent clean up to Roxberry, and away down to Squaw-neck Creek.' I was afeerd he was a-goin' for to give me day and date for every graft, being a terrible long-winded man in his stories, so says I: 'I know that, Minister, but how do you preserve them?' 'Why, I was a-goin' to tell you,' said he, 'when you stopped me. That 'are outward row I grafted myself with the choicest I could find, and I succeeded. They are beautiful, but so eternal sour no human soul can eat them. Well, the boys think the old minister's graftin' has all succeeded about as well as that row, and they sarch no farther. They snicker at my graftin', and I laugh in my sleeve, I guess, at their penetration.'

"Now, Marm Pugwash is like the minister's apples, very temptin' fruit to look at, but desperate sour. If Pugwash had a watery mouth when he married, I guess it's pretty puckery by this time. However, if she goes for to act ugly, I'll give her a dose of *soft sawder,* that will take the frown out of her frontispiece, and make her dial-plate as smooth as a lick of copal varnioh. It's a pity she's such a kickin' devil, too, for she has good points — good eye, good foot, neat pastern, fine chest, a clean set of limbs, and carries a good — But here we are; now you'll see what *soft sawder* will do."

When we entered the house the traveller's room was all in darkness, and on opening the opposite door into the sitting-room, we found the female part of the family extinguishing the fire for the night. Mrs. Pugwash had a broom in her hand, and was in the act (the last act of female housewifery) of sweeping the hearth. The strong flickering light of the fire, as it fell upon her tall fine figure and beautiful face, revealed a creature worthy of the Clockmaker's comments.

"Good evenin', marm," said Mr. Slick, "how do you do, and how's Mr. Pugwash?" "He," said she, "why, he's been abed this hour; you don't expect to disturb him at this time of night, I hope." "Oh, no," said Mr. Slick, "certainly not, and I am sorry to have disturbed you, but we got detained longer than we expected; I am sorry that —" "So am I," said she; "but if Mr. Pugwash will keep an inn when he has no sort of occasion to, his family can't expect no rest."

Here the Clockmaker, seeing the storm gathering, stooped down suddenly, and staring intently, held out his hand, and exclaimed: "Well, if that ain't a beautiful child! Come here, my little man, and shake hands along with me. Well, I declare, if that 'are little fellow ain't the finest child I ever see'd; what, not abed yet? Ah, you rogue, where did you get them 'are pretty rosy cheeks; stole 'em from mamma, eh? Well, I wish my old mother could see that 'are child, it is such a treat! In our country," said he, turning to me, "the children are all as pale as chalk, or as yaller as an orange. Lord, that 'are little fellow would be a show in our country — come to me, my man." Here the "soft sawder" began to operate. Mrs. Pugwash said, in a milder tone than we had yet heard: "Go, my dear, to the gentleman; go, dear." Mr. Slick kissed him, asked him if he would to go the States along with him, told him all the little girls there would fall in love with him, for they didn't see such a beautiful face once in a month of Sundays. "Black eyes — let me see — ah, mamma's eyes too, and black hair also; as I am alive, why you are a mamma's own boy, the very image of mamma." "Do be seated, gentlemen," said Mrs. Pugwash. "Sally, make a fire in the next room." "She ought to be proud of you," he continued. "Well, if I live to return here, I must paint your face, and have it put on my clocks, and our folks will buy the clocks for the sake of the face. Did you ever see," said he, again addressing me, "such a likeness between one human and another as between this beautiful little boy and his mother?" "I am sure you have had no supper," said Mrs. Pugwash to me; "you must be hungry and weary, too — I will get you a cup of tea." "I am sorry to give you so much trouble," said I. "Not the least trouble in the world," she replied, "on the contrary, a pleasure."

We were then shown into the next room, where the fire was now blazing up, but Mr. Slick protested he could not proceed without the little boy, and lingering behind me to ascertain his age, concluded by asking the child if he had any aunts that looked like mamma.

As the door closed, Mr. Slick said: "It's a pity she don't go well in gear. The difficulty with those critters is to get them to start, arter that there is no trouble with them if you don't check 'em too short. If you do, they'll stop again, run back and kick like mad, and then Old Nick himself wouldn't start 'em. Pugwash, I guess, don't onderstand the natur' of the critter: she'll never go kind in harness for him. *When I see a child,*" said the Clockmaker, "*I always feel safe with these women folk; for I have always found that the road to a women's heart lies through her child.*"

"You seem," said I, "to understand the female heart so well, I make no doubt you are a general favorite among the fair sex." "Any man," he replied, "that onderstands horses has a pretty considerable fair knowledge of women, for they are jist alike in temper, and require the very identical same treatment. *Encourage the timid ones, be gentle and steady with the fractious, but lather the sulky ones like blazes.*

"People talk an everlastin' sight of nonsense about wine, women, and horses. I've bought and sold 'em all, I've traded in all of them, and I tell you there ain't one in a thousand that knows a grain about either on 'em. You hear folks say, 'Oh, such a man is an ugly-grained critter, he'll break his wife's heart'; jist as if a woman's heart was as brittle as a pipe-stalk.

"The female heart, as far as my experience goes, is just like a new india rubber shoe; you may pull and pull at it, till it stretches out a yard long, and then let go, and it will fly right back to its old shape. Their hearts are made of stout leather, I tell you; there is a plaguy sight of wear in 'em . . . ."

— The Clockmaker, First Series, 1836

Whoever has read Haliburton's "History of Nova Scotia" — which, next to Mr. Josiah Slick's "History of Cuttyhunk," in five volumes, is the most important account of unimportant things I have ever seen — will recollect that this good city of Annapolis is the most ancient one in North America; but there is one fact omitted by that author, which I trust he will not think an intrusion upon his province if I take the liberty of recording, and that is, that in addition to its being the most ancient, it is also the most loyal city of this Western Hemisphere. This character it has always sustained, and "loyal," as a mark of particular favor, has ever been added to its cognomen by every government that has had dominion over it.

Under the French, with whom it was a great favorite, it was called Port Royal; and the good Queen Anne, who condescended to adopt it, permitted it to be called Annapolis Royal. . . .

"Here it was," said I ,"Mr. Slick, that the egg was laid of that American bird whose progeny have since spread over this immense continent." "Well, it is a'most a beautiful bird too, ain't it?" said he. "What a plumage it has! What a size it is! It is a whopper, that's sartain; it has the courage and the soarin' of the eagle; and the color of the peacock, and his majestic step and keen eye. The world never see'd the beat of it; that's a fact. How streaked the English must feel when they think they once had it in the cage, and couldn't keep it there! It is a pity they are so invious, tho', I declare."

"Not at all, I assure you," I replied; "there is not a man among them who is not ready to admit all you have advanced in favor of your national emblem: the fantastic strut of the peacock, the melodious and attic tones, the gaudy apparel, the fondness for display which is perpetually exhibiting to the world the extended tail with painted stars, the amiable disposition of the bird towards the younger and feebler offspring of others, the unwieldy —"

"I thought so," said he. "I hadn't ought to have spoke of it afore you, for it does seem to rile you, that's sartain; and I don't know as it was jist altogether right to allude to a thin' that is so humblin' to your national pride. But, Squire, ain't this been a hot day? I think it would pass muster among the hot ones of the West Indgies a'most. I do wish I could jist slip off my flesh and sit in my bones for a space, to cool myself, for I ain't see'd such thawy weather this many a year, I know. I calculate I will brew a little lemonade, for Marm Bailey ginerally keeps the materials for that Temperance Society drink.

"This climate o' Nova Scotia does run to extremes; it has the hottest and the coldest days in it I ever see'd. I shall never forget a night I spent here three winters ago. I came very near freezin' to death. The very thought of that night will cool me the hottest day in summer. It was about the latter eend of February, as far as my memory sarves me. I came down here to cross over the bay to St. John, and it was considerable arter daylight down when I arrived. It was the most violent, slippery weather, and the most cruel cold, I think, I ever mind seein' since I was raised.

"Says Marm Bailey to me, 'Mr. Slick,' says she, 'I don't know what onder the sun I'm a-goin' to do with you, or how I shall be able to accommodate you; for there's a whole raft of folks from Halifax here, and a batch of moose-huntin' officers, and I don't know who all; and the house is chock full, I declare.'

" 'Well,' says I, 'I'm no ways partikiler — I can put up with 'most anything. I'll jist take a stretch here afore the fire on the floor; for I'm e'en a'most chilled to death, and awful sleepy too. First come,' says I, 'first sarved, you know's an old rule; and luck's the word nowadays. Yes, I'll jist take the hearthrug for it, and a good warm berth it is too.'

" 'Well,' says she, 'I can't think o' that at no rate. There's old Mrs. Fairns in the next street but one; she's got a spare bed she lets out sometimes. I'll send up to her to get it ready for you, and tomorrow these folks will be off, and then you can have your old quarters again.'

"So, arter supper, old Johnny Farquhar, the English help, showed me up to the widder's. She was considerable in years, but a cheerfulsome old lady and very pleasant; but she had a darter, the prettiest gal I ever see'd since I was created. There was sunthin' or other about her that made a body feel melancholy too. She was a lovely-lookin' critter, but her countenance was sad; she was tall and well-made, had beautiful-lookin' long black hair and black eyes; but oh! how pale she was! — and the only color she had was a little fever-like-lookin' red about her lips. She was dressed in black, which made her countenance look more marble like; and yet, whatever it was — natur', or consumption, or desartion, or settin' on the anxious benches, or what not — that made her look so, yet she hadn't fallen away one morsel, but was full-formed and well-waisted. I couldn't keep my eyes off her.

"I felt a kind o' interest in her. I seemed as if I'd like to hear her story, for sunthin' or another had gone wrong — that was clear; some little story of the heart, most like, for young gals are plaguy apt to have a tender spot thereabouts. She never smiled, and when she looked on me she looked so streaked and so sad, and cold withal, it made me kinder superstitious. Her voice, too, was so sweet, and yet so doleful, that I felt proper sorry, and amazin' curious too. Thinks I, 'I'll jist ax to-morrow all about her, for folks have pretty 'cute ears in Annapolis: there ain't a smack of a kiss that ain't heard all over the town in two twos, and sometimes they think they hear 'em even afore they happen. It's a'most a grand place for news, like all other small places I ever see'd.' Well, I tried jokin' and funny stories, and every kind o' thing to raise a larf, but all wouldn't do; she talked and listened and chatted away as if there was nothin' above partikiler; but still no smile; her face was cold, and clear, and bright as the icy surface of a lake, and so transparent, too, you could see the veins in it.

"Arter a while the old lady showed me to my chamber, and there was a fire in it: but, oh! my sakes, how cold! it was like goin' down into a well in summer; it made my blood fairly thicken agin. — Your tumbler is out, Squire; try a little more of that lemonade; that iced water is grand. —

"Well, I sot over the fire a space, and gathered up the little bits o' brands and kindlin' wood (for the logs were green, and wouldn't burn up at no rate); and then I ondressed and made a desperate jump right into the cold bed, with only half clothes enough on it for such weather, and wrapped up all the clothes round me. Well, I thought I should have died. The frost was in the sheets, and my breath looked like the steam from a boilin' tea-kettle, and it settled right down on the quilt, and froze into white hoar. The nails in the house cracked like a gun with a wet wad, they went off like thunder, and now and then you'd hear someone run along ever so fast, as if he couldn't show his nose to it for one minit, and the snow creakin' and crumplin' onder his feet, like a new shoe with a stiff sole to it. The fire wouldn't blaze no longer, and only gave up a blue smoke, and the glass in the winder looked fuzzy with the frost. Thinks I, 'I'll freeze to death to a sartainty. If I go for to drop off asleep, as sure as the world I'll never wake up agin. I've heerd tell of folks afore now feelin' dozy-like out in the cold, and layin' down to sleep, and goin' for it, and I don't half like to try it, I vow.' Well, I got considerable narvous like, and I kept awake near about all night; first I rubbed one foot agin t'other, then I doubled up all in a heap, and then rubbed all over with my hands. Oh! it was dismal, you may depend. At last I began to nod and doze, and fancy I see'd a flock o' sheep a-takin' a split for it over a wall, and tried to count 'em, one by one, and couldn't; and then I'd start up, and then nod agin. I felt it a-comin' all over, in spite of all I could do; and thinks I, 'It ain't so everlastin' long to daylight now; I'll try it anyhow, I'll be darned if I don't, so here goes!'

"Jist as I shot my eyes, and made up my mind for a nap, I hears a low moan and a sob; well, I sits up and listens, but all was silent agin. Nothin' but them etarnal nails a-goin' off, one arter t'other, like anything. Thinks I to myself, 'The wind's a-gettin' up, I estimate; it's as like as not we shall have a change o' weather.' Presently I heerd a light step on the entry, and the door opens softly, and in walks the widder's darter, on tip-toe, dressed in a long white wrapper; and after peerin' all round to see if I was asleep, she goes and sits down in the chimbly corner, and picks up the coals and fixes the fire, and sits a-lookin' at it for ever so long. Oh! so sad, and so melancholy; it was dreadful to see her. Says I to myself, says I, 'What on airth brings the poor critter here, all alone, this time o' night; and the air so plaguy cold too? I guess she thinks I'll freeze to death; or p'raps she's walkin' in her sleep.' But there she sot lookin' more like a ghost than a human. First she warmed one foot and then the other; and then held her hands over the coals, and moaned bitterly.

" 'Dear! dear!' thinks I, 'that poor critter is a freezin' to death as well as me; I do believe the world is a-comin' to an eend right off, and we shall all die of cold,' and I shivered all over. Presently she got up, and I saw her face, part covered with her long black hair, and the other parts so white and so cold, it chilled me to look at it, and her footsteps I consaited sounded louder, and I cast my eyes down to her feet, and I actilly did fancy they looked froze. Well, she come near the bed, and lookin' at me, stood for a space without stirrin', and then she cried bitterly. 'He, too, is doomed,' said she; 'he is in the sleep of death, and so far from home, and all his friends too.'

" 'Not yet,' said I, 'you dear critter you, not yet, you may depend; but you will be if you don't go to bed.' So says I, 'Do, for gracious' sake, return to your room, or you will perish.'

" 'It's frozen,' says she; 'it's deathly cold. The bed is a snow-wreath, and the piller is ice, and the coverlet is congealed; the chill has struck into my heart, and my blood has ceased to flow. I'm doomed, I'm doomed to die; and oh! how strange, how cold is death!'

"Well, I was all struck up of a heap; I didn't know what on airth to do. Says I to myself, says I, 'Here's this poor gal in my room carryin' on like ravin' distracted mad in the middle of the night here; she's oneasy in her mind, and is a-walkin' as sure as the world, and how it's a-goin' for to eend, I don't know; that's a fact.'

41

'Katey,' says I, 'dear, I'll get up and give you my bed if you are cold, and I'll go and make up a great rousin' big fire, and I'll call up the old lady, and she will see to you, and get you a hot drink; sunthin' must be done, to a sartainty, for I can't bear to hear you talk so.'

" 'No,' says she, 'not for the world! What will my mother say, Mr. Slick? and me here in your room, and nothin' but this wrapper on. It's too late now; it's all over;' and with that she fainted, and fell right across the bed. Oh, how cold she was; the chill struck into me; I feel it yet; the very thought is enough to give one the ague. Well, I'm a modest man, Squire— I was always modest from a boy; but there was no time for ceremony now, for there was a sufferin', dyin' critter — so I drew her in, and folded her in my arms, in hopes she would come to, but death was there.

"I breathed on her icy lips, but life seemed extinct, and every time I pressed her to me, I shrunk from her till my back touched the cold gypsum wall. It felt like a tomb, so chill, so damp, so cold — (you have no notion how cold them 'are kind o' walls are, they beat all natur') — squeezed between this frozen gal on one side, and the icy plaster on the other, I felt as if my own life was a-ebbin' away fast. 'Poor critter!' says I, 'has her care of me brought her to this pass? I'll press her to my heart once more; p'raps the little heat that's left there may revive her, and I can but die a few minutes sooner.' It was a last effort, but it succeeded; she seemed to breathe again. I spoke to her, but she couldn't answer, tho' I felt her tears flow fast on my bosom; but I was actilly sinking fast myself now. I felt my eend approachin'. Then came reflection; bitter and sad thoughts they were too, I tell you. 'Dear, dear!' said I; 'here's a pretty kettle o' fish, ain't there! We shall be both found dead here in the mornin', and what will folks say of this beautiful gal, and one of our free and enlightened citizens, found in such a scrape? Nothin' will be too bad for 'em that they can lay their tongues to, that's a fact: the Yankee villain, the cheatin' Clockmaker, the —'

"The thought gave my heart a jupe, so sharp, so deep, so painful, I awoke and found I was a-huggin' a snow-wreath, that had sifted through a hole in the roof on the bed; part had melted and trickled down my breast, and part had froze to the clothes and chilled me through. I woke up, proper glad it was all a dream, you may depend — but amazin' cold and dreadful stiff; and I was laid up at this place for three weeks, with the 'cute rheumatiz, that's a fact."

"But your pale young friend," said I, "did you ever see her again? Pray, what became of her?"

"Would you believe it?" said he; "the next mornin', when I came down, there sot Katey by the fire, lookin' as bloomin' as a rose, and as chipper as a canary bird. The fact is, I was so uncommon cold, and so sleepy too, the night afore, that I thought everybody and everything looked cold and dismal too.

" 'Mornin', sir,' said she, as I entered the keepin' room; 'mornin' to you, Mr. Slick! How did you sleep last night? I'm most afeerd you found that 'are room dreadful cold, for little Binney opened the window at the head of the bed to make the fire draw and start the smoke up, and forgot to shut it again, and I guess it was wide open all night. I minded it arter I got to bed, and I thought I should ha' died a-larfin'.'

" 'Thank you,' said I, 'for that; but you forgot you came and shot it yourself.'

" 'Me!' said she; 'I never did no such thing. Catch me, indeed, a-goin' into a gentleman's chamber; no, indeed, not for the world.'

" 'If I wasn't cold,' said I, 'it's a pity; that's all! I was e'en a'most frozen as stiff as a poker, and near about frightened to death too, for I see'd you or your ghost last night, as plain as I see you now; that's a fact.'

" 'A ghost!' said she; 'how you talk! do tell. Why, how was that?'

"Well, I told her the whole story from beginning to eend. First she larfed ready to split at my account of the cold room, and my bein' afeerd to go to sleep; but then she stopped pretty short, I guess, and blushed like anything when I told her about her comin' into the chamber, and looked proper frightened, not knowin' what was to come next; but when she heerd of her turnin' first into an icicle, and then a snow-drift she haw-hawed right out. I thought she actilly would have gone into hysterics.

" 'You might have frozen,' said she, 'in real right-down airnest, afore I'd a-gone into your chamber at that time o' night to see arter you, or your fire either,' said she, 'you may depend. I can't think what on airth could have put that 'are crotchet into your head.'

" 'Nor I neither,' said I. . . .

"There's another lemon left, Squire, s'pose we mix a little more sourin' afore we turn in, and take another glass to the widder's darter. "

—*The Clockmaker, Second Series, 1838*

A CURE FOR SMUGGLING

"Wherever *natur' does least, man does most,*" said the Clockmaker. "Jist see the difference atween these folks here to Liverpool and them up the bay of Fundy. There natur' has given them the finest country in the world — she has taken away all the soil from this place, and chucked it out there, and left nothin' but rocks and stones here. There they jist vegetate, but here they go ahead like anything. I was credibly informed, when Liverpool was first settled, folks had to carry little light ladders on their shoulders to climb over the rocks, and now they've got better streets, better houses, better gardens, and a better town than any of the baymen. They carry on a considerable of a fishery here, and do a great stroke in the timber business.

"I shall never forget a talk I had with Ichabod Gates here, and a frolic him and me had with the tide-waiter. Ichabod had a large store o' goods, and I was in there one evenin' a-drinkin' tea along with him, and we got a-talkin' about smugglin'. Says he, 'Mr. Slick, your people ruin the trade here, they *do* smuggle so; I don't know as I ever shall be able to get rid of my stock of goods, and it cost me a considerable of a sum too. What a pity it is them navy people, instead of carryin' freights of money from the West Indgies, warn't employed more a-protectin' of our fisheries and our trade.' 'Why don't you smuggle then, too,' says I, 'and meet 'em in their own way? — tit for tat — diamond cut diamond — smuggle yourselves and seize *them;* — free trade and sailors' rights is our maxim.' 'Why,' says he, 'I ain't jist altogether certified that it's right; it goes agin my conscience to do the like o' that 'are, and I must say I like a fair deal. In a gineral way a'most, I've observed what's got over the devil's back is commonly lost under his belly.

It don't seem to wear well.' 'Well, that's onconvenient too, to be so thin-skinned,' said I; 'for conscience most commonly has a hide as thick as the sole of one's foot; you may cover it with leather to make it look decent-like, but it will bear a considerable hard scrubbin' without anythin' over it. Now,' says I, 'I will put you on a track that will sarve you without bringin' corns on your conscience either. Do you jist pretend to smuggle and make believe as if you were a-goin' the whole hog in it. It's safer and full out as profitable as the raal thing, and, besides, there's no sort o' risk in it in the world. When folks hear a thing is smuggled they always think it's cheap, and never look into the price; they bite directly — it's a grand bait that. Now always onload your vessels at night, and let folks hear a cart a-goin' into your place atween two and three o'clock in the mornin'; fix one o' the axles so it will squeak like a pig, and do you look suspicious, mysterious, and oneasy. Says you (when a chap says, I guess you were up late last night), ax me no questions, and I'll tell you no lies. There are so many pimpin' eyes about now, a body has to be cautious if he don't want to get into the centre of a hobble. If I'm up late, I guess it's nobody's business but my own I'm about, anyhow; but I hope you won't make no remarks about what you see'd or heerd.

"Well, when a feller axes arter a thing, do you jist stand and look at him for a space without sayin' a word, inquirin' like, with a dubersum' look, as if you didn't know as you could trust him or no; then jist wink, put your finger on your nose, and say mum is the word. Take a candle and light it, and say, foller me now, and take him into the cellar. Now, says you, friend, don't betray me, I beseech you, for your life; don't let on to anyone about this place; people will never think o' suspectin' me, if you only keep dark about it. I'll let you see some things, says you, that will please you, I know; but don't blow me — that's a good soul. This article, says you, a-takin' up one that cost three pounds, I can afford to let you have as low as five pounds, and that one as cheap as six pounds, on one condition — but, mind you, it's on them tarms only — and that is, that you don't tell anyone, not even your wife, where you got it; but you must promise me on the word and honor of a man. The critter will fall right into the trap, and swear by all that's good he'll never breathe it to a livin' soul, and then go right off and tell his wife; and you might as well pour a thing into a filterin' stone as into a woman's ear. It will run right thro', and she'll go a-braggin' to her neighbors of the bargain they got, and swear them to secrecy, and they'll tell the whole country in the same way, as a secret, of the cheap things Ichabod Gates has. Well, the excise folks will soon hear o' this, and come and sarch your house from top to bottom, and the sarch will make your fortin'; for, as they can't find nothin', you will get the credit of doin' the officers in great style.

" 'Well, well,' said Ichabod, 'if you Yankees don't beat all natur'. I don't believe on my soul there's a critter in all Nova Scotia would 'a thought o' such a scheme as that; but it's a grand joke, and comports with conscience, for it paralls pretty close with the truth; I'll try it. 'Try it,' says I, 'to be sure; let's go right off this blessed night and hide away a parcel of your goods in the cellar — put some in the garrat and some in the gig-house. Begin and sell tomorrow, and all the time I'm in Liverpool I'll keep a-runnin' in and out o' your house; sometimes I'll jist come to the corner of the fence, put my head over and draw it back agin, as if I didn't want folks to see me, and sometimes I'll make as if I was a-goin' out, and if I see anyone a-comin' I'll spring back and hide behind the door: it will set the whole town on the look-out — and they'll say it's me that's a-smugglin' either on my own hook or your'n.' In three days he had a great run o' custom particularly arter nightfall. It was fun alive to see how the critters were bammed by that hoax.

"On the fifth day the tide-waiter came. 'Mr. Slick,' says he, 'I've information th —' 'Glad to hear it,' says I; 'an officer without information would be a poor tool — that's a fact.' Well, it brought him up all a-standin'. Says he, 'Do you know who you are a-talkin' to?' 'Yes,' says I, 'I guess I do; I'm talkin' to a man of information, and that bein' the case, I'll be so bold as to ax you one question — have you anything to say to me, for I'm in a considerable of a hurry?' 'Yes,' said he, 'I have. I'm informed you have smuggled goods in the house.' 'Well, then,' says I, 'you can say what many gals can't boast on, at any rate.' 'What's that?' says he. 'Why,' says I, 'that you are *miss*informed.'

" 'Mr. Gates,' said he, 'give me a candle — I must go to the cellar,' 'Sartainly, sir,' said Ichabod, 'you may sarch where you please. I've never smuggled yet, and I am not a-goin' now to commence at my time of life.' As soon as he got the candle, and was a-goin' down to the cellar with Gates, I called out to Ichabod. 'Here,' says I, 'Ich, run quick, for your life — now's your time;' and off we ran upstairs as hard as we could leg it, and locked the door; the sarcher heerin' that, up too and arter us hot foot, and bust open it. As soon as we heerd him a-doin' of that, we out o' the other door and locked that also, and down the back stairs to where we started from. It was some time afore he broke in the second door, and then he follered us down, lookin' like a proper fool. 'I'll pay you up for this,' said he to me. 'I hope so,' said I, 'and Ichabod too. A pretty time o' day this, when folks can tare and race over a decent man's house, and smash all afore him this way for nothin', ain't it? Them doors you broke all to pieces will come to sunthin', you may depend; a joke is a joke, but that's no joke.' After that he took his time, searched the cellar, upper rooms, lower rooms, and garrat, and found nothin' to seize; he was all cut up, and amazin' vexed and put out. Says I: 'Friend, if you want to catch a weasel, you must catch him asleep; now, if you want to catch me a-smug-glin', rise considerably airly in the mornin', will you?' This story made Ichabod's fortin' a'most; he had smuggled goods to sell for three years, and yet no one could find him in the act, or tell where onder the sun he had hid 'em away to. At last the secret leaked out, and it fairly broke up smugglin' on the whole shore. That story has done more nor twenty officers — that's a fact.

"There's nothin' a'most," said the Clockmaker, "I like so much as to see folks cheat themselves. I don't know as I ever cheated a man myself in my life. I like to do things above board handsum', and go straight ahead; but if a chap seems bent on cheatin' himself, I like to be neighborly, and help him to do it. . . . "

— The Clockmaker, Second Series, 1838

THE PRINCE DE JOINVILLE'S HORSE

". . . The machinery of the colonies is good enough in itself, but it wants a safety valve," [said the Rev. Mr. Hopewell]. "When the pressure within is too great, there should be something devised to let off the steam. This is a subject well worthy of your consideration; and if you [*i.e.*, the Squire] have an opportunity of conversing with any of the ministry, pray draw their attention to it. By not understanding this, the English have caused one revolution at home, and another in America."

"Exactly," said Mr. Slick, "It reminds me of what I once saw done by the Prince de Joinville's horse, on the Halifax road."

"Pardon me," said Mr. Hopewell, "you shall have an opportunity presently of telling your story of the Prince's horse, but suffer me to proceed.

"England, besides other outlets, has a never-failing one in the colonies, but the colonies have no outlet. Cromwell and Hampden were actually embarked on board of a vessel in the Thames, for Boston, when they were prevented from sailing by an Order in Council. What was the consequence? The sovereign was dethroned. Instead of leading a small sect of fanatical puritans, and being the first men of a village in Massachusetts, they aspired to be the first men in an empire, and succeeded. So in the old colonies. Had Washington been sent abroad in command of a regiment, Adams to govern a colony, Franklin to make experiments in an observatory like that at Greenwich, and a more extended field been opened to colonial talent, the United States would still have continued to be dependencies of Great Britain.

"There is no room for men of talent in British America; and by not affording them an opportunity of distinguishing themselves, or rewarding them when they do, they are always ready to make one, by opposition. In comparing their situation with that of the British Isles, they feel that they labor under disabilities; these disabilities they feel as a degradation; and as those who impose that degradation live a thousand miles off, it becomes a question whether it is better to suffer or resist."

"The Prince de Joinville's horse," said Mr. Slick, "is a case in pint."

"One moment, Sam," said Mr. Hopewell.

"The very word 'dependencies' shows the state of the colonies. If they are to be retained, they should be incorporated with Great Britain. The people should be made to feel, not that they are colonists, but Englishmen. They may tinker at constitutions as much as they please; the root of the evil lies deeper than statesmen are aware of. O'Connell, when he agitates for a repeal of the Union, if he really has no ulterior objects beyond that of an Irish Parliament, does not know what he is talking about. If his request were granted, Ireland would become a province, and descend from being an integral part of the empire, into a dependency. Had he ever lived in a colony, he would have known the tendencies of such a condition.

"What I desire to see is the very reverse. Now that steam has united the two continents of Europe and America, in such a manner that you can travel from Nova Scotia to England in as short a time as it once required to go from Dublin to London, I should hope for a united legislature. Recollect that the distance from New Orleans to the head of the Mississippi River is greater than from Halifax, Nova Scotia, to Liverpool, Great Britain. I do not want to see colonists and Englishmen arrayed against each other, as different races, but united as one people, having the same rights and privileges, each bearing a share of the public burdens, and all having a voice in the general government.

"The love of distinction is natural to man. Three millions of people cannot be shut up in a colony. They will either turn on each other, or unite against their keepers. The road that leads to retirement in the provinces should be open to those whom the hope of distinction invites to return and contend for the honors of the empire. At present the egress is practically closed."

"If you was to talk for ever, Minister," said Mr. Slick, "you couldn't say more than the Prince de Joinville's hoss on that subject."

The interruption was very annoying; for no man I ever met, so thoroughly understands the subject of colonial government as Mr. Hopewell. His experience is greater than that of any man now living, and his views more enlarged and more philosophical.

"Go on, Sam," said he, with great good humor. "Let us hear what the Prince's horse said."

"Well," said Mr. Slick, "I don't jist exactly mean to say he spoke as Balaam's donkey did, in good English or French nother; but he did that that spoke a whole book, with a handsum wood-cut to the fore, and that's a fact.

"About two years ago, one mortal brilin' hot day, as I was a-pokin' along the road from Halifax to Windsor, with Old Clay in the wagon, with my coat off, a-ridin' in my shirtsleeves, and a-thinkin' how slick a mint-julep would travel down red-lane, if I had it, I heard such a chatterin' and laughin' and screamin' as I never a'most heerd afore, since I was raised.

" 'What in natur' is this,' sais I, as I gave Old Clay a crack of the whip, to push on. 'There is some critters here I guess, that have found a haw haw's nest, with a tee hee's egg in it. What's in the wind now?' Well, a sudden turn of the road brought me to where they was, and who should they be but French officers from the Prince's ship, travellin' incog. in plain clothes. But, Lord bless you, cook a Frenchman any way you please, and you can't disguise him. Natur' will out, in spite of all, and the name of a Frencher is written as plain as anything in his whiskers, and his hair, and his skin, and his coat, and his boots, and his air, and his gait, and in everythin', but only let him open his mouth, and the cat's out of the bag in no time, ain't it? They are droll boys, is the French, that's a fact.

"Well, there was four on 'em dismounted, a-holdin' of their hosses by the bridle, and a-standin' near a spring of nice cool water; and there was a fifth, and he was a-layin' down belly flounder on the ground, a-tryin' to drink out of the runnin' spring.

" 'Parley vous French,' sais I, 'Mountsheer?' At that, they sot to, and larfed again more than ever, I thought they would have gone into the high strikes, they hee-hawed so.

"Well, one on 'em, that was a Duke, as I found out arterwards, said 'O yees, Sare, we spoked English too.'

" 'Lawful heart!' sais I, 'what's the joke?'

" 'Why,' sais he, 'look there, Sare.' And then they larfed agin, ready to split; and sure enough, no sooner had the Leftenant layed down to drink, then the Prince's hoss kneeled down, and put his head jist over his neck, and began to drink too. Well, the officer couldn't get up for the hoss, and he couldn't keep his face out of the water for the hoss, and he couldn't drink for the hoss, and he was almost choked to death, and as black in the face as your hat. And the Prince and the officers larfed so, they couldn't help him, if they was to die for it.

"Sais I to myself, 'A joke is a joke, if it tante carried too far, but this critter will be strangled, as sure as a gun, if he lays here splutterin' this way much longer.'

So I jist gives the hoss a dab in the mouth, and made him git up; and then sais I, 'Prince,' sais I, for I know'd him by his beard, he had one exactly like one of the old saints' heads in an Eyetalian pictur', all dressed to a pint, so sais I, 'Prince,' and a plaguy handsum man he is too, and as full of fun as a kitten, so sais I, 'Prince,' and what's better, all his officers seemed plaguy proud and fond of him too; so sais I, 'Prince, voilà le condition of one colonist, which,' sais I, 'Prince, means in English, that leftenant is jist like a colonist.'

" 'Commong,' says he, 'how is dat?'

" 'Why,' sais I, 'Prince, whenever a colonist goes for to drink at a spring of the good things in this world (and plaguy small springs they have here too), and fairly lays down to it, jist as he gets his lips cleverly to it, for a swig, there is some cussed neck or another, of some confounded Britisher, pops right over him, and pins him there. He can't get up, he can't back out, and he can't drink, and he is blacked and blued in the face, and most choked with the weight.'

" 'What country was you man of?' said he, for he spoke very good for a Frenchman.

"With that I straightened myself up, and looked dignified, for I know'd I had a right to be proud, and no mistake; sais I, 'Prince, I am an American citizen.' How them two words altered him. P'raps there beant no two words to ditto 'em. He looked for all the world like a different man when he see'd I wasn't a mean onsarcumsised colonist." . . .

— *The Attaché, First Series, 1843*

["*WE* HAVE NO SLAVES"]

"Yes," said Mr. Slick, pursuing the same subject of conversation; "I like the English sarvant. Sarvice is a trade here, and a house-help sarves an apprenticeship to it, is master of his work, and onderstands his business. He don't feel kinder degraded by it, and ain't therefore above it. Nothin' ain't so bad as a crittur bein' above his business. He is a part of his master here. Among other folks' sarvants he takes his master's title. See these two fellers meet now, and hear them. — 'Ah, Lothian! how are you?' 'All right; how are you, Douro? It's an age since I saw you.' Ain't that droll now? A cotton-spinner's sarvant is a snob to these folks. He ain't a man of fashion. They don't know him — he uses a tallow candle, and drinks beer; he ain't a fit associate for one who uses a wax, and drinks wine. They have their rank and *position* in socie*ty* as well as their masters, them fellers; and to my mind they are the best off of the two, for they have no care. Yes, they are far above our helps, I must say; but their misfortunate niggers here are a long chalk below our slaves to the south, and the cotton-manufacturers are a thousand times harder task-masters than our cotton planters, that's a fact."

"Negroes!" I said in some astonishment; "why, surely you are aware *we* have emancipated our negroes. *We* have no slaves."

"Come, Squire," said he, "now don't git your back up with me; but for goodness gracious sake never say *we*. It would make folks snicker here to hear you say that. It's as bad as a sarvant sayin' 'our castle' — 'our park' — 'our pictur' gallery,' and so on. What right have you to say 'We?' You ain't an Englishman, and old Bull won't thank you for your familiarity, I know. You had better say, 'Our army,'

48

though you have nothin' to do with it; or 'our navy,' though you form no part of it; or 'our House of Lords,' and you can't boast one Lord; or 'our House of Commons,' and you hante a single blessed member there; or 'our authors,' — well, p'raps you may say that, because you are an exception: but the only reason you warn't shot, was that you was the fust colonial bird that flew across the Atlantic, and you was saved as a curiosity, and will be stuffed some day or another, and stuck up in a museum. The next one will be pinked, for fear he should cross the breed. — 'Our!' heavens and airth! I wonder you hante too much pride to say that; it's too sarvanty for the like o' you. How can you call yourself a part of an empire, in the government of which you have no voice? — from whose honors you are excluded, from whose sarvice you are shut out? — by whom you are looked on as a consumer of iron and cotton goods, as a hewer of wood for the timber market, a curer of fish to freight their vessels — as worth havin', because you afford a station for an admiral, a place for a governor, a command for a gineral; because, like the stone steps to a hall door, you enable others to rise, but never move yourselves. 'Our!' It makes me curl inwardly to hear you use that word 'Our.' I'll tell you what a colonial 'Our' is. I'll tell you what awaits you: in the process of a few years, after your death, all your family will probably sink into the class of laborers. Some on 'em may struggle on for a while, and maintain the position you have; but it won't be long. Down, down, down they must go; rise they never can. It is as impossible for a colonist to rise above the surface, as for a stone to float on a river. Every one knows this but yourself, and that is the reason gentlemen will not go and live among you. They lose caste — they descend on the scale of life — they cease to be Romans. Din this for ever in the ears of British statesmen: tell them to make you Englishmen, or to give you a Royal Prince for a King, and make you a new people. But that to be made fun of by the Yankees, to be looked down upon by the English, and to be despised by yourselves, is a condition that you only desarve as long as you tolerate it. No, don't use that word 'Our' till you are entitled to it. Be formal, and everlastin' polite. Say 'your' empire, 'your' army, etc.; and never strut under borrowed feathers and say 'our,' till you can point to your own members in both houses of Parliament — to your own country-men fillin' such posts in the imperial sarvice as they are qualified for by their talents, or entitled to in right of the population they represent; and if anybody is struck up of a heap by your sayin' 'yours' instead of 'ours,' tell them the reason; say — that was a lesson I learnt from Sam Slick, the clockmaker; and one thing is sartin, to give the devil his due, that feller was 'no fool,' at any rate. But to git back to what we was a-talkin' of. We have two kinds of niggers in the States — free niggers and slaves. In the north they are all free, in the south all in bondage. Now the free nigger may be a member of Congress, but he can't get there; he may be President, but he guesses he can't, and he reckons right. He may marry Tyler's darter, but she won't have him; he may be ambassador to the Court of St. James's, Victoria, if he could be only appointed; or he may command the army or the navy if they'd only let him — that's his condition. The slave is a slave, and that's his condition. Now the English have two sorts of niggers — American colonists, who are free white niggers; and manufacturers' laborers at home, and they are white slave niggers. A white colonist, like our free black nigger, may be a member of Parliament, but he can't get there; he may *be* a governor, but he guesses he can't, and he guesses right; he may marry an English nobleman's darter, if she'd only have him; he may be an ambassador to our Court at Washington, if he could be only appointed; he may command the army or the fleet, if he had the commission; and that's his condition. — A colonist and a free nigger don't differ in anythin' but color: both have naked rights, but they have no power given 'em to clothe those rights, and that's the naked truth.

"Your blockheads of Liberals to Canada are for ever yelpin' about 'sponsible government; if it was all they think it is, what would be the good of it? Now, I'll tell you the remedy. Don't repeal the Union, lay down your life fust, but have a closer union. Let 'em form a Colonial council board to London, and appoint some colonists to it, that they may feel they have some voice in the government of the empire. Let 'em raise provincial regiments, and officer them with natives, that you may have somethin' to do with the army. Let 'em have some man-of-war devoted to Colony offices, that you may have somethin' to do with the navy. All you've got in that line is a miserable little cutter, paid by yourselves, commanded by one of yourselves, Captain Darby: and he has sot a proper pattern to your navy. He has seized more Yankee vessels in the last seven years for breakin' the fish treaty, than all the admirals and all the squadrons on the American coast has, put together twice over. He and his vessel costs you a few hundred a-year; them fleets durin' that time has cost more nor all Halifax would sell for tomorrow, if put up to vandu. He desarves a feather in his cap from your Government, which he won't get, and a tar-jacket covered with feathers from us, which he is very likely to get. Yes, have some man-o'-war there with colony officers like him, then say 'our navy,' if you like. Remove the restrictions on colonial clergy, so that if they desarve promotion in the church to Britain, they needn't be shut out among big bogs, black logs, and thick fogs, for ever and ever; and then it tante the Church of England, but 'our church.' If there is a feller everlastin' strong in a colony, don't make it his interest to wrastle with a Governor; but send him to another province, and make him one himself. Let 'em have a Member to Parliament, and he will be a safety valve to let off steam. It's then 'our Parliament.' Open the door to youngsters, and let 'em see stars, ribbons, garters, coronets, and all a-hangin' up agin the wall, and when their mouths water, and they lick their chops as if they'd like a taste of them, then say, — 'Now d--n you, go ahead an win 'em, and if you win the race you shall have 'em, and if you lose, turn to, import some gentlemen and improve the breed, and mind your trainin', and try agin; all you got to do, is to win. Go ahead, I'll bet on you, if you try.' Let 'death or victory' be your colony motto — Westminster Abbey or the House of Lords. Go ahead, my young 'coons, wake snakes, and walk your chalks, streak it off like 'iled lightnin', and whoever gets in first, wins. Yes, that's the remedy. But now they have no chance. . . ."

—*The Attaché, Second Series, 1844*

VALEDICTORY ADDRESS

. . . Neither the "Clockmaker" nor the "Attaché" were ever designed as books of travels, but to portray character — to give practical lessons in morals, and politics — to expose hypocrisy — to uphold the connection between the parent country and the colonies, to develop the resources of the province and to enforce the just claims of my countrymen — to discountenance agitation — to strengthen the union between Church and State — and to foster and excite a love for our own form of government, and a preference of it over all others. So many objects necessarily required several continuations of the work, and although seven volumes warn me not to trespass too long on the patience of the public, yet many excluded topics make me feel, with regret, that I have been either too diffuse, or too presumptuous. Prolixity was unavoidable from another cause. In order to attain my objects, I found it expedient so to intermingle humor with the several topics, so as to render subjects attractive that in themselves are generally considered as too deep and dry for general reading. All these matters, however, high and difficult as they are to discuss properly, are exhausted and hackneyed enough. But little that is new can now be said upon them. The only attraction they are susceptible of is the novelty of a new dress. That I have succeeded in rendering them popular by clothing them in the natural language, and illustrating them by the humor of a shrewd and droll man like Mr. Slick, their unprecedented circulation, on both sides of the Atlantic, leaves me no room to doubt, while I am daily receiving the most gratifying testimony of the beneficial effects they have produced, and are still producing in the colonies, for whose use they were principally designed. Much as I value the popularity of these works, I value their utility much higher, and of the many benefits that have accrued to myself as the author, and they have been most numerous, none have been so grateful as that of knowing that "they have done good."

— The Attaché, Second Series, 1844

JOSEPH HOWE

(1804-1873)

Joseph Howe was born near Halifax. His father, a Loyalist from Boston, was a journalist and printer who for many years held the offices of King's Printer and Postmaster General for the Maritime Provinces. At thirteen, young Howe was apprenticed to the printing trade. In December 1827, after a year's experience as part-owner of the Acadian, *Howe purchased the* Novascotian *and became its sole proprietor and editor. During the next eight years he travelled extensively throughout Nova Scotia, getting to know his province and his readers and becoming well known himself. In 1835 his successful defence of himself in the famous trial for libel led to his election to the local Assembly, where he became leader of the Reform Party and helped win the fight for responsible government in Nova Scotia.*

In later life, Howe held various offices in the public service, including those of Provincial Secretary, Chief Commissioner of the Railway Board, Premier of Nova Scotia, and Cabinet Member under Sir John A. Macdonald. On May 6, 1873, he was appointed Lieutenant-Governor of Nova Scotia, but he died a few weeks later. Howe's publications consist largely of public papers and addresses. His one volume of belletristic writings — Poems and Essays — was published posthumously.

THE FLAG OF OLD ENGLAND

A Centenary Song, written for the one hundredth anniversary of the landing
of Lord Cornwallis at Halifax [in 1749]

All hail to the day when the Britons came over,
   And planted their standard, with sea-foam still wet,
Around and above us their spirits will hover,
   Rejoicing to mark how we honor it yet.
Beneath it the emblems they cherished are waving,
   The Rose of Old England the roadside perfumes;
The Shamrock and Thistle the north winds are braving,
   Securely the Mayflower* blushes and blooms.

Chorus

Hail to the day when the Britons came over,
   And planted their standard with sea-foam still wet,
Around and above us their spirits will hover,
   Rejoicing to mark how we honor it yet.
     We'll honor it yet, we'll honor it yet,
     The flag of Old England! we'll honor it yet.

In the temples they founded, their faith is maintained,
   Every foot of the soil they bequeathed is still ours,
The graves where they moulder, no foe has profaned,
   But we wreathe them with verdure, and strew them with flowers!
The blood of no brother, in civil strife pour'd,
   In this hour of rejoicing, encumbers our souls!
The frontier's the field for the Patriot's sword,
   And curs'd be the weapon that Faction controls!

Chorus — Hail to the day, etc.

Then hail to the day! 'tis with memories crowded,
   Delightful to trace 'midst the mists of the past,
Like the features of Beauty, bewitchingly shrouded,
   They shine through the shadows Time o'er them has cast.
As travellers track to its source in the mountains,
   The stream, which far swelling, expands o'er the plains,
Our hearts, on this day, fondly turn to the fountains
   Whence flow the warm currents that bound in our veins.

Chorus — Hail to the day, etc.

And proudly we trace them: No warrior flying
   From city assaulted, and fanes overthrown,
With the last of his race on the battlements dying,
   And weary with wandering, founded our own.

*The Mayflower is the emblem of the Province of Nova Scotia.

From the Queen of the Islands, then famous in story,
  A century since, our brave forefathers came,
And our kindred yet fill the wide world with her glory,
  Enlarging her Empire, and spreading her name.

Chorus — Hail to the day, etc.

Ev'ry flash of her genius our pathway enlightens —
  Ev'ry field she explores we are beckoned to tread,
Each laurel she gathers, our future day brightens —
  We joy with her living, and mourn for her dead.
Then hail to the day when the Britons came over,
  And planted their standard, with sea-foam still wet,
Above and around us their spirits shall hover,
  Rejoicing to mark how we honor it yet.

Chorus — Hail to the day, etc.

—*1874*

FROM ACADIA

I

[Before the coming of the white man]

But see, where breaking through the leafy
    wood,
The Micmac bends beside the tranquil flood,
Launches his light canoe from off the strand,
And plies his paddle with a dexterous hand;
Or, as his bark along the water glides,
With slender spear his simple meal provides;
Or mark his agile figure, as he leaps
From crag to crag, and still his footing keeps,
For fast before him flies the desp'rate Deer,
For life is sweet, and death she knows is near.
No hound or horse assist him in the chase,
His hardy limbs are equal to the race,
For, since he left, unswathed, his mother's
    back
They've been familiar with each sylvan track;
They've borne him daily, as they bear him now,
Swift through the wood, and o'er the mountain's
    brow —
But mark — his bow is bent, his arrow flies,
And at his feet the bleeding victim dies.

While o'er the fallen tenant of the wild
A moment stands the forest's dusky child
From his dark brow his long and glossy hair
Is softly parted by the gentle air.
The glow of pride has flush'd his manly cheek,

And in his eye his kindled feelings speak.
For, as he casts his proud and fearless glance,
O'er each fair feature of the wide expanse,
The blushing flowers — the groves of stately
    pine —
The glassy lakes that in the sunbeams shine —
The swelling sea — the hills that heavenward
    soar —
The mountain stream, meandering to the shore—
Or hears the birds' blythe song, the woods'
    deep tone —
He feels, yes proudly feels, 'tis all his own . . . .

  With practised skill he soon divides his prey,
Then to his home pursues his devious way . . . .

  Some slender poles, with tops together bound,
And butts inserted firmly in the gound,
Form the rude frames — o'er which are closely
    laid
Birch bark and fir boughs, forming grateful
    shade,
And shelter from the storm, and sunny ray
Of summer noon, or winter's darker day.
A narrow opening, on the leeward side,
O'er which a skin is negligently tied,
Forms the rude entrance to the Indian's home—
Befitting portal for so proud a dome.
A fire is blazing brightly on the ground —

The motley inmates scatter'd careless round.
Some strip the maple, some the dye prepare,
Or weave the basket with assiduous care;
Others, around the box of bark entwine
Quills, pluck'd from off the "fretful porcupine,"
And which may form, when curiously inlaid,
A bridal offering to some dark-eyed maid.
Some shape the bow, some form the feather'd
     dart,
Which soon may quiver in a foeman's heart.
The Squaws proceed, upon the coals to broil,
Steaks cut from off the newly furnished spoil,
And these with lobsters, roasted in the shell,
And eels, by Indian palates loved so well,
Complete their frugal feast, for sweet content,
Which thrones have not, makes rich the Indian's
     tent.

   As to the West the glorious Sun retires,
The Micmacs kindle up their smouldering fires,
The aged Chiefs around the tents repose,
The dark Papoose to laugh and gambol goes;
While youths and maidens to the green advance,
And clustering round, prepare them for the
     dance.
Nor smile ye modern fair, who float along,
The dazzling spirits of the nightly throng,
Wafted by mingled music's softest tone,
With fashion's every grace around ye thrown,
Smile not at those, who, ere your sires were
     born,
Danced on the very spot you now adorn,
Kindling, with laughing eyes, love's hallow'd
     fire,
And swelling gallant hearts with fond desire.

   Crossing his legs upon a mossy seat,
With maple wand a youth begins to beat
On some dried bark, with measured time and
     slow,
A soft low tune — his voice's solemn flow
Mingling with every stroke. The dance begins,
Not such as now the modern fair one wins
To mazy evolutions, wild and free,
Where forms of radiant beauty seem to be
Like heavenly planets, whirling round at will,
Yet by fixed laws controll'd and govern'd still,
But slow and measured as the music's tone,
To which the dancers first beat time alone,

Murm'ring a low response. A broken shout,
To mark the changing time, at times rings out,
When all is soft, and faint, and slow again,
Till, by degrees, the music's swelling strain,
Sweeps through the Warriors' souls with
     rushing tide,
Rousing each thought of glory and of pride;
Then, while the deeds of other days return,
By music's power clothed in words that burn,
When ev'n the Dead, evoked by mem'ry's spell,
Burst into life, to fight where once they fell,
A savage joy the dancers' eyes bespeak,
A deeper tinge pervades each maiden's cheek,
The glossy clusters of their long dark hair
Are floating wildly on the ev'ning air,
As from the earth, with frantic bounds they
     spring,
And rock and grove with shouts of triumph ring.
Thus we may see the River steal along
Noiseless and slow, till growing deep and strong,
Its turbid waters foam, and curve, and leap,
Dashing with startling echo down the steep....

II
[*First settlers*]

   Thus, while Acadia's charms my eye surveys,
My soul, unbidden, turns to other days,
When the stout-hearted rear'd amidst the wood,
Their sylvan Homes, and by their thresholds
     stood
With stern resolve the savage tribes to brave,
And win a peaceful dwelling, or a grave. . . .

   They felled the forest trees with sturdy stroke,
The virgin soil, with gentle culture broke,
Scatter'd the fruitful seeds the stumps between,
And Ceres lured to many a sylvan scene.
Then rose the Log House by the water side,
Its seams by moss and seaweed well supplied,
Its roof with bark o'erspread — its humble
     door
Hung on a twisted withe — the earth its floor,
With stones and harden'd clay its chimney
     form'd,
Its spacious hearth by hissing green wood
     warmed,
Round which, as night her deep'ning shadows
     throws,

The Hamlet's wearied inmates circling close.
The sturdy settler lays his axe aside,
Which all day long has quell'd the forest's
    pride.
The wooden cleats that from the walls extend,
Receive his gun, his oft tried faithful friend,
Which crowns his frugal board with plenteous
    meals,
And guards his rest when sleep his eyelids
    seals . . . .

[*A massacre by Micmac Indians*]

When sleep had closed the weary cottar's eyes,
They sought to take the slumberers by
    surprise —
Essay'd the door, and then the window tried
With gentle pressure, studiously applied,
Nor knew how light a doting mother sleeps,
When near her babes its watch the spirit keeps.
The first faint whisper of alarm within,
Convinced them force, not fraud, their prey
    must win.
'Twas then their shout of fierce defiance rose,
While fast and vehement their heavy blows
On door and shutter diligently fell,
Each followed by a wild tumultuous yell;
Nor are the inmates idle — logs of wood,
Trunks, cribs, whate'er can make defences
    good,
Are piled against the bars that still are true,
Despite the efforts of the howling crew.
This done, the gun is seized — the Father fires,
Chance guides — a groan — one bleeding
    wretch expires.
Again he loads, again a savage dies —
Again the yells upon the welkin rise,
Hope half persuades that till the dawn of day
The fierce besiegers may be kept at bay.
What scene so dark, what stroke of fate so rude,
That Hope cannot a moment's space intrude?
But soon he flies, for now an Indian flings
Himself upon the roof, which loudly rings
To every stroke the polished hatchet lends;
The bark which bears him, to the pressure
    bends,
It yields — it breaks — he falls upon the floor —
One blow — his fleeting term of life is o'er,
The settler's axe has dashed his reeking brain

Upon the hearth his soul had sworn to stain.
Fast through the breach two others downward
    leap,
But, ere they rise, a knife is planted deep
In one dark breast, by gentle Woman's hand,
Who, for her household, wields a household
    brand;
The axe has clove the other to the chin.
But now, *en masse*, the shrieking fiends leap in,
Till wounded, faint, o'erpowered, the Father
    falls
And hears the shout of triumph shake his walls.
The wretched Mother from her babe is torn,
Which on a red right hand aloft is borne,
Then dashed to earth before its Parent's eyes,
And, as its form, deform'd and quivering lies,
Life from its fragile tenement is trod,
And the bruised, senseless, and unsightly clod,
Is flung into the soft but bleeding breast
To which so late in smiling peace 'twas
    press'd.

Nor does the boy escape — the smouldering
    fire
Is stirred, — and, as its feeble flames aspire
In wanton cruelty they thrust his hands
Into the blaze, and on the reddening brands,
Like Montezuma bid him seek repose,
As though his couch were but a perfumed rose.
Sated with blood, at length the scalps they
    tear
Ere life be yet extinct — for these, with care,
The Indian tribes, like precious coins, retain
To count their victories, and the victims slain.

Now plunder follows death—then one applies
Fire to the bed, from which the flames arise
Fiercely and fast, as anxious to efface
All record of so sad, so foul a place.
Around the cot the Indians form a ring,
And songs of joy and triumph wildly sing
With horrid gesture and demoniac strain,
Then plunge into the forest depths again.

Such are the scenes Acadia once display'd;
Such was the price our gallant Fathers paid
For this fair land, where now our footsteps
    rove
From lake to sea, from cliff to shady grove,

Uncheck'd by peril, unrestrained by fear
Of more unfriendly ambush lingering near
Than timid rabbits lurking in the fern
And peeping forth your worst intent to learn;
Or mottled squirrel, frisking round the pines
To seek the buds on which he lightly dines; ...

III

[*Acadia now*]

O'er the stout hearts that death and danger
   braved,
The flag of Britain soon victorious waved,
And races, hostile once, now freely blend
In happy union, each the other's friend;
Striving as nobly for the general good
As once their fathers strove in fields of blood.
Here England's sons, by fortune led to roam,
Now find a peaceful and a happy home;
The Scotchman rears his dwelling by some
   stream,
So like to that which blends with boyhood's
   dream,
That present joys with old world thoughts
   combined
Repress the sigh for those he left behind;
And here the wanderer from green Erin's shore
Tastes of delights he seldom knew before.

He toils beneath no law's unequal weight,
No rival parties tempt his soul to hate;
No lordly Churchman passes o'er his field,
To share the fruits the generous seasons
   yield.
With joy, Acadia welcomes to her strand
These venturous wanderers from their
   Fatherland —
A Mother's love bestows — with pride,
   beholds
Them mark the charms her simple form
   unfolds —
Then to her breast with filial rapture cling,
And cast their lot beneath her pleasant wing.

   With equal pride a numerous race she rears,
Sons of those sires who braved the Indian
   spears;
And those who've sprung from that devoted
   band,
Who, when rebellion reared its impious hand,
Spite of her faults, to Albion's standard true,
Fought 'neath its folds, till fate her power
   o'erthrew;
Then sought amidst Acadia's wilds to claim
A Briton's feelings, and a Briton's name.

                        —*1874*

SUSANNA MOODIE

(1803-1885)

Susanna Strickland was one of a family of nine children, six of whom were to write books of varying importance in such fields as poetry, history, science, biography, and fiction. Three of the six — Susanna, Catharine, and Samuel — emigrated to Canada. Samuel was the first, arriving in Canada in 1825. He later published an account of his experiences under the title: Twenty-Seven Years in Canada West. *Susanna published her first book, a volume of poems, in 1831 — the year in which she married J. W. Dunbar Moodie, a British Army officer retired on half pay after being severely wounded in Holland in 1827. In 1832, the Moodies emigrated to Canada, accompanied by Catharine and her husband, Thomas Traill. Mrs. Traill (see pages 25-27) later won fame for her Canadian botanical studies and her juvenile fiction of animal life.*

Arriving in Canada in August 1832, the Moodies settled briefly on a farm near Port Hope before removing to their grant of four hundred acres north of Peterborough. There, in the backwoods, they spent several laborious years clearing a homestead before the husband was recalled to active military duty to help suppress the Rebellion of 1837.

In 1839, Major Moodie was appointed Sheriff of Hastings County, and moved his family permanently to Belleville.

Mrs. Moodie had done some writing during her years in the bush, but the move to Believille enabled her to engage much more actively in literary pursuits. She was a leading contributor of both prose and verse to The Literary Garland *of Montreal and the author of a number of novels. Unfortunately, her poetry is generally undistinguished and her fiction (in which she avoids Canadian settings) is imitative of the sentimental and melodramatic popular fiction of the day in England. When she draws upon her personal experiences in Canada, however, she is at her best.* Roughing It In The Bush *(1852) is not only her masterpiece, but a work that has a secure place in Canadian literary history as a vigorous, accurate, and humorous account of frontier conditions in Upper Canada. In a somewhat abridged version, it is currently available in the* New Canadian Library *paperback series.*

FROM THE INTRODUCTION TO *Mark Hurdlestone* (1853)

[EARLY CANADIAN PERIODICALS]

Twenty years ago Canada was not in a condition to foster a literature of her own and the upper province had not given to the world a native-born author of any distinction. Peopled almost entirely by U. E. loyalists, or poor emigrants from the mother country, who were forced by necessity to devote all their time and energies to obtain food for their families, they had no leisure for the study of books, and no money to spare for the purchase of them. Besides, the greater portion of such emigrants were perfectly uneducated; many of them unable either to read or write. Their occupation was to handle the axe and the hand-spike, to guide the plough, and kindle the lagging fire; not to drive the pen. Learning would have been of little use to the first pioneers of the great wilderness: it would only have impeded their progress, and filled their minds with disgust while contemplating the difficulties which hard and unremitting labor could alone surmount....

Since 1832 the Colony has made rapid strides in moral and intellectual improvement. It is really wonderful to remark the great change which a few years under a more liberal government has effected in the condition of the people. Education was then confined to a very few; it is now diffused through the whole length and breadth of the land. Every large town has its college and grammar-school, and free schools abound in every district ....

There is now no lack of books in Canada, of money to purchase them, and persons to read and understand them. The reading class is no longer confined to the independent and wealthy: mechanics and artisans are all readers when they have time to spare; and the cheap American reprints of the best European works enable them to gratify their taste, without drawing very largely upon their purse.

The traffic in books from the United States employs a great many young men, who travel through the country, selling and taking up subscriptions for new works; and the astonishingly low price at which they can be obtained is an incalculable benefit to the colony, however it may interfere with the rights of European publishers.

Of books published in the Colony, we have very few indeed; and those which have been issued from a Canadian press have generally been got out, either by subscription, or at the expense of the author. It is almost impossible for any work published in Canada to remunerate the bookseller, while the United States can produce reprints of the works of the first writers in the world, at a quarter the expense. The same may be said of the different magazines which have been published in the Colony.

Shortly after we came to Canada, a magazine was started in Toronto, called the *Canadian Literary Magazine,* edited by Mr. Kent, a gentleman of considerable talent; and his list of contributors embraced some of the cleverest men in the Colony. This periodical, though a very fair specimen of that species of literature, and under the immediate patronage of the Lieutenant-Governor, Sir John Colborne, only reached its third number, and died for want of support.

Another monthly, bearing the same title, minus the *Literary,* was issued the same year; but being inferior in every respect to its predecessor, it never reached a third number.

A long time elapsed between the disappearance of these unfortunate attempts at a national periodical and the appearance of the Montreal *Literary Garland,* which was published at the most exciting period of Canadian history, on the eve of her memorable rebellion, which proved so fatal to its instigators, and of such incalculable benefit to the Colony.

For twelve years the *Literary Garland* obtained a wide circulation in the Colony, and might still have continued to support its character as a popular monthly periodical, had it not been done to death by *Harper's Magazine* and the *International.*

These American monthlies, got up in the first style, handsomely illustrated, and composed of the best articles, selected from European and American magazines, are sold at such a low rate, that one or the other is to be found in almost every decent house in the province. It was utterly impossible for a colonial magazine to compete with them; for, like the boy mentioned by St. Pierre, they enjoyed the advantage of *stealing the brooms ready made.*

It is greatly to the credit of the country that for so many years she supported a publication like the *Garland,* and much to be regretted that a truly Canadian publication should be put to silence by a host of foreign magazines, which were by no means superior in literary merit. The *Literary Garland* languished during the years 1850 and 1851, and finally expired in the December of the latter.

From the period of its outset, until its close, I was a constant contributor to the *Garland,* in which I earned from twenty to forty pounds per annum, as time or inclination tempted me to contribute to its pages. The flattering manner in which all my articles were received by the Canadian public was highly gratifying to my feelings; and as human nature, with very few modifications, is the same everywhere, it induced in me a hope that what had won for me respect in the land of my adoption would not be received unfavorably by my own country; for though my writings must pass through a more severe ordeal, and stand the test of more learned criticism in England, I feel certain that whatever is worthy of notice will not fail to command a generous acknowledgment from her truthful people.

In the January of 1841, a Canadian monthly review was published in Toronto, conducted by John Waudby, Esq., and devoted to the civil government of Canada.

This magazine was strictly political. It contained many admirable, well-written articles, but its existence did not extend beyond a few months.

In the May of 1846, Barker's *Canadian Monthly Magazine* was published in Kingston, and though decidedly a *party* magazine, contained many excellent papers; and as far as *literary merit* was concerned, was entitled to long life and popularity. But it insured neither of these advantages, and its brief career terminated at the expiration of twelve months. This was decidedly the best magazine that had appeared in the Upper Province.

In 1848, Mr. Moodie and myself undertook the joint editorship of a cheap monthly magazine published in Belleville, under the title of the *Victoria Magazine*. This periodical was issued at the low price of five shillings per annum, and was chiefly intended as a periodical for the people. It had a good circulation, for the brief period of its existence, which only lasted until the end of the year, when the failure of its proprietor, who was engaged in several literary speculations, put a stop to its further progress. Our subscription list contained eight hundred names: all of these subscribers had paid their twelve months' subscriptions in advance, and Mr. W—— must have been a considerable gainer by the publication, although we received nothing for our trouble. The greater portion of the articles, and all the reviews and notices of new works, were written by us. Had we been able to purchase the magazine, and carry it on as our own property, I feel very little doubt of its success.

Whilst conducting this periodical, we had many opportunities of judging of the literary taste and capacity of the public, from the articles that we were constantly receiving for insertion. We had some clever contributions offered to us for the magazine, but they were all, with a very few exceptions, from persons born and educated in the mother country, and could scarcely be ranked under the head of Canadian talent. It was our earnest desire to encourage as much as possible native-born authors, and to make our magazine a medium through which they might gain the attention of the public; and we were not a little disappointed that the few articles we received from Canadian writers were not of a character to interest our readers. The Canadian people are more practical than imaginative. Romantic tales and poetry would meet with less favor in their eyes than a good political article from their newspapers. The former they scarcely understand, the latter is a matter of general interest to the community. Yet there are few countries in the world which possess so many natural advantages, and present more striking subjects to fire the genius of the poet, and guide the pencil of the painter.

Beautiful—most beautiful in her rugged grandeur is this vast country. How awful is the sublime solitude of her pathless woods! what eloquent thoughts flow out of the deep silence that broods over them! We feel as if we stood alone in the presence of God, and nature lay at His feet in speechless adoration.

Has Canada no poet to describe the glories of his parent land—no painter that can delineate her matchless scenery of land and wave? Are her children dumb and blind, that they leave to strangers the task of singing her praise? . . .

—*1853*

THE INDIAN FISHERMAN'S LIGHT

[*This poem was first published in* The Literary Garland *in February 1843, and republished in Mrs. Moodie's* Roughing It in the Bush.]

The air is still, the night is dark,
  No ripple breaks the dusky tide;
From isle to isle the fisher's bark
  Like fairy meteor seems to glide;
Now lost in shade—now flashing bright
  On sleeping wave and forest tree;
We hail with joy the ruddy light,
Which far into the darksome night
  Shines red and cheerily!

With spear high poised, and steady hand,
  The centre of that fiery ray,
Behold the Indian fisher stand,
  Prepared to strike the finny prey;
Hurrah! the shaft has sped below—
  Transfix'd the shining prize I see;
On swiftly darts the birch canoe;
Yon black rock shrouding from my view
  Its red light gleaming cheerily!

Around yon bluff, whose pine crest hides
  The noisy rapids from our sight,
Another bark—another glides—
  Red meteors of the murky night.
The bosom of the silent stream
  With mimic stars is dotted free;
The waves reflect the double gleam,
The tall woods lighten in the beam,
  Through darkness shining cheerily!

—*1852*

THOMAS D'ARCY McGEE

(1825-1868)

Thomas D'Arcy McGee was born in Ireland. He emigrated to the United States and lived there three years (1842-1845). He then spent a year in England, after which he returned to Dublin (1846-1848) to support the "Young Ireland" movement and to edit the Dublin Nation. *Forced to flee from Ireland he promoted the Irish and Roman Catholic cause in the United States (1848-1857); in 1857 he moved to Montreal and became one of the "Fathers of Confederation" in 1867. He was assassinated by a Fenian sympathizer in Ottawa in 1868.*

McGee was a very active journalist and the author of numerous books devoted to Irish and Roman Catholic history, politics, and literature. In Canada, however, he is best known as a statesman and orator who ardently fostered a Canadian national spirit, giving it imaginative range and memorable phrases befitting a new northern nation. He had been in Montreal only a year when he published Canadian Ballads and Occasional Verses *(1858), contributing to incipient nationalism by the means he had employed for the cause of "Young Ireland"—the writing of a people's history in prose and in the form of the ballad. "The Arctic Indian's Faith" recognizes myths of the aborigines, and "Jacques Cartier" celebrates heroic events of the distant past.*

THE ARCTIC INDIAN'S FAITH

I

We worship the spirit that walks unseen
Through our land of ice and snow:
We know not His face, we know not His place,
But His presence and power we know.

II

Does the Buffalo need the Pale-face word
To find his pathway far?
What guide has he to the hidden ford,
Or where the green pastures are?
Who teacheth the Moose that the hunter's gun
Is peering out of the shade—
Who teacheth the doe and the fawn to run
In the track the Moose has made?

III

Him do we follow, Him do we fear—
The spirit of earth and sky;—
Who hears with the *Wapiti's* eager ear
His poor red children's cry.
Whose whisper we note in every breeze
That stirs the birch canoe—
Who hangs the reindeer moss on the trees
For the food of the *Caribou*.

IV

That Spirit we worship who walks unseen
Through our land of ice and snow:
We know not His face, we know not His place,
But His presence and power we know.

—1858

JACQUES CARTIER

I

In the sea-port of Saint Malo 'twas a smiling morn in May
When the Commodore Jacques Cartier to the westward sailed away;
In the crowded old Cathedral all the town were on their knees
For the safe return of kinsmen from the undiscover'd seas;
And every autumn blast that swept o'er pinnacle and pier
Filled manly hearts with sorrow and gentle hearts with fear.

II

A year passed o'er Saint Malo—again came round the day
When the Commodore Jacques Cartier to the westward sailed away;

But no tidings from the absent had come the way they went,
And tearful were the vigils that many a maiden spent;
And manly hearts were filled with gloom and gentle hearts with fear
When no tidings came from Cartier at the closing of the year.

III

But the Earth is as the Future, it hath its hidden side,
And the Captain of Saint Malo was rejoicing in his pride
In the forests of the north—while his townsmen mourned his loss
He was rearing on Mount-Royal the *fleur-de-lis* and cross;
And when two months were over and added to the year,
Saint Malo hailed him home again, cheer answering to cheer.

IV

He told them of a region, hard, iron-bound, and cold,
Nor seas of pearl abounded, nor mines of shining gold,
Where the wind from Thule freezes the word upon the lip,
And the ice in spring comes sailing athwart the early ship;
He told them of the frozen scene until they thrill'd with fear,
And piled fresh fuel on the hearth to make him better cheer.

V

But when he chang'd the strain—he told how soon is cast
In early Spring the fetters that hold the waters fast;
How the Winter causeway broken is drifted out to sea,
And the rills and rivers sing with pride the anthem of the free;
How the magic wand of Summer clad the landscape to his eyes,
Like the dry bones of the just, when they wake in Paradise.

VI

He told them of the Algonquin braves—the hunters of the wild,
Of how the Indian mother in the forest rocks her child;
Of how, poor souls, they fancy, in every living thing
A spirit good or evil, that claims their worshipping;
Of how they brought their sick and maim'd for him to breathe upon,
And of the wonders wrought for them thro' the Gospel of St. John.

VII

He told them of the river whose mighty current gave
Its freshness for a hundred leagues to ocean's briny wave;
He told them of the glorious scene presented to his sight,
What time he reared the cross and crown on Hochelaga's height,
And of the fortress cliff that keeps of Canada the key,
And they welcomed back Jacques Cartier from his perils over sea.

—1858

THE MENTAL OUTFIT OF THE NEW DOMINION

Before the Montreal Literary Club,
November 4th, 1867

Mr. President and Gentlemen:

I propose . . . to consider now, on the eve of our first Dominion Parliament, with what intellectual forces and appliances, with what quantity and kind of mental common stock, we are about to set up for ourselves a distinct national existence in North America. . . .

Regarding the New Dominion as an incipient new nation, it seems to me that our mental self-reliance is an essential condition of our political independence; I do not mean a state of public mind puffed up on small things; an exaggerated opinion of ourselves and a barbarian depreciation of foreigners; a controversial state of mind; or a merely imitative apish civilization. I mean a mental condition, thoughtful and true; national in its preferences, but catholic in its sympathies; gravitating inward, not outward; ready to learn from every other people on one sole condition, that the lesson when learned has been worth acquiring. In short, I would desire to see, Gentlemen, our new national character distinguished by a manly modesty as much as by mental independence; by the conscientious exercise of the critical faculties, as well as by the zeal of the inquirer. . . .

God speed the trowel and the plumb-line, as well as the loom, the plough and the anvil. But dream not . . . that great cities are built chiefly by stone-masons. Let me give you an illustration of the contrary fact. Take Boston and Montreal, for example, in their actual relations. Boston has some advantages in size and wealth, but it has another and a nobler sort of superiority; it is the vicinage of native poets like Longfellow and Lowell; of orators like Wendell Phillips; of a sort of Leipsig commerce in books, if not the largest in quantity, the most valuable in quality, of any carried on in the New World. Take a thousand of the most intelligent of our citizens, and you will find that Boston books and Boston utterances sway the minds of one-half of them; while Montreal is, I fear, absolutely unknown and unfelt, as an intellectual community in Boston and elsewhere. Far be it from me to disparage our own city; I cordially concur in the honest pride of every inhabitant, in the strong masonry and fine style of our new edifices. But if "stone walls do not a prison make," still less do they make a capital—a ruling city—a seat of light and guidance, and authority, to a nation or a generation. When the Parliamentary Buildings were finished at Ottawa, one of the first problems was to regulate the heating apparatus, in short to make them habitable for half the year; and this precisely is the problem with us in relation to another and equally necessary kind of plenishing and furnishing, for town and country. It remains for us to learn whether we have the internal heat, and light, to stand alone, and go alone—as go we must, either alone or with a master, leading us by the hand. . . .

Our reading supplies are, as you know, drawn chiefly from two sources; first, books, which are imported from the United States, England and France—a foreign supply likely long to continue foreign. The second source is our newspaper literature, chiefly supplied . . . from among ourselves, but largely supplemented by English and American journals.

I shall not be accused of flattering anyone when I say that I consider our press tolerably free from the licence which too often degrades and enfeebles the authority of the free press of the United States. Ours is chiefly to blame for the provincial narrowness of its views; for its localism and egotism; for the absence of a large and generous catholicity of spirit; both in the selection of its subjects and their treatment; for a rather servile dependence for its opinions of foreign affairs, on the leading newspapers of New York and London. . . .

This newspaper literature forms by much the largest part of our general reading. There are in the four united provinces about one hundred and thirty journals, of which thirty at least are published daily. . . .

As to the other branch of supply I believe our booksellers have nothing to complain of. The sale of books is on the increase, though not at all so largely as the sale of newspapers. Our books are mainly English or American reprints of English originals. In point of price the editions are not so far apart as they were on the other side of the Civil War. As to the classes of books most in request, I have been informed by one of our members well informed on the matter, that the sales may be divided somewhat in these proportions: religious books, 18 per cent.; poetical works, 10 per cent.; books on historical, scientific and literary subjects 28 per cent.; and works of fiction 44 per cent. My obliging informant (Mr. Samuel Dawson) adds in relation to the comparative money value of the several classes of books most in demand, the historical, scientific and literary works would represent about 45 per cent., the works of fiction 22, the poetical 15, and the religious 18 per cent. of the whole. We thus have this striking result that, whereas the works of fiction are, in volume, nearly one-half of all the reading done among us, in cost they come to less than one-fourth what is expended for other and better books. . . .

Mention must be made, Gentlemen, of those institutions of learning, and those learned professional classes which ought, and doubtless do, leaven the whole lump of our material progress. We have already twelve Universities in the Dominion—perhaps more than enough, though dispersed at long distances—as from Windsor and Fredericton to Cobourg and Toronto. . . .

Of the learned professions which represent in the world to a large extent these native colleges and universities, there are, probably, in the Dominion above 3,000 clergyman, 2,500 medical men, and perhaps (this is a guess) from 500 to 600 lawyers; say, apart from collegiate professors, 6,000 essentially "educated men." The special requirements of this large body of men, in languages, laws, history, dialectics, chemistry, and *belles lettres,* ought surely not to be confined solely within the rigid limits of professional occupation; but ought, at least occasionally, to flow out in secular channels for the benefit of lay societies, and the general elevation of the public taste. . . .

From all these sources—our numerous reading classes—our colleges—our learned professions—we ought to be able to give a good account of the mental outfit of the new Dominion. Well, then, for one of those expected to say what he thinks in these matters, I must give it as my opinion that we have as yet but few possessions in this sort that we can call our own. We have not produced in our Colonial era any thinker of the reputation of Jonathan Edwards, or Benjamin Franklin; nor any native poet of the rank of Garcilaso de la Vega—the Spanish American. The only sustained poems we have of which the scenes are laid within the Dominion are both by Americans, Longfellow's "Evangeline" and Mr.

Streets's "Frontenac"—the latter much less read than it deserves. One original humourist we have had, hardly of the highest order, however, in the late Judge Haliburton; one historian of an undoubtedly high order, in the late Mr. Garneau; one geologist, Sir William Logan; but, as yet, no poet, no orator, no critic, of either American or European reputation.

About a century ago an eminent French writer raised a doubt as to whether any German could be a literary man. Not, indeed, to answer that, but many others, arose as a golden cloud that gifted succession of poets, critics, and scholars, whose works have placed the German language in the vanguard of every department of human thought. Thirty years ago a *British Quarterly Review* asked: "Who reads an American book?" Irving had answered that long ago; but Longfellow, Cooper, Emerson, Prescott, Hawthorne, Holmes, and many another, has answered the taunt triumphantly since. Those Americans might, in turn, taunt us to-day with "Who reads a Canadian book?" I should answer frankly, very few, for Canadian books are exceedingly scarce. Still, we are not entirely destitute of resident writers. Dr. Dawson has given the world a work on his favourite science, which has established his name as an authority: Dr. Daniel Wilson's speculations and researches on Prehistoric Man have received the approval of high names; Mr. Alpheus Todd has given us a masterly and original treatise on Parliamentary Government, which will be read and quoted wherever there is constitutional government in the world; Heavysege, Sangster, and McLachlan, are not without honour. An amiable friend of mine, Mr. J. LeMoine of Quebec, has given to the world many "Maple Leaves" worthy of all praise—the only thoroughly Canadian book in point of subject which has appeared of late days, and for which, I am ashamed to say, the author has not received that encouragement his labours deserve. If he were not an enthusiast he might well have become a misanthrope, as to native literature, at least. Another most deserving man in a different walk—a younger man—but a man of very untired industry and laudable ambition—Mr. Henry J. Morgan, now of Ottawa, announces a new book of reference, *The Bibliotheca Canadensis*, which I trust will repay him for the enormous labour of such a compilation. . . .

I believe the existence of a recognized literary class will by and by be felt as a state and social necessity. The books that are made elsewhere, even in England, are not always the best fitted for us; they do not always run on the same mental gauge, nor connect with our trains of thought; they do not take us up at the by-stages of cultivation at which we have arrived, and where we are emptied forth as on a barren, pathless, habitationless heath. They are books of another state of society, bearing traces of controversies, or directed against errors or evils which for us hardly exist, except in the pages of these exotic books. Observe, I do not object to such books, especially when truthfully written; but it seems to me we do much need several other books calculated to our own meridian, and hitting home to our own society, either where it is sluggish or priggish, or wholly defective in its present style of culture.

If English-made books do not mortice closely with our Colonial deficiencies, still less do American national books. I speak not here of such literary universalists as Irving, Emerson and Longfellow; but of such American nationalists as Hawthorne, Bancroft, Brownson, Draper, and their latter prose writers generally. Within the last few years, especially since the era of the Civil War, there has been a craving desire to assert the mental independence of America as against England; to infuse an American philosophy of life, and philosophy of government, into every American writing and work of art. Mr. Bancroft's oration on the death of Mr. Lincoln was an example of this new spirit; and Dr. Draper's *Civil Policy of America* affords another illustration. It is a natural ambition for them to endeavour to Americanize their literature more and more; all nations have felt the same ambition, earlier or later; so Rome wearied of borrowing from the Greeks, and so Germany revolted a century ago against French philosophy, French romances and a Frenchified drama; so the sceptre of mind passed for a time from Berlin to Weimar, and of late only by annexation has it gone back to Berlin. No one complains of this revolution. As long as justice, and courtesy, and magnanimity are not sacrificed to an intolerant nationalism, the growth of new literary States must be to the increase of the universal literary Republic. . . .

It is quite clear to me that if we are to succeed with our new Dominion, it can never be by accepting a ready-made easy literature, which assumes Bostonian culture to be the worship of the future, and the American democratic system to be the manifestly destined form of government for all the civilized world, new as well as old. . . .

It is usual to say of ourselves, Gentlemen, that we are entering on a new area. It may be so, or it may be only the mirage of an era painted on an exhalation of self-opinion. Such eras, however, have come for other civilized States, why not for us also? There came for Germany the Swabian era, the era of Luther, and the era of Goethe; for modern Italy the age of Leo X; for France the age of Louis XIV; in our own history there have been an Elizabethan and a Georgian era; and perhaps there is at hand an American era, in ideas, in manners, and in politics. How far we, who are to represent British ethics and British culture in America—we, whose new Constitution solemnly proclaims "the well-understood principles of the British Constitution"; how far we are to make this probable next era our own—either by adhesion or resistance—is what, Gentlemen, we must all determine for ourselves, and so fare forth, for the Dominion. . . .

—1867

CHARLES SANGSTER

(1822-1893)

Charles Sangster was born at the Navy Yard, Point Frederick, Kingston, Ontario, grandson of a United Empire Loyalist and son of a joiner in the British Navy. The father died when Charles was in his second year. After only a meagre education, Charles had to leave school at fifteen and find work in the Navy Yard and Ordnance Office at Fort Henry (Kingston) so that he could contribute to the support of his mother. In 1849 he went to Amherstburg and edited the Courier. *When the publisher died the following year, Sangster returned to Kingston to become bookkeeper and proofreader in the office of the* Whig *until 1861. In 1864 he was a reporter on the staff of the Kingston* Daily News. *When the Civil Service of the new Dominion was established at Ottawa, Sangster, then forty-six years of age, accepted a position in the Post Office Department. He died in Kingston.*

Some of his first poems appeared in Kingston newspapers and early Canadian magazines; The Literary Garland *published three of them during the years 1849-1851. His two books—*The St. Lawrence and the Saguenay and Other Poems *(1856) and* Hesperus and Other Poems and Lyrics *(1860)—were well received in Canada. Edward Hartley Dewart, in an introductory essay to his* Selections from Canadian Poets *(1864)—the first important anthology of poetry in Canada—hailed Sangster as his brightest star, and he was not alone in this opinion.*

———————◆———————

FROM *The St. Lawrence and the Saguenay*

[THE THOUSAND ISLANDS]

The bark leaps love-fraught from the land; the sea
Lies calm before us. Many an isle is there,
Clad with soft verdure; many a stately tree
Uplifts its leafy branches through the air;
The amorous current bathes the islets fair,
As we skip, youth-like, o'er the limpid waves;
White cloudlets speck the golden atmosphere,
Through which the passionate sun looks down, and graves
His image on the pearls that boil from the deep caves,

And bathe the vessel's prow. Isle after isle
Is passed, as we glide tortuously through
The opening vistas, that uprise and smile
Upon us from the ever-changing view.
Here nature, lavish of her wealth, did strew
Her flocks of panting islets on the breast
Of the admiring River, where they grew,
Like shapes of Beauty, formed to give a zest
To the charmed mind, like waking Visions of the Blest.

The silver-sinewed arms of the proud Lake,
Love-wild, embrace each islet tenderly,
The zephyrs kiss the flowers when they wake
At morn, flushed with a rare simplicity;
See how they bloom around yon birchen tree,
And smile along the bank, by the sandy shore,
In lovely groups—a fair community!
The embossed rocks glitter like golden ore,
And here, the o'erarching trees form a fantastic bower.

Red walls of granite rise on either hand,
Rugged and smooth; a proud young eagle soars
Above the stately evergreens, that stand
Like watchful sentinels on these God-built towers;
And near yon beds of many-colored flowers
Browse two majestic deer, and at their side
A spotted fawn all innocently cowers;
In the rank brushwood it attempts to hide,
While the strong-antlered stag steps forth with lordly stride,

And slakes his thirst, undaunted, at the stream.
Isles of o'erwhelming beauty! surely here
The wild enthusiast might live, and dream
His life away. No Nymphic trains appear,
To charm the pale Ideal Worshipper
Of Beauty; nor Neriads from the deeps below;
Nor hideous Gnomes, to fill the breast with fear:
But crystal streams through endless landscapes flow,
And o'er the clustering Isles the softest breezes blow.

—1856

SONNETS WRITTEN IN THE ORILLIA WOODS

AUGUST, 1859

VIII

Above where I am sitting, o'er these stones,
The ocean waves once heaved their mighty forms;
And vengeful tempests and appalling storms
Wrung from the stricken sea portentous moans,
That rent stupendous icebergs, whose huge heights
Crashed down in fragments through the startled nights.
Change, change, eternal change in all but God!
Mysterious nature! thrice mysterious state
Of body, soul, and spirit! Man is awed,
But triumphs in his littleness. A mote,
He specks the eye of the age and turns to dust,
And is the sport of centuries. We note
More surely nature's ever-changing fate;
Her fossil records tell how she performs her trust.

I've almost grown a portion of this place;
I seem familiar with each mossy stone;
Even the nimble chipmunk passes on,
And looks, but never scolds me. Birds have flown
And almost touched my hand; and I can trace
The wild bees to their hives. I've never known
So sweet a pause from labor. But the tone
Of a past sorrow, like a mournful rill
Threading the heart of some melodious hill,
Or the complainings of the whippoorwill,
Passes through every thought, and hope, and aim.
It has its uses; for it cools the flame
Of ardent love that burns my being up—
Love, life's celestial pearl, diffused through all its cup.

—1860

DANIEL WILSON

(1816-1892)

Daniel Wilson was born and educated in Edinburgh, graduating from the university there in 1837. After publishing several scholarly works in Scotland, he was appointed in 1853 Professor of history and English literature in University College, Toronto; President of the College in 1880; and President of the University of Toronto in 1887. He was knighted the following year. Besides papers in learned journals, he published books on such varied subjects as archeology, local history, biographical and literary studies, as well as a collection of poems.

The following review of Charles Sangster's first volume of poetry appeared in The Canadian Journal of Industry, Science, and Art *in January 1858.*

REVIEW OF SANGSTER'S *The St. Lawrence and the Saguenay*

Poetry is the natural progeny of a nation's youth. It is the eldest as well as the fairest, of the offspring of literature; if indeed it be not rather her parent, for songs were sung long before letters were invented. Our Province, however, occupies a singular position in this its Canadian youth. Our schooling has been too much alongside of the elder of Europe's nations, and our individual thoughts partake too largely of the experience which centuries have accumulated around the old Saxon hearth, to admit of the lyrical or epic muse inspiring for us the lay

that is born of nature in the true poet's heart. We are past the first poetic birth-time, which pertains to the vigorous infancy of races; we have yet to attain to the era of refinement from which a high civilization educes new phases of poetic inspiration. We cannot yet respond, amid these charred stumps and straggling snake-fences of our rough clearings, to Hiawatha's appeal to those:

> Who love the haunts of nature,
> Love the sunshine of the meadow,
> Love the shadow of the forest,
> Love the wind among the branches,
> And the rain-shower and the snow-storm,
> And the rushings of great rivers,
> Through their palisades of pine-trees.

We want our pine-trees for lumber, and so long as they spare us a surplus for kindling wood, we ask no kindling inspiration from them. The rushing of our great rivers we estimate rejoicingly—for their water-privileges. The sunshine of the meadow is very welcome to us—in the hay-harvest; and the poetry of the snow-storm full of the music—of our sleigh-bells. As to our love for the shadow of the forest, that pertains to the romantic simplicity of our squatter stage of infancy, from whence we emerge as fast as possible into the clearing we hew out of it, rejoicing at the crash of falling pines, and keeping time with the music of the axe to the crackling of the logging-pile. We do not mean to say that a poet is an impossibility, amid the rugged realism of this vigorously practical Canada. The ungenial Ayrshire farm of Mosgiel gave no greater promise of a crop of poetry from its bleak and exposed heights before it gave birth to its "Mountain Daisy." But we wonder what would be the estimate of the emigrant settler who should apostrophise the giants of the Canadian back-woods, as they bowed beneath his sturdy stroke, after the fashion of the Ayrshire bard to the "wee, modest, crimson-tipped flower" over which he so reluctantly drove the plough-share. We question much if our minister of agriculture could be induced to rescue from the rapidly dispersing ordnance reserves a Sabine farm for such a Canadian Virgil.

Such being the present prospects of the poet amongst us, it is not greatly to be wondered at that such poetry as we do produce is less redolent of "the odors of the forest" than of the essences of the drawing-room; and more frequently re-echoes the songs that are to be gathered amid the leaves of the library-shelf, than under those with which the wind sports among the branches whereon song-birds warble their nuptial lays. To the class of poetry which thus repeats the old-world music and song we must assign Mr. Sangster's "The St. Lawrence and the Saguenay." It is a pleasant and tasteful depiction of the scenes and associations of our noble river, written in the same stanza as "Childe Harold," and with some echo of its mode of thought, though lacking the force and pathos of its passionate utterances. But, while we may easily cull from it many graceful versifications of such descriptions as the scenery naturally suggests, we have to search carefully through its hundred and ten stanzas to find any such as might be welcome to the jaded fancy of the old world because of their freshness of wild-wood imagery . . . [The] poet of "The St. Lawrence and the Saguenay," sees the river as it is, and not as it was. To him, with all its beauty, it is only the great navigable highway from Ontario to the Sea, with its daily steamers, its wooding stations, its locks and canals. If the Indian lingers among its vanishing woods, it is as the old painted British Druid haunts Avebury or Stonehenge. Here, for example, is the picturing of the Thousand Isles:

> Many a tale of legendary lore
> Is told of these romantic Isles. The feet
> Of the Red Man have pressed each wave-zoned shore,
> And many an eye of beauty oft did greet
> The painted warriors and their birchen fleet,
> As they returned with trophies of the slain.
> That race has passed away; their fair retreat
> In its primeval loneness smiles again,
> Save where some vessel snaps the isle-inwoven chain:

> Save where the echo of the huntsman's gun
> Startles the wild duck from some shallow nook,
> Or the swift hounds' deep baying, as they run,
> Rouses the lounging student from his book;
> Or where, assembled by some sedgy brook,
> A pic-nic party, resting in the shade,
> Spring pleasedly to their feet to catch a look
> At the strong steamer, through the watery glade,
> Ploughing, like a huge serpent from its ambuscade.

Were we to transport the scene to the firth of Clyde, or any other islanded home river, and change only a single term; that of the *Red Man* for the *old Pict*, or even the *Red Gael*, there is nothing in the description that would betray its new-world parentage. At best it is no true Indian, but only the white man dressed in his attire; strip him of his paint and feathers, and it is our old-world familiar acquaintance. The lay of the Whip-poor-will, instead of some romantic Indian legend, is but a commonplace "Willie and Jeannie" love song, though thus heralded by one of the best stanzas in the poem:

> The Whip-poor-will, among the slumberous trees,
> Flingeth her solitary triple cry
> Upon the busy lips of every breeze,
> That wafts it in wild echoes up the sky,
> And through the answering woods, incessantly.
> Surely some pale Ophelia's spirit wails
> In this remorseless bird's impassioned sigh,
> That like a lost soul haunts the lonely dale!
> *Maiden sing me one of thy pleasing madrigals.*

However much taste and refinement may be displayed in such echoes of the old thought and fancy of Europe, the path to success lies not in this direction for the poet of the new world. To Tennyson this nineteenth century is as fresh an *el dorado* as America was to Cortes or Pizarro. To him it is a thing such as Spenser,

71

or Dryden, or Pope, or Campbell, or Byron, had no knowledge of. Its politics, its geology, its philosophy, its utopian aspirations, its homely fashions and fancies, all yield to his poetic eye suggestive imagery rich with pregnant thought. And surely our new world is not less suggestive. It is not a "Hiawatha" song we demand. The Indian Savage is not the sole native product of the wilds, nor the only poetical thing that meets the eye in the clearings. Here is the Saxon doing once again, what Ælla and Cedric did in old centuries in that historic isle of the Britons. Science and politics, and many a picturesque phase of colonial life, all teem with inspiration such as might awake for a Canadian Tennyson another "Sleeping palace" like that from whence he led his happy princess:

> When far across the hills they went;
> In that new world which is the old.

Poetry, however, is not the crop which it can at all be expected, or indeed desired, that Canadian farmers will cultivate at present. And if we can only reproduce exotic thoughts in verse, it is better on the whole that we should take the foreign originals at first hand. Having, however, stated our feeling in regard to the absence of that originality and individuality of character in "The St. Lawrence," which might have made of such a virgin theme a poetic gem of rarest beauty; we may nevertheless, refer with pleasure to some of its stanzas as gracefully commemorating historical features. Here, for example, is a good subject not discreditably dealt with:

> . . . Quebec! how regally it crowns the height,
> Like a tanned giant on a solid throne!
> Unmindful of the sanguinary fight,
> The roar of the cannon mingling with the moan
> Of mutilated soldiers years agone,
> That gave the place a glory and a name
> Among the nations. France was heard to groan;
> England rejoiced, but checked the proud acclaim—
> A brave young chief had fallen to vindicate her fame.

> Wolfe and Montcalm! two nobler names ne'er graced
> The page of history, or the hostile plain;
> No braver souls the storm of battle faced,
> Regardless of the danger or the pain.
> They pass'd unto their rest without a stain
> Upon their nature or their generous hearts.
> One graceful column to the noble twain,
> Speaks of a nation's gratitude and starts
> The tear that valor claims, and feeling's self imparts.

The poem is manifestly designed as a companion, if not a guide-book, for the voyage to the Saguenay; and though it has in it none of those magical passages which stir the heart like the sound of a trumpet, it will nevertheless make an agreeable return to the tourist for the small space it claims in his baggage. —*1858*

EDWARD HARTLEY DEWART

(1828-1903)

Of Irish birth, Edward Hartley Dewart attended the Toronto Normal School and in 1855 was ordained a minister of the Methodist Church. His Selections from Canadian Poets *(1864) was the first published anthology of Canadian verse. Five years later he published a volume of his own poems. For twenty-five years (1869-1894) he was editor of* The Christian Guardian.

———◆———

FROM THE INTRODUCTION TO *Selections from Canadian Poets*

Only the illiterate and unreflecting adopt the sentiment that, because more books have been already produced than can possibly be read in the compass of the longest life, to increase the number of books or the quantity of literature, is undesirable and unnecessary. The literature of the world is the footprints of human progress; and, unless all progress should cease, and mental paralysis arrest all human activity, these way-marks shall continue to be erected along the pathway of the vanishing years. Whatever is discovered as new in the records of creation, in the capacities and relations of things, in the history of the mind's operations, or in the forms of thought and imagery by which in its higher moods soul speaks to soul, will always demand some suitable embodiment in literature.

Equally shallow and reprehensible is the idea, very widely entertained, that, because we can procure sufficient quantities of mental aliment from other lands, it is superfluous to make any attempt to build up a literature of our own. A national literature is an essential element in the formation of national character. It is not merely the record of a country's mental progress: it is the expression of its intellectual life, the bond of national unity, and the guide of national energy. It may be fairly questioned, whether the whole range of history presents the spectacle of a people firmly united politically, without the subtle but powerful cement of a patriotic literature. On the other hand, it is easy to show that, in the older countries of the world, the names of distinguished poets, enshrined in the national heart, are the watchwords of national union. . . .

There is probably no country in the world, making equal pretension to intelligence and progress, where the claims of native literature are so little felt, and where every effort in poetry has been met with so much coldness and indifference, as in Canada. And what is more to be deprecated than neglect of our most meritorious authors, is the almost universal absence of interest and faith in all indigenous literary productions, and the undisturbed satisfaction with a state of things that, rightly viewed, should be regarded as a national reproach. The common method of accounting for this by the fact that almost the whole community is engaged in the pursuit of the necessaries and comforts of life, and that comparatively few possess wealth and leisure to enable them to give much time or thought to the study of poetry and kindred subjects, is by no means satisfactory. This state of things is doubtless unfavorable to the growth of poetry; but there are other causes less palpable, which exert a more subtle and powerful antagonism.

Nothing so seriously militates against the growth and extension of our poetic literature, as the low and false conceptions which extensively prevail respecting the nature and influence of poetry itself. Many regard it as a tissue of misleading fancies, appealing chiefly to superstitious credulity, a silly and trifling thing, the product of the imagination when loosed from the control and direction of reason. These misconceptions may have arisen from a natural incapacity for appreciating the truths which find their highest embodiment in poetry, from familiarity with low styles, or from the frequency with which verse has been degraded to be the vehicle of low and debasing thought. But whatever be their origin, they are false and misleading. They ignore the essential unity of the mind. Poetry is not the product of any one faculty of the mind: it is the offspring of the whole mind, in the full exercise of all its faculties, and in its highest moods of sympathy, with the truths of the worlds of mind and matter. It is not some artificial distortion of thought and language by a capricious fancy: it has its foundation in the mental constitution which our Creator has given us. As fragrance to the sense of smell, music to the ear, or beauty to the eye, so is poetry to the sensibilities of the heart. It ministers to a want of our intellectual nature. This is the secret of its power, and the pledge of its perpetuity. . . .

Our colonial position, whatever may be its political advantages, is not favorable to the growth of an indigenous literature. Not only are our mental wants supplied by the brains of the Mother Country, under circumstances that utterly preclude competition; but the majority of persons of taste and education in Canada are emigrants from the Old Country, whose tenderest affections cling around the land they have left. The memory of the associations of youth, and of the honored names that have won distinction in every department of human activity, throws a charm around everything that comes from their native land, to which the productions of our young and unromantic country can put forth no claim. . . .

In pronouncing judgment on the character of our native poetry, the most partial critic must confess that it is extensively marked by crudity and imperfection. This is to some extent accounted for by the want of educational advantages incident to a new country. Many writers of undoubted genius have been deficient in that thorough literary culture essential to high artistic excellence. But, in many instances, this want of finish may be traced to want of application, resulting from a low estimate of poetry as an art. . . .

To those who are best acquainted with the poetry of Canada, the wonder is, not that so little has been achieved, but that so much true poetry has been written, in spite of such unpropitious circumstances. . . .

Enough however has already been achieved, to be an earnest of better things for the future. . . .

If these anticipations are not realized, it is not because there is anything in the country itself uncongenial to poetry. If we are deprived of many of the advantages of older countries, we have ample compensation in more unshackled freedom of thought, and broader spheres of action. Though poor in historic interest, our past is not altogether devoid of events capable of poetic treatment. But if Memory cannot draw rich materials for poetry from treasures consecrated to fame, Hope unfolds the loftier inspiration of a future bright with promise. If we cannot point to a past rich with historic names, we have the inspiring spectacle of a great country, in her youthful might, girding herself for a race for an honorable place among the nations of the world. In our grand and gloomy forests—in our brilliant skies and varied seasons—in our magnificent lakes and rivers—in our hoary mountains and fruitful valleys, external Nature unveils her most majestic forms to exalt and inspire the truly poetic soul; while human nature—especially human nature in its relation to the spiritual and divine—still presents an exhaustless mine of richest ore, worthy of the most exalted genius, and of the deepest human and spiritual knowledge.

—1864

CHARLES HEAVYSEGE

(1816-1876)

Charles Heavysege was born in England and had published a verse drama, The Revolt of Tartarus, *anonymously, before he settled in Montreal in 1853 to work as a cabinet-maker and carpenter, and later as a journalist. He is generally remembered as an individualist who quietly worked at a humble trade and composed pompous rhetorical dialogue for pseudo-Elizabethan dramas that happened to gain the praise of some British and American reviewers. Extracts from* Saul *(Montreal, 1857) have frequently been printed in anthologies. The selection from* Jephthah's Daughter *(a Biblical dramatic poem, 1865), and the two sonnets presented here, display a different approach to the work of this extraordinary man. Thomas R. Dale, in an article in the* University of Toronto Quarterly *(October 1952) and in an unpublished thesis for the University of Chicago, has found evidence of Heavysege's "rebellious and questioning spirit," his mild but insistent doubts about God's justice in dealing with men and fallen angels. Northrop Frye, in several papers, has recognized, in* Jephthah's Daughter, *the emergence of "the central Canadian tragic theme" — "the indifference of nature to human values" (see pages 599 and 606).*

Jephthah's Daughter is based upon the Book of Judges, XI: 30-40. Jephthah the Gileadite had promised the Lord that, if he were granted victory over the Ammonites, he would offer up as a sacrifice "whatsoever cometh forth of the doors of my house to meet me, when I return . . . and, behold, his daughter came out to meet him . . . his only child."

"Oh, rashly, rashly for my peace, I vowed!
Oh, dearly, dearly was the victory bought!
Its price, your ransom, my dear daughter, — she
Compared (oh, foolish, vain comparison!)
With whom the glory of this victory
Seems utter darkness, misery, and shame. . . .

     . . .

"God, God, oh, God, demand not, stern, thy due!
If I have ever moved thee by my prayers,
If I favor ever found before thine eyes,
If I am father to my daughter, she
The only heir to my affections, — if
I am an heir of Abraham, the sad sire
Who to Moriah went to slay his son,
But for whose need thou didst provide a ram,
Oh, hear me now, dispense, or else provide!
Behold, I am a rash, imperfect man,
With but one cherished child, a daughter, lamb,
Whose life I staked, not knowing what I did.
Forgive, forego; or say what ransom thou
Demand'st, what price. I give thee all I have
Save her: take all, take me; e'en take the mother.
Take my whole household, all that throng my fields;
Choose Tabor for thine altar; I will pile
It with the choice of Bashan's lusty herds,
And flocks of fatlings, and, for fuel, thither
Will bring umbrageous Lebanon to burn;
Whilst, in the stead of wine and oil, there shall
Pour over it the blood of heathen kings,
So her blood thou wilt spare, and, gracious, give
To me some token that my prayer is heard."

He said, and stood awaiting for the sign,
And hears above the hoarse, bough-bending wind,
The hill-wolf howling on the neighboring height,
And bittern booming in the pool below.
Some drops of rain fell from the passing cloud,
That sudden hides the wanly shining moon,
And from the scabbard instant dropped his sword,
And, with long, living leaps and rock-struck clang,
From side to side, and slope to sounding slope,
In gleaming whirls swept down the dim ravine. . . .

—1865

SONNETS

XIII

'Twas on a day, and in high, radiant heaven,
An angel lay beside a lake reclined,
Against whose shores the rolling waves were driven,
And beat the measure to the dancing wind.
There, rapt, he meditated on that story
Of how Jehovah did of yore expel
Heaven's aborigines from grace and glory, —
Those mighty angels that did dare rebel.
And, as he mused upon their dread abode
And endless penance, from his drooping hands
His harp down sank, and scattered all abroad
Its rosy garland on the golden sands;
His soul mute wondering that the All-wise Spirit
Should have allowed the doom of such demerit.

XVIII

How great unto the living seem the dead!
How sacred, solemn; how heroic grown;
How vast and vague, as they obscurely tread
The shadowy confines of the dim unknown! —
For they have met the monster that we dread,
Have learned the secret not to mortal shown.
E'en as gigantic shadows on the wall
The spirit of the daunted child amaze,
So on us thoughts of the departed fall,
And with phantasma fill our gloomy gaze.
Awe and deep wonder lend the living lines,
And hope and ecstasy the borrowed beams;
While fitful fancy the full form divines,
And all is what imagination dreams.

—1865

77

The new nation

ALEXANDER McLACHLAN

(1818-1896)

Alexander McLachlan was born of poor parents living near Glasgow. In 1840 he emigrated to Upper Canada to try pioneer farming in Peel and Perth counties (until 1850); from 1850 to 1877, in Erin township, Wellington County, he devoted himself to tailoring, reading, writing, and lecturing. For a time in the eighteen-sixties he was a Canadian government lecturer and emigration agent in Scotland. After 1877, McLachlan lived on a farm near Orangeville.

The Rev. Edward Hartley Dewart's biographical sketch of McLachlan in The Poetical Works *(1900) makes it apparent that McLachlan was strongly influenced in his early years by the unrest among Glasgow radicals, and, after emigration, by homesickness and the rigors of pioneer farming. His first book was published in 1846, and his most pretentious one,* The Emigrant and Other Poems, *in 1861. Poems and Songs followed* The Emigrant *in 1874. McLachlan's verses are reminiscent of Robert Burns and of that poet's assertive independence. In his later works, he displays pride in his adopted land.*

ACRES OF YOUR OWN

Here's the road to independence!
Who would bow and dance attendance?
Who, with e'er a spark of pride,
While the bush is wild and wide,
Would be but a hanger on,
Begging favors from a throne,
While beneath yon smiling sun
Farms by labor can be won?
Up, be stirring, be alive!
Get upon a farm and thrive!
He's a king upon a throne
Who has acres of his own!

Tho' the cabin's walls are bare,
What of that, if love is there?
What altho' thy back is bent,
There is none to hound for rent;
What tho' thou must chop and plow,
None dare ask, "What doest thou?"

What tho' homespun be thy coat,
Kings might envy thee thy lot.
Up, be stirring, be alive!
Get upon a farm and thrive!
He's a king upon a throne
Who has acres of his own!

Honest labor thou would'st shirk?
Thou art far too good for work?
Such gentility's a fudge—
True men all must toil and drudge.
Nature's true nobility
Scorns such mock gentility!
Fools but talk of blood and birth—
Ev'ry man must prove his worth.
Up, be stirring, be alive!
Get upon a farm and thrive!
He's a king upon a throne
Who has acres of his own!

—1874

Around the world the fame is blown
Of fighting heroes, dead and gone;
But we've a hero of our own—
   The man who rose from nothing.

He's a magician great and grand;
The forests fled at his command;
And here he said, "Let cities stand!"—
   The man who rose from nothing.

And in our legislative hall
He towering stands alone, like Saul,
"A head and shoulders over all,"—
   The man who rose from nothing.

His efforts he will ne'er relax,
His faith in figures and in facts,

And always calls an axe an axe,—
   The man who rose from nothing.

The gentleman in word and deed;
And short and simple in his creed;
"Fear God and help the soul in need!"
   The man who rose from nothing.

In other lands he's hardly known,
For he's a product of our own;
Could grace a shanty or a throne,—
   The man who rose from nothing.

Here's to the land of lakes and pines,
On which the sun of freedom shines,
Because we meet on all our lines
   The man who rose from nothing.

—1874

CHARLES MAIR

(1838-1927)

Charles Mair was born in Lanark, Upper Canada, but lived most of his long life in the western provinces. He died in Victoria, B.C. His first book, Dreamland and Other Poems *(1868) was very favorably reviewed, but under the influence of the nationalism fostered by the Canada First Movement (of which Mair was one of the founders), he became dissatisfied with many of the poems and made extensive revisions before republishing them in 1901. Out of touch with literary developments in eastern Canada, he showed little awareness of the poetry produced by Roberts, Lampman, and others in the 1880's and 1890's. The 1901 volume won only lukewarm attention, and Mair became convinced that his revisions had been a mistake. When his works were collected in 1926 he insisted upon returning to the 1868 versions.*

SUMMER

[excerpts from the original version]

O Day! give me all thy beams,
All thy warm, embodied dreams,
Such as pant in meadow still,
By streamlet brink, or upland hill.

SUMMER

[excerpts from the revised version]

O Day! give me all your gleams,
All your sun-warm, throbbing beams,
Such as pant in meadow-still,
By the brook or upland hill!

O Fields! give me all your flow'rs
Which beguile the wanton Hours,
All sweet dews which night distils,
All your shallow, whisp'ring rills,
All your deeply perfumed breath,
Ev'ry note each small bird hath,
Ev'ry breeze by woods delayed,
Each cool place those woods have made—

So may I thy riches prove
Till Sleep bring me dreams of love,

Dreams of by-gone chivalry,
Wassailing and revelry,
And lordly seasons long since spent
In bout, and joust, and tournament.
And, mid visioned feats of arms,
Fierce attacks and rude alarms,
Let my dreams run back to thee,
Chastely fair Eurydice!
To the lover and the lute,
Which made the mighty torrents mute,
And rumbling hell itself grow meek,
While iron tears from Pluto's cheek
Rolled down. Then let processions pass—
Bacchanals, each with his lass,
Waving mighty clusters round,
Tipsily, until the ground
Purples with the clammy juice,
Spoilt for quaffing, spoilt for use.

And let nymph-attended Pan
Come in habit of a man,
Singing songs of reeds and rushes,
Elder brakes and hazel bushes.
See him swing and jig about,
Whilst the merry, rabble rout
Chases round with joinèd hands,
Twitching slily, when he stands,
At his back, his garments tearing,
All his swart, brute-buttocks baring.

O Fields! give me all your flowers
Which beguile the wanton Hours

All the windrowed meadow's math,
Every note each small bird hath,
Every breeze by woods delayed,
Each cool place those woods have made!

So may I your treasures prove
Richer still at each remove, . . .

Or, in quest of bygone themes,
Lapse into the realm of dreams,—

Dreams of old world chivalry,
Bout and joust and revelry;
Or, more suited to our land,
Dreams of forest chief and band:
Braves in paint and plume arrayed,
Sun-burnt youth and dusky maid
Paddling down, in days gone by,
Spirit lake or haunted snie;
Huddling in their barks in fear
When strange voices hit the ear;
Or encamped where, mountain-throned,
Star-lit, monarch pines intoned
Earth's primeval homage, backt
By wild chute and cataract;
Hearing Nature's Spirits then
Talking to the souls of men!

Or, if Fancy still would trace
Forms ideal, forms of grace,
Still would haunt, in dreamy trance,
Kindred regions of Romance,
Let her now recall the sweet
Image of lorn Marguerite,
In the forest-screened château
Of the ribald, foul Bigot;
Or restore the restless mien
Of hope-fed Evangeline,
Robbed of love's pure ends by fate
At the very altar's gate;
Follow, and recall her quest
In the wide-spread, savage West,
Seeking, through love's living flame,
Him who never came — yet came!

And let Comus and his crew
Shout until the welkin blue
Claps its hands in quick refrain,
And echoes o'er and o'er again.
Flushed and jolly is his face,
With something of Olymp'an grace
Still ling'ring on his beamy brow:
Now lolls he on the ground, and now
His youthful revellers recline,
Draining beakers full of wine,
Or, upstarting from the green,
With a wild, unsteady mien,
Tread a measure on the sod,
In honor of the mirthful god. . . .

—1868

Or let roving Fancy delve
In the fields of "Eighteen-Twelve";
In her dreams recall the sward
Where the wife of lame Secord,
Knowing Boerstler's subtle plan
To surprise the British van
In the far camp where it lay,
Roused her cows at break of day,
Hoaxed the sentry thus, then passed,
Smiling, to the forest vast.
Call up now that sultry morn—
Call up her who sped forlorn
Through the swales and trackless woods,
Wolfish wilds and solitudes,
Till at night, with heart aflame,
To the British camp she came
With her priceless tidings then
For FitzGibbon and his men. . . .

—1901

ISABELLA VALANCY CRAWFORD

(1850-1887)

Isabella Valancy Crawford was born in Dublin, Ireland. Her parents and their four children—all that remained after seven had died of fever while their father was in Australia—emigrated to Canada in 1858 and settled in the village of Paisley in Bruce County, Upper Canada, on the banks of the Saugeen River. Here the father, Stephen Dennis Crawford, practised his profession of medicine, bartering his services, it is said, for farm produce from the pioneer inhabitants. The life described in "Malcolm's Katie" was drawn from Isabella's experiences at Paisley and in the village of Lakefield in the Kawartha Lakes, where the Crawfords moved in 1864. Eight years later they made their home in Peterborough, where Dr. Crawford died in 1875.

Shortly afterwards, Isabella and her mother went to Toronto and on a small allowance from an uncle lived over a grocery store at the corner of King and John Streets. Isabella wrote poems, short stories, and novels, many of which were designed to attract the readers of The Evening Telegram, The Mail, or The Globe through the use of currently popular subject matter: farming, Indians, cowboys, and the opening of the great Northwest. She died of heart failure in 1887 in Toronto but is buried at Peterborough under a Celtic cross erected by friends.

Her one book of verse published in her lifetime appeared in 1884—a little book in cheap paper covers, printed at her own expense, and bearing the title: Old Spookses' Pass, Malcolm's Katie, and Other Poems. It brought her a little fame, but no money.

In 1905, John W. Garvin published a collection of her poems, but a considerable quantity of further manuscript material—novels, poems, and short stories—can be found in the Lorne Pierce Collection at Queen's University.

FROM MALCOLM'S KATIE

PART II

The South Wind laid his moccasins aside,
Broke his gay calumet of flow'rs, and cast
His useless wampum, beaded with cool dews,
Far from him, northward; his long, ruddy spear
Flung sunward, whence it came, and his soft locks
Of warm, fine haze grew silver as the birch.
His wigwam of green leaves began to shake;
The crackling rice-beds scolded harsh like squaws;
The small ponds pouted up their silver lips;
The great lakes ey'd the mountains, whisper'd "Ugh!
Are ye so tall, O chiefs? Not taller than
Our plumes can reach." And rose a little way,
As panthers stretch to try their velvet limbs,
And then retreat to purr and bide their time.
At morn the sharp breath of the night arose
From the wide prairies, in deep-struggling seas,
In rolling breakers, bursting to the sky;
In tumbling surfs, all yellow'd faintly thro'
With the low sun — in mad, conflicting crests,
Voic'd with low thunder from the hairy throats
Of the mist-buried herds; and for a man
To stand amid the cloudy roll and moil,
The phantom waters breaking overhead,
Shades of vex'd billows bursting on his breast,
Torn caves of mist wall'd with a sudden gold,
Reseal'd as swift as seen — broad, shaggy fronts,
Fire-ey'd and tossing on impatient horns
The wave impalpable — was but to think
A dream of phantoms held him as he stood.
The late, last thunders of the summer crash'd,
Where shrieked great eagles, lords of naked cliffs.
The pulseless forest, lock'd and interlock'd
So closely, bough with bough, and leaf with leaf,
So serf'd by its own wealth, that while from high
The moons of summer kiss'd its green-gloss'd locks;
And round its knees the merry West Wind danc'd;
And round its ring, compacted emerald,
The South Wind crept on moccasins of flame;

And the red fingers of th' impatient sun
Pluck'd at its outmost fringes — its dim veins
Beat with no life — its deep and dusky heart,
In a deep trance of shadow, felt no throb
To such soft wooing answer: thro' its dream
Brown rivers of deep waters sunless stole;
Small creeks sprang from its mosses, and amaz'd,
Like children in a wigwam curtain'd close
Above the great, dead heart of some red chief,
Slipp'd on soft feet, swift stealing through the gloom,
Eager for light and for the frolic winds.
   In this shrill moon the scouts of winter ran
From the ice-belted north, and whistling shafts
Struck maple and struck sumach — and a blaze
Ran swift from leaf to leaf, from bough to bough;
Till round the forest flash'd a belt of flame
And inward lick'd its tongues of red and gold
To the deep, tranced, inmost heart of all.
Rous'd the still heart — but all too late, too late.
Too late, the branches welded fast with leaves,
Toss'd, loosen'd, to the winds — too late the sun
Pour'd his last vigor to the deep, dark cells
Of the dim wood. The keen, two-bladed Moon
Of Falling Leaves roll'd up on crested mists
And where the lush, rank boughs had foil'd the sun
In his red prime, her pale, sharp fingers crept
After the wind and felt about the moss,
And seem'd to pluck from shrinking twig and stem
The burning leaves—while groan'd the shudd'ring wood.
   Who journey'd where the prairies made a pause,
Saw burnish'd ramparts flaming in the sun,
With beacon fires, tall on their rustling walls.
And when the vast, horn'd herds at sunset drew
Their sullen masses into one black cloud,
Rolling thund'rous o'er the quick pulsating plain,
They seem'd to sweep between two fierce red suns
Which, hunter-wise, shot at their glaring balls
Keen shafts, with scarlet feathers and gold barbs.
   By round, small lakes with thinner forests fring'd,
More jocund woods that sung about the feet
And crept along the shoulders of great cliffs,
The warrior stags, with does and tripping fawns,
Like shadows black upon the throbbing mist
Of Evening's rose, flash'd thro' the singing woods—
Nor tim'rous, sniff'd the spicy, cone-breath'd air;
For never had the patriarch of the herd
Seen limn'd against the farthest rim of light
Of the low-dipping sky, the plume or bow

Of the red hunter; nor when stoop'd to drink,
Had from the rustling rice-beds heard the shaft
Of the still hunter hidden in its spears;
His bark canoe close-knotted in its bronze,
His form as stirless as the brooding air,
His dusky eyes, too, fix'd, unwinking fires;
His bow-string tighten'd till it subtly sang
To the long throbs, and leaping pulse that roll'd
And beat within his knotted, naked breast.
   There came a morn. The Moon of Falling Leaves,
With her twin silver blades had only hung
Above the low set cedars of the swamp
For one brief quarter, when the sun arose
Lusty with light and full of summer heat,
And pointing with his arrows at the blue,
Clos'd, wigwam curtains of the sleeping moon,
Laugh'd with the noise of arching cataracts,
And with the dove-like cooing of the woods,
And with the shrill cry of the diving loon
And with the wash of saltless, rounded seas,
And mock'd the white Moon of the Falling Leaves:
   "Esa! esa! shame upon you, Pale Face!
Shame upon you, moon of evil witches!
Have you kill'd the happy, laughing Summer?
Have you slain the mother of the Flowers
With your icy spells of might and magic?
Have you laid her dead within my arms?
Wrapp'd her, mocking, in a rainbow blanket?
Drown'd her in the frost mist of your anger?
She is gone a little way before me;
Gone an arrow's flight beyond my vision;
She will turn again and come to meet me,
With the ghosts of all the slain flowers,
In a blue mist round her shining tresses;
In a blue smoke in her naked forests —
She will linger, kissing all the branches,
She will linger, touching all the places,
Bare and naked, with her golden fingers,
Saying,
  'Sleep, and dream of me, my children;
  Dream of me, the mystic Indian Summer;
  I, who slain by the cold Moon of Terror,
  Can return across the path of Spirits,
  Bearing still my heart of love and fire;
  Looking with my eyes of warmth and splendor;
  Whisp'ring lowly thro' your sleep of sunshine.
  I, the laughing Summer, am not turn'd
  Into dry dust, whirling on the prairies,—

Into red clay, crush'd beneath the snowdrifts.
I am still the mother of sweet flowers
Growing but an arrow's flight beyond you —
In the Happy Hunting Ground — the quiver
Of great Manitou, where all the arrows
He has shot from his great bow of Pow'r,
With its clear, bright, singing cord of Wisdom,
Are re-gather'd, plum'd again, and brighten'd,
And shot out, re-barb'd with Love and Wisdom;
Always shot, and evermore returning.
Sleep, my children, smiling in your heart-seeds
At the spirit words of Indian Summer!'
Thus, O Moon of Falling Leaves, I mock you!
Have you slain my gold-ey'd squaw, the Summer?"

   The mighty Morn strode laughing up the land,
And Max, the laborer and the lover, stood
Within the forest's edge, beside a tree,
The mossy king of all the woody tribes,
Whose clatt'ring branches rattl'd, shuddering,
As the bright axe cleav'd moon-like thro' the air,
Waking strange thunders, rousing echoes link'd
From the full, lion-throated roar, to sighs
Stealing on dove-wings thro' the distant aisles.
Swift fell the axe, swift follow'd roar on roar,
Till the bare woodland bellow'd in its rage,
As the first-slain slow toppl'd to his fall.
"O King of Desolation, art thou dead?"
Thought Max, and laughing, heart and lips, leap'd on
The vast prone trunk. "And have I slain a King?
Above his ashes will I build my house —
No slave beneath its pillars, but — a King!"

   Max wrought alone, but for a half-breed lad,
With tough, lithe sinews and deep Indian eyes,
Lit with a Gallic sparkle. Max, the lover, found
The laborer's arms grow mightier day by day —
More iron-welded as he slew the trees;
And with the constant yearning of his heart
Towards little Kate, part of a world away,
His young soul grew and shew'd a virile front,
Full-muscl'd and large statur'd, like his flesh.

   Soon the great heaps of brush were builded high,
And like a victor, Max made pause to clear
His battle-field, high strewn with tangl'd dead.
Then roar'd the crackling mountains, and their fires
Met in high heaven, clasping flame with flame.
The thin winds swept a cosmos of red sparks
Across the bleak, midnight sky; and the sun
Walk'd pale behind the resinous, black smoke.

And Max car'd little for the blotted sun,
And nothing for the startl'd, outshone stars;
For Love, once set within a lover's breast,
Has its own Sun — its own peculiar sky,
All one great daffodil — on which do lie
The sun, the moon, the stars — all seen at once,
And never setting; but all shining straight
Into the faces of the trinity, —
The one belov'd, the lover, and sweet Love!
    It was not all his own, the axe-stirr'd waste.
In these new days men spread about the earth,
With wings at heel — and now the settler hears,
While yet his axe rings on the primal woods,
The shrieks of engines rushing o'er the wastes;
Nor parts his kind to hew his fortunes out.
And as one drop glides down the unknown rock
And the bright-threaded stream leaps after it,
With welded billions, so the settler finds
His solitary footsteps beaten out,
With the quick rush of panting, human waves
Upheav'd by throbs of angry poverty,
And driven by keen blasts of hunger, from
Their native strands — so stern, so dark, so dear!
O, then, to see the troubl'd, groaning waves,
Throb down to peace in kindly valley beds;
Their turbid bosoms clearing in the calm
Of sun-ey'd Plenty — till the stars and moon,
The blessed sun himself, have leave to shine
And laugh in their dark hearts! So shanties grew
Other than his amid the blacken'd stumps;
And children ran with little twigs and leaves
And flung them, shouting, on the forest pyres,
Where burn'd the forest kings — and in the glow
Paus'd men and women when the day was done.
    There the lean weaver ground anew his axe,
Nor backward look'd upon the vanish'd loom,
But forward to the ploughing of his fields;
And to the rose of Plenty in the cheeks
Of wife and children — nor heeded much the pangs
Of the rous'd muscles tuning to new work.
The pallid clerk look'd on his blister'd palms
And sigh'd and smil'd, but girded up his loins
And found new vigor as he felt new hope.
The lab'rer with train'd muscles, grim and grave,
Look'd at the ground and wonder'd in his soul,
What joyous anguish stirr'd his darken'd heart,
At the mere look of the familiar soil,
And found his answer in the words — *"Mine own!"*

Then came smooth-coated men, with eager eyes,
And talk'd of steamers on the cliff-bound lakes;
And iron tracks across the prairie lands;
And mills to crush the quartz of wealthy hills;
And mills to saw the great, wide-arm'd trees;
And mills to grind the singing stream of grain;
And with such busy clamor mingled still
The throbbing music of the bold, bright Axe —
The steel tongue of the Present, and the wail
Of falling forests — voices of the Past.

   Max, social-soul'd, and with his practised thews,
Was happy, boy-like, thinking much of Kate,
And speaking of her to the women-folk;
Who, mostly, happy in new honeymoons
Of hope themselves, were ready still to hear
The thrice-told tale of Katie's sunny eyes
And Katie's yellow hair, and household ways:
And heard so often, "There shall stand our home —
On yonder slope, with vines about the door!"
That the good wives were almost made to see
The snowy walls, deep porches, and the gleam
Of Katie's garments flitting through the rooms;
And the black slope all bristling with burn'd stumps
Was known amongst them all as "Max's House."

   O, Love builds on the azure sea,
     And Love builds on the golden sand;
  And Love builds on the rose-wing'd cloud,
     And sometimes Love builds on the land.

   O, if Love build on sparkling sea —
     And if Love build on golden strand —
  And if Love build on rosy cloud —
     To Love these are the solid land.

   O, Love will build his lily walls,
     And Love his pearly roof will rear, —
  On cloud or land, or mist or sea —
     Love's solid land is everywhere!

.   .   .

PART IV

   From his far wigwam sprang the strong North Wind
And rush'd with war-cry down the steep ravines,
And wrestl'd with the giants of the woods;
And with his ice-club beat the swelling crests
Of the deep watercourses into death,
And with his chill foot froze the whirling leaves
Of dun and gold and fire in icy banks;

And smote the tall reeds to the harden'd earth;
And sent his whistling arrows o'er the plains,
Scatt'ring the ling'ring herds — and sudden paus'd
When he had frozen all the running streams,
And hunted with his war-cry all the things
That breath'd about the woods, or roam'd the bleak
Bare prairies swelling to the mournful sky.
  "White Squaw," he shouted, troubl'd in his soul,
"I slew the dead, wrestl'd with naked chiefs
Unplum'd before, scalped of their leafy plumes;
I bound sick rivers in cold thongs of death,
And shot my arrows over swooning plains,
Bright with the Paint of death — and lean and bare.
And all the braves of my loud tribe will mock
And point at me — when our great chief, the Sun,
Relights his Council fire in the Moon
Of Budding Leaves: 'Ugh, ugh! he is a brave!
He fights with squaws and takes the scalps of babes!'
And the least wind will blow his calumet —
Fill'd with the breath of smallest flow'rs — across
The war-paint on my face, and pointing with
His small, bright pipe, that never moved a spear
Of bearded rice, cry, 'Ugh! he slays the dead!'
O, my white squaw, come from thy wigwam gray,
Spread thy white blanket on the twice-slain dead;
And hide them, ere the waking of the Sun!"
  High grew the snow beneath the low-hung sky,
And all was silent in the Wilderness;
In trance of stillness Nature heard her God
Rebuilding her spent fires, and veil'd her face
While the Great Worker brooded o'er His work.

  "Bite deep and wide, O Axe, the tree,
  What doth thy bold voice promise me?"

  "I promise thee all joyous things,
  That furnish forth the lives of kings!

  For ev'ry silver ringing blow,
  Cities and palaces shall grow!"

  "Bite deep and wide, O Axe, the tree,
  Tell wider prophecies to me."

  "When rust hath gnaw'd me deep and red,
  A nation strong shall lift his head!

  His crown the very Heav'ns shall smite,
  Aeons shall build him in his might!"

  "Bite deep and wide, O Axe, the tree;
  Bright Seer, help on thy prophecy!"

— 1884

THE CANOE

My masters twain made me a bed
Of pine-boughs resinous, and cedar;
Of moss, a soft and gentle breeder
Of dreams of rest; and me they spread
With furry skins, and laughing said,
"Now she shall lay her polish'd sides,
As queens do rest, or dainty brides,
Our slender lady of the tides!"

My masters twain their camp-soul lit,
Streamed incense from the hissing cones,
Large, crimson flashes grew and whirl'd
Thin, golden nerves of sly light curl'd
Round the dun camp, and rose faint zones,
Half way about each grim bole knit,
Like a shy child that would bedeck
With its soft clasp a Brave's red neck;
Yet sees the rough shield on his breast,
The awful plumes shake on his crest,
And fearful drops his timid face,
Nor dares complete the sweet embrace.

Into the hollow hearts of brakes,
Yet warm from sides of does and stags,
Pass'd to the crisp dark river flags;
Sinuous, red as copper snakes,
Sharp-headed serpents, made of light,
Glided and hid themselves in night.

My masters twain, the slaughter'd deer
Hung on fork'd boughs—with thongs of leather.
Bound were his stiff, slim feet together—
His eyes like dead stars cold and drear;
The wand'ring firelight drew near
And laid its wide palm, red and anxious,
On the sharp splendor of his branches;
On the white foam grown hard and sere
    On flank and shoulder.
Death—hard as breast of granite boulder,
    And under his lashes
Peer'd thro' his eyes at his life's grey ashes.

My masters twain sang songs that wove
(As they burnish'd hunting blade and rifle)
A golden thread with a cobweb trifle—
Loud of the chase, and low of love.

"O Love, art thou a silver fish?
Shy of the line and shy of gaffing,
Which we do follow, fierce, yet laughing,
Casting at thee the light-wing'd wish,
And at the last shall we bring thee up
From the crystal darkness under the cup
    Of lily folden,
    On broad leaves golden?

"O Love! art thou a silver deer,
Swift thy starr'd feet as wing of swallow,
While we with rushing arrows follow;
And at the last shall we draw near,
And over thy velvet neck cast thongs—
Woven of roses, of stars, of songs?
    New chains all moulden
    Of rare gems olden!"

They hung the slaughter'd fish like swords
On saplings slender—like scimitars
Bright, and ruddied from new-dead wars,
Blaz'd in the light—the scaly hordes.

They pil'd up boughs beneath the trees,
Of cedar-web and green fir tassel;
Low did the pointed pine tops rustle,
The camp fire blush'd to the tender breeze.

The hounds laid dew-laps on the ground,
With needles of pine sweet, soft and rusty—
Dream'd of the dead stag stout and lusty;
A bat by the red flames wove its round.

The darkness built its wigwam walls
Close round the camp, and at its curtain
Press'd shapes, thin woven and uncertain,
As white locks of tall waterfalls.

—1884

THE CITY TREE

I stand within the stony, arid town,
   I gaze for ever on the narrow street;
I hear for ever passing up and down,
   The ceaseless tramp of feet.

I know no brotherhood with far-lock'd woods,
   Where branches bourgeon from a kindred sap;
Where o'er moss'd roots, in cool, green solitudes,
   Small silver brooklets lap.

No em'rald vines creep wistfully to me,
   And lay their tender fingers on my bark;
High may I toss my boughs, yet never see
   Dawn's first most glorious spark.

When to and fro my branches wave and sway,
   Answ'ring the feeble wind that faintly calls,
They kiss no kindred boughs but touch alway
   The stones of climbing walls.

My heart is never pierc'd with song of bird;
   My leaves know nothing of that glad unrest,
Which makes a flutter in the still woods heard,
   When wild birds build a nest.

There never glance the eyes of violets up,
   Blue into the deep splendour of my green:
Nor falls the sunlight to the primrose cup,
   My quivering leaves between.

Not mine, not mine to turn from soft delight
   Of wood-bine breathings, honey sweet, and warm;
With kin embattl'd rear my glorious height
   To greet the coming storm!

Not mine to watch across the free, broad plains
   The whirl of stormy cohorts sweeping fast;
The level, silver lances of great rains,
   Blown onward by the blast.

Not mine the clamouring tempest to defy,
   Tossing the proud crest of my dusky leaves:
Defender of small flowers that trembling lie
   Against my barky greaves.

Not mine to watch the wild swan drift above,
   Balanced on wings that could not choose between
The wooing sky, blue as the eye of love,
   And my own tender green.

And yet my branches spread, a kingly sight,
  In the close prison of the drooping air:
When sun-vex'd noons are at their fiery height,
  My shade is broad, and there

Come city toilers, who their hour of ease
  Weave out to precious seconds as they lie
Pillow'd on horny hands, to hear the breeze
  Through my great branches die.

I see no flowers, but as the children race
  With noise and clamour through the dusty street,
I see the bud of many an angel face—
  I hear their merry feet.

No violets look up, but shy and grave,
  The children pause and lift their crystal eyes
To where my emerald branches call and wave—
  As to the mystic skies.

—1884

THE CAMP OF SOULS

My white canoe, like the silvery air
  O'er the River of Death that darkly rolls
When the moons of the world are round and fair,
  I paddle back from the "Camp of Souls."
When the wishton-wish in the low swamp grieves
Come the dark plumes of red "Singing Leaves."

Two hundred times have the moons of spring
  Rolled over the bright bay's azure breath
Since they decked me with plumes of an eagle's wing,
  And painted my face with the "paint of death,"
And from their pipes o'er my corpse there broke
The solemn rings of the blue "last smoke."

Two hundred times have the wintry moons
  Wrapped the dead earth in a blanket white;
Two hundred times have the wild sky loons
  Shrieked in the flush of the golden light
Of the first sweet dawn, when the summer weaves
Her dusky wigwam of perfect leaves.

Two hundred moons of the falling leaf
  Since they laid my bow in my dead right hand
And chanted above me the "song of grief"
  As I took my way to the spirit land;

92

Yet when the swallow the blue air cleaves
Come the dark plumes of red "Singing Leaves."

White are the wigwams in that far camp,
    And the star-eyed deer on the plains are found;
No bitter marshes or tangled swamp
    In the Manitou's happy hunting-ground!
And the moon of summer forever rolls
Above the red men in their "Camp of Souls."

Blue are its lakes as the wild dove's breast,
    And their murmurs soft as her gentle note;
As the calm, large stars in the deep sky rest,
    The yellow lilies upon them float;
And canoes, like flakes of the silvery snow,
Thro' the tall, rustling rice-beds come and go.

Green are its forests; no warrior wind
    Rushes on war trail the dusk grove through,
With leaf-scalps of tall trees mourning behind;
    But South Wind, heart friend of Great Manitou,
When ferns and leaves with cool dews are wet,
Blows flowery breaths from his red calumet.

Never upon them the white frosts lie,
    Nor glow their green boughs with the "paint of death";
Manitou smiles in the crystal sky,
    Close breathing above them His life-strong breath;
And He speaks no more in fierce thunder sound,
So near is His happy hunting-ground.

Yet often I love, in my white canoe,
    To come to the forests and camps of earth:
'Twas there death's black arrow pierced me through;
    'Twas there my red-browed mother gave me birth;
There I, in the light of a young man's dawn,
Won the lily heart of dusk "Springing Fawn."

And love is a cord woven out of life,
    And dyed in the red of the living heart;
And time is the hunter's rusty knife,
    That cannot cut the red strands apart:
And I sail from the spirit shore to scan
Where the weaving of that strong cord began.

But I may not come with a giftless hand,
    So richly I pile, in my white canoe,
Flowers that bloom in the spirit land,
    Immortal smiles of Great Manitou.
When I paddle back to the shores of earth
I scatter them over the white man's hearth.

For love is the breath of the soul set free;
    So I cross the river that darkly rolls,
That my spirit may whisper soft to thee
    Of *thine* who wait in the "Camp of Souls."
When the bright day laughs, or the wan night grieves,
Come the dusky plumes of red "Singing Leaves."

— 1905

WILFRED CAMPBELL

(1858-1918)

Wilfred Campbell was born in Kitchener (then Berlin), Ontario, the son of an Anglican clergyman. His boyhood was spent in various parishes in Eastern Ontario and in the Georgian Bay region. Here he began to write poetry and he became known as a romantic poet of the upper lakes. Lake Lyrics (1889) was not published, however, until after he had attended the University of Toronto, Wycliffe College, and the Episcopal Theological School of Cambridge, Massachusetts, and had preached at West Claremont, New Hampshire, and at St. Stephen, New Brunswick.

While he was in the United States, his religious orthodoxy was disturbed by Emersonian transcendentalism and by a study of mythology — both of which he regarded as bulwarks against animal (or nature) worship and other forms of materialism. He retired from the ministry in 1891 and entered the Civil Service at Ottawa. From then until his death on January 1, 1918, he devoted his leisure time to poems about the lakes, fields, and woods of Ontario, the ideals of the British race, and the spirit and destiny of man. He also wrote journalistic articles, poetic dramas, novels, and descriptive books about Canada.

THE WINTER LAKES

Out in a world of death, far to the northward lying,
    Under the sun and the moon, under the dusk and the day;
Under the glimmer of stars and the purple of sunsets dying,
    Wan and waste and white, stretch the great lakes away.

Never a bud of spring, never a laugh of summer,
    Never a dream of love, never a song of bird;
But only the silence and white, the shores that grow chiller and dumber,
    Wherever the ice-winds sob, and the griefs of winter are heard.

Crags that are black and wet out of the gray lake looming,
    Under the sunset's flush, and the pallid, faint glimmer of dawn;
Shadowy, ghost-like shores, where midnight surfs are booming
    Thunders of wintry woe over the spaces wan.

Lands that loom like spectres, whited regions of winter,
  Wastes of desolate woods, deserts of water and shore;
A world of winter and death, within these regions who enter,
  Lost to summer and life, go to return no more.

Moons that glimmer above, waters that lie white under,
  Miles and miles of lake far out under the night;
Foaming crests of waves, surfs that shoreward thunder,
  Shadowy shapes that flee, haunting the spaces white.

Lonely hidden bays, moon-lit, ice-rimmed, winding,
  Fringed by forests and crags, haunted by shadowy shores;
Hushed from the outward strife, where the mighty surf is grinding
  Death and hate on the rocks, as sandward and landward it roars.

— *1889*

INDIAN SUMMER

Along the line of smoky hills
  The crimson forest stands,
And all the day the blue-jay calls
  Throughout the autumn lands.

Now by the brook the maple leans
  With all his glory spread,
And all the sumachs on the hills
  Have turned their green to red.

Now by great marshes wrapt in mist,
  Or past some river's mouth,
Throughout the long, still autumn day
  Wild birds are flying south.

—*1889*

HOW ONE WINTER CAME IN THE LAKE REGION

For weeks and weeks the autumn world stood still,
  Clothed in the shadow of a smoky haze;
The fields were dead, the wind had lost its will,
And all the lands were hushed by wood and hill,
  In those gray, withered days.

Behind a mist the blear sun rose and set,
  At night the moon would nestle in a cloud;
The fisherman, a ghost, did cast his net;
The lake its shores forgot to chafe and fret,
  And hushed its caverns loud.

Far in the smoky woods the birds were mute,
  Save that from blackened tree a jay would scream,
Or far in swamps the lizard's lonesome lute
Would pipe in thirst, or by some gnarlèd root
  The tree-toad trilled his dream.

From day to day still hushed the season's mood,
  The streams stayed in their runnels shrunk and dry;
Suns rose aghast by wave and shore and wood,
And all the world, with ominous silence, stood
  In weird expectancy.

When one strange night the sun like blood went down,
  Flooding the heavens in a ruddy hue;
Red grew the lake, the sere fields parched and brown,
Red grew the marshes where the creeks stole down,
  But never a wind-breath blew.

That night I felt the winter in my veins,
  A joyous tremor of the icy glow;
And woke to hear the North's wild vibrant strains,
While far and wide, by withered woods and plains,
  Fast fell the driving snow.

— 1893

AT EVEN

I sit me moanless in the sombre fields,
The cows come with large udders down the dusk,
One cudless, the other chewing of a husk,
Her eye askance, for that athwart her heels,
Flea-haunted and rib-cavernous, there steals
The yelping farmer-dog. An old hen sits
And blinks her eyes. (Now I must rack my wits
To find a rhyme, while all this landscape reels.)

Yes! I forgot the sky. The stars are out,
There being no clouds; and then the pensive maid!
Of course she comes with tin-pail up the lane.
Mosquitoes hum and June bugs are about.
(That line hath "quality" of loftiest grade.)
And I have eased my soul of its sweet pain.

— 1893

PAN THE FALLEN

He wandered into the market
   With pipes and goatish hoof;
He wandered in a grotesque shape,
   And no one stood aloof.
For the children crowded round him,
   The wives and greybeards, too,
To crack their jokes and have their mirth,
   And see what Pan would do.

The Pan he was they knew him,
   Part man, but mostly beast,
Who drank, and lied, and snatched what bones
   Men threw him from their feast;
Who seemed in sin so merry,
   So careless in his woe,
That men despised, scarce pitied him,
   And still would have it so.

He swelled his pipes and thrilled them,
   And drew the silent tear;
He made the gravest clack with mirth
   By his sardonic leer.
He blew his pipes full sweetly
   At their amused demands,
And caught the scornful, earth-flung pence
   That fell from careless hands.

He saw the mob's derision,
   And took it kindly, too,
And when an epithet was flung,
   A coarser back he threw;
But under all the masking
   Of a brute, unseemly part,
I looked, and saw a wounded soul,
   And a god-like, breaking heart.

And back of the elfin music,
   The burlesque, clownish play,
I knew a wail that the weird pipes made,
   A look that was far away—
A gaze into some far heaven
   Whence a soul had fallen down;
But the mob only saw the grotesque beast
   And the antics of the clown.

For scant-flung pence he paid them
   With mirth and elfin play,
Till, tired for a time of his antics queer,
   They passed and went their way;
Then there in the empty market
   He ate his scanty crust,
And, tired face turned to heaven, down
   He laid him in the dust.

And over his wild, strange features
   A softer light there fell,
And on his worn, earth-driven heart
   A peace ineffable.
And the moon rose over the market,
   But Pan the beast was dead;
While Pan the god lay silent there,
   With his strange, distorted head.

And the people, when they found him,
   Stood still with awesome fear.
No more they saw the beast's rude hoof,
   The furtive, clownish leer;
But the lightest in that audience
   Went silent from the place,
For they knew the look of a god released
   That shone from his dead face.

—1893

SIR CHARLES G. D. ROBERTS

(1860-1943)

Born in the parish of Douglas, about ten miles north of Fredericton, Charles George Douglas Roberts spent his boyhood at the old Westcock Parsonage of St. Ann's, Sackville, overlooking the Tantramar marshes. He was the son of an Anglican clergyman and classical scholar, whose father and grandfather had been teachers of Latin and Greek. His mother traced her lineage back to the grandfather of Ralph Waldo Emerson, the Reverend Daniel Bliss, who was a United Empire Loyalist. The family name was borne by her sister's son, Bliss Carman.

When Charles was fourteen, the family moved to the Rectory at Fredericton. Here he attended the Collegiate School, of which the Headmaster was George R. Parkin. An invaluable friend and guide, Parkin inspired Roberts and Carman with a vital interest in Homer, Virgil, Horace, Keats, Shelley, the Pre-Raphaelites, Tennyson, Browning, and Arnold. At the University of New Brunswick, which Roberts attended from 1876 to 1879, Greek and Latin were still his favorites, but much of his time was now devoted to writing the verses which were to be published in Orion and Other Poems *(1880). "Ode to Drowsihood" is an example of this early verse, and clearly shows the young poet struggling to relate imported poetic imagery to his direct personal experience of Canadian nature.*

From 1879 to 1881 Roberts was headmaster of the Grammar School at Chatham; then he returned to Fredericton as headmaster of a local school. He had married in December 1880.

In 1883, when Goldwin Smith was planning to publish a new Canadian journal, The Week, *Roberts went to Toronto to become its editor, but he disagreed so thoroughly with Smith that he resigned in February 1884. A period of free-lancing came to a close when King's College, of Windsor, Nova Scotia, appointed him to its faculty in 1885 as Professor of English and French, later English and Economics. For ten years he was a college teacher and an author who wrote a number of books in the study of Kingscroft, his home on the edge of the college woods. Bliss Carman came to visit him there and was inspired by the neighboring village of Grand Pré. From Windsor Roberts went to Fredericton, where he worked as a free-lance once again, and in February 1897 he moved to New York to live with Bliss Carman in a rooming house while he held the position of assistant editor of* The Illustrated American. *He was able to drop his editorship the following autumn to devote all his time to successful free-lancing, with a growing list of books in both prose and poetry to his credit. Roberts visited England in 1889, but it was not until November 1907 that he left America for seventeen years abroad. He lived on the continent and in England, with London as his headquarters. During the first months of the War of 1914-1918 he enlisted in the British Army and rose to a captaincy; in 1916 he transferred to the Canadian Forces Overseas with the rank of Major and spent a part of 1916 and 1917 in France. Following the peace, he travelled in Europe and North Africa and lived in many parts of England.*

In 1925, however, he returned to Canada. A series of lectures and recitals took him across the nation. His renewed association with the literary life of his country was marked by the award to him of the Royal Society of Canada's first Lorne Pierce Medal and by his election as President of the Canadian Authors' Association. On June 3, 1935, he was honored by a knighthood. Roberts had taken up residence in Toronto, and there his reputation as a pioneer and a leading spirit in Canadian letters grew steadily, in spite of the rise of new literary movements. He died on November 26, 1943.

ODE TO DROWSIHOOD

Breather of honeyed breath upon my face!
  Teller of balmy tales! Weaver of dreams!
  Sweet conjurer of palpitating gleams
And peopled shadows trooping into place
          In purple streams
Between the drooped lid and the drowsy eye!
  Moth-winged seducer, dusky-soft and brown,
Of bubble gifts and bodiless minstrelsy
  Lavish enough! Of rest the restful crown!
At whose behest are closed the lips that sigh,
  And weary heads lie down.

Thee, Nodding Spirit! Magic Comforter!
  Thee, with faint mouth half speechless, I invoke,
  And straight uplooms through the dead centuries' smoke
The agéd Druid in his robe of fur,
          Beneath the oak
Where hang uncut the paly mistletoes.
  The mistletoe dissolves to Indian willow,
Glassing its red stems in the stream that flows
  Through the broad interval; a lazy billow
Flung from my oar lifts the long grass that grows
  To be the Naiad's pillow.

The startled meadow-hen floats off, to sink
  Into remoter shades and ferny glooms;
  The great bees drone about the thick pea-blooms;
The linkéd bubblings of the bobolink,
          With warm perfumes
From the broad-flowered wild parsnip, drown my brain;
  The grackles bicker in the alder boughs;
The grasshoppers pipe out their thin refrain
  That with intenser heat the noon endows:
Then thy weft weakens, and I wake again
  Out of my dreamful drowse.

Ah! fetch thy poppy-baths, juices exprest
  In fervid sunshine, where the Javan palm
  Stirs scarce awakened from its odorous calm
By the enervate wind, that sinks to rest
          Amid the balm
And sultry silence, murmuring, half asleep,
  Cool fragments of the ocean's foamy roar,
And of the surge's mighty sobs that keep
  Forever yearning up the golden shore,
Mingled with song of Nereids that leap
  Where the curled crests downpour.

Who sips thy wine may float in Baiæ's skies,
    Or flushed Maggiore's ripples, mindless made
    Of storming troubles hard to be allayed.
Who eats thy berries, for his ears and eyes
        May vineyard shade
Melt with soft Tuscan, glow with arms and lips
    Cream-white and crimson, making mock at reason.
Thy balm on brows by care uneaten drips;
    I have thy favors, but I fear thy treason.
Fain would I hold thee by the dusk wing-tips
    Against a grievous season.

—1880

TANTRAMAR REVISITED

Summers and summers have come, and gone with the flight of the swallow;
Sunshine and thunder have been, storm, and winter, and frost;
Many and many a sorrow has all but died from remembrance,
Many a dream of joy fall'n in the shadow of pain.
Hands of chance and change have marred, or molded, or broken,
Busy with spirit or flesh, all I most have adored;
Even the bosom of Earth is strewn with heavier shadows,—
Only in these green hills, aslant to the sea, no change!
Here where the road that has climbed from the inland valleys and woodlands,
Dips from the hilltops down, straight to the base of the hills,—
Here, from my vantage-ground, I can see the scattering houses,
Stained with time, set warm in orchards, meadows, and wheat,

Dotting the broad light slopes outspread to southward and eastward,
Wind-swept all day long, blown by the southeast wind.
Skirting the sunbright uplands stretches a riband of meadow,
Shorn of the laboring grass, bulwarked well from the sea,
Fenced on its seaward border with long clay dykes from the turbid
Surge and flow of the tides vexing the Westmoreland shores.
Yonder, toward the left, lie broad the Westmoreland marshes,—
Miles on miles they extend, level, and grassy, and dim,
Clear from the long red sweep of flats to the sky in the distance,
Save for the outlying heights, green-rampired Cumberland Point;
Miles on miles outrolled, and the river-channels divide them,—
Miles on miles of green, barred by the hurtling gusts.

Miles on miles beyond the tawny bay is Minudie.
There are the low blue hills; villages gleam at their feet.
Nearer a white sail shines across the water, and nearer
Still are the slim, gray masts of fishing boats dry on the flats.
Ah, how well I remember those wide red flats, above tide-mark
Pale with scurf of the salt, seamed and baked in the sun!

Well I remember the piles of blocks and ropes, and the net-reels
Wound with the beaded nets, dripping and dark from the sea!
Now at this season the nets are unwound; they hang from the rafters
Over the fresh-stowed hay in upland barns, and the wind
Blows all day through the chinks, with the streaks of sunlight, and sways them
Softly at will; or they lie heaped in the gloom of a loft.

Now at this season the reels are empty and idle; I see them
Over the lines of the dykes, over the gossiping grass.
Now at this season they swing in the long strong wind, thro' the lonesome
Golden afternoon, shunned by the foraging gulls.
Near about sunset the crane will journey homeward above them;
Round them, under the moon, all the calm night long,
Winnowing soft gray wings of marsh-owls wander and wander,
Now to the broad, lit marsh, now to the dusk of the dike.
Soon, thro' their dew-wet frames, in the live keen freshness of morning,
Out of the teeth of the dawn blows back the awakening wind.
Then, as the blue day mounts, and the low-shot shafts of the sunlight
Glance from the tide to the shore, gossamers jewelled with dew
Sparkle and wave, where late sea-spoiling fathoms of driftnet
Myriad-meshed, uploomed sombrely over the land.

Well I remember it all. The salt raw scent of the margin;
While, with men at the windlass, groaned each reel, and the net,
Surging in ponderous lengths, uprose and coiled in its station;
Then each man to his home,— well I remember it all!

Yet, as I sit and watch, this present peace of the landscape,—
Stranded boats, these reels empty and idle, the hush,
One gray hawk slow-wheeling above yon cluster of haystacks,—
More than the old-time stir this stillness welcomes me home.

Ah, the old-time stir, how once it stung me with rapture,—
Old-time sweetness, the winds freighted with honey and salt!
Yet will I stay my steps and not go down to the marshland,—
Muse and recall far off, rather remember than see,—
Lest on too close sight I miss the darling illusion,
Spy at their task even here the hands of chance and change.

—1887

IN AN OLD BARN

Tons upon tons the brown-green fragrant hay
  O'erbrims the mows beyond the time-warped eaves,
  Up to the rafters where the spider weaves,
Though few flies wander his secluded way.
Through a high chink one lonely golden ray,
  Wherein the dust is dancing, slants unstirred.
  In the dry hush some rustlings light are heard,
Of winter-hidden mice at furtive play.

Far down, the cattle in their shadowed stalls,
  Nose-deep in clover fodder's meadowy scent,
  Forget the snows that whelm their pasture streams,
The frost that bites the world beyond their walls.
  Warm housed, they dream of summer, well content
  In day-long contemplation of their dreams.

"Wild Geese Ostenso

— *1893*

✽ THE FLIGHT OF THE GEESE   *- A Sonnet*

I hear the low wind wash the softening snow,
  The low tide loiter down the shore. The night
  Full filled with April forecast, hath no light.
The salt wave on the sedge-flat pulses slow.
Through the hid furrows lisp in murmurous flow
  The thaw's shy ministers; and hark! The height
  Of heaven grows weird and loud with unseen flight
Of strong hosts prophesying as they go!

blank verse

High through the drenched and hollow night their wings
  Beat northward hard on winter's trail. The sound
Of their confused and solemn voices, borne
Athwart the dark to their long Arctic morn,
  Comes with a sanction and an awe profound,
A boding of unknown, foreshadowed things.

— Iambic — pentameter

—*1893*

IN THE WIDE AWE AND WISDOM OF
THE NIGHT

In the wide awe and wisdom of the night
  I saw the round world rolling on its way,
Beyond significance of depth or height,
  Beyond the interchange of dark and day.
I marked the march to which is set no pause,
  And that stupendous orbit, round whose rim
The great sphere sweeps, obedient unto laws
  That utter the eternal thought of Him.
I compassed time, outstripped the starry speed,
  And in my still soul apprehended space,
Till, weighing laws which these but blindly heed,
  At last I came before Him face to face—
And knew the Universe of no such span
As the august infinitude of Man.

—*1893*

103

THE SKATER

My glad feet shod with the glittering steel
I was the god of the winged heel.

The hills in the far white sky were lost;
The world lay still in the wide white frost;

And the woods hung hushed in their long white dream
By the ghostly, glimmering, ice-blue stream.

Here was a pathway, smooth like glass,
Where I and the wandering wind might pass

To the far-off palaces, drifted deep,
Where Winter's retinue rests in sleep.

I followed the lure, I fled like a bird,
Till the startled hollows awoke and heard

A spinning whisper, a sibilant twang,
As the stroke of the steel on the tense ice rang;

And the wandering wind was left behind
As faster, faster I followed my mind;
Till the blood sang high in my eager brain,
And the joy of my flight was almost pain.

Then I stayed the rush of my eager speed
And silently went as a drifting seed, —

Slowly, furtively, till my eyes
Grew big with the awe of a dim surmise,

And the hair of my neck began to creep
At hearing the wilderness talk in sleep.

Shapes in the fir-gloom drifted near.
In the deep of my heart I heard my fear;

And I turned and fled, like a soul pursued,
From the white, inviolate solitude.

— 1896

KINSHIP

Back to the bewildering vision
  And the borderland of birth;
Back into the looming wonder,
  The companionship of earth;

Back unto the simple kindred —
  Childlike fingers, childlike eyes,
Working, waiting, comprehending,
  Now in patience, now surprise;

Back unto the faithful healing
  And the candor of the sod —
Scent of mold and moisture stirring
  At the secret touch of God;

Back into the ancient stillness
  Where the wise enchanter weaves,
To the twine of questing tree-root,
  The expectancy of leaves;

Back to hear the hushed consulting
  Over bud and blade and germ,
As the Mother's mood apportions
  Each its pattern, each its term;

Back into the grave beginnings
  Where all wonder-tales are true,
Strong enchantments, strange successions,
  Mysteries of old and new;

Back to knowledge and renewal,
  Faith to fashion and reveal,
Take me, Mother, — in compassion
  All thy hurt ones fain to heal.

Back to wisdom take me, Mother;
  Comfort me with kindred hands;
Tell me tales the world's forgetting,
  Till my spirit understands.

Tell me how some sightless impulse,
  Working out a hidden plan,
God for kin and clay for fellow,
  Wakes to find itself a man.

Tell me how the life of mortal,
  Wavering from breath to breath,
Like a web of scarlet pattern
  Hurtles from the loom of death.

How the caged bright bird, desire,
  Which the hands of God deliver,
Beats aloft to drop unheeded
  At the confines of forever.

Faints unheeded for a season,
  Then outwings the farthest star,
To the wisdom and the stillness
  Where thy consummations are.
                              —1896

ORIGINS

Out of the dreams that heap
The hollow hand of sleep;
Out of the dark sublime,
The echoing deeps of time;
From the averted Face
Beyond the bournes of space,
Into the sudden sun
We journey, one by one.
Out of the hidden shade
Wherein desire is made;
Out of the pregnant stir
Where death and life confer;
The dark and mystic heat
Where soul and matter meet;
The enigmatic Will;
We start, and then are still.

    Inexorably decreed
By the ancestral deed,
The puppets of our sires,
We work out blind desires,
And for our sons ordain,
The blessing or the bane.
In ignorance we stand
With fate on either hand,
And question stars and earth
Of life, and death, and birth.
With wonder in our eyes
We scan the kindred skies,
While through the common grass
Our atoms mix and pass.
We feel the sap go free
When spring comes to the tree;
And in our blood is stirred
What warms the brooding bird.

The vital fire we breathe
That bud and blade bequeathe,
And strength of native clay
In our full veins hath sway.
　　But in the urge intense
And fellowship of sense,

Suddenly comes a word
In other ages heard.
On a great wind our souls
Are borne to unknown goals,
And past the bournes of space
To the unaverted Face.

—1896

THE SOLITARY WOODSMAN

When the gray lake-water rushes
Past the dripping alder-bushes,
　　And the bodeful autumn wind
In the fir-tree weeps and hushes, —

When the air is sharply damp
Round the solitary camp,
　　And the moose-bush in the thicket
Glimmers like a scarlet lamp, —

When the birches twinkle yellow,
And the cornel bunches mellow,
　　And the owl across the twilight
Trumpets to his downy fellow, —

When the nut-fed chipmunks romp
Through the maples' crimson pomp,
　　And the slim viburnum flushes
In the darkness of the swamp,—

When the blueberries are dead,
When the rowan clusters red,
　　And the shy bear, summer-sleekened,
In the bracken makes his bed,—

On a day there comes once more
To the latched and lonely door,
　　Down the wood-road striding silent,
One who has been here before.

Green spruce branches for his head,
Here he makes his simple bed,

Crouching with the sun, and rising
When the dawn is frosty red.

All day long he wanders wide
With the gray moss for his guide,
　　And his lonely axe-stroke startles
The expectant forest-side.

Toward the quiet close of day
Back to camp he takes his way,
　　And about his sober footsteps
Unafraid the squirrels play.

On his roof the red leaf falls,
At his door the bluejay calls,
　　And he hears the wood-mice hurry
Up and down his rough log walls;

Hears the laughter of the loon
Thrill the dying afternoon,—
　　Hears the calling of the moose
Echo to the early moon.

And he hears the partridge drumming,
The belated hornet humming,—
　　All the faint, prophetic sounds
That foretell the winter's coming.

And the wind about his eaves
Through the chilly night-wet grieves,
　　And the earth's dumb patience fills him,
Fellow to the falling leaves.

—1898

AS DOWN THE WOODLAND WAYS

As down the woodland ways I went
　　With every wind asleep
I felt the surge of endless life
　　About my footsteps creep.

I felt the urge of quickening mold
　　That had been once a flower
Mount with the sap to bloom again
　　At its appointed hour.

I saw gray stumps go crumbling down
  In sodden, grim decay,
To soar in pillared green again
  On some remoter day.

I saw crushed beetles, mangled grubs,
  All crawling, perished things,
Whirl up in air, an ecstasy
  Of many-colored wings.

Through weed and world, through worm and star,
  The sequence ran the same —
Death but the travail-pang of life,
  Destruction but a name.

—1941

IN THE DEEP OF THE GRASS

Misty gray green, washed with tints of the palest violet, spotted with red clover-blooms, white oxeyes, and hot orange Canada lilies, the deep-grassed levels basked under the July sun. A drowsy hum of bees and flies seemed to distil, with warm aromatic scents, from the sun-steeped blooms and grass-tops. The broad, blooming, tranquil expanse, shimmering and softly radiant in the heat, seemed the very epitome of summer. Now and again a small cloud-shadow sailed across it. Now and again a little wind, swooping down upon it gently, bent the grass-tops all one way, and spread a sudden silvery pallor. Save for the droning bees and flies there seemed to be but one live creature astir between the grass and the blue. A solitary marsh-hawk, far over by the rail fence, was winnowing slowly, slowly, hither and thither, lazily hunting.

All this was in the world above the grass-tops. But below the grass-tops was a very different world — a dense, tangled world of dim green shade, shot with piercing shafts of sun, and populous with small, furtive life. Here, among the brown and white roots, the crowded green stems, and the mottled stalks, the little earth kindreds went busily about their affairs and their desires, giving scant thought to the aerial world above them. All that made life significant to them was here in the warm green gloom; and when anything chanced to part the grass to its depths they would scurry away in unanimous indignation.

On a small stone, over which the green closed so thickly that, when he chanced to look upward, he caught but the scantiest shreds of sky, sat a half-grown field-mouse, washing his whiskers with his dainty claws. His tiny, bead-like eyes kept ceaseless watch, peering through the shadowy tangle for whatever might come near in the shape of foe or prey. Presently two or three stems above his head were beaten down, and a big green grasshopper, alighting clumsily from one of his blind leaps, fell sprawling on the stone. Before he could struggle to his long legs and climb back to the safer region of the grass-tops, the little mouse was upon him. Sharp, white teeth pierced his green mail, his legs kicked convulsively twice or thrice, and the faint iridescence faded out of his big, blank, foolish eyes. The mouse made his meal with relish, daintily discarding the dry legs and wing-cases. Then amid the green debris scattered upon the stone, he sat up, and once more went through his fastidious toilet.

But life for the little mouse in his grass-world was not quite all watching and hunting. When his toilet was complete, and he had amiably let a large black cricket crawl by unmolested, he suddenly began to whirl round on the stone, chasing his own tail. As he was amusing himself with this foolish play, another mouse, about the same size as himself, and probably of the same litter, jumped upon the stone, and knocked him off. He promptly retorted in kind; and for several minutes, as if the game were a well-understood one, the two kept it up, squeaking soft merriment, and apparently forgetful of all peril. The grass-tops above this play rocked and rustled in a way that would certainly have attracted attention had there been any eyes to see. But the marsh-hawk was still hunting lazily at the other side of the field, and no tragedy followed the childishness.

Both seemed to tire of the sport at the same instant; for suddenly they stopped, and hurried away through the grass on opposite sides of the stone, as if remembered business had just called to them. Whatever the business was, the first mouse seemed to forget it very speedily, for in half a minute he was back upon the stone again, combing his fine whiskers and scratching his ears. This done to his satisfaction, he dropped like a flash from his seat, and disappeared into a small hollow beneath it. As he did so, a hairy black spider darted out, and ran away among the roots.

A minute or two after the disappearance of the mouse, a creature came along which appeared gigantic in the diminutive world of the grass folk. It was nearly three feet long, and of the thickness of a man's finger. Of a steely gray-black, striped and reticulated in a mysterious pattern with a clear whitish yellow, it was an ominous shape indeed, as it glided smoothly and swiftly, in graceful curves, through the close green tangle. The cool shadows and thin lights touched it flickeringly as it went, and never a grass-top stirred to mark its sinister approach. Without a sound of warning it came straight up to the stone, and darted its narrow, cruel head into the hole.

There was a sharp squeak, and instantly the narrow head came out again, ejected by the force of the mouse's agonized spring. But the snake's teeth were fastened in the little animal's neck. The doom of the green world had come upon him while he slept.

But doomed though he was, the mouse was game. He knew there was no poison in those fangs that gripped him, and he struggled desperately to break free. His powerful hind legs kicked the ground with a force which the snake, hampered at first by the fact of its length being partly trailed out through the tangle, was unable to quite control. With unerring instinct — though this was the first snake he had ever encountered — the mouse strove to reach its enemy's back and sever the bone with the fine chisels of his teeth. But it was just this that the snake was watchful to prevent. Three times in his convulsive leaps the mouse succeeded in touching the snake's body — but with his feet only, never once with those destructive little teeth. The snake held him inexorably, with a steady, elastic pressure which yielded just so far, and never quite far enough. And in a minute or two the mouse's brave struggles grew more feeble.

All this, however, — the lashing and the wriggling and the jumping — had not gone on without much disturbance to the grass-tops. Timothy head and clover-bloom, oxeye, and feathery plume-grass, they had bowed and swayed and shivered till the commotion, very conspicuous to one looking down upon the tranquil, flowery sea of green, caught the attention of the marsh-hawk, which at that moment chanced to be perching on a high fence stake. The lean-headed, fierce-eyed, trim-feathered bird shot from his perch, and sailed on long wings over the grass to see what was happening. As the swift shadow hovered over the grass-tops, the snake looked up. Well he understood the significance of that sudden shade. Jerking back his fangs with difficulty from the mouse's neck, he started to glide off under the thickest matting of the roots. But lightning-quick though he was, he was not quite quick enough. Just as his narrow head darted under the roots, the hawk, with wings held straight up, and talons reaching down, dropped upon him, and clutched the middle of his back in a grip of steel. The next moment he was jerked into the air, writhing and coiling, and striking in vain frenzy at his captor's mail of hard feathers. The hawk flew off with him over the sea of green to the top of the fence stake, there to devour him at leisure. The mouse, sore wounded but not past recovery, dragged himself back to the hollow under the stone. And over the stone the grass-tops, once more still, hummed with flies, and breathed warm perfumes in the distilling heat.

— *1904*

BLISS CARMAN

(1861-1929)

Bliss Carman was born in Fredericton, New Brunswick, of Loyalist stock. Like Charles G. D. Roberts, he was descended from the Reverend Daniel Bliss of Concord, the grandfather of Ralph Waldo Emerson. Carman was educated at the Collegiate School in Fredericton and the University of New Brunswick. After his graduation in 1881 he studied at Edinburgh for two years. Returning to Canada, he contemplated a career in law or engineering, but instead went to Harvard, where he read philosophy under Royce and met Richard Hovey, who collaborated with him in the "Vagabondia" books that appeared in the years 1894-1912. From 1890 until 1898, Carman worked as a journalist and editor for various American magazines. Low Tide on Grand Pré (1893), his first book, was named for a poem inspired by the Evangeline country in Nova Scotia, near Windsor, where Carman went to visit Roberts.

During the last thirty years of his life Carman devoted himself to poetry and occasional essays. "Subconscious Art," reprinted here from The Kinship of Nature *(1903), clearly states his early poetic theory and practice. After 1908 he lived at New Canaan, Connecticut, in the winter, and in the Catskills during the summer. When Roberts returned to Canada in 1925, Carman also travelled in his homeland and gave many readings, especially in the West. The Lorne Pierce Gold Medal of the Royal Society of Canada was awarded him in 1928. He died in New Canaan, but his ashes were buried in Fredericton.*

Here by the gray north sea,
  In the wintry heart of the wild,
Comes the old dream of thee,
  Guendolen, mistress and child.

The heart of the forest grieves
  In the drift against my door;
A voice is under the eaves,
  A footfall on the floor.

Threshold, mirror, and hall,
  Vacant and strangely aware,
Wait for their soul's recall
  With the dumb expectant air.

Here when the smoldering west
  Burns down into the sea,
I take no heed of rest
  And keep the watch for thee.

I sit by the fire and hear
  The restless wind go by,
On the long dirge and drear
  Under the low bleak sky.

When day puts out to sea
  And night makes in for land,
There is no lock for thee,
  Each door awaits thy hand!

When night goes over the hill
  And dawn comes down the dale,
It's O for the wild sweet will
  That shall no more prevail!

When the zenith moon is round,
  And snow-wraiths gather and run,
And there is set no bound
  To love beneath the sun,

O wayward will, come near
  The old mad wilful way,
The soft mouth at my ear
  With words too sweet to say!

Come, for the night is cold,
  The ghostly moonlight fills
Hollow and rift and fold
  Of the eerie Ardise hills!

The windows of my room
  Are dark with bitter frost,
The stillness aches with doom
  Of something loved and lost.

Outside, the great blue star
  Burns in the ghostland pale,
Where giant Algebar
  Holds on the endless trail.

Come, for the years are long,
  And silence keeps the door,
Where shapes with the shadows throng
  The firelit chamber floor.

Come, for thy kiss was warm,
  With the red embers' glare
Across thy folding arm
  And dark tumultuous hair!

And though thy coming rouse
  The sleep-cry of no bird,
The keepers of the house
  Shall tremble at thy word.

Come, for the soul is free!
  In all the vast dreamland
There is no lock for thee,
  Each door awaits thy hand.

Ah, not in dreams at all,
  Fleering, perishing, dim,
But thy old self, supple and tall,
  Mistress and child of whim!

The proud imperious guise,
  Impetuous and serene,
The sad mysterious eyes,
  And dignity of mien!

Yea, wilt thou not return,
  When the late hill-winds veer,
And the bright hill-flowers burn
  With the reviving year?

When April comes, and the sea
  Sparkles as if it smiled,
Will they restore to me
  My dark Love, empress and child?

The curtains seem to part;
  A sound is on the stair,
As if at the last---I start;
  Only the wind is there.

Lo, now far on the hills
  The crimson fumes uncurled,
Where the cauldron mantles and spills
  Another dawn on the world!

—1893

trochaic tetrameter   *Rhyme Scheme*
a - b - c - b

THE EAVESDROPPER

In a still room at hush of dawn,
  My Love and I lay side by side
And heard the roaming forest wind
  Stir in the paling autumn-tide.

I watched her earth-brown eyes grow glad
  Because the round day was so fair;
While memories of reluctant night
  Lurked in the blue dusk of her hair.

Outside, a yellow maple tree,
  Shifting upon the silvery blue
With tiny multitudinous sound,
  Rustled to let the sunlight through.

The livelong day the elvish leaves
  Danced with their shadows on the floor;
And the lost children of the wind
  Went straying homeward by our door.

And all the swarthy afternoon
  We watched the great deliberate sun
Walk through the crimsoned hazy world,
  Counting his hilltops one by one.

Then as the purple twilight came
  And touched the vines along our eaves,
Another Shadow stood without
  And gloomed the dancing of the leaves.

The silence fell on my Love's lips;
  Her great brown eyes were veiled and sad
With pondering some maze of dream,
  Though all the splendid year was glad.

Restless and vague as a gray wind
  Her heart had grown, she knew not why.
But hurrying to the open door,
  Against the verge of western sky

I saw retreating on the hills,
  Looming and sinister and black,
The stealthy figure swift and huge
  Of One who strode and looked not back.

—1893

LOW TIDE ON GRAND PRÉ

The sun goes down, and over all
  These barren reaches by the tide
Such unelusive glories fall,
  I almost dream they yet will bide
  Until the coming of the tide.

And yet I know that not for us,
  By any ecstasy of dream,
He lingers to keep luminous
  A little while the grievous stream,
  Which frets, uncomforted of dream—

A grievous stream, that to and fro
  Athrough the fields of Acadie
Goes wandering, as if to know
  Why one beloved face should be
  So long from home and Acadie.

Was it a year or lives ago
  We took the grasses in our hands,
And caught the summer flying low
  Over the waving meadow lands,
  And held it there between our hands?

The while the river at our feet—
　A drowsy inland meadow stream—
At set of sun the after-heat
　Made running gold, and in the gleam
　We freed our birch upon the stream.

There down along the elms at dusk
　We lifted dripping blade to drift,
Through twilight scented fine like musk,
　Where night and gloom awhile uplift,
　Nor sunder soul and soul adrift.

And that we took into our hands
　Spirit of life or subtler thing—
Breathed on us there, and loosed the bands
　Of death, and taught us, whispering,
　The secret of some wonder-thing.

Then all your face grew light, and seemed
　To hold the shadow of the sun;
The evening faltered, and I deemed
　That time was ripe, and years had done
　Their wheeling underneath the sun.

So all desire and all regret,
　And fear and memory, were naught;
One to remember or forget
　The keen delight our hands had caught;
　Morrow and yesterday were naught.

The night has fallen, and the tide---
　Now and again comes drifting home,
Across these aching barrens wide,
　A sigh like driven wind or foam:
　In grief the flood is bursting home.

　　　　　　　　　　　　　—1893

SPRING SONG

Make me over, mother April,
When the sap begins to stir!
When thy flowery hand delivers
All the mountain-prisoned rivers,
And thy great heart beats and quivers
To revive the days that were,
Make me over, mother April,
When the sap begins to stir!

Take my dust and all my dreaming,
Count my heart-beats one by one,
Send them where the winters perish;
Then some golden noon recherish
And restore them in the sun,
Flower and scent and dust and dreaming,
With their heart-beats every one!

Set me in the urge and tide-drift
Of the streaming hosts a-wing!
Breast of scarlet, throat of yellow,
Raucous challenge, wooings mellow—
Every migrant is my fellow,
Making northward with the spring.
Loose me in the urge and tide-drift
Of the streaming hosts a-wing!

Shrilling pipe or fluting whistle,
In the valleys come again
Fife of frog and call of tree-toad,
All my brothers, five or three-toed,

With their revel no more vetoed,
Making music in the rain;
Shrilling pipe or fluting whistle,
In the valleys come again.

Make me of thy seed tomorrow,
When the sap beings to stir!
Tawny light-foot, sleepy bruin,
Bright-eyes in the orchard ruin,
Gnarl the good life goes askew in,
Whiskey-jack, or tanager,—
Make me anything tomorrow,
When the sap begins to stir!

Make me even (How do I know?)
Like my friend the gargoyle there;
It may be the heart within him
Swells that doltish hands should pin him
Fixed forever in mid-air.
Make me even sport for swallows,
Like the soaring gargoyle there!

Give me the old clue to follow,
Through the labyrinth of night!
Clod of clay with heart of fire,
Things that burrow and aspire,
With the vanishing desire,
For the perishing delight,—
Only the old clue to follow,
Through the labyrinth of night.

Make me over, mother April,
When the sap begins to stir!
Fashion me from swamp or meadow,
Garden plot or ferny shadow,
Hyacinth or humble burr!
Make me over, mother April,
When the sap begins to stir!

Let me hear the far, low summons,
When the silver winds return;
Rills that run and streams that stammer,
Goldenwing with his loud hammer,
Icy brooks that brawl and clamor,
Where the Indian willows burn;
Let me hearken to the calling,
When the silver winds return,

Till recurring and recurring,
Long since wandered and come back,
Like a whim of Grieg's or Gounod's,
This same self, bird, bud, or Bluenose,
Some day I may capture (Who knows?)
Just the one last joy I lack,
Waking to the far new summons,
When the old spring winds come back.

For I have no choice of being,
When the sap begins to climb,—
Strong insistence, sweet intrusion,
Vasts and verges of illusion,—
So I win, to time's confusion,
The one perfect pearl of time,
Joy and joy and joy forever,
Till the sap forgets to climb!

Make me over in the morning
From the rag-bag of the world!
Scraps of dream and duds of daring,
Home-brought stuff from far sea-faring,
Faded colors once so flaring,
Shreds of banners long since furled!
Hues of ash and glints of glory,
In the rag-bag of the world!

Let me taste the old immortal
Indolence of life once more;
Not recalling nor foreseeing,
Let the great slow joys of being
Well my heart through as of yore!
Let me taste the old immortal
Indolence of life once more!

Give me the old drink for rapture,
The delirium to drain,
All my fellows drank in plenty
At the Three Score Inns and Twenty
From the mountains to the main!
Give me the old drink for rapture,
The delirium to drain!

Only make me over, April,
When the sap begins to stir!
Make me man or make me woman,
Make me oaf or ape or human,
Cup of flower or cone of fir;
Make me anything but neuter
When the sap begins to stir!

—1894

A VAGABOND SONG

There is something in the autumn that is native to my blood —
Touch of manner, hint of mood;
And my heart is like a rhyme,
With the yellow and the purple and the crimson keeping time.

The scarlet of the maples can shake me like a cry
Of bugles going by.
And my lonely spirit thrills
To see the frosty asters like a smoke upon the hills.

There is something in October sets the gypsy blood astir;
We must rise and follow her,
When from every hill of flame
She calls and calls each vagabond by name.

— 1896

THE GRAVEDIGGER

Oh, the shambling sea is a sexton old,
And well his work is done.
With an equal grave for lord and knave,
He buries them every one.

Then hoy and rip, with a rolling hip,
He makes for the nearest shore;
And God, who sent him a thousand ship,
Will send him a thousand more;
But some he'll save for a bleaching grave,
And shoulder them in to shore, —
Shoulder them in, shoulder them in,
Shoulder them in to shore.

Oh, the ships of Greece and the ships of Tyre
Went out, and where are they?
In the port they made, they are delayed
With the ships of yesterday.

He followed the ships of England far,
As the ships of long ago;
And the ships of France they led him a dance,
But he laid them all a-row.

Oh, a loafing, idle lubber to him
Is the sexton of the town;
For sure and swift, with a guiding lift,
He shovels the dead men down.

But though he delves so fierce and grim,
His honest graves are wide,
As well they know who sleep below
The dredge of the deepest tide.

Oh, he works with a rollicking stave at lip,
And loud is the chorus skirled;
With the hurly rote of his rumbling throat
He batters it down the world.

He learned it once in his father's house,
Where the ballads of eld were sung;
And merry enough is the burden rough,
But no man knows the tongue.

Oh, fair, they say, was his bride to see,
And wilful she must have been,
That she could bide at his gruesome side
When the first red dawn came in.

And sweet, they say, is her kiss to those
She greets to his border home;
And softer than sleep her hand's first sweep
That beckons, and they come.

Oh, crooked is he, but strong enough
To handle the tallest mast;
From the royal barque to the slaver dark,
He buries them all at last.

Then hoy and rip, with a rolling hip,
He makes for the nearest shore;
And God, who sent him a thousand ship,
Will send him a thousand more;
But some he'll save for a bleaching grave,
And shoulder them in to shore,—
Shoulder them in, shoulder them in,
Shoulder them in to shore.

— 1897

XXIII

I loved thee, Atthis, in the long ago,
When the great oleanders were in flower
In the broad herded meadows full of sun.
And we would often at the fall of dusk
Wander together by the silver stream,
When the soft grass-heads were all wet with dew
And purple-misted in the fading light.
And joy I knew and sorrow at thy voice,
And the superb magnificence of love, —
The loneliness that saddens solitude,
And the sweet speech that makes it durable, —
The bitter longing and the keen desire,
The sweet companionship through quiet days
In the slow ample beauty of the world,
And the unutterable glad release
Within the temple of the holy night.
O Atthis, how I loved thee long ago
In that fair perished summer by the sea!

LIV

How soon will all my lovely days be over,
And I no more be found beneath the sun —
Neither beside the many-murmuring sea,
Nor where the plain-winds whisper to the reeds,
Nor in the tall beech-woods among the hills
Where roam the bright-lipped Oreads, nor along
The pasture-sides where berry-pickers stray
And harmless shepherds pipe their sheep to fold!
For I am eager, and the flame of life
Burns quickly in the fragile lamp of clay.
Passion and love and longing and hot tears
Consume this mortal Sappho, and too soon
A great wind from the dark will blow upon me,
And I be no more found in the fair world,
For all the search of the revolving moon
And patient shine of everlasting stars.

XCIII

When in the spring the swallows all return,
And the bleak bitter sea grows mild once more,
With all its thunders softened to a sigh;

When to the meadows the young green comes back,
And swelling buds put forth on every bough,
With wild-wood odors on the delicate air;

Ah, then, in that so lovely earth wilt thou
With all thy beauty love me all one way,
And make me all thy lover as before?

Lo, where the white-maned horses of the surge,
Plunging in thunderous onset to the shore,
Trample and break and charge along the sand!

— 1902

OVERLORD

Lord of the grass and hill,
Lord of the rain,
White Overlord of will,
Master of pain,

I who am dust and air
Blown through the halls of death,
Like a pale ghost of prayer, —
I am thy breath.

Lord of the blade and leaf,
Lord of the bloom,
Sheer Overlord of grief,
Master of doom,

Lonely as wind or snow,
Through the vague world and dim,
Vagrant and glad I go;
I am thy whim.

Lord of the storm and lull,
Lord of the sea,
I am thy broken gull,
Blown far alee.

Lord of the harvest dew,
Lord of the dawn,
Star of the paling blue
Darkling and gone,

Lost on the mountain height
Where the first winds are stirred,
Out of the wells of night
I am thy word.

Lord of the haunted hush,
Where raptures throng,
I am thy hermit thrush,
Ending no song.

Lord of the frost and cold,
Lord of the North,
When the red sun grows old
And day goes forth,

I shall put off this girth, —
Go glad and free,
Earth to my mother earth,
Spirit to thee.

— 1902

LORD OF MY HEART'S ELATION

Lord of my heart's elation,
Spirit of things unseen,
Be thou my aspiration
Consuming and serene!

Bear up, bear out, bear onward
This mortal soul alone,
To selfhood or oblivion,
Incredibly thine own, —

As the foamheads are loosened
And blown along the sea,
Or sink and merge forever
In that which bids them be.

I, too, must climb in wonder,
Uplift at thy command, —
Be one with my frail fellows
Beneath the wind's strong hand,

A fleet and shadowy column
Of dust or mountain rain,
To walk the earth a moment
And be dissolved again.

Be thou my exaltation
Or fortitude of mien,
Lord of the world's elation,
Thou breath of things unseen!

— *1903*

THE SHIPS OF YULE

When I was just a little boy,
Before I went to school,
I had a fleet of forty sail
I called the Ships of Yule;

Of every rig, from rakish brig
And gallant barkentine,
To little Fundy fishing boats
With gunwales painted green.

They used to go on trading trips
Around the world for me,
For though I had to stay on shore
My heart was on the sea.

They stopped at every port to call
From Babylon to Rome,
To load with all the lovely things
We never had at home;

With elephants and ivory
Bought from the King of Tyre,

And shells and silks and sandal-wood
That sailor men admire;

With figs and dates from Samarcand,
And squatty ginger-jars,
And scented silver amulets
From Indian bazaars;

With sugar-cane from Port of Spain,
And monkeys from Ceylon,
And paper lanterns from Pekin
With painted dragons on;

With cocoanuts from Zanzibar,
And pines from Singapore;
And when they had unloaded these
They could go back for more.

And even after I was big
And had to go to school,
My mind was often far away
Aboard the Ships of Yule.

— *1912*

THE WORLD VOICE

I heard the summer sea
Murmuring to the shore
Some endless story of a wrong
The whole world must deplore.

I heard the mountain wind
Conversing with the trees
Of an old sorrow of the hills
Mysterious as the sea's.

And all that haunted day
It seemed that I could hear
The echo of an ancient speech
Ring in my listening ear.

And then it came to me,
That all that I had heard
Was my own heart in the sea's voice
And the wind's lonely word.

— *1916*

VESTIGIA

I took a day to search for God,
And found Him not. But as I trod
By rocky ledge, through woods untamed,
Just where one scarlet lily flamed,
I saw His footprint in the sod.

Then suddenly, all unaware,
Far off in the deep shadows, where
A solitary hermit thrush
Sang through the holy twilight hush —
I heard His voice upon the air.

And even as I marvelled how
God gives us Heaven here and now,
In a stir of wind that hardly shook
The poplar leaves beside the brook —
His hand was light upon my brow.

At last with evening as I turned
Homeward, and thought what I had learned
And all that there was still to probe —
I caught the glory of His robe
Where the last fires of sunset burned.

Back to the world with quickening start
I looked and longed for any part
In making saving Beauty be---
And from that kindling ecstasy
I knew God dwelt within my heart.

— 1921

SUBCONSCIOUS ART

There is a general recognition of the fact, but no clear comprehension of the power, of subconsciousness expressing itself in various forms of art. We readily recognize in a painting, a poem, a piece of music, the presence of a force ("a something" we are likely to call it), which we do not readily define. We say perhaps that the picture has soul; it sways us, we know not why; it allures us, we cannot tell how. A too exact critic might perhaps ridicule our susceptibility to a vague charm we could not pretend to understand. His very philosophic and rational mind would insist on clarity, on definiteness. For him the painting must be logical, conclusive, limpid. But somehow, we say, we do not care whether it means anything or not, so long as it moves us pleasurably. We can enjoy Browning's "Childe Roland" or William Morris's "Blue Closet" without asking what they mean. And we are right, too. Art does not always have to mean something obvious. Some poetry is addressed to the mind and some is not. The best poetry, of course, addresses the mind and emotions as well. But just as a deal of good poetry has been written which appeals chiefly to the rational self in us (nearly all of Pope and Dryden, for example), so a good deal has been written which appeals to our irrational instinctive self. And indeed, in all poetry, even the most rational, there are certain qualities which pass the threshold of the outer mind and pass in to sway the mysterious subconscious person who inhabits us.

The most obvious of the qualities in poetry is the metre or rhythm. The measure of verse has an influence on us beyond our reckoning, potent and ever present, though unrecognized, so that the simplest, most unexalted statement of truth, commonplace though it be, if once thrown into regular verse, comes to us with an added force. Perhaps I should say with a new force. It may not make a statement any plainer to our mind, to versify it; it may not make it any stronger mentally; but it gives it a power and influence of a sort it did not possess before. This added power is one of the things that distinguish poetry from prose — art from science. Now the principle of recurrence is the underlying principle of rhythm and metre and rhyme and alliteration. And I wonder whether this constant reiteration, this regular pulsing recurrence in poetry, does not act as a mesmeric or hypnotic agent.

It is quite true that good art is the expression, not only of the rational waking objective self, the self which is clever and intentional and inductive, but of the deeper unreasoning self, as well. It is also true that good art impresses the deeper as well as the shallower self. The outer objective self may be extremely brilliant, may master technique and become skilled in every lore of the craft, may, indeed, become as masterful in execution as the masters themselves, and yet if it have not the aid of a great strong inner subjective unconscious self, it can do nothing of permanent human interest. You know how accurate a draughtsman may be, and how learned in anatomy, and yet how dismal and uninspired his paintings after all. You know what brilliant execution a pianist may have, and yet how cold his recitals may leave you. This is the achievement of intentional mind unassisted by the subconscious spirit. And necessary as it is, it is not alone sufficient.

To attain the best results in art we must have both the personalities of the artist working at once. All the skill which training and study can give must be at his command, to serve as the alphabet or medium of his art, and at the same time the submerged unsleeping self must be set free for active creation. Scientific formulae are an admirable means of communication between mind and mind, but art is a means of communication for the whole being — mind, body, and spirit.

This being so, it is necessary, in doing any creative work, to cultivate the power of submerging our useful, objective self far enough to give free play to the greater subjective self, the self beyond the threshold. This is exactly what occurs in hypnosis, and I dare say the beat and rhythm of poetry serves just such a purpose.

> Dearest, three months ago,
> When the mesmerizer Snow
> With his hand's first sweep
> Put the earth to sleep - - -

In these lines of Browning's there resides, I am certain, a power like that that he describes. It resides in all poetry. It is the magic we feel but cannot fathom, the charm we must follow, discredit it as we may.

Apply this test to any good piece of poetry of which you are fond. Take Tennyson's "Crossing the Bar," for instance. That poem appeals to our mind with a definite idea, a definite image, which you may easily transpose into prose. The poem might be translated without loss of the thought. But what of the magic charm of the lines:

> For though the flood may bear me beyond the boundary of time,
> I hope to see my Pilot's face when I shall have crossed the bar.

I have not altered the thought, but I have destroyed the stanza. The spell has vanished with the metre. The reason that Tennyson's verse is more pleasing than our mangled version of it is this — simply that it speaks to us more completely. It not only appeals to our intelligence, but it appeals to our sense and soul as well. The soul has memories of regions and lives of which we have never heard. The soul dwells with us as tacitly as a silent companion who should share our habitation for years, yet never reveal the secrets of his earlier life. And good poetry and good art have much to say to this work-a-day understanding of ours; yet they have more to say to the soul within us, which comprehends everything. The difficulty is in obtaining access to the soul and securing egress for it. The creative artist must subordinate cunning to intuition, and he must embody his beautiful creations in some form that will be able to elude the too vigilant reason of his fellows and gain instant access to their spirit.

If I were a poet I should not merely wish to set down my conclusions about life and the universe; I could accomplish that better by being a trained philosopher. I should not merely want to convey to you new and important facts of nature; I could do that better by being a scientist. I should not want to convince your mind only, for I could do that better by logic and rhetoric. But I should wish to do all these things and to win your sympathy as well. I should not only wish to make you believe what I say, but to believe it passionately — with your whole heart. In order to do this I should have to secure free communication of spirit, as well as of mind. I should not only have to satisfy reason, I should have to lull and charm it. I should have to hypnotize that good warder of your house before he would allow me to enter. Just as I had to mesmerize myself with the cadence of my lines before I could fully make them express my whole nature, so you in your turn as reader would have to feel their undefinable magic before you could appreciate and enjoy my poems to the utmost capacity of your nature. I could only secure this result through the senses, through the monotonous music of my verse.

This may seem to you nothing more than the wisdom of the snake-charmer. Well, that is all it is. But that is enough.

— *The Kinship of Nature, 1903*

ARCHIBALD LAMPMAN

(1861-1899)

Archibald Lampman was born in Morpeth, Ontario, where his poetry-loving father was rector of Trinity Church. Both his grandfathers were United Empire Loyalists. In 1867 the family moved to Gore's Landing on Rice Lake, where they lived for the next seven years. An attack of rheumatic fever in 1868 lamed young Archibald for four years and probably left a permanent physical weakness. In his early years he was educated at home, but in 1870 he entered a private school where he received a thorough education in Greek and Latin. Later, when the family moved to Cobourg, he attended the Collegiate Institute there for a year and then Trinity College School in Port Hope, where he won many prizes. At Trinity College, Toronto, he won several scholarships despite the fact that he was a somewhat desultory student, fond of beer, tobacco, and boon companionship, as well as being editor of the college paper. He was graduated with second class honors in classics in 1882.

For a few months he taught high school at Orangeville, but then he joined the Post Office Department of the Canadian Civil Service in Ottawa, where he remained until his death. In 1887 he married Maud Playter, by whom he had two children. Canoe trips through the lake regions about Ottawa were his principal recreation, and, according to Duncan Campbell Scott, it was on one of these expeditions, in 1896, that he strained his heart and almost certainly hastened his death.

His first book of poems, Among the Millet, was published in 1888, to be followed seven years later by Lyrics of Earth. He was correcting the proofs of a third volume, to be called Alcyone, at the time of his final illness and death in February, 1899.

HEAT

From plains that reel to southward, dim,
The road runs by me white and bare;
Up the steep hill it seems to swim
Beyond, and melt into the glare.
Upward half-way, or it may be
Nearer the summit, slowly steals
A hay-cart, moving dustily
With idly clacking wheels.

By his cart's side the wagoner
Is slouching slowly at his ease,
Half-hidden in the windless blur
Of white dust puffing to his knees.
This wagon on the height above,
From sky to sky on either hand,
Is the sole thing that seems to move
In all the heat-held land.

Beyond me in the fields the sun
Soaks in the grass and hath his will;
I count the marguerites one by one;
Even the buttercups are still.
On the brook yonder not a breath
Disturbs the spider or the midge.
The water-bugs draw close beneath
The cool gloom of the bridge.

Where the far elm-tree shadows flood
Dark patches in the burning grass,
The cows, each with her peaceful cud,
Lie waiting for the heat to pass.
From somewhere on the slope near by
Into the pale depth of the noon
A wandering thrush slides leisurely
His thin revolving tune.

In intervals of dreams I hear
The cricket from the droughty ground;
The grasshoppers spin into mine ear
A small innumerable sound.
I lift mine eyes sometimes to gaze:
The burning sky-line blinds my sight:
The woods far off are blue with haze:
The hills are drenched in light.

And yet to me not this or that
Is always sharp or always sweet;
In the sloped shadow of my hat
I lean at rest, and drain the heat;
Nay more, I think some blessèd power
Hath brought me wandering idly here:
In the full furnace of this hour
My thoughts grow keen and clear.

— 1888

THE FROGS

I

Breathers of wisdom won without a quest,
Quaint uncouth dreamers, voices high and strange;
Flutists of lands where beauty hath no change,
And wintry grief is a forgotten guest,
Sweet murmurers of everlasting rest,
For whom glad days have ever yet to run,
And moments are as aeons, and the sun
But ever sunken half-way toward the west.
Often to me who heard you in your day,
With close rapt ears, it could not choose but seem
That earth, our mother, searching in what way
Men's hearts might know her spirit's inmost dream;
Ever at rest beneath life's change and stir,
Made you her soul, and bade you pipe for her.

II

In those mute days when spring was in her glee,
And hope was strong, we knew not why or how,
And earth, the mother, dreamed with brooding brow,
Musing on life, and what the hours might be,
When love should ripen to maternity,
Then like high flutes in silvery interchange
Ye piped with voices still and sweet and strange,
And ever as ye piped, on every tree
The great buds swelled; among the pensive woods
The spirits of first flowers awoke and flung
From buried faces the close-fitting hoods,
And listened to your piping till they fell,
The frail spring-beauty with her perfumed bell,
The wind-flower, and the spotted adder-tongue.

III

All the day long, wherever pools might be
Among the golden meadows, where the air
Stood in a dream, as it were moorèd there
For ever in a noon-tide reverie,
Or where the birds made riot of their glee
In the still woods, and the hot sun shone down,
Crossed with warm lucent shadows on the brown
Leaf-paven pools, that bubbled dreamily,
Or far away in whispering river meads
And watery marshes where the brooding noon,
Full with the wonder of its own sweet boon,
Nestled and slept among the noiseless reeds,
Ye sat and murmured, motionless as they,
With eyes that dreamed beyond the night and day.

IV

And when day passed and over heaven's height,
Thin with the many stars and cool with dew,
The fingers of the deep hours slowly drew
The wonder of the ever-healing night,
No grief or loneliness or rapt delight
Or weight of silence ever brought to you
Slumber or rest; only your voices grew
More high and solemn; slowly with hushed flight
Ye saw the echoing hours go by, long-drawn,
Nor ever stirred, watching with fathomless eyes,
And with your countless clear antiphonies
Filling the earth and heaven, even till dawn,
Last-risen, found you with its first pale gleam,
Still with soft throats unaltered in your dream.

V

And slowly as we heard you, day by day,
The stillness of enchanted reveries
Bound brain and spirit and half-closed eyes,
In some divine sweet wonder-dream astray;
To us no sorrow or upreared dismay
Nor any discord came, but evermore
The voices of mankind, the outer roar,
Grew strange and murmurous, faint and far away.
Morning and noon and midnight exquisitely,
Rapt with your voices, this alone we knew,
Cities might change and fall, and men might die,
Secure were we, content to dream with you
That change and pain are shadows faint and fleet,
And dreams are real, and life is only sweet.   — *1888*

OUTLOOK

Not to be conquered by these headlong days,
But to stand free: to keep the mind at brood
On life's deep meaning, nature's altitude
Of loveliness, and time's mysterious ways;
At every thought and deed to clear the haze
Out of our eyes, considering only this,
What man, what life, what love, what beauty is,
This is to live, and win the final praise.
Though strife, ill fortune, and harsh human need
Beat down the soul, at moments blind and dumb
With agony; yet, patience — there shall come
Many great voices from life's outer sea,
Hours of strange triumph, and, when few men heed,
Murmurs and glimpses of eternity.   — *1888*

Far above us where a jay
Screams his matins to the day,
Capped with gold and amethyst,
Like a vapor from the forge
Of a giant somewhere hid,
Out of hearing of the clang
Of his hammer, skirts of mist
Slowly up the woody gorge
Lift and hang.

Softly as a cloud we go,
Sky above and sky below,
Down the river; and the dip
Of the paddles scarcely breaks,
With the little silvery drip
Of the water as it shakes
From the blades, the crystal deep
Of the silence of the morn,
Of the forest yet asleep;
And the river reaches borne
In a mirror, purple gray,
Sheer away
To the misty line of light,

Where the forest and the stream,
In the shadow meet and plight,
Like a dream.

From amid a stretch of reeds,
Where the lazy river sucks
All the water as it bleeds
From a little curling creek,
And the muskrats peer and sneak
In around the sunken wrecks
Of a tree that swept the skies
Long ago,
On a sudden seven ducks
With a splashy rustle rise,
Stretching out their seven necks,
One before, and two behind,
And the others all arow,
And as steady as the wind
With a swivelling whistle go,
Through the purple shadow led,
Till we only hear their whir
In behind a rocky spur,
Just ahead.

— *1888*

STORM

Out of the gray northwest, where many a day gone by
    Ye tugged and howled in your tempestuous grot,
And evermore the huge frost giants lie,
    Your wizard guards in vigilance unforgot,
Out of the gray northwest, for now the bonds are riven,
On wide white wings your thongless flight is driven,
    That lulls but resteth not.

And all the gray day long, and all the dense wild night,
    Ye wheel and hurry with the sheeted snow,
By cedared waste and many a pine-dark height,
    Across white rivers frozen fast below;
Over the lonely forests, where the flowers yet sleeping
Turn in their narrow beds with dreams of weeping
    In some remembered woe;

Across the unfenced wide marsh levels, where the dry
    Brown ferns sigh out, and last year's sedges scold
In some drear language, rustling haggardly
    Their thin dead leaves and dusky hoods of gold;

Across gray beechwoods where the pallid leaves unfalling
In the blind gusts like homeless ghosts are calling
  With voices cracked and old;

Across the solitary clearings, where the low
  Fierce gusts howl through the blinded woods, and round
The buried shanties all day long the snow
  Sifts and piles up in many a spectral mound;
Across lone villages in eerie wildernesses
Whose hidden life no living shape confesses
  Nor any human sound;

Across the serried masses of dim cities, blown
  Full of the snow that ever shifts and swells,
While far above them all their towers of stone
  Stand and beat back your fierce and tyrannous spells,
And hour by hour send out, like voices torn and broken
Of battling giants that have grandly spoken,
  The veering sound of bells;

So day and night, O Wind, with hiss and moan you fleet,
  Where once long gone on many a green-leafed day
Your gentler brethren wandered with light feet
  And sang, with voices soft and sweet as they,
The same blind thought that you with wilder might are speaking,
Seeking the same strange thing that you are seeking
  In this your stormier way.

O Wind, wild-voicèd brother, in your northern cave,
  My spirit also being so beset
With pride and pain, I heard you beat and rave,
  Grinding your chains with furious howl and fret,
Knowing full well that all earth's moving things inherit
The same chained might and madness of the spirit,
  That none may quite forget.

You in your cave of snows, we in our narrow girth
  Of need and sense, for ever chafe and pine;
Only in moods of some demonic birth
  Our souls take fire, our flashing wings untwine;
Even like you, mad Wind, above our broken prison,
With streaming hair and maddened eyes uprisen,
  We dream ourselves divine;

Mad moods that come and go in some mysterious way,
  That flash and fall, none knoweth how or why,
O Wind, our brother, they are yours today,
  The stormy joy, the sweeping mastery;
Deep in our narrow cells, we hear you, we awaken,
With hands afret and bosoms strangely shaken,
  We answer to your cry.

I most that love you, Wind, when you are fierce and free,
  In these dull fetters cannot long remain;
Lo, I will rise and break my thongs and flee
  Forth to your drift and beating, till my brain
Even for an hour grow wild in your divine embraces,
And then creep back into mine earthly traces,
  And bind me with my chain.

Nay, Wind, I hear you, desperate brother, in your might
  Whistle and howl; I shall not tarry long,
And though the day be blind and fierce, the night
  Be dense and wild, I still am glad and strong
To meet you face to face; through all your gust and drifting
With brow held high, my joyous hands uplifting,
  I cry you song for song.

— 1888

MIDNIGHT

From where I sit, I see the stars,
  And down the chilly floor
The moon between the frozen bars
  Is glimmering dim and hoar.

Without in many a peakèd mound
  The glinting snowdrifts lie;
There is no voice or living sound;
  The embers slowly die.

Yet some wild thing is in mine ear;
  I hold my breath and hark;

Out of the depth I seem to hear
  A crying in the dark;

No sound of man or wife or child,
  No sound of beast that groans,
Or of the wind that whistles wild,
  Or of the tree that moans:

I know not what it is I hear;
  I bend my head and hark:
I cannot drive it from mine ear,
  That crying in the dark.

— 1888

LATE NOVEMBER*

The far-off leafless forests slowly yield
To the thick-driving snow. A little while
And night shall darken down. In shouting file
The woodmen's carts go by me homeward-wheeled,
Past the thin fading stubbles, half concealed,
Now golden-gray, sowed softly through with snow,
Where the last ploughman follows still his row,
Turning black furrows through the whitening field.
Far off the village lamps begin to gleam,
Fast drives the snow, and no man comes this way;
The hills grow wintry white, and bleak winds moan
About the naked uplands. I alone
Am neither sad, nor shelterless, nor gray,
Wrapped round with thought, content to watch and dream.

*[Originally entitled "In November."]

— 1888

IN NOVEMBER

With loitering step and quiet eye,
Beneath the low November sky,
I wandered in the woods, and found
A clearing, where the broken ground
Was scattered with black stumps and briers,
And the old wreck of forest fires.
It was a bleak and sandy spot,
And, all about, the vacant plot,
Was peopled and inhabited
By scores of mulleins long since dead.
A silent and forsaken brood
In that mute opening of the wood,
So shrivelled and so thin they were,
So gray, so haggard, and austere,
Not plants at all they seemed to me,
But rather some spare company
Of hermit folk, who long ago,
Wandering in bodies to and fro,
Had chanced upon this lonely way,
And rested thus, till death one day
Surprised them at their compline prayer,
And left them standing lifeless there.

There was no sound about the wood
Save the wind's secret stir. I stood
Among the mullein-stalks as still
As if myself had grown to be
One of their sombre company,

A body without wish or will.
And as I stood, quite suddenly,
Down from a furrow in the sky
The sun shone out a little space
Across that silent sober place,
Over the sand heaps and brown sod,
The mulleins and dead goldenrod,
And passed beyond the thickets gray,
And lit the fallen leaves that lay,
Level and deep within the wood,
A rustling yellow multitude.

And all around me the thin light,
So sere, so melancholy bright,
Fell like the half-reflected gleam
Or shadow of some former dream;
A moment's golden reverie
Poured out on every plant and tree
A semblance of weird joy, or less,
A sort of spectral happiness;
And I, too, standing idly there,
With muffled hands in the chill air,
Felt the warm glow about my feet,
And shuddering betwixt cold and heat,
Drew my thoughts closer, like a cloak,
While something in my blood awoke,
A nameless and unnatural cheer,
A pleasure secret and austere.   — *1895*

COMFORT OF THE FIELDS

What would'st thou have for easement after grief,
When the rude world hath used thee with despite,
And care sits at thine elbow day and night,
Filching thy pleasures like a subtle thief?
To me, when life besets me in such wise,
'Tis sweetest to break forth, to drop the chain,
   And grasp the freedom of this pleasant earth,
   To roam in idleness and sober mirth,
Through summer airs and summer lands, and drain
The comfort of wide fields unto tired eyes.

By hills and waters, farms and solitudes,
　　To wander by the day with wilful feet;
　　Through fielded valleys wide with yellowing wheat;
Along gray roads that run between deep woods,
Murmurous and cool; through hallowed slopes of pine,
　　Where the long daylight dreams, unpierced, unstirred,
　　And only the rich-throated thrush is heard;
By lonely forest brooks that froth and shine
　　In bouldered crannies buried in the hills;
By broken beeches tangled with wild vine,
　　And long-strewn rivers murmurous with mills.

In upland pastures, sown with gold, and sweet
　　With the keen perfume of the ripening grass,
　　Where wings of birds and filmy shadows pass,
Spread thick as stars with shining marguerite:
To haunt old fences overgrown with brier,
　　Muffled in vines, and hawthorns, and wild cherries,
　　Rank poisonous ivies, red-bunched elder-berries,
And pièd blossoms to the heart's desire,
　　Gray mullein towering into yellow bloom,
　　Pink-tasselled milkweed, breathing dense perfume,
And swarthy vervain, tipped with violet fire.

To hear at eve the bleating of far flocks,
　　The mud-hen's whistle from the marsh at morn;
　　To skirt with deafened ears and brain o'erborne
Some foam-filled rapid charging down its rocks
With iron roar of waters; far away
　　Across wide-reeded meres, pensive with noon,
　　To hear the querulous outcry of the loon;
To lie among deep rocks, and watch all day
　　On liquid heights the snowy clouds melt by;
Or hear from wood-capped mountain-brows the jay
　　Pierce the bright morning with his jibing cry.

To feast on summer sounds; the jolted wains,
　　The thresher humming from the farm near by,
　　The prattling cricket's intermittent cry,
The locust's rattle from the sultry lanes;
Or in the shadow of some oaken spray,
　　To watch, as through a mist of light and dreams,
　　The far-off hayfields, where the dusty teams
Drive round and round the lessening squares of hay,
　　And hear upon the wind, now loud, now low,
With drowsy cadence half a summer's day,
　　The clatter of the reapers come and go.

Far violet hills, horizons filmed with showers,
 The murmur of cool streams, the forest's gloom,
 The voices of the breathing grass, the hum
Of ancient gardens overbanked with flowers:
Thus, with a smile as golden as the dawn,
 And cool fair fingers radiantly divine,
 The mighty mother brings us in her hand,
For all tired eyes and foreheads pinched and wan,
Her restful cup, her beaker of bright wine;
 Drink, and be filled, and ye shall understand!

— 1895

WE TOO SHALL SLEEP

Not, not for thee,
Belovèd child, the burning grasp of life
Shall bruise the tender soul. The noise, and strife,
And clamor of midday thou shalt not see;
But wrapped for ever in thy quiet grave,
Too little to have known the earthly lot,
Time's clashing hosts above thine innocent head,
Wave upon wave,
Shall break, or pass as with an army's tread,
And harm thee not.

A few short years
We of the living flesh and restless brain
Shall plumb the deeps of life and know the strain,
The fleeting gleams of joy, the fruitless tears;
And then at last when all is touched and tried,
Our own immutable night shall fall, and deep
In the same silent plot, O little friend,
Side by thy side,
In peace that changeth not, nor knoweth end,
We too shall sleep.

— 1899

THE WOODCUTTER'S HUT

Far up in the wild and wintry hills in the heart of the cliff-broken woods,
Where the mounded drifts lie soft and deep in the noiseless solitudes,
The hut of the lonely woodcutter stands, a few rough beams that show
A blunted peak and a low black line, from the glittering waste of snow.
In the frost-still dawn from his roof goes up in the windless, motionless air,
The thin, pink curl of leisurely smoke; through the forest white and bare

The woodcutter follows his narrow trail, and the morning rings and cracks
With the rhythmic jet of his sharp-blown breath and the echoing shout of his axe.
Only the waft of the wind besides, or the stir of some hardy bird —
The call of the friendly chickadee, or the pat of the nut-hatch — is heard;
Or a rustle comes from a dusky clump, where the busy siskins feed,
And scatter the dimpled sheet of the snow with the shells of the cedar-seed.
Day after day the woodcutter toils untiring with axe and wedge,
Till the jingling teams come up from the road that runs by the valley's edge,
With plunging of horses, and hurling of snow, and many a shouted word,
And carry away the keen-scented fruit of his cutting, cord upon cord.
Not the sound of a living foot comes else, not a moving visitant there,
Save the delicate step of some halting doe, or the sniff of a prowling bear.
And only the stars are above him at night, and the trees that creak and groan,
And the frozen, hard-swept mountain-crests with their silent fronts of stone,
As he watches the sinking glow of his fire and the wavering flames upcaught,
Cleaning his rifle or mending his moccasins, sleepy and slow of thought.
Or when the fierce snow comes, with the rising wind, from the gray north-east,
He lies through the leaguering hours in his bunk like a winter-hidden beast,
Or sits on the hard-packed earth, and smokes by his draught-blown guttering fire,
Without thought or remembrance, hardly awake, and waits for the storm to tire.
Scarcely he hears from the rock-rimmed heights to the wild ravines below,
Near and far off, the limitless wings of the tempest hurl and go
In roaring gusts that plunge through the cracking forest, and lull, and lift,
All day without stint and all night long with the sweep of the hissing drift.
But winter shall pass ere long with its hills of snow and its fettered dreams,
And the forest shall glimmer with living gold, and chime with the gushing
    of streams;
Millions of little points of plants shall prick through its matted floor,
And the wind-flower lift and uncurl her silken buds by the woodman's door;
The sparrow shall see and exult; but lo! as the spring draws gaily on,
The woodcutter's hut is empty and bare, and the master that made it is gone.
He is gone where the gathering of valley men another labor yields,
To handle the plough and the harrow and scythe, in the heat of the summer fields.
He is gone with his corded arms, and his ruddy face, and his moccasined feet,
The animal man in his warmth and vigor, sound, and hard, and complete.
And all summer long, round the lonely hut, the black earth burgeons and breeds,
Till the spaces are filled with the tall-plumed ferns and the triumphing forest weeds;
The thick, wild raspberries hem its walls, and stretching on either hand,
The red-ribbed stems and the giant leaves of the sovereign spikenard stand.
So lonely and silent it is, so withered and warped with the sun and snow,
You would think it the fruit of some dead man's toil a hundred years ago;
And he who finds it suddenly there, as he wanders far and alone,
Is touched with a sweet and beautiful sense of something tender and gone,
The sense of a struggling life in the waste, and the mark of a soul's command,
The going and coming of vanished feet, the touch of a human hand.

— 1899

THE CITY OF THE END OF THINGS

Beside the pounding cataracts
Of midnight streams unknown to us
'Tis builded in the leafless tracts
And valleys huge of Tartarus.
Lurid and lofty and vast it seems;
It hath no rounded name that rings,
But I have heard it called in dreams
The City of the End of Things.

Its roofs and iron towers have grown
None knoweth how high within the night,
But in its murky streets far down
A flaming terrible and bright
Shakes all the stalking shadows there,
Across the walls, across the floors,
And shifts upon the upper air
From out a thousand furnace doors;
And all the while an awful sound
Keeps roaring on continually,
And crashes in the ceaseless round
Of a gigantic harmony.
Through its grim depths re-echoing
And all its weary height of walls,
With measured roar and iron ring,
The inhuman music lifts and falls.
Where no thing rests and no man is,
And only fire and night hold sway,
The beat, the thunder, and the hiss
Cease not, and change not, night nor day.
And moving at unheard commands,
The abysses and vast fires between,
Flit figures that with clanking hands
Obey a hideous routine;
They are not flesh, they are not bone,
They see not with the human eye,
And from their iron lips is blown
A dreadful and monotonous cry;
And whoso of our mortal race
Should find that city unaware,
Lean Death would smite him face to face,
And blanch him with its venomed air:
Or caught by the terrific spell,
Each thread of memory snapt and cut,
His soul would shrivel and its shell
Go rattling like an empty nut.

It was not always so, but once,
In days that no man thinks upon,
Fair voices echoed from its stones,
The light above it leaped and shone:
Once there were multitudes of men,
That built that city in their pride,
Until its might was made, and then
They withered age by age and died.
But now of that prodigious race,
Three only in an iron tower,
Set like carved idols face to face,
Remain the masters of its power;
And at the city gate a fourth,
Gigantic and with dreadful eyes,
Sits looking toward the lightless north,
Beyond the reach of memories;
Fast rooted to the lurid floor,
A bulk that never moves a jot,
In his pale body dwells no more,
Or mind or soul, — an idiot!
But sometime in the end those three
Shall perish and their hands be still,
And with the master's touch shall flee
Their incommunicable skill.
A stillness absolute as death
Along the slacking wheels shall lie,
And, flagging at a single breath,
The fires shall moulder out and die.
The roar shall vanish at its height,
And over that tremendous town
The silence of eternal night
Shall gather close and settle down.
All its grim grandeur, tower and hall,
Shall be abandoned utterly,
And into rust and dust shall fall
From century to century;
Nor ever living thing shall grow,
Nor trunk of tree, nor blade of grass;
No drop shall fall, no wind shall blow,
Nor sound of any foot shall pass:
Alone of its accursèd state,
One thing the hand of Time shall spare,
For the grim Idiot at the gate
Is deathless and eternal there.

— 1899

WINTER EVENING

Tonight the very horses springing by
Toss gold from whitened nostrils. In a dream
The streets that narrow to the westward gleam
Like rows of golden palaces; and high
From all the crowded chimneys tower and die
A thousand aureoles. Down in the west
The brimming plains beneath the sunset rest,
One burning sea of gold. Soon, soon shall fly
The glorious vision, and the hours shall feel
A mightier master; soon from height to height,
With silence and the sharp unpitying stars,
Stern creeping frosts, and winds that touch like
    steel,
Out of the depth beyond the eastern bars,
Glittering and still shall come the awful night.

                 — 1899

VOICES OF EARTH

We have not heard the music of the spheres,
The song of star to star, but there are sounds
More deep than human joy and human tears,
That Nature uses in her common rounds;
The fall of streams, the cry of winds that strain
The oak, the roaring of the sea's surge, might
Of thunder breaking afar off, or rain
That falls by minutes in the summer night.
These are the voices of earth's secret soul,
Uttering the mystery from which she came.
To him who hears them grief beyond control,
Or joy inscrutable without a name,
Wakes in his heart thoughts bedded there,
      impearled,
Before the birth and making of the world.

                 — 1899

EVENING

From upland slopes I see the cows file by,
Lowing, great-chested, down the homeward trail,
By dusking fields and meadows shining pale
With moon-tipped dandelions. Flickering high,
A peevish night-hawk in the western sky
Beats up into the lucent solitudes,
Or drops with griding wing. The stilly woods
Grow dark and deep, and gloom mysteriously.
Cool night winds creep, and whisper in mine ear.
The homely cricket gossips at my feet.
From far-off pools and wastes of reeds I hear,
Clear and soft-piped, the chanting frogs break sweet
In full Pandean chorus. One by one
Shine out the stars, and the great night comes on.

                 — 1899

A THUNDERSTORM

A moment the wild swallows like a flight
Of withered gust-caught leaves, serenely high,
Toss in the windrack up the muttering sky.
The leaves hang still. Above the weird twilight,
The hurrying centres of the storm unite
And spreading with huge trunk and rolling fringe,
Each wheeled upon its own tremendous hinge,
Tower darkening on. And now from heaven's height,

With the long roar of elm-trees swept and swayed,
And pelted waters, on the vanished plain
Plunges the blast. Behind the wild white flash
That splits abroad the pealing thunder-crash,
Over bleared fields and gardens disarrayed,
Column on column comes the drenching rain.

— 1899

WINTER UPLANDS*

The frost that stings like fire upon my cheek,
The loneliness of this forsaken ground,
The long white drift upon whose powdered peak
I sit in the great silence as one bound;
The rippled sheet of snow where the wind blew
Across the open fields for miles ahead;
The far-off city towered and roofed in blue
A tender line upon the western red;
The stars that singly, then in flocks appear,
Like jets of silver from the violet dome,
So wonderful, so many, and so near,
And then the golden moon to light me home;
The crunching snowshoes and the stinging air,
And silence, frost, and beauty everywhere.

*[According to D. C. Scott this was the last poem
written by Lampman, fourteen days before his death.]

— 1900

TO A MILLIONAIRE

The world in gloom and splendor passes by,
And thou in the midst of it with brows that
    gleam,
A creature of that old distorted dream
That makes the sound of life an evil cry.
Good men perform just deeds, and brave men
    die,
And win not honor such as gold can give,
While the vain multitudes plod on, and live,
And serve the curse that pins them down:
    But I
Think only of the unnumbered broken hearts,
The hunger and the mortal strife for bread,
Old age and youth alike mistaught, misfed,
By want and rags and homelessness made vile,
The griefs and hates, and all the meaner parts
That balance thy one grim misgotten pile.

— 1900

ON THE COMPANIONSHIP WITH NATURE

Let us be much with Nature; not as they
That labor without seeing, that employ
Her unloved forces, blindly without joy;
Nor those whose hands and crude delights obey
The old brute passion to hunt down and slay;
But rather as children of one common birth,
Discerning in each natural fruit of earth
Kinship and bond with this diviner clay.
Let us be with her wholly at all hours,
With the fond lover's zest, who is content
If his ear hears, and if his eye but sees;
So shall we grow like her in mold and bent,
Our bodies stately as her blessèd trees,
Our thoughts as sweet and sumptuous as her flowers.

— 1900

A SUNSET AT LES EBOULEMENTS

Broad shadows fall. On all the mountain side
The scythe-swept fields are silent. Slowly home
By the long beach the high-piled hay-carts come,
Splashing the pale salt shallows. Over wide
Fawn-colored wastes of mud the slipping tide,
Round the dun rocks and wattled fisheries,
Creeps murmuring in. And now by twos and threes,
O'er the slow spreading pools with clamorous chide,
Belated crows from strip to strip take flight.
Soon will the first star shine; yet ere the night
Reach onward to the pale-green distances,
The sun's last shaft beyond the gray sea-floor
Still dreams upon the Kamouraska shore,
And the long line of golden villages.

— 1900

A JANUARY MORNING

The glittering roofs are still with frost; each worn
Black chimney builds into the quiet sky
Its curling pile to crumble silently.
Far out to westward on the edge of morn,
The slender misty city towers up-borne
Glimmer faint rose against the pallid blue;
And yonder on those northern hills, the hue
Of amethyst, hang fleeces dull as horn.
And here behind me come the woodmen's sleighs
With shouts and clamorous squeakings; might and main
Up the steep slope the horses stamp and strain,
Urged on by hoarse-tongued drivers — cheeks ablaze,
Iced beards and frozen eyelids — team by team,
With frost-fringed flanks, and nostrils jetting steam.

— 1900

REALITY

I stand at noon upon the heated flags
At the bleached crossing of two streets, and
    dream
With brain scarce conscious now the hurrying
    stream
Of noonday passengers is done. Two hags
Stand at an open doorway piled with bags
And jabber hideously. Just at their feet
A small, half-naked child screams in the street,
A blind man yonder, a mere hunch of rags,

Keeps the scant shadow of the eaves, and scowls,
Counting his coppers. Through the open glare
Thunders an empty wagon, from whose trail
A lean dog shoots into the startled square,
Wildly revolves and soothes his hapless tail,
Piercing the noon with intermittent howls.

— 1925

WINTER-SOLITUDE

I saw the city's towers on a luminous pale-gray sky;
Beyond them a hill of the softest mistiest green,
With naught but frost and the coming of night between,
And a long thin cloud above it the color of August rye.

I sat in the midst of a plain on my snowshoes with bended knee
Where the thin wind stung my cheeks,
And the hard snow ran in little ripples and peaks,
Like the fretted floor of a white and petrified sea.

And a strange peace gathered about my soul and shone,
As I sat reflecting there,
In a world so mystically fair,
So deathly silent — I so utterly alone.

February 1893   *— 1943*

[FOUR REGIONAL BALLADS]

Despite some topical references, the dating of the four regional ballads that follow remains uncertain. "Ye Maidens of Ontario" reflects the life of the raftsmen in the square-timber trade, which reached its peak about 1865 but declined rapidly and had practically disappeared by about 1900. The geographical references in "The Alberta Homesteader" and "The Poor Little Girls of Ontario" suggest that these songs were written some years after 1882, when the Districts of Alberta and Saskatchewan were created; just how long afterwards remains in doubt. "A Noble Fleet of Sealers" probably dates from the nineteenth century. In the process of oral transmission, changes were frequently made in both local and topical allusions. The versions given here are taken from Canada's Story in Song *(Toronto, Gage, 1960) edited by Edith Fowke, except "Ye Maidens of Ontario" which is taken from* Folk Songs of Canada *(Waterloo, Waterloo Music Co., 1954) also edited by Edith Fowke.*

YE MAIDENS OF ONTARIO

anonymous

Ye maidens of Ontario, give ear to what I write,
In driving down these rapid streams where raftsmen take delight,
In driving down these rapid streams as jolly raftsmen do,
While your lowland loafing farmer boys can stay at home with you.

These lowland loafing farmer boys, they tell the girls great tales
Of all the dangers they go through in crossing o'er their fields.
The cutting of the grass so green is all that they can do,
While we poor jolly raftsmen are running the Long Soo.

And when the sun is going down, their plows they'll cast aside.
They'll jump upon their horses' backs and homeward they will ride,
And when the clock strikes eight or nine, then into bed they'll crawl,
While down on Lake St. Peter we stand many a bitter squall.

The wind blew from the south and east; it blew our cribs along.
It blew so very hard it shook our timbers up and down,
And put us in confusion for fear we should all drown.
Our pilot cried, "Cheer up, brave boys! Your red pine oars bring on."

When we get down to Quebec town, the girls all dance for joy.
Says one unto another one, "Here comes a shanty-boy!"
One treats us to a bottle, and another to a dram,
While toasts go 'round the table for the jolly shantyman.

Before I'd been in Quebec long—in weeks 'twas scarcely three,
The landlord's lovely daughter did fall in love with me.
She told me that she loved me, and she took me by the hand,
And shyly told her mother that she loved a shantyman.

"O daughter, dearest daughter, you grieve my heart full sore,
 To fall in love with a shantyman you never saw before."
"Well, mother, I don't care for that, so do the best you can,
 For I'm bound to go to Ottawa with my roving shantyman."

THE ALBERTA HOMESTEADER

anonymous

My name is Dan Gold, an old bach'lor I am,
I'm keeping old batch on an elegant plan.
You'll find me out here on Alberta's bush plain
A-starving to death on a government claim.

So come to Alberta, there's room for you all
Where the wind never ceases and the rain always falls,

136

Where the sun always sets and there it remains
Till we get frozen out on our government claims.

My house it is built of the natural soil,
My walls are erected according to Hoyle,
My roof has no pitch, it is level and plain,
And I always get wet when it happens to rain.

My clothes are all ragged, my language is rough,
My bread is case-hardened and solid and tough,
My dishes are scattered all over the room,
My floor gets afraid at the sight of a broom.

How happy I feel when I roll into bed,
The rattlesnake rattles a tune at my head.
The little mosquito devoid of all fear
Crawls over my face and into my ear.

The little bed-bug so cheerful and bright,
It keeps me up laughing two-thirds of the night,
And the smart little flea with tacks in his toes
Crawls up through my whiskers and tickles my nose.

You may try to raise wheat, you may try to raise rye,
You may stay there and live, you may stay there and die,
But as for myself, I'll no longer remain
A-starving to death on a government claim.

So farewell to Alberta, farewell to the west,
It's backwards I'll go to the girl I love best.
I'll go back to the east and get me a wife
And never eat cornbread the rest of my life.

THE POOR LITTLE GIRLS OF ONTARIO

anonymous

I'll sing you a song of that plaguey pest,
It goes by the name of the Great North-West.
I cannot have a beau at all,
They all skip out there in the fall.

Refrain: One by one they all clear out,
            Thinking to better themselves, no doubt,
            Caring little how far they go
            From the poor little girls of Ontario.

First I got mashed on Charlie Brown,
The nicest fellow in all the town.
He tipped his hat and sailed away,
And now he's settled in Manitobay.

Then Henry Mayner with his white cravat,
His high stiff collar and his new plug hat,
He said if he stayed he'd have to beg,
And now he's settled in Winnipeg.

Then my long-legged druggist with his specs on his nose,
I really thought he would propose,
But he's sold his bottle-shop and now he's gone
Clear out to little Saskatchewan.

I'll pack my clothes in a carpet sack,
I'll go out there and I'll never come back,
I'll find me a husband and a good one, too,
If I have to go through to Cariboo.

Last refrain: One by one we'll all clear out,
            Thinking to better ourselves, no doubt,
            Caring little how far we go
            From the old, old folks of Ontario.

A NOBLE FLEET OF SEALERS

anonymous

There's a noble fleet of sealers being fitted for the ice.
They'll take a chance again this year tho' fat's gone down in price,
And the owners will supply them as in the days of old,
For in Newfoundland the sealing voyage means something more than gold.

Refrain: For the ice is drifting "suddard," it's getting near the Funks,
      And men will leave their feather beds to sleep in wooden bunks.
      Tho' times are getting hard again our men have not gone soft;
      They'll haul their tows o'er icy floes or briskly go aloft.

The *Algerine* is first to sail, she's steaming out the Harbor,
With eager sealers on her deck, and on the bridge, Wilf Barbour.
The Viking blood runs in his veins, as in the days of yore
When the Barbours fought the seal and whale and fished the Labrador.

The *Terra Nova's* next to sail in charge of Charlie Kean.
In the history of our fisheries that's a grand and worthy name.
His crew of bully northern men can handle gaff or gun,
To get their share, they'll risk and dare, and think it all great fun.

And now they're back in old St. John's a-sharing out the flippers.
Let's wish good luck to sealers all, likewise their gallant skippers.
Tho' Newfoundland is changing fast, some things we must not lose:
May we always have our flipper pie, and codfish for our brewis.*

---

*[Edith Fowke writes: " 'Brewis' is a popular Newfoundland dish made from broken hard biscuit boiled with small pieces of salt codfish and served with melted pork fat," and "The Barbours and Keans are two of the famous sealing families of Newfoundland." *Canada's Story in Song* (1960), p.164.]

SARA JEANNETTE DUNCAN

(1861-1922)

Born and educated in Brantford, Ontario, Sara Jeannette Duncan for a short time taught junior school. In 1885, however, having arranged with Canadian newspapers for a series of travel letters, she set off for the New Orleans Exposition on the first of her writing journeys. Subsequently she wrote for the Washington Post *also. Then, returning to Canada, she worked as a journalist for the Toronto* Globe *and the Montreal* Star, *writing under the pseudonym of Garth Grafton. During 1888 she was parliamentary correspondent in Ottawa for the Montreal* Star. *The following year she and another woman journalist, Mrs. Lilian Rood, started west on the recently completed Canadian Pacific Railway for a tour round the world, sending back letters and special articles for newspapers in Canada and the United States. Sara Jeannette Duncan's first book,* A Social Departure *(1890), was an outgrowth of this journey. Thereafter books flowed steadily from her pen, some two dozen in all.*

In India she met Everard Charles Cotes of the Indian Museum; they were married in 1891. Much of her later life she spent in Calcutta and Simla, but with frequent and lengthy visits to both England and Canada. Many of her books have been published under her married name of Mrs. Everard Cotes. She died at Ashtead in England in 1922.

*One of her novels—*The Imperialist *(1904)—has Ontario as its principal setting. Several others, however, focus with both humor and insight upon what might be called the Canadian-British-American triangle. In* An American Girl in London, *published in 1891 (to which* A Voyage of Consolation *is a sequel), the point of view taken by the author is that of a self-reliant American girl travelling alone. In* Those Delightful Americans *(1902) the story is told from the point of view of a proper young Englishwoman visiting the United States with her husband. In* Cousin Cinderella *(1908)— subtitled "A Canadian Girl in London"—an unmarried Canadian girl, accompanied by her brother, interprets the English (and Americans abroad) through Canadian eyes.*

FROM *An American Girl in London*

I am an American Girl. Therefore, perhaps, you will not be surprised at anything further I may have to say for myself. I have observed, since I came to England, that this statement, made by a third person in connection with any question of my own conduct, is always broadly explanatory. And as my own conduct will naturally enter more or less into this volume, I may as well make it in the beginning, to save complications.

It may be necessary at this point to explain further. I know that in England an unmarried person, of my age, is not expected to talk much, especially about herself. This was a little difficult for me to understand at first, as I have always talked a great deal, and, one might say, been encouraged to do it; but I have at length been brought to understand it, and lately I have spoken with becoming infrequency, and chiefly about the Zoo. I find the Zoo to be a subject which is almost certain to be received with approval; and in animal nature there is, fortunately, a good deal of variety. I do not intend, however, in this book, to talk about the Zoo, or anything connected with it, but about the general impressions and experiences I have received in your country; and one of my reasons for departing from approved models of discussion for young ladies and striking out, as it were, into subject-matter on my own account, is that I think you may find it more or less interesting. I have noticed that you are pleased, over here, to bestow rather more attention upon the American Girl than upon any other kind of American that we produce. You have taken the trouble to form opinions about her—I have heard quantities of them. Her behavior and her bringing-up, her idioms and her "accent"—above all her "accent"—have made themes for you, and you have been good enough to discuss them—Mr. James, in your midst, correcting and modifying your impressions—with a good deal of animation, for you. I observe that she is almost the only frivolous subject that ever gets into your newspapers. . . .

My father is Mr. Joshua P. Wick, of Chicago, Ill.—you may have seen his name in connection with the baking-powder interest in that city. That is how he made his fortune—in baking-powder; as he has often said, it is to baking-powder that we owe everything. He began by putting it up in small quantities, but it is an article that is so much used in the United States, and ours was such a very good kind, that the demand for it increased like anything; and though we have not become so rich as a great many people in America, it is years since poppa gave his personal superintendence to the business. You will excuse my spelling it "poppa"; I have called him that all my life, and "papa" doesn't seem to mean anything to me. Lately he has devoted himself to politics; he is in Congress now, and at the next election momma particularly wishes him to run for Senator. There is a great deal of compliance about poppa, and I think he will run. . . .

My father's father lived in England, and was also a manufacturer, poppa says, always adding, "in a plain way"; so I suppose whatever he made he made himself. It may have been boots, or umbrellas, or pastry—poppa never states; though I should be disposed to think, from his taking up the baking-powder idea, that it was pastry. . . .

And there is Mrs. Portheris, of Half-Moon Street, Hyde Park, who is poppa's aunt by her first marriage. . . . None of us had ever seen her, and there had been very little correspondence. . . . She sent us every year a Christmas card, . . . inscribed "To my nephew and niece, Joshua Peter and Mary Wick, and all their dear ones." . . .

I started to see Mrs. Portheris at eleven o'clock on the morning of the 9th of April—a lovely day, a day which augured brightly and hopefully. I waited carefully till eleven, thinking by that time my relation would have had her breakfast in bed and been dressed, and perhaps have been helped downstairs to her own particular sunny window, where I thought I might see her faded, placid, sweet old face looking up from her knitting and out into the busy street. Words have such an inspiring effect upon the imagination. All this had emanated from the "dear ones," and I felt confident and pleased and happy beforehand to be a dear one. I wore one of my plainest walking-dresses—I love simplicity in dress—so as to mitigate the shock to my relation as far as I could; but it was a New York one, and it gave me a great deal of moral support. It may be weakminded in me, but I simply couldn't have gone to see my relation in a hat and gloves that didn't match. Clothes and courage have so much to do with each other.

The porter said that I had better take "a 'ansom," or if I walked to Charing Cross I could get "a 'Ammersmith 'bus" which would take me to Half-Moon Street, Piccadilly. . . .

I did not think, before, that anything could wobble like an Atlantic steamer, but I experienced nothing more trying coming over than that Hammersmith 'bus. And there were no straps from the roof to hold on by—nothing but a very high and inconvenient handrail; and the vehicle seemed quite full of stout old gentlemen with white whiskers, who looked deeply annoyed when I upset their umbrellas and unintentionally plunged upon their feet. "More room houtside miss!" the conductor said—which I considered impertinent, thinking that he meant in the road. "Is there any room on top?" I asked him, because I had walked on so many of the old gentlemen's feet that I felt uncomfortable about it. "Yes, miss; that's wot I'm a-saying'—lots o' room houtside!" So I took advantage of a lame man's getting off to mount the spiral staircase at the back of the 'bus and take a seat on top. It is a pity, isn't it, that Noah didn't think of an outside spiral staircase like that to his ark. He might have accommodated so many more of the animals, providing them, of course, with oilskin covers to keep off the wet, as you do. But even coming from a brand new and irreverent country, where nobody thinks of consulting the Old Testament for models of public conveyances, anybody can see that in many respects you have improved immensely upon Noah.

It was lovely up there—exactly like coming on deck after being in a stuffy little cabin in the steamer—a good deal of motion, but lots of fresh air. I was a little nervous at first, but as nobody fell off the tops of any of the other 'buses, I concluded that it was not a thing you were expected to do, and presently forgot all about it looking at the people swarming below me. My position made me feel immeasurably superior—at such a swinging height above them all—and I found myself speculating about them and criticizing them, as I never should have done walking. I had never ridden on the top of anything before; it gave me an entirely new revelation of my fellow-creatures—if your monarchical feelings will allow that expression from a Republican. I must say I liked it—looking down upon people who were travelling in the same direction as I was, only on a level below. I began to understand the agreeableness of class distinctions, and I wondered whether the arrangement of seats on the tops of the 'buses was not, probably, a material result of aristocratic prejudices.

Oh, I liked it through and through, that first ride on a London 'bus! To know just how I liked it, and why, and how and why we all like it from the other side of the Atlantic, you must be born and brought up, as most of us have been, in a city twenty-five or fifty years old, where the houses are all made of clean white or red brick, with clean green lawns and geranium beds and painted iron fences; where rows of nice new maple trees are planted in the clean-shaved boulevards, and fresh-planed wooden sidewalks run straight for a mile or two at a time, and all the city blocks stand in their proper right angles—which are among our advantages, I have no doubt; but our advantages have a way of making your disadvantages more interesting. Having been monarchists all your lives, however, you can't possibly understand what it is to have been brought up in fresh paint. . . .

We find the irregularity of London so gratifying, too. The way the streets turn and twist and jostle each other, and lead up into nothing, and turn around and come back again, and assume aliases, and break out into circuses and stray into queer dark courts, where small boys go round on one roller skate, or little green churchyards only a few yards from the cabs and the crowd, where there is nobody but the dead people, who have grown tired of it all. From the top of the Hammersmith 'bus, as it went through the Strand that morning, I saw funny little openings that made me long to get down and look into them; but I had my relation to think of, so I didn't.

Then there is the well-settled, well-founded look of everything, as if it had all come ages ago, and meant to stay for ever, and just go on the way it had before. We like that—the security and the permanence of it, which seems to be in some way connected with the big policemen, and the orderly crowd, and "Keep to the Left" on the signboards, and the British coat of arms over so many of the shops. I thought that morning that those shops were probably the property of the Crown, but I was very soon corrected about that. At home I am afraid we fluctuate considerably, especially in connection with cyclones and railway interests—we are here today, and there is no telling where we shall be tomorrow. So the abiding kind of city gives us a comfortable feeling of confidence. It was not very long before even I, on the top of the Hammersmith 'bus, felt that I was riding an Institution, and no matter to what extent it wobbled it might be relied upon not to come down. . . .

From the outside I didn't think much of Mrs. Portheris's house. It was very tall, and very plain, and very narrow, and quite expressionless, except that it wore a sort of dirty brown frown. Like its neighbors, it had a well in front of it, and steps leading down into the well, and an iron fence round the steps, and a brass bell-handle lettered "Tradesmen." Like its neighbors, too, it wore boxes of spotty black greenery on the window-sills—in fact, it was very like its neighbors, except that it had one or two solemn little black balconies that looked as if nobody ever sat in them running across the face of it, and a tall shallow porch, with two or three extremely white stone steps before the front door. Half-Moon Street, to me, looked like a family of houses—a family differing in heights and complexions and the color of its hair, but sharing all the characteristics of a family—of an old family. A person draws a great many conclusions from the outside of a house, and my conclusion from the outside of my relation's house was that she couldn't be very well off to be obliged to live in such a plain and gloomy locality, with "Tradesmen" on the ground-floor; and I hoped they were not any noisy kind of tradesmen, such as shoemakers or carpenters, who would disturb her early in the morning. The clean-scrubbed stone steps reflected very favorably, I thought, upon Mrs. Portheris, and gave the house, in spite of its grimy, old-fashioned, cramped appearance, a look of respectability which redeemed it. But I did not see at any window, behind the spotty evergreens, the sweet sad face of my relation, though there were a hand-organ and a monkey and a German band all operating within twenty yards of the house.

I rang the bell. The door opened a great deal more quickly than you might imagine from the time I am taking to tell about it, and I was confronted by my first surprise in London. It was a man—a neat, smooth, pale, round-faced man in livery, rather fat and very sad. It was also Mrs. Portheris's interior. This was very dark and very quiet, but what light there was fell richly, through a square stained-glass window at the end of the hall, upon the red and blue of some old china above a door, and a collection of Indian spears, and a twisting old oak staircase that glowed with color. Mrs. Portheris's exterior had prepared me for something different. I did not know then that in London everything is a matter of the inside— I had not seen a Duchess living crowded up to her ears with other people's windows. With us the outside counts so tremendously. An American duchess, if you can imagine such a person, would consider it only due to the fitness of things that she should have an imposing front yard, and at least room enough at the back for the clothes-lines. But this has nothing to do with Half-Moon Street.

"Does Mrs. Portheris live here?" I asked, thinking it was just possible she might have moved.

"Yes, miss," said the footman, with a subdued note of interrogation.

I felt relieved. "Is she—is she well?" I inquired.

"*Quite* well, miss," he replied, with a note of interrogation a little more obvious.

"I should like to see her. Is she in?"

"I'll h'inquire, miss. 'Oo shall I sai, miss?"

I thought I would prepare my relation gradually. "A lady from Chicago," said I.

"Very well, miss. Will you walk upstairs, miss?"

In America drawing-rooms are on the ground-floor. I thought he wanted to usher me into Mrs. Portheris's bedroom. "No, sir," I said; "I'll wait here." Then I thought of Mr. Mafferton, and of what he had said about saying "sir" to people, and my sensations were awful. I have never done it once since.

The footman reappeared in a few minutes with a troubled and apologetic countenance. "Mrs. Portheris says as she doesn't want anythink, miss! I told her as I didn't understand you were disposin' of anythink; but that was 'er message, miss."

I couldn't help laughing—it was so very funny to think of my being taken for a lady-pedlar in the house of my relation. "I'm very glad she's in," I said. "That is quite a mistake! Tell her it's Miss Mamie Wick, daughter of Colonel Joshua P. Wick, of Chicago; but if she's lying down, or anything, I can drop in again."

He was away so long that I began to wonder if my relation suspected me of dynamite in any form, and he came back looking more anxious than ever. "Mrs. Portheris says she's very sorry, miss, and will you please to walk up?" "Certainly," I said, "but I hope I won't be disturbing her!"

And I walked up.

It was a big square room, with a big square piano in it, and long lace curtains, and two or three gilt-framed mirrors, and a great many old-fashioned ornaments under glass cases, and a tinkling glass chandelier in the middle. There were several oil-paintings on the walls—low-necked portraits and landscapes, principally dark-green and black and yellow, with cows, and quantities of lovely china. The furniture was red brocade, with spindly legs, and there was a tall palm in a pot, which had nothing to do with the rest of the room, by itself in a corner. I remembered these things afterwards. At the time I noticed chiefly two young persons with the pinkest cheeks I ever saw, out of a picturebook, sitting near a window. They were dressed exactly alike, and their hair hung down their backs to their waists, although they must have been seventeen; and they sat up very nicely indeed on two of the red chairs, one occupied with worsted work, and the other apparently reading aloud to her, though she stopped when I came in. I have seen something since at Madame Tussaud's—but I daresay you have often noticed it yourself. And standing in the middle of the room, with her hand on a centre-table, was Mrs. Portheris.

My first impression was that she had been standing there for the last hour in that immovable way, with exactly that remarkable expression; and it struck me that she could go on standing for the next without altering it, quite comfortably— she seemed to be so solidly placed there, with her hand upon the table. Though I wouldn't call Mrs. Portheris stout, she was massive—rather, of an impressive build. Her skirt fell in a commanding way from her waist, though it hitched up a little in front, which spoiled the effect. She had broad square shoulders, and a lace collar, and a cap with pink ribbons in it, and gray hair smooth on each side of her face, and large well-cut features, and the expression I spoke of. I've seen the expression since among the Egyptian antiquities in the British Museum, but I am unable to describe it. "Armed neutrality" is the only phrase that occurs to me in connection with it, and that by no means does it justice. For there was curiosity in it, as well as hostility and reserve—but I won't try. And she kept her hand—it was her right hand—upon the table.

"Miss *Wick*," she said, bowing, and dwelling upon the name with strong doubt. "I believe I have a connection of that name in America. Is your father's name Joshua *Peter*?"

"Yes, Mrs. Portheris," I replied; "and he says he is your nephew. I've just come. How do you do?" I said this because it was the only thing the situation seemed to warrant me saying.

"Oh, I am quite in my usual health, thank you! My nephew by marriage—a former marriage—a very distant connection."

"Three thousand five hundred miles," said I; "he lives in Chicago. You have never been over to see us, Mrs. Portheris." At this point I walked across to one of the spindly red chairs and sat down. I thought then that she had forgotten to ask me; but even now, when I know she hadn't, I am not at all sorry I sat down. I find it is possible to stand up too much in this country.

The old lady gathered herself up and looked at me. "Where are your father and mother?" she said.

"In Chicago, Mrs. Portheris. All very well, thank you! I had a cable from them this morning, before I left the hotel. Kind regards to you."

Mrs. Portheris looked at me in absolute silence. Then she deliberately arranged her back draperies and sat down too—not in any amiable way, but as if the situation must be faced.

"Margaret and Isabel," she said to the two young pink persons, "go to your rooms, dears!" And she waited till the damsels, each with a little shy smile and blush, gathered up their effects and went, before she continued the conversation. As they left the room I observed that they wore short dresses, buttoned down the back. It began to grow very interesting to me, after the first shock of finding this kind of relation was over. I found myself waiting for what was to come next with the deepest interest. In America we are very fond of types—perhaps because we have so few among ourselves—and it seemed to me, as I sat there on Mrs. Portheris's spindly red chair, that I had come into violent contact with a type of the most valuable and pronounced description. Privately I resolved to stay as long as I could, and lose no opportunity of observing it. And my first observation was that Mrs. Portheris's expression was changing—losing its neutrality and beginning to radiate active opposition and stern criticism, with an uncompromising sense of duty twisted in at the corners of the mouth. There was no agitation whatever, and I thought with an inward smile of my relation's nerves.

"Then I suppose," said Mrs. Portheris—the supposition being of the vaguest possible importance—"that you are with a party of Americans. It seems to be an American idea to go about in hordes. I never could understand it—to me it would be most obnoxious. How many are there of you?"

"One, Mrs. Portheris—and I'm the one. Poppa and momma had set their hearts on coming. Poppa thought of getting up an Anglo-American Soda Trust, and momma wanted particularly to make your acquaintance—your various Christmas cards have given us all such a charming idea of you—but at the last minute something interfered with their plans and they had to give it up. They told me to tell you how sorry they were."

"Something interfered with their plans! But nothing interfered with *your* plans!"

"Oh, no; it was some political business of poppa's—nothing to keep me!'

"Then do I actually understand that your parents, of their *own free will* permitted you to cross the Atlantic *alone*?"

"I hope you do, Mrs. Portheris; but if it's not quite clear to you, I don't mind explaining it again."

"Upon my word! And you are at an hotel—which hotel?"

When I told Mrs. Portheris the Métropole, her indignation mounted to her cap, and one of the pink ribbons shook violently.

"It is very American!" she said; and I felt that Mrs. Portheris could rise to no more forcible a climax of disapproval.

But I did not mind Mrs. Portheris's disapproval; in fact, according to my classification of her, I should have been disappointed if she had not disapproved—it would have been out of character. So I only smiled as sweetly as I could, and said, "So am I."

"Is it not very expensive?" There was a note of angry wonder as well as horror in this.

"I don't know, Mrs. Portheris. It's very comfortable."

"I never heard of such a thing in my life!" said Mrs. Portheris. "It's—it's outrageous! It's—it's not customary! I call it criminal lenience on the part of my nephew to allow it. He must have taken leave of his senses!"

"Don't say anything nasty about poppa, Mrs. Portheris," I remarked; and she paused.

"As to your mother—"

"Momma is a lady of great intelligence and advanced views," I interrupted, "though she isn't very strong. And she is very well acquainted with me."

"Advanced views are your ruin in America! May I ask how you found your way here?"

"On a 'bus, Mrs. Portheris—the red Hammersmith kind. On two 'buses, rather, because I took the wrong one first, and went miles straight away from here; but I didn't mind it—I liked it."

"*In* an omnibus I suppose you mean. You couldn't very well be *on* it, unless you went on the top!" And Mrs. Portheris smiled rather derisively.

"I did; I went on the top," I returned calmly. "And it was lovely."

Mrs. Portheris very nearly lost her self-control in her effort to grasp this enormity. Her cap bristled again, and the muscles round her mouth twitched quite perceptibly.

"Careering all over London on the top of an omnibus!" she ejaculated. "Looking for my house! And in that frock!" I felt about ten when she talked about my "frock." "Couldn't you *feel* that you were altogether too smart for such a position?"

"No, indeed, Mrs. Portheris!" I replied, unacquainted with the idiom. "When I got down off the first omnibus in Cheapside I felt as if I hadn't been half smart enough!"

She did not notice my misunderstanding. By the time I had finished my sentence she was rapping the table with suppressed excitement.

"Miss Wick!" she said—and I had expected her to call me Mamie, and say I was the image of poppa!—"you are the daughter of my nephew—which can hardly be called a connection at all—but on that account I will give you a piece of advice. The top of an omnibus is not a proper place for you—I might say, for any connection of mine, however distant! I would not feel that I was doing my duty toward my nephew's daughter if I did not tell you that you *must not* go there! Don't on any account do it again! It is a thing people *never* do!"

"Do they upset?" I asked.

"They might. But apart from that, I must ask you, on personal—on family grounds—*always* to go inside. In Chicago you may go outside as much as you like, but in London—"

"Oh, no!" I interrupted, "I wouldn't for the world—in Chicago!" which Mrs. Portheris didn't seem to understand.

I had stayed dauntlessly for a half an hour—I was so much interested in Mrs. Portheris—and I began to feel my ability to prolong the interview growing weaker. I was sorry—I would have given anything to have heard her views upon higher education and female suffrage, and the Future State and the Irish Question; but it seemed impossible to get her thoughts away from the appalling Impropriety which I, on her spindly red chair, represented. I couldn't blame her for that—I suppose no impropriety bigger than a spider had ever got into her drawing-room before. So I got up to go. Mrs. Portheris also rose, with majesty. I think she wanted to show me what, if I had been properly brought up, I might have expected reasonably to develop into. She stood in the midst of her red brocaded furniture, with her hands folded, a model of what bringing up can do if it is unflinchingly persevered in, and all the mirrors reflected the ideal she presented. I felt, beside her, as if I had never been brought up at all. . . .

—*1891*

DUNCAN CAMPBELL SCOTT

(1862-1947)

Duncan Campbell Scott was the son of a Methodist minister, the Reverend William Scott. Throughout Duncan's childhood, the family moved frequently from one small community to another in eastern Ontario and western Quebec. By 1877 the family was in Stanstead, where the boy attended the recently founded Wesleyan College. Inadequate family resources dashed his hope for a medical career, and in 1879 he entered the Civil Service in Ottawa as a temporary copying clerk in the Department of Indian Affairs. He found his duties congenial and by 1913 had risen to the highest position in the Department. His interest in the Indians and the knowledge of their way of life that he gained on his many visits and journeys among them are clearly reflected in his writings.

Although his father had encouraged his reading and his mother his study of piano, Scott experienced no inclination to write poetry until he was about twenty-five and had met and been influenced by Archibald Lampman. A few years later, Scott, along with Lampman and Wilfred Campbell, joined in the writing of an informal weekly column for the Toronto Globe. *Under the title "At the Mermaid Inn," it ran from February 1892 to July 1893. After Lampman's death, Scott served as literary executor, and his labors and enthusiasm did much to preserve and promote his friend's reputation.*

In 1894 Scott married Belle Warner Botsford, a concert violinist from Boston whom he had met when he was her accompanist at a recital in Ottawa. The following year their only child, a daughter, was born. When the little girl, to whom the father was intensely devoted, died suddenly in 1907, the shock was profound and lasting. His poem "The Closed Door" is an elegy in her memory, not published until nine years afterwards. In 1929 his wife died, having been frequently ill for long periods, and two years later Scott married Elise Aylen of Ottawa, also a poet.

Scott's first collection of poems appeared in 1893 under the title of The Magic House and Other Poems. *Three years later his second book was published—a collection of short stories and sketches, some of which had already appeared in* Scribner's Magazine, *now gathered under the title of* In the Village of Viger *(1896). His second volume of poetry was published in 1898 and was followed by a number of other books of verse as well as prose. In 1932 Scott retired from the Civil Service and, with his wife, took a long holiday in Europe. Many of the poems published in* The Green Cloister *(1935) were written abroad. Between 1936 and 1942 he travelled extensively.* The Circle of Affection, *his last book, appeared in the summer of 1947—only a few months before his death at the age of 85.*

AT THE CEDARS

You had two girls—Baptiste—
One is Virginie—
Hold hard—Baptiste!
Listen to me.

The whole drive was jammed
In that bend at the Cedars,
The rapids were dammed
With the logs tight rammed
And crammed; you might know
The Devil had clinched them below.

We worked three days—not a budge,
"She's as tight as a wedge, on the ledge,"
Says our foreman;
"Mon Dieu! boys, look here,
We must get this thing clear."
He cursed at the men
And we went for it then;
With our cant-dogs arow,
We just gave he-yo-ho;
When she gave a big shove
From above.

The gang yelled and tore
For the shore,
The logs gave a grind
Like a wolf's jaws behind,
And as quick as a flash,

With a shove and a crash,
They were down in a mash,
But I and ten more,
All but Isaac Dufour,
Were ashore.

He leaped on a log in the front of the rush,
And shot out from the bind
While the jam roared behind;
As he floated along
He balanced his pole
And tossed us a song.

But just as we cheered,
Up darted a log from the bottom,
Leaped thirty feet square and fair,
And came down on his own.

He went up like a block
With the shock,
And when he was there
In the air,
Kissed his hand
To the land;
When he dropped
My heart stopped,
For the first logs had caught him
And crushed him;
When he rose in his place
There was blood on his face.

There were some girls, Baptiste,
Picking berries on the hillside,
Where the river curls, Baptiste,
You know—on the still side
One was down by the water,
She saw Isaac
Fall back.

She did not scream, Baptiste,
She launched her canoe;
It did seem, Baptiste,

That she wanted to die too,
For before you could think
The birch cracked like a shell
In that rush of hell,
And I saw them both sink—

Baptiste!—
He had two girls,
One is Virginie,
What God calls the other
Is not known to me.

—*1893*

148

THE ONONDAGA MADONNA

She stands full-throated and with careless pose,
This woman of a weird and waning race,
The tragic savage lurking in her face,
Where all her pagan passion burns and glows;
Her blood is mingled with her ancient foes,
And thrills with war and wildness in her veins;
Her rebel lips are dabbled with the stains
Of feuds and forays and her father's woes.

And closer in the shawl about her breast,
The latest promise of her nation's doom,
Paler than she her baby clings and lies,
The primal warrior gleaming from his eyes;
He sulks, and burdened with his infant gloom,
He draws his heavy brows and will not rest.

—1898

THE PIPER OF ARLL

There was in Arll a little cove
Where the salt wind came cool and free:
A foamy beach that one would love,
If he were longing for the sea.

A brook hung sparkling on the hill,
The hill swept far to ring the bay;
The bay was faithful, wild or still,
To the heart of the ocean far away.

There were three pines above the comb
That, when the sun flared and went down,
Grew like three warriors reaving home
The plunder of a burning town.

A piper lived within the grove,
Tending the pasture of his sheep;
His heart was swayed with faithful love,
From the springs of God's ocean clear and deep.

And there a ship one evening stood,
Where ship had never stood before;
A pennon bickered red as blood,
An angel glimmered at the prore.

About the coming on of dew,
The sails burned rosy, and the spars
Were gold, and all the tackle grew
Alive with ruby-hearted stars.

The piper heard an outland tongue,
With music in the cadenced fall;
And when the fairy lights were hung,
The sailors gathered one and all,

And leaning on the gunwales dark,
Crusted with shells and dashed with foam,
With all the dreaming hills to hark,
They sang their longing songs of home.

When the sweet airs had fled away,
The piper, with a gentle breath,
Molded a tranquil melody
Of lonely love and longed-for death.

When the fair sound began to lull,
From out the fireflies and the dew,
A silence held the shadowy hull,
Until the eerie tune was through.

149

Then from the dark and dreamy deck
An alien song began to thrill;
It mingled with the drumming beck,
And stirred the braird upon the hill.

Beneath the stars each sent to each
A message tender, till at last
The piper slept upon the beach,
The sailors slumbered round the mast.

Still as a dream till nearly dawn,
The ship was bosomed on the tide;
The streamlet, murmuring on and on,
Bore the sweet water to her side.

Then shaking out her lawny sails,
Forth on the misty sea she crept;
She left the dawning of the dales,
Yet in his cloak the piper slept.

And when he woke he saw the ship,
Limned black against the crimson sun;
Then from the disc he saw her slip,
A wraith of shadow—she was gone.

He threw his mantle on the beach,
He went apart like one distraught,
His lips were moved—his desperate speech
Stormed his inviolable thought.

He broke his human-throated reed,
And threw it in the idle rill;
But when his passion had its mead,
He found it in the eddy still.

He mended well the patient flue,
Again he tried its varied stops;
The closures answered right and true,
And starting out in piercing drops,

A melody began to drip
That mingled with a ghostly thrill
The vision-spirit of the ship,
The secret of his broken will.

Beneath the pines he piped and swayed,
Master of passion and of power;
He was his soul and what he played,
Immortal for a happy hour.

He, singing into nature's heart,
Guiding his will by the world's will,
With deep, unconscious, childlike art
Had sung his soul out and was still.

And then at evening came the bark
That stirred his dreaming heart's desire;
It burned slow lights along the dark
That died in glooms of crimson fire.

The sailors launched a sombre boat,
And bent with music at the oars;
The rhythm throbbing every throat,
And lapsing round the liquid shores,

Was that true tune the piper sent,
Unto the wave-worn mariners,
When with the beck and ripple blent
He heard that outland song of theirs.

Silent they rowed him, dip and drip,
The oars beat out an exequy,
They laid him down within the ship,
They loosed a rocket to the sky.

It broke in many a crimson sphere
That grew to gold and floated far,
And left the sudden shore-line clear,
With one slow-changing, drifting star.

Then out they shook the magic sails,
That charmed the wind in other seas,
From where the west line pearls and pales,
They waited for a ruffling breeze.

But in the world there was no stir,
The cordage slacked with never a creak,
They heard the flame begin to purr
Within the lantern at the peak.

They could not cry, they could not move,
They felt the lure from the charmed sea;
They could not think of home or love
Or any pleasant land to be.

They felt the vessel dip and trim,
And settle down from list to list;
They saw the sea-plain heave and swim
As gently as a rising mist.

And down so slowly, down and down,
Rivet by rivet, plank by plank;
A little flood of ocean flown
Across the deck, she sank and sank.

From knee to breast the water wore,
It crept and crept; ere they were ware
Gone was the angel at the prore,
They felt the water float their hair.

They saw the salt plain spark and shine,
They threw their faces to the sky;
Beneath a deepening film of brine
They saw the star-flash blur and die.

She sank and sank by yard and mast,
Sank down the shimmering gradual dark;
A little drooping pennon last
Showed like the black fin of a shark.

And down she sank till, keeled in sand,
She rested safely balanced true,
With all her upward gazing band,
The piper and the dreaming crew.

And there, unmarked of any chart,
In unrecorded deeps they lie,
Empearled within the purple heart
Of the great sea for aye and aye.

Their eyes are ruby in the green
Long shaft of sun that spreads and rays,
And upward with a wizard sheen
A fan of sea-light leaps and plays.

Tendrils of or and azure creep,
And globes of amber light are rolled,
And in the gloaming of the deep
Their eyes are starry pits of gold.

And sometimes in the liquid night
The hull is changed, a solid gem,
That glows with a soft stony light,
The lost prince of a diadem.

And at the keel a vine is quick,
That spreads its bines and works and weaves
O'er all the timbers veining thick
A plenitude of silver leaves.

—1898

THE FORSAKEN

I

Once in the winter
Out on a lake
In the heart of the northland,
Far from the Fort
And far from the hunters,
A Chippewa woman
With her sick baby,
Crouched in the last hours
Of a great storm.
Frozen and hungry,
She fished through the ice
With a line of the twisted
Bark of the cedar,
And a rabbit-bone hook
Polished and barbed;

Fished with the bare hook
All through the wild day,
Fished and caught nothing;
While the young chieftain
Tugged at her breasts,
Or slept in the lacings
Of the warm *tikanagan*.
All the lake-surface
Streamed with the hissing
Of millions of iceflakes
Hurled by the wind;
Behind her the round
Of a lonely island
Roared like a fire
With the voice of the storm
In the deeps of the cedars.
Valiant, unshaken,
She took of her own flesh,
Baited the fish-hook,
Drew in a gray-trout,
Drew in his fellows,
Heaped them beside her,
Dead in the snow.
Valiant, unshaken,
She faced the long distance,
Wolf-haunted and lonely,
Sure of her goal
And the life of her dear one:
Tramped for two days,
On the third in the morning,
Saw the strong bulk
Of the Fort by the river,
Saw the wood-smoke
Hang soft in the spruces,
Heard the keen yelp
Of the ravenous huskies
Fighting for whitefish:
Then she had rest.

II

Years and years after,
When she was old and withered,
When her son was an old man
And his children filled with vigor,
They came in their northern tour on the verge of winter,
To an island in a lonely lake.

There one night they camped, and on the morrow
Gathered their kettles and birch-bark
Their rabbit-skin robes and their mink-traps,
Launched their canoes and slunk away through the islands,
Left her alone forever,
Without a word of farewell,
Because she was old and useless,
Like a paddle broken and warped,
Or a pole that was splintered.
Then, without a sigh,
Valiant, unshaken,
She smoothed her dark locks under her kerchief,
Composed her shawl in state,
Then folded her hands ridged with sinews and corded with veins,
Folded them across her breasts spent with the nourishing of children,
Gazed at the sky past the tops of the cedars,
Saw two spangled nights arise out of the twilight,
Saw two days go by filled with the tranquil sunshine,
Saw, without pain, or dread, or even a moment of longing:
Then on the third great night there came thronging and thronging
Millions of snowflakes out of a windless cloud;
They covered her close with a beautiful crystal shroud,
Covered her deep and silent.
But in the frost of the dawn,
Up from the life below,
Rose a column of breath
Through a tiny cleft in the snow,
Fragile, delicately drawn,
Wavering with its own weakness,
In the wilderness a sign of the spirit,
Persisting still in the sight of the sun
Till day was done.
Then all light was gathered up by the hand of God and hid in His breast,
Then there was born a silence deeper than silence,
Then she had rest.

—1905

NIGHT HYMNS ON LAKE NIPIGON

Here in the midnight, where the dark mainland and island
Shadows mingle in shadow deeper, profounder,
Sing we the hymns of the churches, while the dead water
          Whispers before us.

Thunder is travelling slow on the path of the lightning;
One after one the stars and the beaming planets
Look serene in the lake from the edge of the storm-cloud,
          Then have they vanished.

153

While our canoe, that floats dumb in the bursting thunder,
Gathers her voice in the quiet and thrills and whispers,
Presses her prow in the star-gleam, and all her ripple
        Lapses in blackness.

Sing we the sacred ancient hymns of the churches,
Chanted first in old-world nooks of the desert,
While in the wild, pellucid Nipigon reaches
        Hunted the savage.

Now have the ages met in the Northern midnight,
And on the lonely, loon-haunted Nipigon reaches
Rises the hymn of triumph and courage and comfort,
        Adeste Fideles.

Tones that were fashioned when the faith brooded in darkness,
Joined with sonorous vowels in the noble Latin,
Now are married with the long-drawn Ojibwa,
        Uncouth and mournful.

Soft with the silver drip of the regular paddles
Falling in rhythm, timed with the liquid, plangent
Sounds from the blades where the whirlpools break and are carried
        Down into darkness;

Each long cadence, flying like a dove from her shelter
Deep in the shadow, wheels for a throbbing moment,
Poises in utterance, returning in circles of silver
        To nest in the silence.

All wild nature stirs with the infinite tender
Plaint of a bygone age whose soul is eternal,
Bound in the lonely phrases that thrill and falter
        Back into quiet.

Back they falter as the deep storm overtakes them,
Whelms them in splendid hollows of booming thunder,
Wraps them in rain, that sweeping, breaks and onrushes
        Ringing like cymbals.

                —1905

THE SEA BY THE WOOD

I dwell in the sea that is wild and deep,
  But afar in a shadow still,
I can see the trees that gather and sleep
  In the wood upon the hill.

The deeps are green as an emerald's face,
  The caves are crystal calm,
But I wish the sea were a little trace
  Of moisture in God's palm.

The waves are weary of hiding pearls,
  Are aweary of smothering gold,
They would all be air that sweeps and swirls
  In the branches manifold.

They are weary of laving the seaman's eyes
  With their passion prayer unsaid,
They are weary of sobs and the sudden sighs
  And movements of the dead.

All the sea is haunted with human lips
 Ashen and sere and gray,
You can hear the sails of the sunken ships
 Stir and shiver and sway,

In the weary solitude;
  If mine were the will of God, the main
Should melt away in the rustling wood
  Like a mist that follows the rain.

  But I dwell in the sea that is wild and deep
   And afar in the shadow still,
  I can see the trees that gather and sleep
   In the wood upon the hill.

       —1905

THE WOOD BY THE SEA

I dwell in the wood that is dark and kind
 But afar off tolls the main,
Afar, far off I hear the wind,
 And the roving of the rain.

Weary are all the birds of sleep,
  The nests are weary of wings,
The whole wood yearns to the swaying deep,
  The mother of restful things.

The shade is dark as a palmer's hood,
 The air with balm is bland:
But I wish the trees that breathe in the wood
 Were ashes in God's hand.

The wood is very old and still,
  So still when the dead cones fall,
Near in the vale or away on the hill,
  You can hear them one and all,

The pines are weary of holding nests,
 Are aweary of casting shade;
Wearily smoulder the resin crests
 In the pungent gloom of the glade.

And their falling wearies me;
  If mine were the will of God—O, then
The wood should tramp to the sounding sea,
  Like a marching army of men!

  But I dwell in the wood that is dark and kind,
   Afar off tolls the main;
  Afar, far off I hear the wind
   And the roving of the rain.

       —1905

NIGHT BURIAL IN THE FOREST

Lay him down where the fern is thick and fair.
Fain was he for life, here lies he low:
With the blood washed clean from his brow and his beautiful hair,
Lay him here in the dell where the orchids grow.

Let the birch-bark torches roar in the gloom,
And the trees crowd up in a quiet startled ring
So lone is the land that in this lonely room
Never before has breathed a human thing.

Cover him well in his canvas shroud, and the moss
Part and heap again on his quiet breast,
What recks he now of gain, or love, or loss
Who for love gained rest?

While she who caused it all hides her insolent eyes
Or braids her hair with the ribbons of lust and of lies,
And he who did the deed fares out like a hunted beast
To lurk where the musk-ox tramples the barren ground
Where the stroke of his coward heart is the only sound.

Haunting the tamarac shade,
Hear them up-thronging
Memories foredoomed
Of strife and of longing:
Haggard or bright
By the tamaracs and birches,
Where the red torch light
Trembles and searches,
The wilderness teems
With inscrutable eyes
Of ghosts that are dreams
Commingled with memories.

Leave him here in his secret ferny tomb,
Withdraw the little light from the ocean of gloom,
He who feared nought will fear aught never,
Left alone in the forest forever and ever.

Then, as we fare on our way to the shore
Sudden the torches cease to roar:
For cleaving the darkness remote and still
Comes a wind with a rushing, harp-like thrill,
The sound of wings hurled and furled and unfurled,
The wings of the Angel who gathers the souls from the wastes of the world.

—1906

FROM THE HEIGHT OF LAND

Now the Indian guides are dead asleep;
There is no sound unless the soul can hear
The gathering of the waters in their sources.
    We have come up through the spreading lakes
From level to level,—
Pitching our tents sometimes over a revel
Of roses that nodded all night,
Dreaming within our dreams,

To wake at dawn and find that they were captured
With no dew on their leaves;
Sometimes mid sheaves
Of bracken and dwarf-cornel, and again
On a wide blueberry plain
Brushed with the shimmer of a bluebird's wing;
A rocky islet followed
With one lone poplar and a single nest
Of white-throat-sparrows that took no rest
But sang in dreams or woke to sing,—
To the last portage and the height of land:
Upon one hand
The lonely north enlaced with lakes and streams,
And the enormous targe of Hudson Bay,
Glimmering all night
In the cold arctic light;
On the other hand
The crowded southern land
With all the welter of the lives of men.
But here is peace, and again
That Something comes by flashes
Deeper than peace,— a spell
Golden and inappellable
That gives the inarticulate part
Of our strange being one moment of release
That seems more native than the touch of time,
And we must answer in chime;
Though yet no man may tell
The secret of that spell
Golden and inappellable. . . .

—1916

THE CLOSED DOOR

The dew falls and the stars fall,
The sun falls in the west,
But never more
Through the closed door,
Shall the one that I loved best
Return to me:
A salt tear is the sea,
All earth's air is a sigh,
But they never can mourn for me
With my heart's cry,
For the one that I loved best
Who caressed me with her eyes,
And every morning came to me,
With the beauty of sunrise,
Who was health and wealth and all,
Who never shall answer my call,
While the sun falls in the west,
The dew falls and the stars fall.

—1916

Gull Lake set in the rolling prairie—
Still there are reeds on the shore,
As of old the poplars shimmer
As summer passes;
Winter freezes the shallow lake to the core;
Storm passes,
Heat parches the sedges and grasses,
Night comes with moon-glimmer,
Dawn with the morning-star;
All proceeds in the flow of Time
As a hundred years ago.
Then two camps were pitched on the shore,
The clustered teepees
Of Tabashaw Chief of the Saulteaux.
And on a knoll tufted with poplars
Two gray tents of a trader—
Nairne of the Orkneys.
Before his tents under the shade of the poplars
Sat Keejigo, third of the wives
Of Tabashaw Chief of the Saulteaux;
Clad in the skins of antelopes
Broidered with porcupine quills
Colored with vivid dyes,
Vermilion here and there
In the roots of her hair,
A half-moon of powder-blue
On her brow, her cheeks
Scored with light ochre streaks.
Keejigo daughter of Launay
The Normandy hunter
And Oshawan of the Saulteaux,
Troubled by fugitive visions
In the smoke of the camp-fires,
In the close dark of the teepee,
Flutterings of color
Along the flow of the prairies,
Spangles of flower tints
Caught in the wonder of dawn,
Dreams of sounds unheard—
The echoes of echo,
Star she was named for
Keejigo, star of the morning,
Voices of storm—
Wind-rush and lightning—
The beauty of terror;
The twilight moon

Colored like a prairie lily,
The round moon of pure snow,
The beauty of peace;
Premonitions of love and of beauty
Vague as shadows cast by a shadow.
Now she had found her hero,
And offered her body and spirit
With abject unreasoning passion,
As Earth abandons herself
To the sun and the thrust of the lightning.
Quiet were all the leaves of the poplars,
Breathless the air under their shadow,
As Keejigo spoke of these things to her heart
In the beautiful speech of the Saulteaux.

The flower lives on the prairie,
The wind in the sky,
I am here my beloved;
The wind and the flower.

The crane hides in the sand-hills,
Where does the wolverine hide?
I am here my beloved,
Heart's-blood on the feathers
The foot caught in the trap.

Take the flower in your hand,
The wind in your nostrils;
I am here my beloved;
Release the captive,
Heal the wound under the feathers.

A storm-cloud was marching
Vast on the prairie,
Scored with livid ropes of hail,
Quick with nervous vines of lightning—
Twice had Nairne turned her away
Afraid of the venom of Tabashaw,
Twice had the Chief fired at his tents
And now when two bullets
Whistled above the encampment
He yelled "Drive this bitch to her master."

Keejigo went down a path by the lake;
Thick at the tangled edges,
The reeds and the sedges
Were gray as ashes

Against the death-black water;
The lightning scored with double flashes
The dark lake-mirror and loud
Came the instant thunder.
Her lips still moved to the words of her music,
"Release the captive,
Heal the wound under the feathers."

At the top of the bank
The old wives caught her and cast her down
Where Tabashaw crouched by his camp-fire.
He snatched a live branch from the embers,
Seared her cheeks,
Blinded her eyes,
Destroyed her beauty with fire,
Screaming, "Take that face to your lover."
Keejigo held her face to the fury
And made no sound.
The old wives dragged her away
And threw her over the bank
Like a dead dog.

Then burst the storm—
The Indians' screams and the howls of the dogs
Lost in the crash of hail
That smashed the sedges and reeds,
Stripped the poplars of leaves,

Tore and blazed onwards,
Wasting itself with riot and tumult—
Supreme in the beauty of terror.

The setting sun struck the retreating cloud
With a rainbow, not an arc but a column
Built with the glory of seven metals;
Beyond in the purple deeps of the vortex
Fell the quivering vines of the lightning.
The wind withdrew the veil from the shrine
    of the moon,
She rose changing her dusky shade for the
    glow
Of the prairie lily, till free of all blemish
    of color
She came to her zenith without a cloud or a star,
A lovely perfection, snow-pure in the heaven
    of midnight.
After the beauty of terror the beauty of peace.

But Keejigo came no more to the camps of
    her people;
Only the midnight moon knew where she
    felt her way,
Only the leaves of autumn, the snows of winter
Knew where she lay.

                                        —1935

THE PEDLAR

He used to come in the early spring-time, when, in sunny hollows, banks of coarse snow lie thawing, shrinking with almost inaudible tinklings, when the upper grassbanks are covered thickly with the film left by the melted snow, when the old leaves about the gray trees are wet and sodden, when the pools lie bare and clear, without grasses, very limpid with snow-water, when the swollen streams rush insolently by, when the grosbeaks try the cedar buds shyly, and a colony of little birds take a sunny tree slope, and sing songs there.

He used to come with the awakening of life in the woods, with the strange cohosh, and the dog-tooth violet, piercing the damp leaf which it would wear as a ruff about its neck in blossom time. He used to come up the road from St. Valérie, trudging heavily, bearing his packs. To most of the Viger people he seemed to appear suddenly in the midst of the street, clothed with power, and surrounded by an attentive crowd of boys, and a whirling fringe of dogs, barking and throwing up dust.

I speak of what has become tradition, for the pedlar walks no more up the St. Valérie road, bearing those magical baskets of his.

There was something powerful, compelling, about him; his short, heavy figure, his hair-covered, expressionless face, the quick hands in which he seemed to weigh everything that he touched, his voluminous, indescribable clothes, the great umbrella he carried strapped to his back, the green spectacles that hid his eyes, all these commanded attention. But his powers seemed to lie in those inscrutable guards to his eyes. They were such goggles as are commonly used by threshers, and were bound firmly about his face by a leather lace; with their setting of iron they completely covered his eye-sockets, not permitting a glimpse of those eyes that seemed to glare out of their depths. They seemed never to have been removed, but to have grown there, rooted by time in his cheek-bones.

He carried a large wicker-basket covered with oiled cloth, slung to his shoulder by a strap; in one hand he carried a light stick, in the other a large oval bandbox of black shiny cloth. From the initials "J. F.," which appeared in faded white letters on the bandbox, the village people had christened him Jean-François.

Coming into the village, he stopped in the middle of the road, set his bandbox between his feet, and took the oiled cloth from the basket. He never went from house to house, his customers came to him. He stood there and sold, almost without a word, as calm as a sphinx, and as powerful. There was something compelling about him; the people bought things they did not want, but they had to buy. The goods lay before them, the handkerchiefs, the laces, the jewellery, the little sacred pictures, matches in colored boxes, little cased looking-glasses, combs, mouth-organs, pins, and hairpins; and over all, this figure with the inscrutable eyes. As he took in the money and made change, he uttered the word, "Good," continually, "good, good." There was something exciting in the way he pronounced that word, something that goaded the hearers into extravagance.

It happened one day in April, when the weather was doubtful and moody, and storms flew low, scattering cold rain, and after that day Jean-François, the pedlar, was a shape in memory, a fact no longer. He was blown into the village unwetted by a shower that left the streets untouched, and that went through the northern fields sharply, and lost itself in the far woods. He stopped in front of the post office. The Widow Laroque slammed her door and went upstairs to peep through the curtain; "these pedlars spoiled trade," she said, and hated them in consequence. Soon a crowd collected, and great talk arose, with laughter and some jostling. Everyone tried to see into the basket, those behind stood on tiptoe and asked questions, those in front held the crowd back and tried to look at the goods. The air was full of the staccato of surprise and admiration. The late comers on the edge of the crowd commenced to jostle, and somebody tossed a handful of dust into the air over the group. "What a wretched wind," cried someone, "it blows all ways."

The dust seemed to irritate the pedlar; besides, no one had bought anything. He called out sharply, "Buy—buy." He sold two papers of hairpins, a little brass shrine of La Bonne St. Anne, a colored handkerchief, a horn comb, and a mouth-organ. While these purchases were going on, Henri Lamoureux was eyeing the little red purses, and fingering a coin in his pocket. The coin was a doubtful one, and he was weighing carefully the chances of passing it. At last he said, carelessly, "How much?" touching the purses. The pedlar's answer called out the coin from his pocket; it lay in the man's hand. Henri took the purse and moved hurriedly back. At once the pedlar grasped after him, reaching as well as his basket would allow; he caught him by the coat; but Henri's dog darted in, nipped the pedlar's leg, and got away, showing his teeth. Lamoureux struggled, the pedlar swore; in a moment everyone was jostling to get out of the way, wondering what was the matter. As Henri swung his arm around he swept his hand across the pedlar's eyes; the shoe-string gave way, and the green goggles fell into the basket. Then a curious change came over the man. He let his enemy go, and stood dazed for a moment; he passed his hand across his eyes, and in that interval of quiet the people saw, where they expected to see flash the two rapacious eyes of their imaginings, only the seared, fleshy seams where those eyes should have been.

That was the vision of a moment, for the pedlar, like a fiend in fury, threw up his long arms and cursed in a voice so powerful and sudden that the dismayed crowd shrunk away, clinging to one another and looking over their shoulders at the violent figure. "God have mercy!—Holy St. Anne protect us!—He curses his Baptism!" screamed the women. In a second he was alone; the dog that had assailed him was snarling from under the sidewalk, and the women were in the nearest houses. Henri Lamoureux, in the nearest lane, stood pale, with a stone in his hand. It was only for one moment; in the second, the pedlar had gathered his things, blind as he was, had turned his back, and was striding up the street; in the third, one of the sudden storms had gathered the dust at the end of the village and came down with it, driving everyone indoors. It shrouded the retreating figure, and a crack of unexpected thunder came like a pistol shot, and then the pelting rain.

Some venturesome souls who looked out when the storm was nearly over, declared they saw, large on the hills, the figure of the pedlar, walking enraged in the fringes of the storm. One of these was Henri Lamoureux, who, to this day, has never found the little red purse.

"I would have sworn I had it in this hand when he caught me; but I felt it fly away like a bird."

"But what made the man curse everyone so when you just bought that little purse—say that?"

"Well, I know not, do you? Anyway he has my quarter, and he was blind—blind as a stone fence."

"Blind! Not he!" cried the Widow Laroque. "He was the Old Boy himself, I told you—it is always as I say, you see now—it was the old Devil himself."

However that might be, there are yet people in Viger who, when the dust blows, and a sharp storm comes up from the southeast, see the figure of the enraged pedlar, large upon the hills, striding violently along the fringes of the storm.

—1896

The twentieth century

STEPHEN LEACOCK

(1869-1944)

Four years after the death in England of Canada's first internationally known humorist, Thomas Chandler Haliburton, Stephen Butler Leacock was born in Hampshire. In 1876 his parents emigrated to Canada and settled on an unproductive farm near Lake Simcoe in Ontario. Occasional financial assistance from England enabled the family to survive and to send young Stephen to Upper Canada College and the University of Toronto, from which he was graduated in 1891. He returned to Upper Canada College and taught there until 1899. Then, having acquired some savings, partly through writing humorous sketches for various periodicals in Canada and the United States, he left to pursue graduate studies in economics and politics at the University of Chicago, where he held a Fellowship in Political Economy. After obtaining his Doctor's degree in 1903, he was appointed to the staff of McGill University, and eventually rose to be Head of the Department of Political Science and Economics there. He was retired, much against his wishes, in 1936. Retirement age at McGill was 65.

His first book of humor—Literary Lapses—was published in Montreal in 1910, the year in which Mark Twain died. Like the American humorist, Leacock was a very gifted raconteur and platform speaker, in great demand for public addresses and readings from his works. His reputation is world-wide, since some of his books have appeared in translation in countries ranging from Norway to Japan. While he is best known for his humorous writing, Leacock has also written books on political science, history, economics, sociology, education, and biography. Despite the length of the bibliography on pages 685-689, considerable uncollected material still remains in newspapers and magazines.

REFLECTIONS ON RIDING

The writing of this paper has been inspired by a debate recently held at the literary society of my native town on the question, "Resolved: that the bicycle is a nobler animal than the horse." In order to speak for the negative with proper authority, I have spent some weeks in completely addicting myself to the use of the horse. I find that the difference between the horse and the bicycle is greater than I had supposed.

The horse is entirely covered with hair; the bicycle is not entirely covered with hair, except the '89 model they are using in Idaho.

In riding a horse the performer finds that the pedals in which he puts his feet will not allow of a good circular stroke. He will observe, however, that there is a saddle in which—especially while the horse is trotting—he is expected to seat himself from time to time. But it is simpler to ride standing up, with the feet in the pedals.

There are no handles to a horse, but the 1910 model has a string to each side of its face for turning its head when there is anything you want it to see.

Coasting on a good horse is superb, but should be under control. I have known a horse to suddenly begin to coast with me about two miles from home, coast down the main street of my native town at a terrific rate, and finally coast through a platoon of the Salvation Army into its very stable.

I cannot honestly deny that it takes a good deal of physical courage to ride a horse. This, however, I have. I get it at about forty cents a flask, and take it as required.

I find that in riding a horse up the long street of a country town, it is not well to proceed at a trot. It excites unkindly comment. It is better to let the horse walk the whole distance. This may be made to seem natural by turning half round in the saddle with the hand on the horse's back, and gazing intently about two miles up the road. It then appears that you are the first in of about fourteen men.

Since learning to ride, I have taken to noticing the things that people do on horseback in books. Some of these I can manage, but most of them are entirely beyond me. Here, for instance, is a form of equestrian performance that every reader will recognize and for which I have only a despairing admiration:

"With a hasty gesture of farewell, the rider set spurs to his horse and disappeared in a cloud of dust."

With a little practice in the matter of adjustment, I think I could set spurs to any size of horse, but I could never disappear in a cloud of dust—at least, not with any guarantee of remaining disappeared when the dust cleared away.

Here, however, is one that I certainly can do:

"The bridle rein dropped from Lord Everard's listless hand and, with his head bowed upon his bosom, he suffered his horse to move at a foot's pace up the sombre avenue. Deep in thought, he heeded not the movement of the steed which bore him."

That is, he looked as if he didn't; but in my case Lord Everard has his eyes on the steed pretty closely, just the same.

This next I am doubtful about:

" 'To horse! to horse!' cried the knight, and leaped into the saddle."

I think I could manage it if it read:

" 'To horse!' cried the knight and, snatching a stepladder from the hands of his trusty attendant, he rushed into the saddle."

As a concluding remark, I may mention that my experience of riding has thrown a very interesting sidelight upon a rather puzzling point in history. It is recorded of the famous Henry the Second that he was "almost constantly in the saddle, and of so restless a disposition that he never sat down, even at meals." I had hitherto been unable to understand Henry's idea about his meals, but I think I can appreciate it now.

—Literary Lapses, 1910

MY FINANCIAL CAREER

When I go into a bank I get rattled. The clerks rattle me; the wickets rattle me; the sight of the money rattles me; everything rattles me.

The moment I cross the threshold of a bank and attempt to transact business there, I become an irresponsible idiot.

I knew this beforehand, but my salary had been raised to fifty dollars a month and I felt that the bank was the only place for it.

So I shambled in and looked timidly round at the clerks. I had an idea that a person about to open an account must needs consult the manager.

I went up to a wicket marked "Accountant." The accountant was a tall, cool devil. The very sight of him rattled me. My voice was sepulchral.

"Can I see the manager?" I said, and added solemnly, "alone." I don't know why I said "alone."

"Certainly," said the accountant, and fetched him.

The manager was a grave, calm man. I held my fifty-six dollars clutched in a crumpled ball in my pocket.

"Are you the manager?" I said. God knows I didn't doubt it.

"Yes," he said.

"Can I see you," I asked, "alone?" I didn't want to say "alone" again, but without it the thing seemed self-evident.

The manager looked at me in some alarm. He felt that I had an awful secret to reveal.

"Come in here," he said, and led the way to a private room. He turned the key in the lock.

"We are safe from interruption here," he said; "sit down."

We both sat down and looked at each other. I found no voice to speak.

"You are one of Pinkerton's men, I presume," he said.

He had gathered from my mysterious manner that I was a detective. I knew what he was thinking, and it made me worse.

"No, not from Pinkerton's," I said, seeming to imply that I came from a rival agency.

"To tell the truth," I went on, as if I had been prompted to lie about it, "I am not a detective at all. I have come to open an account. I intend to keep all my money in this bank."

The manager looked relieved but still serious; he concluded now that I was a son of Baron Rothschild or a young Gould.

"A large account, I suppose," he said.

"Fairly large," I whispered, "I propose to deposit fifty-six dollars now and fifty dollars a month regularly."

The manager got up and opened the door. He called to the accountant.

"Mr. Montgomery," he said unkindly loud, "this gentleman is opening an account; he will deposit fifty-six dollars. Good morning."

I rose.

A big iron door stood open at the side of the room.

"Good morning," I said, and stepped into the safe.

"Come out," said the manager coldly, and showed me the other way.

I went up to the accountant's wicket and poked the ball of money at him with a quick convulsive movement as if I were doing a conjuring trick.

My face was ghastly pale.

"Here," I said, "deposit it." The tone of the words seemed to mean, "Let us do this painful thing while the fit is on us."

He took the money and gave it to another clerk.

He made me write the sum on a slip and sign my name in a book. I no longer knew what I was doing. The bank swam before my eyes.

"Is it deposited?" I asked in a hollow, vibrating voice.

"It is," said the accountant.

"Then I want to draw a cheque."

My idea was to draw out six dollars of it for present use. Someone gave me a cheque book through a wicket and someone else began telling me how to write it out. The people in the bank had the impression that I was an invalid millionaire. I wrote something on the cheque and thrust it in at the clerk. He looked at it.

"What! are you drawing it all out again?" he asked in surprise. Then I realized that I had written fifty-six instead of six. I was too far gone to reason now. I had a feeling that it was impossible to explain the thing. All the clerks had stopped writing to look at me.

Reckless with misery, I made a plunge.

"Yes, the whole thing."

"You withdraw your money from the bank?"

"Every cent of it."

"Are you not going to deposit any more?" said the clerk, astonished.

"Never."

An idiot hope struck me that they might think something had insulted me while I was writing the cheque and that I had changed my mind. I made a wretched attempt to look like a man with a fearfully quick temper.

The clerk prepared to pay the money.

"How will you have it?" he said.

"What?"

"How will you have it?"

"Oh"—I caught his meaning and answered without even trying to think—"in fifties."

He gave me a fifty-dollar bill.

"And the six?" he asked dryly.

"In sixes," I said.

He gave it to me and I rushed out.

As the big door swung behind me I caught the echo of a roar of laughter that went up to the ceiling of the bank. Since then I bank no more. I keep my money in cash in my trousers' pocket and my savings in silver dollars in a sock.

—Literary Lapses, 1910

THE AWFUL FATE OF MELPOMENUS JONES

Some people—not you nor I, because we are so awfully self-possessed—but some people, find great difficulty in saying good-bye when making a call or spending the evening. As the moment draws near when the visitor feels that he is fairly entitled to go away he rises and says abruptly, "Well, I think I——" Then the people say, "Oh, must you go now? Surely it's early yet!" and a pitiful struggle ensues.

I think the saddest case of this kind of thing that I ever knew was that of my poor friend Melpomenus Jones, a curate—such a dear young man, and only

166

twenty-three! He simply couldn't get away from people. He was too modest to tell a lie, and too religious to wish to appear rude. Now it happened that he went to call on some friends of his on the very first afternoon of his summer vacation. The next six weeks were entirely his own—absolutely nothing to do. He chatted awhile, drank two cups of tea, then braced himself for the effort and said suddenly:

"Well, I think I——"

But the lady of the house said, "Oh, no! Mr. Jones, can't you really stay a little longer?"

Jones was always truthful. "Oh yes," he said, "of course, I—er—can stay."

"Then please don't go."

He stayed. He drank eleven cups of tea. Night was falling. He rose again.

"Well now," he said shyly, "I think I really——"

"You must go?" said the lady politely. "I thought perhaps you could have stayed to dinner——"

"Oh well, so I could, you know," Jones said, "if——"

"Then please stay; I'm sure my husband will be delighted."

"All right," he said feebly, "I'll stay," and he sank back into his chair, just full of tea, and miserable.

Papa came home. They had dinner. All through the meal Jones sat planning to leave at eight-thirty. All the family wondered whether Mr. Jones was stupid and sulky, or only stupid.

After dinner mamma undertook to "draw him out," and showed him photographs. She showed him all the family museum, several gross of them—photos of papa's uncle and his wife, and mamma's brother and his little boy, an awfully interesting photo of papa's uncle's friend in his Bengal uniform, an awfully well-taken photo of papa's grandfather's partner's dog, and an awfully wicked one of papa as the devil for a fancy-dress ball.

At eight-thirty Jones had examined seventy-one photographs. There were about sixty-nine more that he hadn't. Jones rose.

"I must say good night now," he pleaded.

"Say good night!" they said; "why, it's only half-past eight! Have you anything to do?"

"Nothing," he admitted, and muttered something about staying six weeks, and then laughed miserably.

Just then it turned out that the favorite child of the family, such a dear little romp, had hidden Mr. Jones's hat; so papa said that he must stay, and invited him to a pipe and a chat. Papa had the pipe and gave Jones the chat, and still he stayed. Every moment he meant to take the plunge, but couldn't. Then papa began to get very tired of Jones, and fidgeted and finally said, with jocular irony, that Jones had better stay all night; they could give him a shakedown. Jones mistook his meaning and thanked him with tears in his eyes, and papa put Jones to bed in the spare room and cursed him heartily.

After breakfast next day, papa went off to his work in the City, and left Jones playing with the baby, broken-hearted. His nerve was utterly gone. He was meaning to leave all day, but the thing had got on his mind and he simply couldn't. When papa came home in the evening he was surprised and chagrined to find Jones still there. He thought to jockey him out with a jest, and said he thought he'd have to charge him for his board, he! he! The unhappy young man stared wildly for a moment, then wrung papa's hand, paid him a month's board in advance, and broke down and sobbed like a child.

In the days that followed he was moody and unapproachable. He lived, of course, entirely in the drawing room, and the lack of air and exercise began to tell sadly on his health. He passed his time in drinking tea and looking at the photographs. He would stand for hours gazing at the photographs of papa's uncle's friend in his Bengal uniform—talking to it, sometimes swearing bitterly at it. His mind was visibly failing.

At length the crash came. They carried him upstairs in a raging delirium of fever. The illness that followed was terrible. He recognized no one, not even papa's uncle's friend in his Bengal uniform. At times he would start up from his bed and shriek, "Well, I think I——" and then fall back upon the pillow with a horrible laugh. Then, again, he would leap up and cry, "Another cup of tea and more photographs! More photographs! Har! Har!"

At length, after a month of agony, on the last day of his vacation, he passed away. They say that when the last moment came, he sat up in bed with a beautiful smile of confidence playing upon his face, and said, "Well — the angels are calling me; I'm afraid I really must go now. Good afternoon."

And the rushing of his spirit from its prison-house was as rapid as a hunted cat passing over a garden fence.

—Literary Lapses, 1910

THE RETROACTIVE EXISTENCE OF MR. JUGGINS

I first met Juggins—really to notice him—years and years ago as a boy out camping. Somebody was trying to nail up a board on a tree for a shelf and Juggins interfered to help him.

"Stop a minute," he said, "you need to saw the end of that board off before you put it up." Then Juggins looked round for a saw, and when he got it he had hardly made more than a stroke or two with it before he stopped. "This saw," he said, "needs to be filed up a bit." So he went and hunted up a file to sharpen the saw, but found that before he could use the file he needed to put a proper handle on it, and to make a handle he went to look for a sapling in the bush, but to cut the sapling he found that he needed to sharpen up the axe. To do this, of course, he had to fix the grindstone so as to make it run properly. This involved making wooden legs for the grindstone. To do this decently Juggins decided to make a carpenter's bench. This was quite impossible without a better set of tools. Juggins went to the village to get the tools required, and, of course, he never came back.

He was re-discovered—weeks later—in the city, getting prices on wholesale tool machinery.

After that first episode I got to know Juggins very well. For some time we were students at college together. But Juggins somehow never got far with his studies. He always began with great enthusiasm and then something happened. For a time he studied French with tremendous eagerness. But he soon found that for a real knowledge of French you need first to get a thorough grasp of Old French and Provençal. But it proved impossible to do anything with these without an absolutely complete command of Latin. This Juggins discovered could only be obtained, in any thorough way, through Sanskrit, which of course lies at the base of it. So Juggins devoted himself to Sanskrit until he realized that for a proper understanding of Sanskrit one needs to study the ancient Iranian, the root-language underneath. This language however is lost.

So Juggins had to begin over again. He did, it is true, make some progress in natural science. He studied physics and rushed rapidly backwards from forces to molecules, and from molecules to atoms, and from atoms to electrons, and then his whole studies exploded backward into the infinities of space, still searching a first cause.

Juggins, of course, never took a degree, so he made no practical use of his education. But it didn't matter. He was very well off and was able to go straight into business with a capital of about a hundred thousand dollars. He put it at first into a gas plant, but found that he lost money at that because of the high price of the coal needed to make gas. So he sold out for ninety thousand dollars and went into coal mining. This was unsuccessful because of the awful cost of mining machinery. So Juggins sold his share in the mine for eighty thousand dollars and went in for manufacturing mining machinery. At this he would have undoubtedly made money but for the enormous cost of gas needed as motive-power for the plant. Juggins sold out of the manufacture for seventy thousand, and after that he went whirling in a circle, like skating backwards, through the different branches of allied industry.

He lost a certain amount of money each year, especially in good years when trade was brisk. In dull times when everything was unsalable he did fairly well.

Juggins' domestic life was very quiet.

Of course, he never married. He did, it is true, fall in love several times; but each time it ended without result. I remember well his first love story for I was very intimate with him at the time. He had fallen in love with the girl in question utterly and immediately. It was literally love at first sight. There was no doubt of his intentions. As soon as he had met her he was quite frank about it. "I intend," he said, "to ask her to be my wife."

"When?" I asked. "Right away?"

"No," he said, "I want first to fit myself to be worthy of her."

So he went into moral training to fit himself. He taught in a Sunday School for six weeks, till he realized that a man has no business in Divine work of that sort without first preparing himself by serious study of the history of Palestine. And he felt that a man was a cad to force his society on a girl while he is still only half acquainted with the history of the Israelites. So Juggins stayed away. It was nearly two years before he was fit to propose. By the time he was fit, the girl had already married a brainless thing in patent leather boots who didn't even know who Moses was.

Of course Juggins fell in love again. People always do. And at any rate by this time he was in a state of moral fitness that made it imperative.

So he fell in love—deeply in love this time—with a charming girl, commonly known as the eldest Miss Thorneycroft. She was only called eldest because she had five younger sisters; and she was very poor and awfully clever and trimmed all her own hats. Any man, if he's worth the name, falls in love with that sort of thing at first sight. So, of course, Juggins would have proposed to her; only when he went to the house he met her next sister: and of course she was younger still; and, I suppose, poorer: and made not only her own hats but her own blouses. So Juggins fell in love with her. But one night when he went to call, the door was opened by the sister younger still, who not only made her own blouses and trimmed her own hats, but even made her own tailor-made suits. After that Juggins backed up from sister to sister till he went through the whole family, and in the end got none of them.

Perhaps it was just as well that Juggins never married. It would have made things very difficult because, of course, he got poorer all the time. You see, after he sold out his last share in his last business he bought with it a diminishing life annuity, so planned that he always got rather less next year than this year, and still less the year after. Thus, if he lived long enough, he would starve to death.

Meantime he has become a quaint-looking elderly man, with coats a little too short and trousers a little above his boots—like a boy. His face too is like that of a boy, with wrinkles.

And his talk now has grown to be always reminiscent. He is perpetually telling long stories of amusing times that he has had with different people that he names.

He says for example—

"I remember a rather queer thing that happened to me in a train one day——"

And if you say "When was that, Juggins?" he looks at you in a vague way as if calculating and says, "In 1875, or 1876, I think, as near as I recall it——"

I notice, too, that his reminiscences are going further and further back. He used to base his stories on his recollections as a young man; now they are further back.

The other day he told me a story about himself and two people that he called the Harper brothers—Ned and Joe. Ned, he said, was a tremendously powerful fellow.

I asked how old Ned was and Juggins said that he was three. He added that there was another brother not so old, but a very clever fellow about—here Juggins paused and calculated—about eighteen months.

So then I realized where Juggins' retroactive existence is carrying him to. He has passed back through childhood into infancy, and presently, just as his annuity runs to a point and vanishes, he will back up clear through the Curtain of Existence and die,—or be born, I don't know which to call it.

Meantime he remains to me as one of the most illuminating allegories I have met.

—*Behind the Beyond, 1913*

THE RIVAL CHURCHES OF ST. ASAPH AND ST. OSOPH

The church of St. Asaph, more properly called St. Asaph's in the Fields, stands among the elm trees of Plutoria Avenue opposite the university, its tall spire pointing to the blue sky. Its rector is fond of saying that it seems to him to point, as it were, a warning against the sins of a commercial age. More particularly does he say this in his Lenten services at noonday, when the business men sit in front of him in rows, their bald heads uncovered and their faces stamped with contrition as they think of mergers that they should have made, and real estate that they failed to buy for lack of faith.

The ground on which St. Asaph's stands is worth seven dollars and a half a foot. The mortgagees, as they kneel in prayer in their long frock-coats, feel that they have built upon a rock. It is a beautifully appointed church. There are windows with priceless stained glass that were imported from Normandy, the rector himself swearing out the invoices to save the congregation the grievous burden of the customs' duty. There is a pipe organ in the transept that cost ten thousand dollars to install. The debenture-holders, as they join in the morning anthem, love to hear the dulcet notes of the great organ and to reflect that it is as good as new. Just behind the church is St. Asaph's Sunday School, with a ten thousand dollar mortgage of its own. And below that again, on the side street, is the building of the Young Men's Guild, with a bowling-alley and a swimming-bath deep enough to drown two young men at a time, and a billiard-room with seven tables. It is the rector's boast that with a Guild House such as that there is no need for any young man of the congregation to frequent a saloon. Nor is there.

And on Sunday mornings, when the great organ plays, and the mortgagees and the bondholders and the debenture-holders and the Sunday School teachers and the billiard-markers all lift up their voices together, there is emitted from St. Asaph's a volume of praise that is practically as fine and effective as paid professional work.

St. Asaph's is episcopal. As a consequence it has in it and about it all those things which go to make up the episcopal church—brass tablets let into its walls, blackbirds singing in its elm trees, parishioners who dine at eight o'clock, and a rector who wears a little crucifix and dances the tango.

On the other hand, there stands upon the same street, not a hundred yards away, the rival church of St. Osoph—presbyterian down to its very foundations in bed-rock, thirty feet below the level of the avenue. It has a short squat tower—and a low roof, and its narrow windows are glazed with frosted glass. It has dark spruce trees instead of elms, crows instead of blackbirds, and a gloomy minister with a shovel hat who lectures on philosophy on week-days at the university. He loves to think that his congregation is made up of the lowly and the meek in spirit, and to reflect that, lowly and meek as they are, there are men among them that could buy out half the congregation of St. Asaph's.

St. Osoph's is only presbyterian in a special sense. It is, in fact, too presbyterian to be any longer connected with any other body whatsoever. It seceded some forty years ago from the original body to which it belonged, and later on, with three other churches, it seceded from the group of seceding congregations. Still later it fell into a difference with the three other churches on the question of eternal punishment, the word "eternal" not appearing to the elders of St. Osoph's to designate a sufficiently long period. The dispute ended in a secession which left the church of St. Osoph practically isolated in a world of sin whose approaching fate it neither denied nor deplored.

In one respect the rival churches of Plutoria Avenue had had a similar history. Each of them had moved up by successive stages from the lower and poorer parts of the city. Forty years ago, St. Asaph's had been nothing more than a little frame church with a tin spire, away in the west of the slums, and St. Osoph's a square diminutive building away in the east. But the site of St. Asaph's had been bought by a brewing company, and the trustees, shrewd men of business, themselves rising into wealth, had rebuilt it right in the track of the advancing tide of a real estate boom. The elders of St. Osoph, quiet men, but illumined by an inner light, had followed suit and moved their church right against the side of an expanding distillery. Thus both the churches, as decade followed decade, made their way up the slope of the City till St. Asaph's was presently gloriously expropriated by the street railway company, and planted its spire in triumph on Plutoria Avenue itself. But St. Osoph's followed. With each change of site it moved nearer and nearer to St. Asaph's. Its elders were shrewd men. With each move of their church they took careful thought in the rebuilding. In the manufacturing district it was built with sixteen windows on each side and was converted at a huge profit into a bicycle factory. On the residential street it was made long and deep and was sold to a moving picture company without the alteration of so much as a pew. As a last step a syndicate, formed among the members of the congregation themselves, bought ground on Plutoria Avenue, and sublet it to themselves as a site for the church, at a nominal interest of five per cent per annum, payable nominally every three months and secured by a nominal mortgage.

As the two churches moved, their congregations, or at least all that was best of them—such members as were sharing in the rising fortunes of the City—moved also, and now for some six or seven years the two churches and the two congregations had confronted one another among the elm trees of the Avenue opposite to the university.

But at this point the fortunes of the churches had diverged. St. Asaph's was a brilliant success; St. Osoph's was a failure. Even its own trustees couldn't deny it. At a time when St. Asaph's was not only paying its interest but showing a handsome surplus on everything it undertook, the church of St. Osoph was moving steadily backwards.

There was no doubt, of course, as to the cause. Everybody knew it. It was simply a question of men, and, as everybody said, one had only to compare the two men conducting the churches to see why one succeeded and the other failed.

The Reverend Edward Fareforth Furlong of St. Asaph's was a man who threw his whole energy into his parish work. The subtleties of theological controversy he left to minds less active than his own. His creed was one of works rather than of words, and whatever he was doing he did it with his whole heart. Whether he was lunching at the Mausoleum Club with one of his churchwardens, or playing the flute—which he played as only the episcopal clergy can play it—accompanied on the harp by one of the fairest of the ladies of his choir, or whether he was dancing the new episcopal tango with the younger daughters of the elder parishioners, he threw himself into it with all his might. He could drink tea more gracefully and play tennis better than any clergyman on this side of the Atlantic. He could stand beside the white stone font of St. Asaph's in his long white surplice holding a white-robed infant, worth half a million dollars, looking as beautifully innocent as the child itself, and drawing from every matron of the congregation with unmarried daughters the despairing cry, "What a pity that he has no children of his own!"

Equally sound was his theology. No man was known to preach shorter sermons or to explain away the book of Genesis more agreeably than the rector of St. Asaph's; and if he found it necessary to refer to the Deity he did so under the name of Jehovah or Jah, or even Yaweh, in a manner calculated not to hurt the sensitiveness of any of the parishioners . . . . Hell itself was spoken of as She-ol, and it appeared that it was not a place of burning, but rather of what one might describe as moral torment. This settled She-ol once and for all: nobody minds moral torment. In short, there was nothing in the theological system of Mr. Furlong that need have occasioned in any of his congregation a moment's discomfort.

There could be no greater contrast with Mr. Fareforth Furlong than the minister of St. Osoph's, the Reverend Dr. McTeague, who was also honorary professor of philosophy at the university. The one was young, the other was old; the one could dance, the other could not; the one moved about at church picnics and lawn teas among a bevy of disciples in pink and blue sashes; the other moped around under the trees of the university campus, with blinking eyes that saw nothing and an abstracted mind that had spent fifty years in trying to reconcile Hegel with St. Paul, and was still busy with it. Mr. Furlong went forward with the times; Dr. McTeague slid quietly backwards with the centuries.

Dr. McTeague was a failure, and all his congregation knew it. "He is not up to date," they said. That was his crowning sin. "He don't go forward any," said the business members of the congregation. "That old man believes just exactly the same sort of stuff now that he did forty years ago. What's more, he *preaches* it. You can't run a church that way, can you?"

His trustees had done their best to meet the difficulty. They had offered Dr. McTeague a two-years' vacation to go and see the Holy Land. He refused; he said he could picture it. They reduced his salary by fifty per cent; he never noticed it. They offered him an assistant; but he shook his head, saying that he didn't know where he could find a man to do just the work that he was doing. Meantime he mooned about among the trees concocting a mixture of St. Paul with Hegel, three parts to one for his Sunday sermon, and one part to three for his Monday lecture.

No doubt it was his dual function that was to blame for his failure. And this, perhaps, was the fault of Dr. Boomer, the president of the university. Dr. Boomer, like all university presidents of today, belonged to the presbyterian church; or rather, to state it more correctly, he included presbyterianism within himself. He was, of course, a member of the board of management of St. Osoph's, and it was he who had urged, very strongly, the appointment of Dr. McTeague, then senior professor of philosophy, as minister.

"A saintly man," he said, "the very man for the post. If you should ask me whether he is entirely at home as a professor of philosophy on our staff at the university, I should be compelled to say no. We are forced to admit that as a lecturer he does not meet our views. He appears to find it difficult to keep religion out of his teaching. In fact, his lectures are suffused with a rather dangerous attempt at moral teaching which is apt to contaminate our students. But in the Church I should imagine that would be, if anything, an advantage. Indeed, if you were to come to me and say, 'Boomer, we wish to appoint Dr. McTeague as our minister,' I should say, quite frankly, 'Take him.' "

So Dr. McTeague had been appointed. Then, to the surprise of everybody, he refused to give up his lectures in philosophy. He said he felt a call to give them. The salary, he said, was of no consequence. He wrote to Mr. Furlong senior (the father of the episcopal rector, and honorary treasurer of the Plutoria University), and stated that he proposed to give his lectures for nothing. The trustees of the college protested; they urged that the case might set a dangerous precedent which other professors might follow. While fully admitting that Dr. McTeague's

173

lectures were well worth giving for nothing, they begged him to reconsider his offer. But he refused; and from that day on, in spite of all offers that he should retire on double his salary, that he should visit the Holy Land, or Syria, or Armenia, where the dreadful massacres of Christians were taking place, Dr. McTeague clung to his post with a tenacity worthy of the best traditions of Scotland. His only internal perplexity was that he didn't see how, when the time came for him to die, twenty or thirty years hence, they would ever be able to replace him.

Such was the situation of the two churches on a certain beautiful morning in June, when an unforeseen event altered entirely the current of their fortunes . . . .

It appeared to the rector afterwards as almost a shocking coincidence that the first person whom he met [that morning] upon the avenue should have been the Reverend Dr. McTeague himself. Mr. Furlong gave him the form of amiable "good morning" that the episcopal church always extends to those in error. But he did not hear it. The minister's head was bent low, his eyes gazed into vacancy, and from the movements of his lips and from the fact that he carried a leather case of notes, he was plainly on his way to his philosophical lecture. But the rector had no time to muse upon the abstracted appearance of his rival. For, as always happened to him, he was no sooner upon the street than his parish work of the day began. In fact, he had hardly taken a dozen steps after passing Dr. McTeague when he was brought up standing by two beautiful parishioners with pink parasols.

"Oh, Mr. Furlong," exclaimed one of them, "so fortunate to happen to catch you; we were just going into the rectory to consult you. Should the girls—for the lawn tea for the Guild on Friday, you know—wear white dresses with light blue sashes all the same, or do you think we might allow them to wear any colored sashes that they like? What do you think?"

This was an important problem. In fact, there was a piece of parish work here that it took the Reverend Fareforth half an hour to attend to, standing the while in earnest colloquy with the two ladies under the shadow of the elm trees. But a clergyman must never be grudging of his time.

"Good-bye, then," they said at last. "Are you coming to the Browning Club this morning? Oh, so sorry! but we shall see you at the musicale this afternoon, shall we not?"

"Oh, I trust so," said the rector.

"How dreadfully hard he works," said the ladies to one another as they moved away.

Thus slowly and with many interruptions the rector made his progress along the avenue. At times he stopped to permit a pink-cheeked infant in a perambulator to beat him with a rattle while he inquired its age of an episcopal nurse, gay with flowing ribbons. He lifted his hat to the bright parasols of his parishioners passing in glistening motors, bowed to episcopalians, nodded amiably to presbyterians, and even acknowledged with his lifted hat the passing of persons of graver forms of error.

Thus he took his way along the avenue and down a side street towards the business district of the City, until just at the edge of it, where the trees were about to stop and the shops were about to begin, he found himself at the door of the Hymnal Supply Corporation, Limited. The premises as seen from the outside combined the idea of an office with an ecclesiastical appearance. The door was as that of a chancel or vestry; there was a large plate-glass window filled with Bibles and Testaments, all spread open and showing every variety of language in their pages. These were marked "Arabic," "Syriac," "Coptic," "Ojibway," "Irish," and so forth. On the window in small white lettering were the words, "Hymnal Supply Corporation," and below that, "Hosanna Pipe and Steam Organ Incorporated," and still lower the legend, "Bible Society of the Good Shepherd Limited."

There was no doubt of the sacred character of the place.

Here labored Mr. Furlong senior, the father of the Reverend Edward Fareforth. He was a man of many activities, president and managing director of the companies just mentioned, trustee and secretary of St. Asaph's, honorary treasurer of the university, etc.; and each of his occupations and offices was marked by something of a supramundane character, something higher than ordinary business. His different official positions naturally overlapped and brought him into contact with himself from a variety of angles. Thus he sold himself hymn-books at a price per thousand, made as a business favor to himself, negotiated with himself the purchase of the ten thousand dollar organ (making a price on it to himself that he begged himself to regard as confidential), and as treasurer of the college he sent himself an informal note of enquiry asking if he knew of any sound investment for the annual deficit of the college funds, a matter of some sixty thousand dollars a year, which needed very careful handling. Any man—and there are many such—who has been concerned with business dealings of this sort with himself realizes that they are more satisfactory than any other kind.

To what better person then could the rector of St. Asaph's bring the quarterly accounts and statements of his church than to Mr. Furlong senior . . . .

Mr. Furlong senior spread the papers on the table before him and adjusted his spectacles to a more convenient angle. He smiled indulgently as he looked at the documents before him.

"I am afraid you would never make an accountant, Edward," he said.

"I fear not," said the rector.

"Your items," said his father, "are entered wrongly. Here, for example, in the general statement, you put down Distribution of Coals to the Poor to your credit. In the same way, Bibles and Prizes to the Sunday School you again mark to your credit. Why? Don't you see, my boy, that these things are debits? When you give out Bibles or distribute fuel to the poor you give out something for which you get no return. It is a debit. On the other hand, such items as Church Offertory, Scholars' Pennies, etc., are pure profit. Surely the principle is clear."

"I think I see it better now," said the Reverend Edward.

"Perfectly plain, isn't it?" his father went on. "And here again, Paupers' Burial Fund, a loss; enter it as such. Christmas Gift to Verger and Sexton, an absolute loss—you get nothing in return. Widow's Mite, Fines inflicted in Sunday School, etc., these are profit; write them down as such. By this method, you see, in ordinary business we can tell exactly where we stand: anything that we give out without return or reward we count as a debit; all that we take from others without giving in return we count as so much to our credit."

"Ah, yes," murmured the rector. "I begin to understand."

"Very good. But after all, Edward, I mustn't quarrel with the mere form of your accounts; the statement is really a splendid showing. I see that not only is our mortgage and debenture interest all paid to date, but that a number of our enter-- prises are making a handsome return. I notice, for example, that the Girls' Friendly Society of the church not only pays for itself, but that you are able to take something out of its funds and transfer it to the Men's Book Club. Excellent! And I observe that you have been able to take a large portion of the Soup Kitchen Fund and put it into the Rector's Picnic Account. Very good indeed. In this respect your figures are a model for church accounts anywhere."

Mr. Furlong continued his scrutiny of the accounts. "Excellent," he murmured, "and on the whole an annual surplus, I see, of several thousands. But stop a bit," he continued, checking himself; "what's this? Are you aware, Edward, that you are losing money on your Foreign Missions Account?"

"I feared as much," said Edward.

"It's incontestable. Look at the figures for yourself: missionary's salary so much, clothes and books to converts so much, voluntary and other offerings of converts so much—why, you're losing on it, Edward!" exclaimed Mr. Furlong, and he shook his head dubiously at the accounts before him.

"I thought," protested his son, "that in view of the character of the work itself——"

"Quite so," answered his father, "quite so. I fully admit the force of that. I am only asking you, is it worth it? Mind you, I am not speaking now as a Christian, but as a business man. Is it worth it?"

"I thought that perhaps, in view of the fact of our large surplus in other direc- tions——"

"Exactly," said his father, "a heavy surplus. It is precisely on that point that I wished to speak to you this morning. You have at present a large annual surplus, and there is every prospect under Providence—in fact, I think in any case—of it continuing for years to come. If I may speak very frankly I should say that as long as our reverend friend Dr. McTeague continues in his charge of St. Osoph's— and I trust that he may be spared for many years to come—you are likely to enjoy the present prosperity of your church. Very good. The question arises, what disposition are we to make of our accumulating funds?"

"Yes," said the rector, hesitating.

"I am speaking to you now," said his father, "not as the secretary of your church, but as president of the Hymnal Supply Company which I represent here. Now please understand, Edward, I don't want in any way to force or control your judgment. I merely wish to show you certain—shall I say certain opportunities that present themselves for the disposal of our funds? The matter can be taken up later, formally, by yourself and the trustees of the church. As a matter of fact, I have already written to myself as secretary in the matter, and I have received what I consider a quite encouraging answer. Let me explain what I propose." . . .

[*His proposal is interrupted, however, by the delivery of a newspaper reporting that Dr. McTeague had just been stricken with paralysis. Then the president of the university also arrives.*]

Dr. Boomer entered, shook hands in silence and sat down.

"You have heard our sad news, I suppose?" he said. He used the word "our" as between the university president and his honorary treasurer.

"How did it happen?" asked Mr. Furlong.

"Most distressing," said the president. "Dr. McTeague, it seems, had just entered his ten o'clock class (the hour was about ten-twenty) and was about to open his lecture, when one of his students rose in his seat and asked a question. It is a practice," continued Dr. Boomer, "which, I need hardly say, we do not encourage; the young man, I believe, was a newcomer in the philosophy class. At any rate, he asked Dr. McTeague, quite suddenly it appears, how he could reconcile his theory of transcendental immaterialism with a scheme of rigid moral determinism. Dr. McTeague stared for a moment, his mouth, so the class assert, painfully open. The student repeated the question, and poor McTeague fell forward over his desk, paralyzed."

"Is he dead?" gasped Mr. Furlong.

"No," said the president. "But we expect his death at any moment. Dr. Slyder, I may say, is with him now and is doing all he can."

"In any case, I suppose, he could hardly recover enough to continue his college duties," said the young rector.

"Out of the question," said the president. "I should not like to state that of itself mere paralysis need incapacitate a professor. Dr. Thrum, our professor of the theory of music, is, as you know, paralyzed in his ears, and Mr. Slant, our professor of optics, is paralyzed in his right eye. But this is a case of paralysis of the brain. I fear it is incompatible with professorial work."

"Then, I suppose," said Mr. Furlong senior, "we shall have to think of the question of a successor."

They had both *been* thinking of it for at least three minutes.

"We must," said the president. "For the moment I feel too stunned by the sad news to act. I have merely telegraphed to two or three leading colleges for a *locum tenens* and sent out a few advertisements announcing the chair as vacant . . . ."

And after it all, at the close of the third day, Dr. McTeague feebly opened his eyes.

But when he opened them the world had already passed on, and left him behind . . . .

Within a few weeks of this date the Reverend Uttermust Dumfarthing moved into the manse of St. Osoph's and assumed his charge. And forthwith he became the sole topic of conversation on Plutoria Avenue. "Have you seen the new minister of St. Osoph's?" everybody asked. "Have you been to hear Dr. Dumfarthing?" "Were you at St. Osoph's Church on Sunday morning? Ah, you really should go! most striking sermon I ever listened to."

The effect of him was absolute and instantaneous; there was no doubt of it.

"My dear," said Mrs. Buncomhearst to one of her friends, in describing how she had met him, "I never saw a more striking man. Such power in his face! Mr. Boulder introduced him to me on the avenue, and he hardly seemed to see me at all, simply scowled! I was never so favorably impressed with any man."

On his very first Sunday he preached to his congregation on eternal punishment, leaning forward in his black gown and shaking his fist at them. Dr. McTeague had never shaken his fist in thirty years, and as for the Reverend Fareforth Furlong, he was incapable of it.

But the Reverend Uttermust Dumfarthing told his congregation that he was convinced that at least seventy per cent of them were destined for eternal punishment; and he didn't call it by that name, but labelled it simply and forcibly "hell." The word had not been heard in any church in the better part of the City for a generation. The congregation was so swelled next Sunday that the minister raised the percentage to eighty-five, and everybody went away delighted. Young and old flocked to St. Osoph's. Before a month had passed the congregation at the evening service at St. Asaph's Church was so slender that the offertory, as Mr. Furlong senior himself calculated, was scarcely sufficient to pay the overhead charge of collecting it . . . .

Everything [the Reverend Mr. Dumfarthing] did was calculated to please. He preached sermons to the rich and told them they were mere cobwebs, and they liked it; he preached a special sermon to the poor and warned them to be mighty careful; he gave a series of weekly talks to working men, and knocked them sideways; and in the Sunday School he gave the children so fierce a talk on charity and the need of giving freely and quickly that such a stream of pennies and nickels poured into Catherine Dumfarthing's Sunday School Fund as hadn't been seen in the church in fifty years . . . .

Meantime the handsome face of the Reverend Edward Fareforth Furlong began to wear a sad and weary look that had never been seen on it before. He watched his congregation drifting from St. Asaph's to St. Osoph's and was powerless to prevent it. His sadness reached its climax one bright afternoon in the late summer, when he noticed that even his episcopal blackbirds were leaving his elms and moving westward to the spruce trees of the manse . . . .

"Edward," said the rector's father on the occasion of their next quarterly discussion, "I cannot conceal from you that the position of things is very serious. Your statements show a falling off in every direction. Your interest is everywhere in arrears; your current account overdrawn to the limit. At this rate, you know, the end is inevitable. Your debenture and bondholders will decide to foreclose; and if they do, you know, there is no power that can stop them. Even with your limited knowledge of business you are probably aware that there is no higher power that can influence or control the holder of a first mortgage."

"I fear so," said the Reverend Edward very sadly . . . .

Such was the situation of the rival churches of St. Asaph and St. Osoph as the autumn slowly faded into winter: during which time the elm trees on Plutoria Avenue shivered and dropped their leaves and the chauffeurs of the motors first turned blue in their faces and then, when the great snows came, were suddenly converted into liveried coachmen with tall bearskins and whiskers like Russian horseguards, changing back again to blue-nosed chauffeurs the very moment of a thaw. During this time also the congregation of the Reverend Fareforth Furlong was diminishing month by month, and that of the Reverend Uttermust Dumfarthing was so numerous that they filled up the aisles at the back of the church. Here the worshippers stood and froze, for the minister had abandoned the use of steam heat in St. Osoph's on the ground that he could find no warrant for it . . . .

It was noted also that the broken figure of Dr. McTeague had reappeared upon the street, leaning heavily upon a stick and greeting those he met with such a meek and willing affability, as if in apology for his stroke of paralysis, that all who talked with him agreed that McTeague's mind was a wreck.

"He stood and spoke to me about the children for at least a quarter of an hour," related one of his former parishioners, "asking after them by name, and whether they were going to school yet and a lot of questions like that. He never used to speak of such things. Poor old McTeague, I'm afraid he is getting soft in the head." "I know," said the person addressed. "His mind is no good. He stopped me the other day to say how sorry he was to hear about my brother's illness. I could see from the way he spoke that his brain is getting feeble. He's losing his grip. He was speaking of how kind people had been to him after his accident and there were tears in his eyes. I think he's getting batty."

Nor were even these things the most momentous happenings of the period. For as winter slowly changed to early spring it became known that something of great portent was under way. It was rumored that the trustees of St. Asaph's Church were putting their heads together. This was striking news. The last time that the head of Mr. Lucullus Fyshe, for example, had been placed side by side with that of Mr. Newberry, there had resulted a merger of four soda-water companies, bringing what was called industrial peace over an area as big as Texas and raising the price of soda by three peaceful cents per bottle. And the last time that Mr. Furlong senior's head had been laid side by side with those of Mr. Rasselyer-Brown and Mr. Skinyer, they had practically saved the country from the horrors of a coal famine by the simple process of raising the price of nut coal seventy-five cents a ton and thus guaranteeing its abundance.

Naturally, therefore, when it became known that such redoubtable heads as those of the trustees and the underlying mortgagees of St. Asaph's were being put together, it was fully expected that some important development would follow. It was not accurately known from which of the assembled heads first proceeded the great idea which was presently to solve the difficulties of the church. It may well have come from that of Mr. Lucullus Fyshe. Certainly a head which had brought peace out of civil war in the hardware business by amalgamating ten rival stores and had saved the very lives of five hundred employees by reducing their wages fourteen per cent was capable of it.

At any rate it was Mr. Fyshe who first gave the idea a definite utterance.

"It's the only thing, Furlong," he said, across the lunch table at the Mausoleum Club. "It's the one solution. The two churches can't live under the present conditions of competition. We have here practically the same situation as we had with the two rum distilleries — the output is too large for the demand. One or both of the two concerns must go under. It's their turn just now, but these fellows are business men enough to know that it may be ours tomorrow. We'll offer them a business solution. We'll propose a merger."

"I've been thinking of it," said Mr. Furlong senior. "I suppose it's feasible?"

"Feasible!" exclaimed Mr. Fyshe. "Why look what's being done every day everywhere, from the Standard Oil Company downwards."

"You would hardly, I think," said Mr. Furlong, with a quiet smile, "compare the Standard Oil Company to a church?"

"Well, no, I suppose not," said Mr. Fyshe, and he too smiled — in fact he almost laughed. The notion was too ridiculous. One could hardly compare a mere church to a thing of the magnitude and importance of the Standard Oil Company.

"But on a lesser scale," continued Mr. Fyshe, "it's the same sort of thing.". . .

The preliminary stages of the making of the merger followed along familiar business lines. The trustees of St. Asaph's went through the process known as "approaching" the trustees of St. Osoph's. First of all, for example, Mr. Lucullus Fyshe invited Mr. Asmodeus Boulder of St. Osoph's to lunch with him at the Mausoleum Club; the cost of the lunch, as is usual in such cases, was charged to the general expense account of the church. Of course nothing whatever was said during the lunch about the churches or their finances or anything concerning them. Such discussion would have been a gross business impropriety. A few days later the two brothers Overend dined with Mr. Furlong senior, the dinner being charged directly to the contingencies account of St. Asaph's. After which Mr. Skinyer and his partner, Mr. Beatem, went to the spring races together on the Profit and Loss account of St. Osoph's, and Philippa Overend and Catherine Dumfarthing were taken (by the Unforeseen Disbursements Account) to the grand opera, followed by a midnight supper.

All of these things constituted what was called the promotion of the merger and were almost exactly identical with the successive stages of the making of the Amalgamated Distilleries and the Associated Tin Pot Corporation; which was considered a most hopeful sign.

"Do you think they'll go into it?" asked Mr. Newberry of Mr. Furlong senior, anxiously. "After all, what inducement have they?"

"Every inducement," said Mr. Furlong. "All said and done they've only one large asset — Dr. Dumfarthing. We're really offering to buy up Dr. Dumfarthing by pooling our assets with theirs."

"And what does Dr. Dumfarthing himself say to it?"

"Ah, there I am not so sure," said Mr. Furlong; "that may be a difficulty. So far there hasn't been a word from him, and his trustees are absolutely silent about his views. However, we shall soon know all about it. Skinyer is asking us all to come together one evening next week to draw up the articles of agreement."

"Has he got the financial basis arranged then?"

"I believe so," said Mr. Furlong. "His idea is to form a new corporation to be known as the United Church Limited or by some similar name. All the present mortgagees will be converted into unified bondholders, the pew rents will be capitalized into preferred stock and the common stock, drawing its dividend from the offertory, will be distributed among all members in standing. Skinyer says that it is really an ideal form of church union, one that he thinks is likely to be widely adopted. It has the advantage of removing all questions of religion, which he says are practically the only remaining obstacle to a union of all the churches. In fact it puts the churches once and for all on a business basis."

"But what about the question of doctrine, of belief?" asked Mr. Newberry.

"Skinyer says he can settle it," answered Mr. Furlong.

About a week after the above conversation the united trustees of St. Asaph's and St. Osoph's were gathered about a huge egg-shaped table in the board room of the Mausoleum Club. They were seated in intermingled fashion after the precedent of the recent Tin Pot Amalgamation and were smoking huge black cigars specially kept by the club for the promotion of companies and chargeable to expenses of organization at fifty cents a cigar. There was an air of deep peace brooding over the assembly, as among men who have accomplished a difficult and meritorious task.

"Well, then," said Mr. Skinyer, who was in the chair, with a pile of documents in front of him, "I think that our general basis of financial union may be viewed as settled."

A murmur of assent went round the meeting. "The terms are set forth in the memorandum before us, which you have already signed. Only one other point — a minor one — remains to be considered. I refer to the doctrines or the religious belief of the new amalgamation."

"Is it necessary to go into that?" asked Mr. Boulder.

"Not entirely, perhaps," said Mr. Skinyer. "Still there have been, as you all know, certain points — I won't say of disagreement — but let us say of friendly argument — between the members of the different churches — such things for example," here he consulted his papers, "as the theory of the creation, the salvation of the soul, and so forth, have been mentioned in this connection. I have a memorandum of them here, though the points escape me for the moment. These, you may say, are not matters of first importance, especially as compared with the intricate financial questions which we have already settled in a satisfactory manner. Still I think it might be well if I were permitted with your unanimous approval to jot down a memorandum or two to be afterwards embodied in our articles."

There was a general murmur of approval.

"Very good," said Mr. Skinyer, settling himself back in his chair. "Now, first, in regard to the creation," — here he looked all round the meeting in a way to command attention — "is it your wish that we should leave that merely to a gentlemen's agreement or do you want an explicit clause?"

"I think it might be well," said Mr. Dick Overend, "to leave no doubt about the theory of the creation."

"Good," said Mr. Skinyer. "I am going to put it down then something after this fashion: 'On and after, let us say, August first proximo, the process of the creation shall be held, and is hereby held, to be such and such only as is acceptable to a majority of the holders of common and preferred stock voting pro rata.' Is that agreed?"

"Carried," cried several at once.

"Carried," repeated Mr. Skinyer. "Now let us pass on" — here he consulted his notes — "to item two, eternal punishment. I have made a memorandum as follows, 'Should any doubts arise, on or after August first proximo, as to the existence of eternal punishment they shall be settled absolutely and finally by a pro rata vote of all the holders of common and preferred stock.' Is that agreed?"

"One moment!" said Mr. Fyshe, "do you think that quite fair to the bondholders? After all, as the virtual holders of the property, they are the persons most interested. I should like to amend your clause and make it read — I am not phrasing it exactly but merely giving the sense of it — that eternal punishment should be reserved for the mortgagees and bondholders."

At this there was an outbreak of mingled approval and dissent, several persons speaking at once. In the opinion of some, the stockholders of the company, especially the preferred stockholders, had as good a right to eternal punishment as the bondholders. Presently Mr. Skinyer, who had been busily writing notes, held up his hand for silence.

"Gentlemen," he said, "will you accept this as a compromise? We will keep the original clause but merely add to it the words, 'but no form of eternal punishment shall be declared valid if displeasing to a three-fifths majority of the holders of bonds.'"

"Carried, carried," cried everybody.

"To which I think we need only add," said Mr. Skinyer, "a clause to the effect that all other points of doctrine, belief, or religious principle may be freely altered, amended, reversed, or entirely abolished at any general annual meeting!"

There was a renewed chorus of "Carried, carried," and the trustees rose from the table shaking hands with one another, and lighting fresh cigars as they passed out of the club into the night air.

"The only thing that I don't understand," said Mr. Newberry to Dr. Boomer as they went out from the club arm in arm (for they might now walk in that fashion with the same propriety as two of the principals in a distillery merger), "the only thing that I don't understand is why the Reverend Mr. Dumfarthing should be willing to consent to the amalgamation."

"Do you really not know?" said Dr. Boomer.

"No."

"You have heard nothing?"

"Not a word," said Mr. Newberry.

"Ah," rejoined the president, "I see that our men have kept it very quiet — naturally so, in view of the circumstances. The truth is that the Reverend Mr. Dumfarthing is leaving us."

"Leaving St. Osoph's!" exclaimed Mr. Newberry in utter astonishment.

"To our great regret. He has had a call — a most inviting field of work, he says, a splendid opportunity. They offered him ten thousand one hundred; we were only giving him ten thousand here, though of course that feature of the situation would not weigh at all with a man like Dumfarthing."

"Oh no, of course not," said Mr. Newberry.

"As soon as we heard of the call we offered him ten thousand three hundred — not that that would make any difference to a man of his character. Indeed Dumfarthing was still waiting and looking for guidance when they offered him eleven thousand. We couldn't meet it. It was beyond us, though we had the consolation of knowing that with such a man as Dumfarthing the money made no difference."

"And he has accepted the call?"

"Yes. He accepted it today. He sent word to Mr. Dick Overend, our chairman, that he would remain in his manse, looking for light, until two-thirty, after which, if we had not communicated with him by that hour, he would cease to look for it."

"Dear me," said Mr. Newberry, deep in reflection, "so that when your trustees came to the meeting ——"

"Exactly," said Dr. Boomer — and something like a smile passed across his features for a moment — "Dr. Dumfarthing had already sent away his telegram of acceptance."

"Why, then," said Mr. Newberry, "at the time of our discussion tonight, you were in the position of having no minister."

"Not at all. We had already appointed a successor."

"A successor?"

"Certainly. It will be in tomorrow morning's papers. The fact is that we decided to ask Dr. McTeague to resume his charge."

"Dr. McTeague!" repeated Mr. Newberry in amazement. "But surely his mind is understood to be ——"

"Oh, not at all," interrupted Dr. Boomer. "His mind appears, if anything, to be clearer and stronger than ever. Dr. Slyder tells us that paralysis of the brain very frequently has this effect; it soothes the brain — clears it, as it were, so that very often intellectual problems which occasioned the greatest perplexity before present no difficulty whatever afterward. Dr. McTeague, I believe, finds no trouble now in reconciling St. Paul's dialectic with Hegel as he used to. He says that so far as he can see they both mean the same thing."

"Well, well," said Mr. Newberry, "and will Dr. McTeague also resume his philosophical lectures at the university?"

"We think it wiser not," said the president. "While we feel that Dr. McTeague's mind is in admirable condition for clerical work we fear that professorial duties might strain it. In order to get the full value of his remarkable intelligence, we propose to elect him to the governing body of the university. There his brain will be safe from any shock. As a professor there would always be the fear that one of his students might raise a question in his class. This of course is not a difficulty that arises in the pulpit or among the governors of the university." . . .

Thus was constituted the famous union or merger of the churches of St. Asaph and St. Osoph, viewed by many of those who made it as the beginning of a new era in the history of the modern church.

There is no doubt that it has been in every way an eminent success.

Rivalry, competition, and controversies over points of dogma have become unknown on Plutoria Avenue. The parishioners of the two churches may now attend either of them just as they like. As the trustees are fond of explaining, it doesn't make the slightest difference. The entire receipts of the churches being now pooled are divided without reference to individual attendance. At each half year there is issued a printed statement which is addressed to the shareholders of the United Churches Limited and is hardly to be distinguished in style or material from the annual and semi-annual reports of the Tin Pot Amalgamation and the United Hardware and other quasi-religious bodies of the sort. "Your directors," the last of these documents states, "are happy to inform you that in spite of the prevailing industrial depression the gross receipts of the corporation have shown such an increase as to justify the distribution of a stock dividend of special Offertory Stock Cumulative, which will be offered at par to all holders of common or preferred shares . . . . "

So the two churches of St. Asaph and St. Osoph stand side by side united and at peace. Their bells call softly back and forward to one another on Sunday mornings, and such is the harmony between them that even the episcopal rooks in the elm trees of St. Asaph's and the presbyterian crows in the spruce trees of St. Osoph's are known to exchange perches on alternate Sundays.

—*Arcadian Adventures with the Idle Rich, 1914*

THE DEVIL AND THE DEEP SEA:
A DISCUSSION OF MODERN MORALITY

The devil is passing out of fashion. After a long and honorable career he has fallen into an ungrateful oblivion. His existence has become shadowy, his outline attenuated, and his personality displeasing to a complacent generation. So he stands now leaning on the handle of his three-pronged oyster fork and looking into the ashes of his smothered fire. Theology will have none of him. Genial clergy of ample girth, stuffed with the buttered toast of a rectory tea, are preaching him out of existence. The fires of his material hell are replaced by the steam heat of moral torture. This even the most sensitive of sinners faces with equanimity . . . .

Now that the Devil is passing away an unappreciative generation fails to realize the high social function that he once performed. There he stood for ages a simple and workable basis of human morality; an admirable first-hand reason for being good, which needed no ulterior explanation. The rude peasant of the Middle Ages, the illiterate artisan of the shop, and the long-haired hind of the fields, had no need to speculate upon the problem of existence and the tangled skein of moral enquiry. The Devil took all that off their hands. He had either to "be good" or else he "got the fork," just as in our time the unsuccessful comedian of amateur night in the vaudeville houses "gets the bird." Humanity, with the Devil to prod it from behind, moved steadily upwards on the path of moral development. Then having attained a certain elevation, it turned upon its tracks, denied that there had been any Devil, rubbed itself for a moment by way of investigation, said that there had been no prodding, and then fell to wandering about on the hilltops without any fixed idea of goal or direction.

In other words, with the disappearance of the Devil there still remains unsolved the problem of conduct, and behind it the riddle of the universe. How are we getting along without the Devil? How are we managing to be good without the fork? What is happening to our conception of goodness itself? . . .

I suppose that most of us would have the general idea that there never was an age which displayed so high a standard of morality, or at least of ordinary human decency, as our own. We look back with a shudder to the blood-stained history of our ancestors: the fires of Smithfield with the poor martyr writhing about his post, frenzied and hysterical in the flames; the underground cell where the poor remnant of humanity turned its haggard face to the torch of the entering jailer; the mad-house itself with its gibbering occupants converted into a show for the idle fools of London. We may well look back on it all and say that, at least, we are better than we were. The history of our little human race would make but sorry reading were not its every page imprinted with the fact that human ingenuity has invented no torment too great for human fortitude to bear.

In general decency—sympathy—we have undoubtedly progressed. Our courts of law have forgotten the use of the thumbkins and boot; we do not press a criminal under "weights greater than he can bear" in order to induce him to plead; nor flog to ribands the bleeding back of the malefactor dragged at the cart's tail through the thoroughfares of a crowded city. Our public, objectionable though it is as it fights its way to its ball games, breathes peanuts and peppermint upon the offended atmosphere, and shrieks aloud its chronic and collective hysteria, is at all events better than the leering oafs of the Elizabethan century, who put hard-boiled eggs in their pockets and sat around upon the grass waiting for the "burning" to begin.

But when we have admitted that we are better than we were as far as the facts of our moral conduct go, we may well ask as to the principles upon which our conduct is based. In past ages there was the authoritative moral code as a guide — thou shalt and thou shalt not — and behind it the pains, and the penalties, and the three-pronged oyster fork. Under that influence, humanity, or a large part of it, slowly and painfully acquired the moral habit. At present it goes on, as far as its actions are concerned, with the momentum of the old beliefs.

But when we turn from the actions on the surface to the ideas underneath, we find in our time a strange confusion of beliefs out of which is presently to be made the new morality. Let us look at some of the varied ideas manifested in the cross-sections of the moral tendencies of our time.

Here we have first of all the creed and cult of self-development. It arrogates to itself the title of New Thought, but contains in reality nothing but the Old Selfishness. According to this particular outlook the goal of morality is found in fully developing oneself. Be large, says the votary of this creed, be high, be broad. He gives a shilling to a starving man, not that the man may be fed but that he himself may be a shilling-giver. He cultivates sympathy with the destitute for the sake of being sympathetic. The whole of his virtue and his creed of conduct runs to a cheap and easy egomania in which his blind passion for himself causes him to use external people and things as mere reactions upon his own personality. The immoral little toad swells itself to the bursting point in its desire to be a moral ox.

In its more ecstatic form, this creed expresses itself in a sort of general feeling of "uplift," or the desire for internal moral expansion. The votary is haunted by the idea of his own elevation. He wants to get into touch with nature, to swim in the Greater Being, "to tune himself," harmonize himself, and generally to perform on himself as on a sort of moral accordion. He gets himself somehow mixed up with natural objects, with the sadness of autumn, falls with the leaves and drips with the dew. Were it not for the complacent self-sufficiency which he induces, his refined morality might easily verge into simple idiocy. Yet, odd though it may seem, this creed of self-development struts about with its head high as one of the chief moral factors which have replaced the authoritative dogma of the older time.

The vague and hysterical desire to "uplift" oneself merely for exaltation's sake is about as effective an engine of moral progress as the effort to lift oneself in the air by a terrific hitching up of the breeches.

The same creed has its physical side. It parades the Body, with a capital B, as also a thing that must be developed; and this, not for any ulterior thing that may be effected by it but presumably as an end in itself. The Monk or the Good Man of the older day despised the body as a thing that must learn to know its betters. He spiked it down with a hair shirt to teach it the virtue of submission. He was of course very wrong and very objectionable. But one doubts if he was much worse than his modern successor who joys consciously in the operation of his pores and his glands, and the correct rhythmical contraction of his abdominal muscles, as if he constituted simply a sort of superior sewage system.

I once knew a man called Juggins who exemplified this point of view. He used to ride a bicycle every day to train his muscles and to clear his brain. He looked at all the scenery that he passed to develop his taste for scenery. He gave to the poor to develop his sympathy with poverty. He read the Bible regularly in order to cultivate the faculty of reading the Bible, and visited picture galleries with painful assiduity in order to give himself a feeling for art. He passed through life with a strained and haunted expression waiting for clarity of intellect, greatness of soul, and a passion for art to descend upon him like a flock of doves. He is now dead. He died presumably in order to cultivate the sense of being a corpse.

No doubt, in the general scheme or purpose of things the cult of self-development and the botheration about the Body may, through the actions which it induces, be working for a good end. It plays a part, no doubt, in whatever is to be the general evolution of morality.

And there, in that very word evolution, we are brought face to face with another of the widespread creeds of our day, which seek to replace the older. This one is not so much a guide to conduct as a theory, and a particularly cheap and easy one, of a general meaning and movement of morality. The person of this persuasion is willing to explain everything in terms of its having been once something else and being about to pass into something further still. Evolution, as the natural scientists know it, is a plain and straightforward matter, not so much a theory as a view of a succession of facts taken in organic relation. It assumes no purposes whatever. It is not — if I may be allowed a professor's luxury of using a word which will not be understood — in any degree teleological.

The social philosopher who adopts the evolutionary theory of morals is generally one who is quite in the dark as to the true conception of evolution itself. He understands from Darwin, Huxley, and other great writers whom he has not read, that the animals have been fashioned into their present shape by a long process of twisting, contortion, and selection, at once laborious and deserving. The giraffe lengthened its neck by conscientious stretching; the frog webbed its feet by perpetual swimming; and the bird broke out in feathers by unremitting flying. "Nature," by weeding out the short giraffe, the inadequate frog, and the top-heavy bird, encouraged by selection the ones most "fit to survive." Hence the origin of species, the differentiation of organs — hence, in fact, everything.

Here, too, when the theory is taken over and mistranslated from pure science to the humanities, is found the explanation of all our social and moral growth. Each of our religious customs is like the giraffe's neck. A manifestation such as the growth of Christianity is regarded as if humanity broke out into a new social organism, in the same way as the ascending amoeba breaks out into a stomach. With this view of human relations, nothing in the past is said to be either good or bad. Everything is a movement. Cannibalism is a sort of apprenticeship in meat-eating. The institution of slavery is seen as an evolutionary stage towards free citizenship, and "Uncle Tom's" overseer is no longer a nigger-driver but a social force tending towards the survival of the Booker Washington type of negro.

With his brain saturated with the chloroform of this social dogma, the moral philosopher ceases to be able to condemn anything at all, measures all things with a centimetre scale of his little doctrine, and finds them all of the same length. Whereupon he presently desists from thought altogether, calls everything bad or good an evolution, and falls asleep with his hands folded upon his stomach, murmuring "survival of the fittest."

Anybody who will look at the thing candidly, will see that the evolutionary explanation of morals is meaningless, and presupposes the existence of the very thing it ought to prove. It starts from a misconception of the biological doctrine. Biology has nothing to say as to what ought to survive and what ought not to survive; it merely speaks of what does survive. The burdock easily kills the violet, and the Canadian skunk lingers where the hummingbird has died. In biology the test of fitness to survive is the fact of the survival itself — nothing else. To apply this doctrine to the moral field brings out grotesque results. The successful burglar ought to be presented by society with a nickel-plated "jemmy," and the starving cripple left to die in the ditch. Everything — any phase of movement or religion — which succeeds, is right. Anything which does not is wrong. Everything which is, is right; everything which was, is right; everything which will be, is right. All we have to do is to sit still and watch it come. This is moral evolution.

On such a basis, we might expect to find, as the general outcome of the new moral code now in the making, the simple worship of success. This is exactly what is happening. The morality which the Devil with his oyster fork was commissioned to inculcate was essentially altruistic. Things were to be done for other people. The new ideas, if you combine them in a sort of moral amalgam — to develop oneself, to evolve, to measure things by their success — weigh on the other side of the scale. So it comes about that the scale begins to turn and the new morality shows signs of exalting the old-fashioned Badness in place of the discredited Goodness. Hence we find, saturating our contemporary literature, the new worship of the Strong Man, the easy pardon of the Unscrupulous, the Apotheosis of the Jungle, and the Deification of the Detective. Force, brute force, is what we now turn to as the moral ideal, and Mastery and Success are the sole tests of excellence. The nation cuddles its multi-millionaires, cinematographs itself silly with the pictures of its prize-fighters, and even casts an eye of slant-wise admiration through the bars of its penitentiaries. Beside these things the oimple Good Man of the older dispensation, with his worn alpaca coat and his obvious inefficiency, is nowhere.

Truly, if we go far enough with it, the Devil may come to his own again, and more than his own, not merely as Head Stoker but as what is called an End in IIimself. . . .

Our poor Devil then is gone. We cannot have him back for the whistling. For generations, as yet unlearned in social philosophy, he played a useful part — a dual part in a way, for it was his function to illustrate at once the pleasures and the penalties of life. Merriment in the scheme of things was his, and for those drawn too far in pleasure and merriment, retribution and the oyster fork. . . .

So with his twin incentives of pain and pleasure he coaxed and prodded humanity on its path, till it reached the point where it repudiated him, called itself a Superman, and headed straight for the cliff over which is the deep sea. *Quo Vadimus?*

—Essays and Literary Studies, 1916

The basis of the humorous, the amusing, the ludicrous, lies in the incongruity, the unfittingness, the want of harmony among things; and this incongruity, according to the various stages of evolution of human society and of the art of speech, may appear in primitive form, or may assume a more complex manifestation. The crudest and most primitive form of all "disharmonies" is that offered by the aspect of something smashed, broken, defeated, knocked out of its original shape and purpose. Hence it is that Hobbes tells us that the prototype of human amusement is found in the exulting laugh of the savage over his fallen foe whose head he has cracked with a club. This represents the very origin and fountain source of laughter. "The passion of laughter," says Hobbes, "springs from a sudden glory arising from a conception of some eminence in ourselves, as compared with the misfortunes of others." It seems but a sad commentary upon the history of humanity to think that the original basis of our amusement should appear in the form which is called demoniacal merriment. But there is much to support this view. "The pleasure of the ludicrous," says Plato, "originates in the sight of another's misfortune." Nay, we have but to consider the cruder forms of humor even among civilized people to realize that the original type still persists. The laughter of a street urchin at the sight of a fat gentleman slipping on a banana peel, the amusement of a child in knocking down ninepins, or demolishing a snow-man, the joy of a schoolboy in breaking window-panes—all such cases indicate the principle of original demoniacal amusement at work. . . .

Now this primitive form of fun is of a decidedly anti-social character. It runs counter to other instincts, those of affection, pity, unselfishness, upon which the progressive development of the race has largely depended. As a consequence of this, the basis of humor tends in the course of social evolution to alter its original character. It becomes a condition of amusement that no serious harm or injury shall be inflicted, but that only the appearance or simulation of it shall appear. Indeed Plato himself adds, as a proviso to the definition which I have quoted above, that the misfortune which excites mirth in question must involve no serious harm. Hence it comes about that the sight of a humped back, or a crooked foot, is droll only to the mind of a savage or a child; while the queer gyrations of a person whose foot has gone to sleep, and who tries in vain to walk, may excite laughter in the civilized adult by affording the appearance of crooked limbs without the reality. . . .

When the development of humor reaches this stage its basis is shifted from the appearance of destructiveness and demolition to that of the *incongruous*. Man's advancing view of what is harmonious, purposeful, and properly adjusted to its surroundings begins to cause him a sense of intellectual superiority, a tickling of amused vanity at the sight of that which misses its mark, which betrays a maladjustment of means to end, a departure from the proper type of things. The idea of contrast, incongruity, of the false semblance between the correct and the incorrect, becomes the basic principle of the ludicrous.

To this stage of the development of the ludicrous belongs the amusement one feels at the sight of a juggler swallowing yards of tape, or of a circus clown wearing a little round hat the size of a pill-box. . . .

To this secondary stage of development is to be assigned the first appearance of the mode of humor called wit. Wit depends upon a contrast or incongruity effected by calling in the art of words. "It is," says Professor Bain, "a sudden and unexpected form of humor, involving a play upon words." "Wit," writes Walter Pater, "is that unreal and transitory form of mirth, which is like the crackling of thorns under a pot." "It consists," says another modern authority, Mr. Lilly, "in the discoveries of incongruities in the province of the understanding." If the view here presented be correct, wit is properly to be regarded not as something contrasted with the humorous but offering merely a special and, relatively speaking, unimportant subdivision of a general mode of intellectual operation: it presents a humorous idea by means of the happy juxtaposition of verbal forms.

Now this principle of intellectual pleasure excited by contrast or incongruity, once started on an upward path of development, loses more and more its antisocial character, until at length it appears no longer antagonistic to the social feelings, but contributory to them. The final stage of the development of humor is reached when amusement no longer arises from a single "funny" idea, meaningless contrast, or odd play upon words, but rests upon a prolonged and sustained conception of the incongruities of human life itself. The shortcomings of our existence, the sad contrast of our aims and our achievements, the little fretting aspiration of the day that fades into the nothingness of tomorrow, kindle in the mellowed mind a sense of gentle amusement from which all selfish exultation has been chastened by the realization of our common lot of sorrow. On this higher plane humor and pathos mingle and become one. To the Creator perhaps in retrospect the little story of man's creation and his fall seems sadly droll.

It is of this final stage of the evolution of amusement that one of the keenest of modern analysts has written thus — "when men become too sympathetic to laugh at each other for individual defects or infirmities which once moved their mirth, it is surely not strange that sympathy should then begin to unite them, not in common lamentation for their common defects and inferiorities, but in common amusement at them." This is the sentiment that has inspired the greater masterpieces of humorous literature — this is the humor of Cervantes smiling sadly at the passing of the older chivalry, and of Hawthorne depicting the sombre melancholies of Puritanism against the background of the silent woods of New England. This is the really great humor — unquotable in single phrases and paragraphs, but producing its effect in a long-drawn picture of human life, in which the universal element of human imperfection — alike in all ages and places — excites at once our laughter and our tears.

—"American Humour," *Essays and Literary Studies, 1916*

EMILY CARR

(1871-1945)

Emily Carr was born on December 12, 1871, in Victoria, British Columbia. She attended the local high school and then studied at the Mark Hopkins School of Art in San Francisco (1889-1892) and later at the Westminster School of Art in England (1899-1904). On her return to Canada she taught art privately for a number of years both in Victoria and Vancouver. Unable to make a living from art, she turned to other activities. Her book, House of All Sorts *(1942), describes some of her experiences while she kept a boarding house in Victoria (1913-1936).*

During these years she had made many trips to the Indian villages of the West Coast, where she sketched the totem poles and the people. She developed an individualistic style in painting which later made her famous. At the same time, these trips provided her with material for the prose sketches included in her first book, Klee Wyck *(1941), which won a Governor-General's Gold Medal. The* Book of Small *(1942) and the posthumous* Growing Pains *were autobiographical. Emily Carr died in Victoria on March 2, 1945.*

JUICE

It was unbelievably hot. We three women came out of the store each eating a juicy pear. There was ten cents' express on every pound of freight that came up the Cariboo road. Fruit weighs heavy. Everything came in by mule-train.

The first bite into those Bartletts was intoxicating. The juice met your teeth with a gush.

I was considering the most advantageous spot to set my bite next when I saw Dr. Cabbage's eyes over the top of my pear, feasting on the fruit with unquenched longing.

I was on the store step, so I could look right into his eyes. They were dry and filmed. The skin of his hands and face was shrivelled, his clothes nothing but a bunch of tatters hanging on a dry stick. I believe the wind could have tossed him like a dead leaf, and that nothing juicy had ever happened in Doctor Cabbage's life.

"Is it a good apple?"

After he had asked, his dry tongue made a slow trip across his lips and went back into his mouth hotter and dryer for thinking of the fruit.

"Would you like it?"

A gleam burst through his filmed eyes. He drew the hot air into his throat with a gasp, held his hand out for the pear and then took a deep greedy bite beside mine.

The juice trickled down his chin—his tongue jumped out and caught it; he sipped the oozing juice from the hole our bites had made. He licked the drops running down the rind, then with his eyes still on the pear, he held it out for me to take back.

"No, it's all yours."

"Me eat him every bit?"

"Yes."

His eyes squinted at the fruit as if he could not quite believe his ears and that all the pear in his hands belonged to him. Then he took bite after bite, rolling each bite slowly round his mouth, catching every drop of juice with loud suckings. He ate the core. He ate the tail, and licked his fingers over and over like a cat.

"Hyas Klosshe (very good)," he said, and trotted up the hill as though his joints had been oiled.

Some days later I had occasion to ride through the Indian village. All the cow ponies were busy—the only mount available was an old, old mare who resented each step she took, and if you stopped one instant she went fast asleep.

Indian boys were playing football in the street of their village. I drew up to ask direction. The ball bounced exactly under my horse's stomach. The animal had already gone to sleep and did not notice. Out of a cabin shot a whirl of a little man, riddled with anger. It was Doctor Cabbage.

He confiscated the ball and scolded the boys so furiously that the whole team melted away—you'd think there was not a boy left in the world.

Laying his hand on my sleeping steed, Doctor Cabbage smiled up at me.

"You brave good rider," he said. "Skookum tumtum (good heart)!"

I thanked Doctor Cabbage for the compliment and for his gallant rescue.

I woke my horse with great difficulty, and decided that honour for conspicuous bravery was sometimes very easily won.

—1941

THE STARE

Millie's stare was the biggest thing in the hut. It dimmed for a moment as we stood in its way—but in us it had no interest. The moment we moved from its path it tightened again—this tense, living stare glowing in the sunken eyes of a sick Indian child.

All the life that remained in the emaciated, shrivelled little creature was concentrated in that stare. It burned a path for itself right across the sea to the horizon, burning with longing focused upon the return of her father's whaling-boat.

The missionary bent over the child.

"Millie!"

Millie's eyes lifted grudgingly, then hastened back to their watching.

Turning to the old crone who took the place of a mother who was dead and cared for the little girl, the missionary asked, "How is she, Granny?"

"I t'ink 'spose boat no come quick, Milly die plitty soon now."

"Is there no word of the boats?"

"No, maybe all Injun-man dead. Whale fishin' heap, heap bad for make die."

They brought the child food. She struggled to force down enough to keep the life in her till her father came. Squatted on her mat on the earth floor, her chin resting on the sharp knees and circled by her sticks of arms, she sat from dawn till dark, watching. When light was gone the stare fought its way, helped by Millie's ears, listening, listening out into black night.

It was in the early morning that the whaling-boats came home. When the mist lifted, Millie saw eight specks out on the horizon. Taut, motionless, uttering no word, she watched them grow.

"The boats are coming!" The cry rang through the village. Women left their bannock-baking, their basket-weaving and hurried to the shore. The old crone who tended Millie hobbled to the beach with the rest.

"The boats are coming!" Old men warming their stiff bodies in the sun shaded dull eyes with their hands to look far out to sea, groaning for joy that their sons were safe.

"The boats are coming!" Quick ears of children heard the cry in the school-house and, squeezing from their desks without leave, pattered down to the shore. The missionary followed. It was the event of the year, this return of the whaling-boats.

Millie's father was the first to land. His eyes searched among the people.

"My child?"

His feet followed the women's pointing fingers. Racing up the bank, his bulk filled the doorway of the hut. The stare enveloped him, Millie swayed towards him. Her arms fell down. The heavy plaits of her hair swung forward. Brittle with long watching, the stare had snapped.

—1941

FREDERICK PHILIP GROVE

(1879-1948)

According to Frederick Philip Grove's own account, his grandfather was an Englishman who had emigrated to Sweden, married a Swedish woman, and eventually established the family fortune and a large estate in southern Sweden. Grove's father, born in Sweden, married a Scotswoman with a considerable personal fortune. Grove himself was born in 1871, the eighth child and only son of a marriage which was destined to result in a separation. His childhood was largely spent in the company of his mother, whose travels in search of the society of writers, musicians, and intellectuals took her through countries from Russia to England, Sweden to Egypt. In consequence, the boy's formal education was desultory, but private tutoring and wide reading in various languages were compensations. By 1886 his mother's private means were exhausted, and the two settled in Berlin, where she died of cancer in 1887.

No hint of the father's declining fortunes, Grove says, intruded upon the son's life as artistic dilettante and casual archeologist. In the years after 1887 he journeyed through Siberia to the Pacific, studied at universities in Paris, Rome, and Munich, and travelled to North Africa and Australasia. He had become intimate with the most sophisticated literary circles of Paris and the centre of a cosmopolitan group of young Europeans before he began a tour of North America in 1892. In Toronto, according to his In Search of Myself, *word came of the father's death and bankruptcy, leaving the son stranded. The next twenty years, Grove tells us, he spent as a wandering labourer and harvest hand, when he followed the season north from Kansas to Alberta, and during the winters worked doggedly at his writing. But no publisher would accept any of his ten or more manuscripts. Then in January 1913 he took an appointment as a school teacher in rural Manitoba.*

It can now be said, following publication of D. O. Spettigue's FPG: The European Years *(1973), that this account is largely fiction. Grove's real name was Felix Paul Greve. Born in 1879 on the border of West Prussia and Russia, he was German, not Anglo-Swedish. His parents were not wealthy, he did not travel as a child but grew up in Hamburg, where his mother died in 1898. He attended the universities of Bonn and Munich before becoming a free-lance writer and translator. His first book was a slim volume of poems, published privately in 1902. The European years were not happy ones. Poverty, indebtedness, and misfortune, including imprisonment, drove Greve to fake a suicide and flee to Canada in 1909.*

Still a mystery are the three years after 1909. We do not even know what name Greve used when he entered Manitoba. But he called himself Grove when he became a teacher and, in 1914, married a fellow teacher. For the next decade, undaunted by ill luck and ill health, Grove struggled to combine writing and teaching. By extramural study he earned a B.A. in 1922 from the University of Manitoba, but within a couple of years his increasing deafness forced him to abandon teaching. In 1929 the Groves moved to Ontario, where for a while he was with the Graphic Press in Ottawa, an ambitious but short-lived publishing firm. After 1931 the Groves settled on a farm near Simcoe, Ontario.

Grove's first Canadian work, Over Prairie Trails *(1922) was followed the next year by* The Turn of the Year. *Both books had been written in 1919-1920, and they consist of descriptive and narrative essays which incorporate Grove's observations and experiences during his residence in several districts of Manitoba and during travel on weekends between school and family in different seasons and weather. His first Canadian novel—though two previous novels and a large assortment of other books had appeared in Germany—was* Settlers of the Marsh *(1925) often called our first realistic novel. Of his fifteen Canadian books,* A Search for America *(1927) was the most popular. Some seven or eight volumes remained unpublished at his death. A collection of his manuscripts and papers is deposited at the University of Manitoba.*

In 1934 the Royal Society awarded him the Lorne Pierce Gold Medal; in 1945 the University of Manitoba made him an honorary Doctor of Letters. Shortly before his death, his "autobiography" In Search of Myself *won a Governor-General's award.*

THE SOWER

The field behind the yard which is flanked by dense thickets of young poplar growth stretches away to the north, perfectly level, flat like a table-top as far as it is cleared. Beyond it, the bush of second-growth poplar forms the horizon.

On the large roomy yard which is covered by a sward of short grass, an old man goes about, puttering at his chores in the light of the rising sun. First he splits wood and carries it to the door of the log shack that stands some fifty feet or so from the winding bush-trail in front. Then he tinkers about at the old rickety seeder, trying the shafts to which two axe-squared poplar poles are spliced. And at last he goes to the stable where three horses are munching away at their straw, mixed with some hay. Two of the horses are old; the third is a colt a little over three years old. The colt nickers when the old man enters and impetuously turns to the oat-box in the corner of his stall and licks it. He is the only one of the three that throws his head when the harness descends on his back.

As the man moves about, an onlooker would be struck by a peculiarity of his gait. His legs seem too short for his body, his arms too long: there is something ape-like in his movements. His face is framed by a gray scraggy beard; but his upper lip and the front of his chin are bare though not freshly shaved; in fact, they look as if they were clipped with a pair of scissors rather, for the bristly stubble that covers them is of uneven length. The type is unmistakable: it is Icelandic.

*   *   *

He was a sailor once, in his own far country. Inconceivable though it is, he once was young: young at least in years, though never young in life, for he went to work and to toil at the age of twelve. And one day, when he had thus been a toiler for almost a lifetime, he took a wife to himself, much younger than he was; and she bore him three children. It was when the children had arrived that the desire to give up his wandering life became overpowering. He gave himself over to brooding; and slowly his brooding became articulate. He thought of his own youth and how he had gone out to toil on the sea when merely a child. He hated to think that his little ones should have to do the same. He shared the prejudice of his class that, if he could give them what he considered to be an education, they would not have to do hard work. He heard of Canada and the United States: homes of freedom across the seas. He longed to go on the land. Land was given away there to those who would till it. He pondered over that for three more years.

And then, one day, he announced to his wife that he had made up his mind to emigrate. The young woman who was about thirty at the time did not like this plan. But, for another year, at every home-coming from his trips across the northern sea, he kept talking about it till the thought became familiar and less repulsive to her. And at last they came and settled on the prairie of the west.

He took up the homestead in the bush and built a log hut. And he began at once to clear some land. But in summer he worked out for such of his countrymen as were already established, while his wife stayed at home with the children; and in winter, when he could look after the little ones, his wife went out, to the city, to work in the homes of well-to-do people.

In a money-sense, she did better than he; she was capable, honest, and clean; and the work was like play to her. But he, meanwhile, was clearing land and began to break it. A cow and a team of oxen appeared on the farm. The trouble was that she began to like the city: the company she found and the shallow ease of life. She could not see that he was building up capital; wages that come and go looked alluring to her. And so she began nagging at him to leave the farm and to come with her to the city. He listened and shook his head.

194

Thus a few more years went by. And there came a time when the work on the field demanded his full unstinted strength. That summer the work of milking three cows, of feeding the pigs, and of tending the kitchen-garden fell to the woman's share. He, too, it is true, worked from four in the morning till after dark. But while he worked, his vision was of the farm; her vision was a comparison between this slavery and the city. Man and wife found themselves estranged.

The children meanwhile had grown; and there was no school as yet, for there were only three settlers in the bush so far, and they were miles apart. The woman had become acclimated in speech and thought; and as summer went on, this dumb Icelandic man became a horror to her.

In the fall, when he proposed that she should stay for the winter, she refused. She went; and she took the oldest girl, who was sixteen by now, along; and shortly after, she came back for the other two children. He did not put up a fight; he drove them to town in an all-day trip with his slow oxen; but he looked wistfully after the midnight-train that took them away; and he never saw any of them again. He was sixty years old at the time.

Next spring he found that he could not handle all the work on the farm; and so he disposed of the cattle, the oxen, and pigs; and with the money he bought two mares.

Henceforth he worked on, clearing a little every year, buying mower and binder, and seeding the land that was broken. In the beginning, he was still thinking of his children in all he did. But he ceased dreaming of a better house: the log shack was good enough for him, now that he was all alone. Then he heard, in one of the yearly letters which he received, that his wife was doing well in the city, she and the girls hiring out as domestic servants, and the boy working in a garage; and so they began to fade from his life and became a memory, detached from himself; and their place was taken by a strange idea in his mind: he was working for God, not for Man. Seeding and reaping became an obsession with him; or, better, perhaps, a religious exercise.

*   *   *

The sun rises higher; and the surface of the soil becomes moist as the frost of the night leaves the ground. The old man, in his swinging sailor-gait, leads the horses out of the low log stable, one by one, the old mares first, and then the colt; and he hooks them together. And when he is finished with that, he drives them over to the seeder and hitches them up. A bag with the seed-grain stands behind the machine, leaning against the covering discs. He empties it into the seeder-box and reaches in with his hand that has only three fingers left, caressing it, lifting it up, and allowing it to run down in a smooth golden stream, his lips muttering the while.

Then he mounts on the seat and takes the lines. The horse between the shafts — the colt — is the first to move. The two old mares are slow to start, reluctant; but at last all three are slowly walking away. He drives to the back of the yard where alongside the stable a pole-gate marks off the field. An old rheumatic dog, a collie, almost black, but gray about the mouth, has limped over and fallen in line behind the seeder. The horses stop.

Slowly and stiffly the old man gets off his seat; and then he opens the gate, pulling out the poles one by one and laying them down, methodically, along the fence to the east of the gate. The colt paws the ground with one foot and snorts, stepping back and forth; but the two old mares stand still.

When the gate is open, the old man goes a few steps beyond and bends down to pick up a clod of the freshly harrowed soil and to crumble it between the thumb and the two remaining fingers of his hand. Then he looks wistfully out. To the east and the west of his farm huge, low-lying, bluish clouds of smoke curl along the ground, slowly rolling southward in the slight, cool morning breeze. They mark the spots where recent settlers are burning the bush, preliminary to the clearing of their first land. The air has the acrid smell of the smoke of green poplar-brush which the old man breathes in with a sort of deliberate relish.

Behind the log stable, north of it, there still lies a snowdrift, caught in a poplar thicket left for protection. The old man walks over there; he kicks against the snow which has consolidated into ice, glassy and hard, so that his foot glances off.

Then he turns back to the seeder. The dog behind has lain down and is reposing his head on his paws. But when he sees his master mounting the seat, he gets up and gives one single wag with the stump of his tail. The horses lean forward; and the seeder rolls on to the field and turns to the east, skirting the ground that is plowed. When it reaches the edge of the clearing, it stops once more; and the old man gets off again.

He bares and bows his head, as he stands between horses and seeder, and mutters a prayer. "God," he says in his own Icelandic tongue, "I do as thou bidst me that those who are hungry be fed. I bring this offering to thy broad altar. Let it grow and prosper that it may become bread for those who will ask thee to give to their need. Amen."

And then for the third time, he gets back on his seat; and after pulling the lever that opens the grain-spouts, he turns north on his first long row.

Slowly, slowly the two old mares step out, hesitating at every move, while the colt between them frets and champs at his bit. Humped over, the old man sits on his seat, holding the lines and clicking his tongue from time to time. And slowly, slowly the old rheumatic dog plods behind, like the two old horses hanging his graying head.

And so they go up and down, up and down, over that thirty-acre field, while the sun climbs slowly over the vault of sparkling, cool spring air with its smell of smoke, and then sinks west again, thus marking a pulse-beat in the season.

* * *

If you were to ask the old man why he does not rest, why he goes on seeding and reaping, he would look at you with uncomprehending bleary eye; and perhaps he would stutter out a word or two of, "God —— the children —— and the land." And interpreted, those words would mean: So long as the land was not cleared, it was God's and supported that life which He had planted there. When man came and cleared it, he drove the wild life out to support man's life with what it could produce. To clear the land and leave it untilled would be sin. And the children, even though they may be, as it is called, making their living, yet need bread; and so they may not take that bread from others who need it and for whom there is no one to grow it, he must still grow it for them that their life remain free of sin. This country is the granary of a world. To put it to that use for which it was meant is serving God; not to do so is defying God.

—1923

THE MIDWIFE

It was the evening of a warm, cloudy day late in March. The thaw had been on for over a week; and the snow on the flat prairie had become rotten.

Dave Chisholm, a short, round shouldered man with an enormous, ball-shaped head and a clean-shaven face with large sky-blue eyes, was working away in silence on top of the load of hay. Kruger, his neighbour on whose place they were, was fully aware of the silence, which was unusual: for Dave was a sociable man as can be. He knew the reason too. The fact was that Kruger had, along in the fall, borrowed five loads of hay from Dave, promising to return them as soon as there was snow on the ground so that he could haul from his own meadow which was some twenty miles away. Now spring was coming, and the hay had not been returned, though Kruger had long since transferred his haystack to a point east of the house. At last Dave, who needed the hay for seeding, had had to go after it himself. Kruger had offered to bring the four remaining loads but Dave had said he had better take them all himself "he guessed."

However, Dave was not in the best humour over it.

When the horses at last pulled the completed load over the field where pools of water were gathering in the hollows, and across the culvert on to the road, Dave stopped the team of bay mares, and Kruger slipped off the hay, climbing down between the horses over the tongue of the sleigh. There he stood but a moment, a great big hulking figure of a man, in goloshes and threadbare mackinaw.

"You ain't mad, Dave, are you?" he said at last.

"Don't talk nonsense," Dave replied. "It makes me nothing out," imitating in these words the speech of certain of his neighbours whose words were English though their phrases and idioms had remained German. It makes me nothing out meant, it does not matter to me.

"You see," Kruger went on, "the wife—well, you know—I was thinking, if you ain't mad, you'd maybe go for Betsy again when the time comes. You've done so before."

"Yes," Dave said slowly, "I guess I'll go."

And he clicked his tongue to his horses, and wearily they plodded home through the slush and the gathering dusk, while Kruger picked his way to his yard where a single huge building stood, a barn with a house built on its side.

Dave was the one farmer in the district who, because he had half a dozen buildings in his yard, and a four-roomed house, white painted, was considered well-to-do. The district was flat prairie, flat as a table top. Yet, when the water came from the hills to the west, in the thaw-up, it drained eastward. There was always too much water when the snow went, so that even the enormous ditches which the municipality had drawn from east to west could not carry it away to the river. For days, often for weeks, it stood on the land, leaving it wet, sour, and infested with weed-seeds when at last it subsided.

A week or two went by.

Dave was sitting in the living room of his house, late at night after dark—having done his chores in hip boots, for the water stood twelve inches deep all over his yard and there was an inch or so of it on the driveway of his barn. He was sitting in a leather-upholstered easy-chair, a big roomy thing bought at an auction sale. He sat crosswise in it, his shoulder blades propped against one of the arm-rests, his stockinged feet perched on the other. He was reading a book: his little library held a curious assortment of books, Tolstoi, Swift, Thoreau, Hamsun. But, while reading, he yawned and yawned. He had overhauled, that day, what implements would be needed for spring work, and winter had made him soft.

The children, overwhelmed with sleepiness, had at last been put to bed: and his wife had followed them. It was always thus. Now Dave sat alone. He was yawning, yawning.

Suddenly, from the room beyond, his wife's voice rang out. "There's somebody coming on horseback."

"Dawggone it!" David yawned. "I bet that's Kruger." He, too, heard by this time the splashing of a horse's feet in the yard.

And Kruger it was. He tied his horse to a post outside and came to the house afoot, through the dark. He knocked at the door and opened it, but did not enter.

Dave got up and went in his stockinged feet into the kitchen. "Eh!"

"Dave," the big hulking man said apologetically spitting behind him between words. "It's coming, you know, what I was talking to you about."

"Yea. I'm tired like a horse. But I'll go."

"I'll help you hitch up."

"Naw," Dave yawned through a whole gamut of notes. "Get back home. Your wife's afraid alone. I'll manage, I guess."

"Well," Kruger said, hesitated, and turned, "all right."

And, as Dave still stood in the dark kitchen, he heard the man outside going back to his horse, and mounting: and the horse went splashing away through the flood.

Half an hour later Dave was pulling out of the yard, leaving the gate open. His two horses were big, bony brutes, picked from among his ten or twelve head because they knew the road and would not get scared should anything untoward happen: his vehicle was a topless buggy.

The night was dark: clouds were hiding even the stars. Yet the water, which covered everything, seemed to help. First there was Kruger's farm with a dim light shining from a window to the west. This light was reflected by the water, tracing dimly a thin yellow path. There would be another farm, halfway to the station, on the north-south road. Next the station would come, where a grain elevator stood and where small signal-lights burned all night though never a train came rumbling by over this little frequented line with its two mixed trains a week. Beyond, the road ran straight east, a good high grade which would not be flooded and, therefore, would show black against the grey gleam of the water on both sides. It would be muddy, to be sure; almost bottom; and the mud would be sticky gumbo which would make the thin wheels of the buggy look like the pneumatic tires of a car. But the horses were used to that. They were not ambitious to run anyway.

Dave had hours of driving ahead of him, "heaps of time"; he might not get to town before midnight, possibly later. Well, he would make himself comfortable, at any rate.

Slowly he pulled his big boots off.

The horses were gingerly plodding along, splash, splash, through the water.

Dave hung the lines over the dashboard, tying them to the whip-socket. He stood up, put his greatcoat on, and shook his tanned horsehides out, wrapping them about his legs. At last, picking the lines up again, he disposed himself on the seat of the buggy as he had been sitting in the chair at home, his shoulder blades pressed against the arm-rest to the right.

He was now passing Kruger's place; no doubt the man was walking up and down in the house, stopping to listen to the splashing of Dave's horses through the water.

"There's Dave going now," he probably said to the woman to comfort her. "In a few hours he'll be back. All will be well."

The horses nodded on. Dave was dozing. Every now and then he yawned, opening his mouth like a wild beast threatening: and he snuggled deeper into his horsehides. Every now and then, too, turning his head, he peered into the darkness over the road.

The horses made the turn to the south. Four miles now to the station, then ten to town. It was like driving through a lake: even the road was covered to a depth of six inches; the wheels picked up the mud from underneath; and as it rose through the water, it melted and dripped back. To both sides were ditches, five, six feet deep, enough for a man to drown in.

Dave dozed, not a thought in his head. An hour went by. Ahead, when he sat up, the lights of the station, red and green.

Dave knew the agent well, a young, unmarried fellow, who often, on the "jigger" of the station-boss, speeded to town for a few hours of a "good time." To Dave, the settled farmer, these lights symbolized distance and far-bound traffic. Years ago, when he himself had been given to going to town, Doyle and he had been a queer pair of friends, talking, disputing, and chaffing each other, and spending money recklessly. Doyle was still living in "single blessedness." No doubt he was sleeping right now on his little cot in the office where he preferred to stay on account of the good, warm stove, leaving the living quarters provided in the building vacant, to be haunted by mice.

Dave wondered whether Doyle was happier that way. But perhaps he was even now dreaming of taking a wife to himself as he, Dave, had done some six, seven years ago. He liked to have the kiddies crawling up on his knee, of an evening in winter. He liked to come home from the field in summer and to pick them up and toss them into the air.

Suddenly, in these thoughts, he saw himself in the days of his courtship, in store clothes with a white collar on: and he grinned all over his face in the dark: then he had taken the little teacher of the district school out in his buggy on Sunday afternoons: till she had married him. Funny business that.

When he had made the turn to the east, he settled back again. There was no need for him watching any longer. The horses would keep going. They were fresh:

he was tired. It was hard pulling through the mud: but the road, here, was not under water, at least, and there was no room to turn without going into the ditch: they wouldn't do that, nor would they stop. They knew they were going to town.

In a drowsy effort Dave fumbled for his pipe which he had thrust half filled into the pocket of his coat. But it was too much work: he gave up and dozed. An hour went by: two hours.

When he awoke, it was from the fact that the horses were stepping out more briskly than before. He must be in town. He sat up. Not a light in any of the cottages betrayed the direction of the road. But leafless cottonwoods outlined themselves dimly, blackly, against the less black sky.

Then came the railroad crossing: beyond it the trees disappeared. The buildings were larger here: bank, department store, hotel. In the lobby of the hotel at the corner a single electric bulb glowed feebly down on the hatless polished skull of the night clerk, sleeping in a chair. Then came the turn into the chief street of the town, running south, past town-hall and garage, drug store, confectionery, cobbler's stall, harnessmaker's shop; all were benighted and asleep. It must be very late indeed. Even the street lights, supposed to be burning till one o'clock, were turned off.

Dave neared the end of the town and made his last turn, into the northernmost side street, toward the river, going on till he reached the last house to his right. A few rods beyond the road was under water again: a grey lake stretched ahead, the flood.

He stopped in front of the gate, shook himself out of his robes, and climbed to the ground. He tied the horses to a fence post and spread the robes over them. At last he went through the little gate to the door and knocked. The house seemed to squat on the mud, almost to float on it.

Dave knocked and knocked, at first with the knuckles of his fingers, after that with his fist. He knocked for fully five minutes. Then came a response.

"Wait a minute, will you?" a high pitched, girlish voice called from within.

He desisted and waited. Through the crack between frame and blind of one of the windows trembled the flickering light of a match, then the steadier gleam of a coal oil lamp. Steps within, slurring, be-slippered steps. The grating of a key in the lock, and at last the door opened an inch or so.

"Who's there?" the same girlish voice enquired.

"Chisholm," said Dave. "Kruger wants you. You know him, I guess."

"All right. Come in, Dave, sit down."

The door opened altogether: and in front of Dave, now illumined in outline by the light of the lamp which fell through the open door of the parlour into the hall, stood a giant woman, a faded kimono thrown over her night-gown. With one hand she held the kimono in at the waist while with the other she held the door. Her bust overflowed that arm at the waist.

Dave, scraping the mud off his feet, entered the little hall which was almost filled by the female presence. He looked like a dwarf in front of her, a crippled mis-shapen dwarf. But although the whole house seemed to fit her like a glove, she managed to step back and let him pass into the parlour, which was scarcely larger than the hall.

"Sit down," the girlish-voiced woman repeated. "You've got robes have you?"

"Sure I've got robes."

"I'll be ready in a few minutes." And with that she drew the parlour door shut, leaving him alone.

The slurring steps passed into the room behind. There followed the groan and squeak of a bed as the woman sat down. Then her own groans, puffing and breathless as she began to dress. They were in a differing key from her voice. The voice was a tenor: the groans a male bass.

Dave waited and dozed, reclining in a creaky, upholstered armchair. His head fell now forward, now backward, as his eyes closed on him. Whenever he fell back, he began to snore, and the noise awakened him. He waited and waited. At last, in the fight against sleep, he began to take an inventory of the furnishings in the room. But the sleepiness made him see things in a queer way. There was a piano, standing slantways in the corner, and it seemed to fill the whole room. Then a sofa covered with nice cream coloured damask below the front edge: this damask was worn into shreds: only the warp remained: the woof had been consumed by time. Next four gigantic upholstered chairs, showing the skeletons of their springs. And finally, in front of the low window, a scaffolding supporting scores upon scores of house plants, each of the size of a good-sized tree.

How had the lamp got on the piano? It was clear that the woman could never enter this room: she would lift the ceiling off. The south wall, however, was hung with a dusty portiere. Reaching around, from where he sat, his legs crossed, Dave lifted the portiere with a lazy finger: there was a door behind it, which explained the mystery.

"I'll be coming in a minute," the girlish voice said impatiently. Probably the woman had been aware of the fact that he had lifted the curtain.

He was fully awake for a moment: and things seemed to fall back into their natural proportions. "All right," he grumbled. "Take your time. Take your time."

All this, he suddenly thought, must be stylish in the way of a town. Stylish! He looked down at himself. He wasn't stylish. His greatcoat was bespattered with mud. It did not fit his peculiar figure very well. Almost audibly he grumbled. "It's a bit small round about. Plenty long up and down. A bit small round about—"

That moment his head hit the piano bench in front of him: he had been asleep again. And at the same time a noise as of an earthquake and of tumbling down houses assailed his ear. He sat up and looked about, dazed and astonished.

Behind him stood the woman, enormous and lowering, filling the door space that had been hidden by the portiere. The noise had been made by the opening of the sliding door.

"You go into the hall," the woman's girlish voice said. "I'll turn the lamp out."

Dave rose to his feet and went out into the hall. There he opened the outside door. "All right," he said. And the house seemed to sink into a pit of darkness. He went through the mud to the gate, and hence to his horses.

They stood on three legs, their heads hanging down.

He felt his way to the buggy, and finding that the wheels on the right side almost touched, he went to the back and lifted it, throwing it over to the left.

Meanwhile the woman had locked and barricaded her door and hidden the key in the voluminous folds of her wrappings. Gingerly she picked her way through the dark to the side of the buggy.

"Why can you never bring a wagon?" she nagged.

"Too heavy, mother. In the mud. With you aboard."

"How am I going to get into this?"

"You've done it before," said Dave. "That buggy should know you. Just wait. Wait a minute. Wait. I've taken you to Kruger's ere this. I know how. I've taken you to Kruger's ten times. I'll hoist you up."

And, having picked the robes off the horses' backs and dropped them into the box, and having untied the halter-shanks from the fence-post, he climbed over the wheels on his own side into the buggy.

"Will the horses stand?" the girlish voice asked in alarm.

"They'll stand," said Dave. "They'll stand till doomsday. They stood when they were colts, the first time I got you. They know you." He put his right knee on the seat, braced his left foot in front, and reached forward with his hands for her arms. "Put your foot on the step," he directed.

"Won't it break?"

"It won't break. I specially reinforced it for you years ago."

But when she put her foot on it, the buggy tilted, the springs on her side going flat.

"Now," Dave shouted. "Now for a good pull, a king pull, a strong pull: up, up, you come."

And he pulled, and she pulled, and up she came.

Unseen in the dark, the horses laid their ears back on their heads and listened.

A few minutes later the woman sat in the seat, puffing and breathless from the exertion. Dave spread the robe about her and squeezed into the scanty space left on the seat. The woman was soft and almost overflowed him. Her left arm, thick as a man's thigh, was in front of his chest.

"Ted, Beaut," he called to his horses and tugged at the lines.

The horses almost sat down in the mud as they backed on to the road. Then they pulled: and the buggy, squeaking and groaning under its load, went west.

Back to Main St. it went: and then south: and finally west again on the long ten mile stretch. They passed the hotel where the dim light of one electric bulb was still reflected from the polished skull of the night clerk sleeping in his chair, and they crossed the track and filed between the cottonwoods that stood sentinel over the cottages in their little yards. And at last they were engulfed again in the mud of the open road between the drowned fields. It was mild, spring, warm: and Dave began to sweat.

"Eleven," the woman suddenly said, half asleep.

"What's that?" Dave asked startled.

"Eleven times you've taken me out to Kruger's. You're a good faithful soul."

"I sure am," Dave said between a yawn and a chuckle. "Good and faithful I should say. . . ."

But the woman by his side, or rather in front of him, did not hear. Her head had fallen forward: she was asleep.

The horses, knowing they were going home, stepped out a little more briskly than before: the buggy squeaked, groaned and jolted along.

Soon the heat of the body that half enveloped him made Dave drowsy again. At first he fought against sleep: he yawned and yawned, drawing in the night air which seemed to refresh his lungs. But slowly, slowly sleep conquered. There was no sound except the sucking and smacking of the mud under the horses' steps, and the grinding of the wheels when they hit a stone embedded in the mud, and the squeaking of the springs on his, Dave's side: for on the other, they lay flat on the reaches of the buggy.

And Dave, too, slept, again. An hour went by, two hours.

There was the station, benighted, with Doyle on his cot in the office, and a few red and green lights high in the air, seen by the horses, unseen by Dave. Here was the turn.

Now, in summer, when Dave went to town, and in the fall, when he hauled his wheat, he did not follow the grade as he had done today in going out. He crossed a culvert farther on, went through a farmyard and over the open prairie across a trail he himself had worn into the sod. That way he angled, hitting two other culverts, a mile west, where they bridged the two huge master ditches. In winter, too, he shortened his road that way: there snow lay all along instead of in patches only as on the wind-swept grade. The only time, in fact, when he could not use the trail was the thaw-up: for the wind shifted the ditches, and these ditches were ten, twelve feet deep and twenty feet wide, and filled with water, of course.

But the horses, unguided by any hand, went past the turn and through the farmyard and over the prairie which was covered with water ten or twelve inches deep. The sod underneath had still some "back-bone." The frost was still in it, covered as it was by the mulch of last year's grass. It was not like the grade, almost bottomless mud: the pulling was easy. Dave and the enormous woman slept and snored, and the horses' ears kept twitching and turning at every note.

But there came a time when the horses stopped. With infallible homing instinct they had held to the trail under the water. They had come to the first of the ditches: there was no culvert.

Dave awoke and tried to stretch and yawn. Dawgonne it. Where was he? Oh yes! Oh no! Yes, sure. He clicked his tongue. What were the horses stopping for? Where were they? He looked about, as much as he could. At last he forced his whole body around. He saw nothing, nothing. . . .

Again he clicked his tongue: the horses merely fidgeted on their feet. Where were they? Where in Sam Blazes were they? He had been dozing. One of his legs had gone to sleep. He rubbed it with his left hand and pressed it against the floor of the box. It hurt. He grew angry. What was the matter with them that they wouldn't go? Eh, yea! It was a bother all right! Traipsing through the country at night, in the thaw-up during the flood, for other people. He pushed his elbow into the soft side of the woman.

"Hi!" he shouted. "You'll have to wake up and let me get out."

A sleep-drowned yawn. A ripple through the mountain of flesh. "Eh?"

"We've lost the road. I must get my hip boots."

A wave of motion through the mountain of flesh released the pressure on him. "Lost the road?"

Dave reached into the back of the box, found the hip boots, and threw them forward. Then he lifted himself out of the seat. It took several minutes before he had divested himself of his greatcoat and pulled the big boots on over his legs. Then he climbed gingerly out over the wheels into the water. It struck him that the wheels were clean: that the bottom was firm.

"Gosh!" he said. "We're on the prairie."

Splashing through the water he went to the horses' heads and felt with his foot for the edge of the ditch. He found it. There was no culvert. "Yea," he said to himself, "that's what you get for it."

But he patted the horses' noses before he went east, along the course. The wind had been west. The water was ice-cold: it chilled his feet through boots, shoes and stockings.

He found the culvert, a couple of rods out of place. It was afloat. But when he stepped on it, it sank till it touched bottom, bridging the ditch.

He returned to the horses and backed them away from the edge taking hold of their bridles. The snoring of the woman beat time. Then, still leading the horses, he made for the culvert.

They snorted and raised their heads as, under his step, the planks sank away to the bottom. But he held them and coaxed them to follow him: and slowly, nervously, in jerks and starts, they crossed the ditch. Dave led them till, with his groping feet, he had found the trail under the water: he was wet all through, for the horses had splashed in rearing and jumping forward.

Then he climbed back into the buggy, squatting down in front, without taking his hip-boots off, or putting his greatcoat on again: and also without waking the woman. "Well," he said slowly, clicking his tongue, speaking to the horses, "it's up to you babies. You've got us into this: you've got to get us out."

And the horses went, stepping briskly: they knew the road: they were going home: and the water splashed. Though he held the lines, Dave was careful not to exert any pull.

The minutes went by: and the quarter hours. Black night was all about.

Then the second ditch came, the last to be crossed. The horses stopped.

Again Dave got out, went to the horses' heads, and felt for the culvert. Like the first, it was gone. The horses had held to the trail. Again Dave went east till he had found the culvert: and again he made sure that it took hold of the ground as it sank.

Again he backed the horses away from the edge of the ditch and led them forward to the floating bridge. Again they reared and plunged as the culvert moved underfoot. Slowly he stepped back, holding them in an iron grip by their bridles. He was in the centre.

Then something went wrong. Something slipped underfoot. The horses plunged. No holding them this time. He jumped back. They came to with a crash. He held them.

From behind, out of the buggy came a yell. "What's happened? I'm drowning!"

"No, no," said Dave. "Just hold on. You couldn't yell if you were drowning."

"I'm right in the water. It's up to my hips." The voice was shrill with fright.

"Just hold on," Dave repeated. "I'll see in a minute." He stroked the horses' noses till they quieted down. They stood, their legs braced backward holding the buggy. He let go of their bridles and watched: they stood. He went back on their right and felt for the front wheel: it stood square against the almost perpendicular wall of the ditch, cutting into the mud there. No pull of the horses could lift it over the edge. He bent forward, reaching into the box.

"Yes," said the woman, "that's me. I'm right in the water. Can't you get me out?"

"Wait, wait," said Dave. "Sure I'll get you out."

He went to the other side and found that the culvert was slanting up at an angle of thirty degrees. The back of the box was entirely in water. He straightened and felt for the rump of the off-horse. Its muscles were taut.

"Whoa," he said softly. And carefully he climbed up on the wheel, and the edge of the box.

He felt for the woman. She had been jerked forward with the cushions and was wedged in between dashboard and seat. Her hands were holding for dear life to arm and back rest.

"Now," Dave said, "we've got to get you back on the seat and on this side here, so's to take the weight off the other wheel. I'll count. At three you pull for all you're worth."

"Dear me!" groaned the woman. "What next?"

He put his arm about her and took a firm hold. "One, two, three!"

They both heaved. Dave was as strong as a mule and twice as stubborn. Up she came slowly but surely. He jumped back into the water, which splashed up high.

He returned to the other side and felt for the rump of the horse: its muscles were taut. So he groped for the lines, found them, took them slack, and bent forward to take hold of the wheel. He braced himself for the lift: and when he was ready, he gave a powerful heave, shouting to the horses and the woman at the same time.

"Get up there, you brutes! Hold on now, Betsy! Hold on for dear life!"

And, as the horses plunged forward and he lifted the wheel, the buggy went over the edge of the ditch with a violent lurch. The lines, tightening, nearly jerked Dave off his feet: but he held on and began stepping out. Then he stopped the horses and climbed back into the buggy, squatting down in front.

"Well," sighed the woman. "It's a dog's life. I'll say that much."

"What's the matter with it? A dog's life isn't a bad life by any means. We're both up and doing. While there's life, there's hope; and while hope lasts, it isn't all wrong."

"Yes," said the woman and bent forward, feeling his back, "you're a good faithful soul, Dave. You're wet all through, like myself. But you don't complain."

"What's there to complain about? We're nearly there. If we'd have drowned there in the ditch, we could not complain. As long as you can, you haven't any reason."

"That's true," said the woman. "True as gospel, Dave. You're a brick. We two should have hitched up together when we were young. I'd have made you a wife!"

"Maybe you would," Dave said callously. "I don't say no. But you're too big. Too big all round. And up and down, too. Up and down and round about."

They drove in silence over the last mile to Kruger's.

The east was streaked with grey when they pulled up in the yard.

Kruger was there, a big hulking figure. In hip-boots and mackinaw, carrying a lantern. He brought a saw-buck and a plank, for the woman to alight on in going to the house.

"Was it a hard trip?" he asked, as the two of them supported the enormous woman on her way over the plank to the stone slabs in front of the door.

"Naw," Dave said. "It was all right. Well, I'll get and hit the hay."

When, in his own yard, he had unhitched and stabled and fed his horses, he went to his house and pulled his hip-boots off in the shed.

Then, in the kitchen, he lighted a lamp and rummaged about in the kitchen cabinet for some biscuits.

His wife awoke. "I hope," she called, "you took your muddy shoes off before you went into the kitchen. My floors are freshly washed."

"Sure, sure," Dave said and looked at his shoes as he stood, leaning against the rail. "My sweater's freshly washed too: and my coat: and my pants: and my shirt, too, for that matter. The whole fellow's freshly washed if you want to know. . . ."

—1971

JOHN McCRAE

(1872-1918)

Born in Guelph, Ontario, John McCrae studied medicine at the University of Toronto and later had a distinguished career as a physician in Montreal. He served in the South African War as an artillery subaltern but in 1914 enlisted as a medical officer with the first Canadian contingent. He died in France of pneumonia in January 1918. "In Flanders Fields" was first published in Punch *in 1915, and became probably the most famous poem in English written during the First World War. His collected verses were published posthumously.*

IN FLANDERS FIELDS

In Flanders fields the poppies blow
Between the crosses, row on row,
   That mark our place; and in the sky
   The larks, still bravely singing, fly
Scarce heard amid the guns below.

We are the Dead. Short days ago
We lived, felt dawn, saw sunset glow,
   Loved and were loved, and now we lie
     In Flanders fields.

Take up our quarrel with the foe:
To you from failing hands we throw
   The torch; be yours to hold it high.
   If ye break faith with us who die
We shall not sleep, though poppies grow
     In Flanders fields.

—1919

ROBERT W. SERVICE

(1874-1958)

Robert William Service was born in Lancashire and spent his youth in Glasgow. His father was a Scottish bank teller and his mother the daughter of an English owner of cotton mills. Wanderlust carried Robert across the Atlantic and over the continent: in 1895 to a backwoods ranch in British Columbia, and after that to a roving life up and down the Pacific Coast. He reached the Yukon as a bank clerk and lived in Whitehorse or Dawson from 1904 until 1912. There he saw the latter days of the great Gold Rush of 1898, and his rhymes of the Yukon brought him fame and fortune after the publication in Toronto of Songs of a Sourdough *(1907).*

When he adopted writing as a lifetime career, he had further success with Ballads of a Cheechako *(1909) and* Rhymes of a Rolling Stone *(1912).* Rhymes of a Red-Cross Man *(1916) was one of the most popular books of the First World War. By this time Service had chosen to live in France, although he remained a British subject. After his marriage to a French girl in 1913, he had homes in Paris, Brittany, and on the Riviera. His love of the exotic lured him to study life in Paris's Latin Quarter and to travel to the Balkans, Hollywood, Tahiti, and Russia. His melodramatic novels were unsuccessful, but there was always a public for many books of "roughneck" verse written by this gentleman of leisure who kept out of the limelight and was not at all the rough person his readers supposed. During the Second World War he and his family lived quietly in Hollywood. He died in Brittany in 1958. The two volumes of his collected verse contain more than 1700 pages; thousands of his books are still sold every year.*

THE CREMATION OF SAM McGEE

> *There are strange things done in the midnight sun*
> *By the men who moil for gold;*
> *The Arctic trails have their secret tales*
> *That would make your blood run cold;*
> *The Northern Lights have seen queer sights;*
> *But the queerest they ever did see*
> *Was that night on the marge of Lake Lebarge*
> *I cremated Sam McGee.*

Now Sam McGee was from Tennessee, where the cotton blooms and blows.
Why he left his home in the South to roam round the Pole God only knows.
He was always cold, but the land of gold seemed to hold him like a spell;
Though he'd often say in his homely way that he'd "sooner live in hell."

On a Christmas Day we were mushing our way over the Dawson trail.
Talk of your cold! through the parka's fold it stabbed like a driven nail.

If our eyes we'd close, then the lashes froze, till sometimes we couldn't see;
It wasn't much fun, but the only one to whimper was Sam McGee.

And that very night as we lay packed tight in our robes beneath the snow,
And the dogs were fed, and the stars o'erhead were dancing heel and toe,
He turned to me, and, "Cap," says he, "I'll cash in this trip, I guess;
And if I do, I'm asking that you won't refuse my last request."

Well, he seemed so low that I couldn't say no; then he says with a sort of moan;
"It's the cursèd cold, and it's got right hold till I'm chilled clean through to the bone.
Yet 'taint being dead, it's my awful dread of the icy grave that pains;
So I want you to swear that, foul or fair, you'll cremate my last remains."

A pal's last need is a thing to heed, so I swore I would not fail;
And we started on at the streak of dawn, but God! he looked ghastly pale.
He crouched on the sleigh, and he raved all day of his home in Tennessee;
And before nightfall a corpse was all that was left of Sam McGee.

There wasn't a breath in that land of death, and I hurried, horror driven,
With a corpse half-hid that I couldn't get rid because of a promise given;
It was lashed to the sleigh, and it seemed to say: "You may tax your brawn and brains,
But you promised true, and it's up to you to cremate those last remains."

Now a promise made is a debt unpaid, and the trail has its own stern code.
In the days to come, though my lips were dumb, in my heart how I cursed that load.
In the long, long night, by the lone firelight, while the huskies, round in a ring,
Howled out their woes to the homeless snows — O God! how I loathed the thing.

And every day that quiet clay seemed to heavy and heavier grow;
And on I went, though the dogs were spent and the grub was getting low;
The trail was bad, and I felt half mad, but I swore I would not give in;
And I'd often sing to the hateful thing, and it hearkened with a grin.

Till I came to the marge of Lake Lebarge, and a derelict there lay;
It was jammed in the ice, but I saw in a trice it was called the "Alice May."
And I looked at it, and I thought a bit, and I looked at my frozen chum:
Then, "Here," said I, with a sudden cry, "is my cre-ma-tor-eum!"

Some planks I tore from the cabin floor, and I lit the boiler fire;
Some coal I found that was lying around, and I heaped the fuel higher;
The flames just soared, and the furnace roared — such a blaze you seldom see;
And I burrowed a hole in the glowing coal, and I stuffed in Sam McGee.

Then I made a hike, for I didn't like to hear him sizzle so;
And the heavens scowled, and the huskies howled, and the wind began to blow.
It was icy cold, but the hot sweat rolled down my cheeks, and I don't know why;
And the greasy smoke in an inky cloak went streaking down the sky.

I do not know how long in the snow I wrestled with grisly fear;
But the stars came out and they danced about ere again I ventured near;
I was sick with dread, but I bravely said: "I'll just take a peep inside.
I guess he's cooked, and it's time I looked," --- then the door I opened wide —

And there sat Sam, looking cool and calm, in the heart of the furnace roar;
And he wore a smile you could see a mile, and he said: "Please close that door.
It's fine in here, but I greatly fear you'll let in the cold and storm —
Since I left Plumtree, down in Tennessee, it's the first time I've been warm."

> *There are strange things done in the midnight sun*
> *By the men who moil for gold;*
> *The Arctic trails have their secret tales*
> *That would make your blood run cold;*
> *The Northern Lights have seen queer sights,*
> *But the queerest they ever did see*
> *Was that night on the marge of Lake Lebarge*
> *I cremated Sam McGee.*

—1907

THE SHOOTING OF DAN McGREW

A bunch of the boys were whooping it up in the Malamute saloon;
The kid that handles the music-box was hitting a jag-time tune;
Back of the bar, in a solo game, sat Dangerous Dan McGrew,
And watching his luck was his light-o'-love, the lady that's known as Lou.

When out of the night, which was fifty below, and into the din and the glare,
There stumbled a miner fresh from the creeks, dog-dirty, and loaded for bear.
He looked like a man with a foot in the grave, and scarcely the strength of a louse,
Yet he tilted a poke of dust on the bar, and he called for drinks for the house.
There was none could place the stranger's face, though we searched ourselves for a clue;
But we drank his health, and the last to drink was Dangerous Dan McGrew.

There's men that somehow just grip your eyes, and hold them hard like a spell;
And such was he, and he looked to me like a man who had lived in hell;
With a face most hair, and the dreary stare of a dog whose day is done,
As he watered the green stuff in his glass, and the drops fell one by one.
Then I got to figgering who he was, and wondering what he'd do,
And I turned my head — and there watching him was the lady that's known as Lou.

His eyes went rubbering round the room, and he seemed in a kind of daze,
Till at last that old piano fell in the way of his wandering gaze.
The rag-time kid was having a drink; there was no one else on the stool,
So the stranger stumbles across the room, and flops down there like a fool.
In a buckskin shirt that was glazed with dirt he sat, and I saw him sway;
Then he clutched the keys with his talon hands — my God! but that man could play!

Were you ever out in the Great Alone, when the moon was awful clear,
And the icy mountains hemmed you in with a silence you most could *hear;*
With only the howl of a timber wolf, and you camped there in the cold,
A half-dead thing in a stark, dead world, clean mad for the muck called gold;
While high overhead, green, yellow, and red, the North Lights swept in bars? —
Then you've a haunch what the music meant --- hunger and night and the stars.

And hunger not of the belly kind, that's banished with bacon and beans;
But the gnawing hunger of lonely men for a home and all that it means;
For a fireside far from the cares that are, four walls and a roof above;
But oh! so cramful of cosy joy, and crowned with a woman's love;
A woman dearer than all the world, and true as Heaven is true —
(God! how ghastly she looks through her rouge — the lady that's known as Lou.)

Then on a sudden the music changed, so soft that you scarce could hear;
But you felt that your life had been looted clean of all that it once held dear;
That someone had stolen the woman you loved; that her love was a devil's lie;
That your guts were gone, and the best for you was to crawl away and die.
'Twas the crowning cry of a heart's despair, and it thrilled you through and through —
"I guess I'll make it a spread misere," said Dangerous Dan McGrew.
The music almost died away --- then it burst like a pent-up flood;
And it seemed to say, "Repay, repay," and my eyes were blind with blood.
The thought came back of an ancient wrong, and it stung like a frozen lash,
And the lust awoke to kill, to kill --- then the music stopped with a crash.

And the stranger turned, and his eyes they burned in a most peculiar way;
In a buckskin shirt that was glazed with dirt he sat, and I saw him sway;
Then his lips went in in a kind of grin, and he spoke, and his voice was calm;
And, "Boys," says he, "you don't know me, and none of you care a damn;
But I want to state, and my words are straight, and I'll bet my poke they're true,
That one of you is a hound of hell --- and that one is Dan McGrew."

Then I ducked my head, and the lights went out, and two guns blazed in the dark;
And a woman screamed, and the lights went up, and two men lay stiff and stark;
Pitched on his head, and pumped full of lead, was Dangerous Dan McGrew,
While the man from the creeks lay clutched to the breast of the lady that's known as Lou.

These are the simple facts of the case, and I guess I ought to know;
They say that the stranger was crazed with "hooch," and I'm not denying it's so.
I'm not so wise as the lawyer guys, but strictly between us two —
The woman that kissed him and — pinched his poke — was the lady that's known as Lou.
—1907

THE SPELL OF THE YUKON

I wanted the gold, and I sought it;
  I scrabbled and mucked like a slave.
Was it famine or scurvy—I fought it;
  I hurled my youth into a grave.
I wanted the gold and I got it—
  Came out with a fortune last fall,—
Yet somehow life's not what I thought it,
  And somehow the gold isn't all.

No! There's the land. (Have you seen it?)
  It's the cussedest land that I know,
From the big, dizzy mountains that screen it
  To the deep, deathlike valleys below.
Some say God was tired when He made it:
  Some say it's a fine land to shun;
Maybe: but there's some as would trade it
  For no land on earth—and I'm one.

You come to get rich (damned good reason),
    You feel like an exile at first;
You hate it like hell for a season,
    And then you are worse than the worst.
It grips you like some kinds of sinning;
    It twists you from foe to a friend;
It seems it's been since the beginning;
    It seems it will be to the end.

I've stood in some mighty-mouthed hollow
    That's plumb-full of hush to the brim;
I've watched the big, husky sun wallow
    In crimson and gold, and grow dim,
Till the moon set the pearly peaks gleaming,
    And the stars tumbled out, neck and crop;
And I've thought that I surely was dreaming,
    With the peace o' the world piled on top.

The summer—no sweeter was ever;
    The sunshiny woods all athrill;
The greyling aleap in the river,
    The bighorn asleep on the hill.
The strong life that never knows harness;
    The wilds where the caribou call;
The freshness, the freedom, the farness—
    O God! how I'm stuck on it all.

The winter! the brightness that blinds you,
    The white land locked tight as a drum,
The cold fear that follows and finds you,
    The silence that bludgeons you dumb.
The snows that are older than history,
    The woods where the weird shadows slant;
The stillness, the moonlight, the mystery,
    I've bade 'em good-bye—but I can't.

There's a land where the mountains are nameless,
    And the rivers all run God knows where;
There are lives that are erring and aimless,
    And deaths that just hang by a hair;
There are hardships that nobody reckons;
    There are valleys unpeopled and still;
There's a land—oh, it beckons and beckons,
    And I want to go back—and I will.

They're making my money diminish;
    I'm sick of the taste of champagne.
Thank God! when I'm skinned to a finish
    I'll pike to the Yukon again.
I'll fight—and you bet it's no sham-fight;
    It's hell!—but I've been there before;
And it's better than this by a damsite—
    So me for the Yukon once more.

There's gold, and it's haunting and haunting;
    It's luring me on as of old;
Yet it isn't the gold that I'm wanting,
    So much as just finding the gold.
It's the great, big, broad land 'way up yonder,
    It's the forests where silence has lease;
It's the beauty that thrills me with wonder,
    It's the stillness that fills me with peace.   —1907

THE LAND GOD FORGOT*

The lonely sunsets flare forlorn
    Down valleys dreadly desolate;
The lordly mountains soar in scorn,
    As still as death, as stern as fate.

The lonely sunsets flame and die;
    The giant valleys gulp the night;
The monster mountains scrape the sky,
    Where eager stars are diamond-bright.

So gaunt against the gibbous moon,
    Piercing the silence velvet-piled,
A lone wolf howls his ancient rune,
    The fell arch-spirit of the Wild.

O outcast land! O leper land!
    Let the lone wolf-cry all express—
The hate insensate of thy hand,
    Thy heart's abysmal loneliness.   —1907

*[In the Canadian edition of Songs of a Sourdough (Toronto, Briggs, 1907) this prefatory poem
was untitled. The American imprint appeared as The Spell of the Yukon and Other Verses
(New York, Barse, 1907); in it this title was attached to the poem.]

MARJORIE PICKTHALL

(1883-1922)

Born near Chiswick, in Middlesex, England, Marjorie Lowry Christie Pickthall came with her parents to Toronto when she was six years old. She was educated in private schools in that city. At the age of fifteen she sold her first story to the Toronto Globe *and shortly thereafter won prizes in a competition conducted by the* Mail and Empire. *Soon she became a regular contributor to newspapers and magazines while she made a world of fancy for herself, full of beautiful scenes, twilight melodies, Indian legends, Biblical stories, and Celtic lore.* The Drift of Pinions, *her first book of poems, appeared in 1913. Thereafter she lived in England for a number of years, continuing her work in poetry and prose while she tried, in spite of ill health, to do useful war work as an ambulance driver, gardener, and assistant librarian in a meteorological office. She returned to Canada in May 1920, and made her home in British Columbia until her death two years later. Besides poems, she published two novels, a book of short stories, and a poetic tragedy.*

THE POOL

Come with me, follow me, swift as a moth,
Ere the wood-doves waken.
Lift the long leaves and look down, look down
Where the light is shaken,
Amber and brown,
On the woven ivory roots of the reed,
On a floating flower and a weft of weed
And a feather of froth.

Here in the night all wonders are,
Lapped in the lift of the ripple's swing, —
A silver shell and a shaken star,
And a white moth's wing.
Here the young moon when the mists unclose
Swims like the bud of a golden rose.

I would live like an elf where the wild grapes cling,
I would chase the thrush
From the red rose-berries.
All the day long I would laugh and swing
With the black choke-cherries.

I would shake the bees from the milkweed blooms,
And cool, O cool,
Night after night I would leap in the pool,
And sleep with the fish in the roots of the rush.
Clear, O clear my dreams should be made
Of emerald light and amber shade,
Of silver shallows and golden glooms.
Sweet, O sweet my dreams should be
As the dark, sweet water enfolding me
Safe as a blind shell under the sea.

—1913

PERE LALEMENT

I lift the Lord on high,
Under the murmuring hemlock boughs, and see
The small birds of the forest lingering by
And making melody.
These are mine acolytes and these my choir,
And this mine altar in the cool green shade,
Where the wild soft-eyed does draw nigh
Wondering, as in the byre
Of Bethlehem the oxen heard Thy cry
And saw Thee, unafraid.

My boatmen sit apart,
Wolf-eyed, wolf-sinewed, stiller than the trees.
Help me, O Lord, for very slow of heart
And hard of faith are these.
Cruel are they, yet Thy children. Foul are they,
Yet wert Thou born to save them utterly.
Then make me as I pray
Just to their hates, kind to their sorrows, wise
After their speech, and strong before their free
Indomitable eyes.

Do the French lilies reign
Over Mont Royal and Stadacona still?
Up the St. Lawrence comes the spring again,
Crowning each southward hill
And blossoming pool with beauty, while I roam
Far from the perilous folds that are my home,

There where we built St. Ignace for our needs,
Shaped the rough roof tree, turned the first
    sweet sod,
St. Ignace and St. Louis, little beads
On the rosary of God.

Pines shall Thy pillars be,
Fairer than those Sidonian cedars brought
By Hiram out of Tyre, and each birch-tree
Shines like a holy thought.
But come no worshippers; shall I confess,
St. Francis-like, the birds of the wilderness?
O, with Thy love my lonely head uphold.
A wandering shepherd I, who hath no sheep;
A wandering soul, who hath no scrip, nor gold,
Nor anywhere to sleep.

My hour of rest is done;
On the smooth ripple lifts the long canoe;
The hemlocks murmur sadly as the sun
Slants his dim arrows through.
Whither I go I know not, nor the way,
Dark with strange passions, vexed with
    heathen charms,
Holding I know not what of life or death;
Only be Thou beside me day by day,
Thy rod my guide and comfort, underneath
Thy everlasting arms.

—1913

E. J. PRATT

(1883-1964)

Edwin John Pratt was born on February 4, 1883, at Western Bay, a Newfoundland village on Conception Bay, twenty-five miles from Harbour Grace. He grew up in the coastal settlements and was trained to follow his father in the Methodist ministry. At the denominational college in St. John's he qualified for the London Matriculation, and in his early twenties he preached and taught at Moreton's Harbour, Clarke's Beach, Bell Island, and Portugal Cove, the scenes for the poems later published in Newfoundland Verse. *In 1907 he came to Toronto and enrolled in Victoria, the college with which he was to be identified until his retirement from the Department of English in 1953. He earned various degrees — his B.A. in 1911, his B.D. in 1913, and his Ph.D in 1917 — specializing at first in theology, but turning soon to psychology and literature. In 1919 he joined Professor Pelham Edgar's department as an Associate Professor of English. He influenced the reading habits of generations of Victoria students, and he became an independent force in modern Canadian poetry, honored as a man and as a writer. He won the Governor-General's Award for Poetry in 1937, 1940, and 1952; the Lorne Pierce Gold Medal of the Royal Society of Canada in 1940; royal recognition as a Companion of the Order of St. Michael and St. George in 1946; and honorary degrees from many universities.*

Pratt was forty years old when he published his first book of poetry. Newfoundland Verse *(1923) contains his early ballads and lyrics of the sea and of the rugged life along the coast of England's oldest colony, now Canada's newest province. His second book,* The Witches' Brew *(1925), reveals his gift of humor and his allegorical method. On the surface a fantasy about a drunken spree enjoyed by fish and denied to thirsty warm-blooded creatures,* The Witches' Brew *is also a Hudibrastic satire on the era of the prohibition of liquor in the various Canadian provinces. Other volumes followed in rapid succession — epics of great marine animals, long allegorical, elegiac, and narrative peoms, as well as collections of shorter pieces.* The Titanic *(1935), an epic conceived in terms of a five-act tragedy, treats ironically of man's too great reliance upon mechanisms.*

After the middle nineteen-thirties Pratt's poetry displayed a richer awareness of human society. Brébeuf and his Brethren *(1940) recounts the story of the last days of the Jesuit martyrs at Fort Ste. Marie, and is a revelation of the deep roots of Canadian history, where French and English differences disappear in common admiration of sacrifice and courage.* Dunkirk *(1941),* They are Returning *(1946), and* Behind the Log *(1947) demonstrate this historical principle in contemporary terms, treating of exploits showing the characteristic blend of nature, men, and ships.* Towards the Last Spike *(1952) describes the building of the transcontinental Canadian Pacific Railway and suggests that men and machines have only begun to co-operate with nature in the making of a great nation. The second edition of Pratt's* Collected Poems *(1958) contains a valuable Introduction by Northrop Frye.*

Pratt died 26 April, 1964, in Toronto.

THE SHARK

He seemed to know the harbor,
So leisurely he swam;
His fin,
Like a piece of sheet-iron,
Three-cornered,
And with knife-edge,
Stirred not a bubble
As it moved
With its base-line on the water.

His body was tubular
And tapered
And smoke-blue,
And as he passed the wharf
He turned,
And snapped at a flat-fish

That was dead and floating.
And I saw the flash of a white throat,
And a double row of white teeth,
And eyes of metallic gray,
Hard and narrow and slit.

Then out of the harbor,
With that three-cornered fin
Shearing without a bubble the water
Lithely,
Leisurely,
He swam —
That strange fish,
Tubular, tapered, smoke-blue,
Part vulture, part wolf,
Part neither — for his blood was cold.

—1923

THE GROUND SWELL

Three times we heard it calling with a low,
Insistent note; at ebb-tide on the noon;
And at the hour of dusk, when the red moon
Was rising and the tide was on the flow;
Then, at the hour of midnight once again,
Though we had entered in and shut the door
And drawn the blinds, it crept up from the shore
And smote upon a bedroom window-pane;
Then passed away as some dull pang that grew
Out of the void before Eternity
Had fashioned out an edge for human grief;
Before the winds of God had learned to strew
His harvest-sweepings on a winter sea
To feed the primal hungers of a reef.

—1923

SEA-GULLS

For one carved instant as they flew,
The language had no simile —
Silver, crystal, ivory
Were tarnished. Etched upon the horizon blue,
The frieze must go unchallenged, for the lift
And carriage of the wings would stain the drift
Of stars against a tropic indigo
Or dull the parable of snow.

Now settling one by one
Within green hollows or where curled
Crests caught the spectrum from the sun,
A thousand wings are furled.
No clay-born lilies of the world
Could blow as free
As those wild orchids of the sea.

—1932

EROSION

It took the sea a thousand years,
A thousand years to trace
The granite features of this cliff,
In crag and scarp and base.

It took the sea an hour one night,
An hour of storm to place
The sculpture of these granite seams
Upon a woman's face.

—1932

FROM STONE TO STEEL

From stone to bronze, from bronze to steel
Along the road-dust of the sun,
Two revolutions of the wheel
From Java to Geneva run.

The snarl Neanderthal is worn
Close to the smiling Aryan lips,
The civil polish of the horn
Gleams from our praying finger tips.

The evolution of desire
Has but matured a toxic wine,
Drunk long before its heady fire
Reddened Euphrates or the Rhine.

Between the temple and the cave
The boundary lies tissue-thin:
The yearlings still the altars crave
As satisfaction for a sin.

The road goes up, the road goes down —
Let Java or Geneva be —
But whether to the cross or crown,
The path lies through Gethsemane.

—1932

THE MAN AND THE MACHINE

By right of fires that smelted ore
Which he had tended years before,
The man whose hands were on the wheel
Could trace his kinship through her steel,
Between his body warped and bent
In every bone and ligament,
And this "eight-cylinder" stream-lined,
The finest model yet designed.

He felt his lesioned pulses strum
Against the rhythm of her hum,
And found his nerves and sinews knot
With sharper spasm as she climbed
The steeper grades, so neatly timed
From storage tank to piston shot —
This creature with the cougar grace,
This man with slag upon his face.

—1932

THE 6000

For creatures of this modern breed,
Reared from the element of flame,
Designed to match a storm for speed,
Ionia would have found a name,
Like Mercury or Bucephalus —
Some picturesque immortal label
That lifts a story into fable,
Out of the myths of Uranus;
Then changed its root to demonize
The nature of its strength and size
With fictions out of Tartarus.

Those giants of Vulcan, leather-skinned,
Whose frightful stare monocular
Made mad the coursers of the wind,
And chased the light of the morning star
Away from the Sicilian shore,
Would have been terror-blind before
This forehead which, had it been known
In Greek or Scandinavian lore,
Had turned the hierarchs to stone,
Had battered down the Martian walls,
Reduced to dust Jove's arsenals,
Or rammed the battlements of Thor.

His body black as Erebus
Accorded with the hue of night;
His central eye self-luminous
Threw out a cone of noon-day light,
Which split the gloom and then flashed back
The diamond levels of the track.
No ancient poet ever saw
Just such a monster as could draw
The Olympian tonnage of a load
Like this along an iron road;

Or ever thought that such a birth —
The issue of an inventor's dream —
With breath of fire and blood of steam,
Could find delivery on this earth.
In his vast belly was a pit,
Which even Homer would admit,
Or Dante, searching earth and hell,
Possessed no perfect parallel.
Evolved from no Plutonian forge,
The tender, like a slave, that followed,
Conveyed bitumen to his gorge,
Which on the instant it was swallowed
Ran black through crimson on to white.
Above the mass floated a swirl
Of crystal shapes, agate and pearl
And rose, like imps a-chase, and light
As thistledown, while the blast roared
With angry temperatures that soared
To seven hundred Fahrenheit.
Outside, the engine's dorsal plate,
Above the furnace door ajar,
Revealed the boiler's throbbing rate,
By dial fingers animate,
Like pulses at the jugular.

For every vital inch of steel,
A vibrant indicator read
Two hundred pounds plus twenty-five,
Waiting for the hour to drive
Their energy upon the wheel
In punches from the piston head.

And there another one supplied
The measure of the irrigation,
Whereby the lubricating tide,

Through linear runs and axle curves
Made perfect his articulation.
And ramifying copper wire
Made up the system of his nerves,
In keeping with his lungs of fire.

Now with his armored carapace
On head and belly, back and breast,
The Taurian prepared to face
The blurring stretches of the west.
To him it was of no concern
The evening gale was soon to turn
To the full stature of a storm
That would within an hour transform
The ranges for a thousand miles,

Close up all human thoroughfares,
Sweep down through canyons and defiles,
And drive the cougars to their lairs.

A lantern flashed out a command,
A bell was ringing as a hand
Clutched at a throttle, and the bull,
At once obedient to the pull,
Began with bellowing throat to lead
By slow accelerating speed
Six thousand tons of caravan
Out to the spaces — there to toss
The blizzard from his path across
The prairies of Saskatchewan.

—*1932*

THE HIGHWAY

What aeons passed without a count or name,
Before the cosmic seneschal,
Succeeding with a plan
Of weaving stellar patterns from a flame,
Announced at his high carnival
An orbit — with Aldebaran!

And when the drifting years had sighted land,
And hills and plains declared their birth
Amid volcanic throes,
What was the lapse before the marshal's hand
Had found a garden on the earth,
And led forth June with her first rose?

And what the gulf between that and the hour,
Late in the simian-human day,
When Nature kept her tryst
With the unfoldment of the star and flower —
When in her sacrificial way
Judaea blossomed with her Christ!

But what made *our* feet miss the road that brought
The world to such a golden trove,
In our so brief a span?
How may we grasp again the hand that wrought
Such light, such fragrance, and such love,
O star! O rose! O Son of Man?

—*1932*

218

The Titanic

HARLAND & WOLFF WORKS, BELFAST,
MAY 31, 1911

The hammers silent and the derricks still,
And high-tide in the harbor! Mind and will
In open test with time and steel had run
The first lap of a schedule and had won.
Although a shell of what was yet to be
Before another year was over, she,
Poised for the launching signal, had surpassed
The dreams of builder or of navigator.
The Primate of the Lines, she had out-classed
That rival effort to eliminate her
Beyond the North Sea where the air shots played
The laggard rhythms of their fusillade
Upon the rivets of the *Imperator*.
The wedges in, the shores removed, a girl's
Hand at a sign released a ribbon braid;
Glass crashed against the plates; a wine cascade,
Netting the sunlight in a shower of pearls,
Baptized the bow and gave the ship her name;
A slight push of the rams as a switch set free
The triggers in the slots, and her proud claim
On size — to be the first to reach the sea —
Was vindicated, for whatever fears
Stalked with her down the tallow of the slips
Were smothered under by the harbor cheers,
By flags strung to the halyards of the ships.

MARCH 31, 1912

Completed! Waiting for her trial spin —
Levers and telegraphs and valves within
Her intercostal spaces ready to start
The power pulsing through her lungs and heart.
An ocean lifeboat in herself — so ran
The architectural comment on her plan.
No wave could sweep those upper decks —
    unthinkable!
No storm could hurt that hull — the papers
    said so.
The perfect ship at last — the first unsinkable,
Proved in advance — had not the folders read so ?
Such was the steel strength of her double floors
Along the whole length of the keel, and such
The fine adjustment of the bulkhead doors

Geared to the rams, responsive to a touch,
That in collision with iceberg or rock
Or passing ship she could survive the shock,
Absorb the double impact, for despite
The bows stove in, with forward holds aleak,
Her aft compartments buoyant, watertight,
Would keep her floating steady for a week.
And this belief had reached its climax when,
Through wireless waves as yet unstaled by use,
The wonder of the ether had begun
To fold the heavens up and reinduce
That ancient *hubris* in the dreams of men,
Which would have slain the cattle of the sun,
And filched the lightnings from the fist of Zeus.
What mattered that her boats were but a third
Of full provision — caution was absurd:
Then let the ocean roll and the winds blow
While the risk at Lloyds remained a record low.

THE ICEBERG

Calved from a glacier near Godhaven coast,
It left the fiord for the sea — a host
Of white flotillas gathering in its wake,
And joined by fragments from a Behring floe,
Had circumnavigated it to make
It centre of an archipelago.
Its lateral motion on the Davis Strait
Was casual and indeterminate,
And each advance to southward was as blind
As each recession to the north. No smoke
Of steamships nor the hoist of mainsails broke
The polar wastes — no sounds except the grind
Of ice, the cry of curlews and the lore
Of winds from mesas of eternal snow;
Until caught by the western undertow,
It struck the current of the Labrador
Which swung it to its definite southern stride.
Pressure and glacial time had stratified
The berg to the consistency of flint,
And kept inviolate, through clash of tide
And gale, façade and columns with their hint
Of inward altars and of steepled bells
Ringing the passage of the parallels.
But when with months of voyaging it came

To where both streams — the Gulf and Polar —
  met,
The sun which left its crystal peaks aflame
In the sub-arctic noons, began to fret
The arches, flute the spires and deform
The features, till the batteries of storm,
Playing above the slow-eroding base,
Demolished the last temple touch of grace.
Another month, and nothing but the brute
And palaeolithic outline of a face
Fronted the transatlantic shipping route.
A sloping spur that tapered to a claw
And lying twenty feet below had made
It lurch and shamble like a plantigrade;
But with an impulse governed by the raw
Mechanics of its birth, it drifted where
Ambushed, fog-gray, it stumbled on its lair,
North forty-one degrees and forty-four,
Fifty and fourteen west the longitude,
Waiting a world-memorial hour, its rude
Corundum form stripped to its Greenland core.

SOUTHAMPTON, WEDNESDAY, APRIL 10, 1912

An omen struck the thousands on the shore —
A double accident! And as the ship
Swung down the river on her maiden trip,
Old sailors of the clipper decades, wise
To the sea's incantations, muttered fables
About careening vessels with their cables
Snapped in their harbors under peaceful skies.
Was it just suction or fatality
Which caused the *New York* at the dock to
  turn,
Her seven mooring ropes to break at the stern
And writhe like anacondas on the quay,
While tugs and fenders answered the collision
Signals with such trim margin of precision?
And was it backwash from the starboard screw
Which, tearing at the big *Teutonic*, drew
Her to the limit of her hawser strain,
And made the smaller tethered craft behave
Like frightened harbor ducks? And no one knew
For many days the reason to explain
The rise and wash of one inordinate wave,
When a sunken barge on the Southampton bed
Was dragged through mire eight hundred
  yards ahead,

As the *Titanic* passed above its grave.
But many of those sailors wise and old,
Who pondered on this weird mesmeric power,
Gathered together, lit their pipes and told
Of portents hidden in the natal hour,
Told of the launching of some square-rigged
  ships,
When water flowed from the inverted tips
Of a waning moon, of sun-hounds, of the shrieks
Of whirling shags around the mizzen peaks.
And was there not this morning's augury
For the big one now heading for the sea?
So long after she passed from landsmen's sight,
They watched her with their Mother Carey eyes
Through Spithead smoke, through mists of
  Isle of Wight,
Through clouds of sea-gulls following with
  their cries.

WEDNESDAY EVENING

Electric elements were glowing down
In the long galley passages where scores
Of white-capped cooks stood at the oven doors
To feed the population of a town.
Cauldrons of stock, purées and consommés,
Simmered with peppercorns and marjoram.
The sea-shore smells from bisque and crab
  and clam
Blended with odors from the fricassées.
Refrigerators, hung with a week's toll
Of the stockyards, delivered sides of lamb
And veal, beef quarters to be roasted whole.
Hundreds of capons and halibut. A shoal
Of Blue-Points waited to be served on shell.
The boards were loaded with pimolas, pails
Of lobster coral, jars of Béchamel,
To garnish tiers of rows of chilled timbales
And aspics. On the shelves were pyramids
Of truffles, sprigs of thyme and water-cress,
Bay leaf and parsley, savories to dress
Shad roes and sweetbreads broiling on the grids.
And then in diamond, square, crescent and star,
Hors d'oeuvres were fashioned from the
  toasted bread,
With paste of anchovy and caviare,
Paprika sprinkled and pimento spread,
All ready, for the hour was seven!

Meanwhile,
Rivalling the engines with their steady tread,
Thousands of feet were taking overhead
The fourth lap round the deck to make the mile.
Squash racquet, shuffle board and quoits; the cool
Tang of the plunge in the gymnasium pool,
The rub, the crisp air of the April night,
The salt of the breeze made by the liner's rate,
Worked with an even keel to stimulate
Saliva for an ocean appetite:
And like storm troops before a citadel,
At the first summons of a bugle, soon
The army massed the stairs towards the saloon,
And though twelve courses on the cards
    might well
Measure themselves against Falstaffian juices,
But few were found presenting their excuses,
When stewards offered on the lacquered trays
The Savoy chasers and the canapés.

The dinner gave the sense that all was well:
That touch of ballast in the tanks; the feel
Of peace from ramparts unassailable,
Which, added to her seven decks of steel,
Had constituted the *Titanic* less
A ship than a Gibraltar under heel.
And night had placed a lazy lusciousness
Upon a surfeit of security.
Science responded to a button press.
The three electric lifts that ran through tiers
Of decks, the reading lamps, the brilliancy
Of mirrors from the tungsten chandeliers,
Had driven out all phantoms which the mind
Had loosed from ocean closets, and assigned
To the dry earth the custody of fears.
The crowds poured through the sumptuous
    rooms and halls,
And tapped the tables of the Regency;
Smirked at the caryatids on the walls;
Talked Jacobean-wise; canvassed the range
Of taste within the Louis dynasty.
Gray-templed Caesars of the world's Exchange
Swallowed liqueurs and coffee as they sat
Under the Georgian carved mahogany,
Dictating wireless hieroglyphics that
Would on the opening of the Board Rooms rock
The pillared dollars of a railroad stock.

IN THE GYMNASIUM

A group had gathered round a mat to watch
The pressure of a Russian hammerlock,
A Polish scissors and a German crotch,
Broken by the toe-hold of Frank Gotch;
Or listened while a young Y.M.C.A.
Instructor demonstrated the left-hook,
And that right upper-cut which Jeffries took
From Johnson in the polished Reno way.
By midnight in the spacious dancing hall,
Hundreds were at the Masqueraders' Ball,
The high potential of the liner's pleasures,
Where mellow lights from Chinese lanterns
    glowed
Upon the scene, and the *Blue Danube* flowed
In andantino rhythms through the measures.

By three the silence that proceeded from
The night-caps and the soporific hum
Of the engines was far deeper than a town's:
The starlight and the low wash of the sea
Against the hull bore the serenity
Of sleep at rural hearths with eiderdowns.

The quiet on the decks was scarcely less
Than in the berths: no symptoms of the toil
Down in the holds; no evidence of stress
From gears drenched in the lubricating oil.
She seemed to swim in oil, so smooth the sea.
And quiet on the bridge: the great machine
Called for laconic speech, close-fitting, clean,
And whittled to the ship's economy.
Even the judgment stood in little need
Of reason, for the Watch had but to read
Levels and lights, meter or card or bell
To find the pressures, temperatures, or tell
Magnetic North within a binnacle,
Or gauge the hour of docking; for the speed
Was fixed abaft where under the Ensign,
Like a flashing trolling spoon, the log rotator
Transmitted through a governor its fine
Gradations on a dial indicator

Morning of Sunday promised cool and clear,
Flawless horizon, crystal atmosphere;
Not a cat's paw on the ocean, not a guy
Rope murmuring: the steamer's columned
    smoke
Climbed like extensions of her funnels high

Into the upper zones, then warped and broke
Through the resistance of her speed — blue
    sky,
Blue water rifted only by the wedge
Of the bow where the double foam line ran
Diverging from the beam to join the edge
Of the stern wake like a white unfolding fan.
Her maiden voyage was being sweetly run,
Adding a half-knot here, a quarter there,
Gliding from twenty into twenty-one.
She seemed so native to her thoroughfare,
One turned from contemplation of her size,
Her sixty thousand tons of sheer flotation,
To wonder at the human enterprise
That took a gamble on her navigation —
Joining the mastiff strength with whippet grace
In this head-strained, world-watched Atlantic
    race:
Her less than six days' passage would combine
Achievement with the architect's design.

9 A.M.

A message from *Caronia: advice*
From ships proceeding west; sighted field ice
And growlers; forty-two north; forty-nine
To fifty-one west longitude. S.S.
'Mesaba' of Atlantic Transport Line
Reports encountering solid pack: would guess
The stretch five miles in width from west to east,
And forty-five to fifty miles at least
In length.

1 P.M.

    Amerika obliged to slow
Down: warns all steamships in vicinity
Presence of bergs, especially of three
Upon the southern outskirts of the floe.

1.42 P.M.

The *Baltic* warns *Titanic:* so *Touraine;*
Reports of numerous icebergs on the Banks,
The floe across the southern traffic lane.

5 P.M.

The *Californian* and *Baltic* again
Present their compliments to Captain.

"TITANIC"

        Thanks.

THREE MEN TALKING ON DECK

"That spark's been busy all the afternoon —
Warnings! The Hydrographic charts are strewn
With crosses showing bergs and pack-ice all
Along the routes, more south than usual
For this time of the year."
        "She's hitting a clip
Instead of letting up while passing through
This belt. She's gone beyond the twenty-two."

"Don't worry — Smith's an old dog, knows his
    ship,
No finer in the mercantile marine
Than Smith with thirty years of service, clean
Record, honored with highest of all commands,
'Majestic,' then 'Olympic' on his hands,
Now the 'Titanic.' "
        " 'Twas a lucky streak
That at Southampton dock he didn't lose her,
And the 'Olympic' had a narrow squeak
Some months before rammed by the British
    Cruiser,
The 'Hawke.' "
"Straight accident. No one to blame:
'Twas suction — Board absolved them both. The
    same
With the 'Teutonic' and 'New York.' No need
To fear she's trying to out-reach her speed.
There isn't a sign of fog. Besides by now
The watch is doubled at crow's nest and bow."
"People are talking of that apparition,
When we were leaving Queenstown — that head
    showing
Above the funnel rim, and the fires going!
A stoker's face — sounds like a superstition.
But he was there within the stack, all right;
Climbed up the ladder and grinned. The
    explanation
Was given by an engineer last night —
A dummy funnel built for ventilation."

"That's queer enough, but nothing so absurd
As the latest story two old ladies heard
At a rubber o' bridge. They nearly died with fright;
Wanted to tell the captain — of all things!

The others sneered a bit but just the same
It did the trick of breaking up the game.
A mummy from The Valley of the Kings
Was brought from Thebes to London. Excavators
Passed out from cholera, black plague or worse.
Egyptians understood — an ancient curse
Was visited on all the violators.
One fellow was run over, one was drowned,
And one went crazy. When in time it found
Its way to the Museum, the last man
In charge — a mothy Aberdonian —
Exploding the whole legend with a laugh,
Lost all his humor when the skeleton
Appeared within the family photograph,
And leered down from a corner just like one
Of his uncles."

      "Holy Hades!"

            "The B.M.
Authorities themselves were scared and sold
It to New York. That's how the tale is told."
"The joke is on the Yanks."

           "No, not on them,
Nor on The Valley of the Kings. What's rummy
About it is — we're carrying the mummy."

7.30 P.M. AT A TABLE IN THE DINING SALOON

Green Turtle!

      Potage Romanoff!

          "White Star
Is out this time to press Cunarders close,
Got them on tonnage — fifty thousand gross.
Preferred has never paid a dividend.
The common's down to five — one hundred par.
The double ribbon — size and speed — would send
Them soaring."

      "Speed is not in her design,
But comfort and security. The Line
Has never advertised it — 'twould be mania
To smash the record of the 'Mauretania.' "
Sherry!

    "The rumor's out."

        "There's nothing in it."
"Bet you she docks on Tuesday night."

        "I'll take it."
"She's hitting twenty-two this very minute."
"That's four behind — She hasn't a chance to
    make it."

Brook Trout!

      Fried Dover Sole!

          "Her rate will climb
From twenty-two to twenty-six in time.
The Company's known never to rush their ships
At first or try to rip the bed-bolts off.
They run them gently half-a-dozen trips,
A few work-outs around the track to let
Them find their breathing, take the boiler cough
Out of them. She's not racing for a cup."
Claret!

    "Steamships like sprinters have to get
Their second wind before they open up."

"That group of men around the captain's table,
Look at them, count the aggregate — the House
Of Astor, Guggenheim, and Harris, Straus,
That's Frohman, isn't it? Between them able
To halve the national debt with a cool billion!
Sir Hugh is over there, and Hays and Stead.
That woman third from captain's right, it's said,
Those diamonds round her neck — a quarter
    million!"

Mignon of Beef!

      Quail!

        "I heard Phillips say
He had the finest outfit on the sea;
The new Marconi valve; the range by day
Five hundred miles, by night a thousand. Three
Sources of power. If some crash below
Should hit the engines, flood the dynamo,
He had the batteries: in emergency,
He could switch through to the auxiliary
On the boat deck."

      Woodcock and Burgundy!
"Say waiter, I said RARE, you understand."
Escallope of Veal!

      Roast Duckling!

        Snipe! More Rhine!
"Marconi made the sea as safe as land:
Remember the 'Republic' — White Star Line —
Rammed off Nantucket by the 'Florida,'
One thousand saved — the 'Baltic' heard the call.
Two steamers answered the 'Slavonia,'
Disabled off the Azores. They got them all,
And when the 'Minnehaha' ran aground
Near Bishop's Rock, they never would have found
Her — not a chance without the wireless. Same

Thing happened to that boat — what was her
  name?
The one that foundered off the Alaska Coast —
Her signals brought a steamer in the nick
Of time. Yes, sir — Marconi turned the trick."

The Barcelona salad; *no,* Beaucaire;
That Russian dressing;
               Avocado pear;

"They wound her up at the Southampton dock,
And then the tugs gave her a push to start
Her off — as automatic as a clock."

Moselle!
      "For all the hand work there's to do
Aboard this liner up on deck, the crew
Might just as well have stopped ashore. Apart
From stokers and the engineers, she's run
By gadgets from the bridge — a thousand and one
Of them with a hundred miles of copper wire.
A filament glows at the first sign of fire,
A buzzer sounds, a number gives the spot,
A deck-hand makes a coupling of the hose.
That's all there's to it; not a whistle; not
A passenger upon the ship that knows
What's happened. The whole thing is done without
So much as calling up the fire brigade.
They don't need even the pumps — a gas is
  sprayed,
Carbon dioxide —and the blaze is out."

A Cherry Flan!
          Champagne!
                    Chocolate parfait!

"How about a poker crowd tonight?
Get Jones, an awful grouch — no good to play,
But has the coin. Get hold of Larry."
                        "Right."
"You fetch Van Raalte: I'll bring in MacRae.
In Cabin D, one hundred seventy-nine.
In half-an-hour we start playing."
                        "Fine."

ON DECK

The sky was moonless but the sea flung back
With greater brilliance half the zodiac.
As clear below as clear above, the Lion

Far on the eastern quarter stalked the Bear:
Polaris off the starboard beam — and there
Upon the port the Dog-star trailed Orion.
Capella was so close, a hand might seize
The sapphire with the silver Pleiades.
And further to the south — a finger span,
Swam Betelgeuse and red Aldebaran.
Right through from east to west the ocean
  glassed
The billions of that snowy caravan
Ranging the highway which the Milkmaid
  passed.

9.05 P.M.

"CALIFORNIAN" FLASHING

I say, old man, we're stuck fast in this place,
More than an hour. Field ice for miles about.

"TITANIC"

Say, 'Californian,' shut up, keep out,
You're jamming all my signals with Cape Race.

10 P.M.

A group of boys had gathered round a spot
Upon the rail where a dial registered
The speed, and waiting each three minutes
  heard
The taffrail log bell tallying off a knot.

11.20 P.M.

BEHIND A DECK HOUSE

First act to fifth act in a tragic plan,
Stage time, real time — a woman and a man,
Entering a play within a play, dismiss
The pageant on the ocean with a kiss.
Eleven-twenty curtain! Whether true
Or false the pantomimic vows they make
Will not be known till at the *fifth* they take
Their mutual exit twenty after two.

11.25 P.M.

Position half-a-mile from edge of floe,
Hove-to for many hours, bored with delay,
The *Californian* fifteen miles away,

224

And fearful of the pack, has now begun
To turn her engines over under slow
Bell, and the operator, his task done,
Unclamps the 'phones and ends his dullest day.

The ocean sinuous, half-past eleven;
A silence broken only by the seven
Bells and the look-out calls, the log-book
    showing
Knots forty-five within two hours — not quite
The expected best as yet — but she was going
With all her bulkheads open through the night,
For not a bridge induction light was glowing.
Over the stern zenith and nadir met
In the wash of the reciprocating set.
The foam in bevelled mirrors multiplied
And shattered constellations. In between,
The pitch from the main drive of the turbine
Emerged like tuna breaches to divide
Against the rudder, only to unite
With the converging wake from either side.
Under the counter, blending with the spill
Of stars — the white and blue — the yellow light
Of Jupiter hung like a daffodil.

D-179

"Ace full! A long time since I had a pot."

*"Good boy, Van Raalte. That's the juiciest haul
'Tonight. Calls for a round of roodles, what?
Let's whoop her up. Double the limit. All
In."* (Jones, heard muttering as usual,
Demurs, but over-ruled.) *"Jones sore again."*

VAN RAALTE (DEALER):
"Ten dollars and all in!
                    The sea's like glass
Tonight. That fin-keel keeps her steady."

JONES: *"Pass."*
(Not looking at his hand.)

LARRY: *"Pass."*

CRIPPS: *"Open for ten."*
(Holding a pair of aces.) *"Say, who won
The sweep today?"*
                *"A Minnesota guy
With olive-colored spats and a mauve tie.
Five hundred and eighty miles — Beat last
    day's run."*

MAC: *"My ten."*

HARRY: (Taking a gamble on his four
Spades for a flush) *"I'll raise the bet ten more."*

VAN R.: (Two queens) *"AND ten."*

JONES: (Discovering three kings)
"Raise you to forty" (face expressing doubt.)

LARRY:
(Looking hard at a pair of nines) *"I'm out."*

CRIPPS:
(Flirts for a moment with his aces, flings
His thirty dollars to the pot.)

MAC: (The same.)

HARRY: *"My twenty. Might as well stay with
    the game."*

VAN R.: *"I'm in. Draw! Jones, how bloody long
    you wait."*

JONES: (Withholds an eight) *"One."* (And then
    draws an eight.)

CRIPPS: *"Three."* (Gets another pair.)
                        "How many, Mac?"

MAC: *"Guess I'll take two, no, three."* (Gets a
    third Jack.)

HARRY: *"One."* (Draws the ace of spades.)

VAN R.:   *"Dealer takes three."*

CRIPPS (THE OPENER): (Throws in a dollar chip.)

MAC: (The same.)

HARRY: *"I'll raise
You ten."*

VAN R.:   *"I'll see you."*

JONES: (Hesitates, surveys
The chips.) *"Another ten."*

CRIPPS: *"I'll call you."*

MAC: *"See."*

HARRY:
"White livers! Here she goes to thirty."

VAN R.:   *"Just
The devil's luck."* (Throws cards down
    in disgust.)

JONES: *"Might as well raise."* (Counts twenty
   sluggishly,
Tosses them to the centre.)
                         "Staying, Cripps?"

CRIPPS: *"No, and be damned to it."*

MAC: *"My ten."* (With groans.)

HARRY:
(Looks at the pyramid and swears at Jones,
Then calls, pitching ten dollars on the chips.)

JONES: (Cards down.) *"A full house tops
   the flush."* (He spreads
His arms around the whites and blues and reds.)

MAC:
*"As the Scotchman once said to the Sphinx,
I'd like just to know what he thinks,
I'll ask him, he cried,
And the Sphinx — he replied,
It's the hell of a time between drinks."*

CRIPPS (WATCH IN HAND):
"Time? Eleven forty-four, to be precise."

HARRY:
*"Jones — that will fatten up your pocket-book.
My throat's like charcoal. Ring for soda and ice."*

VAN R.: *"Ice: God! Look — take it through the
   port-hole — look!"*

11.45 P.M.

A signal from the crow's nest. Three bells pealed:
The look-out telephoned — *Something ahead,
Hard to make out, sir; looks like - - - iceberg dead
On starboard bow!*

MURDOCH HOLDING THE BRIDGE-WATCH

                    Starboard your helm: ship heeled
To port. From bridge to engine-room the clang
Of the telegraph. *Danger. Stop.* A hand sprang
To the throttle; the valves closed, and with
   the churn
Of the reverse the sea boiled at the stern.
Smith hurried to the bridge and Murdoch
   closed

The bulkheads of the ship as he supposed,
But could not know that with those riven floors
The electro-magnets failed upon the doors.
No shock! No more than if something alive
Had brushed her as she passed. The bow had
   missed.
Under the vast momentum of her drive
She went a mile. But why that ominous five
Degrees (within five minutes) of a list?

IN A CABIN:

"What was that, steward?"
                    "Seems like she hit a sea, sir."
*"But there's no sea; calm as a landlocked bay
It is; lost a propeller blade?"*
                              "Maybe, sir."
"She's stopped."
                    *"Just cautious like, feeling her way,
There's ice about. It's dark, no moon tonight,
Nothing to fear, I'm sure, sir."*
                              For so slight
The answer of the helm, it did not break
The sleep of hundreds: some who were awake
Went up on deck, but soon were satisfied
That nothing in the shape of wind or tide
Or rock or ice could harm that huge bulk spread
On the Atlantic, and went back to bed.

CAPTAIN IN WIRELESS ROOM:

*"We've struck an iceberg — glancing blow: as yet
Don't know extent; looks serious; so get
Ready to send out general call for aid;
I'll tell you when — having inspection made."*

REPORT OF SHIP'S CARPENTER AND FOURTH
   OFFICER:

A starboard cut three hundred feet or more
From foremast to amidships. Iceberg tore
Right at the bilge turn through the double skin:
Some boiler rooms and bunkers driven in;
The forward five compartments flooded — mail
Bags floating. Would the engine power avail
To stem the rush?

WIRELESS ROOM, FIRST OFFICER PHILLIPS AT KEY:
                    Titanic, C.Q.D.
Collision: iceberg: damaged starboard side:

Distinct list forward. (Had Smith magnified
The danger? Over-anxious certainly.)
The second (joking) — *"Try new call, maybe
Last chance you'll have to send it."*
                                                    S.O.S.
Then back to older signal of distress.

On the same instant the *Carpathia* called,
The distance sixty miles — *Putting about,
And heading for you; Double watch installed
In engine-room, in stokehold and look-out.
Four hours the run, should not the ice retard
The speed; but taking chances: Coming hard!*

THE BRIDGE

As leaning on her side to ease a pain,
The tilted ship had stopped the captain's breath:
The inconceivable had stabbed his brain,
This thing unfelt — her visceral wound of
        death?
Another message — this time to report her
Filling, taxing the pumps beyond their strain.
Had that blow rent her from the bow to
        quarter?
Or would the aft compartments still intact
Give buoyancy enough to counteract
The open forward holds?
                                        The carpenter's
Second report had offered little chance,
And panic — heart of God — the passengers,
The fourteen hundred — seven hundred packed
In steerage — seven hundred immigrants!
Smith thought of panic clutching at their throats,
And feared that Balkan scramble for the boats.

No call from bridge, no whistle, no alarm
Was sounded. Have the stewards quietly
Inform the passengers: no vital harm,
Precautions merely for emergency;
Collision? Yes, but nature of the blow
Must not be told: not even the crew must know:
Yet all on deck with lifebelts, and boats ready,
The sailors at the falls, and all hands steady.

WIRELESS ROOM

The lilac spark was crackling at the gap,
Eight ships within the radius of the call
From fifteen to five hundred miles, and all

But one answering the operator's tap.
Olympic twenty hours away had heard;
The *Baltic* next and the *Virginian* third;
Frankfurt and *Burma* distant one-half day;
Mount Temple nearer, but the ice-field lay
Between the two ships like a wall of stone;
The *Californian* deaf to signals though
Supreme deliverer an hour ago:
The hope was on *Carpathia* alone.

ON THE DECKS

So suave the fool-proof sense of life that fear
Had like the unforeseen become a mere
Illusion — vanquished by the towering height
Of funnels pouring smoke through thirty feet
Of bore; the solid deck planks and the light
From a thousand lamps as on a city street;
The feel of numbers; the security
Of wealth; the placid surface of the sea,
Reflecting on the ship the outwardness
Of calm and leisure of the passengers;
Deck-hands obedient to their officers;
Pearl-throated women in their evening dress
And wrapped in sables and minks; the silhouettes
Of men in dinner jackets staging an act
In which delusion passed, deriding fact
Behind the cupped flare of the cigarettes.

Women and children first! Slowly the men
Stepped backward from the rails where
        number ten,
Its cover off, and lifted from the chocks,
Moved outward as the Welin davits swung.
The new ropes creaking through the unused
        blocks,
The boat was lowered to B deck and hung
There while her load of sixty stepped inside,
Convinced the order was not justified.

Rockets, one, two, God! Smith — what does
        he mean?
The sounding of the bilges could not show
This reason for alarm — the sky serene
And not a ripple on the water — no
Collision. What report came from below?
No leak accounts for this — looks like a drill,
A bit of exhibition play — but still
Stopped in mid-ocean! and those rockets — *three!*

More urgent even than a tapping key
And more immediate as a protocol
To a disaster. *There!* An arrow of fire,
A fourth sped towards the sky, its bursting spire
Topping the foremast like a parasol
With fringe of fuchsia, — more a parody
Upon the tragic summons of the sea
Than the real script of unacknowledged fears
Known to the bridge and to the engineers.

Midnight! The Master of the ship presents
To the Master of the Band his compliments,
Desiring that the Band should play right
    through;
No intermission.

CONDUCTOR: "Bad?"

OFFICER: "*Yes, bad enough,*
The half not known yet even to the crew;
For God's sake, cut the sentimental stuff,
The BLUE BELLS *and Kentucky lullabies.*
Murdoch will have a barrel of work to do,
Holding the steerage back, once they get wise;
They're jumpy now under the rockets' glare;
So put the ginger in the fiddles — Zip
Her up."

CONDUCTOR: "*Sure, number forty-seven:*" E-Yip
I Addy-I-A, I Ay - - - I don't care - - -

NUMBER TEN GOES OVER THE SIDE

Full noon and midnight by a weird design
Both met and parted at the median line.
Beyond the starboard gunwale was outspread
The jet expanse of water islanded
By fragments of the berg which struck the blow.
And further off towards the horizon lay
The loom of the uncharted parent floe,
Merging the black with an amorphous gray.
On the port gunwale the meridian
Shone from the terraced rows of decks that ran
From gudgeon to the stem nine hundred feet;
And as the boat now tilted by the stern,
Or now resumed her levels with the turn
Of the controlling ropes at block and cleat,
How easy seemed the step and how secure
Back to the comfort and the warmth — the lure
Of sheltered promenade and sun decks starred
By hanging bulbs, amber and rose and blue,

The trellis and palms lining an avenue
With all the vista of a boulevard:
The mirror of the ceilings with festoon
Of pennants, flags and streamers — and now
    through
The leaded windows of the grand saloon,
Through parted curtains and the open doors
Of vestibules, glint of deserted floors
And tables, and under the sorcery
Of light excelling their facsimile,
The periods returning to relume
The panels of the lounge and smoking-room,
Holding the mind in its abandonment
During those sixty seconds of descent.
Lower away! The boat with its four tons
Of freight went down with jerks and stops
    and runs
Beyond the glare of the cabins and below
The slanting parallels of port-holes, clear
Of the exhaust from the condenser flow:
But with the uneven falls she canted near
The water line; the stern rose; the bow dipped;
The crew groped for the link-releasing gear;
The lever jammed; a stoker's jack-knife ripped
The aft ropes through, which on the instant
    brought her
With rocking keel though safe upon the water.

THE "CARPATHIA"

Fifteen, sixteen, seventeen, eighteen — three
Full knots beyond her running limit, she
Was feeling out her port and starboard points,
And testing rivets on her boiler joints.
The needle on the gauge beyond the red,
The blow-offs feathered at the funnel head.
The draught-fans roaring at their loudest, now
The quartermaster jams the helm hard-over,
As the revolving searchlight beams uncover
The columns of an iceberg on the bow,
Then compensates this loss by daring gains
Made by her passage through the open lanes.

THE BAND

East side, West side, all around the town,
The tots sang "Ring-a-Rosie"
"London Bridge is falling down,"
Boys and girls together - - -

228

The cranks turn and the sixth and seventh
  swing
Over and down, the "tiller" answering
"*Aye, Aye, sir*" to the shouts of officers —
"*Row to the cargo ports for passengers.*"
The water line is reached, but the ports fail
To open, and the crews of the boats hail
The decks; receiving no response they pull
Away from the ship's side, less than half full.
The eighth caught in the tackle foul is stuck
Half-way. With sixty-five capacity,
Yet holding twenty-four, goes number three.

The sharp unnatural deflection, struck
By the sea-level with the under row
Of dipping port-holes at the forward, show
How much she's going by the head. Behind
The bulkheads, sapping out their steel control,
Is the warp of the bunker press inclined
By many thousand tons of shifting coal.

The smoothest, safest passage to the sea
Is made by number one — the next to go —
Her space is forty — twelve her company:
"*Pull like the devil from her — harder — row!*
The minute that she founders, not a boat
Within a mile around that will not follow.
What nearly happened at Southampton? So
Pull, pull, I tell you — not a chip afloat,
God knows how far, her suction will not swallow."

Alexander's rag-time band---
It's the best band in the land---

VOICES FROM THE DECK:

"*There goes the Special with the toffs. You'll make*
New York tonight rowing like that. You'll take
Your death o' cold out there with all the fish
And ice around."
                 "*Make sure your butlers dish*
You up your toddies now, and bring hot rolls
For breakfast."
                 "*Don't forget the finger bowls.*"

The engineering staff of thirty-five
Are at their stations: those off-duty go
Of their free will to join their mates below
In the grim fight for steam, more steam, to drive
The pressure through the pumps and dynamo.

Knee-deep, waist-deep in water they remain,
Not one of them seen on the decks again.
The under braces of the rudder showing,
The wing propeller blades began to rise,
And with them, through the hawse-holes,
  water flowing —
The angle could not but assault the eyes.
A fifteen minutes, and the fo'c'sle head
Was under. And five more, the sea had shut
The lower entrance to the stairs that led
From C deck to the boat deck — the short cut
For the crew. Another five, the upward flow
Had covered the wall brackets where the glow
Diffusing from the frosted bulbs turned green
Uncannily through their translucent screen.

ON THE "CARPATHIA"

White Star — Cunarder, forty miles apart,
Still eighteen knots! From coal to flame to
  steam —
Decision of a captain to redeem
Errors of brain by hazards of the heart!
Showers of sparks danced through the funnel
  smoke,
The firemen's shovels, rakes and slice-bars broke
The clinkers, fed the fires, and ceaselessly
The hoppers dumped the ashes on the sea.

As yet no panic, but none might foretell
The moment when the sight of that oblique
Breath-taking lift of the taffrail and the sleek
And foamless undulation of the swell
Might break in meaning on those diverse races,
And give them common language. As the throng
Came to the upper decks and moved along
The incline, the contagion struck the faces
With every lowering of a boat and backed
Them towards the stern. And twice between
  the hush
Of fear and utterance the gamut cracked,
When with the call for women and the flare
Of an exploding rocket, a short rush
Was made for the boats — fifteen and two.
'Twas nearly done — the sudden clutch and tear
Of canvas, a flurry of fists and curses met
By swift decisive action from the crew,
Supported by a quartermaster's threat
Of three revolver shots fired on the air.

But still the fifteenth went with five inside,
Who, seeking out the shadows, climbed aboard
And, lying prone and still, managed to hide
Under the thwarts long after she was lowered.

Jingle bells, jingle bells,
Jingle all the way,
O what fun---

"*Some men in number two, sir!*"
                              The boat swung
Back.
      "*Chuck the fellows out.*"
                              Grabbed by the feet,
The lot were pulled over the gunwale and flung
Upon the deck.
              "*Hard at that forward cleat!*
A hand there for that after fall. Lower
Away — port side, the second hatch, and wait."

With six hands of his watch, the bosun's mate,
Sent down to open up the gangway door,
Was trapped and lost in a flooded alley way,
And like the seventh, impatient of delay,
The second left with room for twenty more.

The fiddley leading from a boiler room
Lay like a tortuous exit from a tomb.
A stoker climbed it, feeling by the twist
From vertical how steep must be the list.
He reached the main deck where the cold
      night airs
Enswathed his flesh with steam. Taking the
      stairs,
He heard the babel by the davits, faced
The forward, noticed how the waters raced
To the break of the fo'c'sle and lapped
The foremast root. He climbed again and saw
The resolute manner in which Murdoch's
      rapped
Command put a herd instinct under law;
No life-preserver on, he stealthily
Watched Phillips in his room, bent at the key,
And thinking him alone, he sprang to tear
The jacket off. He leaped too soon. "*Take that!*"
The second stove him with a wrench. "*Lie there,*
Till hell begins to singe your lids — you rat!"

But set against those scenes where order failed,
Was the fine muster at the fourteenth where,

Like a zone of calm along a thoroughfare,
The discipline of sea-worn laws prevailed.
No women answering the repeated calls,
The men filled up the vacant seats: the falls
Were slipping through the sailors' hands,
When a steerage group of women, having fought
Their way over five flights of stairs, were
      brought
Bewildered to the rails. Without commands
Barked from the lips of officers; without
A protest registered in voice or face,
The boat was drawn up and the men stepped
      out
Back to the crowded stations with that free
Barter of life for life done with the grace
And air of a Castilian courtesy.

I've just got here through Paris,
From the sunny Southern shore,
I to Monte Carlo went---

ISIDOR AND IDA STRAUS

At the sixteenth — a woman wrapped her coat
Around her maid and placed her in the boat;
Was ordered in but seen to hesitate
At the gunwale, and more conscious of her pride
Than of her danger swiftly took her fate
With open hands, and without show of tears
Returned unmurmuring to her husband's side;
"*We've been together now for forty years,*
Whither you go, I go."
                              A boy of ten,
Ranking himself within the class of men,
Though given a seat, made up his mind to waive
The privilege of his youth and size, and piled
The inches on his stature as he gave
Place to a Magyar woman and her child.

And men who had in the world's run of trade,
Or in pursuit of the professions, made
Their reputation, looked upon the scene
Merely as drama in a life's routine:
Millet was studying eyes as he would draw them
Upon a canvas; Butt, as though he saw them
In the ranks; Astor, social, debonair,
Waved "*Good-bye*" to his bride — "*See you*
      tomorrow,"
And tapped a cigarette on a silver case;
Men came to Guggenheim as he stood there

In evening suit, coming this time to borrow
Nothing but courage from his calm, cool face.

And others unobserved, of unknown name
And race, just stood behind, pressing no claim
Upon priority but rendering proof
Of their oblation, quiet and aloof
Within the maelstrom towards the rails. And
     some
Wavered a moment with the panic urge,
But rallied to attention on the verge
Of flight as if the rattle of a drum
From quarters faint but unmistakable
Had put the stiffening in the blood to check
The impulse of the feet, leaving the will
No choice between the lifeboats and the deck.

The four collapsibles, their lashings ripped,
Half-dragged, half-lifted by the hooks, were
     slipped
Over the side. The first two luckily
Had but the forward distance to the sea.
Its canvas edges crumpled up, the third
Began to fill with water and transferred
Its cargo to the twelfth, while number four,
Abaft and higher, nose-dived and swamped
     its score.

The wireless cabin — Phillips in his place,
Guessing the knots of the Cunarder's race.
Water was swirling up the slanted floor
Around the chair and sucking at his feet.
Carpathia's call — the last one heard complete—
Expect to reach position half-past four.
The operators turned — Smith at the door
With drawn incredulous face. *"Men, you have
     done*
Your duty. I release you. Everyone
Now for himself." They stayed ten minutes yet,
The power growing fainter with each blue
Crackle of flame. Another stammering jet —
Virginian heard "a tattering C.Q."
Again a try for contact but the code's
Last jest had died between the electrodes.

Even yet the spell was on the ship: although
The last lifeboat had vanished, there was no
Besieging of the heavens with a crescendo
Of fears passing through terror into riot —

But on all lips the strange narcotic quiet
Of an unruffled ocean's innuendo.
In spite of her deformity of line,
Emergent like a crag out of the sea,
She had the semblance of stability,
Moment by moment furnishing no sign,
So far as visible, of that decline
Made up of inches crawling into feet.
Then, with the electric circuit still complete,
The miracle of day displacing night
Had worked its fascination to beguile
Direction of the hours and cheat the sight.
Inside the recreation rooms the gold
From Arab lamps shone on the burnished tile.
What hindered the return to shelter while
The ship clothed in that irony of light
Offered her berths and cabins as a fold?
And, was there not the *Californian*?
Many had seen her smoke just over there,
But two hours past — it seemed a harbor span —
So big, so close, she could be hailed, they said;
She must have heard the signals, seen the flare
Of those white stars and changed at once her
     course.
There under the *Titanic's* foremast head,
A lamp from the look-out cage was flashing
     Morse.
No ship afloat unless deaf, blind and dumb
To those three sets of signals but would come.
And when the whiz of a rocket bade men turn
Their faces to each other in concern
At shattering facts upon the deck, they found
Their hearts take reassurance with the sound
Of the violins from the gymnasium, where
The bandsmen in their blithe insouciance
Discharged the sudden tension of the air
With the fox-trot's sublime irrelevance.

The fo'c'sle had gone under the creep
Of the water. Though without a wind, a lop
Was forming on the wells now fathoms deep.
The seventy feet — the boat deck's normal
     drop —
Was down to ten. Rising, falling, and waiting,
Rising again, the swell that edged and curled
Around the second bridge, over the top
Of the air-shafts, backed, resurged and whirled
Into the stokehold through the fiddley grating.

Under the final strain the two wire guys
Of the forward funnel tugged and broke at
    the eyes:
With buckled plates the stack leaned, fell and
    smashed
The starboard wing of the flying bridge, went
    through
The lower, then tilting at the davits crashed
Over, driving a wave aboard that drew
Back to the sea some fifty sailors and
The captain with the last of the bridge command.

Out on the water was the same display
Of fear and self-control as on the deck —
Challenge and hesitation and delay,
The quick return, the will to save, the race
Of snapping oars to put the realm of space
Between the half-filled lifeboats and the wreck.
The swimmers whom the waters did not take
With their instant death-chill struck out for
    the wake
Of the nearer boats, gained on them, hailed
The steersmen and were saved: the weaker failed
And fagged and sank. A man clutched at the rim
Of a gunwale, and a woman's jewelled fist
Struck at his face: two others seized his wrist,
As he released his hold, and gathering him
Over the side, they staunched the cut from the
    ring.
And there were many deeds envisaging
Volitions where self-preservation fought
Its red primordial struggle with the "ought,"
In those high moments when the gambler tossed
Upon the chance and uncomplaining lost.

Aboard the ship, whatever hope of dawn
Gleamed from the *Carpathia's* riding lights was
    gone,
For every knot was matched by each degree
Of list. The stern was lifted bodily
When the bow had sunk three hundred feet,
    and set
Against the horizon stars in silhouette

Were the blade curves of the screws, hump
    of the rudder.
The downward pull and after buoyancy
Held her a minute poised but for a shudder
That caught her frame as with the upward stroke
Of the sea a boiler or a bulkhead broke.

Climbing the ladders, gripping shroud and stay,
Storm-rail, ringbolt or fairlead, every place
That might befriend the clutch of hand or brace
Of foot, the fourteen hundred made their way
To the heights of the aft decks, crowding the
    inches
Around the docking bridge and cargo winches.
And now that last salt tonic which had kept
The valor of the heart alive — the bows
Of the immortal seven that had swept
The strings to outplay, outdie their orders,
    ceased.
Five minutes more, the angle had increased
From eighty on to ninety when the rows
Of deck and port-hole lights went out, flashed
    back
A brilliant second and again went black.
Another bulkhead crashed, then following
The passage of the engines as they tore
From their foundations, taking everything
Clean through the bows from 'midships with a
    roar
Which drowned all cries upon the deck and
    shook
The watchers in the boats, the liner took
Her thousand fathoms journey to her grave.

*   *   *

And out there in the starlight, with no trace
Upon it of its deed but the last wave
From the *Titanic* fretting at its base,
Silent, composed, ringed by its icy broods,
The gray shape with the palaeolithic face
Was still the master of the longitudes.
                                        —1935, 1958

THE PRIZE CAT

Pure blood domestic, guaranteed,
Soft-mannered, musical in purr,

The ribbon had declared the breed,
Gentility was in the fur.

Such feline culture in the gads
No anger ever arched her back —
What distance since those velvet pads
Departed from the leopard's track!

And when I mused how Time had thinned
The jungle strains within the cells,
How human hands had disciplined
Those prowling optic parallels;

I saw the generations pass
Along the reflex of a spring,
A bird had rustled in the grass,
The tab had caught it on the wing:

Behind the leap so furtive-wild
Was such ignition in the gleam,
I thought an Abyssinian child
Had cried out in the whitethroat's scream.

—1937

SILENCES

There is no silence upon the earth or under the earth like the silence under the sea;
No cries announcing birth,
No sounds declaring death.
There is silence when the milt is laid on the spawn in the weeds and fungus
    of the rock-clefts;
And silence in the growth and struggle for life.
The bonitoes pounce upon the mackerel,
And are themselves caught by the barracudas,
The sharks kill the barracudas
And the great molluscs rend the sharks,
And all noiselessly —
Though swift be the action and final the conflict,
The drama is silent.

There is no fury upon the earth like the fury under the sea.
For growl and cough and snarl are the tokens of spendthrifts who know not
    the ultimate economy of rage.
Moreover, the pace of the blood is too fast.
But under the waves the blood is sluggard and has the same temperature as
    that of the sea.

There is something pre-reptilian about a silent kill.

Two men may end their hostilities just with their battle-cries.
"The devil take you," says one.
"I'll see you in hell first," says the other.
And these introductory salutes followed by a hail of gutturals and sibilants are
    often the beginning of friendship, for who would not prefer to be lustily
    damned than to be half-heartedly blessed?
No one need fear oaths that are properly enunciated, for they belong to the
    inheritance of just men made perfect, and, for all we know, of such may
    be the Kingdom of Heaven.
But let silent hate be put away for it feeds upon the heart of the hater.
Today I watched two pairs of eyes. One pair was black and the other gray. And
    while the owners thereof, for the space of five seconds, walked past each
    other, the gray snapped at the black and the black riddled the gray.

One looked to say — "The cat,"
And the other — "The cur."
But no words were spoken;
Not so much as a hiss or a murmur came through the perfect enamel of the
     teeth; not so much as a gesture of enmity.
If the right upper lip curled over the canine, it went unnoticed.
The lashes veiled the eyes not for an instant in the passing.
And as between the two in respect to candor of intention or eternity of wish,
     there was no choice, for the stare was mutual and absolute.
A word would have dulled the exquisite edge of the feeling,
An oath would have flawed the crystallization of the hate.
For only such culture could grow in a climate of silence, —
Away back before the emergence of fur or feather, back to the unvocal sea and
     down deep where the darkness spills its wash on the threshold of light, where
     the lids never close upon the eyes, where the inhabitants slay in silence and
     are as silently slain.

—1937

FROM *Brébeuf and his Brethren*

I

The winds of God were blowing over France,
Kindling the hearths and altars, changing vows
Of rote into an alphabet of flame.
The air was charged with song beyond the range
Of larks, with wings beyond the stretch of
     eagles.
Skylines unknown to maps broke from the mists
And there was laughter on the seas. With sound
Of bugles from the Roman catacombs,
The saints came back in their incarnate forms.
Across the Alps St. Francis of Assisi
In his brown tunic girt with hempen cord,
Revisited the plague-infected towns.
The monks were summoned from their
     monasteries,
Nuns from their convents; apostolic hands
Had touched the priests; foundlings and galley
     slaves
Became the charges of Vincent de Paul;
Francis de Sales put his heroic stamp
Upon his order of the Visitation.
Out of Numidia by way of Rome,
The architect of palaces, unbuilt
Of hand, again was busy with his plans,
Reshaping for the world his *City of God*.
Out of the Netherlands was heard the call
Of Kempis through the *Imitatio*

To leave the dusty marts and city streets
And stray along the shores of Galilee.
The flame had spread across the Pyrenees —
The visions of Theresa burning through
The adorations of the Carmelites;
The very clouds at night to John of the Cross
Being cruciform — chancel, transept and aisle
Blazing with light and holy oracle.
Xavier had risen from his knees to drive
His dreams full-sail under an ocean compass.
Loyola, soldier-priest, staggering with wounds
At Pampeluna, guided by a voice,
Had travelled to the Montserrata Abbey
To leave his sword and dagger on an altar
That he might lead the *Company of Jesus*.

The story of the frontier like a saga
Sang through the cells and cloisters of the
     nation,
Made silver flutes out of the parish spires,
Troubled the ashes of the canonized
In the cathedral crypts, soared through the nave
To stir the foliations on the columns,
Roll through the belfries, and give deeper tongue
To the *Magnificat* in Notre Dame.
It brought to earth the prophets and apostles
Out of their static shrines in the stained glass.
It caught the ear of Christ, reveined his hands

And feet, bidding his marble saints to leave
Their pedestals for chartless seas and coasts
And the vast blunders of the forest glooms.
So, in the footsteps of their patrons came
A group of men asking the hardest tasks
At the new outposts of the Huron bounds
Held in the stern hand of the Jesuit Order.

And in Bayeux a neophyte while rapt
In contemplation saw a bleeding form
Falling beneath the instrument of death,
Rising under the quickening of the thongs,
Stumbling along the Via Dolorosa.
No play upon the fancy was this scene,
But the Real Presence to the naked sense.
The fingers of Brébeuf were at his breast,
Closing and tightening on a crucifix,
While voices spoke aloud unto his ear
And to his heart — *Per ignem et per aquam.*
Forests and streams and trails thronged
      through his mind,
The painted faces of the Iroquois,
Nomadic bands and smoking bivouacs
Along the shores of western inland seas,
With forts and palisades and fiery stakes.
The stories of Champlain, Brulé, Viel,
Sagard and Le Caron had reached his town —
The stories of those northern boundaries
Where in the winter the white pines could brush
The Pleiades, and at the equinoxes
Under the gold and green of the auroras
Wild geese drove wedges through the zodiac.
The vows were deep he laid upon his soul.
"I shall be broken first before I break them."
He knew by heart the manual that had stirred
The world — the clarion calling through the
      notes
Of the Ignatian preludes. On the prayers,
The meditations, points and colloquies,
Was built the soldier and the martyr program.
This is the end of man — *Deum laudet,*
To seek and find the will of God, to act
Upon it for the ordering of life,
And for the soul's beatitude. This is
To do, this not to do. To weigh the sin;
The interior understanding to be followed
By the amendment of the deed through grace;
The abnegation of the evil thought

And act; the trampling of the body under;
The daily practice of the *counter virtues.*
*"In time of desolation to be firm
And constant in the soul's determination,
Desire and sense obedient to the reason."*

The oath Brébeuf was taking had its root
Firm in his generations of descent.
The family name was known to chivalry —
In the Crusades; at Hastings; through the blood
Of the English Howards; called out on the rungs
Of the siege ladders; at the castle breaches;
Proclaimed by heralds at the lists, and heard
In Council Halls: — the coat-of-arms a bull
In black with horns of gold on a silver shield.
So on that toughened pedigree of fibre
Were strung the pledges. From the novice stage
To the vow-day he passed on to the priesthood,
And on the anniversary of his birth
He celebrated his first mass at Rouen. . . .

III

[*In 1626 Brébeuf had embarked for the New
World, but this first venture ended in 1629 with
little to show for it. Following four years in France,
Brébeuf returned with renewed zeal. Experience
gave him a better understanding both of the Indians
and of what was needed for a successful mission.*]

. . . The other need was urgent — laborers!
The villages were numerous and were spread
Through such a vast expanse of wilderness
And shore. Only a bell with a bronze throat
Must summon missionaries to these fields.
With the last cry of the captive in his ears,
Brébeuf strode from his cabin to the woods
To be alone. He found his tabernacle
Within a grove, picked up a stone flat-faced,
And going to a cedar-crotch, he jammed
It in, and on this table wrote his letter.
*"Herein I show you what you have to suffer.
I shall say nothing of the voyage — that
You know already. If you have the courage
To try it, that is only the beginning,
For when after a month of river travel
You reach our village, we can offer you
The shelter of a cabin lowlier
Than any hovel you have seen in France.*

As tired as you may be, only a mat
Laid on the ground will be your bed. Your food
May be for weeks a gruel of crushed corn
That has the look and smell of mortar paste.
This country is the breeding place of vermin.
Sandflies, mosquitoes haunt the summer months.
In France you may have been a theologian,
A scholar, master, preacher, but out here
You must attend a savage school; for months
Will pass before you learn even to lisp
The language. Here barbarians shall be
Your Aristotle and Saint Thomas. Mute
Before those teachers you shall take your lessons.
What of the winter? Half the year is winter.
Inside your cabins will be smoke so thick
You may not read your Breviary for days.
Around your fireplace at mealtime arrive
The uninvited guests with whom you share
Your stint of food. And in the fall and winter,
You tramp unbeaten trails to reach the missions,
Carrying your luggage on your back. Your life
Hangs by a thread. Of all calamities
You are the cause — the scarcity of game,
A fire, famine or an epidemic.
There are no natural reasons for a drought
And for the earth's sterility. You are
The reasons, and at any time a savage
May burn your cabin down or split your head.
I tell you of the enemies that live
Among our Huron friends. I have not told
You of the Iroquois our constant foes.
Only a week ago in open fight
They killed twelve of our men at Contarea,
A day's march from the village where we live.
Treacherous and stealthy in their ambuscades,

They terrorize the country, for the Hurons
Are very slothful in defence, never
On guard and always seeking flight for safety.

"Wherein the gain, you ask, of this acceptance?
There is no gain but this — that what you suffer
Shall be of God: your loneliness in travel
Will be relieved by angels overhead;
Your silence will be sweet for you will learn
How to commune with God; rapids and rocks
Are easier than the steeps of Calvary.
There is a consolation in your hunger
And in abandonment upon the road,
For once there was a greater loneliness
And deeper hunger. As regards the soul
There are no dangers here, with means of grace
At every turn, for if we go outside
Our cabin, is not heaven over us?
No buildings block the clouds. We say our prayers
Freely before a noble oratory.
Here is the place to practise faith and hope
And charity where human art has brought
No comforts, where we strive to bring to God
A race so unlike men that we must live
Daily expecting murder at their hands,
Did we not open up the skies or close
Them at command, giving them sun or rain.
So if despite these trials you are ready
To share our labors, come; for you will find
A consolation in the cross that far outweighs
Its burdens. Though in many an hour your soul
Will echo — 'Why hast Thou forsaken me?',
Yet evening will descend upon you when,
Your heart too full of holy exultation,
You call like Xavier — 'Enough, O Lord!'"...

XII

[In March, 1649, the Iroquois routed the Hurons around Sainte Marie
and triumphantly brought Brébeuf and Lalemant back to St. Ignace as captives
for mockery and torture.]

. . . Now three o'clock, and capping the height of the passion,
Confusing the sacraments under the pines of the forest,
Under the incense of balsam, under the smoke
Of the pitch, was offered the rite of the font. On the head,
The breast, the loins and the legs, the boiling water!
While the mocking paraphrase of the symbols was hurled
At their faces like shards of flint from the arrow heads —

236

"We baptize thee with water---
               That thou mayest be led

To Heaven---
               To that end we do anoint thee.
We treat thee as a friend: we are the cause
Of thy happiness; we are thy priests; the more
Thou sufferest, the more thy God will reward thee,
So give us thanks for our kind offices."

The fury of taunt was followed by fury of blow.
Why did not the flesh of Brébeuf cringe to the scourge,
Respond to the heat, for rarely the Iroquois found
A victim that would not cry out in such pain — yet here
The fire was on the wrong fuel. Whenever he spoke,
It was to rally the soul of his friend whose turn
Was to come through the night while the eyes were uplifted in prayer,
Imploring the Lady of Sorrows, the mother of Christ,
As pain brimmed over the cup and the will was called
To stand the test of the coals. And sometimes the speech
Of Brébeuf struck out, thundering reproof to his foes,
Half-rebuke, half-defiance, giving them roar for roar.
Was it because the chancel became the arena,
Brébeuf a lion at bay, not a lamb on the altar,
As if the might of a Roman were joined to the cause
Of Judaea? Speech they could stop for they girdled his lips,
But never a moan could they get. Where was the source
Of his strength, the home of his courage that topped the best
Of their bravos and even out fabled the lore of their legends?
In the bunch of his shoulders which often had carried a load
Extorting the envy of guides at an Ottawa portage?
The heat of the hatchets was finding a path to that source.
In the thews of his thighs which had mastered the trails of the Neutrals?
They would gash and beribbon those muscles. Was it the blood?
They would draw it fresh from its fountain. Was it the heart?
They dug for it, fought for the scraps in the way of the wolves.
But not in these was the valor or stamina lodged;
Nor in the symbol of Richelieu's robes or the seals
Of Mazarin's charters, nor in the stir of the *lilies*
Upon the Imperial folds; nor yet in the words
Loyola wrote on a table of lava-stone
In the cave of Manresa — not in these the source —
But in the sound of invisible trumpets blowing
Around two slabs of board, right-angled, hammered
By Roman nails and hung on a Jewish hill. . . .

—1940, 1958

COME AWAY, DEATH

Willy-nilly, he comes or goes, with the clown's
    logic,
Comic in epitaph, tragic in epithalamium,
And unseduced by any mused rhyme.
However blow the winds over the pollen,
Whatever the course of the garden variables,
He remains the constant,
Ever flowering from the poppy seeds.

There was a time he came in formal dress,
Announced by Silence tapping at the panels
In deep apology.
A touch of chivalry in his approach,
He offered sacramental wine,
And with acanthus leaf
And petals of the hyacinth
He took the fever from the temples
And closed the eyelids,
Then led the way to his cool longitudes
In the dignity of the candles.

His medieval grace is gone —
Gone with the flame of the capitals
And the leisured turn of the thumb
Leafing the manuscripts,
Gone with the marbles
And the Venetian mosaics,
With the bend of the knee
Before the rose-strewn feet of the Virgin.
The *paternosters* of his priests,
Committing clay to clay,
Have rattled in their throats

Under the gride of his traction tread.

One night we heard his footfall — one
    September night —
In the outskirts of a village near the sea.
There was a moment when the storm
Delayed its fist, when the surf fell
Like velvet on the rocks — a moment only;
The strangest lull we ever knew!
A sudden truce among the oaks
Released their fratricidal arms;
The poplars straightened to attention
As the winds stopped to listen
To the sound of a motor drone —
And then the drone was still.
We heard the tick-tock on the shelf,
And the leak of valves in our hearts.
A calm condensed and lidded
As at the core of a cyclone ended breathing.
This was the monologue of Silence
Grave and unequivocal.

What followed was a bolt
Outside the range and target of the thunder,
And human speech curved back upon itself
Through Druid runways and the Piltdown
    scarps,
Beyond the stammers of the Java caves,
To find its origins in hieroglyphs
On mouths and eyes and cheeks
Etched by a foreign stylus never used
On the outmoded page of the Apocalypse.

—1943

THE TRUANT

"What have you there?" the great Panjandrum
    said
To the Master of the Revels who had led
A bucking truant with a stiff backbone
Close to the foot of the Almighty's throne.

"Right Reverend, most adored,
And forcibly acknowledged Lord
By the keen logic of your two-edged sword!

This creature has presumed to classify
Himself — a biped, rational, six feet high
And two feet wide; weighs fourteen stone;
Is guilty of a multitude of sins.
He has abjured his choric origins,
And like an undomesticated slattern,
Walks with tangential step unknown
Within the weave of the atomic pattern.
He has developed concepts, grins

Obscenely at your Royal bulletins,
Possesses what he calls a will
Which challenges your power to kill."

"What is his pedigree?"

"The base is guaranteed, your Majesty —
Calcium, carbon, phosphorus, vapor
And other fundamentals spun
From the umbilicus of the sun,
And yet he says he will not caper
Around your throne, nor toe the rules
For the ballet of the fiery molecules."

"His concepts and denials — scrap them, burn
    them —
To the chemists with them promptly."

                              "Sire,
The stuff is not amenable to fire.
Nothing but their own kind can overturn them.
The chemists have sent back the same
        old story—
'With our extreme gelatinous apology,
We beg to inform your Imperial Majesty,
Unto whom be dominion and power and glory,
There still remains that strange precipitate
Which has the quality to resist
Our oldest and most trusted catalyst.
It is a substance we cannot cremate
By temperatures known to our Laboratory.' "

And the great Panjandrum's face grew dark—
"I'll put those chemists to their annual purge,
And I myself shall be the thaumaturge
To find the nature of this fellow's spark.
Come, bring him nearer by yon halter rope:
I'll analyse him with the cosmoscope."

Pulled forward with his neck awry,
The little fellow six feet short,
Aware he was about to die,
Committed grave contempt of court
By answering with a flinchless stare
The Awful Presence seated there.

The ALL HIGH swore until his face was black.
He called him a coprophagite,
A genus *homo*, egomaniac,
Third cousin to the family of worms,

A sporozoan from the ooze of night,
Spawn of a spavined troglodyte:
He swore by all the catalogue of terms
Known since the slang of carboniferous Time.
He said that he could trace him back
To pollywogs and earwigs in the slime.
And in his shrillest tenor he began
Reciting his indictment of the man,
Until he closed upon this capital crime —
"You are accused of singing out of key
(A foul unmitigated dissonance),
Of shuffling in the measures of the dance,
Then walking out with that defiant, free
Toss of your head, banging the doors,
Leaving a stench upon the jacinth floors.
You have fallen like a curse
On the mechanics of my Universe.

"Herewith I measure out your penalty —
Hearken while you hear, look while you see:
I send you now upon your homeward route
Where you shall find
Humiliation for your pride of mind.
I shall make deaf the ear, and dim the eye,
Put palsy in your touch, make mute
Your speech, intoxicate your cells and dry
Your blood and marrow, shoot
Arthritic needles through your cartilage,
And having parched you with old age,
I'll pass you wormwise through the mire;
And when your rebel will
Is mouldered, all desire
Shrivelled, all your concepts broken,
Backward in dust I'll blow you till
You join my spiral festival of fire.
Go, Master of the Revels — I have spoken."

And the little genus *homo*, six feet high,
Standing erect, countered with this reply —
"You dumb insouciant invertebrate,
You rule a lower than a feudal state —
A realm of flunkey decimals that run,
Return; return and run; again return,
Each group around its little sun,
And every sun a satellite.
There they go by day and night,
Nothing to do but run and burn,
Taking turn and turn about,

Light-year in and light-year out,
Dancing, dancing in quadrillions,
Never leaving their pavilions.

"Your astronomical conceit
Of bulk and power is anserine.
Your ignorance so thick,
You did not know your own arithmetic.
We flung the graphs about your flying feet;
We measured your diameter —
Merely a line
Of zeros prefaced by an integer.
Before we came
You had no name.
You did not know direction or your pace;
We taught you all you ever knew
Of motion, time, and space.
We healed you of your vertigo
And put you in our kindergarten show,
Perambulated you through prisms, drew
Your mileage through the Milky Way,
Lassoed your comets when they ran astray,
Yoked Leo, Taurus, and your team of Bears
To pull our kiddy cars of inverse squares.

"Boast not about your harmony,
Your perfect curves, your rings
Of *pure and endless light* — 'Twas we
Who pinned upon your Seraphim their wings,
And when your brassy heavens rang
With joy that morning while the planets sang
Their choruses of archangelic lore,
'Twas we who ordered the notes upon their score
Out of our winds and strings.
Yes! all your shapely forms
Are ours — parabolas of silver light,
Those blueprints of your spiral stairs
From nadir depth to zenith height,
Coronas, rainbows after storms,
Auroras on your eastern tapestries
And constellations over western seas.

"And when, one day, grown conscious of your age,
While pondering an eolith,
We turned a human page
And blotted out a cosmic myth
With all its baby symbols to explain
The sunlight in Apollo's eyes,
Our rising pulses and the birth of pain,

Fear, and that fern-and-fungus breath
Stalking our nostrils to our caves of death —
That day we learned how to anatomize
Your body, calibrate your size
And set a mirror up before your face
To show you what you really were — a rain
Of dull Lucretian atoms crowding space,
A series of concentric waves which any fool
Might make by dropping stones within a pool,
Or an exploding bomb forever in flight
Bursting like hell through Chaos and Old Night.

"You oldest of the hierarchs
Composed of electronic sparks,
We grant you speed,
We grant you power, and fire
That ends in ash, but we concede
To you no pain nor joy nor love nor hate,
No final tableau of desire,
No causes won or lost, no free
Adventure at the outposts — only
The degradation of your energy
When at some late
Slow number of your dance your sergeant-
     major Fate
Will catch you blind and groping and will send
You reeling on that long and lonely
Lockstep of your wave-lengths towards your
     end.

"We who have met
With stubborn calm the dawn's hot fusillades;
Who have seen the forehead sweat
Under the tug of pulleys on the joints,
Under the liquidating tally
Of the cat-and-truncheon bastinades;
Who have taught our souls to rally
To mountain horns and the sea's rockets
When the needle ran demented through the
     points;
We who have learned to clench
Our fists and raise our lightless sockets
To morning skies after the midnight raids,
Yet cocked our ears to bugles on the barricades,
And in cathedral rubble found a way to quench
A dying thirst within a Galilean valley —
No! by the Rood, we will not join your ballet."

—1943

240

The Canadian Pacific Railway had to traverse three regions: Number One was the prairie; Two was North of Lake Superior; Three was the mountainous area of British Columbia.

NUMBER TWO

On the North Shore a reptile lay asleep —
A hybrid that the myths might have conceived,
But not delivered, as progenitor
Of crawling, gliding things upon the earth.
She lay snug in the folds of a huge boa
Whose tail had covered Labrador and swished
Atlantic tides, whose body coiled itself
Around the Hudson Bay, then curled up north
Through Manitoba and Saskatchewan
To Great Slave Lake. In continental reach
The neck went past the Great Bear Lake until
Its head was hidden in the Arctic Seas.
This folded reptile was asleep or dead:
So motionless, she seemed stone dead — just seemed:
She was too old for death, too old for life,
For as if jealous of all living forms
She had lain there before bivalves began
To catacomb their shells on western mountains.
Somewhere within this life-death zone she sprawled,
Torpid upon a rock-and-mineral mattress.
Ice-ages had passed by and over her,
But these, for all their motion, had but sheared
Her spotty carboniferous hair or made
Her ridges stand out like the spikes of moloche.
Her back grown stronger every million years,
She had shed water by the longer rivers
To Hudson Bay and by the shorter streams
To the great basins to the south, had filled
Them up, would keep them filled until the end
Of Time.

        Was this the thing Van Horne set out
To conquer? When Superior lay there
With its inviting levels? Blake, Mackenzie,
Offered this water like a postulate.
"Why those twelve thousand men sent to the North?
Nonsense and waste with utter bankruptcy."
And the Laurentian monster at the first
Was undisturbed, presenting but her bulk
To the invasion. All she had to do
Was lie there neither yielding nor resisting.
Top-heavy with accumulated power
And overgrown survival without function,
She changed her spots as though brute rudiments

Of feeling foreign to her native hour
Surprised her with a sense of violation
From an existence other than her own —
Or why take notice of this unknown breed,
This horde of bipeds that could toil like ants,
Could wake her up and keep her irritated?
They tickled her with shovels, dug pickaxes
Into her scales and got under her skin,
And potted holes in her with drills and filled
Them up with what looked like fine grains of sand,
Black sand. It wasn't noise that bothered her,
For thunder she was used to from her cradle —
The head-push and nose-blowing of the ice,
The height and pressure of its body: these
Like winds native to clime and habitat
Had served only to lull her drowsing coils.
It was not size or numbers that concerned her.
It was their foreign build, their gait of movement.
They did not crawl — nor were they born with wings.
They stood upright and walked, shouted and sang;
They needed air — that much was true — their mouths
Were open but the tongue was alien.
The sounds were not the voice of winds and waters,
Nor that of any beasts upon the earth.
She took them first with lethargy, suffered
The rubbing of her back — those little jabs
Of steel were like the burrowing of ticks
In an elk's hide needing an antler point,
Or else left in a numb monotony.
These she could stand but when the breed
Advanced west on her higher vertebrae,
Kicking most insolently at her ribs,
Pouring black powder in her cavities,
And making not the clouds but her insides
The home of fire and thunder, then she gave
Them trial of her strength: the trestles tottered;
Abutments, bridges broke; her rivers flooded:
She summoned snow and ice, and then fell back
On the last weapon in her armory —
The first and last — her passive corporal bulk,
To stay or wreck the schedule of Van Horne.

NUMBER THREE

The big one was the mountains — seas indeed!
With crests whiter than foam: they poured like seas,
Fluting the green banks of the pines and spruces.
An eagle-flight above they hid themselves
In clouds. They carried space upon their ledges.

Could these be overidden frontally,
Or like typhoons outsmarted on the flanks?
And what were on the flanks? The troughs and canyons,
Passes more dangerous to the navigator
Than to Magellan when he tried to read
The barbarous language of his Strait by calling
For echoes from the rocky hieroglyphs
Playing their pranks of hide-and-seek in fog:
As stubborn too as the old North-West Passage,
More difficult, for ice-packs could break up;
And as for bergs, what polar architect
Could stretch his compass points to draught such peaks
As kept on rising there beyond the foothills?
And should the bastions of the Rockies yield
To this new human and unnatural foe,
Would not the Selkirks stand? This was a range
That looked like some strange dread outside a door
Which gave its name but would not show its features,
Leaving them to the mind to guess at. This
Meant tunnels — would there be no end to boring?
There must be some day. Fleming and his men
Had nosed their paths like hounds; but paths and trails,
Measured in every inch by chain and transit,
Looked easy and seductive on a chart.
The rivers out there did not flow: they tumbled.
The cataracts were fed by glaciers;
Eddies were thought as whirlpools in the Gorges,
And gradients had paws that tore up tracks.

Terror and beauty like twin signal flags
Flew on the peaks for men to keep their distance.
The two combined as in a storm at sea —
"Stay on the shore and take your fill of breathing,
But come not to the decks and climb the rigging."
The Ranges could put cramps in hands and feet
Merely by the suggestion of the venture.
They needed miles to render up their beauty,
As if the gods in high aesthetic moments,
Resenting the profanity of touch,
Chiselled this sculpture for the eye alone. . . .

INTERNECINE STRIFE

The men were fighting foes which had themselves
Waged elemental civil wars and still
Were hammering one another at this moment.
The peaks and ranges flung from ocean beds
Had wakened up one geologic morning

To find their scalps raked off, their lips punched in,
The color of their skins charged' with new dyes.
Some of them did not wake or but half-woke;
Prone or recumbent with the eerie shapes
Of creatures that would follow them. Weather
Had acted on their spines and frozen them
To stegosaurs or, taking longer cycles,
Divining human features, had blown back
Their hair and, pressing on their cheeks and temples,
Bestowed on them the gravity of mummies.
But there was life and power which belied
The tombs. Guerilla evergreens were climbing
In military order: at the base
The *ponderosa* pine; the fir backed up
The spruce; and it the Stoney Indian lodge-poles;
And these the white-barks; then, deciduous,
The outpost suicidal Lyell larches
Aiming at summits, digging scraggy roots
Around the boulders in the thinning soil,
Till they were stopped dead at the timber limit —
Rock *versus* forest with the rock prevailing.

Or with the summer warmth it was the ice,
In treaty with the rock to hold a line
As stubborn as a Balkan boundary,
That left its caves to score the Douglases,
And smother them with half a mile of dirt,
And making snow-sheds, covering the camps,
Futile as parasols in polar storms.
One enemy alone had battled rock
And triumphed: searching levels like lost broods,
Keen on their ocean scent, the rivers cut
The quartzite, licked the slate and softened it,
Till mud solidified was mud again,
And then, digesting it like earthworms, squirmed
Along the furrows with one steering urge —
To navigate the mountains in due time
Back to their home in worm-casts on the tides.

Into this scrimmage came the fighting men,
And all but rivers were their enemies.
Whether alive or dead the bush resisted:
Alive, it must be slain with axe and saw,
If dead, it was in tangle at their feet.
The ice could hit men as it hit the spruces.
Even the rivers had betraying tricks,
Watched like professed allies across a border.

They smiled from fertile plains and easy runs
Of valley gradients: their eyes got narrow,
Full of suspicion at the gorges where
They leaped and put the rickets in the trestles.
Though natively in conflict with the rock,
Both leagued against invasion. At Hell's Gate
A mountain labored and brought forth a bull
Which, stranded in mid-stream, was fighting back
The river, and the fight turned on the men,
Demanding from this route their bread and steel.
And there below the Gate was the Black Canyon
With twenty-miles-an-hour burst of speed.

(ONDERDONK BUILDS THE "SKUZZY"
TO FORCE THE PASSAGE.)

'Twas more than navigation: only eagles
Might follow up this run; the spawning salmon
Gulled by the mill-race had returned to rot
Their upturned bellies in the canyon eddies.
Two engines at the stern, a forrard winch,
Steam-powered, failed to stem the cataract.
The last resource was shoulders, arms and hands.
Fifteen men at the capstan, creaking hawsers,
Two hundred Chinese tugging at shore ropes
To keep her bow-on from the broadside drift,
The *Skuzzy* under steam and muscle took
The shoals and rapids, and warped through the Gate,
Until she reached the navigable water —
The adventure was not sailing: it was climbing.

As hard a challenge were the precipices
Worn water-smooth and sheer a thousand feet.
Surveyors from the edges looked for footholds,
But, finding none, they tried marine maneuvres.
Out of a hundred men they drafted sailors
Whose toes as supple as their fingers knew
The wash of reeling decks, whose knees were hardened
Through tying gaskets at the royal yards:
They lowered them with knotted ropes and drew them
Along the face until the lines were strung
Between the juts. Barefooted, dynamite
Strapped to their waists, the sappers followed, treading
The spider films and chipping holes for blasts,
Until the cliffs delivered up their features
Under the civil discipline of roads.

.   .   .

—1952

245

Let the mind rest awhile, lower the eyes,
Relieve the spirit of its Faustian clamor:
An atom holds more secrets than the skies;
Be patient with the earth and do not cram her

With seed beyond the wisdom of her soil.
She knows the foot and hoof of man and ox,
She learned the variations of their toil —
The ploughshare's sensitivity to rocks.

Gather the stones for field and garden walls,
Build cellars for your vegetable stores,
Forgo the architecture of your halls,
Until your hands have fashioned stable doors.

She likes the smell of nitrates from the stalls,
She hates a disciplined tread, the scorching roar
At the grain's roots: she is nervous at the calls
Of men in panic at a strike of ore.

Patient she is in her flesh servitude,
Tolerant to curry ticklings of the harrow,
But do not scratch past her agrarian mood
To cut the calcium in her bone and marrow.

Hold that synthetic seed, for underneath
Deep down she'll answer to your horticulture:
She has a way of germinating teeth
And yielding crops of carrion for the vulture.

—1958

ETHEL WILSON

(1888-   )

Ethel Davis (Bryant) Wilson was born in Port Elizabeth, South Africa, the daughter of a Methodist missionary. Most of her early childhood, however, was spent in England. Both of her parents died before she was eight years old, and in 1898 she was brought to Canada to live with relatives in Vancouver. Four years of schooling there were followed by four more at a boarding school in England. Achieving her London Matriculation at seventeen, she returned to Vancouver, attended Normal School, and became a teacher. In 1920 she married Dr. Wallace Wilson, a distinguished physician. Mrs. Wilson has been honored with the degree of Doctor of Letters from the University of British Columbia (1955), the Canada Council Medal (1961), and the Lorne Pierce Medal (1964).

The first of her writing to appear in print was a short story in the New Statesman and Nation *(December 4, 1937), republished the following year in E. J. O'Brien's* Best British Short Stories *(1938). Two other stories appeared in 1939, but with the onset of war she turned most of her available time to the editing of a Red Cross magazine. Only after the war ended did her career as author really become established. Her first book was a novel,* Hetty Dorval *(1947). This has been followed by five other books, including a collection of her short stories,* Mrs. Golightly and Other Stories *(1961).*

A DRINK WITH ADOLPHUS

"Well I can't do both," said Anne Gormley. "If I go with you I can't go to the Moxons' " ("What you mean is you can't go with that Thibeaudeau boy to the Moxons'," said her mother) "and if I don't go with you I *can* go with Tibby and I like going to the Moxons' and it *is* a party and it'll go on and on the way I like it. I'm sorry of course," said the beautiful girl shaking back her hair, "that you'll have to take a taxi but I do hate that kind of party that goes home at seven, sheer waste, and you know that's when you'll want to come home because you're scared of being late for dinner — you darling darling," she said, almost surrounding her mother with sudden cajoling love, "we like different parties. Okay by you?"

"I suppose so but this isn't a party. It's just us." And, as so often, she stopped herself saying out loud to her youngest child, "I'd like you to have been brought up in my generation, my young lass, just for about two years."

"I'll order your taxi for you."

"Not yet," said Mrs. Gormley who was lame and had to do her hair and make the best of herself and go downstairs rather slowly.

"Oh why do you go!" said Anne, her affection smiting her a little. "You don't *haf*to!"

"Yes," said her mother at the mirror, "that's three Saturdays now. I do have to. It's just us. To see the view. The house is old but he's mad about the view on Capitol hill. That's why Adolphus bought it. I can't *not* go and your father'll be delighted not to have to."

Before walking downstairs, crabwise, Mrs. Gormley looked in on her husband but there was nothing to see except a great lump in the bed. "I'm going to have a drink with Old Adolphus. Goodbye Hamish," she said, but only a muffled sound came from the bed. In the hall she met Ah Sing the cook.

"I takem hot lum Mister Doctor," said Ah Sing. "I fixem he cold."

"Yes do, Ah Sing," said Mrs. Gormley in the rather effusive way that she had the habit of employing to the Chinese cook whom she and the children had loved, feared, and placated for twenty years.

The taxi, proceeding eastwards, sped through mean streets and then began to climb. Mrs. Gormley looked towards the north at the salt waters of the inlet, gently snoring against the foot of the hill. The thought of going all this way to have a drink with Adolphus bored her and the fact of paying for a taxi both ways bored her still more; but she would enjoy the view. Adolphus was not a friend by selection, rather by happening. He was the kind of person that she had known, fortuitously, for so many years that he was designated "friend." They had lived near each other in childhood and Dolly had played with her big brothers and had survived to be called Adolphus. That was all. Therefore Mrs. Gormley was bored in anticipation and it was expecting too much of Hamish who had not been brought up with Dolly Bond to want to spend one of his precious Saturday afternoons admiring Dolly's new house. Now that the years spun faster and faster, Saturdays came hurtling towards Mrs. Gormley like apples thrown. She was still a fool for optimism and thought each week (after all these years with the children), But next Saturday Hamish and I will really "do" something, even if it's only staying at home. But come Saturday, and Hamish would say "I may be late home from the hospital and then I have some calls to make." He would arrive home late for dinner (he — the only one permitted by Ah Sing) and Saturday spun past them again without even being seen.

"Please stop," said Mrs. Gormley to the taxi-man, "and I'll have ten cents' worth of view."

The view was certainly superb and worth more than ten cents. She looked down the slope at the configuration of the inlet and on the wooded shores which now were broken by dwellings, by sawmills, by small wharves, by squatters' houseboats that were not supposed to be there, by many little tugs and fishboats moored and moving with vees of water in their wakes. But her eyes left the shores and looked down across the inlet, shimmering like silk with crawling waves where the tidal currents through the Second Narrows disturbed the waters. She looked farther on to where the dark park lay, dark green and black with pines and cedars against the bright skies of coming evening, at the ocean and islands beyond (so high she was above the scene), and across at the great escarpment of mountains still white with winter's snow. In ten cents' worth of time, she thought—and she was very happy islanded, lost, alone in this sight — there's nearly all the glory of the world and no despair, and then she told the taxi-man to drive on.

Adolphus Bond's new house was nice and rather shabby but, Mrs. Gormley told herself, it was a credit to Adolphus and it had something that these flat caricatures of houses hadn't got, although their insides were charming. The taxi arrived, and she was greeted by Adolphus and other sounds.

"It's so good of you to come," said Adolphus kindly as he helped her out of the car.

"So sorry about Hamish," said Mrs. Gormley at the same moment, stepping down not gracefully but with care.

"Too bad you had to get a taxi, someone would have fetched you," said Adolphus, kindest of men.

"You see it came on so suddenly," said Mrs. Gormley simultaneously. "One moment no cold, the next moment the worst cold you ever saw in your life but as usual he refuses inhalations. Ah Sing is giving him a hot rum and lemon and butter and honey, good enough to make anyone have a cold on purpose," but Adolphus did not hear. Neither of them listened to the other.

"This is the cupboard," he said. "Let me."

"I see you have a party," said Mrs. Gormley, "I thought it was just us. If I'd known I'd have worn a smarter dress. In honor of the new house. Who have you?"

"Oh, some people," said Adolphus vaguely. "So I see," she said, for how could it be otherwise; but Adolphus was steering her towards wide and wide-open doors and then across a room towards a fine long and deep window which intimated a sloping lawn, a fir tree perhaps, and some lovely scene beyond. "This is the library," he said although nothing corroborated the statement.

Sounds of voices came from all around. Guests had scattered, and some had gone out of the french windows on to the lawn, adding to and subtracting from the view. Mrs. Gormley felt herself seized round the waist from behind. Two hands clasped themselves in front of her and a man's voice said (breath fanning

248

the back of her neck), "At last, little one, at last! At last I have you!"

"Well really! How unfamiliar!" said Mrs. Gormley, wishing she were still slender, "this is very pleasant but who do you suppose it is ? Is there some mistake ?"

"Pay no attention. He's been to a wedding," murmured Adolphus rather crossly in her ear. Mrs. Gormley stood still and tried to avoid falling over backwards upon the person to whose body she was firmly clamped in an unusual manner.

"Perhaps if you'd tell me——" she began, unable to do anything about it.

"This is the view, you see," said Adolphus frowning at the view.

"Yes but ——" said Mrs. Gormley perceiving that she was now unclasped. A tall slight fair man in a gray suit stood in front of her.

"Jonathan Pascoe——" remarked Adolphus, —— "you see how the garden slopes away, affording ——"

"How do you do Mr. Pascoe —— Yes I do see, Dolly, and what trees!"

"At last we have met!" said the man in the gray suit, indicating something somewhere with his long hands and smiling gently.

"But I have never seen you before!" said Mrs. Gormley.

"Neither have I," said the wedding guest and was no longer there. Adolphus explained the view.

"It is beautiful, beautiful, but I should like to sit down somewhere," said Mrs. Gormley and Adolphus led her back into the centre of the room and to a large high chair from which she could see out of the window. A black poodle dog, walking on his hind legs, pushed past them, strode down the library, out of the french windows, and disappeared.

"What a peculiar thing for a dog to do! I didn't know you had a dog, or whose dog is it ?" she asked.

"What dog," said Adolphus, "this is Mr. Leaper."

"How do you do," said Mrs. Gormley and was surprised when Mr. Leaper said he was well, He's very literal, she thought. She sat down upon the high comfortable chair and looked around her. The wedding guest was not among the vivacious strangers in the room which though solid enough had a dream-like irrelevance. The large black rims of Mr. Leaper's glasses intimidated her.

"I have just been in Spain and my wife has been in Portugal," he said.

"Have you a dog ?" asked Mrs. Gormley and Mr. Leaper said, "We used to have a monkey but it stole and we became involved in legal difficulties." Someone put a glass in her hand. Adolphus was fulfilling his duties elsewhere.

A young man who had the appearance of a hired waiter stood in front of her. On the tray were familiar-looking pieces of colored food that she had seen somewhere before and some small spheres unfamiliar in appearance but, it seemed, edible.

"What are these do you suppose ?" asked Mrs. Gormley tentatively. The young man became suffused by a dark spreading blush.

"I think," he said, speaking very low, "I heard some person call them hot ovaries."

"Did you really say hot ovaries ?" said Mrs. Gormley very much interested and looking at him affectionately because he was so young, so awkward, blushing there. "Uh-huh," said the young waiter who was some mother's son.

"I wouldn't if I were you," said Mr. Leaper as if to a child. "When we were in Spain ——"

"Parmee parmee" said a maid with a tray, pushing between them.

"What does she mean — 'parmee' ?" asked Mr. Leaper.

"I think she means 'pardon me,' " said Mrs. Gormley. "You were saying when you were in Spain ?"

"We had too many eggs.".

"I thought so too," she said, "but" (warmly) "there are compensations — what about the El Grecos ?"

"We never had any of those," said Mr. Leaper gloomily. "Of that I am sure, as I noted down our meals very carefully in my diary."

"In your diary ?" enquired Mrs. Gormley. "What else do you write in your diary ?"

"I write my personal reflections and impressions," said Mr. Leaper looking very queer.

"Do you mean after a party like this ? How alarming."

Mr. Leaper looked at her intently through his black-rimmed glasses and Mrs. Gormley felt uneasy. From the next room came shrieks of laughter.

"Parmee parmee," said the maid, pushing back again. There was Adolphus, looking engagingly kind. He brought up a nut-brown girl, a sad man, and a young friend of Mrs. Gormley's with a dark beard. Beards are usually dark, she thought, why. They do not even know they have legs, these people, she thought with a pang, smiling at them. They do not know how pleasant it is at a party to move, move on, move on, negotiate yourself elsewhere, get away from Mr. Leaper who does not like eggs in Spain and will write about us in his diary, give him a chance poor thing. "I am going to show them the house," said Adolphus.

"Oh do!" said Mrs. Gormley in her gushing way, and Adolphus, the nut-brown girl, the sad young man, and the young man with the beard went to look at the house. Mrs. Gormley and Mr. Leaper began to talk in earnest about Spain and the prices there. God, thought Mrs. Gormley, what would I give to have Hamish's cold, "—— but cheaper still in Portugal!" she said, smiling, mustering pleasure and charm if any.

Evening had really fallen now. People had drifted away, to look at the house, to fill their glasses again in the dining-room, and wasn't the drawing-room full of music or something ? The maid stood at the library door and threw a quick glance into the nearly empty room. Then she turned away. Mrs. Gormley, talking to Mr. Leaper, looked beyond him through the long windows unobscured now by people, on to the garden which was only faintly green in the twilight. A pale moon hung high, and upon the inlet the moonlight fell, and fell upon the garden, casting still faint shadows from a great cedar tree. The garden and the moonlight and the cedar shadows were made to walk in, but Mrs. Gormley, continuing to sit, continued also to fabricate things like "the Savoy —— Dorchester —— a quite humble little place on Ebury Street —— Claridge's" (how snob can we get, talking like this, impressing each other but probably not. I sound as if Hamish and I stayed in these places, and she mimicked herself "a quite humble little place"). In the garden something moved. It could not be a large moth, but like a large moth the wedding guest danced all alone under the moon. His gray flannel arms rose and fell again. Perhaps he was flying. He advanced, flapping his arms in the haunted mystical evening, he retreated, stepping high and slowly below the cedar tree. How beautiful he was and he must have been happy. Mrs. Gormley longed to be out there dancing with the free slowly dancing wedding guest. She longed it until (sitting there smiling, with immobile hips and legs) she nearly burst, but she did not say to Mr. Leaper, "Look, there is Jonathan Pascoe whoever he is dancing in the scented moonlight like a large gray flannel moth." She could not share the wedding guest (whom she loved to see dancing under the moon) with Mr. Leaper. As she turned to agree that one could not do better than a good small hotel she saw that the young man with a beard had come to sit as if exhausted in a large chair opposite.

"Where's Anne, I suppose she wouldn't come. Your dog bit me," he said morosely.

"It's not my dog whose dog is it?" said Mrs. Gormley, "you know I haven't got a dog, Ozzie!"

"I think the government will be out in six weeks," he said, "and serve them right."

"Oh why do you think that? Whatever makes you think that?" she asked eagerly but he looked suspicious and did not answer.

"Let me fill your glass," said Mr. Leaper and did not return. Mrs. Gormley and the young man with a beard sat at peace and looked for some time at the very good carpet. She raised her head and saw that Jonathan Pascoe was leaning against the doorway.

"Little one," he said, "you are so beautiful, may I kiss you?"

"Yes, please do," said Mrs. Gormley laughing, "I need a kiss badly. I think it would do me good. How did the moonlight feel? And then will you get me a taxi. I want to go home."

11

Upon his return home from Mr. Bond's party, Mr. Leaper did not write in his diary as usual. He was agitated. Perhaps some part of his thin protective covering had been abrased, split, broken. However, a few nights later, he wrote:

"As you know, I make it a rule to write up my diary just before retiring at night. Mabel knows this and respects my privacy for a time which varies from a few minutes (I make registers of the seasons, bursting of buds, etc.) to quite a protracted period, even an hour. She then knocks and says in that clear voice of hers Beddy-byes and I bring my writing to a conclusion, that is, I stop writing. I hesitate to commit to paper the effect of that word Beddy-byes (which I even find it difficult to write) upon me. There may have been a time when it did not cause me to wince, but I do not remember. I cannot bring myself to tell Mabel (for whom I have such a regard) to say something else, nor can I be unmoved by it. I have no doubt that in the larger things of life Religion is a great comfort, but I do not think that Religion provides an answer in a relatively small matter like this. However.

"Some years ago Mabel gave me a nicely bound book with the specially embossed words Diary — S. B. Leaper upon the cover. Although I appreciated the gift, it has not been useful, as I find a pad of typing paper easier on the whole. The book had a feeling of permanence which did not put me at my ease, and I found that I could not cross out what I had written without a sensation of waste.

"Last night I was in a disturbed frame of mind owing to an unpleasant experience on the previous evening and I did not write my diary. However, tonight I have adjusted my feelings somewhat and will record the evening party which Mabel and I attended, given by my friend Mr. Adolphus Bond, one of the kindest of men. When I say 'my friend,' perhaps I overstep and should rather say acquaintance. A cousin of mine married a cousin of his who has since passed away.

"Mr. Bond lives in a charming house complete with garden. He is a bachelor of many interests and has a wide and scattered social and business acquaintance and so Mabel and I did not see many familiar faces. In fact none. Mr. Bond, a genial host, introduced me to a young man with a dark beard whose name seemed to be Ozzie who was talking to a handsome lively girl. I did not hear Ozzie's other name but I thought I heard Mr. Bond say before he left us that he was a nephew of the Leader of the House. I was going to say by way of joke What House? because I had noticed in the telephone book that very day the House of Liqueurs, the House of Charm, the House of Drapes, and the House of Sport but decided not to. Although I make it a rule never to bring up the subjects of politics and religion in strange company, it seemed safe to refer to my satisfaction at the recent elections, with a passing reference to the young man's uncle Mr. Robertshaw. The young man Ozzie became almost violent and referred to his uncle's party as a lot of bloody fools. I was silent, but the girl was amused and laughed heartily. It seems that Ozzie is an artist which one might have suspected from his beard, but as Mabel says, that is no proof.

"There was a slight lull in the conversation and turning to the window I remarked on the lengthening of the days. I said that I made the practice of recording the position of the sun in my diary. The young man Ozzie said, very rudely I thought, 'Your *what?* Do you mean you write a diary?'

"I said, 'Certainly I write a diary,' whereupon he said, 'If I can believe that I can believe anything.' Silence fell and then the girl said, 'Ozzie you great oaf some day somebody's going to hit you. You'd better apologize,' and Ozzie said to me, 'I beg your pardon. I had no business to say that but I never met anyone who wrote a diary before.'

"I received his apology as best I could and as I heard Mabel's clear voice ringing out from the neighboring room I thought I would join her. I smiled and withdrew but I must confess that I was shaken as I had always regarded the writing of a diary as a natural affair and apparently there are some people who find it strange. The uncomfortable feeling of not resembling other people persisted with me and that is one reason why I did not feel in the mood for writing yesterday.

"Before I reached the door I was stopped by my host who had on his arm an elderly woman who appeared to be lame, by the name I think of Gormley or Gormer. He introduced us and found her a chair and we were left together. Thinking the matter over later, I came to the conclusion that Mr. Bond, unintentionally no doubt, had left me — as Mabel sometimes says — holding the bag, for owing to Mrs. Gormley's lameness a certain sense of 'noblesse oblige' made me spend most of the rest of the time at the party conversing with her. I did not find her an interesting woman and Mabel remarked afterwards that I seemed embittered at the close of the evening.

"In an endeavor to avoid inflammable subjects I told this Mrs. Gormley that we had recently been in Spain. That conversational opening usually promotes lively response. People either wish to go to Spain or they have been in Spain, and a certain enthusiasm follows. Mrs. Gormley's only response was to make some enquiry about a dog. I saw at once that she must be a very unintelligent woman. I mentioned the monkey Chiko which we had some years ago but did not go further as Chiko led us into very unfortunate legal proceedings. I well remember that we had to give Chiko to the Monkey House in Stanley Park. Mabel and I have often remarked that when we went to visit Chiko there, it was impossible to distinguish him from the other monkeys. They all seemed to have the same anxious expression and a similarity of feature. I did not tell Mrs. Gormer anything further.

"An embarrassing moment occurred at once. Owing to the strike among waiters, all available experienced waiters are employed in the various hotels and restaurants and very few can be found for private parties. This accounts, I think, for the young hobbledehoy who served us at Mr. Adolphus Bond's party. When this Mrs. Gormer asked him (very rudely, I thought) what certain of the hors d'oeuvres contained, he said he did not know but thought they were hot ovaries. Mrs. Gormer seemed very much amused at this, but that shows the kind of woman she is.

"We then had a long conversation on foreign travel. I said that in Spain we had too many eggs and she said Yes, but what about the el grecos. I had to admit that we did not have any. We then spoke about hotel accommodation. While I was telling her my impressions of the hotels in London she looked past me and at the windows behind my head, looking into the garden. I would, at any other time, have thought she was in a trance, but she responded with moderate intelligence to my remarks. I think it must be a bad habit of hers and I must say it is very disagreeable.

"We were just discussing the Royal York Hotel in Toronto when the young man Ozzie entered the room. He flung himself down in a large chair opposite us and appeared quite exhausted. He too said something about a dog. I did not stay to enquire but gladly made this an opportunity to leave on the pretext of bringing Mrs. Gormer another drink. When I arrived at the bar which had been set up in the dining-room I saw Mabel leaning against the bar surrounded by other people, and talking very loudly. I was instantly alarmed, remembering that occasion in Winnipeg. She saw me and shouted 'Hi!' (a greeting I particularly dislike) and went on laughing and talking. I did not join them but filled Mrs. Gormer's glass and my own. I drank my own and then decided to have a refill. I then carried Mrs. Gormer's glass and my own back to the library. I stopped at the door because it was partially blocked by a tall thin man in a gray suit who spoke the following words to someone in the room: 'Little one, little one, you are so beautiful, may I kiss you?'

"I looked under the extended arm of the man in gray, taking care not to spill the drinks, in order to see whom he might be addressing, but only Mrs. Gormer looking different and the man called Ozzie were in the room. The remark of the man in the gray suit then seemed unintelligible as Mrs. Gormer is far from beautiful but he may not have been quite sober.

"What was my surprise to hear this Mrs. Gormer thereupon urge the man in gray to kiss her which he did with, I must say, considerable respect, but without passion which was understandable. She made the plea that she needed a kiss. I found the whole episode quite incomprehensible. I decided to drink Mrs. Gormer's whiskey as well as my own — did not re-enter the room but returned to the bar.

"On the way home I have never known Mabel so outrageous except on that occasion in Winnipeg. She called me a sourpuss and used other terms which I shall never be able to forget. I went so far as to say that a little attention always goes to her head which seemed to annoy her excessively. She was driving the car and I must confess that some very strange thoughts came into my mind. You can imagine that on our arrival at home I was in no condition to write my diary. I sometimes think that whereas some people are born to joy, I was born to sorrow.

"This morning I purchased a small safe and brought it home. I told Mabel that I had been asked to keep some of the Firm's papers in a safe in our house. I shall also keep my diary there which permits me the freedom of expression that I sometimes require but which in daily life I seem unable to enjoy. A man must have a friend even if it is only himself.

"Before I stop, I will mention an item in the paper that has touched and moved me very much tonight. A man in Illinois or is it Iowa is undergoing trial for the murder of his wife. The thing that impressed me was that he and his wife had seemed to live a devoted and harmonious life together."

"I must have another party," said Adolphus, busy with his lists.

—1961

PAUL HIEBERT

(1892-   )

Paul Gerhardt Hiebert was born in Pilot Mound, Manitoba. He was educated at the Universities of Manitoba (B.A. in Philosophy, 1916), Toronto (M.A. in German, 1917), and McGill (M.Sc., 1923; Ph.D. in Chemistry, 1924). From 1924 to 1953 he taught in the Department of Chemistry of the University of Manitoba. He retired to Carman, Manitoba.

In 1947 Hiebert published the "full-length portrait" of a fictitious prairie poetess, Sarah Binks. In it he satirized the pretensions of Canadian poetasters and their heavy-handed supporters. Numerous examples of what purported to be Sarah's verse were included in the volume. Sarah Binks was awarded the 1947 Leacock Medal for Humour. Twenty years later, Willows Revisited *was published as a kind of sequel, continuing Hiebert's deadpan exposure of inflated poets, inept critics, pretentious politicians, and cultural hangers-on.*

Sarah Binks, the Sweet Songstress of Saskatchewan, as she is often called, no longer needs any introduction to her ever-growing list of admirers. In fact, it may be asked why another book should be added to the already voluminous and continually growing literature which deals with the work of this great Canadian. We already know about her life—we know about her tragic death. We know about her early struggles for recognition and her rise to fame. We know about the honors that were showered upon her, culminating finally in that highest award in the bestowal of the Saskatchewan people, the Wheat Pool Medal. But what is not known, or at least what is so often overlooked, is that quite apart from the Saskatchewan for which Sarah speaks, she was pre-eminently a poetess in her own right, that in a life so poor in incident and surrounded on all sides by the pastoral simplicity, if not actual severity, of the Municipality of Willows, she developed a character so rich and a personality so winsome and diverse. There is, too, a profound personal philosophy, which speaks to us quite apart from the sweep and beauty of the prairies with which she is associated. It is this theme which the Author has developed. It definitely strikes a new note.

From Shakespeare's "England, my England," to a Saskatchewan wheat farm may seem to be a far cry. But that same patriotism, that same confidence and joy in his native land which is the heritage of all poets, is also Sarah's. And when she cries out in a sudden awareness of her own gumbo stretch, "The Farmer is King!" or when she sings in full throat, "The Song of the Chore," or hymns the joy of "Spreading Time," or discusses with deep understanding but with impersonal detachment, as in "To My Father, Jacob Binks," the fine economic adjustment between the farmer and the cutworm, we know that she speaks for the Canadian West in the language of all poets at all times. It is this which has given her the high place in the world of literature and in the hearts of her countrymen.

But there is much more to Sarah Binks than being the Laureate of Saskatchewan. Sarah was not only the expression of her day and age, she was also the product of her immediate environment. She was the product of her friends, of her books, and of the little incidents which shaped her life. She was the product of the Grade School, of her neighbors, of Mathilda Schwantzhacker, of Ole the hired man, of her grandfather the philosophical herbalist, of William Greenglow who taught her Geology, of Henry Welkin who took her to Regina. From all of these Sarah emerges as a character, as a personality, and, above all, as a woman.

It has been no light task to gather together the many threads of personal and literary influence and to reconstruct from them, as in fine needlepoint, a truer, more intimate picture of Sarah Binks than we have hitherto known. Sarah, on the larger canvas, as a national figure, loses nothing thereby. But for those who like to look beyond the poetry to the poetess, for those who would see beyond the high achievement the unfolding and blossoming of the poetic spirit, this new life of Sarah Binks has been written.

There is an age in Western Canada which is fast disappearing before our very eyes: an age which began with the turn of the century and lasted at its best about thirty years. Sarah's dates, 1906 to 1929, practically define it. They were the halcyon days of Western Canada, the golden days of the dirt farmer. It was an age sandwiched between the romantic West of the "cow country" and the West of drought and relief and economic experiment. It was a prosperous age for Saskatchewan, and such periods of prosperity and commercial expansion are always accompanied by literary and artistic blossoming. On a small scale the Golden Age of Pericles in Greece, or the Elizabethan age of England, finds its counterpart in Canada's fairest and flattest province. Already in brief historical perspective that age is beginning to take on an aura of romance. Sarah Binks was its artistic expression.

Those most productive years of Sarah's also mark the high-water mark of Saskatchewan's prosperity. The price of wheat rose to fabulous heights; clean eggs, not over three days old, sold in the general stores at prices ranging all the way from twenty to twenty-six cents a dozen, whilst at the Willows and Quagmire elevators the classifications of both screenings and Durum, No. 4, Smutty, were raised to No. 3, Smutty. Liver also showed signs of a rise.

To the west the frontier had been rolled back; the tumbleweed had yielded to the sow-thistle, the coyote had vanished from the plains, and with the disappearance of these great herds, his last source of Vitamin B gone, disappeared also the prairie Indian, a proud and picturesque figure in overalls and plug hat—swept away before the ruthless march of civilization. The land was open for wheat. No economic cloud marked the Saskatchewan horizon; mortgage money could be had at any time for twelve per cent, and the dry belt, which years later was to creep north and eastwards over a country already desiccated by prohibition laws, still lay in the heart of the Great American desert.

It is claimed by some writers that Sarah Binks sprang spontaneously from Saskatchewan's alkaline soil, that she was an isolated genius such as the ages have produced from time to time with no significance beyond her unparalleled talent. With this view the Author takes exception. Sarah Binks was the product of her soil and her roots go deep. But more than that, she was an expression of her environment and her age. Without Saskatchewan at its greatest, at its golden age, Sarah would have been just another poetess. Sarah was the daughter and the grand-daughter of a dirt farmer; she loved the soil and much of Jacob Binks' passion for another quarter section flowed in her veins. Her love for the paternal acres was a real love, she believed in the rotation of crops, and in the fall, after the plowing was done, she spread the fertilizer with a lavish hand. "The farmer is king!" she cries,

> The farmer is king of his packer and plow,
> Of his harrows and binders and breakers,
> He is lord of the pig, and Czar of the cow
> On his hundred and sixty-odd acres.

> The farmer is monarch in high estate,
> Of his barn and his back-house and byre,
> And all the buildings behind the gate
> Of his two-odd miles of barbed wire.

> The farmer is even Caesar of freight
> And tariff and tax, comes election,
> And from then until then he can abdicate,
> And be king on his own quarter section.

256

The farmer is king, oh, the farmer is king,
And except for his wife and his daughter,
Who boss him around, he runs the thing,
Come drought, come hell, or high water.

It is significant, too, that Sarah Binks should have seized upon Warden and Rockbuster's *First Steps in Geology* and made it so singularly her own. Geology to her was the farm extended to the outer world, to the larger life. Any other book at that period of her life would have left her cold. It is undoubtedly true, to quote Principal Pinhole, "If the benign fates which rule the lives of men had passed William Greenglow in Geology II and had given him a supplemental in Maths II instead, Sarah's songs would not have been touched to the same extent. The binomial theorem as I understand it is by no means the same as the theory of crustal movements, and it is just because the one deals with rocks and the other has to do with figures without rocks, that the whole Neo-Geo-Literary school of literature is different by just that much. In fact some other province might have got the credit."

Sarah Binks has raised her home province of Saskatchewan to its highest prairie level. Unschooled, but unspoiled, this simple country girl has captured in her net of poesy the flatness of that great province. Like a sylph she wanders through its bluffs and coulees, across its hay lands, its alkali flats, its gumbo stretches, its gopher meadows:

Hark! Like a mellow fiddle moaning,
Through the reed-grass sighing,
Through a gnarled branch groaning,
Comes the Poet—
Sylph-like,
Gaunt-like,
Poeming—
And his eyes are stars,
And his mouth is foaming.

Thus, Sarah herself, in the divine frenzy. No wonder she is called the Sweet Songstress of Saskatchewan. Indeed she could be called much more. No other poet has so expressed the Saskatchewan soul. No other poet has caught in deathless lines so much of its elusive spirit, the baldness of its prairies, the alkalinity of its soil, the richness of its insect life.

In presenting this new study of the life and works of the Sweet Songstress the Author feels that he is filling a long-felt want. Much has already been written, much more remains to be written, but hitherto no such complete sudy of the life and character of Sarah Binks has been published. The papers which have appeared from time to time have been fragmentary, generally critical studies dealing with one phase of her life or with a group of poems. Special mention must be made of the numerous papers of Horace P. Marrowfat, B.A., Professor Emeritus of English and Swimming, of St. Midget's College; of Dr. Taj Mahal, D.O., of British Columbia; and of the Proceedings of the Ladies' Literary League of Quagmire. These papers and publications have been of especial value in the preparation of this book, and proper acknowledgments have been made wherever it was considered absolutely necessary.

The Author also wishes to express his indebtedness to the recent work, *Great Lives and Great Loves,* by Miss Rosalind Drool, and to the publishers, Bunnybooks Ltd., for permission to quote therefrom. Miss Drool's intense and even introspective searchings into certain phases of Sarah Binks' life have been of great interest, more especially since her own personal offer to pursue further studies "at considerable lengths" has also heightened an interest in Miss Drool.

The great source of material for the student of Sarah Binks is, of course, the Binksian Collection in the Provincial Archives of Saskatchewan. This, together with the letters of Mathilda, has been the supply upon which all other students have hitherto drawn. But much inference has been published as fact. Many of the details of Sarah's life are still vague and have still to be filled in. There is, however, a great wealth of material still unturned and unexploited around Willows, Sarah's birthplace. The Author has not hesitated to make use of this material where it could be published.

It has been the aim of the Author at all times to give a deeper, truer meaning to the poetic heritage which belongs to Sarah, the unspoiled child of the soil. Sarah's lyrical poetry, small as it is in bulk, ranks among the rarest treasures of Canadian literature. The poems which have been included in this work are most of them well known, but no apology need be made for their repetition. Quite apart from their intrinsic beauty, they are significant in that they are expressions of facts and events in her life. Sarah, more than most poets, seizes upon the trivial, or what to lesser souls would appear trivial, incident and experience, for example the loss of Ole's ear by a duck, as an occasion for a lyrical outburst of pulsating beauty. These poems can only be understood within the context of Sarah's life, and free use has therefore been made of them. No one has ever wanted to copyright any of Sarah's poems, and they have therefore been quoted at length—wholly, partly, or just simply quoted.

In addition to the field work done in and around Willows the Author has made a special journey to Quorum, Sask., at which place Mrs. Steve Grizzlykick (Mathilda) was interviewed, and to Vertigo, Manitoba, where Mrs. Pete Cattalo was questioned concerning Ole. Although the actual field data obtained in these investigations cannot be published, they have been of much value in giving atmosphere and in interpreting the scene around Willows and Quagmire during and immediately preceding the time when Sarah wrote *Wash Out on the Line.*

The Author is greatly indebted to the Editor of *The Horsebreeder's Gazette* for the opportunity of going through his files, and also, when he was out to lunch, his desk. Much interesting information was available there.

In the case of the Editor of *Swine and Kine* no files had been kept, but permission was given to interview the secretary and later on to take her out to the local dance. The information here was exceptionally good.

The Author in particular wishes to express his indebtedness to the Quagmire Malting and Brewing Company for much of the material embodied in this book, and to the Dominion Distillers, Limited, who so kindly read the proofs.

—1947

F. R. SCOTT

(1899-   )

Francis Reginald Scott was born in Quebec City, the son of Archdeacon Frederick George Scott, a well-known poet. He received his B.A. from Bishop's College (1919), taught for a time at the Quebec High School and at Bishop's College, and then spent three years at Oxford University on a Rhodes Scholarship. Returning to Canada, he studied láw at McGill University, and in 1927 was called to the Quebec bar. After a year in law practice, he joined the McGill Faculty of Law as a full-time teacher; from 1961-1964 he was Dean of the Faculty. He is now retired. He has received numerous honors, including in 1967 that of Companion of the Order of Canada.

Scott was one of the founders of the League for Social Reconstruction in 1932, and served as C.C.F. National Chairman from 1942 to 1950. In 1952 he was Resident Representative in Burma for the United Nations Technical Assistance Program. In 1963 he was made a member of the Royal Commission on Bilingualism and Bicul-turalism. He has written not only poetry, but also several works concerning law, economics, and international relations, and he has edited or helped to edit such journals as The McGill Fortnightly Review, The Canadian Mercury, Preview, The Canadian Forum, *and* Northern Review.

His earliest poems appeared in The McGill Fortnightly Review *in the mid nineteen-twenties. With A. J. M. Smith he edited* New Provinces: Poems of Several Authors *in 1936, and* The Blasted Pine: An Anthology of Satire, Invective and Disrespectful Verse *in 1957 (2nd. ed. 1967). His own books of poetry are:* Overture *(1945),* Events & Signals *(1954),* The Eye of the Needle *(1957),* Saint-Denys Garneau & Anne Hébert: Translations/traductions *(1963),* Signature *(1964),* Selected Poems *(1966),* Trouvailles *(1967), and* The Dance is One *(1973).*

SURFACES

This rock-bound river, ever flowing
Obedient to the ineluctable laws,
Brings a reminder from the barren north
Of the eternal lifeless processes.
There is an argument that will prevail
In this calm stretch of current, slowly drawn
Toward its final equilibrium.

Come, flaunt the brief prerogative of life,
Dip your small civilized foot in this cold water
And ripple, for a moment, the smooth surface of time.

—1936

THE CANADIAN AUTHORS MEET

Expansive puppets percolate self-unction
Beneath a portrait of the Prince of Wales.
Miss Crotchet's muse has somehow failed to function,
Yet she's a poetess. Beaming, she sails

From group to chattering group, with such a dear
Victorian saintliness, as is her fashion,
Greeting the other unknowns with a cheer —
Virgins of sixty who still write of passion.

The air is heavy with "Canadian" topics,
And Carman, Lampman, Roberts, Campbell, Scott,
Are measured for their faith and philanthropics,
Their zeal for God and King, their earnest thought.

The cakes are sweet, but sweeter is the feeling
That one is mixing with the *literati*;
It warms the old, and melts the most congealing.
Really, it is a most delightful party.

Shall we go round the mulberry bush, or shall
We gather at the river, or shall we
Appoint a poet laureate this Fall,
Or shall we have another cup of tea?

O Canada, O Canada, Oh can
A day go by without new authors springing
To paint the native maple, and to plan
More ways to set the selfsame welkin ringing?

—1936

OVERTURE

In the dark room, under a cone of light
You precisely play the Mozart sonata. The bright
Clear notes fly like sparks through the air
And trace a flickering pattern of music there.

Your hands dart in the light, your fingers flow —
They are ten careful operatives in a row
That pick their packets of sound from steel bars,
Constructing harmonies as sharp as stars.

But how shall I hear old music? This is an hour
Of new beginnings, concepts warring for power,
Decay of systems — the tissue of art is torn
With overtures of an era being born.

And this perfection which is less yourself
Than Mozart, seems a trinket on a shelf,
A pretty octave played before a window
Beyond whose curtain grows a world crescendo.

—1936

MARCH FIELD

Now the old folded snow
Shrinks from black earth.
Now is thrust forth
Heavy and still
The field's dark furrow.

Not yet the flowing
The mound-stirring
Not yet the inevitable flow.

There is a warm wind, stealing
From blunt brown hills, loosening
Sod and cold loam
Round rigid root and stem.

But no seed stirs
In this bare prison
Under the hollow sky.
The stone is not yet rolled away
Nor the body risen.

—1936

VAGRANT

he fled beyond the outer star
to spaces whcrc no systems are

beyond the last accepted norm
the final vestiges of form

the compass of his mind   astute
to find a polar absolute
patrolled a mute circumference

the present seemed the only tense
there was no downwards for his feet
even his lust was obsolete

and he   the last dot in the sky
did but accentuate an i

infinity became his own
liiuiself the sole criterion

now you may see him   virginal
content to live in montreal

—1936

CALVARY

Where crag and loose stone
stand bare to wind and sky
there come armed men. Steel
clangs upon rock, and bone
breaks under nail. They drag
him here to die, whose frail
young body, being human,

born of a man and a woman,
lies so easy to wound.
The tree is planted in ground
barren and dry, and a creed
roots in the cruel mound.

So with the body broken
blood becomes token
eras are stricken.

—1936

OLD SONG

far voices
and fretting leaves
this music the
hillside gives

but in the deep
Laurentian river
an elemental song
for ever

a quiet calling
of no mind
out of long aeons
when dust was blind
and ice hid sound

only a moving
with no note
granite lips
a stone throat

—1945

UNION

Come to me
Not as a river willingly downward falls
To be lost in a wide ocean
But come to me
As flood-tide comes to shore-line
Filling empty bays
With a white stillness
Mating earth and sea.

Union
Exact and complete
Of still separate identities.

—1945

MURAL

When shepherds cease to watch their flocks
And tend instead bacterial stocks;
When farmers learn in chemic schools
To architect the molecules;
When all our food comes fresh and clean
From some unbreakable machine,
And crops are raised in metal trays
Beneath the ultra-violet rays;
When eggs are laid in numbered tens
Without the aid of pregnant hens,
And from the cool assembly-lines
Come wormless fruits and vintaged wines;
When honey drips in plastic cone
With none but a mechanic drone,
And vitamins by legal right
Are bedded in each measured bite;
When clothes are spun from glass and trees
And girls are clad with engine ease,
And men in rockets leave the ground
To fly the pole with single bound;
When ova swell in Huxleyan tubes,
Paternal sperm is sold in cubes,
And babies nuzzle buna taps
As sucklings now the unsterile paps;
When rules of health need not espouse
The ventral processes of cows,
And man is parasite no more
On some less clever herbivore;
When sheep and cattle graze at will

As decorations on the hill,
And all the natural creatures roam
As pets within their zoo-like home;
When by some microscopic means
Genetecists control the genes
And colored skin and crinkly hair
Are choices for each bridal pair;
Then, on the Eden air, shall come
A gentle, low, electric hum,
Apotheosis of the Wheel
That cannot think and cannot feel,
A lingering echo of the strife
That crushed the old pre-technic life.
Then poverty shall be a word
Philologists alone have heard,
The slightest want shall know its fill,
Desire shall culminate in skill.
The carefree lovers shall repair
To halls of air-conditioned air
And tune-in colored symphonies
To prick their elongated bliss.
Man shall arise from dialled feast
Without the slaughter of a beast;
His conscience smooth as metal plate
Shall magnify his stainless state;
His bloodless background shall be blest
With a prolonged, inventive rest.
All violence streamlined into zeal
For one colossal commonweal.

1945

SATURDAY SUNDAE

The triple-decker and the double-cone
I side-swipe swiftly, suck the coke-straws dry.
Ride toadstool seat beside the slab of morgue —
Sweet corner drug-store, sweet pie in the sky.

Him of the front-flap apron, him I sing,
The counter-clockwise clerk in underalls.
Swing low, sweet chocolate, Oh swing, swing,
While cheek by juke the jitter chatter falls.

I swivel on my axle and survey
The latex tintex kotex cutex land.

Soft kingdoms sell for dimes, Life Pic Look Click
Inflate the male with conquest girly grand.

My brothers and my sisters, two by two,
Sit sipping succulence and sighing sex.
Each tiny adolescent universe
A world the vested interests annex.

Such bread and circuses these times allow,
Opium most popular, life so small and slick,
Perhaps with candy is the new world born
And cellophane shall wrap the heretic.

—1945

263

SOCIAL NOTES

Here is a lovely little camp
Built among the Laurentian hills
By a Children's Welfare Society,
Which is entirely supported by voluntary contributions.
All summer long underprivileged children scamper about
And it is astonishing how soon they look happy and well.
Two weeks here in the sun and air
Through the charity of our wealthy citizens
Will be a wonderful help to the little tots
When they return for a winter in the slums.

The efficiency of the capitalist system
Is rightly admired by important people.
Our huge steel mills
Operating at 25% of capacity
Are the last word in organization.
The new grain elevators
Stored with superfluous wheat
Can load a grain-boat in two hours.
Marvellous card-sorting machines
Make it easy to keep track of the unemployed.
There is not one unnecessary worker
In these textile plants
That require a 75% tariff protection.
And when our closed shoe-factories re-open
They will produce more footwear than we can possibly buy.
So don't let us start experimenting with socialism
Which everyone knows means inefficiency and waste.

—*1945*

TRANS CANADA

Pulled from our ruts by the made-to-order gale
We sprang upward into a wider prairie
And dropped Regina below like a pile of bones.

Sky tumbled upon us in waterfalls,
But we were smarter than a Skeena salmon
And shot our silver body over the lip of air
To rest in a pool of space
On the top storey of our adventure.

A solar peace
And a six-way choice.

Clouds, now, are the solid substance,
A floor of wool roughed by the wind
Standing in waves that halt in their fall.
A still of troughs.

The plane, our planet,
Travels on roads that are not seen or laid
But sound in instruments on pilots' ears,
While underneath,

The sure wings
Are the everlasting arms of science.

Man, the lofty worm, tunnels his latest clay,
And bores his new career.

This frontier, too, is ours.
This everywhere whose life can only be led
At the pace of a rocket
Is common to man and man,
And every country below is an I land.

The sun sets on its top shelf,

And stars seem farther from our nearer grasp.

I have sat by night beside a cold lake
And touched things smoother than moonlight
   on still water,
But the moon on this cloud sea is not human,
And here is no shore, no intimacy,
Only the start of space, the road to suns.

—1945

LAST RITES

Inside his tent of pain and oxygen
This man is dying; grave, he mutters prayers,
Stares at the bedside altar through the screens,
Lies still for invocation and for hands.
Priest takes his symbols from a leather bag,
Surplice and stole, the pyx and marks of faith,
And makes a chancel in the ether air.
Nurse too is minister. Tall cylinders,
Her altar-boys, press out rich draughts for lungs
The fluid slowly fills. The trick device
Keeps the worn heart from failing, and bright dials
Flicker their needles as the pressures change
Like eyelids on his eyes. Priest moves in peace,
Part of his other world. Nurse prays with skills
Serving her Lord with rites and acts of love.
Both acolytes are uniformed in white
And wear a holy look, for both are near
The very point and purpose of their art.
Nurse is precise and careful. She will fail
In the end, and lose her battle. Death will block
The channels of her aid, and brush aside
All her exact inventions, leaving priest
Triumphant on his ground. But nurse will stare
This evil in the face, will not accept,
Will come with stranger and more cunning tools
To other bedsides, adding skill to skill
Till death is driven slowly farther back.
How far? She does not ask.
              Priest does not fight.
He lives through death and death is proof of him.
In the perpetual, unanswerable why
Are born the symbol and the sacrifice.
The warring creeds run past the boundary
And stake their claims to heaven; science drives

The boundary back, and claims the living land,
A revelation growing, piece by piece,
Wonder and mystery as true as God.
And I who watch this rightness and these rites,
I see my father in the dying man,
I am his son who dwells upon the earth,
There is a holy spirit in this room,
And straight toward me from both sides of time
Endless the known and unknown roadways run.

—1954

SOCIAL SONNET

II

Take a look at the *Sat Eve Post,*
Get a load of its thick slick ads
That have turned our ancestors into Mums and Dads
And reduced living to the level of making toast.
Have an eyeful of its long slim girls
Selling themselves with lipstick and whiskey and cars
To any man whose distinction is drinking in bars
Using a dictaphone, or buying false pearls.

Hail to the huckster! Knight errant of our time!
Proudly he rides to war for the barons of soap,
Perpetually storming the castles of the home.
This gives our bathrooms a touch of the sublime
So be not discouraged, never give up hope,
And please — no escaping to Moscow or to Rome.

—1954

CARING

Caring is loving, motionless,
An interval of more and less
Between the stress and the distress.

After the present falls the past,
After the festival, the fast.
Always the deepest is the last.

This is the circle we must trace,
Not spiralled outward, but a space
Returning to its starting place.

Centre of all we mourn and bless,
Centre of calm beyond excess,
Who cares for caring, has caress.

—1954

EDEN

Adam stood by a sleeping lion
Feeling its fur with his toes.
He did not hear Eve approaching,
Like a shy fawn she crept close.

The stillness deepened. He turned.
She stood there, too solemn for speech.
He knew that something had happened
Or she never would stay out of reach.

"What is it? What have you found?"
He stared as she held out her hand.
The innocent fruit was shining.
The truth burned like a brand.

"It is good to eat," she said,
"And pleasant to the eyes,
And — this is the reason I took it —
It is going to make us wise!"

She was like that, the beauty,
Always simple and strong.
She was leading him into trouble
But he could not say she was wrong.

Anyway, what could he do?
She'd already eaten it first.
She could not have all the wisdom.
He'd have to eat and be cursed.

So he ate, and their eyes were opened.
In a flash they knew they were nude.
Their ignorant innocence vanished.
Taste began shaping the crude.

This was no Fall, but Creation,
For although the Terrible Voice
Condemned them to sweat and to labor,
They had conquered the power of choice.

Even God was astonished.
"This man is become one of Us.
If he eat of the Tree of Life --- !"
Out they went in a rush.

As the Flaming Sword receded
Eve walked a little ahead.
"If we keep on using this knowledge
I think we'll be back," she said.

—1954

DIAGONALS

LIPS

who   gave   you   yours
taught   more   than
you   surer
lips
never   are
built   just   so
kissing   is   always   certain

HANDS

hammer   in   whose   hands
these   wounded   gods
glittering   fastening
nails
driving   into
arms   open   the
cross   forever   upon   sky

—1964

Rounding a look
Her lightened tips
Tackled my fincy
So I gave her the um con.
She was right, all tight,
But clan, did she have mass!

Hatting her pair
She rossed off her tum
Barred at the leer-tender
Tumbled her way to my fable
And cholding my hair
Lissed me on the kips.

I skoated in the fly!

—1964

A. J. M. SMITH

(1902-   )

A. J. M. Smith was born and educated in Montreal. After obtaining a B.Sc. degree from McGill University, he switched to Arts and wrote his M.A. thesis on the poetry of W. B. Yeats. A new Canadian school of poets—inspired by the Group of Seven, the Imagists, the Symbolists, Frazer's Golden Bough, John Donne, Yeats, and Edith Sitwell—grew up around Smith and F. R. Scott while they wrote for university journals and served on their editorial boards. His earliest verses appeared in the weekly Literary Supplement of the McGill Daily, which he founded and edited, and in The Canadian Forum in 1924; he was founder and editor with others of The McGill Fortnightly Review (1925-1927). He went abroad to study at Edinburgh University under Professor H. J. C. Grierson, whose edition of Donne was a milestone in modern criticism and poetry; there Smith obtained a Ph.D. in 1931.

He became a member of the English Department at Michigan State University in 1936, and he remained there as Professor and Poet-in-Residence until his retirement in 1971.

In addition to textbooks, Smith has compiled and edited several Canadian anthologies and, with F. R. Scott, The Blasted Pine (1957, 1967), a collection of "disrespectful" verse. His notes and commentaries in these volumes and in numerous articles in various journals have established him as a major critic of English-Canadian literature.

The first book of his own poems, News of the Phoenix *(1943), won a Governor-General's Award. Three other volumes have followed, the latest being* Poems: New and Collected *(1967).*

His "A Rejected Preface" appears in Canadian Anthology, *pages 585-588.*

THE LONELY LAND

Cedar and jagged fir
uplift sharp barbs
against the gray
and cloud-piled sky;
and in the bay
blown spume and windrift
and thin, bitter spray
snap
at the whirling sky;
and the pine trees
lean one way.

A wild duck calls
to her mate,
and the ragged
and passionate tones
stagger and fall,
and recover,
and stagger and fall,
on these stones —

are lost
in the lapping of water
on smooth, flat stones.

This is a beauty
of dissonance,
this resonance
of stony strand,
this smoky cry
curled over a black pine
like a broken
and wind-battered branch
when the wind
bends the tops of the pines
and curdles the sky
from the north.

This is the beauty
of strength
broken by strength
and still strong.

—*1936*

SWIFT CURRENT

This is a visible
and crystal wind:
no ragged edge,
no splash of foam,
no whirlpool's scar;
only
       — in the narrows,
sharpness cutting sharpness,
arrows of direction,
spears of speed.

—*1943*

A HYACINTH FOR EDITH

Now that the ashen rain of gummy April
Clacks like a weedy and stain'd mill,

So that all the tall purple trees
Are pied porpoises in swishing seas,

And the yellow horses and milch cows
Come out of their long frosty house

To gape at the straining flags
The brown pompous hill wags,

I'll seek within the woods' black plinth
A candy-sweet sleek wooden hyacinth —

And in its creaking naked glaze,
And in the varnish of its blaze,

The bird of ecstasy shall sing again,
The bearded sun shall spring again,

— A new ripe fruit upon the sky's high tree,
A flowery island in the sky's wide sea —

And childish cold ballades, long dead, long mute,
Shall mingle with the gayety of bird and fruit,

And fall like cool and soothing rain
On all the ardor, all the pain

Lurking within this tinsel paradise
Of trams and cinemas and manufactured ice,

Till I am grown again my own lost ghost
Of joy, long lost, long given up for lost,

And walk again the wild and sweet wildwood
Of our lost innocence, our ghostly childhood.

—1943

FAR WEST

Among the cigarettes and the peppermint creams
Came the flowers of fingers, luxurious and bland,
Incredibly blossoming in the little breast.
And in the Far West
The tremendous cowboys in goatskin pants
Shot up the town of her ignorant wish.

In the gun flash she saw the long light shake
Across the lake, repeating that poem
At Finsbury Park.
But the echo was drowned in the roll of the trams —
Anyway, who would have heard? Not a soul!
Not one noble and toxic like Buffalo Bill.

In the holy name *bang! bang!* the flowers came
With the marvellous touch of fingers
Gentler than the fuzzy goats
Moving up and down up and down as if in ecstasy
As the cowboys rode their skin-tight stallions
Over the barbarous hills of California.

—1943, 1962

SEA CLIFF

Wave on wave
and green on rock
and white between
the splash and black
the crash and hiss
of the feathery fall,
the snap and shock
of the water wall
and the wall of rock:
after —
after the ebb-flow,
wet rock,
high —
high over the slapping green,
water sliding away
and the rock abiding,
new rock riding
out of the spray.

—1943

NEWS OF THE PHOENIX

They say the Phoenix is dying, some say dead.
Dead without issue is what one message said,
But that has been suppressed, officially denied.

I think, myself, the man who sent it lied.
In any case, I'm told, he has been shot,
As a precautionary measure, whether he did or not.

—1943

THE ARCHER

Bend back thy bow, O Archer, till the string
Is level with thine ear, thy body taut,
Its nature art, thyself thy statue wrought
Of marble blood, thy weapon the poised wing
Of coiled and acquiline Fate. Then, loosening, fling
The hissing arrow like a burning thought
Into the empty sky that smokes as the hot
Shaft plunges to the bullseye's quenching ring.

So for a moment, motionless, serene,
Fixed between time and time, I aim and wait;
Nothing remains for breath now but to waive
His prior claim and let the barb fly clean
Into the heart of what I know and hate —
That central black, the ringed and targeted grave.

—1943

SON-AND-HEIR

The nine-months-long-awaited heir is born,
And the parents are pretty proud of the thing.
Instinct censors any real, as too forlorn,
Preview of coming attractions. Angels sing

Like press agents the praises of their lamb
In minds as polite as a mezzanine floor.
They do concoct a brave, politic sham
To ravel the plot, feature the smirking star.

They see him innocency's Jaeger pelt
Hide in the wolf's coat of angry youth,
Striding over the very veldtlike veldt
In a bandolier full of Kodak films.

They make him up in the attractive role
Of a he-god in the next episode,
Bringing his woman dividends to roll
A cigarette with, giving his old dad

Market tips, and cigars on Father's Day,
And his Mother telegrams and roses,
Walking in rightwiseness, always au fait,
Always sure of the thing he supposes.

Who will turn the lights up on this show?
You will find something has gone wrong with the switch,
Or their eyes, used to horse opera, cannot grow
Used to an ordinary son-of-a-bitch

Like you or me for a son, or the doom
We discern — the empty years, the hand to mouth,
The moving cog, the unattended loom,
The breastless street, and lolling summer's drouth,

Or zero's shears at paper window pane---
And so forth and so forth and so forth.
Let us keep melodrama out of this scene,
Eye open to daylight, foot on the firm earth.

—1943

THE FOUNTAIN

This fountain sheds her flowery spray
Like some enchanted tree of May
Immortalized in feathery frost
With nothing but its fragrance lost;
Yet nothing has been done amiss
In this white metamorphosis,
For fragrance here has grown to form,
And Time is fooled, although he storm.

Through Autumn's sodden disarray
These blossoms fall, but not away;
They rear a lattice-work of light
On which black roses twine with white;
And while chaotic darkness broods
The golden groves to solitudes,
Here shines, in this transfigured spray,
The cold, immortal ghost of day.

—1943

THE SORCERER

There is a sorcerer in Lachine
Who for a small fee will put a spell
On my beloved, who has sea-green
Eyes, and on my doting self as well.

He will transform us, if we like, to goldfish:
We shall swim in a crystal bowl,
And the bright water will go swish
Over our naked bodies; we shall have no soul.

In the morning the syrupy sunshine
Will dance on our tails and fins.
I shall have her then all for mine,
And Father LeBeau will hear no more of her sins.

Come along, good sir, change us into goldfish.
I would put away intellect and lust,
Be but a red gleam in a crystal dish,
But kin of the trembling ocean, not of the dust.

—1954

TO HOLD IN A POEM

I would take words
As crisp and as white
As our snow; as our birds
Swift and sure in their flight;

As clear and as cold
As our ice; as strong as a jack pine;
As young as a trillium, and old
As Laurentia's long undulant line;

Sweet-smelling and bright
As new rain; as hard
And as smooth and as white
As a brook pebble cold and unmarred;

To hold in a poem of words
Like water in colorless glass
The spirit of mountains like birds,
Of forests as pointed as grass;

To hold in a verse as austere
As the spirit of prairie and river,
Lonely, unbuyable, dear,
The North, as a deed, and forever.

—1954

BIRD AND FLOWER

A spiritual pigeon catapults the
Air around you; a loaded violet
Is dangerous in your fur. Tenderness, set
Like a mousetrap or poised like a bee,
Falls from you (God's angry love). Lucky
The lean communicant whose table's set
With you; he banquets well, and rises fed
With innocence and Apollonian energy.

Some holy men so love their cells they make
Their four gray walls the whole damned
    stinking world,
And God comes in and fills it easily.
Your Christian bird and Grecian flower twirled
In gamblers' spirals sets a trickier stake,
Grounded, o Love, in holiness and joy.

—*1962*

ON KNOWING *Nothing*

Others have seen men die
Or heard a woman scream
One last word *Never!*
How do I know the horror
That breaks the dream,
Hateful yet clung to
As the image hugs the mirror
With such a silver shiver
As chills and almost kills?

I know: but how or why
Out of this savory fatness I
Should suck the sharp surmise
That strangles dying eyes

I do not know. What have I done
To bring the Angel round my head
That I can smell his pinion
(Bond or wing?)
Whom I must hate and love?

The surgeon's jab, a woman's thigh
Give blank surcease
For short or long.
I cannot let the hollow
Interval alone,
But pick it like a scab
To probe the wound within —
As deep, as nothing, as the grave.

—*1962*

THE HIPPOPOTAMUS

After Théophile Gautier

The hippo with his massive gut
Frequents the jungle-land of Java;
More monsters than you'd dream of root
In caves or grots of lime or lava.

The boa colubrates and hisses.
Before he springs the tiger creeps.
The charging bison rarely misses.
The hippo crops the grass or sleeps.

He fears no kris or pointed staff;
He looks on Man without chagrin;
The huntsman's balls just make him laugh;
They bounce against his leather skin.

I am like the hippopot-
amus, in my conviction strong;
In armour thick as he has got
I walk the waste and fear no wrong.

—*1967*

ROY DANIELLS

(1902-   )

Roy Daniells was born in London, England, and came to Canada in 1910. He graduated from the University of British Columbia in 1930 and received his Ph.D. at the University of Toronto in 1936. After teaching at Victoria College, Toronto, and at the University of Manitoba, he became Head of the Department of English at the University of British Columbia in 1948. In 1965 he was appointed as University Professor there. His first book of verse, Deeper into the Forest, *was published in 1948. His second,* The Chequered Shade, *appeared in 1963, shortly after he returned from a year in France and England. Distinguished as a Milton scholar, he has also served as an editor and a principal contributor to* Literary History of Canada *(1965). In 1972 he was made a Companion of the Order of Canada.*

"SO THEY WENT DEEPER INTO THE FOREST..."

"So they went deeper into the forest," said Jacob Grimm,
And the child sat listening with all his ears,
While the angry queen passed. And in after years
The voice and the fall of words came back to him
(Though the fish and the faithful servant were grown dim,
The aproned witch, the door that disappears,
The lovely maid weeping delicious tears
And the youngest brother, with one bright-feathered limb)—
"Deeper into the forest."
                              There are oaks and beeches
And green high hollies. The multitudinous tree
Stands on the hill and clothes the valley, reaches
Over long lands, down to a roaring sea.
And the child moved onward, into the heart of the wood,
Unhindered, unresisted, unwithstood.

—*1948*

"THREE LECTURE HOURS PER WEEK"

Take care when you lift the little copper bottle
You do not wake the genie. He is drowned
In your old drugs and safely under throttle,
Darkened and deadened, all his powers bound.
Pour gently into the teaspoon's silver bowl
And give in lukewarm water thrice a week
The thick dark liquor that might incite the soul
But O take care he does not wake or speak.
Put the top back on quickly. He is a spirit
Able to raise your prostrate crew as kings
And priests that his imperial halls inherit
Filled with unspeakable and glorious things.
Able to wither you with one slight breath.
All they who bound him go down into death.

—*1963*

MORLEY CALLAGHAN

(1903-   )

Edward Morley Callaghan was born in Toronto of Irish parents, and educated at St. Michael's College and Osgoode Law School. While he was studying he also worked as a reporter on the Toronto Daily Star *and was encouraged in his ambition to write by another member of its staff, Ernest Hemingway. Callaghan's first published story appeared in a 1926 issue of* This Quarter, *edited in Paris. He was admitted to the bar in 1928, the same year in which his novel* Strange Fugitive *was published by Scribner's of New York. The success of this book and of his first collection of stories,* A Native Argosy *(1929), enabled Callaghan to spend several months in Paris in the year 1929. There he associated with such writers as Ernest Hemingway, Scott Fitzgerald, and James Joyce, and finished a second novel,* It's Never Over *(1930), several short stories, and a short privately printed novella,* No Man's Meat *(1931).*

After returning home to Toronto, Callaghan published A Broken Journey *(1932),* Such Is My Beloved *(1934),* They Shall Inherit the Earth *(1935), and* More Joy in Heaven *(1937), all novels, and a collection of his best short stories of the period,* Now That April's Here *(1936). All of these works reveal his increasing preoccupation with the plight of the individual who is yearning for love and recognition yet is unable to adjust to society. Callaghan was concerned, too, with the tension between spiritual and material values in a temporal world. In 1939 he wrote two unpublished stage plays,* "Just Ask for George" *and* "Turn Again Home," *which were produced in Toronto under the titles* "To Tell the Truth" *(1949) and* "Going Home" *(1950).*

During the Second World War Callaghan spent much of his time in journalism and radio. He travelled across Canada as Chairman of the Canadian Broadcasting Corporation's program "Citizens' Forum" *and he participated in other popular radio series. When he turned seriously to writing fiction again, he produced in 1948 a juvenile novel,* Luke Baldwin's Vow, *and* The Varsity Story, *a nostalgic description of the University of Toronto.*

His first major novel after the war, The Loved and The Lost *(1951), won a Governor-General's Award. Four years later* The Man With The Coat *won a Maclean's $5000 Novel Award. Out of this long novella grew* The Many Colored Coat *(1960). A third collection of stories,* Morley Callaghan's Stories, *appeared in 1959, and another novel,* A Passion in Rome, *in 1961. In* That Summer in Paris *(1963) Callaghan recalls his youthful career and association with other famous literary figures of an earlier period. Callaghan's reputation is international and his books have been translated into several European languages.*

AN ESCAPADE

Snow fell softly and the sidewalks were wet but Mrs. Rose Carey had on her galoshes and enjoyed feeling thick snow crunching underfoot. She walked slowly, big flakes falling on her lamb coat and clinging to hair over her ears, the lazily falling snow giving her, in her thick warm coat, a fine feeling of self-indulgence. She stood on the corner of Bloor and Yonge, an impressive build of a woman, tall, stout, good-looking for forty-two, and watched the traffic-signal.

Few people were on this corner at half past eight, Sunday evening. A policeman, leaning against a big plate-glass window, idly watched her cross the road and look up the street to the clock on the firehall and down the street at the theatre lights, where Reverend John Simpson held Sunday service. She had kept herself late deliberately, intending to enter the theatre quietly and unnoticed, and sit in a back seat, ready to leave as soon as the service was over. She walked with dignity, bothered by her own shyness, and thinking of her husband asking if Father Conley was speaking tonight in the Cathedral. She didn't want to think of Father Conley, or at least she didn't want to compare him with Mr. Simpson, who was simply interesting because all her bridge friends were talking about him. It was altogether different about Father Conley.

She was under the theatre lights, turning in, and someone said to her: "This way, lady. Step this way, right along now."

She stopped abruptly, nervously watching the little man with the long nose and green sweater, pacing up and down in front of the entrance, waving his hands. He saw her hesitating and came close to her. He had on a funny flat black hat, and walked with his toes turned way out. "Step lively, lady," he muttered, wagging his head at her.

She was scared of him and would have turned away but a man got out of a car at the curb and smiled at her. "Don't be afraid of Dick," he said. The man had on a christie and had gray hair and a tie-pin in a wide black tie. He was going into the theatre, but had noticed her embarrassment.

"Run along, Dick," he said to the silly fellow, and turning to Mrs. Carey, he explained. "He's absolutely harmless. They call him Crazy Dick."

"Thank you very much," Mrs. Carey said.

"I hope he didn't keep you from going in," he said, taking off his hat. His hair was quite thick and he had a generous smile.

"I didn't know him, that was all," she said, feeling foolish as he opened the door for her. She heard Crazy Dick talking rapidly, then the door closed.

The minister was moving on the stage and talking quietly. She knew it was the minister because she had seen his picture in the papers and recognized the Prince Albert coat and the four-in-hand tie with the collar open at the throat. She took three steps down the aisle, fearfully aware that many people were looking at her, and sat down, four rows from the back. Only once before had she been in a strange church when a friend of her husband had got married, and it hadn't seemed like church. She unbuttoned her coat carefully, leaving a green and black scarf lying across her full breasts, and relaxed in the seat, getting her big body comfortable. Someone sat down beside her. The man with the gray hair and red face was sitting down beside her. She was annoyed because she knew she was too definitely aware of him sitting beside her. The minister walked the length of the platform, his voice pleasant and soothing, one of the city's most interesting ministers, and she tried to follow the flow of words but was too restless. She had come in too late, that was the trouble. So she tried concentrating, closing her eyes, but at once thought of a trivial and amusing argument she had had with her husband, and three or four words she might have used effectively. The minister was giving an idea of an after life and some words seemed beautiful, but she was disappointed because it was not what she had expected, and she had never intended to take his religious notions seriously.

The seat was becoming uncomfortable, and she stretched a little, crossing her legs at the ankles. The minister had a lovely voice but, so far, wasn't a bit sensational, and she might just as well have gone to the Cathedral. She felt slightly ashamed, and out of place in the theatre.

The man on her right was sniffling. Puzzled, she watched him out of the corner of her eye, as he gently rubbed his eyes with a large white handkerchief. The handkerchief was fresh and the creases firm. One plump hand held four corners, making a pad, and he dabbed his eyes, watching the minister intently.

Mrs. Carey was anxious not to appear ill-bred, but a respectable man, moved by the minister's words, or an old thought, was sitting beside her, crying. She tried to adjust her thoughts so the man's misery would belong to a pattern of a Sunday service in a theatre, and did not glance at him again till she realized that his elbow was on the arm of her seat, supporting his chin, while he blinked his eyes and slowly moved his head. He was feeling so bad she was uncomfortable, but thought that he looked gentlemanly, even though feeling so miserable. He was probably a nice man, and she was sorry for him.

She expected him to get up and go out. Other people were noticing him. A fat woman, in the seat ahead, craned her neck so much Mrs. Carey wanted to slap her. The man put the handkerchief over his face and didn't lift his head. The minister was talking rapidly, but Mrs. Carey suddenly felt absolutely alone in the theatre, rows of heads simply sloped down to the orchestra. Impulsively she touched the man's arm, leaning toward him, whispering, "I'm awfully sorry for you, sir."

She patted his arm a second time and he looked at her helplessly, and went to speak, but merely shook his head and patted the back of her hand.

"I'm sorry," she repeated gently.

"Thank you very much," he said sincerely.

"I hope it's all right now," she whispered.

He spoke quietly and slowly: "Something the minister said reminded me of my brother who died last week. My younger brother."

People in the row ahead were turning angrily, annoyed by Mrs. Carey. She became embarrassed, and leaned back in her seat, very dignified, and looked directly ahead till aware that the man was holding her hand. Startled, she twitched it nervously, but he didn't notice. His eyes were still moist. His thoughts seemed so far away. She reflected it could do no harm to let him hold her hand a moment, if it helped him.

She listened to the minister but didn't understand a word he was saying, and glanced curiously at the gray-haired man, who didn't look at her but still held her hand. He was good-looking and a feeling she had not had for years was inside her, her hand had suddenly become so sensitive. She closed her eyes. Then the minister stopped speaking and she opened them, knowing the congregation was ready to sing a hymn. She looked directly at him. He had put away the handkerchief and now was smiling sadly. Uneasily, she avoided his eyes, firmly removing her hand, as she stood up to sing the last hymn. Her cheeks were warm. She tried to stop thinking altogether. It was necessary to leave at once only she had to squeeze by his knees to reach the aisle.

She buttoned her coat while they were singing, ready to slip past him. She was surprised when he stepped out to the aisle, allowing her to pass, but didn't look at him. Erect and dignified, she walked slowly up the aisle, her eyes on the door.

Then she heard steps behind her and knew definitely he was following. An usher held open the door and she smiled awkwardly. The usher smiled. Outside, she took a few quick steps, then stood still, bewildered, expecting Crazy Dick to be on the street. She thought of the green sweater and funny flat hat, then looked back hurriedly. Through the doorway she saw him smiling at the usher and putting on his hat, the tie-pin shining in the light. Sinking her chin into her high fur collar she walked rapidly down the street, looking only at the ground immediately ahead of her. It was snowing harder, driving along on a wind.

When she got to a car stop she looked back and saw the gray-haired man standing on the sidewalk in front of the theatre doors. A street-car was coming. She was sure he took a few steps toward her, but she got on the car.

The conductor said, "Fares please," but hardly glancing at him, she shook wet snow from her coat, and sat down, taking three deep breaths while her cheeks tingled. She felt tired suddenly, and her heart was thumping unevenly.

She got off the car at Shuter Street. She didn't want to go straight home, and was determined to visit the Cathedral.

On the side streets snow was thick. Men from some of the rooming-houses were shovelling it from the sidewalks, the shovels scraping on concrete. She lifted her eyes occasionally to the illuminated cross on the Cathedral spire.

One light was over the church door. The congregation had come out half an hour ago, and she felt lonely walking in the dark toward the single light.

Inside the Cathedral she knelt down half-way up the centre aisle, her eyes on the altar lights. She closed her eyes to pray, and remembered midnight mass in the Cathedral, the Archbishop with his mitre and staff, and the choir of boys' voices. A vestry door opened, a priest passed in the shadow beside the altar, took a book from a pew, and went out. She closed her eyes again and said many prayers, repeating her favorite ones over and over, but often she thought of her husband at home. She prayed hard so she could go home and not be bothered by anything that had happened in the theatre. She prayed for half an hour, feeling better gradually, till she hardly remembered the man in the theatre, and fairly satisfied, she got up and left the Cathedral.

—1929

TWO FISHERMEN

The only reporter on the town paper, the *Examiner,* was Michael Foster, a tall, long-legged, eager young fellow, who wanted to go to the city some day and work on an important newspaper.

The morning he went into Bagley's hotel, he wasn't at all sure of himself. He went over to the desk and whispered to the proprietor, Ted Bagley, "Did he come here, Mr. Bagley?"

Bagley said slowly, "Two men came here from this morning's train. They're registered." He put his spatulate forefinger on the open book and said, "Two men. One of them's a drummer. This one here, T. Woodley. I know because he was through this way last year and just a minute ago he walked across the road to Molson's hardware store. The other one —— here's his name, K. Smith."

"Who's K. Smith?" Michael asked.

"I don't know. A mild, harmless-looking little guy."

"Did he look like the hangman, Mr. Bagley?"

"I couldn't say that, seeing as I never saw one. He was awfully polite and asked where he could get a boat so he could go fishing on the lake this evening, so I said likely down at Smollet's place by the power house."

"Well, thanks. I guess if he was the hangman, he'd go over to the jail first," Michael said.

He went along the street, past the Baptist church to the old jail with the high brick fence around it. Two tall maple trees, with branches drooping low over the sidewalk, shaded one of the walls from the morning sunlight. Last night, behind those walls, three carpenters, working by lamplight, had nailed the timbers for the scaffold. In the morning, young Thomas Delaney, who had grown up in the town, was being hanged: he had killed old Mathew Rhinehart whom he had caught molesting his wife when she had been berrypicking in the hills behind the town. There had been a struggle and Thomas Delaney had taken a bad beating before he had killed Rhinehart. Last night a crowd had gathered on the sidewalk by the lamp post, and while moths and smaller insects swarmed around the high blue carbon light, the crowd had thrown sticks and bottles and small stones at the out-of-town workmen in the jail yard. Billy Hilton, the town constable, had stood under the light with his head down, pretending not to notice anything. Thomas Delaney was only three years older than Michael Foster.

Michael went straight to the jail office, where Henry Steadman, the sheriff, a squat, heavy man, was sitting on the desk idly wetting his long black mustaches with his tongue. "Hello, Michael, what do you want?" he asked.

"Hello, Mr. Steadman. The *Examiner* would like to know if the hangman arrived yet."

"Why ask me?"

"I thought he'd come here to test the gallows. Won't he?"

"My, you're a smart young fellow, Michael, thinking of that."

"Is he in there now, Mr. Steadman?"

"Don't ask me. I'm saying nothing. Say Michael, do you think there's going to be trouble? You ought to know. Does anybody seem sore at me? I can't do nothing. You can see that."

"I don't think anybody blames you, Mr. Steadman. Look here, can't I see the hangman? Is his name K. Smith?"

"What does it matter to you, Michael? Be a sport, go on away and don't bother us any more."

"All right, Mr. Steadman," Michael said very competently, "just leave it to me."

Early that evening, when the sun was setting, Michael Foster walked south of the town on the dusty road leading to the power house and Smollet's fishing pier. He knew that if Mr. K. Smith wanted to get a boat he would go down to the pier. Fine powdered road dust whitened Michael's shoes. Ahead of him he saw the power plant, square and low, and the smooth lake water. Behind him the sun was hanging over the blue hills beyond the town and shining brilliantly on square patches of farm land. The air around the power house smelt of steam.

Out on the jutting, tumbledown pier of rock and logs, Michael saw a little fellow without a hat, sitting down with his knees hunched up to his chin, a very small man with little gray baby curls on the back of his neck, who stared steadily far out over the water. In his hand he was holding a stick with a heavy fishing line twined around it and a gleaming copper spoon bait, the hooks brightened with bits of feathers such as they used in the neighborhood when trolling for lake trout. Apprehensively Michael walked out over the rocks toward the stranger and called, "Were you thinking of going fishing, mister?" Standing up, the man smiled. He had a large head, tapering down to a small chin, a birdlike neck, and a very wistful smile. Puckering his mouth up, he said shyly to Michael, "Did you intend to go fishing?"

"That's what I came down here for. I was going to get a boat back at the boat house there. How would you like if we went together?"

"I'd like it first rate," the shy little man said eagerly. "We could take turns rowing. Does that appeal to you?"

"Fine. Fine. You wait here and I'll go back to Smollet's place and ask for a rowboat and I'll row around here and get you."

"Thanks. Thanks very much," the mild little man said as he began to untie his line. He seemed very enthusiastic.

When Michael brought the boat around to the end of the old pier and invited the stranger to make himself comfortable so he could handle the line, the stranger protested comically that he ought to be allowed to row.

Pulling strongly at the oars, Michael was soon out in the deep water and the little man was letting his line out slowly. In one furtive glance, he had noticed that the man's hair, gray at the temples, was inclined to curl to his ears. The line was out full length. It was twisted around the little man's forefinger, which he let drag in the water. And then Michael looked full at him and smiled because he thought he seemed so meek and quizzical. "He's a nice little guy," Michael assured himself and he said, "I work on the town paper, the *Examiner*."

"Is it a good paper? Do you like the work?"

"Yes. But it's nothing like a first-class city paper and I don't expect to be working on it long. I want to get a reporter's job on a city paper. My name's Michael Foster."

"Mine's Smith. Just call me Smitty."

"I was wondering if you'd been over to the jail yet."

Up to this time the little man had been smiling with the charming ease of a small boy who finds himself free, but now he became furtive and disappointed. Hesitating, he said, "Yes, I was over at the jail. I didn't think you knew. I tested the trap. I went there first thing this morning."

"Oh, I just knew you'd go there," Michael said. They were a bit afraid of each other. By this time they were far out on the water which had a millpond smoothness. The town seemed to get smaller, with white houses in rows and streets forming geometric patterns, just as the blue hills behind the town seemed to get larger at sundown.

Finally Michael said, "Do you know this Thomas Delaney that's dying in the morning?" He knew his voice was slow and resentful.

"No. I don't know anything about him. I never read about them. Aren't there any fish at all in this old lake? I'd like to catch some fish," he said rapidly. "I told my wife I'd bring her home some fish." Glancing at Michael, he was appealing, without speaking, that they should do nothing to spoil an evening's fishing.

The little man began to talk eagerly about fishing as he pulled out a small flask from his hip pocket. "Scotch," he said, chuckling with delight. "Here, take a swig." Michael drank from the flask and passed it back. Tilting his head back and saying "Here's to you, Michael," the little man took a long pull at the flask. "The only time I take a drink," he said still chuckling, "is when I go on a fishing trip by myself. I usually go by myself," he added apologetically as if he wanted the young fellow to see how much he appreciated his company.

They had gone far out on the water but they had caught nothing. It began to get dark. "No fish tonight, I guess, Smitty," Michael said.

"It's a crying shame," Smitty said. "I looked forward to coming up here when I found out the place was on the lake. I wanted to get some fishing in. I promised my wife I'd bring her back some fish. She'd often like to go fishing with me, but of course, she can't because she can't travel around from place to place like I do. Whenever I get a call to go some place, I always look at the map to see if it's by a lake or on a river, then I take my lines and hooks along."

"If you took another job, you and your wife could probably go fishing together," Michael suggested.

"I don't know about that. We sometimes go fishing together anyway." He looked away, waiting for Michael to be repelled and insist that he ought to give up the job. And he wasn't ashamed as he looked down at the water, but he knew that Michael thought he ought to be ashamed. "Somebody's got to do my job. There's got to be a hangman," he said.

"I just meant that if it was such disagreeable work, Smitty."

The little man did not answer for a long time. Michael rowed steadily with sweeping, tireless strokes. Huddled at the end of the boat, Smitty suddenly looked up with a kind of melancholy hopelessness and said mildly, "The job hasn't been so disagreeable."

"Good God, man, you don't mean you like it?"

"Oh, no," he said, to be obliging, as if he knew what Michael expected him to say. "I mean you get used to it, that's all." But he looked down again at the water, knowing he ought to be ashamed of himself.

"Have you got any children?"

"I sure have. Five. The oldest boy is fourteen. It's funny, but they're all a lot bigger and taller than I am. Isn't that funny?"

They started a conversation about fishing rivers that ran into the lake farther north. They felt friendly again. The little man, who had an extraordinary gift for story telling, made many quaint faces, puckered up his lips, screwed up his eyes, and moved around restlessly as if he wanted to get up in the boat and stride around for the sake of more expression. Again he brought out the whiskey flask and Michael stopped rowing. Grinning, they toasted each other and said together, "Happy days." The boat remained motionless on the placid water. Far out, the sun's last rays gleamed on the water line. And then it got dark and they could only see the town lights. It was time to turn around and pull for the shore. The little man tried to take the oars from Michael, who shook his head resolutely and insisted that he would prefer to have his friend catch a fish on the way back to the shore.

"It's too late now, and we may have scared all the fish away," Smitty laughed happily. "But we're having a grand time, aren't we?"

When they reached the old pier by the power house, it was full night and they hadn't caught a single fish. As the boat bumped against the rocks Michael said, "You can get out here. I'll take the boat around to Smollet's."

"Won't you be coming my way?"

"Not just now. I'll probably talk with Smollet a while."

The little man got out of the boat and stood on the pier looking down at Michael. "I was thinking dawn would be the best time to catch some fish," he said. "At about five o'clock. I'll have an hour and a half to spare anyway. How would you like that?" He was speaking with so much eagerness that Michael found himself saying, "I could try. But if I'm not here at dawn, you go on without me."

"All right. I'll walk back to the hotel now."

"Good night, Smitty."

"Good night, Michael. We had a fine neighborly time, didn't we?"

As Michael rowed the boat around to the boat house, he hoped that Smitty wouldn't realize he didn't want to be seen walking back to town with him. And later, when he was going slowly along the dusty road in the dark and hearing all the crickets chirping in the ditches, he couldn't figure out why he felt so ashamed of himself.

At seven o'clock next morning Thomas Delaney was hanged in the town jail yard. There was hardly a breeze on that leaden gray morning and there were no small whitecaps out over the lake. It would have been a fine morning for fishing. Michael went down to the jail, for he thought it his duty as a newspaperman to have all the facts, but he was afraid he might get sick. He hardly spoke to all the men and women who were crowded under the maple trees by the jail wall. Everybody he knew was staring at the wall and muttering angrily. Two of Thomas Delaney's brothers, big strapping fellows with bearded faces, were there on the sidewalk. Three automobiles were at the front of the jail.

Michael, the town newspaperman, was admitted into the courtyard by old Willie Mathews, one of the guards, who said that two newspapermen from the city were at the gallows on the other side of the building. "I guess you can go around there, too, if you want to," Mathews said, as he sat down slowly on the step. White-faced, and afraid, Michael sat down on the step with Mathews and they waited and said nothing.

At last the old fellow said, "Those people outside there are pretty sore, ain't they?"

"They're pretty sullen, all right. I saw two of Delaney's brothers there."

"I wish they'd go," Mathews said. "I don't want to see anything. I didn't even look at Delaney. I don't want to hear anything. I'm sick." He put his head back against the wall and closed his eyes.

The old fellow and Michael sat close together till a small procession came around the corner from the other side of the yard. First came Mr. Steadman, the sheriff, with his head down as though he were crying, then Dr. Parker, the physician, then two hard-looking young newspapermen from the city, walking with their hats on the backs of their heads, and behind them came the little hangman, erect, stepping out with military precision and carrying himself with a strange cocky dignity. He was dressed in a long black cutaway coat with gray striped trousers, a gates-ajar collar and a narrow red tie, as if he alone felt the formal importance of the occasion. He walked with brusque precision till he saw Michael, who was standing up, staring at him with his mouth open.

The little hangman grinned and as soon as the procession reached the door step, he shook hands with Michael. They were all looking at Michael. As though his work were over now, the hangman said eagerly to Michael, "I thought I'd see you here. You didn't get down to the pier at dawn?"

"No. I couldn't make it."

"That was tough, Michael. I looked for you," he said. "But never mind. I've got something for you." As they all went into the jail, Dr. Parker glanced angrily at Michael, then turned his back on him. In the office, where the doctor prepared to sign a certificate, Smitty was bending down over his fishing basket which was in the corner. Then he pulled out two good-sized salmon-bellied lake trout, folded in a newspaper, and said, "I was saving these for you, Michael. I got four in an hour's fishing." Then he said, "I'll talk about that later, if you'll wait. We'll be busy here, and I've got to change my clothes."

Michael went out to the street with Dr. Parker and the two city newspapermen. Under his arm he was carrying the fish, folded in the newspaper. Outside, at the jail door, Michael thought that the doctor and the two newspapermen were standing a little apart from him. Then the small crowd, with their clothes all dust-soiled from the road, surged forward, and the doctor said to them, "You might as well go home, boys. It's all over."

"Where's old Steadman?" somebody called.

"We'll wait for the hangman," somebody else shouted.

The doctor walked away by himself. For a while Michael stood beside the two city newspapermen, and tried to look as nonchalant as they were looking, but he lost confidence in them when he smelled whiskey. They only talked to each other. Then they mingled with the crowd, and Michael stood alone. At last he could stand there no longer looking at all those people he knew so well, so he, too, moved out and joined the crowd.

When the sheriff came out with the hangman and two of the guards, they got half way down to one of the automobiles before someone threw an old boot. Steadman ducked into one of the cars, as the boot hit him on the shoulder, and the two guards followed him. The hangman, dismayed, stood alone on the side-walk. Those in the car must have thought at first that the hangman was with them for the car suddenly shot forward, leaving him alone on the sidewalk. The crowd threw small rocks and sticks, hooting at him as the automobile backed up slowly towards him. One small stone hit him on the head. Blood trickled from the side of his head as he looked around helplessly at all the angry people. He had the same expression on his face, Michael thought, as he had last night when he had seemed ashamed and had looked down steadily at the water. Once now, he looked around wildly, looking for someone to help him as the crowd kept pelting him. Farther and farther Michael backed into the crowd and all the time he felt dreadfully ashamed as though he were betraying Smitty, who last night had had such a good neighborly time with him. "It's different now, it's different," he kept thinking, as he held the fish in the newspaper tight under his arm. Smitty started to run toward the automobile, but James Mortimer, a big fisherman, shot out his foot and tripped him and sent him sprawling on his face.

Mortimer, the big fisherman, looking for something to throw, said to Michael, "Sock him, sock him."

Michael shook his head and felt sick.

"What's the matter with you, Michael?"

"Nothing. I got nothing against him."

The big fisherman started pounding his fists up and down in the air. "He just doesn't mean anything to me at all," Michael said quickly. The fisherman, bending down, kicked a small rock loose from the road bed and heaved it at the hangman. Then he said, "What are you holding there, Michael, what's under your arm? Fish. Pitch them at him. Here, give them to me." Still in a fury, he snatched the fish, and threw them one at a time at the little man just as he was getting up from the road. The fish fell in the thick dust in front of him, sending up a little cloud. Smitty seemed to stare at the fish with his mouth hanging open, then he didn't even look at the crowd. That expression on Smitty's face as he saw the fish on the road made Michael hot with shame and he tried to get out of the crowd.

Smitty had his hands over his head, to shield his face as the crowd pelted him, yelling "Sock the little rat. Throw the runt in the lake." The sheriff pulled him into the automobile. The car shot forward in a cloud of dust.

—1936

AUTHOR'S COMMENT

Morley Callaghan's explanation of why he chose "Two Fishermen" to represent him in the anthology This Is My Best, *edited by Whit Burnett (Cleveland, Ohio, World Publishing Co., 1942):*

When I wrote this story, I found I was liking the material because there was a certain grim contrast between the nice human and warm relationship of the young fellow and the hangman and the actual vocation of the hangman. Also I liked the hangman's rather wistful attachment to his despised job and his realization that it gave him an opportunity to get around the country and enjoy himself as a human being and a fisherman. And then after I had written it I saw that it had a certain social implication that I liked. The hangman, a necessary figure in society, a man definitely serving the public and the ends of justice, was entitled to a little human dignity. In fact he saw himself as a dignified human being. But of course as an instrument of justice he became a despised person, and even his young friend, who understood his wistful humanity, betrayed that humanity when the chips were down. If I had started out to write the story with that in mind it might have become very involved but I wrote it very easily and naturally and without any trouble at all. At the time I wrote it, I let the editor of *Esquire*, who published it, know that I thought it was one of my best stories. He was very dubious about it. I find looking back on it that the story seems to stand up well and I was right in my judgment of it.

—1942

THE SHINING RED APPLE

It was the look of longing on the boy's face that made Joe Cosentino, dealer in fruits and vegetables, notice him. Joe was sitting on his high stool at the end of the counter where he sat every afternoon looking out the window at the bunches of bananas and the cauliflowers and the tomatoes and apples piled outside on the street stand, and he was watching to see that the kids on the way home from school didn't touch any of the fruit.

This skinny little boy, who was wearing a red sweater and blue overalls, stood near the end of the fruit stand where there was a pyramid of big red apples. With his hands linked loosely together in front of him, and his head, with the straight, untidy brown hair that hung almost down to his blue eyes, cocked over to one side, he stood looking with longing at the apples. If he moved a little to the right, he would be out of sight of the window, but even so if he reached his hand out to take an apple, Joe, sitting at the end of the counter and watching, would surely see the hand. The sleeves of Joe's khaki shirt were rolled up, and as he sat on his stool he folded his hairy forearms across his deep chest. There wasn't much business, there seemed to be a little less every day, and sitting there week after week, he grew a little fatter and a little slower and ever so much more meditative. The store was untidy, and the fruit and the vegetables no longer had the cool fresh appearance they had in the stores of merchants who were prosperous.

If the kid, standing outside, had been a big, resolute-looking boy, Joe would have been alert and suspicious, but as it was, it was amusing to sit there and pretend he could feel the kid's longing for the apple growing stronger. As though making the first move in a game, Joe leaned forward suddenly, and the boy, lowering his head, shuffled a few feet away. Then Joe, whistling thinly, as if he hadn't noticed anything, got up and went out, took out his handkerchief, and started to polish a few of the apples on the pile. They were big, juicy-looking apples, a little over-ripe and going soft. He polished them till they gleamed and glistened in the sun. Then he said to the kid, "Fine day, eh, son?"

"Yeh," the kid said timidly.

"You live around here?"

"No."

"New around here, eh?" Joe said.

The kid, nodding his head shyly, didn't offer to tell where he lived, so Joe, chuckling to himself, and feeling powerful because he knew so surely just what would happen, went back to the store and sat down on the stool.

At first the little kid, holding his hands behind his back now, shuffled away out of sight, but Joe knew he would go no further than the end of the stand; he knew the kid would be there looking up and down the street furtively, stretching his hand out a little, then withdrawing it in fear before he touched an apple, and always staring, wanting the apple more and more.

Joe got up and yawned lazily, wetting his lips and rubbing his hand across them, and then he deliberately turned his back to the window. But at the moment when he was sure the kid would make up his mind and shoot out his hand, he swung around, and he was delighted to see how the child's hand, empty and faltering, was pulled back. "Ah, it goes just like a clock. I know just what he'll do," Joe thought. "He wants it, but he doesn't know how to take it because he's scared.

Soon he wants it so much, he'll have to take it. Then I catch him. That's the way it goes," and he grinned.

But in a little while Joe began to feel that maybe he was making it far too hard for the kid, as though the apples were something precious and untouchable. So, doing a thing he hardly ever did, he went out onto the street and, paying no attention to the kid, who had jumped away nervously, he mopped his shining forehead and wiped his red mouth and lazily picked up one of the apples from the top of the pile, as though all such luxuries of the world were within his reach. He munched it slowly with great relish, spitting out bits of red skin, and gnawing it down to the core. The kid must have been very hungry, for his mouth dropped open helplessly, and his blue eyes were innocent and hopeless.

After tossing the core in a wide arc far out on the street, where it lay in the sunlight and was attacked by two big flies, Joe started back into the store thinking, "Now for sure he'll grab one. He won't wait now. He can't." Yet to tantalize him, he didn't go right into the store; he turned at the door, looked up at the sky, as though expecting it to rain suddenly.

The frightened kid had really been ready to take an apple then. He had been so ready that he couldn't turn his head away, even though he knew Joe was watching him, for the apple seemed to belong to him now that he had made up his mind to take it and it was so close to him.

While Joe was grinning and feeling pleased with his cunning, his wife came in from the room at the back of the store. She was a black-haired woman, wide-hipped and slow-moving now, with tired brown eyes. When she stood beside her husband, with her hands on her hips, she looked determined and sensible. "The baby's sleeping now, I think, Joe. It's been pretty bad the way she's been going on."

"That's good," Joe said.

"She feels a lot better today."

"She's all right."

"I feel pretty tired. I think I'll lie down," she said, but she walked over to the window and looked out at the street.

Then she said sharply, "There's a kid out there near the apples. One's gone from the top."

"I sold it," Joe lied.

"Watch the kid," she said.

"O.K.," Joe said, and she went back to the bedroom.

Eagerly Joe looked again for the kid, who stood rooted there in spite of the hostile glance of the woman. "I guess he doesn't know how to do it," Joe thought. Yet the look of helpless longing was becoming so strong in the kid's face, so bold and unashamed, that it bothered Joe and made him irritable. He wanted to quarrel openly with the boy. "Look at the face on you. Look out, kid, you'll start and cry in a minute," he said to himself. "So you think you can have everything you want, do you?" The agony of wanting was so plain in the boy's face that Joe was indignant. "Who does the kid think he is?" he muttered.

In the room back of the store there was a faint whimpering and the sound of a baby stirring. "Look at that, son," Joe said to himself, as though still lecturing the kid. "It's a nice baby, but it's not a boy. See what I mean? If you go round with that look on your face when you want things and can't get them, people'll only laugh at you." As he spoke Joe grew restless and unhappy, and he looked helplessly around the untidy store, as if looking upon his own fate.

The kid on the sidewalk, who had shuffled away till he was out of sight, came edging back slowly. And Joe, getting excited, whispered, "Why doesn't he take it when he wants it so much? I couldn't catch him if he took it and ran," and he got up to be near the corner of the window, where he could see the boy's hand if it came reaching out. "Now. Right now," he muttered, really hoping it would happen.

Then he thought, "What's the matter with him?" for the kid was walking away, brushing by the fruit stand. One of his hands was swinging loose at his side. Then Joe realized that the swinging hand was to knock an apple off the pile and send it rolling along the sidewalk, and he got up eagerly and leaned forward with his head close to the window.

The kid, looking up warily, saw Joe's face and he grew frightened. His own face was full of terror. Ducking, he ran.

"Hey!" Joe yelled, running out to the sidewalk.

In a wild way the kid looked around, but he kept on running, his legs in the blue overalls pumping up and down.

Grabbing an apple and yelling, "Hey, hey, kid, you can have it!" Joe followed a few steps, but the kid wouldn't look back.

Joe stood on the sidewalk, an awful eagerness growing in him as he stared at the shiny red apple and wondered what would happen to the kid he was sure he would never see again.

—1936

EARLE BIRNEY

(1904-   )

Born in Calgary, Alberta, Earle Birney attended public school in the mountain village of Banff and high school in Creston, British Columbia. He graduated from the University of British Columbia in 1926 with first class honors in English. He has held a teaching fellowship at the University of California, an instructorship in English at the University of Utah, and a Royal Society of Canada Fellowship at the University of London. He obtained the degrees of M.A. (1927) and Ph. D. (1936) at the University of Toronto, and in 1936 was appointed to the staff there in the Department of English, University College. From 1936 to 1940 he was also literary editor of the Canadian Forum.

During the war he served in the Canadian Army as a personnel selection officer in Britain and Holland. Afterwards, in 1946, following a period in which he was supervisor of European-language broadcasts for CBC's Radio Canada, *he joined the staff of the University of British Columbia as Professor of English. In 1963 he became Chairman of the Department of Creative Writing there. For two years, from 1946 to 1948, he was also editor of* The Canadian Poetry Magazine. *As one of the first recipients of a Canadian Government Overseas Award, he spent the year 1953 in France working on his second novel,* Down the Long Table *(1955). Research into* aspects of Chaucer's poetry took him to London in 1958-1959 as a Nuffield Foundation Fellow. During 1962-1963 he was a Canada Council Senior Arts Fellow and Lecturer on Contemporary Canadian Poetry in Latin America and the West Indies. Birney assisted in the posthumous publication of the manuscripts of his friend Malcolm Lowry: he was editor of the Selected Poems (1962) and co-editor of Lunar Caustic (1968). In 1961 he had been co-compiler of a Lowry bibliography.

He has been Writer-in-Residence at various universities: Toronto (1965-1967), Waterloo (1967-1968), and California (1968). More recently, he has made "reading tours" of Australia, New Zealand, the United States, Canada, the British Isles, West and East Africa, and South Asia. He has written a large number of radio plays (for the CBC), talks, articles, stories and reviews, as well as some academic articles on Chaucer and medieval English literature. The Creative Writer (1966) is an important contribution to Canadian criticism. Trial of a City, a poetic play in verse, was published in 1952. He also wrote two novels, the picaresque Turvey (1953) and Down the Long Table (1955).

In addition to an honorary degree from the University of Alberta, Birney has received the 1951 Leacock Medal for Humor (for his novel Turvey), the Lorne Pierce Medal of the Royal Society of Canada (1952) and the Canada Council Medal (1968).

Birney's fame as a poet began with his publication of David and Other Poems (1942) and Now is Time (1945), both of which won Governor-General's awards. Altogether, Birney has published more than a dozen collections of poetry, including his Selected Poems 1940-1966 (1966) and his most recent book The Bear on the Delhi Road (1973).

His "[Recent Poetic] Experimentation" appears in this book, pages 615-619.

DAVID

I

David and I that summer cut trails on the Survey,
All week in the valley for wages, in air that was steeped
In the wail of mosquitoes, but over the sunalive weekends
We climbed, to get from the ruck of the camp, the surly

Poker, the wrangling, the snoring under the fetid
Tents, and because we had joy in our lengthening coltish
Muscles, and mountains for David were made to see over,
Stairs from the valleys and steps to the sun's retreats.

II

Our first was Mount Gleam. We hiked in the long afternoon
To a curling lake and lost the lure of the faceted
Cone in the swell of its sprawling shoulders. Past
The inlet we grilled our bacon, the strips festooned

On a poplar prong, in the hurrying slant of the sunset.
Then the two of us rolled in the blanket while round us the cold
Pines thrust at the stars. The dawn was a floating
Of mists till we reached to the slopes above timber, and won

To snow like fire in the sunlight. The peak was upthrust
Like a fist in a frozen ocean of rock that swirled
Into valleys the moon could be rolled in. Remotely unfurling
Eastward the alien prairie glittered. Down through the dusty

Skree on the west we descended, and David showed me
How to use the give of shale for giant incredible
Strides. I remember, before the larches' edge,
That I jumped a long green surf of juniper flowing

Away from the wind, and landed in gentian and saxifrage
Spilled on the moss. Then the darkening firs
And the sudden whirring of water that knifed down a fern-hidden
Cliff and splashed unseen into mist in the shadows.

III

One Sunday on Rampart's arête a rainsquall caught us,
And passed, and we clung by our blueing fingers and bootnails
An endless hour in the sun, not daring to move
Till the ice had steamed from the slate. And David taught me

How time on a knife-edge can pass with the guessing of fragments
Remembered from poets, the naming of strata beside one,
And matching of stories from schooldays.---We crawled astride
The peak to feast on the marching ranges flagged

By the fading shreds of the shattered stormcloud. Lingering
There it was David who spied to the south, remote,
And unmapped, a sunlit spire on Sawback, an overhang
Crooked like a talon. David named it the Finger.

That day we chanced on the skull and the splayed white ribs
Of a mountain goat underneath a cliff, caught tight
On a rock. Around were the silken feathers of kites.
And that was the first I knew that a goat could slip.

IV

And then Inglismaldie. Now I remember only
The long ascent of the lonely valley, the live
Pine spirally scarred by lightning, the slicing pipe
Of invisible pika, and great prints, by the lowest

Snow, of a grizzly. There it was too that David
Taught me to read the scroll of coral in limestone
And the beetle-seal in the shale of ghostly trilobites,
Letters delivered to man from the Cambrian waves.

V

On Sundance we tried from the col and the going was hard.
The air howled from our feet to the smudged rocks
And the papery lake below. At an outthrust we balked
Till David clung with his left to a dint in the scarp,

Lobbed the iceaxe over the rocky lip,
Slipped from his holds and hung by the quivering pick,
Twisted his long legs up into space and kicked
To the crest. Then grinning, he reached with his freckled wrist

And drew me up after. We set a new time for that climb.
That day returning we found a robin gyrating
In grass, wing-broken. I caught it to tame but David
Took and killed it, and said, "Could you teach it to fly?"

VI

In August, the second attempt, we ascended The Fortress.
By the forks of the Spray we caught five trout and fried them
Over a balsam fire. The woods were alive
With the vaulting of mule-deer and drenched with clouds all the morning,

Till we burst at noon to the flashing and floating round
Of the peaks. Coming down we picked in our hats the bright
And sunhot raspberries, eating them under a mighty
Spruce, while a marten moving like quicksilver scouted us.

VII

But always we talked of the Finger on Sawback, unknown
And hooked, till the first afternoon in September we slogged
Through the musky woods, past a swamp that quivered with frog-song
And camped by a bottle-green lake. But under the cold

Breath of the glacier sleep would not come, the moonlight
Etching the Finger. We rose and trod past the feathery
Larch, while the stars went out, and the quiet heather
Flushed, and the skyline pulsed with the surging bloom

Of incredible dawn in the Rockies. David spotted
Bighorns across the moraine and sent them leaping
With yodels the ramparts redoubled and rolled to the peaks
And the peaks to the sun. The ice in the morning thaw

Was a gurgling world of crystal and cold blue chasms,
And seracs that shone like frozen saltgreen waves.
At the base of the Finger we tried once and failed. Then David
Edged to the west and discovered the chimney; the last

Hundred feet we fought the rock and shouldered and kneed
Our way for an hour and made it. Unroping we formed
A cairn on the rotting tip. Then I turned to look north
At the glistening wedge of giant Assiniboine, heedless

Of handhold. And one foot gave. I swayed and shouted.
David turned sharp and reached out his arm and steadied me
Turning again with a grin and his lips ready
To jest. But the strain crumbled his foothold. Without

A gasp he was gone. I froze to the sound of grating
Edge-nails and fingers, the slither of stones, the lone
Second of silence, the nightmare thud. Then only
The wind and the muted beat of unknowing cascades.

VIII

Somehow I worked down the fifty impossible feet
To the ledge, calling and getting no answer but echoes
Released in the cirque, and trying not to reflect
What an answer would mean. He lay still, with his lean

Young face upturned and strangely unmarred, but his legs
Splayed beneath him, beside the final drop,
Six hundred feet sheer to the ice. My throat stopped
When I reached him, for he was alive. He opened his gray

Straight eyes and brokenly murmured "over---over."
And I, feeling beneath him a cruel fang
Of the ledge thrust in his back, but not understanding,
Mumbled stupidly, "Best not to move," and spoke

Of his pain. But he said, "I can't move.---If only I felt
Some pain." Then my shame stung the tears to my eyes
As I crouched, and I cursed myself, but he cried,
Louder, "No, Bobbie! Don't ever blame yourself.

I didn't test my foothold." He shut the lids
Of his eyes to the stare of the sky, while I moistened his lips
From our water flask and tearing my shirt into strips
I swabbed the shredded hands. But the blood slid

From his side and stained the stone and the thirsting lichens,
And yet I dared not lift him up from the gore
Of the rock. Then he whispered, "Bob, I want to go over!"
This time I knew what he meant and I grasped for a lie

And said, "I'll be back here by midnight with ropes
And men from the camp and we'll cradle you out." But I knew
That the day and the night must pass and the cold dews
Of another morning before such men unknowing

The ways of mountains could win to the chimney's top.
And then, how long? And he knew---and the hell of hours
After that, if he lived till we came, roping him out.
But I curled beside him and whispered, "The bleeding will stop.

You can last." He said only, "Perhaps---. For what? A wheelchair,
Bob?" His eyes brightening with fever upbraided me.
I could not look at him more and said, "Then I'll stay
With you." But he did not speak, for the clouding fever.

I lay dazed and stared at the long valley,
The glistening hair of a creek on the rug stretched
By the firs, while the sun leaned round and flooded the ledge,
The moss, and David still as a broken doll.

I hunched to my knees to leave, but he called and his voice
Now was sharpened with fear. "For Christ's sake push me over!
If I could move---. Or die---." The sweat ran from his forehead,
But only his eyes moved. A kite was buoying

Blackly its wings over the wrinkled ice.
The purr of a waterfall rose and sank with the wind.
Above us climbed the last joint of the Finger
Beckoning bleakly the wide indifferent sky.

Even then in the sun it grew cold lying there.---And I knew
He had tested his holds. It was I who had not.---I looked
At the blood on the ledge, and the far valley. I looked
At last in his eyes. He breathed, "I'd do it for you, Bob."

IX

I will not remember how nor why I could twist
Up the wind-devilled peak, and down through the chimney's empty
Horror, and over the traverse alone. I remember
Only the pounding fear I would stumble on It

When I came to the grave-cold maw of the bergschrund---reeling
Over the sun-cankered snowbridge, shying the caves
In the névé---the fear, and the need to make sure It was there
On the ice, the running and falling and running, leaping

Of gaping greenthroated crevasses, alone and pursued
By the Finger's lengthening shadow. At last through the fanged
And blinding seracs I slid to the milky wrangling
Falls at the glacier's snout, through the rocks piled huge

On the humped moraine, and into the spectral larches,
Alone. By the glooming lake I sank and chilled
My mouth but I could not rest and stumbled still
To the valley, losing my way in the ragged marsh.

I was glad of the mire that covered the stains, on my ripped
Boots, of his blood, but panic was on me, the reek
Of the bog, the purple glimmer of toadstools obscene
In the twilight. I staggered clear to a firewaste, tripped

And fell with a shriek on my shoulder. It somehow eased
My heart to know I was hurt, but I did not faint
And I could not stop while over me hung the range
Of the Sawback. In blackness I searched for the trail by the creek

And found it. --- My feet squelched a slug and horror
Rose again in my nostrils. I hurled myself
Down the path. In the woods behind some animal yelped.
Then I saw the glimmer of tents and babbled my story.

I said that he fell straight to the ice where they found him,
And none but the sun and incurious clouds have lingered
Around the marks of that day on the ledge of the Finger,
That day, the last of my youth, on the last of our mountains.

—1942

VANCOUVER LIGHTS

About me the night, moonless, wimples the mountains,
wraps ocean, land, air, and mounting
sucks at the stars. The city, throbbing below,
webs the sable peninsula. Streaming, the golden
strands overleap the seajet, by bridge, and buoy,
vault the shears of the inlet, climb the woods
toward me, falter and halt. Across to the firefly
haze of a ship on the gulf's erased horizon
roll the lambent spokes of a restless lighthouse.

Now through the feckless years we have come to the time
when to look on this quilt of lamps is a troubling delight.
Welling from Europe's bog, through Africa flowing
and Asia, drowning the lonely lumes on the oceans,
tiding up over Halifax, and now to this winking
outpost, comes flooding the primal ink.

On this mountain's brutish forehead, with terror of space
I stir, of the changeless night and the stark ranges
of nothing, pulsing down from beyond and between
the fragile planets. We are a spark beleaguered
by darkness; this twinkle we make in a corner of emptiness,
how shall we utter our fear that the black Experimentress
will never in the range of her microscope find it? Our Phoebus
himself is a bubble that dries on Her slide, while the Nubian
wears for an evening's whim a necklace of nebulae.

Yet we must speak, we the unique glowworms.
Out of the waters and rocks of our little world
we cunningly conjured these flames, hooped these sparks
by our will. From blankness and cold we fashioned stars
to our size, rulered with manplot the velvet chaos
and signalled Aldebaran. This must we say,
whoever may be to hear us, if murk devour,
and none weave again in gossamer:

These rays were ours,

we made and unmade them. Not the shudder of continents
doused us, the moon's passion, nor crash of comets.
In the fathomless heat of our dwarfdom, our dream's combustion,
we contrived the power, the blast that snuffed us.
No one bound Prometheus. Himself he chained
and consumed his own bright liver. O Stranger,
Plutonian, descendant, or beast in the stretching night —
there was light.

—1942, 1948

ANGLOSAXON STREET

Dawndrizzle ended,   dampness steams from
blotching brick and   blank plasterwaste.
Faded housepatterns,   hoary and finicky,
unfold stuttering,   stick like a phonograph.
Over the eaves and   over dank roofs
peep giraffetowers,   pasted planless
against graysky,   great dronecliffs
like cutouts for kids,   clipped in two dimensions.

Here is a ghetto   gotten for goyim,
O with care denuded   of nigger and kike.
No coonsmell rankles,   reeks only cellarrot,
attar of carexhaust,   catcorpse and cookinggrease.
Imperial hearts   heave in this haven.
Cracks across windows   are welded with slogans:
There'll Always Be An England   enhances geraniums,
and *V's* for a *Victory*   vanquish the housefly.

Ho! with climbing sun,   heading from cocoons,
go bleached beldames,   garnished in bargainbasements,
festooned with shoppingbags,   farded, flatarched,
bigthewed Saxonwives,   stepping over buttrivers,
waddling back to suckle   smallfry, wienerladen.

Hoy! with sunslope,   shrieking over hydrants,
flood from learninghall   the lean fingerlings,
Nordic, nobblecheeked,   not all clean of nose,
leaping Commando-wise   into leprous lanes.

What! after whistleblow,   spewed from wheelboat,
after daylong doughtiness,   dire handplay
in sewertrench or sandpit,   come Saxonthegns,
Junebrown Jutekings,   jawslack for meat.

Sit after supper   on smeared doorsteps,
not humbly swearing   hatedeeds on Huns,
profiteers, politicians,   pacifists, Jews.

Then by twobit magic   to muse in movie,
unlock picturehoard,   or lope to alehall,
soaking bleakly   in beer, skittleless.

Home again to hotbox   and humid husbandhood,
in slumbertrough adding   sleepily to Anglekin.
Alongside in lanenooks   carling and leman
caterwaul and clip,   careless of Saxonry,
with moonglow and haste   and a higher heartbeat.

Slumbers now slumtrack,   unstinks, cooling,
waiting brief for milkhind,   mornstar and worldrise.

Toronto 1942   —*1942, 1948*

THE ROAD TO NIJMEGEN*

(For Gabrielle)

December, my dear, on the road to Nijmegen,
between the stones and the bitter skies was your face.

At first only the gatherings of graves
along the lank canals, each with a frosted
billy-tin for motto; the bones of tanks
beside the stoven bridges; old men in the mist
knifing chips from a boulevard of stumps;
or women riding into the wind on the rims of their cycles,
like tattered sailboats tossing over the cobbles.

These at first, and the fangs of homes, but more
the clusters of children, like flies, at the back of mess-huts,
or groping in gravel for knobs of coal,
their legs standing like dead stems out of their clogs.

Numbed on the long road to mangled Nijmegen,
I thought that only the living of others assures us;
we remember the gentle and true as trees walking,
as the men and women whose breath is a garment about us;
that we who are stretched now in this tomb of time
may remount like Lazarus into the light of kindness
by a hold in the hands of the kind.

*Pronounced Ny-*may*-gen.

296

And so in the sleet as we neared Nijmegen,
searching my heart for the hope of our minds,
for the proof in the flesh of the words we wish,
for laughter outrising at last the rockets,
I saw the rainbow answer of you,
of you and your seed who, peopling the earth, would distil
our not impossible dreamed horizon,
and who, moving within the nightmare Now,
give us what creed we have for our daily crimes,
for this road that arrives at no future,
for this guilt
in the griefs of the old and the graves of the young.

Holland, January, 1945   *—1945*

WORLD CONFERENCE

The quiet diesel in the breast
   propels a trusting keel
whether we swing toward a port
   or crocodiles of steel.

The compassed mind must quiver north
   though every chart defective;
there is no fog but in the will,
   the iceberg is elective.

Troopship 1943   *—1945*

FROM THE HAZEL BOUGH

He met a lady
   on a lazy street
hazel eyes
   and little plush feet

her legs swam by
   like lovely trout
eyes were trees
   where boys leant out

hands in the dark and
   a river side
round breasts rising
   with the finger's tide

she was plump as a finch
   and live as a salmon
gay as silk and
   proud as a Brahmin

they winked when they met
   and laughed when they parted
never took time
   to be brokenhearted

but no man sees
   where the trout lie now
or what leans out
   from the hazel bough

—1948

THE EBB BEGINS FROM DREAM

The stars like stranded starfish pale and die
and tinted sands of dawning dry.
The ebb begins from dream, leaving a border
of milk and morning paper on the porches.

From homes like crusted reefs behind the
    Danforth,
from Peele, and all the suburbs' unkempt shores
the workers slip reluctant, half-asleep,
lapse back into the city's deep.
The waves of factory hands and heads, of
    salesman
eyes and dulling waitress faces,
slide soughing out from night's brief crannies,
suck back along the strand of streets, rattling
pebbled smalltalk. O then the curves and curls
of girl stenographers, the loops and purls
of children foaming in the ooze
that by the ceaseless moon of living moves
through heaving flats of habit down the day.

And late, from tortuous coves in Forest Hill
and Rosedale, sets the sinuous undertow
of brokers, and the rolling politicians flow
to welter in the one pelagic motion.
Housewives, beached like crabs in staling pools,

crisscross, are swashed in search of food
down to the booming caves of Queen and
    Bloor.

Ah, then, with turning earth, relentless moon,
slow, but flooding, comes the swell once more;
with gurge and laughter's plash and murmur
back to the fraying rocks, far-freighted now
with briny flotsam of each morning vow,
with wrack of deeds that dull with neaping,
dead sins that float again to sea,
frustrations like long weeds that lie
and rot between the cracks of life,
and hopes that waterlogged will never link
to land but will be borne until they sink.

Now tide is full and sighing creeps
into the clean sought coigns of sleep.
And yet in sleep begins to stir,
to mutter in the dark its yearning,
and to the round possessive mother turning
dreams of vaster wellings, makes the last cliff
    totter,
cradles all the globe in swaying water.

The ebb begins from dream. - - -

Toronto

—1948

MAPPEMOUNDE

No not this old whalehall can whelm us,
shiptamed, gullgraced, soft to our glidings.
Harrows that mere more that squares our map.
See in its north where scribe has marked *mermen*,
shore-sneakers who croon, to the seafarer's girl,
next year's gleewords. East and west *nadders*,
flamefanged bale-twisters; their breath dries up tears,
chars in the breast-hoard the dear face-charm.
Southward *Cetegrande*, that sly beast who sucks
in with whirlwind also the wanderer's pledges.
That sea is hight Time, it hems all hearts' landtrace.
Men say the redeless, reaching its bounds,
topple in maelstrom, tread back never.
Adread in that mere we drift to map's end.

—1948

MAN IS A SNOW

Not the cougar leaping to myth
from the orange lynx of our flame
not the timber swooning to death
in the shock of the saw's bright whine
but the rotograved lie
the pine resurrected in slum
and a nursery of crosses in Europe

Not the death of the prairie grass
in the wheat's monotonous flooding
but the harvest mildewed with doubt

and the starved in the hour of hoarding
not the rivers we foul but our blood
o cold and more devious rushing

Man is a snow that cracks
the trees' red resinous arches
that winters his cabined heart
till the chilled nail shrinks in the wall
and pistols the brittle air
till frost like ferns of the world that is lost
unfurls on the darkening windows

—1949

WIND-CHIMES IN A TEMPLE RUIN

This is the moment
   for two glass leaves
dangling dumb
   from the temple eaves
This is the instant
   when the sly air breathes
and the tremblers touch
   where no man sees

Who is the moving
   or moved is no matter
but the birth of the possible
   song in the rafter
that dies as the wind goes
   nudging other
broken eaves
   for waiting lovers

—1962

EL GRECO: *ESPOLIO*

The carpenter is intent on the pressure of his hand
on the awl, and the trick of pinpointing his strength
through the awl to the wood, which is tough.
He has no effort to spare for despoilings
nor to worry if he'll be cut in on the dice.
His skill is vital to the scene, and the safety of the state.
Anyone can perform the indignities; it is his hard arms
and craft that hold the eyes of the convict's women.
There is the problem of getting the holes straight
(in the middle of this shoving crowd)
and deep enough to hold the spikes
after they've sunk through those soft feet
and wrists waiting behind him.
The carpenter isnt aware that one of the hands
is held in a curious beseechment over him —
but what is besought, forgiveness or blessing? —
nor if he saw would he take the time to be puzzled.

Criminals come in all sorts, as anyone knows who makes crosses,
are as mad or sane as those who decide on their killings.
Our one at least has been quiet so far
though they say he has talked himself into this trouble —
a carpenter's son who got notions of preaching.
Well here's a carpenter's son who'll have carpenter's sons,
God willing, and build what's wanted, temples or tables,
mangers or crosses, and shape them decently,
working alone in that firm and profound abstraction
which blots out the bawling of rag-snatchers.
To construct with hands, knee-weight, braced thigh,
keeps the back turned from death.
But it's too late now for the other carpenter's boy
to return to this peace before the nails are hammered.

—*1962*

ELLESMERELAND

Explorers say that harebells rise
from the cracks of Ellesmereland
and cod swim fat beneath the ice
that grinds its meagre sands

No man is settled on that coast
The harebells are alone
Nor is there talk of making man
from ice cod bell or stone   —*1962*

ELLESMERELAND II

And now in Ellesmereland there sits
a town of twenty men
They guard the floes that reach to the Pole
a hundred leagues and ten
The warders watch the sky watch them
the stricken hills eye both
A Mountie visits twice a year
And there is talk of growth

—*1965*

THE BEAR ON THE DELHI ROAD

Unreal, tall as a myth
by the road the Himalayan bear
is beating the brilliant air
with his crooked arms.
About him two men, bare,
spindly as locusts, leap.
One pulls on a ring
in the great soft nose; his mate
flicks, flicks with a stick
up at the rolling eyes.

They have not led him here,
down from the fabulous hills
to this bald, alien plain
and the clamorous world, to kill
but simply to teach him to dance.

They are peaceful both, these spare
men of Kashmir, and the bear
alive is their living too.
If far on the Delhi way
around him galvanic they dance
it is merely to wear, wear
from his shaggy body the tranced
wish forever to stay
only an ambling bear
four-footed in berries.

It is no more joyous for them
in this hot dust to prance
out of reach of the praying claws
sharpened to paw for ants
in the shadows of deodars.

It is not easy to free
myth from reality
or rear this fellow up

to lurch, lurch with them
in the tranced dancing of men.

—1962

FOR GEORGE LAMMING

To you
    I can risk words about this

Mastering them you know
    they are dull
        servants
who say less
    and worse
        than we feel

That party above Kingston Town
    we stood   five (six ?) couples
linked singing
    more than rum happy

I was giddy
    from sudden friendship
    wanted   undeserved

black tulip faces
self swaying forgotten
laughter in dance

Suddenly on a wall mirror
    my face assaulted me
stunned to see itself
    like a white snail
    in the supple dark flowers

Always now
    I move grateful
        to all of you
who let me walk thoughtless
    and unchallenged
in the gardens
    in the castles
        of your skins

Jamaica, November, 1963

—1964

BUILDINGS 2

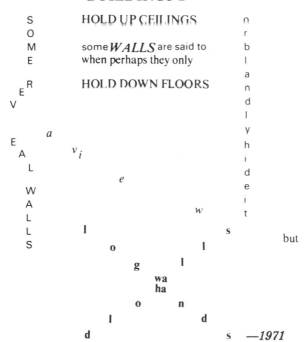

—1971

LEO KENNEDY

(1907-   )

Leo Kennedy, who came to Canada from England when he was a child five years old, attended the University of Montreal, but was associated with the young McGill poets of the 1920's while contributing to The McGill Fortnightly Review *and* The Canadian Mercury. *He was one of the editors of the latter in 1928. Kennedy left Canada to live in the United States, but his one book of poems,* The Shrouding *(1933), remains as a significant contribution to Canadian literature. Some of his poems were also included in* New Provinces *(1936), edited by F. R. Scott. He is now on the staff of* Reader's Digest *in Pleasantville, New York.*

EPITHALAMIUM

This body of my mother, pierced by me,
In grim fulfilment of our destiny,
Now dry and quiet as her fallow womb
Is laid beside the shell of that bridegroom
My father, who with eyes towards the wall
Sleeps evenly; his dust stirs not at all,
No syllable of greeting curls his lips,
As to that shrunken side his leman slips.

Lo! these are two of unabated worth
Who in the shallow bridal bed of earth
Find youth's fecundity, and of their swift
Comminglement of bone and sinew, lift
— A lover's seasonable gift to blood
Made bitter by a parchèd widowhood —
This bloom of tansy from the fertile ground:
My sister, heralded by no moan, no sound.

—1933

WORDS FOR A RESURRECTION

Each pale Christ stirring underground
Splits the brown casket of its root,
Wherefrom the rousing soil upthrusts
A narrow, pointed shoot,

And bones long quiet under frost
Rejoice as bells precipitate
The loud, ecstatic sundering,
The hour inviolate.

This Man of April walks again —
Such marvel does the time allow —
With laughter in His blessèd bones,
And lilies on His brow.

—1933

HUGH MacLENNAN

(1907-   )

Hugh MacLennan was born in Cape Breton Island, the son of a physician of Highland Scot antecedents. The family moved to Halifax in 1914, and survived the great explosion in 1917, when the Mont Blanc, *with its cargo of explosives, collided with the* Imo *in Halifax harbor. One-tenth of the city was destroyed, and about three thousand persons were killed. The memories stored up by the ten-year-old boy found expression later in MacLennan's first novel,* Barometer Rising *(1941).*

In 1929 MacLennan earned a B.A. in Classics from Dalhousie University, and then he proceeded to Oriel College, Oxford, on a Rhodes Scholarship. Gaining his degree from Oxford in 1932, he continued his studies at Princeton University, where he obtained his Ph.D. in 1935 with the completion of his thesis: Oxyrhynchus, An Economic and Social Study. *Between 1935 and 1945 he taught classics and history at Lower Canada College in Montreal while establishing himself as a novelist. The award of a Guggenheim Fellowship in Creative Writing (1943-1944) enabled him to complete his second novel,* Two Solitudes, *which won the Governor-General's Award for fiction in 1945. His third novel,* The Precipice *(1948), and his fifth novel,* The Watch That Ends the Night *(1959), also won the award. Since two of his books of essays,* Cross Country *(1949) and* Thirty and Three *(1954), have also won in their class, MacLennan has the distinction of having received more Governor-General's awards than any other writer. He has received honorary degrees from four universities. and been appointed a Companion of the Order of Canada.*

In 1936 he married the writer Dorothy Duncan, who died in 1957 after long being ill with an incurable heart disease. He is now remarried. He was appointed to the staff of McGill University in 1951 and is now a Professor in the Department of English. His sixth novel, Return of the Sphinx, *was published in 1967.*

THE RIVERS THAT MADE A NATION

If any modern Canadian is curious to know how his country was valued two centuries ago, all he need do is recall some of the sentiments it inspired among famous men at that time. Voltaire's dismissal of the St. Lawrence Valley as "a few acres of snow" is almost too well known to repeat; it is less well known that Montcalm, who now is a Canadian hero, loathed the country he fought to defend. The British never valued Canada for herself. Just before the peace conference which ended the Seven Years War there was strong pressure in England in favour of trading Canada back to France in return for Guadeloupe. This little Carib isle grew sugar which makes rum, and because many people like rum, rum will always have an economic future.

But in early days few people liked the Land of Cain or the Land of Snows, nor did many believe that it could possibly have an economic future worth mentioning. Had it not been for the strategic necessity of securing the St. Lawrence as a high-road into the Ohio Territory, and also of protecting the northern flank of the rich Thirteen Colonies, Guadeloupe might easily have been England's choice.

Nor would the British of that time have been absurd if they had made such a choice. Canada may have had, as Dr. Johnson remarked of Lapland and the Scottish Highlands, "prodigious wild and noble prospects," but the Age of Reason saw nothing beautiful in wild and noble prospects, and certainly nothing useful. Least of all could the British recognize any economic future in a terrain shaggy with evergreens and horrid (to them the word meant "bristling") with the rocky outcroppings of the Pre-Cambrian Shield. In addition to all these disadvantages there was the Canadian climate.

Once more we cannot consider the British to have been stupid. The gold and practical metals of the Shield were still locked there, hidden, awaiting a twentieth-century technology to make them available to men. Two centuries ago nobody understood the value of petroleum, least of all did they know that a lake of it existed under the Alberta plain. From the servants of the Hudson's Bay Company the English might have picked up some vague information about prairie soils, but they would have presumed them unfavourable to any large creatures except the buffalo which browsed and multiplied in the knee-high grass of a pasture a thousand miles wide. After fearful hardships the Selkirk settlers managed to keep themselves alive in Manitoba, but for decades they were the most isolated farmers in North America. Railways had to be built, farm implements mechanized, grain elevators invented before wheat growing could become the huge industry it is today. As for the timber of the Canadian east, it never transcended a local use before Napoleon sealed off the Baltic ports from British shipping and made it profitable for Canadian business men to export timber for the masts and decks of the Royal Navy. Most of Canada, just like Siberia, had to wait for the age of technology before it could be developed.

Two centuries ago—and this the English understood when they toyed with the idea of exchanging Canada for Guadeloupe—the sole profitable Canadian enterprises were fur trading and the coastal fisheries. Of these, only the former was of real and continuing interest to the capitals of Europe.

Far different was the situation south of what is now the Canadian-American border. With climates ranging from temperate to sub-tropical, the American English soon developed an economy of considerable variety. Towns and cities flourished on the fertile lands between the sea and the Appalachians. The ports were all ice-free and in easy contact with Europe and the West Indies. By the middle of the eighteenth century a mature urban culture had grown in cities like Boston, New York, Philadelphia, Baltimore and Charleston, and its capacity to offer outlets to a variety of human resources and talents was soon proved by the kind of men it produced. The careers, interests and abilities of men like Benjamin Franklin, Thomas Jefferson and John Jay were of a kind that could not have been developed in the Canada of that time, any more than the careers and abilities of men like Peter Pond and Alexander Mackenzie could have been developed within the Thirteen Colonies. Sophistication is the product of universities and the variety of urban life, epic adventures of a society much more primitive.

In the early days the Canadian experience was epic, and the price of such an experience is roughness and lack of education. As late as 1800, James McGill wrote to the Governor of Lower Canada that not one boy in five in the Montreal area could write his own name. Reading and writing was of no use to a canoe man (nearly all the *engagés* in the fur trade signed with an X), and for a hundred and fifty years young French Canadians had been growing up along the St. Lawrence expecting to earn their livings on the rivers leading into the west.

For this reason alone, urban growth in Canada was extremely slow, and the seniority of a few Canadian cities is no indication whatever of a cultural maturity. Though Quebec was founded some dozen years before the landing of the Pilgrims in Massachusetts, and in the mid-eighteenth century had an imposing presence on its rock above the river, it was really more fortress than city. Louisbourg in Cape Breton Island was rightly named the Gibraltar of America: nearly all of its citizens were soldiers. Halifax, founded in 1749, was originally intended as a naval and military base and only developed into a true city after the American Revolution. As for Montreal, up to the end of the Napoleonic Wars, when its population was verging on 20,000, it could almost be described as a supply depot and base camp for the fur trade carried on in the interior.

But early Canada possessed one asset the Americans lacked: the St. Lawrence River. Its rapids halted sailing ships just above Montreal, but the river struck directly through the gap between the Laurentian and Appalachian chains, and the French Canadians used it. While the Americans remained penned between the mountains and the sea, it was the high honour of the French Canadians that their boldest spirits sallied out from the St. Lawrence to explore and map nearly all·of the continental interior which Americans and English-speaking Canadians now occupy. Many Americans today believe that their own West was unknown before the mountain men went up the Missouri, but French-Canadian voyageurs had been there long before the mountain men. When Francis Parkman went out on the Oregon Trail in 1846, the epic period of French-Scottish-Canadian exploration was over. But the reliable guides Parkman found in the Missouri country were all French Canadians. They were the last in a long chain of frontier adventurers whose abilities had been developed by the fur trade.

By its very nature this was a river trade. The rivers brought the traders and the Indians into contact with each other, and from the beginning the French had a wonderful naturalness in getting on with the Indians. The tributaries and back-waters of the great river systems were breeding grounds for the animals, and most of the valuable fur-bearing animals are amphibious. In early times the beaver was the animal whose fur was most highly valued in Europe, and for a curious reason: it served as raw material for the hat trade in a period when the wearing of costly hats was deemed essential to a man's status as a fine gentleman. By another of history's ironies—and Canadian history has been a huge congeries of ironies—this wild and dangerous trade owed its support to a temporary fashion in the capitals of Europe.

The dominance of the fur trade conspired with conditions of soil and climate to retard the development of a true Canadian culture. Not only was fur trading a nomadic occupation; it discouraged settlement everywhere because settlement drove off the animals. It could never afford to employ a large body of workers in the field, and the great majority of these were ignorant men who regarded themselves as a class apart, very much like mercenary soldiers in the old days. Since some of the leaders—Alexander Mackenzie, for instance, David Thompson, Alexander Henry and William McGillivray—had intelligence and sensitivity, they hated the harshness and semi-savagery of life in the field, though the goal that urged them onward never failed to give them a mental and moral dominance over the men they led.

Even the habits of the beaver tribe conspired to turn the early Canadians into rovers who departed further and further from civilization. The beaver is not a remarkably prolific animal: if let alone, the beaver population never increases by more than 20% annually. When the Europeans first arrived in America there were, according to later computations, about ten million beaver on the continent, their numbers varying between ten to fifty per square mile in the regions where they bred. This was not a large number considering the destructiveness of the trade. The beaver's habits made it impossible for him to escape his enemies because he was not a migrant. He lived in lodges. As David Thompson noted, the beaver "could be attacked at any convenient time and in all seasons, and thus their numbers were reduced."

They were reduced so rapidly that in the Maritime Provinces the fur trade was virtually dead after a few years of European depredation. As early as 1635, only twenty-seven years after the founding of Quebec, beaver had almost vanished in the region about Three Rivers, despite the fact that the St. Maurice is a great tributary which still, for most of its course, flows through uninhabited land. Champlain himself recognized that if he hoped to retain the interest of his home government in the colony of New France, the fur trade would have to be carried into the interior. *His* primary interest may have been to find the Northwest Passage to the sea of Japan, but he was practical enough to see that if this venture was to be financed, it would have to be paid for in beaver.

It was Champlain who was the first European to recognize that if Canadians were to move in a forested country they would have to forget about horses and even about European methods of navigation. Cartier had been stopped at Lachine, and so was he:

"The water here is so swift that it could not be more so . . . so that it is impossible to imagine one's being able to go by boats through these falls. But anyone desiring to pass them, should provide himself with the canoe of the savages, which a man can easily carry."

So began, with Champlain's first tentative journey in a crazy birch-bark canoe above Montreal, the first chapter in the long saga of voyaging. The canoe, as has sometimes been suggested, would make as accurate a symbol on our coat of arms as the beaver, and the birch tree a truer emblem than the maple. Canada is one of the few countries which did not depend for its early development on the horse. In the Canadian bush a horse could neither eat nor move; if you merely tethered him there the mosquitoes and blackflies would kill him or drive him mad. But the birch-bark canoe could go wherever there was a foot of water to float it, and was so light that even the largest could be carried by a few men. The canoe made possible the careers of generation after generation of explorers who were to follow the rivers of America from Montreal to the Gulf of Mexico, to the Beaufort Sea, and finally to the Pacific Ocean.

It was Champlain, as Bartlet Brebner suggests, who invented the strange trade of voyageur, with its even stranger derivative, the *coureur de bois*. The difference between them was technically a legal one. The *coureur de bois* was an individualist who operated without a licence, and when he first appeared in the west, the servants of the Hudson's Bay Company called him a pedlar. But voyaging, as it was conceived by some of the greater spirits who engaged in it, was more than fur trading. Though men like Radisson, LaSalle, LaVérendrye, Samuel Hearne, Alexander Mackenzie, David Thompson and Simon Fraser were certainly in the fur-trading business, essentially they were explorers.

Once Champlain had begun the fur trade along the interior waterways, the voyages multiplied with a rapidity which still astonishes the historian. So mobile was the canoe, so enticing the next bend around the river, so dominant the human instinct to know what lay around it, that within the course of a very few years the voyageurs of French Canada were in the heartland of the continent. The names of some of them ring like bugle calls in the North American story—some of them the greatest in continental history before the age of Washington.

Etienne Brûlé, one of Champlain's "young men," almost certainly reached the Chaudière Falls on the Ottawa as early as 1610. Two years afterwards he became the first European to reach the Sweetwater Sea, as Lake Huron was then called.

Radisson, with his brother-in-law Groseilliers, was probably west of Lake Michigan by the mid-1650s. During this period (the dates are uncertain) the pair entered Lake Superior and *discovered a portage over which other unknown voyageurs, possibly French, had passed before them!* Soon after this they were in Minnesota at the top of the drainage basin of the greatest river on the continent. When the government of New France, which seldom had the quality of its greatest subjects, confiscated the furs of Radisson and Groseilliers on the excuse that they lacked a licence to trade, they went over to the English, and one result of their doing so was the founding of the Hudson's Bay Company.

The two priests, Marquette and Jolliet, descended the Mississippi as far as the Arkansas in 1673, and thereby established beyond doubt the existence of a practicable water avenue from the St. Lawrence to the Gulf of Mexico.

They were followed a decade later by Cavelier de la Salle. In 1680, LaSalle was on the upper Mississippi with Père Hennepin, and in 1682 he reached the delta of the river and claimed the region later known as the Louisiana Territory for the French king.

About two decades later Sieur de Bienville, who may have been born in Montreal, became the first official governor of Louisiana. A road had been found and developed, though it was very thinly held, from Quebec City to the Gulf of Mexico. The French, using the rivers as only they knew how, had drawn a vast loop about the English colonists who still were confined to the Atlantic seaboard.

The last of the supremely great French discoverers, and surely one of the most interesting, was Pierre Gaultier de Varennes, Sieur de la Vérendrye. Born in Three Rivers in 1685 (the same year, incidentally, in which Handel and Johann Sebastian Bach were born) LaVérendrye first served in colonial wars, then went to Europe to fight in the War of the Spanish Succession. After his final return to Canada, a man over forty, he took to the rivers. Armed with a monopoly for the far western fur trade, LaVérendrye was at Grand Portage in 1731 with a party of fifty including three of his sons. He worked out a successful route through the maze of small streams, lakes and muskeg of the western Shield, and in 1734 the first white man's fort stood on the black earth of Manitoba. The vast central plain lay open to him. The Assiniboine and the South Saskatchewan wound across it and led men of the LaVérendrye party to a sight of mountains, possibly the Rockies, a little more than one hundred and thirty years after Brûlé reached the Chaudière Falls.

Nothing in later years was as epic as the sustained efforts of these early Frenchmen. It could not be. In later years the white men were better armed, and though the Indians in the Canadian west could be dangerous, they seldom if ever displayed the appalling cruelty and military vigour of the eastern savages who tortured Brébeuf to death. After the Hurons killed Etienne Brûlé, they ate him.

These facts are familiar: I repeat them only to underline the desperate nature of the early Canadian experience. There was no discharge from this war, at least not for the dedicated man. The isolation of the voyageurs, the knowledge that they were self-condemned to a life of hardship and danger before which, ultimately, their physical and moral powers were bound to fail—these thoughts haunted the bravest and boldest among them. They lacked the consolation of soldiers who risk their lives, for what they did was done without an audience, without the support of a disciplined regiment or army. They could not even communicate their experiences to civilized men, because civilized men lacked the knowledge and background to understand what they meant when they told them that the winter had descended before they could reach a base camp, or that such and such a number of portages had been made or rapids run in such and such a number of days.

Thoughts like these were in Radisson's mind when he wrote a passage with the force of poetry:

"What fairer bastion than a good tongue, especially when one sees his owne chimney smoak, or when we can kisse our owne wife or kisse our neighbour's wife with ease and delight? It is a different thing when victuals are wanting, worke whole nights & dayes, lye down on the bare ground, & not always that hap, the breech in the water, the feare in the buttocks, to have the belly empty, the wearinesse in the bones, the drowsinesse in the body by the bad weather you are to suffer, having nothing to keep you from such calamity."

When New France fell and was ceded to England in 1763, the control of the Canadian fur trade passed from the French forever. English-speaking men, most of them Scottish Highlanders, now appear in the trade working with the experienced French-Canadian voyageurs who served under them in the North West Company as *engagés*. It was a partnership vital for the future of Canada, and the beginning of the Scottish influence in Canadian affairs.

For it was about this time that the Highland Scotch had finally reached the end of their long, brave but self-damaging struggle for independence against the Anglo-Saxons of the south. The English had conquered them in 1745 and doomed the clansman's way of life. At the best of times it had been a poor life in a poor country: it has been remarked more than once that only the Highlanders and the French Canadians had the necessary background of poverty to qualify them for work on the Canadian rivers. Already the Hudson's Bay Company, scouring the British Isles for men hardy, desperate and disciplined enough to entice into the trade, had been recruiting Orkneymen from the rocks of Ultima Thule, shipping them by the northern route into Hudson Bay and putting them to work there.

Simon McTavish, the master of the North West Company, lived in Montreal like a lord and had something of the temperament and style of a highland chief of the better sort, though his Scottish ancestry was probably less exalted than he liked to pretend. All of these Highlanders — as distinct from the patient Orkneymen — had the intense personal pride of a race never noted for its emotional balance. This may have been one reason why they had so little sympathy for the slogans of the democratic revolution then brewing in the Thirteen Colonies. That revolution came out of the middle classes, and the Highlands had never had a middle class.

The fire, the imagination and the boldness of these Highland leaders transformed the whole character of the fur trade and turned it into an enterprise in which business considerations, at least as seen by a cool-headed man, very often took a second place to dreams. When the American Revolution broke out, James McGill (a Glasgow man originally) instantly recognized that if the Americans won the war the south-west of the continent would soon be closed to the Canadian fur trade. When he realized that the Americans were on the point of victory, he sold his shares in the company. But Simon McTavish met the challenge by pushing it right over the edge of the map. He bet his fortune on the Athabaska region. The tenacity of McTavish and his colleagues in the face of appalling obstacles can almost be called sublime. Under the best of circumstances, fur trading was a gamble in which the margin of profit over cost was never very great. Though a few large fortunes were made in it, they were acquired by pennypinching and a driving of the *engagés* to a degree which would horrify a modern labour union. But McTavish and his associates did not hesitate. Not even the complete success of the American Revolution lessened their compulsion to expand. Ironically, it was the blind obstinacy of these Highlanders which limited the plans of some of the shrewdest American statesmen who ever lived.

When Benjamin Franklin, John Adams and John Jay met the English diplomats in Versailles in 1783 to draft the treaty which ended the Revolutionary War, one of their chief objects was to destroy permanently the British ability to threaten the new Republic. The British were still entrenched in Nova Scotia and the St. Lawrence; the Americans had not yet moved out in any large degree beyond the Appalachians. The question of the boundary between the United States and what remained of British North America was therefore the most vital question at this conference.

The boundary to which the British finally agreed was a triumph for the United States and a permanent disaster for Canada. The British were so ignorant of North American geography they did not understand what they were giving away, and they had invited no Canadians to the conference who might have told them. Ever since 1783, the Canadian population has been penned between the Shield and the border in narrow strips. The St. Lawrence and the four northern Great Lakes were split down the middle between the two countries. Montreal was cut off, totally from the Ohio Territory and the Mississippi Valley, and as a final touch Grand Portage was slipped in just underneath the new border so that it reposed in the United States. However, the British did insist on gaining equal rights along the Pigeon and Rainy rivers, and this was to be of vital importance to Canada. It left open a canoe route to the prairies and the far west.

The Montreal fur-traders had few illusions about what this border would mean to them. In time, and the time would not be long, they would be forbidden to do any business at all in the wilderness south of the border which Canadians had explored and opened up to trade. Even Grand Portage would be closed to them. So the North West Company moved their inland base to a new site at Fort William. The cost of doing so came to £10,000.

From this time until the North West Company was absorbed by the Bay in 1821, the Montreal traders met one of the most remarkable challenges in the history of commerce. As they depended on the far north-west for their furs, they were now committed to an operation in which the supply lines were stretched to a limit which would make any normal, hard-headed man of commerce turn pale. The pelts had to be paid for in trade goods conveyed three-quarters of the way across the continent in birchbark canoes. The pay loads had to be paddled and portaged back to Montreal over a distance of some three thousand miles. The market, nearly all of it in Europe, was still another three thousand miles to the east across the Atlantic Ocean.

Speed and efficiency of the highest kind, supported by an *esprit de corps* among the canoemen as intense as that of a championship hockey team, were the sole possible replies to a challenge so stern. The travel schedules set for the voyageurs seem incredible to the modern imagination.

Leaving Lachine in "brigades" of three to four canoes, with an experienced guide in the leading craft, the voyageurs from Montreal first set out for the Grand River, as the Ottawa was then called. At Sainte-Anne-de-Bellevue they always stopped to pray in the chapel to the saint who protects travellers on water, and this rite gave rise to Thomas Moore's famous poem:

> *Faintly as tolls the evening chime*
> *Our voices keep tune and our oars keep time.*
> *Soon as the woods on the shore look dim*
> *We'll sing at St. Ann's our parting hymn.*
> *Row, brothers, row! The stream runs fast,*
> *The rapids are near and the daylight's past . . . .*

This poem, written in soft music by a cultivated visitor to Canada, using the word "oars" instead of "paddles," depreciates its subject. The Homer of the *Iliad* might have risen to the experience of the voyageurs, but not the sweet poet of Ireland.

After paddling and portaging the Ottawa as far as Mattawa, the canoes turned south toward Lake Nipissing, crossed it, and descended the French River into Georgian Bay. Then they paddled west along the North Channel above Manitoulin Island, working in the dead or choppy waters of the lake and often losing several days if the winds were contrary. They called the wind *la vieille* (the old woman), and if she was behind them they could raise a sail. But if she was heavy against them — and the prevailing winds in the region are contrary to west-bound canoes

— they often had to put up on the shore because the high, steep waves of the inland lakes would break the backs of their canoes. When they went to Michilimackinac they were expected to reach their destination within a period of from thirty-five to forty days, and the same time was expected when they were bound for Grand Portage and Fort William. This voyage was accomplished with canoes fully loaded with trade goods, and there were thirty-six portages between Lachine and the Lakehead, some of them longer than a "league." In the voyageur's language, a "league" was roughly two miles. If express canoes without cargo were used, as they sometimes were on special occasions, the time was much faster. A letter survives dated in Montreal on May 6, 1817, which was received at Rainy Lake beyond Fort William on June 3.

What these voyages involved in hardship, labour and moral stamina can no more be revealed by the historian's method of stating the facts than the truth of a battle can be conveyed by the communiqué issued by the high command after the fighting is over and the dead have been counted. From Julius Caesar to the P.R.s of the Pentagon, the truth of life and death has always been hidden behind facts and statistics. That is the trouble with history. It is probably an unavoidable trouble, but it certainly explains why so few people learn much from it.

"Our men moved their camp, marched twenty miles, and at night they placed their camp in a suitable place"—how many of us welcomed lines like these when we studied the *Gallic War* in school! They occurred so often we did not have to pause to work out the grammar. But they told us nothing of the realities.

On every step of that twenty-mile march, probably through hostile country, the legionaries had to carry their weapons and food, their armour and personal necessities, a total weight close to a hundred pounds per man. When the "suitable place" was reached, it was usually on a hill with a forest nearby. While one detachment marked out the lines of the camp, another dug a trench about it and still another went into the woods to cut trees. After the trunks had been trimmed, sawn up and sharpened at one end, they were dragged to the suitable place and staked into the ground just behind the lip of the trench. Only after all this work was done could the soldier wrap himself in his cloak and fall asleep on the ground.

A similar recovery of reality is essential if any modern man is to understand the truth about life on the Canadian rivers in the voyaging days.

On May 25, 1793, a young Scot called John Macdonell set out from Lachine on his first voyage with a brigade of the North West Company. He has left a diary of that voyage written in the usual terse language of the communiqué, and he has also recorded, with the distances distinctly stated, the nature of each of the thirty-six portages between Montreal and Grand Portage — here the carrying place was nine miles long — as well as the character of the streams and lakes. With the help of the imagination, the record is a fascinating one, the more so because this was a routine voyage.

On this stage of the journey into the west, the larger canoes carried loads varying from three to four tons and were manned by crews of eight or ten men. The middle men, using short paddles, sat two abreast while the bowman and steersman were placed higher and were equipped with paddles much longer. The Montreal canoe was thirty-five to forty feet long made entirely of the bark of yellow birch placed over ribs of thin white cedar with thwarts numbering between four and nine and boards four inches wide secured just below the gunwales as seats for the paddlemen. The bark was secured by melted pine gum, and after a heavy rapid or a day's paddling the seams had to be re-gummed to prevent leaking. The canoe used by Alexander Mackenzie, and specially designed for his exploration of the Rockies, was so light that it could be carried by two men. But the weight of a large canoe out of Montreal was much greater than this, and required at least four men on the portage. The whole operation of portaging brings up an interesting calculation in the mathematics of labour, sweat and tired muscles.

Superlatives have bothered me all through the writing of this book, but I cannot avoid them without diminishing what seems to me the truth. Every new thing I have learned about the Canadian voyageur seems to me more incredible than the last. His deeds originated the Paul Bunyan myths of the American north-west, and Paul Bunyan was an inheritor of Hercules and Mercury in folklore. But the true and proved facts concerning the life of the voyageur are such that I can only say that if I, physically, am a man, he, physically, was a superman.

On portages the load that had to be moved, divided up among the crew, usually totalled more than four hundred pounds per man not counting the canoe. Every man of the crew was expected to carry at least two "pieces" of goods, each weighing ninety pounds, but so great was the emulation among them that some individuals often carried three pieces or even four. They did not walk with these loads: *they carried them at a dog trot* bent half-double with the pieces on their backs and secured there by a leather band, called a tumpline, which was passed around their foreheads. More than one traveller conveyed by voyageurs in the canoes has testified that without any load at all he could barely move as fast as these men did with two hundred pounds on their backs. Finally, because they worked at the height of the insect season, the voyageurs were encased over the carrying places in humming, stinging envelopes of mosquitoes and blackflies.

In addition to the portaging there was the tracking of canoes against heavy currents and the running of rapids. The rapids were always risky, and crosses marked the graves of drowned voyageurs on the banks, clusters of them all the way from the Long Sault on the Ottawa to the mouth of the Winnipeg River. Tracking could be a nightmare. The men had to get out and haul by ropes attached to bow and stern (two ropes were essential to prevent the canoe from yawing in against the shore) and this meant slithering over wet rocks slimy with vegetable growth, stumbling over the usual litter of fallen trees and sometimes wading breast high in the stream. As I know from personal experience, the silt along the banks of the Assiniboine, Saskatchewan and Mackenzie is deep and soft, and after rain it has the consistence of porridge and sometimes the texture of axle grease. Along the Fraser when the men had to do a great deal of tracking under appalling difficulties, they wore out a pair of moccasins a day and had to make themselves new ones. While tracking canoes, the men were more plagued by insects even than when they portaged, because there were usually more of them along the water's edge. So paddling in a free river or in an open lake came as a marvellous release, and when the men swung into the stroke they broke into song. That was when time was made up. The mileage from Montreal to Georgian Bay was little more than the mileage from the mouth of French River through the Sault to the head of Lake Superior, and here the figures of John Macdonell tell their own story. It took his brigade thirty-one days to reach Lake Huron from Sainte-Anne. But though they lost a day through a storm on the lake, they reached Grand Portage from French River in just under ten days! Look at the map, remember that most of the time they were travelling against the wind, and try to believe that this was merely a routine voyage!

At Grand Portage or Fort William the Montreal men ended their runs. The Company's agent met the wintering partners from the north-west, and the trade goods were forwarded over the height of land by a special body of men to the Company's fort on Rainy Lake, the eastern terminus of *les vrais hommes du nord* who had come down across the plains from the Athabaska country. At Grand Portage or Fort William the Montreal crews had a brief time for carousing and eating, then they re-loaded their canoes with the furs and set out on the return trail to Montreal with the pay loads. If they did not get back before winter, they were frozen in and had to survive as best they could. A failure to return in time also meant a disastrous financial loss to the Company.

At Rainy Lake the true Northmen took over, and these were the élite of the service. They paddled through Lake of the Woods and by a series of smaller lakes and interconnecting streams (the Winnipeg River was exhaustingly cursed by rapids) into Lake Winnipeg itself. In earlier times canoe parties used to paddle from there up the Red River into Minnesota toward the sources of the Mississippi, but after the American Revolution the goal was the north-western edge of the North American map, Lake Athabaska and the Peace River country. The Saskatchewan and Athabaskan brigades paddled north up Lake Winnipeg to the mouth of the Saskatchewan River and then—after some very severe portages—they worked up against the current of the North Branch to Cumberland Lake and thence to Frog Portage, which made a bridge to the Churchill River. This powerful stream, against which they also had to paddle, led them to the Methye Portage (or Portage LaLoche), a very tough one with a sharp height of land at the end of it. The Methye took them to the Clearwater, a tributary of the Athabaska, and then they coasted down that great river of the north-west into Lake Athabaska and reached their chief north-western base at Fort Chipewyan. In the later years of the North West Company the brigades went even beyond this. They paddled up to Fort Vermilion on the Peace, and later still the fur-traders established themselves in forts on the Fraser and the Columbia.

This final leap across two-fifths of Ontario, across Manitoba, Saskatchewan and some or all of Alberta, all of it trending north, was a race against time even more intense than the run from Montreal to the head of Lake Superior. So close was the margin between the meeting with the Montreal canoes and the coming of frost that a delay of a few days might ruin a whole voyage. According to Alexander Mackenzie, the Athabaskan brigades generally left Rainy Lake on the first of August, and had to reach Chipewyan inside two months.

What of the canoes and of the men themselves?

By the time the North West Company was established, the art of canoe-handling had so matured on the rivers that the French Canadians were much more mobile than the men of the Hudson's Bay Company. British as they were, the Bay men clung for a long time to wooden *bateaux*. The Nor'westers used two types of canoe which they called the *canot du maître* and the *canot du nord*, the former for the run out of Montreal, the latter, which was lighter and carried less than a ton and a half of cargo, for the run west of Fort William where the streams were shallower and tracking more frequent. The *canot du nord* often carried a crew of no more than five men.

But the *canot du maître* was a considerable craft. It had a wide beam, a remarkably high strake and high, curved bows. It was gaily painted and travelled with a pennant blowing out from its stern and often with the picture of an Indian's head on its bows. A variety of pictures of these larger canoes survive and one of them has a feature which—at least to me—was more interesting than the canoe itself.

This was no less a personage than Sir George Simpson, the "Big Bourgeois" of the Hudson's Bay Company, the chief destroyer of the Nor'westers, and in his old age one of the richest men in Montreal. After the Bay absorbed the North West Company they not only employed the skilled Canadian voyageurs; even before that time they had adopted the classic Canadian canoes. In this picture Simpson sits in the middle wearing a top hat of massive proportions, as did many of the bourgeois (this was the old French name for the proprietor or company partner) while *en voyage*. The top hat was a mark of their quality and station. In Simpson's canoe the paddlemen are seated as usual two abreast and the bowman and steersman are in their usual places. But directly behind Simpson, who wears a grim expression on one of the most haughty faces in Canadian history, are a pair of undersized, wild-looking characters blowing bagpipes.

The presence of these pipers in Simpson's canoe gives the Big Bourgeois an extra dimension. People who worked for him knew that he was the toughest employer there ever was in a notoriously tough trade. He pinched pennies, he was ruthless, he squeezed out of his servants the last ounce of work, he paid them as little as he possibly could. One knows that Simpson understood the value of every square foot of every canoe or York boat in the service of his company. And yet, there sits that pair of private pipers! The Scotch are a peculiar people, and never more so than when they try to out-English the English in cold calculation after they have gone into business and made a success of it. But the old wildness never quite leaves the pure Scot. Behind the granite features of George Simpson, underneath his brutal surface callousness, the primitive heat burned, and hence that pair of pipers. Without them, the *canot du maître* could have carried at least two hundred more pounds of trade goods. Yet Simpson sacrificed money for the pipers, and I like to think of him sitting there in his stove-pipe hat, the mosquitoes buzzing in his hair, the canoe swaying down a rapid through the forest wilderness, and that pair of wee pipers behind him blowing his ears off.

But there were no pipers, no luxuries, for the average *engagé* — the paid voyageur of the fur-trading companies. Day after day from dawn to dusk, sometimes for eighteen hours daily, they drove those loaded canoes back and forth across the continent. As they paddled they sang the old French songs and some others of their own making. In favouring currents they could swing the stroke easily, but in adverse currents or dead water their paddles bit hard. The average rate of stroking was forty to the minute, but often they stroked at the rate of one per second, in perfect time and with only a few stops in the course of the day. The stops were called "a pipe," and their length depended on the state of the men. Travellers carried in canoes have testified that after twelve hours' paddling, with only three rests of ten to fifteen minutes each, those incredible French Canadians refused to stop because they were still "fresh." Their sense of competition with one another was Homeric. Duncan McGillivray once witnessed a race in Lake Winnipeg between Athabaska men and a rival brigade. The men paddled all out *for forty-eight consecutive hours without once leaving their canoes!* A steersman collapsed into sleep, fell overboard and would have been drowned had not his own canoe gone back to pick him up; he was sinking under the weight of his clothes and in a state of shock from the frigid water. In this race as the men stroked, the guides cut off hunks of pemmican and thrust them into the mouths of the paddlers.

What manner of men were these—giants? Actually, they were built more like gnomes. In 1826 an American, Thomas L. McKenney, visited the trading routes of Canada and described the voyageurs as follows:

"They are short, thick set, and active, and never tire. A Canadian, if born to be a labourer, deems himself to be very unfortunate if he should chance to grow over five feet five, or six inches—and if he shall reach five feet ten or eleven, it forever excludes him from the privilege of becoming voyageur. There is no room for the legs of such people, in these canoes. But if he shall stop growing at about five feet four inches, and be gifted with a good voice, and lungs that never tire, he is considered as having been born under a most favourable star."

Freedom, T. E. Lawrence once wrote, is man's second need: here is the sole explanation of those men's willingness to engage in a trade like this, which in time was sure to break them. Though there were many instances of river men keeping on working into late middle-age, the voyageurs as a rule died young. They were lucky if they were not double-ruptured and suffering from spastic backs before they were forty. But at least they were free from the forelock-tugging kind of poverty their class had to endure in Europe. They had the pride of champions which is the surest of all proofs of an inner sense of personal value. Freedom has always been the most expensive possession in the world, and the price for it has been paid in different coin from age to age. In the early days of Canada, the coin was hardship and endurance.

There were rains and cold nights, and the only women of the interior were virtual savages. The food the men ate on the rivers makes the diet of a modern Canadian work camp seem like the fare of a Roman emperor of the decadence. On the eastern run to the Lakehead the voyageurs were called *mangeurs de lard*, or pork-eaters, and the French word gives us a good idea of the quality of the pork. In the west pemmican was the stable diet, and no more nourishing one was ever invented, but even with wild rice added, boiled pemmican at the end of sixteen hours of labour is not much to look forward to. If the schedule was not too exacting, the men fished and hunted and searched for birds' eggs, but if food ran out they would eat anything. Often they literally ate crow. The poor French voyageur, especially in the early days, usually had nothing better to eat than a kind of hominy made of split dried peas or corn impregnated with fat.

But of all the ordeals faced by the river men, that of the winterer was the worst. He was the one who had to stay out in the wilderness perhaps two thousand miles from his base. The Indians brought him furs, and though he often had an Indian wife, he sometimes was entirely alone. If game was abundant he ate well, and there was usually plenty of fish preserved from the fall through the winter. But if game failed or fish rotted, starvation or dysentery was his fate. If he fell sick there was no help for him, and his loneliness was total in a six months' winter when the prairie was nothing but a white death.

Narrow this life was, uncivilized and uneducated, but on the whole it was less brutalizing than the life in the lumber camps in the Victorian era. At the principal bases of the Hudson's Bay Company all the men were required to attend prayers regularly. There is a poignant memorandum dating from the early eighteenth-century records of the Bay which enjoins the Company's servants "to live lovingly with one another not to swear or quarrel but to live peaceably without drunkenness or profaneness." The Nor'westers had a rougher tradition but more personal independence within the service; less consciousness, perhaps, that they were suffering a thankless exploitation by rich men who never troubled themselves to know at what price of human stamina and hardship the profits were earned. Nearly all the Montreal partners in the Company had served at least some time on the rivers. The French-Canadian voyageur, though not fond of washing *en route*, was a considerable dandy whenever he neared a post. Even though the only women in the post were savages, he washed and put on his best clothes. He had a Gallic courtesy to counteract his almost incredible toughness, and Francis Parkman writes feelingly of the human quality of his *Canadien* guides along the Missouri. As for the Highlanders in the service of the fur trade, one of them wrote the "Lone Shieling" poem, possibly the most haunting verses ever composed in Canada.

The fur trade failed in the end; it was doomed the moment the settlers began moving into the west to farm. Long before that time there were men engaged in it who had seen the writing on the wall. Sometimes when I walk up the avenue of the McGill campus and reach the Founder's tomb, I think back on the life he led and the shrewd Lowland caution which prompted James McGill to take his money out of the fur trade in time. He had never been a true voyageur, merely a poor boy from Scotland who had entered the only Canadian trade which offered him a living. He had earned his place in the Beaver Club by a winter spent alone near the headwaters of the Mississippi, but he got off the rivers before the life on them broke him. McGill lacked the transcendent imagination of Simon McTavish and the last-ditch loyalty of William McGillivray, but he had much common sense. Unlike most of his old colleagues in the fur trade, he did not die broke. His life had taught him that civilization could never grow in Canada under the conditions he had known in his youth. Though he was well off by colonial standards, he would never have been accounted an especially rich man in England. He left just enough to make it possible to found a college. Today McGill University lies like a quiet pattern of order in the roaring tumult of modern Montreal, and is by far the most important visible monument to the North West Company's great adventure.

For the economic contribution of the fur trade after the American Revolution has surely been exaggerated. It is a common argument that furs saved the country from being absorbed by the United States because they provided an east-west trade, all Canadian, in a continent where the normal lines of economic communication run north and south with the greater power and population of the United States sucking the wealth of Canada southward. I cannot believe this. The fur trade may have bridged an economic gap for a number of years, but the true reason why it saved Canada from absorption was not economic. It was political.

Not only did the voyageurs explore most of North America; after 1783 they staked out Canadian — or, at that time, British — claims to the whole north-western hinterland from the head of the Lakes to the Pacific. When the tide of homesteaders fanned out from the railheads in the American mid-west in the nineteenth century, the Canadian west would surely have been occupied by them, and subsequently claimed as American territory by the American government, had not the ancient rights of prior exploration, which the Americans respected, bound the land to Canada. The lonely posts were on the plains, in the Fraser and Columbia valleys, on the Pacific coast, and the Union Jack flew over all of them. Yet only a handful of men achieved this result. At the height of its power the North West Company may have employed as many as five thousand men, but less than two thousand were in service in the field between Montreal and Chipewyan. It was not their numbers that counted, but what they did. And in the long run what was done by the dreamers mattered the most.

David Thompson was probably the greatest geographer ever developed in North America; without his work, backed by Simon Fraser's voyage down the river which bears his name, it is hard to believe that British Columbia would now be a Canadian province. And of course there was Alexander Mackenzie, the prince of all the Canadian explorers.

A dozen years before Lewis and Clark, Mackenzie reached the Pacific through North America. He threaded to the end of the Northwest Passage. Its reality bore no resemblance to the European dream of a great gorge which would float sailing ships from the Old World through the continental land mass of the New. It was simply the chain of rivers, lakes and portages which enabled canoes from Montreal to move all the way from the St. Lawrence across Canada to the northern and western oceans.

"Alexander Mackenzie, from Canada, by land, the twenty-second of July, one thousand seven hundred and ninety-three" — this celebrated understatement scrawled in a mixture of vermillion and grease on a rock in Dean Channel after Mackenzie's passage down the Bella Coola, wrote *finis* to a quest begun exactly three hundred and one years earlier when Christopher Columbus set out across the Atlantic from Palos. The reality found by Mackenzie served only to dissipate the dream. But it introduced a new reality, just as Columbus' lost quest drew an entire hemisphere into the story of civilization. How strange that a Canadian birch-bark canoe without a name, last in a long succession of canoes from Champlain's first one, should have earned a place in the company of ships like the *Santa Maria* and the *Golden Hind!*

—1961

317

SINCLAIR ROSS

(1908-   )

Sinclair Ross was born in Saskatchewan, near Prince Albert, where his parents were homesteading. He was twelve years old when his father died. In 1924 he became a bank clerk and was employed in various small towns in Saskatchewan before being transferred to Winnipeg. During the war he served overseas with the Royal Canadian Ordnance Corps. Upon his return he was employed in the Royal Bank in Montreal. Since his retirement, he has lived in Greece and Spain. One of his earliest stories, "No Other Way," appeared in 1935 in Nash's Magazine, *London, winning third prize in a competition which drew some eight thousand entries. Subsequently he has published most of his stories in* Queen's Quarterly. *The distinguishing mark of his fiction— including his first novel,* As For Me and My House *(1941) — is its preoccupation with the psychological effects of life in the small communities and on the farms of his native province. A second novel,* The Well, *appeared in 1958,* The Lamp at Noon and Other Stories *in 1968, and a third novel in 1970.*

ONE'S A HEIFER

My uncle was laid up that winter with sciatica, so when the blizzard stopped and still two of the yearlings hadn't come home with the other cattle, Aunt Ellen said I'd better saddle Tim and start out looking for them.

"Then maybe I'll not be back tonight," I told her firmly. "Likely they've drifted as far as the sandhills. There's no use coming home without them."

I was thirteen, and had never been away like that all night before, but, busy with the breakfast, Aunt Ellen said yes, that sounded sensible enough, and while I ate, hunted up a dollar in silver for my meals.

"Most people wouldn't take it from a lad, but they're strangers up towards the hills. Bring it out independent-like, but don't insist too much. They're more likely to grudge you a feed of oats for Tim."

After breakfast I had to undress again, and put on two suits of underwear and two pairs of thick home-knitted stockings. It was a clear bitter morning. After the storm the drifts lay clean and unbroken to the horizon. Distant farm buildings stood out distinct against the prairie as if the thin sharp atmosphere were a magnifying glass. As I started off Aunt Ellen peered cautiously out of the door a moment through a cloud of steam, and waved a red and white checkered dish-towel. I didn't wave back, but conscious of her uneasiness rode erect, as jaunty as the sheepskin and two suits of underwear would permit.

We took the road straight south about three miles. The calves, I reasoned, would have by this time found their way home if the blizzard hadn't carried them at least that far. Then we started catercornering across fields, riding over to straw-stacks where we could see cattle sheltering, calling at farmhouses to ask had they seen any strays. "Yearlings," I said each time politely. "Red with white spots and faces. The same almost except that one's a heifer and the other isn't."

Nobody had seen them. There was a crust on the snow not quite hard enough to carry Tim, and despite the cold his flanks and shoulders soon were steaming. He walked with his head down, and sometimes, taking my sympathy for granted, drew up a minute for breath.

My spirits, too, began to flag. The deadly cold and the flat white silent miles of prairie asserted themselves like a disapproving presence. The cattle round the straw-stacks stared when we rode up as if we were intruders. The fields stared, and the sky stared. People shivered in their doorways, and said they'd seen no strays.

At about one o'clock we stopped at a farmhouse for dinner. It was a single oat sheaf half thistles for Tim, and fried eggs and bread and tea for me. Crops had been poor that year, they apologized, and though they shook their heads when I brought out my money I saw the woman's eyes light greedily a second, as if her instincts of hospitality were struggling hard against some urgent need. We too, I said, had had poor crops lately. That was why it was so important that I find the calves.

We rested an hour, then went on again. "Yearlings," I kept on describing them. "Red with white spots and faces. The same except that one's a heifer and the other isn't."

Still no one had seen them, still it was cold, still Tim protested what a fool I was.

The country began to roll a little. A few miles ahead I could see the first low line of sandhills. "They'll be there for sure," I said aloud, more to encourage myself than Tim. "Keeping straight to the road it won't take a quarter as long to get home again."

But home now seemed a long way off. A thin white sheet of cloud spread across the sky, and though there had been no warmth in the sun the fields looked colder and bleaker without the glitter on the snow. Straw-stacks were fewer here, as if the land were poor, and every house we stopped at seemed more dilapidated than the one before.

A nagging wind rose as the afternoon wore on. Dogs yelped and bayed at us, and sometimes from the hills, like the signal of our approach, there was a thin, wavering howl of a coyote. I began to dread the miles home again almost as much as those still ahead. There were so many cattle straggling across the fields, so many yearlings just like ours. I saw them for sure a dozen times, and as often choked my disappointment down and clicked Tim on again.

2

And at last I really saw them. It was nearly dusk, and along with fifteen or twenty other cattle they were making their way towards some buildings that lay huddled at the foot of the sandhills. They passed in single file less than fifty yards away, but when I pricked Tim forward to turn them back he floundered in a snowed-in water-cut. By the time we were out they were a little distance ahead, and on account of the drifts it was impossible to put on a spurt of speed and pass them.

319

All we could do was take our place at the end of the file, and proceed at their pace towards the buildings.

It was about half a mile. As we drew near I debated with Tim whether we should ask to spend the night or start off right away for home. We were hungry and tired, but it was a poor shiftless-looking place. The yard was littered with old wagons and machinery; the house was scarcely distinguishable from the stables. Darkness was beginning to close in, but there was no light in the windows.

Then as we crossed the yard we heard a shout, "Stay where you are," and a man came running towards us from the stable. He was tall and ungainly, and, instead of the short sheepskin that most farmers wear, had on a long black overcoat nearly to his feet. He seized Tim's bridle when he reached us and glared for a minute as if he were going to pull me out of the saddle. "I told you to stay out," he said in a harsh excited voice. "You heard me, didn't you? What do you want coming round here anyway?"

I steeled myself and said, "Our two calves."

The muscles of his face were drawn together threateningly, but close to him like this and looking straight into his eyes I felt that for all their fierce look there was something about them wavering and uneasy. "The two red ones with the white faces," I continued. "They've just gone into the shed over there with yours. If you'll give me a hand getting them out again I'll start for home now right away."

He peered at me a minute, let go the bridle, then clutched it again. "They're all mine," he countered. "I was over by the gate. I watched them coming in."

His voice was harsh and thick. The strange wavering look in his eyes steadied itself for a minute to a dare. I forced myself to meet it and insisted, "I saw them back a piece in the field. They're ours all right. Let me go over a minute and I'll show you."

With a crafty tilt of his head he leered, "You didn't see any calves. And now, if you know what's good for you, you'll be on your way."

"You're trying to steal them," I flared rashly. "I'll go home and get my uncle and the police after you — then you'll see whether they're our calves or not."

My threat seemed to impress him a little. With a shifty glance in the direction of the stable he said, "All right, come along and look them over. Then maybe you'll be satisfied." But all the way across the yard he kept his hand on Tim's bridle, and at the shed made me wait a few minutes while he went inside.

The cattle shed was a lean-to on the horse stable. It was plain enough: he was hiding the calves before letting me inside to look around. While waiting for him, however, I had time to realize that he was a lot bigger and stronger than I was, and that it might be prudent just to keep my eyes open, and not give him too much insolence.

He reappeared carrying a smoky lantern. "All right," he said pleasantly enough, "Come in and look around. Will your horse stand, or do you want to tie him?"

We put Tim in an empty stall in the horse stable, then went through a narrow doorway with a bar across it to the cattle shed. Just as I expected, our calves weren't there. There were two red ones with white markings that he tried to make me believe were the ones I had seen, but, positive I hadn't been mistaken, I shook my head and glanced at the doorway we had just come through. It was narrow, but not too narrow. He read my expression and said, "You think they're in there. Come on, then, and look around."

The horse stable consisted of two rows of open stalls with a passage down the centre like an aisle. At the far end were two box-stalls, one with a sick colt in it, the other closed. They were both boarded up to the ceiling, so that you could see inside them only through the doors. Again he read my expression, and with a nod towards the closed one said, "It's just a kind of harness room now. Up till a year ago I kept a stallion."

But he spoke furtively, and seemed anxious to get me away from that end of the stable. His smoky lantern threw great swaying shadows over us; and the deep clefts and triangles of shadow on his face sent a little chill through me, and made me think what a dark and evil face it was.

I was afraid, but not too afraid. "If it's just a harness room," I said recklessly, "why not let me see inside? Then I'll be satisfied and believe you."

He wheeled at my question, and sidled over swiftly to the stall. He stood in front of the door, crouched down a little, the lantern in front of him like a shield. There was a sudden stillness through the stable as we faced each other. Behind the light from his lantern the darkness hovered vast and sinister. It seemed to hold its breath, to watch and listen. I felt a clutch of fear now at my throat, but I didn't move. My eyes were fixed on him so intently that he seemed to lose substance, to loom up close a moment, then recede. At last he disappeared completely, and there was only the lantern like a hard hypnotic eye.

It held me. It held me rooted, against my will. I wanted to run from the stable, but I wanted even more to see inside the stall. And yet I was afraid to see inside the stall. So afraid that it was a relief when at last he gave a shamefaced laugh and said, "There's a hole in the floor — that's why I keep the door closed. If you didn't know, you might step into it — twist your foot. That's what happened to one of my horses a while ago."

I nodded as if I believed him, and went back tractably to Tim. But regaining control of myself as I tried the saddle girths, beginning to feel that my fear had been unwarranted, I looked up and said, "It's ten miles home, and we've been riding hard all day. If we could stay a while — have something to eat, and then get started —"

The wavering light came into his eyes again. He held the lantern up to see me better, such a long, intent scrutiny that it seemed he must discover my designs. But he gave a nod finally, as if reassured, brought oats and hay for Tim, and suggested, companionably, "After supper we can have a game of checkers."

Then, as if I were a grown-up, he put out his hand and said "My name is Arthur Vickers."

3

Inside the house, rid of his hat and coat, he looked less forbidding. He had a white nervous face, thin lips, a large straight nose, and deep uneasy eyes. When the lamp was lit I fancied I could still see the wavering expression in them, and decided it was what you called a guilty look.

"You won't think much of it," he said apologetically, following my glance around the room. "I ought to be getting things cleaned up again. Come over to the stove. Supper won't take long."

It was a large low-ceilinged room that for the first moment or two struck me more like a shed or granary than a house. The table in the centre was littered with tools and harness. On a rusty cook-stove were two big steaming pots of bran. Next to the stove stood a grindstone, then a white iron bed covered with coats and horse blankets. At the end opposite the bed, weasel and coyote skins were drying. There were guns and traps on the wall, a horse collar, a pair of rubber boots. The floor was bare and grimy. Ashes were littered around the stove. In a corner squatted a live owl with a broken wing.

He walked back and forth a few times looking helplessly at the disorder, then cleared off the table and lifted the pots of bran to the back of the stove. "I've been mending harness," he explained. "You get careless, living alone like this. It takes a woman anyway."

My presence, apparently, was making him take stock of the room. He picked up a broom and swept for a minute, made an ineffective attempt to straighten the blankets on the bed, brought another lamp out of a cupboard and lit it. There was an ungainly haste to all his movements. He started unbuckling my sheepskin for me, then turned away suddenly to take off his own coat. "Now we'll have supper," he said with an effort at self-possession. "Coffee and beans is all I can give you — maybe a little molasses."

I replied diplomatically that that sounded pretty good. It didn't seem right, accepting hospitality this way from a man who was trying to steal your calves, but theft, I reflected, surely justified deceit. I held my hands out to the warmth, and asked if I could help.

There was a kettle of plain navy beans already cooked. He dipped out enough for our supper into a frying pan, and on top laid rashers of fat salt pork. While I watched that they didn't burn he rinsed off a few dishes. Then he set out sugar and canned milk, butter, molasses, and dark heavy biscuits that he had baked himself the day before. He kept glancing at me so apologetically all the while that I leaned over and sniffed the beans, and said at home I ate a lot of them.

"It takes a woman," he repeated as we sat down to the table. "I don't often have anyone here to eat with me. If I'd known, I'd have cleaned things up a little."

I was too intent on my plateful of beans to answer. All through the meal he sat watching me, but made no further attempts at conversation. Hungry as I was, I noticed that the wavering uneasy look was still in his eyes. A guilty look, I told myself again, and wondered what I was going to do to get the calves away. I finished my coffee and he continued:

"It's worse even than this in the summer. No time for meals — and the heat and flies. Last summer I had a girl cooking for a few weeks, but it didn't last. Just a cow she was — just a big stupid cow — and she wanted to stay on. There's a family of them back in the hills. I had to send her home."

I wondered should I suggest starting now, or ask to spend the night. Maybe when he's asleep, I thought, I can slip out of the house and get away with the calves. He went on, "You don't know how bad it is sometimes. Weeks on end and no one to talk to. You're not yourself — you're not sure what you're going to say or do."

I remembered hearing my uncle talk about a man who had gone crazy living alone. And this fellow Vickers had queer eyes all right. And there was the live owl over in the corner, and the grindstone standing right beside the bed. "Maybe

I'd better go now," I decided aloud. "Tim'll be rested, and it's ten miles home."

But he said no, it was colder now, with the wind getting stronger, and seemed so kindly and concerned that I half forgot my fears. "Likely he's just starting to go crazy," I told myself, "and it's only by staying that I'll have a chance to get the calves away."

When the table was cleared and the dishes washed he said he would go out and bed down the stable for the night. I picked up my sheepskin to go with him, but he told me sharply to stay inside. Just for a minute he looked crafty and forbidding as when I first rode up on Tim, and to allay his suspicions I nodded compliantly and put my sheepskin down again. It was better like that anyway, I decided. In a few minutes I could follow him, and perhaps, taking advantage of the shadows and his smoky lantern, make my way to the box-stall unobserved.

But when I reached the stable he had closed the door after him and hooked it from the inside. I walked round a while, tried to slip in by way of the cattle shed, and then had to go back to the house. I went with a vague feeling of relief again. There was still time, I told myself, and it would be safer anyway when he was sleeping.

So that it would be easier to keep from falling asleep myself I planned to suggest coffee again just before we went to bed. I knew that the guest didn't ordinarily suggest such things, but it was no time to remember manners when there was someone trying to steal your calves.

4

When he came in from the stable we played checkers. I was no match for him, but to encourage me he repeatedly let me win. "It's a long time now since I've had a chance to play," he kept on saying, trying to convince me that his short-sighted moves weren't intentional. "Sometimes I used to ask her to play, but I had to tell her every move to make. If she didn't win she'd upset the board and go off and sulk."

"My aunt is a little like that too," I said. "She cheats sometimes when we're playing cribbage — and, when I catch her, says her eyes aren't good."

"Women talk too much ever to make good checker players. It takes concentration. This one, though, couldn't even talk like anybody else."

After my long day in the cold I was starting to yawn already. He noticed it, and spoke in a rapid earnest voice, as if afraid I might lose interest soon and want to go to bed. It was important for me too to stay awake, so I crowned a king and said, "Why don't you get someone, then, to stay with you?"

"Too many of them want to do that." His face darkened a little, almost as if warning me. "Too many of the kind you'll never get rid of again. She did, last summer when she was here. I had to put her out."

There was silence for a minute, his eyes flashing, and wanting to placate him I suggested, "She liked you, maybe."

He laughed a moment, harshly. "She liked me all right. Just two weeks ago she came back — walked over with an old suitcase and said she was going to stay. It was cold at home, and she had to work too hard, and she didn't mind even if I couldn't pay her wages."

I was getting sleepier. To keep awake I sat on the edge of the chair where it was uncomfortable and said, "Hadn't you asked her to come?"

His eyes narrowed. "I'd had trouble enough getting rid of her the first time. There were six of them at home, and she said her father thought it time that someone married her."

"Then she must be a funny one," I said. "Everyone knows that the man's supposed to ask the girl."

My remark seemed to please him. "I told you, didn't I ?" he said, straightening a little, jumping two of my men. "She was so stupid that at checkers she'd forget whether she was black or red."

We stopped playing now. I glanced at the owl in the corner and the ashes littered on the floor, and thought that keeping her would maybe have been a good idea after all. He read it in my face and said, "I used to think that too sometimes. I used to look at her and think nobody knew now anyway and that she'd maybe do. You need a woman on a farm all right. And night after night she'd be sitting there where you are — right there where you are, looking at me, not even trying to play —"

The fire was low, and we could hear the wind. "But then I'd go up in the hills, away from her for a while, and start thinking back the way things used to be, and it wasn't right even for the sake of your meals ready and your house kept clean. When she came back I tried to tell her that, but all the family are the same, and I realized it wasn't any use. There's nothing you can do when you're up against that sort of thing. The mother talks just like a child of ten. When she sees you coming she runs and hides. There are six of them, and it's come out in every one."

It was getting cold, but I couldn't bring myself to go over to the stove. There was the same stillness now as when he was standing at the box-stall door. And I felt the same illogical fear, the same powerlessness to move. It was the way his voice had lowered, the glassy cold look in his eyes. The rest of his face disappeared; all I could see were his eyes. And they held me as the lantern had held me, held me intent, rigid, even as they filled me with a vague and overpowering dread. My voice gone a whisper on me I asked, "And when you wouldn't marry her — what happened then ?"

He remained motionless a moment, as if answering silently; then with an unexpected laugh like a breaking dish said, "Why, nothing happened. I just told her she couldn't stay. I went to town for a few days — and when I came back she was gone."

"Has she been back to bother you since ?" I asked.

He made a little silo of checkers. "No — she took her suitcase with her."

To remind him that the fire was going down I went over to the stove and stood warming myself. He raked the coals with the lifter and put in poplar, two split pieces for a base and a thick round log on top. I yawned again. He said maybe I'd like to go to bed now, and I shivered and asked him could I have a drink of coffee first. While it boiled he stood stirring the two big pots of bran. The trouble with coffee, I realized, was that it would keep him from getting sleepy too.

I undressed finally and got into bed, but he blew out only one of the lamps, and sat on playing checkers with himself. I dozed a while, then sat up with a start, afraid it was morning already and that I'd lost my chance to get the calves away. He came over and looked at me a minute, then gently pushed my shoulders back on the pillow, "Why don't you come to bed too?" I asked, and he said,

"Later I will — I don't feel sleepy yet."

It was like that all night. I kept dozing on and off, wakening in a fright each time to find him still there sitting at his checker board. He would raise his head sharply when I stirred, then tiptoe over to the bed and stand close to me listening till satisfied again I was asleep. The owl kept wakening too. It was down in the corner still where the lamplight scarcely reached, and I could see its eyes go on and off like yellow bulbs. The wind whistled drearily around the house. The blankets smelled like an old granary. He suspected what I was planning to do, evidently, and was staying awake to make sure I didn't get outside.

Each time I dozed I dreamed I was on Tim again. The calves were in sight, but far ahead of us, and with the drifts so deep we couldn't overtake them. Then instead of Tim it was the grindstone I was straddling, and that was the reason, not the drifts, that we weren't making better progress.

I wondered what would happen to the calves if I didn't get away with them. My uncle had sciatica, and it would be at least a day before I could be home and back again with some of the neighbors. By then Vickers might have butchered the calves, or driven them up to a hiding place in the hills where we'd never find them. There was the possibility, too, that Aunt Ellen and the neighbors wouldn't believe me. I dozed and woke — dozed and woke — always he was sitting at the checker board. I could hear the dry tinny ticking of an alarm clock, but from where I was lying couldn't see it. He seemed to be listening to it too. The wind would sometimes creak the house, and then he would give a start and sit rigid a moment with his eyes fixed on the window. It was always the window, as if there was nothing he was afraid of that could reach him by the door.

Most of the time he played checkers with himself, moving his lips, muttering words I couldn't hear, but once I woke to find him staring fixedly across the table as if he had a partner sitting there. His hands were clenched in front of him, there was a sharp metallic glitter in his eyes. I lay transfixed, unbreathing. His eyes as I watched seemed to dilate, to brighten, to harden like a bird's. For a long time he sat contracted, motionless, as if gathering himself to strike, then furtively he slid his hand an inch or two along the table towards some checkers that were piled beside the board. It was as if he were reaching for a weapon, as if his invisible partner were an enemy. He clutched the checkers, slipped slowly from his chair and straightened. His movements were sure, stealthy, silent like a cat's. His face had taken on a desperate, contorted look. As he raised his hand the tension was unbearable.

It was a long time — a long time watching him the way you watch a finger tightening slowly on the trigger of a gun — and then suddenly wrenching himself to action he hurled the checkers with such vicious fury that they struck the wall in front of him and clattered back across the room.

And then everything was quiet again. I started a little, mumbled to myself as if half-awakened, lay quite still. But he seemed to have forgotten me, and after standing limp and dazed a minute got down on his knees and started looking for the checkers. When he had them all, he put more wood in the stove, then returned quietly to the table and sat down. We were alone again; everything was exactly as before. I relaxed gradually, telling myself that he'd just been seeing things.

The next time I woke he was sitting with his head sunk forward on the table.

It looked as if he had fallen asleep at last, and huddling alert among the bed-clothes I decided to watch a minute to make sure, then dress and try to slip out to the stable.

While I watched, I planned exactly every movement I was going to make. Rehearsing it in my mind as carefully as if I were actually doing it, I climbed out of bed, put on my clothes, tiptoed stealthily to the door and slipped outside. By this time, though, I was getting drowsy, and relaxing among the blankets I decided that for safety's sake I should rehearse it still again. I rehearsed it four times altogether, and the fourth time dreamed that I hurried on successfully to the stable.

I fumbled with the door a while, then went inside and felt my way through the darkness to the box-stall. There was a bright light suddenly and the owl was sitting over the door with his yellow eyes like a pair of lanterns. The calves, he told me, were in the other stall with the sick colt. I looked and they were there all right, but Tim came up and said it might be better not to start for home till morning. He reminded me that I hadn't paid for his feed or my own supper yet, and that if I slipped off this way it would mean that I was stealing too. I agreed, realizing now that it wasn't the calves I was looking for after all, and that I still had to see inside the stall that was guarded by the owl. "Wait here," Tim said, "I'll tell you if he flies away," and without further questioning I lay down in the straw and went to sleep again. —— When I woke coffee and beans were on the stove already, and though the lamp was still lit I could tell by the window that it was nearly morning.

5

We were silent during breakfast. Two or three times I caught him watching me, and it seemed his eyes were shiftier than before. After his sleepless night he looked tired and haggard. He left the table while I was still eating and fed raw rabbit to the owl, then came back and drank another cup of coffee. He had been friendly and communicative the night before, but now, just as when he first came running out of the stable in his long black coat, his expression was sullen and resentful. I began to feel that he was in a hurry to be rid of me.

I took my time, however, racking my brains to outwit him still and get the calves away. It looked pretty hopeless now, his eyes on me so suspiciously, my imagination at low ebb. Even if I did get inside the box-stall to see the calves — was he going to stand back then and let me start off home with them? Might it not more likely frighten him, make him do something desperate, so that I couldn't reach my uncle or the police? There was the owl over in the corner, the grindstone by the bed. And with such a queer fellow you could never tell. You could never tell, and you had to think about your own skin too. So I said politely, "Thank you, Mr. Vickers, for letting me stay all night," and remembering what Tim had told me took out my dollar's worth of silver.

He gave a short dry laugh and wouldn't take it. "Maybe you'll come back," he said, "and next time stay longer. We'll go shooting up in the hills if you like — and I'll make a trip to town for things so that we can have better meals. You need company sometimes for a change. There's been no one here now quite a while."

His face softened again as he spoke. There was an expression in his eyes as if he wished that I could stay on now. It puzzled me. I wanted to be indignant, and it was impossible. He held my sheepskin for me while I put it on, and tied the scarf around the collar with a solicitude and determination equal to Aunt Ellen's. And then he gave his short dry laugh again, and hoped I'd find my calves all right.

He had been out to the stable before I was awake, and Tim was ready for me, fed and saddled. But I delayed a few minutes, pretending to be interested in his horses and the sick colt. It would be worth something after all, I realized, to get just a glimpse of the calves. Aunt Ellen was going to be sceptical enough of my story as it was. It could only confirm her doubts to hear me say I hadn't seen the calves in the box-stall, and was just pretty sure that they were there.

So I went from stall to stall, stroking the horses and making comparisons with the ones we had at home. The door, I noticed, he had left wide open, ready for me to lead out Tim. He was walking up and down the aisle, telling me which horses were quiet, which to be careful of. I came to a nervous chestnut mare, and realized she was my only chance.

She crushed her hips against the side of the stall as I slipped up to her manger, almost pinning me, then gave her head a toss and pulled back hard on the halter shank. The shank, I noticed, was tied with an easy slip-knot that the right twist and a sharp tug would undo in half a second. And the door was wide open, ready for me to lead out Tim — and standing as she was with her body across the stall diagonally, I was for the moment screened from sight.

It happened quickly. There wasn't time to think of consequences. I just pulled the knot, in the same instant struck the mare across the nose. With a snort she threw herself backwards, almost trampling Vickers, then flung up her head to keep from tripping on the shank and plunged outside.

It worked as I hoped it would. "Quick," Vickers yelled to me, "the gate's open — try and head her off" — but instead I just waited till he himself was gone, then fairly flew to the box-stall.

The door was fastened with two tight-fitting slide-bolts, one so high that I could scarcely reach it standing on my toes. It wouldn't yield. There was a piece of broken whiffle-tree beside the other box-stall door. I snatched it up and started hammering on the pin. Still it wouldn't yield. The head of the pin was small and round, and the whiffle-tree kept glancing off. I was too terrified to pause a moment and take careful aim.

Terrified of the stall though, not of Vickers. Terrified of the stall, yet compelled by a frantic need to get inside. For the moment I had forgotten Vickers, forgotten even the danger of his catching me. I worked blindly, helplessly, as if I were confined and smothering. For a moment I yielded to panic, dropped the piece of whiffle-tree and started kicking at the door. Then, collected again, I forced back the lower bolt, and picking up the whiffle-tree tried to pry the door out a little at the bottom. But I had wasted too much time. Just as I dropped to my knees to peer through the opening Vickers seized me. I struggled to my feet and fought a moment, but it was such a hard strangling clutch at my throat that I felt myself go limp and blind. In desperation then I kicked him, and with a blow like a reflex he sent me staggering to the floor.

But it wasn't the blow that frightened me. It was the fierce wild light in his eyes.

Stunned as I was, I looked up and saw him watching me, and, sick with terror, made a bolt for Tim. I untied him with hands that moved incredibly, galvanized for escape. I knew now for sure that Vickers was crazy. He followed me outside, and, just as I mounted, seized Tim again by the bridle. For a second or two it made me crazy too. Gathering up the free ends of the reins I lashed him hard across the face. He let go of the bridle, and, frightened and excited too now, Tim made a dash across the yard and out of the gate. Deep as the snow was, I kept him galloping for half a mile, pommelling him with my fists, kicking my heels against his sides. Then of his own accord he drew up short for breath, and I looked around to see whether Vickers was following. He wasn't — there was only the snow and the hills, his buildings a lonely little smudge against the whiteness — and the relief was like a stick pulled out that's been holding up tomato vines or peas. I slumped across the saddle weakly, and till Tim started on again lay there whimpering like a baby.

6

We were home by noon. We didn't have to cross fields or stop at houses now, and there had been teams on the road packing down the snow so that Tim could trot part of the way and even canter. I put him in the stable without taking time to tie or unbridle him, and ran to the house to tell Aunt Ellen. But I was still frightened, cold, and a little hysterical, and it was a while before she could understand how everything had happened. She was silent a minute, indulgent, then helping me off with my sheepskin said kindly, "You'd better forget about it now, and come over and get warm. The calves came home themselves yesterday. Just about an hour after you set out."

I looked up at her. "But the stall, then — just because I wanted to look inside he knocked me down — and if it wasn't the calves in there —"

She didn't answer. She was busy building up the fire and looking at the stew.

—1944

ERNEST BUCKLER

(1908-   )

Ernest Buckler was born at Dalhousie West, a small Nova Scotian village. Educated first at the local one-room school, he later won scholarships that enabled him to take his B.A. at Dalhousie University in 1929. He obtained an M.A. in philosophy from Toronto in 1930 and was offered a fellowship to pursue a Ph.D., but reasons of health sent him back to the family farm. From 1931 to 1936 he worked in Toronto in the actuarial department of an insurance company. Then he returned to Nova Scotia, and in 1939 moved to a farm of his own outside Bridgetown, where he now lives.

He began his career as author with an article which won a prize in a Coronet contest. In 1948 one of his short stories won the Maclean's fiction award. Later short stories have been judged best Canadian stories of their year. He has also published both light and serious verse and articles in various periodicals, and has written talks and radio plays for the CBC. His best-known work is his first novel, The Mountain and the Valley, *which has received steadily widening critical acclaim since its publication in 1952. A Canada Council Arts Scholarship was awarded him to assist in the completion of his second novel,* The Cruelest Month *(1963). He has honorary doctorates from both Dalhousie and New Brunswick. His latest book is* Nova Scotia: Window on the Sea *(1973).*

DAVID COMES HOME

There was a stillness in Joseph's mind as he plowed the first furrows on the side-hill below the orchard; not the stillness of the weary, because it was only midafternoon and his muscles were without weight; but the stillness which comes over the mind when it has searched so long, silently, for the answer to a question not itself quite clear.

When David, his son, had been there to guide the horses, sometimes there would be no sound between them either, not even the building together of small jokes. Yet then the thoughts in his mind had seemed to make a little current moving shapelessly but as with a gentle ringing through the quiet minutes, the way the plow shelved its soft path through the long, curling sod.

At the top of the hill, Joseph paused to give the horses their wind. He could see his own house now—the neat, low clapboard house that had been his father's—with the large chimneys showing white and clean above the chestnut trees. He turned over a sod, absently, with his heavy boot.

And when he did, he noticed something fall away cleanly from its tight pocket in the earth. It was not a stone. Joseph picked it up and looked at it. It was a spinner he had plowed up, and it had lain there, lost, for seven years. He and David had searched for it but they could never find it.

He remembered so clearly the morning David had lost that spinner. It was the morning he had taken him back in the woods fishing and David had stayed all night in the camp for the first time. He could remember how David looked then, the hair heavy and moist but the face and the body almost thin. He could see the strange quickness in David's face and the eyes which always seemed to have the heat of fever in them. He knew David was excited that day, in a secret sort of way. And that night Joseph could tell that he was lying awake, quietly, in the dark.

But he was not sure whether David had been happy or just tired. He could not ask him, even then. And when David grew up, his strange quiet had still been there. Joseph had been proud of the many new things that David could read and understand easily. But he had always felt that David must leave the farm which he loved so much himself. The steps in the field, the slower steps in the field as the day tired and grew dark . . . and then the quiet kitchen walled in from the swing of the ax and the shoulder-bending and the sun-bright sweep of the scythe and the heavy plow handles and the day-movement and the man-business . . . the small, walled-in place to come to at noon when the sun was still high, and the food warmed in you like a slow wine . . . and soberly the evening when the lamp was lit, for peace . . . things like these . . . these would be small things for David's bright mind, and Joseph was not sure they were enough to hold him.*

It was hard for a clumsy man to show his own son a thing like that. And yet, sometimes when they would be plowing in the field together, he had hoped that the silence between them might not be a strangeness at all: had hoped that David was quiet because he knew his father's thoughts were not word-shaped and bright like his own but of one flesh just the same. In that way the silence became a bond. But Joseph could not be sure that this was so.

If your son went away in anger, even, then no matter what happened, he would be your son still. But his son had seemingly gone away with no keepsake at all of the things they had had together. He had tried desperately, that last morning as David went off to camp, to say some simple thing that might make it plain between them, but the slow erosion of minutes had dumbed his tongue. And Joseph knew that if they had loved nothing in the same way, death would leave him no part of his son to cherish.

Joseph had read the first letters that David sent, hoping desperately for some sign, but there had been none. Now he would never know, for the phone call had ended that. The facts were all gathered, all there would ever be, and no matter how long he thought, the answer was in none of them.

Joseph sighed a little, quickly, and turned the horses. He set the plow in the furrow again and followed it patiently down the long face of the hill.

In the kitchen, Ellen, his wife, was sitting quiet, waiting a few minutes before she called to him. The wrappings from the package were on the table before her, and one sheet of the papers inside she held in her hands still. She was letting the tears come a little, easily, before she called Joseph.

The kitchen was small, but the soft-wood floor was scrubbed and white as cotton, and the sun seemed always to be in it. It had been the heart of the whole house. It had been Ellen's whole world—close and quiet like the presence of a friend—until that day weeks ago the phone rang and the strange voice told her in curiously flat words about David. Ever since that day, the kitchen had seemed quite strange and, when she worked there, it had seemed as if she were not home at all.

Now she placed the papers together again, tenderly, and went to call her husband.

Joseph could not think what Ellen could want in the middle of the afternoon. He glanced at her face as he came through the door, but there seemed to be nothing wrong.

"There were some papers," Ellen said softly, pointing to the table, "of David's. They are little things—notes he must have just put down sometime, as one would who lacks someone close to talk with."

There was a date at the top of the page: August 30, 1944. That was the very day before, Joseph thought suddenly . . . it would be the very last. And then, as he began to read, all the awkwardness seemed to leave his hands at once.

"I guess the day I remember best of all was the day I lost the spinner . . . the day Father and I went back in the woods and I stayed all night in the camp for the first

*[In this story the use of the three dots (. . .) does not indicate an editorial omission but rather the author's own punctuation.]

330

time. I could not eat my breakfast for thinking about it. And when we were all ready I started off, wanting to run, wanting to leave the pasture road behind and get onto the strange, exciting log road that went where I had never been, deep and deeper into the still woods.

"The log road was so beautiful to walk along it. made a song in one's feet, and there was no need to say anything, with all the bright running things happening inside. . . . . There would be little patches of snow, still, under the big trees, and I could feel the cool breath of it as I walked along, but when I sat on the big rock and looked at the line so steadily in the current, it felt after a while as though I were floating along with it. The sun came out on the back of my shirt.

"And then, later, when the whole night was cool, there was the dry wood Father could always find somewhere for the fire. And with Father there, it was dark and quiet and warm in the camp, and the big trees whispered together their drowsy talk outside in the dark. It was the first night I had slept in the woods, and there had never been anything like it. . . . . I guess that was the best day there ever was. I guess a guy should be satisfied to have had just one day like that.

"I remember lying awake a long time that night. And I think Dad was awake, too. He didn't say anything, but I think he knew how it was. Somehow I think Dad always knew how it was . . . ."

"The horses," Joseph said suddenly in a low voice. "I forgot the horses."

Ellen had seen him tie the horses before he came over to the house. But she didn't say anything.

David! David! Joseph said his son's name over and over in his mind when he was again in the fields. He said it with an exaltation, for the stillness was all gone now from his mind, and the good kind of tears were tight in his throat. It had been *David* who loved this place best of all. And if your son loved the place he went away from, then he could never leave it. If he died even for these things you both loved, then you could hear his voice in their voice still.

He took the spinner from his pocket and made a hole deep in the ground. Then he covered it over gently with earth where the plow could never reach it. That would be David's spot, always. He stood for a minute, looking across the valley from mountain to mountain, and then he turned the horses again into the furrow. The field had looked long and wide. But now it seemed an easy field to plow. It seemed as if everywhere he looked, David had come home.

—1944

PENNY IN THE DUST

My sister and I were walking through the old sun-still fields the evening before the funeral, recalling this or that thing which had happened in this or that place, turning over memories after the fashion of families who gather again in the place where they were born — trying to disclose and identify themselves with the strange children they must have been.

"Do you remember the afternoon we thought you were lost?" my sister said. I did. That was as long ago as the day I was seven.

"We searched everywhere," she said, "up in the meetinghouse, back in the blueberry barrens —— we even looked in the well. I think it's the only time I ever saw Father really upset. He didn't even stop to tie up the horse's reins. He raced right through the chopping where Tom Reeve was burning brush, looking for you —— right through the flames almost. They couldn't do a thing with him. And you up in your bed, sound asleep!

"It was all over losing a penny or something, wasn't it?" she went on, when I didn't answer. It was. She laughed indulgently. "You were a crazy kid, weren't you?"

I was. But there was more to it than that. I had never seen a brand-new penny before. I thought they were all black. This one was bright as gold. And my father had given it to me.

You would have to understand about my father and that is the hard thing to tell. If I say that he worked all day long, but I had never seen him hurry, that would make him sound like a stupid man. If I say that he never held me on his knee and that I never heard him laugh out loud in his life, it would make him sound humorless and severe. If I said that whenever I'd be telling mother some of my fancy plans and he'd come into the kitchen I'd stop, like someone hiding the pages of a foolish book, you'd think that he was distant and that in some kind of way I was afraid of him. None of that would be true.

There's no way you can tell it to make it sound like anything more than an inarticulate man a little at sea with an imaginative child. You'll have to take my word for it that there was more to it than that. It was as if his sure-footed way in the fields forsook him the instant he came near the door of my child's world and that he must wipe off his feet before he stood inside, awkward and conscious of trespass; and that I, sensing that but not understanding it, felt, at the sound of his solid step outside, my world's foolish fragility.

He would fix the small spot where I planted beans and other quick-sprouting seeds before he prepared the big garden, even if the spring was late; but he wouldn't ask me how many rows I wanted and, if he made three tiny rows and I wanted four, I couldn't ask him to change them. If I walked behind the load of hay, longing to ride, and he walked ahead of the oxen, I couldn't ask him to put me up and he wouldn't make any move to do so, until he saw me trying to grasp the binder.

He, my father, had just given me a new penny, bright as gold.

He took it from his pocket several times, pretending to examine the date on it, waiting for me to notice it. He couldn't offer me *anything* until I had shown some sign that the gift would be welcome.

"You can have it if you want it, Dan," he said at last.

I said, "Oh, thanks." Nothing more.

I started with it to the store. For a penny you could buy the magic cylinder of "Long Tom" popcorn, with Heaven knows what colored jewel on the ring inside. But the more I thought of my bright penny disappearing forever into the black drawstring pouch the Assyrian merchant kept his money in, the slower my steps lagged as the store came nearer and nearer. I sat down in the road.

It was that time of magic suspension in an August afternoon. The lifting smells of leaves and cut clover hung still in the sun. The sun drowsed, like a kitten curled upon my shoulder. The deep flour-fine dust in the road puffed about my bare ankles, warm and soft as sleep. A swallow-tailed butterfly clung to the road, its bright-banded wings spreading and converging like the movements of breathing. The sound of the cowbells came sharp and hollow from the cool swamp.

I began to play with the penny, postponing the decision. I would close my eyes and bury it deep in the sand and then, with my eyes still closed, get up and walk around and then come back to search for it, tantalizing myself each time with the thrill of discovering afresh its bright shining edge. I did that again and again. Alas, once too often.

It was almost dark when their excited talking in the room woke me. It was mother who had found me. I suppose when it came dusk she thought of me in the bed other nights and I suppose she looked there without any reasonable hope, but as you do when the search has become desperate, in every place where the thing lost has ever lain before. And now suddenly she was crying.

"Danny!" she cried, with the pointlessness of sudden relief, "*where* have you been!"

"I lost my penny," I said.

"You lost your penny —— ? But what made you come up here and hide?"

If my father hadn't been there, I might have told her. But when I looked up at my father, standing there like the shape of everything sound and straight, it was like daylight shredding the memory of a foolish dream. How could I bear the shame of repeating before him the soft twisting visions I had built in my head in the magic August afternoon when almost anything could be made to seem real, as I buried the penny and dug it up again? How could I explain that pit-of-the-stomach sickness which struck through the whole day when I had to believe, at last, that it was really lost? How could I explain that I wasn't really hiding from *them*? How, with the words and the understanding I had then, that the only possible place to run from that awful feeling of loss was the soft, absorbing, dark safeness of bed? That I had cried myself asleep?

"I lost my penny," I said. I looked at father and turned my face into the pillow. "I want to go to sleep."

"Danny," my mother said, "it's almost nine o'clock. You haven't had a bite of supper. Do you know you almost scared the *life* out of us!"

"You better git some supper," my father said. It was the only time he had spoken.

I knew mother would talk about it and talk about it, but I never dreamed of father ever mentioning it again. But the next morning when we had the forks in our hands, ready to toss out the hay, he seemed to hold up the moment of actually leaving for the field. He stuck his fork in the ground and brought in another pail of water, though the kettle was chock-full. He took out the shingle nail that held his broken brace together and put it back in exactly the same hole. He went into the shop to see if the pigs had cleaned up all their breakfast.

"Ain't you got no idea where you lost your penny?" he said suddenly.

"Yes," I said, "I know just about."

"Let's see if we can't find it," he said.

We walked down the road together, stiff with awareness. He didn't hold my hand.

"It's right here somewheres," I said. "I was playin' with it in the dust." He looked at me, questioningly but he didn't ask me what game anyone could possibly play with a penny in the dust.

I might have known he would find it. In making a whistle he could tap alder bark with his jackknife just exactly hard enough so it wouldn't break but so it would twist free from the wood beneath, though I couldn't believe he had ever made a whistle for himself when he was a child. His great fingers could trace loose the hopeless snarl of a fishing line that I could only succeed in tangling tighter and tighter. If I broke the handle of my wheelbarrow ragged beyond sight of any possible repair, he could take it and bring it back to me so you could hardly see the place if you weren't looking for it.

He got down on his knees and drew his fingers carefully through the dust, like a harrow; not clawing it frantically in heaps as I had done, covering even while I uncovered. He found the penny almost at once.

He held it in his hand, as if the moment of passing it to me were a deadline for something he dreaded to say, but must. Something that could not be postponed any longer if it were to be spoken at all.

"Dan," he said, "You needn'ta hid. I wouldn'ta beat you."

"*Beat* me? Oh, Father! You didn't think *that* was the reason —— ?" I felt almost sick.

Do you know how I felt then? I felt as if I had beaten *him*. His face looked like I had seen it of an evening when mother wasn't speaking and he would pick up a schoolbook or a paper and follow the lines patiently, though he never read any other time at all. I had to tell him the truth then. Because only the truth, no matter how foolish it was, would have the unmistakable sound of truth, to scatter that awful idea out of his head.

"I wasn't hidin', father," I said, "honest —— I was —— I was buryin' my penny and makin' out I was diggin' up treasure. I was makin' out I was findin' gold. I didn't know what to *do* when I lost it, I just didn't know where to *go* ——"
His head was bent forward, like mere listening. I had to make it truer still.

"I made out it was gold," I said desperately, "and I —— I was making out I bought you a mowin' machine so's you could get your work done early every day so's you and I could go into town in the big automobile I made out I bought and everyone'd turn around and look at us drivin' down the streets ——" His head was perfectly still, as if he were only waiting with patience for me to finish.

"——*laughin'* and *talkin'* ——" I said, louder, smiling intensely, compelling him, by the absolute conviction of some true particular, to believe me. ——

He looked up then. It was the only time I had ever seen tears in his eyes.

I wondered, though, why he hesitated and then put the penny back in his own pocket.

Yesterday I knew. I never found any fortune and we never had a car to ride in together. But I think he knew what that would be like, just the same. I found the penny again yesterday, when we were getting out his good clothes — in an upper vest pocket where no one ever carries change. It was still shining. He must have kept it polished.

I left it there.

—1948

A. M. KLEIN

(1909-1972)

Abraham Moses Klein was born into an orthodox Jewish family in Montreal. At one time he studied for the rabbinate, which made him a master of the Hebrew language and richly learned in Jewish theology and culture. While attending McGill University, Klein contributed to the McGill Fortnightly Review. *He was graduated with a B.A. in 1930; three years later he took a law degree at the University of Montreal. In addition to his law practice in Montreal, he was for many years an active supporter of the Canadian Zionist organization and was editor of* The Canadian Jewish Chronicle. *At one time he campaigned for civic office in Montreal as a C.C.F. candidate.*

During the years 1945 to 1948 he was Visiting Lecturer in Poetry at McGill University. His volume, The Rocking Chair and Other Poems, *was awarded the Governor-General's Medal for poetry in 1948. Besides poetry, he published reviews and articles on various subjects in* The Canadian Jewish Chronicle *and other periodicals. His special interest in the Irish novelist James Joyce was shown in published studies. His* The Second Scroll *(1951) — a work mainly prose but incorporating much poetry — has been called a novel but may perhaps more usefully be considered a philosophical parable about the search for a way of life amidst conflicting ideologies. Klein died, after a long illness, in Montreal in 1972.*

SONNETS SEMITIC

I

Would that three centuries past had seen us born!
When youngest sons, with mappemounde for chart,
Sought them golcondas at its farthest bourn, —
Then had my gifts indeed declared my heart!
From foreign coasts, in the teeth of piracies,
Elixirs and gems to you I would have brought!
Small tokens: mystic mirror--- magic keys ---
A parrot praising you in polyglot---
— Myself had hoisted up the skull-and-bones,
And bearded corsairs, cutlass'd aft and fore,
Battened down booty, ingots, silks, rare stones, —
Tribute of love. --- Such deeds my daring! ---or
I would have been a humble thin-voiced Jew
Hawking old clo'es, in ghetto lanes, for you.

I shall not bear much burden when I cross
My father's threshold to our common door;
Only some odds I would not count as loss,
Only some ends old days can not ignore:
The prayer-shawl my mother cast upon
My shoulders, blessing Israel with a man;
Phylacteries my father gave his son;
The Bible over which my young eyes ran;
And Talmud huge, once shield from heathen stones.
I bring these as mementos; also, verse
Scribbled in rhymes their honesty condones;
And a capacious though still empty purse.
For your old age I keep a psalter-book
From which to read on Sabbaths, in perruque.

V

Now we will suffer loss of memory:
We will forget the things we must eschew.
We will eat ham, despite our tribe's tabu,
Ham buttered---and on fast-days---publicly---
Null, then, and void, the kike nativity.
Our family albums we will hide from view.
Ourselves, we'll do what all pretenders do,
And like the ethnics mightily strive to be.
Our recompense?---Emancipation-day!
We will find friend where once we found but foe.
Impugning epithets will glance astray.
To gentile parties we will proudly go;
And Christians, anecdoting us, will say:
"Mr. and Mrs. Klein — the Jews, you know---"

—1940

GREETING ON THIS DAY*

VI

O who is this, rising from the Sharon, bearing a basket of grapes, vaunting
the golden apples? And who is he, that other, hand on his plough, breaking
the soil, hard as the heart of Pharaoh?

*["Greeting on This Day," and "Sonnets Semitic," are reprinted with the
permission of the publishers from *Hath Not a Jew* (New York, Behrman's Jewish Book
House, 1940). The poet's subsequent revisions have been incorporated here.]

If this be a Jew, — where is the crook of his spine? and the quiver of lip, where?
Behold his knees are not callous through kneeling; he is proud, he is erect.
There is in his eyes no fear; in his mind no memory of faggots.
And these are not words to parable a Jew.

But truly this is such an one; he has left his hump in Ashkinaz; in
Sphorad his maimed limb; beyond the seas his terror.
He has said to the sun, Thou art my father that gives me strength; and to the
   cloud, Thou art my mother suckling me my milk.

The sign of his father is on his brow, and the breath of his mother renders
   him fragrant. No legion affrights him, no flame in the dark, no sword in
   the sun. For a thousand shall come upon him, and a thousand be carried away.

A son has returned to her that bare him; at her hearth he grows comely; he is
   goodly to behold.
Behind the bony cage there beats the bird of joy; within the golden cup is
   wine that overflows.

—1940

REB LEVI YITSCHOK TALKS TO GOD

Reb Levi Yitschok, crony of the Lord,
Familiar of heaven, broods these days.
His heart erupts in sighs. He will have a word
At last, with Him of the mysterious ways.

He will go to the synagogue of Berditchev,
And there sieve out his plaints in a dolorous
   sieve.

Rebono shel Olam — he begins —
Who helps you count our little sins?
Whosoever it be, saving Your grace,
I would declare before his face,
He knows no ethics,
No, nor arithmetics.

For if from punishments we judge the sins,
Thy midget Hebrews, even when they snore,
Are most malefic djinns,
And wicked to the core of their heart's core;
Not so didst thou consider them,
Thy favorite sons of yore.

How long wilt thou ordain it, Lord, how long
Will Satan fill his mickle-mouth with mirth,
Beholding him free, the knave who carned the
   thong,
And Israel made the buttocks of the earth?

The moon grinned from the window-pane; a cat
Standing upon a gable, humped and spat;
Somewhere a loud mouse nibbled at a board,
A spider wove a niche in the House of the Lord.

Reb Levi Yitschok talking to himself,
Addressed his infant arguments to God:
Why has thou scattered him like biblic dust,
To make a union with unhallowed sod,
Building him temples underneath a mound,
Compatriot of the worm in rain-soaked ground?

The lion of Judah! no such parable
Is on my lips; no lion, nor lion's whelp,
But a poor bag'o'bones goat which seeks thy
   help,
A scrawny goat, its rebel horns both broken,
Its beard uncouthly plucked, its tongue so
   dumbly lolling
Even its melancholy ma-a- remains unspoken.

The candles flicker,
And peeping through the windows, the winds
   snicker.
The mice digest some holy rune,
And gossip of the cheeses of the moon---

Where is the trumpeted Messiah? Where
The wine long-soured into vinegar?
Have cobwebs stifled his mighty shofar? Have
Chilblains weakened his ass's one good hoof?

So all night long Reb Levi Yitschok talked,
Preparing words on which the Lord might brood.
How long did even angels guard a feud?
When would malign Satanas be unfrocked?
Why were the tortured by their echoes mocked?
Who put Death in his ever-ravenous mood?

Good men groaned: Hunger; bad men belched
    of food;
Wherefore? And why? Reb Levi Yitschok
    talked---
Vociferous was he in his monologue.
He raged, he wept. He suddenly went mild
Begging the Lord to lead him through the fog;
Reb Levi Yitschok, an ever-querulous child,
Sitting on God's knees in the synagogue,
Unanswered even when the sunrise smiled.

—1940

A Psalm of Abraham,
concerning that which he beheld

UPON THE HEAVENLY SCARP*

I

And on that day, upon the heavenly scarp,
The hosannahs ceased, the hallelujahs died,
And music trembled on the silenced harp.
An angel, doffing his seraphic pride,
Wept; and his tears so bitter were, and sharp,
That where they fell, the blossoms shrivelled and died.

II

Another with such voice intoned his psalm
It sang forth blasphemy against the Lord.
Oh, that was a very imp in angeldom,
Who, thinking evil, said no evil word —
But only pointed, at each *Te Deum*
Down to the earth, and its abhorrèd horde.

III

The Lord looked down, and saw the cattle-cars:
Men ululating to a frozen land.
He saw a man tear at his flogged scars,
And saw a babe look for its blown-off hand.
Scholars, he saw, sniffing their bottled wars,
And doctors who had geniuses unmanned.

*[This poem and "A Psalm Touching Genealogy" are reprinted by permission of the publishers from *Poems* (Philadelphia, Jewish Publication Society of America, 1944). The poet's subsequent revisions are incorporated here.]

The gentle violinist whose fingers played
Such godly music, washing a pavement, with lye,
He saw. He heard the priest who called His aid.
He heard the agnostic's undirected cry.
Unto Him came the odor Hunger made,
And the odor of blood before it is quite dry.

V

The angel who wept looked into the eyes of God.
The angel who sang ceased pointing to the earth.
A little cherub, now glimpsing God's work flaw'd,
Went mad, and flapped his wings in crazy mirth.
And the good Lord said nothing, but with a nod
Summoned the angels of Sodom down to earth.

—1944

A PSALM TOUCHING GENEALOGY

Not sole was I born, but entire genesis:
For to the fathers that begat me, this
Body is residence. Corpuscular,
They dwell in my veins, they eavesdrop at my ear,
They circle, as with Torahs, round my skull,
In exit and in entrance all day pull
The latches of my heart, descend, and rise —
And there look generations through my eyes.

—1944

FOR THE SISTERS OF THE HOTEL DIEU

In pairs,
as if to illustrate their sisterhood,
the sisters pace the hospital garden walks.
In their robes black and white immaculate hoods
they are like birds,
the safe domestic fowl of the House of God.

O biblic birds,
who fluttered to me in my childhood illnesses
— me little, afraid, ill, not of your race, —
the cool wing for my fever, the hovering solace,
the sense of angels —
be thanked, O plumage of paradise, be praised.

—1948

PASTORAL OF THE CITY STREETS

I

Between distorted forests, clapped into geometry,
in meadows of macadam,
heat-fluff-a-host-of-dandelions dances on the air.
Everywhere glares the sun's glare,
the asphalt shows hooves.

                        In meadows of macadam
grazes the dray horse, nozzles his bag of pasture,
is peaceful. Now and then flicks through farmer straw
his ears, like pulpit-flowers; quivers
his hide; swishes his tempest tail
a black and sudden nightmare for the fly.
The sun shines, sun shines down
new harness on his withers, saddle, and rump.

On curbrock and on stairstump the clustered kids
resting let slide some afternoon: then restless
hop to the game of the sprung haunches; skid
to the safe place; jump up: stir a wind in the heats:
laugh, puffed and sweat-streaked.

O for the crystal stream!

Comes a friend's father
with his pet of a hose,
and plays the sidewalk black
cavelike and cool.

O crisscross beneath the spray, those pelting petals and peas
those white soft whisks
brushing off heat!
O underneath these acrobatic fountains
among the crystal,
like raindrops a sunshower of youngsters dance:
small-nippled self-hugged boys
and girls with water sheer, going *Ah* and *Ah*.

II

And at twilight,
the sun like a strayed neighborhood creature
having been chased
back to its cover
the children count a last game, or talk, or rest,
beneath the bole of the tree of the single fruit of glass
now ripening,
a last game, talk, or rest,
until mothers like evening birds call from the stoops.

                                                  —1948

POLITICAL MEETING

(for Camillien Houde)

On the school platform, draping the folding seats,
they wait the chairman's praise and glass of water.
Upon the wall the agonized Y initials their faith.

Here all are laic; the skirted brothers have gone.
Still, their equivocal absence is felt, like a breeze
that gives curtains the sounds of surplices.

The hall is yellow with light, and jocular;
suddenly some one lets loose upon the air
the ritual bird which the crowd in snares of singing

catches and plucks, throat, wings, and little limbs.
Fall the feathers of sound, like *alouette's*.
The chairman, now, is charming, full of asides and wit,

building his orators, and chipping off
the heckling gargoyles popping in the hall.
(Outside, in the dark, the street is body-tall,

flowered with faces intent on the scarecrow thing
that shouts to thousands the echoing
of their own wishes.) The Orator has risen!

Worshipped and loved, their favorite visitor,
a country uncle with sunflower seeds in his pockets,
full of wonderful moods, tricks, imitative talk,

he is their idol: like themselves, not handsome,
not snobbish, not of the *Grande Allée! Un homme!*
Intimate, informal, he makes bear's compliments

to the ladies; is gallant; and grins;
goes for the balloon, his opposition, with pins;
jokes also on himself, speaks of himself

in the third person, slings slang, and winks with folklore;
and knows now that he has them, kith and kin.
Calmly, therefore, he begins to speak of war,

praises the virtue of being *Canadien*,
of being at peace, of faith, of family,
and suddenly his other voice: *Where are your sons?*

He is tearful, choking tears; but not he
would blame the clever English; in their place
he'd do the same; maybe.

Where *are* your sons?
                    The whole street wears one face,
shadowed and grim; and in the darkness rises
the body-odor of race.

                                        —1948

INDIAN RESERVATION: CAUGHNAWAGA

Where are the braves, the faces like autumn fruit,
who stared at the child from the colored frontispiece?
And the monosyllabic chief who spoke with his throat?
Where are the tribes, the feathered bestiaries? —
Rank Aesop's animals erect and red,
with fur on their names to make all live things kin, —
Chief Running Deer, Black Bear, Old Buffalo Head?

Childhood, that wished me Indian, hoped that
one afterschool I'd leave the classroom chalk,
the varnish smell, the watered dust of the street,
to join the clean outdoors and the Iroquois track.
Childhood; but always, — as on a calendar, —
there stood that chief, with arms akimbo, waiting
the runaway mascot paddling to his shore.

With what strange moccasin stealth that scene is changed!
With French names, without paint, in overalls,
their bronze, like their nobility expunged, —
the men. Beneath their alimentary shawls
sit like black tents their squaws; while for the tourist's
brown pennies scattered at the old church door,
the ragged papooses jump, and bite the dust.

Their past is sold in a shop: the beaded shoes,
the sweetgrass basket, the curio Indian,
burnt wood and gaudy cloth and inch-canoes —
trophies and scalpings for a traveller's den.
Sometimes, it's true, they dance, but for a bribe;
after a deal don the bedraggled feather
and welcome a white mayor to the tribe.

This is a grassy ghetto, and no home.
These are but fauna in a museum kept.
The better hunters have prevailed. The game,
losing its blood, now makes these grounds its crypt.
The animals pale, the shine of the fur is lost,
bleached are their living bones. About them watch
as through a mist, the pious prosperous ghosts.

                                        —1948

MONSIEUR GASTON

You remember the big Gaston, for whom everyone predicted
a bad end? —
Gaston, the neighbor's gossip and his mother's cross?
You remember him *vaurien,* always out of a job,
with just enough clinking coinage
for pool, bright neckties, and blondes, —
the scented Gaston in the poolroom lolling
in meadows of green baize?
In clover now. Through politics. *Monsieur* Gaston.

They say the Minister of a certain department does not move
without him; and they say, to make it innocent, —
chauffeur.
But everyone understands. Why, wherever our Gaston smiles
a nightclub rises and the neons flash.
To his slightest whisper
the bottled rye, like a fawning pet-dog, gurgles.

The burlesque queen will not undress
unless Monsieur Gaston says yes.
And the Madame will shake her head behind the curtain-rods
unless he nods.

A changed man, Gaston; almost a civil servant,
keeps records, appointments, women; speaks tough English;
is very much respected.
You should hear with what greetings his distinguished approach is greeted;
you should see the gifts he gets,
with compliments for his season.

—1948

LONE BATHER

Upon the ecstatic diving board the diver,
poised for parabolas, lets go
lets go his manshape to become a bird.
Is bird, and topsy-turvy
the pool floats overhead, and the white tiles snow
their crazy hexagons. Is dolphin. Then
is plant with lilies bursting from his heels.

Himself, suddenly mysterious and marine,
bobs up a merman leaning on his hills.
Splashes and plays alone the deserted pool;
as those, is free, who think themselves unseen.

343

He rolls in his heap of fruit,
he slides his belly over
the melonrinds of water, curved and smooth and green.
Feels good: and trains, like little acrobats
his echoes dropping from the galleries;
circles himself over a rung of water;
swims fancy and gay; taking a notion, hides
under the satins of his great big bed, —
and then comes up to float until he thinks
the ceiling at his brow, and nowhere any sides.

His thighs are a shoal of fishes: scattered: he
turns with many gloves of greeting
towards the sunnier water and the tiles.

Upon the tiles he dangles from his toes
lazily the eight reins of his ponies.

An afternoon, far from the world
a street sound throws like a stone, with paper, through the glass.
Up, he is chipped enamel, grained with hair.
The gloss of his footsteps follows him to the showers,
the showers, and the male room, and the towel
which rubs the bird, the plant, the dolphin back again
personable plain.

—1948

PORTRAIT OF THE POET AS LANDSCAPE

I

Not an editorial-writer, bereaved with bartlett,
mourns him, the shelved Lycidas.
No actress squeezes a glycerine tear for him.
The radio broadcast lets his passing pass.
And with the police, no record. Nobody, it appears,
either under his real name or his alias,
missed him enough to report.

It is possible that he is dead, and not discovered.
It is possible that he can be found some place
in a narrow closet, like the corpse in a detective story,
standing, his eyes staring, and ready to fall on his face.
It is also possible that he is alive
and amnesiac, or mad, or in retired disgrace,
or beyond recognition lost in love.

We are sure only that from our real society
he has disappeared; he simply does not count,
except in the pullulation of vital statistics —
somebody's vote, perhaps, an anonymous taunt
of the Gallup poll, a dot in a government table —
but not felt, and certainly far from eminent —
in a shouting mob, somebody's sigh.

O, he who unrolled our culture from his scroll —
the prince's quote, the rostrum-rounding roar —
who under one name made articulate
heaven, and under another the seven-circled air,
is, if he is at all, a number, an X,
a Mr. Smith in a hotel register, —
incognito, lost, lacunal.

II

The truth is he's not dead, but only ignored —
like the mirroring lenses forgotten on a brow
that shine with the guilt of their unnoticed world.
The truth is he lives among neighbors, who, though they will allow
him a passable fellow, think him eccentric, not solid,
a type that one can forgive, and for that matter, forego.

Himself he has his moods, just like a poet.
Sometimes, depressed to nadir, he will think all lost,
will see himself as throwback, relict, freak,
his mother's miscarriage, his great-grandfather's ghost,
and he will curse his quintuplet senses, and their tutors
in whom he put, as he should not have put, his trust.

Then he will remember his travels over that body —
the torso verb, the beautiful face of the noun,
and all those shaped and warm auxiliaries!
A first love it was, the recognition of his own.
Dear limbs adverbial, complexion of adjective,
dimple and dip of conjugation!

And then remember how this made a change in him
affecting for always the glow and growth of his being;
how suddenly was aware of the air, like shaken tinfoil,
of the patents of nature, the shock of belated seeing,
the lonelinesses peering from the eyes of crowds;
the integers of thought; the cube-roots of feeling.

Thus, zoomed to zenith, sometimes he hopes again,
and sees himself as a character, with a rehearsed role:
the Count of Monte Cristo, come for his revenges;
the unsuspected heir, with papers; the risen soul;
or the chloroformed prince awaking from his flowers;
or — deflated again — the convict on parole.

III

He is alone; yet not completely alone.
Pins on a map of a color similar to his,
each city has one, sometimes more than one;
here, caretakers of art, in colleges;
in offices, there, with arm-bands, and green-shaded;
and there, pounding their catalogued beats in libraries, —

everywhere menial, a shadow's shadow.
And always for their egos — their outmoded art.
Thus, having lost the bevel in the ear,
they know neither up nor down, mistake the part
for the whole, curl themselves in a comma,
talk technics, make a colon their eyes. They distort —

such is the pain of their frustration — truth
to something convolute and cerebral.
How they do fear the slap of the flat of the platitude!
Now Pavlov's victims, their mouths water at bell,
the platter empty.
                        See they set twenty-one jewels
into their watches; the time they do not tell!

Some, patagonian in their own esteem,
and longing for the multiplying word,
join party and wear pins, now have a message,
an ear, and the convention-hall's regard.
Upon the knees of ventriloquists, they own,
of their dandled brightness, only the paint and board.

And some go mystical, and some go mad.
One stares at a mirror all day long, as if
to recognize himself; another courts
angels — for here he does not fear rebuff;
and a third, alone, and sick with sex, and rapt,
doodles him symbols convex and concave.

O schizoid solitudes! O purities
curdling upon themselves! Who live for themselves,
or for each other, but for nobody else;
desire affection, private and public loves;
are friendly, and then quarrel and surmise
the secret perversions of each other's lives.

He suspects that something has happened, a law
been passed, a nightmare ordered. Set apart,
he finds himself, with special haircut and dress,
as on a reservation. Introvert.

He does not understand this; sad conjecture
muscles and palls thrombotic on his heart.

He thinks an impostor, having studied his personal biography,
his gestures, his moods, now has come forward to pose
in the shivering vacuums his absence leaves.
Wigged with his laurel, that other, and faked with his face,
he pats the heads of his children, pecks his wife,
and is at home, and slippered, in his house.

So he guesses at the impertinent silhouette
that talks to his phone-piece and slits open his mail.
Is it the local tycoon who for a hobby
plays poet, he so epical in steel?
The orator, making a pause? Or is that man
he who blows his flash of brass in the jittering hall?

Or is he cuckolded by the troubador
rich and successful out of celluloid?
Or by the don who unrhymes atoms? Or
the chemist death built up? Pride, lost impostor'd pride,
it is another, another, whoever he is,
who rides where he should ride.

V

Fame, the adrenalin: to be talked about;
to be a verb; to be introduced as *The*:
to smile with endorsement from slick paper; make
caprices anecdotal; to nod to the world; to see
one's name like a song upon the marquees played;
to be forgotten with embarrassment; to be —
to be.

It has its attractions, but is not the thing;
nor is it the ape mimesis who speaks from the tree
ancestral; nor the merkin joy - - -
Rather it is stark infelicity
which stirs him from his sleep, undressed, asleep
to walk upon roofs and window-sills and defy
the gape of gravity.

VI

Therefore he seeds illusions. Look, he is
the nth Adam taking a green inventory
in world but scarcely uttered, naming, praising,
the flowering fiats in the meadow, the
syllabled fur, stars aspirate, the pollen
whose sweet collision sounds eternally.
For to praise

the world — he, solitary man — is breath
to him. Until it has been praised, that part
has not been. Item by exciting item —
air to his lungs, and pressured blood to his heart, —
they are pulsated, and breathed, until they map,
not the world's, but his own body's chart!

And now in imagination he has climbed
another planet, the better to look
with single camera view upon this earth —
its total scope, and each afflated tick,
its talk, its trick, its tracklessness — and this,
this he would like to write down in a book!

To find a new function for the déclassé craft
archaic like the fletcher's; to make a new thing;
to say the word that will become sixth sense;
perhaps by necessity and indirection bring
new forms to life, anonymously, new creeds —
O, somehow pay back the daily larcenies of the lung!

These are not mean ambitions. It is already something
merely to entertain them. Meanwhile, he
makes of his status as zero a rich garland,
a halo of his anonymity,
and lives alone, and in his secret shines
like phosphorus. At the bottom of the sea.

—1948

AUTOBIOGRAPHICAL*

Out of the ghetto streets where a Jewboy
Dreamed pavement into pleasant Bible-land,
Out of the Yiddish slums where childhood met
The friendly beard, the loutish Sabbath-goy,
Or followed, proud, the Torah-escorting band
Out of the jargoning city I regret
Rise memories, like sparrows rising from
The gutter-scattered oats,
Like sadness sweet of synagogal hum,
Like Hebrew violins
Sobbing delight upon their eastern notes.

Again they ring their little bells, those doors
Deemed by the tender-year'd, magnificent:
Old Ashkenazi's cellar, sharp with spice;

The widows' double-parlored candy-stores
And nuggets sweet bought for one sweaty cent;
The warm fresh-smelling bakery, its pies,
Its cakes, its navel'd bellies of black bread;
The lintels candy-poled
Of barber-shop, bright-bottled, green, blue,
    red;
And fruit-stall piled, exotic,
And the big synagogue door, with letters of
    gold.

Again my kindergarten home is full —
Saturday night — with kin and compatriot:
My brothers playing Russian card-games; my
Mirroring sisters looking beautiful,

*[Reprinted by permission of Alfred A. Knopf Inc. from *The Second Scroll*. Copyright 1951 by A. M. Klein. Published in Canada by McClelland and Stewart, Toronto.]

Humming the evening's imminent fox-trot;
My uncle Mayer, of blessed memory,
Still murmuring maariv, counting holy
    words;
And the two strangers, come
Fiery from Volhynia's murderous hordes —
The cards and humming stop.
And I too swear revenge for that pogrom.

Occasions dear: the four-legged aleph named
And angel pennies dropping on my book;
The rabbi patting a coming scholar-head;
My mother, blessing candles, Sabbath-flamed,
Queenly in her Warsovian perruque;
My father pickabacking me to bed
To tell tall tales about the Baal Shem Tov,
Letting me curl his beard.
Oh memory of unsurpassing love,
Love leading a brave child
Through childhood's ogred corridors, unfear'd!

The week in the country at my brother's — (May
He own fat cattle in the fields of heaven!)
Its picking of strawberries from grassy ditch,
Its odor of dogrose and of yellowing hay, —
Dusty, adventurous, sunny days, all seven! —
Still follow me, still warm me, still are rich
With the cow-tinkling peace of pastureland.
The meadow'd memory
Is sodded with its clover, and is spanned
By that same pillow'd sky
A boy on his back one day watched enviously.

And paved again the street; the shouting boys
Oblivious of mothers on the stoops
Playing the robust robbers and police,
The corncob battle, — all high-spirited noise
Competitive among the lot-drawn groups.
Another day, of shaken apple-trees
In the rich suburbs, and a furious dog
And guilty boys in flight;
Hazelnut games, and games in the synagogue,—
The burrs, the Haman rattle,
The Torah-dance on Simchas Torah night.

Immortal days of the picture-calendar
Dear to me always with the virgin joy
Of the first flowering of senses five
Discovering birds, or textures, or a star,
Or tastes sweet, sour, acid, those that cloy,
And perfumes. Never was I more alive.

All days thereafter are a dying-off,
A wandering away
From home and the familiar. The years doff
Their innocence.
No other day is ever like that day.

I am no old man fatuously intent
On memoirs, but in memory I seek
The strength and vividness of nonage days,
Not tranquil recollection of event.
It is a fabled city that I seek;
It stands in space's vapors and Time's haze;
Thence comes my sadness in remembered joy
Constrictive of the throat;
Thence do I hear, as heard by a Jewboy,
The Hebrew violins,
Delighting in the sobbed oriental note.

—1951

349

RALPH GUSTAFSON

(1909-   )

Ralph Gustafson was born of Anglo-Swedish stock at Lime Ridge, in the Eastern Townships of Quebec. He graduated from Bishop's University in Lennoxville and took his M.A. at Oxford University. He lived and worked as a journalist in England (1935-1938) and New York (1942-1946), and published several influential Penguin anthologies of Canadian writing, Anthology of Canadian Poetry *(English) (1942),* Canadian Accent *(1944) and* The Penguin Book of Canadian Verse *(1958) as well as* A Little Anthology of Canadian Poetry *(Norfolk, Connecticut, 1943). His own* Selected Poems, *drawn from five earlier books of poetry, appeared in 1972. Subsequently he has published* Theme & Variations for Sounding Brass *(1972). His many broadcasts on music have made him widely known. A book of his short stories,* Summer Storm, *and of poems,* Fire on Stone, *will appear in 1974. He is now Professor of English at Bishop's University and University Poet-in-Residence.*

QUEBEC WINTERSCENE

And the snow trodden round the yard,
Soiled with boots and fetched cordwood,
Straw ravelled near the barn —
The long snow of the fourfold land.
At dusk, acres clamped cold,
Threshold and clearing everywhere white
To the distant scribble of alders, across
The frozen field snakefence
Like charred music; sky only harvest
Helps over, buckled, with taste of tin
Dipper icy a man drinks gasping,
Sweat of warm barn-work a hazard
Once out, door-to, headed for house.

At eight, night now pitch, the train,
Halted for mailsacks at the swung
Lantern — the far horizontals
A moment, a history happening
The hills — alongside, pants, monstrous,
Pistons poised.   Then pulls past.

At the cutting, heard warning

                                    whose only
Answer is the local heart.

                                        —1960

350

MY LOVE EATS AN APPLE

She bites into the red skin
Of the white hard apple in bed
And there is joy in heaven
Like innocence and whitefalls
Of snow and waters dancing up
In among green trees perched with more
Apples in tight skin
Hard as a bite and containing
Seven-eighths applesap deadpan.
I try to distil this knowledgeable joy
In crunching heaven.
God sits up there amongst
His shamefully nude nudgers,
Praising sin,
The juice of the plucked
Happy apple
In great psalms and paeans
Dripping down His testamentary beard.

—1966

THE GRANDEUR WAS WHEN

The grandeur was when men adapted to nature,
Sophisticated grunts and there was the wheel,
Fire, his woman big-bellied while
He fought the mastodon, got the better
Of whatever it was, roof against rain, shod
In leather, then against breast-thumping
Conquered himself. A script of some humour.
Yet love got in and love of where he was,
And therefore science paring redundancies, errors,
Moons, a millionth of an inch by laser-beam.
The paring done: knowledge from mystery, poetry
From fact as hide from bearer to be cured,
Problem from protein, trouble from sickness, the paring
Done, he threw away beer-cans, safes,
Old cars, containers, plastic, exhaust
From pipes, tinfoil, cellophane, urine, spit,
Papers, wrappers from products, chewing-gum,
Wads, excrement, damned nature beaten.

—1974

Animals and children are
What gets me these days.
The two-year-old with mud pies.
Faith! It takes him
Two hours to exhaust
A white stone.
What's so wonderful about a rock
Circling white sun?
Green and mud?
I also recall
A wet kitten in
The rain.

Oh I laugh with grief!
Pies and stone and
Slim cats like the Lord's.

—1974

DOROTHY LIVESAY

(1909-   )

Dorothy Livesay was born in Winnipeg, of parents who were themselves writers — her father in journalism and her mother in poetry. After studying modern languages at Trinity College, Toronto, and in France, she was graduated with a Bachelor of Arts degree from the University of Toronto in 1931. Returning to France, she studied at the Sorbonne, where she wrote a dissertation on "The influence of symbolism and the metaphysical tradition on modern English poetry." Later she earned a diploma in Social Science at the University of Toronto, and served as a social worker in New Jersey and Vancouver. In 1937 she married Duncan Cameron Macnair (who died in 1959). She has worked as a reporter for several newspapers—in Winnipeg, Toronto, and Vancouver. During the war Mrs. Macnair was for three months on European assignment for the Toronto Star. Later she became Director of Adult Education for the Vancouver Branch of the Y.W.C.A., and then a high school teacher. With the help of the Canada Council, she went to England to study in 1958 and spent four years subsequently working for UNESCO, in connection with its educational program, first in Paris, then in Northern Rhodesia. Mrs. Macnair has taught creative writing at the University of British Columbia, has been Writer-in-Residence in the University of New Brunswick, and has most recently held a position in the Department of English of the University of Alberta.

As an undergraduate in her second year at Toronto she won the Jardine Memorial Prize for her poem, "City Wife," and while she was still in her teens The Macmillan Company published a brochure of her poems: Green Pitcher (1928). She won her first Governor-General's Award in 1944 for Day and Night, and her second in 1947 for Poems for People. In 1948 she received the Lorne Pierce Medal of the Royal Society of Canada. Selected Poems, with an Introduction by Desmond Pacey, was published in 1957. Her Collected Poems, The Two Seasons appeared in 1972.

THE DIFFERENCE

Your way of loving is too slow for me.
For you, I think, must know a tree by heart
Four seasons through, and note each single leaf
With microscopic glance before it falls—
And after watching soberly the turn
Of autumn into winter and the slow
Awakening again, the rise of sap—
Then only will you cry: "I love this tree!"

As if the beauty of the thing could be
Made lovelier or marred by any mood
Of wind, or by the sun's caprice; as if
All beauty had not sprung up with the seed.—
With such slow ways you find no time to love
A falling flame, a flower's brevity

—*1932*

"NIGHT'S SOFT ARMOR . . ."

Night's soft armor welds me into thought
Pliant and all engaging; warm dark,
No scintillations to distract
Nor any restless ray, moon-shot.
I am still of all but breathing —
No throbbing eye, no pulse; and a hushed heart.

* * *

Sometimes at rest, the bones assume
World's weight, hold us dumb
We cannot lift a finger, flick
An eyelash, wag a tongue:
Breath is the only fluctuation in
Death's posture, stoney, dumb.

Then is all sound fled
Flown from the fluted ear
Wind in the heavy head
Can find no corridor

And then is sight so bound
Lids petrified to earth
Only one light is found —
Imagination's going forth!

Only the heaven sent
Pulse of the universe
Beats through the buried heart
Its steady course.

—*1944*

The child looks out from doors too high and wide for him
On words spun large as suns, huge meanings sprayed on tree
And roadway, spreading fields, not to be caught and clapped
Together in a rosy nave, the sun no coin
For fingers to indent.
                The child runs out to stare
At masterful young men who bat a tennis ball
At giants in kilt skirts whose march is purposeful
At mothers in cool gowns who move about like moons
Upon the eternal lawns, low laughter shimmering
About their curving mouths.
                The child leans on the future,
Slender tree ungainly rooted there by private worlds
Who knew a private ecstasy unshared by him
But let the memory slip and reared a hedge
Of bristling phrases, last year's bills, and week-ends snatched
In secret hate; his room laid waste when radios
Are tuned, when rumor's blatant voice hits nerve,
Dries tissue, brittles down
The new unmolded bone.
                The child in cities toddling up
A stifling reach of stair, gains window-seat:
How consternation puckers up his eyes—at space
Unplanted, seed unwanted, wars unwarranted
Consuming his small thankless growing place!

—1944

OF MOURNERS

Mourn not for man, speeding to lay waste
The essence of a countryside's most chaste
And ageless contour; her cool-breasted hills,
Purled streams, bare choirs in wood, fair daffodils —

Mourn not, as maudlin singers did, the scars
Left by the slag, industrial wars,
Men tearing fields apart for railway towns
Wresting the silly sheep from sleepy downs:

And sing no more the sentimental song
Of spinning jenny holding lads too long,
Of children toiling underground, or laws
For hanging witches, burning corn for cause.

Sing only with the gibing Chaucer's tongue
Of foible and grave fault; of words unsung,
More pungent victory than battles won:
Sing deeds neglected, desecrations done

Not on the lovely body of the world
But on man's building heart, his shaping soul.
Mourn, with me, the intolerant, hater of sun:
Child's mind maimed before he learns to run.

—1952

GENERATION*

I see them moving on the other shore
The young men, baffled, with no fruit in store
And winter coming on. They have not fished
Nor hunted; manna fell; they lapped it to their lips,
Made snowballs of the residue, and aimed
Their easy blow, like bear-cubs tamed,

     Baring no cruel intent.

They're stranded now. The ice floes move
Inexorably toward their fading grove;
I see them herded on the farther ridge
Who never knew the meaning of a bridge:
Our signals flashed in code of human kind
They never learned; they see us, but are blind.
In vain our struggling tongues convey the news —
No use to battle, where we cannot bruise.

     The ice floes circumvent.

—1955, 1957

BARTOK AND THE GERANIUM

She lifts her green umbrellas
Towards the pane
Seeking her fill of sunlight
Or of rain;
Whatever falls
She has no commentary
Accepts, extends,
Blows out her furbelows
Her bustling boughs;

*[In this and the following poems the revisions of the 1955 versions
subsequently made by the author have been incorporated. The revised
versions appear in *Selected Poems* (1957).]

And all the while he whirls
Explodes in space,
Never content with this small room;
Not even can he be
Confined to sky
But must speed high
From galaxy to galaxy,
Wrench from the stars their momentary calm,
Stir music on the moon.

She's daylight;
He is dark.
She's heaven's held breath;
He storms and crackles
Spits with hell's own spark.

Yet in this room, this moment now
These together breathe and be:
She, essence of serenity,
He in a mad intensity
Soars beyond sight
Then hurls, lost Lucifer,
From heaven's height.
And when he's done, he's out:

She lays a lip against the glass
And preens herself in light.

—1955, 1957

LAMENT

(for J.F.B.L.)

What moved me, was the way your hand
Lay in my hand, not withering,
But warm, like a hand cooled in a stream
And purling still; or a bird caught in a snare
Wings folded stiff, eyes in a stare,
But still alive with the fear,
Heart hoarse with hope —
So your hand, your dead hand, my dear.

And the veins, still mounting as blue rivers,
Mounting towards the tentative finger-tips,
The delta where four seas come in —

Your fingers promontories into colorless air
Were rosy still — not chalk (like cliffs
You knew in boyhood, Isle of Wight):
But blushed with color from the sun you sought
And muscular from garden toil;
Stained with the purple of an iris bloom,
Violas grown for a certain room;
Hands seeking faïence, filagree,
Chinese lacquer and ivory, —
Brussels lace; and a walnut piece
Carved by a hand now phosphorus.

What moved me, was the way your hand
Held life, although the pulse was gone.
The hand that carpentered a children's chair,
Carved out a stair
Held leash upon a dog in strain
Gripped wheel, swung sail,
Flicked horse's rein
And then again
Moved kings and queens meticulous on a board,
Slashed out the cards, cut bread, and poured
A purring cup of tea;
The hand so neat and nimble
Could make a tennis partner tremble,
Write a resounding round
Of sonorous verbs and nouns —
Hand that would not strike a child, and yet
Could ring a bell and send a man to doom.

And now unmoving in this Spartan room
The hand still speaks:
After the brain was fogged
And the tight lips tighter shut,
After the shy appraising eyes
Relinquished fire for the sea's green gaze —
The hand still breathes, fastens its hold on life;
Demands the whole, establishes the strife.

What moved me, was the way your hand
Lay cool in mine, not withering;
As bird still breathes, and stream runs clear —
So your hand; your dead hand, my dear.

—1957

FOR ABE KLEIN: POET

And lives alone, and in his secret shines
like phosphorus. At the bottom of the sea.
                              A.K.

Drowned? Were you the one
drowned
or do I dream again
and do I hold your hand across a table
in a Chinese restaurant
Leo and Art gesticulating chopsticks?
Hand reaching to affirm
against the goyish laughter?

A drowned man now . . . Your hand
that delicate instrument
long servant to
the fervent ferment of thought
your hand lies twitching out
a spider's mark
on the bare table

And in the hive, your head
the golden bowl
bees buzz and bumble
fumble for honey amidst empty cells
where the slain poems
wingless, tremble.

—1967

357

THE UNQUIET BED

The woman I am
is not what you see
I'm not just bones
and crockery

the woman I am
knew love and hate
hating the chains
that parents make

longing that love
might set men free
yet hold them fast
in loyalty

the woman I am
is not what you see
move over love
make room for me   —1967

THE INCENDIARY

for Duncan

Now that the poetry's bursting out
all over the place
firecrackers setting off explosions
under train wheels
bombs
under hydrants

"bloody marvellous"
I can hear you saying
your eyes bulging and blazing
with that flinty excitement

as if every bone in your body
though burnt now to ashes
had started a conflagration
had gone off crackling
and shooting poems
all over the bloody map
Canada—

      country you came to, late
      and loved with hate
      and longed to set fire to

—1967

EVE

Beside the highway
at the motel door
      it roots
the last survivor of a pioneer
      orchard
miraculously   still
      bearing.

A thud   another apple falls
      I stoop   and O
that scent, gnarled, ciderish
      with sun in it
that woody pulp
      for teeth and tongue
      to bite and curl around
that spurting juice
      earth-sweet!

In fifty seconds, fifty summers sweep
      and shake me—
I am alive! can stand
      up still
hoarding this apple
      in my hand.

—1967

358

MALCOLM LOWRY

(1909-1957)

Malcolm Boden Lowry was born on Merseyside in England and educated at a private school in Cambridge. From the time he was ten until he was fourteen he was prevented from reading by an eye condition, but following an operation he was able to resume his schooling. Later, under the influence of Eugene O'Neill and Joseph Conrad, he worked his way to the Far East on a freighter. He entered Cambridge University in 1929 and was graduated in 1932. Two of his short stories, based on notes made during his travels, were printed in the undergraduate magazine Experiment. *One of these, "Seductio ad Absurdum," was chosen by E. J. O'Brien for inclusion in his* Best British Short Stories *(1931). Both stories became part of his first novel,* Ultramarine, *written during his Cambridge years. However, the novel had to be entirely rewritten after an editor lost the only completed manuscript. After* Ultramarine *was published in 1933, Lowry became dissatisfied with it, and in the years that followed he made various changes in his own copy and projected extensive revisions. In 1963 the novel was republished (posthumously), incorporating many changes and additions. Many of the themes in* Ultramarine *were developed in later writings.*

For half a dozen years after 1933 Lowry lived in France, the United States, and Mexico, meanwhile writing three novels, including the first draft of Under the Volcano, *but failing to get them accepted for publication. In 1939 he came to Canada and established himself in a squatter's house on the beach at Dollarton, near Vancouver. There he completed the third version of* Under the Volcano *(published in 1947) and wrote most of the novella and short stories contained in* Hear Us O Lord from Heaven Thy Dwelling Place, *which won the Governor-General's Award for fiction in 1961.*

In 1954 Lowry and his wife, the novelist Margerie Bonner, left Canada for an extended visit to Europe; after their departure, their beach home was lost to them when the adjacent property was converted to public use as a natural parkland. In it a signpost points to the "Malcolm Lowry Walk"! An inveterate reviser of whatever he wrote, Lowry had just completed work on the manuscript of Hear Us O Lord . . . *when he died in England in the summer of 1957. He had also been working on, and had nearly completed, another novel,* October Ferry to Gabriola. *This was edited by Margerie Lowry and published in 1970. Lowry's* Selected Poems *was edited by his friend Earle Birney in 1962. A novella,* Lunar Caustic, *edited from the manuscripts by Mrs. Lowry and Dr. Birney, appeared in* The Paris Review *in 1963, and as a separate publication in London in 1968. Another novel,* Dark As the Grave Wherein My Friend is Laid, *edited by Douglas Day and Mrs. Lowry, was published in 1968. Among the collection of Lowry manuscripts presented by Mrs. Lowry to the library of the University of British Columbia, and still awaiting publication, are more poems, some short stories and plays, several other works in various stages, and numerous letters.*

The short story, "Strange Comfort . . . ," was originally published in the Partisan Review *in 1953. The character Sigbjørn Wilderness appears in other stories in* Hear

Us O Lord. . . *based on Lowry's own experiences, and is perhaps to be regarded as a kind of* alter ego. *The "Seattle" episode in the story reflects Lowry's own situation during his first months in Vancouver.* *

STRANGE COMFORT AFFORDED BY THE PROFESSION

Sigbjørn Wilderness, an American writer in Rome on a Guggenheim fellowship, paused on the steps above the flower stall and wrote, glancing from time to time at the house before him, in a black notebook:

ll poeta inglese Giovanni Keats mente maravigliosa quanto precoce mori in questa casa il 24 Febraio 1821 nel ventiseesimo anno dell' eta sua.

Here, in a sudden access of nervousness, glancing now not only at the house, but behind him at the church of Trinità dei Monti, at the woman in the flower stall, the Romans drifting up and down the steps, or passing in the Piazza di Spagna below (for though it was several years after the war he was afraid of being taken for a spy), he drew, as well as he was able, the lyre, similar to the one on the poet's tomb, that appeared on the house between the Italian and its translation:

Then he added swiftly the words below the lyre:

The young English poet, John Keats, died in this house on the 24th of February 1821, aged 26.

This accomplished, he put the notebook and pencil back in his pocket, glanced round him again with a heavier, more penetrating look—that in fact was informed by such a malaise he saw nothing at all but which was intended to say "I have a perfect right to do this," or "If you saw me do that, very well then, I *am* some sort of detective, perhaps even some kind of painter"—descended the remaining steps, looked around wildly once more, and entered, with a sigh of relief like a man going to bed, the comforting darkness of Keats's house.

Here, having climbed the narrow staircase, he was almost instantly confronted by a legend in a glass case which said:

Remnants of aromatic gums used by Trelawny when cremating the body of Shelley.

And these words, for his notebook with which he was already rearmed felt ratified in this place, he also copied down, though he failed to comment on the gums themselves, which largely escaped his notice, as indeed did the house itself—

*[Explanatory notes on the biographical and literary allusions in this story may be found in *The Creative Reader,* Second Edition (New York, 1962), edited by R. W. Stallman and R. E. Watters.]

there had been those stairs, there was a balcony, it was dark, there were many pictures, and these glass cases, it was a bit like a library—in which he saw no books of his—these made about the sum of Sigbjørn's unrecorded perceptions. From the aromatic gums he moved to the enshrined marriage licence of the same poet, and Sigbjørn transcribed this document too, writing rapidly as his eyes became more used to the dim light:

Percy Bysshe Shelley of the Parish *of* Saint Mildred, Bread Street, London, Widower, *and* Mary Wollstonecraft Godwin *of* the City of Bath, Spinster, a minor, *were married in this* Church *by* Licence *with Consent of* William Godwin her father *this* Thirtieth *Day of December in the year one thousand eight hundred and sixteen.* By me Mr. Heydon, Curate. This marriage was solemnized between us.

Percy Bysshe Shelley
Mary Wollstonecraft Godwin

In the presence of:

William Godwin
M. J. Godwin

Beneath this Sigbjørn added mysteriously:

Nemesis. Marriage of drowned Phoenician sailor. A bit odd here at all. Sad — feel swine to look at such things.

Then he passed on quickly—not so quickly he hadn't time to wonder with a remote twinge why, if there was no reason for any of his own books to be there on the shelves above him, the presence was justified of *In Memoriam, All Quiet on the Western Front, Green Light,* and the *Field Book of Western Birds*—to another glass case in which appeared a framed and unfinished letter, evidently from Severn, Keats's friend, which Sigbjørn copied down as before:

My dear Sir:
    Keats has changed somewhat for the worse — at least his mind has much — very much — yet the blood has ceased to come, his digestion is better and but for a cough he must be improving, that is as respects his body — but the fatal prospect of consumption hangs before his mind yet — and turns everything to despair and wretchedness — he will not hear a word about living — nay, I seem to lose his confidence by trying to give him this hope [the following lines had been crossed out by Severn but Sigbjørn ruthlessly wrote them down just the same: *for his knowledge of internal anatomy enables him to judge of any change accurately and largely adds to his torture*], he will not think his future prospect favorable — he says the continued stretch of his imagination has already killed him and were he to recover he would not write another line — he will not hear of his good friends in England except for what they have done — and this is another load — but of their high hopes of him — his certain success — his experience — he will not hear a word — then the want of some kind of hope to feed his vivacious imagination —

The letter having broken off here, Sigbjørn, notebook in hand, tiptoed lingeringly to another glass case where, another letter from Severn appearing, he wrote:

My dear Brown — He is gone — he died with the most perfect ease — he seemed to go to sleep. On the 23rd at half past four the approaches of death came on. "Severn — lift me up for I am dying — I shall die easy — don't be frightened, I thank God it has come." I lifted him upon my arms and the phlegm seemed boiling in his throat. This increased until 11 at night when he gradually sank into death so quiet I still thought he slept — But I cannot say more now. I am broken down beyond my strength. I cannot be left alone. I have not slept for nine days — the days since. On Saturday a gentleman came to cast his hand and foot. On Thursday the body was opened. The lungs were completely gone. The doctors would not —

Much moved, Sigbjørn reread this as it now appeared in his notebook, then added beneath it:

On Saturday a gentleman came to cast his hand and foot — that is the most sinister line to me. Who is this gentleman?

Once outside Keats's house Wilderness did not pause nor look to left or right, not even at the American Express, until he had reached a bar which he entered, however, without stopping to copy down its name. He felt he had progressed in one movement, in one stride, from Keats's house to this bar, partly just because he had wished to avoid signing his own name in the visitor's book. Sigbjørn Wilderness! The very sound of his name was like a bell-buoy—or more euphoniously a light-ship—broken adrift, and washing in from the Atlantic on a reef. Yet how he hated to write it down (loved to see it in print?)—though like so much else with him it had little reality unless he did. Without hesitating to ask himself why, if he was so disturbed by it, he did not choose another name under which to write, such as his second name which was Henry, or his mother's, which was Sanderson-Smith, he selected the most isolated booth he could find in the bar, that was itself an underground grotto, and drank two grappas in quick succession. Over his third he began to experience some of the emotions one might have expected him to undergo in Keats's house. He felt fully the surprise which had barely affected him that some of Shelley's relics were to be found there, if a fact no more astonishing than that Shelley—whose skull moreover had narrowly escaped appropriation by Byron as a drinking goblet, and whose heart, snatched out of the flames by Trelawny, he seemed to recollect from Proust, was interred in England — should have been buried in Rome at all (where the bit of Ariel's song inscribed on his gravestone might have anyway prepared one for the rich and strange), and he was touched by the chivalry of those Italians who, during the war, it was said, had preserved, at considerable risk to themselves, the contents of that house from the Germans. Moreover he now thought he began to see the house itself more clearly, though no doubt not as it was, and he produced his notebook again with the object of adding to the notes already taken these impressions that came to him in retrospect.

"Mamertine Prison," he read —— He'd opened it at the wrong place, at some observations made yesterday upon a visit to the historic dungeon, but being gloomily entertained by what he saw, he read on, as he did so feeling the clammy confined horror of that underground cell, or other underground cell, not, he suspected, really sensed at the time, rise heavily about him.

MAMERTINE PRISON [ran the heading]
  The lower is the true prison
of Mamertine, the state prison of ancient Rome.
    The lower cell called Tullianus is probably the most ancient building in Rome. The prison was used to imprison malefactors and enemies of the State. In the lower cell is seen the well where according to tradition St. Peter miraculously made a spring to baptize the gaolers Processus and Martinianus.

Victims: politicians. Pontius, King of the Sanniti. Died 290 B.C. Giurgurath (Jugurtha), Aristobulus, Vercingetorix. — The Holy Martyrs, Peter and Paul. Apostles imprisoned in the reign of Nero. — Processus, Abondius, *and many others unknown* were:

> decapitato
> suppliziato (suffocated)
> strangolato
> morto per fame.

Vercingetorix, the King of the Gauls, was certainly strangolato 49 B.C. and Jugurtha, King of Numidia, dead by starvation 104 B.C.

The lower is the true prison—why had he underlined that? Sigbjørn wondered. He ordered another grappa and, while awaiting it, turned back to his notebook where, beneath his remarks on the Mamertine prison, and added as he now recalled in the dungeon itself, this memorandum met his eyes:

Find Gogol's house — where wrote part of Dead Souls — 1838. Where died Vielgorsky? "They do not heed me, nor see me, nor listen to me," wrote Gogol. "What have I done to them? Why do they torture me? What do they want of poor me? What can I give them? I have nothing. My strength is gone. I cannot endure all this." Suppliziato. Strangolato. In wonderful-horrible book of Nabokov's when Gogol was dying — he says — "you could feel his spine through his stomach." Leeches dangling from nose: "Lift them up, keep them away . . ." Henrik Ibsen, Thomas Mann, ditto brother: Buddenbrooks and Pippo Spano. A — where lived? became sunburned? Perhaps happy here. Prosper Mérimée and Schiller. Suppliziato. Fitzgerald in Forum. Eliot in Colosseum?

And underneath this was written enigmatically:

And many others.

And beneath this:

Perhaps Maxim Gorky too. This is funny. Encounter between Volga Boatman and saintly Fisherman.

What was funny? While Sigbjørn, turning over his pages toward Keats's house again was wondering what he had meant, beyond the fact that Gorky, like most of those other distinguished individuals, had at one time lived in Rome, if not in the Mamertine prison—though with another part of his mind he knew perfectly well—he realized that the peculiar stichometry of his observations, jotted down as if he imagined he were writing a species of poem, had caused him prematurely to finish the notebook:

On Saturday a gentleman came to cast his hand and foot — that is the most sinister line to me — who is this gentleman?

With these words his notebook concluded.

That didn't mean there was no more space, for his notebooks, he reflected avuncularly, just like his candles, tended to consume themselves at both ends; yes, as he thought, there was some writing at the beginning. Reversing this, for it was upside down, he smiled and forgot about looking for space, since he immediately recognized these notes as having been taken in America two years ago upon a visit to Richmond, Virginia, a pleasant time for him. So, amused, he composed himself to read, delighted also, in an Italian bar, to be thus transported back to the

South. He had made nothing of these notes, hadn't even known they were there, and it was not always easy accurately to visualize the scenes they conjured up:

> The wonderful slanting square in Richmond and the tragic silhouette of inter-laced leafless trees.
> On a wall: *dirty stinking Degenerate Bobs was here from Boston, North End, Mass. Warp son of a bitch.*

Sigbjørn chuckled. Now he clearly remembered the biting winter day in Richmond, the dramatic courthouse in the precipitous park, the long climb up to it, and the caustic attestation to solidarity with the North in the (white) men's washroom. Smiling he read on:

> In Poe's shrine, strange preserved newsclipping: CAPACITY CROWD HEARS TRIBUTE TO POE'S WORKS. *University student, who ended life, buried at Wytherville.*

Yes, yes, and this he remembered too, in Poe's house, or one of Poe's houses, the one with the great dark wing of shadow on it at sunset, where the dear old lady who kept it, who'd showed him the news clipping, had said to him in a whisper: "So you see, *we* think these stories of his drinking can't *all* be true." He continued:

> Opposite Craig house, where Poe's Helen lived, these words, upon façade, windows, stoop of the place from which E.A.P. — if I am right — must have watched the lady with the agate lamp: Headache — A.B.C. — Neuralgia: LIC-OFF-PREM — enjoy Pepsi — Drink Royal Crown Cola — Dr. Swell's Root Beer — "Furnish room for rent": did Poe really live here? Must have, could only have spotted Psyche from the regions which are Lic-Off-Prem. — Better than no Lic at all though. Bet Poe does not still live in Lic-Off-Prem. Else might account for "Furnish room for rent"?
> Mem: Consult Talking Horse Friday.
> — Give me Liberty or give me death [Sigbjørn now read]. In churchyard, with Patrick Henry's grave; a notice: No smoking within ten feet of the church; then:
> Outside Robert E. Lee's house:
> Please pull the bell
> To make it ring.
> — Inside Valentine Museum, with Poe's relics —

Sigbjørn paused. Now he remembered that winter day still more clearly. Robert E. Lee's house was of course far below the courthouse, remote from Patrick Henry and the Craig house and the other Poe shrine, and it would have been a good step hence to the Valentine Museum, even had not Richmond, a city whose Hellenic character was not confined to its architecture, but would have been recognized in its gradients by a Greek mountain goat, been grouped about streets so steep it was painful to think of Poe toiling up them. Sigbjørn's notes were in the wrong order, and it must have been morning then, and not sunset as it was in the other house with the old lady, when he went to the Valentine Museum. He saw Lee's house again, and a faint feeling of the beauty of the whole frostbound city outside came to his mind, then a picture of a Confederate white house, near a gigantic red-brick factory chimney, with far below a glimpse of an old cobbled street, and a lone figure crossing a waste, as between three centuries, from the house toward the railway tracks and this chimney, which belonged to the Bone Dry Fertilizer Company. But in the sequence of his notes "Please pull the bell, to make it ring," on Lee's house, had seemed to provide a certain musical effect of solemnity, yet ushering him instead into the Poe museum which Sigbjørn now in memory re-entered.

> Inside Valentine Museum, with Poe's relics [he read once more]
> Please
> Do not smoke
> Do not run
> Do not touch walls or exhibits
> Observation of these rules will insure your own and others' enjoyment of the museum.
> — Blue silk coat and waistcoat, gift of the Misses Boykin, that belonged to one of George Washington's dentists.

Sigbjørn closed his eyes, in his mind Shelley's crematory gums and the gift of the Misses Boykin struggling for a moment helplessly, then he returned to the words that followed. They were Poe's own, and formed part of some letters once presumably written in anguished and private desperation, but which were now to be perused at leisure by anyone whose enjoyment of them would be "insured" so long as they neither smoked nor ran nor touched the glass case in which, like the gums (on the other side of the world), they were preserved. He read:

> Excerpt from a letter by Poe — after having been dismissed from West Point — to his foster father. Feb. 21, 1831.
> "It will however be the last time I ever trouble any human being — I feel I am on a sick bed from which I shall never get up."

Sigbjørn calculated with a pang that Poe must have written these words almost seven years to the day after Keats's death, then, that far from never having got up from his sick bed, he had risen from it to change, thanks to Baudelaire, the whole course of European literature, yes, and not merely to trouble, but to frighten the wits out of several generations of human beings with such choice pieces as "King Pest," "The Pit and the Pendulum," and "A Descent into the Maelstrom," not to speak of the effect produced by the compendious and prophetic *Eureka*.

> My *ear* has been too shocking for any description — I am wearing away every day, even if my last sickness had not completed it.

Sigbjørn finished his grappa and ordered another. The sensation produced by reading these notes was really very curious. First, he was conscious of himself reading them here in this Roman bar, then of himself in the Valentine Museum in Richmond, Virginia, reading the letters through the glass case and copying fragments from these down, then of poor Poe sitting blackly somewhere writing them. Beyond this was the vision of Poe's foster father likewise reading some of these letters, for all he knew unheedingly, yet solemnly putting them away for what turned out to be posterity, these letters which, whatever they might not be, were certainly—he thought again—intended to be private. But were they indeed? Even here at this extremity Poe must have felt that he was transcribing the story that was E. A. Poe, at this very moment of what he conceived to be his greatest need, his final—however consciously engineered—disgrace, felt a certain reluctance, perhaps, to send what he wrote, as if he were thinking: Damn it, I could use some of that, it may not be so hot, but it is at least too good to waste on my foster father. Some of Keats's own published letters were not different. And yet it was almost bizarre how, among these glass cases, in these museums, to what extent one revolved about, was hemmed in by, this cinereous evidence of anguish. Where was Poe's astrolabe, Keats's tankard of claret, Shelley's "Useful Knots for the Yachtsman"? It was true that Shelley himself might not have been aware of the aromatic gums, but even that beautiful and irrelevant circumstantiality that was the gift of the Misses Boykin seemed not without its suggestion of suffering, at least for George Washington.

Baltimore, April 12, 1833.

> I am perishing — absolutely perishing for want of aid. And yet I am not idle — nor have I committed any offence against society which would render me deserving of so hard a fate. For God's sake pity me and save me from destruction.
>
> E. A. Poe

Oh, God, thought Sigbjørn. But Poe had held out another sixteen years. He had died in Baltimore at the age of forty. Sigbjørn himself was nine behind on that game so far, and—with luck — should win easily. Perhaps if Poe had held out a little longer—perhaps if Keats—he turned over the pages of his notebook rapidly, only to be confronted by the letter from Severn:

> My dear Sir:
>
> Keats has changed somewhat for the worse — at least his mind has much — very much — yet the blood has ceased to come . . . but the fatal prospect hangs . . . *for his knowledge of internal anatomy . . . largely adds to his torture.*

Suppliziato, strangolato, he thought—— *The lower is the true prison. And many others.* Nor have I committed any offence against society. Not much you hadn't, brother. Society might pay you the highest honors, even to putting your relics in the company of the waistcoat belonging to George Washington's dentist, but in its heart it cried:—*dirty stinking Degenerate Bobs was here from Boston, North End, Mass. Warp son of a bitch!*—— "On Saturday a gentleman came to cast his hand and foot . . ." Had anybody done that, Sigbjørn wondered, tasting his new grappa, and suddenly cognizant of his diminishing Guggenheim, compared, that was, Keats and Poe?—But compare in what sense, Keats, with what, in what sense, with Poe? What was it he wanted to compare? Not the aesthetic of the two poets, nor the breakdown of *Hyperion,* in relation to Poe's conception of the short poem, nor yet the philosophic ambition of the one, with the philosophic achievement of the other. Or could that more properly be discerned as negative capability, as opposed to negative achievement? Or did he merely wish to relate their melancholias? potations? hangovers? Their sheer guts—which commentators so obligingly forgot!—character, in a high sense of that word, the sense in which Conrad sometimes understood it, for were they not in their souls like hapless shipmasters, determined to drive their leaky commands full of valuable treasure at all costs, somehow, into port, and always against time, yet through all but interminable tempest, typhoons that so rarely abated? Or merely what seemed funereally analogous within the mutuality of their shrines? Or he could even speculate, starting with Baudelaire again, upon what the French movie director Epstein who had made *La Chute de la Maison Usher* in a way that would have delighted Poe himself, might have done with *The Eve of St. Agnes: And they are gone!*—— "For God's sake pity me and save me from destruction!"

Ah ha, now he thought he had it: did not the preservation of such relics betoken —beyond the filing cabinet of the malicious foster father who wanted to catch one out—less an obscure revenge for the poet's nonconformity, than for his magical monopoly, his possession of words? On the one hand he could write his translunar "Ulalume," his enchanted "To a Nightingale" (which might account for the *Field Book of Western Birds),* on the other was capable of saying, simply, "I am perishing.... For God's sake pity me...." You see, after all, he's just like folks—— What's this?—— Conversely there might appear almost a tragic condescension in remarks such as Flaubert's often quoted "Ils sont dans le vrai" perpetuated by Kafka—Kaf—and others, and addressed to child-bearing rosy-cheeked and jolly humanity at large. Condescension, nay, inverse self-approval, something downright unnecessary. And Flaub — Why should they be dans le vrai any more than the artist was dans le vrai? All people and poets are much the same but some poets are more the same than others, as George Orwell might have said. George Or— And yet, what modern poet would be caught dead (though they'd do their best to catch him all right) with his "For Christ's sake send aid," unrepossessed, unincinerated, to be put in a glass case? It was a truism to say that poets not only were, but looked like folks these days. Far from ostensible nonconformists, as the daily papers, the very writers themselves—more shame to them—took every opportunity triumphantly to point out, they dressed like, and as often as not were, bank clerks, or, marvellous paradox, engaged in advertising. It was true. He, Sigbjørn, dressed like a bank clerk himself—how else should he have courage to go into a bank? It was questionable whether poets especially, in uttermost private, any longer allowed themselves to say things like "For God's sake pity me!" Yes, they had become more like folks even than folks. And the despair in the glass case, all private correspondence carefully destroyed, yet destined to become ten thousand times more public than ever, viewed through the great glass case of art, was now transmuted into hieroglyphics, masterly compressions, obscurities to be deciphered by experts—yes, and poets—like Sigbjørn Wilderness. Wil—

And many others. Probably there was a good idea somewhere, lurking among these arrant self-contradictions; pity could not keep him from using it, nor a certain sense of horror that he felt all over again that these mummified and naked cries of agony should lie thus exposed to human view in permanent incorruption, as if embalmed evermore in their separate eternal funeral parlors: separate, yet not separate, for was it not as if Poe's cry from Baltimore, in a mysterious manner, in the manner that the octet of a sonnet, say, is answered by its sestet, had already been answered, seven years before, by Keats's cry from Rome; so that according to the special reality of Sigbjørn's notebook at least, Poe's own death appeared like something extraformal, almost extraprofessional, an afterthought. Yet inerrably it was part of the same poem, the same story. "And yet the fatal prospect hangs...." "Severn, lift me up, for I am dying." "Lift them up, keep them away." Dr. Swell's Root Beer.

Good idea or not, there was no more room to implement his thoughts within this notebook (the notes on Poe and Richmond ran, through Fredericksburg, into his remarks upon Rome, the Mamertine Prison, and Keats's house, and vice versa), so Sigbjørn brought out another one from his trousers pocket.

This was a bigger notebook altogether, its paper stiffer and stronger, showing it dated from before the war, and he had brought it from America at the last minute, fearing that such might be hard to come by abroad.

In those days he had almost given up taking notes: every new notebook bought represented an impulse, soon to be overlaid, to write afresh; as a consequence he had accumulated a number of notebooks like this one at home, yet which were almost empty, which he had never taken with him on his more recent travels since the war, else a given trip would have seemed to start off with a destructive stoop, from the past, in its soul: this one had looked an exception so he'd packed it.

Just the same, he saw, it was not innocent of writing: several pages at the beginning were covered with his handwriting, so shaky and hysterical of appearance, that Sigbjørn had to put on his spectacles to read it. Seattle, he made out. July? 1939. Seattle! Sigbjørn swallowed some grappa hastily. Lo, death hath reared himself a throne in a strange city lying alone far down within the dim west, where the good and the bad and the best and the rest, have gone to their eternal worst! The lower is the true Seattle— Sigbjørn felt he could be excused for not fully appreciating Seattle, its mountain graces, in those days. For these were not notes he had found but the draft of a letter, written in the notebook because it was that type of letter possible for him to write only in a bar. A bar? Well, one might have called it a bar. For in those days, in Seattle, in the State of Washington, they still did not sell hard liquor in bars—as, for that matter to this day they did not, in Richmond, in the State of Virginia—which was half the gruesome and pointless point of his having been in the State of Washington. LIC-OFF-PREM, he thought. No, no, go not to Virginia Dare— Neither twist Pepso—tight-rooted! —for its poisonous bane. The letter dated—no question of his recognition of it, though whether he'd made another version and posted it he had forgotten—from absolutely the lowest ebb of those low tides of his life, a time marked by the baleful circumstance that the small legacy on which he then lived had been suddenly put in charge of a Los Angeles lawyer, to whom this letter indeed was written, his family, who considered him incompetent, having refused to have anything further to do with him, as, in effect, did the lawyer, who had sent him to a religious-minded family of Buchmanite tendencies in Seattle on the understanding he be entrusted with not more than 25¢ a day.

Dear Mr. Van Bosch:

It is, psychologically, apart from anything else, of extreme urgency that I leave Seattle and come to Los Angeles to see you. I fear a complete mental collapse else. I have co-operated far beyond what I thought was the best of my ability here in the matter of liquor and I have also tried to work hard, so far, alas, without selling anything. I cannot say either that my ways have been as circumscribed exactly as I thought they would be by the Mackorkindales, who at least have seen my point of view on some matters, and if they pray for guidance on the very few occasions when they do see fit to exceed the stipulated 25¢ a day, they are at least sympathetic with my wishes to return. This may be because the elder Mackorkindale is literally and physically worn out following me through Seattle, or because you have failed to supply sufficient means for my board, but this is certainly as far as the sympathy goes. In short, they sympathize, but cannot honestly agree; nor will they advise you I should return. And in anything that applies to my writing — and this I find almost the hardest to bear — I am met with the opinion that I "should put all that behind me." If they merely claimed to be abetting yourself or my parents in this it would be understandable, but this judgment is presented to me independently, somewhat blasphemously in my view — though without question they believe it — as coming directly from God, who stoops daily from on high to inform the Mackorkindales, if not in so many words, that as a serious writer I am lousy. Scenting some hidden truth about this, things being what they are, I would find it discouraging enough if it stopped there, and were not beyond that the hope held out, miraculously congruent also with that of my parents and yourself, that I could instead turn myself into a successful writer of advertisements. Since I cannot but feel, I repeat, and feel respectfully, that they are sincere in their beliefs, all I can say is that in this daily rapprochement with their Almighty in Seattle I hope some prayer that has slipped in by mistake to let the dreadful man for heaven's sake return to Los Angeles may eventually be answered. For I find it impossible to describe my spiritual isolation in this place, nor the gloom into which I have sunk. I enjoyed of course the seaside — the Mackorkindales doubtless reported to you that the Group were having a small rally in Bellingham (I wish you could go to Bellingham one day) — but I have completely exhausted any therapeutic value in my stay. God knows I ought to know, I shall never recover in this place, isolated as I am from Primrose who, whatever you may say, I want with all my heart to make my wife. It was with the greatest of anguish that I discovered that her letters to me were being opened, finally, even having to hear lectures on her moral character by those who had read these letters, which I had thus been prevented from replying to, causing such pain to her as I cannot think of. This separation from her would be an unendurable agony, without anything else, but as things stand I can only say I would be better off in a prison, in the worst dungeon that could be imagined, than to be incarcerated in this damnable place with the highest suicide rate in the Union. Literally I am dying in this macabre hole and I appeal to you to send me, out of the money that is after all mine, enough that I may return. Surely I am not the only writer, there have been others in history whose ways have been misconstrued and who have failed —— who have won through —— success —— publicans and sinners —— I have no intention —

Sigbjørn broke off reading, and resisting an impulse to tear the letter out of the notebook, for that would loosen the pages, began meticulously to cross it out, line by line.

And now this was half done he began to be sorry. For now, damn it, he wouldn't be able to use it. Even when he'd written it he must have thought it a bit too good for poor old Van Bosch, though one admitted that wasn't saying much. Wherever or however he could have used it. And yet, what if they had found this letter— whoever "they" were—and put it, glass-encased, in a museum among *his* relics ? Not much — Still, you never knew! Well, they wouldn't do it now. Anyhow, perhaps he would remember enough of it—— "I am dying, absolutely perishing." "What have I done to them ?" "My dear Sir." "The worst dungeon." And many others: and *dirty stinking Degenerate Bobs was here from Boston, North End, Mass. Warp son—!*

Sigbjørn finished his fifth unregenerate grappa and suddenly gave a loud laugh, a laugh which, as if it had realized itself it should become something more respectable, turned immediately into a prolonged—though on the whole relatively pleasurable—fit of coughing.——

—1961

UNDER THE VOLCANO*

As they walked up the Calle Nicaragua toward the bus stop Hugh and Yvonne turned to watch the marmalade-colored birds trapezing in the vines. But her father, afflicted by their raucous cries, strode on austerely through the blue, hot November afternoon.

The bus was not very full at first and soon was rolling like a ship in a heavy sea.

Now out of one window, now out of another, they could see the great mountain, Popocatapetl, round whose base clouds curled like smoke drawn from a train.

They passed tall, hexagonal stands with advertisements for the Morelos Cinema: Los Manos de Orlac: con Peter Lorre. Elsewhere, as they clattered through the little town, they noticed posters of the same film, showing a murderer's hands laced with blood.

"Like Paris," Yvonne said to Hugh, pointing to the kiosks, "Kub, Oxygenee, do you remember ?"

Hugh nodded, stammering out something, and the careening of the bus made him swallow every syllable.

"—— Do you remember Peter Lorre in 'M' ?"

But they had to give it up. The patient floor boards were creaking too loudly. They were passing the undertakers: *Inhumaciones*. A parrot, head cocked, eyed them from its perch at the entrance. Quo Vadis ? asked a notice above it.

"Marvellous," the Consul said.

At the market they stopped for Indian women with baskets of poultry. They had strong faces, the color of dark earthenware. There was a massiveness in their movements as they settled themselves. Two or three had cigarette stubs behind their ears, another chewed an old pipe. Their good humored faces of old idols were wrinkled with sun but they did not smile.

Then someone laughed, the faces of the others slowly cracked into mirth, the camion was welding the old women into a community. Two even managed to hold an anxious conversation in spite of the racket.

The Consul, nodding to them politely, wished he too were going home. And he wondered who had suggested making this ghastly trip to the fiesta at Chapultepec when their car was laid up and there were no taxis to be had! The effort of going without a drink for a day, even for the benefit of his daughter and her young man who had arrived that morning from Acapulco, was far greater than he had expected. Perhaps it was not the effort of merely being sober that told so much as that of coping with the legacy of impending doom recent unprecedented bouts had left him. When Yvonne pointed out Popocatapetl to him for the fifth time he smiled wanly. Chimborozo, Cotopaxi—and there it was! To the Consul the volcano had taken on a sinister aspect: like a sort of Moby Dick, it had the air of beckoning them on, as it swung from one side of the horizon to the other, to some disaster, unique and immedicable.

The bus lurched away from the mercado where the clock on the main building

---

*["Under the Volcano " is the first version of what later grew into the novel of the same name. The short story was written in Cuernavaca, Mexico, about 1936, but remained unpublished until its appearance in the Lowry issue of *Prairie Schooner* (Winter 1963-64).]

sheltering the stalls stood at seven minutes past two—it had just struck eleven, the Consul's watch said a quarter to four—then bumped down a steep cobbled incline and began to cross a little bridge over a ravine.

Was this the same arras, Yvonne wondered, that cut through her father's garden? The Consul was indicating that it was. The bottom was immensely far below, one looked down at it as from the maintruck of a sailing ship, though dense foliage and wide leaves partly concealed the real treachery of the drop. Its steep banks were piled with refuse, which even hung on the foliage; from the precipitous slope beyond the bridge, turning round, Yvonne could see a dead dog right down at the bottom, with white bones showing through, nuzzling the refuse.

"How's the rajah hangover, Dad?" she asked smiling.

" 'Taut over chaos,' " the Consul gritted his teeth, " 'crammed with serried masks.' "

"Just a little longer."

"No. I shall *never* drink again. Nevermore."

The bus went on. Halfway up the slope, beyond the ravine, outside a gaudily decorated little cantina named the El Amor de los Amores, waited a man in a blue suit, swaying gently and eating a melon.

As they approached, the Consul thought he recognized him as the part owner of the cantina, which was not, however, on his beat: from the interior came the sound of drunken singing.

When the bus stopped, the Consul thirstily caught sight, over the jalousied doors, of a bartender leaning over the bar and talking with intensity to a number of roaring policemen.

The camion throbbed away to itself while the driver went into the cantina. He emerged almost immediately to hurl himself back on his vehicle. Then, with an amused glance at the man in the blue suit, whom he apparently knew, he jammed the bus into gear and drove away.

The Consul watched the man, fascinated. The latter was very drunk indeed, and he felt a queer envy of him, albeit it was perhaps a stir of fellowship. As the bus drew in sight of the brewery, the Cerveceria de Quahnahuac, the Consul, his too sober gaze on the other's large, trembling hands, thrust his own hands into his pocket guiltily, but he had found the word he wanted to describe him: pelado.

Pelados, he thought, the peeled ones, were those who did not have to be rich to prey on the really poor. They were also those half-breed politicians who work like slaves to get into office for one year, just one year, in which year they hope to put by enough to forswear work for the rest of their lives. Pelado—it was an ambiguous word, to be sure! The Consul chuckled. A Spaniard could interpret it as meaning Indian, the Indian whom he despised, used, and filled with —ah—"poisonous" liquor. While to that Indian it might mean the Spaniard, or, employed by either with an amiable contempt, simply anyone who made a show of himself.

But whatever it might or might not mean, the Consul judged, his eyes still fixed on his man with the blue suit, it was fair to consider that the word could have been distilled only from such a venture as the Conquest, suggesting as it did on the one hand exploiter, and on the other, thief: and neither was it difficult to understand why it had come in time to describe the invaders as well as their victims. Interchangeable ever were the terms of abuse with which the aggressor publicly discredited those about to be ravaged!

The pelado then, who for a time had been talking thickly to himself, was now sunk in stupor. There was no conductor this trip, fares were paid to the driver on getting off, none bothered him. The dusty blue suit with its coat, tight at the waist but open, the broad trousers, pointed shoes shined that morning and soiled with the saloon's sawdust, indicated a confusion in his mind the Consul well understood: who shall I be today, Jekyll or Hyde? His purple shirt, open at the neck and showing a crucifix, had been torn and was partially hanging out over the top of his trousers. For some reason he wore two hats, a kind of cheap Homberg fitting neatly over the broad crown of his sombrero.

Soon they were passing the Hotel Casino de la Selva and they stopped once more. Colts with glossy coats were rolling on a slope. The Consul recognized Dr. Vigil's back moving among the trees on the tennis court; it was as if he were dancing a grotesque dance all by himself there.

Presently they were getting out into the country. At first there were rough stone walls on either side: then, after crossing the narrow gauge railway, where the Pearce oil tanks were pillowed along the embankment against the trees, leafy hedges full of bright wildflowers with deep royal blue bells. Green and white clothing hung on the cornstalks outside the low, grass-roofed houses. Now the bright blue flowers grew right into the trees, already snowy with blooms, and all this beauty the Consul noted with horror.

The road became smoother for a time so that it was possible for Hugh and Yvonne to talk: then, just as Hugh was saying something about the "convolvuli," it grew much worse again.

"It's like a canterbury bell," the Consul was trying to say, only the camion bumped over a pothole at that moment and it was as if the jolt had thrown his soul up into his teeth. He steadied himself on the seat and the wood sent a piercing pain through his body. His knees knocked together. With Popocatapetl always following or preceding them they jogged into very rough country indeed. The Consul felt that his head had become an open basket swarming with crabs. Now it was the ravine that was haunting him, creeping after them with a gruesome patience, he thought, winding always around the road on one side or the other. The crabs were at the back of his eyes, yet he forced himself to be hearty.

"Where's old Popeye gone to now?" he would exclaim as the volcano slid out of sight past the window to the left, for though he was afraid of it, he felt somehow better when it was there.

"This is like driving over the moon," Hugh tried to whisper to Yvonne, but ended up by shouting.

"Maybe all covered with spinach!" Yvonne was answering her father.

"Right down Archimedes this time! Look out!"

Then for a while they were passing through flat, wooded country with no volcano in sight, nothing to be seen but pines, stones, fircones, black earth. But when they looked more closely they noticed that the stones were volcanic, the earth was parched looking, that everywhere were attestations to Popocatapetl's presence and antiquity.

After, the mountain itself would stride into view again, magnificent, or appearing sad, slate-gray as despair, poised over his sleeping woman, Ixtaccihuatl, now permanently contiguous, which perhaps accounted for it, the Consul decided, feeling that Popo had also an annoying quality of looking as though it knew people expected it to be about to do, or mean, something—as if to be the most beautiful mountain in the world were not enough.

Gazing round the camion, which was somewhat fuller, Hugh took stock of his surroundings. He noticed the drunk, the old women, the men in their white trousers with purple shirts, and now the men in black trousers with their white Sunday shirts—for it was a holiday—and one or two younger women in mourning. He attempted to take an interest in the poultry. The hens and cocks and turkeys imprisoned in their baskets, and those that were still loose, had all alike submitted. With only an occasional flutter to show they were alive they crouched passively under the seats, their emphatic spindly claws bound with cord. Two pullets lay, frightened and quivering, between the handbrake and the clutch, their wings linked, it seemed, with the levers. Hugh was bored with all this finally. The thought of Yvonne sagged down his mind, shook his brain, permeating the camion, the very day itself, with nervous passion.

He turned away from her nearness and looked out, only to see her clear profile and sleeked fair hair sailing along reflected in the window.

The Consul was suffering more and more intensely. Each object on which his glance fell appeared touched with a cruel, supersensual significance. He knew the very wood of the seat to be capable of hurting his hands. And the words which ran across the entire breadth of the bus over the windscreen: *su salva estara a salvo no escapiendo en el interior de esta vehiculo:* the driver's round mirror, the legend above it, *Cooperacion de la Crux Roja,* beside which hung three postcards of the Virgin Mary and a fire-extinguisher, the two slim vases of marguerites fixed over the dashboard, the dungaree jacket and whiskbroom under the seat opposite where the pelado was sitting, all seemed to him actually to be alive, to be participating, with evil animation, in their journey.

And the pelado? The shaking of the camion was making it difficult for him to remain seated. With his eyes shut, and swaying from side to side, he was trying to tuck his shirt in. Now he was methodically buttoning his coat on the wrong buttons. The Consul smiled, knowing how meticulous one could be when drunk: clothes mysteriously hung up, cars driven by a seventh sense, police eluded by an eighth. Now the pelado had found room to lie down full length on the seat. And all this had been superbly accomplished without once opening his eyes!

Stretched out—a corpse—he still preserved the appearance of being uncannily aware of all that was going on. In spite of his stupor, he was a man on his guard; half a melon slipped out of his hand, the segments full of seeds like raisins rolled to and fro on the seat, yet with eyeless sight those dead eyes saw it: his crucifix was slipping off, but he was conscious of it: the Homberg fell from his sombrero, slipped to the floor, and though making no attempt to pick it up, he obviously knew it was there. He was guarding himself against theft while gathering strength for more debauchery. In order to get into somebody's else cantina he might have to walk straight. His prescience was worthy of admiration.

Yvonne was enjoying herself. For the time being she was freed by the fact of Hugh's presence from the tyranny of thinking exclusively about him. The camion was travelling very much faster, rolling, swaying, jumping; the men were smiling and nodding, two boys, hanging at the back of the bus were whistling; and the bright shirts, the brighter serpentine confetti of tickets, red, yellow, green, blue, dangling from a loop on the ceiling, all contributed a certain sense of gaiety to their trip. They might have been going to a wedding.

But when the boys dropped off some of this gaiety departed. That predominance of purple in the men's shirts gave a disquieting glare to the day. There seemed something brutal to her too about those candelabra cactus swinging by. And about those other cactus, further away, like an army advancing uphill under machine-gun fire. All at once there was nothing to see outside but a ruined church full of pumpkins, caves for doors, windows bearded with grass. The exterior was blackened as by fire and it had an air of being damned. It was as though Hugh had left her again, and the pain of him slid back into her heart, momentarily possessing her.

Buses bobbed by in the other direction: buses to Tetecala, to Jujuta; buses to Xiutepec, to Xochitepec, to Xocxitepec —

At a great pace they swerved into a side road. Popocatapetl appeared, off to the right, with one side beautifully curved as a woman's breast, the other jagged and ferocious. The drifted clouds were massing, high-piled, behind it.

Everyone felt at last that they were really going somewhere: they had become self-enclosed, abandoned to the tumultuous will of the vehicle.

They thundered on, passing little pigs trotting along the road, an Indian screening sand. Advertisements on ruined walls swam by. Atchis! Instantia! Resfria dos Dolores. Cafiaspirina. Rechaches Imitaciones. Los Manos de Orlac: con Peter Lorre.

When there was a bad patch the bus rattled ominously and sometimes they ran off the road. But its determination outweighed these waverings: all were pleased to have transferred their responsibilities to it, and to be lulled into a state from which it would be pain to awaken.

As a partner in this, it was with a freezing, detached calm that the Consul found himself able to think, as they bucked and bounded over an interminable series of teeth-rattling potholes, even of the terrible night which doubtless awaited him, of his room shaking with daemonic orchestras, of the snatches of fearful sleep, interrupted by imaginary voices outside which were dogs barking, or by his own name being continually repeated with scorn by imaginary parties arriving.

The camion pitched and rolled on.

They spelt out the word *Deviacion* but made the detour too quickly with a yelping of tires and brakes. As they swerved into alignment once more the Consul noticed a man apparently lying fast asleep under the hedge by the right side of the road.

Both Hugh and Yvonne appeared oblivious to this. Nor did it seem likely to the Consul that in this country anyone else was going to think it extraordinary a man should choose to sleep in the sun by the side of the road, or even in the middle of the road.

The Consul looked back again. No mistake. The man, receding quickly now, lay with his hat over his eyes, his arms stretched out toward a wayside cross. Now they were passing a riderless horse, munching the hedge.

The Consul leaned forward to call out but hesitated. What if it were simply an hallucination? This might prove very embarrassing. However he did call out, tapping the driver on the shoulder; almost at the same moment the bus leaped to a standstill.

Guiding the whining vehicle swiftly, steering an erratic course with one hand, the driver, who was craning right out of his seat watching the corners behind and before with quick yet reluctant turns of the head, reversed along the dusty detour.

There was the friendly, overpowering smell of exhaust gases tempered with the hot smell of tar from the repairs, though no one was at work on the road, everybody having knocked off, and there was nothing to be seen there, just the soft indigo carpet sparkling and sweating by itself. But a little further back, to one side by the hedge, was a stone cross and beneath it were a milk bottle, a funnel, a sock, and part of an old suitcase.

Now they could see the man quite plainly, lying with his arms stretched out toward this wayside cross.

II

As the bus jerked to another stop the pelado almost slid from his seat to the floor but, managing to recover himself, not only reached his feet and an equilibrium he contrived remarkably to maintain, but in doing so had arrived halfway to the door in one strong movement, crucifix fallen safely into place around his neck, hats in one hand, melon in the other. He nodded gravely and with a look that might have withered at its inception any thought of stealing them, placed the hats carefully on a vacant seat near the door, and with exaggerated care let himself down to the road. His eyes were still only half-open, preserving that dead glaze, yet there could be no doubt he had taken in the whole situation. Throwing away the melon he walked over toward the man in the road. Even though he stepped as if over imaginary obstacles his course was straight and he held himself erect.

Yvonne, Hugh, the Consul, and two of the passengers followed him. None of the old women had moved from their seats.

Halfway across the road Yvonne gave a nervous cry, turning on her heel abruptly. Hugh gripped her arm.

"Are you all right?"

"Yes," she said, freeing herself. "Go on. It's just that I can't stand the sight of blood, damn it."

She was climbing back into the camion as Hugh came up with the Consul and the two passengers.

The pelado was swaying gently over the recumbent man.

Although the latter's face was covered by his hat it could be seen that he was an Indian of the peon class. There seemed no doubt that he was dying. His chest heaved like a spent swimmer's, his stomach contracted and dilated rapidly, yet there was no sign of blood. One clenched fist spastically thumped the dust.

The two foreigners stood there helplessly, each waiting for the other to remove the peon's hat, to expose the wound they all felt must be there, each checked from some such action by a common reluctance, an obscure courtesy. Each knew the other was also thinking it would be, naturally, even better still should the pelado or one of the passengers examine the man. But as nobody made any move Hugh became impatient. He shifted from foot to foot. He looked at the Consul with supplication. The Consul had been here long enough to know what could be done; moreover he was the one among them most nearly representing authority.

375

But the Consul, who was trying to prevent himself saying, "Go ahead, after all, Spain invaded Mexico first," made no move either. At last Hugh could stand it no longer. Stepping forward impulsively he made to bend over the peon when one of the passengers plucked at his sleeve.

"Mistair, have you throw away your cigarette?"

"What!" Hugh turned around, astonished.

"I don't know," said the Consul. "Forest fires, probably."

"Better throw your cigarette, Senor. They have prohibidated it."

Hugh dropped his cigarette and stamped it out, bewildered and irritated. He was about to bend over the man once more when the passenger plucked his sleeve again. Hugh straightened up.

"They have prohibidated it, Senor," the other said politely, tapping his nose. He gave an odd little laugh. "Positivemente!"

"I no comprendo, gnädige Senor." Hugh tried desperately to produce some Spanish.

"He means you can't touch this chap because you'd be an accessory after the fact," nodded the Consul, beginning to sweat and wishing profoundly he could get as far away from this scene as possible, if necessary even by means of the peon's horse, to somewhere where great gourds of mescal crouched. "Leave well enough alone is not only the watchword, Hugh, it's the law."

The man's breathing and thumping was like the sea dragging itself down a stone beach.

Then the pelado went down on one knee and whipped off the dying man's hat.

They all peered over, seeing the terrible wound in the side of his head, the blood from which had almost coagulated, and before they stood back, before the pelado replaced the hat and, drawing himself erect, made a hopeless gesture with hands blotched with half dried blood, they caught a glimpse of a sum of money, four or five silver pesos and a handful of centavos, which had been placed neatly under the man's collar, by which it was partly obscured.

"But we can't let the poor fellow die," Hugh said despairingly, looking after the pelado as he returned to the bus, and then down once more at this life gasping away from them all. "We'll have to get a doctor."

This time from the camion, the pelado again made that gesture of hopelessness, which might have been also a gesture of sympathy.

The Consul was relieved to see that by now their presence had exampled approach to the extent that two peasants, hitherto unnoticed, had come up to the dying man, while another passenger was also standing beside the body.

"Pobrecito," said one.

"Chingarn," muttered the other.

And gradually the others took up these remarks as a kind of refrain, a quiet seething of futility, of whispers, in which the dust, the heat, the bus with its load of immobile old women and doomed poultry, even the terrible beauty and mystery of the country itself, seemed to be conspiring: while only these two words, the one of tender compassion, the other of fiendish contempt, were audible above the thudding and the gasping, until the driver, as if satisfied that all was now as it should be, began impatiently blowing his horn.

A passenger shouted to him to shut up, but possibly thinking the admonition was in jesting approval, the driver continued to blow, punctuating the seething, which soon developed into a general argument in which suspicions and suggestions cancelled each other out, to a heckling accompaniment of contemptuous blasts.

Was it murder? Was it robbery? Or both? The peon had ridden from the market with more than that four or five pesos, possibly he'd been in possession of mucho dinero, so that a good way to avoid suspicion of theft was to leave a little of the money, as had been done. Perhaps it was not robbery at all; he had only been thrown from his horse? The horse had kicked him? Possible? Impossible! Had the police been called? An ambulance — the Crux Roja? Where was the nearest phone? One of them, now, should go for the police? But it was absurd to suppose they were not on their way. How could they be on their way when half of them were on strike? They would be on their way all right, though. An ambulance? But here it was impertinent of a gringo to interfere. Surely the Red Cross were perfectly capable of looking after such a matter themselves? But was there any truth in the rumor that the Servicio de Ambulante had been suspended? It was not a red but a green cross and their business began only when they were informed. Perhaps it was imprudent of a gringo to assume they hadn't been informed? A personal friend, Dr. Vigil, why not call him? He was playing tennis. Call the Casino de la Selva then? There was no phone; oh, there was one once but it had decomposed. Get another doctor, Dr. Gomez. Un hombre noble. Too far, and anyhow, probably he was out; well, perhaps he was back!

At last Hugh and the Consul became aware that they had reached an impasse upon which the driver's horn still made a most adequate comment. Neither could presume, from the appearance of it, that the peon's fate was not being taken care of in some way "by one of his own kind." Well, it certainly didn't look as though · his own kind had been any too generous to him! On the contrary, the same person who placed him at the side of the road, who placed the money in the peon's collar, was probably even now going for help!

These sentiments got up and knocked each other down again and although their voices were not raised, although Hugh and the Consul were not quarrelling, it was as if they were actually knocking each other down physically and getting up again, each time more weary than the last time down, each time with a practical or psychic obstruction toward co-operating or even acting singly, the most potent and final of all of which obstructions being that it was not their business at all but somebody else's.

Yet on looking around them they realized that this too was only what the others were arguing. It is not my business, nor yours, they said as they shook their heads, but someone else's, their answers becoming more and more involved, more and more theoretical, so that finally the discussion began to take a political turn.

To the Consul, time suddenly seemed to be moving at different speeds: the speed at which the peon was dying contrasting oddly with that at which everyone was arriving at the conclusion it was impossible to make up their minds. Aware that the discussion was by no means closed and that the driver, who had stopped blowing his horn, and was conversing with some of the women over his shoulder, would not think of leaving without first taking their fares, the Consul excused himself to Hugh and walked over to the Indian's horse, which, with its bucket saddle and heavy iron sheathes for stirrups, was calmly chewing the "convolvulus" in the hedge, looking as innocent as only one of its species can when suspected, even wrongfully, of throwing its rider or kicking a man to death. He examined it carefully, without touching it, noticing its wicked, friendly, plausible eyes, the sore on its hipbone, the number seven branded on its rump, as if for some clue to what had happened. Well, what *had* happened? Parable of a too late hour! More important, what was going to happen — to them all? What was going to happen to him was that he was going to have fifty-seven drinks at the earliest opportunity.

The bus was hooting with real finality now that two cars were held up behind it; and the Consul, observing that Hugh was standing on the step of one of them, walked back shaking his head as the camion came toward him to stop at a wider part of the road. The cars, wild with impatience, thrust past and Hugh dropped off the second one. Bearing tin plates under their numbers with the warning "Diplomatico" they disappeared ahead in a cloud of dust.

"It's the diplomatic thing, doubtless," said the Consul, with one foot on the step of the camion. "Come on, Hugh, there's nothing we can do."

The other passengers were getting on board and the Consul stood to one side to talk to Hugh. The periodicity of the honking now had become much slower. There was a bored, almost amused resignation in the sound.

"You'll only be hauled into gaol and entangled in red tape for God knows how long," the Consul persisted. "Come *on*, Hugh. What do you think you're going to do?"

"If I can't get a doctor here, God damn it, I'll take him to one."

"They won't let you on the bus."

"The hell they won't! Oh—here come the police," he added, as three smiling vigilantes came tramping through the dust at that moment, their holsters slapping their thighs.

"No, they're not," the Consul said unfortunately. "At least, they're just from the policia de seguridad, I think. They can't do anything much either, just tell you to go away or —"

Hugh began to expostulate with them while the Consul watched him from the step of the camion apprehensively. The driver was wearily honking. One of the policemen began to push Hugh toward the bus. Hugh pushed back. The policeman drew back his hand. Hugh raised his fist. The policeman dropped his hand and began to fumble with his holster.

"Come on Hugh, for God's sake," the Consul pleaded, grasping him again. "Do you want to land us all in the gaol? Yvonne —"

The policeman was still fumbling with his holster when suddenly Hugh's face collapsed like a heap of ashes, he let his hands fall limply to his sides, and with a scornful laugh boarded the bus, which was already moving away.

"Never mind, Hugh," said the Consul, on the step with him, a drop of sweat falling on his toe, "it would have been worse than the windmills."

"What windmills?" Hugh looked about him, startled.

"No, no," the Consul said, "I meant something else, only that Don Quixote wouldn't have hesitated that long."

And he began to laugh.

Hugh stood for a moment cursing under his breath and looking back at the scene, the peon's horse munching the hedge, the police enveloped in the dust, the peon far beyond thumping the road, and now, hovering high above all, what he hadn't noticed before, the obvious cartoon birds, the xopilotes, who wait only for the ratification of death.

III

The bus plunged on.

Yvonne was flaccid with shame and relief. She tried to catch Hugh's eyes but he crammed himself into his seat so furiously she was afraid to speak to him or even to touch him.

She sought some excuse for her own behavior in the thought of the silent, communal decision of the old women to have nothing to do with the whole affair. With what sodality, scenting danger, they had clenched their baskets of poultry to them, or peered around to identify their property! Then they had sat, as now, motionless. It was as if, for them, through the various tragedies of Mexican history, pity, the impulse to approach, and terror, the impulse to escape, (as she had learned at college), had been reconciled finally by prudence, the conviction it is better to stay where you are.

And the other passengers? The men in their purple shirts who had a good look at what was going on but didn't get out either? Who wanted to be arrested as an accomplice, they seemed to be saying to her now. Frijoles for all; Tierra, Libertad, Justica y Ley. Did all that mean anything? Quien sabe. They were not sure of anything save that it was foolish to get mixed up with the police, who had their own way of looking at the law.

Yvonne clutched Hugh's arm but he did not look at her. The camion rolled and swayed as before, some more boys jumped on the back of the bus; they began to whistle, the bright tickets winked with their bright colors and the men looked at each other with an air as of agreement that the bus was outdoing itself, it had never before gone so fast, which must be because it too knew today was a holiday.

Dust filtered in through the windows, a soft invasion of dissolution, filling the vehicle

Then they were at Chapultepec.

The driver kept his hand on the screaming emergency brake as they circled down into the town, which was already invested with the Consul's abhorrence because of his past excesses there. Popocatapetl seemed impossibly close to them now, crouching over the jungle, which had begun to draw the evening over its knees.

For a moment there was a sort of twilight calm in the bus. The stars were out now: the Scorpion had come out of its hole and waited low on the horizon.

The Consul leaned forward and nudged Hugh: "Do you see what I see?" he asked him, inclining his head toward the pelado, who had been sitting bolt upright all this time, fidgeting with something in his lap, and wearing much the same expression as before, though he was evidently somewhat rested and sobered.

As the bus stopped in the square, pitching Hugh to his feet, he saw that the pelado clutched in his fist a sad, blood-stained pile of silver pesos and centavos, the dying man's money —

The passengers began to crowd out. Some of them looked at the pelado, incredulous but always preoccupied. Grinning round at them he perhaps half hoped that some comment would be made. But there was no comment.

379

The pelado paid his fare with part of the blood-stained money, and the driver accepted it. Then he went on taking the other fares.

The three of them stood in the warm evening in the little zocalo. The old women had disappeared: it was as if they had been sucked down into the earth.

From a street near by the crashing, plangent chords of a guitar sounded. And from further away came the bangs and cries of the fiesta.

Yvonne took Hugh's arm. As they walked away they saw the driver, now ostensibly knocked off for the day, and the pelado, stepping high and with a fatuous smile of triumph on his face, swagger into a pulqueria. The three stared after them and at the name of the saloon, after its doors had swung shut: the Todos-Contentos-y-yo-Tambien.

"Everybody happy," said the Consul, the certainty that he would drink a million tequilas between now and the end of his life stealing over him like a benison and postponing for the moment the necessity for the first one, "including me."

A bell somewhere compounded sudden wild triphthongs.

They moved in the direction of the fiesta, their shadows falling across the square, bending upward on the door of the Todos-Contentos-y-yo-Tambien, below which the bottom of a crutch had appeared.

They lingered curiously, noticing that the crutch rested for some time where it was, its owner having an argument at the door, or a last drink perhaps.

Presently, the crutch disappeared, as if it had been hoisted away. The door of the Todos-Contentos-y-yo-Tambien, through which they could see the bus driver and the pelado getting their drinks, was propped back, they saw something emerge.

Bent double and groaning with the weight, an old, lame Indian was carrying out another Indian, yet older and more decrepit, on his back, by means of a strap clamped to his forehead. He carried the older man and his crutches — he carried both their burdens —

They all stood in the dusk watching the Indian as he disappeared with the old man around a bend in the road, shuffling through the gray white dust in his poor sandals.   *—1964*

ANNE WILKINSON

(1910-1961)

Mrs. Anne (Gibbons) Wilkinson was born in Toronto, spent her early years in London (Ontario) and Toronto, and was educated abroad. Her memories of her childhood are charmingly related in "Four Corners of My World," a prose sketch that appeared in The Tamarack Review *(1961). She was an editor of that magazine. She also wrote* Lions in the Way *(1956), a history of the famous Osler family from which she was descended.* Swann and Daphne *(1960) was a fable for children. In addition to poems in periodicals during the last fifteen years of her life, she published two books of verse,* Counterpoint to Sleep *(1951) and* The Hangman Ties the Holly *(1955).*

Mrs. Wilkinson died in Toronto on May 10, 1961. Her Collected Poems *were edited, with an Introduction, by A. J. M. Smith in 1968.*

SUMMER ACRES

I

These acres breathe my family,
Holiday with seventy summers' history.
My blood lives here,
Sunned and veined three generations red
Before my bones were formed.

My eyes are wired to the willow
That wept for my father,
My heart is boughed by the cedar
That covers with green limbs the bones of my children,
My hands are white with a daisy, sired
By the selfsame flower my grandfather loved;

My ears are tied to the tattle of water
That echoes the vows of ancestral lovers,
My skin is washed by a lather of waves
That bathed the blond bodies of uncles and aunts
And curled on the long flaxen hair of my mother;

My feet step soft on descendants of grass
That was barely brushed
By the wary boots of a hummingbird woman,
The Great Great Grandmother
Of my mid-century children.

II

September born, reared in the sunset hour,
I was the child of old men heavy with honor;
I mourned the half mast time of their death and sorrowed
A season for leaves, shaking their scarlet flags
From green virility of trees.

As ears spring cartilaged from skulls
So my ears spring from the sound of water
And the whine of autumn in the family tree.
How tired, how tall grow the trees
Where the trees and the family are temples
Whose columns will tumble, leaf over root to their ruin.

Here, in my body's home my heart dyes red
The last hard maple in their acres.
Where birch and elm and willow turn,
Gently bred, to gold against the conifers,
I hail my fathers, sing their blood to the leaf.

—1951

A POET'S-EYE VIEW

You are earth, loam, actual fields
And we the green reed growing from your body;
You are solid, we are porous, ringed with chatter,
Stalks that echo water
Running in your under-worldly springs;
Your ribs crack in the sun, ridge with rain,
We lie boneless when our tissues fade;
You are stiff against the wind, we
Bend, arc'd with ague, by the storm
Are properly bowed down a day
Then up a daisy, green stalk straight, unbroken;
You, the earth, are bound to earth's own axis,
We, who grow our down roots deep in you
Are multi-headed, spray out seed like dandipuff
To tickle the fabulous thin highborn skin of air
Before we fall, point every potent feather
Back into its spawning bed, your tethered body;
You are warped with rock, the woof of you
Is ore; in soul's rough weather
Rock splits open at the giant tremor of the soil;
We, the green ones, laugh and add an inch
For each storm's death, our knowing nonsense blowing
On and off the lode of your mortality.

—1951

SOUTH, NORTH

Countries where the olive
And the orange ripen
Grow their men
On slopes unpuritan;
Joy a food
Deserving rites of measure.

Where winter pulls the blind
A bliss as keen —
On native stone of sin
Cold men whet their pleasure
Cussed by the black north wind.

—1955

382

EASTER SKETCHES, MONTREAL

1

South of North
Men grow soft with summer,
Lack the winter muscle
Set to tauten at the miracle;
Boom and shrapnel,
Riot of Easter, loud
Where guns of ice salute
The cracking god.

Vision dims where flowers
Blur the lens
But here, intemperate
The ropes of air
Whip the optic nerve
Till eyes are clean with crying
For the melting hour
When flocks of snow stampede
And rocks are split by spring
And intimations of fertility
In water ring.

South of North
Men grow deaf with summer,
Sound is muffled by the pile of lawns,
But where the air is seeded fresh
And skies can stretch their cloudy loins
To the back of the long north wind
The ear is royal pitched
And hears the dying snows
Sing like swans.

2

Where campanile of rock steeples the town
Water bells the buoy of all our birthdays;
Rivers swell in tumbling towers of praise,
Ice in aqua risen hails
The bearing down in labor of the sun.

And after sun, guards of northern lights
Stand their swords; green fires kindled
By the green shoots in our wood
Cut the natal cord,

Freeing the animal sensual man with astral
Spears of grass.
Cerebral ore conceives when pollen
Falls from heaven in a buzz of stars

And time and the rolling world
Fold the birthday children in their arms.

3

North of South
Winter is Jehovah, we
The Jobs who scold the frosty Lord
Till wings of weather
Clap the air
And crows unfrock the melting God.

On our nativity
The mellowed sun is grown,
A man to kill our father,
A sun with breath so warm
It seeds the body of our summer.

—*1955*

THE PRESSURE OF NIGHT

The pressure of night is on her.
She lies stiff against her saviour sleep.
Vicious as a scratch her cry
"I love the light, I'll have no traffic
With the nigger world of night."
And her white flesh creeps.

But night is, and blazed with eyes.
Night has no shudder in
Its whole dark hemisphere of skin

And night replies
"I am your shepherd lover,
Root of daisy and the seed of clover,
I am the poet's pasture."

But she lies dumb
Ice and fire die tepid on her tongue
Scorched with cold, the unbeliever
Resists her saviour.

—*1955*

IN JUNE AND GENTLE OVEN

In June and gentle oven
Summer kingdoms simmer
As they come
And flower and leaf and love
Release
Their sweetest juice.

No wind at all
On the wide green world
Where fields go stroll-
Ing by
And in and out
An adder of a stream
Parts the daisies
On a small Ontario farm.

And where, in curve of meadow,
Lovers, touching, lie,
A church of grass stands up
And walls them, holy, in.

Fabulous the insects
Stud the air
Or walk on running water,

Klee-drawn saints
And bright as angels are.

Honeysuckle here
Is more than bees can bear
And time turns pale
And stops to catch its breath
And lovers slip their flesh
And light as pollen
Play on treble water
Till bodies reappear
And a shower of sun
To dry their languor.

Then two in one the lovers lie
And peel the skin of summer
With their teeth
And suck its marrow from a kiss
So charged with grace
The tongue, all knowing
Holds the sap of June
Aloof from seasons, flowing.

—1955

THE RED AND THE GREEN

Here, where summer slips
Its sovereigns through my fingers
I put on my body and go forth
To seek my blood.

I walk the hollow subway
Of the ear; its tunnel
Clean of blare
Echoes the lost red syllable.

Free from cramp and chap of winter
Skin is minstrel, sings
Tall tales and shady
Of the kings of Nemi Wood.

I walk an ancient path
Wearing my warmth and singing
The notes of a Druid song
In the ear of Jack-in-the-Green.

But the quest turns round, the goal,
My human red centre
Goes whey in the wind,
Mislaid in the curd and why of memory.

Confused, I gather rosemary
And stitch the leaves
To green hearts on my sleeve;
My new green arteries

Fly streamers from the maypole of my arms,
From head to toe
My blood sings green,
From every heart a green amnesia rings.

—1955

LETTER TO MY CHILDREN

I guided you by rote—
Nipple to spoon, from spoon
To knife and fork,
And many a weak maternal morning
Bored the breakfast hour
With "manners make the man,"
And cleanliness I kissed
But shunned its neighbour,
Puzzled all my days
By the "I" in godliness.

Before you turn
And bare your faultless teeth at me
Accept a useless gift, apology,
Admit I churched you in the rites

Of trivia
And burned the family incense
At a false god's altar.

If we could start again,
You, newbegotten, I
A clean stick peeled
Of twenty paper layers of years
I'd tell you only what you know
But barely know you know,
Teach one commandment,
"Mind the senses and the soul
Will take care of itself,
Being five times blessed."

—1955

ADAM AND GOD

On Monday man gave God
Dominion of the sky;
On Tuesday swore Him
President of waves;
On Wednesday crowned
Him Emperor
Of every creeping thing,
A monarch of the night
And King of day;
On Thursday
Man breathed into God
Man's anger, charged His gun
That God might fire from heaven;
On Friday
Bade Him eat the apple, fallen
From the Good and Evil
Tree in Eden;
On Saturday
Man grumbled, "God
Is lonely, has no peer
To share His fate"
And cut the Devil
From a sleeping woman's rib;
On Sunday
God cried, "Rest! Enough!"
And ran from man and hid.

—1968

4. WHEN A BODY BREAKS

I

When a body breaks or is
Cast off from its hemisphere
Something grave has gone amiss.
Danger, danger, everywhere.

Moon broke loose, or was she thrown
Altar high that none dare doubt
Her powers, now more potent grown,
As Helen's have, with chant and rhyming?
No man puts to sea without
Her tides' consent; and at her waning
Virgins pale, and bribe with moon-blood
Goddess of their maidenhead
Whose light can stone or warp a womb
Or send the lovers mad.

II

It happened on a Tuesday, noon
(A body breaks or is cast off),
And being neither moon nor Helen
I fell down a well,
Commonplace abyss,
Black and waterless,
And in the falling turned to stone.

I shot through earth; now am come
Right back where I started from
In outer space,
Our point of genesis.
A tunnel travelled indicates
Some kind of birth, a milky way,
But not to me; my mouth
Is stone and sucks on meteors.

Twinkle twinkle how I wonder
What I'm falling from up yonder.
Virtue? Vice? Abstract nouns?
If vice, it is my sloth, my own,
My slug in hiding under a stone
But not under me anymore
For I am on all sides exposed
And falling down,
On through graveyards where the dead
Stars lie cold, their glitter gone.

*[In a footnote Anne Wilkinson explained her title was a country
saying for a graveyard.]

I hail white Jupiter.
God-white Jupiter, I call,
But he is king and need not stare
At stone, except in monuments.
Venus combs her copper hair
As I come plunging by,
And Mercury, the slippery one,
Talks to redfaced Mars,
But none of them talk to me. O
Try another tongue, cry *Marduk*
Ishtar Nebo Nergal.
They pay me no heed as I drop,
No more than Sin and Shamash.

It is other than I had imagined. I thought
To travel behind two plumed white horses,
I thought to lie like cream in a long black hearse
I had not calculated on this
Fall without end.

—1968

NATURE BE DAMNED

I

Pray where would lamb and lion be
If they lay down in amity?
Could lamb then nibble living grass?
Lamb and lion both must starve;
Bird and flower, too, must die of love.

II

I go a new dry way, permit no weather
Here, on undertaker's false green sod
Where I sit down beneath my false tin tree.
There's too much danger in a cloud,
In wood or field, or close to moving water.
With my black blood—who can tell?
The dart of one mosquito might be fatal;

Or in the flitting dusk a bat
Might carry away my destiny,
Hang it upside down from a rafter
In a barn unknown to me.

I hide my skin within the barren city
Where artificial moons pull no man's tide,
And so escape my green love till the day
Vine breaks through brick and strangles me.

III

I was witch and I could be
Bird or leaf
Or branch and bark of tree.

In rain and two by two my powers left me;
Instead of curling down as root and worm
My feet walked on the surface of the earth,
And I remember a day of evil sun
When forty green leaves withered on my arm.

And so I damn the font where I was blessed,
Am unbeliever; was deluded lover; never
Bird or leaf or branch and bark of tree.
Each, separate as curds from whey,
Has signature to prove identity.

And yet we're kin in appetite;
Tree, bird in the tree and I.
We feed on dung, a fly, a lamb
And burst with seed
Of tree, of bird, of man,
Till tree is bare
And bird and I are bone
And feaster is reborn
The feast, and feasted on.

Once a year in the smoking bush
A little west of where I sit
I burn my winter caul to a green ash.
This is an annual festival,
Nothing to stun or startle;
A coming together — water and sun
In summer's first communion.

Today again I burned my winter caul
Though senses nodded, dulled by ritual.

One hundred singing orioles
And five old angels wakened me;
Morning sky rained butterflies
And simple fish, bass and perch,
Leapt from the lake in salutation.
St. Francis, drunk among the daisies,
Opened his ecstatic eye.

Then roused from this reality I saw
Nothing, anywhere, but snow.

—1968

IRVING LAYTON

(1912-   )

Irving Layton was born in Rumania and emigrated to Montreal with his family (Lazarovitch) when he was an infant. He graduated from Macdonald College (B.Sc.Agric.) in 1939. After serving in the army during the war, he earned an M.A. degree from McGill in Political Science and Economics, taught in a high school in Montreal, and lectured part-time at Sir George Williams University.

In her article, "Montreal Poets of the Forties," (Canadian Literature No. 14), *Wynne Francis has told how John Sutherland, Irving Layton, and Louis Dudek formed a* First Statement *group (so-called after the little magazine which they published) in opposition to the rival* Preview *group of Patrick Anderson, P. K. Page, F. R. Scott, Neufville Shaw, Bruce Ruddick, and (later) A. J. M. Smith and A. M. Klein. Layton's first published volume was* Here and Now *(1945), the first chapbook in a* New Writers Series *to be published by First Statement Press. Since that time Layton has been a prolific writer and publisher of privately-printed books of verse. Among his volumes, which have circulated widely, are such collections as* The Improved Binoculars *(1956),* A Red Carpet for the Sun *(1959),* The Swinging Flesh *(1961), and* Balls for a One-Armed Juggler *(1963). By that year he had published fifteen volumes of verse.*

During the next decade he added another ten volumes, including the Collected Poems *(1971) and* Lovers and Lesser Men *(1973).* Love Where the Nights Are Long *(1962), which Layton edited, is an anthology of Canadian love songs.* Engagements: The Prose of Irving Layton, *was edited by Seymour Mayne (1972).*

The prefaces to such volumes as A Red Carpet for the Sun *express Layton's passion for experience, his literary principles, and his defence of his own distinctive poetry. Like his poems, they also reveal his acquaintance with literary tradition and help to explain* a later softening in his attitude toward English studies in the universities. He was Poet-in-Residence at Sir George Williams University in 1966, and Writer Consultant at the University of Guelph in 1969. He has given readings throughout Canada and the United States. Layton is now a Professor of English in York University. He has won many awards, including two Governor-General's awards.

NEWSBOY

Neither tribal nor trivial he shouts
From the city's centre where tramcars move
Like stained bacilli across the eyeballs,
Where people spore in composite buildings
From their protective gelatine of doubts,
Old ills, and incapacity to love
While he, a Joshua before their walls,
Sells newspapers to the gods and geldings.

Intrusive as a collision, he is
The Zeitgeist's too public interpreter,
A voice multiplex and democratic,
The people's voice or the monopolists';
Who with last-edition omniscience
Plays Clotho to each gaping customer
With halcyon colt, sex crime in an attic,
The story of a twice-jailed bigamist.

For him the mitred cardinals sweat in
Conclaves domed; the spy is shot. Empiric;
And obstreperous confidant of kings,
Rude despiser of the anonymous,
Danubes of blood wash up his bulletins
While he domesticates disaster like
A wheat in pampas of prescriptive things
With cries animal and ambiguous.

His dialectics will assault the brain,
Contrive men to voyages or murder,
Dip the periscope of their public lives
To the green levels of acidic caves;
Fever their health, or heal them with ruin,
Or with lies dangerous as a letter;
Finally enfold the season's cloves,
Cover a somnolent face on Sundays.

—1945

THE BLACK HUNTSMEN

Before ever I knew men were hunting me
I knew delight as water in a glass in a pool;
The childish heart then
Was ears nose eyes twiceten fingers,
And the torpid slum street, in summer,
A cut vein of the sun
That shed goldmotes by the million
Against a boy's bare toe foot ankle knee.

Then when the old year fell out the window
To break into snowflakes on the cold stones of City Hall,
I discovered Tennyson in a secondhand bookstore;
He put his bugle for me to his bearded mouth,
And down his Aquitaine nose a diminutive King Arthur
Rode out of our grocery shop bowing to left and to right,
Bearing my mother's *sheitel* with him;
And for a whole week after that
I called my cat Launcelot.

Now I look out for the evil retinue
Making their sortie out of a forest of gold;
Afterwards their dames shall weave my *tzitzith*
Into a tapestry,
Though for myself I had preferred
A death by water or sky.

—1951

THE BIRTH OF TRAGEDY

And me happiest when I compose poems.
  Love, power, the huzza of battle
  are something, are much;
yet a poem includes them like a pool
  water and reflection.
In me, nature's divided things —
  tree, mold on tree —
  have their fruition;
I am their core. Let them swap,
bandy, like a flame swerve
I am their mouth; as a mouth I serve.

And I observe how the sensual moths
  big with odor and sunshine
  dart into the perilous shrubbery;
or drop their visiting shadows
  upon the garden I one year made
of flowering stone to be a footstool

for the perfect gods:
  who, friends to the ascending orders,
sustain all passionate meditations
and call down pardons
for the insurgent blood.

A quiet madman, never far from tears,
  I lie like a slain thing
  under the green air the trees
inhabit, or rest upon a chair
  towards which the inflammable air
tumbles on many robins' wings;
  noting how seasonably
  leaf and blossom uncurl
and living things arrange their death,
while someone from afar off
blows birthday candles for the world.

—1954

MISUNDERSTANDING

I placed
my hand
upon
her thigh.

By the way
she moved
away
I could see
her devotion
to literature
was not
perfect.

—1954

THE COLD GREEN ELEMENT

At the end of the garden walk
the wind and its satellite wait for me;
their meaning I will not know
    until I go there,
but the black-hatted undertaker

who, passing, saw my heart beating in the grass,
is also going there. Hi, I tell him,
a great squall in the Pacific blew a dead poet
    out of the water,
who now hangs from the city's gates.

Crowds depart daily to see it, and return
with grimaces and incomprehension;
if its limbs twitched in the air
    they would sit at its feet
peeling their oranges.

And turning over I embrace like a lover
the trunk of a tree, one of those
for whom the lightning was too much
    and grew a brilliant
hunchback with a crown of leaves.

The ailments escaped from the labels
of medicine bottles are all fled to the wind;
I've seen myself lately in the eyes
    of old women,
spent streams mourning my manhood,

in whose old pupils the sun became
a bloodsmear on broad catalpa leaves
and hanging from ancient twigs,
    my murdered selves
sparked the air like the muted collisions

of fruit. A black dog howls down my blood,
a black dog with yellow eyes;
he too by someone's inadvertence
    saw the bloodsmear
on the broad catalpa leaves.

But the furies clear a path for me to the worm
who sang for an hour in the throat of a robin,
and misled by the cries of young boys
    I am again
a breathless swimmer in that cold green element.

—1955

SONG FOR NAOMI

Who is that in the tall grasses singing
By herself, near the water?
I can not see her
But can it be her
Than whom the grasses so tall
Are taller,
My daughter,
My lovely daughter?

Who is that in the tall grasses running
Beside her, near the water?
She can not see there
Time that pursued her
In the deep grasses so fast
And faster
And caught her,
My foolish daughter.

What is the wind in the fair grass saying
Like a verse, near the water?
Saviours that over
All things have power
Make Time himself grow kind
And kinder
That sought her,
My little daughter.

Who is that at the close of the summer
Near the deep lake? Who wrought her
Comely and slender?
Time but attends and befriends her
Than whom the grasses though tall
Are not taller,
My daughter,
My gentle daughter.

—1956

391

THE BULL CALF

The thing could barely stand. Yet taken
from his mother and the barn smells
he still impressed with his pride,
with the promise of sovereignty in the way
his head moved to take us in.
The fierce sunlight tugging the maize from the ground
licked at his shapely flanks.
He was too young for all that pride.
I thought of the deposed Richard II.

"No money in bull calves," Freeman had said.
The visiting clergyman rubbed the nostrils
now snuffing pathetically at the windless day.
"A pity," he sighed.
My gaze slipped off his hat toward the empty sky
that circled over the black knot of men,
over us and the calf waiting for the first blow.

Struck,
the bull calf drew in his thin forelegs
as if gathering strength for a mad rush — — —
tottered — — — raised his darkening eyes to us,
and I saw we were at the far end
of his frightened look, growing smaller and smaller
till we were only the ponderous mallet
that flicked his bleeding ear
and pushed him over on his side, stiffly,
like a block of wood.

Below the hill's crest
the river snuffled on the improvised beach.
We dug a deep pit and threw the dead calf into it.
It made a wet sound, a sepulchral gurgle,
as the warm sides bulged and flattened.
Settled, the bull calf lay as if asleep,
one foreleg over the other,
bereft of pride and so beautiful now,
without movement, perfectly still in the cool pit,
I turned away and wept.

—1956

CAT DYING IN AUTUMN

I put the cat outside to die,
Laying her down
Into a rut of leaves
Cold and bloodsoaked;
Her moan
Coming now more quiet
And brief in October's economy
Till the jaws
Opened and shut on no sound.

And I was thinking
Of melting snow in spring
Or a strip of gauze
When a sparrow
Dropped down beside it
Leaning his clean beak
Into the hollow;
Then whirred away, his wings,
You may suppose, shuddering.

Behind the wide pane
I watched the dying cat
Whose fur like a veil of air
The autumn wind stirred
Indifferently with the leaves;
Her form (or was it the wind?)
Still breathing —
A surprise of white.

Letting me see
From my house
The twisted petal
That fell
Between the ruined paws
To hold or play with,
And the tight smile
Cats have for meeting death.

—1958

BERRY PICKING

Silently my wife walks on the still wet furze
Now darkgreen the leaves are full of metaphors
Now lit up is each tiny lamp of blueberry.
The white nails of rain have dropped and the sun is free.

And whether she bends or straightens to each bush
To find the children's laughter among the leaves
Her quiet hands seem to make the quiet summer hush —
Berries or children, patient she is with these.

I only vex and perplex her; madness, rage
Are endearing perhaps put down upon the page;
Even silence daylong and sullen can then
Enamour as restraint or classic discipline.

So I envy the berries she puts in her mouth,
The red and succulent juice that stains her lips;
I shall never taste that good to her, nor will they
Displease her with a thousand barbarous jests.

How they lie easily for her hand to take,
Part of the unoffending world that is hers;
Here beyond complexity she stands and stares
And leans her marvellous head as if for answers.

No more the easy soul my childish craft deceives
Nor the simpler one for whom yes is always yes;
No, now her voice comes to me from a far way off
Though her lips are redder than the raspberries.

—*1958*

WHATEVER ELSE
POETRY IS FREEDOM

Whatever else poetry is freedom.
Forget the rhetoric, the trick of lying
All poets pick up sooner or later. From the river,
Rising like the thin voice of grey castratos—the mist;
Poplars and pines grow straight but oaks are gnarled;
Old codgers must speak of death, boys break windows;
Women lie honestly by their men at last.

And I who gave my Kate a blackened eye
Did to its vivid changing colours
Make up an incredible musical scale;
And now I balance on wooden stilts and dance
And thereby sing to the loftiest casements.
See how with polish I bow from the waist.
Space for these stilts! More space or I fail!

And a crown I say for my buffoon's head.
Yet no more fool am I than King Canute,
Lord of our tribe, who scanned and scorned;
Who half-deceived, believed; and, poet, missed
The first white waves come nuzzling at his feet;
Then damned the courtiers and the foolish trial
With a most bewildering and unkingly jest.

It was the mist. It lies inside one like a destiny.
A real Jonah it lies rotting like a lung.
And I know myself undone who am a clown
And wear a wreath of mist for a crown;
Mist with the scent of dead apples,
Mist swirling from black oily waters at evening.
Mist from the fraternal graves of cemeteries.

It shall drive me to beg my food and at last
Hurl me broken I know and prostrate on the road:
Like a huge toad I saw, entire but dead,
That Time mordantly had blacked; O pressed
To the moist earth is pled for entry.
I shall be I say that stiff toad for sick with mist
And crazed I smell the odour of mortality.

And Time flames like a paraffin stove
And what it burns are the minutes I live.
At certain middays I have watched the cars
Bring me from afar their windshield suns;
What lay to my hand were blue fenders,
The suns extinguished, the drivers wearing sunglasses
And it made me think I had touched a hearse.

So whatever else poetry is freedom. Let
Far off the impatient cadences reveal
A padding for my breathless stilts. Swivel,
O hero, in the fleshy groves, skin and glycerine,
And sing of lust, the sun's accompanying shadow
Like a vampire's wing, the stillness in dead feet—
Your stave brings resurrection, O aggrievèd king.

—1959

KEINE LAZAROVITCH, 1870-1959

When I saw my mother's head on the cold pillow,
Her white waterfalling hair in the cheeks' hollows,
I thought, quietly circling my grief, of how
She had loved God but cursed extravagantly His creatures.

For her final mouth was not water but a curse,
A small black hole, a black rent in the universe,
Which damned the green earth, stars and trees in its stillness
And the inescapable lousiness of growing old.

And I record she was comfortless, vituperative,
Ignorant, glad, and much else besides; I believe
She endlessly praised her black eyebrows, their thick weave,
Till plagiarizing Death leaned down and took them for his mold.

And spoiled a dignity I shall not again find,
And the fury of her stubborn limited mind;
Now none will shake her amber beads and call God blind,
Or wear them upon a breast so radiantly.

O fierce she was, mean and unaccommodating;
But I think now of the toss of her gold earrings,
Their proud carnal assertion, and her youngest sings
While all the rivers of her red veins move into the sea.

—1961

A TALL MAN EXECUTES A JIG

For Malcolm Ross

I

So the man spread his blanket on the field
And watched the shafts of light between the tufts
And felt the sun push the grass towards him;
The noise he heard was that of whizzing flies,
The whistlings of some small imprudent birds,
And the ambiguous rumbles of cars
That made him look up at the sky, aware
Of the gnats that tilted against the wind
And in the sunlight turned to jigging motes.
Fruitflies he'd call them except there was no
    fruit
About, spoiling to hatch these glitterings,
These nervous dots for which the mind supplied
The closing sentences from Thucydides,
Or from Euclid having a savage nightmare.

II

Jig, jig, jig, jig. Like minuscule black links
Of a chain played with by some playful
Unapparent hand or the palpitant
Summer haze bored with the hour's stillness.
He felt the sting and tingle afterwards
Of those leaving their orthodox unrest,
Leaving their undulant excitation
To drop upon his sleeveless arm. The
    grass,
Even the wildflowers became black hairs
And himself a maddened speck among them.
Still the assaults of the small flies made him
Glad at last, until he saw purest joy
In their frantic jiggings under a hair,
So changed from those in the unrestraining air.

III

He stood up and felt himself enormous.
Felt as might Donatello over stone,

Or Plato, or as a man who has held
A loved and lovely woman in his arms
And feels his forehead touch the emptied sky
Where all antinomies flood into light.
Yet jig jig jig, the haloing black jots
Meshed with the wheeling fire of the sun:
Motion without meaning, disquietude
Without sense or purpose, ephemerides
That mottled the resting summer air till
Gusts swept them from his sight like wisps of
    smoke.
Yet they returned, bringing a bee who, seeing
But a tall man, left him for a marigold.

IV

He doffed his aureole of gnats and moved
Out of the field as the sun sank down,
A dying god upon the blood-red hills.
Ambition, pride, the ecstasy of sex,
And all circumstance of delight and grief,
That blood upon the mountain's side, that flood
Washed into a clear incredible pool
Below the ruddied peaks that pierced the sun.
He stood still and waited. If ever
The hour of revelation was come
It was now, here on the transfigured steep.
The sky darkened. Some birds chirped.
    Nothing else.
He thought the dying god had gone to sleep:
An Indian fakir on his mat of nails.

V

And on the summit of the asphalt road
Which stretched towards the fiery town, the man
Saw one hill raised like a hairy arm, dark
With pines and cedars against the stricken sun
— The arm of Moses or of Joshua.

He dropped his head and let fall the halo
Of mountains, purpling and silent as time,
To see temptation coiled before his feet:
A violated grass snake that lugged
Its intestine like a small red valise.
A cold-eyed skinflint it now was, and not
The manifest of that joyful wisdom,
The mirth and arrogant green flame of life;
Or earth's vivid tongue that flicked in praise
    of earth.

VI

And the man wept because pity was useless.
"Your jig's up; the flies come like kites," he
    said
And watched the grass snake crawl towards
    the hedge,
Convulsing and dragging into the dark
The satchel filled with curses for the earth,
For the odors of warm sedge, and the sun,
A blood-red organ in the dying sky.
Backwards it fell into a grassy ditch
Exposing its underside, white as milk,
And mocked by wisps of hay between its jaws;

And then it stiffened to its final length.
But though it opened its thin mouth to scream
A last silent scream that shook the black sky,
Adamant and fierce, the tall man did not curse.

VII

Beside the rigid snake the man stretched out
In fellowship of death; he lay silent
And stiff in the heavy grass with eyes shut,
Inhaling the moist odors of the night
Through which his mind tunnelled with
      flicking tongue
Backwards to caves, mounds, and sunken ledges
And desolate cliffs where come only kites,
And where of perished badgers and racoons
The claws alone remain, gripping the earth.
Meanwhile the green snake crept upon the sky,
Huge, his mailed coat glittering with stars
    that made
The night bright, and blowing thin wreaths
    of cloud
Athwart the moon; and as the weary man
Stood up, coiled above his head, transforming
    all.

—*1963*

BUTTERFLY ON ROCK

The large yellow wings, black-fringed,
were motionless

They say the soul of a dead person
will settle like that on the still face

But I thought: the rock has borne this;
this butterfly is the rock's grace,
its most obstinate and secret desire
to be a thing alive made manifest

Forgot were the two shattered porcupines
I had seen die in the bleak forest.
Pain is unreal; death, an illusion:
There is no death in all the land,
I heard my voice cry;
And brought my hand down on the butterfly
And felt the rock move beneath my hand.

—*1963*

Cemeteries
      are thrown away
on North Americans
they behave
      as if they are going
to live forever
      ignoring
in their walks and car-drives
these discreet dumps
with their sad embarrassed slabs
that advertise
      human refuse

Yet death's certain ignominy's
the one sure pull of sanity
and eternity
      in their lives
a tranquil interlude
      in the senseless ceaseless
biological froth
   where finally and mercifully
there are no answers
      and no lies
no absurd rebellion
but – shattering paradox – dignity
and, as bonus, rest

—1971

FOREWORD TO *A Red Carpet for the Sun*

This volume contains all the poems I wrote between 1942 and 1958 that I wish to preserve. They are taken from twelve collections I have published during this period . . . . Looking back upon this period—how to say this tongue-in-cheek yet mean it; how to make love with a hot potato in one's mouth—I see my work as an effort to achieve a definition of independence. Not, though, of disaffiliation. Aristotle was surely wrong; it isn't reason but cruelty distinguishes our species. Man is not a rational animal, he's a dull-witted animal who loves to torture. However, I have my share in the common disgrace; project along with others the fearful rigidities, crippling and comforting, of family, state, and religion. The free individual—independent and gay—is farther from realization than he ever was. Still, in a world where corruption is the norm and enslavement universal, all art celebrates him, prepares the way for his coming. Poetry, by giving dignity and utterance to our distress, enables us to hope, makes compassion reasonable.

Why are people destructive and joy-hating? Is it perception of the unimportance of their lives finally penetrating the bark of their complacency and egotism? The slow martyrdom of sexual frustration? The feeling they're objects of use and not of love? The knowledge they're marked out for death, their resentment hardening with their arteries? Whichever is the reason, they can't for long endure the sight of a happy man. You might as wisely light a match in a room filled with cyclopropane as go among them with a pleased expression. Tear it off your face they must, let their fingers be crushed in the attempt. Because many poets have averted their eyes from this radical evil, they strike me as insufferable blabbermouths. They did not retch enough; were too patient, courteous, civilized. A little brutality would have made them almost men.

My extraction has made me suspicious of both literature and reality. Let me explain. My father was an ineffectual visionary; he saw God's footprint in a cloud and lived only for his books and meditations. A small bedroom in a slum tenement, which in the torrid days steamed and blistered and sweated, he converted into a tabernacle for the Lord of Israel; and here, like the patriarch Abraham, he received his messengers. Since there was nothing angelic about me or his other children, he no more noticed us than if we had been flies on a wall. Had my mother been as otherworldly as he was, we should have starved. Luckily for us, she was not; she was tougher than nails, shrewd and indomitable. Moreover, she had a gift for cadenced vituperation; to which, doubtless, I owe my impeccable ear for rhythm. With parents so poorly matched and dissimilar, small wonder my entelechy was given a terrible squint from the outset. I am not at ease in the world (what poet ever is?); but neither am I fully at ease in the world of the imagination. I require some third realm, as yet undiscovered, in which to live. My dis-ease has spurred me on to bridge the two with the stilts of poetry, or to create inside me an ironic balance of tensions. Unlike Keats, I have not wished to escape into the unreal domain of the nightingale nor to flee, as the more cowardly do, from imagination to fact. Mercifully all poetry, in the final analysis, is about poetry itself; creating through its myriad forms a world in which the elements of reality are sundered; are, as it were, preserved for a time in suspension.

Yet this rift reflects something actual and objective, is as tensing and generative as that of the Hebrew and pagan in Occidental civilization. A real division exists in the human world where at certain points art and life, like thought and instinct, are hostile to each other. It's a truism to say normal people do not write poetry. Philistinism is the permanent basis of human existence: a world in which everyone was an artist or a philosopher would perish in a week. The Canadian philistine, of course, enjoys advantages—his Anglo-Saxon connection, numbers, natural resources, prosperity—philistines of other countries may perhaps envy. But human life anywhere on this planet very wisely preserves itself by spawning more stenographers, trade-union bosses, military leaders, hashslingers, and second-rate presidents than it does poets. The aesthete, nursing incurable ego-wounds, has the relationship down pat—life is the raw material for art! I can't persuade myself this is so. In my very bones I feel it isn't. Art also finally crumbles and falls back into life as the water-lily's brightness crumbles into the pondscum that surrounds it. Though art transcends pain and tragedy, it does not negate them, does not make them disappear. Whatever its more perfervid devotees may think and write, poetry does not exorcise historical dynamism, macabre cruelty, guilt, perversity, and the pain of consciousness.

Each poem that thumbs its nose at death is a fusion of accident and destiny. As such it is a structure in which the bronzed, athletic philistine is not interested. In any event, he can live without it. For accidents he has insurance policies; for destiny, his image of Napoleon, should he be a profound intellectual suburbanite; the assurances of dialectical materialism, if he is a Marxist proletarian. Before these, the poet unwilling to act as choirboy or morale-builder must appear ailing, furtive, hysterical; one who bumps his forehead against a wall, then exclaims: "Look at the lovely bump I have! Isn't the shape of it glorious? Aren't the colours extraordinarily beautiful?" (That's the sort of poetry the genteel and "cultured" especially like. The poet, of course, *should* strike his head against the wall of men's ferocity and senselessness, but let him yell and curse; not whimper, not bleat.) At this point Byron's contempt and Nietzsche's for the poet becomes understandable; my mother's commonsensical expletives begin ringing in my ears. And so rapturously, too, does he sing of his griefs, this poet, while the dull muttonheads pick their teeth or mount their females. Miserable clown! Can one think of anything more ludicrous? ironic? zany? Squeaking and throbbing, chittering and twittering; demon-driven or driven by their peacock vanity—so the poets, or so I sometimes see them, even the best of them. "What have these jigging fools to do with wars?" Shakespeare understood. Patricians or mob, what have they to do with the joy and wonder that is poetry: they are far happier killing or intriguing to kill. Too long have poets sung with blocked noses, their suffocating complaints and sudden euphoric sneezes filling the indifferent air. They deceive themselves—would they might deceive the hard-faced and heartless. Nevertheless the world remembers them, needs them. They alone are authentic. Bypassing the philistine suburbs of purgatory, they alone have the imagination to commute between heaven and hell.

So what I've written—besides my joy in being alive to write about them—has been about this singular business of human evil; the tension between Hebrew and pagan, between the ideal and real. The disorder and glory of passion. The modern tragedy of the depersonalization of men and women. About a hideously commercial civilization spawning hideously deformed monstrosities. Modern women I see cast in the role of furies striving to castrate the male; their efforts aided by all the malignant forces of a technological civilization that has rendered the male's creative role of revelation superfluous—if not an industrial hazard and a nuisance. We're being feminized and proletarianized at one and the same time. This is the inglorious age of the mass-woman. Her tastes are dominant everywhere—in theatres, stores, art, fiction, houses, furniture—and these tastes are dainty and trivial. Dionysus is dead: his corpse seethes white-maggotty with social workers and analysts. Not who is winning the Cold War is the big issue confronting mankind, but this: Will the Poet, as a type, join the Priest, the Warrior, the Hero, and the Saint as melancholy museum pieces for the titillation of a universal babbitry? It could happen.

The poems in this collection are all leaves from the same tree. A certain man living between 1942 and 1958 wrote them. That man is now dead, and even if he could be resurrected wouldn't be able to write them in the way they were written. Nor would he want to. They belong to a period of my life that is now behind me: a period of testing, confusion, ecstasy. Now there is only the ecstasy of an angry middle-aged man growing into courage and truth. Unlike the scholar or literary historian who writes about life, the poet enjoys it, *lives* it. Lives it with such intensity that he is often unable to say coherently or in plain words what the experience was like. I have in these paragraphs tried to set down those things that have most violently engaged my feelings and entered into the composition of my poems. For me, a poet is one who explores new areas of sensibility. If he has the true vocation he will take risks; for him there can be no "dogmatic slumbers." It will not do to repeat oneself, life is fluid and complex, and become with Housman or Jeffers a one-note Johnny. Or having grown respectable, to trot out a sterile moralism or religiosity, that favourite straw of poets with declining powers. I too have seen the footprint in the cloud, though somewhat gorier than my father saw it. When all is said, I have no choice but to walk after it.

—*1959*

ROBERTSON DAVIES

(1913-   )

Robertson Davies is the son of Senator William Rupert Davies, newspaper owner and publisher of the Kingston Whig-Standard. *Born in 1913, he was educated at Upper Canada College, Toronto, and at Queen's University, Kingston, where because of a deficiency in mathematics he was admitted as a "special student." From Queen's he went to Balliol College, Oxford. On leaving Oxford he sought work in the British theatre. After experience as an actor in the English provinces, Davies joined the Old Vic Company to act and teach in its drama school and to do literary work for the Director. He married Brenda Mathews, who had been stage manager at the Old Vic. Rejected for war service, he returned to Canada as Literary Editor of* Saturday Night *(1940-1942). He became Editor of the Peterborough* Examiner *in 1942 and Publisher (1958-1968). He was Chancellor's Professor in Trinity College (Toronto) in 1960-1961, and he is now Master of Massey College of the University of Toronto. He has received many honors, including seven honorary degrees and appointment as Companion of the Order of Canada (1972).*

It was in the columns of the Peterborough Examiner *that Davies' alter ego or Doppelgänger, Samuel Marchbanks, was born.* The Diary of Samuel Marchbanks *(1947) and* The Table Talk *(1949) were collections from the newspaper column.*

The writing of plays (most of which have been performed) has occupied Davies' attention throughout his career. The plays have been published in some half-dozen volumes, the earliest, Eros at Breakfast and Other Plays *(1949) and the latest,* Hunting Stuart and Other Plays *(1972). In collaboration with Sir Tyrone Guthrie, Davies also wrote three books on the Stratford (Ontario) Shakespeare Festival.*

Davies' series of satiric novels about Salterton (Kingston) began with Tempest-Tost *(1951), and continued with* Leaven of Malice *(1954) and* A Mixture of Frailties *(1958). Another group, displaying a marked difference in settings, tone, and characters, has appeared in* Fifth Business *(1970) and its sequel* The Manticore *(1972).*

FROM *Leaven of Malice*

. . . From a shelf above his desk [Solly Bridgetower] took down a book bound in dingy brown cloth, upon the front of which, inside a border of ornamental stamping, was printed the title, *Saul.* Inside, on the title page was:

SAUL

A DRAMA

IN THREE PARTS

———

Montreal

Henry Rose, Great St James Street

MDCCCLVII

This was it, the principal work of Canada's earliest, and in the opinion of many people, greatest dramatist, Charles Heavysege. Had not Longfellow, moved by we know not what impulse, declared that Heavysege was the greatest dramatist since Shakespeare?

Solly had not been drawn toward Heavysege by any kinship of spirit. Heavysege had been given to him, with overwhelming academic generosity, by the head of the English Faculty, Dr. Darcy Sengreen. He remembered the occasion vividly when, a few months before, Dr. Sengreen had asked him to lunch. And, when they had eaten, and were sitting at the table from which everything had been removed but a bouquet of paper roses, Dr. Sengreen had said: "Now, Bridgetower, you've got to get down to work. What are you going to do?"

Solly had muttered something about having a lot to learn about lecturing and the preparation of his courses.

"Ah, yes," Dr. Sengreen had said, "but that isn't enough, you know. You've got to work on something that will make your name known in scholastic circles. You've got to publish. Unless you publish, you'll never be heard of. You've nothing in mind?"

Solly had nothing in mind save apprehension as to what Dr. Sengreen might say next.

"Well, if I were a young fellow in your position, I wouldn't hesitate for an instant. I'd jump right into Amcan."

Solly knew that Dr. Sengreen meant the scholarly disembowelling of whatever seemed durable in American-Canadian literature.

"Amcan's the coming thing, and particularly the Canadian end of it. But there isn't much to be done, and the field is being filled up very quickly. Now, I'll tell you what I'm going to do. I'm going to give you Heavysege."

And half an hour later Solly had left Dr. Sengreen's house carrying first editions of the two plays, the three long narrative poems, and the single novel of Charles Heavysege, which Dr. Sengreen had let him have at the prices which they had cost him. And, within a week, he had written to several learned papers asking for information about Heavysege, to be used in connection with a critical edition of that author upon which he was at work. Not, of course, that he expected any information, but this was a recognized way of warning other eager delvers in the dustheaps of Amcan that he had put his brand on Heavysege, had staked out a claim on him, so to speak, and that anybody trespassing on his property was committing an offence against the powerful, though unwritten, rules of academic research.

And here he was, landed with Heavysege. Within a year at most Dr. Sengreen would expect a learned and provocative article on Heavysege, from his pen, in some journal or quarterly of recognized academic standing.

Amcan. A new field in literary study, particularly the Can half. In twenty years they would be saying, "Dr. Bridgetower? The big man in the Heavysege field; yes, the collected edition is pretty much all his own work, you know, though he let X and Y do the bibliography, and Z did a lot of the digging on Heavysege's newspaper writings; yes, a monument in Canadian scholarship; wonderful tribute to old Darcy Sengreen in the general introduction, but the dedication is 'To my Mother, who first taught me to love Amcan, *Si Monumentem requiris, circumspice*'; yes, one of the very biggest things in Canadian literary studies." Holding the brown book in his hand, a sudden nausea swept over Solly, and he gagged.

Why do countries have to have literatures? Why does a country like Canada, so late upon the international scene, feel that it must rapidly acquire the trappings of older countries—music of its own, pictures of its own, books of its own—and why does it fuss and stew, and storm the heavens with its outcries when it does not have them? Solly pondered bitterly upon these problems, knowing full well how firmly he was caught in the strong, close mesh of his country's cultural ambitions. Already he was being asked for advice by hopeful creators of culture. Who was that fellow, that reporter on *The Bellman,* who had been at him only a few days ago? Bumble, was that his name? No; Rumball; that was it. Poor Rumball, toiling every spare minute of his time at what he was certain would be the great Canadian prose epic, *The Plain That Broke the Plough.*

Rumball had approached him with great humility, explaining that he had no education, and wanted to find out a few things about epics. Solly, capriciously, had said that he had more education than he could comfortably hold, and he was damned if *he* could write an epic. He had advised Rumball to model himself on Homer, who had no education either. He had expressed admiration for Rumball's theme. God knows it had sounded dreary enough, but Solly felt humble in the presence of Rumball. Here, at least, was a man who was trying to create something, to spin something out of his own guts and his own experience. He was not a scholarly werewolf, digging up the corpse of poor Charles Heavysege, hoping to make a few meals on the putrefying flesh of the dead poet.

But this was not getting anything done. He looked at his watch. Nine o'clock. He put *Saul* back on the shelf, removed his shoes and crept downstairs with them in his hand. Outside his mother's door he listened; though the light was still on, thin, tremulous snores assured him that she was asleep and would probably remain so for many hours. He stole down to the ground floor, shut himself into the telephone cupboard and dialled a number.

"Yes?"

"Is that you, Molly? It's Solly. Is Humphrey at home?"

"Yes."

"May I come over? I need you."

"Righto, ducks. . . ."

The Cobblers lived in a row of small, impermanent-looking houses, all exactly alike and all—though not more than a few years old—with an air of weariness, like children who have never been strong from birth, and have a poor chance of reaching maturity. Molly Cobbler opened the door to Solly's knock, and in her usual silent fashion nodded to him to follow her upstairs.

When they entered the bedroom Humphrey Cobbler was invisible, but in the old-fashioned bed, shaped rather like an elegant sleigh, a heap of bedclothes showed that he was sitting up and bending forward, and a strong smell, and some very loud sniffings and exhalations, made it clear that he was inhaling the fumes of Friar's Balsam.

"Come along, now; you've had enough of that," said his wife, unveiling him. His mop of black curls was more untidy than ever, and the steam had given his face a boiled look.

"Bridgetower, you find me very low," said he.

Solly said that he was sorry.

"I have a cold. It would be nothing in another man, but in me it is an affliction of the utmost seriousness. I cannot sing. Suppose I lose my voice entirely? I am not one of your fraudulent choirmasters who *tells* people how to sing; I *show* 'em. I'm at a very low ebb. Don't come near me, or you may catch it. You wouldn't like a precautionary sniff of this, I suppose?" He held out the steaming jug of balsam.

"I've brought you the only reliable cold cure," said Solly, producing a bottle of rye from his pocket.

"Bridgetower, this is an act of positively Roman nobility. This is unquestionably the kind of thing that Brutus used to do for Marc Antony when *he* had a cold. God bless you, my dear fellow. We'll have it hot, for our colds. Molly, let's have hot water and lemon and sugar. Would you believe it, Bridgetower, I have been so improvident as to fall ill without a drop of anything in the house?"

The invalid looked very much better already, and was now sitting up in bed in a ragged dressing-gown, wrapping up his head in a silk square which obviously belonged to his wife.

"Have a chair, my dear fellow. Just throw that stuff on the floor. I can't tell you how much I appreciate this visit." He fetched a large and unpleasant-looking rag from under his pillow and blew his nose loud and long. "E flat," said he, when he had finished. "Funny, I never seem to blow twice on the same note. You'd think that the nose, under equal pressure, and all that, would behave predictably, but it doesn't. See this?" He held out the rag. "Piece of an old bedsheet; never blow your nose on paper, Bridgetower. Save old bedsheets for when you have a cold. They're the only comfort in a really bad cold, and the only way of reckoning its virulence. I consider this to be a two-sheet cold."

By this time his wife had returned, with glasses, lemon and sugar, and an electric kettle which she plugged into an outlet in the floor. Solly chatted to her, and Cobbler plied the bedsheet, until the water was hot and the toddies mixed.

"Aha," roared the invalid, who seemed to grow more cheerful every minute. . . .

"Molly, my pet, I need another length of old sheeting."

Molly took the sodden rag from his hand and left the room.

"What would you do if you were me?" said Solly.

"What would I do in your place?"

"No, no; you'd do something fantastic and get farther into the soup. I want to know what you would do if you were intelligent but prudent. What would you do if you were me?"

Cobbler pondered for a moment. "Well," he said, "I suppose if I were you— that's to say a somewhat inert chap, half content to be the football of fate—I'd go right on doing whatever I was doing at the moment, and hope the whole thing would blow over."

"Yes, but I can't do that. I'm absolutely fed up with what I'm doing. I'm a bad teacher; I loathe teaching; I'm expected to teach English literature to people who don't want to know about it; I'm expected to make a name for myself in Amcan; damn it, sometimes I think seriously about suicide."

"Lots of people do," said Cobbler, "but don't delude yourself. You're not the suicidal type."

"Why not?"

"You're too gabby. People who talk a lot about their troubles never commit suicide; talk's the greatest safety-valve there is. I always laugh at that bit in *Hamlet* where he pretends to despise himself because he unpacks his heart with words, and falls a-scolding like a very drab; that's why the soliloquy about suicide is just Hamlet putting on intellectual airs. A chatterbox like that would never pop himself off with a bare bodkin. No, the suicides are the quiet ones, who can't find the words to fit their misery. We talkers will never take that way out. Anyway, you wouldn't dare commit suicide, because it would upset your mother; she'd need more than six kinds of medicine to get her out of that."

Molly came back into the room. She had put on her nightdress in the bathroom, and her black hair hung loose about her shoulders. Solly had never seen her look so striking.

"You look like one of those wonderful Cretan women," said he, in honest admiration.

"Thanks. I'm going to go to bed, if you don't mind. The furnace is out. But don't think that means you have to go. We'll be very jolly like this."

And with a flash of legs she was in bed with Cobbler, and settled back against her pillows with a basket of socks to mend.

"Solly is thinking of suicide," said her husband, making a beginning on his new piece of sheeting.

"Solly needs a wife," said Molly.

"But not Pearl Vambrace," said Cobbler, with great decision. "She's too much like him in temperament. Married couples should complement each other, and not merely double their losses. There's much to be said for the square peg in the round hole, as the Cubist told the Vorticist."

"I don't want a wife," said Solly, passionately. "I've got a mother, and that, God knows, is enough to warn me off the female sex for life. I don't want a wife, and I don't want my job, and I don't want Charles Heavysege."

"You want to run away to sea," said Cobbler. "But you wouldn't like it, you know."

"I suppose not," said Solly. "Don't pay attention to anything I say tonight. I'm utterly fed up." He looked into his glass, which was empty.

"Perhaps you are beflustered by the blabsome wine," said Molly Cobbler.

"Impossible. I've only had one. But where did you get that business about being beflustered by the blabsome etcetera."

"You used it last time you were here."

"That was weeks ago."

"Yes. But it stuck in my mind."

"Molly, do you realize that you have been quoting from the great Charles Heavysege?"

"Oh? Never heard of him. Yes I have, too. You've mentioned him."

"I've mentioned him! What an understatement! He obsesses me. He is my incubus—my succubus. He is becoming part of the fabric of my being. I expect that within ten years there will be more of Heavysege in me than of the original material. Do you realize what Heavysege is? He is my path to fame, my immortality and the tomb of my youth. I wish I'd never heard of him."

"Mix us some more toddies, like a dear," said Molly. "If he's so important to you, why do you wish you'd never heard of him?"

Solly busied himself with the glasses. "Do you really want to know why?" said he.

"If it's not too long, and not a bore," said Molly.

"It is very long, and it is a bore, but I'll tell you anyhow. You can go to sleep if you like. Fortunately you are in a position to do so. It's getting cold in here." And Solly lifted a red eiderdown from the bed and draped himself in it.

"I am now gowned as Dr. Bridgetower, the eminent authority on the works of Heavysege," said he. "The great scholar in the Heavysege field will now address you.

"It was on May 2nd, 1816, that Charles Heavysege first saw the light of day in Liverpool. When I write my introduction to his *Collected Works* I shall embellish that statement by pointing out that the shadow of the Corsican Ogre had but lately faded from the chancelleries of Europe, that the Industrial Revolution was in full flower in England, that Byron had been accused of incest by his wife, that Russia's millions still groaned under the knout, and that in Portland, Maine, the nine-year-old Longfellow had not, so far, written a line. I'll make it appear that little Heavysege hopped right into the middle of a very interesting time, which is a lie, but absolutely vital to any scholarly biography.

"What happened between 1816 and 1853, when Heavysege came to Canada, I don't know, but I'll fake up something. He was a wood-carver by trade, which is good for a few hundred words of hokum about craftsmanship, but he soon became a reporter on the Montreal *Witness*."

"That was the trumpet-call of the Muse," said Cobbler, and blew his nose triumphantly.

"Exactly. From there on it's plain sailing, as scholarship goes. Heavysege's major work was his great triple-drama, *Saul*. Now *Saul*, ladies and gentlemen, presents the scholar with the widest possible variety of those literary problems which scholars seize upon as dogs seize upon bones. The first of these, of course, is: What is *Saul*? It is in three parts, and fills 315 closely-printed pages. Therefore we may fittingly describe it as 'epic in scope'—meaning damned long. It is brilliantly unactable, but it is fair to call it a 'closet drama'? Is it not, rather, a vast philosophical poem, like *Faust*? We dismiss with contempt any suggestion that it is just a plain mess; once scholarship has its grappling-hooks on a writer's work there is no room for doubt."

"Nobody has ever written a great play on a Biblical theme," said Cobbler. "Milton couldn't pull it off. Even Ibsen steered clear of Holy Writ. There's something about it that defies dramatization."

"Please do not interrupt the lecturer," said Solly. "Heavysege did not write a mere Biblical drama; he wrote a vast, cosmic poem, like a fruit-cake with three layers. Only the middle layer concerns Saul and mankind; the top layer is all about angels, and like everything that has ever been written about angels, it is of a deadly dreariness; the bottom layer, which is thicker than the others, is about devils, and much the best of the three. Heavysege was awed by angels, sobered by Saul, but right in his element with the devils. He makes them comic, in a jaunty, slangy, nineteenth-century way; he provides love-affairs for them. In fact, he is at his best with his devils. This obviously suggests a parallel with Milton; in scholarly work of this kind, you've got to have plenty of parallels, and Heavysege provides them by the bushel. Heavysege reveals traces of every influence that even the greediest scholar could require.

"But in your eyes I see the question of the greatest import. Was Heavysege, in the truest sense, a Canadian writer? I hear you ask. Set your minds at rest. Who but a Canadian could have written Saul's speech:

> *If Prompted, follow me and be the ball*
> *Tiny at first, that shall, like one of snow,*
> *Gather in rolling.*

Does not Jehoiadah behave like a Canadian when he refuses to cheer when his neighbours are watching him? Is it not typically Canadian of Heavysege's Hebrews that they take exception to Saul's 'raging in a public place'? Is it not Canadian self-control that David displays when, instead of making a noisy fuss he 'lets his spittle fall upon his beard, and scrabbles on the door-post'? Friends, these are the first evidences of the action of our climate and our temperament upon the native drama.

"I could go on at some length about the beauties of Heavysege, as they appear to the scholar. *Saul* is full of misprints. Correcting misprints is the scholar's delight. On page 17 we find the word 'returniag.' Did Heavysege mean 'returning'? That's good for a footnote. On page 19 we find the word 'clods' where we might expect 'clouds.' But can Heavysege have meant something deeply poetic by 'clods'? That's good for a paragraph of speculation, for we must be true to the printed text at all costs, and avoid any mischievous emendations. Does the poet allow anything of his own life to colour his drama? Well, at one point Saul speaks of 'poignant emerods,' and the adjective opens up an alluring avenue of speculation; we must find out all we can about Heavysege's state of health in 1857, when *Saul* was published. Had Heavysege a personal philosophy? What else can we call the four lines which he gives to an Israelite Peasant? (Incidentally, this peasant makes his appearance smoking a pipe; Heavysege has not even denied the editor the luxury of a nice, juicy anachronism.) This Peasant says:

> *Man is a pipe that life doth smoke*
> *As saunters it the earth about;*
> *And when 'tis wearied of the joke,*
> *Death comes and knocks the ashes out.*

Can we hear that unmoved?"

"I can hear it totally unmoved," said Cobbler.

"Then you have no soul, and do not deserve the intellectual feast that I am spreading before you," said Solly. "But there, in a nutshell, is Heavysege. I spare you his other play, his two long poems and his newspaper writings, which it will be my duty to find and sift. There, my friends, is the ash-heap upon which I must lavish my efforts and thought, in order that I may loom large in the firmament of Amcan. It's devilish cold."

"Poor Solly, you look miserable," said Molly Cobbler. "You'd better get in with us."

Solly looked at the bed dubiously. "But how?" said he.

"Give us all nice hot drinks again. Then loosen the covers at the foot, take off your shoes and hop in. You can put your legs up between us. We'll warm you. And I'll spare you one of my pillows."

Solly did as he was bidden, and a few minutes later was surprised to find himself snugly tucked in, facing the Cobblers, and with his feet in the remarkable warmth which they had created.

"I feel like the sword which Launcelot laid between him and whoever it was," said he. Molly Cobbler said nothing, but laughed and tickled one of his feet, which made him blush.

"You know, you tell a very pathetic story," said Cobbler, who had been blowing his nose and pondering, "but it doesn't hold water. You want us to be sorry for you because you're tied to Heavysege and teaching people who don't want to learn. But you're not tied, you know. Nobody has to teach if they don't want to. I remember my own fiasco as a teacher of music appreciation at Waverley. That repulsive Tessie Forgie came to me one day and said, 'Mr. Cobbler, do I understand that I am responsible for all the operas of Mozart?' I said, 'Miss Forgie, if you were responsible even for one of Mozart's overtures I should clasp you to my bosom, but you aren't; if you mean, do you need to have a knowledge of Mozart's work to appreciate music, the answer is yes.' That finished me as a teacher. I expected my students to know something, instead of being examination passers. That's why I only see a few of the university brats privately now, as on that memorable Hallowe'en. If you don't like teaching, get out of it."

"But what else can I do?"

"How do I know? But you won't find out while you are hugging your miserable job. And why do you bother with Heavysege? Why don't you write something yourself?"

"Me? What could I write?"

"How should I know? Write a novel."

"There's no money in novels."

"Is there any money in Heavysege?"

"No, but there are jobs in Heavysege. Get a solid piece of scholarship under your belt and some diploma-mill will always want you. Don't think I haven't considered writing something original. But what? Everything's been written. There aren't any plots that haven't been worked to death."

"You've read too much, that's what ails you. All the originality has been educated out of you. The world is full of plots. I'll give you one. In a town like

Salterton lives a wealthy, talented and physically beautiful couple who have two beautiful and talented children. Arthur is a boy of twenty-one and Alice is a girl of eighteen. Although they live in wealthy seclusion the news leaks out that Alice has had a child, and that Arthur is the father. There is a scandal, but nobody can do anything because no charge has been laid. Then Alice and Arthur enter their child in an international baby contest sponsored by UN, and it sweeps off all the first prizes. They explain that this is because incest strengthens the predominating strains in stock, and as their physical and mental predominating strains are all good, they have produced a model child. Their parents reveal that they also are brother and sister, and that the family has six generations of calculated incest, practised on the highest moral and eugenic grounds, behind it. UN takes up the scheme and the free world has a race with Russia as to which can produce the most superior beings in the shortest time. Amusingly written, it would sell like hot-cakes."

"You don't think it a little lacking in love-interest, do you?" said Molly.

"Oh, that could be taken care of, somehow. What I am saying is that it is an original plot. If every story has to be a love-story, you'll never have any originality, for a less original creature than a human being in love cannot be found. But I get sick of hearing people crying for originality, and rejecting it when it turns up."

"Your plot is utterly impossible," said Solly, "it would offend against the high moral tone of Canadian letters, for it is at once frivolous and indecent."

"Oh, very well," said Cobbler. "Go on ransacking the cupboards of oblivion for such musty left-overs as Heavysege; that is all you are good for. I have a horrible feeling that in two or three more years I shall despise you. Quite without prejudice, mind."

The hot toddy and the bed were working strongly upon Solly's spirit. "I have a strong sense of being ill-used," said he murmurously. "I am in seven kinds of a mess. I am trapped in a profession I hate, and I am saddled with a professional task I hate. I am the victim of a practical joke which puts me into a very delicate relationship with a girl I hardly know and whom I don't think I like. I ask advice of the one man I know who seems to be free of petty considerations, and all he does is mock me. Very well. Loaded as I am with indignity I can bear this also."

"Hogwash!" said Cobbler, groping under his pillow for his piece of bedsheet. "Don't come the noble sufferer over me, Bridgetower. You are in a richly varied mess, true enough. But, much as I like you, I am clear-eyed enough to see that it is the outward and visible reflection of the inward and invisible mess which is your soul. You think life has trapped you, do you? Well, my friend, everybody is trapped, more or less. The best thing you can hope for is to understand your trap and make terms with it, tooth by tooth. If this seems hard, reflect that I speak from what may well be my deathbed." He blew his nose resoundingly. "B natural," said he, "my cold drops more than a full tone every hour. Obviously I am dying. Well, accept these hard words as a parting gift. You are the prisoner of circumstance, Bridgetower, and it is my considered view that you are not one of the tiny minority of mankind that can grapple with circumstance and give it a fall."

Solly pondered. "We'll see about that," he said, after a time, but his host and hostess were both asleep.

—1954

HUGH GARNER

(1913-   )

*Hugh Garner was born in Batley, Yorkshire. His school days were spent in Toronto,
and he has lived mainly in that city. He has described his early employment as copy boy
for the Toronto* Daily Star, *messenger for CN Telegraph, harvest hand in Saskatchewan and Ontario, packer of Lux soap flakes, store-manager, haberdashery salesman,
public relations director, assistant editor of* Saturday Night *(1952-1953), daily
columnist for the* Toronto Telegram *(1966), "etc., etc."*

Garner's literary career began in the Canadian Forum *in June 1936. A year later
he was in Spain, fighting for the Loyalists in the Mackenzie-Papineau Battalion of the
XVth International Brigade on the Jarama and Brunette fronts. His first book,* Storm
Below *(1949), reflected his experience on a Canadian corvette in World War II. Most
of his novels, however, are set in a working-class district of Toronto. The first of these
was* Cabbagetown, *written in 1946 and published in a drastically shortened form as a
paperback in 1950, but in its full version in 1968.* The Silence on the Shore *appeared
in 1962, and* The Sin Sniper *in 1970.* A Nice Place to Visit, *also published in 1970,
had a small Ontario town as its setting.*

*To date Garner has written eighty-five short stories, twelve TV plays, and four
hundred and forty magazine essays and articles. His* Best Stories *(1963) won the
Governor-General's Award.* Men and Women *(1966) and* Violation of the Virgins
(1971) are later collections of short stories.

ANOTHER TIME, ANOTHER PLACE, ANOTHER ME

I don't know why I should think back again after all these years to the night
spent with the dying old man, but I do. It was really only an incident out of many
in my first youthful confrontations with disease and death. Perhaps, I sometimes
think, it is because I have now reached the age that the old man had reached
when he died; sometimes it seems to be something that happened to somebody
else.

The cold October rain came down in ragged sheets across the railroad yards
filled with empty coal gondolas, and now and then you could catch a glimpse of
the black bulk of the hills in the distance, but how far away they were you couldn't
tell. The red and green switch lamps twinkled through the darkness like a lighted
Christmas tree seen from outside a rain-drenched window. The sign on the soot-
covered stone station read, PARKERSBURG W.V.

I was soaked to the skin and cold with a feverish shivering cold that my wet
shirt and thin windbreaker pressed against my skin. The water ran from the broken
peak of my cap making rivulets, I guess, through the coal dust on my cheeks. The

trip through the mountains on top of a B & O freight, through the old stone-lined tunnels, hadn't improved my looks, but blackface was a common disguise in 1933.

I'd been released from the county can in Keyser, West Virginia the day before, after doing seven days on a vag charge. I'd hurried through the jailhouse yard and the turnkey's house into the street, hating every hillbilly bastard prisoner in the place since it was built. They'd known from my accent that I wasn't from around there, and had put me through a kangaroo court on the charge of "breaking into jail as a vagrant bum." If you've never done hard time in a hillbilly can during the Depression it's no use me telling you what it was like. You wouldn't believe it. By the time I was sprung I hated the whole goddam coal-dusted state of West Virginia, and the Baltimore & Ohio Railroad too.

Now the noise of the splashing rain shut out the smaller noises of the nearby town and the railroad shops, and as I stumbled along the tracks and across the switch ties I felt more alone than I'd ever felt before in my life. The only other human being in sight was a man in a lighted switch tower near the coal-tipple, who was staring in the direction of the yard diamond, at the same time taking gulps of something that looked warm and good from a thermos cup.

I steered clear of the lights from the station, passed by the coal-tipple and the water tower, and kept on until I spied a low windowless shack that showed a crack of light beneath its door. I crossed the mainline tracks, opened the door an inch or two, and glanced inside. It was the sand-house, as I'd expected it to be, its piles of warm dry sand banked high against the bubbling radiators that lined the walls. I stepped into the welcoming warmth, shutting the door quickly behind me.

For a minute or two I just stood there enjoying the heat, leaning with my wet face pressed against the door frame, letting the heat seep through my clothes as it raised small wisps of steam from my shoulders. The steam carried with it the familiar smell of months of boxcars, flophouses, and the new stink I'd learned in the Keyser county can.

A low moan from somewhere behind me raised the uncut hair from my neck and I swung around to see who or what it was. Sprawled on a pile of sand in a dim corner of the shack was a ragged old hobo, his legs thrust out at an awkward angle from his body and his arms thrashing at his sides. My sudden fright was replaced by a happiness to find I was not alone, as I'd been alone all day. I stumbled through the sand to his side, feeling its stickiness cake on my sodden shoes and crunch like sugar under my broken soles.

"Anything wrong, Cap?" I asked, staring down at the old man's sweating twisted face. A battered felt hat had rolled away from him and his thin dirty grey hair was sand-filled and stuck to his forehead.

His rheumy old eyes opened, and looking at me without hope he said, "Wa'er."
"Water?"
He closed his eyes again but managed to nod.
I looked around me for a cup or a tin can, but there was nothing.
"What'll I get it in, Cap?" I asked him.
The rheumy old eyes opened again and he pointed to a pocket of his oversize wrinkled coat. "Bottle," he said.
I groped in a pocket and found a small bottle. Holding it up to the light I could read the heavy print on the label, RUBBING ALCOHOL.

Going outside again into the cold and rain was the last thing I wanted to do, but I slipped out and ran down the yards to a standpipe near the water tank. After rinsing out the bottle a couple of times I filled it with water. By the time I returned to the sand-house the old man had passed out, his legs twitching and kicking in the sand and his face grimacing like a kid in a nightmare. I sat down in the warm sand beside him, waiting for him to wake up.

I guess my weariness and the life-giving warmth of the shack made me doze off myself, but I was awakened by the wheezing voice of my companion pleading for water again. I held his head in my arms, put the bottle to his lips and let him take a long slow drink.

When he'd finished he stared at me and then said, "Tell Edna May—Springfield —" and passed out again. Springfield! There must be a score of towns with that name in the U.S., scattered over as many states. I sat staring at the poor old guy, listening to his labored breathing against the knocking of the hot radiator pipes. After a while his legs stopped twitching and his breathing quieted down. I picked a fresh pile of sand against the wall and fell asleep myself.

The loud scraping of a shovel woke me and I sat up and stared scared at an overalled workman turning over some sand near the door. When he noticed I was awake and staring at him he said, "It's okay, Bud, nobody'll bother you here. The yard bull's home with the flu." His accent was neither Yankee nor cornpone Southern but a mountain mixture of the two, just like those of the prisoners in the county can.

"What time is it please, mister?"

"Nearly two o'clock."

The shack trembled as a heavy manifest freight pounded through a few feet outside the door.

When the train had passed the workman asked, "What's wrong with your friend over there?"

"I don't know. He was there when I came in."

"I seen him earlier. He looks po'ly."

I glanced at the old man. His face was dead white now against the yellow sand, and his mouth had fallen open revealing his rotten teeth. His breath was being forced out of his chest in long shuddering gasps and he'd slipped from the pile of sand and was lying huddled on the sandy floor.

I talked to the workman, trying to keep him there, not wanting to be left alone with the sick old man. My pack of *Bugler* tobacco from the county can was damp but I managed to roll an uneven cigarette. In a minute or two the workman finished his shovelling and left the shack, while I sat with my back against a radiator unable to take my eyes off the old man.

After a while he croaked, "Water!" again.

I was glad to leave the sand-house this time even though it meant getting wet all over again. I ran down to the standpipe, filled the bottle and ran back to the shack again.

I managed to lift the old man's head but I had to pour the water slowly down his throat. A lot of it spilled over his chin and chest but he didn't even open his eyes.

His breathing had now become harsh and uneven and I knew he was going to die. I prayed that somebody would come and take him out of there, not for his sake but for mine. Until then I'd never seen anyone die and my own death was something I was still too young to contemplate. I was scared to be left alone with a dying old man in a railroad sand-house, a long way from home and shut off from the rest of the world by the pelting rain. Crawling to him warily I placed him on his back and loosened his dirty collar. He looked more comfortable but his breath still escaped in long tortured sobs. I crawled back to my own place against the wall.

I guess it was more than an hour before the workman returned with his shovel to the sand-house. This time I told him I was certain the old hobo was dying. He walked over to the side of the old man and stared down at him briefly. Then he left, saying, "I guess I'll go call the doctor."

Left alone with the dying old man again I put my fingers in my ears to shut out the terrible sound of his breathing. From the corner of my eye I saw him raise himself off the floor, his body arched so only his heels and the back of his head touched the sand. Then he collapsed and lay still, looking like a pile of old clothes thrown into a corner. I took my fingers from my ears and found the room was quiet again, and I knew the old man was dead.

It was a long time before the doctor arrived, followed by two ambulance men carrying a stretcher. The doctor shook the rain from his yellow slicker, unbuttoned it to reveal he was wearing a pajama top pushed into his pants, and took his stethoscope from his bag. He opened the man's shirt and listened for a heartbeat, then pushed up the old man's eyelids and closed the eyes again. Some yard workers crowded into the sand-house.

"What was it, Doc?" one of the railroad men asked.

The doctor shrugged and held up the rubbing alcohol bottle, which he placed in his slicker pocket. The ambulance men lifted the body from the floor to their stretcher, and the workmen stepped aside as the old hobo was carried out into the rain.

After the ambulance men had gone the workman who had been turning over the sand said to me, "You hungry, kid?"

I nodded. I was always hungry.

"Come with us down to the roundhouse an' I'll give you a sandwich."

The workman and I followed the others down the yards.

In the roundhouse locker room I sat with my friend and three or four yardmen and ate a lettuce-and-baloney sandwich washed down with a mug of coffee one of the others gave me.

When I was finished and was rolling a cigarette I said, "I feel sorry for that old guy. He sure scared me though. It was the first time in my life I actually saw anybody die."

"How old are you, boy?" asked the man who'd given me the coffee.

"Nineteen."

He looked around at the others and shook his head.

"It's an awful way to die," I said.

"It's a hell of a way for people to have to live too," another man said.

The man who'd given me the coffee said, "I heered they're closin' down No. 6 colliery over the near Deerwalk. That'll mean a couple a hunnerd more families on county aid."

"An' less coal to haul, so who can tell who'll be next?"

When I thanked the men and got up to leave the roundhouse one of them said, "If you're heading west there's a way freight pulls out for Chillicothe at eight in the mornin, an' you can catch her easy at the diamond. A 'bo told me las week that they're givin out free meals at dinnertime at the nuthouse in Athens, Ohio. That's not too far along the main line."

I thanked him, and said I'd make the way freight for sure.

When I reached the sand-house again I threw myself down in the sand and fell asleep. When I woke up in the morning I saw that the rain had stopped, and that the sun was just coming over the top of a wooded hill to the east. As I was leaving the shack I looked back at the place where the old man had died a few hours before. The sand had shifted and settled into different shapes since I'd fallen asleep. My eye caught a silvery glitter just about where the old hobo had been lying, and thinking it might be a quarter that had fallen from his pocket I hurried over and picked it up. It was much bigger than a half-dollar even, a World War I medal attached to a torn shabby ribbon. Around its edge had been cut the name *J. C. Waltham* and a service number.

It may have belonged to the old hobo, or maybe not. It was no good to me so I hung it by its ribbon on a nail above the inside of the sand-house door. If it *had* been the old man's that had died it was probably the only thing he'd left behind to show that he too had once lived as a member of the human race.

When the westbound way freight had been made up and was leaving the yards I jumped her. We reached Athens just in time for me to hurry to the state mental hospital and join the line-up of men waiting outside the kitchen door. After a long wait a kitchen worker handed us each a tin plate of macaroni-and-cheese, and we squatted on our haunches in the yard and ate it. It sure tasted good.

There's an awful lot of cities and towns called Springfield in the United States, but I can't drive through one even yet, almost forty years later, without remembering the dying old man in the sand-house in Parkersburg, West Virginia, and some girl or woman in his life named Edna May.

—1971

GEORGE JOHNSTON

(1913-   )

George Benson Johnston was born in Hamilton, Ontario, and pursued undergraduate and postgraduate studies at the University of Toronto. During the War he served as a pilot in the R.C.A.F. In 1946 he became Assistant Professor of English at Mount Allison University, but since 1950 he has taught at Carleton University in Ottawa. Much of his poetry has been published in periodicals, such as London Mercury, Atlantic Monthly, Queen's Quarterly, The New Yorker, *and* The Tamarack Review. The Cruising Auk *(1959) was his first volume of poems. His collected poems appeared in 1972 under the title* Happy Enough: Poems 1935-1972.

ELAINE IN A BIKINI

Mrs. McGonigle's boys enjoy the sun
By gogglesful, and stare along the beach
Whose innocence is almost all Elaine,
   Almost, but not quite, all.

Felicitously she comes in every eye
Bending her knees and tender finger nails
While the incalculable strings gather in
   What's hers to gather in.

Her feet entice themselves across the sands
Down to the water's edge, and the old sea
Fumbles about the naked afternoon
   As though in paradise.

I am felicitous too on the bright shore
Waiting for darkness with the roving boys
And all but gathered in myself with strings,
   What's mine to gather in.

—1959

NIGHT NOISES

Late at night in night's neglected places
The busy diesel shunter thumps and grinds
As to and fro he singles out and chases
The helpless cars whose businesses he minds.

He enters dreams in unexpected guises
Suggesting jungles, jungle laughter, screams,
Telephone calls, pursuits and wild surprises,
Desperate croquet games and froggy streams.

A noise of idling river water comes
Across the cindered yard that's his demesne
And qualifies his busy to's and from's,
Mumbling of spongy pastures, far and green.

A solitary streetcar, deep in town,
Pesters the late sky with electric sparks.
Behind a million windows Sleep, the clown,
Draws out his turn. The cats are in the parks.

—1959

ART AND LIFE

Sadie McGonigle, Mrs. McGonigle's daughter,
Is in a state of art from head to foot;
She's spent the afternoon with suds and water
And creams and mud; her lines and points are put
And every inch is tender to the view—
Elegant work of art and artist too.

Sweet love, that takes a master piece like this
And rumples it and tumbles it about,
Why can he not be happy with a kiss?
He turns the shimmering object inside out
And all for life, that's enemy to art.
Now where's your treasure, little scented heart?

—1959

O EARTH, TURN!

The little blessed Earth that turns
Does so on its own concerns
As though it weren't my home at all;
It turns me winter, summer, fall
Without a thought of me.

I love the slightly flattened sphere,
Its restless, wrinkled crust's my here,
Its slightly wobbling spin's my now
But not my why and not my how:
My why and how are me.

—1959

US TOGETHER

I do not like anything the way I
like you in your underwear I like you
and in your party clothes o my in your
party clothes and with nothing on at all
you do not need to wear a thing at all
for me to like you and you may talk or
not talk I like you either way nothing
makes me feel so nearly at home on Earth
as just to be with you and say nothing.

—1966

AN AFFLUENT GRACE

I sit before my splendid thawed-out meal
And thank God for the hunger that I feel.
Grace before meat still speaks its firm amen:
Dear God I am luckier than most men.
My children are not hungry, maimed or lost,
By and large my ambitions are not crossed,
By and large I have good works yet to do
Being one of God's dwindling favoured few:
I can spare from my table blest and crammed
Thawed-out crumbs for God's multiplying damned.

—1966

The less said about Edward's slut the better,
Nobody knows who she is or how he met her
With her waterfall of yellow-coloured hair
And feet like scissor points, a spiky pair.

Melancholy of love improves her lies,
Melancholy of gin makes deep her eyes,
Melancholy of streets refines her touch,
Sweet melancholy of tongue and teeth and such.

When summer evenings come across the tracks
We spread ourselves with beer and paperbacks:
Down comes Edward, powder on his face,
To take his slut out smooching every place.

Bliss is nice, but a little bit will do;
Edward has had too much, and his slut has too:
Only to see the hoof-marks in their eyes
And hear them wheeze would make a fellow wise.

—1966

DOUGLAS LE PAN

(1914-   )

Douglas Le Pan was born and educated in Toronto. He received his B.A. degree with first class honors in English and History from the University of Toronto in 1935. After two years at Oxford University on a scholarship, he was appointed Lecturer in English, first at Toronto and then at Harvard University during 1939-1941. During the following years he acted as an adviser on army education to General A. G. McNaughton and later served in the artillery during the Italian campaign. In 1945 he was transferred to the staff of the High Commissioner in London and attended most of the big international conferences during the next few years. In 1948 he held a Guggenheim Fellowship in Creative Writing, but in the following year he joined the Department of External Affairs, acting as head of the Department's UN Division in Ottawa; later he became Special Assistant to Lester Pearson, Minister of External Affairs, and then served as Counsellor in the Canadian Embassy in Washington. In 1955 he was appointed secretary to the Gordon Commission on Canada's economic prospects. From 1959 to 1964 he was Professor of English at Queen's University. He was Principal of University College in the University of Toronto from 1964-1970. He is now a University Professor of the University of Toronto.

His second volume of poems, The Net and the Sword, *won the Governor-General's Award for 1953, and his first novel,* The Deserter, *won the Governor-General's Award for 1964.*

CANOE-TRIP

What of this fabulous country
Now that we have it reduced to a few hot hours
And sun-burn on our backs?
On this south side the countless archipelagoes,
The slipway where titans sent splashing the last great glaciers;
And then up to the foot of the blue pole star
A wilderness,
The pinelands whose limits seem distant as Thule,
The millions of lakes once cached and forgotten,
The clearings enamelled with blueberries, rank silence about them;
And skies that roll all day with cloud-chimeras
To baffle the eye with portents and unwritten myths,
The flames of sunset, the lions of gold and gules.
Into this reservoir we dipped and pulled out lakes and rivers,
We strung them together and made our circuit.
Now what shall be our word as we return,
What word of this curious country?
It is good,
It is a good stock to own though it seldom pays dividends.
There are holes here and there for a gold-mine or a hydro-plant.
But the tartan of river and rock spreads undisturbed,
The plaid of a land with little desire to buy or sell.
The dawning light skirls out its independence;
At noon the brazen trumpets slash the air;
Night falls, the gulls scream sharp defiance;
Let whoever comes to tame this land, beware!
Can you put a bit to the lunging wind?
Can you hold wild horses by the hair?
Then have no hope to harness the energy here,
It gallops along the wind away.
But here are crooked nerves made straight,
The fracture cured no doctor could correct.
The hand and mind, reknit, stand whole for work;
The fable proves no cul-de-sac.
Now from the maze we circle back;
The map suggested a wealth of cloudy escapes;
That was a dream, we have converted the dream to act.
And what we now expect is not simplicity,
No steady breeze, or any surprise,
Orchids along the portage, white water, crimson leaves.
Content, we face again the complex task.

And yet the marvels we have seen remain.
We think of the eagles, of the fawns at the river bend,
The storms, the sudden sun, the clouds sheered downwards.
O so to move! With such immaculate decision!
O proudly as waterfalls curling like cumulus!   —*1948*

A COUNTRY WITHOUT A MYTHOLOGY

No monuments or landmarks guide the stranger
Going among this savage people, masks
Taciturn or babbling out an alien jargon
And moody as barbaric skies are moody.

Berries must be his food. Hurriedly
He shakes the bushes, plucks pickerel from the river,
Forgetting every grace and ceremony,
Feeds like an Indian, and is on his way.

And yet, for all his haste, time is worth nothing.
The abbey clock, the dial in the garden,
Fade like saint's days and festivals.
Months, years, are here unbroken virgin forests.

There is no law—even no atmosphere
To smooth the anger of the flagrant sun.
November skies sting sting like icicles.
The land is open to all violent weathers.

Passion is not more quick. Lightnings in August
Stagger, rocks split, tongues in the forest hiss,
As fire drinks up the lovely sea-dream coolness,
This is the land the passionate man must travel.

Sometimes—perhaps at the tentative fall of twilight—
A belief will settle that waiting around the bend
Are sanctities of childhood, that melting birds
Will sing him into a limpid gracious Presence.

The hills will fall in folds, the wilderness
Will be a garment innocent and lustrous
To wear upon a birthday, under a light
That curls and smiles, a golden-haired Archangel.

And now the channel opens. But nothing alters.
Mile after mile of tangled struggling roots,
Wild-rice, stumps, weeds, that clutch at the canoe,
Wild birds hysterical in tangled trees.

And not a sign, no emblem in the sky
Or boughs to friend him as he goes; for who
Will stop where, clumsily contrived, daubed
With war-paint, teeters some lust-red manitou?

—1948

FINALE

Always the path leads back.
The spy who has spun his web as subtly as an artist,
Living in a perpetual cellar, a prey to whispers,

Finds at last that the schemes he has excreted, the work of the spider,
Are fastened at some point to the visible world; and endangered and violable.
Or the criminal, working at night,
Who slunk as a boy into crime like an endless subway,
Somewhere is careless and, caught by his finger-tips,
Must leave the gray light of no-man's land and stagger back,
Back through humanity's brutal barriers.
Always the path leads back.

Or the counterfeiter, following his species of madness.
His eyes, enflamed by the color of coins,
His imagination, corroded by golden calculations,
Tell him his room, transmuted by spurious flames to gold,
Is an image of the whole dark golden globe
Where his fears are irrelevant. Yet there in the darkness,
Surrounded by greed as by a neurosis, he still is afraid.
For always, though sooner or later, will come the knock on the door;
Always the path leads back.

In hospitals too there are those who live underground,
Who thrill to the delightful chills of fever,
Sweating in the sweet drift of chloroform or ether.
And there they have time for their hobbies. Turning the hospital into a hot-house,
Where their dreams can sprout to enormous blooms,
Lilies, overpowering lilacs, fleshly dahlias,
They feed their flowers with the flesh of their friends.
But sometime the longest convalescence must come to an end.

Even the lovers living on their island
Must kiss the friendly earth good-bye like children.
All summer long they swooned an ecstasy away,
Bound in a mesh the warblers wove with their bright bits of song.
But now the leaves are falling, the distant surf is calling,
The summer sun is over.
Always the path leads back;
The islands are a prelude to the shore,
The dawn wind stirs the curtains and blows in the light,
The subway opens on the public square.

On dust. On sparrows bathing in the dust. On dust, heat, noise.
There in the market-place where tongues clack and chaffer
Under the actual sun, to the sound of clocks,
Are brass bursts of light, and draymen cursing,
Sharps of sirens, and brakes and gears, and pistons drumming.
Are shouts—and not the long voluptuous silence
Or bird-calls issuing from the arras of a dream.
But there steel-bright necessity. Out of those notes,
That sound so improbable, to weld a music like a school-boy's song,
Out of those metals to hammer, to conquer, the new and strenuous song.

—1948

IMAGE OF SILENUS

"He [Socrates] is like one of the images of Silenus.
They are made to open in the middle,
and inside them are figures of the gods."

— A remark by Alcibiades in Plato's *Symposium.*

Suddenly lifting and rising heavily from the reeds,
Its bent legs trailing and bent neck outstretched,
With wide wings set like sails,
Comes the great blue heron.
It is as if, in the twilight, a whole ship should be startled from the stream
And, limping a little at first, then gaining assurance,
Should continue across the sky imperturbably;
Equally at home in the brown shadows of evening and the moss-soft shadowy trees
As among the fish-haunted weeds and the lily-pads.
It leaves no wake, it makes no noise,
It flaps in time with the slow fall of night.
And yet unmistakably a wonder,
Unmistakably blue among the indistinguishable limbs and boughs.

So that the weather-beaten mask, that sees everything,
That has the air of having seen it all before,
Is taken by surprise.
The strained grin has been rivered by marks of rain
Since first it was set up in the garden; it is not so bright now
As when it left the hands of the makers; one would not know
It had any treasures to show, it opens so seldom.
But its population is many and waiting.
They are lodged underground among tombs,
Baffled, bewildered, at a turn of the catacombs.
Now, as the mask relaxes and the door unaccountably opens,
They appear.

See them, the shrunken figures of desire,
Swarming complete as when they were first here deposited,
But not heroic, filling all the sky,
Miniatures rather, toys in a toy shop window.
See Dionysus and the golden Christopher,
Francis circled by a charm of birds,
Apollo of the large loose limbs and gauze-gold nimbus,
Foam-born Aphrodite.
And all the other roles that men have pictured for themselves,
The figures fashioned out of desperation,
The plants they grew to feed their failure,
All throng behind the ironic mask.
The runner here is always first to breast the tape,
The infant Hercules compels the snake,
The surgeon cuts the flesh to an exquisite thinness,
The climber stands triumphant over Everest.

And other figures, neither gold nor simple,
Tell of the ultimate wish to do and suffer.
Green light escaping from clouds portending thunder
Shines on the prince at Elsinore, shines on the dungeoned Oedipus.

(Stand off a little, or you will see those blasted eyes.)

And even far off there will come,
Faintly perhaps, dissonant, confused,
But gradually forming into words,
Complaint of captives,
Lament of long-denied desires,
Strange heave and swell, unmusical, of all this ill-assorted choir.

> *O where is the realm of promised good,*
> *The hint of content we have felt in the blood?*
> *We have been told of the bird on the bough,*
> *Of the misted land where time goes slow.*
> *Sometimes we thought that high in the air*
> *We saw it drift. But where? O where?*
>
> *The mask has said, "Your hopes defer;*
> *As seeds are still, do do not stir."*
> *But sweet in the dark is the sickly doubt,*
> *What if we never should blossom out?*
> *What if the promise were puffs of air?*
> *Where is our city? Nowhere? Nowhere?*
>
> *And the bird? Is it only a blue mirage,*
> *To waken desire and helpless rage?*
> *There is no secret to which it flies.*
> *There is no bird; the wonder dies.*
> *Let us go down the deathward stair,*
> *Give us your hand, despair, despair.*

The song scatters.
The words are dissolved like a cloud into snowflakes.

And then out of the silence comes answering, not a song—
It has no words, it is animal, inarticulate—
A ground swell continually making for the shores of speech
And never arriving. And like the sea variable,
Unpredictable, not fixed in one place,
But gathering everywhere a vagrant strength.
From whispers in narrow alleys,
From sighs confided to lonely pillows,
From mutterings and grumblings as the bars are closing.
Yes, this is the real and suffering city.
Turn and look down from the railway viaduct.
They are souls underground, buried under miles of brick,
Under miles of chimneys. They are rows of jostling seeds,
Planted too close, unlikely to come to maturity.

Some will shoot up (germs are brave things and hard to kill)
But most will be crushed; and, living, will not even know
Why they had no chance to break and expand;
Will not even be able to put their discontent into words.
Only sometimes at nightfall, like this, they will sigh and know they are beaten.

Their sigh comes and goes with the night-wind.
The wind drops.
And now the whole city is quiet,
Under the halo of man-made twilight.

And to the inner city, the city of phantoms,
The winds of chance at last are charitable.
Open it has been, but guarded by guiling glass
By an invisible barrier. The puppets have looked out
Like sick children with their faces pressed to the window.
Now the blind drops, the shop shuts, the mask grins again.

For the great bird
With wings stretched wide as love
Has disappeared.
It is travelling on slow through the clinging darkness,
Or somewhere has found its home
And moored
In its nest that quietly floats on the sea-dark forest,
Now everywhere perfectly sealed and secret.

—1948

"NO MUSIC IS ABROAD"

No music is abroad except your breath,
That comes and goes and gives the night its dream.
The hawks have done their sun-down flights, the wind
Drops down now Scorpio's coils are on the trees;
Cones dropping and the far-off whip-poor-wills
Are bubbles in a deep and noiseless stream.

The blush of moonlight lasts and lightens,
The queen of heaven makes the water blue
As birds; the sky bends down, the islands gather,
The hour's repose is deep as yours. I turn
To where your head is lying, dreaming of skies
As calm as these; and see you motionless
In moonlight, a quiet isle in quiet seas.

—1948

THE NET AND THE SWORD

Who could dispute his choice
That in the nets and toils of violence
Strangled his leafing voice
Enforced his own compassionate heart to silence,
Hunted no more to find the untangling word
And took a short, straight sword?

In this sandy arena, littered
And looped with telephone wires, tank-traps, mine-fields,
Twining about the embittered
Debris of history, the people whom he shields
Would quail before a stranger if they could see
His smooth as silk ferocity.

Where billowing skies suspend
Smoke-latticed rumors, enmeshed hypotheses
And mad transmitters send
Impossible orders on crossed frequencies,
His eyes thrust concentrated and austere.
Behind his lids, the skies are clear.

Not that he ever hopes
To strike the vitals of the knotted cloud.
But, to the condemned, those ropes
At least let in the sun. And he, grown proud,
Among the sun's bright retinue would die,
Whose care is how they fall, not why.

—1953

ELEGY IN THE ROMAGNA

I

How villainous the empty wine-vats grow
Here in the candlelight as I wait for fire-orders,
How cloaked and felted with shadows. The brown and bat-
Winged air has thickened to a brackish silence,
Brimming over old rakes and harness in the corner,
Filling the empty stalls, gathering and settling,
Swung from the storm on the gimbals of an ancient house.
So melancholy-still it is, so distant seems
The wash of shell-fire overhead, I hear
Adrift in the squandered grain the discourse of mice
Like filaments strung through this clouded calm,
Think I can even hear the cellar-spiders
Tugging from their guts their viscous webs.
I am the only other animal awake.

No messages. No new intelligence
Conducted to the low-plucked gloom unriddles
The suspense or signals changing weather;
Superior to clumsy hands, the fire-programme
Continues, the shells interweaving, theirs and ours
In a maze of literal madness. The lines are quiet.
But in the smother something strains to speak.
In the clammy touch that wakes my throat there is
Entreaty, is entrance of an amnestied familiar,
Summons and recognition from a withering hand.
Commingled in the air the sweat and sighs
Of fifteen soldiers sleeping withers and grieves
About me. Exiled. Sour with the taint of exile.
Sour with the taint of surfeit. The heavy breath
Of men who have gorged all day on fear and danger,
Have supped with devils, dabbled in stews of corruption.
I smell the crooked nomadic ways they came.

II

Cut-throats, the shadows lead me with black knives
To vulnerable flesh. There the argument continues,
Lost seigneuries of childhood in wilderness
Engulfed, limbs gross with the leaves of darkness, and vines
Infesting the ruined chapel. My eye-balls are
Skewered forward to hang peering, shuddering. How far
The settlements are recessed! the candle almost out!
One of the sleepers moving in his sleep
Is tangled in a mess of gear, and groans;
One shows his back as brown as a tobacco leaf;
One sighs; one lies as though his neck were broken.

Dim spires far down the rapid river.

After the festivals of savagery (loud bodies
Writhing with vermilion), after flares and flames
And the stare of madness—this stupor of leather,
Where derangement of the subtlest tissues, still
Smouldering, creeps underground; and the breath
Of the burning bark, that innocence encased
And faggoted, seduces still in absence.
After the long traverse. The mind sunk sceptreless
In flesh till heat, cold, hunger, pain
As tetrarchs reigned, arbitrary usurpers.
After the ultimate rapids where the cargo was lightened,
The white caesura that stripped down longings
To the compass of these serviceable packs of greasy memories,
At the white mist where finally faded the bells—

Bells break the joists of swaying towers.

425

This rest in the meagre feast of deep necessity:
Grain spilled on the floor, the empty wine-vats, dirty straw,
Enthusiasts and thieves together lying
Awkwardly in a bare thieves' kitchen.
Ache down, my eyes, along with closing vista
From prodigals and children pell-mell scattered
Through the choked pores and rivers, the paths blood-speckled,
Where animals fought infatuate and leaves
Are waiting for rain, to the shrunk estuary
By spires and settlements surrounded . . . so distant!
The bay spread small and smooth as milk, a seed
Of cloud troubling the savage voyagers,
Trouble of birth in the winter-strangled tree
That can flower again and again through embarrassed bark
With buds and bells beclouded.

                    Bells buried in the earth and broken.

Leaves cursed with blood, voluptuous fronds of darkness,
O aboriginal heaviness in which
My gaze is limed and exiled! The wilderness
Laocoöns this ancient settlement.
Rusts and broods by the wall the heavy mattock,
The sickle tarnishes. And the husbandmen,
Cast out to see what wisdom there may be
In husks, stumble through trip-wires. If I should find
An emblem of order, a scythe that year after year
Mooned through the grass, disparaged it is
By shadows, in feverish growth sick metal sweats.
Or caves where the heart of the sleeping wine was warmed
And the sunburnt melody of summer extended
As a link in the seemingly endless garland of harvests,
They are gutted those caves, and hollow as gourds.
The song of the seasons is broken, the diadem
Star-studded, revolving in patient ecstasy
Over bent backs and rotated furrows, cracked.

                    Down fading spires stars trickle out.

The guns have shaken the stars from their sockets,
The weeping certainties of generation, cracked,
The voice of consolation, cracked.
Tonight the wilderness is here and everywhere.
And here sluggishly drifting (but seined by my candle
That sails mildly fishing through the dark)
Welters a gentle crew. Mangered in unease,
By sombre streams reduccd, stripped naked,
Relation leaves them and identity,
Though childhood still is lilied in closed lids.
Dim to me

eyelids that fleur-de-lis the dark
Impeach the absent stars. O much traduced
And tarnished flesh, where guns and hungers peal,
Abandoned here beneath the blow of history,
But silvered still and still imperial
In the phosphored wash what quick life starts,
What filaments are spawned from misery?

III

Awake and conscious, and god-like so.
But the impotent god of a lost creation.
To pacify this brawl of whispers
My breath goes from me, and is impotent.

Spirits that weave the petals of the weeping flowers
Speak for me, speak natural powers,
While at the base of my brain
An ampoule of pity
Swells like a trillium.
Would break, would break in a cedar breath
From untarnished lakes and rivers,
Lakes of sweet water, skies of unsullied godhead.
Would suck in through the blanket at the door
Fresh breezes to this fetid lair
To wash all trace of cordite from the air.

Enters, though, as the blanket stirs aside
The scent of death, the sentinel,
Scent of dead horses and dead men,
O sickly sweet! The scent of nitre.

If there were stars and skies accessible,
A brightly tented system to bless
And diadem them whole like glistening hills at evening . . .
If there were heavens to call to,
A promontory of comfort, some peak of comprehension . . .
But dark, dark.

Guards of the house:
A dead horse with turds half-bulging from its rump,
A sergeant dead in the ditch, half-buried,
Green as his tunic. Verdigris blots him.
The whites of his eyes are scrawled with flies,
The hair of his head now dead and excremental.
These termini of nature picketing the nether pit
Impose a stern perimeter,
Guard the thick ferment, thought-threaded nakedness,
Clouding the fallible, fallen star in its own brightness.

427

In gusts redound on my diminished light
With foul air reeking, and send me back defeated.

IV

Absorbed. Given over to their silence. A membrane listening.
Misery is moving like the mother of a liquid.
"What will become of me?" Wash of the wilderness
Folds a thin filament, a white dissected nerve
In isolation. "How like a knife in my guts
His glance has stayed." Hangs in the air a moment
That cry, a dagger, slits open my ear. Thin fronds
Sharpened by scalpels sway in the brown bat-light.
Flesh has been cut by leaves of bitter laurel,
Tissue been cut away and the sheaths of brightness,
Environing lymph lapped up by fire
Till insidious fibres twitch their charged message
Nakedly, publish their lamentation. "Lost.
O something that I lost as I was wandering."

Struggling in the consistory of silence
To clothe their fallen anonymity
These limbs now never to be free from lesion
Cry through white nerves, cry seeking themselves
In a nameless ferment. Strand after strand I hear,
Phrase after phrase blown one way by the muffled wind.
And so the air is peopled. One breathes, "I've seen too much."
Another, "Let me be lucky and be killed."
These threads and hairs combed into a theme of nerves
Paint with so fine a brush the tympanum
Of a temple where the divinity is dying
I think of trees that sigh as the night wind rises
Of boughs lifting, quivering, green and black and grey
As bats and night-hawks pluck the sky's stretched membrane.
A theme of nerves, a downward branching tree
Where single fibres snap and link, are joined
In a system downwards, misery to misery linked,
Are interlaced in a light and delicate embrace.
These whispers harp to a proud king softly.
Joined . . . joined . . . joined in a tree of animal
Heaviness, of animal kindness.
I hear the sighing of a dark green tree.
White filaments compose a live green tree.
O I have listened long enough! My brain
Runs ruining down the desired descent, descent
Desired and paid for, down to the weedy dungeon
Where their cries are prisoned, where their breath is mist,
Where I myself am lying. Their cries are mine,
Their miseries thrill through my impoverished nerves,
People the dungeon of my bowels with fancies.

428

These are my villain fancies also.
No others would I have as my familiars,
No other company than this. In the ooze
And reeking vapours of a barren cellar,
I would have only such still and subterranean music,
Blind fingering of mice through destitution
And spidery tentacles as a covering for the brain,
A kind of comfort. Beneath a crumbling house
I sift the detritus of dreams with a goodly company.
In the heart-sick earth these clammy manacles,
These tendrils straggling in a turbid stream
Are furnishing enough as the night wind rises.
Rises to a muffled roar as the nearest guns
Resume methodical vituperation,
The whole house wheezing like a bellows,
And imprisoned tendrils, lifting, blowing all one way.

V

The candle starts and flickers
Interrogates the shadows, leaves them still more secret
The candle of the lord gone over to the captive voices
Enfolded in foul air,
Unkinged, uncrowned, and minion now
To every gust that blows the spider's wreckage.

Still the slow spider weaves.
And so make to trial. To imitate the spider,
From our unravelled tissues,
To spin an intellectual thread, no more
Mercurial nor more pure than this so precious crew,
That mounting, mounting, breaking, respun, as thin
As starlight, perhaps at last might clasp the upper air
And there restore relation and identity.
With webs dilating in lucid dialectic
Might jewel and justify limbs weak as gossamer,
Perhaps with eloquence of stars might stud
The drift of animal affection, and so make fast
A habitation in the wilderness.
Perhaps.
          But thick dew falls on my face.
I am gummed all over with a strange balsam.
I am sticky with sweat and with humankind
That fastens and laces me here. I am content.
Here is my place in a friendly heaven for a night
Where they have built a word- and star-less system
Perfectly. Our sighs like the milk
Of the milky way arch over us. Corrupted
Our lungs breathe out a new heaven of pity and concern.

—1953

429

THE GREEN MAN

Leaves twist out of his mouth, of his eyes, of his ears,
twine down over his thighs, spring out of his heels,
as he runs through the woods as a deer or an outlaw, or curled
up in moss and bracken, light speckling him feckless,
he watches the other animals, himself hidden
like an animal, although so strangely human
that if you surprise him you might think yourself looking
into the eyes of the mad but all-wise Merlin.

Boreal forest his most natural habitat
from the edge of our cities up to the tree-line
where at summer's end in the spongy Mackenzie Delta
he glides through pale yellowing poplars before the snow flies
or at Northwest River slips out of the spruce to play
with the huskies, chained on the shingle. His territory
spreads far and wide beneath the Bear. Morose
and frolic and savage his sports where the forests are.

But I have glimpsed him almost everywhere.
In pool-rooms and bargain-basements. In the glance of the dark
prisoner in the dock, not knowing how to plead,
passionate the criss-cross light that sifts through leaves.
In pale changing-rooms at the atomic energy plant
the young technician is changed into a sylvan man,
shadowed with mystery, and suffering from the sap
like a young green tree, quick thrall of earth and frenzy.

And quick he runs through my dreams, so quick and grieving,
to banish grey calculations of tomorrow,
to banish old gods with gay assurance,
impatient of bounds and all mere definition,
but sometimes himself a god, now minor, marginal,
now reigning sovereign over an empty tomb,
the incised leaves on his flesh now wounds, now blood,
now flame. The forest reeks now with vermilion.

There is a shade that glides beneath the skyscrapers
and makes those papery steeples soar and tremble
like poplars in the breeze, a green man's shade
who came before Champlain, green traveller, trader,
debauchee, wearing around his neck
gull's feathers and four new sweetwater seas,
interpreting the woods to Europe and Europe to
the woods—till finally he was cooked and eaten.

430

His taciturnities were our title-deeds,
his heart divided food that our hearts have fed on,
so many morsels from that seething pot,
some for the merchant princes in their lofty
board-rooms (a long long way from poor Etienne Brûlé!),
but more for more ravenous hunters through other wastes,
lost, lost, and wild in utter inner dark
where the hunters and the circling hunted are the same.

And so I circle on the green man's tracks,
allured, bewildered by the bright green shoots
and headsman's axe he holds, those baffling icons
(for all the subtle theories that I half believe in)
that lead me on and down. But past all doubt
there thrives an underworld where life and death
are woven. And it is bright and dark and savage,
as speckled and as rippling as a snakeskin.

Outlaw or god this cunning harlequin?
I feel him darkening my glittering veins,
he kennels in my loins, knows every crevice
of my half-breed heart, and yet eludes me still,
though rumours reach me of him fugitive,
laughing and drinking behind an empty warehouse,
disguised in rags, and tossing empty bottles
to splash and sparkle on the cindery railway-siding.

Scion of the undergrowth and underworld
but a prince of darkness in all daylight polity.
I could lead you on a perfect summer afternoon
into a clearing where the trees are still and lucid
and have you stare and listen till a rustle comes
of a serpent moving underneath the columns.
Light slows. Leaves tremble—with Marsyas' blood as much
as Apollo's brightness. Now break a branch, it bleeds.

Some nights and seasons are his own, and sacred.
Then dreams flow into the woods, woods flow
into dreams, the whole pent city dreaming of a carnal
wood, confluence that empties into the streets
with a scurry of leaves and carnival drums and flutes,
and torches that set fire to the leaves and the city, a blaze
of harlequin crimson, skyward, as quick he still winds
among the masquers mocking, a green man with green wounds.

—1971

431

P. K. PAGE

(1916-   )

Patricia K. Page, the daughter of the late Major General L. F. Page, C.B., D.S.O., was born in England but brought to Canada at the age of two. Educated at St. Hilda's School, in Calgary, she has lived at one time or another in many parts of Canada. From Saint John, N.B., she went to Montreal in 1941 and became associated with the Preview *group of poets, including Patrick Anderson and F. R. Scott. Later she lived in Victoria, British Columbia. During World War II she worked as sales clerk, filing clerk, radio actress, and historical researcher. For a number of years following 1947 she was employed as script writer with the National Film Board in Ottawa. In 1950 she married W. Arthur Irwin, then Chairman of the Film Board, but from 1953 a member of Canada's diplomatic service, first as Canadian High Commissioner to Australia, and subsequently as Ambassador to Brazil and then Mexico. From 1964 until he retired he was publisher of the* Victoria Times *and vice-president of Victoria Press.*

Although P. K. Page had written verse from her childhood, the first collection of her work appeared in 1944—in Unit of Five, *edited by Ronald Hambleton. In the same year, under the pseudonym of "Judith Cape," she published a novel entitled* The Sun and the Moon. *Two years later her first volume of poems,* As Ten as Twenty, *was published. A second volume,* The Metal and the Flower, *won the Governor-General's Award for 1954. A number of her short stories have appeared in various magazines, but they have not as yet been issued in book form.*

Between 1954 and 1967, P. K. Page published very few poems; she was devoting most of her creative energies to painting and drawing. Her work has been exhibited in many galleries, and black-and-white reproductions of four of her drawings have been published in The Tamarack Review *(Spring, 1960). There she is quoted as saying: "As to why I began to draw—there must be one hundred reasons . . . . I don't suppose I knew before I began that drawing is the perfect medium for metaphor. But it is. For my kind of a poet, my kind of drawing seems inevitable. It's the same pen."* Cry Ararat! Poems New and Selected *was published in 1967.*

SUMMER RESORT

They lie on beaches and are proud to tan —
climb banks in search of flowers for their hair,
change colors like chameleons and seem
indolent and somehow flat and sad.

Search out the trees for love, the beach umbrellas,
the bar, the dining-room; flash as they walk,
are pretty-mouthed and careful as they talk;

send picture post-cards to their offices
brittle with ink and soft with daily phrases.

Find Sunday empty without churches — loll
not yet unwound in deck chair and by pool,
cannot do nothing neatly, while in lap,
periscope ready, scan the scene for love.

Under the near leaves or the sailing water
eyes hoist flags and handkerchiefs between the breasts, alive,
flutter like pallid bats at the least eddy.

Dread the return which magnifies the want —
wind in high places soaring round the heart
and carried like a star-fish in a pail
through dunes and fields and lonely mountain paths.
But memory, which is thinner than the senses,
is only a wave in grass that the kiss erases.
And love once found their metabolism changes
the kiss is worn like a badge upon the mouth —
pinned there in darkness, emphasized in daylight.

Now all the scene is flying. Before the face
people and trees are swift; the enormous pool
brims like a crying eye. The immediate flesh
is real and night no curtain.

There, together, the swift exchange of badges
accelerates to a personal prize giving
while pulse and leaf rustle and grow climactic.

—1944

FOREIGNER

Between strange walls,
you, foreigner, walk in silence,
sheltered from eyes
by the shady hands of fear
and suddenly dropped
blinds of embarrassment.

A room will hold you a smile
but you will not look;
from a long past of walking you have come
wearing blinkers and the balanced book.
Now, pressed in a corner by words
you have no face
and cry for love
in the leaning tower of self.   —*1944*

THE CONDEMNED

(For L. O.)

In separate cells they tapped the forbidden message.
Even the wide-eared warden could never hear
their miniature conversation
though he slipped the bolt of his hearing and walked the passage.

Then feeling the walls would dissolve with love they planned
the inevitable and leisurely excavation;
tap grew into chip behind the bed
as darkness hid the activities of the hand.

In an area a cigarette could light, everything lived.
The intricate machinery of the head
stopped and the heart's attention
increased the circumference of what they loved.

Then as the wall grew thin they wore their hopes
inwardly like a name they must never mention;
the riots of the skin were still to listen
for the warden's silent black-and-white approach.

And as their fingers groped and came together
it was so suddenly tender in that prison
birds might have sung from water — just as if
two mouths meeting and melting had become each other.

Later the whole hand grasped and the ultimate escape
plunging through velvet to an earth so stiff
their footfall left no mark
though their feet felt sharp, resuming use and shape.

Their lungs, in all that air, filled like balloons,
pastel and luminous against the dark:
no angels could have had more grace
in a children's heaven full of clouds and moons.

But light destroyed their splendor, all their soft
movements jerked to woodcuts and the lace
of their imagination atrophied.
Their stark identities — all they had left —

were mirrored upon fence and parish hall
and plastered on the staring countryside
till each became a terror and a face
and everywhere they went was nowhere at all.

—1946

ADOLESCENCE

In love they wore themselves in a green embrace.
A silken rain fell through the spring upon them.
In the park she fed the swans and he
whittled nervously with his strange hands.
And white was mixed with all their colors
as if they drew it from the flowering trees.

At night his two-finger whistle brought her down
the waterfall stairs to his shy smile
which, like an eddy, turned her round and round
lazily and slowly so her will
was nowhere — as in dreams things are and aren't.

Walking along the avenues in the dark
street lamps sang like sopranos in their heads
with a violence they never understood
and all their movements when they were together
had no conclusion.

Only leaning into the question had they motion:
after they parted were savage and swift as gulls.
Asking and asking the hostile emptiness
they were as sharp as partly sculptured stone
and all who watched, forgetting, were amazed
to see them form and fade before their eyes.

—1946

THE STENOGRAPHERS

After the brief bivouac of Sunday,
their eyes, in the forced march of Monday to Saturday,
hoist the white flag, flutter in the snow storm of paper,
haul it down and crack in the midsun of temper.

In the pause between the first draft and the carbon
they glimpse the smooth hours when they were children —
the ride in the ice-cart, the ice-man's name,
the end of the route and the long walk home;

remember the sea where floats at high tide
were sea marrows growing on the scatter-green vine
or spools of gray toffee, or wasps' nests on water;
remember the sand and the leaves of the country.

Bell rings and they go and the voice draws their pencil
like a sled across snow; when its runners are frozen
rope snaps and the voice then is pulling no burden
but runs like a dog on the winter of paper.

Their climates are winter and summer — no wind
for the kites of their hearts — no wind for a flight;
a breeze at the most, to tumble them over
and leave them like rubbish — the boy-friends of blood.

In the inch of the noon as they move they are stagnant.
The terrible calm of the noon is their anguish;
the lip of the counter, the shapes of the straws
like icicles breaking their tongues are invaders.

Their beds are their oceans — salt water of weeping
the waves that they know — the tide before sleep;
and fighting to drown they assemble their sheep
in columns and watch them leap desks for their fences
and stare at them with their own mirror-worn faces.

In the felt of the morning the calico minded,
sufficiently starched, insert papers, hit keys,
efficient and sure as their adding machines;
yet they weep in the vault, they are taut as net curtains
stretched upon frames. In their eyes I have seen
the pin men of madness in marathon trim
race round the track of the stadium pupil.

—1946

LANDLADY

Through sepia air the boarders come and go,
impersonal as trains. Pass silently
the craving silence swallowing her speech;
click doors like shutters on her camera eye.

Because of her their lives become exact:
their entrances and exits are designed;
phone calls are cryptic. Oh, her ticklish ears
advance and fall back stunned.

Nothing is unprepared. They hold the walls
about them when they weep or laugh. Each face
is dialled to zero publicly. She peers
stippled with curious flesh;

pads on the patient landing like a pulse,
unlocks their keyholes with the wire of sight,
searches their rooms for clues when they are out,
pricks when they come home late.

Wonders when they are quiet, jumps when they
        move,
dreams that they dope or drink, trembles to know
the traffic of their brains, jaywalks their street
in clumsy shoes.

Yet knows them better than their closest friends:
their cupboards and the secrets of their drawers,
their books, their private mail, their photographs
are theirs and hers.

Knows when they wash, how frequently their
        clothes
go to the cleaners, what they like to eat,
their curvature of health, but even so
is not content.

For, like a lover, must know all, all, all.
Prays she may catch them unprepared at last
and palm the dreadful riddle of their skulls —
hoping the worst.

—1946

ISOLATIONIST

When the many move, the man
in the cubicle of content
cowers, suddenly discovered, suddenly rent
by the reality of crowds.
He has trained the climbing vine,
written "roses" on his ledger,
lived like a saint and finds himself a leper.

Immaculate of belief and violent on Mondays,
thinking no evil and thanking no second party
he has leaned in the evenings on the low-lipped window
and learned of his saintliness from outlines of lovers.

Now lovers leap the sash and the many winnow
his penny bank of wisdom and set it swirling
down the unclogged drain in the hidden scullery.
People take solid shape and are vividly human,
smash walls, uproot chairs and juggle cutlery
while he sits with gloved hands in a buttoned confusion.

—1946

REFLECTION IN A TRAIN WINDOW

There is a woman floating in a window —
transparent —
Christmas wreaths in passing houses
shine now in eye and now in hair, in heart.
How like a saint with visions, the stigmata
marking her like a martyr.

Merged with a background of mosaic
she drifts
through tenement transoms, independent stars,
while in between her and herself the sharp
frost crystals prick the pane with thorns.

She without substance, ectoplasmic, still,
is haloed with the reading lamps of strangers
while brass and brick pass through her.
                                    Yet she stirs
to some soft soundless grieving and tears well
in her unseeing eyes and from the sill
her trembling bosom falls, rises and falls.

—1954

PORTRAIT OF MARINA

Far out the sea has never moved. It is
prussian forever, rough as teazled wool
some antique skipper worked into a frame
to bear his lost four-master.
                    Where it hangs
now in a sunny parlor, none recalls

how all his stitches, interspersed with oaths
had made his one pale spinster daughter grow
transparent with migraines — and how his call
fretted her more than waves.
                    Her name,
Marina, for his youthful wish —

boomed at the font of that small salty church
where sailors lurched like drunkards, would,
    he felt
make her a water woman, rich with bells.
To her, the name Marina simply meant
he held his furious needle for her thin
fingers to thread again with more blue wool
to sew the ocean of his memory.
Now, where the picture hangs, a dimity
young inland housewife with inherited
clocks under bells and ostrich eggs on shelves
pours amber tea in small rice china cups
and reconstructs
how great-great-grandpappa at ninety-three
his fingers knotted with arthritis, his
old eyes grown agatey with cataracts
became as docile as a child again—
that fearful salty man—
and sat, wrapped round with faded paisley
    shawls
gently embroidering.
While Aunt Marina in gray worsted, warped
without a smack of salt, came to his call
the sole survivor of his last shipwreck.

           *   *   *

Slightly offshore, it glints. Each wave is
    capped
with broken mirrors. Like Marina's head
the glinting of these waves.
She walked forever antlered with migraines
her pain forever putting forth new shoots

until her strange unlovely head became
a kind of candelabra—delicate—
where all her tears were perilously hung
and caught the light as waves that catch the sun.
The salt upon the panes, the grains of sand
that crunched beneath her heel
her father's voice, "Marina!"—all these broke
her trembling edifice. The needle shook
like ice between her fingers.
In her head
too many mirrors dizzied her and broke.

           *   *   *

But where the wave breaks, where it rises
    green
turns into gelatine, becomes a glass
simply for seeing stones through, runs across
the colored shells and pebbles of the shore
and makes an aspic of them
then sucks back
in foam and undertow—
this aspect of the sea
Marina never knew.
For her the sea was Father's Fearful Sea
harsh with sea serpents
winds and drowning men.
For her it held no spiral of a shell
for her descent to dreams,
it held no bells.
And where it moved in shallows it was more
imminently a danger, more alive
than where it lay off shore full fathom five.
                                —1954

THE PERMANENT TOURISTS

Somnolent through landscapes and by trees
nondescript, almost anonymous,
they alter as they enter foreign cities—
the terrible tourists with their empty eyes
longing to be filled with monuments.

Verge upon statues in the public squares
remembering the promise of memorials
yet never enter the entire event
as dogs, abroad in any kind of weather,
move perfectly within their rainy climate.

Lock themselves into snapshots on the steps
of monolithic bronze as if suspecting
the subtle mourning of the photograph
might later, conjure in the memory
all they are now incapable of feeling.

And track all heroes down: the boy who gave
his life to save a town: the stolid queen;
forgotten politicians minus names;
the plunging war dead, permanently brave,
forever and ever going down to death.

Look, you can see them nude in any café
reading their histories from the bill of fare,
creating futures from a foreign teacup.
Philosophies like ferns bloom from the fable
that travel is broadening at the café table.

Yet, somehow beautiful, they stamp the plaza.
Classic in their anxiety they call
all the memorials of naked stone
into their passive eyes, as placid rivers
are always calling to the ruined columns.

—*1954*

SISTERS

These children split each other open like nuts,
break and crack in the small house,
are doors slamming.
Still, on the whole, are gentle for mother, take
her simple comfort like a drink of milk.

Fierce on the street they own the sun and spin
on separate axes
attract about them in their motion all

the shrieking neighborhood of little earths;
in violence hold hatred in their mouths.

With evening their joint gentle laughter leads
them into pastures of each other's eyes;
beyond, the world is barren; they contract
tenderness from each other like disease
and talk as if each word had just been born—
a butterfly, and soft from its cocoon.

—*1954*

MIRIAM WADDINGTON

(1917-   )

Miriam (Dworkin) Waddington, whose parents were Russian immigrants, was born in Winnipeg and spent her early years in that city. She attended an Ottawa high school and the University of Toronto. Upon graduation in 1939 from a general arts course she married Patrick Waddington. Turning now to Social Work, she took special training in the university and worked for several years in a Family Service agency. In 1945 she completed an advanced course in a children's psychiatric clinic at the University of Pennsylvania. Then she lived in Montreal, teaching for a few years at McGill but later giving up her professional work because of her young children. Since 1964 she has been in the Department of English at York University in Toronto.

Mrs. Waddington's first book of poems was Green World *published in 1945 by John Sutherland's First Statement Press. Other volumes have followed, the most recent being* Driving Home: New & Selected Poems *(1973).*

As a Professor of Canadian literature at York University, Mrs. Waddington has published various scholarly articles and books in the subject, including a monograph on A. M. Klein (1970) and John Sutherland: Essays, Controversies, Poems *(1973). Her address on "Canadian Tradition and Canadian Literature" appears in* Canadian Anthology, *pages 627-638.*

INVESTIGATOR

I who am street-known am also street knowing:
Just ask me —
I know the tangle of hot streets behind the poorhouse
Pouring from the city like coiled intestines,
The smell of the brewery as it splays long fumes in the alleys,
And the streets pushed against the zoo
With litter of peanut shells and empty candy boxes.
Also the streets climbing crazily up the river bank
Between bridge and jail.

My hand knows the familiar gesture
Of measuring a child's height in passing.
Even if I were blind I would see the gray figure
Hear the thin high call of the city's authorized salvage collector.
I could tell you and no exaggeration
Of the in and out of houses twenty times a day,
Of the lace antimacassars, the pictures of kings and queens,
The pious mottoes, the printed blessings, the dust piling up on bureaus,
The velour interiors, the Niagara souvenirs,
The faded needlepoint, the hair pulled tight
And the blinds drawn against day and the feel of sun.

Then down between lake and railway tracks
The old houses running to seed, the grass grown tall,
The once mansion made into quaint apartments
Where a foul granny with warts all over her face
Sits counting last year's newspapers lost in a timeless litter
And her hunchback son runs nimble messages with covetous eyes.

Out on the street again into the fainting heat
Where bloom the rank garbage cans to the jazz of trolleys,
Past the garden where the old man drooling senile decay

Lets the sun slip ceaselessly through his fingers,
And for humor
A long lean lap-eared dog sitting on a roof
Blinks wet eyes at me.

—1945

IN THE BIG CITY

On South and Fourteenth street
Wind assaulted her
Dark voices shuttered her
Chaos threatened her,

Then fear exploded
Brilliant on trolley tracks,

A motor-cycle leaped
Against a wall of flame;

A forest of faces grew
Thick on the edge of the night
Hot smiles crowded her
Loose elbows jostled her

Among faces anonymous
Was one she recognized,
The hunter loneliness
Had stalked and followed her

She turns now and runs
To buildings to shelter her,
Her feet hold to earth
The mother who nourished her

Relentless the hunter
Through the night follows her,
Hate his ragged hound
Knows love is her camouflage,

Furious they stalk the night
Through the jungle streets
Terror spills its stars
Over her leopard flight

And fear now feels its shape
Alter with every hour,
Child of itself in her
Fear is reborn

New and apart from her,
At dawn they separate
Childless in empty streets
Hunter covers his sightless eyes.

—*1945*

NIGHT IN OCTOBER

(The dream, the dream, where did it begin?
In the downpour of light that flooded through
   the sky?
Where was the key that opened up the door
To a white room with candles burning?)

At midnight the wind
Stretched long leathery fingers
Against the warm night,
Lifted the roof of torment and sang
Lullabies from an old book
Of apples and nutmegs and peacocks that
   flew
Ceaselessly circling a golden sea.
(It was dream, it was dream,
Light echoed and keys were lost in the sea.)

Then pain came with its symphony
With its many players
Who tuned forceps and scissors
And the sharp cruel dancers
Who whirled and galloped
All over my girlhood, shipwrecked and bitter.
(There was an answer, I heard it through
   water
Through the coils and columns,
But it was lost in the weather
The genesis of snow.)

The dream the dream
That nested like a dove
In evergreens and eaves
That fed on angel honey
And loaves of silky bread,
The dream still nameless,
Wandering and restless,
Searching for me.

I in my torment was chained to the moment,
Heard the harsh rasp of wire
And the ring of steel
On vast white porcelain—
All over the prairie my prayers were empty,
All over the ocean my hands had spread
And the doctors were dancing

Fandangoes, boleros,
They sang commands in a chorus
Of feverish laughter, "Once more and again,"
"And now die again, yes die, yes die,"
So I died just to please them.

(But the dream, the dream, where did it
   begin?
In jewels, in stars, in powdery snow
Or sin? Oh lullabies be quiet and still,

The dandelions do die and on my graveyard
   green
Their white petticoats of lace upon the
   hilltop blow,
And pebbles bleached and dry
Neatly line the path.)

From far away a voice
Calls me from the dead,
"Are you there, are you there,

Are you there?" Urgently jolted
Out of death without warning
I wake to the new child's crying.
It is morning, morning—
Full of problems and sorrow.

(Light fades from the window,
And the dream, nameless and wandering
Goes to sleep in its echoes
Unsolved and insoluble.)

—1955

SOMEONE WHO USED TO HAVE SOMEONE

There used to be someone
to whom I could say do you
love me and be sure that the
answer would always be yes;
there used to be someone to
whom I could telephone and
be sure when the operator
said do you accept the charges
the answer would always be yes;
but now there is no one to ask
no one to telephone from the
strangeness of cities in the
lateness of nightness now there
is no-one always now no-one
no someone no never at all.

Can you imagine what it is
like to live in a world where
there is no-one now always no
no-one and never some some-

one to ask do you love me and
be sure that the answer would
always be yes? I live in a world
where only the billboards are
always   they're twenty feet tall
and they circle the city they
coax and caress me they heat
me and cool me they promise and
plead me with colour and comfort:
you can get to sleep with me
tonight (the me being ovaltine)
but who wants to get to sleep
with a cup of ovaltine what
kind of sleep is that for someone who used to have someone
to ask do you love me and
be sure that the answer
would always be yes?

—1966

SEA BELLS

Five fathoms deep my father lies,
and of his bones are my bones made,
this is his blindness in my eyes,
his limping paced my grave.

Oh daughter toll the sea-green bell
and shake the coral from your hair,
the sea was once your bed of birth,
your given name your knell.

My body was your sepulchre,
the wide world was your cell,
my hand as written in your blood
what time and tide will tell.

The tide has since cast up its scroll,
and told what time could tell;
five fathoms deep my father lies
his daughter deeper fell

To see the seeing of his eyes
and take what pearls might have to give;
five fathoms deep in sleep he lies
whose death waked me to live.

—1966

SAD WINTER IN THE LAND OF CAN. LIT.

I tell myself
I am sad because
it is winter:
but Nelly Sachs
lived through
many such winters
and poured biblical
summer through the
blackest chimneys.

Madame Nathalie
lived through them
too; she comes from
Moscow like my
grandmother and now
she will visit
Toronto and speak
to us in English.
Will I learn
anything from her?

There are many
things I must learn
in order to write
better in Canada.
I must learn to
write & for *and*
and *wll* for *will*:
to put : at the
beginning of a line
instead of at the end;

to spell everything
my own swt way just
to prve my indep
endens of all thr
shtty authrty.

I must learn to
write about dead
horses with myths
in my mouth, dead
birds and frogs
that I shot with
tears in my eyes
but compassion in
my heart just
because I'm human
and was born to
original sin.

I must learn to
sing the joy of
penises and all
their frequencies;
the gloriousness
of blow jobs and
how avant garde
is everything in
London Ontario;
they will then
maybe mistake me
for a 26-year-old

white-protestant-
anglo-saxon-or-
duddy-kravitz-ok-
type-jew — a man — or
someone who at least
reads comic books
and was once a cree
indian or a wistful
eskimo.

Dear Nelly Sachs,
dear Nathalie Sarraute,
isn't there anything
you can teach me
about how to write
better in Canada?

—*1972*

POLEMICS

I am not interested
in the polemics of art
you can keep your cosmic
gossip I don't care if
poetry is dying if the
language is debased if
you stuff people's ears
with bananas and their
mouths with dead elm
trees; to hell with style!
I'm in favour of living
I reject dying while
I'm still alive I don't
want to analyse the process
of how we disappear from
the world; I care only
how we appear; I want
to build apparitions
a million monuments
to the future completely
uncool, to shout from
the rooftops: *history
is not so fleeting!*

There were heroes, wars
were halted, men were
healed, children were
born, people sang,
worlds were changed;
I don't want to be ashamed
of the word *courage* or
choke on the word *love*
or deny the category
of being human any more;
I want to say *brother* and
see when I close my eyes
not ploughs of riot or
fields of burning people
or the bones of smoking
cities: I want to see
vistas of all that is
being made impossible—
civilization.

—*1972*

FRED COGSWELL

(1917-   )

Fred Cogswell was born in East Centreville, N. B., and educated at the University of New Brunswick and Edinburgh University (Ph.D., 1952). He served in the Canadian army from 1940-1945. He has taught English in the University of New Brunswick since 1952 and he is now Professor and Head of the Department. From 1952 until 1966 he edited The Fiddlehead, *an excellent and durable "little magazine" of verse. He now edits and publishes the Fiddlehead Poetry Series. His first book of verse,* The Stunted Strong *(1954), was followed by half a dozen more, the latest being* The House Without A Door *(1973).*

A BALLAD OF LOVING

We stripped our bodies naked
When we were lass and lad,
And still I've not forgotten
The white, clean flesh we had.

And had we gone no further
We both had stayed content,
For flesh to flesh in nature
Is fair and innocent.

But our rash, youthful loving,
Its flesh-look satisfied,
Then stripped our souls as naked
To feed our mutual pride.

And love died out in horror
That flesh could not control—
God's love alone, I'm thinking,
Should see a naked soul!

—1956

ODE TO FREDERICTON

White are your housetops, white too your vaulted elms
That make your stately streets long aisles of prayer,
And white your thirteen spires that point your God
Who reigns afar in pure and whiter air,
And white the dome of your democracy —
The snow has pitied you and made you fair,
O snow-washed city of cold, white Christians,
So white you will not cut a black man's hair.   —1959

A SUNBEAM ROLLED THE STONE AWAY

A sunbeam rolled the stone away
From off the grave of murdered love,
And from these walls of bone and clay
There rose by miracle a dove.

It gave a little joyous cry
And flew, all light and free from pain:
Nor can I coax, for all I try,
It back to death with me again.

—1959

THE WIDOWER

Not lonely now in bed the widower lies
Who late at night has felt the smooth-skinned swell
Of rounded sheets arouse his skin to flame
Or in his dreams, like Ixion in hell,
Has clasped a curve of softness that became
A cloudy pillow to his morning eyes.
Such nightmare waking not tonight applies;
It is warm flesh that meets his warmer thighs.

Warm flesh and tendered in such tender wise
He feels his love return and all the black
Life-loneliness lie conquered on its back
There in the dark one passion-breathing space
Before his mind recalls the raddled face
Of his love-machine and her hard, glazed eyes.

—1959

THE SENSES

My mind opens the windows of my eyes
and I see you standing straight and clear
although you are
                   miles and years away

When memory moves the inner ear
deep inside
              I hear your voice
and smile with sudden joy

And sometimes in a vacant room
the familiar scent of you
                      now and then
as from a flower breathes

But what my mind loves most
the touch and taste of you
                      is dead
except through masks of other women

—1968

BUT SOMETIMES RISING

when I close my eyes
a deep ocean swells to drown
the dry shapes of day

but sometimes rising
in the waters of my mind
flesh faces waver

into clarity—
tantalizing cameos
like quicksilver fish

that gleam and vanish
as the current twists and shifts,
or mermaids groping

from the wrong side of
time's translucent element
for what might have been

—1968

MARGARET AVISON

(*1918-   *)

Margaret Avison was born in Galt (now Cambridge), Ontario. Her first poems were written in childhood. She graduated from the University of Toronto (Victoria College) in 1940, and returned during 1964-1966 for further study. Meanwhile, she attended schools of creative writing in the Universities of Indiana (1955) and Chicago (1956-1957). She has worked variously as librarian, secretary, university lecturer in English, and social worker in Toronto while she contributed a few poems to magazines; a selection of these appeared in The Book of Canadian Poetry, *edited by A. J. M. Smith, who described her poetry as "metaphysical . . . passionate, intellectual, and essentially religious."*

Miss Avison's first volume was Winter Sun *(1960); most of the contents date from 1956 to 1959. Her second book was* The Dumbfounding *(1966). She also took part, with others, in translations of poetry and prose from Hungarian.*

In 1972-1973 she was Poet-in-Residence at the University of Western Ontario.

THE APEX ANIMAL

A Horse, thin-colored as oranges ripened in freight-cars
which have shaken casements through the miles of night
across three nights of field and waterfront ware-houses—
rather, the narrow Head of the Horse
with the teeth shining and white ear-tufts:
It, I fancy, and from experience
commend the fancy to your inner eye,
It is the One, in a patch of altitude
troubled only by clarity of weather,
Who sees, the ultimate Recipient
of what happens, the One Who is aware
when, in the administrative wing
a clerk returns from noon-day, though
the ointment of mortality
for one strange hour, in all his lustreless life,
has touched his face.

(For that Head of a Horse there is no question
whether he spent the noon-hour with a friend,
below street-level, or on the parapet—
a matter which may safely rest
in mortal memory.)

—1960

NEW YEAR'S POEM

The Christmas twigs crispen and needles rattle
Along the windowledge.
      A solitary pearl
Shed from the necklace spilled at last week's party
Lies in the suety, snow-luminous plainness
Of morning, on the windowledge beside them.
And all the furniture that circled stately
And hospitable when these rooms were brimmed
With perfumes, furs, and black-and-silver
Crisscross of seasonal conversation, lapses
Into its previous largeness.
      I remember
Anne's rose-sweet gravity, and the stiff grave
Where cold so little can contain;
I mark the queer delightful skull and crossbones
Starlings and sparrows left, taking the crust,
And the long loop of winter wind
Smoothing its arc from dark Arcturus down
To the bricked corner of the drifted courtyard,
And the still windowledge.
      Gentle and just pleasure
It is, being human, to have won from space
This unchill, habitable interior
Which mirrors quietly the light
Of the snow, and the new year.

—1960

THE WORLD STILL NEEDS

Frivolity is out of season.
Yet, in this poetry, let it be admitted
The world still needs piano-tuners
And has fewer, and more of these
Gray fellows prone to liquor
On an unlikely Tuesday, gritty with wind,
When somewhere, behind windows,
A housewife stays for him until the
      Hour of the uneasy bridge-club cocktails
      And the office rush at the groceteria
      And the vesper-bell and lit-up buses passing
      And the supper trays along the hospital corridor,
Suffering from
Sore throat and dusty curtains.

Not all alone on the deserted boathouse
Or even on the prairie freight
(The engineer leaned out, watchful and blank
And had no Christmas worries
Mainly because it was the eve of April),
Is like the moment
When the piano in the concert-hall
Finds texture absolute, a single solitude
For those hundreds in rows, half out of overcoats,
Their eyes swimming with sleep.

From this communal cramp of understanding
Springs up suburbia, where every man would build
A clapboard in a well of Russian forest
With yard enough for a high clothesline strung
To a small balcony . . .
A woman whose eyes shine like evening's star
Takes in the freshblown linen
While sky a lonely wash of pink is still
Reflected in brown mud
Where lettuces will grow, another spring.

—1960

BUTTERFLY BONES; OR, SONNET
AGAINST SONNETS

The cyanide jar seals life, as sonnets move
towards final stiffness. Cased in a white glare
these specimens stare for peering boys, to prove
strange certainties. Plane dogsled and safari
assure continuing range. The sweep-net skill,
the patience, learning, leave all living stranger.
Insect—or poem—waits for the fix, the frill
precision can effect, brilliant with danger.
What law and wonder the museum spectres
bespeak is cryptic for the shivery wings,
the world cut-diamond-eyed, those eyes' reflectors,
or herbal grass, sunned motes, fierce listening.
Might sheened and rigid trophies strike men blind
like Adam's lexicon locked in the mind?

—1960

PERSPECTIVE

A sport, an adventitious sprout
These eyeballs, that have somehow slipped
The mesh of generations since Mantegna?

Yet I declare, your seeing is diseased
That cripples space. The fear has eaten back
Through sockets to the caverns of the brain
   And made of it a sifty habitation.

We stand beholding the one plain
And in your face I see the chastening
Of its small tapering design
That brings up *punkt*.
   (The Infinite, you say,
     Is an unthinkable—and pointless too—
       Extension of that *punkt*.)

But, ho, you miss the impact of that fierce
Raw boulder five miles off? You are not pierced
By that great spear of grass on the horizon?
    You are not smitten with the shock
      Of that great thundering sky?

Your law of optics is a quarrel
Of chickenfeet on paper. Does a train
Run pigeon-toed?

I took a train from here to Ottawa
On tracks that did not meet. We swelled and roared
Mile upon mightier mile, and when we clanged
Into the vasty station we were indeed
Brave company for giants.

  Keep your eyes though,
You, and not I, will travel safer back
         To Union Station.

Your fear has me infected, and my eyes
That were my sport so long, will soon be apt
Like yours to press out dwindling vistas from
The massive flux massive Mantegna knew
And all its sturdy everlasting foregrounds.

—1960

FROM "THE EARTH THAT FALLS AWAY"*

XIV

I knew how to live
by hearing and touch
and sense of place. I could pre-judge
obstacles too: at first the couch,
lamp, table; you have to have
them mapped in your mind—you clutch
notions, till you trust sense. Then I could move
out among trees and traffic, a march
in Nomansland to risk it, a dive
into invisible interdependence, no crutch
needed, for all the dread. I knew how to live.
Please. Leave me alone.
Bandage my eyes again.
The dream of seeing
I want, as it has been, open
daybreak blue, with the sting
of the far-off; not this urging
of person, color, thing.
Unclutter me. Relieve
me of this visible. Give
back my sealed-off dayshine. . . .

XV

The broken prism of noise,
pure air (in buildings), pour
of night-wind on a choir of
loosed, elbowing, lift-looney shelters,
traffic-sift, wall-tower,
echo-chambers and hoo-ing
scattering street-boys in the pursuing
murmur haunted stillness, city's unquiet,
the flipped flight
of park pigeons, heavy with knowing
tame food and kicked wing-flop, brewing
in-cringing crowds: Who broke it
in words, fire-pure?

*["The Earth That Falls Away" begins with a passage from Beddoes, *Death's Jest-Book,*
II ii, 39-40:
    Can a man die? Ay, as the sun doth set:
    It is the earth that falls away from light.
Sections XIV and XV constitute the conclusion of this poem, which was published in *The
Dumbfounding.*]

on lips wine-bright?
so that night was in clear
oases lit, not a smokey flare,
no illusory gleam-and-gone?

Your beauty and holiness,
Your fair-seeing, scald.

In the intolerable hour
our fingers and fists
blunder for blindfolds
to have you in our power!

"He does not resist you,"
said James
looking to
Him who, in his hour,
comes.

—1966

WE THE POOR WHO ARE ALWAYS WITH US

The cumbering hungry
and the uncaring ill
become too many
try as we will.

Try on and on, still?
In fury, fly
out, smash shards (and quail
at tomorrow's new supply,
and fail anew to find and smash the why?)

It is not hopeless.
One can crawling move
in useless recognition
there, still free to love
past use, where none survive.

And there is reason in
the hope that then can shine
when other hope is none.

—1974

LOUIS DUDEK

(1918-   )

Louis Dudek was born in Montreal of parents who had emigrated from Poland to Canada before the First World War; he grew up in the industrialized East End of the city. After his graduation from McGill University in 1939, he worked as an advertising copy-writer for five years, then resumed his studies at Columbia University, where he took his M.A. in history before finally transferring to English (Ph.D., 1955).

He joined the First Statement *group shortly after the magazine was founded by John Sutherland in 1942. Some of his poems were published in Ronald Hambleton's* Unit of Five *(1944). From 1946 until 1951, Dudek taught English at City College in New York. On his return to Montreal to teach at McGill University he engaged in several literary ventures, founding and editing various "little magazines" and "little presses," often in collaboration with Souster and Layton: Contact Press (1952-1967); CIV/n (1955-1956); McGill Poetry Series;* Delta *(1957-1966); and Delta Canada, which continues. Ten volumes of his own poetry had appeared before he published his* Collected Poetry *in 1971.*

With Michael Gnarowski, Dudek edited in 1967 an important collection of articles about the Canadian literary history of his time, The Making of Modern Poetry in Canada. *Dudek is now a Professor at McGill University.*

NIGHT TRAIN

The heads of these people—baggage—paper—fur—
And the great flares of matches lighted in the train.
                Outside, smoke crossing the country
Fretted with oil tanks and forgotten freight cars,
                        then the river
Frozen under the bridge, whose banging black girders
Break across the snow-swept shrubbery of the river shallows;
Then the singing wires of telegraphs
And the silent fences
                at the beginnings and endings of forests
A milky emulsion of sky—the motion
Of the railroad's belly pounding under us—
While within the lighted car, in the loudness,
Girls sit, their heads bowed over books,
Ferreting the pages of love, unsatisfied.

—1946

PUERTO RICAN SIDE STREET

Morning came at me like a flung snowball,
the light flaked out of a chalk-blue sky;
and I was walking down the dilapidated side-street
like a grasshopper in a field, just born;
all the rails and pails glistened and deceived me
with bunches of blue flowers and with silk of corn.

The yellow shades were mostly down, some up, some torn;
and I went looking into windows, into rooms,
looking for the breakfasters, and the cluttered dressers
and cracked walls; watching the black doorways and the dim
charred halls, for the baby carriages and the kids;
and as I walked, they came, like shots in a foreign film.

And then, in a blue window, lifted like a cross,
her legs straight, hair flat, and arms strung wide,
gazing out at the daylight out of coal-black
glassy eyes, I saw the twelve-year child—a saint
upon a stained-glass window—with her blue sash dress
hanging on her, thinly, and her small face thin and faint.

As I passed looking at her eyes held far away,
she almost turned; but the sun suddenly came
from behind some chimney stack, and I went ahead:
the street blazed up again. The morning hour
that made the ashes shine and the stones burst out in flame,
had shown me in her face the sad, dark human flower.

—1951, 1971

DANGER

The poet, living in a cloud of violent dream,
congested with energy,
illuminates only as lightning does, fitfully,
with less light than thunder;
he flings plums at your feet as if they were boulders.
You will not learn from him of your danger,
you must fear a more mean and mechanical murder—
Greed, with arithmetic in his fangs, coils near you,
his tail in time and the grave;
you can hardly hear his sliding as he crawls
among the shining faces of the dead and living who sleep.

—1952

POEM FOR SPRING

Mother Earth's belly is broken,
      the spring begins.
Sap flows into deadened arteries,
      branches open,
the lamb bleats, the pussy willow
      puts out;
green is her blood —
      the white scab of winter is washed away.

O let this new birth be
      into a fertile year!
Let the summer fruit be a full scrotum
      between the desired branches
and not fall to the ground,
      wrinkled apples.

Let the horn of morning
      awaken sleeping feathers
        all the long summer,
and if winter comes,
      let it be a sleep
hungry, and dreamful
      of unforgotten spring.

—1952

A CHILD BLOWING BUBBLES

Against the storefronts, by the loud buses whose
blue exhaust in its clean colored worlds
made moving clouds and many a blossoming rose,
the child laughed, blowing its small breath
into a curved wire, a magic circle for a cent.

Blowing more, and catching the globes, it laughed
at me bemused in wheels of floating foam,
crisp and crystal fortune balls about my head—
when looking at the future there I lost my thread
of childlike sense, and brutish saw each bubble burst.

—1952

CITY AND FIELD

The bridge's black girders, the spread street and the factory like a crater,
the round tubes of distilleries,
the swoop of wires and stores as they leap into a spot of sky,
the perspectives of the residential quarters,
the red coat of a skipping child,
strung and shining branches against the sky, watery blue,
the splashing spade of quicksilver light on a passing car,
the dust blown like coughing smoke, like poison gas
along the street, into a crowd of kids,
the half-prism of a church steeple in sunlight,
waste paper patchy among the shrubs
of the gray islands of the boulevard,
and there, everywhere, the commercialized
houses, the mineral-water advertised—
I remember these, and the gulled pattern of the streetcar floor,
as I sit on the hill's arm, threading the twisted hair of the fields,
tracing the meanders of streams
to the skyline.

—1952

COMING SUDDENLY TO THE SEA

Coming suddenly to the sea in my twenty-eighth year,
to the mother of all things that breathe, of mussels and whales,
I could not see anything but sand at first
and burning bits of mother-of-pearl.
But this was the sea, terrible as a torch
which the winter sun had lit,
flaming in the blue and salt sea-air
under my twenty-eight-year infant eyes.
And then I saw the spray smashing the rocks
and the angry gulls cutting the air,
the heads of fish and the hands of crabs on stones:
the carnivorous sea, sower of life,
battering a granite rock to make it a pebble—
love and pity needless as the ferny froth on its long smooth waves.
The sea, with its border of crinkly weed,
the inverted Atlantic of our unstable planet,
froze me into a circle of marble, sending the icy air out in lukewarm waves.
And so I brought home, as an emblem of the day
ending my long blind years, a fistful of blood-red weed in my hand.

—1956

AL PURDY

(1918-   )

Alfred (Al) Purdy was born near Wooler, Ontario. His father, a farmer who had been educated at an agricultural college, died when Alfred was two years of age. His mother, a very religious person, then moved the family to nearby Trenton. The boy's schooling ended when, as he claims, he "failed Grade 10 and quit."

He did "a little of everything . . . Bata Shoe Factory, picking apples, six years in R.C.A.F. [1940-1945], store clerk in a foundry, in a Vancouver mattress factory, six months making box springs in Montreal. Visiting professor at Simon Fraser U . . . Creative writing teacher at Banff School of Fine Arts [1971-1973]." In addition he wrote and travelled; in 1964 he was in Cuba, and in the summer of 1965 in Baffin Island.

Purdy dislikes his first book, The Enchanted Echo *(1944). His writing changed drastically about 1953, the "year of Dylan Thomas' death," and also because of "people [he] knew in Vancouver," and a new interest in reading very widely.* Poems for all the Annettes *(1962) was a popular success; the second edition in 1968 included also selected poems from earlier books. Another book* Selected Poems *appeared in 1972. Meanwhile, other individual volumes had appeared. Besides poetry, Purdy has published several short stories and written since 1955 at least fifteen plays, produced on radio and television for the CBC.*

ELEGY FOR A GRANDFATHER

Well, he died, didn't he? They said he did.
His wide whalebone hips will make a prehistoric barrow,
A kitchen midden for mice under the rough sod,
Where relatives stood in real and pretended sorrow
For the dearly beloved gone at last to God,
After a bad century—a tough, turbulent Pharaoh
With a deck of cards in his pocket and a Presbyterian grin.

Well, maybe he did die, but the boy didn't see it.
The man knows now and the whimsical tale is told
Of a lying lumberjack with a fist like a piece of suet,
A temper like toppling timber and splintering words to scald
The holy ears of an angel—and a beautiful man in a riot:
But a bright, bragging boy's hero with a pocketful of gold.
Like a neolith swear word from the opposite end of time.

No doubt at all that he's dead: a sadly virtuous voice
Folded tragedy sideways and glossed his glittering sins.
Old in his ancient barrow and no one could ever guess
If the shy fox people play with his gnarled grey bones,
Or a green Glengarry river sluices his grave and sighs.
And earth has another tenant involved in her muttering plans,
With a deck of cards in his pocket and a Presbyterian grin.

—1956

THE CARIBOO HORSES

At 100 Mile House the cowboys ride in rolling
stagey cigarettes with one hand reining
half-tame bronco rebels on a morning grey as stone
—so much like riding dangerous women
   with whiskey coloured eyes—
such women as once fell dead with their lovers
with fire in their heads and slippery froth on thighs
—Beaver or Carrier women maybe or
   Blackfoot squaws far past the edge of this valley
on the other side of those two toy mountain ranges
   from the sunfierce plains beyond

But only horses
    waiting in stables
hitched at taverns
    standing at dawn
pastured outside the town with
jeeps and fords and chevvys and
busy muttering stake trucks rushing
importantly over roads of man's devising
over the safe known roads of the ranchers
families and merchants of the town
    On the high prairie
are only horse and rider
    wind in dry grass
clopping in silence under the toy mountains
dropping sometimes and
    lost in the dry grass
    golden oranges of dung

Only horses
   no stopwatch memories or palace ancestors

not Kiangs hauling undressed stone in the Nile Valley
and having stubborn Egyptian tantrums or
Onagers racing thru Hither Asia and
the last Quagga screaming in African highlands
            lost relatives of these
            whose hooves were thunder
the ghosts of horses battering thru the wind
whose names were the wind's common usage
whose life was the sun's
            arriving here at chilly noon
            in the gasoline smell of the
            dust and waiting 15 minutes
            at the grocer's

                                —*1965, 1972*

COUNTRY SNOWPLOW

                    Tyrannosaurus
comes lumbering around the stalled
Quaternary glaciers to deliver his ancient
                    thundering manifesto
modified to suit the times—
                    Tyrannosaurus
roaming the bed clothes of earth—
Warm in the cold hutch rabbits endure
their scarcities
            owls survive a dream
of pterodactyls—
            SNOW
engendering in marsupial darkness
the fierce equations of light—
                  To rescue
the perishing
            married woman expecting
strength from snowshovel husband
he knowing and searching the shapes of self
to seize the disparate ghost that strength is
baby about to be born or old man dying
without help
            in diesel thunder
the transistor's and sick woman's bones
            dance
                neuter together—

Others
          with all the resources of not-needing
(the white dust being merely white dust) hold
steadfast in the pouring
                    millrace of cold
marshal around them magazines
                    collections of postage stamps
and all the old absorbing hobbies of
                    getting and keeping and counting
barricade themselves in themselves and
wait
          indignant at the lateness of the hour—
                    Thunder dies
and in the monster's milky wake
                    come separate and severally
the chattering mammals—
                                        —1965

INNUIT

An old man carving soapstone
at the co-op in Frobisher Bay
and in his faded eyes
it is possible to see them
shadowy figures
past the Dorset and pre-Dorset Cultures
5,000 years ago
if you look closely
But the race-soul has drawn back
drawn back
from settlements and landing fields
from white men
into secret vaults
and catacombs of marrow
bone rooms
that reveal nothing
The Innuit which is to say
          THE PEOPLE
as the Greeks called all foreigners
          barbaroi
something other than themselves
          un-GREEK
so the Innuit
          The People

these unknowable human beings
who have endured 5,000 years
on the edge of the world
a myth from long ago
that reaches into the past
but touches an old man still living
Looking into his eyes
it is possible to see the first hunters
(if you have your own vision)
after the last ice age
moving eastward from Siberia
without dogs or equipment
toward the new country
pausing on the sea-ice
for a moment of rest
then pushing on thru the white smother
—Flying generations
leap and converge on this face
an old man carving soapstone
with the race-soul of The People
THE PEOPLE
moving somewhere
behind his eyes

Pangnirtung   —1967

460

ARCTIC RHODODENDRONS

They are small purple surprises
in the river's white racket
and after you've seen them
a number of times
in water-places
where their silence seems
related to river-thunder
you think of them as "noisy flowers"
Years ago
it may have been
that lovers came this way
stopped in the outdoor hotel
to watch the water floorshow
and lying prone together
where the purged green
boils to a white heart
and the shore trembles
like a stone song
with bodies touching
flowers were their conversation
and love the sound of a colour
that lasts two weeks in August
and then dies
except for the three or four
I pressed in a letter
and sent whispering to you

Pangnirtung   *—1967*

ELEGY FOR A GRANDFATHER

Well, he died I guess. They said he did.
His wide whalebone hips will make a prehistoric barrow
men of the future may find and perhaps may not:
where this man's relatives ducked their heads
in real and pretended sorrow
for the dearly beloved gone thank Christ to God,
after a bad century: a tough big-bellied Pharaoh,
with a deck of cards in his pocket and a Presbyterian grin—

461

Maybe he did die, but the boy didn't understand it,
the man knows now and the scandal never grows old
of a happy lumberjack who lived on rotten whiskey,
and died of sin and Quaker oats age 90 or so.
But all he was was too much for any man to be,
a life so full he couldn't include one more thing,
not tell the same story twice if he'd wanted to,
and didn't and didn't—

Just the same he's dead. A sticky religious voice
folded his century sideways to get it out of sight,
and lowered him into the ground like someone still alive
who made other people uncomfortable:
barn raiser and backwoods farmer,
become an old man in a one-room apartment
over a drygoods store—
And earth takes him as it takes more beautiful things:
populations of whole countries,
museums and works of art,
and women with such a glow
it makes their background vanish
                    they vanish too,
and Lesbia's singer in her sunny islands
stopped when the sun went down—

No, my grandfather was decidedly unbeautiful,
250 pounds of scarred slag.
And I've somehow become his memory,
taking on flesh and blood again
the way he imagined me,
floating among the pictures in his mind
where his dead body is,
laid deep in the earth—
and such a relayed picture perhaps
outlives any work of art,
survives among its alternatives.

—1968

WILDERNESS GOTHIC

Across Roblin Lake, two shores away,
they are sheathing the church spire
with new metal. Someone hangs in the sky
over there from a piece of rope,
hammering and fitting God's belly-scratcher,

462

working his way up along the spire
until there's nothing left to nail on—
Perhaps the workman's faith reaches beyond:
touches intangibles, wrestles with Jacob,
replacing rotten timber with pine thews,
pounds hard in the blue cave of the sky,
contends heroically with difficult problems
of gravity, sky navigation and mythopeia,
his volunteer time and labor donated to God,
minus sick benefits of course on a non-union job—

Fields around are yellowing into harvest,
nestling and fingerling are sky and water borne,
death is yodeling quiet in green woodlots,
and bodies of three young birds have disappeared
in the sub-surface of the new county highway—

That picture is incomplete, part left out
that might alter the whole Dürer landscape:
gothic ancestors peer from medieval sky,
dour faces trapped in photograph albums escaping
to clop down iron roads with matched greys:
work-sodden wives groping inside their flesh
for what keeps moving and changing and flashing
beyond and past the long frozen Victorian day.
A sign of fire and brimstone? A two-headed calf
born in the barn last night? A sharp female agony?
An age and a faith moving into transition,
the dinner cold and new-baked bread a failure,
deep woods shiver and water drops hang pendant,
double yolked eggs and the house creaks a little—
Something is about to happen. Leaves are still.
Two shores away, a man hammering in the sky.
Perhaps he will fall.

                                             —1968

LAMENT FOR THE DORSETS

(Eskimos extinct in the 14th century A.D.*)*

Animal bones and some mossy tent rings
scrapers and spearheads   carved ivory swans
all that remains of the Dorset giants
who drove the Vikings back to their long ships
talked to spirits of earth and water
—a picture of terrifying old men

so large they broke the backs of bears
so small they lurk behind bone rafters
in the brain of modern hunters
among good thoughts and warm things
and come out at night
to spit on the stars

The big men with clever fingers
who had no dogs and hauled their sleds
over the frozen northern oceans
awkward giants
                    killers of seal
they couldn't compete with little men
who came from the west with dogs
Or else in a warm climatic cycle
the seals went back to cold waters
and the puzzled Dorsets scratched their heads
with hairy thumbs around 1350 A.D.
—couldn't figure it out
went around saying to each other
plaintively
            "What's wrong? What happened?
            Where are the seals gone?"
And died

Twentieth century people
apartment dwellers
executives of neon death
warmakers with things that explode
—they have never imagined us in their future
how could we imagine them in the past
squatting among the moving glaciers
six hundred years ago
with glowing lamps?
As remote or nearly
as the trilobites and swamps
when coal became
or the last great reptile hissed
at a mammal the size of a mouse
that squeaked and fled

Did they ever realize at all
what was happening to them?
Some old hunter with one lame leg
a bear had chewed
sitting in a caribou skin tent
—the last Dorset?
Let's say his name was Kudluk
carving 2-inch ivory swans

for a dead grand-daughter
taking them out of his mind
the places in his mind
where pictures are
He selects a sharp stone tool
to gouge a parallel pattern of lines
on both sides of the swan
holding it with his left hand
bearing down and transmitting
his body's weight
from brain to arm and right hand
and one of his thoughts
turns to ivory
The carving is laid aside
in beginning darkness
at the end of hunger
after a while wind
blows down the tent and snow
begins to cover him
After 600 years
the ivory thought
is still warm

—1968

RAYMOND SOUSTER

(1921-   )

Raymond Souster was born and educated in Toronto. He served in the R.C.A.F., 1941-1945. Since the war he has lived in his native city. He is married and works for a chartered bank. His first volume, When We Are Young, *was published in 1946; his twentieth book of poetry,* Change-up, *will appear in 1974. One of these collections,* The Colour of the Times, *won the Governor-General's Award for 1964. He is also the editor and co-editor of a number of anthologies of verse, and has edited two "little magazines" of verse,* Contact *(1952-1953) and* Combustion *(1957-1960). Along with Louis Dudek, Peter Miller and Irving Layton, he helped to keep Contact Press alive from 1952-1967. In 1973 he published* On Target, *a novel about a Canadian bomber squadron in England in World War II, under the pseudonym "John Holmes." For a previous novel he used "Raymond Holmes" as his pseudonym.*

Souster's Preface to Cerberus *(1952) expresses his hopes of "a clue" to "a possible road for the future" of poetry in Ezra Pound's* Cantos *and in Charles Olson's "basic idea,* Composition by Field, *as opposed to inherited line." One may also see Souster's titles,* A Local Pride *(1962) and* The Colour of the Times *(1964), as agreement with the aims and poetic experiments of William Carlos Williams, especially in the American poet's city epic,* Paterson. *Souster's* Selected Poems *appeared in 1972.*

THE ENEMIES

What do they care for your books, will they ever read a chapter through or
    a verse without yawning,
Do you ever think they will stand before your painting and enjoy it
Without something lewd to suggest to the mind, or something they do not
    understand to be laughed at,
What do they care how you eat your heart out, how you kill yourself slowly
    or quickly, how you go mad.

You are not of their world, you are strangers, you are enemies, the hated,
Because you laugh at their money, their women, the cheapness of their lives,

Because they cannot laugh off, cannot pay off, the epitaph you have written.

—1944

YOUNG GIRLS

With the night full of spring and stars we stand
here in the dark doorway and watch the young
girls pass, two, three together, hand in hand.
Like flowers they are whose fragrance has not sprung
or awakened, whose bodies dimly feel
the flooding upward welling of the trees;
whose senses, caressed by the wind's soft fingers, reel
with a delirium that makes them ill at ease.

They lie awake at night unable to sleep
and walk the streets kindled by strange desires;
they steal glances at us, unable to keep
control upon those subterranean fires.
We whistle after them, then laugh, for they
stiffen, not knowing what to do or say.

—1946, 1964

KITES

Young boy
With your kite down the wind
Dipping and twisting as the breeze
Plays with it, sending it up and up
Into the sun, then as suddenly
Pitching earthward, almost
Touching the ground, then dashing it up again,

Watch well how your kite
Flies on this bright afternoon in the park
In the golden morning of your life:
Some day when you are older you'll remember
The kite in the wind — your life
Played with by the world, sending your heart
Up to the sky in passion, in the great happiness,
And the next the air-pocket, the fall to earth
Or almost earth — but the both of them are hell.

Some day you'll remember this —
But today
Today only the sun among the trees
And your kite at the end of your cord
Dancing in the playtime air.

—1947

IN PRAISE OF LONELINESS

Loneliness of men makes poets.
The great poem is a hymn to loneliness,
a crying out in the night with no ear bent to.

This is a breeding-ground for poets.
Here the spawning, glittering rivers of poetry.
Here is loneliness to live with, sleep with, eat with,
Loneliness of streets, of the coyote.

O Mistress Loneliness, heed your worshipper.
Give him the voice to be heard in this land
Loud with the cluck of the hen and the croak of the frog.

—1951, 1964

ROLLER SKATE MAN

A freak of the city,
little man with big head,
shrivelled body, stumps of legs
clamped to a block of wood
running on roller-skate wheels.

On his hands gloves
because the Queen Street pavements
are rough when your hands are paddles
and you speed between
silk-stockinged legs
and extravagant pleats,

steering through familiar waters
of spit, old butts, chewed gum,
flotsam among the jetsam of your world.

—1952, 1964

LA BELLE DAME

O it's not hard to see why these poets
seek the university,
they're clever and young and ambitious,
each with the right degree.

O it's not hard to see why these poets
give us little poetry,
nourished, sustained by the dried-up dugs
of the university.

(Seduced by an old bitch they'd probably call
La Belle Dame Sans Merci.)

—1954, 1964

DOWNTOWN CORNER NEWS STAND

It will need all of death to take you from this corner.
It has become your world, and you its unshaved
bleary-eyed, foot-stamping king. In winter
you curse the cold, huddled in your coat from the wind,
you fry in summer like an egg hopping on a griddle;
and always the whining voice, the nervous-flinging arms,
the red face, shifting eyes watching, waiting
under the grimy cap for God knows what
to happen. (But nothing ever does, downtown Toronto
goes to sleep and wakes the next morning
always the same, except a little dirtier.)
And you stand with your armful of Stars and Telys,
the peak of your cap well down against the sun,
and all the city's restless seething river
surges beside you, but not once do you plunge
into its flood, are carried or tossed away:
but reappear always, beard longer than ever, nose running,
to catch the noon editions at King and Bay.

—1954, 1964

BEAUTIFUL CHILDREN

Beautiful children
conceived in lust and despair,
beautiful children,
                    the boy
in blue jeans, the girl the same,
age ten and eleven, the boy ugly
in three or four years who'll have every
boy for miles round tossing sleepless
at night wondering how
to get her into the bush - - -
                    bush lying
a hundred yards in from the road,
running on into useless swamp
or lakes reflecting empty skies
and leafless trees rotting at their trunks,
that every year inches in closer
to the cleared land lying largely idle,
land slaved over fifty years ago
in hope, now abandoned for what it is,
a bitter joke: land where the rock jags through
at every rise, land never clear of stones,
land worked out, waiting to be swept back
into bush, into death.
                    The parents
young once, now terribly old,
turning to the bottle more and more
as they turn from each other, he
with a pension from shrapnel
in the stomach, lion with booze in him,
sick dog the rest, she
once girl-beautiful, now with the care-lines
branching her face, figure turned

but if knowing it yet
not caring, the girl beautiful
and aware of it by the way she tosses
that dark hair down her back, by the way
she walks in the tight-fitting
shiny jeans — O she'll be a beauty
shapeless as her life, brooding
on the four lost children, beating
the two live ones to atone for it.

These beautiful children
conceived in lust and despair,
beautiful children —
                    going by them on the road
you want to stop, take them with you far
to some place, any place but this patch of death
on the back roads:
                    but with any luck
they'll make it away themselves, the boy
maybe into the army, the stories
of his father ringing in his ears,
where they'll teach him to kill and be a man:
the girl, if she stays that beautiful
and doesn't get pregnant first,
may make Barrie or even Toronto
as a waitress, a factory hand,
may end up respectable and married:

but for now they are only
beautiful children moving through the weeds
of an uprooted pasture towards a sort of barn
hidden behind their tar-papered shack of a home
on a back-road nobody ever uses.

—1964

COLONIAL SATURDAY NIGHT

for Ken and Geneviève

"You're the best audience in the world,"
Big T says as the last kick of jazz dies
on the stand and we gulp our drinks
and spill down into the street:

Yonge Street twelve o'clock Saturday night
all the bars emptying
up and down the block
color suddenly filling
the sidewalks, everyone hurrying —
where ? — to find girls for the night
an alley to be sick in
a cop to pick a fight with ? —

or maybe like the four of us
just walking northward, savoring the night air
after the cigarette haze, going really nowhere
in no particular hurry, looking for nothing
we haven't already put hands or minds around,

with a little jazz still singing in our heads
as we greet the new day, Christ's day,
but not yet our own.

—1964

THE DAY BEFORE CHRISTMAS

My best Christmases
are all behind me. Grandmother
lifting the done-to-perfection bird
grease-dripping from the pan. My brother

and I Christmas morning
out of bed at six-thirty. I suppose
the house shivered to the sudden sharp
tearing of gift-wrap by excited fingers.

This Christmas Eve mid-afternoon,
too many years later, I wander downtown,
feeling worse than most drunks
set adrift from their office parties.

Birk's windows bulge and glow
with the totally inconspicuous. There's something
fairy-queer about coloured lights
hung above the stink of bus exhausts.

Every store hums, an angry honey-hive,
as if wartime and rationing were back.
I picture patient clerks behind counters
walking on what they can't believe are feet.

Skaters on the fancy rink at City Hall
seem impatient of old waltzes. They dart,
sudden bright goldfish below Revell's
scooped clam-shells blinking underwater eyes.

My heart's with the skaters, though my mood
is more with Adam Beck, bronzed sober head
splitting the traffic of the Avenue,
where on that Republic's black Consul door I see

or seem to see a holly wreath hung, through which
napalm-skinned face and dying eyes stare out
at me, this city, and core-rotted world,
to riddle us with bleeding, gaping questions.

—1967

ELIZABETH BREWSTER

(1922-   )

Elizabeth Brewster was born at Chipman, New Brunswick. Her education began in a one-room school and she later attended the University of New Brunswick (B.A., 1946), Radcliffe College (A.M., 1947), King's College, University of London (1949-1950), University of Toronto Library School (B.L.S., 1953), and Indiana University (Ph.D., 1962). She has worked as a librarian in various universities across Canada and has taught in the English Department of Victoria University, British Columbia and of the University of Alberta. She is now an Assistant Professor in the University of Saskatchewan (Saskatoon). She has published five books of poems, beginning with East Coast *(1951).* Sunrise North *(1972) is her latest volume.*

THE IDIOT

The idiot with his slobbering mouth, half shoved,
Half led by his younger brother, slowly moved
Across my childhood's April. Stammering,
He handed me the violets of the spring,
And wished to please; but fright so sped my feet,
A timid child intolerant of the strange,
I dropped the flowers and ran, out of the range
Of slobber on petals blue and delicate.

Out of his range, in the white and wooden church,
I prayed, and felt my heart still work
Like churning butter. Why should an idiot
Be to the blossom like the blossom's rot?
My bowels turned that the ugly should be human,
That a boy should be like a white, unhealthy grub
Sliming the violets, yet be flesh and blood
And born to be a man from flesh of woman.

—1969

COACH CLASS

Now the train,
Swaying towards the sunset, moves immense,
A wheezing monster. In the gathering dusk
I glimpse through fly-specked windows ragged children
Sitting on doorsteps staring with grave eyes . . .
A barking dog . . . boys playing ball, lithe-muscled . . .
And suddenly, at a crossing, a pallid face,
Gleaming up strangely among clustering moths,
And lost at once in darkness, to be vainly sought for . . .

Night settles down, and the bored travellers turn
From the empty dark to the empty brightness of novels,
Or eat ham sandwiches with listless hunger
And scatter candy wrappings on the floor.
A baby cries . . . Two sailors quarrel loudly . . .
The man in the egg-stained suit
Snores, handkerchief over eyes,
And his wife pulls his topcoat round her shoulders . . .

The train jerks to a halt, and the sleepers, dazed,
Sit up, stretch, yawn, blink drowsiness from their lashes.
Another train moves past them, and they watch
The unconscious inhabitants of this new-found planet
Sitting in dazzling light. In the reflecting faces
They see themselves as suave and seasoned travellers,
Adventurers in strange lands. They sit erect,
Casual but gallant; then they plunge on,
Feeling space sliding from beneath their world.

—1969

ELI MANDEL

(1922-   )

Eli Mandel was born in Estevan, Saskatchewan. During the war he served for several years abroad in the Army Medical Corps. He took his M.A. degree at the University of Saskatchewan and his Ph.D. at the University of Toronto. He has taught at the Collège Militaire Royal de Saint Jean and at the University of Alberta (1957-1968). He is now a Professor in the Division of Humanities at York University. His poems have been published in magazines in Canada and abroad, but his first collection was made for Trio (1954), in which Gael Turnbull and Phyllis Webb were also represented. Fuseli Poems (1960) is his first book of verse. Henry Fuseli, for whom the book was named, was a Swiss-British painter, a friend of William Blake. An Idiot Joy (1967) won a Governor-General's Award. Mandel has edited or co-edited four anthologies of poetry and Contexts of Canadian Criticism, a collection of significant essays by a variety of Canadian scholars and critics, with a valuable Introduction by Mandel. His most recent volumes of poetry are Crusoe: Poems Selected and New and Stony Plain, both published in 1973.

THE MINOTAUR POEMS

II

My father was always out in the garage
building a shining wing, a wing
that curved and flew along the edge of blue air
in that streamed and sunlit room
that smelled of oil and engines
and crankcase grease, and especially
the lemon smell of polish and cedar.
Outside there were sharp rocks, and trees,
cold air where birds fell like rocks
and screams, hawks, kites, and cranes.
The air was filled with a buzzing and flying
and the invisible hum of a bee's wings was honey
in my father's framed and engined mind.
Last Saturday we saw him at the horizon
screaming like a hawk as he fell into the sun.

CHILDREN OF THE SUN

Light falls upon them and they see the form
That gave them birth and praise it with the names
Of northern trees, the cedar and the pine and fir,
The wood within the wood to build the form
That all may praise what the eye sees and the ear
Hears amid the rock and in the weary hills
Over the sleeping land where night falls.

I think about my past and try to change
Into a singing metaphor a silent heart,
A frail red parrot perched within its cage
Repeating what it hears and cackling without change
All that ear hears and tongue speaks. I form in thought
The singing form that forms the silent heart.

But parrots bring in sleep only the surly shape
Of images of men turned into beasts
Carrying their loads of shame upon their backs,
That forest where the trees are shapes of girls
And every stone an image of a face, and eyes
Are in the flowers, and I could weep for all
Those lost and stoned and silent faces.

Such images rise up in thought as out of dreams
Rose from the sea, still hung in weeds,
To haunt poor Shelley or to torment Yeats,
Such as, oh fury of the winged and hopeful mind,
Could wear this great world and show to naught,
One, that would drive among the children of the sun
Bearing a singing sword, and in his hands,
Held for the eyes of all to see, the head
Of that great bull and all to hear his bellowing.   —*1960*

MARINA

Because she spoke often of the sea we thought she had known
    another country, her people distant, not forgotten

We did not know then who was calling her or what songs she
    listened to or why the sea-birds came to rest
    upon her long fingers.

Or why she would shudder like a sea-bird about to take flight,
    her eyes changing with the changing light

474

As the sea-changing opal changes, as a shell takes its
　　　colours from the sea as if it were the sea

As if the great sea itself were held in the palm of a hand

They say the daughters of the sea know the language of birds,
　　　that in their restless eyes the most fortunate learn
　　　how the moon rises and sets

We do not know who is calling her or why her eyes change
　　　or what shore she will set her foot upon

—1967

HOUDINI

I suspect he knew that trunks are metaphors,
could distinguish between the finest rhythms
unrolled on rope or singing in a chain
and knew the metrics of the deepest pools

I think of him listening to the words
spoken by manacles, cells, handcuffs,
chests, hampers, roll-top desks, vaults,
especially the deep words spoken by coffins

escape, escape: quaint Harry in his suit
his chains, his desk, attached to all attachments
how he'd sweat in that precise struggle
with those binding words, wrapped around him
like that mannered style, his formal suit

and spoken when? by whom? What thing first said
"there's no way out?"; so that he'd free himself,
leap, squirm, no matter how, to chain himself again,
once more jump out of the deep alive
with all his chains singing around his feet
like the bound crowds who sigh, who sigh.

—1967

THE SPEAKING EARTH

grandfathers fall into it
their mighty beards muffled in grass

and admirals, the sea-sounding men

lovers fall into the earth
like rain on wet dark bodies

475

listen, our lady earth flowers
into the sea-green language
of grass and drowned admirals

listen: in bearded branches
clasped like broken hands
admiring birds
lovers singing of their kiss
before and after all the words

—*1967*

MILTON ACORN

(1923-   )

Milton Acorn was born in Charlottetown, Prince Edward Island, and attended public and secondary schools there. He served in the Canadian Army from 1939 to 1945. He has lived in various cities across Canada. Trained as a carpenter, he decided one day in Montreal to sell all his tools and be a writer. When he was living in Vancouver, he helped to found the Georgia Straight. *He now makes his home in Toronto.*

He published his first book of poems in 1956, but it was his fifth book, I've Tasted My Blood *(1969), that established his reputation. This was a selection made by Al Purdy from Acorn's earlier volumes.* More Poems for People *appeared in 1972.*

I'VE TASTED MY BLOOD

If this brain's over-tempered
consider that the fire was want
and the hammers were fists.
I've tasted my blood too much
to love what I was born to.

But my mother's look
was a field of brown oats, soft-bearded;
her voice rain and air rich with lilacs:
and I loved her too much to like
how she dragged her days like a sled over gravel.

Playmates? I remember where their skulls roll!
One died hungry, gnawing grey perch-planks;
one fell, and landed so hard he splashed;
and many and many
come up atom by atom
in the worm-casts of Europe.

My deep prayer a curse.
My deep prayer the promise that this won't be.
My deep prayer my cunning,
my love, my anger,
and often even my forgiveness
that this won't be and be.
I've tasted my blood too much
to abide what I was born to.

—1963

DETAIL OF A CITYSCAPE

Have you noticed
how the cripple
struggles
onto the bus?

From where I sit
a hand,
white-knuckled
on the rail
io all I oee;

and then the parts,
a head, an aimless
cane flopping,
hooked to a wrist,
levering elbows,
the poor twist
of a torso,
finally those disobedient
feet.

Once on, he lurches
onto the unrailed bench
next to the driver
. . . the most uncomfortable seat;

because if he tried for another
the surge of the bus starting
would upend him.

—1969

As the orange-
striped cat
hunches,
glaring down,

the pale-fluffed
nestlings
he's discovered
feel cooled
in the shadow,

and

stretch their thin
necks, heavy
heads up,
hungry
beaks open,

wide
on hinges.

—1969

MARGARET LAURENCE

(1926-   )

Jean Margaret Wemyss was born in Neepawa, Manitoba. Being a member of a family of storytellers, she "began to fictionalize early." She graduated from the University of Manitoba (United College) in 1947. Her marriage to John Ferguson Laurence took her to Africa in the course of her husband's duties as a civil engineer.

Mrs. Laurence lived in Somaliland from 1950 to 1952 and collected folk tales. From 1952 until 1957 she was in Ghana. Her first novel, This Side Jordan *(1960), and her book of short stories,* The Tomorrow-Tamer *(1963), have settings in Ghana. The Prophet's Camel Bell (1963) refers to her experiences in Somaliland.*

From 1957-1962 she lived in Vancouver, and for ten years thereafter her residence was in England, although during the first five years (1962-1967) she travelled in Greece, Crete, Palestine, India, Egypt, and Spain. Mrs. Laurence was Writer-in-Residence at the University of Toronto in the academic year 1969-1970, and for 1973-1974 has been appointed to similar positions at Western Ontario and at Trent. Her home is now near Peterborough, Ontario. She won the Governor-General's Award in 1967, has received honorary degrees from four universities, and in 1972 was made a Companion of the Order of Canada.

"Manawaka," in Manitoba, is the setting of her most famous novel, The Stone Angel *(1964), which presents a remarkable character-study of an old woman named Hagar. A* Jest of God *(1966)—which was filmed as* Rachel, Rachel *in 1968—is related to* The Stone Angel *by also being set in Manawaka; the narrator and chief character is Rachel, a schoolteacher.* The Fire-Dwellers *(1969), about Rachel's sister Stacey, is set in Vancouver. The Vanessa MacLeod short stories, published in various magazines and collected in* A Bird in the House *(1970), are again set in Manawaka. Another novel,* The Diviners, *is to be published in 1974.*

THE MASK OF THE BEAR

In winter my Grandfather Connor used to wear an enormous coat made out of the pelt of a bear. So shaggy and coarse-furred was this coat, so unevenly coloured in patches ranging from amber to near-black, and so vile-smelling when it had become wet with snow, that it seemed to have belonged when it was alive to some lonely and giant kodiak crankily roaming a high frozen plateau, or an ancient grizzly scarred with battles in the sinister forests of the north. In actuality, it had been an ordinary brown bear and it had come, sad to say, from no more fabled a place than Galloping Mountain, only a hundred miles from Manawaka. The skin had once been given to my grandfather as payment, in the days when he was a blacksmith, before he became a hardware merchant and developed the policy of cash only. He had had it cobbled into a coat by the local shoemaker, and Grandmother Connor had managed to sew in the lining. How long ago that was, no one could say for sure, but my mother, the eldest of his family, said she could not remember a time when he had not worn it. To me, at the age of ten and a half, this meant it must be about a century old. The coat was so heavy that I could not even lift it by myself. I never used to wonder how he could carry that phenomenal weight on himself, or why he would choose to, because it was obvious that although he was old he was still an extraordinarily strong man, built to shoulder weights.

Whenever I went into Simlow's Ladies' Wear with my mother, and made grotesque faces at myself in the long mirror while she tried on dresses, Millie Christopherson who worked there would croon a phrase which made me break into snickering until my mother, who was death on bad manners, tapped anxiously at my shoulders with her slender, nervous hands. *It's you, Mrs. MacLeod,* Millie would say feelingly, *no kidding it's absolutely you.* I appropriated the phrase for my grandfather's winter coat. *It's you,* I would simper nastily at him, although never, of course, aloud.

In my head I sometimes called him "The Great Bear." The name had many associations other than his coat and his surliness. It was the way he would stalk around the Brick House as though it were a cage, on Sundays, impatient for the new week's beginning that would release him into the only freedom he knew, the acts of work. It was the way he would take to the basement whenever a man came to call upon Aunt Edna, which in those days was not often, because—as I had overheard my mother outlining in sighs to my father— most of the single men her age in Manawaka considered that the time she had spent working in Winnipeg had made more difference than it really had, and the situation wasn't helped by her flyaway manner (whatever that might mean). But if ever she was asked out to a movie, and the man was waiting and making stilted weather-chat with Grandmother Connor, Grandfather would prowl through the living room as though seeking a place of rest and not finding it, would stare fixedly without speaking, and would then descend the basement steps to the rocking chair which sat beside the furnace. Above ground, he would not have been found dead sitting in a rocking chair, which he considered a piece of furniture suitable only for the elderly, of whom he was never in his own eyes one. From his cave, however, the angry crunching of the wooden rockers against the cement floor would reverberate throughout the house, a kind of sub-verbal Esperanto, a disapproval which even the most obtuse person could not fail to comprehend.

In some unformulated way, I also associated the secret name with Great Bear Lake, which I had seen only on maps and which I imagined to be a deep vastness of black water, lying somewhere very far beyond our known prairies of tamed fields and barbed-wire fences, somewhere in the regions of jagged rock and eternal ice, where human voices would be drawn into a cold and shadowed stillness without leaving even a trace of warmth.

One Saturday afternoon in January, I was at the rink when my grandfather appeared unexpectedly. He was wearing his formidable coat, and to say he looked out of place among the skaters thronging around the edges of the ice would be putting it mildly. Embarrassed, I whizzed over to him.

"There you are, Vanessa—about time," he said, as though he had been searching for me for hours. "Get your skates off now, and come along. You're to come home with me for supper. You'll be staying the night at our place. Your dad's gone away out to Freehold, and your mother's gone with him. Fine time to pick for it. It's blowing up for a blizzard, if you ask me. They'll not get back for a couple of days, more than likely. Don't see why he don't just tell people to make their own way in to the hospital. Ewen's too easy-going. He'll not get a penny nor a word of thanks for it, you can bet your life on that."

My father and Dr. Cates used to take the country calls in turn. Often when my father went out in the winter, my mother would go with him, in case the old Nash got stuck in the snow and also to talk and thus prevent my father from going to sleep at the wheel, for falling snow has a hypnotic effect.

"What about Roddie?" I asked, for my brother was only a few months old.

"The old lady's keeping care of him," Grandfather Connor replied abruptly.

The old lady meant my Grandmother MacLeod, who was actually a few years younger than Grandfather Connor. He always referred to her in this way, however, as a calculated insult, and here my sympathies were with him for once. He maintained, quite correctly, that she gave herself airs because her husband had been a doctor and now her son was one, and that she looked down on the Connors because they had come from famine Irish (although at least, thank God, Protestant). The two of them seldom met, except at Christmas, and never exchanged more than a few words. If they had ever really clashed, it would have been like a brontosaurus running headlong into a tyrannosaurus.

"Hurry along now," he said, when I had taken off my skates and put on my snow boots. "You've got to learn not to dawdle. You're an awful dawdler, Vanessa."

I did not reply. Instead, when we left the rink I began to take exaggeratedly long strides. But he paid no attention to my attempt to reproach him with my speed. He walked beside me steadily and silently, wrapped in his great fur coat and his authority.

The Brick House was at the other end of town, so while I shuffled through the snow and pulled my navy wool scarf up around my nose against the steel cutting edge of the wind, I thought about the story I was setting down in a five-cent scribbler at nights in my room. I was much occupied by the themes of love and death, although my experience of both had so far been gained principally from the Bible, which I read in the same way as I read Eaton's Catalogue or the collected works of Rudyard Kipling—because I had to read something, and the family's finances in the thirties did not permit the purchase of enough volumes of *Doctor Doolittle* or the *Oz* books to keep me going.

For the love scenes, I gained useful material from The Song of Solomon. *Let him kiss me with the kisses of his mouth, for thy love is better than wine*, or *By night on my bed I sought him whom my soul loveth; I sought him but I found him not*. My interpretation was somewhat vague, and I was not helped to any appreciable extent by the explanatory bits in small print at the beginning of each chapter—*The church's love unto Christ. The church's fight and victory in temptation*, et cetera. These explanations did not puzzle me, though, for I assumed even then that they had simply been put there for the benefit of gentle and unworldly people such as my Grandmother Connor, so that they could read the Holy Writ without becoming upset. To me, the woman in The Song was some barbaric queen, beautiful and terrible, and I could imagine her, wearing a long robe of leopard skin and one or two heavy gold bracelets, pacing an alabaster courtyard and keening her unrequited love.

The heroine in my story (which took place in ancient Egypt—my ignorance of this era did not trouble me) was very like the woman in The Song of Solomon, except that mine had long wavy auburn hair, and when her beloved left her, the only thing she could bring herself to eat was an avocado, which seemed to me considerably more stylish and exotic than apples in lieu of love. Her young man was a gifted carver, who had been sent out into the desert by the cruel pharaoh (pharaohs were always cruel — of this I was positive) in order to carve a giant sphinx for the royal tomb. Should I have her die while he was away? Or would it be better if he perished out in the desert? Which of them did I like the least? With the characters whom I liked best, things always turned out right in the end. Yet the death scenes had an undeniable appeal, a sombre splendour, with (as it said in Ecclesiastes) the mourners going about the streets and all the daughters of music brought low. Both death and love seemed regrettably far from Manawaka and the snow, and my grandfather stamping his feet on the front porch of the Brick House and telling me to do the same or I'd be tracking the wet in all over the hardwood floor.

The house was too warm, almost stifling. Grandfather burned mainly birch in the furnace, although it cost twice as much as poplar, and now that he had retired from the hardware store, the furnace gave him something to do and so he was forever stoking it. Grandmother Connor was in the dining room, her stout body in its brown rayon dress bending over the canary's cage.

"Hello, pet," she greeted me. "You should have heard Birdie just a minute ago —one of those real long trills. He's been moulting lately, and this is the first time he's sung in weeks."

"Gee," I said enthusiastically, for although I was not fond of canaries, I was extremely fond of my grandmother. "That's swell. Maybe he'll do it again."

"Messy things, them birds," my grandfather commented. "I can never see what you see in a fool thing like that, Agnes."

My grandmother did not attempt to reply to this.

"Would you like a cup of tea, Timothy?" she asked.

"Nearly supper-time, ain't it?"

"Well, not for a little while yet."

"It's away past five," my grandfather said. "What's Edna been doing with herself?"

"She's got the pot-roast in," my grandmother answered, "but it's not done yet."

"You'd think a person could get a meal on time," he said, "considering she's got

481

precious little else to do."

I felt, as so often in the Brick House, that my lungs were in danger of exploding, that the pressure of silence would become too great to be borne. I wanted to point out, as I knew Grandmother Connor would never do, that it wasn't Aunt Edna's fault there were no jobs anywhere these days, and that, as my mother often said of her, she worked her fingers to the bone here so she wouldn't need to feel beholden to him for her keep, and that they would have had to get a hired girl if she hadn't been here, because Grandmother Connor couldn't look after a place this size any more. Also, that the dining-room clock said precisely ten minutes past five, and the evening meal in the Connor house was always at six o'clock on the dot. And—and—a thousand other arguments rose up and nearly choked me. But I did not say anything. I was not that stupid. Instead, I went out to the kitchen.

Aunt Edna was wearing her coral sweater and grey pleated skirt, and I thought she looked lovely, even with her apron on. I always thought she looked lovely, though, whatever she was wearing, but if ever I told her so, she would only laugh and say it was lucky she had a cheering section of one.

"Hello, kiddo," she said. "Do you want to sleep in my room tonight, or shall I make up the bed in the spare room?"

"In your room," I said quickly, for this meant she would let me try out her lipstick and use some of her Jergens hand-lotion, and if I could stay awake until she came to bed, we would whisper after the light was out.

"How's *The Pillars of the Nation* coming along?" she asked.

That had been my epic on pioneer life. I had proceeded to the point in the story where the husband, coming back to the cabin one evening, discovered to his surprise that he was going to become a father. The way he ascertained this interesting fact was that he found his wife constructing a birch-bark cradle. Then came the discovery that Grandfather Connor had been a pioneer, and the story had lost its interest for me. If pioneers were like *that*, I had thought, my pen would be better employed elsewhere.

"I quit that one," I replied laconically. "I'm making up another—it's miles better. It's called *The Silver Sphinx*. I'll bet you can't guess what it's about."

"The desert? Buried treasure? Murder mystery?"

I shook my head.

"Love," I said.

"Good Glory," Aunt Edna said, straight-faced. "That sounds fascinating. Where do you get your ideas, Vanessa?"

I could not bring myself to say the Bible. I was afraid she might think this sounded funny.

"Oh, here and there," I replied noncommittally. "You know."

She gave me an inquisitive glance, as though she meant to question me further, but just then the telephone rang, and I rushed to answer it, thinking it might be my mother or father phoning from Freehold. But it wasn't. It was a voice I didn't know, a man's.

"Is Edna Connor there?"

"Just a minute, please," I cupped one hand over the mouthpiece fixed on the wall, and the other over the receiver.

"For you," I hissed, grinning at her. "A strange man!"

"Mercy," Aunt Edna said ironically, "these hordes of admirers will be the death of me yet. Probably Todd Jeffries from Burns' Electric about that busted lamp."

Nevertheless, she hurried over. Then, as she listened, her face became startled, and something else which I could not fathom.

"Heavens, where are you?" she cried at last. "At the station *here*? Oh Lord. Why didn't you write to say you were—well, sure I am, but—oh, never mind. No, you wait there. I'll come and meet you. You'd never find the house—"

I had never heard her talk this way before, rattlingly. Finally she hung up. Her face looked like a stranger's, and for some reason this hurt me.

"It's Jimmy Lorimer," she said. "He's at the C.P.R. station. He's coming here. Oh my God, I wish Beth were here."

"Why?" I wished my mother were here, too, but I could not see what difference it made to Aunt Edna. I knew who Jimmy Lorimer was. He was a man Aunt Edna had gone around with when she was in Winnipeg. He had given her the Attar of Roses in an atomiser bottle with a green net-covered bulb—the scent she always sprayed around her room after she had had a cigarette there. Jimmy Lorimer had been invested with a remote glamour in my imagination, but all at once I felt I was going to hate him.

I realised that Aunt Edna was referring to what Grandfather Connor might do or say, and instantly I was ashamed for having felt churlishly disposed towards Jimmy Lorimer. Even if he was a cad, a heel, or a nitwit, I swore I would welcome him. I visualised him as having a flashy appearance, like a riverboat gambler in a movie I had seen once, a checkered suit, a slender oiled moustache, a diamond tie-pin, a dangerous leer. Never mind. Never mind if he was Lucifer himself.

"I'm glad he's coming," I said staunchly.

Aunt Edna looked at me queerly, her mouth wavering as though she were about to smile. Then, quickly, she bent and hugged me, and I could feel her trembling. At this moment, Grandmother Connor came into the kitchen.

"You all right, pet?" she asked Aunt Edna. "Nothing's the matter, is it?"

"Mother, that was an old friend of mine on the phone just now. Jimmy Lorimer. He's from Winnipeg. He's passing through Manawaka. Is it all right if he comes here for dinner?"

"Well, of course, dear," Grandmother said. "What a lucky thing we're having the pot-roast. There's plenty. Vanessa, pet, you run down to the fruit cellar and bring up a jar of strawberries, will you? Oh, and a small jar of chili sauce. No, maybe the sweet mustard pickle would go better with the pot-roast. What do you think, Edna?"

She spoke as though this were the only important issue in the whole situation. But all the time her eyes were on Aunt Edna's face.

"Edna—" she said, with great effort, "is he—is he a good man, Edna?"

Aunt Edna blinked and looked confused, as though she had been spoken to in some foreign language.

"Yes," she replied.

"You're sure, pet?"

"Yes," Aunt Edna repeated, a little more emphatically than before.

Grandmother Connor nodded, smiled reassuringly, and patted Aunt Edna lightly on the wrist.

"Well, that's fine, dear. I'll just tell Father. Everything will be all right, so don't you worry about a thing."

When Grandmother had gone back to the living room, Aunt Edna began pulling on her black fur-topped overshoes. When she spoke, I didn't know whether it was to me or not.

"I didn't tell her a damn thing," she said in a surprised tone. "I wonder how she knows, or if she really does? *Good.* What a word. I wish I didn't know what she means when she says that. Or else that she knew what I mean when I say it. Glory, I wish Beth were here."

I understood then that she was not speaking to me, and that what she had to say could not be spoken to me. I felt chilled by my childhood, unable to touch her because of the freezing burden of my inexperience. I was about to say something, anything, however mistaken, when my aunt said *Sh*, and we both listened to the talk from the living room.

"A friend of Edna's is coming for dinner, Timothy," Grandmother was saying quietly. "A young man from Winnipeg."

A silence. Then, "Winnipeg!" my grandfather exclaimed, making it sound as though Jimmy Lorimer were coming here straight from his harem in Casablanca.

"What's he do?" Grandfather demanded next.

"Edna didn't say."

"I'm not surprised," Grandfather said darkly. "Well, I won't have her running around with that sort of fellow. She's got no more sense than a sparrow."

"She's twenty-eight," Grandmother said, almost apologetically. "Anyway, this is just a friend."

"Friend!" my grandfather said, annihilating the word. Then, not loudly, but with an odd vehemence, "You don't know a blame thing about men, Agnes. You never have."

Even I could think of several well-placed replies that my grandmother might have made, but she did not do so. She did not say anything. I looked at Aunt Edna, and saw that she had closed her eyes the way people do when they have a headache. Then we heard Grandmother's voice, speaking at last, not in her usual placid and unruffled way, but hesitantly.

"Timothy—please. Be nice to him. For my sake."

For my sake. This was so unlike my grandmother that I was stunned. She was not a person who begged you to be kind for her sake, or even for God's sake. If you were kind, in my grandmother's view, it was for its own sake, and the judgement of whether you had done well or not was up to the Almighty. *Judge not, that ye be not judged*—this was her favourite admonition to me when I lost my temper with one of my friends. As a devout Baptist, she believed it was a sin to pray for anything for yourself. You ought to pray only for strength to bear whatever the Lord saw fit to send you, she thought. I was never able to follow this advice, for although I would often feel a sense of uneasiness over the tone of my prayers, I was the kind of person who prayed frantically—"Please, God, please, please *please* let Ross MacVey like me better than Mavis." Grandmother Connor was not self-effacing in her lack of demands either upon God or upon her family. She merely believed that what happened to a person in this life was in Other Hands. Acceptance was at the heart of her. I don't think in her own eyes she ever lived in a state of bondage. To the rest of the family, thrashing furiously and uselessly in various snarled dilemmas, she must often have appeared to live in a state of perpetual grace, but I am certain she didn't think of it that way, either.

Grandfather Connor did not seem to have heard her.

"We won't get our dinner until all hours, I daresay," he said.

But we got our dinner as soon as Aunt Edna had arrived back with Jimmy Lorimer, for she flew immediately out to the kitchen and before we knew it we were all sitting at the big circular table in the dining room.

Jimmy Lorimer was not at all what I had expected. Far from looking like a Mississippi gambler, he looked just like anybody else, any uncle or grown-up cousin, unexceptional in every way. He was neither overwhelmingly handsome nor interestingly ugly. He was okay to look at, but as I said to myself, feeling at the same time a twinge of betrayal towards Aunt Edna, he was nothing to write home about. He wore a brown suit and a green tie. The only thing about him which struck fire was that he had a joking manner similar to Aunt Edna's, but whereas I felt at ease with this quality in her, I could never feel comfortable with the laughter of strangers, being uncertain where an including laughter stopped and taunting began.

"You're from Winnipeg, eh?" Grandfather Connor began. "Well, I guess you fellows don't put much store in a town like Manawaka."

Without waiting for affirmation or denial of this sentiment, he continued in an unbroken line.

"I got no patience with these people who think a small town is just nothing. You take a city, now. You could live in one of them places for twenty years, and you'd not get to know your next-door neighbour. Trouble comes along—who's going to give you a hand? Not a blamed soul."

Grandfather Connor had never in his life lived in a city, so his first-hand knowledge of their ways was, to say the least, limited. As for trouble—the thought of my grandfather asking any soul in Manawaka to give aid and support to him in any way whatsoever was inconceivable. He would have died of starvation, physical or spiritual, rather than put himself in any man's debt by so much as a dime or a word.

"Hey, hold on a minute," Jimmy Lorimer protested. "I never said that about small towns. As a matter of fact, I grew up in one myself. I came from McConnell's Landing. Ever heard of it?"

"I heard of it all right," Grandfather said brusquely, and no one could have told from his tone whether McConnell's Landing was a place of ill-repute or whether he simply felt his knowledge of geography was being doubted. "Why'd you leave, then?"

Jimmy shrugged. "Not much opportunity there. Had to seek my fortune, you know. Can't say I've found it, but I'm still looking."

"Oh, you'll be a tycoon yet, no doubt," Aunt Edna put in.

"You bet your life, kiddo," Jimmy replied. "You wait. Times'll change."

I didn't like to hear him say "kiddo." It was Aunt Edna's word, the one she called me by. It didn't belong to him.

"Mercy, they can't change fast enough for me," Aunt Edna said. "I guess I haven't got your optimism, though."

"Well, I haven't got it, either," he said, laughing, "but keep it under your hat, eh?"

Grandfather Connor had listened to this exchange with some impatience. Now he turned to Jimmy once more.

"What's your line of work?"

"I'm with Reliable Loan Company right now, Mr. Connor, but I don't aim to stay there permanently. I'd like to have my own business. Cars are what I'm really interested in. But it's not so easy to start up these days."

Grandfather Connor's normal opinions on social issues possessed such a high degree of clarity and were so frequently stated that they were well known even to me—all labour unions were composed of thugs and crooks; if people were unemployed it was due to their own laziness; if people were broke it was because they were not thrifty. Now, however, a look of intense and brooding sorrow came into his face, as he became all at once the champion of the poor and oppressed.

"Loan company!" he said. "Them blood-suckers. They wouldn't pay no mind to how hard-up a man might be. Take everything he has, without batting an eye. By the Lord Harry, I never thought the day would come when I'd sit down to a meal alongside one of them fellows."

Aunt Edna's face was rigid.

"Jimmy," she said. "Ignore him."

Grandfather turned on her, and they stared at one another with a kind of inexpressible rage but neither of them spoke. I could not help feeling sorry for Jimmy Lorimer, who mumbled something about his train leaving and began eating hurriedly. Grandfather rose to his feet.

"I've had enough," he said.

"Don't you want your dessert, Timothy?" Grandmother asked, as though it never occurred to her that he could be referring to anything other than the meal. It was only then that I realised that this was the first time she had spoken since we sat down at the table. Grandfather did not reply. He went down to the basement. Predictably, in a moment we could hear the wooden rockers of his chair thudding like retreating thunder. After dinner, Grandmother sat in the living room, but she did not get out the red cardigan she was knitting for me. She sat without doing anything, quite still, her hands folded in her lap.

"I'll let you off the dishes tonight, honey," Aunt Edna said to me. "Jimmy will help with them. You can try out my lipstick, if you like, only for Pete's sake wash it off before you come down again."

I went upstairs, but I did not go to Aunt Edna's room. I went into the back bedroom to one of my listening posts. In the floor there was a round hole which had once been used for a stove-pipe leading up from the kitchen. Now it was covered with a piece of brown-painted tin full of small perforations which had apparently been noticed only by me.

"Where does he get his lines, Edna?" Jimmy was saying. "He's like old-time melodrama."

"Yeh, I know." Aunt Edna sounded annoyed. "But let me say it, eh?"

"Sorry. Honest. Listen, can't you even—"

Scuffling sounds, then my aunt's nervous whisper.

"Not here, Jimmy. Please. You don't understand what they're—"

"I understand, all right. Why in God's name do you stay, Edna? Aren't you ever coming back? That's what I want to know."

"With no job? Don't make me laugh."

"I could help out, at first anyway—"

"Jimmy, don't talk like a lunatic. Do you really think I could?"

"Oh hell, I suppose not. Well, look at it this way. What if I wasn't cut out for the unattached life after all? What if the old leopard actually changed his spots, kiddo? What would you say to that?"

A pause, as though Aunt Edna were mulling over his words.

"That'll be the day," she replied. "I'll believe it when I see it."

"Well, Jesus, lady," he said, "I'm not getting down on my knees. Tell me one thing, though—don't you miss me at all? Don't you miss—everything? C'mon now—don't you? Not even a little bit?"

Another pause. She could not seem to make up her mind how to respond to the teasing quality of his voice.

"Yeh, I lie awake nights," she said at last, sarcastically.

He laughed. "Same old Edna. Want me to tell you something, kiddo? I think you're scared."

"Scared?" she said scornfully. "Me? That'll be the fair and frosty Friday."

Although I spent so much of my life listening to conversations which I was not meant to overhear, all at once I felt, for the first time, sickened by what I was doing. I left my listening post and tiptoed into Aunt Edna's room. I wondered if someday I would be the one who was doing the talking, while another child would be doing the listening. This gave me an unpleasantly eerie feeling. I tried on Aunt Edna's lipstick and rouge, but my heart was not in it.

When I went downstairs again, Jimmy Lorimer was just leaving. Aunt Edna went to her room and closed the door. After a while she came out and asked me if I would mind sleeping in the spare bedroom that night after all, so that was what I did.

I woke in the middle of the night. When I sat up, feeling strange because I was not in my own bed at home, I saw through the window a glancing light on the snow. I got up and peered out, and there were the northern lights whirling across the top of the sky like lightning that never descended to earth. The yard of the Brick House looked huge, a white desert, and the pale gashing streaks of light pointed up the caverns and the hollowed places where the wind had sculptured the snow.

I could not stand being alone another second, so I walked in my bare feet along the hall. From Grandfather's room came the sound of grumbling snores, and from Grandmother's room no sound at all. I stopped beside the door of Aunt Edna's room. It seemed to me that she would not mind if I entered quietly, so as not to disturb her, and crawled in beside her. Maybe she would even waken and say, "It's okay, kiddo—your dad phoned after you'd gone to sleep—they got back from Freehold all right."

Then I heard her voice, and the held-in way she was crying, and the name she spoke, as though it hurt her to speak it even in a whisper.

Like some terrified poltergeist, I flitted back to the spare room and whipped into bed. I wanted only to forget that I had heard anything, but I knew I would not forget. There arose in my mind, mysteriously, the picture of a barbaric queen, someone who had lived a long time ago. I could not reconcile this image with the known face, nor could I disconnect it. I thought of my aunt, her sturdy laughter, the way she tore into the housework, her hands and feet which she always disparagingly joked about, believing them to be clumsy. I thought of the story in the scribbler at home. I wanted to get home quickly, so I could destroy it.

Whenever Grandmother Connor was ill, she would not see any doctor except my father. She did not believe in surgery, for she thought it was tampering with the Divine Intention, and she was always afraid that Dr. Cates would operate on her without her consent. She trusted my father implicitly, and when he went into the room where she lay propped up on pillows, she would say, "Here's Ewen—now everything will be fine," which both touched and alarmed my father, who said he hoped she wasn't putting her faith in a broken reed.

Late that winter, she became ill again. She did not go into hospital, so my mother, who had been a nurse, moved down to the Brick House to look after her. My brother and I were left in the adamant care of Grandmother MacLeod. Without my mother, our house seemed like a museum, full of dead and meaningless objects, vases and gilt-framed pictures and looming furniture, all of which had to be dusted and catered to, for reasons which everyone had forgotten. I was not allowed to see Grandmother Connor, but every day after school I went to the Brick House to see my mother. I always asked impatiently, "When is Grandmother going to be better?" and my mother would reply, "I don't know, dear. Soon, I hope." But she did not sound very certain, and I imagined the leaden weeks going by like this, with her away, and Grandmother MacLeod poking her head into my bedroom doorway each morning and telling me to be sure to make my bed because a slovenly room meant a slovenly heart.

But the weeks did not go by like this. One afternoon when I arrived at the Brick House, Grandfather Connor was standing out on the front porch. I was startled, because he was not wearing his great bear coat. He wore no coat at all, only his dingy serge suit, although the day was fifteen below zero. The blown snow had sifted onto the porch and lay in thin drifts. He stood there by himself, his yellowish-white hair plumed by a wind which he seemed not to notice, his bony and still-handsome face not averted at all from the winter. He looked at me as I plodded up the path and the front steps.

"Vanessa, your grandmother's dead," he said.

Then, as I gazed at him, unable to take in the significance of what he had said, he did a horrifying thing. He gathered me into the relentless grip of his arms. He bent low over me, and sobbed against the cold skin of my face.

I wanted only to get away, to get as far away as possible and never come back. I wanted desperately to see my mother, yet I felt I could not enter the house, not ever again. Then my mother opened the front door and stood there in the doorway, her slight body shivering. Grandfather released me, straightened, became again the carved face I had seen when I approached the house.

"Father," my mother said. "Come into the house. Please."

"In a while, Beth," he replied tonelessly. "Never you mind."

My mother held out her hands to me, and I ran to her. She closed the door and led me into the living room. We both cried, and yet I think I cried mainly because she did, and because I had been shocked by my grandfather. I still could not believe that anyone I cared about could really die.

Aunt Edna came in to the living room. She hesitated, looking at my mother and me. Then she turned and went back to the kitchen, stumblingly. My mother's hands made hovering movements and she half rose from the chesterfield, then she held me closely again.

"It's worse for Edna," she said. "I've got you and Roddie, and your dad."

I did not fully realise yet that Grandmother Connor would never move around this house again, preserving its uncertain peace somehow. Yet all at once I knew how it would be for Aunt Edna, without her, alone in the Brick House with Grandfather Connor. I had not known at all that a death would be like this, not only one's own pain, but the almost unbearable knowledge of that other pain which could not be reached nor lessened.

My mother and I went out to the kitchen, and the three of us sat around the oilcloth-covered table, scarcely talking but needing one another at least to be there. We heard the front door open, and Grandfather Connor came back into the house. He did not come out to the kitchen, though. He went, as though instinctively, to his old cavern. We heard him walking heavily down the basement steps.

"Edna—should we ask him if he wants to come and have some tea?" my mother said. "I hate to see him going like that—there—"

Aunt Edna's face hardened.

"I don't want to see him, Beth," she replied, forcing the words out. "I can't. Not yet. All I'd be able to think of is how he was—with her."

"Oh honey, I know," my mother said. "But you mustn't let yourself dwell on that now."

"The night Jimmy was here," my aunt said distinctly, "she asked Father to be nice, for her sake. For her sake, Beth. For the sake of all the years, if they'd meant anything at all. But he couldn't even do that. Not even that."

Then she put her head down on the table and cried in a way I had never heard any person cry before, as though there were no end to it anywhere.

I was not allowed to attend Grandmother Connor's funeral, and for this I was profoundly grateful, for I had dreaded going. The day of the funeral, I stayed alone in the Brick House, waiting for the family to return. My Uncle Terence, who lived in Toronto, was the only one who had come from a distance. Uncle Will lived in Florida, and Aunt Florence was in England, both too far away. Aunt Edna and my mother were always criticising Uncle Terence and also making excuses for him. He drank more than was good for him—this was one of the numerous fractured bones in the family skeleton which I was not supposed to know about. I was fond of him for the same reason I was fond of Grandfather's horse-trader brother, my Great-Uncle Dan—because he had gaiety and was publicly reckoned to be no good.

I sat in the dining room beside the gilt-boned cage that housed the canary. Yesterday, Aunt Edna, cleaning here, had said, "What on earth are we going to do with the canary? Maybe we can find somebody who would like it."

Grandfather Connor had immediately lit into her. "Edna, your mother liked that bird, so it's staying, do you hear?"

When my mother and Aunt Edna went upstairs to have a cigarette, Aunt Edna had said, "Well, it's dandy that he's so set on the bird now, isn't it? He might have considered that a few years earlier, if you ask me."

"Try to be patient with him," my mother had said. "He's feeling it, too."

"I guess so," Aunt Edna had said in a discouraged voice. "I haven't got Mother's patience, that's all. Not with him, nor with any man."

And I had been reminded then of the item I had seen not long before in the Winnipeg *Free Press*, on the social page, telling of the marriage of James Reilly Lorimer to Somebody-or-other. I had rushed to my mother with the paper in my hand, and she had said, "I know, Vanessa. She knows, too. So let's not bring it up, eh?"

The canary, as usual, was not in a vocal mood, and I sat beside the cage dully, not caring, not even trying to prod the creature into song. I wondered if Grandmother Connor was at this very moment in heaven, that dubious place.

"She believed, Edna," my mother had said defensively. "What right have we to say it isn't so?"

"Oh, I know," Aunt Edna had replied. "But can you take it in, really, Beth?"

"No, not really. But you feel, with someone like her—it would be so awful if it didn't happen, after she'd thought like that for so long."

"She wouldn't know," Aunt Edna had pointed out.

"I guess that's what I can't accept," my mother had said slowly. "I still feel she must be somewhere."

I wanted now to hold my own funeral service for my grandmother, in the presence only of the canary. I went to the bookcase where she kept her Bible, and looked up Ecclesiastes. I intended to read the part about the mourners going about the streets, and the silver cord loosed and the golden bowl broken, and the dust returning to the earth as it was and the spirit unto God who gave it. But I got stuck on the first few lines, because it seemed to me, frighteningly, that they were being spoken in my grandmother's mild voice — *Remember now thy Creator in the days of thy youth, while the evil days come not—*

Then, with a burst of opening doors, the family had returned from the funeral. While they were taking off their coats, I slammed the Bible shut and sneaked it back into the bookcase without anyone's having noticed.

Grandfather Connor walked over to me and placed his hands on my shoulders, and I could do nothing except endure his touch.

"Vanessa—" he said gruffly, and I had at the time no idea how much it cost him to speak at all, "she was an angel. You remember that."

Then he went down to the basement by himself. No one attempted to follow him, or to ask him to come and join the rest of us. Even I, in the confusion of my lack of years, realised that this would have been an impossibility. He was, in some way, untouchable. Whatever his grief was, he did not want us to look at it and we did not want to look at it, either.

Uncle Terence went straight into the kitchen, brought out his pocket flask, and poured a hefty slug of whiskey for himself. He did the same for my mother and father and Aunt Edna.

"Oh Glory," Aunt Edna said with a sigh, "do I ever need this. All the same, I feel we shouldn't, right immediately afterwards. You know—considering how she always felt about it. Supposing Father comes up—"

"It's about time you quit thinking that way, Edna," Uncle Terence said.

Aunt Edna felt in her purse for a cigarette. Uncle Terence reached over and lit it for her. Her hands were unsteady.

"You're telling me," she said.

Uncle Terence gave me a quizzical and yet resigned look, and I knew then that my presence was placing a constraint upon them. When my father said he had to go back to the hospital, I used his departure to slip upstairs to my old post, the deserted stove-pipe hole. I could no longer eavesdrop with a clear conscience, but I justified it now by the fact that I had voluntarily removed myself from the kitchen, knowing they would not have told me to run along, not today.

"An angel," Aunt Edna said bitterly. "Did you hear what he said to Vanessa? It's a pity he never said as much to Mother once or twice, isn't it?"

"She knew how much he thought of her," my mother said.

"Did she?" Aunt Edna said. "I don't believe she ever knew he cared about her at all. I don't think I knew it myself, until I saw how her death hit him."

"That's an awful thing to say!" my mother cried. "Of course she knew, Edna."

"How would she know," Aunt Edna persisted, "if he never let on?"

"How do you know he didn't?" my mother countered. "When they were by themselves."

"I don't know, of course," Aunt Edna said. "But I have my damn shrewd suspicions."

"Did you ever know, Beth," Uncle Terence enquired, pouring himself another drink, "that she almost left him once? That was before you were born, Edna."

"No," my mother said incredulously. "Surely not."

"Yeh. Aunt Mattie told me. Apparently Father carried on for a while with some girl in Winnipeg, and Mother found out about it. She never told him she'd considered leaving him. She only told God and Aunt Mattie. The three of them thrashed it out together, I suppose. Too bad she never told him. It would've been a relief to him, no doubt, to see she wasn't all calm forgiveness."

"How could he?" my mother said in a low voice. "Oh Terence. How could he have done that? To Mother, of all people."

"You know something, Beth?" Uncle Terence said. "I think he honestly believed that about her being some kind of angel. She'd never have thought of herself like that, so I don't suppose it ever would have occurred to her that he did. But I have a notion that he felt all along she was far and away too good for him. Can you feature going to bed with an angel, honey? It doesn't bear thinking about."

"Terence, you're drunk," my mother said sharply. "As usual."

"Maybe so," he admitted. Then he burst out, "I only felt, Beth, that somebody might have said to Vanessa just now, *Look, baby, she was terrific and we thought the world of her, but let's not say angel, eh?* All this angel business gets us into really deep water, you know that?"

"I don't see how you can talk like that, Terence," my mother said, trying not to cry. "Now all of a sudden everything was her fault. I just don't see how you can."

"I'm not saying it was her fault," Uncle Terence said wearily. "That's not what I meant. Give me credit for one or two brains, Beth. I'm only saying it might have been rough for him, as well, that's all. How do any of us know what he's had to carry on his shoulders? Another person's virtues could be an awful weight to tote around. We all loved her. Whoever loved him? Who in hell could? Don't you think he knew that? Maybe he even thought sometimes it was no more than was coming to him."

"Oh—" my mother said bleakly. "That can't be so. That would be—oh, Terence, do you really think he might have thought that way?"

"I don't know any more than you do, Beth. I think he knew quite well that she had something he didn't, but I'd be willing to bet he always imagined it must be righteousness. It wasn't. It was—well, I guess it was tenderness, really. Unfair as you always are about him, Edna, I think you hit the nail on the head about one thing. I don't believe Mother ever realised he might have wanted her tenderness. Why should she? He could never show any of his own. All he could ever come out with was anger. Well, everybody to his own shield in this family. I guess I carry mine in my hip pocket. I don't know what yours is, Beth, but Edna's is more like his than you might think."

"Oh yeh?" Aunt Edna said, her voice suddenly rough. "What is it, then, if I may be so bold as to enquire?"

"Wisecracks, honey," Uncle Terence replied, very gently. "Just wisecracks."

They stopped talking, and all I could hear was my aunt's uneven breathing, with no one saying a word. Then I could hear her blowing her nose.

"Mercy. I must look like the wreck of the Hesperus," she said briskly. "I'll bet I haven't got a speck of powder left on. Never mind. I'll repair the ravages later. What about putting the kettle on, Beth? Maybe I should go down and see if he'll have a cup of tea now."

"Yes," my mother said. "That's a good idea. You do that, Edna."

I heard my aunt's footsteps on the basement stairs as she went down into Grandfather Connor's solitary place.

Many years later, when Manawaka was far away from me, in miles and in time, I saw one day in a museum the Bear Mask of the Haida Indians. It was a weird mask. The features were ugly and yet powerful. The mouth was turned down in an expression of sullen rage. The eyes were empty caverns, revealing nothing. Yet as I looked, they seemed to draw my own eyes towards them, until I imagined I could see somewhere within that darkness a look which I knew, a lurking bewilderment. I remembered then that in the days before it became a museum piece, the mask had concealed a man.

—1970

JAMES REANEY

(1926-   )

James Reaney was born in Stratford, Ontario, and grew up on a farm near that city. He was educated at the Stratford Collegiate Institute and the University of Toronto (B.A., 1948; M.A., 1949; Ph.D., 1959). His poems and short stories first appeared in Canadian Poetry Magazine *and* The Canadian Forum *during the years 1947 and 1948. In 1949 he brought his poems together in a book,* The Red Heart, *which won a Governor-General's award for that year. His wife, Colleen Thibaudeau, has also published poetry and short stories in many Canadian magazines. Reaney has taught English at the University of Manitoba and is now a Professor in the University of Western Ontario.*

A Suit of Nettles *(1958), a satirical work, contains a dozen pastoral poems reminiscent of Spenser's* Shepherd's Calendar, *but is based on farmyard scenes in Ontario. Reaney won Governor-General's awards for these books and for* The Killdeer and Other Plays *(1962). He founded, edited, and set type for a "little magazine" called* Alphabet *(1960-1971), "devoted to the Iconography of the Imagination."* Twelve Letters to a Small Town *(1962), which also won a Governor-General's Award, presents his memories of Stratford, Ontario. His collected poetry has been edited by Germaine Warkentin under the title:* Poems/James Reaney *(1972).*

Many of Reaney's dramatic works have been produced on the stage or heard on radio. In addition to The Killdeer, The Sun and the Moon, One-Man Masque, *and* Night Blooming Cereus *(all in 1962), he has published* Colours in the Dark *(1969)— which was produced at the Stratford Festival and the National Arts Centre—*Listen to the Wind *(1971), and a collection of* The Easter Egg, Three Desks, *and* The Killdeer *in* Masks of Childhood *(1972).*

THE SCHOOL GLOBE

Sometimes when I hold
Our faded old globe
That we used at school
To see where oceans were
And the five continents,
The lines of latitude and longitude,
The North Pole, the Equator and the South
    Pole —
Sometimes when I hold this
Wrecked blue cardboard pumpkin
I think: here in my hands
Rest the fair fields and lands
Of my childhood
Where still lie or still wander
Old games, tops and pets;
A house where I was little
And afraid to swear
Because God might hear and
Send a bear
To eat me up;
Rooms where I was as old
As I was high;
Where I loved the pink clenches,
The white, red and pink fists
Of roses; where I watched the rain
That Heaven's clouds threw down

In puddles and rutfuls
And irregular mirrors
Of soft brown glass upon the ground.
This school globe is a parcel of my past,
A basket of pluperfect things.
And here I stand with it
Sometime in the summertime
All alone in an empty schoolroom
Where about me hang
Old maps, an abacus, pictures,
Blackboards, empty desks.
If I raise my hand
No tall teacher will demand
What I want.
But if someone in authority
Were here, I'd say
Give me this old world back
Whose husk I clasp
And I'll give you in exchange
The great sad real one
That's filled
Not with a child's remembered and pleasant
    skies,
But with blood, pus, horror, death, step-
    mothers, and lies.

                 —*1949*

THE HEART AND THE SUN

"Come to me!" cried the Heart to the Star.
The Heart like a lute, like a red guitar
Thus sang out to its golden lover.
"Stand here within me and kindle
My beating, pulsive breathing;
Pray start those soft footsteps
That in my streets
May march a century."

"Come to me!" gasped the Heart to the Star.
The Heart like a red bell
Hanging in a walking steeple
Thus sang to its gold beloved.
"Ring me, begin my beating
So that my new, peculiar voice
May sing at last."

Into the Heart's red cage
Then ran the young Sun.
Into its blood-filled dungeon
Where like the prisoner of a Maze
His footsteps of Sunsets and Sunrises
Did ticktock five times 5,000 days.

"You are mine! I have caught you!"
Cried the Heart
In her love for the trapped yellow wanderer.

Then came, long after, the winter
When ripely heavy with age
The Heart like a red leaf
Fell from the branch
Into a grave and gray grave.
Pulled by the fierce winter wind
Plucked down by the bold winter cold
The Heart fell from life
And the gold prisoner within her
With swift rust
Wore away her red, russet walls.
When out of that broken heart he flew
He wept and did sadly survey
His dead red mistress
Whose sweet rooms and dungeons
Now swarmed and whirred with decay.
"Alas, my Love, it is your fate and mine
That I someday smother whom I kindle
And give birth to those I'll someday kill."

—1949

CLOUDS

These clouds are soft fat horses
That draw Weather in his wagon
Who bears in his old hands
Streaked whips and strokes of lightning.
The hooves of his cattle are made
Of limp water, that stamp
Upon the roof during a storm
And fall from dripping eaves;
Yet these hooves have worn away mountains
In their trotting over Earth.
And for manes these clouds
Have the soft and various winds
That still can push
A ship into the sea
And for neighs, the sable thunder.

—1949

ANTICHRIST AS A CHILD

When Antichrist was a child
He caught himself tracing
The capital letter A
On a window sill
And wondered why
Because his name contained no A.
And as he crookedly stood
In his mother's flower-garden
He wondered why she looked so sadly
Out of an upstairs window at him.
He wondered why his father stared so
Whenever he saw his little son

Walking in his soot-colored suit.
He wondered why the flowers
And even the ugliest weeds
Avoided his fingers and his touch.
And when his shoes began to hurt
Because his feet were becoming hooves
He did not let on to anyone
For fear they would shoot him for a monster.
He wondered why he more and more
Dreamed of eclipses of the sun,
Of sunsets, ruined towns and zeppelins,
And especially inverted, upside down churches.

—1949

THE TWO KITES

Our kites seem
Flat fish that swim
In a high, loud river of the wind
That flows, far above us, from the lungs
Of one of the four directions.
We fly them every windy day
So that they know the North Wind's way
Of armoring all with snow and ice;
And how the South Wind
Sweet as licorice
Paints the summer streets of trees
With white, sweet dust;
Also they know the East Wind
That ruins the Spring;
And the West Wind whose sunset sundogs
Growl for a storm and a rainbow.

But although they wander the windy sky
Like any bird or cloud
These kites are hinged to us
Who never let them go
But, cruelly, must
Always pull them down
To a place where no winds blow.
How they must cry out there
Against the still, playbox air,
How they must desire to fly
Up the glass stairs of a windy sky
To where stands that cloud-nailed door
Whose doorknob sometimes is the Moon,

Whose gold latch sometimes is the Sun.

Those that fly kites are also kites
Carried upon a wind that comes
From nowhere,
Hurried in a direction that depends
Upon which wind of Love or Hate is blowing;
Pulled down from all our life:
Of loving, talking, singing, sighing,
Of watching the weather through windowpanes,
Of howing, hating, whethering, whying;
Pulled down from all this
To a grave.

Someday, for us, the Wind will stop
And, like kites, we'll listless drop,
Or a Someone will say,
"You've flown enough,
You've suffered sufficient huffpuff,"
And wind us back
To a place where no winds blow.
How we'll groan there
Against the still coffin air,
How we'll long to be blown
Back to the jostle of fates and plights
Of a life beneath the sun
Where the dust whirls up
Beneath the summer trees
And where every windy day,
In the bare fields, we flew our kites.

—1949

THE COFFINS

These coffins are submarines
That will sail beneath the slopes
Of gray-green old graveyards.

One white lone sailor to each
Submarine that navigates
The wormy seas of earth.

With shrouds for uniforms
Stitched by weeping tailors

These bony sailors
Shall sail deep field and morass
Without periscope or compass
They'll only dimly know
That someday they must flow
Into the final harbor
On some high gray shore
Where the Lord shall weigh
Men's wicked souls on Doomsday.

—1949

KLAXON

All day cars mooed and shrieked,
Hollered and bellowed and wept
Upon the road.
They slid by with bits of fur attached,
Fox-tails and rabbit-legs,
The skulls and horns of deer,
Cars with yellow spectacles
Or motorcycle monocle,
Cars whose gold eyes burnt
With a too-rich battery,
Murderous cars and manslaughter cars,
Chariots from whose foreheads leapt
Silver women of ardent bosom.
Ownerless, passengerless, driverless,
They came to anyone

And with headlights full of tears
Begged for a master,
For someone to drive them
For the familiar chauffeur.
Limousines covered with pink slime
Of children's blood
Turned into the open fields
And fell over into ditches,
The wheels kicking helplessly.
Taxis begged trees to step inside,
Automobiles begged of posts
The whereabouts of their mother.
But no one wished to own them any more,
Everyone wished to walk.

—1949

FROM *A Suit of Nettles*

INVOCATION TO THE MUSE OF SATIRE

With Punch's stick (he holds it in his hand)
Beat fertility into a sterile land,
With hands of hawthorn branches in the winter,
And teeth of cold March rain that bite the soft snow,
And bristly porcupines on which the hunter sits for hair;
With skin of mildew and botfly holes poked through
In hide of long impounded, ancient cow,
With eyes whose tears have quotaed out to ice long ago,
Eyes bright as the critical light upon the white snow;

With arms of gallows wood beneath the bark
And torso made of a million hooked unhooking things,
And legs of stainless steel, knives & scythes bunched together,
And feet with harrows, and with discs for shoes —
Speak, Muse of Satire, to this broken pen
And from its blots and dribbling letter-strings
Unloose upon our fame & barnyard—medicine.

With those feet, dance upon their toes
With those legs, grasp them lovingly about the thighs
With that torso, press against their breasts
With those arms, hug them black and blue
With those eyes, look at them you love
With that cheek, rub against their cheeks
With that hair, put your head down in their laps
With those teeth, give forth playful bites
And shake their hands with hour-long explorations
Of their life and heart and mind-line,
But with that stick of which new ones spring ever
From that vine where it was barbarously cut off,
Beat them about the ears and the four senses
Until, like criminals lashed in famine time,
They bring forth something; until thy goad
Grows so warm it bursts into blossoms.

Here, lady, almost blind with seeing too much
Here is the land with spires and chimneys prickly,
Here is the east of the board and here the west,
Here may you enter and there, before you depart,
May you make the sky red with doom and axey wrath.

Has no one seen the country where your cure has nursed?
It is a land of upturned privies with occupants inside them
Crawling out through new tops like astonished moths
Bursting from their unusual, foul and dark cocoons.

—1958

WINNIPEG SEEN AS A BODY OF TIME AND SPACE

Winnipeg, what once were you? You were,
Your hair was grass by the river ten feet tall,
Your arms were burr oaks and ash leaf maples,
Your backbone was a crooked silver muddy river,
Your thoughts were ravens in flocks, your bones were snow,
Your legs were trails and your blood was a people
    Who did what the stars did and the sun.

Then what were you? You were cracked enamel like
Into parishes and strips that come down to the river.
Convents were built, the river lined with nuns
Praying and windmills turning and your people
Had a blood that did what a star did and a Son.

Then on top of you fell
A Boneyard wrecked auto gent, his hair
Made of rusted car door handles, his fingernails
Of red Snowflake Pastry signs, his belly
Of buildings downtown; his arms of sewers,
His nerves electric wires, his mouth a telephone,
His backbone — a cracked cement street. His heart
An orange pendulum bus crawling with the human fleas
Of a so-so civilization — half gadget, half flesh —
   I don't know what I would have instead —
  And they did what they did more or less.

SPEAKER:

In the past it was decided. While the English beat
the French at Waterloo the French Métis beat the
English at the Battle of Seven Oaks but then in the
end, dear listener, Waterloo counted for more than
Seven Oaks.

—1962

THE BICYCLE

  Halfway between childhood & manhood,
    More than a hoop but never a car,
  The bicycle talks gravel and rain pavement
    On the highway where the dead frogs are.

  Like sharkfish the cars blur by,
    Filled with the two-backed beast
  One dreams of, yet knows not the word for,
    The accumulating sexual yeast.

  Past the house where the bees winter,
    I climb on the stairs of my pedals
  To school murmuring irregular verbs
    Past the lion with legs like a table's.

  Autumn blows the windfalls down
    With a twilight horn of dead leaves.
  I pick them up in the fence of November
    And burrs on my sweater sleeves.

Where a secret robin is wintering
  By the lake in the fir grove dark
Through the fresh new snow we stumble
  That Winter has whistled sharp.

The March wind blows me ruts over,
  Puddles past, under red maple buds,
Over culvert of streamling, under
  White clouds and beside bluebirds.

Fireflies tell their blinking player
  Piano hesitant tales
Down at the bridge through the swamp
  Where the ogre clips his rusty nails.

Between the highschool & the farmhouse
  In the country and the town
It was a world of love and of feeling
  Continually floating down.

On a soul whose only knowledge
  Was that everything was something,
This was like that, that was like this —
  In short, everything was
  The bicycle of which I sing.

—1962

HUGH HOOD

(1928-   )

Hugh Hood was born in Toronto, the son of a Nova Scotian father and a French-Canadian mother. He attended parochial and high schools in Toronto, graduated from the University of Toronto, and also received his Ph.D. from that institution in 1955. Married, with four children, he teaches Canadian literature at the Université de Montréal.

His first book was a collection of his short stories, Flying a Red Kite *(1962). This has been followed by four novels and two more collections of short stories. Hood is also a sports enthusiast, especially hockey, and has written a biography of the great Jean Béliveau, published in both English and French.*

WHOS PAYING FOR THIS CALL

For Sam Tata

im a poet   have been for quite a while   a fact difficult to explain
now im a celebrity   thats impossible to explain or even defend   dont just
know how that happened   i went a year to college   became literate when
light shows were the right thing   going against the grain   there was this
man played broomstick through a washtub   broomstick through a hole in
the bottom of the tub   piece of cord from the edge of the tub to the top of
the stick   could really blow on the one string   looking for the place hed
say   now ive found it zum zum zum   this fellow bought out an old fun-
fair ride   one of those rooms with the floor in collapsible sections when you
stepped on one it went down and the next one went up   very disorientating
he put in lights   accompanying loud records on his tub   hollered a good bit

that was two years after zimmerman changed his name

i would go there and read   wrote a long poem in prose about fronds   all
the different kinds of fronds   saw a number of pictures by an amateur painter
rousseau   full of fucking fronds frightened you to look at them big green
things about to grab you   i put in orange peacocks and jokes about orange
peacock tea   next thing the phrase turned up on a beatles track *Orange
Peacock Tea*

words that end in cock are pronounced coe in england as it happens and the
reference did me a power of good i had a book come out with that on the cover
saying i had invented the phrase   i dont suppose i had   anybody could
have thought of it but i did first then I realized those things i would say in fun were
poetry stopped giving my jokes away   now people tell me orange peacock
tea was one of the significant phrases of the sixties uniting in holy grandeur sex
urine pot   then i thought of a song called urinalysis restaurant   that
went very well   very big as we say in showbusiness

MARSHAL DYLAN AND HIS DEPUTY CLYDE

lived twelve years in a twentyone inch tube
jest a driftin gunsmoke through a woodstock
win chester win the marshal would holler and
my names clyde chester lied as he lay down and died

la lo la lo la lo the marshal rode on the poetry circuit
pickin and grinnin and pluckin at good little girls
my bobby lies over the ocean
dylan cried as he lay down and died as he died

come all you good people and learn of my poems and songs
about marshal dylan and marshall mcluhan and clyde
the deputy dying who sighed as he cried about
doubting thomas with his hand in his own bloody side

when i read that to finish my program i would read the last line very slow
even at that few people got the message at first

i still use it to finish my program though   a real wow now because its so
well known i dont like the music its too loud and monotonous i didnt intend it for
music   a song is one thing a poem is something else   im a poet i wont sing
i might chant now and then they all want a little chanting these days i wont do
hare krishna though   if jesus christ wont do it for you krishna wont either
the guys doing krishna are shitting on christ doesnt seem right somehow
i have certain loyalties

loyalties pay no royalties   i thought id say that quick and establish its mine
before some other poet says it   if you come right down to it anyway loyalties
do pay royalties the way you wouldnt believe it   i never did anything but
compose poems reading them first in the funhouse   when id disorientated

enough college kids i got in an anthology i was in an anthology before i printed anything anywhere   everybody says books are going out it looks to me theyre
coming in the back door   i dont like giving readings because i dont smoke and
it gets in my eyes i have to stay up late those places are noisy   what i wanted
was a book something that you could pick up anytime   now thats true fame

i mean like theres a difference between fame and celebrity i dont believe anybody
will look at me on the street when im thirtyfive but they might read a book anyway
the book is there   fact is i hate readings and you have to have a book to get
on the circuit anyway anthologies wont make it for you or poems in *Trace New
Image Up Arse with One Ear Showing Poor Old Tired Horse Poetry Review Poetry
Chicago Prism Delta Contact Prism* i said that one *Evergreen*

somebody should have a magazine *Deciduous* running   nothing but sweet
clean stuff for a switch   thats an   idea ill tell it to my agent shell love
that   vanessa is smart as a   not a whip thats a tired metaphor and
after all im a pro   smart as a bitter worm in the white thighs of a trip

good but not great

im tired tonight or id think of something better   smart as salt in christs
blood   how does that grab you   better than krishna

girls outside the readings after
        me first im prettiest
        write PIG on my arm in ballpoint   please
        why not in blood
        whose
        yours
i said and gave her the old lugosi   she ran off   what a stupid thing
write PIG on my arm i mean where do they come up with this stuff   one
of them asked me to brand her on her rump at a party in detroit with a cigarette
        how did you think of that
        isnt it a good idea

501

no for krishnas sakes its a stupid idea im not   here for to go hurting
somebody whered you get that idea what do i look like
heavenly you look heavenly

i may look heavenly but i feel like hell a considerable part of the time on the circuit
edmonton alberta aspen colorado northfield minnesota eugene oregon   thats
the northwest circuit of course theres many of them you arrive and they ask where
are the lights and the amplifiers then after youve explained you dont sing and you
dont need special lights just a spot and a PA system such as they have in any highschool after all that the chairman of the creative writing department takes you to a
roadside steakhouse just outside of town on route whatever   fine thing
the dean never comes or the head of the english department just the creative
writing man   he wants to know if youve ever run into dylan
        im too young
        your beard gives you authority i suppose especially with young people the
reading is at eightthirty would you like one for the road well be going out after
thats understood   the bars dont close till two AM
        we have to go out after do we
        you dont want to
        naw ive got a train to catch
        lets have two for the road then

those chairmen of creative writing departments drink quite a bit its the strain of the
creative life does it to them   that and sitting up night after night after readings
where there is always pushing and shoving   as a rule they arent young guys
must be exhausting for them its exhausting for me and im still young   well
fairly young   not old anyway

the day *Life* came we were in vermont   just a small college nobody knows
about kids all dressed up in ski clothes   tried to get me up a big fucking
mountain in the afternoon i went to the bottom of the ski tow and looked up
you have to sit on like a bar and hang on for your life all the way up this milelong
ride with your skis and poles sticking out in all directions   i took one look
said fuck that went back to the college with a crowd of kids after me yelling
peace peace   the *Life* photographer killing himself laughing

        you want a picture of me on skis
        with the beard it would go great
        on skis
        great publicity for your record

i put on skis and felt ridiculous ive got a beard two feet long pretty near and i looked
out of place   the photographer wanted me to bless them like the pope on
the balcony   hold out my arms and give the multitude my blessing

THE SNOW POPE

        one must have a mind of winter   xmas trees in the head
        pinecones sticking out of the ears   carrot nose

502

buttons of charcoal   things never mentioned by wallace
and a snow overcoat

to see LIFE steadily and see its hole
ecumenically charismatically eschatologically scatologically
     rome thoughts from a broad   shagged with ice
cream in the hole of the whole of the something not there

in the something that is

good poets steal all the time   its the only way to go   they printed *The Snow Pope* in *Life* and other poems from my record father abraham   that was my first big hit   now im famous as shit people stop and stare on the street expecting the message all call me father or lord   sometimes my guru even the police take a respectful tone when they come to the hotel   they come all the time looking for kids who have left home to come to my readings   i always try to help the police ive got nothing against them secretly i still think of a police-man as well like my father but i dont say that to anybody i have a respect for them because i was taught the policeman is your friend   in the fourth grade that was   now i cant get the idea out of my mind   when they visit the hotelim always cooperative
          any distinguishing marks officer
          he has a long beard something like yours if you dont mind my mentioning
it   his parents say he worships you
          and the girl
          yeah well the girl is only fourteen   if we find her with the boy hes in bad trouble they came from wisconsin
          anything else
          she has an appendix scar and a big vaccination
          im not likely to see it
          with this girl you might   she likes to get her   clothes off whenever she can   were told shes a bit of an exhibitionist
          a what
          an exhibitionist   you know
          if i see them youll be the first to know

if youve seen one beard youve seen them all only some seem longer and hairier than others but by and large theres not much difference between beards if youre looking down at them from a platform with lights in your eyes   still i do what i can to help   the mothers call me up   i dont mean mothers i mean real mothers people who have children that are lost or have run away wanting me to find them and save them its beginning to be a strain on me be-cause i cant save anybody from anything i dont believe

all comes of being wellknown   the *Life* cover changed everything people rip your sleeves off   they did that on my triumphal entry into new york
          booked you into the big town baby   youre the hottest poet in the business

who needs a hot poet
im speaking metaphorically   you of all people should know that
now we start looking for a new recording contract
i ought to take some voice lessons   my throat hurts

good thing you stopped smoking
i dont smoke anything   anything   put that in the papers

i got up to my hotel room with both sleeves missing would you believe it just pulled
right away at the seam   last i saw they were fighting over the pieces in the
lobby   i lay on the bed and started to dream   ive been dreaming all the time
im asleep this last year i was on a stage with this great band they were really great
and i wanted to play with them   you know im not musical   if you hit me
i dont ring i just go bonk   but i wanted to play and i had a kazoo in my
pocket a blue kazoo and i hummed into it real loud   i was having all these
musical ideas and wanted to get them out so the people could hear but no matter
how loud i hummed and sang i didnt get that real kazoo sound to blend in with the
band   that za za tissue paper sound and when i looked at the kazoo between choruses i saw what was wrong there was a pinhole in the tissue paper i
couldnt think of a way to repair it

i was dreaming hard and knew it was a dream the way you do but i didnt want to
wake up because there was this big sound and i had all these ideas   no matter
what i couldnt fix my instrument and i started to shout and howl theres a hole in
my blue kazoo at the same time thinking it was a wonderful title for a poem theres
a hole in my blue kazoo   as soon as i thought it would make a title i started to
wake up with the sound of the telephone ringing in my ears   naturally i
thought it was a telephone in the dream a siren or an alarm or a new instrument
for the band telephone bells ringing at intervals   fierce notion   but i
found as i woke up the telephone was really ringing in my ear   i grabbed at
it all mixed in with the blue kazoo when i put it to my ear and grunted this human
voice burst right through the operator or maybe operators i believe there were two
girls talking in there but this mans voice rode right over them speaking very fast
getting a driving rhythm i admired

mister somebody somebody from tampa florida
      tampa what
      tampa florida ive been a fan of yours since you   read your poems here
i bought the record   the first one then i bought the second ive played them
so much theyre worn out the needle jumps all the time   like me   worn
right out i do believe   im calling you for help master   help   i need
help tell you why im at the end of my rope im desperate if you cant give me some
word i dont know where ill turn   what it is is

wailing and crying noises

i saw the picture of you reciting *The Snow Pope* in the snow with those kids around
you saying peace   peace   my sister said why dont you speak to him he

will understand i thought i would try im dying of leukemia   just found out
on monday of this week   thats last monday i mean im a young man only
twentyfour dont know what to do they say it will be a year or less   might
be a remission   but usually under a year i feel all right i look all right you
wouldnt know from looking at me now im dying all of a sudden it doesnt seem
right   i thought id try to get in contact with you   master   lord
because you are the one who can give me your word   the word i surely need
at this time
i surely need at this time

the operators were talking to each other and i was waking up
        what is the word

i just said the first thing came into my head
        whos paying for this call
        you are   the doctors have taken all my money
   i have nothing

i got right awake and felt ashamed   heres this guy desperate asking me for
the word   and i havent got the word   what am i going to tell him and
at that he has stuck me with the toll which i dont mind i can afford it but i have
nothing else to give   im empty   i tried to think of something to say that
would fit the case   never been in such a box before   what do you tell
a guy in his spot   be of good cheer i will not desert you i am the man i suffered
i was there doesnt do him any good
        i cant hear you master
        im thinking
        well say something for christs sake

naturally i didnt want to say i had nothing to say i had it in mind to help him but
i didnt want to break in on his suffering which is his alone maybe the only thing
he has for himself i wonder what the buddha would say in my place or jesus
its a mistake to make such large claims if youre a poet   i see that
        the end is the beginning   death is the door to life
        dont put me down with paradoxes guru   i want to know why it has
to be me and will it hurt
        everything dies   yet everything lives
        not in some fucking coffin it doesnt   you got to admit theres a difference
between running around in a dune buggy and being unconscious in a coffin underground
        answer me that one
        to tell the truth i cant

there was crying then he hung up   the operator came on saying that the charge
for the call was eleven ninetyfive and would be billed to my room account
        sure sure thanks

now i am sitting in this hotel room thinking its wrong to go out on the platform

505

tonight and come on like god it makes me think of god being alone up there in his hotel room maybe hes like me just wanting to eat a sandwich and lie down for a while but keeps getting bothered by mister somebody somebody from someplace he cant remember visiting even if he is in all places at all times for   god must get tired of all the complaints

if you look at it that way you can see that every prayer is a collect call   all these collect calls drifting up out of nowhere for god to accept the charges maybe hes feeling dead tonight and hasnt anything to say   we ask too much of god i see that now   having been in the same spot   somebody depending on me to give him the word of life and me with nothing to say   that dream put me off   if it hadnt been for the pinhole in my kazoo id have been able to give him the message only there was nothing there but air escaping through a hole in tissue paper   im going to scale down my ambitions and maybe shorten up my beard   i ought to stop acting so saintly and just be a poet thats good enough for openers

krishna and christ   probably same word

—1971

THE HOLE

Laidlaw sat at the counter on a wobbly stool in Sam and Kitty's diner, looking at the hole in a doughnut, wondering if it was correct to speak of the hole as if it really existed. How could he be looking at a hole? There was nothing to see. He was of the opinion, without having thought the matter through with rigour, that the doughnut was actually comprised of the solid brown mass of cooked batter forming the ringlike object he held in his hand, which undeniably circled a space. Surely you couldn't claim that this space was in the batter, exactly . . . could you?

The doughnut did not include the space; the doughnut was what you could eat. When you had eaten the fried dough you hadn't consumed a hole.

He meditated upon crullers, straight uncircular twists of material, and upon doughnuts with no holes, more like cakes than anything else, blobs, droppings, twists.

Kitty the waitress, an old friend, spoke to him. "Something the matter with that?"

Laidlaw said, "I'm thinking about it."

This speech made the other customers in the diner laugh very hard. "What's to think?" said Berger from the hardware store. "Too big of a hole for such a little doughnut?" asked a burly truckdriver, one of the regulars.

"Shhh," warned Kitty, who had a reverence for Laidlaw because he was a professor, "leave him be." Silence fell; there were a few further half-hearted attempts at mirth and eating, but in a little while all the other customers filed out one after another, leaving Laidlaw almost alone with Kitty, in silent reflection.

When the doughnut machine extrudes the batter, he thought, just as it is being squeezed out of the tip of the batter-squeezer, no hole exists. There is no hole

506

already in being, waiting for the mix to be wrapped around it. He remembered some comedians' proposals for the sale of different kinds of stoppers, like Henry Morgan's imaginary product, Morgan's Minty Middles, designed to go with Life Savers. If you inserted a Minty Middle in a Life Saver you were not really filling a hole, you were bringing together two pieces of matter which had no existential connection. They were mutually alienated.

If you changed a flat tire, you didn't consider the hub as being inside the new wheel, exactly. That seemed to be because the surface of neither the wheel nor the hub was broken. But suppose you put a Minty Middle into a Life Saver, then sucked the two candies till they ran together, couldn't you then say that the one candy had gotten inside the other?

Laidlaw stuck his forefinger through the hole in his doughnut in a gesture of distinct erotic substance; the waitress snickered.

He ate the doughnut. "Give me a fresh one," he mumbled with his mouth full. Kitty brought another, and fresh coffee, and looked deep into his eyes, which were glazed somewhat alarmingly.

He was now thinking about surfaces, and the impenetrability of matter, and wondering finally, as he had many times before, whether any one thing could ever be said really to get inside anything else, whether any surface was ever penetrated. For if two things grew together, or were so united as not to be distinguishable in space, they seemed to be a single thing.

Married people were only metaphorically said to be sexually united. Sexual congress consisted merely in the insertion of one body in a vacant space, with surfaces which defined it all around, to be sure, but quite impenetrable surfaces. It was characteristic of Laidlaw in all innocence to consider sexuality strictly within the confines of the married state. His cosmological point, however, was sound.

Inside and outside: purely relative. He imagined a cube of polished granite, one foot by one foot by one foot. Suppose you wanted to get inside that stone. You might take a sledgehammer and break it apart. Then all you would have would be several irregularly shaped smaller pieces of granite, and you would not be inside any of them. You might then reduce these pieces to a fine crystalline powder. And then suppose you picked out a single speck of the powder and magnified it under a powerful microscope—it would still exist, solid and complete, an impenetrable thing.

Laidlaw now began to be aware of a phenomenon which had always disturbed his thinking: he felt strongly tempted to fall asleep. There was something powerfully soporific about this kind of speculation: perhaps it was dangerous, and this was nature's warning.

He shook his head vigorously, and fought off the urge to sleep or self-hypnosis. From the kitchen, the waitress and her husband, the short-order cook, watched him anxiously.

"I wish he wouldn't do that here," said Sam, the cook, in some distress of mind. Once or twice before Laidlaw had meditated so deeply in the diner that he had put himself into a state of catalepsy, and had had to be carried off, stiff as a board, in a condition which terrified Kitty and Sam. They were afraid they might have poisoned him.

"He's falling into another trance," said Kitty.

But this was not so. Under his appearance of immobility and near-trance,

Laidlaw had never been so active; his mind raced backwards, round and round circling avenues of reasoning, trying to think of some mode of being in which one thing was inside another thing and yet distinct from it. He briefly considered the condition of the child in the womb, then rejected it as unacceptable. He began to guess that individual bits of matter were incommunicable; but if that were so, how did they associate themselves together so as to form what we call things?

Whenever he reached this stage in a sequence of reasoning long familiar to him, Laidlaw felt a dreadful shudder of revulsion from his own body, which at these moments he considered a loose and arbitrary, accidental, coming-together of bits of stuff that had no reason to coalesce. His body was a ghastly irrational accident. The notion made him want to vomit, and he always used the same stratagem to repress nausea.

> But in thy beauties orient deep
> These flowers, as in their causes, sleep.

He would recite these lines from Carew's beautiful poem over and over to himself, like an incantation or prayer, until the notion of a thing's existing in its cause seized his imagination and banished his nausea.

Now he began to think of containment in other than merely physical terms. Instead of seeing physical proximity, like that of the water against the sides of a well, as a terrifying puzzle (how could any bit of water be next to any other bit, as all water seemed to be sliding around all the time), his mind resigned matter to its own peculiar conditions of inscrutability and ascended to the consideration of immaterial things. Matter was likely better left unthought; he could make nothing of it. He smiled.

"Now he's going to be all right," said the waitress. "He won't pass out on us this time." She came out of the kitchen and rattled saucers on the Masonite counter. "Professor," she said softly, then louder, "Professor Laidlaw."

Coming to with a jump he mumbled,

> Ask me no more where Jove bestows,
> When June is past, the fading rose.

"Fading?" said Kitty. "Fading? Sex! That's all you ever think about." She gave a discreet cough.

"More coffee. I need to stay awake."

"It's early afternoon."

"Never mind that. I feel sleepy."

"That is what we all feel very much concerned about," said Kitty.

The professor said, "Don't be frightened. There's no danger."

"Are you certain?"

"Perfectly. A harmless matter of metaphysical speculation."

For some reason this alarmed Kitty a lot. She wished he would do his metaphysical speculations somewhere else, but hesitated to speak out. She watched with fascination and perplexity as his face cleared, his eyes rounded, and he sank into meditation.

"This isn't the place," she said irritably, but he couldn't hear. He was far off down a new chain of thought. "In their causes. *In* their causes." In what way could a flower be said to be in its cause? Bits of traditional philosophical language rose up in memory. Causality, necessary and sufficient, formal, material, efficient and final. Suppose a musician had composed a whole overture in his head, without ever having written it down, could you then say that this was a genuine case of something's being inside something else? Or was it inaccurate to say that the piece of music existed before it was written down in an observable public state on music manuscript paper? Did the act of publication then create the work? It seemed ridiculous to maintain that an overture, unperformable because not in score, nevertheless existed somehow or other. And yet it did, because the composer could hear it. This had notoriously been the case of W. A. Mozart.

How about poems, or the ideas for paintings?

"*In* their causes."

Naturally this kind of thinking led Laidlaw, trained as a philosopher for many years, to the notion of the Deity, a notion which had always at once fascinated and repelled him. His idea of Deity was wholly impersonal, an Aristotelian Unmoved Mover, the pattern of all things, perhaps the physical source of motion and biological change, but not personal—simply the stopgap by which philosophers avoided an unthinkable infinite regress, when they speculated about the age of the universe.

"In their *causes*?"

Uncaused causes, unmoved movers, same thing. Obviously you couldn't think of more than one uncaused cause, or unmoved mover. Why not? Why couldn't you have parallel series of infinite regression, without contact between the series? That would be absurd, wouldn't it? For it would presuppose two, perhaps more than two, infinite things, which appeared to be contradictory; there could not be two or more infinite things. If they were really multiple, they would be limited by one another.

His chest heaved; he screwed his eyes tightly shut in an effort to concentrate. He didn't want to be interrupted.

Sam went to the door and hung a sign in the window. It said CLOSED. Over his shoulder he asked Kitty, "Has anybody ever ruptured themselves just thinking?"

With his eyes shut tight like that, and his chest inflated, the Waynflete Professor of Mental and Moral Philosophy at the provincial university resembled a bullfrog. He would have been pleased by this resemblance, never liking to consider himself removed from the other elements of creation. Blown up so, hardly breathing, he looked like a balloon or a big puffball which might suddenly float up into the air and away out the window. Outside it was early June, about two-thirty in the afternoon of a hazy, mildly sunny day. Students from the university came and went, their faces twisted in the agony of the examination season.

Professor Laidlaw was supposed to be in his office, grading exam papers; some students, observing that he philosophized most intensely at this time of year, claimed that metaphysics was a form of escape for him.

"His intense apprehension of the real is a crutch," they would say, and the brighter students would go on to propose some paradox about illusion being socially more real than an intuitive perception of a higher truth. To do him justice, Professor Laidlaw would not have entertained such a paradox for an instant if he had been around to hear it.

As things were, sitting in Sam and Kitty's place, the stink of rancid deep-fry in his nose, the faint creaking of the stool under him suggesting that he might fall off it at any moment, he had passed beyond the level of easy paradox into a region of severe and taxing concentration, a kind of effort not many people are called upon to make. Real thought is rare, and feels funny; it's hard on you, and you can't keep it up too long.

Why could there be no more than one infinite entity? Obviously because there couldn't be anything outside of it. If some being were infinite, it would be infinite throughout time and space, or rather it would extend beyond time and space and enclose them; but it would not enclose them as finite things are enclosed in space. The way an infinite being surrounded things would be different from the way space defined cubes of granite, or human beings or bullfrogs. An infinite being would be omnipresent; therefore it would extend itself necessarily through all other things, and nothing would be separate from it.

In God we live and move and have our being.

Was it unthinkable that there might be two universes, two infinite beings which acted as unmoved movers, each in its own universe? Perhaps it was unthinkable. The word "universe" appeared to entail unity. "Universe" could only mean the sum total of what exists in space and time. How could there be more than one universe?

The professor remembered that some physicists had put it forward that there might be more than one universe, and that the laws of different universes might have nothing in common. In another universe there might be more truth-values open to propositions than simply truth on the one hand, and falsehood on the other. There could be a universe where sentences could be both true and false at the same time, where things might both exist and not exist at the same time, where a being might be both finite and infinite. Where, for example, the unmoved mover might be both present and absent. Such a universe would be indeed perplexing to live in. He wondered if he were not perhaps in fact living in such a universe, and not in the one he'd always imagined himself in, where contradictions excluded one another, where God either existed or He didn't, and no nonsense about it.

Sam the short-order man took hold of the professor's wrist and felt for a pulse. It was there, but much slowed.

"He's gone into a state of suspended animation," said Sam, in a tone of extreme annoyance. "No, really now, this has got to stop."

How could Sam tell that the professor had just taken an extreme metaphysical step, that of denying the possibility of there being more than one universe. As he did this, his pulse slowed to practically nothing; his body temperature dropped below ninety-five; his respiration grew deep and slow and his eyeballs rolled way back into his head. Now he stopped thinking and began to imagine.

At first it seemed to him as if he were standing in the middle of the sky, unsupported in any way. Yet he had no inclination to fall. He was simply at a point, with nothing around him. He couldn't see his arms or legs, and had no sensation of possessing a body, but he was at a point which he would describe as "there." He was located, and he could move.

To move he simply thought about changing the point where he was, but it wasn't like floating around at all, as you might in a science-fiction movie. It was more like passing through a whole series of intervening there-points without moving in space, like a series of projected slides. No, not like that. Like a series of completely unconnected states of existing. Hard to express.

No sensation of strain or using the muscles, but he hadn't become an angel or anything like that. He was human, and what's more he was himself, though he had no name. But he was himself, and completely himself, not a baby. This wasn't a womb. Not dark.

It wasn't light either—there didn't seem to be any darkness or light or the intervening shades. The closest he could come to describing where he was might be to say that it was all a pale silver gray, but it would be wrong to say that. He thought of colorlessness as a pale silver gray but of course it wasn't that at all. Not at all. He began to imagine he'd arrived at an unconditioned state of pre-existence where he was in his cause, that is, in or annexed to or issuing from or conceived by or held in the Divine Mind, in a state of unmixed creaturehood before locality caught him. Not before birth. More like in the idea of himself in the Creator's eternal contemplation of His Essence.

This was colorless but not invisible nor outside the possibility of experience. It was not an annihilation of himself. It was like finally grasping the definition of himself, seeing everything he meant, unconditionally and in an instant.

Outside, students came and went, expecting the professor to hand back their papers, neatly graded, but he never did. He wasn't dead, not what you'd call dead precisely. But a lot of people came to somebody's funeral.

—1974

AUTHOR'S COMMENT

In an article in Canadian Literature *(No. 49, Summer 1971), entitled "Sober Colouring: The Ontology of Super Realism," Hugh Hood set forth some of the ideas and principles governing his own fiction, and also commented upon the foregoing story, "The Hole," then not yet published:*

I have also written some stories about a kind of experience close to that of the artist: metaphysical thought . . . . "The Hole" . . . tries to show a philosopher's intelligence actually at work, a hard thing to do. Like musical thought, metaphysical thought seems to take place in a non-verbal region of consciousness, if there is such a thing, and it is therefore hard to write about, but to me an irresistible challenge...

A transcendentalist must first study the things of this world, and get as far inside them as possible. My story "The Hole" tries to show a philosopher working out this idea in his own experience. Here, as everywhere in my writing, I have studied as closely and intensely as I can the *insides* of things which are not me. The great metaphor in human experience for truly apprehending another being is sexual practice. Here, perhaps only here, do we get inside another being. Alas, the entrance is only metaphorical. In plain fact no true penetration happens in lovemaking. It is not possible for one physical being to merge into another, as D. H. Lawrence finally realized. Bodies occupy different places; there is nothing to be done about this. Sex is a metaphor for union, not itself achieved union.

What we are united to in this world is not the physical insides of persons or things, but the knowable principle in them. Inside everything that exists is essence, not in physical space and time, but as forming space and time and the perceptions possible within them. What I know, love, and desire in another person isn't inside him like a nut in its shell, but it is everywhere that he is, forming him. My identity isn't inside me—it is *how I am*. It is hard to express the way we know the forms of things, but this is the knowing that art exercises ...

I'm not a Platonist or a dualist of any kind. I think with Aristotle that the body and the soul are one; the form of a thing is totally united to its matter. The soul is the body....

—*1971*

When asked by one of the present editors why Laidlaw, in the story, rejected as unacceptable "the condition of the child in the womb," Dr. Hood replied: "I would say that, once the soul has been infused into the embryo, the child is a separate moral identity, even if still in the womb. It's a question of the soul's separateness. For that matter, how is created being in God? I don't know! But I suspect that we are more united to God than the child in the womb to the mother....

"Did you notice the pun on the name Laidlaw? He is meditating on God's Law, as laid down for the universe."

D. G. JONES

(1929-   )

Douglas Gordon Jones was born in Bancroft, Ontario, and educated at McGill and Queen's Universities. He was a lecturer in English at the Royal Military College in Kingston, at the Ontario Agricultural College in Guelph, and at Bishop's University, Lennoxville, Quebec. He is now an Associate Professor in the University of Sherbrooke.

He began writing poems while he was an undergraduate at McGill and he was a contributor to Poetry 56. *His first volumes were* Frost on the Sun *(1957) and* The Sun is Axeman *(1961). In 1967 he published* Phrases from Orpheus.

Jones edited Ellipse: Oeuvres en traduction/Writers in translation *from its beginnings until 1972. His critical work,* Butterfly on Rock: A Study of Themes and Images in Canadian Literature, *was published in 1970.*

BEAUTIFUL CREATURES BRIEF AS THESE

Like butterflies but lately come
From long cocoons of summer
These little girls start back to school
To swarm the sidewalks, playing-fields,
And litter air with color.

So slight they look within their clothes,
Their dresses looser than the Sulphur's wings,
It seems that even if the wind alone
Were not to break them in the lofty trees,
They could not bear the weight of *things*.

And yet they cry into the morning air
And hang from railings upside down
And laugh, as though the world were theirs
And all its buildings, trees, and stones
Were toys, were gifts of a benignant sun.   —*1961*

LIKE ONE OF BOTTICELLI'S DAUGHTERS

The flesh is such a sweet thing
the tooth longs to engage it:

the pubescent limbs
run in the wind, and the hair
streams in the mouth.

But the apple bitten is destroyed;
broken to the hungry air, the flesh
turns brown at once.

The flesh is lonely and its beauty serves
but nuns; it welters in the wind
and will not be.

The girl in green and yellow
sings on the grass;

her hair, like the Primavera,
blows in her mouth —

and I am lost.

I welter in the sun
and like a mortal man rejoice
to be so moved —

to apprehend, but hardly,
what cannot be caught:

the wind that streaks the waters
and the shadows
in the bright flesh - - -

O angels, what has heaven lost!
                    —*1961*

TO EVE IN BITTERNESS

All the gardens and green trees,
Gnarled blossoming boughs
And sweet grass I shall burn,

Burn, for I will have
Stumps and in the sweet earth ash
And no flowers, none,

No petals, scented, or green sap
In tender foliage or grass
But rock and charred boughs etched

Against the sky, all that,
And hardly proof against the soft
Air of summer, season's ghost

That haunts me with a memory of flowers,
Memory of a garden and your breath
That haunts all words.

Anemone, the one
Pale windflower scattered over earth!
I'll leave . . . ah, God!

No Adam in your banishment
But angel who must watch you go,
Brandishing a sword, I leave

Ember and ash and scarred rock
Against the paling sky.
And let it be cold.

                    —*1967*

513

SUMMER IS A POEM BY OVID

For Michael Ondaatje

The fire falls, the night
Grows more profound.
The music is composed
Of clear chords
And silence. We become
Clear and simple as the forms
Of music; we are dumb
As water
Mirroring the stars.

Then summer is
Ovidian, and every sun
Is but a moth evolving
In the large gloom,
An excerpt from
Ars Amoris: flame
Is no more fleeting than the limbs
Of boy and girl: the conflagration
Is the same.

While the fire falls, and night
Grows more profound, the flesh,
The music and the flame
All undergo
Metamorphosis. The sounds
Of music make a close,
So with our several selves,
Together, until silence shall compose
All but the ashes in the pale dawn
And even those.

—1967

JAY MACPHERSON

(1931-   )

Jay Macpherson was born in England and came to Canada at the age of nine. She studied at Carleton College (B.A., 1951), the University of London (1951-1952), McGill (1953) and the University of Toronto (M.A., 1955; Ph.D., 1964). She is now a Professor at Victoria College, Toronto. Robert Graves' press in Majorca published her first book, Nineteen Poems, *in 1952.* O Earth Return *(1954) appeared in Toronto. A substantial collection,* The Boatman *(1957), gave her a well-established position among Canadian poets, and a Governor-General's Award. This book was revised in 1968.* Four Ages of Man: the classical myths *(1962) is an illustrated volume for older children.*

TRUE NORTH

All other winters shall break against hers,
Such fire is wedded to her frost.
She is harsh as the blizzard that scrapes and strains,
Firm as the mountains, crowned as the firs,
Rich as the earth's old smouldering veins,
And to the level mild world locked and lost.   —*1952*

ORDINARY PEOPLE IN THE LAST DAYS

My mother was taken up to heaven in a pink
    cloud.
She was talking to a friend on the telephone
When we saw her depart through the ceiling
Still murmuring about bridge.

The white bull ran away with my sister.
My father sent me to find her
But the oracle maundered on about a cow
And I came home disgruntled.

My father prophesied.
He looked out from behind his newspaper
And said, "Johnny-Boy will win the Derby."
The odds against were fifteen to one, and
    he won.

The dove descended on my brother.
He was working in the garden
When the air became too bright for comfort
And the glory of the bird scorched his roses.

The unicorn yielded to my sweetheart.
She was giggling with some girls
When the unicorn walked carefully up to her
And laid his head in her lap.

A mouse ran away in my wainscot.
I study all day and pray all night.
My God, send me a sign of Thy coming
Or let me die.

My mother was taken up to heaven in a pink cloud,
My father prophesied,
The unicorn yielded to my sweetheart,
The white bull ran away with my sister,
The dove descended on my brother,
And a mouse ran away in my wainscot.

        —*1957*

THE THIRD EYE

Of three eyes, I would still give two for one.
The third eye clouds: its light is nearly gone.
The two saw green, saw sky, saw people pass:
The third eye saw through order like a glass
To concentrate, refine and rarify
And make a Cosmos of miscellany.
Sight, world and all to save alive that one
Fading so fast! Ah love, its light is done.

        —*1957*

515

COLD STONE

I lay my cheek against cold stone
And feel my self returned to me
As soft my flesh and firm my bone
By it declare their quality.
I hear my distant blood drive still
Its obscure purpose with clear will.

The stone's unordered rigor stands
Remote and heavy as a star.
My returned self in cheek and hands
Regards as yet not very far
The leap from shape to living form;
For where I rested, the stone is warm.

—1957

THE CAVERNED WOMAN

What's packed about her ivory bones
Is cruel to the wondering touch;
Her hard skull rounds the roots of stones
And cannot give or comfort much;

Her lap is sealed to summer showers,
Ice-bound, and ringed in iron hold:
Her breast puts forth its love like flowers
Astonished into hills of cold.

Not here the Sun that frees and warms,
Cherishes between fire and flood:
But far within are Seraph forms,
Are flowers, fountains, milk, blood.

—1957

THE BOATMAN

You might suppose it easy
For a maker not too lazy
To convert the gentle reader to an Ark:
But it takes a willing pupil
To admit both gnat and camel
—Quite an eyeful, all the crew that must embark.

After me when comes the deluge
And you're looking round for refuge
From God's anger pouring down in gush and spout,
Then you take the tender creature
—You remember, that's the reader—
And you pull him through his navel inside out.

That's to get his beasts outside him,
For they've got to come aboard him,
As the best directions have it, two by two.
When you've taken all their tickets
And you've marched them through his sockets,
Let the tempest bust Creation: heed not you.

For you're riding high and mighty
In a gale that's pushing ninety
With a solid bottom under you—that's his.
Fellow flesh affords a rampart,
And you've got along for comfort
All the world there ever shall be, was, and is.

—1957

THE ANAGOGIC MAN

Noah walks with head bent down;
For between his nape and crown
He carries, balancing with care,
A golden bubble round and rare.

Its gently shimmering sides surround
All us and our worlds, and bound
Art and life, and wit and sense,
Innocence and Experience.

Forbear to startle him, lest some
Poor soul to its destruction come,
Slipped out of mind and past recall
As if it never was at all.

O you that pass, if still he seems
One absent-minded or in dreams,
Consider that your senses keep
A death far deeper than his sleep.

Angel, declare: what sways when Noah nods?
The sun, the stars, the figures of the gods.

—1957

THE INWARD ANGEL

A diamond self, more clear and hard
Than breath can cloud or touch can stain,
About my wall keeps mounted guard,
Maintaining an impervious reign.

But planted as an inward eye
And nourishing my patient mold,
He's soft with sense, and round him I
Ingather sun where all was cold.

Look, inward Angel, cast your light:
My dark is crystal in your sight.

—1957

THE FISHERMAN

The world was first a private park
Until the angel, after dark,
Scattered afar to wests and easts
The lovers and the friendly beasts.

And later still a home-made boat
Contained Creation set afloat,
No rift nor leak that might betray
The creatures to a hostile day.

But now beside the midnight lake
One single fisher sits awake
And casts and fights and hauls to land
A myriad forms upon the sand.

Old Adam on the naming-day
Blessed each and let it slip away:
The fisher of the fallen mind
Sees no occasion to be kind,

But on his catch proceeds to sup;
Then bends, and at one slurp sucks up
The lake and all that therein is
To slake that hungry gut of his,

Then whistling makes for home and bed
As the last morning breaks in red;
But God the Lord with patient grin
Lets down his hook and hoicks him in.

—1957

MERMAID

The fish-tailed lady offering her breast
Has nothing else to give.
She'll render only brine, if pressed,
That none can drink and live.

She has a magic glass, whose spell
Makes bone look wondrous white.
By day she sings, though, travellers like to tell,
She weeps at night.

—1957

THE BEAUTY OF JOB'S DAUGHTERS

The old, the mad, the blind have fairest daughters.
Take Job: the beasts the accuser sends at evening
Shoulder his house and shake it; he's not there,
Attained in age to inwardness of daughters,
In all the land no women found so fair.

Angels and sons of God are nearest neighbours,
And even the accuser may repair
To walk with Job in pleasures of his daughters:
Wide shining rooms more warmly lit at evening,
Gardens beyond whose secrets scent the air.

Not wiles of men nor envy of the neighbours,
Riches of earth, nor what heaven holds more rare,
Can take from Job the beauty of his daughters,
The gardens in the rock, music at evening,
And cup so full that all who come must share.

Perhaps we passed them? it was late, or evening,
And surely those were desert stumps, not daughters,
In fact we doubt that they were ever there.
The old, the mad, the blind have fairest daughters.
In all the land no women found so fair.

—1968

ALICE MUNRO

(1931-   )

Alice Anne Laidlaw was born in Wingham, Ontario. Her father was a farmer and her mother a teacher. Alice graduated from the University of Western Ontario in 1951, and married a classmate, James Armstrong Munro. They have three daughters. Mrs. Munro worked as an assistant in the Vancouver Public Library from 1952-1955, and began publishing short stories in The Canadian Forum, The Montrealer, Queen's Quarterly, *and* The Tamarack Review.

Although her stories were sometimes anthologized, she did not publish a collection of her own until The Dance of the Happy Shades *(1968), which won a Governor-General's Award. Her second book,* Lives of Girls and Women, *which appeared in 1971, is being re-published in the United States and in Britain. In the early 1960's Mr. and Mrs. Munro left Vancouver to establish a successful book store in Victoria, British Columbia.*

THE SHINING HOUSES

Mary sat on the back steps of Mrs. Fullerton's house, talking—or really listening—to Mrs. Fullerton, who sold her eggs. She had come in to pay the egg money, on her way to Edith's Debbie's birthday party. Mrs. Fullerton did not pay calls herself and she did not invite them, but, once a business pretext was established, she liked to talk. And Mary found herself exploring her neighbour's life as she had once explored the lives of grandmothers and aunts—by pretending to know less than she did, asking for some story she had heard before; this way, remembered episodes emerged each time with slight differences of content, meaning, colour, yet with a pure reality that usually attaches to things which are at least part legend. She had almost forgotten that there are people whose lives can be seen like this. She did not talk to many old people any more. Most of the people she knew had lives like her own, in which things were not sorted out yet, and it is not certain if this thing, or that, should be taken seriously. Mrs. Fullerton had no doubts or questions of this kind. How was it possible, for instance, not to take seriously the broad blithe back of Mr. Fullerton, disappearing down the road on a summer day, not to return?

"I didn't know that," said Mary. "I always thought Mr. Fullerton was dead."

"He's no more dead than I am," said Mrs. Fullerton, sitting up straight. A bold Plymouth Rock walked across the bottom step and Mary's little boy, Danny, got up to give rather cautious chase. "He's just gone off on his travels, that's what he is. May of gone up north, may of gone to the States, I don't know. But he's not dead. I would of felt it. He's not old neither, you know, not old like I am. He was my second husband, he was younger. I never made any secret of it. I had this place and raised my children and buried my first husband, before ever Mr. Fullerton came upon the scene. Why, one time down in the post office we was standing together by the wicket and I went over to put a letter in the box and left my bag behind me, and Mr. Fullerton turns to go after me and the girl calls to him, she says, here, your mother's left her purse!"

Mary smiled, answering Mrs. Fullerton's high-pitched and not trustful laughter. Mrs. Fullerton was old, as she had said—older than you might think, seeing her hair still fuzzy and black, her clothes slatternly-gay, dime-store brooches pinned to her ravelling sweater. Her eyes showed it, black as plums, with a soft inanimate sheen; things sank into them and they never changed. The life in her face was all in the nose and mouth, which were always twitching, fluttering, drawing tight grimace-lines down her cheeks. When she came around every Friday on her egg deliveries her hair was curled, her blouse held together by a bunch of cotton flowers, her mouth painted, a spidery and ferocious line of red; she would not show herself to her new neighbours in any sad old-womanish disarray.

"Thought I was his mother," she said. "I didn't care. I had a good laugh. But what I was telling you," she said, "a day in summer, he was off work. He had the ladder up and he was picking me the cherries off of my black-cherry tree. I came out to hang my clothes and there was this man I never seen before in my life, taking the pail of cherries my husband hands down to him. Helping himself, too, not backward, he sat down and ate cherries out of my pail. Who's that, I said to my husband, and he says, just a fellow passing. If he's a friend of yours, I said, he's welcome to stay for supper. What are you talking about, he says, I never seen him before. So I never said another thing. Mr. Fullerton went and talked to him, eating my cherries I intended for a pie, but that man would talk to anybody, tramp, Jehovah's Witness, anybody—that didn't need to mean anything."

"And half an hour after that fellow went off," she said, "Mr. Fullerton comes out in his brown jacket and his hat on. I have to meet a man downtown. How long will you be, I said. Oh, not long. So off he goes down the road, walking down to where the old tram went—we was all in the bush then—and something made me look after him. He must be hot in that coat, I said. And that's when I knew he wasn't coming back. Yet I couldn't've expected it, he liked it here. He was talking about putting chinchillas in the back yard. What's in a man's mind even when you're living with him you will never know."

"Was it long ago?" said Mary.

"Twelve years. My boys wanted me to sell then and go and live in rooms. But I said no. I had my hens and a nanny goat too at that time. More or less a pet. I had a pet coon too for a while, used to feed him chewing gum. Well, I said, husbands maybe come and go, but a place you've lived fifty years is something else. Making a joke of it with my family. Besides, I thought, if Mr. Fullerton was to come back, he'd come back here, not knowing where else to go. Of course he'd hardly know where to find me, the way it's changed now. But I always had the idea he might of suffered a loss of memory and it might come back. That has happened.

"I'm not complaining. Sometimes it seems to me about as reasonable a man should go as stay. I don't mind changes, either, that helps out my egg business. But this baby-sitting. All the time one or the other is asking me about baby-sitting. I tell them I got my own house to sit in and I raised my share of children."

Mary, remembering the birthday party, got up and called to her little boy. "I thought I might offer my black cherries for sale next summer," Mrs. Fullerton said. "Come and pick your own and they're fifty cents a box. I can't risk my old bones up a ladder no more."

"That's too much," Mary said, smiling. "They're cheaper than that at the supermarket." Mrs. Fullerton already hated the supermarket for lowering the price of eggs. Mary shook out her last cigarette and left it with her, saying she had another package in her purse. Mrs. Fullerton was fond of a cigarette but would not accept one unless you took her by surprise. Baby-sitting would pay for them, Mary thought. At the same time she was rather pleased with Mrs. Fullerton for being so unaccommodating. When Mary came out of this place, she always felt as if she were passing through barricades. The house and its surroundings were so self-sufficient, with their complicated and seemingly unalterable layout of vegetables and flower beds, apple and cherry trees, wired chicken-run, berry patch and wooden walks, woodpile, a great many roughly built dark little sheds, for hens or rabbits or a goat. Here was no open or straightforward plan, no order that an outsider could understand; yet what was haphazard time had made final. The place had become fixed, impregnable, all its accumulations necessary, until it seemed that even the washtubs, mops, couch springs and stacks of old police magazines on the back porch were there to stay.

Mary and Danny walked down the road that had been called, in Mrs. Fullerton's time, Wicks Road, but was now marked on the maps of the subdivision as Heather Drive. The name of the subdivision was Garden Place, and its streets were named for flowers. On either side of the road the earth was raw; the ditches were running full. Planks were laid across the open ditches, planks approached the doors of the newest houses. The new, white and shining houses, set side by side in long rows in the wound of the earth. She always thought of them as white houses, though of course they were not entirely white. They were stucco and siding, and only the stucco was white; the siding was painted in shades of blue, pink, green and yellow, all fresh and vivid colours. Last year, just at this time, in March, the bulldozers had come in to clear away the brush and second-growth and great trees of the mountain forest; in a little while the houses were going up among the boulders, the huge torn stumps, the unimaginable upheavals of that earth. The houses were frail at first, skeletons of new wood standing up in the dusk of the cold spring days. But the roofs went on, black and green, blue and red, and the stucco, the siding; the windows were put in, and plastered with signs that said, Murry's Glass, French's Hardwood Floors; it could be seen that the houses were real. People who would live in them came out and tramped around in the mud on Sundays. They were for people like Mary and her husband and their child, with not much money but expectations of more; Garden Place was already put down, in the minds of people who understood addresses, as less luxurious than Pine Hills but more desirable than Wellington Park. The bathrooms were beautiful, with three-part mirrors, ceramic tile, and coloured plumbing. The cupboards in the kitchen were light birch or mahogany, and there were copper lighting fixtures there and in the dining ells. Brick planters, matching the fireplaces, separated the living rooms and halls. The rooms were all large and light and the basements dry, and all this soundness and excellence seemed to be clearly, proudly indicated on the face of each house—those ingenuously similar houses that looked calmly out at each other, all the way down the street.

Today, since it was Saturday, all the men were out working around their houses.

They were digging drainage ditches and making rockeries and clearing off and burning torn branches and brush. They worked with competitive violence and energy, all this being new to them; they were not men who made their livings by physical work. All day Saturday and Sunday they worked like this, so that in a year or two there should be green terraces, rock walls, shapely flower beds and ornamental shrubs. The earth must be heavy to dig now; it had been raining last night and this morning. But the day was brightening; the clouds had broken, revealing a long thin triangle of sky, its blue still cold and delicate, a winter colour. Behind the houses on one side of the road were pine trees, their ponderous symmetry not much stirred by any wind. These were to be cut down any day now, to make room for a shopping centre, which had been promised when the houses were sold.

And under the structure of this new subdivision, there was still something else to be seen; that was the old city, the old wilderness city that had lain on the side of the mountain. It had to be called a city because there were tramlines running into the woods, the houses had numbers and there were all the public buildings of a city, down by the water. But houses like Mrs. Fullerton's had been separated from each other by uncut forest and a jungle of wild blackberry and salmonberry bushes; these surviving houses, with thick smoke coming out of their chimneys, walls unpainted and patched and showing different degrees of age and darkening, rough sheds and stacked wood and compost heaps and grey board fences around them—these appeared every so often among the large new houses of Mimosa and Marigold and Heather Drive—dark, enclosed, expressing something like savagery in their disorder and the steep, unmatched angles of roofs and lean-tos; not possible on these streets, but there.

"What are they saying," said Edith, putting on more coffee. She was surrounded in her kitchen by the ruins of the birthday party—cake and molded jellies and cookies with animal faces. A balloon rolled underfoot. The children had been fed, had posed for flash cameras and endured the birthday games; now they were playing in the back bedrooms and the basement, while their parents had coffee. "What are they saying in there?" said Edith.

"I wasn't listening," Mary said, holding the empty cream pitcher in her hand. She went to the sink window. The rent in the clouds had been torn wide open and the sun was shining. The house seemed too hot.

"Mrs. Fullerton's house," said Edith, hurrying back to the living-room. Mary knew what they were talking about. Her neighbours' conversation, otherwise not troubling, might at any moment snag itself on this subject and eddy menacingly in familiar circles of complaint, causing her to look despairingly out of windows, or down into her lap, trying to find some wonderful explanatory word to bring it to a a stop; she did not succeed. She had to go back; they were waiting for cream.

A dozen neighbourhood women sat around the living room, absently holding the balloons they had been given by their children. Because the children on the street were so young, and also because any gathering-together of the people who lived there was considered a healthy thing in itself, most birthday parties were attended by mothers as well as children. Women who saw each other every day met now in earrings, nylons and skirts, with their hair fixed and faces applied. Some of the men were there too—Steve, who was Edith's husband, and others he had invited in for beer; they were all in their work clothes. The subject just introduced was one of the few on which male and female interest came together.

"I tell you what I'd do if I was next door to it," Steve said, beaming good-naturedly in expectation of laughter. "I'd send my kids over there to play with matches."

"Oh, funny," Edith said. "It's past joking. You joke, I try to do something. I even phoned the Municipal Hall."

"What did they say?" said Mary Lou Ross.

"Well *I* said couldn't they get her to paint it, at least, or pull down some of the shacks, and they said no they couldn't. I said I thought there must be some kind of ordinance applied to people like that and they said they knew how I *felt* and they were very *sorry*—"

"But no?"

"But no."

"But what about the chickens, I thought—"

"Oh, they wouldn't let you or me keep chickens, but she has some special dispensation about that too, I forgot how it goes."

"I'm going to stop buying them," Janie Inger said. "The supermarket's cheaper and who cares that much about fresh? And my God, the smell. I said to Carl I knew we were coming to the sticks but I somehow didn't picture us next door to a barnyard."

"Across the street is worse than next door. It makes me wonder why we ever bothered with a picture window, whenever anybody comes to see us I want to draw the drapes so they won't see what's across from us."

"Okay, okay," Steve said, cutting heavily through these female voices. "What Carl and I started out to tell you was that, if we can work this lane deal, she has got to go. It's simple and it's legal. That's the beauty of it."

"What lane deal?"

"We are getting to that. Carl and I been cooking this for a couple of weeks, but we didn't like to say anything in case it didn't work out. Take it, Carl."

"Well she's on the lane allowance, that's all," Carl said. He was a real estate salesman, stocky, earnest, successful. "I had an idea it might be that way, so I went down to the Municipal Hall and looked it up."

"What does that mean, dear?" said Janie, casual, wifely.

"This is it," Carl said. "There's an allowance for a lane, there always has been, the idea being if the area ever got built up they would put a lane through. But they never thought that would happen, people just built where they liked. She's got part of her house and half a dozen shacks sitting right where the lane has to go through. So what we do now, we get the municipality to put through a lane. We need a lane anyway. Then she has to get out. It's the law."

"It's the law," said Steve, radiating admiration. "What a smart boy. These real estate operators are smart boys."

"Does she get anything?" said Mary Lou. "I'm sick of looking at it and all but I don't want to see anybody in the poorhouse."

"Oh, she'll get paid. More than it's worth. Look, it's to her advantage. She'll get paid for it, and she couldn't sell it, she couldn't give it away."

Mary set her coffee cup down before she spoke and hoped her voice would sound all right, not emotional or scared. "But remember she's been here a long time," she said. "She was here before most of us were born." She was trying desperately to think of other words, words more sound and reasonable than these; she could not expose to this positive tide any notion that they might think flimsy and romantic, or she would destroy her argument. But she had no argument. She could try all night and never find any words to stand up to their words, which came at her now invincibly from all sides: *shack, eyesore, filthy, property, value.*

"Do you honestly think that people who let their property get so rundown have that much claim to our consideration?" Janie said, feeling her husband's plan was being attacked.

"She's been here forty years, now we're here," Carl said. "So it goes. And whether you realize it or not, just standing there that house is bringing down the resale value of every house on this street. I'm in the business, I know."

And these were joined by other voices; it did not matter much what they said as long as they were full of self-assertion and anger. That was their strength, proof of their adulthood, of themselves and their seriousness. The spirit of anger rose among them, bearing up their young voices, sweeping them together as on a flood of intoxication, and they admired each other in this new behaviour as property-owners as people admire each other for being drunk.

"We might as well get everybody now," Steve said. "Save going around to so many places."

It was supper time, getting dark out. Everybody was preparing to go home, mothers buttoning their children's coats, children clutching, without much delight, their balloons and whistles and paper baskets full of jelly beans. They had stopped fighting, almost stopped noticing each other; the party had disintegrated: The adults too had grown calmer and felt tired.

"Edith! Edith, have you got a pen?"

Edith brought a pen and they spread the petition for the lane, which Carl had drawn up, on the dining-room table, clearing away the paper plates with smears of dried ice cream. People began to sign mechanically as they said goodbye. Steve was still scowling slightly; Carl stood with one hand on the paper, businesslike, but proud. Mary knelt on the floor and struggled with Danny's zipper. She got up and put on her own coat, smoothed her hair, put on her gloves and took them off again. When she could not think of anything else to do she walked past the dining-room table on her way to the door. Carl held out the pen.

"I can't sign that," she said. Her face flushed up, at once, her voice was trembling. Steve touched her shoulder.

"What's the matter, honey?"

"I don't think we have the right. We haven't the right."

"Mary, don't you care how things look? You live here too."

"No, I—I don't care." Oh, wasn't it strange, how in your imagination, when you stood up for something, your voice rang, people started, abashed; but in real life they all smiled in rather a special way and you saw that what you had really done was serve yourself up as a conversational delight for the next coffee party.

"Don't worry, Mary, she's got money in the bank," Janie said. "She must have. I asked her to baby-sit for me once and she practically spit in my face. She isn't exactly a charming old lady, you know."

"I know she isn't a charming old lady," Mary said.

Steve's hand still rested on her shoulder. "Hey what do you think we are, a bunch of ogres?"

"Nobody wants to turn her out just for the fun of it," Carl said. "It's unfortunate. We all know that. But we have to think of the community."

"Yes," said Mary. But she put her hands in the pockets of her coat and turned to say thank you to Edith, thank you for the birthday party. It occurred to her that they were right, for themselves, for whatever it was they had to be. And Mrs. Fullerton was old, she had dead eyes, nothing could touch her. Mary went out and walked with Danny up the street. She saw the curtains being drawn across living-room windows; cascades of flowers, of leaves, of geometrical designs, shut off these rooms from the night. Outside it was quite dark, the white houses were growing dim, the clouds breaking and breaking, and smoke blowing from Mrs. Fullerton's chimney. The pattern of Garden Place, so assertive in the daytime, seemed to shrink at night into the raw black mountainside.

The voices in the living room have blown away, Mary thought. If they would blow away and their plans be forgotten, if one thing could be left alone. But these are people who win, and they are good people; they want homes for their children, they help each other when there is trouble, they plan a community—saying that word as if they found a modern and well-proportioned magic in it, and no possibility anywhere of a mistake.

There is nothing you can do at present but put your hands in your pockets and keep a disaffected heart.

—1968

MORDECAI RICHLER

(1931-   )

Mordecai Richler was born in Montreal and spent his youth in that city's St. Urbains section. He attended Sir George Williams College for two years, and worked as a news editor for the CBC. When he went abroad in the early 1950's he spent eight months in Spain, and wrote The Acrobats, *a novel about a lost generation of expatriates. A year later he published* Son of a Smaller Hero *(1955) set in the Montreal ghetto. Making his home in England, he wrote scripts for such films as,* Life at the Top, *and* No Love for Johnny.

Between 1957 and 1971 Richler published five novels, of which the best are The Apprenticeship of Duddy Kravitz *(1959) and* St. Urbain's Horseman *(1971), the latter winning a Governor-General's Award.* The Street *(1969) is a collection of his short stories and memoirs. Besides fiction, he has published two volumes of essays and articles.*

Richler was appointed Writer-in-Residence at Sir George Williams University, 1968-1969. He has received a Guggenheim Fellowship and two Canada Council Senior Arts Fellowships. He returned to live in Canada in 1972 and has been appointed Visiting Professor of English at Carleton University.

Two streets below our own came the Main. Rich in delights, but also squalid, filthy, and hollering with stores whose wares, whether furniture or fruit, were ugly or damaged. The signs still say FANTASTIC DISCOUNTS or FORCED TO SELL PRICES HERE, but the bargains so bitterly sought after are illusory—and perhaps they always were.

The Main, with something for all our appetites, was dedicated to pinching pennies from the poor, but it was there to entertain, educate and comfort us too. Across the street from the synagogue you could see THE PICTURE THEY CLAIMED COULD NEVER BE MADE. A little further down the street there was the Workman's Circle and, if you liked, a strip show. Peaches, Margo, Lili St. Cyr. Around the corner there was the ritual baths, the *shvitz* or *mikva*, where my grandfather and his cronies went before the High Holidays, emerging boiling red from the highest reaches of the steam rooms to happily flog each other with brushes fashioned of pine tree branches. Where supremely orthodox women went once a month to purify themselves.

It was to the Main, once a year before the High Holidays, that I was taken for a new suit (the itch of the cheap tweed was excruciating) and shoes (with a built-in squeak). We also shopped for fruit on the Main, meat and fish, and here the important thing was to watch the man at the scales. On the Main, too, was the Chinese laundry—"Have you ever seen such hard workers?"—the Italian hat-blocker— "Tony's a good goy, you know. Against Mussolini from the very first."—and strolling French Canadian priests—"Some of them speak Hebrew now." "Well, if you ask me, it's none of their business. Enough's enough, you know." Kids like myself were dragged along on shopping expeditions to carry parcels. Old men gave us snuff, at the delicatessens we were allowed salami butts, card players pushed candies on us for luck, and everywhere we were poked and pinched by the mothers. Absolutely the best that could be said of us was, "He eats well, knock wood," and later, as we went off to school, "He's a rank-one boy."

After the shopping, once our errands had been done, we returned to the Main once more, either for part-time jobs or to study with our *melamud*. Jobs going on the Main included spotting pins in a bowling alley, collecting butcher bills and, best of all, working at a newsstand, where you could devour the *Police Gazette* free and pick up a little extra short-changing strangers during the rush hour. Work was supposed to be good for our character development and the fact that we were paid was incidental. To qualify for a job we were supposed to be "bright, ambitious, and willing to learn." An ad I once saw in a shoe store window read:

PART-TIME BOY WANTED FOR EXPANDING BUSINESS.
EXPERIENCE ABSOLUTELY NECESSARY, BUT NOT ESSENTIAL

Our jobs and lessons finished, we would wander the street in small groups smoking Turret cigarettes and telling jokes.

"Hey, *shmo-hawk*, what's the difference between a mail box and an elephant's ass?"

"I dunno."

"Well, I wouldn't send *you* to mail my letters."

As the French Canadian factory girls passed arm-in-arm we would call out, "I've got the time, if you've got the place."

Shabus it was back to the Main again and the original Young Israel synagogue. While our grandfathers and fathers prayed and gossiped and speculated about the war in Europe in the musty room below, we played chin the bar in the upstairs attic and told jokes that began, "Confucius say. . . ." or, "Once there was an Englishman, an Irishman, and a Hebe . . . . "

We would return to the Main once more when we wanted a fight with the pea-soups. Winter, as I recall it, was best for this type of sport. We could throw snowballs packed with ice or frozen horse buns, and with darkness falling early, it was easier to elude pursuers. Soon, however, we developed a technique of battle that served us well even in the spring. Three of us would hide under an outside staircase while the fourth member of our group, a kid named Eddy, would idle provocatively on the sidewalk. Eddy was a good head-and-a-half shorter than the rest of us. (For this, it was rumoured, his mother was to blame. She wouldn't let Eddy have his tonsils removed and that's why he was such a runt. It was not that Eddy's mother feared surgery, but Eddy sang in the choir of a rich synagogue, bringing in some thirty dollars a month, and if his tonsils were removed it was feared that his voice would go too.) Anyway, Eddy would stand out there alone and when the first solitary pea-soup passed he would kick him in the shins. "Your mother fucks," he'd say.

The pea-soup, looking down on little Eddy, would naturally knock him one on the head. Then, and only then, would we emerge from under the staircase.

"Hey, that's my kid brother you just slugged."

And before the bewildered pea-soup could protest, we were scrambling all over him.

These and other fights, however, sprang more out of boredom than from racial hatred, not that there were no racial problems on the Main.

If the Main was a poor man's street, it was also a dividing line. Below, the French Canadians. Above, some distance above, the dreaded WASPS. On the Main itself there were some Italians, Yugoslavs and Ukrainians, but they did not count as true Gentiles. Even the French Canadians, who were our enemies, were not entirely unloved. Like us, they were poor and coarse with large families and spoke English badly.

Looking back, it's easy to see that the real trouble was there was no dialogue between us and the French Canadians, each elbowing the other, striving for WASP acceptance. We fought the French Canadians stereotype for stereotype. If many of them believed that the St. Urbain Street Jews were secretly rich, manipulating the black market, then my typical French Canadian was a moronic gum-chewer. He wore his greasy black hair parted down the middle and also affected an eyebrow moustache. His zoot trousers were belted just under the breastbone and ended in a peg hugging his ankles. He was the dolt who held up your uncle endlessly at the liquor commission while he tried unsuccessfully to add three figures or, if he was employed at the customs office, never knew which form to give you. Furthermore, he only held his liquor commission or customs or any other government job because he was the second cousin of a backwoods notary who had delivered the village vote to the *Union Nationale* for a generation. Other French

Canadians were speed cops, and if any of these ever stopped you on the highway you made sure to hand him a folded two dollar bill with your licence.

Wartime shortages, the admirable Protestant spirit of making-do, benefited both Jews and French Canadians. Jews with clean fingernails were allowed to teach within the Protestant School system and French Canadians off the Atwater League and provincial sandlots broke into the International Baseball League. Jean-Pierre Roy won twenty-five games for the Montreal Royals one year and a young man named Stan Breard enjoyed a season as a stylish but no-hit shortstop. Come to think of it, the only French Canadians I heard of were athletes. Of course there was Maurice Richard, the superb hockey player, but there was also Dave Castiloux, a cunning welterweight, and, above all, the wrestler-hero, Yvon Robert, who week after week gave the blond Anglo-Saxon wrestlers what for at the Forum.

Aside from boyhood street fights and what I read on the sports pages, all I knew of French Canadians was that they were clearly hilarious. Our Scots schoolmaster would always raise a laugh in class by reading us the atrocious Uncle Tom-like dialect verse of William Henry Drummond: *Little Baptiste & Co.*

> On wan dark night on Lac St. Pierre,
> De win' she blow, blow, blow,
> An' de crew of de wood scow "Julie Plante"
> Got scar't and' run below—
> Bimeby she blow some more,
> An' de scow bus' up on Lac St. Pierre
> Wan arpent from de shore.

Actually, it was only the WASPS who were truly hated and feared. "Among them," I heard it said, "with those porridge faces, who can tell what they're thinking?" It was, we felt, their country, and given sufficient liquor who knew when they would make trouble?

We were a rude, aggressive bunch round the Main. Cocky too. But bring down the most insignificant, pinched WASP fire insurance inspector and even the most arrogant merchant on the street would dip into the drawer for a ten spot or a bottle and bow and say, "Sir."

After school we used to race down to the Main to play snooker at the Rachel or the Mount Royal. Other days, when we chose to avoid school altogether, we would take the No. 55 streetcar as far as St. Catherine Street, where there was a variety of amusements offered. We could play the pinball machines and watch archaic strip-tease movies for a nickel at the Silver Gameland. At the Midway or the Crystal Palace we could see a double feature and a girlie show for as little as thirty-five cents. The Main, at this juncture, was thick with drifters, panhandlers and whores. Available on both sides of the street were "Tourist Rooms by Day and Night," and everywhere there was the smell of french fried potatoes cooking in stale oil. Tough, unshaven men in checked shirts stood in knots outside the taverns and cheap cafés. There was the promise of violence.

As I recall it, we were always being warned about the Main. Our grandparents and parents had come there by steerage from Rumania or by cattleboat from Poland by way of Liverpool. No sooner had they unpacked their bundles and cardboard suitcases than they were planning a better, brighter life for us, the Canadian-born children. The Main, good enough for them, was not to be for us, and that they told us again and again was what the struggle was for. The Main was for *bummers*, drinkers, and (heaven forbid) failures.

During the years leading up to the war, the ideal of the ghetto, no different from any other in America, was the doctor. This, mistakenly, was taken to be the very apogee of learning and refinement. In those days there also began the familiar and agonizing process of alienation between immigrant parents and Canadian-born children. Our older brothers and cousins, off to university, came home to realize that our parents spoke with embarrassing accents. Even the younger boys, like myself, were going to "their" schools. According to them, the priests had made a tremendous contribution to the exploration and development of this country. Some were heroes. But our parents had other memories, different ideas, about the priesthood. At school we were taught about the glory of the Crusades and at home we were instructed in the bloodier side of the story. Though we wished Lord Tweedsmuir, the Governor-General, a long life each Saturday morning in the synagogue, there were those among us who knew him as John Buchan. From the very beginning there was their history, and ours. Our heroes, and theirs.

Our parents used to apply a special standard to all men and events. "Is it good for the Jews?" By this test they interpreted the policies of Mackenzie King and the Stanley Cup play-offs and earthquakes in Japan. To take one example—if the Montreal *Canadiens* won the Stanley Cup it would infuriate the WASPS in Toronto, and as long as the English and French were going at each other they left us alone: *ergo*, it was good for the Jews if the *Canadiens* won the Stanley Cup.

We were convinced that we gained from dissension between Canada's two cultures, the English and the French, and we looked neither to England nor France for guidance. We turned to the United States. The real America.

America was Roosevelt, the Yeshiva College, Max Baer, Mickey Katz records, Danny Kaye, a Jew in the Supreme Court, the *Jewish Daily Forward*, Dubinsky, Mrs. Nussbaum of Allen's Alley, and Gregory Peck looking so cute in *Gentleman's Agreement*. Why, in the United States a Jew even wrote speeches for the president. Returning cousins swore they had heard a cop speak Yiddish in Brooklyn. There were the Catskill hotels, Jewish soap operas on the radio and, above all earthly pleasure grounds, Florida. Miami. No manufacturer had quite made it in Montreal until he was able to spend a month each winter in Miami.

We were governed by Ottawa, we were also British subjects, but our true capital was certainly New York. Success was (and still is) acceptance by the United States. For a boxer this meant a main bout at Madison Square Garden, for a writer or an artist, praise from New York critics, for a businessman, a Miami tan and, today, for comics, an appearance on the Ed Sullivan Show or for actors, not an important part at the Stratford Festival, but Broadway, or the lead in a Hollywood TV series (Lorne Green in *Bonanza*). The outside world, "their" Canada, only concerned us insofar as it affected our living conditions. All the same, we liked to impress the *goyim*. A knock on the knuckles from time to time wouldn't hurt them. So, while we secretly believed that the baseball field or the prize-fighting ring was no place for a Jewish boy, we took enormous pleasure in the accomplishments of, say, Kermit Kitman, the Montreal Royals outfielder, and Maxie Berger, the welterweight.

Streets such as ours and Outremont, where the emergent middle-class and the rich lived, comprised an almost self-contained world. Outside of business there was a minimal contact with the Gentiles. This was hardly petulant clannishness or naive fear. In the years leading up to the war neo-fascist groups were extremely active in Canada. In the United States there was Father Coughlin, Lindberg, and others. We had Adrian Arcand. The upshot was almost the same. So I can recall seeing swastikas and "*A bas les Juifs*" painted on the Laurentian highway. There were suburbs and hotels in the mountains and country clubs where we were not wanted, beaches with signs that read GENTILES ONLY, quotas at the universities, and occasional racial altercations on Park Avenue. The democracy we were being invited to defend was flawed and hostile to us. Without question it was better for us in Canada than in Europe, but this was still their country, not ours.

I was only a boy during the war. I can remember signs in cigar stores that warned us THE WALLS HAVE EARS and THE ENEMY IS EVERYWHERE. I can also recall my parents, uncles and aunts, cracking peanuts on a Friday night and waiting for those two unequalled friends of the Jews, Roosevelt and Walter Winchell, to come off it and get into the war. We admired the British, they were gutsy, but we had more confidence in the United States Marines. Educated by Hollywood, we could see the likes of John Wayne, Gable, and Robert Taylor making minced meat out of the Panzers, while Noel Coward, Laurence Olivier, and others, seen in a spate of British war films, looked all too humanly vulnerable to us. Briefly, then, Pearl Harbour was a day of jubilation, but the war itself made for some confusions. In another country, relatives recalled by my grandparents were being murdered. But on the street in our air cadet uniforms, we F.F.H.S. boys were more interested in seeking out the fabulously wicked v-girls ("They go the limit with guys in uniform, see.") we had read about in the *Herald*. True, we made some sacrifices. American comic books were banned for the duration due, I think, to a shortage of U.S. funds. So we had to put up a quarter on the black market for copies of the *Batman* and *Tip-Top Comics*. But at the same newsstand we bought a page on which four pigs had been printed. When we folded the paper together, as directed, the four pigs' behinds made up Hitler's hateful face. Outside Cooperman's Superior Provisions, where if you were a regular customer you could get sugar without ration coupons, we would chant "Black-market Cooperman! Black-market Cooperman!" until the old man came out, wielding his broom, and sent us flying down the street.

The war in Europe brought about considerable changes within the Jewish community in Montreal. To begin with, there was the coming of the refugees. These men, interned in England as enemy aliens and sent to Canada where they were eventually released, were to make a profound impact on us. I think we had conjured up a picture of the refugees as penurious *hassidim* with packs on their backs. We were eager to be helpful, our gestures were large, but in return we expected more than a little gratitude. As it turned out, the refugees, mostly German and Austrian Jews, were far more sophisticated and better educated than we were. They had not, like our immigrant grandparents, come from *shtetls* in Galicia or Russia. Neither did they despise Europe. On the contrary, they found our culture thin, the city provincial, and the Jews narrow. This bewildered and stung us. But what cut deepest, I suppose, was that the refugees spoke English better than many of us did and, among themselves, had the effrontery to talk in the abhorred German language. Many of them also made it clear that Canada was no more than a frozen place to stop over until a U.S. visa was forthcoming. So for a while we real Canadians were hostile.

For our grandparents who remembered those left behind in Rumania and Poland the war was a time of unspeakable grief. Parents watched their sons grow up too quickly and stood by helplessly as the boys went off to the fighting one by one. They didn't have to go, either, for until the last days of the war Canadians could only be drafted for service within Canada. A boy had to volunteer before he could be sent overseas.

For those of my age the war was something else. I cannot remember it as a black time, and I think it must be so for most boys of my generation. The truth is that for many of us to look back on the war is to recall the first time our fathers earned a good living. Even as the bombs fell and the ships went down, always elsewhere, our country was bursting out of a depression into a period of hitherto unknown prosperity. For my generation the war was hearing of death and sacrifice but seeing with our own eyes the departure from cold-water flats to apartments in Outremont, duplexes and split-levels in the suburbs. It was when we read of the uprising in the Warsaw ghetto and saw, in Montreal, the changeover from poky little *shuls* to big synagogue-cum-parochial schools with stained glass windows and mosaics outside. During the war some of us lost brothers and cousins but in Canada we had never had it so good, and we began the run from rented summer shacks with outhouses in Shawbridge to Colonial-style summer houses of our own and speedboats on the lake in Ste Agathe.

—1969

ALDEN NOWLAN

(1933-   )

Alden Nowlan was born near Windsor, Nova Scotia. Leaving school in grade 5, he worked at a variety of occupations, mainly manual, before becoming a newspaper reporter in 1952 and later an editor of The Observer, *a weekly newspaper published in Hartland, New Brunswick. In 1963 he transferred to the* Telegraph Journal *in Saint John. He is the author of nine books of poetry, one of which—Bread, Wine and Salt—won the Governor-General's Award for 1967.* Playing the Jesus Game *(1970) is a selection of his poems. It has been followed by* Between Tears and Laughter *(1971). He has also published a collection of short stories,* Miracle at Indian River *(1968), and a novel,* Various Persons Named Kevin O'Brien *(1973). He was a Guggenheim Fellow in Poetry in 1968. Since 1968 he has been Writer-in-Residence at the University of New Brunswick, which awarded him an honorary degree of Doctor of Letters in 1971.*

ALL DOWN THE MORNING

All down the morning, women sprinkled crumbs
Of musty laughter, watching Janice Smith
In brazen languor smear her husband's lips
With public kisses, while he glared or blushed.

And when the Sunday village itched in church,
They thought of Janice, hot as Babylon,
Who lured her Jimmie to the porch and bared
His people's blanket-buried secrecies.

Or dancing to the snarl of feline strings,
Each Friday at the school, they leered at jokes
That made obscenities of her taut breasts
Against her startled husband's sweating suit.

For she was city-bred and unaware
That love was bordered by the rumpled quilts
And children bred from duty as the soil
Was ploughed to hide the seed and not for joy.

So taunted by harsh laughter, half-ashamed,
Enraged with rum and manhood late one night,
And shouting like betrayal, Jim came home
To bruise his knuckles on her shameless face.

—1958

A POEM TO MY MOTHER

I being twelve and scared, my lantern shook,
shrunk to string my stomach knotted,
breathing the sultry mustiness of hay
and dung in the cowbarn,
and the heifer calving.

Ours was a windy country and its crops
were never frivolous, malicious rocks
kicked at the plough and skinny cattle broke
ditch ice for mud to drink and pigs were axed.

Finding the young bull drowned, his shoulders
wedged
into a sunken hogshead in the pasture,
I vomited, my mother, yet the flies
around his dull eyes vanished with the kiss
your fingers sang into my hair all night.

Mother, O gentler Christ, O warmest bed,
hearing the wind at bay your heart was milk;
under the crazy quilting of such love,
needles of adoration knit
bandages for my babied eyes; I slept.

—1958

THE EGOTIST

A gushing carousel, the cock
Revolved around the axeman's block.

Sweet Christ, he kicked his severed head
And drenched the summer where he bled.

And terrible with pain, the scream
Of blood engulfed his desperate dream—

He knew (and knowing could not die)
That dawn depended on his cry.

—*1958*

GOD SOUR THE MILK OF THE KNACKING WENCH

God sour the milk of the knacking wench
with razor and twine she comes
to stanchion our blond and bucking bull,
pluck out his lovely plumbs.

God shiver the prunes on her bark of chest,
who capons the prancing young.
Let maggots befoul her alive in bed,
and dibble thorns in her tongue.

—*1962*

THE BULL MOOSE

Down from the purple mist of trees on the mountain,
lurching through forests of white spruce and cedar,
stumbling through tamarack swamps.
came the bull moose
to be stopped at last by a pole-fenced pasture.

Too tired to turn or, perhaps, aware
there was no place left to go, he stood with the cattle.
They, scenting the musk of death, seeing his great head
like the ritual mask of a blood god, moved to the other end
of the field, and waited.

The neighbours heard of it, and by afternoon
cars lined the road. The children teased him
with alder switches and he gazed at them
like an old, tolerant collie. The women asked
if he could have escaped from a Fair.

The oldest man in the parish remembered seeing
a gelded moose yoked with an ox for plowing.
The young men snickered and tried to pour beer
down his throat, while their girl friends took their pictures.

And the bull moose let them stroke his tick-ravaged flanks,
let them pry open his jaws with bottles, let a giggling girl
plant a little purple cap
of thistles on his head.

When the wardens came, everyone agreed it was a shame
to shoot anything so shaggy and cuddlesome.
He looked like the kind of pet
women put to bed with their sons.

So they held their fire. But just as the sun dropped in the river
the bull moose gathered his strength
like a scaffolded king, straightened and lifted his horns
so that even the wardens backed away as they raised their rifles.
When he roared, people ran to their cars. All the young men
leaned on their automobile horns as he toppled.

—1962

THE LONELINESS OF THE LONG-DISTANCE RUNNER

My wife bursts into the room
where I'm writing well
of my love for her

and because now
the poem is lost

I silently curse her.

—1967

THE GOLDEN APPLES OF THE SUN

Both as mere children see a tinsel star
(with undivided wonder) and as men
observe the ornaments they've fashioned when
their art is clumsier than their desire:
I see you, all my love, a tree afire
in the cold forests of me, and again
a tree I made from staves torn from the pen
of loneliness, and all its roots are wire.

My love, with so much hatred in the earth,
a thousand bats against the burning sky,
I think it seldom matters why the seed
of love was planted if it comes to birth.
Love is too rare to kill (though it will die)
whether it grows in you or in my need.

—1969

FOR CLAUDINE BECAUSE I LOVE HER

Love is also
my finding this house
emptier than a stranger
ever could.

Is it the sound of your movements
enlivening the chairs
although I hear nothing, is it the weight
of your small body moving the house
so little no machine
could ever assess it,

though my mind knows,
is it some old
wholly animal instinct

that fills every room with you,
gently, so I am aware of it only

when I come home
and there is nothing here.

—1969

HYMN TO DIONYSUS

The trick is to loose
the wild bear
but hold tight
to the chain,
woe
when the bear
snatches up
the links
and the man dances.

—1969

HURT

"When I grow up there ain't nothin' ever gonna hurt me. Not ever," Stevie used to tell me, doubling up his grimy fists until his knuckles whitened, and snarling like a small, trapped animal, a fox or a feral cat maybe, as he squeezed back the tears at the corners of the eyes that looked ridiculously huge in his peaked ten-year-old's face.

He'd say that after the health nurse sent him home from school because there were lice in his whiskey-coloured mop of hair again or after one of the kids teased him about his old man getting drunk and losing his job at the mill for probably the tenth time that summer, and maybe after Mom or somebody tried to give him a second-hand polo shirt.

The only plans I'd made for growing up were that I was going to be a cowboy, a locomotive engineer, a pirate and maybe pitcher for the Brooklyn Dodgers. Stevie lived in a trailer across the bridge from our farm. I thought it must be wonderful to live in a trailer and not have somebody yelling at you all the time to take off your rubbers when you came in the house.

Stevie's old man yelled at him plenty but only when he was drunk. When he was sober he let him do whatever he liked. Stevie went to school when he wanted to go and when he was bored with it he stayed home or spent the day on the marsh or in the woods. He fixed his own meals and sometimes ate six chocolate bars and a bottle of pop for supper.

Stevie wasn't like any of the other kids who came to school in dirty sweat shirts and were sent home lousy. There were a dozen kids in Hastings Mills public school like that. Muscular thirteen-year-olds spending their fifth year in Grade V, knowing that next year they'd be free to chuck their exercise books and get a job on somebody's farm or at the mill. Wet-nosed little girls who wore wrinkled dresses that almost tickled their ankles and stole everything from the Junior Red Cross treasury to the buttons on the teacher's coat. Stevie never studied and he was usually at the head of the class. When he wasn't in first place it was because he'd stayed home the week we had exams, lying on his belly in the grass in front of the trailer reading a book old man Simms had given him, or picking lady's slippers in the swamp or building the biggest kite we'd ever seen, or something like that. Old man Simms was supposed to be crazy and rich. Eventually he was buried by the parish. Every Hallowe'en he patrolled his farm with a shotgun loaded with rock salt. Naturally, stealing his mail box was the finest adventure of the year. He liked Stevie and gave him a book called *The Boy's Book of Heroes*, all about people like Xerxes and Xenophon and Achilles and Napoleon. Stevie read it all that summer we were ten. When I went over to the trailer after school or on Saturdays and suggested we play war, I always wanted to fight Nazis and Japs but Stevie wouldn't play unless we fought Persians or Trojans.

The more Trojans we killed in the games the better Stevie liked it. We picked cat-tails in the swamp, dried them in the sun and used them as torches when we razed Troy. Stevie sprinkled half a box of salt on the burnt grass and said that's what you were supposed to do when you conquered a city because then "there won't never be anything grow there anymore." At the end I always had to be Hector and he was Achilles and killed me with a wooden sword. He swung the sword with furious intensity, forcing me to back away from him. His teeth clenched and his eyes were slits in his white face. He was quick as a cat and sometimes sharp smacks from the sword on my arms and chest goaded me into bringing my stave down on his shoulder or wrist with all my strength and anger behind the blow so that it left a red blotch that gradually turned blue wherever it hit. After hitting him I was always ashamed. But he'd say, "That's the way, Skip, that's the way to do it," and keep boring in until we agreed that I was dead and went swimming.

Stevie couldn't bear to see real things die. My brother Chuck let us go out with him to try out a new .22 and Stevie liked watching him shoot holes through a tomato can and knock chips off the fence posts but when he sent a squirrel spinning out of a tree and we walked over and looked down at the little limp bundle of fur and blood, Stevie's lips were shivering as if someone had dropped an icicle down the neck of his shirt and his eyes looked exactly like those of a fawn the dogs killed one winter in the field back of our house.

"Why did you have to kill it?" he said and Chuck looked down at him, not knowing what to say, and Stevie started crying, pressing his palms into his eyes.

The winter after that, he found all of Bill Taylor's rabbit snares and stole them.

Sometimes when I went over to the trailer, Stevie's old man was drunk on moonshine or homebrew or vanilla extract. One Saturday he'd be lying on the sofa with his shirt and boots off, singing at the top of his voice and ending each verse with an explosion of laughter. Then next Saturday he'd be pounding the walls with his fists and swearing and crying at the same time or maybe lying on the floor or in the grass, snoring and mumbling in his sleep, waking up every little while to vomit.

When he was happy-drunk and wanted to sing he gave Stevie cigarettes. When it was summer we sat on the ground behind the trailer, with our bare knees drawn up under our chins, and smoked, with Stevie inhaling like a man and me just letting the cigarette burn down as I held it in my mouth. Stevie had no "respect" for his old man, not the kind of respect Pop was always telling me I was supposed to have for him, but when he passed out and started shivering Stevie threw a coat over his shoulders. And Sunday mornings when the old man was too sick to go himself, Stevie went down to the store and got him a couple of bottles of vanilla to sober up on.

Sometimes I met him on my way to Sunday School, me itching and sweating in my starched shirt and my toes aching in leather shoes. He'd be barefoot and wearing a pair of dirty denim shorts. He'd have the vanilla bottles in a paper bag and maybe be carrying something crazy like a big bouquet of daisies in the other hand. Once or twice I went back to the trailer with him and after the old man drank the vanilla he'd give us whatever change he had in his pockets and we'd go back to the store and buy some chocolate bars with old Mason, the storekeeper, teasing me about what Pop would do to me if he found out about me running around with Stevie when I was supposed to be in Sunday School, and then short-changing us because he knew I wouldn't dare tell. Stevie wasn't afraid to tell, but he ignored it. He took it for granted that people were going to cheat him every chance they got.

Then we'd go swimming in the creek and I'd feel free and fine, pulling my torturing Sunday clothes off and feeling the soreness ooze out of my feet when we ran across the cool mud toward the water. One Sunday on the creek bank Stevie tried to teach me to play cards, giving me half his money and then manipulating the pieces of greasy pasteboard until he'd won it all back.

He didn't laugh when he won. Stevie seldom laughed at anything. When he smiled it wasn't a kid's grin. I thought it was like Mom smiled sometimes when you weren't quite sure she was smiling at you or at anything you could see but maybe at something inside her you couldn't understand, something that was even a little sad. Stevie found a duck with a broken leg and made it a splint out of a shingle and kept it in a box in the trailer, trying to get it to eat bread crumbs, and after a week it died. When he knelt down to coax it to eat he always had that funny, sad little smile.

When he did laugh his whole body vibrated with it and he'd roll on the ground hugging himself and laughing, until tears ran down his cheeks and he blew his nose and rocked back and forth, trying to get his breath. His laughter always scared me a little and I'd punch him in the chest and yell at him and once I threw a dipperful of cold water in his face and he only laughed harder.

When Stevie cried it was never for the reasons the rest of the kids cried. Miss Grant, who taught school at Hastings Mills the year I was ten, strapped him every time he skipped school and while she was smacking him he bit his lower lip and blinked at the blackboard and after it was over he went back to his desk and spat on his palms and thumbed his nose at her elaborately as she turned her back, so that everyone laughed.

But one noon hour when he had nothing for lunch except a gooey chocolate bar and she offered him some of her sandwiches, he bolted away from her and afterwards I found him in the woodshed, lying face down in the sawdust, his shoulders shaking with sobs.

That was one of the times that he told me when he grew up nothing was ever going to hurt him.

"When I grow up, Skip, there ain't nothin' ever gonna hurt me," he said. But he didn't stop crying.

—1968

LEONARD COHEN

(1934-   )

Leonard Cohen was born in the Westmount section of Montreal, graduated from McGill University, and continued his studies at Columbia University. He has lived for varying periods in such countries as England, Norway, Cuba, and Greece, but has declared, "I have to keep coming back to Montreal to renew my neurotic affiliations."

Cohen's first book of poems, Let Us Compare Mythologies, *was published in 1956, a year after his graduation from McGill. Other books followed. His* Selected Poems 1956-1968 *won a Governor-General's Award in 1968.* The Energy of Slaves *appeared in 1972.*

Cohen has won an international reputation as a poet and songwriter. He has made numerous appearances as a reader and singer before enthusiastic popular and university audiences in Canada, the United States, and Europe.

Besides poetry, he has published two novels, The Favourite Game *(1963) and* Beautiful Losers *(1966), both of which have been also published in Great Britain and the United States.*

I HAVE NOT LINGERED IN EUROPEAN MONASTERIES

I have not lingered in European monasteries
and discovered among the tall grasses tombs of knights
who fell as beautifully as their ballads tell;
I have not parted the grasses
or purposefully left them thatched.

I have not released my mind to wander and wait
in those great distances
between the snowy mountains and the fishermen,
like a moon,
or a shell beneath the moving water.

I have not held my breath
so that I might hear the breathing of God,
or tamed my heartbeat with an exercise,
or starved for visions.
Although I have watched him often
I have not become the heron,
leaving my body on the shore,
and I have not become the luminous trout,
leaving my body in the air.

I have not worshipped the wounds and relics,
or combs of iron,
or bodies wrapped and burnt in scrolls.

I have not been unhappy for ten thousand years.
During the day I laugh and during the night I sleep.
My favorite cooks prepare my meals,
my body cleans and repairs itself,
and all my work goes well.

—1961

THE SLEEPING BEAUTY

"You are brave," I told the Sleeping Beauty,
"to climb these steps into my home,
but I regret your man, the Kissing Prince, is gone."
      "You don't understand what story I am from," she said,
"we both know who lives in this garden."
      Still, all those following nights
she never knew to call me Beast or Swan.

—1961

YOU HAVE THE LOVERS

You have the lovers,
they are nameless, their histories only for each other,
and you have the room, the bed and the windows.
Pretend it is a ritual.
Unfurl the bed, bury the lovers, blacken the windows,
let them live in that house for a generation or two.
No one dares disturb them.

Visitors in the corridor tip-toe past the long closed door,
they listen for sounds, for a moan, for a song:
nothing is heard, not even breathing.
You know they are not dead,
you can feel the presence of their intense love.
Your children grow up, they leave you,
they have become soldiers and riders.
Your mate dies after a life of service.
Who knows you? Who remembers you?
But in your house a ritual is in progress:
it is not finished: it needs more people.
One day the door is opened to the lovers' chamber.
The room has become a dense garden,
full of colors, smells, sounds you have never known.
The bed is smooth as a wafer of sunlight,
in the midst of the garden it stands alone.
In the bed the lovers, slowly and deliberately and silently,
perform the act of love.
Their eyes are closed,
as tightly as if heavy coins of flesh lay on them.
Their lips are bruised with new and old bruises.
Her hair and his beard are hopelessly tangled.
When he puts his mouth against her shoulder
she is uncertain whether her shoulder
has given or received the kiss.
All her flesh is like a mouth.
He carries his fingers along her waist
and feels his own waist caressed.
She holds him closer and his own arms tighten around her.
She kisses the hand beside her mouth.
It is his hand or her hand, it hardly matters,
there are so many more kisses.
You stand beside the bed, weeping with happiness,
you carefully peel away the sheets
from the slow-moving bodies.
Your eyes are filled with tears, you barely make out the lovers.
As you undress you sing out, and your voice is magnificent
because now you believe it is the first human voice
heard in that room.
The garments you let fall grow into vines.
You climb into bed and recover the flesh.
You close your eyes and allow them to be sewn shut.
You create an embrace and fall into it.
There is only one moment of pain or doubt
as you wonder how many multitudes are lying beside your body,
but a mouth kisses and a hand soothes the moment away.

—1961

541

SONG

When with lust I am smitten
To my books I then repair
And read what men have written
Of flesh forbid but fair

But in these saintly stories
Of gleaming thigh and breast
Of sainthood and its glories
Alas I find no rest

For at each body rare
The saintly man disdains
I stare O God I stare
My heart is stained with stains

And casting down the holy tomes
I lead my eyes to where
The naked girls with silver combs
Are combing out their hair

Then each pain my hermits sing
Flies upward like a spark
I live with the mortal ring
Of flesh on flesh in dark

—1961

I BELIEVE YOU HEARD YOUR MASTER SING

I believe you heard your master sing
while I lay sick in bed
I believe he told you everything
I keep locked in my head
Your master took you traveling
at least that's what you said
O love did you come back to bring
your prisoner wine and bread

You met him at a nightclub where
they take your clothes at the door
He was just a numberless man of a pair
who has just come back from the war
You wrap his quiet face in your hair
and he hands you the apple core
and he touches your mouth now so suddenly bare
of the kisses you had on before

He gave you a German Shepherd to walk
with a collar of leather and nails
He never once made you explain or talk
about all of the little details
such as who had a worm and who had a rock
and who had you through the mails
Your love is a secret all over the block
and it never stops when he fails

He took you on his air-o-plane
which he flew without any hands
and you cruised above the ribbons of rain
that drove the crowd from the stands
Then he killed the lights on a lonely lane
where an ape with angel glands
erased the final wisps of pain
with the music of rubber bands

And now I hear your master sing
You pray for him to come
His body is a golden string
that your body is hanging from
His body is a golden string
My body is growing numb
O love I hear your master sing
Your shirt is all undone

Will you kneel beside the bed
we polished long ago
before your master chose instead
to make my bed of snow
Your hair is wild your knuckles red
and you're speaking much too low
I can't make out what your master said
before he made you go

I think you're playing far too rough
For a lady who's been to the moon
I've lain by the window long enough
(you get used to an empty room)
Your love is some dust in an old man's cuff
who is tapping his foot to a tune
and your thighs are a ruin and you want too much
Let's say you came back too soon

I loved your master perfectly
I taught him all he knew
He was starving in a mystery
like a man who is sure what is true
I sent you to him with my guarantee
I could teach him something new
I taught him how you would long for me
No matter what he said no matter what you do

—1966

543

SUZANNE TAKES YOU DOWN

Suzanne takes you down
to her place near the river,
you can hear the boats go by
you can stay the night beside her.
And you know that she's half crazy
but that's why you want to be there
and she feeds you tea and oranges
that come all the way from China.
Just when you mean to tell her
that you have no gifts to give her,
she gets you on her wave-length
and she lets the river answer
that you've always been her lover.
> And you want to travel with her,
> you want to travel blind
> and you know that she can trust you
> because you've touched her perfect body
> with your mind.

Jesus was a sailor
when he walked upon the water
and he spent a long time watching
from a lonely wooden tower
and when he knew for certain
only drowning men could see him
he said All men will be sailors then
until the sea shall free them,
but he himself was broken
long before the sky would open,
forsaken, almost human,
he sank beneath your wisdom like a stone.
> And you want to travel with him,
> you want to travel blind
> and you think maybe you'll trust him
> because he touched your perfect body
> with his mind.

Suzanne takes your hand
and she leads you to the river,
she is wearing rags and feathers
from Salvation Army counters.
The sun pours down like honey
on our lady of the harbour
as she shows you where to look
among the garbage and the flowers,

there are heroes in the seaweed
there are children in the morning,
they are leaning out for love
they will lean that way forever
while Suzanne she holds the mirror.
> And you want to travel with her
> and you want to travel blind
> and you're sure that she can find you
> because she's touched her perfect body
> with her mind.

—1966

FROM *The Energy of Slaves*

I am no longer at my best practising
the craft of verse
I do better
in the cloakroom with Sara
But even in this alternate realm
I am no longer at my best
I need
the mercy of my own attention
Who could have foretold
the heart grows old
from touching others

I perceived the outline of your breasts
through your Hallowe'en costume
I knew you were falling in love with me
because no other man could perceive
the advance of your bosom into his imagination
It was a rupture of your unusual modesty
for me and me alone
through which you impressed upon my shapeless hunger
the incomparable and final outline of your breasts
like two deep fossil shells
which remained all night long and probably forever

I dress in black
I have green eyes
          in certain light

If others try to write this
death to them
death to anyone
if he or she unseal this poem
in which I dress in black

and bless your eyes
who hurry from this page
Put a green-eyed man
out of his misery and rage

I am dying
   because you have not
died for me
   and the world
still loves you

I write this because I know
that your kisses
   are born blind
on the songs that touch you

I don't want a purpose
   in your life
I want to be lost among
         your thoughts
the way you listen to New York City
when you fall asleep

I make this song for thee
Lord of the World
who has everything in the world
except this song

—1972

GEORGE BOWERING

(1935-   )

George Harry Bowering was born in Osoyoos, British Columbia, attended primary school in Greenwood, high school in Oliver, and then proceeded to Victoria [B.C.] College (1953-1954); the University of British Columbia (B.A. 1960; M.A. 1963); and the University of Western Ontario (1966-1967). He has lived in a dozen different Canadian cities, and his writings reflect a variety of experiences: as an aerial photographer with the R.C.A.F. (1954-1957); a "fruit-picker"; a British Columbia Forest Service worker; a recorder of unconventional life and language (Mirror on the Floor, *a novel, 1967); an editor and contributor to "little magazines"* (Kulchur, Tish, Imago, *and others) and to other ones in Canada and the United States. Bowering is an enthusiast for the poetic theory and practice of William Carlos Williams and the Black Mountain Poets, some of whom he met in Vancouver. He has been a Writer-in-Residence and lecturer at Sir George Williams University (1967-1971); he is now in the Department of English at Simon Fraser University in Burnaby, and he is still publishing books, chiefly through smaller presses.*

He is the author of more than a dozen books of poetry, one novel (with another forthcoming), a short story anthology, and a critical study of Al Purdy. Rocky Mountain Foot *and* The Gangs of Kosmos, *both published in 1969, won him a Governor-General's Award. In 1971 he published* Touch: Selected Poems 1960-1970. *A Senior Arts Award was given him by the Canada Council (1971-1972).*

GRANDFATHER

Grandfather
       Jabez Harry Bowering
strode acrosss the Canadian prairie
hacking down trees
          and building churches
delivering personal baptist sermons in them
leading Holy holy holy lord god almighty songs in them
red haired man squared off in the pulpit
reading Saul on the road to Damascus at them

Left home
       big walled Bristol town
at age eight
        to make a living
buried his stubby fingers in root snarled earth
for a suit of clothes and seven hundred gruelly meals a year

taking an anabaptist cane across the back every day
for four years till he was whipped out of England

Twelve years old
                    and across the ocean alone
to apocalyptic Canada
                              Ontario of bone bending child labor
six years on the road to Damascus till his eyes were blinded
with the blast of Christ and he wandered west
to Brandon among the wheat kings and heathen Saturday nights
young red haired Bristol boy shoveling coal
in the basement of Brandon College five in the morning

Then built his first wooden church and married
a sick girl who bore two live children and died
leaving several pitiful letters and the Manitoba night
He moved west with another wife and built children and churches
Saskatchewan Alberta British Columbia Holy holy holy
lord god almighty
                        struck his labored bones with pain
and left him a postmaster prodding grandchildren with crutches
another dead wife and a glass bowl of photographs
and holy books unopened save the bible by the bed

Till he died the day before his eighty fifth birthday
in a Catholic hospital of sheets white as his hair

—1964

FOR WCW

I

Language lifted
            out of the ordinary
                              into the illumination
of poetry.
                    Objects: sticks & stones
                                    coming together
you place before
                  our eyes
                        exposed bare to the weather
rained on and
            crackt dry in the sun
A stick a stone
            a river cutting thru clay
a white barn in a field
                    a cat coiled
                        on a box

Words
>   coming together
>   moving at one another
> traction for the tongue

>   Look at that! American
> language shouting
>   across the Potomac
>   ring coins over the river
> open out western states
>   —anywhere a man can
>   hear his voice

>   In the machines of Paterson
> rattling ten million words a day
>   a voice moves
>   physical—not understood
>   as lit-er-ary, but moving

>   as a machine, with traction
>   fitting itself against resistance

>   —Song understood by
>   the banging ear

II

A sparrow   The wind blows
balances in the wind   the wire snaps underfoot

voicing song   the feet hold
into the shifting air   the feathers have no time

It is a small thing   to compose themselves
but big as all creation
                                   It is
to its mate beside it   as it should be or
on the wire, balancing   as it is

III

> I heard he askt the excavators
>   for a boulder
>   dumpt in his
>   front yard

> They must have thought
>   he was some old nut

> I mean you dig a boulder
>   out of the ground you dont
>   leave it in your front yard

I mean what good is a big rock?
                          all you can do
                                    is look at it
                          or lean on it

I mean if youve got a lawn
                    youve got to mow around
                                        the damn thing
                          and clip the bloody grass

I mean I hear he used to be
                    a doctor what'd he do
                with the gallstones he cut out
                          put them on the bloody mantle?

                          IV

The descent beckons
                    as the ascent beckoned
                                    I understand that

till the point of
                What now?
                    He is dead gone forever

and to where?
            Into the black which is
                            blacker than the memory
of black?
        It is as it should be
                        or as it is.

He is a part of the history
                    he brought poems together
                                    clutcht out of chaos

he will be the reason
                behind a language where
                            epics can be clutcht
he will be sticks & stones
                    hewer of wood
                            drawer of water

            William
                Carlos
                    Williams

                          —1965

                          550

CADENCE

And an idea   clusters
    at the end of the line

thought   becoming
    a servant of the ego
        hanging onto a perpetual mind
listening to the foot
stepping down

The idea of   becoming
depending on the spending
of the value of the very next following

step

          Rhythm; measured move-
ment, esp. of sound; full of voice, esp. at
end of period; intonation; close of musi-
cal phrase.

so that it is the walking of the voice

the

opening of doors and the walking
on floors
and the closing of doors

the swinging of arms

and the talking of the voice

the cadet marching of the legs all
straight and bending in the sun   *—1966*

NEWS

Every day I add an inch
to the pile of old newspapers
in the closet.

In that three foot pile now
a dozen airliner crashes,
one earthquake in Alaska,
seventeen American soldiers
face down in Asian mud.

I could go on enumerating
like newsprint—we record
violent death & hockey scores
& keep the front room neat.

In front of me, on the table
my empty coffee cup, somewhat melted
butter, carbon copy of an old poem,
familiar things, nothing unexpected.

A plane could crash into the kitchen—
a fissure could jag the floor open—
some olive faced paratrooper bash
his rifle butt thru the window—

It would be news, somewhere.

—1966

DAVE GODFREY

(1938-   )

Dave Godfrey was born in Manitoba, and attended the Universities of Toronto, Iowa, and, Stanford. He now lives in Toronto pursuing careers in writing, publishing, and teaching. He lectures at both Trinity and Erindale Colleges in the University of Toronto, and runs a small publishing house, Press Porcépic. In 1967 he was co-founder with Dennis Lee of the House of Anansi providing an outlet to new Canadian writers. Later, he helped found New Press, another advocate of young writers. His career reflects his deep concern for contemporary Canadian issues. In 1970 he published Gordon to Watkins to You, *and in 1972 co-edited with Robert Fulford and Abraham Rotstein* Read Canadian. *Both books explore American encroachment upon Canadian affairs, particularly economic and cultural.*

His novel, The New Ancestors, *based on his teaching experiences in Ghana under the auspices of the Canadian University Service Overseas, won the Governor-General's Award in 1971.*

NIGHT TRIPPER

When I can, I fly at night, for I dislike the thought of crashing into sunlight. So I arrived in Chicago very early this time and I just walked around, after riding in the airport bus down to the Palmer House and drinking coffee there, because I had so recently done a lot of things which I had enjoyed and I was about to make a visit in which there would be absolutely no enjoyment, and I was in search of a certain neutrality.

Walking around, I did not want to remember Tony Hasper and how he had once been, or to think about the rightness or wrongness of the situation: I simply arranged a few things that had recently happened in a list so that I would have something to say. For that had been the trouble, not having such things arranged, the previous time.

Tony was with his friends on the fourth floor of a tenement in the 50's between Greenwood and Cottage Grove. They were eating a breakfast of corn flakes and scrambled eggs, at a table which was a Bell Telephone cable-spool laid on its side and painted in very bright oranges and blues. One of them, who was a photographer and had money, was just returned from a trip to India and there were photographs of starving Harijans in Bihar on all the walls. Some of the prints were still drying. He was a clever photographer and you saw not only the burnt, unresponsive eyes of children whose minds were damaged by malnutrition, but also, next to these, photographs of a Rajput man whose hair was carefully combed, and oiled, and dust free. Another of them, who was a painter, was working on a munitions series, but he was too clever. He was doing paintings, on 4 x 4 poplar, of men feeding Nike missiles, and of the Phoenix system for the F-111B. But he had gone too far; he was too overt. He was not sure of his own art. In the corner of the painting he had printed: *HUGHES: Creating a New World with Electronics*. And over another he had printed: *A QUOTE FROM McNAMARA'S BAND: FY 1962 through FY 1966 sales of arms abroad of $8.1 billion . . . 1.4 million man-years of employment spread throughout the 50 states and over $1 billion in profits to American Industry*.

"Is Tony still in the back?" I said.

"Sure man," the painter said. "Did you bring us some bread?"

"With clever stuff like that you should be able to sell all over the place." I said. "*Life* should come and pay five thousand just to shoot you all in your new, creative, underground way of life."

"Your friend is in the back room," the painter said. He had on a green shirt with red flowers and wore white jockey shorts and assumed an expression of great peacefulness as though he had suffered to an extent of which I could never become aware. As though my sarcasm was beneath his notice.

Tony was still in the room that had been a sunroom before they had had to plywood up all the windows and put in fluorescent lighting. On the plywood his own early sunflowers were marred by nailholes and damp and by the peeling of the paint around the imperfections of the board. Tony had a bed and there was a hand-woven rug on the floor.

"How's it going, Ton?" I said.

I looked at him very closely and then I just wanted to talk and I was glad that I had my list arranged.

"I was coming back from the coast," I said, "and I just thought I'd drop by and tell you what it was like."

Doom is dark and deeper than any sea-dingle, I thought. And what cage is like the iron-cage of despair?

"You'd have done some wild paintings," I said. "We'll have to go sometime. It's not exactly the Vineyard, but it's beautiful. And far from spoiled."

And the sea there was omar deep and ephah wide, I thought. But that made little sense.

"I fished a little but you know how it is—never enough time to get at ease. I was only really lucky the first time. Took a bus right out of the city, not very far up the coast, to a little bay where there were ferries going past—like buses on Wabash. I didn't even want to catch anything there. It's already late May out on the coast. I just wanted to sit there, bobbing, off a little cave that ran right into the mountains, called Hole-in-the-Wall, and that looked like it owned a spirit or two. But I had the herring strips down, almost by habit, and I got a nice Spring. Hard to carry on a trip though, and I would have given it away or something, but a boy with his father in a rowboat down the way got one too, larger, and I decided then to keep mine. I went up to the restaurant over the bay and watched the weather and watched the father and son clean their salmon while I ate some shrimps, and then I went and borrowed their gear to clean mine. They weren't very impressed that I had to borrow gear, but the boy was very proud of what he had caught. The two of them were very short and they looked like one another.

"The next day I went out on the island, but the wind was blowing right down the strait so I couldn't go out. Talked to an old navy-man fisherman for a while and we quoted Pope at one another. *Horace still charms with graceful negligence*. That was his favourite, standing on the boards of the pier with the boats rocking along each side and a small flock of Goldeneyes spiraling high and wary off the far shore. *Horace still charms with graceful negligence and without method talks us into sense; will, like a friend, familiarly convey the truest notions in the easiest way.* It's hard to believe when you meet someone who thinks in that way and still has a memory to use.

"He suggested I might try one of the rivers, and drift-fish it, so I did, but that was a mistake. The river was open, but it shouldn't have been. Not this early in March. I had a good guide, it wasn't that. But there were so many black fish, spent from spawning, that the clean ones you picked up were in your mind tarnished by contagion. I only drifted down for one afternoon and then I came here. Through Seattle.

"Seattle is a bad time now. I had to wait until past midnight for my connecting flight. The place was full of soldiers and whores, as though it were the Forties again, but there was one mess of unsureness in the air, Ton. I talked to them, but I couldn't talk to them about certain things. About the father and son, for instance. And the not talking of it made it almost an image of old calendar art for me. I'll have to take you up there and have you do it modern for me in the summer, when the fresh run comes."

Tony did not reply, of course, to any of this. The switch is off. The grey is monked. His cow took an overdose. This train is full, Charlie. Grass from a lyed mine. Etc. Etc. For more than a year, gentle amateur physicians and readers, he has been convinced that he is a pawpaw tree and its fruit, and says so, with additions and variation, when he talks. If there had been any change, his friends would have told me about it.

They haven't taken him into a hospital. That is what we fought about the previous time, when I hadn't prepared my list and when I blew up at them after I had seen him. One of the friends is a spoiled social worker, if there is such a category, and doesn't trust the system into which Tony would be placed if they gave him up. They were all with him when he took the last bad trip, although they all pretend to know that it was bad stuff and nothing else that switched him out. They take good care of him. Tony's father was a tailgunner in a bomber. His mother raised him until he was fifteen and then she married her Dreyfus Fund salesman. When I knew him he was in his early twenties and just bursting into a creative life. He was an action painter, and would paint sometimes for five or six hours straight, hurling, scraping, lashing paint onto canvas as though it too were alive and quickened by his own energy. He took peyote the first time simply because he could not conceive of himself as somebody who didn't. We turned it at a funeral chapel, an old, refurbished Victorian house. When he first tried to chew it he got sick and couldn't keep it down. We had to wander around town and find some gelatin capsules so he could get the small chunks of peyote into his stomach without retching. Then he went off and on. At times he could swear I was trying to knife him, or that I was coming at him with an axe, and he would crouch in terror and run away down black alleys; at times he would become euphoric and warble about the blue guitars he was hearing and the tomato skies that embraced him and the vitality of the golden blood he could feel carousing through him and speaking to him of wisdoms. When he came down off the mountain he remembered the fear and he swore never to take it again. For two or three months he refrained and worked on his sunflower series. Then he turned his head to acid and I went to another continent. Now his friends take good care of him. They have seen minds burned out in other ways. They have chosen their reasons; they do for him what they would have done for themselves. Under the circumstances.

Mais moi, I am glad that I have a list prepared, my mind at least roughly organized so that I need not think of old measures, of omars and ephahs, so that I can continue talking.

"If you come out there to that coast with me sometime, Ton, we'll go all the way up into one of the sounds and just fish and live on the boat and argue. We'll take about a hundred of the big Ryecrisp cartwheels you can get out there and a sack of spinach for greens. The sea is full of fish for the asking: rockfish, perch, oysters and mussels. And when the spinach is gone we can get our greens from lamb's quarters, sheep sorrel, nettle greens, sea plantain, Indian consumption plant. Or have Labrador Tea on the shore."

This list of things I talk about to an old friend, a man of only twenty-six, a man of whom I have good memories, a man whose eyes are as blear as any famined Harijan child's, whose face is as without character now as the split globe of a lemon-half, scuffed into an alley's soot.

"If we go up maybe you'll get that for me, the way the two of them looked like one another. Like my ancestral spirits walking up from the sea. They both wore those black, red-soled, rubber boots, turned down half so that the thin grey cloth inside showed visible to the sun, with their red-and-black bush shirts open at the collar to the warmth of the day. And something in their faces, something of a human similarity when they looked at one another. The boy carrying his salmon in his arms like a flopping treasure."

When I finish the list, I simply repeat it, with few variations, almost singing parts of it, gazing at the sunflowers and at memories, at the sun-streaked alleys outside beyond the plywood. Gazing at that great dead mass of flopping salmon as the boy struggled to keep his arms straight beneath it and struggled to be able to assume its entire weight as he moved up slowly from the sea.

—1967

DAVID HELWIG

(1938-   )

David Helwig was born in Toronto, but in 1948 his family moved to the old town of Niagara-on-the-Lake. He obtained his B.A. degree from the University of Toronto, and an M.A. from the University of Liverpool. Married, with two children, he now lives in Kingston and teaches in the Department of English at Queen's University. He has also worked with prisoners in Kingston Penitentiary who had interest in writing, and has edited Words from Inside, *a magazine of writing by inmates of Canadian prisons.*

His own writing includes poetry, drama, and fiction. His first two books were volumes of poetry, the next two were a collection of his short stories (The Streets of Summer) *and a novel* (The Day Before Tomorrow). *In* The Best Name of Silence *(1972), he returned to poetry.*

SONGS FOR PAPAGENO

I

Dark in the rain,
black on the broken
walls of the grey
castle and shaken

by God's wet weather,
the jackdaws strut
and cackle. Bother
in the bone hut

of my singing brain
are the black-jack daws,
talking of rain,
of darkness that gnaws

at castle walls.
And I am stung
by small tales,
pointed tongue.

II

Crow, my gay birds,
strut, my dandies,
with your eyes on fire
cry your gay plumage.

With blood on your head
strut to your love,
dance on your thin feet,
flash your colours.

Fling out, my bravoes,
the cry that tears
the air into fragments
of fire and feathers.

Cry out the light
each coming of morning.
Crow for the sun
as red as your wattles.

Cry all night long
the coming of brightness.   *—1967*

ON A TRAIN

We have laid out our country in lines,
highways, telephone wires, the invisible
network of television signals,
a system of exacerbated nerves,
vibrating, seeking a torture, a drug.

This is our city, this is what we have built,
a short-circuit for the burning brain.
A city of thin lines.

                    And the hands
twitch that might have touched
snow, the muck of spring earth,
body's hair, breasts,
brick, wood, asphalt, lived
in touch, texture. Whole.

—1967

THE BUGBEAR

A kind of fuzzy shambling beetle,
he can be heard at night,
fumbling his way upstairs in the dark,
blundering down hallways,
chuckling in closets,
mumbling and fumbling
around the dark house.

He is blind, no-eyed,
and cannot hear,
only fumbles, fumbles
with his hairy paws.

Adam
naming the multitude of beasts
left him unnamed
and tried to forget him,
but when the two children
left the garden,
the bugbear was waiting for them
at the gate
and shambled and bounded
after their feet
as they walked on
through the disconsolate wood
of unknown trees.
Still he runs behind us.

When the wind parts his hair,
we see beneath it
the shell shining,
and turn away
from his soft hug.

He is blind, no-eyed,
and cannot hear.
Our tears and our pleas
are useless, unseen,
unheard.

We may lock the closet,
but the fuzzy creature
giggles
and appears
beside the bed
in a shambling dance,
seeking praise
he cannot hear.

A hundred times
we wish that Adam
had named him
so that he might be real and die.

Always he is near,
running at our heels,
deathless, no-eyed,
fumbling, fumbling.   *—1967*

As Catherine stood by the open window and felt the damp air, she glanced at the books on the shelf by her hand. She picked up one that looked familiar and held it in her hand as she watched a light far off across the city. Her brother lay still.

"Do you ever stop drinking?" she asked.

"No," her brother answered from the bed.

"Who brings you home nowadays?"

"Any one of a number of friends."

"Do you have an arrest to your credit yet?"

"No. My youthful charm seems to hold the police in abeyance."

"I used to wish that I was going to school in the city so I could look after you and bring you home."

Catherine looked down at the book and opened it. On the title page there was an inscription that read "To Hawkeye from Chingachgook."

"I'm probably the only law student in the city with the complete works of Fenimore Cooper. You gave me all the decent books I own," Mike said.

Catherine looked out the window and down the hill at the moving lights below. She remembered the times at home when she had covered for her brother when he was drunk.

"That building with the red sign is the Park Plaza," her brother said. "The building is a kind of beacon. Red in the winter to make you feel warm, and blue in the summer to make you feel cool. It's really very comforting. Seems they haven't discovered that it's spring."

The book reminded Catherine of the first time she had bought lipstick. The man in the store had been kind, not made a joke or teased her. She had put her two quarters on the counter with what she hoped was mature know-how, taken the bag and her one-cent change and walked carefully and slowly out of the store.

"Can I get you a drink, Cathy?" Mike said. "It's about all I have to offer."

"Why did she come to me, Mike?"

"You have a kind face."

When Catherine had reached home with her lipstick, she had put her hand in her jacket pocket to cover it before going into the house.

"Catherine," her mother had called as she came in.

"Yes?" Her mother had appeared down the hall.

"You're not letting what I told you bother you?"

"No."

"It may not happen to you for a long time. Some girls are older than others. But when it happens, it means you're becoming a woman and that is something quite wonderful."

"Yes mother, I know." She had hurried upstairs to her room and shut the door. After making sure that everything was quiet, she had taken the lipstick out of her pocket and settled herself in front of the mirror to draw dark red circles on both her cheeks and then begin a series of heavy checkmarks on her forehead. The lipstick had started to crumble when she pressed too hard. To finish off her makeup, she had put large spots on her nose and chin. When she had carefully considered her image in the mirror, she had hidden the lipstick in a drawer and slipped out by the back stairs.

"There might be some food in the refrigerator," Mike said, but Catherine didn't turn away from the window.

"What are you going to do?" she said.

"Get sober to apologize and then stay drunk."

"She's in love with you."

"I'm sorry about that."

"Why did you pick one of my friends?"

"I've always admired your taste in people. I thought at first she was like you. She isn't though. Not a bit."

As Catherine had hurried down the back stairs with the lipstick on her face, she had listened carefully so that her mother wouldn't intercept her. She had reached the back door safely and raced across the yard.

"Hawkeye," she had called, "Hawkeye, Hawkeye."

There had been no answer from the tree house.

"It's me. It's Chingachgook." Catherine had hoisted herself up the trunk of the tree and banged on the door. "Hawkeye," she had called, "it's Chingachgook. Come on and open up. The Mingoes aren't around. It's safe." She had dropped to the ground as the door of the tree house opened. Mike had come to the door.

"Can't you be quiet, we're trying to work. What's wrong with your face?"

"It's war paint."

"Chingachgook didn't wear war paint."

"We can pretend we did."

"You can if you like. Me and Murray are making a rabbit trap."

"Drop down the ladder and let me see."

"There isn't enough room for three people."

"But I'm Chingachgook. There's got to be room for me."

Murray was standing at the door.

"What's that your sister has on her face?"

"She says it's war paint."

"I'm Chingachgook and he's Hawkeye."

"Who're they?"

"From a book," Mike had said. "Let's go back to the trap. I'll see you later, Chingachgook," he had said and closed the door.

Catherine had turned away and gone back into the house and up to her room. She had taken off the lipstick and lain on the bed, and after a while her mother had come in to see if she was upset and explain about growing up.

Catherine put down the book and turned from the window. She looked at her brother.

"Sorry Pathfinder," he said.

"I was Chingachgook, Mike."

"So you were."

Catherine picked up her coat and walked to the door.

"And as far as I'm concerned," she said, "you can go to hell." When she left the room her brother had not said another word.

—1969

559

JOHN NEWLOVE

(1938-   )

*John Herbert Newlove was born in Regina, and has lived in various farming com-
munities of eastern Saskatchewan, where his mother was a schoolteacher. He has himself taught in a high school, served as a social worker, a radio copywriter, a music and
news editor, and a lecturer on poetry. He has lived in both the Maritimes and on the
West Coast. He is now Senior Editor of McClelland and Stewart, the Toronto publishers. He has contributed to magazines and anthologies in Canada, the United States,
Mexico, England, France, Roumania, India, and Australia.*

His first volume of poetry was Grave Sirs *(1962). Since then he has published eight
more volumes, including* The Cave *(1970) and* Lies *(1972). The latter won a
Governor-General's Award.*

THE PRIDE

I

The image/   the pawnees
in their earth-lodge villages,
the clear image
of teton sioux, wild
fickle people the chronicler says,

the crazy dogs, men
tethered with leather dog-thongs
to a stake, fighting until dead,

image: arikaras
with traded spanish sabre blades
mounted on the long
heavy buffalo lances,
riding the sioux
down, the centaurs, the horsemen
scouring the level plains
in war or hunt
until smallpox got them,
4,000 warriors,

image – of a desolate country,
a long way between fires,
unfound lakes, mirages, cold rocks,
and lone men going through it,
cree with good guns
creating terror in athabaska
among the inhabitants, frightened
stone-age people, "so that
they fled at the mere sight
of a strange smoke miles away."

II

This western country crammed
with the ghosts of indians,
haunting the coastal stones and shores,
the forested pacific islands,
mountains, hills and plains:

beside the ocean ethlinga,
man in the moon, empties
his bucket, on
a sign from Spirit

of the Wind ethlinga
empties his bucket, refreshing
the earth, and it rains
on the white cities;

that black joker, broken-
jawed raven, most prominent
among haida and tsimshyan tribes,
is in the kwakiutl
dance masks too —
it was he who brought fire,
food and water to man,
the trickster;

and thunderbird hilunga,
little thought of
by haida for lack of thunderstorms
in their district, goes
by many names, exquisite disguises
carved in the painted wood,

he is nootka tootooch, the wings
causing thunder and the tongue
or flashing eyes engendering
rabid white lightning,
whose food was whales,
called kwunusela by the kwakiutl,
it was he who laid down the house-logs
for the people at Place
Where Kwunusela Alighted;

in full force and virtue
and terror of the law, eagle —
he is authority, the sun
assumed his form once,
the sun which used to be
a flicker's egg, success-
fully transformed;

and malevolence comes to the land,
the wild woman of the woods;
grinning, she wears
a hummingbird in her hair,
d'sonoqua, the furious one —

they are all ready
to be found, the legends
and the people, or
all their ghosts and memories,
whatever is strong enough
to be remembered.

III

But what image, bewildered
son of all men
under the hot sun,
do you worship,
what completeness
do you hope to have
from these tales,
a half-understood massiveness, mirage,
in men's minds — what
is your purpose;

with what force
will you proceed
along a line
neither straight nor short,
whose future
you cannot know
or result foretell,
whose meaning is still
obscured as the incidents
occur and accumulate?

IV

The country moves on;
there are orchards in the interior,
the mountain passes
are broken, the foothills
covered with cattle and fences,
and the fading hills covered;

but the plains are bare,
not barren, easy
for me to love their people
for me to love their people
without selection.

V

In 1787, the old cree saukamappee,
aged 75 or thereabout, speaking then
of things that had happened when he was 16,
just a man, told david thompson,
of the raids the shoshonis,
the snakes, had made on the westward-
reaching peigan, of their war-parties
sometimes sent 10 days journey to enemy camps,

the men all afoot in battle array for
the encounter, crouching
behind their giant shields;

the peigan armed with guns
drove these snakes out of the plains,
the plains where their strength had been,
where they had been settled since living
memory (though nothing is remembered
beyond a grandfather's time),
to the west of the rockies;

these people moved without rest,
backward and forward with the wind,
the seasons, the game, great herds,
in hunger and abundance—

in summer and in the bloody fall
they gathered on the killing grounds,
fat and shining with fat, amused
with the luxuries of war and death,

relieved from the steam of knowledge,
consoled by the stream of blood
and steam rising from the fresh hides
and tired horses, wheeling in their pride
on the sweating horses, their pride.

we stand alone,
we are no longer lonely
but have roots,
and the rooted words
recur in the mind, mirror, so that
we dwell on nothing else, in nothing else,
touched, repeating them,
at home freely
at last, in amazement;

"the unyielding phrase
in tune with the epoch,"
the thing made up
of our desires,
not of its words, not only
of them, but of something else,
as well, that which we desire
so ardently, that which
will not come when
it is summoned alone,
but grows in us
and idles about and hides
until the moment is due—

the knowledge of
our origins, and where
we are in truth,
whose land this is
and is to be.

VI

Those are all stories;
the pride, the grand poem
of our land, of the earth itself,
will come, welcome, and
sought for, and found,
in a line of running verse,
sweating, our pride;

we seize on
what has happened before,
one line only
will be enough,
a single line and
then the sunlit brilliant image suddenly
floods us
with understanding, shocks our
attentions, and all desire
stops, stands alone;

VII

The unyielding phrase:
when the moment is due, then
it springs upon us
out of our own mouths,
unconsidered, overwhelming
in its knowledge, complete—

not this handful
of fragments, as the indians
are not composed of
the romantic stories
about them, or of the stories
they tell only, but
still ride the soil
in us, dry bones a part

of the dust in our eyes,
needed and troubling
in the glare, in
our breath, in our
ears, in our mouths,
in our bodies entire, in our minds, until at
last we become them

in our desires, our desires,
mirages, mirrors, that are theirs, hard-
riding desires, and they
become our true forbears, moulded
by the same wind or rain,
and in this land we
are their people, come
back to life.   —*1968*

MARGARET ATWOOD

(1939-   )

Margaret Atwood was born of Nova Scotian parents in Ottawa, and lived there until she moved to Sault Ste. Marie (1945) and Toronto (1946-1961). As the daughter of an entomologist specializing in forest insects, she learned to know the Northern Ontario and Quebec bush in spring, summer, and fall. She graduated from Victoria College with a B.A. (1961) and Radcliffe College (Harvard) with an A.M. (1962). She has also lived in Vancouver (1964-1965), Montreal (1967-1968), and Edmonton (1968-1970), and travelled in England, France, and Italy (1970-1971). Miss Atwood has taught at British Columbia, Sir George Williams, Alberta, and York Universities In 1972-1973 she was Writer-in-Residence at the University of Toronto. She was a board member and editor with House of Anansi Press, Toronto.

Her first book of poems was Double Persephone *(1961); her second book,* The Circle Game *(1966), won a Governor-General's Award. Besides four subsequent volumes of poetry, she has published two novels:* The Edible Woman *(1969) and* Surfacing *(1972). Survival (1972) is a provocative, even controversial "thematic guide to Canadian Literature."*

JOURNEY TO THE INTERIOR

There are similarities
I notice: that the hills
which the eyes make flat as a wall, welded
together, open as I move
to let me through; become
endless as prairies; that the trees
grow spindly, have their roots
often in swamps; that this is a poor country;
that a cliff is not known
as rough except by hand, and is
therefore inaccessible. Mostly

that travel is not the easy going
from point to point, a dotted
line on a map, location
plotted on a square surface
but that I move surrounded by a tangle
of branches, a net of air and alternate
light and dark, at all times;
that there are no destinations
apart from this.

There are differences
of course: the lack of reliable charts;
more important, the distraction of small details:
your shoe among the brambles under the chair
where it shouldn't be; lucent
white mushrooms and a paring knife
on the kitchen table; a sentence
crossing my path, sodden as a fallen log
I'm sure I passed yesterday
                              (have I been

walking in circles again?)

but mostly the danger:
many have been here, but only
some have returned safely.

A compass is useless; also
trying to take directions
from the movements of the sun,
which are erratic;
and words here are as pointless
as calling in a vacant
wilderness.
              Whatever I do I must
keep my head. I know
it is easier for me to lose my way
forever here, than in other landscapes

                                        —1966

THIS IS A PHOTOGRAPH OF ME

It was taken some time ago.
At first it seems to be
a smeared
print: blurred lines and grey flecks
blended with the paper;

then, as you scan
it, you see in the left-hand corner
a thing that is like a branch: part of a tree
(balsam or spruce) emerging
and, to the right, halfway up
what ought to be a gentle
slope, a small frame house.

In the background there is a lake,
and beyond that, some low hills.

(The photograph was taken
the day after I drowned.

I am in the lake, in the center
of the picture, just under the surface.

It is difficult to say where
precisely, or to say
how large or small I am:
the effect of water
on light is a distortion

but if you look long enough,
eventually
you will be able to see me).

—1966

THE LANDLADY

This is the lair of the landlady.

She is
a raw voice
loose in the rooms beneath me,

the continuous henyard
squabble going on below
thought in this house like
the bicker of blood through the head.

She is everywhere, intrusive as the smells
that bulge in under my doorsill;
she presides over my
meagre eating, generates
the light for eyestrain.

From her I rent my time:
she slams
my days like doors.
Nothing is mine

and when I dream images
of daring escapes through the snow
I find myself walking
always over a vast face
which is the land-
lady's, and wake up shouting.

She is a bulk, a knot
swollen in space. Though I have tried
to find some way around
her, my senses
are cluttered by perception
and can't see through her.

She stands there, a raucous fact
blocking my way:
immutable, a slab
of what is real,

solid as bacon.

—1968

THE IMMIGRANTS

They are allowed to inherit
the sidewalks involved as palmlines, bricks
exhausted and soft, the deep
lawnsmells, orchards whorled
to the land's contours, the inflected weather

only to be told they are too poor
to keep it up, or someone
has noticed and wants to kill them; or the towns
pass laws which declare them obsolete.

I see them coming
up from the hold smelling of vomit,
infested, emaciated, their skins grey
with travel; as they step on shore

the old countries recede, become
perfect, thumbnail castles preserved
like gallstones in a glass bottle, the
towns dwindle upon the hillsides
in a light paperweight-clear.

They carry their carpetbags and trunks
with clothes, dishes, the family pictures;
they think they will make an order
like the old one, sow miniature orchards,
carve children and flocks out of wood

but always they are too poor, the sky
is flat, the green fruit shrivels
in the prairie sun, wood is for burning;
and if they go back, the towns

in time have crumbled, their tongues
stumble among awkward teeth, their ears
are filled with the sound of breaking glass.
I wish I could forget them
and so forget myself:

my mind is a wide pink map
across which move year after year
arrows and dotted lines, further and further,
people in railway cars

their heads stuck out of the windows
at stations, drinking milk or singing,
their features hidden with beards or shawls
day and night riding across an ocean of unknown
land to an unknown land.

—1970

DREAM 1: THE BUSH GARDEN

I stood once more in that garden
sold, deserted and
gone to seed

In the dream I could
see down through the earth, could see
the potatoes curled
like pale grubs in the soil
the radishes thrusting down
their fleshy snouts, the beets
pulsing like slow amphibian hearts

Around my feet
the strawberries were surging, huge
and shining

When I bent
to pick, my hands
came away red and wet

In the dream I said
I should have known
anything planted here
would come up blood

—1970

THE PLANTERS

They move between the jagged edge
of the forest and the jagged river
on a stumpy patch of cleared land

my husband, a neighbour, another man
weeding the few rows
of string beans and dusty potatoes.

They bend, straighten: the sun
lights up their faces and hands, candles
flickering in the wind against the

unbright earth. I see them: I know
none of them believe they are here.
They deny the ground they stand on.

pretend this dirt is the future.
And they are right. If they let go
of that illusion solid to them as a shovel,

open their eyes even for a moment
to these trees, to this particular sun
they would be surrounded, stormed, broken

in upon by branches, roots, tendrils, the dark
side of light
as I am.

—1970

FOR ARCHEOLOGISTS

Deep under, far back
the early horses run
on rock   /   the buffalo, the deer
the other animals (extinct)
run with spears in their backs

Made with blood, with coloured
dirt, with smoke, not meant
to be seen but to remain
there hidden, potent
in the dark, the link between
the buried will and the upper
world of the sun and green feeding,
chase and the hungry kill

drawn by a hand hard
even to imagine

but passed on
in us, part of us now
part of the structure of the bones

existing still in us
as fossil skulls
of the bear, spearheads, bowls and
folded skeletons arranged
in ritual patterns, waiting
for the patient searcher to find them

exist in caves of the earth.

—1970

WOMAN SKATING

A lake sunken among
cedar and black spruce hills;
late afternoon.

On the ice a woman skating,
jacket sudden
red against the white,

concentrating on moving
in perfect circles.

>   (actually she is my mother, she is
>   over at the outdoor skating rink
>   near the cemetery. On three sides
>   of her there are streets of brown
>   brick houses; cars go by; on the
>   fourth side is the park building.
>   The snow banked around the rink
>   is grey with soot. She never skates
>   here. She's wearing a sweater and
>   faded maroon earmuffs, she has
>   taken off her gloves)

Now near the horizon
the enlarged pink sun swings down.
Soon it will be zero.

With arms wide the skater
turns, leaving her breath like a diver's
trail of bubbles.

Seeing the ice
as what it is, water:
seeing the months
as they are, the years
in sequence occurring
underfoot, watching
the miniature human
figure balanced on steel
needles (those compasses
floated in saucers) on time
sustained, above
time circling: miracle

Over all I place
a glass bell

—1970

YOU HAVE MADE YOUR ESCAPE

You have made your escape,
your known addresses
crumple in the wind, the city
unfreezes with relief

traffic shifts back
to its routines, the swollen
buildings return to

normal, I walk believably
from house to store, nothing

remembers you but the bruises
on my thighs and the inside of my skull.

—1971

GWENDOLYN MacEWEN

(1941-   )

Toronto-born Gwendolyn MacEwen has been a prolific writer from an early age. She was only fifteen when her work first appeared in print. She attended public school in Winnipeg, high school in Toronto. At eighteen, although she was a scholarship student, she left school to devote more time to her writing. In 1961 she published two privately-printed booklets of verse. These were followed by her first published novel, Julian, the Magician, *and her first full book of poetry,* The Rising Fire, *both published in 1963. The latter book established her reputation as a poet. Three later volumes of poetry followed, the latest being* The Armies of the Moon *(1972). Between 1965 and 1968 four of her radio plays were broadcast by the CBC. Her second novel was* King of Egypt, King of Dreams *(1971).* Noman *(1972) is a collection of short stories. A brief marriage with Milton Acorn was followed by a decade of single life, during which she travelled often to the Middle and Near East, since she has long been interested in Islamic studies. She has since remarried and lives in Toronto.*

EXPLORATION AND DISCOVERY

We must sing much to master wind's loud
love of land
in insistence of dimension,
and be bards ever
on green earth under
clear-cut sun cutting yellow dolls of us
in the morning.

In an orphan valley between
two tossed parental mountains
boys blow reed pipes where the water is
and string days around their necks
like painted beads;
in a city's rabbit hours
in lightning streets three children
trisect a dragonfly, taste air on their tongues,
and find it sweet and run after wind,
their hands wide open like beggars.

A white bonhomme smokes the years in his pipe;
his woman knits socks for the feet in her daughter's womb,
day like a blond bear leans down their shoulders.

There are sixteen sails on the sea's face.
The waves drink the water.
A moon is happening in the high sky
and the grass prays greenly.

The butter of the sun is spread on world
thick as all summer in this time.
All gay seeds are split for primordial light
to enter.
            Welcome to the earth.

                                        —1963

SKULLS AND DRUMS

you talked about sound, not
footstep sound, shiphorn, nightcry,
                              but

strings collecting, silver
and catgut, violas riding
the waves of May like soft ships,
                              yes

and the anchoring senses,
the range, the register,
the index
          in the ear; the long
measure from the drums of our skulls
to the heart (and its particular tempo);
the music anchored there, gathered
in.

you will hear me now, I think,
while my skin still gathers tones of the sun in,
while we ride the bars, the slow passages
of these first minutes;

while the taut drums of our skulls
open
and all sounds enter
and the pores of our skin like slow valves open.

we will hear each other now, I think,
while nothing is known, while sound
and statement in the ear
leave all alternatives;
                our skulls like drums,
                like tonal caves
                echo, enclose

while the ribs of our bodies are great hulls
and the separate ships of our senses
for a minute
anchor,
for a minute in the same harbor
anchor.

                                  —*1963*

THE HOUSE

in this house poems are broken,
I would invent the end of poetry;
we are only complete when

           that image of me in you
           that image of you in me
           breaks, repairs itself.

you are the earth and the earth;
release those cosmic hands which held you
while I set out on my urgent journeys—

           in this house we repair
           torn walls together and do not
           ask how they were torn.

we work slowly, for
the house is the earth
and the earth—

           the delicate people in you
           move
           from room to room.   —*1966*

POEMS IN BRAILLE

I

all your hands are verbs,
now you touch worlds and feel their names-
thru the thing to the name
not the other way thru (in winter
I am Midas, I name gold)

the chair and table and book
extend from your fingers;
all your movements
command these things back to their
places; a fight against familiarity
makes me resume my distance

II

they knew what it meant,
those egyptian scribes who drew
eyes right into their hieroglyphs,
you read them dispassionate until
the eye stumbles upon itself
blinking back from the papyrus

outside, the articulate wind
annotates this; I read carefully
lest I go blind in both eyes, reading with
that other eye the final hieroglyph

III

the shortest distance between 2 points
on a revolving circumference
is a curved line; O let me follow you,
Wenceslas

IV

with legs and arms I make alphabets
like in those children's books
where people bend into letters and signs,
yet I do not read the long cabbala of my bones
truthfully; I need only to move
to alter the design

V

I name all things in my room
and they rehearse their names,
gather in groups, form tesseracts,
discussing their names among themselves

I will not say the cast is less than the print
I will not say the curve is longer than the line,
I should read all things like braille in this season
with my fingers I should read them
lest I go blind in both eyes reading with
that other eye the final hieroglyph

—*1966*

ARCANUM ONE

and in the morning the king loved you most
and wrote your name with a sun and a beetle
and a crooked ankh, and in the morning
you wore gold mainly, and the king adorned you
with many more names

beside fountains, both of you slender
as women, circled and walked together
like bracelets circling water, both of you
slender as women, wrote your names with
beetles and with suns, and spoke together
in the golden mornings

and the king entered your body
into the bracelet of his name
and you became a living syllable
in his golden script, and your body
escaped from me like founting water
all the daylong

but in the evenings you wrote my name
with a beetle and a moon, and lay upon me
like a long broken necklace which had fallen
from my throat, and the king loved you
most in the morning, and his glamorous love
lay lengthwise along us all the evening

—*1966*

POEM IMPROVISED AROUND A FIRST LINE

the smoke in my bedroom which is always burning
worsens you, motorcycle Icarus;
you are black and leathery and lean and
you cannot distinguish between sex and nicotine

anytime, it's all one thing for you—
cigarette, phallus, sacrificial fire—
all part of that grimy flight
on wings axlegreased from Toronto to Buffalo
for the secret beer over the border—

now I long to see you fullblown and black
over Niagara, your bike burning and in full flame
and twisting and pivoting over Niagara
and falling finally into Niagara,
and tourists coming to see your black leather wings
hiss and swirl in the steaming current—

now I long to give up cigarettes
and change the sheets on my carboniferous bed;
O baby, what Hell to be Greek in this country—
without wings, but burning anyway

—1966

THE SHADOW-MAKER

I have come to possess your darkness, only this.

My legs surround your black, wrestle it
As the flames of day wrestle night
And everywhere you paint the necessary shadows
On my flesh and darken the fibres of my nerve;
Without these shadows I would be
In air one wave of ruinous light
And night with many mouths would close
Around my infinite and sterile curve.

Shadow-maker create me everywhere
Dark spaces (your face is my chosen abyss),
For I said I have come to possess your darkness,
Only this.

—1970

THE DISCOVERY

do not imagine that the exploration
ends, that she has yielded all her mystery
or that the map you hold
cancels further discovery

I tell you her uncovering takes years,
takes centuries, and when you find her naked
look again,
admit there is something else you cannot name,
a veil, a coating just above the flesh
which you cannot remove by your mere wish

when you see the land naked, look again
(burn your maps, that is not what I mean),
I mean the moment when it seems most plain
is the moment when you must begin again

—1970

SEA THINGS

I've been giving a lot of thought
to shellfish and sponges and those
half-plant half-animal things that go
flump flump on the seafloor, also
a funny thing shaped like a pyramid
which spends all its life
buried in the sand upside-down
and has no friends.

And because I know nothing
about the sea I worry
about how they're finding their food
or making love, or for that matter
if they have anything to make love with.

I open a can of oysters
and see them all lying there, lying there
naked and embryonic, and wonder
how long I can go on worrying about things
that creep around miles below my eye
beneath tons of black water

With their hopes and fears and hungers
and their attempts to better themselves
and the secret brains or pearls they keep
protected in their shells.

I've been giving them a lot of thought
but I do not really want to know them,
for they flung me forth, a nuisance in their midst
with my mind and complex hungers
crashing on the high white beaches of the world.   *—1972*

She, of course, was used to it. Twenty-five years of parkas, fur-lined snowboots, mittens, scarves and crunching, slushing, sliding through it on the way to work or school. It was a Thing that covered the country four or five months a year, not unlike that billowy white corpuscle or whatever it was that went mad and smothered the villain of the film *Incredible Journey*. But for *him*, fresh from the Mediterranean, it was a kind of heavenly confetti, ambrosia or manna, and he rushed out half-mad at the first snowfall and lost himself in the sweet salt cold. He even dreamed of snow and he had a weird talent for predicting the next snowfall. He'd sleep and see tiny people coming down from the sky in parachutes that were snowflakes, a rain of infinitesimally small doves, ejaculations of white blossoms— the sperm of the great sleeping sky tree.

All through September and October his blood rose in anticipation of the cold, while all around him people lost their summer energy and grew weary and irritable as they thought of the long white siege ahead.

In December he trudged around frozen and delirious with joy in his soft Italian leather shoes with the pointed European toes, while she, bundled up to the chin with countless nameless pieces of wool and fur, hardly able to turn her head to see him, wondered how he could stand having to take his pants to the cleaner's twice a week to get the slush and wintry crud cleaned off of the cuffs. He made snowballs with his *bare hands*, if you can imagine, and when the tips of his ears turned a ghastly white from the cold, it never occurred to him to buy a hat. Coming indoors after an hour or two of strolling through a blizzard he would be *laughing* and freezing as if the winter were a great white clown someone had created solely for his amusement. She meanwhile, huddled in front of the oven or even the toaster, would try to unnerve him with horrendous tales of winter in Winnipeg. "If you think *this* is something," she would gasp, "you should see what it's like out *west!*" and go on to describe how as a child she used to walk to school in the morning through shoulder-high snowbanks and by the time she got to the schoolyard there would be icicles in her nose and all round her mouth and her lips were so frozen she couldn't speak, and all the kids would be trying to laugh with their wooden lips. But he laughed too when he heard the story, and told her he wished he'd been with her out there, because, he explained, what thrilled him wasn't feeling the cold but letting the cold feel *him*.

Actually, she was quite a good sport with him that first winter he was in Kanada. At midnight after a heavy snowfall, they'd go into a little park where the swings and slides stood like skeletons in the blackness, and he, trembling with excitement, would put his foot into a fresh snowscape and examine the footprint of man marring the virgin whiteness. "A giant step for mankind," she'd say, as if the park were a moonscape, and slowly slowly they would walk forward pretending they were astronauts, clumsy and weightless in the midnight park, pouncing with glee on a swing or a slide or a water-fountain and radioing back to Earth that they had found evidence of an intelligent civilization. She would pick up a boulder—which turned out once to be somebody's frozen bowling shoe—and he, zooming in with his invisible TV camera, would relay the image to the millions of viewers in Tokyo and New York and Paris and London and Montreal. Then they would take imaginary pictures of each other standing triumphantly in front of the swings, or gazing rapturously at a gleaming slide, which seemed to be giving off inter-galactic signals, like the rectangular slab in *Space Odyssey*.

For the first half hour or so she found it fun; they made cryptic triangles and squares in the snow and she even taught him how to make an "angel" by lying on his back in the snow and swinging his arms up and down on both sides. But he was always wanting to prolong the excursions long after the cold had crept into her bones and she, wet through and shivering horribly, would have to wait for him to finish his angels—sometimes five, six, even seven of them all done in a neat circle around the water-fountain with their wings facing many points of the compass.

Gradually they became quite serious about what they should make of each fresh snowscape. They would stand on the brink of the park sometimes for five or ten whole minutes debating what they should inscribe there with their feet or hands, not wanting to waste the cleanness, the newness of the snow on trivial ventures. Moonscapes and angels started to pall on them, so one night they decided to do a series of gigantic initials, which seemed easy but was actually quite difficult because they had to make tremendous Nureyev-like leaps between the various strokes of the letters. When they still had some space left he decided to write his name, but he got all fouled up in the middle trying to do the splits between the bottom of an "O" and the top of an "R." So he fell down flat in the middle of his name and got up protesting that it all came of not knowing how to write English well.

Another night they made a magic circle with segments bearing Cabbalistic Hebrew letters, and they both leapt into the centre of the circle and stood there under the stars and made secret wishes that are not our business to know.

Another night they were tired and spent the time throwing snowballs at tree trunks, which left hazy white circles like the fist-marks of avenging angels.

Another night they did Fantastic Footprints and Imaginary Beast tracks, trying to make the park look as if it has been the battleground between three-footed humans and hideous monsters who walked sideways like crabs. It took two hours to finish and though she had serious doubts as to whether it had been worth the effort, he was swollen with pride. You'd think he'd just completed a painting or a novel.

He was forever thinking up new things to be done with the snow. He considered (seriously) painting it, even flavouring it with sacks full of lime or lemon powder, and would have gone ahead with his plan had she not discouraged him by informing him you couldn't buy lime or lemon powder by the sack. So they made snowmen and snowwomen and snowchildren and snowanimals and snowstars. (A snowstar is a big ball of snow with long icicles—if you can find them—protruding out of the sides.) They made snowstars until her hands hurt. They made snowtrenches—where they lay in wait for the invisible army of abominable snowmen to come—until she thought she'd go mad, screaming mad. They made white fairy castles, they made white futuristic city-scapes, and they made footprints, footprints, footprints.

So I suppose what developed was, after all, to be expected. Which is not to say that she herself expected it in the least. When the night of the blizzard came and he hadn't showed up at his usual time, she got worried, very worried. And so she put on her fur-lined boots and her parka and her scarf and her mittens and went

577

trudging out in the direction of the park. The snowfall that night was like a rapid descent of stars; they came down obliquely, razor-sharp, and her face stung and reddened and burned. *Snowfire,* she thought. Another word.

And she *was* surprised, though not totally, to find Grigori lying there at the bottom of the slide that gave off signals like the metal slab in *Space Odyssey*, with his Mediterranean hair all aflurry from the wind and his absolutely naked stone dead body wedged somehow into the snowdrift, and his arms outstretched at his sides as if he'd been making his last *angel*.

But what really got her was the smile on his face. He never did feel the cold.

—1972

MICHAEL ONDAATJE

(1943-   )

Philip Michael Ondaatje was born in Colombo, Ceylon, and came to Canada by way of England. He is now a Canadian citizen. He was educated at Bishop's University, Toronto, and Queen's (M.A.).

Ondaatje has taught at the University of Western Ontario and he is now in the English Department of Glendon College, York University. As well as being a writer he makes films: Sons of Captain Poetry *is on the concrete poet, b.p. Nichol. His poems have appeared in most Canadian periodicals.*

Ondaatje's first book of poetry was The Dainty Monsters *(1967). His third volume,* The Collected Works of Billy the Kid: Left Handed Poems, *won the Governor-General's Award for 1970.* Rat Jelly *(1973) is his most recent volume. Ondaatje has also written a short critical monograph (1970) on Leonard Cohen.*

BIOGRAPHY

The dog scatters her body in sleep,
paws, finding no ground, whip at air,
the unseen eyeballs reel deep, within.
And waking—crouches,
tacked to humility all day,
children ride her, stretch,
display the black purple lips,
pull hind legs to dance;
unaware that she
tore bulls apart, loosed
heads of partridges,
dreamt blood.   *—1967*

I HAVE SEEN PICTURES OF GREAT STARS

I have seen pictures of great stars,
drawings which show them straining to the centre
that would explode their white
if temperature and the speed they moved at
shifted one degree.

Or in the East have seen
the dark grey yards where trains are fitted
and the clean speed of machines
that make machines, their
red golden pouring which when cooled
mists out to rust or grey.

The beautiful machines pivoting on themselves
sealing and fusing to others
and men throwing levers like coins at them.
And there is there the same stress as with stars,
the one altered move that will make them maniac.

—1970

POSTCARD FROM PICCADILLY STREET

Dogs are the unheralded voyeurs of this world.
When we make love
the spaniel shudders
walks out of the room,
she's had her fill of children now.

but the bassett—for whom
we've pretty soon got to find a love object
apart from furniture or visitors' legs—
jumps on the bed and watches.

It is a catching habit having a spectator
and appeals to the actor in both of us,
in spite of irate phone calls from the SPCA
who claim we are corrupting minors
(the dog being one and a half).

We have moved to elaborate audiences now.
At midnight we open the curtains
turn out the light
and imagine the tree outside
full of sparrows
with infra red eyes.

—1970, 1973

Selected criticism

Lionel Stevenson

Appraisals of Canadian Literature, published in 1926 when its author was only 24, is by far the best general study of its subject before the appearance (in 1943) of E. K. Brown's On Canadian Poetry. *Born in Scotland, Stevenson has pursued his career as Professor of English in American universities. He has published two volumes of poetry, but most of his many books are studies of British authors.*

———◆———

A Manifesto for a National Literature

To admit the existence or define the character of a distinctive literature deserving the term "national" for more cogent reasons than the accidental locality of production, is in the case of Canada a very different problem from that entailed in making the same analysis for other countries. This is due to the linguistic and cultural relation in which Canada stands to the Mother Country, complicated by the proximity of another English-speaking nation. Most people are disposed to evade the discussion by denying that a Canadian literature exists or can exist. Certainly the assertion that only native-born Canadians can produce the national literature, or that only Canadian scenes can constitute it, rests on an entire ignoring of what literature is. Boundary lines have no existence for the things of the mind and imagination; languages are incidental variations of the medium, rather than primary factors. But to assert that a true national literature, in the correct sense of both terms, can never develop in Canada, is, as I shall attempt to indicate, equally fallacious.

How far the tradition of English literature in America is a harmful domination and how far

essential, is too complex a problem to be discussed here. It is an aspect of the deep correlations of "convention and revolt" in literature. Every literary production depends, more or less palpably, on a long and diverse ancestry, in which can be traced not only the whole foregoing literary development of the country where it is written, but the outstanding achievements of human thought and genius everywhere. Each author is an "heir of the ages," and it is impossible to imagine a literary masterpiece appearing full-blown without this evolution having preceded it. Merely because Canadians employ the language and literary forms of English literature, there is no more justification in denying them distinctive qualities than in gainsaying Chaucer's originality because he used French metres and conventions, Italian and classical stories. . . .

On this continent the language and the whole cultural system are not, as in older civilisations, the product of many centuries during which the natural influences of the country have moulded the soul of the people, who have grown out of the soil and through countless generations have lived in intimate communion with it. In this country the civilisation is not thus indigenous: it is a perfected mechanism, evolved under very different conditions and introduced ready-made. It has gradually become modified to some extent by the inherent character of this continent, but the change has been delayed and disrupted by the constant transfusion of peoples from varied races, each with a different mental background, as well as by unbroken intercourse with the Mother Country. In the United States the outcome is a situation still anomalous enough; Canada, a newer country with more scattered population, has had even less chance of developing a homogenous outlook. . . .

Without going into all Taine's analyses of the effects of climate, scenery and living conditions on literature, one may assume that while a race is developing its particular national culture and temper of mind these factors are of first importance. The inhabitants of Canada brought in their whole system of civilisation ready-made. They have erected a barrier against the natural influences of the country; but those with the poetic gift of seeing and feeling cannot be quite oblivious to Canada's immensity and power. I think that this perception is gradually increasing and taking form in Canadian poetry, from the days of George Frederick Cameron through Lampman and Bliss Carman and Duncan Campbell Scott, to the generation of Robert Norwood and Wilson MacDonald.

This individuality is not at all like that which is coming to be embodied in the literature of the United States. There is between the two countries a significant difference, not only geographically, but socially and spiritually. The first great interpreter of the new world, Walt Whitman, wrote scarcely a poem that could apply to Canada without modification, so pervasive is the distinctive quality of "Americanism," and in his successors, such as Carl Sandburg, this feature is still more pronounced. It resides not so much in the contrast of Canada's forests and plains and mountains with those of the United States, as in two other considerations: the preoccupation, even in Whitman's time, with cities and factories and immigrating swarms; and the studied emphasis which our southern neighbours set upon the externals of national consciousness —what is colloquially known as "flag-waving." The latter point may seem paradoxical, so I repeat that an explicit and encouraged sense of nationality does not necessarily produce great literature. Patriotic poetry is seldom on the high plane in which the spirit moves freely among the supreme minds of all nations. It is only when the poet's country has become for him a living being, endowed with a soul, and not an abstraction of economists, that his love for her can raise his work to that lofty region. Then at last the barriers of convention, of alien or obsolete traditions, are utterly cleared away, and the poet's communion with his country is manifest in all his work. But the intercourse is subconscious, if one may use the slang of the psychologist for something that is really, in this case, more rare and exalted than the movements of the conscious intelligence. The poet draws his life from the latent forces of the country, and in his turn he gives form to that which must otherwise remain unrevealed to men.

In Canada the configurations of nature have scarcely been modified as yet by the presence of humanity. Scenes are pervaded, in the Old World, by the sense of the past, the atmosphere of countless settled generations. Fostered in such an atmosphere, the poetic mind assumes a very different cast from that influenced by the sense of space and of nature's permanence. In Canada the primordial forces are still dominant. So Canadian art is almost entirely devoted to landscape, Canadian poetry to the presentation of nature. But there are deeper implications than that. The distinctive type of landscape painting which has established itself in the country is anything but the photographic type; it is essentially interpretative. And Canadian poetry is equally concerned with the apocalyptic. The poetic mind, placed in the midst of natural grandeur, can scarcely avoid mysticism. It is not the sectarian mysticism of the Old World, steeped in religion and philosophy, but an instinctive pantheism, recognising a spiritual meaning in nature and its identity with the soul of man.

I am not asserting that the ultimate message of Canadian literature will be precisely this. I merely point out that analysis of the Canadian poetry already existing shows that the tendency is towards the expression of this attitude, and that it is consistent with the psychology of the relation between the poet and his surroundings in this country. Of course, I do not assume that genius—or even, if you will, talent —can be marshalled in categories. Among the Canadian poets who have done genuine and original work there are no two who have approached the vision from the same quarter. Lampman's primary concern was with the landscape, Bliss Carman's is with the ecstasy of communion. Duncan Campbell Scott is preoccupied with the beauty and perfection of the form in which the vision is to be embodied, and this applies also to Marjorie Pickthall . . . .

Canadian literature [can be read for what it reveals about the Canadian landscape and Canadian experience]. But this is only one half of the two-fold attraction of literature—the dual appeal that Aristotle distinguishes as the individual and the universal. That is to say, literature not only represents particular scenes and conditions which are interesting for their unfamiliarity, but also uses them as the vehicle for a fresh illumination of the mysteries common to man's existence in every age and clime. Some attention must therefore be paid to this second attribute of Canadian literature, its "universal" value as a contribution to man's comprehension—or rather to his intuitive and imaginative conception—of his place in the world.

Some idea of this quality of Canadian literature has already been suggested in the preceding chapter, but another effort at definition must be made in the light of general tendencies in modern thought. It may be summed up as a revaluation of mental equipment by fresh contact with the primordial natural forces. As I have pointed out, the contrast in Canada of man's puny powers and achievements with Nature's permanence and immensity render ludicrous the anthropomorphic attitude which has become traditional in older civilisations. Tested by the rigours of such a country, the institutions and fashions of civilisation take on new semblances. Whether this reversion to the primitive is preferable to the involutions of a highly developed society has been a topic of debate since the days of Rousseau; but, setting aside theories of "les temps d'innocence et d'égalité," there can be no doubt that the human imagination was acting in such an environment when it evolved some of its loftiest conceptions of the supernatural. The great basic achievements of the human spirit have come out of races in close contact with earth. The Old Testament springs from the barren hills of Judah and the burning sands of the desert. The Greek Pantheon points back to the shepherd Dorians making their first effort to equate the powers of external nature

with the human personality. The Scandinavian mythology has its root in even more desperate conflicts of man against his physical surroundings. But in Europe all these concepts have long ago ceased to be vitalised by the Antaeus-contact with earth. They are shadowy, intellectual figments, symbols which have survived their significance. Even Puck and the rest of the English fairy hierarchy have for centuries been the puppets of literary convention.

In Canada the modern mind is placed in circumstances approximating those of the primitive myth-makers; and as indicating its reaction, shown in its attitude towards contemporary movements in the world of "civilisation," Canadian literature has a value to anyone interested in the history of culture. Canadian authors are familiar with the whole body of tradition in which the imaginative faculty of the race has manifested itself. But they see it in a new perspective. As I have already suggested, the European author is brought up in an atmosphere saturated with history. The country is overlaid with monuments of human handiwork, and even the natural landmarks gain their importance from the events or legends associated with them. Added to this are the restricted traditions pertaining to each nation and to each caste of society. The individual is early equipped with a complete system of national, social, and religious dogmas, and even the unusual man who later attempts to reorganise the system according to his own rational faculty can seldom get rid entirely of preconceptions.

In the last couple of generations there has been a certain emancipation of the mind in one at least of these fields—the religious. As we all know, anthropology, archaeology, and the physical sciences have precipitated a reaction from the strict doctrinal religion of previous centuries. The Hebraic antecedents of Christianity are seen in a new light, and Paganism is no longer a synonym for iniquity. Canadian writers have the benefit of this new sense of proportion, and in addition they have a similar advantage in regard to social and national dogmas. Theirs is a country where the immigrant of aristocratic descent has had to compete on equal terms with the humblest crofter or artisan, and the latter classes have contributed much that is finest in the developed national stock. Similarly, barriers of nationality have diminished: in addition to the three-fold populace of Indian, French, and British, there are settlers from many European countries, and all have found co-operation imperative in the struggle for existence.

So the Canadian has an opportunity of estimating dispassionately the vast accumulation of tradition which forms modern civilisation, in order to select and retain whatever appeals to him as appropriate to the new country. And he has the further advantage of making this estimate by standards derived from an intimate knowledge of primitive nature. In Canada three hundred years of history have scarcely made an impression on the immense and ancient mountains and lakes and plains. Tracts as large as European countries are still unexplored. The inhabitants seem to be precariously perched on a monster not yet conscious of their presence, and if they were to relinquish the perpetual effort of maintaining a foothold their mushroom cities and sporadic cultivation would vanish more rapidly then they have appeared. From childhood surrounded by this vastness and potentiality of nature, the Canadian becomes aware of it long before his education in the traditions of culture begins. Since his sympathy with nature is practically an inbred trait he instinctively responds to those features of religion, myth, or philosophy that retain some meaning as interpretations of Ancient Earth and man's relationship to her . . . .

Canadian Poets and the New Universe

About the middle of the nineteenth century the intellectual world was rocked by an earthquake which shattered or undermined practically all the symmetrical and traditionally authenticated edifices into which knowledge was at that time partitioned. Too much bewildered to recognise the extent of the damage, most men set about patching up their tottering concepts, and buttressing them against one another;

indeed, many of these makeshift ideas survive today, but they are rapidly falling into complete ruin. The "Victorian compromise," to use Mr. Chesterton's phrase, has been in a process of gradual dissolution ever since the great event of 1859.

The publication of Darwin's "Origin of Species" was, of course, merely the focal point of forces which had long been maturing in scientific research and philosophic speculation. But as Darwin put the idea of evolution into a concrete form which appealed to the public mind, he stands as the instigator of the vast controversies and readjustments which invaded not only physical science but also ethics, politics, sociology, and religion. The simultaneous publication of "Essays and Reviews" led to the great "higher criticism" battle in the churches; large numbers of people deserted the traditional faiths, resorting first to positivism, agnosticism, and free thinking, and many later reacting towards more mystical creeds which took the idea of evolution into account.

The new theory, embracing in its wider implications an entire revolution in our concept of the universe and man's place in it, had an immediate and profound effect on literature, particularly on poetry. Indeed the poets led the way toward the new evolutionary mysticism, when the orthodox clerics and materialistic scientists showed no signs of coming to terms . . . .

In short, the evolutionary idea has been the greatest factor in the development of English poetic thought during the nineteenth century, so that contemporary poetry is demarcated from that of the Romantic Revival by an entire change in outlook on nature and human life.

Exactly concurrent with this development has been the other interesting and little studied movement, upon which the present book is based—the extension of English literature into the other parts of the Empire. The years of the great Darwinian controversies witnessed the birth of that generation of poets who have given Canada a voice in literature. Brought up in a country comparatively free from established "schools of thought," they had a chance to learn the new principle of evolution without being distracted by the dust and uproar of the combat. Although by reason of this isolation Canada may have been slower to perceive the importance of the new doctrine, yet by the time our poets were receiving their education, evolution had so far emerged from the conflict that a young man of enquiring and independent mind could scarcely fail to encounter it and recognise its vital importance. I do not mean that the Canadian poets consciously adopted the evolutionary theory as a definite concept to be disseminated didactically in verse; but it seems to me highly probable that their outlook would be fundamentally influenced by the new spirit. In support of this "a priori" assumption I intend to examine some typical examples of Canadian poetry for evidence that the evolutionary concept is in the very heart of their philosophy, necessarily transmuted into poetic forms.

In Canada the theory would not impress itself merely as an intellectual exercise, a hypothesis to be co-ordinated with a whole system of philosophy and culture: to a young man confronting with awe and almost with dismay the vastness of nature in Canada, and committed to the task of adjusting to it his own self-consciousness in a relationship not utterly ridiculous—a task which must often have seemed veritably overwhelming—the principle of evolution must have come as nothing short of a revelation. Nature could not be to him an assemblage of physical objects, a mere landscape picture, as it was to the eighteenth century; but neither could it be the benevolent and sympathetic attendant on human emotions, as Wordsworth pictured it. To a Canadian of poetic perceptions, nature is an entity, embodying vast and inconceivable forces, shadowing forth some mighty purpose beyond human comprehension. Realising this overwhelming might of nature, the poet's sensitive spirit would be in serious danger of quailing in horror and withdrawing itself to less terrific themes. But the idea of evolution allowed a glimpse of unity pervading nature and control directing her mysterious ways. Intuitively rather than rationally the poet perceived that from such a stand-point he might obtain a vision of life in which man's puny figure and nature's brooding power assumed a conceivable proportion, both subordinated to a supernal plan.

In the forests he could see in both vegetable and animal life the struggle for survival in actual operation; in the mountains and cataracts he could trace the very processes by which the face of the globe had been shaped through aeonian action; so the physical arguments in favour of evolution gave him little trouble. He was concerned straightway with the spiritual significance; and the mystical interpretation which he derived partly from philosophy (including the English poetry of the generation which was so seriously preoccupied with evolutionary theorising) but more largely from the influence of his environment, merges consistently into the scientific arguments. Accordingly we do not find Canadian poets approaching evolution with doubts and misgivings, weighing the "pros and cons" as Tennyson did; nor proclaiming it as a definite doctrine, developed to a logical conclusion, like Meredith's "racial immortality" or Hardy's "Godhead dying downward"; they arrive immediately at the third stage, using evolution implicitly as the basis for their treatment of life and nature. . . .

—1926

A REJECTED PREFACE

A. J. M. Smith

The appearance in 1936 of New Provinces *marked a turning point in Canadian poetry. This anthology contained poems by six poets: Robert Finch, A. M. Klein, Leo Kennedy, E. J. Pratt, F. R. Scott, and A. J. M. Smith. Except for Kennedy and Pratt, this was first publication in book form. Smith wrote the original preface for the volume, but Pratt objected and it was withdrawn; another and shorter preface was then written by Scott. Smith's rejected preface was*

first published in Canadian Literature *No. 24:*
6-9 (Spring 1965). A biographical note on Smith
appears with some of his poetry on pages 268-274.

The bulk of Canadian verse is romantic in conception and conventional in form. Its two great themes are Nature and Love—nature humanized, endowed with feeling, and made sentimental; love idealized, sanctified, and inflated. Its characteristic type is the lyric. Its rhythms are definite, mechanically correct, and obvious; its rhymes are commonplace.

The exigencies of rhyme and rhythm are allowed to determine the choice of a word so often that a sensible reader is compelled to conclude that the plain sense of the matter is of only minor importance. It is the arbitrarily chosen verse pattern that counts. One has the uncomfortable feeling in reading such an anthology as W.W. Campbell's *The Oxford Book of Canadian Verse* or J.W. Garvin's *Canadian Poets* that the writers included are not interested in saying anything in particular; they merely wish to show that they are capable of turning out a number of regular stanzas in which statements are made about the writer's emotions, say "In Winter," or "At Montmorenci Falls," or "In A Birch Bark Canoe." Other exercises are concerned with pine trees, the open road, God, snowshoes or Pan. The most popular experience is to be pained, hurt, stabbed or seared by Beauty—preferably by the yellow flame of a crocus in the spring or the red flame of a maple leaf in autumn.

There would be less objection to these poems if the observation were accurate and its expression vivid, or if we could feel that the emotion was a genuine and intense one. We could then go on to ask if it were a valuable one. But, with a negligible number of exceptions, the observation is general in these poems and the descriptions are vague. The poet's emotions are unbounded, and are consequently lacking in the intensity which results from discipline and compression; his thinking is of a transcendental or theosophical sort that has to be taken on faith. The fundamental criticism that must be brought against Canadian poetry as a whole is that it ignores the intelligence. And as a result it is dead.

Our grievance, however, against the great dead body of poetry laid out in the mortuary of the *Oxford Book* or interred under Garvin's florid epitaphs is not so much that it is dead but that its sponsors in Canada pretend that it is alive. Yet it should be obvious to any person of taste that this poetry cannot now, and in most cases never could, give the impression of being vitally concerned with real experience. The Canadian poet, if this kind of thing truly represents his feelings and his thoughts, is a half-baked, hyper-sensitive, poorly adjusted, and frequently neurotic individual that no one in his senses would trust to drive a car or light a furnace. He is the victim of his feelings and fancies, or of what he fancies his feelings ought to be, and his emotional aberrations are out of all proportion to the experience that brings them into being. He has a soft heart and a soft soul; and a soft head. No wonder nobody respects him, and few show even the most casual interest in his poetry. A few patriotic professors, one or two hack journalist critics, and a handful of earnest anthologists—these have tried to put the idea across that there exists a healthy national Canadian poetry which expresses the vigorous hope of this young Dominion in a characteristically Canadian style, etc., etc., but the idea is so demonstrably false that no one but the interested parties has been taken in.

We do not pretend that this volume contains any verse that might not have been written in the United States or in Great Britain. There is certainly nothing specially Canadian about more than one or two poems. Why should there be? Poetry today is written for the most part by people whose emotional and intellectual heritage is not a national one; it is either cosmopolitan or provincial, and, for good or evil, the forces of civilization are rapidly making the latter scarce.

A large number of the verses in this book were written at a time when the contributors were inclined to dwell too exclusively on the fact that the chief thing wrong with Canadian poetry was its conventional and insensitive technique. Consequently, we sometimes thought we had produced a good poem when all we had done in reality was not produce a conventional one. In Canada this is a deed of some merit.

In attempting to get rid of the facile word, the stereotyped phrase and the mechanical rhythm, and in seeking, as the poet today must, to combine colloquialism and rhetoric, we were of course only following in the path of the more significant poets in England and the United States. And it led, for a time, to the creation of what, for the sake of brevity, I will call "pure poetry."

A theory of pure poetry might be constructed on the assumption that a poem exists as a thing in itself. It is not a copy of anything or an expression of anything, but is an individuality as unique as a flower, an elephant or a man on a flying trapeze. Archibald MacLeish expressed the idea in *Ars Poetica* when he wrote,

A poem should not mean, but be.

Such poetry is objective, impersonal and in a sense timeless and absolute. It stands by itself, unconcerned with anything save its own existence.

Not unconnected with the disinterested motives that produce "pure" poetry are those which give rise to imagist poetry. The imagist seeks with perfect objectivity and impersonality to recreate a thing or arrest an experience as precisely and vividly and simply as possible. Mr. Kennedy's *Shore,* Mr. Scott's *trees in ice,* my own *Creek* are examples of the simpler kind of imagist verse; Mr. Finch's *Teacher,* tiny as it is, of the more complex. In *Shore* and *Creek* the reader may notice that the development of the poem depends upon metrical devices as much as on images; the music is harsh and the rhythm difficult.

Most of the verses in this book are not, however, so unconcerned with thought as those mentioned. In poems like *Epithalamium, the Five Kine, Words for a Resurrection* and *Like An Old Proud King* an attempt has been made to fuse thought and feeling. Such a fusion is characteristic of the kind of poetry usually called metaphysical. Good metaphysical verse is not, it must be understood, concerned with the communication of ideas. It is far removed from didactic poetry. What it is concerned with is the emotional effect of ideas that have entered so deeply into the blood as never to be questioned. Such poetry is primarily lyrical; it should seem spontaneous. Something of the quality I am suggesting is to be found in such lines as

The wall was there, oh perilous blade of glass

or

This Man of April walks again

In the poems just mentioned thought is the root, but it flowers in the feeling. They are essentially poems of the sensibility, a little bit melancholy, perhaps a little too musical. A healthier robustness is found in satirical verse, such as Mr. Scott's much needed counterblast against the Canadian Authors Association, or in the anti-romanticism of Mr. Klein's

And my true love,
She combs and combs,
The lice from off
My children's domes.

The appearance of satire, and also of didactic poetry that does not depend upon wit, would be a healthy sign in Canadian poetry. For it would indicate that our poets are realizing, even if in an elementary way, that poetry is more concerned with expressing exact ideas than wishy-washy "dreams." It would indicate, too, that the poet's lofty isolation from events that are of vital significance to everybody was coming to an end.

Detachment, indeed, or self-absorption is (for a time only, I hope) becoming impossible. The era of individual liberty is in eclipse. Capitalism can hardly be expected to survive the cataclysm its most interested adherents are blindly steering towards, and the artist who is concerned with the most intense of experiences must be concerned with the world situation in which, whether he likes it or not, he finds himself. For the moment at least he has something more important to do than to record his private emotions. He must try to perfect a technique that will combine power with simplicity and sympathy with intelligence so that he may play his part in developing mental and emotional attitudes that will facilitate the creation of a more practical social system.

Of poetry such as this, there is here only the faintest foreshadowing — a fact that is not unconnected with the backwardness politically and economically of Canada — but that Canadian poetry in the future must become increasingly aware of its duty to take cognizance of what is going on in the world of affairs we are sure.

That the poet is not a dreamer, but a man of sense; that poetry is a discipline because it is an art; and that it is further a useful art; these are propositions which it is intended this volume shall suggest. We are not deceiving ourselves that it has proved them.

—(1936) 1965

CULTURE WITHOUT LITERACY

Marshall McLuhan

Marshall McLuhan, a Professor of English at St. Michael's College, Toronto, has written a number of books concerned with the cultural aspects of communication. "Culture Without Literacy" appeared in the first number of Explorations *(1953-1959), edited by Marshall McLuhan and E. S. Carpenter.*

The ordinary desire of everybody to have everybody else think alike with himself has some explosive implications today. The perfection of the *means* of communication has given this average power-complex of the human being an enormous extension of expression.

The telephone, the teleprinter, and the wireless made it possible for orders from the highest levels to be given direct to the lowest levels, where, on account of the absolute authority behind them, they were carried out uncritically; or brought it about that numerous offices and command centres were directly connected with the supreme leadership from which they received their sinister orders without any intermediary; or resulted in a widespread surveillance of the citizen, or in a high degree of secrecy surrounding criminal happenings. To the outside observer this governmental apparatus may have resembled the apparently chaotic confusion of lines at a telephone exchange, but like the latter it could be controlled and operated from one central source. Former dictatorships needed collaborators of high quality even in the lower levels of leadership, men who could think and act independently. In the era of modern technique an authoritarian system can do without this. The means of communication alone permit it to mechanize the work of subordinate leadership. As a consequence a new type develops: the uncritical recipient of orders.[1]

Perfection of the *means* of communication has meant instantaneity. Such an instantaneous network of communication is the body-mind unity of each of us. When a city or a society achieves a diversity and equilibrium of awareness analogous to the body-mind network, it has what we tend to regard as a high culture.

But the instantaneity of communication makes free speech and thought difficult if not impossible and for many reasons. Radio extends the range of the casual speaking voice, but it forbids that many should speak. And when what is said has such range of control it is forbidden to speak any but the most acceptable words and notions. Power and control are in all cases paid for by loss of freedom and flexibility.

Today the entire globe has a unity in point of mutual inter-awareness which exceeds in rapidity the former flow of information in a small city—say Elizabethan London with its eighty or ninety thousand inhabitants. What happens to existing societies when they are brought into

---

1. Albert Speer, German Armament Minister in 1942, in a speech at the Nuremburg trials, quoted in Hjalmar Schacht, *Account Settled* (London, 1949), p. 240.

such intimate contact by press, picture stories, newsreels, and jet propulsion? What happens when the neolithic Eskimo is compelled to share the time and space arrangements of technological man? What happens in our minds as we become familiar with the diversity of human cultures which have come into existence under innumerable circumstances, historical and geographical? Is not what happens comparable to that social revolution which we call the American melting-pot?

When the telegraph made possible a daily cross-section of the globe transferred to the page of newsprint, we already had our mental melting-pot for cosmic man—the world citizen. The mere format of the page of newsprint was more revolutionary in its intellectual and emotional consequences than anything that could be *said* about any part of the globe.

When we juxtapose news items from Tokyo, London, New York, Chile, Africa, and New Zealand we are not just manipulating space. The events so brought together belong to cultures widely separated in time. The modern world abridges all historical times as readily as it reduces space. Every *where* and every *age* have become *here* and *now*. History has been abolished by our new media. If prehistoric man is simply preliterate man living in a timeless world of seasonal recurrence, may not posthistoric man find himself in a similar situation? May not the upshot of our technology be the awakening from the historically conditioned nightmare of the past into a timeless present? Historic man may turn out to have been literate man. An episode.

Robert Redfield in his recent book *The Primitive World and Its Transformations* points to the timeless character of preliterate societies where exclusively oral communication ensures intimacy, homogeneity, and fixity of social experience. It is the advent of writing that sets in motion the urban revolution. Writing breaks up the fixity and homogeneity of preliterate societies. Writing creates that inner dialogue or dialectic, that psychic withdrawal which makes possible the reflexive analysis of thought via the stasis of the audible made spatial. Writing is the translation of the audible into the spatial as reading is the reverse of this reciprocal process. And the complex shuttling of eye, ear, and speech factors once engaged in this ballet necessarily reshape the entire communal life, both inner and outer, creating not only the "stream of consciousness" rediscovered by contemporary art, but ensuring multiple impediments to the activities of perception and recall.

So far as writing is the spatializing and arrest of oral speech, however, it implies that further command of space made possible by the written message and its attendant road system. With writing, therefore, comes logical analysis and specialism, but also militarism and bureaucracy. And with writing comes the break in that direct intuitive relationship between men and their surroundings which modern art has begun to uncover.

"Compared with the evidence afforded by living tradition," says Sir James Frazer, "the testimony of ancient books on the subject of the early religion is worth very little. For literature accelerates the advance of thought at a rate which leaves the slow progress of opinion by word of mouth at an immeasurable distance behind. Two or three generations of literature may do more to change thought than two or three thousand years of traditional life."[2] But literature, as we know today, is a relatively conservative time-binding medium compared with press, radio, and movie. So the thought is now beginning to occur: How many thousands of years of change can we afford every ten years? May not a spot of culture-lag here and there in the great time-flux prove to be a kind of social and psychological oasis?

Involved with the loss of memory and the psychic withdrawal of alphabetic cultures, there is a decline of sensuous perception and adequacy of social responsiveness. The preternatural sensuous faculties of Sherlock Holmes or the modern sleuth are simply those of preliterate man who can retain the details of a hundred-mile trail as easily as a movie camera can record

---

2. J. Frazer, *Man, God and Immortality*, (1927), p. 318.

it. Today our detailed knowledge of societies existing within the oral tradition enables us to estimate accurately the advantages and disadvantages of writing. Without writing there is little control of space, but perfect control of accumulated experience. The misunderstandings of Ireland and England can be seen in some basic respects as the clash of oral and written cultures. And the strange thing to us is that the written culture has very little historical sense. The English could never remember; the Irish could never forget. Today the university as a community is in large degree one in which the members are in regular oral communication. And whereas the university has a highly developed time sense, the business community operates on the very short-run and exists mainly by the control of space. The present divorce between these two worlds is only accentuated by the perfection of the media peculiar to each.

Faced with the consequence of writing, Plato notes in the *Phaedrus:*

> This discovery of yours will create forgetfulness in the learners' souls, because they will not use their memories; they will trust to the external written characters and not remember of themselves. The specific which you have discovered is an aid not to memory, but to reminiscence, and you give your disciples not truth but only the semblance of truth; they will be hearers of many things and have learned nothing; they will appear to be omniscient and will generally know nothing; they will be tiresome company, having the show of wisdom without the reality.

Two thousand years of manuscript culture lay ahead of the Western world when Plato made this observation. But nobody has yet studied the rise and decline of Greece in terms of the change from oral to written culture. Patrick Geddes said that the road destroyed the Greek city-state. But writing made the road possible, just as printing was later to pay for the roads of England and America.

In order to understand the printed-book culture which today is yielding, after four hundred years, to the impact of visual and auditory media, it is helpful to note a few of the characteristics of that manuscript culture which persisted from the fifth century B.C. to the fifteenth century A.D. I shall merely mention a few of the principal observations of scholars like Pierce Butler and H. J. Chaytor. In the first place, manuscript culture never made a sharp break with oral speech because everybody read manuscripts aloud. Swift silent reading came with the macadamized surfaces of the printed page. Manuscript readers memorized most of what they read since in the nature of things they had to carry their learning with them. Fewness of manuscripts and difficulty of access made for utterly different habits of mind with regard to what was written. One result was encyclopedism. Men of learning tried, at least, to learn everything, so that if learning was oral, teaching was even more so. Solitary learning and study came only with the printed page. And today when learning and study are switching more and more to the seminar, the round-table, and the discussion group, we have to note these developments as due to the decline of the printed page as the dominant art form.

The manuscript page was a very flexible affair. It was not only in close rapport with the oral speech but with plastic design and color illustration. So the ornate examples of manuscript art easily rival and resemble those books in stone and glass, the cathedrals and abbeys. In our own time James Joyce, seeking a means to orchestrate and control the various verbivoco-visual media of our own age, resorted to the page format of the *Book of Kells* as a means thereto. And even the early romantic poets, painters, and novelists expressed their preference for gothic in terms of rebellion against book culture.

Recently Rosamund Tuve, in elucidating the art of George Herbert, discovered that the characteristic effects of metaphysical wit in the seventeenth century poetry resulted from the translation of visual effects from medieval manuscript and woodcut into the more abstract form of the printed word. If the seventeenth century was receding from a visual plastic culture towards an abstract literary culture, today we seem to be receding from an abstract book culture towards a highly sensuous, plastic pictorial culture. Recent poets have used simultaneously effects from both extremes to achieve witty results not unlike those of the seventeenth century. The impact of Mr. Eliot's very first lines of poetry has been felt everywhere:

Let us go then, you and I,
When the evening is spread out against the sky
Like a patient etherized upon a table.

It is the overlayering of perspectives, the simultaneous use of two kinds of space which creates the shock of dislocation here. For if all art is a contrived trap for the attention, all art and all language are techniques for looking at one situation through another one.

The printed page is a sixteenth century art form which obliterated two thousand years of manuscript culture in a few decades. Yet it is hard for us to see the printed page or any other current medium except in contrast to some other form. The mechanical clock, for example, created a wholly artificial image of time as a uniform linear structure. This artificial form gradually changed habits of work, feeling, and thought which are only being rejected today. We know that in our own lives each event exists in its own time. Time is not the same for the speaker as for the audience. To the speaker it is too, too brief for what he has to say. For the audience it is grim foretaste of eternity. Ultimately the medieval clock made Newtonian physics possible. It may also have initiated those orderly linear habits which made possible the rectilinear page of print created from movable type, as well as the method of commerce. At any rate the mechanization of writing was as revolutionary in its consequences as the mechanization of time. And this, quite apart from thoughts or ideas conveyed by the printed page. Movable type was already the modern assembly line in embryo.

Harold Innis explored some of the consequences of the printed page: the break-down of international communication; the impetus given to nationalism by the commercial exploitation of vernaculars; the loss of contact between writers and audience; the depressing effect on music, architecture, and the plastic arts.

Bela Balazs in his *Theory of the Film* notes some of the changes in visual habits resulting from the printing press on one hand and the camera on the other:

The discovery of printing gradually rendered illegible the faces of men. So much could be read from paper that the method of conveying meaning by facial expression fell into desuetude. Victor Hugo wrote once that the printed book took over the part played by the cathedral in the Middle Ages and became the carrier of the spirit of the people. But the thousands of books tore the one spirit . . . into thousands of opinions . . . tore the church into a thousand books. The visual spirit was thus turned into a legible spirit and visual culture into a culture of concepts. . . . But we paid little attention to the fact that, in conformity with this, the faces of individual men, their foreheads, their eyes, their mouths, had also of necessity and quite correctly to suffer a change.

At present a new discovery, a new machine, is at work to turn the attention of men back to a visual culture and to give them new faces. This machine is the cinematographic camera. Like the printing press it is a technical device for the multiplication and distribution of products of the human spirit; its effect on human culture will not be less than that of the printing press. . . . The gestures of visual man are not intended to convey concepts which can be expressed in words, but such . . . non-rational emotions which would still remain unexpressed when everything that can be told has been told. . . . Just as our musical experiences cannot be expressed in rationalized concepts, what appears on the face and in facial expression is a spiritual experience which is rendered immediately visible without the intermediary of words.

The printed page in rendering the language of the face and gesture illegible has also caused the abstract media of printed words to become the main bridge for the inter-awareness of spiritual and mental states. In the epoch of print and word culture the body ceased to have much expressive value and the human spirit became audible but invisible. The camera eye has reversed this process in reacquainting the masses of men once more with the grammar of gesture. Today commerce has channelled much of this change along sex lines. But even there the power of the camera eye to change physical attitudes and make-up is familiar to all. In the 'nineties Oscar Wilde noted how the pale, long-necked, consumptive red-heads painted by Rossetti and Burne-Jones were for a short time an exotic and visual experience. But soon in every London salon these creatures sprouted up where none had been before. The fact that human nature, at least, imitates art is too obvious to labor. But the fact that with modern technology the entire material of the globe as well as the thoughts and feelings of its human inhabitants have become the matter of art and of man's factive intelligence means that there is no more nature. At least there is no more external nature. Everything from politics to bottle-feeding, global landscape, and the subconscious of the infant is subject to the manipulation of conscious artistic control — the BBC carries the unrehearsed voice of the nightingale to the Congo, the Eskimo sits entranced by the hill-billy music from West Tennessee. Under these conditions the activities of Senator McCarthy belong with the adventures of the Pickwick Club and our talk about the Iron Curtain is a convenient smoke-screen likely to divert our attention from much greater problems. The Russians differ from us in being much more aware of the non-commercial impact of the new media. We have been so hypnotized with the commercial and entertainment qualities of press, radio, movie, and TV that we have been blind to the revolutionary character of these toys. The Russians after a few years of playing with these radio-active toys have tried to neutralize them by imposing various stereotypes on their content and messages. They have forced their press to stick to an 1850 format. They have imposed similar time-locks on music and literature. They hope, thereby, to abate the revolutionary fury of these instruments. But the fury for change is in the form and not the message of the new media, a fact which seems almost inevitably to escape men trained in our abstract literary culture. The culture of print has rendered people extremely insensitive to the language and meaning of spatial forms—one reason for the architectural and city horrors tolerated by predominantly book cultures. Thus the English and American cultures in particular were overwhelmed by print, since in the sixteenth century they had only rudimentary defences to set up against the new printed word. The rest of Europe, richer in plastic and oral culture, was less blitzed by the printing press. And the Orient has so far had many kinds of resistance to offer. But the curious thing is that Spaniards like Picasso or Salvador Dali are much more at home amidst the new visual culture of North America than we ourselves.

This division between visual and literary languages is a fact which has also set a great abyss between science and the humanities. Thinking as we do of culture in book terms, we are unable to read the language of technological forms. And since our earliest aesthetic responses are to such forms, this has set up numerous cleavages between official and idiomatic cultural response within our own experience. We are all of us persons of divided and sub-divided sensibility through failure to recognize the multiple languages with which our world speaks to us. Above all it is the multiplicity of messages with which we are hourly bombarded by our environment that renders us ineffectual. Karl Deutsch has argued that a people shaped by oral tradition will respond to an alien challenge like a suicidal torpedo. The wild Celtic charge. A people shaped by a written tradition will not charge, but drift, pulled in a thousand different directions.

One obvious feature of the printed book is its republicanism. The page of print is not only a leveller of other forms of expression; it is a social leveller as well. Anyone who can read has at least the illusion of associating on equal terms with anyone who has written. And that fact gave the printed word a privileged place in American society and politics. The Duke of Gloucester could say casually to Edward Gibbon, on the completion of his *History*: "Another damned fat square book. Scribble, scribble,

scribble, eh, Mr. Gibbon!" But there were no fox-hunters in America to put the literary upstart in his place.

So far as quantity goes, the printed book was the first instrument of mass culture. Erasmus was the first to see its meaning and turned his genius to the manufacture of textbooks for the classroom. He saw, above all, that the printing press was a device for reproducing the past in the present, much like a Hollywood movie set. The nouveaux riches of Italy began to enact on a tiny scale the past that was being unearthed and printed. Hastily they ran up villas and palazzas in ancient style. Assisted by the newly printed exemplars they began to imitate the language of Cicero and Seneca. In England the new print mingled with the old oral tradition to produce the new forms of sermon and drama which were hybrids of written and spoken culture. But in the printing press there is one great feature of mass culture which is lacking. Namely, the instantaneous. From one point of view, language itself is the greatest of all mass media. The spoken word instantly evokes not only some recently conceived idea but reverberates with the total history of its own experience with man. We may be oblivious of such overtones as of the spectrum of color in a lump of coal. But the poet by exact rhythmic adjustment can flood our consciousness with this knowledge. The artist is older than the fish.

Reading the history of the newspaper retrospectively we can see that it was not a mere extension of the art form of the book page. As used by Rimbaud, Mallarmé, and Joyce the newspaper page is a revolution in itself, juxtaposing many book pages on a single sheet. And the news page was, moreover, more nearly a mass medium not only in reaching more people than the book, but in being more instantaneous in its coverage and communication. Once linked to the telegraph, the press achieved the speed of light, as radio and TV have done since then. Total global coverage in space, instantaneity in time. Those are the two basic characters that I can detect in a mechanical mass medium. There are other characteristics derivative from these, namely anonymity of those originating the messages or forms, and anonymity in the recipients. But in respect of this anonymity it is necessary to regard not only words and metaphors as mass media but buildings and cities as well.

The modern newspaper page is not a mere extension of the book page because the speed with which the telegraph feeds news to the press today precludes any possibility of organizing a sheet of news by any but the most impressionistic devices. Each item lives in its own kind of space totally discontinuous from all other items. A particularly vigorous item will sprout a headline and provide a kind of aura or theme for surrounding items. So that, if the book page could imitate visual perspective as in Renaissance painting, setting facts and concepts in proportions that reproduced the optical image of the three-dimensional object-world, the uninhibited world of the press and modern advertising abandoned such realistic properties in favor of weighting news and commercial objects by every dynamic and structural device of size and color, bringing words and pictures back into a plastic and meaningful connection. If the book page tends to perspective, the news page tends to cubism and surrealism. So that every page of newspapers and magazines, like every section of our cities, is a jungle of multiple, simultaneous perspectives which make the world of hot-jazz and be-bop seem relatively sedate and classical. Our intellectual world, by virtue of the same proliferation of books (over 18,000 new titles in England alone last year) has achieved the same entanglement which is easier to assess through the complexity of our visual environment. It is not just a quantitative problem, of course. As Gyorgy Kepes states it in his *Language of Vision*:

> The environment of man living today has a complexity which cannot be compared with any environment of any previous age. The skyscrapers, the street with its kaleidoscopic vibration of colors, the window-displays with their multiple mirroring images, the street cars and motor cars, produce a dynamic simultaneity of visual impression which cannot be perceived in the terms of inherited visual habits. In this optical turmoil the fixed objects

appear utterly insufficient as the measuring tape of the events. The artificial light, the flashing of electric bulbs, and the mobile game of the many new types of light-sources bombard man with kinetic color sensations having a keyboard never before experienced. Man, the spectator, is himself more mobile than ever before. He rides in streetcars, motorcars, and aeroplanes and his own motion gives to optical impacts a tempo far beyond the threshold of a clear object-perception. The machine man operates adds its own demand for a new way of seeing. The complicated interactions of its mechanical parts cannot be conceived in a static way; they must be perceived by understanding of their movements. The motion picture, television, and, in a great degree, the radio, require a new thinking, *i.e.*, seeing, that takes into account qualities of change, interpenetration, and simultaneity.[3]

That situation can be snapshotted from many angles. But it always adds up to the need to discover means for translating the experience of one medium or one culture into another, of translating Confucius into Western terms and Kant into Eastern terms. Of seeing our old literary culture in the new plastic terms in order to enable it to become a constitutive part of the new culture created by the orchestral voices and gestures of new media. Of seeing that modern physics and painting and poetry speak a common language and of acquiring that language at once in order that our world may possess consciously the coherence that it really has in latency, and which for lack of our recognition has created not new orchestral harmonies but mere noise.

Perhaps the terrifying thing about the new media for most of us is their inevitable evocation of irrational response. The irrational has become the major dimension of experience in our world. And yet this is a mere by-product of the instantaneous character in communication. It can be brought under rational control. It is the perfection of the means which has so far defeated the end, and removed the time necessary for assimilation and reflection. We are now compelled to develop new techniques of perception and judgment, new ways of reading the languages of our environment with its multiplicity of cultures and disciplines. And these needs are not just desperate remedies but roads to unimagined cultural enrichment.

All the types of linear approach to situations past, present, or future are useless. Already in the sciences there is recognition of the need for a unified field theory which would enable scientists to use one continuous set of terms by way of relating the various scientific universes. Thus the basic requirement of any system of communication is that it be circular, with, of course, the possibility of self-correction. That is why presumably the human dialogue is and must ever be the basic form of all civilization. For the dialogue compels each participant to see and recreate his own vision through another sensibility. And the radical imperfection in mechanical media is that they are not circular. So far they have become one-way affairs with audience research taking the place of genuine human vision, heckling, and response. There is not only the anonymity of press, movies, and radio but the factor of scale. The individual cannot discuss a problem with a huge mindless bureaucracy like a movie studio or a radio corporation. On the other hand a figure like Roosevelt could mobilize the networks for a war with the press. He could even make the microphone more effective by having the press against him, because the intimacy of the microphone preserved his human dimension while the national scale of the press attack could only appear as a tank corps converging on a telephone booth.

Thus the microphone invites chat, not oratory. It is a new art form which transforms all the existing relations between speakers and their audiences and speakers and their material of discourse. "The great rhetorical tradition which begins with Halifax and runs through Pitt to Channing, sent up its expiring flash in Macaulay."[4] The modern manner was less declamatory and more closely reasoned. And

---

3. *The Language of Vision,* edited by S. Giedion and S. J. Hayakawa (Chicago, Theobald, 1944).

4. G. M. Young, *Victorian England,* (1944), p. 31.

the new manner which Gladstone handled like a Tenth Muse was based on facts and figures. Statistics represents a branch of pictorial expression. If the rise of bureaucracy and finance changed the style of public and private speech, how much more radical a change is daily worked in our habits of thought and discourse by the microphone and the loudspeaker.

Perhaps we could sum up our problem by saying that technological man must betake himself to visual metaphor in contriving a new unified language for the multiverse of cultures of the entire globe. All language or expression is metaphorical because metaphor is the seeing of one situation through another one. Right on the beam. I'll take a rain check on that.

One's vernacular is best seen and felt through another tongue. And for us, at least, society is only appreciated by comparing and contrasting it with others. Pictorial and other experience today is filled with metaphors from all the cultures of the globe. Whereas the written vernaculars have always locked men up within their own cultural monad, the language of technological man, while drawing on all the cultures of the world, will necessarily prefer those media which are least national. The language of visual form is, therefore, one which lies to hand as an unused Esperanto at everybody's command. The language of vision has already been adopted in the pictograms of scientific formulae and logistics. These ideograms transcend national barriers as easily as Chaplin or Disney and would seem to have no rivals as the cultural base for cosmic man.

—1953

PREFACE TO AN UNCOLLECTED ANTHOLOGY

Northrop Frye

Northrop Frye is internationally renowned as a literary critic and author of Fearful Symmetry, A Study of William Blake *(1947),* Anatomy of Criticism *(1957), and many other volumes. He*

was from 1950 to 1960 author of the annual surveys of Canadian poetry in "Letters in Canada" in the University of Toronto Quarterly. *"Preface to an Uncollected Anthology" was first presented to Section II of the Royal Society of Canada in June 1956, and was printed in expanded form in* Studia Varia, *edited by E.G.D. Murray (University of Toronto Press, 1957). Frye explained that, as author, he "imagines that he has collected his ideal anthology of English-Canadian poetry, with no difficulties about permissions, publishers, or expense, and is writing his preface." The author has revised and shortened this Preface for reprinting here.*

———◆———

While the reason for collecting an anthology can only be the merit of the individual poems, still, having made such a collection, one may legitimately look at the proportioning of interests, at the pattern of the themes that seem to make Canadian poets eloquent. It is not a nation but an environment that makes an impact on poets, and poetry can deal only with the imaginative aspect of that environment. A country with almost no Atlantic seaboard, which for most of its history has existed in practically one dimension; a country divided by two languages and great stretches of wilderness, so that its frontier is a circumference rather than a boundary; a country with huge rivers and islands that most of its natives have never seen; a country that has made a nation out of the stops on two of the world's longest railway lines: this is the environment that Canadian poets have to grapple with, and many of the imaginative problems it presents have no counterpart in the United States, or anywhere else.

In older countries the works of man and of nature, the city and the garden of civilization, have usually reached some kind of imaginative harmony. But the land of the Rockies and the Precambrian Shield impresses painter and poet alike by its raw colors and angular rhythms, its profoundly unhumanized isolation. It is still "The Lonely Land" to A. J. M. Smith, still "A Country without a Mythology" to Douglas Le

595

Pan. The works of man are even more imaginatively undigested. Irving Layton says, looking at an abstract picture,

When I got the hang of it
I saw a continent of railway tracks
coiling about the sad Modigliani necks
like disused tickertape, the streets
exploding in the air
with disaffected subway cars.

The Wordsworth who saw nature as exquisitely fitted to the human mind would be lost in Canada, where what the poets see is a violent collision of two forces, both monstrous. Earle Birney describes the bulldozers of a logging camp as "iron brontosaurs"; Klein compares grain elevators to leviathans.

Poets are a fastidious race, and in Canadian poetry we have to give some place, at least at the beginning, to the anti-Canadian, the poet who has taken one horrified look at the country and fled. Thus Standish O'Grady, writing of *The Emigrant*:

Here forests crowd, unprofitable lumber,
O'er fruitless lands indefinite as number;
Where birds scarce light, and with the north
     winds veer
On wings of wind, and quickly disappear,
Here the rough Bear subsists his winter year,
And licks his paw and finds no better fare. . . .
The lank Canadian eager trims his fire,
And all around their simpering stoves retire;
With fur-clad friends their progenies abound,
And thus regale their buffaloes around;
Unlettered race, how few the number tells,
Their only pride a cariole and bells. . . .
Perchance they revel; still around they creep,
And talk, and smoke, and spit, and drink, and
     sleep!

There is a great deal of polished wit in these couplets of the modern ambiguous kind: the word "lumber," for example, has both its Canadian meaning of wood and its English meaning of junk. We notice that "Canadian" in this poem means French-Canadian habitant: O'Grady no more thinks of himself as Canadian than an Anglo-Indian colonel would think of himself as Hindu. Here is an American opinion, the close of a folk song about a construction gang that spent a winter in Three Rivers:

And now the winter's over, it's homeward we
     are bound,
And in this cursed country we'll never more
     be found.
Go back to your wives and sweethearts, tell
     others not to go
To that God-forsaken country called
     Canaday-I-O.

Thanks to the efforts of those who remained, this particular theme is now obsolete, although Norman Levine in 1950 spoke of leaving the land of "parchment summers and merchant eyes" for "the loveliest of fogs," meaning England. Still, it will serve as an introduction to two central themes in Canadian poetry: one a primarily comic theme of satire and exuberance, the other a primarily tragic theme of loneliness and terror.

It is often said that a pioneering country is interested in material rather than spiritual or cultural values. This is a cliché, and it has become a cliché because it is not really true, as seventeenth-century Massachusetts indicates. What is true is that the imaginative energy of an expanding economy is likely to be mainly technological. As a rule it is the oppressed or beleaguered peoples, like the Celts and the Hebrews, whose culture makes the greatest imaginative efforts: successful nations usually express a restraint or a matter-of-fact realism in their culture and keep their exuberance for their engineering. If we are looking for imaginative exuberance in American life, we shall find it not in its fiction but in its advertising; not in Broadway drama but in Broadway skyscrapers; not in the good movies but in the vista-visioned and technicolored silly ones. The extension of this life into Canada is described by Frank Scott in "Saturday Sundae," by James Reaney in "Klaxon," a fantasy of automobiles wandering over the highways without drivers, "Limousines covered with pink slime /Of children's blood," and by many other poets.

The poet dealing with the strident shallowness of much Canadian life is naturally aware that there is no imaginative change when we cross the American border in either direction. Yet there is, I think, a more distinctive attitude in Canadian poetry than in Canadian life, a more withdrawn and detached view of that life which may go back to the central fact of Canadian history: the rejection of the American Revolution. What won the American Revolution was the spirit of entrepreneur capitalism, an enthusiastic plundering of the natural resources of a continent and an unrestricted energy of manufacturing and exchanging them. In *A Search for America,* which is quite a profound book if we take the precaution of reading it as a work of fiction, Grove speaks of there being two Americas, an ideal one that has something to do with the philosophy of Thoreau and the personality of Lincoln, and an actual one that made the narrator a parasitic salesman of superfluous goods and finally a hobo. At the end of the book he remarks in a footnote that his ideal America has been preserved better in Canada than in the United States. The truth of this statement is not my concern, but some features of my anthology seem to reflect similar attitudes.

In the United States, with its more intensively indoctrinated educational system, there has been much rugged prophecy in praise of the common man, a tradition that runs from Whitman through Sandburg and peters out in the lugubrious inspirationalism of the Norman Corwin school. Its chief characteristics are the praise of the uncritical life and a manly contempt of prosody. One might call it the Whitmanic-depressive tradition, in view of the fact that it contains Robinson Jeffers. It seems to me significant that this tradition has had so little influence in Canada. I find in my anthology a much higher proportion of humor than I expected when I began: a humor of a quiet, reflective, observant type, usually in a fairly strict metre, and clearly coming from a country with a ringside seat on the revolutionary sidelines.

A song from a poem by Alexander McLachlan called, like O'Grady's, *The Emigrant,* will illustrate what I mean:

I love my own country and race,
  Nor lightly I fled from them both,
Yet who would remain in a place
  Where there's too many spoons for the broth.

The squire's preserving his game.
  He says that God gave it to him,
And he'll banish the poor without shame,
  For touching a feather or limb. . . .
The Bishop he preaches and prays,
  And talks of a heavenly birth,
But somehow, for all that he says,
  He grabs a good share of the earth.

In this poem there is nothing of the typically American identification of freedom with national independence: the poet is still preoccupied with the old land and thinks of himself as still within its tradition. There is even less of the American sense of economic competition as the antidote to social inequality. The spirit in McLachlan's poem is that of a tough British radicalism, the radicalism of the Glasgow dock worker or the Lancashire coal miner, the background of the Tom Paine who has never quite fitted the American way of life.

It is not surprising to find a good deal of satiric light verse in this imaginative resistance to industrial expansion and the gum-chewing way of life. Frank Scott we have mentioned: his "Canadian Social Register" is a ferocious paraphrase of an advertising prospectus, and his "Social Notes" are also something un-American, social poems with an unmistakably socialist moral. The observations of Toronto by Raymond Souster and of Montreal by Louis Dudek, Miriam Waddington, and Irving Layton have much to the same effect: of golfers Layton remarks "that no theory of pessimism is complete /Which altogether ignores them." But of course it is easy for the same satiric tone to turn bitter and nightmarish. Lampman's terrible poem, "The City of the End of Things," is not only social but psychological, and warns of the dangers not simply of exploiting labor but of washing our own brains. There are other sinister visions in A. J. M. Smith's "The Bridegroom," in Dudek's "East of the City," in Dorothy Livesay's "Day and Night," in P. K. Page's "The Stenographers," and elsewhere. Canadian poems of depression and drought, like Dorothy Livesay's "Outrider" or Anne Marriott's "The Wind Our Enemy," often have in them the protest of a food-producing community cheated out of its labor not simply by hail and grasshoppers but by some mysterious financial finagling at the other end of the country, reminding us of the man in Balzac's parable who could make his fortune by killing somebody in China. The same feeling comes out in a poignant folk song that could have come from only one part of the world, southeastern Newfoundland:

"Oh, mother dear, I wants a sack
With beads and buttons down the back. . . .
Me boot is broke, me frock is tore,
But Georgie Snooks I do adore. . . .
Oh, fish is low and flour is high,
So Georgie Snooks he can't have I."

There are of course more positive aspects of industrial expansion. In Canada the enormous difficulties and the central importance of communication and transport, the tremendous energy that developed the fur trade routes, the empire of the St. Lawrence, the transcontinental railways, and the northwest police patrols have given it the dominating role in the Canadian imagination. E. J. Pratt is the poet who has best grasped this fact, and his *Towards the Last Spike* expresses the central comic theme of Canadian life, using the term "comic" in its literary sense as concerned with the successful accomplishing of a human act.

The imagery of technology and primary communication is usually either avoided by poets or employed out of a sense of duty: its easy and unforced appearance in Pratt is part of the reason why Pratt is one of the few good popular poets of our time. Technology appears all through his work, not only in the poems whose subjects demand it, but in other and more unexpected contexts. Thus in "Come Away, Death":

We heard the tick-tock on the shelf,
And the leak of valves in our hearts.

In "The Prize Cat," where a cat pounces on a bird and reminds the poet of the deliberately summoned-up brutality of the Fascist conquest of Ethiopia, the two themes are brought together by the inspired flash of a technical word:

Behind the leap so furtive-wild
Was such ignition in the gleam
I thought an Abyssinian child
Had cried out in the whitethroat's scream.

As a student of psychology, before he wrote poetry at all, he was preoccupied with the problems of sensory response to signals, and the interest still lingers in the wireless messages of *The Titanic,* the radar and asdic of *Behind the Log,* and the amiable joggle of "No. 6000," one of the liveliest of all railway poems:

A lantern flashed out a command,
A bell was ringing as a hand
Clutched at a throttle, and the bull,
At once obedient to the pull,
Began with bellowing throat to lead
By slow accelerating speed
Six thousand tons of caravan
Out to the spaces — there to toss
The blizzard from his path across
The prairies of Saskatchewan.

In *Behind the Log,* Canadians undertake a mission of war in much the spirit of an exploration: there is a long journey full of perils, many members of the expedition drop off, and those that reach the goal feel nothing but a numb relief. Nothing could be less like the charge of the Light Brigade. Yet perhaps in this poem we may find a clue to the fact that Canada, a country that has never found much virtue in war and has certainly never started one, has in its military history a long list of ferocious conflicts against desperate odds. Douglas Le Pan's "The Net and the Sword," the title poem of a book dealing with the Italian campaign of the Second World War, mentions something similar:

In this sandy arena, littered
And looped with telephone wires, tank-traps,
        mine-fields,
Twined about the embittered
Debris of history, the people whom he shields
Would quail before a stranger if they could see
His smooth as silk ferocity.

Le Pan finds the source of the ferocity in the simplicity of the Canadian soldier's vision: "Skating at Scarborough, summers at the

Island," but perhaps it is also a by-product of engineering exuberance. We notice that the looped litter of telephone wires and the like belongs here to Europe, not to Canada, and the same kind of energy is employed to deal with it.

The tragic themes of Canadian poetry have much the same origin as the comic ones. The cold winter may suggest tragedy, but it may equally well suggest other moods, and does so in Lampman's sonnet "Winter Evening," in Patrick Anderson's "Song of Intense Cold," in Roberts' "The Brook in February," in Klein's "Winter Night: Mount Royal," and elsewhere. Other seasons too have their sinister aspects: none of Lampman's landscape poems is finer than his wonderful Hallowe'en vision of "In November," where a harmless pasture full of dead mullein stalks rises and seizes the poet with the spirit of an eerie witches' sabbath:

> And I, too, standing idly there,
> With muffled hands in the chill air
> Felt the warm glow about my feet,
> And shuddering betwixt cold and heat,
> Drew my thoughts closer, like a cloak,
> While something in my blood awoke,
> A nameless and unnatural cheer,
> A pleasure secret and austere.

Still, the winter, with its long shadows and its abstract black and white pattern, does reinforce themes of desolation and loneliness, and, more particularly, of the indifference of nature to human values, which I should say was the central Canadian tragic theme. The first poet who really came to grips with this theme was, as we should expect, Charles Heavysege. Heavysege's first two long poems, *Saul* and *Count Filippo,* are Victorian dinosaurs in the usual idiom: *Count Filippo,* in particular, like the Albert Memorial, achieves a curious perverted beauty by the integrity of its ugliness. His third poem, *Jephthah's Daughter,* seems to me to reflect more directly the influence of his Canadian environment, for what Jephthah is really sacrificing his daughter to is nature, nature as a mystery of mindless power, with endless resources for killing man but with nothing to respond to his moral or intellectual feelings. The evolutionary pessimism of the nineteenth century awoke an unusual number of echoes in Canada, many of them of course incidental. In a well-known passage from Charles Mair's *Tecumseh,* Lefroy is describing the West to Brock, and Brock comments: "What charming solitudes! And life was there!" and Lefroy answers: "Yes, life was there! inexplicable life,/Still wasted by inexorable death"; and the sombre Tennysonian vision of nature red in tooth and claw blots out the sentimental Rousseauist fantasy of the charming solitudes.

In the next generation the tragic theme has all the more eloquence for being somewhat unwanted, interfering with the resolutely cheerful praise of the newborn giant of the north. Roberts, Wilfred Campbell, Wilson MacDonald, and Bliss Carman are all romantics whose ordinary tone is nostalgic, but who seem most deeply convincing when they are darkest in tone, most preoccupied with pain, loss, loneliness, or waste. We notice this in the poems which would go immediately into anyone's anthology, such as Campbell's "The Winter Lakes," Wilson MacDonald's "Exit," Carman's "Low Tide on Grand Pré." It is even more striking when Carman or Roberts writes a long metrical gabble that occasionally drops into poetry, like Silas Wegg, as it is almost invariably this mood that it drops into. Thus in Roberts' "The Great and the Little Weavers":

> The cloud-rose dies into shadow,
> The earth-rose dies into dust.

The "great gray shape with the paleolithic face" of Pratt's *Titanic* and the glacier of Birney's "David" are in much the same tradition as the gloomy and unresponsive nature of *Jephthah's Daughter.* In fact the tragic features in Pratt mainly derive from his more complex view of the situation of Heavysege's poem. Man is also a child of nature, in whom the mindlessness of the animal has developed into cruelty and malice. He sees two men glare in hatred at one another on the street, and his mind goes

> Away back before the emergence of fur or
> feather, back to the unvocal sea and down

deep where the darkness spills its wash on the threshold of light, where the lids never close upon the eyes, where the inhabitants slay in silence and are as silently slain.

From the very beginning, in *Newfoundland Verse*, Pratt was fascinated by the relentless pounding of waves on the rocks, a movement which strangely seems to combine a purpose with a lack of it. This rhythm recurs several times in Pratt's work: in the charge of the swordfish in *The Witches Brew*; in the "queries rained upon the iron plate" of "The Iron Door"; in the torpedo launched from "The Submarine"; in the sinking of the *Titanic* itself, this disaster being caused by a vainglorious hybris which in a sense deliberately aimed at the iceberg. In *Brébeuf* the same theme comes into focus as the half-mindless, half-demonic curiosity which drives the Iroquois on through torture after torture to find the secret of a spiritual reality that keeps eluding them.

It is Pratt who has expressed in *Towards the Last Spike* the central comic theme, and in *Brébeuf* the central tragic theme, of the Canadian imagination, and it is Pratt who combines the two in "The Truant," which is in my anthology because it is the greatest poem in Canadian literature. In it the representative of mankind confronts a "great Panjandrum," a demon of the mathematical order of nature of a type often confused with God. In the dialectic of their conflict it becomes clear that the great Panjandrum of nature is fundamentally death, and that the intelligence that fights him, comprehends him, harnesses him, and yet finally yields to his power is the ultimate principle of life, and capable of the comedy of achievement only because capable also of the tragedy of enduring him:

> We who have learned to clench
> Our fists and raise our lightless sockets
> To morning skies after the midnight raids,
> Yet cocked our ears to bugles on the barricades,
> And in cathedral rubble found a way to quench
> A dying thirst within a Galilean valley —
> No! by the Rood, we will not join your ballet.

While literature may have life, reality, experience, nature, or what you will for its content, the forms of literature cannot exist outside literature, just as the forms of sonata and fugue cannot exist outside music. When a poet is confronted by a new life or environment, the new life may suggest a new content, but obviously cannot provide him with a new form. The forms of poetry can be derived only from other poems, the forms of novels from other novels. The imaginative content of Canadian poetry, which is often primitive, frequently makes extraordinary demands on forms derived from romantic or later traditions. Pratt's attempt to introduce the imagery of dragon-killing into a poem about the Canadian Pacific Railway is a good example; and I have much sympathy for the student who informed me in the examinations last May that Pratt had written a poem called Beowulf and his Brothers.

I think it is partly an obscure feeling for more primitive forms that accounts for the large number of narratives in Canadian poetry. I am aware, of course, that the narrative was a favorite romantic form, but the themes of Canadian narrative have a primeval grimness about them that is not romantic or even modern fashion. Pratt has also turned to older and more primitive types of narrative: Chaucerian beast-fable in the "Pliocene Armageddon" and "The Fable of the Goats," saint's legend in *Brébeuf*, heroic rescue in *The Roosevelt and the Antinoe*.

It is more common for a Canadian poet to solve his problem of form by some kind of erudite parody, using that term, as many critics now do, to mean adaptation in general rather than simply a lampoon, although adaptation usually has humorous overtones. In Charles Mair's "Winter" some wisps of Shakespearean song are delicately echoed in a new context, and Drummond's best poem, "The Wreck of the Julie Plante," is an admirable parody of the ballad, with its tough oblique narration, its moralizing conclusion, and its use of what is called incremental repetition:

> For de win' she blow lak' hurricane,
> Bimeby she blow some more.

According to his own account, Pratt, after his college studies in theology, psychology, literature, and the natural sciences, put everything he knew into his first major poetic effort, an epic named "Clay," which he promptly burnt. Soon afterwards all this erudition went into reverse and came out as the fantasy of *The Witches Brew,* in which parody has a central place. Since then, we have parody in Anne Wilkinson and Wilfred Watson, who use nursery rhymes and ballads as a basis; Birney's "Trial of a City" is among other things a fine collection of parodied styles; and Klein's devotion to one of the world's greatest parodists, James Joyce, has produced his brilliant bilingual panegyric on Montreal:

> Grand port of navigations, multiple
> The lexicons uncargo'd at your quays,
> Sonnant though strange to me; but chiefest, I,
> Auditor of your music, cherish the
> Joined double-melodied vocabulaire
> Where English vocable and roll Ecossic,
> Mollified by the parle of French
> Bilinguefact your air!

Much of Canada's best poetry is now written by professors or others in close contact with universities. There are disadvantages in this, but one of the advantages is the diversifying of the literary tradition by a number of scholarly interests. Earle Birney's "Anglo-Saxon Street" reminds us that its author is a professor of Anglo-Saxon. Louis Mackay, professor of Classics, confronts an unmistakably Canadian landscape with a myth of Eros derived from Virgil:

> The hard rock was his mother; he retains
> Only her kind, nor answers any sire.
> His hand is the black basalt, and his veins
> Are rocky veins, ablaze with gold and fire.

Robert Finch, professor of French, carries on the tradition of Mallarmé and other *symbolistes;* one of his most successful poems, "The Peacock and the Nightingale," goes back to the older tradition of the medieval *débat.* Klein, of course, has brought echoes from the Talmud, the Old Testament, and the whole range of Jewish thought and history; and the erudition necessary to read Roy Daniells and Alfred Bailey with full appreciation is little short of formidable. It may be said, however, that echoes and influences are not a virtue in Canadian poetry, but one of its major weaknesses. Canadian poetry may echo Hopkins or Auden today as it echoed Tom Moore a century ago, but in every age Echo is merely the discarded mistress of Narcissus. This question brings up the most hackneyed subject in Canadian literature, which I have left for that reason to the end.

Political and economic units tend to expand as history goes on; cultural units tend to remain decentralized. Culture, like wine, seems to need a specific locality, and no major poet has been inspired by an empire, Virgil being, as the *Georgics* show, an exception that proves the rule. In this age of world-states we have two extreme forms of the relationship between culture and politics. When cultural developments follow political ones, we get an anonymous international art, such as we have in many aspects of modern architecture, abstract painting, and twelve-tone music. When a cultural development acquires a political aspect, we frequently get that curious modern phenomenon of the political language, where a minor language normally headed for extinction is deliberately revived for political purposes. Examples are Irish, Norwegian, Hebrew, and Afrikaans, and there are parallel tendencies elsewhere. I understand that there is a school of Australian poets dedicated to putting as many aboriginal words into their poems as possible. As the emotional attachments to political languages are very violent, I shall say here only that this problem has affected the French but not the English part of Canadian culture. As we all know, however, English Canada has escaped the political language only to become involved in a unique problem of self-identification, vis-à-vis the British and American poets writing in the same tongue. Hence in every generation there has been the feeling that whether poetry itself needs any defence or manifesto, Canadian poetry certainly does.

The main result of this has been that Canadian poets have been urged in every generation to search for appropriate themes, in other words to look for content. The themes have been characterized as national, international, traditional, experimental, iconic, iconoclastic: in short, as whatever the propounder of them would like to write if he were a poet, or to read if he were a critic. But the poet's quest is for form, not content. The poet who tries to make content the informing principle of his poetry can write only versified rhetoric, and versified rhetoric has a moral but not an imaginative significance: its place is on the social periphery of poetry, not in its articulate centre. The rhetorician, Quintilian tells us, ought to be a learned and good man, but the critic is concerned only with poets.

By form I do not of course mean external form, such as the use of a standard metre or convention. A sonnet has form only if it really is fourteen lines long: a ten-line sonnet padded out to fourteen is still a part of chaos, waiting for the creative word. I mean by form the shaping principle of the individual poem, which is derived from the shaping principles of poetry itself. Of these latter the most important is metaphor, and metaphor, in its radical form, is a statement of identity: this is that, A is B. Metaphor is at its purest and most primitive in myth, where we have immediate and total identifications. Primitive poetry, being mythical, tends to be erudite and allusive, and to the extent that modern poetry takes on the same qualities it becomes primitive too. Here is a poem by Lampman, written in 1894:

So it is with us all; we have our friends
    Who keep the outer chambers, and guard well
Our common path; but there their service ends,
    For far within us lies an iron cell
Soundless and secret, where we laugh or moan
    Beyond all succor, terribly alone.

And here is a poem by E. W. Mandel, published in 1954:

It has been hours in these rooms,
the opening to which, door or sash,
I have lost. I have gone from room to room
asking the janitors who were sweeping up
the brains that lay on the floors,
the bones shining in the wastebaskets,
and once I asked a suit of clothes
that collapsed at my breath and bundled
and crawled on the floor like a coward.
Finally, after several stories,
in the staired and eyed hall,
I came upon a man with the face of a bull.

Lampman's poem is certainly simpler, closer to prose and to the direct statement of emotion. All these are characteristics of a highly developed and sophisticated literary tradition. If we ask which is the more primitive, the answer is certainly the second poem, as we can see by turning to the opening pages of the anthology to see what primitive poetry is really like. Here is a Haida song translated by Hermia Fraser:

I cannot stay, I cannot stay!
I must take my canoe and fight the waves,
For the Wanderer spirit is seeking me.

The beating of great, black wings on the sun,
The Raven has stolen the ball of the sun,
From the Kingdom of Light he has stolen the
    sun. . . .

The Slave Wife born from the first clam shell
Is in love with the boy who was stolen away,
The lovers have taken the Raven's fire.

When we look for the qualities in Canadian poetry that illustrate the poet's response to the specific environment that we call approximately Canada, we are really looking for the mythopoeic qualities in that poetry. This is easiest to see, of course, when the poetry is mythical in content as well as form. In the long mythopoeic passage from Isabella Crawford's "Malcolm's Katie," beginning "The South Wind laid his moccasins aside," we see how the poet is, first, taming the landscape imaginatively, as settlement tames it physically, by animating the lifeless scene with humanized figures, and, second, integrating the literary tradition of the country by deliberately re-establishing the broken cultural link with Indian civilization:

                    . . . for a man
To stand amid the cloudy roll and moil,
The phantom waters breaking overhead,
Shades of vex'd billows bursting on his breast,
Torn caves of mist wall'd with a sudden gold,
Reseal'd as swift as seen—broad, shaggy fronts,
Fire-ey'd and tossing on impatient horns
The wave impalpable — was but to think
A dream of phantoms held him as he stood.

And in the mythical figures of Pratt, the snorting iron horses of the railways, the lumbering dinosaurs of "The Great Feud," the dragon of *Towards the Last Spike,* and above all Tom the Cat from Zanzibar, the Canadian cousin of Roy Campbell's flaming terrapin, we clearly have other denizens of the monstrous zoo that produced Paul Bunyan's ox Babe, Paul Bunyan himself being perhaps a descendant of the giants who roamed the French countryside and were recorded by the great contemporary of Jacques Cartier, Rabelais.

We are concerned here, however, not so much with mythopoeic poetry as with myth as a shaping principle of poetry. Every good lyrical poet has a certain structure of imagery as typical of him as his handwriting, held together by certain recurring metaphors, and sooner or later he will produce one or more poems that seem to be at the centre of that structure. These poems are in the formal sense his mythical poems, and they are for the critic the imaginative keys to his work. The poet himself often recognizes such a poem by making it the title poem of a collection. They are not necessarily his best poems, but they often are, and in a Canadian poet they display those distinctive themes we have been looking for which reveal his reaction to his natural and social environment. Nobody but a genuine poet ever produces such a poem, and they cannot be faked or imitated or voluntarily constructed. My anthology is largely held together by such poems: they start approximately with D. C. Scott's "Piper of Arll," and continue in increasing numbers to our own day. I note among others Leo Kennedy's "Words for a Resurrection," Margaret Avison's "Neverness," Irving Layton's "Cold Green Element," Douglas Le Pan's "Idyll," Wilfred Watson's "Canticle of Darkness," P. K. Page's "Metal and the Flower," and similar poems forming among a younger group that includes James Reaney, Jay Macpherson, and Daryl Hine. Such poems enrich not only our poetic experience but our cultural knowledge as well, and as time goes on they become increasingly the only form of knowledge that does not date and continues to hold its interest for future generations.

—*1957, 1966*

THE NARRATIVE TRADITION IN ENGLISH-CANADIAN POETRY

Northrop Frye

An article by Professor Frye entitled "La Tradition narrative dans la poésie canadienne-anglaise" appeared in the Spring issue, 1946, of Gants du Ciel, a journal edited by Guy Sylvestre and published in Montreal. The essay which follows here is Frye's original English version, appearing in print for the first time in this anthology.

The Canadian poet cannot write in a distinctively Canadian language; he is compelled to take the language he was brought up to speak, whether French, English, or Icelandic, and attempt to adjust that language to an environment which is foreign to it, if not foreign to himself. Once he accepts a language, however, he joins the line of poets in the tradition of that language, at the point nearest to his immediate predecessors. A nineteenth-century Canadian poet writing in English will be emulating Keats and Tennyson; writing in French, he will be emulating Victor Hugo or Baudelaire. It may be thought that it would be a pure advantage to the Canadian poet to put an old tongue into a new face; that the mere fact of his being a Canadian would give him something distinctive to say, and enable him to be original without effort. But it is not as simple as that. His poetry cannot be "young," for it is written in a European language with a thousand years of disciplined utterance behind it, and any attempt to ignore that tradition can only lead to disaster. Nor is Canada a "young" country in the sense that its industrial conditions, its political issues, or the general level of its civilization, are significantly different from contemporary Europe. Nevertheless, to the imaginative eye of the creative artist, whether painter or poet, certain aspects of Canada must, for a long time yet, make it appear young. Its landscape does not have, as that of Europe has, that indefinable quality which shows that it has been lived in by civilized human beings for millennia. Its villages do not "nestle"; they sprawl awkwardly into rectangular lines along roads and railways. Its buildings do not melt into their backgrounds; they stand out with a garish and tasteless defiance. It is full of human and natural ruins, of abandoned buildings and despoiled countrysides, such as are found only with the vigorous wastefulness of young countries. And, above all, it is a country in which nature makes a direct impression on the artist's mind, an impression of its primeval lawlessness and moral nihilism, its indifference to the supreme value placed on life within human society, its faceless, mindless unconsciousness, which fosters life without benevolence and destroys it without malice. There is, of course, much more to be said about nature than this, even by the Canadian artist, but this is an aspect of nature which the sensitive Canadian finds it impossible to avoid. It is all very well for a European poet to see nature in terms of a settled order which the mind can interpret, like Wordsworth, or even in terms of oracular hints and suggestions, like Baudelaire in *Correspondences*; but the Canadian poet receives all his initial impressions in the environment of Rimbaud's *Bateau Ivre*.

What the poet sees in Canada, therefore, is very different from what the politician or business man sees, and different again from what his European contemporaries see. He may be a younger man than Yeats or Eliot, but he has to deal with a poetic and imaginative environment for which, to find any parallel in England, we should have to go back to a period earlier than Chaucer. In certain Old English poems, notably "The Wanderer" and "The Seafarer," there is a feeling which seems to a modern reader more Canadian than English: a feeling of the melancholy of a thinly settled country under a bleak northern sky, of the terrible isolation of the creative mind in such a country, of resigning oneself to hardship and loneliness as the only means of attaining, if not serenity, at least a kind of rigid calm. It is a feeling which in later centuries becomes very rare, though there is something of it in some romantic poems, such

as Keats's "La Belle Dame Sans Merci." And the landscape of this poem, we are told, is of Canadian inspiration.

Now of course modern Canadian life is far less simple and homogeneous than Old English life. The Canadian poet, though he must try to express something of what the Old English poet felt, cannot afford to forget either that a highly sophisticated civilization is as much a part of Canadian life as deep snow and barren spaces. If we can imagine a contemporary of the *Beowulf* poet, with equal genius and an equally strong urge to write an archaic epic of the defeat of a monster of darkness by a hero of immense strength and endurance—a theme which should appeal powerfully to a Canadian—yet writing for the same public as Ovid and Catullus, and forced to adapt their sophisticated witticisms and emotional refinements to his own work, we shall begin to get some idea of what the Canadian poet is up against.

This is why nearly all good Canadian poets (a notable exception is Bliss Carman) have much less simple poetic natures than they appear to have at first glance. The "framework" of Lampman, for instance, is that of a placid romantic nature poet beating the track of Wordsworth and Keats. But there are also in Lampman many very different characteristics. He has, for instance, a spiritual loneliness, a repugnance to organized social life, which goes far beyond mere discontent with his provincial environment. This is a quality in Lampman which links him to the great Canadian explorers, the solitary adventurers among solitudes, and to the explorer-painters like Thomson and Emily Carr who followed them, with their eyes continually straining into the depths of nature. And in the terrible clairvoyance of "The City of the End of Things," a vision of the Machine Age slowly freezing into idiocy and despair, something lives again of the spirit of the Old English Wanderer, who, trudging from castle to castle in the hope of finding food and shelter in exchange for his songs, turned to the great Roman ruins, the "eald enta geweorc" (the ancient work of giants), to brood over a greater oppression of man by nature than his own.

Similarly, the "framework" of Isabella Crawford is that of an intelligent and industrious female songbird of the kind who filled so many anthologies in the last century. Yet the "South Wind" passage from *Malcolm's Katie* is only the most famous example of the most remarkable mythopoeic imagination in Canadian poetry. She puts her myth in an Indian form, which reminds us of the resemblance between white and Indian legendary heroes in the New World, between Paul Bunyan and Davy Crockett on the one hand and Glooscap on the other. The white myths are not necessarily imitated from the Indian ones, but they may have sprung from an unconscious feeling that the primitive myth expressed the imaginative impact of the country as more artificial literature could never do.

Some of the same affinities appear in those aspects of our literature [history?] that a poet would naturally be most interested in, though very few of them have received adequate poetic treatment. The martyrdom of the Jesuit missionaries, the holding of the Long Sault against the Iroquois, the victories over incredible odds in the War of 1812, the desperate courage of the Indians who died with Tecumseh and Riel, the 1837 outbreak, the fight without gas masks against gas at St. Julien, the spear-heading of the plunge into Amiens, the forlorn hope at Dieppe—there is a certain family resemblance among all these events which makes each one somehow typical of Canadian history. Is there not something in the character of such themes that recalls the earliest poetry of our mother countries, of the lost battle of Maldon where courage grew greater as the strength ebbed away, or of the reckless heroism at Roncesvalles which laid the cornerstone of French literature? It is perhaps not an accident that the best known of all Canadian poems, "In Flanders' Fields," should express, in a tight, compressed, grim little rondeau, the same spirit of an inexorable ferocity which even death cannot relax, like the old Norse warrior whose head continued to gnash and bite the dust long after it had been severed from his body.

Hence it is at least possible that some of the poetic forms employed in the earlier centuries of English literature would have been more appropriate for the expression of Canadian themes and moods than the nineteenth-century romantic lyric or its twentieth-century metaphysical successor. It is inevitable that Canadian poetry should have been cast in the conventional forms of our own day; but though the bulk of it is lyrical in form, a great deal of it is not lyrical in spirit, and when a Canadian poem has failed to achieve adequate expression, this may often be the reason. It has been remarked, for instance, that sexual passion is a theme that our poets have not treated very convincingly. This emotion is also lacking in Old English poetry, and perhaps for some of the same reasons. But sexual passion is one of the essential themes of the lyric. Canadian poetry is lyrical in form and Old English poetry is not, hence the failure to deal with sexual passion is felt as a lack in Canadian poetry but is not missed in Old English. On the other hand, it occasionally happens that a successful Canadian poem has owed its success to its coincidence, deliberate or otherwise, with one of the forms of pre-Chaucerian literature. Thus Drummond's best poem, "The Wreck of the Julie Plante," is not merely a modern imitation of the ballad; it has the tough humor and syncopated narrative of the authentic ballad at its best. Consider, too, the subjects of many of D. C. Scott's finest poems, the lovers destroyed in a log jam, the lonely Indian murdered in the forest for his furs, the squaw who baits a fish hook with her own flesh to feed her children. These [are] ballad themes; and his longest poem, "Dominique de Gourgues," a narrative filled with the sombre exultation of revenge, is curiously archaic in spirit for the author of a poem on Debussy. Something medieval has also crept into the religious emotions of A. J. M. Smith and into Leo Kennedy's exercises in the macabre.

All this may help to explain a phenomenon of our poetry which must have puzzled many of its students. In looking over the best poems of our best poets, while of course the great majority are lyrical, we are surprised to find how often the narrative poem has been attempted, and attempted with uneven but frequently remarkable success. I say surprised, because good narratives are exceedingly rare in English poetry—except in the period that ended with the death of Chaucer. And this unusual prominence of the narrative is one of the things that make Canadian poetry so hard to criticize with the right combination of sympathy and judgment. We tend to form our canons of criticism on carefully polished poetry, but such standards do not always apply to the narrative, for the test of the great narrative is its ability to give the flat prose statement a poetic value. And as there has been no connected tradition of narrative in English literature since 1400, the Canadian poet who attempts the form has to depend largely on his own originality, and no one except Pratt has worked hard enough and long enough at the form to discover its inherent genius. Hence among Canadian narratives there are many failures and many errors of taste and stretches of bad writing, but to anyone who cares about poetry there may be something more interesting in the failure than in a less ambitious success.

At the outset of Canadian literature we find many long poems: Goldsmith's *Rising Village*, O'Grady's brilliant but unfinished "Emigrant," Howe's "Acadia," also unfinished, and two dramatic poems by Duvar, *The Enamorado* and *De Roberval*, the last of which illustrate the fact that the Canadian narrative is frequently cast in the form of dialogue or literary drama. All of these follow well-established European conventions, and so do the first two productions of the clumsy but powerfully built genius of Heavysege. *Saul* belongs to the tradition of the Victorian leviathan, the discursive poem combining Biblical subject with middle-class morality, represented by the better known Bailey's *Festus. Count Filippo*, too, is in the manner of nineteenth-century reactions to Jacobean drama and the Italian Renaissance, and might almost have served as the model for Max Beerbohm's *Savonarola Brown*. But *Jephthah's Daughter*, his third effort, strikes its roots deeply into Canada, and is the real commencement of a distinctively Canadian form of the narrative poem.

Heavysege begins by saying that the story of Jephthah's daughter is very similar to the story of Iphigenia, and that he has chosen the Hebrew legend because there is a spiritual loneliness about it which attracts him more profoundly. Iphigenia was sacrificed in the midst of great bustle and excitement, and was, as Samuel Johnson said of the victim at a public hanging, sustained by her audience: Jephthah's daughter is destroyed by the mute anguish of uncomprehending superstition. To Heavysege, a man who, like Jephthah, worships a God who demands fulfilment of a rash vow of sacrifice even if it involves his own daughter, is really a man in the state of nature: he has identified his God, if not with nature, at any rate with a mindless force of inscrutable mystery like nature, and all Jephthah's questionings and searchings of spirit are the looks of intelligence directed at blankness, the attempts of a religious pioneer to find a spiritual portage through the heart of darkness. The passage in which Heavysege describes this most clearly cannot be beaten in James Thomson for the sheer starkness of its mood, a grimness that is far deeper than any ghost-haunted horrors. Jephthah prays to be delivered from the blood of his daughter, and asks for a sign of divine mercy. There is a slight pause, then Jephthah hears:

The hill-wolf howling on the neighboring
   height,
And bittern booming in the pool below.

That is all the answer he gets.

In this poem Heavysege has put together certain essential ideas: the contrast of human and civilized values with nature's disregard of them in a primitive country, the tendency in the religion of such a country for God to disappear behind the mask of nature, and the symbolic significance, when that happens, of human sacrifice and the mutilation of the body (a theme already elaborated by Heavysege in the episode in *Saul* about the hewing of Agag in pieces). Once one has carefully read this narrative, the essential meaning of many fine Canadian poems leaps out of its derivative and conventional context. Thus in Isabella Crawford's *Malcolm's Katie* there is a superbly ironic scene in which the hero sings of the irresistible advance of capitalist civilization and its conquest of nature, symbolized by the axe, and links his exuberant belief in the enduring power of the nation he is building with his belief in the enduring power of his love for the heroine. He is answered by the villain, in a passage of far greater eloquence, who points out the cyclic progress of all empires from rise to decline and the instability of woman's love. As the hero turns indignantly to refute his slanders, the tree which he has not quite chopped down falls on him and crushes him. True, he recovers and marries the heroine and forgives the villain and lives happily ever after and love conquers all and nature is grand, but somehow the poem reaches an imaginative concentration in that scene which it never afterwards recaptures. In the same poem the heroine is caught in a log jam, and, though of course she is rescued, the sudden glimpse of the trap of nature, the endless resources it has for suddenly and unconsciously destroying a fragile and beautiful human life is far more effective without the rescue, and is so developed in D. C. Scott's "At the Cedars."

Mair's *Tecumseh* and Lampman's "At the Long Sault" apply the same pattern to Canadian history. The former has been charged with lack of unity, but the theme of the drama is the sacrifice of Tecumseh, to which everything else leads up, the various conflicts between his own fierce loyalties and the vacillations of his friends and enemies being merely the struggles of a doomed victim who now arouses and now disappoints our hopes for his escape. Lampman, too, seems most deeply impressed, not only by the sacrificial nature of what the Long Sault heroes did, which is obvious enough, but by its symbolic connection with, again, a state of nature in which the higher forms of life are so often destroyed by the lower. That is why he introduces the beautiful picture of the moose pulled down by wolves, the symbol of the exceptional and unblemished hero who falls a victim to the agents of a careless fate.

Pratt has studied the technique and resources of the narrative form more carefully than his predecessors, and so it is not surprising to find the themes we have been tracing much more explicitly set forth in his work. He delights in describing big and even monstrous things, and whenever he can he shows them exulting in their strength. In the antics of Tom the Cat from Zanzibar in *The Witches' Brew,* in the most equally feline sense of relaxed power in "The 6000," in the ferocious but somehow exuberant massacres in "The Great Feud," there is more enthusiasm than in his other works, for naturally he greatly prefers the Othellos of this world to the Iagos, and hates to see the latter victorious. But the Canadian narrative demands a tragic resolution. "The Cachalot" is not perhaps a tragic poem, but is there really so much moral difference between the whale caught by men and the moose in Lampman pulled down by wolves ? In *The Titanic* the mindlessness of the agent of destruction is the imaginative centre of the poem: the tragic theme of hybris, the punishment of man by fate for his presumption in defying it, is, though a very obvious and in fact ready-made aspect of the theme, deliberately played down. If *Dunkirk* seems less wholly convincing than some of his other narratives, it may well be because the absence of the theme of wasted life gives it a resolutely optimistic quality which seems rather forced, more the glossed and edited reporter's story than the poet's complete and tragic vision.

Brébeuf is not only the greatest but the most complete Canadian narrative, and brings together into a single pattern all the themes we have been tracing. Here the mutilation and destruction of the gigantic Brébeuf and the other missionaries is a sacrificial rite in which the Indians represent humanity in the state of nature and are agents of its unconscious barbarity. It is curious that, just as the poet minimizes the theme of hybris in *The Titanic,* so in *Brébeuf* he minimizes the awareness of the Indians, their feeling that they are disposing of a real enemy, a black-coated emissary of an unknown God and an unknown race that may soon wipe them out. In any case, Indians, even Iroquois, are not merely wolves; and while the conflict of mental and physical values is certainly present, there is a greater range of suggestiveness. In the first place, the scene is related to its universal archetype: Brébeuf is given the courage to endure the breaking of his body because the body of God was in a very similar way broken for him. Thus the essential tragedy of Jephthah's daughter, as a pointless and useless waste of life, ceases to exist. In the second place, the Indians represent the fact that the unconscious cruelty of nature is recreated by the partly conscious cruelties of ignorant and frightened men. This point is already implicit in *Jephthah's Daughter*; we have seen that Jephthah is really sacrificing his daughter to nature. But it is clearer here, and it is clear too that the monsters of "The Great Feud," who are animated only by an impulse to mutual destruction, prefigure the stampeding and maniacal fury of Naziism as much as their descendants in *The Fable of the Goats* do.

In *Brébeuf* the poet makes a comment which may well be prophetic for the future of Canadian poetry:

> The wheel had come full circle with the visions
> In France of Brébeuf poured through the mold
>   of St. Ignace.

For a wheel does come full circle here: a narrative tradition begotten in the nineteenth century, and heir to all the philosophical pessimism and moral nihilism of that century, reaches its culmination in *Brébeuf* and is hardly capable of much future development. True, Birney's "David" is a fine example of the same sort of tragedy that is in "At the Cedars" or even *The Titanic,* and in the phrase "the last of my youth" with which the poem ends there is even a faint suggestion of a sacrificial symbolism. And in Anne Marriott's "The Wind Our Enemy," it is significant that the enemy is still the wind rather than the forces of economic breakdown that helped to create the wind. But neither of these poets seem likely to go on with this theme, and in such poems as "The Truant," where man confronts the order of nature undismayed, it is evident that Pratt is abandoning it too. The poet's vision of Canada as a pioneer country in which man stands face to face with nature is bound to be superseded by a vision of Canada as a settled and civilized country, part of an international order, in which men confront the social and spiritual problems of men. That this development is now taking place and will greatly increase in future needs no detailed proof: but it is to be hoped that the poets who do deal with it will maintain an interest in the traditional narrative form. For the lyric, if cultivated too exclusively, tends to become too entangled with the printed page: in an age when new contacts between a poet and his public are opening up through radio, the narrative, as a form peculiarly well adapted for public reading, may play an important role in reawakening a public respect for and response to poetry. There are values in both tradition and experiment, and in both the narrative has important claims as Canadian poetry hesitates on the threshold of a new era.

—(1946) 1966

STEPHEN LEACOCK'S CANADIAN HUMOR

R. E. Watters

The following article appeared under the title "A Special Tang" in Canadian Literature *(Summer, 1960). The author has subsequently made a few minor changes and added a number of footnotes.* (For a biographical note on Stephen Leacock, see page 163.)*

———◆———

A well-known oddity of Canadian literature is the fact that, out of all our authors, the two who have achieved the greatest reputations in the English-speaking world have been humorists. We ourselves have tirelessly repeated that the best of our literature is our poetry, but that world has paid our poets little attention on either the popular or critical levels. Abroad, even our fiction has made greater impact than our poetry. Our humorists are fewer than either

———
*[Where necessary, permission to quote has been obtained from the publisher.]

our poets or novelists, yet two of them have caught the ear of the world. Thomas Chandler Haliburton was in his day this continent's best-known author on both sides of the Atlantic; and in the present century Stephen Leacock is read almost everywhere. To explain all this as simply the "mystery of genius" or perhaps an "accident of international preference" may be nothing more than obscurantism. Perhaps one should ask whether or not there is something in the soil or environment of Canada especially favorable to humor, something that perhaps imparts a special "tang" to it, a flavor obtainable from no other source and therefore valued abroad for its uniqueness, detectable even if undefined. A close examination of some of Leacock's humor may reveal some characteristics which produce whatever special "tang" or flavor it has, and at the same time may suggest how this unique quality is related to Canadian life.

"Canadianness" is not something which I believe either increases or lessens the literary merit of a work. Although a literary evaluation of Leacock's humor is outside the direct concern of this paper, the point of view taken here must be explained. As everyone knows, national qualities in a work of literature—especially when they are Canadian—have been praised by some as a strength, denounced by others as a weakness, and disregarded by many as irrelevant. The first attitude is usually considered the most objectionable, but in my view all three are equally wrong. The third attitude ("irrelevance") is, in criticism, particularly mischievous because superficially it seems so impeccable. Nevertheless it is seriously wrong, because it fails to discriminate between the processes of understanding a work and of judging its excellence, and whenever the understanding is incomplete the judgment will be unsound. Precisely because the "content" of a work is really inseparable from its "form" or "expression," no aspect of that "content" can be irrelevant to the complete critical process. National differences are readily acknowledged and even carefully analyzed in an author's language; even when his language is English, attention is paid to idiomatic variations between, let us say, usage in Great Britain, the United States, and Australia. But little or no attention has been given to national differences in less tangible but more significant matters such as general outlook, unspoken assumptions about motivation and behavior, and attitudes toward certain issues of human existence. While the facts of life may be much the same everywhere, their interpretation may differ in extremely significant ways.

My conviction is that Leacock wrote Canadian humor, that our national characteristics shaped it, and that they are, in turn, revealed by it. Just as American humor can be distinguished from English, so can Leacock's be distinguished from both. Since Leacock himself was interested in the national characteristics of humor he cannot be numbered among those who consider the "national" quality of a work of literature as either regrettable or irrelevant. Of course, he readily admitted that humor everywhere has a common basis and warned that national distinctions could be overdrawn. Nevertheless, he firmly believed that "the various circumstances of environment, of national character, and of language, at least emphasize and make salient certain aspects of national humour."[1] Repeatedly he addressed himself to the challenge of distinguishing between English and American humor. In 1914 he saw in the jokes of the two countries a "divergence of national taste" which he considered "really fundamental": "The Englishman loves what is literal. . . .The American . . . tries to convey the same idea by exaggeration."[2] His remarks here were followed over the years by many more, too many for me to summarize. For instance, he is reported to have once told Cyril Clemens that "English humour is always based on fact, whereas American humour often deals with what really could never have happened except in the imagination."[3] He has an entire chapter on "National Characteristics" in his *Humour, Its Theory and Technique*

1. His article on "Humour" in *Encyclopedia Britannica* (1945), 11:885.
2. "American Humour," *Nineteenth Century,* 76:455-456 (August 1914).
3. Cyril Clemens, "An Evening with Stephen Leacock," *Catholic World,* 159:240 (June 1940).

(1935), and he had further comments to make a couple of years later in *Humour and Humanity* (1937). In this book he goes into social history to explain the greater popularity of the pun in English humor than in American, and to explain why the humor of bad spelling, once so prevalent in the United States, never caught on in England.[4] He analyzes typical English and American jokes to demonstrate the national differences. "There is," he says, "a broad distinction to be made between jokes that proceed by telling the truth and thus landing us in a sort of impossibility, and jokes that proceed to state an impossibility and land us in a truth. These contrasted types correspond very much to the formal aspect (not the inner) of typical British and American jokes."[5]

Unfortunately, Leacock seldom talked directly about the characteristics of his own humor, and said even less about Canadian humor generally. It is certain, however, that he never grouped himself with English humorists. Instead, he spoke of himself as an "American" humorist, though he used the word in its continental rather than national sense.[6]

Critics and reviewers in England seem more perceptive than those in the United States of certain differences in Leacock's humor from both British and American. As with Canadian speech, the "American" characteristics in things Canadian are plainly evident to Englishmen. But British characteristics were also readily found in the humor, perhaps because English readers wished to have some claim on the man (after all, his first six years were lived in England!). The Americans felt no such need to look for differences.

But the perceptiveness of English critics, with one notable exception, had more width than depth. Leacock was regarded as something like a literary mason, skilfully applying English craftsmanship to American materials. No thought was given to the possibility that he might have quarried some of his own stone, invented some of his own methods, originated some of the final design. Sir Owen Seaman (of *Punch*) once spoke of Leacock's humor as being "British by heredity" with "something of the spirit of American humour by force of association."[7] Another English critic described Canada as "a sort of half-way house in letters between U.K. and U.S.A.," and therefore found no surprise in Leacock's having discovered "the hilarious mean between American and English humour":

> His fantastical ideas are often in the nature of American hyperbole — but they are developed in English fashion as a rule, in a quiet and close-knit narrative which has none of the exuberance of the typical American humorist.[8]

The notable exception is J. B. Priestley, who finds specific and positive Canadian qualities in Leacock's "outlook, manner, and style," which, he says, not only "belong to the man but . . . to the nation":

> Very adroitly he aimed at both British and American audiences, but he never identified himself with either; always, at least when he is at his best, he remains a Canadian . . . .

> The best of Leacock exists somewhere between — though at a slight angle from — the amiable nonsense of characteristic British humour (e.g. Wodehouse) and the hard cutting wit and almost vindictive satire of much American humour . . . .

> It is in fact the satirical humour of a very shrewd but essentially good-natured and eupeptic man, anything but an angry reformer. And two sorts of readers may find it unsatisfactory; namely, those who prefer humour to be the nonsense of dreamland, in the Wodehouse manner, and

---

4. *Humour and Humanity* (London, Butterworth, 1937), pp. 42-49.
5. *Ibid.,* p. 219.
6. For example, in *Humour and Humanity* (p. 239) he writes: "A great many of us in North America (the United States and Canada, which last the word America *seems* to omit), will admit that on the whole *our* literature . . . has not equalled in volume or value that of the older English-speaking world. . . . But many of us think that humour is an exception to this, and that here the *American product* . . . is equal to anything." [Italics added.]

---

7. Quoted by Ralph L. Curry in *Stephen Leacock, Humorist and Humanist* (Garden City, N.Y., Doubleday, 1959), p. 152.
8. *The Living Age,* 311:353 (November 1921). [An anonymous article reprinted in *The Living Age* from *The Morning Post* of September 29, 1921.]

those who regard humour as a weapon with which to attack the world.[9]

Beside these words we might place an extract from Lister Sinclair's essay entitled "The Canadian Idiom":

> We are beginning to realize our position in the world, and it is precarious. We lie between the greatest and grimmest of the Grim Great Powers . . . and in the middle of the night we sometimes dream of hot breath quietly playing on the backs of our necks . . . . We are very small in population . . . [yet] we wish to be influential; we have a small voice, but we wish to make it heard.[10]

Mr. Sinclair also refers to what he calls the "calculated diffidence" of Canadians as being a kind of "protective coloration," and goes on to assert that the characteristic Canadian method of making our small voice heard is the use of irony, "the jiu-jitsu of literature . . . the weapon of Socrates . . . the principle of letting the giants destroy one another by their strength."[11]

Not only in the mid-twentieth century but throughout our history Canada's position has been "precarious." With inner tensions between our bi-racial cultures and provincial sectionalisms; with geographic, economic, and military forces pulling vertically within the continent, and with historical, nostalgic, and institutional ones pulling horizontally across the Atlantic; with our vast territory and strenuous climate dwarfing and threatening our numbers and our energies; with all the complexities, in short, which we fully recognize but cannot wholly command, the outlook of Canadians on the world and on human relations is far from identical with that of Englishmen or Americans. We have never known the easy national security and laurelled self-confidence out of which may issue the "amiable nonsense" of a Wodehouse, nor have we ever had the wealth and strength which can both provoke and withstand the iconoclastic satire of a Sinclair Lewis. While one's home is being shaken by violent winds, one neither blows bubbles nor batters another member of the household.

As a people bent on self-preservation, Canadians have had to forego two luxuries: that of forgetting themselves in gay abandon and that of losing their tempers in righteous wrath. Yet there is a kind of humor that combines full understanding of the contending forces with a wry recognition of one's ineffectiveness in controlling them — a humor in which one sees himself as others see him but without any admission that this outer man is a truer portrait than the inner — a humor based on the incongruity between the real and the ideal, in which the ideal is repeatedly thwarted by the real but never quite annihilated. Such humor is Canadian.

What Lister Sinclair calls our "calculated diffidence" would never draw attention to itself in humor by exuberant slapstick or by linguistic pranks in the form of explosive wisecracks — and there is little of either in Leacock. The Socratic irony of letting the giants destroy themselves by their own utterances is a standard device of Leacock — witness, for example, the self-destruction so wrought amongst university administrators and professors, high financiers, clean-government reformers, and church boardmen in his *Arcadian Adventures With the Idle Rich*. Here Leacock may be, in Priestley's phrase, "anything but an angry reformer," yet a reformer he unmistakably is. So also with the *Sunshine Sketches*. Both these books display neither the "amiable nonsense" of a Wodehouse nor the "hard cutting wit and almost vindictive satire of much American humour." Good-tempered restraint is less easy to detect than slashing attack, and is perhaps less colorful to watch, but it has its own unique value. Given Canada's "precarious" situation of inner and outer relationships, self-restraint means self-preservation. We cannot enforce change or reform with a scourge or bludgeon, because the tightrope we walk is no place for flailing arms.

---

9. *The Bodley Head Leacock,* edited and introduced by J. B. Priestley (London, The Bodley Head, 1957), pp. 10-12. [Published in Canada under the title *The Best of Leacock* (Toronto, McClelland, 1957).]
10. Malcolm Ross (ed.), *Our Sense of Identity* (Toronto, Ryerson, 1954), pp. 236-237.
11. *Ibid.,* p. 240.

The Canadian satirical weapon is, of necessity, the scalpel of the cool surgeon or the quick flip of the judo expert.

In his recent biography of Leacock, Ralph L. Curry frequently refers to Leacock's "favorite character, the little man in the society too complex for him," who preserves "his dignity by continuing, in his ignorance, to act like a man."[12] Wearing his American spectacles, Mr. Curry has misread Leacock, for the "little man" he describes is portrayed by various American humorists but not by Leacock. In the light of his own description, it is rather surprising that Mr. Curry cites "My Financial Career" as a good portrait of Leacock's "little man." The protagonist of this most famous of all Leacock's sketches is certainly not an innocent overwhelmed by an environment too complex for his understanding.

The truth is very simple: Leacock's "favorite character" was indeed a "little man" but he was a Canadian type, not an American; and "My Financial Career" *is* a good portrait of him but only when its Canadian subject is properly identified and described. In this sketch Leacock introduces us to a somewhat diffident young man who, he tells us, knows "beforehand" what is likely to happen but who nevertheless enters the bank undeterred by this knowledge. The young man has formed an ideal of saving his money and he considers the bank the best place to accomplish his purpose. He understands the essentials of banking, if not the details; he understands how he appears to others (confused, incompetent, helpless, etc.) and also *why* he appears so; he understands what he does wrong while he does it; and above all he understands himself thoroughly, past and present, both his inner self and his outer appearance. Far from preserving any "dignity" by "continuing, in his ignorance, to act like a man," he is acutely handicapped by the very completeness of his knowledge. It is true that he cannot control his nervous reactions any more than he can change the atmosphere of

_____
12. *Op. cit.*, p. 242 *et al.*

the bank—the humor lies in just this ineffectiveness.

Throughout the sketch the humor sparkles from the changing facets of the young man's "identity": how others see him and how he sees himself, the incongruities between appearance and reality. Besides his own true identity there is mistaken identity, assumed identity, and apparent identity. For instance, the bankers mistake him at first for "one of Pinkerton's men," and then for "a son of Baron Rothchild or a young Gould"; later he himself tries to act or look like an insulted depositor or an irascible curmudgeon; and at the end he appears to the bankers as an utter fool. All the while his essential nature remains intact and unchanged, despite all the environmental entanglements. Unable to adjust his inner self to an environment too powerful for him, he retreats under a barrage of laughter. But consider the ending of the story. Following the description of the roar of laughter he hears as the bank doors close behind him come two concluding sentences:

> Since then I bank no more. I keep my money in cash in my trousers' pocket and my savings in silver dollars in a sock.

In short, this diffident young Canadian's initial intention of saving his money has been quite unaffected by what has happened to him in the bank. Wryly recognizing *once more* his inability to cope with the overpowering atmosphere of the banking world, he changes his method of money-saving to one which is free from external pressures and is entirely within his own control. In his own way this "little man" has solved his problem—a richly humorous solution for the reader, to be sure, because of the incongruity between the ideal of his intention and the reality of his sock.

I have labored the analysis of this story not because I think that Leacock while writing it intended consciously anything like a commentary on the Canadian national character, but because I believe that we have here a prime example of how an author's outlook on life, including his interpretation of the ridiculous or amusing, is colored by the social environment and the people he knows best. And for Leacock these were not English, not American, but Canadian. That last sentence of "My Financial Career" is pure Canadian.

The little Canadian of this sketch is encountered elsewhere in Leacock. Take, for example, "The Awful Fate of Melpomenus Jones." Here the protagonist again finds himself caught in an environment not of his own making — the social context of expected "white lies" — for which he is again morally and emotionally unconstituted. Jones is introduced as "a curate — such a dear young man, and only twenty-three," whose problem was that he "simply couldn't get away from people." As Leacock brilliantly explains the difficulty: "He was too modest to tell a lie and too religious to wish to appear rude." Here is the scalpel stroke, laying bare the twisted values in modern society — the reversal of sanctions between the ideal and the real, where the white lies of social politeness demand and receive the homage due only to religious truths. The dilemma is funny to us because of the incongruity between the momentousness of the ideal principle and the apparent triviality of the real predicament. But consider the significance of this little Canadian's "exit line":

> ... he sat up in bed with a beautiful smile of confidence playing upon his face, and said, "Well — the angels are calling me; I'm afraid I really must go now. Good afternoon."

In that beatific "Good afternoon" the little curate finally departs *on his own terms:* truth and politeness here at last coincide. Though he must die to be true to himself, he has solved his problem to his perfect satisfaction! And again there is the ironic incongruity between the ideal of his simple intention and the reality of his drastic method.

Again and again in Leacock's humor — particularly in the writings of his best years, between 1910 and the early 1920's — we encounter this same "little man" exposed to pressures of various kinds from our complex society, yet maintaining both his dignity and his identity. He is not baffled by the complex world, though he may be frustrated by its overwhelming powers; he is sustained not by ignorance but by his integral understanding of his own nature and position within the world he inhabits. It is of course not a world peculiar to Canadians, as Leacock's wide popularity attests, but perhaps from longer experience Canadians have learned how to treat it humorously.

The diffidence of Leacock's little Canadian must not be misinterpreted as an unreadiness to set forth his own clear convictions. Take, for example, "Are The Rich Happy?" Here the little man reports faithfully the answers given by the rich themselves to his inquiries, but he is not for a moment taken in by the sob stories he hears. He is merely allowing the giants of wealth to destroy themselves with their own tongues, just as they had in another sketch entitled "Self-Made Men." The observant little inquirer in "Are the Rich Happy?" delightedly helps in the rout, indeed, by quietly loosing such barbed shafts as these:

> My judgment is that the rich undergo cruel trials and bitter tragedies of which the poor know nothing. . . .
> The rich are troubled by money all the time. . . .
> I have seen Spugg put aside his glass of champagne — or his glass after he had drunk his champagne — with an expression of something like contempt
> Yet one must not draw a picture of the rich in colors altogether gloomy.

And then comes the ending of the report, which shows the little man's full ironic understanding. The rich Overjoy family, he is told, is now "absolutely cleaned out — not a cent left." On closer inquiry, however, he finds that the Overjoys haven't sold their mansion — "they were too much attached to it" — nor given up their box at the opera — they were "too musical" for that. Nevertheless by general report they are "absolutely ruined.... You could buy Overjoy — so I am informed — for ten dollars." Then he shifts from his ironic reporting to a final direct comment of his own: "But I observe that he still wears a seal-lined coat worth at least five hundred."

In "We Have With Us Tonight" the little man is a travelling lecturer subjected night after night to the bumbling rudenesses and absurdities of pompous chairmen. The world of the lecture circuit bothers but does not baffle him. Though he cannot evade the institutionalized rules and procedures, he can analyze and classify them. He can even extract from them a wry amusement at his occasional discomfitures as well as his petty triumphs. In "The Man in Asbestos" he refuses to yield to persuasion or example that a future Utopian society free from toil and risk and tension is preferable to our own; whatever the stresses and strains of our present world he has no desire to escape to a brand new one. In "Homer and Humbug" he is again resisting the pressure of organized opinion — the demand on him to admire as supreme genius what in his personal judgment is nothing but "primitive literature." In "Roughing It in the Bush" he is opposing such conventional patterns as that physical discomfort is a requisite for proper moose-hunting; he has been quite content for ten years with his own pattern of high living in the wilderness. And for a final example consider "The Transit of Venus," a short story about a professor of astronomy in love with a student. This "little man" — Leacock's own term for Lancelot Kitter — is inexperienced in the ways of love rather than ignorant of them; he lacks knowledge of women but not of his own state of mind. When he is inept in a situation he knows he **has** "failed again." He is fully aware of what he should do, of what is expected of him; he just cannot do it. The story has the conventional happy ending, not because he is forced or maneuvred into something he does not want, but only because an opportunity comes along with no distracting cross-currents to prevent his grasping it. No doubt the girl makes it easy for him — but again the ending is significant. This little professor of astronomy does not weakly join the girl's orbit; instead, she is swung into his to become indistinguishable from "any other professor's wife."

All these "little men" know their environment, know themselves, know what is expected of them; sometimes they cannot conform, sometimes they will not, but invariably they draw their strength from within themselves. The world they choose to live in is a huge one, just as the clothes Stephen Leacock chose to wear were always several sizes too big for him. Yet the essential size and identity of the man inside is unaffected by the bigness outside, even though to outsiders the appearance may seem ridiculously dwarfing.

Leacock's Canadian archetype is therefore radically different in outlook from such a character as Benchley's befuddled little man in an incomprehensible world, or Thurber's Walter Mitty, who can live only by escaping into a fantasy of his own making. To Leacock's "little man" the world is not incomprehensible, nor does he want to escape into fantasy. He wants to continue living in this complex world, preferably by making changes in it to suit himself, but if this is impossible — as it usually is — then to live in this world somehow without sacrificing his self-respect, his principles, or his continuing identity. In an ideal world one should be able to reconcile, through knowledge of both, the outer pressures and the inner desires. But in the real world the actual power to shape and achieve may be lacking. Incongruity between the real and the ideal is everywhere a basis of humor — but which aspect of the real and which aspect of the ideal are not everywhere given the same emphasis. As Leacock said: "The various circumstances of environment, of national character, and of language, at least emphasize and make salient certain aspects of national humour."[13] If my analysis of some pieces of Leacock's work is valid, then certain salient characteristics of his humor are unmistakably national. In our precarious and complicated circumstances, and given our national character, Canadians must either cry with frustration or laugh with Leacock.

All through our history, the favorite intellectual game of Canadians has been to measure ourselves against the British on the one hand and the Americans on the other. We have tended to define what we are almost exclusively by detecting our differences from both. Conse-

_____

13. See footnote [1], *supra*.

quently, if any people anywhere should be especially skilled in the comparative study of human beings considered as groups or types rather than as individuals, it should be us. And we should also be equipped to tell the world whatever insights into general human nature such processes provide. Now consider what Leacock says:

> Comparison is the very soul of humour . . . . It is the discovery of resemblance and the lack of it that builds up the contrasts, discrepancies and incongruities on which . . . humour depends.[14]

As Leacock well knew, poetic imagery also springs from the perception of similarities and differences; but humor, not poetry, builds upon the resultant discrepancies and incongruities, particularly as applied to types of human nature and typical human behavior. For generations, then, Canadians have cultivated the soil from which humor springs, and we therefore should not be surprised that out of Canada have come two great humorists to whom the world has given its approval. Men everywhere can detect and savor a special "tang" without caring about its special ingredients or even its origins.

It is noteworthy that Haliburton's humor is almost entirely the result of scrutinizing the differences between Americans, Nova Scotians, and Englishmen. The neglect into which Haliburton's humor has fallen is usually attributed to the lost appeal of dialect humor. A better reason may be that he concocted his Canadian humor for too restricted a contemporary market — for the provincial societies of England, the Eastern United States, and Nova Scotia; his "tang" is too crude for general modern taste. Leacock's blending is much subtler — he left out almost entirely such a strong ingredient as dialectical differences—and thereby he provided a refined seasoning for the humorous feasts of the entire western world, not merely for the Atlantic fringe. Canada has other humorists besides Haliburton and Leacock; they are lesser men, perhaps, but some day the world may discover them too.

—1960

_____
14. *Humour and Humanity*, p. 212.

[RECENT POETIC] EXPERIMENTATION

Earle Birney

What follows is an abridged version of a talk given by Earle Birney on CBC radio, and subsequently published in his The Creative Writer *(1966). Dr. Birney has made about a dozen minor changes in this abridged text. For a biographical note on Earle Birney and selection of his poetry, see pages 288-301.*

———————◆———————

Marshall McLuhan, our acknowledged philosopher of communications, is also one of our unacknowledged poets. He writes in rhythms and he thinks in images. In his *Understanding Media* McLuhan remarks that art, when it's most significant, "is a DEW line, a Distant Early Warning system that can always be relied on to tell the old culture what is beginning to happen to it." I think this is a truth not often faced, especially by Canadian literary critics, and one that must be accepted if we are to understand the creative process.

Living art, like anything else, stays alive only by changing. The young artist must constantly examine the forms and the aesthetic theories he has inherited; he must reject most of them, and he must search for new ones. Literature is all the more alive today because it is changing so rapidly. In fact it's adjusting to the possibility that the printed page is no longer the chief disseminator of ideas, and that authors must find ways to bend the new technological media to artistic purposes. The rebels and experimenters who are forcing these changes are, of course, having to fight the same battles against the same kind of academic critics who attacked the literary revolutionaries of the last generation. In their beginnings, Joyce, Kafka, Rimbaud, Rilke, Pound, Brecht, even Eliot, were pooh-poohed or ignored as cheap and sensational, as mad or frivolous destroyers of sacred tradition. Now these men are the ancient great — and the young writers who find them inadequate are getting the same treatment. Of course, many literary movements in every generation turn out to be blind alleys, but no critic should think himself so perceptive he can always tell the passing fashion from the significant breakthrough. I don't know exactly where the literary DEW Line is this moment, but I'm sure it lies somewhere in the complicated world of today's little-little magazines and small-press chapbooks.

In that world you'll find that many of the poetic and prose techniques which were regarded a few years ago as merely far out and probably inconsequential are now customary and established ones. To begin with a small example, punctuation in poetry is now used functionally only — or not at all. Syntactical ambiguities are either permitted, or obviated by artful breakings between lines, and blanks or breathing spaces between phrases. Or, if punctuation is used, it may be in company with spelling distortions and enormous variations of type faces and sizes, to signal voice tones simultaneously with visual effects, to reinforce the feeling and meaning of the poem. One Latin-american poet, José Garcia Villa, is particularly known for a series of short verses he called *Comma Poems,* in which all words are separated by commas, to force the reader to accept each word as of equal importance. Here is the conclusion of one of these pieces (in which the poet has been visioning God dancing on a bed of strawberries): "Yet, He, hurt, not, the littlest, one,/ But, gave, them, ripeness, all."[1]

Behind such apparently trivial oddities often lie serious and influential theories. Today there's been going on a great affirmation of poetry as something inescapably auditory as well as visual, a creation successful only when it conveys its maker's unique inner voice, a thing to be spoken or chanted or sung, as in the beginnings, with craft and with care, and yet still a poem in space, working on the eye. Why not give the

eye as much as it can use to extend the experience of the poem? Modern xerox and photo-offset processes, for example, make it possible, without extra expense, for a poet to order almost anything visually he wants on the page, to paint his work in the Oriental tradition, or, following and extending on e. e. cummings, to make the poem itself a sort of etching in print, so adding both to the range and the intensity of the aesthetic communication.

Some of these attitudes lie behind the Projective Verse theories of Charles Olson and the Black Mountain movement—so-called because its chief figures were associated briefly with an experimental college of that name in the United States. Following leads from Ezra Pound and William Carlos Williams, these poets decided to make the single line of a poem its basic unit for sound as well as sight. Like nearly all young American poets, by the end of the Fifties, they had inherited a belief that rhyming and traditional metrical counting are artificial impediments to honest expression; the poet must write to his own inner melody, his unique "voice." But if the line were no longer to set off rhyme or attest to a regular beat, what use was it at all? The Black Mountain poets rejected the anarchism of the old Free Verse writers, whose lines were never good guides to how they read their poems anyway, and they could not accept the indifference to form of any kind shown by the newer Beat poets, who were content to have their longer efforts set as prose, and their shorter pieces in Whitmanesque lines whose length was decreed by the width of the printer's page. Instead, Olson, Robert Creeley and others sought to develop an exact line whose length and accentuation would be determined organically, by the rhythm of the heart beat and by the natural separate exhalations of human breath. This has led them to rather short-line poems, containing only one strong stress, and it has created an agreeable effect of space, simple intensity, and delicate patterning on the page. At least the superficialities of Black Mountain poetry have caught on, and the "look" of it now dominates all the magazines. The Black Mountain in fact has moved from cult to fashion to establish-

---

1. *Comma Poems No. 145;* Signals, June/July, 1965.

ment, in a decade. It's easy, however, to over-simplify its technique and its influence. For some, the theories behind it involve certain principles of Yoga, anti-rational mysticism, and what Ginsberg calls "mind jerks." Some of the best young poets in Canada have emerged out of the Black Mountain movement: George Bowering, Lionel Kearns and John Newlove among others.

As for old-fashioned rhyming and stanza forms, such as the sonnet, no *avant garde* magazines would be caught dead publishing them, or worry a moment about their loss. Robert Duncan, the San Francisco poet and theorist, teaches his followers that "rime" is simply a way of "showing measurable distances between corresponding elements in a poem" and that this can be more subtly and instinctively achieved by a balancing of images and themes in the poem than by the contriving of sound-echoes.

The insistence on the importance of the image is still probably basic to poetic theorizing, though W. C. Williams and some of the Black Mountain writers have tended to begin with the "thing," the precise object from immediate experience which presumably sets the poem going, and to describe that thing as simply and yet minutely and predicatively as possible; if that is well done, the poem itself may be complete, without need of fortification by metaphor or comment or warping into a conscious form. Others, however, following in the mythopoeic movement associated with Robert Graves and going back to Jung, strive to come upon a primordial emblem or a symbol, some call it a "deep image," which can permeate a whole poem and stir that racial memory going back to the cavemen, that Collective Unconscious we are all supposed to have inherited. An exploration of this sort may perhaps be heard going on in these lines fom a recent poem of a Canadian writer, James Reaney:

Existence gives to me . . .
What does it give to thee?

He gives to me: a pebble
He gives to me   a dewdrop
He gives to me   a piece of string
He gives to me   a straw

The pebble is a huge dark hill I must climb
The dewdrop's a great stormy lake you must cross
The string was a road he could not find
The straw will be a sign whose meaning they forgot

Hill   lake   road   sign

What was it that quite changed the scene?

The answer is that they met a Tiger
The answer is that he met a Balloon

Who was the Tiger?   Christ
Who was the Balloon?   Buddha[2]

. . . The machine, of course, affects us all. Most poets I know, including myself, compose on a typewriter if one is handy, and we don't feel sure the poem will look right till we see it in type. We may also like to voice it and play it back on a tape-recorder, and hope to broadcast it over radio. I even think that the present universal fashion for poetry readings is partly a dividend from radio, television, and film, the media which have re-accustomed new poets and new audiences to the fact that poetry can be as public an experience as can any other art. I've no doubt too, that the radio, the tape-recorder and the playback have been influences hastening the very evident change-over in poetic styles from the obscure, gnarled and over-concentrated poetry of Hart Crane and the earlier Dylan Thomas to the direct and plain modes of today, the age of the so-called modern folksong. . . .

There's also of course the so-called computer poetry. Recipe: feed the basic rules of syntax and some recurrent rhythmic patterns into a computer, add vocabulary loaded with image words, run the machine long enough, and out come enormous lengths of word-tape arranged in lines. By the operation of statistical chance, such tapes will occasionally produce passages with sufficient unity of theme and image and enough provocative overtones to warrant their being clipped out and presented as rudimentary poems. English professors who are outraged or terror-struck by such affairs, or reject them scornfully as machine-made, betray their misunderstanding of the nature of poetry. The com-

---

2. *Gifts (Literary Review,* Summer, 1965), by permission of James Reaney and *The Literary Review.*

puter, used this way, becomes only an enormously complicated typewriter. The poem is still being made by poetically-sensitized human beings—by the linguistic expert who chooses the data words and, above all, by the editor of the tape, the critic-perceiver who extracts the poem from the surrounding gibberish. Even when you "make" your own poem longhand, you don't make its form, you find it. Some of these poems are, in fact, much better than many I've been reading recently in such fashionable American poetry journals as Chicago *Poetry*, under the signatures of so-called leading American poets.

In any case, I see nothing sacrilegious or unpoetic in any search by a creatively-minded person into the total resources of his society as aids towards the expression of what he wants to say to that society, or even to himself. When it comes to taking LSD or other drugs, new or old, the poet, of course, must be careful that he really is understanding and controlling the power he's invoking for the stimulation of his imagination and the releasing of the doors of his perception. Smoking marihuana, for example, will certainly not turn him into a drug-addict, despite what Canadian law-makers appear to think, and it may induce highly poetic experiences in the smokers; but it may also put him in a state where he becomes temporarily indifferent to pursuing the hard work of converting the experience to poems. As to the actually addictive drugs, the artist who uses them, legally or illegally, seems to be caught in a self-deteriorating process in which creativity is ultimately one of the casualties.

There's still another world of poetic experimentation today, based on a growing awareness of the primitive unity of all the arts. For example, an increasing number of poets and solo dancers are entering into collaborations for dance-reading productions, in which the recited poem forms the script for the choreography of the dancer. . . .

Again, though the matching of words and music is as old as the clanging of shields to the war-song, and the blowing of reeds to the sorcerer's chant, we mid-century westerners have displayed far more than traditional delight in poetry-music, in the neo-realistic operas of composers like Menotti, in the invention of a whole new mode of "folk-song" and the rise to fame of the Beatles and Bob Dylan, the most widely heard poets alive in the English-speaking world.

Poets have also been working with the film-makers, when they get a chance, from as early at least as the Auden-Grierson combination which produced that fine English documentary, the *Night Mail*. On the whole, however, neither television nor cinema seems as yet to have inspired the sort of collaboration with writers which leads to literature of permanence. On the other hand through tapes and recordings and radio broadcasts the poet has acquired an enormous amplifier for his voice, and mass-circulation opportunities.

Sculptors are even inviting poets to write on their statuary these days, and poems are also turning up on furniture. Why not in weaving and on dress designs? The October, 1965, issue of the *Bulletin* for the London Institute of Contemporary Arts has a full page illustration of a poem in bold face newstype printed on poster-size sheets pasted in such a way as to cover entirely a large sewing machine. Personally I'm still trying to get time to construct a poem from clippings out of a single issue of the *Toronto Daily Star* which will be pasted onto a mobile specially constructed by a team of sculptors. Perhaps we can make something that will create a spell to haul the warm spring sun back sooner in Canada, the way Eskimo poets make chants to go with string figures they weave, to exorcize the Arctic night and make sure that daylight returns at all. At any rate, I seriously and happily look forward to the day when rooms will swing with mobile poems, and the lobbies of our public buildings will be hung with verses inworked with murals, and engraved with things more verbally exciting and more "depth involving" than the names of founders, or sinister fingers pointing to toilets.

What about poems and paintings? Oriental cultures married these thousands of years ago and a proper Chinese poem, to this day, is something painted on the paper as a visual design (which includes both title and signature), and is in harmony with the poet's theme. Moreover, the units of the design, the carefully executed, brush-stroked and beautiful ideographs, carry not only the meaning but often the formalized vestiges of the original picture still behind the word itself. I think the great renewal of interest by the west in Chinese and Japanese poetry has in turn been one of the influences at work in the new emphasis on visuality in poetry today. The Gutenberg world forgot the close relation of painter and writer that existed in the great manuscript pages of medieval bookmakers, but the profusion of visual media now at the writer's back, and the exciting pioneering of artists themselves, have brought us into an era that is neither Gutenberg's nor Caxton's. Yet, despite what my friend Marshall McLuhan is saying, I contend it is still a world of literature. So far we haven't found new William Blakes or Rossettis, with the ability to create great books that are both poems and paintings, but we do have hundreds of poets today who are "swinging" with the visual arts, writing poems *about* paintings, particularly non-objective paintings, or poems *to* painters, or, as I've said, making designs of all sorts out of the poems themselves, even shimmering moire designs (following the lead of OP Art), or designs so visual only the titles require us to think of them as poems. The cool movements of the moment in this connection are what are known as Concrete Poetry and Found Poetry.

Although some dismiss concrete poems as nothing more than acrostics and crossword puzzles, this vogue contains some serious aesthetic theorizings. To quote its chief British practitioner, the Scot, Ian Hamilton Finlay, concrete poetry is "concerned with a structure of small nuances."[3] A single word may be taken, broken into syllables or letters but so arranged as to suggest many other words which extend the force of the original one, and the whole made into a design of a provocative nature in itself. One of the French concrete poets, Pierre Garnier, cheerfully admits that his work cannot be read out loud. You take it in with the eye, as you do with a billboard; the total effect is the accumulation of words as seen. The word itself is the magic, as Charles Olson once said. An American proponent of concrete poetry explains that "letters and junctures retain their physical identities . . . ; poetry here aspires not to the condition of music but to that of spatial art."[4] It doesn't seek to demolish language but to make language yield those enjoyments offered the viewer of non-objective painting.

Found poetry, on the other hand, seems at first glance an anarchist rather than collectivist fashion. Certainly it assaults the very idea of creation as a slow controlled shaping, and asserts art to be a subjective, even momentary, illusion in the eye of the individual beholder. Aesthetic form is, in a sense, always there; the artist merely isolates it. Just as a stone, or a rusted pair of braces off a garbage dump, once an artist frees them from their typical environment, can be offered as *objets d'art*, (if the artist sees them as such), so poems may be "created" merely by extracting paragraphs from newspapers, phrases from advertisements, fragments of novels, letters, scientific articles, anything. Even as a can of Campbell Soup became, when Andy Warhol meticulously duplicated it on canvas, a famous modern painting, so the text of the label of the same can might emerge as a Found Poem. . . .

If all this leaves you convinced at the end that writers are mad, dissatisfied, rebellious, restless, word-obsessed, emotional non-conformists, this is partly what I've been trying to say all these times. I hope, however, that you have also come to agree with me that the artist-writer is on life's side nevertheless, and essential to its victory.

—*1966*

---

3. Letter in *Glasgow Review* (Summer, 1965). See also the special concrete number of *Extra Verse* London, (Summer, 1965).

4. Barbara Smith (Bennington College) in the same issue of the *Glasgow Review*.

THE PRAIRIE:
A STATE OF MIND

Henry Kreisel

Henry Kreisel was born in Vienna, Austria, and had virtually all of his early education there before emigrating to England and then to Canada. He began to write very early in Vienna; his first story (in German) was published when he was 15 years of age. He matriculated from Harbord Collegiate, Toronto, and earned a B.A. and M.A. at the University of Toronto, before taking his doctorate at the University of London. Dr. Kreisel, now Academic Vice-President of the University of Alberta in Edmonton, has published in many journals and is the author of two novels, The Rich Man *(1948) and* The Betrayal *(1964).*

Soon after I first arrived in Alberta, now over twenty years ago, there appeared in the *Edmonton Journal* a letter in which the writer, replying to some article which had appeared some time earlier, asserted with passionate conviction that the earth was flat. Now in itself that would have been quite unremarkable, the expression merely of some cranky and eccentric old man. Normally, then, one would not have been likely to pay very much attention to such a letter, and one would have passed it over with an amused smile. Nothing pleases us more than to be able to feel superior to pre-scientific man, secure behind the fortress of our knowledge. I am no different in this respect from most other people. But there was something in the tone of that letter that would not allow me that kind of response. Far from feeling superior, I felt awed. Even as I write these lines, the emotion evoked in me by that letter that appeared in a newspaper more than twenty years ago comes back to me, tangible and palpable.

The tone of the letter was imperious. Surveying his vast domains, a giant with feet firmly rooted in the earth, a lord of the land asserted what his eyes saw, what his heart felt, and what his mind perceived. I cut the letter out and for some time carried it about with me in my wallet. I don't really know why I did that. I do know that in my travels round the prairie in those early years of my life in the Canadian west I looked at the great landscape through the eyes of that unknown man. At last I threw the clipping away, but the imagined figure of that giant remained to haunt my mind.

Years later I finally came to terms with that vision in a story that I called "The Broken Globe." This story deals with the clash between a father and his young son. The son, who is eventually to become a scientist, comes home from school one day and tells his father that the earth moves. The father, a Ukrainian settler, secure in something very like a mediaeval faith, asserts passionately that it does not and that his son is being tempted and corrupted by the devil. The story is told by a narrator, an academic who goes to visit the father, now an old man, to bring him greetings from his estranged scientist-son. At the end of the story, after the narrator has heard from the father about the conflict that alienated him from his son, the narrator rises to leave:

Together we walked out of the house. When I was about to get into my car, he touched me lightly on the arm. I turned. His eyes surveyed the vast expanse of sky and land, stretching far into the distance, reddish clouds in the sky and blue shadows on the land. With a gesture of great dignity and power he lifted his arm and stood pointing into the distance, at the flat land and the low-hanging sky.

"Look," he said, very slowly and very quietly, "she is flat and she stands still."

It was impossible not to feel a kind of admiration for the old man. There was something heroic about him. I held out my hand and he took it. He looked at me steadily, then averted his eyes and said, "Send greetings to my son." I drove off quickly, but had to stop again in order to open the wooden gate. I looked back at the house, and saw him still standing there, still looking at his beloved land, a lonely, towering figure framed against the darkening evening sky.[1]

You will have noted that the images I used to describe my imagined man seem extravagant —"a lord of the land," "a giant." These were in fact the images that came to me and I should myself have regarded them as purely subjective, if I had not afterwards in my reading encountered similar images in the work of other writers who write about the appearance of men on the prairie at certain times. Thus in Martha Ostenso's *Wild Geese* a young school teacher sees "against the strange pearly distance . . . the giant figure of a man beside his horse," and when he comes closer he recognizes Fusi Aronson, "the great Icelander . . . . He was grand in his demeanor, and somehow lonely, as a towering mountain is lonely, or as a solitary oak on the prairie." (31)[2] On the very first page of *Settlers of the Marsh*, Philip Grove, describing two men "fighting their way through the gathering dusk," calls one of them, Lars Nelson, "a giant, of three years' standing in the country." (11)[3] And in his autobiography, *In Search of Myself*, Grove, recalling the origin of *Fruits of the Earth* and his first encounter with the figure who was to become Abe Spalding, describes the arresting and startling sight of a man ploughing land generally thought to be unfit for farming. "Outlined as he was against a tilted and spoked sunset in the western sky," he writes, "he looked like a giant. Never before had I seen, between farm and town, a human being in all my drives." Grove goes on to tell how he stopped his horses and learned that this man had only that very afternoon arrived from Ontario, after a train journey of two thousand miles, had at once filed a claim for a homestead of a hundred and sixty acres, had unloaded his horses from the freight-car, and was now ploughing his first field. And when Grove expresses his surprise at the speed with which this newcomer set to work, the man replies, "Nothing else to do." (259)[4]

I set the image of the giant in the landscape over against the more familiar one of man pitted against a vast and frequently hostile natural environment that tends to dwarf him, at the mercy of what Grove calls, in *Settlers of the Marsh*, "a dumb shifting of forces." (152) Man, the giant-conqueror, and man, the insignificant dwarf always threatened by defeat, form the two polarities of the state of mind produced by the sheer physical fact of the prairie.

There are moments when the two images coalesce. So the observant Mrs. Bentley, whose diary forms the substance of Sinclair Ross' novel *As for Me and My House*, records the response of a prairie congregation during the bleak and drought-haunted 1930s:

> The last hymn was staidly orthodox, but through it there seemed to mount something primitive, something that was less a response to Philip's sermon and scripture reading than to the grim futility of their own lives. Five years in succession now they've been blown out, dried out, hailed out, and it was as if in the face of so blind and uncaring a universe they were trying to assert themselves, to insist upon their own meaning and importance. (19)[5]

All discussion of the literature produced in the Canadian west must of necessity begin with the impact of the landscape upon the mind. "Only a great artist," records Mrs. Bentley, "could ever paint the prairie, the vacancy and stillness of it, the bare essentials of a landscape, sky and earth." (59) W. O. Mitchell, in the opening sentences of *Who Has Seen the Wind*, speaks of the "least common denominator of nature, the skeleton requirements simply, of

1. Henry Kreisel, "The Broken Globe," in *The Best American Short Stories 1966*, edited by Martha Foley and David Burnett (Boston: Houghton Mifflin Co., 1966), p. 165.
2. Martha Ostenso, *Wild Geese* (originally published 1925). References in parentheses are to the New Canadian Library edition (Toronto, McClelland, 1961).
3. Frederick Philip Grove, *Settlers of the Marsh*. References in parentheses are to the first edition (Toronto, Ryerson, 1925).
4. Frederick Philip Grove, *In Search of Myself*. References in parentheses are to the first edition (Toronto, Macmillan, 1946).
5. Sinclair Ross, *As for Me and My House* (originally published 1947). References in parentheses are to the New Canadian Library edition (Toronto, McClelland, 1957).

land and sky." (3)[6] He goes on to describe the impact of the landscape on Gerald O'Connal, a four-year-old boy, living in a little prairie town and venturing for the first time to the edge of town:

> He looked up to find that the street had stopped. Ahead lay the sudden emptiness of the prairie. For the first time in his four years of life he was alone on the prairie.
>
> He had seen it often, from the veranda of his uncle's farmhouse, or at the end of a long street, but till now he had never heard it. The hum of telephone wires along the road, the ring of hidden crickets, the stitching sound of grasshoppers, the sudden relief of a meadow lark's song, were deliciously strange to him . . . .
>
> A gopher squeaked questioningly as Brian sat down upon a rock warm to the back of his thigh . . . . The gopher squeaked again, and he saw it a few yards away, sitting up, and watching him from its pulpit hole. A suave-winged hawk chose that moment to slip its shadow over the face of the prairie.
>
> And all about him was the wind now, a pervasive sighing through great emptiness, unhampered by the buildings of the town, warm and living against his face and in his hair. (11)

Only one other kind of landscape gives us the same skeleton requirements, the same vacancy and stillness, the same movement of wind through space—and that is the sea. So when Mrs. Bentley records in her diary that "there's a high, rocking wind that rattles the windows and creaks the walls. It's strong and steady like a great tide after the winter pouring north again, and I have a queer, helpless sense of being lost miles out in the middle of it," (35) she might well be tossing in heavy seas, protected only by a small and fragile little bark. In Grove's *Over Prairie Trails,* that remarkable book of impressionistic essays describing seven trips that Grove made in 1917 and 1918 between Gladstone and Falmouth near the western shore of Lake Manitoba, the prairie as sea becomes one of the controlling patterns shaping the imagination of the observer. On one of these trips—in the dead of winter—Grove prepares his horse-drawn cutter as if it were a boat being readied for a fairly long and possibly dangerous journey:

> Not a bolt but I tested it with a wrench; and before the stores were closed, I bought myself enough canned goods to feed me for a week should through any untoward accident the need arise. I always carried a little alcohol stove, and with my tarpaulin I could convert my cutter within three minutes into a windproof tent. Cramped quarters, to be sure, but better than being given over to the wind at thirty below. (60–61)[7]

Soon the cutter, the horses, and the man meet the first test—very like a Conradian crew coming to grips with a storm at sea. A mountainous snowdrift bars the way. The horses, Dan and Peter, who become wonderful characters in their own right, panic. They plunge wildly, rear on their hind legs, pull apart, try to turn and retrace their steps. "And meanwhile the cutter went sharply up at first, as if on the vast crest of a wave, then toppled over into a hole made by Dan, and altogether behaved like a boat tossed on a stormy sea. Then order returned into the chaos . . . . I spoke to the horses in a soft, quiet, purring voice; and at last I pulled in." (69)

He becomes aware of the sun, cold and high in the sky, a relentless inexorable force, and suddenly two Greek words come into his mind: Homer's *pontos atrygetos*—the barren sea. A half hour later he understands why:

> This was indeed like nothing so much as like being out in rough waters and in a troubled sea, with nothing to brace the storm with but a wind-tossed nutshell of a one-man sailing craft . . . . When the snow reached its extreme in depth, it gave you the feeling which a drowning man may have when fighting his desperate fight with the salty waves. But more impressive than that was the frequent outer resemblance. The waves of the ocean rise up and reach out and batter against the rocks and battlements of the shore, retreating again and ever returning

---

6. W. O. Mitchell, *Who Has Seen the Wind* (originally published 1947). References in parentheses are to a new edition (Toronto, Macmillan, 1960).

7. Frederick Philip Grove, *Over Prairie Trails* (originally published 1922). References in parentheses are to the New Canadian Library edition (Toronto, McClelland, 1957).

to the assault.... And if such a high crest wave had suddenly been frozen into solidity, its outline would have mimicked to perfection many a one of the snow shapes that I saw around. (77)

And when, at the end of another journey, the narrator reaches home, he is like a sailor reaching harbour after a long voyage:

> ... there was the signal put out for me. A lamp in one of the windows of the school.... And in the most friendly and welcoming way it looked with its single eye across at the nocturnal guest.
>
> I could not see the cottage, but I knew that my little girl lay sleeping in her cosy bed, and that a young woman was sitting there in the dark, her face glued to the window-pane, to be ready with a lantern which burned in the kitchen whenever I might pull up between school and house. And there, no doubt, she had been sitting for a long while already; and there she was destined to sit during the winter that came, on Friday nights — full often for many and many an hour — full often until midnight — and sometimes longer. (18)

The prairie, like the sea, thus often produces an extraordinary sensation of confinement within a vast and seemingly unlimited space. The isolated farm-houses, the towns and settlements, even the great cities that eventually sprang up on the prairies, become islands in that land-sea, areas of relatively safe refuge from the great and lonely spaces. In *Wild Geese* Martha Ostenso describes a moment when the sensation of safety and of abandonment are felt to be evenly balanced:

> Fine whips of rain lashed about the little house, and the wind whistled in the birch trees outside, bleak as a lost bird. These sounds defined the feelings of enclosed warmth and safety.... But they did also the opposed thing. They stirred the fear of loneliness, the ancient dread of abandonment in the wilderness in the profounder natures of these two who found shelter here. For an imponderable moment they sought beyond each other's eyes, sought for understanding, for communion under the vast terrestrial influence that bound them, an inevitable part and form of the earth, inseparable one from the other. (64)

At the same time the knowledge of the vast space outside brings to the surface anxieties that have their roots elsewhere and thus sharpens and crystallizes a state of mind. In *As for Me and My House* Mrs. Bentley uses the prairie constantly as a mirror of her own fears, frustrations, and helplessness:

> It's an immense night out there, wheeling and windy. The lights on the street and in the houses are helpless against the black wetness, little unilluminating glints that might be painted on it. The town seems huddled together, cowering on a high, tiny perch, afraid to move lest it topple into the wind. Close to the parsonage is the church, black even against the darkness, towering ominously up through the night and merging with it. There's a soft steady swish of rain on the roof, and a gurgle of eave troughs running over. Above, in the high cold night, the wind goes swinging past, indifferent, liplessly mournful. It frightens me, makes me feel lost, dropped on this little perch of town and abandoned. I wish Philip would waken. (5)

That, however, is not the only, perhaps not even the most significant response to the challenge of lonely and forbidden spaces. It is easy to see Mrs. Bentley's reaction as prototypical of the state of mind induced by the prairie, but it would not be altogether accurate. It is one kind of response, but set over against it there is the response typified in Grove's *Settlers of the Marsh* by Niels Lindstedt, who, like a Conradian adventurer, a Lord Jim or a Stein, is driven to follow a dream. It expresses itself in "a longing to leave and go to the very margin of civilization, there to clear a new place; and when it is cleared and people began to settle about it, to move on once more, again to the very edge of pioneerdom, to start it all over anew.... That way his enormous strength would still have a meaning." (180)

To conquer a piece of the continent, to put one's imprint upon virgin land, to say, "Here I am, for that I came," is as much a way of defining oneself, of proving one's existence, as is Descartes' *Cogito, ergo sum*. That is surely why that man whom Grove saw ploughing a field barely two hours after his arrival was driven to do it. He had to prove to himself that he was in some way master of his destiny, that he was fully alive, and that his strength had meaning. When he told Grove that he was doing what he was doing because there was nothing else to do, he was telling him the simple truth, but leaving a more complex truth unspoken, and probably even unperceived.

The conquest of territory is by definition a violent process. In the Canadian west, as elsewhere on this continent, it involved the displacement of the indigenous population by often scandalous means, and then the taming of the land itself. The displacement, the conquest, of the Indians, and later the rising of the Métis under Louis Riel, are events significantly absent from the literature I am discussing. Occasionally Riel breaks into the consciousness of one or another of the characters, usually an old man or an old woman remembering troubled times; occasionally the figure of an Indian appears briefly, but is soon gone. No doubt that is how things appeared to the European settlers on the prairie; no doubt our writers did not really make themselves too familiar with the indigenous people of the prairie, seeing them either as noble savages or not seeing them at all, but it is likely that a conscious or subconscious process of suppression is also at work here.

The conquest of the land itself is by contrast a dominant theme, and the price paid for the conquest by the conqueror or the would-be conqueror is clearly and memorably established. The attempt to conquer the land is a huge gamble. Many lose, and there are everywhere mute emblems testifying to defeat. "Once I passed the skeleton of a stable," Grove records in *Over Prairie Trails,* "the remnant of the buildings put up by a pioneer settler who had to give in after having wasted effort and substance and worn his knuckles to the bone. The wilderness uses human material up." (11) But into the attempted conquest, whether ultimately successful or not, men pour an awesome, concentrated passion. The breaking of the land becomes a kind of rape, a passionate seduction. The earth is at once a willing and unwilling mistress, accepting and rejecting her seducer, the cause of his frustration and fulfilment, and either way the shaper and controller of his mind, exacting servitude.

The most powerful statement of that condition in the literature of the Canadian west is, I think, to be found in Martha Ostenso's *Wild Geese,* the story of Caleb Gare, a tyrannical man who, himself enslaved to the land, in turn enslaves his whole family to serve his own obsession. Characteristically, Ostenso sees him as a gigantic figure. "His tremendous shoulders and massive head, which loomed forward from the rest of his body like a rough projection of rock from the edge of a cliff," she writes, "gave him a towering appearance." (13) He is conceived in a way which makes it difficult to speak of him in conventional terms of human virtue or human vice, for he is conceived as "a spiritual counterpart of the land, as harsh, as demanding, as tyrannical as the very soil from which he drew his existence." (33) He can only define himself in terms of the land, and paradoxically it is the land and not his children that bears testimony to his potency and manhood. As he supervises his sons and daughters, grown up, but still only extensions of himself, working in the fields, he is gratified by the knowledge that what they are producing is the product of *his* land, the result of *his* industry, "as undeniably his as his right hand, testifying to the outer world that Caleb Gare was a successful owner and user of the soil." (171) At night he frequently goes out with a lantern swinging low along the earth. No one knows where he goes or why he goes, and no one dares to ask him, but his daughter Judith once remarks scornfully "that it was to assure himself that his land was still there." (18) Only the land can ultimately give him the assurance that he is alive: "Before him glimmered the silver grey sheet of the flax—rich, beautiful, strong. All unto itself, complete, demanding everything, and in turn yielding everything—growth of the earth, the only thing on the earth worthy of respect, of homage." (126-7)

Being so possessed by the prairie, his mind and body as it were an extension of it, he cannot give himself to anyone else. Since he is incapable of loving another human being, he can receive no love in return. He marries his wife knowing that she has had a child born out of wedlock because this gives him the power of blackmail over her and, in a stern and puritan society, chains her forever to him and to his land. He knows that she once gave herself to another man in a way in which she can never give herself to him, but he cannot see that he chose her because he wanted someone who could not demand from him a love he is incapable of giving. Having committed his mind and his body to the land, greedily acquiring more and more, he can only use other human beings as instruments to help feed an appetite that can never be satisfied. His human feelings must therefore be suppressed, and the passion of his blood must remain forever frustrated, sublimated in his passion for the acquisition of more and more land. Man, the would-be conqueror, is thus also man, the supreme egoist, subordinating everything to the flow of a powerful ambition. "Caleb Gare—he does not feel," says Fusi Aronson, the Icelander. "I shall kill him one day. But even that he will not feel." (31)

He does feel for his land. But the land is a fickle mistress, and he must live in perpetual fear, for he can never be sure that this mistress will remain faithful. She may, and indeed she does, with hail and fire destroy in minutes all that he has laboured to build.

Caleb Gare's obsession may be extreme, and yet a measure of egocentricity, though more often found in less virulent form, is perhaps necessary if the huge task of taming a continent is to be successfully accomplished. At the same time the necessity of survival dictates cooperative undertakings. So it is not surprising that the prairie has produced the most right-wing as well as the most left-wing provincial governments in Canada. But whether conservative or radical, these governments have always been puritan in outlook, a true reflection of their constituencies.

The prairie settlements, insecure islands in that vast land-sea, have been austere, intensely puritan societies. Not that puritanism in Canada is confined to the prairie, of course, but on the prairie it has been more solidly entrenched than even in rural Ontario, and can be observed in something very like a distilled form.

It can be argued that in order to tame the land and begin the building, however tentatively, of something approaching a civilization, the men and women who settled on the prairie had to tame themselves, had to curb their passions and contain them within a tight neo-Calvinist framework. But it is not surprising that there should be sudden eruptions and that the passions, long suppressed, should burst violently into the open and threaten the framework that was meant to contain them. In the literature with which I am dealing this violence often takes the form of melodrama, and though this sudden eruption of violence sometimes seems contrived for the sake of a novel's plot, it is also clearly inherent in the life the novelists observed. It is natural that novelists should exploit the tensions which invariably arise when a rigid moral code attempts to set strict limits on the instinctual life, if not indeed to suppress it altogether. Thus illicit love affairs, conducted furtively, without much joy, quickly begun and quickly ended, and sometimes complicated by the birth of illegitimate children, can be used as a perhaps obvious but nevertheless effective centre for a novel's structure, as for example in Stead's *Grain*, in Ostenso's *Wild Geese*, in Laurence's *A Jest of God*, in Ross's *As for Me and My House*.

It is because *As for Me and My House* contains the most uncompromising rendering of the puritan state of mind produced on the prairie that the novel has been accorded a central place in prairie literature. In the figure of Philip Bentley, a Presbyterian minister and artist *manqué*, we have—at least as he emerges from the diary of his wife—an embodiment of the puritan temperament, the product of his environment and much more a part of it than he would ever admit, angry not really because the communities in which he serves are puritan, but because they are not puritan enough, because they expect him to purvey a genteel kind of piety that will serve as a respectable front to hide a shallow morality. But his own emotions remain frozen within the puritan framework from which he cannot free his spirit. So he draws more and more into himself, becomes aloof and unknowable, not in the end so different from Caleb Gare, though in temperament and sensibility they seem at first glance to move in totally different worlds. Philip's wife is certain that "there's some twisted, stumbling power locked up within him, so blind and helpless still it can't find outlet, so clenched with urgency it can't release itself." (80) His drawing and painting reflect an inner paralysis. He draws endless prairie scenes that mirror his own frustration—the false fronts on the stores, doors and windows that are crooked and pinched, a little schoolhouse standing lonely and defiant in a landscape that is like a desert, "almost a lunar desert, with queer, fantastic pits and drifts of sand encroaching right to the doorstep." (80) Philip Bentley's emotional paralysis affects of course his relationship with his wife. Thus she describes in her diary how he lies beside her, his muscles rigid, and she presses closer to him, pretending to stir in her sleep, "but when I put my hand on his arm there was a sharp little contraction against my touch, and after a minute I shifted again, and went back to my own pillow." (116)

Only once does the twisted power that's locked up within him find some kind of outlet— and then disastrously, when he seduces the young girl Judith who has come to help in the house during his wife's illness.

Prairie puritanism is one result of the conquest of the land, part of the price exacted for the conquest. Like the theme of the conquest of the land, the theme of the imprisoned spirit dominates serious prairie writing, and is connected with it. We find this theme developed not only in Ross's novel, where it is seen at its bleakest and most uncompromising, not only in Grove's and Ostenso's work, but also in more recent novels, such as Margaret Laurence's two novels, *The Stone Angel* and *A Jest of God*, and in George Ryga's *Ballad of a Stone Picker*,

and, surprisingly perhaps, in W. O. Mitchell's *Who Has Seen the Wind*, which is conceived as a celebration and lyrical evocation of a prairie childhood. Brian O'Connel is initiated into the mysteries of God and nature, of life and death, but he is also brought face to face with the strange figure of the young Ben, a curious amalgam of noble savage and Wordsworthian child of nature. Again and again he appears, seemingly out of nowhere, soundlessly, the embodiment of a kind of free prairie spirit. His hair is "bleached as the dead prairie grass itself," (12) his trousers are always torn, he never wears shoes. He has "about as much moral conscience as the prairie wind that lifted over the edge of the prairie world to sing mortality to every living thing." (31) He does not play with other children, takes no part in organized school games. Though he can run "with the swiftness of a prairie chicken," and jump like an antelope, he refuses to have anything to do with athletic competitions. School itself is "an intolerable incarceration for him, made bearable only by flights of freedom which totaled up to almost the same number as the days he attended." (147) The solid burghers of the town, strait-laced and proper, try desperately to tame him, for his wild spirit represents a danger to them. But they cannot control him any more than they can control the wind. Brian O'Connel is drawn to the young Ben, and though they rarely speak to each other, there grows up between them a strong bond, what Mitchell calls "an extrasensory brotherhood." (89) The young Ben is Brian's double, the free spirit Brian would like to be, but dare not be. For Brian, one feels, will ultimately conform to the demands of his society and he will subdue the young Ben within himself.

Most of the works that I have dealt with were conceived and written more than a quarter of a century ago. There have been great social and industrial changes on the prairie since then, and the tempo of these changes has been rapidly accelerating in the past ten years or so. Yet it is surprising that such novels as Adele Wiseman's *The Sacrifice* and John Marlyn's *Under the Ribs of Death*, published in the 1950s, and Margaret

Laurence's *The Stone Angel* and *A Jest of God* and George Ryga's *Ballad of a Stone Picker,* published in the 1960s, should still adhere to the general pattern of the earlier works. The Winnipeg of Wiseman and Marlyn is the city of the 1920s and 1930s, a city of newly arrived immigrants, and the small towns of the Laurence and Ryga novels are clearly the small towns Ross and Ostenso knew.

For though much has changed in the west, much also still remains unchanged. Prairie puritanism is now somewhat beleaguered and shows signs of crumbling, but it remains a potent force still, and the vast land itself has not yet been finally subdued and altered. On a hot summer day it does not take long before, having left the paved streets of the great cities where hundreds of thousands of people now live, one can still see, outlined against the sky, the lonely, giant-appearing figures of men like Caleb Gare or the Ukrainian farmer in my story. And on a winter day one can turn off the great superhighways that now cross the prairies and drive along narrow, snow-covered roads, and there it still lies, the great, vast land-sea, and it is not difficult to imagine Philip Grove in his fragile cutter, speaking softly to Dan and Peter, his gentle, faithful horses, and preparing them to hurl themselves once more against that barren sea, those drifts of snow.

—1968

CANADIAN TRADITION AND CANADIAN LITERATURE

Miriam Waddington

*Besides her poetry, Miriam Waddington has critical and scholarly writings to her credit, such as her study of A. M. Klein (1970) and her edition of the essays and poems of John Sutherland (1973). The following essay is a revised version of a paper presented at the Conference on Commonwealth Literature, Brisbane, Australia, August, 1968, and was first published in the Journal of Commonwealth Literature No. 8: 125-141 (December 1969). A biographical note on Professor Waddington appears with some of her poetry on pages 439-444.***

———◆———

Very deep is the well of the past; should we say almost bottomless?
Thomas Mann, *Joseph and his Brothers.*

Before talking about tradition I would first like to define it, or at least come as close to defining it as possible. Harold Rosenberg suggests that "the attempt to define is like a game in which you cannot possibly reach the goal from the starting point but can only close in on it by picking up each time from where the last play landed."[1] With the word "tradition" it is especially necessary to circle the target, if only because it has so many general as well as specific meanings. I intend to offer several tentative ideas about the word itself, and then to talk briefly about what I understand by tradition in the context of Canadian literature.

Tradition has, first of all, to do with belief or custom, and, secondly, with the handing down of belief or custom to posterity, orally or in writing. Usually the origins are indeterminate, ancient, and unspecific. These very conditions of being unspecified and vague are favourable for the development of traditional customs and beliefs in the realms of art, religion, and nationalism.

In art, tradition tends to emphasize the historical element because it is understood largely as an agglomeration of artistic and literary principles based on continuous usage. But in theology tradition has a narrower and more technical meaning. There, "the traditional element consists of a sacred scripture . . . the verbal revelation of a god."[2]

The trouble is that the revelatory values that derive from theology are apt to get mixed up

*[Footnotes to this article appear on pages 637-638.]

627

with historical secular values that refer to art and literature. We then begin to associate traditionalism with orthodoxy in religion, conservation in politics, and resistance to innovation in art. Often enough, of course, these conjunctions do exist, and then we find tradition working not only as a means of conserving, but also as a way of fossilizing certain aspects of a culture which have crystallized out of the conflicts of opposing forces, and which honour certain values more than others, even to the point of investing them with magical authority. Literary traditions can thus grow out of a series of revolts against authority, and Irving Howe understands it in just this way:

> ... literary tradition can be fruitfully seen as a series of revolts, literary, but sometimes more than literary, of generation against generation, age against age.... Basically it has served as a means of asserting conservative or reactionary moral-ideological views.[3]

But W. R. Sorley stresses the desirability of permanence and continuity which operate in tradition.[4] He holds, however, that tradition embodies only *average* values, that it does not take into sufficient account what may be exceptional either in society or in its members. Valéry touches on this problem too when he complains about ordinary language:

> ... the science of language has, I know not why, taken up a very biased position in questions concerning literature. It tends to consider sacred the average results of the ill-regarded practices of all.[5]

But in spite of certain disadvantages, such as the tendency for the authoritative aspects of tradition to link up with forces which resist experiment and change, and its unsuitability for carrying exceptional values rather than average ones, tradition does fulfil at least two important functions for the individual. First, it extends his life-range beyond his own mere span, backward into the collective past and forward into the collective future. It offers:

> a certain compensation for the brevity and limited powers of individual life. It links gen-

eration to generation in the realm of the mind, so that, in Pascal's figure, we may regard the whole procession of the ages as one man always living and always learning.[6]

Or, as happens with the writer, the procession of the ages may be regarded as one man always reading and always writing in a company which is not limited either by time or place.

The second function of tradition is so pervasive in our lives that we are scarcely ever aware of it. It carries certain kinds of knowledge, makes itself "superior to ... arts of consciousness" and makes "thinking unnecessary, or at least safe."[7] This economy frees the individual's energies for other activities. Indeed, this is one of the notions that is so central in Yeats's essay on "Poetry and Tradition," where he argues that only the inheritors of a tradition, such as aristocrats, country folk, and artists — "because Providence has filled them with recklessness" — are able to make beautiful things. "The others [middle-classes and linen drapers], being always anxious, have come to possess little that is good in itself, and are always changing from thing to thing."[8]

What emerges most clearly from the foregoing is that tradition is hard to define because it is an internal and abstract value as much as an external concrete pressure:

> ... tradition does not operate upon the individual as an external force which merely hampers his freedom of movement. It may rather be described as a birthright into which he enters; it is formed in him by what he sees and hears; the actions he has been taught to do and the language he uses are part of it; it forms the mental atmosphere which he has breathed long before he began to reflect ... from the beginning he is himself part of the tradition to which he belongs.[9]

Finally, I think we can say that tradition is a body of practice in a certain area, accumulated over a certain period of time, which for one reason or another is considered meaningful enough to be passed on from one generation to the next. How and why a people come to value certain things and not others is a real question, for tradition does not only work positively. It expresses its negative aspects by displacing them to some other culture or to a despised aspect of its own culture. Thus Negroes for a long time accepted and lived out the negative tradition of American culture foisted upon them by the white people, and in the same way Jews submitted to the negative stereotype invented by the Christians among whom they lived.

I have made a wide circle around the notion of tradition, and, so far, I have remained at the outer edges of the problem. I now propose to move in closer to the centre, and to examine Canadian tradition more specifically. The question "Is there a Canadian tradition?" is rhetorical. No one is sure that there is such a thing at all, yet everyone acts as if it must exist. In his preface to *Other Canadians* John Sutherland suggests that "the critic has a penchant for the word tradition" because of "the wide field of speculation which it throws open to him." He goes on to criticize A. J. M. Smith for his speculative use of the concept:

Mr Smith knows it is utter nonsense to talk about a "tradition" of Canadian poetry. We could only use the word tradition if we believed that the poetry was so blended with the life of the country that it was able to reach out into the present and influence its course.[10]

C. Wright Mills focusses the problem more sharply when he says: "There is no such thing as 'the' tradition — as if it were a harmonious homogeneous whole—there is a historical movement, and within it, a number of traditions."[11] Mills is right; there is no such thing as a single tradition in Canadian literature. There are numerous traditions, both culturally and politically. I use the word "numerous" because I hope to avoid imposing unworkable theoretical dichotomies in the way Professor Smith and Professor Matthews have already done.

In his introduction to *The Book of Canadian Poetry*[12] Smith postulated a dichotomy between the "native" and "cosmopolitan" traditions, and divided the poets up into two teams. Time has shown that the two traditions are seldom separate in the work of individual Canadian writers. Nativeness and cosmopolitanism are not even true polarities since one can scarcely exist without the other. According to Smith's division it would be possible to argue that pre-Confederation poets were cosmopolitan because their models were European. Or is Smith really referring to T. S. Eliot's French models of the nineteenth century when he uses the word "cosmopolitan" as a critical category? Finally, the essential absurdity of Smith's position is pinpointed by John Sutherland's question:

...where has this hilarious Catholicism of Mr Smith's landed us? Are we really located somewhere abroad, busy improving our minds, or are we sitting in a remote section of the Canadian backwoods? Is the native dust shaken off our shoes or not?[13]

The truth is that the Canadian writer is neither abroad nor in the backwoods. He is, as A. M. Klein understood twenty years ago, in the world with other men, other writers. Klein held that "the proper study of mankind is men — not paysage." And as for the use of local colour, Klein wrote that:

...the writer who is concerned with his writing and not with his passport neither stresses nor ignores that background....This business of indicating longitudes and postal addresses is a procedure so superficial that far from stressing the Canadian background, it merely caresses it. Not in this way does one give a literature a national identity; in this way one writes only Baedekers.[14]

There can probably be no general agreement about a definition of Canadian tradition as such, but existing criticism reveals that there are certain historical facts which are indisputable. The efforts to integrate facts, impressions, and observations into a theoretical framework have so far been scattered and fragmentary. A scrutiny of these interpretations shows that there seem to be two major ways of interpreting the historical issues, and each way leads not only to a widely divergent definition of Canadian tradition and national identity, but also to a very different view of the future direction of literature. The two views I have in mind can be summed up by the terms "historical-social" and "apocalyptic-mythic." The first view has never been more completely articulated than by Archibald MacMechan in *Headwaters of Canadian Literature* (1924), and the second found one of its earliest champions in Lionel Stevenson's *Appraisals of Canadian Literature* (1926).

Each of these attitudes has its modern followers. As might be expected, the apocalyptic school is the dominant one. Its reliance on magic thinking and prophetic knowledge, along with its distrust of empiricism and its rejection of history, answers to a deep need in our depersonalized society. The chief exponents of the apocalyptic critical position are Northrop Frye, Roy Daniells, Malcolm Ross, and James Reaney. Somewhere in between the two positions, but closer to the apocalyptic one, is Milton Wilson. A. J. M. Smith seems hard to place because his method is historical; but his attitudes are Christian-mythic, so on the whole he belongs with the apocalyptic group. On the historical-social side we have, in the wake of MacMechan, such figures as E. K. Brown, John Sutherland, Carl Klinck, Frank W. Watt, John P. Matthews, Desmond Pacey, and A. M. Klein.

Both schools of criticism agree about certain facts and basic issues. They differ only in their interpretation of the facts. The facts which are discussed over and over again as being crucial in the development of our literature are three: geographic location, colonial origins, and the bilingualism and multiculturalism of the Canadian environment. There is also a fourth and perhaps less important area of agreement which centres on the soberness or the northness of the national character. But there is no general agreement (by default rather than through controversy) that our literature may have been influenced by economics and politics as well as by metaphysics.

But before going on to show how the interpretations vary, I will digress for a moment to note that most critics also agree about certain dominant themes. It is far easier to agree on the themes of Canadian literature and on the sobriety of the Canadian character than it is to reach a common interpretation about them. Thus we find Stevenson noting that the themes of our early writers displayed a "zeal for landscape," Klinck and Watt stressing the emigrants' theme of exile, and all the critics noting how out literature for a long time extolled nationalism and the moral qualities of loyalty, courage, resourcefulness, and independence — all the virtues, in fact, that were needed for pioneer life.

The themes of any literature, including ours, are much easier to discern than the forces which shaped them, and so literary historians are in accord that the imaginative writing up to the end of the nineteenth century was concerned with themes which originated in the "zeal for landscape," a self-conscious and colonial nationalism, and the pioneer pattern of family life which required the moral virtues of courage, loyalty, and resourcefulness. The resulting national character has never been better or more Canadianly described than by MacMechan:

> They [Canadians] are, in the main, a forest-felling, railway-building, plowing, sowing, reaping, butter-and-cheese making people, busied with mines and fisheries and factories, intent on making their share of the world a place of human habitation. They are a law-abiding, church-going, school-attending, debt-paying people who, after a long hard struggle with material conditions, are beginning to prosper.[15]

Perhaps that long hard struggle with material conditions is not yet over. E. K. Brown considered it to be still very much present in 1941 when, in an astringent little essay, he wrote sadly about the "survival in the national character of qualities which in our pioneer past have been tried and found precious" but which in his time resulted in a practical nation where art was for leisure only and where the aesthetic life was "not a recognized form of the good life."[16] To E. K. Brown this concentration on practical matters created a definite barrier to the development of great national literature. But W. L. Morton (a historian and not a literary critic) sees this practicality as the deep permanent result of a special combination of geographic and historic factors which he characterizes as "northness":

The discovery and occupation of Canada was separate and distinct from the occupation of the Americas .... It was the outcome of the piecemeal ventures of Norse seamen-farmers probing the northern seas for new harbors and fisheries, new hay meadows and timber stands .... Because of this separate origin in the northern frontier, economy and approach, Canadian life is to this day marked by a northern quality .... the greatest of joys, the return from the lonely savagery of the wilderness to the peace of the home; the puritanical restraint which masks the psychological tensions set up by the contrast of wilderness roughness and home discipline. The line which marks off the frontier from the farmstead, the wilderness from the baseland, the hinterland from the metropolis, runs through every Canadian psyche.[17]

Let me now consider in a general way the matter of colonialism which has been such an important influence in our culture. Carl Klinck draws a lively picture of the comings and goings in Colonial Canada during the early part of the nineteenth century:

Lower Canada ... was almost wholly French in language, culture, religion and laws. The term "Canadian" was equivalent to "*Canadien*," that is North American French, and the image of Canada was made up of seigneurs, habitants, black-clothed clergy, advocates, *coureurs de bois*, *voyageurs*, French Hurons at Lorette, Gallic gaiety, rides in *calèches* or sleighs, folk singing, farm labour, lumbering, church-going, and villages scattered along the St. Lawrence. The English image, significant of power, but also picturesque, included vice-regal display, military colour and bustle, polite sport, harbours full of transatlantic ships, vast stores for continental trade and development, political quarrelling, and high social life.[18]

But the colourful kaleidoscope depicted here also contained other shapes and blacker colours that have since cast a shadow and darkened the twentieth century. E. K. Brown listed emotional colonialism as one of the barriers to the development of Canadian literature;[19] but Roy Daniells takes a different view. He can hardly say enough in praise of the "spirit of high colonialism" (what is low colonialism?) as it operated in the group of post-Confederation writers:

... the principle of loyalty to British cultural tradition provided a *milieu* within which Canadians could hope in time to achieve a national nexus .... British models were accorded the sincerest form of flattery .... This visible dependence upon British tradition, however, had no element of subservience.[20]

Speaking more specifically about New Brunswick writers, Daniells grows eloquent about the isolation which protected the poets from the contaminating industrial influence of the rest of Canada:

Here Loyalist traditions persisted; the very isolation of the community from the expansive and disruptive development of the timber industry was a safeguard of intellectual pursuits and the values of a class structure .... In Fredericton the conservation of British values and the preservation of a colonial culture were no deterrents to the acceptance of nineteenth century liberal ideas and Romantic literature .... Here was the origin of Canada's "dolce stil nuovo" and the source of our first national improvement.[21]

Daniells is not writing only about the past. He ends his essay in a way that leaves no doubt about the assumptions underlying his critical approach to the present:

To turn the pages of the old *Canadian Monthly* is to enter a lost world. Courage and loyalty were its pre-eminent virtues; it demonstrated that liberal views, critical standards, and religious faith could strengthen one another. A handful of people set themselves to form the ideas of a new nation ... they achieved a vision of national greatness and an intellectual method more serviceable, more coherent, more beautiful than any other in English-Canadian history.[22]

It is interesting, as well as baffling, to see how this very same "spirit of high colonialism" receives a very different treatment in other pages of *The Literary History of Canada*. Far from praising the handfuls of people who, in isolation from the rest of the country, set themselves up as arbiters of the national consciousness, Klinck censures them, although his censure applies to an earlier social context than the one Daniells is discussing. He speaks of the "pretentious level" at which official literature operated when "Name, rank, British background and political connections received unusual respect...."[23] And in discussing *The Garland* as a periodical typical of the genteel tradition at the time just preceding Confederation, he has this to say about it:

The Garland kept up its own supply of didactically charged society tales together with the inevitable Biblical narratives, dramatic sketches and poems. The temptation to be English in the aristocratic or upper-gentlefolk manner was, of course, especially strong in the British colonies where class distinctions lived a precarious life among only the favored few. W. D. Howells would have seen much positive harm being done by literature catering to the dreams of this minority. The life portrayed was obviously foreign to most Canadian readers who had shared in these things neither before nor after emigration. As the expression of a social goal or as a palliative it was deplorable.[24]

It is only fair to add that Carl Klinck's disapproving attitude towards the genteel tradition is more representative than is that of Roy Daniells. MacMechan in discussing the verse of his own time was another who harshly condemned the effects of the genteel tradition: "Canadian verse shows its amateurness in defective technique, the forced rhyme, the padded line, the otiose epithet, the cloudy syntax, the lack of rule and proportion, the inability to handle a chosen meter consistently."[25] Although few contemporary critics would speak of the colonial heritage in the glowing terms used by Daniells, we find a curious echo, if not a conscious avowal, in James Reaney's article about the predicament of the Canadian poet. One of the characteristics of a colonial attitude is the way it persists in attaching more importance to what's made outside the country than inside it — whether it's jam or poetry;[26] and Reaney bears this out when he declares: "There's no doubt at all that if a Canadian poet wants to be terrific he has to assimilate what Yeats, Rilke, Eliot and all have done, or else."[27] Why Yeats, Rilke, and Eliot rather than Whitman, Crane, and Stevens? Or Apollinaire and Mayakovsky? In an earlier article in *Poetry*,

Reaney deplored the fact that Canadian poets were failing to use Northrop Frye's *Anatomy of Criticism* as a sourcebook for their works, as a kind of poet's "Plotto" or divine directive. But why can't it happen that a Canadian poet should be terrific in his own way and hit a homerun without an assist from the umpire-critic? Reaney's comment reveals that he sees tradition as something categorical, and as a value system that must be chosen by all poets. Similarly Eliot, in "Tradition and the Individual Talent," singles out the figures of Dante and Baudelaire, neglecting Anglo-Saxon poets and presenting Milton as a discord rather than a resonance.

It seems then that unconscious colonial attitudes of cultural subservience may still persist in our critics even though they may at the same time be aware of its culturally inhibiting effects. P. E. More identified one of the central problems of a colonial culture when he pointed out how only a fragment of the mother tradition was transplanted to New England:

They [the New England Colonists] did not bring with them the full temper of the English people, or even that part of its character which has given us Chaucer and Shakespeare and Dryden and Swift and Johnson and Byron and Tennyson. Their poetry . . . must be criticized, not as belonging to the main current of English literature, but as a slender branch, so to speak, running to one side, and deprived of the broader nourishment of tradition. It is the prolongation of a mood . . . at home under the sway of this same mood the imagination was distrusted, the theatres were closed, the picture collections of Charles dispersed or destroyed, the churches made barren of their beauty.[28]

And in Canada, the fragments were varied. The British fragment was largely a politically conservative one; of the French fragment I do not know enough to be able to describe it. But what Canadians inherited was not, as in New England, one parochialism, but several. In this sense we can claim to be a mosaic of parochialisms.

I have shown how critics differ in their attitudes to our colonial origins. To some it is anathema, to others the very fountainhead of national salvation. I will now discuss varied interpretations of geography and the bicultural situation.

In *Appraisals of Canadian Literature* Stevenson, who is one of the early formulators of the apocalyptic attitude, discusses Canadian landscape painters. He comments that "in Canada the Primordial forces are still dominant" and goes on to say:

> Canadian poetry [like painting] is equally concerned with the apocalyptic. The poetic mind, placed in the midst of natural grandeur, can scarcely avoid mysticism. It is . . . an instinctive pantheism, recognizing a spiritual meaning in nature and its identity with the soul of man.[29]

In much the same spirit is Stevenson's notion that "The poet draws his life from the latent forces of the country, and in his turn he gives form to that which must otherwise remain unrevealed to man."[30]

Few would quarrel with Stevenson's assumption that the poet draws his life from the latent forces of the country or that he makes them visible to all men. For Stevenson, these latent forces reside in the poet's recognition of a spiritual meaning in nature. Stevenson's latent forces, which await the poet's interpretation, seem to have much in common with Jung's collective unconscious. But an understanding of collective unconscious is not too different from an understanding of tradition. Both words incorporate the notions of community, continuity, and of varying degrees of unconsciousness. In each case the critic can people the empty conceptual spaces with his own best friends, very much as Eliot did. For Reaney the collective unconscious is filled with Indian legends, low-church sinning (inter-denominational), spooks, and found objects from rural Ontario. For many of the younger poets of the sixties, the collective unconscious contains whatever can be gathered from a rummage through the surrealist cellars of Europe. The Black Mountain poets of Vancouver seem to be waiting for an electric charge from the United States that will somehow result in a language of bare feelingful words, stripped of all image-bearing powers and freed from social context. For Northrop Frye the collective unconscious remains, as for Jung, an inexhaustible source of universal myth, the source of ever-forming and ever-reforming verbal equivalences and mystical correspondences which find their embodiment in the empirical world.

For the critical attitude that I have called historical-social, there is a different sort of content waiting to be apprehended in this latent consciousness. For Watt and Matthews the latently conscious is not so much latent as it is denied: they speak of the wilful suppression of dissident aspects of our tradition. Watt, for example, believes in the existence of a continuing suppressed radical tradition in Canadian literature.[31] He shows how the radical tradition drew its first inspiration from British Fabianism and continued to exist and grow along with our expanding industrialism until it finally found expression and a measure of acceptance in the intellectual periodicals of the thirties. John Matthews has suggested that it is the folk tradition, in contrast to the academic one, that has always been undervalued in Canada and that has therefore gone unhonoured and almost unrecorded in most histories of Canadian literature.[32] Watt and Matthews both insist on the primacy, indeed on the centrality, of the historical fact in literary criticism.

Lionel Stevenson believes in the power of revelation, but he never denies the historical fact: he often backs up magic with history, and supports prophecy with appropriate social realities. He makes an especially interesting and subtle point when he shows how strong is the human inclination towards illusion. He suggests that the early Canadian immigrant was prevented from seeing his real environment (that is, the true Canada) by two obstructions: his own culture which he brought with him, and second, the stereotyped myth of the north which was foisted on him by commercial interests: "The formula comprises a landscape of illimitable snow, peopled with a Bayard of the Mounted Police, a trapper or two, and a beautiful half-breed girl, all equipped with dog-sleds and rifles!"[33]

But the fact is that Canadian nature *is* unusually impressive, even if not quite in the way that Hollywood sees it: "the contrast in Canada of man's puny powers and achievements with Nature's permanence and immensity render ludicrous the anthropomorphic attitude which has become traditional in older civilizations."[34]

But Stevenson is careful not to make geography the *only* determinant in the development of a Canadian literature. He points out that neighbouring parts of the United States have a similar geography and suggests that the real difference in the development of the two cultures is to be found in their differing industrial pace. Whitman's poetry could not have been written here because Canadians did not have the same "preoccupation . . . with cities and factories and immigrating swarms"; and neither did we have, until recently, the same "studied emphasis which our southern neighbours set upon the externals of national consciousness."[35]

Stevenson's final interpretation of how Canadian tradition manifests itself in literature can be summed up in his own words:

In Canada the modern mind is placed in circumstances approximating those of the primitive myth makers....From childhood surrounded by this vastness and potentiality of nature, the Canadian becomes aware of it long before his education in the traditions of culture begins. Since his sympathy with nature is practically an inbred trait he instinctively responds to those features of religion, myth, or philosophy that retain some meaning as interpretations of Ancient Earth and man's relationship to her.[36]

In contrast to Stevenson's reliance on the power of myth, MacMechan relies almost entirely on historical method and social context to further his insight. He deals with French-language literature as well as English, and declares the factuality of biculturalism without apology:

The history of Canada involves the destiny of two races. They speak different languages; they practise, in the main, different religions. They do not mingle except for the purpose of commerce and politics. They remain separate and distinct like the brown water of the Ottawa and the blue water of the St. Lawrence when their floods meet and join above the island of Montreal. Still they are both affected by the genius of the land they live in, and by the political institutions they have framed. In spite of their unlikeness, they have also a certain likeness; and any account of the beginnings of Canadian literature must reckon with these facts. If the streams of creative impulse are different in color, French and English, still they move in the same direction and under the same conditions.[37]

W. L. Morton also believes that a common political, economic, and historical experience binds the two major cultures of Canada, and that this "common experience has created a common psychology of endurance and survival."[38] He ascribes a good deal of importance to the psychological aspects of endurance and survival, since he sees Canada as a land which emerged from the bitter struggles and sad defeats of two empires; a land which, at different times, was rejected by both, and which nevertheless survived defeat, and learned to tolerate, if not to embrace, the reality of at least two cultures.

The duality and diversity of the Canadian tradition is easy enough to distinguish in the matter of language. Less visible, but just as important, is the duality of political thought which produced, in English Canada at least, a literature of colonial conservatism on the one hand, and a suppressed literature of dissenting radicalism on the other. We have seen how F. W. Watt has traced the course of the dissident radical literature, and J. P. Matthews in his *Tradition in Exile* has pointed out the duality of a folk tradition on the one hand, and an academic one on the other. But these dualities have often remained nebulous and confused, and it has been hard to understand precisely where to locate them. Are Canadian dualities psychological, aesthetic, moral, political or regional? One has to understand not only the origin but the continuing life of each duality in order to deal with it intelligently. It is no use advocating the psychological feeling of unity when the political situation demands certain action. Humanitarian and moral feelings like Arnold's "change of heart" have seldom been effective in transforming social or political arrangements.

Still less effective as agents of social change are aesthetic values and manifestos. Aesthetic categories are always theoretical, and a difference of opinion in that sphere remains abstract and does not change the course of national affairs. And it is a well-known fact that aesthetic categories blend more easily with mythopoeic interpretations of literature than do historical or political ones. There is therefore less risk of change, and less necessity for political action in adopting the apocalyptic approach to Canadian tradition, rather than the historic one.

Malcolm Ross's work is a good example of an original, powerfully articulated, apocalyptic and (to my mind) erroneous interpretation of the Canadian bicultural situation. In a review of Klein's *Second Scroll* he wrote:

We acknowledge that the racial memories of our multi-dimensional culture are much too deep and broad to be filled by Cartier and Wolfe and the U.E. Loyalists. *It is not the item but the pattern which is Canadian.* As persons we live by the varied and separate spiritual inheritances and loyalties and we preserve our differences. But at another level, as Canadians, we take our life from the fruitful collision and interpretation of many inheritances. And thus we grow.[39]

But, as we have seen, MacMechan had postulated the real question whether the collision of many inheritances is always fruitful. He saw dangers in the collision between French and English, and was aware of painful elements in our national life. That did not prevent him from affirming that the two cultural streams were bound to mingle, whether they wanted to or not. And Stephen Leacock also found a less morally exalted way of expressing his perception of cultural pluralism:

Our situation in Canada is peculiar. From England and from America a flood of language washes over us. Telegraphic reports from London and Washington bury our breakfast table. We have to help to elect both Stanley Baldwin and Herbert Hoover. We have to listen in to the Oxford and Cambridge boat race and the World Baseball series. American and London publishers shower their bounties into our lap. Our primary education pours itself into the mould of Massachusetts; our colleges reflect Oxford and Harvard, and we import our theology, like our whiskey, direct from Scotland.[40]

What a dilemma! There are so many different interpretations of the same issue, that the reader is driven to echo John Sutherland's earlier question: "Has the native dust been shaken off our shoes or not?"

Malcolm Ross would probably reply that our native dust still clings and that it enhances our natures and coats us with a dusty film of glory. What MacMechan and Abbé Roy mourned as the ascetic and "irreproachable bearing" of the Canadian muse, is, by other observers, interpreted as a talent for meditation, a skill in finding and adhering to the *via media,* while to still others this same quality appears to be due to a lack of emotion, an inhuman cautiousness and a life-sapping prudence. Once again, Malcolm Ross offers an ingenious lyrical interpretation of Canadian national identity, the chief characteristic of which turns out, through linguistic magic, to be irony.

But there is a North Americanism which is Canadian not "American".... The dual cultural and religious tradition. And the tension, the dynamic and fruitful tension, in play between the two — Baldwin, Lafontaine, Macdonald-Cartier, King-Lapointe. We are inescapably, and almost from the first, the bifocal people. The people of the second thought. To remain a people at all we have had to think before we speak, even to think before we think. Our "characteristic prudence" is not the Scot in us, or the Puritan, or the "North Irish." It is this bifocalism, this necessity for taking second thought, for keeping one foot on each bank of the Ottawa . . . this prudence of ours is *not* a negative virtue. It lies in us coiled like a spring. The resilient prudence of Mackenzie King has been fused in a terrifying furnace. If it seems to suggest immobility, let us think of the immobility at the centre of a moving wheel. . . . Prudence is thus central to our experience *without being typical* of it. . . . In art we break through academic formalism for a moment into the distant perspectives of the Group of Seven, only to cry out that this is not enough, not nearly enough. . . . Our natural mode is therefore not compromise but "irony" — the inescapable response to the presence and pressures of *opposites in tension.* Irony is the key to our identity. . . . Think of the ultimate irony of Lemelin's *Les Plouffes* — the identification by feeling with the *Canadien,* and simultaneously, the distanced intellectual appraisal of him as though from a vantage point across the Ottawa. Feeling and appraisal occur in the same instant and in the grip of tension. We are at once inside and outside the Plouffe family. And there is no simple reconciliation of inside and outside, no "solution." Instead there is the collision of opposites. The sparks that fly illuminate the situation in an ironic awareness. This is the Canadian mode.[41]

Yet, despite Ross's eloquence, I am not convinced that irony is the characteristic Canadian mode or that the flying sparks are really so illuminating. One could just as easily make out a case for tragedy. The possibilities are so many and so bewildering that one can only reiterate Mark Twain's longing to be assured, that whatever else a man is, he's at least human and so can't be any worse. The same is true of our literature; whatever it is, it's Canadian and can't be any worse. But even within this broad framework, some sort of limit must be found, and that limit is, of necessity, always arbitrary.

Speaking arbitrarily then, there seem to be two main approaches to the understanding of Canadian tradition as it affects our literature — the mythopoeic and the historical one. The mythopoeic approach is explicitly stated by Ross and implicitly by Reaney. Both see Canada as a vast geographic form and a mystical presence that has pattern, and if it has content at all, has a content that is both fragmentary and irrelevant. From this point of view, geography

itself becomes the pattern and even the content. Ross talks in more modern and dynamic terms than the early Canadian nature poets ever did, but his notion of pattern seems just as superficial and empty as the old poems about maple leaves in autumn.

I believe that content does exist, that it is important, and that the content of literature is inseparable from its pattern. I even believe that pattern and content may be relevantly and not just paradoxically related. There is a reluctance to discuss content among our critics perhaps it is because our content is neither glamorous, nor romantic, and far from heroic. If our political nationality emerged out of defeat and negative historical events, has our literature really confronted this painful reality? We haven't had a revolution like the Americans; and our thinkers have had to make the most out of random rather than purposeful origins. If there is such a thing as the Canadian dream, it is coming late to Canada and Canadians, and at a time in world history that does not permit the same kind of illusion about individual freedom that the Americans found so ready to hand after the First World War.

Canadian history is neither Greek nor Byronic in its temper. It did not kill its father and has no desire to marry its sister. Which is another way of saying that our history is not distinguished by gothic grandeur nor even tragedy. At least not yet.

There are also many ugly aspects of our history that have never been accounted for in literature. Some of these aspects are still buried in the suppressed radical tradition, which has somehow failed to appeal to the Canadian literary imagination. The story of the long struggle of the dissenting minority against the forces of colonial conservatism, and of the inevitable defeats on political, social, and personal levels, has never really been told. Our poor people, our Indians, our lonely immigrants, our prisoners, our Métis in Manitoba — few of these have found a place in serious Canadian literature; they are only just beginning to find a place in our culture through the mass media.

It seems to me that all the many aspects of the Canadian tradition have not yet emerged or made themselves fully felt in the literary life of the country. There are some who will argue that this is due to the scarcity of great writers; but as E. K. Brown has pointed out, "the line taken here depends on the belief that literature is an autonomous thing .... Thinking of this sort ignores a fundamental fact: That literature develops in close association with society."[42]

There are then a number of traditions that exist in Canada side by side, and the apocalyptic critics like to call these traditions a mosaic. To me they seem more like a collection of solitary fragments. I cannot share Ross's eloquent belief that every fragment is moving and colliding with and energizing its neighbour fragment.

There is, in fact, no real Canadian literary tradition but only a social matrix, an accumulation of historical events, full of contradictions, forces, and counter-forces; we live in a sort of vast cultural chaos upon which all are free to draw. We possess a promiscuous history, which contains not just abstract patterns, but specific items. There will be, perhaps even now there are, poets and critics who will not only acknowledge, but accept this promiscuity, this randomness, without having to make it glorious or even mythic. There will surely come poets who will reclaim and bring to the surface the cast-off and denied elements in our national life. Klein made a beginning when he showed that there is more depth and human suffering in the Canadian tradition than can be ascribed to the mere power of place or the longing for the motherland.

Confederation was only the beginning of a far-reaching process. It furnished the structure and the frame for nationhood. But the fragments of various cultures and interests still move blindly and chaotically within it. There is no mysterious force, no possible dialectic which guarantees that the collisions between opposites will be constructive and energizing. Such collisions, as we have seen, may as easily result in hatred and destruction as in unity and growth.

But the lack of a guaranteed outcome in the matter of national identity is no reason to lose hope. When Canadian writers become willing to examine the denied realities and admit them back into our national life (with emotional as well as with historical and political awareness) then, and only then, will we be able to speak of "the" Canadian tradition.

—*1969*

---

1. Harold Rosenberg, "American Painting," *Tradition of the New* (New York, 1965), p. 23.
2. Max Radin, "Tradition," *Encyclopedia of the Social Sciences,* edited by E. R. A. Seligman and A. Johnson (New York, 1937), 15:62-67.
3. Irving Howe, "The Age of Conformity," *A World More Attractive* (New York, 1963), pp. 251–2.
4. W. R. Sorley, *Tradition* (Oxford, 1926), p. 11.
5. Paul Valéry, "The Poet's Rights over Language," *The Art of Poetry,* translated by D. Folliot (New York, 1957), p.172.
6. W. R. Sorley, *Op. cit.,* p. 23.
7. H. Rosenberg, *Op. cit.,* p. 23.
8. W. B. Yeats, "Poetry and Tradition," *Essays and Introductions* (New York, 1961), pp. 251, 253.
9. W. R. Sorley, *Op. cit.,* p. 10.
10. John Sutherland (ed.), *Other Canadians* (Montreal, n.d.), pp. 5–20.
11. See C. Wright Mills, "Culture and Politics," *The Collected Essays of C. Wright Mills,* edited by I. L. Horowitz (New York, 1963), pp. 236–46.
12. A. J. M. Smith, *The Book of Canadian Poetry* (Chicago, 1943), pp. 3–31.
13. J. Sutherland, *Op. cit.,* p. 11.
14. A. M. Klein, "Writing in Canada," *The Canadian Jewish Chronicle* (22 February 1946), p. 3.
15. Archibald MacMechan, *Head-Waters of Canadian Literature* (Toronto, 1924), pp. 15–16.
16. E. K. Brown, "The Development of Poetry in Canada, 1880–1940," *Poetry,* 58:1 (April 1941), pp. 34–7.
17. W. L. Morton, *The Canadian Identity* (Madison, 1961), pp. 92, 93.
18. Carl F. Klinck, "Literary Activity in the Canadas 1812–1841," *Literary History of Canada* (Toronto, 1965), pp. 125–151.
19. E. K. Brown, *On Canadian Poetry.* Revised edition (Toronto, 1944).
20. Roy Daniels, "Confederation to the First World War," *Literary History of Canada,* edited by Carl F. Klinck (Toronto, 1965), p. 203.
21. *Ibid.,* p. 205.
22. *Ibid.,* p. 207.
23. C. F. Klinck, *Literary History of Canada,* p. 127.
24. *Ibid.,* p. 146.
25. A. MacMechan, *Op. cit.,* p. 119.

26. See. E. K. Brown, *On Canadian Poetry*.
27. James Reaney, "The Canadian Poet's Predicament," *University of Toronto Quarterly*, 26:284–95 (April 1957).
28. Paul Elmer More, "The Spirit and Poetry of Early New England," *Shelburne Essays in American Literature* (New York, 1963), pp. 3–32. First published Houghton Mifflin, 1921.
29. Lionel Stevenson, *Appraisals of Canadian Literature* (Toronto, 1926), p. 12.
30. *Ibid.*, p. 11.
31. F. W. Watt, "Literature of Protest," *Literary History of Canada*, edited by Carl F. Klinck (Toronto, 1965), pp. 457–73.

32. John P. Matthews, *Tradition in Exile* (Toronto, 1962).
33. L. Stevenson, *Op. cit.*, pp. 30–31.
34. *Ibid.*, p. 37.
35. *Ibid.*, p. 10.
36. *Ibid.*, pp. 39, 41.
37. A. MacMechan, *Op. cit.*, p. 53.
38. W. L. Morton, *Op. cit.*, p. 92.
39. *Canadian Forum*, 32:234 (January 1952). [Italics added.]
40. "The National Literature Problem in Canada," *Canadian Mercury*, Vol. 1, No. 1 (1928), pp. 8–9.
41. *Our Sense of Identity*, edited with an Introduction by Malcolm Ross (Toronto, 1954), pp. vii, xii.
42. E. K. Brown, *On Canadian Poetry*, p. 26.

THE BIZARRE AND THE FREAKY IN RECENT CANADIAN FICTION

Donald Cameron

Donald Cameron, formerly Associate Professor of English at the University of New Brunswick and now a freelance writer and broadcaster, was a founder of the magazine The Mysterious East, *and has been a frequent contributor to a variety of periodicals, as well as to CBC radio and television. He has also published a book on Stephen Leacock and a collection of interviews entitled* Conversations with Canadian Novelists *(1973). The article which follows appeared in* Saturday Night, *in July 1972, under the title "Novelists of the Seventies: Through Chaos to the Truth; The Bizarre Images of a New Generation in Canadian Fiction."*

———◆———

Look, I've got this great idea for a cheerful novel:

This big, rangy guy is sitting in a psychologist's office in Winnipeg. He's had dozens of jobs in the last fifteen years — actor, entertainer, editor, broadcaster, businessman — and though he's always successful, he never stays more than a year or so. So he's asking the psychologist, what can I do to make me nice and stable like everybody else?

The psychologist gives him a battery of tests, which show that our hero has an amazing array of aptitudes. His trouble is that he's easily bored, easily interested in new directions. The trick is to get into something he can't easily master. Deep down in your heart, says the psychologist, what would you *really* like to be?

"A famous novelist."

Great, says the psychologist, great! You can never master *that*. Why don't you get on with it? Because I can't afford it, says our hero. So the psychologist suggests that he move to Toronto, make some money in advertising, and then write his novel . . .

Six years later, the highly successful advertising executive sells up everything and enrols in creative writing at Johns Hopkins University. He finishes the novel and submits it to a New York agent, who thinks it splendid but warns that it may well take a year or more to place it with a publisher.

Ten days later, back in Toronto, the phone rings. The agent has sent the book to Harper and Row, who have just bought it. When it is published, the New York *Times* reviewer calls it "a perfect imitation of the exitless maze of human consciousness" and finds in its protagonist "the most charming and amusing character" since Leopold Bloom.

Well, sure, I admit the plot isn't very probable. But then reality isn't conspicuously realistic these days, either. Man on the moon; oil on the water; the Vietnamese beating the Americans; buy a new Mercury but the mercury's in the fish. My plot's just as true. The novelist is Martin Myers, the novel is *The Assignment,* and the question is reality. Who is the hero of the novel, Spiegel, and why has he been assigned to be a junkman? Who is J. J. Jonas, "philanthropy fetishist" and head of the Junk Foundation which employs Spiegel — who never gets any junk, until one day he finds a baby named (but why?) Ling? Why does Spiegel say he "collects decaying civilizations"? What about these previous assignments, speaking at the Parthenon, writing electronic music, working with the cabala, inventing typefaces? Does Spiegel really have a daughter in Buffalo? Is he really a professor from Gimli, Man.? And *really,* now, can we *really* take them seriously, these people like Dr. Plassibeau, Desiree Poodendim, Harry Betnwar? Really, what do we mean by *really?*

Do I exist? the junkman asked himself. Is there really an assignment? Or is the whole thing a dream? Jonas' dream? Or perhaps my own dream? Or worse, could it be someone else's dream? A third party? A sinister third party? Who are you, sinister third party? What do you want with Spiegel? I am just a failed junkman. Couldn't you dream about somebody else? How long must I wait till you wake me up and set me free?

Myers has said that the lens through which he views the world seems to have some kind of wobble in it. Words become as real as anything else; things connect verbally and emotionally, psychologically but not logically. Spiegel winds up in the Reality Resumption Institute, where God (who may be a computer, unless he's the author) talks to him directly.

"Don't think of me as sinister," the third party says. "Don't think of me at all. Forget me. I'm not saying any more. Your redemption is in your own hands. You won't be able to contact me again." Yes, says the God/computer/author, "you are real. In context. Get it through your head. You have your own reality. Don't confuse the two realities."

Two realities? Only two? Then where does Hazard Lepage live, or Bartleby?

Martin Myers is a provocative and entertaining writer, and *The Assignment* is an exceptionally sophisticated first novel. All the same, it is only one of a clutch of substantial first novels published in 1971. Not great novels. Not Melville or Tolstoy. Just novels which can occupy to some profit a few of the hours of which life offers you such a tiny ration. Novels good enough that you feel their authors might conceivably — with luck and discipline and experience and labour and still more luck — wind up one day putting a volume into the permanent body of literature. Books by people who don't think it's worth their trouble to shoot for anything less than a masterpiece. Small successes and honourable failures. A nation's literature, after all, is not composed of masterpieces only. The steady flow of small successes and honourable failures creates an environment in which masterpieces are not too shy to appear.

Canada has never had such a flow. Once in a while, a novel like *Barometer Rising* or *His Majesty's Yankees* or *Hetty Dorval* would announce the appearance of a writer. By the 1950s, the still-isolated work of Gabrielle Roy, Ernest Buckler, Robertson Davies and others made up a hesitant trickle, and as the 1960s dawned, it was swollen by such younger writers as Margaret Laurence, Mordecai Richler and Brian Moore.

Since 1960, though, hardly a year has passed without a few new novelists and a good many substantial novels. Look at 1971: Chris Scott weighed in with an adventurous fiction-about-fiction called *Bartleby,* a romp through fantasy and comedy with some parallels to the boisterous eighteenth-century fiction of Fielding and Sterne. Leo Simpson's *Arkwright* purports to be a more realistic comedy about a cheerful loser named Addison Arkwright, whose incredible uncle controls a vast financial empire and wouldn't hesitate to control Addison as well. But the only person Addison really cares about any more is his daughter Jens, whom he wants to retrieve from the custody of his movie-star wife — and does, happily, as the book ends.

Alice Munro has been writing a long time, and published a highly-praised collection of stories, *Dance of the Happy Shades,* four years ago. Last year she published her first novel, *Lives of Girls and Women,* a sensitive account of Del Jordan's growth into womanhood illuminated by a series of contrasts with her mother, her aunts, and various other women. Similarly, in 1969 David Helwig had published collections both of short stories *(The Streets of Summer)* and of poems *(The Sign of the Gunman).* In 1971 he published a spy-story-plus, *The Day Before Tomorrow,* which was not the novel I had hoped it might be — but which was, like all Helwig's work, craftsmanlike and readable.

Ronald Sutherland, who had earlier presented himself as a scholar and critic of sorts *(Frederick Philip Grove,* 1969; *Second Image,* 1971) also published his first novel last year. *Lark des Neiges* recounted a day in the life of a Montreal housewife whose name, Suzanne MacDonald Laflamme, reveals her uneasy perch betwixt solitudes. Another professor, David Knight, set his novel in the opening days of the Nigerian civil war, mingling love, murder and the confrontation of cultures in a solid if traditional début. *Farquharson's Physique: And What It Did To His Mind* is the story of Henry Farquharson, Canadian exchange lecturer at the University of Ibadan, a solid and uncomplicated man who does what he can and suffers what he must, one of the most likeable characters I have encountered in a long time.

Those are *some* of the first novels of last year. There were others, by Joan Haggerty and Gerald Lampert, for instance. Gwendolyn MacEwen, Matt Cohen and Roch Carrier, among others, published second novels in 1971, while Mordecai Richler carried off the Governor-General's Award for *Saint Urbain's Horseman,* his seventh and best.

A fluke year? Hardly. Look at 1970: Brian Moore's *Fergus,* Robertson Davies' *Fifth Business,* Marian Engel's *The Honeyman Festival.* New novels from Sinclair Ross, Hugh Garner, Norman Levine, Jane Rule, Rudy Wiebe, Hugh Hood. First novels from Percy Janes, Richard Wright, and Dave Godfrey. Short story collec-

tions from Margaret Laurence and John Metcalf.

Since 1960, I am arguing, Canadian novelists have for the first time been working in a reasonably sturdy literary environment. Nobody is surprised any more when a Canadian publishes a novel; and a Canadian novelist can count on informed interest from a goodly number of readers.

More interesting than the mere volume of writers, however, is what they're up to — and the most striking quality of the new fiction is its variety, the multiple lenses, in Myers' image, through which they regard experience. The realistic novel, which has dominated Canadian writing for decades, has largely fallen out of favour. A deep interest in fantasy, myth, humour, history and politics marks the new fiction. Our writers are moving away from realism, perhaps because they no longer feel any more certain than the rest of us about what constitutes reality.

Consider, for instance, Leonard Cohen, poet, singer, novelist, and guru for all seasons. *The Favourite Game* (1963) disclosed a certain freakiness, like a mutation not quite prepared to take the plunge, but readers accustomed to the assumption that the external world was real and that we all broadly agreed on its nature could still find plenty to hold onto. Breavman, its hero, may have been a bit idiosyncratic, but he was always Breavman. Three years later, *Beautiful Losers* offers a hero with no name, obsessed with a Mohawk martyr who is in some subterranean way associated with his Indian wife Edith. Romping through sanctity, mysticism, free-form eroticism, politics and technology, the book concludes with the metamorphosis of the hero, now a stinking old man, into a Ray Charles movie projected on the sky. Breavman, O Breavman, how solid you seem now!

But though the Cohen case is spectacular, it is by no means unique. Harold Horwood's first novel, *Tomorrow Will Be Sunday* (1966), was exceptionally libertarian in outlook, but offered no startling departures in form, no doubts about the nature of reality; his Newfoundland outport remained as solidly realistic as Grove's prairie farms. In *The Toslow Fire Sutra,* one of two new novels now in the process of publication, Horwood emerges as a full-blown freak, zonked on acid, dancing to visions, singing the apocalypse in the rhythms of rock. David Lewis Stein's *Scratch One Dreamer* (1967) was an updated version of 1930s leftist fiction, a shrewd description of an anti-Bomarc protest. *My Sexual and Other Revolutions* (1971) is political fantasy, abrasive and pornographic, pitting the Fork Freaks against the Uglies against the Resistance in a nightmarish and unending series of revolutions. Robert Hunter published one traditional novel, *Erebus* (1968), before turning to cultural journalism with *The Enemies of Anarchy* (1970) and *The Storming of the Mind* (1971). When he returned to fiction this spring, it was as the author of a comic book, *The Time of the Clockmen,* published by the *Georgia Straight.* Radical and indecent, *The Time of the Clockmen* is in the worst possible taste; I enjoyed it thoroughly and I intend to nominate it for the Governor-General's Award. Timothy Findley's *Last of the Crazy People* (1967) was a Southern Gothic tale set — oddly, though not unconvincingly — in Southern Ontario, which has always seemed a pretty spooky place to me. His second novel, *The Butterfly Plague* (1969), set in Hollywood, features infestations of butterflies, disturbing images of knives and wounds, and a strange sexual encounter with a Nordic buck known only as Race; and it is never entirely clear how many of these horrors are imaginary.

Whatever is behind these forays into the rich and strange has its effects on the more established writers, too. After three satiric novels and a long silence, Robertson Davies upsets all possible applecarts with *Fifth Business* (1970), in which a cripple obsessed with a saint travels with a magician when he isn't teaching at a private school in Ontario. Brian Moore introduces fictional revenants in *Fergus* (1970). In *Ox Bells and Fireflies* (1968), Ernest Buckler adopts a form he describes as a "fictive memoir."

Our fiction is reflecting what Brian Moore calls "the overkill which fact presents"; it is also coming of age, in that it allows the imagination of novelists to confront the sometimes bizarre contents of their consciousnesses in whatever form or style may appeal to them. As the world seems to crumble, as the bourgeois liberal outlook increasingly reveals itself as the ideological justification for a vicious assault on life, love and all their support systems, the novelists turn fantastic and satirical both to attack it and to explore the alternatives. What can we learn from the natural world, from drugs, from the lives of the native peoples, from past rebellions, from religious experience mystic and otherwise? What have we done to ourselves psychologically, emotionally, sexually? What is the actual texture of the contemporary urban nightmare? No novelist worth a damn sets out to illustrate such questions, of course: but we who read his work can hardly help noticing what sort of thing excites his imagination.

"I'm fascinated right now by the effects of moving away from realism," says Robert Kroetsch, one of the best of the new novelists, "the kinds of freedom you get, and the kinds of truth you get at, by departing from the sterner varieties of realism. I'm not so sure anyone has a 'realistic' experience; it's a literary convention to begin with, the notion of realism."

That belief shows up in Kroetsch's fiction. *But We Are Exiles* (1965) seems at first to be straightforward enough, an account of riverboatman Peter Guy's trip up the Mackenzie with the body and the widow of Mike Hornyak, his drowned boss. The widow is Peter's former girl, stolen from him by Hornyak, which makes for a lively trip. Only in retrospect does one realize how the book is dominated by images of people above and below the water; by the pervasive and still authoritative presence of the magnetic Hornyak, which ultimately drives various characters variously out of their minds; by an ambiguity in the apparently stalwart Peter about life and death, commitment and withdrawal, love and isolation.

With *The Words of My Roaring* (1967), the rhetoric of Prairie politics and the ironically vital undertaker Johnnie Backstrom — Kroetsch is something of a connoisseur of corpses — constantly tilt the novel towards myth. Backstrom accidentally becomes a candidate in a general election by rashly promising rain to the drought-stricken district, makes love to his opponent's daughter in an inhabited goldfish pond, and tries to understand how in the name of Aberhart he got into the campaign in the first place. The book still pays ritual homage to realism, but the extraordinary nature of its events and the muscular exuberance of Kroetsch's style lend it a dimension of tall tale, legend, comic fantasy.

With *The Studhorse Man* — winner of the 1969 Governor-General's Award, just re-issued in paperback — the chief character, Hazard Lepage, becomes almost openly mythical, a roving seeker for perfection in horsebreeding and simultaneously a sexual adventurer and exploiter himself. In form the book is a thoroughly funny parody of scholarship undertaken by a biographer who sits motionless in a dry bathtub, inadvertently recording his own fussy madness as well as the fantastic exploits of his subject. Says a footnote:

For an excellent treatment of the penis of the horse, see *The Horse Its Treatment in Health and Disease*, Prof. J. Wortley Axe, M.R.C.V.S., editor, 9 volumes (London, The Gresham Publishing Company, 1905-06). See especially Volume IV, p. 69, for: 1. Transverse Section of Penis, 2. Longitudinal Section of Glans Penis, 3. Penis unsheathed. I have here in my bathtub with me the complete set, bound in the original decadent green covers; a set I felt free to acquire by stealth from a local university due to the general neglect accorded hippological studies in the modern centre of learning.

Now really, are we to trust such a reporter? Is Hazard real at all? Is myth the final reality? Or fantasy?

The Weekend Man (1970), Richard Wright's first novel, is an astringent portrayal of a thirty-year-old publisher's salesman who has become "a weekend man" — in other words, "a person who has abandoned the present in favour of the past or the future," who is "forever looking backwards and being affected by a painful sense of loss or . . . looking forward and being continually disappointed." Wes Wakeham's wife has left him, furious at his total lack of ambition — but she still sleeps with him occasionally. Ironic, resigned, mildly amused, Wes remembers the ancient Oriental sex manual Molly bought during their first weeks of marriage:

All those variations on a theme, but after much monkeying around Molly is partial to sitting on it. I don't mind. Any way is fine with me so long as the organ isn't permanently damaged or even badly bent.

Nothing really happens in *The Weekend Man* — or, more accurately, the things that try to happen are so distanced by Wes' wondering sensibility that they somehow never materialize as much more than possibilities. At one point he refers to the "octagonal" stop signs, apparently refusing to assume that anyone has ever seen one before. The more he tries to speak simply, the more trouble he gets into.

Molly believes that the only reason I am not successful is because I am wilfully opposed to worldly success. In her eyes I am a thwarted idealist who has difficulty coming to terms with life as it is lived in our day and age. This is not so. I am not opposed to worldly success and am no more a thwarted idealist than a pygmy's uncle. The truth is that I am not a success because I cannot think straight for days on end, bemused as I am by the weird trance of this life and the invisible passage of time.

Why, one wonders, did a book practically without plot, without any rare or exciting events, without any curious characters, without much, in fact, but the voice of a puzzled and likeable salesman living in some place like Don Mills, achieve the kind of recognition which the reviewers accorded *The Weekend Man?* The answer, I think, lies in Wright's virtually perfect control of tone, the complete submergence of his own voice in Wes'. For Wes is in many ways an Everyman for our day. He simply doesn't understand why people attach such importance to trivial things, and fail to furrow their brows over the "thundering ironies." Stepping out on his apartment balcony as the book ends, Wes stares at the stars and strikes the perfect note for a great many of us.

Right now it is enough to gaze upward and bear witness to all this light, travelling from its fiery origins with a perfect indifference, across the immensities of space and time, to strike the retinas of my eyes at this moment — to bear witness to this remarkable light and wait for sleep and try to remember what it is I was supposed to do.

If *The Weekend Man* is luminously clear, *The New Ancestors,* winner of the Governor-General's Award that same year, seems at points deliberately obscure. James Joyce is supposed to have said that the man who would understand him must devote his life to the study of Joyce's work; Dave Godfrey at some points seems to take the same tack. Otherwise, why the snatches of African languages left untranslated in the text, for instance? Is every bit of that densely-packed detail necessary? When we move from realism, so-called, into surrealism, wouldn't it be kind to hint to the reader that the rules have changed?

Philistine though I may be, I don't intend to devote my life to the study of anybody's work; when there's time, I'm going to read some novels, and they'd better give me as much rapture per hour as the other things I do, or I won't finish them. If I had one single comment to make to several of the new novelists — Chris Scott, Leo Simpson, David Knight, Godfrey — it would be, cut, cut and cut again. Your readership doesn't cheerfully swill down four or five hundred pages.

Despite that, Godfrey is a novelist of the most remarkable gifts. Subtle and flamboyant in its use of language, nightmarish, multiple and impassioned in theme, *The New Ancestors* suggests that there are no meaningful boundaries between public and private life, between myth and ideology, between dream and wakefulness, even between reality and unreality. Who are the new ancestors? By what processes do historical figures assume the status of myth? What bearing does the private life of Kruman the Redeemer have on the public affairs of Lost Coast, Godfrey's fictional West African republic? How different really is the surrealistic section "In The Fifth City" from the rest of the novel?

All this sounds as though *The New Ancestors* were desperately hard work — and it's certainly no lazy read. But it's fun, too, witty, brisk and moving. In the Fifth City sequence, an American agent named Rusk is assassinated again and again, in a different way each time. First it's knifing, then poison; later it's an exploding basketball; on another occasion Rusk watches two women making love, via television, but the image is delayed, and as he watches them couple one of them emerges with a pistol and shoots him. Later, Rusk is putting the case for the American Dream:

> We have heard this many times, of course, the Chelsea Drug Store Argument, this defence of Americanism in terms of "genuine" scientific socialism, genuine people's capitalism, the greater production rates, the vast flexibility, the peasant's territorial instinct which can be verified and must therefore be quantified and melded, Stalin's essential Czarism, the rape of Hungary, the people's slaughter of the Indonesian communists, the sheer impossibility of a collapse of post-Keynesian capitalism, the advanced sexlife of the Detroit auto-workers, etc., etc., etc.
>
> What we are interested in now is the dirty-faced, tooth-gapping urchin in khaki shorts who enters with a wooden tray of small pineapples.

Rusk buys a pineapple, sticks a knife into it, and it explodes — killing him yet again. How can one but love such a book?

Perhaps the most impressive feature of *The New Ancestors* is Godfrey's ability to trust his talent with so wide and — for a Canadian — exotic a range of characters. The strange, warped English Marxist, Michael Burdener; his African wife, Ama, and her brother Gamaliel Harding, former jazz drummer turned defender of the Redeemer; their mother, the madwoman Delicacy; their bastard half-brother, "the irreverent First Samuels, Doublefees Boy, Boler Boy, Marxman Spoker Number One" — these are hardly the people Godfrey grew up with in Manitoba and Ontario, but he seems to know them inside out. To enter so completely into the lives and concerns of people solidly rooted in cultures so different as these is a substantial and mysterious achievement. Essentially it constitutes nothing less than entry into another reality.

If there is a general drift to be seen, it is broadly in the direction of freakiness and radicalism, the equivalent in fiction of the underground press. But that direction itself is composed of so many distinguishable currents that it is anything but a new orthodoxy. In Canada today there is practically no cultural pressure on the novelist: he has something nearer absolute freedom in subject and form than he has ever had. After *The Toslow Fire Sutra*, for instance, Harold Horwood calmly turned out *White Eskimo*, a Labrador novel more or less in the manner of Conrad, which for mysterious reasons will be published first. As any of the novelists might point out, though, it is hopelessly sentimental to admire the polish on the binnacle during the shipwreck of the whole human enterprise.

> Who are you, sinister third party? What do you want with Spiegel? I am just a failed junkman. Couldn't you dream about somebody else? How long must I wait till you wake me up and set me free?

Start talking like that, and you wind up in the Reality Resumption Institute. If it's still in business, if you can find it, and if it's not just another fraud or illusion.

—1972

Bibliography

COMPILED BY

R. E. WATTERS

I. GENERAL REFERENCES AND BIBLIOGRAPHIES

A SELECTIVE LIST

Amtmann, Bernard, *Contributions to a Short-Title Catalogue of Canadiana* (Montreal, Author, 1971-73) 4 vols.

Avis, Walter S. (Editor-in-Chief), *A Dictionary of Canadianisms on Historical Principles.* (Toronto, Gage, 1967) 927p.

Bell, Inglis F. (ed.) *et al*, "Canadian Literature: A Checklist," *Canadian Literature*, 1960-1971 [An annual compilation, covering the years 1959-1970.]

—— and Susan W. Port, *Canadian Literature . . . 1959-1963.* A Checklist of Creative and Critical Writings. . . . (Vancouver, U.B.C. Publications Centre, 1966) 140p.

Bohne, Harold (ed.), *Canadian Books in Print* (Toronto, University of Toronto Press, 1972) 1092p. [Also earlier editions.]

Boyle, Gertrude M. (ed.), *A Bibliography of Canadiana — First Supplement* (Toronto, The Public Library, 1959) 333p. [supplements the Staton and Tremaine *Bibliography* listed below]

The Brock Bibliography of Published Canadian Stage Plays in English 1900-1972 (St. Catherines, Brock University, 1972) 83p. [*First Supplement* (1973) 43p.]

Canadian Catalogue of Books Published in Canada, About Canada, as well as Those Written by Canadians [with Imprints 1921-1949] (Toronto, Public Libraries, 1923-1950) [consolidated into two volumes, with Cumulated Author Index (Toronto, Public Libraries, 1959]

Canadian Periodical Index, 1929-1932; 1938- (Windsor, Public Library, 1929-1932; Toronto, Public Libraries, 1938-   ) [a continuing serial]

Canadiana. A List of Publications of Canadian Interest (Ottawa, National Library of Canada, 1951-   ) [an annual publication which in 1950 superseded the *Canadian Catalogue of Books*]

Fulford, Robert, Dave Godfrey, and Abraham Rotstein, *Read Canadian: A Book about Canadian Books* (Toronto, James Lewis & Samuel, 1972) xi + 275p.

Goggio, Emilio, Beatrice Corrigan, and Jack H. Parker (comps.), *A Bibliography of Canadian Cultural Periodicals (English and French) from Colonial Times to 1950 in Canadian Libraries* (Toronto, University of Toronto Press, 1955) 45p.

Harlowe, Dorothy (comp.), *A Catalogue of Canadian Manuscripts Collected by Lorne Pierce and Presented to Queen's University* (Toronto, Ryerson, 1946) 164p.

Klinck, Carl F. (comp.), "Canada" in "Annual Bibliography of Commonwealth Literature 1965," *Journal of Commonwealth Literature* No. 2: 39-55 (December 1966) [A continuing annual series, with changing compilers.]

Kyte, E. C., *A Note on the Manuscript Collection in the Douglas Library* (Kingston, Queen's University, 1943) 26p.

"Letters in Canada," *University of Toronto Quarterly*, 1936-   [An annual survey which began with the year 1935 — edited by A.S.P. Woodhouse, *et al.*]

Lochhead, Douglas, *Bibliography of Canadian Bibliographies.* 2nd ed., rev. and enl. (Toronto, Bibliographical Society of Canada and the University of Toronto Press, 1972) xiv + 312p.

Long, Robert J., *Bibliography of Nova Scotia* (Orange, N.J., 1918) 312p.

Lowther, Barbara J., *A Bibliography of British Columbia.* Laying the Foundations 1849-1899 (Victoria, B.C., University of Victoria, 1968) 328p.

McFarlane, William G., *New Brunswick Bibliography* . . . (Saint John, N.B., Sun Printing, 1895) 98p.

Milne, W. S., *Canadian Full-Length Plays in English.* A Preliminary Annotated Catalogue ([Ottawa], Dominion Drama Festival, [1964]) 47p. [Part II, Supplement, 1966. 39p.]

Morgan, Henry J., *Bibliotheca Canadensis, or, A Manual of Canadian Literature* (Ottawa, Desbarats, 1867) 411p. [Reprinted: Detroit, Gale Research, 1968]

——, *The Canadian Men and Women of the Time.* A Handbook of Canadian Biography (Toronto, Briggs, 1898) 1118p. [revised and enlarged edition (Toronto, Briggs, 1912) 1218p.]

Morse, W. Inglis, *The Canadian Collection at Harvard University* (Cambridge, Mass., The University, 1944-1949) 6 vols.

Nesbitt, Bruce (ed.), "Canadian Literature/ Littérature Canadienne, 1972. An Annotated Bibliography/Une Bibliographie avec Commentaire," *Journal of Canadian Fiction* 2: 97-159 (Spring 1973) [A continuing annual series]

New Brunswick. University Library, *A Catalogue of the Rufus Hathaway Collection of Canadian Literature, University of New Brunswick* (Fredericton, University of New Brunswick, 1935) 53p.

Park, Julian (ed.), *The Culture of Contemporary Canada* (Ithaca, Cornell University Press, 1957) 404p.

Peel, Bruce Braden (comp.), *A Bibliography of the Prairie Provinces to 1953* (Toronto, University of Toronto Press, 1956) 680p. [*Supplement* (Toronto, University of Toronto Press, 1963) 130p.]

Porteous, Janet S. (comp.), *Canadiana 1689-1900 in the Possession of the Douglas Library, Queen's University* (Kingston, Queen's University, 1932) 86p.

Reference Division, McPherson Library, University of Victoria, B.C., *Creative Canada. A Biographical Dictionary of Twentieth Century Creative and Performing Artists.* 2 vols. + (Toronto, University of Toronto Press, 1971, 1972) [A continuing serial]

Report, Royal Commission on National Development in the Arts, Letters and Sciences (Ottawa, King's Printer, 1951) 517p.

Rhodenizer, V. B., *At the Sign of the Hand and Pen: Nova-Scotian Authors* (N.p., Canadian Authors' Association — Nova Scotia Branch, 1948) 43p. [Reprinted: Toronto, Canadiana House, 1968]

——, *Canadian Literature in English* (Montreal, Quality Press, 1965) 1055p. [*Index to Vernon Blair Rhodenizer's* "Canadian Literature in English," comp. by Lois Mary Thierman (Edmonton, La Survivance Print. [1969?]) 469p.]

Robbins, John E. (ed.), *Encyclopedia Canadiana* (Ottawa, The Canadiana Company, 1957-1958) 10 vols. [Revised edition, 1972]

Roberts, Charles G. D. and Arthur L. Tunnell, (eds.), *A Standard Dictionary of Canadian Biography: The Canadian Who Was Who* (Toronto, Trans-Canada Press, 1934, 1938) 2 vols.

——*et al*, *The Canadian Who's Who* (Toronto, Trans-Canada Press, 1936-) [a continuing serial]

Rome, David, *Jews in Canadian Literature. A Bibliography*. Revised edition (Montreal, Canadian Jewish Congress and Jewish Public Library, 1963) 2 vols.

Ross, Malcolm (ed.), *The Arts in Canada* (Toronto, Macmillan, 1958) 176p.

Staton, Frances M. and Marie Tremaine (eds.), *A Bibliography of Canadiana*. Being Items in the Public Library of Toronto, Canada, Relating to the Early History and Development of Canada (Toronto, Public Library, 1934) 828p. [see above under Boyle, Gertrude M., for *First Supplement*]

Story, Norah, *The Oxford Companion to Canadian History and Literature* (Toronto, Oxford University Press, 1967) 935p.

Sylvestre, Guy, Brandon Conron, and Carl F. Klinck, *Canadian Writers/Écrivains Canadiens. A Biographical Distionary* (Toronto, University of Toronto Press, 1964) 163p. [Rev. and enl. edition, 1966. 186p.]

Thomas, Clara, *Canadian Novelists, 1920-1945* (Toronto, Longmans, 1946) 129p.

Tod, Dorothea D. and Audrey M. Cordingley, *A Check-List of Canadian Imprints 1900-1925* (Ottawa, King's Printer, 1950) 370p.

Tremaine, Marie (comp.), *A Bibliography of Canadian Imprints, 1751 1800* (Toronto, University of Toronto Press, 1952) 705p.

Wallace, W. Stewart, *A Dictionary of North American Authors Deceased before 1950* (Toronto, Ryerson, 1951) 525p.

——, *The Macmillan Dictionary of Canadian Biography*. Third edition — revised and enlarged (Toronto, Macmillan, 1963) 822p.

——, *The Ryerson Imprint*. A Check-List of the Books and Pamphlets Published by the Ryerson Press since . . . 1829 (Toronto, Ryerson. [1954], 141p.

Watters, Reginald Eyre (comp.), *A Checklist of Canadian Literature and Background Materials, 1628-1960* (Toronto, University of Toronto Press, 1972) 1085p. [First edition, 1628-1950, was published in 1959.]

Watters, Reginald Eyre and Inglis Freeman Bell, (comps.), *On Canadian Literature, 1806-1960*. A Check List of Articles, Books, and Theses on English-Canadian Literature, Its Authors, and Language (Toronto,

University of Toronto Press, 1966) 165p. [Reprinted with corrections and additions, 1973.]

II. GENERAL STUDIES OF CANADIAN LITERATURE

Atwood, Margaret, *Survival*. A Thematic Guide to Canadian Literature (Toronto, Anansi, 1972) 208p.

Baker, Ray Palmer, *A History of English-Canadian Literature to the Confederation* . . . (Cambridge, Mass., Harvard University Press, 1920) 200p. [Reprinted: New York, Russell & Russell, 1968]

Bourinot, Arthur S. (ed.), *At the Mermaid Inn*. Being Selections from Essays on Life and Literature which Appeared in the Toronto *Globe* 1892-1893 (Ottawa, Bourinot, 1958) 96p. [selections from a column series conducted by A. Lampman, W. W. Campbell, and D. C. Scott]

Bourinot, Sir John G., *The Intellectual Development of the Canadian People*. An Historical Review (Toronto, Hunter Rose, 1881) 128p.

——, . . . *Our Intellectual Strength and Weakness*. A Short Historical and Critical Review of Literature, Art, and Education in Canada (Montreal, Brown, 1893) 99p.

Brown, E. K., *On Canadian Poetry*. Revised edition (Toronto, Ryerson, 1944) 172p.

Burpee, Lawrence J., *A Little Book of Canadian Essays* (Toronto, Musson, 1909) 87p.

Collin, W. E., *The White Savannahs* (Toronto Macmillan, 1936) 288p.

Colombo, John R., *New Direction in Canadian Poetry* (Toronto, Holt Rinehart, 1971) 87p.

Drolet, Gilbert, *The National Identities in Canada's English and French War Novels, 1935-1965* (Thesis, Université de Montréal, 1971).

Dudek, Louis, and Michael Gnarowski (eds.), *The Making of Modern Poetry in Canada* (Toronto, Ryerson, 1971) 303p.

Edgar, Pelham, "English-Canadian Literature,"

in *Cambridge History of English Literature* Cambridge, England, University Press, 1917) 14: 380-400

Eggleston, Wilfrid, *The Frontier and Canadian Letters* (Toronto, Ryerson, 1957) 164p.

Frye, Northrop, *The Bush Garden*. Essays on the Canadian Imagination (Toronto, Anansi, 1971) 256p.

Fulford, Robert *et al* (eds.), *Read Canadian: A Book about Canadian Books* (Toronto, James Lewis & Samuel, 1972) xi + 275p.

Jones, Douglas Gordon, *Butterfly on Rock*. A Study of Themes and Images in Canadian Literature (Toronto, University of Toronto Press, 1970) 197p.

Klinck, Carl F. *et al*, *Literary History of Canada*. Canadian Literature in English (Toronto, University of Toronto Press, 1965) 945p.

Kline, Marcia, *Beyond the Land Itself*. Views of Nature in Canada and the United States (Cambridge, Mass., Harvard University Press, 1970) 75p.

Logan, J. D. and Donald G. French, *Highways of Canadian Literature*. A Synoptic Introduction to the Literary History of Canada . . . (Toronto, McClelland, 1924) 418p.

McCourt, Edward A., *The Canadian West in Fiction* (Toronto, Ryerson, 1949) 131p.

MacMechan, Archibald M., *Head-Waters of Canadian Literature* (Toronto, McClelland, 1924) 247p. [Reprinted: Toronto, Canadiana House, 1968.]

MacMurchy, Archibald, *Handbook of Canadian Literature (English)* (Toronto, Briggs, 1906) 23p.

Mandel, Eli (ed.), *Contexts of Canadian Criticism* (Toronto, University of Toronto Press, 1971) 304p.

Marquis, Thomas G., *English-Canadian Literature* (Toronto, Glasgow Brook, 1913) 103p. [reprinted from *Canada and its Provinces*, edited by Adam Shortt and Arthur G. Doughty (Toronto, Glasgow Brook, 1914–1917) 12: 493-589]

Matthews, John P., *Tradition in Exile*. A Comparative Study of Social Influences on the Development of Australian and Canadian Poetry in the Nineteenth Century (Toronto, University of Toronto Press, 1962) 197p.

New, William H., *Articulating West*. Essays on Purpose and Form in Modern Canadian Literature (Toronto, New Press, 1972) xxvi + 282p.

—— (ed.), *Dramatists in Canada*. Selected Essays (Vancouver, University of British Columbia Press, 1972) 204p.

Pacey, Desmond, *Creative Writing in Canada*. A Short History of English-Canadian Literature. Revised and enlarged edition (Toronto, Ryerson, 1961) 314p.

——, *Essays in Canadian Criticism 1938-1968* (Toronto, Ryerson, 1969) 294p.

——, *Ten Canadian Poets*. A Group of Biographical and Critical Essays (Toronto, Ryerson, 1958) 350p.

Palmer, Tamara J., *Ethnic Character and Social Themes in Novels about Prairie Canada and the Period from 1900 to 1940* (Thesis, York University, 1972)

Percival, Walter P. (ed.), *Leading Canadian Poets* (Toronto, Ryerson, 1948) 271p.

Phelps, Arthur S., *Canadian Writers* (Toronto, McClelland, 1952) 119p.

Pierce, Lorne A., *An Outline of Canadian Literature (French and English)* (Toronto, Ryerson, 1927) 251p.

Rashley, R. E., *Poetry in Canada: The First Three Steps* (Toronto, Ryerson, 1958) 166p.

Rhodenizer, V. B., *A Handbook of Canadian Literature* (Ottawa, Graphic, 1930) 295p.

Ricou, Laurence R., *Canadian Prairie Fiction: The Significance of Landscape* (Thesis, University of Toronto, 1971)

——, *Vertical Man/Horizontal World* (Vancouver, University of British Columbia Press, 1973)

Rogers, Amos Robert, *American Recognition of Canadian Authors Writing in English, 1890-1960* (Ann Arbor, Mich., University of Michigan, 1964) 2 vols. (813p.)

Smith, A. J. M. (ed.), *Masks of Fiction*. Canadian Critics on Canadian Prose (Toronto, McClelland, 1961) 175p.

——(ed.), *Masks of Poetry*. Canadian Critics on Canadian Verse (Toronto, McClelland, 1962) 143p.

——, *Towards a View of Canadian Letters*. Selected Critical Essays, 1928-1971 (Vancouver, University of British Columbia Press, 1973)

Stephens, Donald (ed.), *Writers of the Prairies* (Vancouver, University of British Columbia Press, 1973)

Stevenson, Lionel, *Appraisals of Canadian Literature* (Toronto, Macmillan, 1926) 272p.

Stevenson, Orlando J., *A People's Best . . .* (Toronto, Musson, 1927) 266p.

Sutherland, Ronald, *Second Image*. Comparative Studies in Québec/Canadian Literature (Toronto, New Press, 1971) 189p.

Thomas, Clara, *Our Nature, Our Voices*, Vol. 1 (Toronto, New Press, 1973) 240p.

Waterston, Elizabeth, *Survey*. A Short History of Canadian Literature (Toronto, Methuen, 1973) 215p. [The bibliographies include Canadian literature on records, tapes, and films]

Wilson, Edmund, *O Canada: An American's Notes on Canadian Culture* (New York, Farrar Straus, 1964) 245p.

Woodcock, George (ed.), *A Choice of Critics* (Toronto, Oxford University Press, 1966)

——, *Odysseus Ever Returning*. Essays on Canadian Writers and Writing, with an Introduction by W. H. New (Toronto, McClelland, 1970) 158p. [New Canadian Library No. 71]

—— (ed.), *The Sixties*. Writers and Writings of the Decade (Vancouver, U.B.C. Publications, 1969) 138p.

III. INDIVIDUAL AUTHORS

Some of the books listed in the following bibliographies can be found bearing the imprints of publishers in three countries: Canada, Britain, and the United States. No attempt, however, is made to indicate this fact about any specific title, nor is any attempt made to prefer the Canadian edition or imprint unless it actually preceded the British or American by a full year.

Generally, first editions only are listed; later reprintings, whether from the same plates or from new plates (as in paperback editions), are not normally listed. Translations of a work into languages other than English are also excluded.

The biographical and critical items listed for each author under the heading "Selected criticism" are of varying quality and importance, and reveal some of the weaknesses as well as the strengths of Canadian critical writing. Nevertheless, even a thin or a rhapsodic piece may sometimes contribute an insight or a fact about an author that could or should be incorporated in any considered study of the author. Biographical or critical comment upon major writers in the standard reference books or literary histories is normally not listed, since such material is readily found. Similarly, book reviews also are normally excluded, except those dealing with the work of the youngest writers, about whom little else has yet been written.

The books of each author are listed chronologically. The selected criticism about each author is also listed chronologically.

MILTON ACORN (1923-)

In Love and Anger (Montreal, Author, 1956) 20p.
The Brain's the Target (Toronto, Ryerson, 1960) 16p.
Against a League of Liars (Toronto, Hawkshead Press, 1961) 1 sheet
Jawbreakers (Toronto, Contact Press, 1963) 54p.
I've Tasted My Blood. Poems 1956 to 1968. Selected by Al Purdy (Toronto, Ryerson, 1969) 136p.
More Poems for People (Toronto, NC Press, 1972) 112p.

Selected criticism:

Cogswell, Fred, "Three Arc-Light Gaps," *Fiddlehead* No. 56: 57-58 (Spring 1963)
Livesay, Dorothy, "Search for a Style: The Poetry of Milton Acorn," *Canadian Literature* No. 40: 33-42 (Spring 1969)
Bowering, George, "Acorn Blood," *Canadian Literature* No. 42: 84-86 (Autumn 1969)

LEVI ADAMS (? -1832)

The Charivari; or, Canadian Poetics. A Tale after the Manner of Beppo [Anonymous] (Montreal, 1824) 48p.
Jean Baptiste. A Poetic Olio in II Cantos (Montreal, 1825) 34p.
Tales of Chivalry and Romance [Anonymous] (Edinburgh, Robertson; London, Baldwin, Cradock & Joy, 1826) 306p.

Selected criticism:

Anonymous, "The Charivari, or Canadian Poetics," *Canadian Review and Literary and Historical Journal* I: 183-201 (July 1824)
Lande, Lawrence M., "Levi Adams," "The Charivari," [and] "Tecumthé" in his *Old Lamps Aglow* (Montreal, the Author, 1957) pp. 108-112, 130-143
Klinck, Carl F., "The Charivari and Levi Adams," *Dalhousie Review* 40: 34-42 (Spring 1960)

MARGARET ATWOOD (1939-)

Double Persephone (Toronto, Hawkshead Press, 1961) 16p.
The Circle Game (Toronto, Contact Press, 1966) 80p.
The Animals in That Country (Toronto, Oxford University Press, 1968) 80p.
The Edible Woman (Toronto, McClelland, 1969) 281p.
Blewointment press occupation issew [By Margaret Atwood *et al*] (Vancouver, Blewointment Press, 1970) 109p.
The Journals of Susanna Moodie (Toronto, Oxford University Press, 1970) 64p.
Procedures for Underground (Toronto, Oxford University Press, 1970) 80p.
Power Politics (Toronto, Anansi, 1971) 58p.
Surfacing (Toronto, McClelland, 1972) 192p.
Survival. A Thematic Guide to Canadian Literature (Toronto, Anansi, 1972) 208p.

Selected criticism:

Yeo, Margaret E., *The Living Landscape: Nature Imagery in the Poetry of Margaret Atwood and Other Modern Canadian Lyric Poets* (Thesis, Carleton University, 1969)
Purdy, A. W., "Atwood's Moodie," *Canadian Literature* No. 47: 80-84 (Winter 1971)
Ayre, John, "Margaret Atwood and the End of Colonialism," *Saturday Night* 87, No. 11: 23-26 (November 1972)
Stephen, Sid, "The Journals of Susanna Moodie: A Self Portrait of Margaret Atwood," *White Pelican* 2: 32-36 (1972)
Woodcock, George, "Margaret Atwood," *The Literary Half-Yearly* 13: 233-242 (July 1972)

Dawe, Alan, Introduction to *The Edible Woman* by Margaret Atwood (Toronto, McClelland, 1973) [New Canadian Library No. 93]

Gibson, Graeme, "Margaret Atwood," *Eleven Canadian Novelists* (Toronto, Anansi, 1973) pp. 1-31

MARGARET AVISON (1918-   )

History of Ontario (Toronto, Gage, 1951) 138p.

Winter Sun and Other Poems (Toronto, University of Toronto Press, 1960) 89p.

The Plough and the Pen, edited by Ilone Duczynska and Karl Polanyi (Toronto, McClelland, 1963) [Avison translations of poems by six Hungarian poets]

The Dumbfounding (New York, Norton, 1966) 99p.

Acta Sanctorum and Other Tales, by Jozsef Lengyel (London, Peter Owen, 1970) [Translations from the Hungarian, in collaboration with Ilona Duczynska]

Selected criticism:

Ghiselin, Brewster, "The Architecture of Vision," *Poetry* (Chicago) 70: 324-328 (September 1947)

Wilson, Milton, "The Poetry of Margaret Avison," *Canadian Literature* No. 2: 47-58 (Autumn 1959)

Smith, A. J. M., "Critical Improvisations on Margaret Avison's *Winter Sun,*" *Tamarack Review* No. 18:81-86 (Winter 1961)

Ade, Janet, *The Poetry of Margaret Avison* (Thesis, Trinity, University of Toronto, 1966)

Smith, A. J. M., "Margaret Avison's New Book," *Canadian Forum* 46: 132-134 (September 1966)

Colombo, J. R., "Avison and Wevill," *Canadian Literature* No. 34: 72-76 (Autumn 1967)

Jones, Lawrence M., "A Core of Brilliance: Margaret Avison's Achievement," *Canadian Literature* No. 38: 50-57 (Autumn 1968)

New, W. H., "The Mind's Eyes (I's) (Ice): The Poetry of Margaret Avison," *Twentieth Century Literature* 16: 185-202 (July 1970)

Redekop, Ernest, *Margaret Avison* (Toronto, Copp Clark, 1970) 152 p. [Studies in Canadian Literature No. 9]

Bowering, George, "Avison's Imitation of Christ the Artist," *Canadian Literature* No. 54: 56-69 (Autumn 1972)

Klus, Chris, *The Religious Poetry of Margaret Avison* (Thesis, McMaster University, 1972).

Redekop, Ernest, "The Only Political Duty: Margaret Avison's Translations of Hungarian Poems," *Literary Half-Yearly* 13: 157-170 (July 1972)

EARLE BIRNEY (1904-   )

David and Other Poems (Toronto, Ryerson, 1942) 40p.

Now is Time (Toronto, Ryerson, 1945) 56p.

The Strait of Anian (Toronto, Ryerson, 1948) 84p.

Turvey: A Military Picaresque (Toronto, McClelland, 1949) 288p. [also published under the title: *The Kootenay Highlander* (London, Landsborough Publications, 1960) 253p.]

Trial of a City, and Other Verse (Toronto, Ryerson, 1952) 71p.

Twentieth Century Canadian Poetry, edited by Earle Birney (Toronto, Ryerson, 1953) 169p.

Down the Long Table (Toronto, McClelland, 1955) 298p.

Ice Cod Bell or Stone. A Collection of New Poems (Toronto, McClelland, 1962) 62p

Near False Creek Mouth. New Poems (Toronto, McClelland, 1964) 35p.

Selected Poems of Malcolm Lowry, edited by Earle Birney with the assistance of Margerie Lowry (San Francisco, City Lights Books, 1962) 79p.

The Creative Writer (Toronto, Canadian Broadcasting Corporation, 1966) 85p.

Selected Poems, 1940-1966 (Toronto, McClelland 1966) 222p.

Lunar Caustic by Malcolm Lowry, edited by Earle Birney and Margerie Lowry (London, Cape, 1968) 76p.

Memory No Servant (Trumansburg, N.Y., New Books, 1968) 52p.

Pnomes Jukollages & other Stunzas [Toronto, Ganglia Press, 1969] 13 pieces

The Poems of Earle Birney (Toronto, McClelland, 1969) 64p.

Rag and Bone Shop (Toronto, McClelland, 1970) 64p.

Four Parts Sand, by Earle Birney *et al* (Ottawa, Oberon, 1972) 54p. [concrete poems]

The Cow Jumped Over the Moon. The Writing and Reading of Poetry (Toronto, Holt Rinehart, 1972) 112p.

The Bear on the Delhi Road. Selected Poems (London, Chatto & Windus, 1973)

What's So Big about Green (Toronto, McClelland, 1973)

Selected criticism:

Sutherland, John, "Earle Birney's *David,*" *First Statement* Vol. 1, No. 9: 6-8 [undated]

Frye, Northrop, Review of *David and Other Poems, Canadian Forum* 22: 278-279 (December 1942)

Pratt, E. J., Review of *David and Other Poems, Canadian Poetry Magazine 6: 34-35* (March 1943)

Brown, E. K., "To the North: a Wall against Canadian Poetry," *Saturday Review of Literature* 27: 9-11 (April 29, 1944)

Daniells, Roy, "Earle Birney et Robert Finch," *Gants du Ciel* 11: 83-96 (Printemps 1946)

Anon., "Two Canadian Poets," *London Times Literary Supplement* No. 2419: 332 (June 12, 1948)

Clay, Charles, "Earle Birney, Canadian Spokesman," in *Leading Canadian Poets,* edited by W. P. Percival (Toronto, Ryerson, 1948) pp. 23-29

Bailey, A. G., [Review article on *The Strait of Anian*] in *Dalhousie Review* 30: 205-208 (July 1950)

Pacey, Desmond, "Earle Birney," in his *Ten Canadian Poets* (Toronto, Ryerson, 1958) pp. 293-326

Elliott, Brian, "Earle Birney: Canadian Poet," *Meanjin* [Australia] No. 78: 338-347 (1959)

Fredeman, William E., "Earle Birney— Author, Poet," *British Columbia Library Quarterly* 23: 8-15 (January 1960)

West, Paul, "Earle Birney and the Compound Ghost," *Canadian Literature* No. 13: 5-14 (Summer 1962)

Colombo, J. R., "Poetic Ambassador," *Canadian Literature* No. 24: 55-59 (Spring 1965) [Review of *Near False Creek Mouth*]

Birney, Earle, "Turvey and the Critics," *Canadian Literature* No. 30: 21-25 (Autumn 1966)

Noel-Bentley, Peter, *A Chronological Study of the Poetry of Earle Birney* (Thesis, Trinity, University of Toronto, 1966)

Smith, A. J. M., "A Unified Personality, Birney's Poems," *Canadian Literature* No. 30: 4-13 (Autumn 1966)

Wilson, Milton, "Poet without a Muse," *Canadian Literature* No. 30: 14-20 Autumn 1966)

Carruth, Hayden, "Up, Over, and Out: The Poetry of Distraction," *Tamarack Review* 42: 61-69 (Winter 1967)

Bélanger, Reynald, *Canadian Humorists: Leacock, Haliburton, Earle Birney, W. O. Mitchell* (Thesis, Université Laval, 1968)

Noel-Bentley, Peter C. and Earle Birney, "Earle Birney: a Bibliography in Progress, 1923-1969," *West Coast Review* 5: 45-53 (October 1970)

Davey, Frank, *Earle Birney* (Toronto, Copp Clark, 1971) vii + 128p.

New, W. H., "Prisoner of Dreams: The Poetry of Earle Birney," *Canadian Forum* 51: 29-32 (September 1972)

Robillard, Richard H., *Earle Birney* (Toronto McClelland, 1972) 64p. [Canadian Writers Series No. 9]

GEORGE BOWERING (1935-   )

Sticks and Stones (Vancouver, Tishbooks, 1963)

Points on the Grid (Toronto, Contact Press, 1964) 67p.

The Man in the Yellow Boots . . . (Mexico, Ediciones el Corno Emplumado, 1965) 112p.

The Silver Wire (Kingston, Quarry Press, 1966) 72p.

Baseball. A Poem in the Magic Number 9 (Toronto, Coach House Press, 1967) 21p.

Mirror on the Floor [A Novel] (Toronto, McClelland, 1967) 160p.

Rocky Mountain Foot: A Lyric, A Memoir (Toronto, McClelland, 1968) 126p.

Solitary Walk. A Book of Longer Poems. By —— *et al* (Toronto, Ryerson, 1968) 75p.

The Gangs of Kosmos (Toronto, Anansi, 1969) 64p.

How I Hear Howl (Montreal, Author 1969) 19p.

Two Police Poems (Vancouver, Talonbooks, 1969) 23p.

Al Purdy (Toronto, Copp Clark, 1970) 117p. [Studies in Canadian Literature No. 6]

George Vancouver. A Discovery Poem
(Toronto, Weed/flower Press, 1970) 39p.
Sitting in Mexico (Montreal, Imago, 1970)
Vibrations. Poems of Youth, edited by ——
(Toronto, Gage, 1970) 53p.
Genève (Toronto, Coach House Press, 1971) 45p.
The Story So Far. [Canadian Short Stories]
edited by —— (Toronto, Coach House Press,
1971) 112p.
Touch. Selected Poems, 1960-1970 (Toronto,
McClelland, 1971) 128p.
Autobiology (Vancouver series 7) (Vancouver,
Georgia Straight Writing Supplement, 1972)
103p.
The Sensible (Toronto, Massasauga Editions,
1972) 23p.

Selected criticism:

Woodcock, George, "Mod Murders" [A review
article] *Canadian Literature* No. 36: 74-77
(Spring 1968)
Davey, Frank, "The Message of George
Bowering: Play Ball," *U.B.C. Alumni
Chronicle* 24: 13-15 (Summer 1970)
Colombo, John R., *Rhymes and Reasons:* Nine
Canadian Poets Discuss their Work . . .
(Toronto, Holt Rinehart, 1971) 117p.
Garnet, Eldon, "Two Bowerings Embrace
Past, Present, Future," *Saturday Night*
86: 46, 49-50 (November 1971)
Davey, Frank, "A Note on Bowering's
Genève," *Open Letter,* 2nd series, No. 1:
42-44 (Winter 1971-72)
Cameron, Donald, "George Bowering: The
Test of Real is the Language," *Conversations
with Canadian Novelists,* Part II (Toronto,
Macmillan, 1973) pp. 3-16.

ELIZABETH BREWSTER (1922-   )

East Coast (Toronto, Ryerson, 1951) 8p.
Lillooet (Toronto, Ryerson, 1954) 28p.
Roads and Other Poems (Toronto, Ryerson,
1957) 12p.
Five New Brunswick Poets: Brewster, Cogswell,
Nowlan, *et al* (Fredericton, Fiddlehead,
1962) 64p.
Passage of Summer. Selected Poems (Toronto,
Ryerson, 1969) 129p.
Sunrise North (Toronto, Clarke Irwin, 1972) 87p.

Selected criticism:

Bauer, W. A., Review of *Passage of Summer,*
Fiddlehead No. 80: 102-104 (May/June/July
1969)
Bartlett, Brian, Review of *Sunrise North,*
Fiddlehead No. 95: 118-122 (Fall 1972)

FRANCES BROOKE (1724-1789)

*Virginia, a Tragedy, with Odes, Pastorals, and
Translations* (London, the Author, 1756) 159p.
The History of Lady Julia Mandeville (1763),
edited by E. P. Poole, with Introduction and
Bibliographical List (London, Partridge,
1930) 218p.
The History of Emily Montague (1769), edited
with Introduction and Notes by L. J. Burpee,
and Appendix by F. P. Grove (Ottawa,
Graphic, 1931) 333p. [also published with
an Introduction and Bibliography by Carl F.
Klinck (Toronto, McClelland, 1961) 317p.
New Canadian Library No. 27]
The Memoirs of the Marquis de St. Forlaix
(London, 1770) 4 vols.
The Excursion [a novel] (London, Cadell, 1777)
2 vols.
The Siege of Sinope. A Tragedy (London,
Cadell, 1781) 71p.
Rosina. A Comic Opera in Two Acts (London,
Cadell, 1783) 46p.
Marian. A Comic Opera in Two Acts (1700)
(London, Longmans, 1800) 31p.

Selected criticism:

Le Moine, James, *Picturesque Quebec* (Montreal,
Dawson, 1882) pp. 375-378
Chateauclair, Wilfrid, "The First Canadian
Novel," *Dominion Illustrated* 4: 31 (January
11, 1890)
Burwash, Ida, "An Old Time Novel," *Canadian
Magazine* 28: 252-256 (January 1907)
Wallace, W. S. (ed.), *The Maseres Letters
1766-1768* (Toronto, University Library,
1919) 131p.
Blue, Charles S., "Canada's First Novelist,"
Canadian Magazine 58: 3-12 (November 1921)
Humphreys, J., "Mrs. Frances Brooke,"
Dictionary of National Biography (London,
Oxford, 1921) 2: 1328-1329
Morgan, H. R., "Frances Brooke: A Canadian

Pioneer," Supplement to the *McGill News* (June 1930) 5p.

Baker, Ernest A., "Mrs. Frances Brooke," in his *The History of the English Novel* (London, Witherby, 1934) 5: 144-146

Woodley, E. C., "The First Canadian Novel and Its Author," *Educational Record* (Quebec) 57: 31-36 (January 1941)

Pacey, Desmond, "The First Canadian Novel," *Dalhousie Review* 26: 143-150 (July 1946)

Klinck, Carl F., Introduction to *The History of Emily Montague* by Frances Brooke (Toronto, McClelland, 1961) pp. v-xiv [New Canadian Library No. 27]

New, W. H., "Frances Brooke's Chequered Gardens," *Canadian Literature* No. 52: 24-38 (Spring 1972)

ERNEST BUCKLER (1908-   )

The Mountain and the Valley (New York, Holt, 1952) 373p.

The Cruelest Month (Toronto, McClelland, 1963) 298p.

Ox Bells and Fireflies. A Memoir (Toronto, McClelland, 1968) 302p.

Window on the Sea. By —— and Hans Weber (Toronto, McClelland, 1973)

Selected criticism:

Anon., Biographical Note, *Maclean's* 62: 2-3 (January 1, 1949)

Douglas, Katherine, Review of *The Mountain and the Valley*, *Dalhousie Review* 32: iii, v (Winter 1953)

Bissell, Claude T., Review of *The Mountain and the Valley*, *University of Toronto Quarterly* 22: 290-292 (April 1953)

——, Introduction to *The Mountain and the Valley* by Ernest Buckler (Toronto, McClelland, 1961) pp. vii-xii [New Canadian Library No. 23]

Cook, Gregory M., *Ernest Buckler: His Creed and His Craft* (Thesis, Acadia University, 1967)

Spettigue, D. O., "The Way It Was: Ernest Buckler," *Canadian Literature* No. 32: 40-56 (Spring 1967)

Cameron, Donald, "Letter from Halifax," *Canadian Literature* No. 40: 55-60 (Spring 1969)

Orange, John C., *Ernest Buckler: The Masks of the Artist* (Thesis, University of Toronto, 1969)

Cook, Gregory (ed.) *On Ernest Buckler* (Toronto, McGraw-Hill, 1972) 145p. [Critical Views on Canadian Writers No. 7]

Reichert, Richard, *"The Mountain and the Valley" Reconsidered* (Thesis, University of New Brunswick, 1972)

Cameron, Donald, "Ernest Buckler: A Conversation with an Irritated Oyster," *Conversations with Canadian Novelists*, Part I (Toronto, Macmillan, 1973) pp. 3-12

ADAM HOOD BURWELL (1790-1849)

Doctrine of the Holy Spirit . . . (Toronto, Coates, 1835) 124p.

A Voice of Warning and Instruction Concerning the Signs of the Times (Kingston, Herald, 1835) 225p.

Summer Evening Contemplations (Montreal, Lovell, 1849) 12p.

The Poems of Adam Hood Burwell, Pioneer Poet of Upper Canada, edited by Carl F. Klinck (London, Ont., Lawson Memorial Library, University of Western Ontario, 1963) 110p.

Selected criticism:

Lande, Lawrence M., "Adam Hood Burwell," in his *Old Lamps Aglow* (Montreal, the Author, 1957) pp. 242-253

Klinck, Carl F., "Adam Hood Burwell, 1790-1849," in *The Poems of Adam Hood Burwell* . . . (London, Ont., Lawson Memorial Library, University of Western Ontario, 1963) pp. iii-ix

MORLEY CALLAGHAN (1903-   )

Strange Fugitive (New York, Scribner, 1928) 264p.

A Native Argosy (New York, Scribner, 1929) 371p.

It's Never Over (New York, Scribner, 1930) 225p.

No Man's Meat (Paris [France], E. W. Titus, Black Manikin Press, 1931) 42p.

A Broken Journey (New York, Scribner, 1932) 270p.

Such is My Beloved (New York, Scribner, 1934) 288p.

They Shall Inherit the Earth (Toronto, Macmillan, 1935) 337p.

Now That April's Here and Other Stories (New York, Random House, 1936) 316p.

More Joy In Heaven (New York, Random House, 1937) 278p.

Luke Baldwin's Vow [juvenile] (Philadelphia, Winston, 1948) 187p.

The Varsity Story (Toronto, Macmillan, 1948) 172p.

The Loved and the Lost (Toronto, Macmillan, 1951) 234p.

Morley Callaghan's Stories (Toronto, Macmillan, 1959) 364p.

The Many Colored Coat (Toronto, Macmillan, 1960) 318p.

A Passion in Rome. A Novel (Toronto, Macmillan, 1961) 352p.

That Summer in Paris (Toronto, Macmillan, 1963) 255p.

An Autumn Penitent and *In His Own Country* [Two short novels] (Toronto, Macmillan, 1973) 192p. [Laurentian Library No. 16]

In addition, Mr. Callaghan is the author of two plays (apparently still unpublished) and a number of short stories still uncollected.

Selected criticism:

Steinhauer, H., "Canadian Writers of To-Day," *Canadian Forum* 12: 177-178 (February 1932)

Davis, H. J., "Morley Callaghan," *Canadian Forum* 15: 398-399 (December 1935)

Preston, B., "Toronto's Callaghan," *Saturday Night* 51: 12 (January 18, 1936)

Callaghan, Morley, "The Plight of Canadian Fiction," *University of Toronto Quarterly* 7: 152-161 (January 1938)

Koch, E. A., "Callaghan: Lend-Lease from the Bohemians," *Saturday Night* 60: 16-17 (October 21, 1944)

Phelps, Arthur L., "Morley Callaghan," in his *Canadian Writers* (Toronto, McClelland, 1951) pp. 10-18

McCarvell, Joan, *Morley Callaghan as a Short Story Writer* (Thesis, Laval University, 1957)

McPherson, Hugo, "The Two Worlds of Morley Callaghan," *Queen's Quarterly* 64: 350-365 (Autumn 1957)

Ross, Malcolm, Introduction to *Such Is My Beloved* by Morley Callaghan (Toronto, McClelland, 1957) pp. v-xiii [New Canadian Library No. 2]

Weaver, Robert, "A Talk with Morley Callaghan," *Tamarack Review* No. 7: 3-29 (Spring 1958)

Ripley, J. D., *A Critical Study of Morley Callaghan* (Thesis, University of New Brunswick, 1959)

Watt, Frank W., "Morley Callaghan as Thinker," *Dalhousie Review* 39: 305-313 (Autumn 1959) [Also in *Masks of Fiction*, edited by A. J. M. Smith (Toronto, McClelland, 1961) pp. 116-127]

Weaver, Robert, "Stories by Callaghan," *Canadian Literature* No. 2: 67-70 (Autumn 1959)

Avison, Margaret, "Callaghan Revisited," *Canadian Forum* 39: 276-277 (March 1960)

Wilson, Edmund, "Morley Callaghan of Toronto," *New Yorker* 36: 224-236 (November 26, 1960)

McPherson, Hugo, Introduction to *More Joy in Heaven* by Morley Callaghan (Toronto, McClelland, 1960) pp. v-x [New Canadian Library No. 17]

Moon, Barbara, "The Second Coming of Morley Callaghan," *Maclean's* 73: 19, 62-64 (December 3, 1960)

McPherson, Hugo, "A Tale Retold," *Canadian Literature* No. 7: 59-61 (Winter 1961)

Wilson, Milton, "Callaghan's Caviare," *Tamarack Review* No. 22: 88-92 (Winter 1962)

Watt, Frank W., Introduction to *They Shall Inherit the Earth* by Morley Callaghan (Toronto, McClelland, 1962) pp. v-x [New Canadian Library No. 33]

Woodcock, George, "The Callaghan Case," *Canadian Literature* No. 12: 60-64 (Spring 1962)

Callaghan, Morley, "Those Summers in Toronto," *Maclean's* 76: 25-27, 37-40 (January 5, 1963)

Weaver, Robert, "A Golden Year," *Canadian Literature* No. 16: 55-57 (Spring 1963)

Woodcock, George, "Lost Eurydice,"

Canadian Literature No. 21: 21-35 (Summer 1964)

Wilson, Edmund, *O Canada*. An American's Notes on Canadian Culture (New York, Farrar Straus, 1965) 245p.

Callaghan, Morley, "The Imaginative Writer," *Tamarack Review* No. 41: 5-11 (Autumn 1966)

Conron, Brandon, *Morley Callaghan* (New York, Twayne, 1966) 188p.

Orange, John, *Morley Callaghan's Catholic Conscience* (Thesis, Trinity, University of Toronto, 1966)

Arthur, Constance J., *A Comparative Study of the Short Stories of Morley Callaghan and Hugh Garner* (Thesis, University of New Brunswick, 1967)

Conron, Brandon, "Morley Callaghan as a Short Story Writer," *Journal of Commonwealth Literature* 3: 58-75 (July 1967)

McGregor, Robert G., *A Comparative Study of the Short Stories of Morley Callaghan and Ernest Hemingway* (Thesis, University of New Brunswick, 1967)

McKellar, Iain H., *The Innocents of Morley Callaghan* (Thesis, Carleton University, 1968)

Hoar, Victor, *Morley Callaghan* (Toronto, Copp Clark, 1969) 123p.

Walsh, William, "Morley Callaghan." in *A Manifold Voice*. Studies in Commonwealth Literature (London, Chatto & Windus, 1970) pp. 185-212

——"Streets of Life: Novels of Morley Callaghan," *Ariel, A Review of International English Literature* 1 : 31-42 (January 1970)

Weaver, Robert, Introduction to *Strange Fugitive* by Morley Callaghan (Edmonton, Hurtig, 1970) [Canadian Reprint Series]

Grenier, Marie-Gertrude, *Contrasted Views of Life Presented in the Short Series of Labege and Callaghan* (Thesis, Université de Sherbrooke, 1971)

Cameron, Donald, "Defending the Inner Light: An Interview with Morley Callaghan," *Saturday Night* 87: 17-22 (July 1972)

Dahlie, Hallvard, "Destructive Innocence in the Novels of Morley Callaghan," *Journal of Canadian Fiction* 1 : 39-42 (Summer 1972)

Ishkanian, Vahan Aram, "Symbolism in Morley Callaghan's Short Stories," in *Three Essays* (Burnaby, B.C., Simon Fraser University, 1972) 168p.

Sutherland, Fraser, "Hemingway and Callaghan: Friends and Writers," *Canadian Literature* No. 53: 8-17 (Summer 1972)

——, *The Style of Innocence: A Study of Hemingway and Callaghan* (Toronto, Clarke Irwin, 1972) 120p.

Cameron, Donald, "Morley Callaghan: There Are Gurus in the Woodwork," *Conversations with Canadian Novelists,* Part II (Toronto, Macmillan, 1973) pp. 17-33

WILFRED CAMPBELL (1858-1918)

Snowflakes and Sunbeams (St. Stephen, N.B., St. Croix Courrier, 1888) 36p.

Lake Lyrics and Other Poems (Saint John, N.B., McMillan, 1889) 160p.

The Dread Voyage and Other Poems (Toronto, Briggs, 1893) 190p.

Mordred and Hildebrand. A Book of Tragedies (Ottawa, Durie, 1895) 168p.

Beyond the Hills of Dream (Boston, Houghton, 1899) 137p.

The Poems of Wilfred Campbell (Toronto, Briggs, 1905) 354p.

Ian of the Orcades, or The Armourer of Girnigoe [a novel] (Edinburgh, Oliphant, etc., 1906) 320p.

Canada. Painted by T. Mower Martin; described by Wilfred Campbell (London, Black, 1907) 272p.

Poetical Tragedies (Toronto, Briggs, 1908) 316p.

A Beautiful Rebel. A Romance of Upper Canada in 1812 (Toronto, Westminster, 1909) 317p.

The Beauty, History, Romance, and Mystery of the Canadian Lake Region (Toronto Musson, 1910) 191p. [enlarged and revised edition 1914, 215p.]

The Scotsman in Canada. Vol. 1: Eastern Canada (Toronto, Musson, [1911]) 423p.

Sagas of Vaster Britain. Poems of the Race, the Empire, and the Divinity of Man (Toronto, Musson, 1914) 163p.

Langemarck, and Other War Poems. With an Introduction by the Rev. Dr. Herridge (Ottawa, St. Andrew's Church, [1917]) 14p.

The Poetical Works of Wilfred Campbell, edited

with a Memoir by W. J. Sykes (London, Hodder, 1923) 363p.

At the Mermaid Inn, Conducted by A. Lampman, W. W. Campbell, Duncan C. Scott. Being Selections from Essays . . . which appeared in the Toronto *Globe*, 1892-1893, edited by Arthur S. Bourinot (Ottawa, Bourinot, 1958) 96p.

A collection of manuscripts and letters (some bound) exists in the Douglas Library at Queen's University.

Selected criticism:

Scott, Colin A., "William Wilfred Campbell," *Canadian Magazine* 2: 270-274 (January 1894)

Tucker, J. A., "The Poems of William Wilfred Campbell," *University of Toronto Quarterly* 1 : 140-145 (May 1895)

Burpee, L. J., "Canadian Poet: W. W. Campbell," *Sewanee Review* 8: 425-436 (October 1900)

Graham, Jean, "Canadian Celebrities. 66: Mr. Wilfred Campbell," *Canadian Magazine* 26: 109-111 (December 1905)

Yeigh, Frank, "William Wilfred Campbell, a Scotch-Canadian Poet," *Book News Monthly* [Phila.] pp. 897-900 (August 1910)

Allison, W. T., "William Wilfred Campbell," *Canadian Bookman* 1: 65-66 (April 1919)

Muddiman, Bernard, "William Wilfred Campbell," *Queen's Quarterly* 27: 201-210 (October 1919)

Knister, Raymond, "The Poetical Works of Wilfred Campbell," *Queen's Quarterly* 31: 435-449 (May 1924)

Stevenson, O. J. "A Pre-War Message," in his *A People's Best* (Toronto, Musson, 1927) pp. 241-248

———, "Who's Who in Canadian Literature: William Wilfred Campbell," *Canadian Bookman* 9: 67-71 (March 1927)

MacKay, L. A., "W. W. Campbell," *Canadian Forum* 14: 66-67 (November 1933)

Barnett, E. S., "The Poetry of William Wilfred Campbell," *Canadian Bookman* 17: 93-94 (August 1935)

Klinck, Carl F., "William Wilfred Campbell: Poet of Lakes," *Canadian Bookman* 21: 34-37 (August 1939)

———, *Wilfred Campbell.* A Study in Late Provincial Victorianism (Toronto, Ryerson, 1942) 289p.

———, *A Complete Bibliography of Wilfred Campbell* [available at Queen's University and at the University of Western Ontario] 36p. [typewritten]

Sykes, W. J., "Wilfred Campbell," *Educational Record* (Quebec) 62: 93-97 (April-June 1946) [also in *Leading Canadian Poets,* edited by W. P. Percival (Toronto, Ryerson, 1948) pp. 37-44]

Tait, Michael, "Playwrights in a Vacuum: English-Canadian Drama in the Nineteenth Century," *Canadian Literature* No. 16: 3-18 (Spring 1963)

Miller, Judith, *Towards a Canadian Aesthetic: Descriptive Colour in the Landscape Poetry of Duncan Campbell Scott, Archibald Lampman, and William Wilfred Campbell* (Thesis, University of Waterloo, 1970)

Ower, J., "Portraits of the Landscape as Poet: Canadian Nature as Aesthetic Symbol in Three Confederation Writers" [Lampman, Campbell, Roberts], *Journal of Canadian Studies* 6: 27-32 (February 1971)

BLISS CARMAN (1861-1929)

Low Tide on Grand Pré, by Bliss Carmen [*sic*] (Canadian Series of Pamphlets) (Toronto, Copp Clark, [1889]) 26p. [an unauthorized publication]

Flower of the Rose, by Louis Norman [pseud.] (New York, Primrose Bindery, 1892) [another edition (Cambridge, Mass., 1938) 4p.]

Low Tide on Grand Pré. A Book of Lyrics (New York, Webster, 1893) 120p.

Saint Kavin. A Ballad (Cambridge, Mass., Wilson, 1894) 9p.

Songs from Vagabondia, by Bliss Carman and Richard Hovey (Boston, Copeland, 1894) 54p.

At Michaelmas. A Lyric (Wolfville, N.S., Acadian Press, 1895) 11p.

Behind the Arras. A Book of the Unseen (Boston, Lamson Wolffe, 1895) 102p.

A Seamark. A Threnody for Robert Louis Stevenson (Boston, Copeland, 1895) 10p.

More Songs from Vagabondia, by Bliss Carman

and Richard Hovey (Boston, Copeland, 1896) 72p.

Ballads of Lost Haven. A Book of the Sea (Boston, Lamson Wolffe, 1897) 117p.

The Girl in the Poster. For a Design by Miss Ethel Reed ([Springfield, Mass.], Wayside Press, 1897) 9p.

By the Aurelian Wall, and Other Elegies (Boston, Lamson Wolffe, 1898) 132p.

Corydon. A Trilogy in Commemoration of Matthew Arnold . . . (Fredericton, MacNutt, 1898) 15p.

The Green Book of the Bards (Cambridge, Mass., University Press, 1898) 12p.

The Vengeance of Noel Brassard. A Tale of the Acadian Expulsion (Cambridge, Mass., Bradley, 1899) 23p. [mis-dated MDCCCXIX]

A Winter Holiday [and Other Poems] (Boston, Small Maynard, 1899) 43p.

Christmas Eve at S. Kavin's (New York, Kimball, 1901) 15p.

Last Songs from Vagabondia, by Bliss Carman and Richard Hovey (Boston, Small Maynard, 1901) 79p.

Ballads and Lyrics (London, A. H. Bullen, 1902) 79p. [a different selection from the one published under same title in 1923]

Coronation Ode (Boston, Page, 1902) 12p.

. . . *From the Book of Myths* (Boston, Page, 1902) 88p.

Ode on the Coronation of King Edward (Boston, Page, 1902) 34p.

Sappho. Lyrics. With Excerpts from a Literal Rendering by H. T. Wharton (N.p., the Author, 1902) 8p.

. . . *From the Green Book of the Bards* (Boston Page, 1903) 137p.

A Vision of Sappho ([New York], the Author, 1903) 7p. [Reprinted: Toronto, Canadiana House, 1968]

The Word at St. Kavin's (Nelson, N.H., Monadnock Press, 1903) 28p.

The Friendship of Art (Boston, Page, 1904) 303p.

The Kinship of Nature (Boston, Page, 1904) 298p. [published in 1903]

. . . *Poems* (New York, Scott-Thaw; London, Murray, 1904) 2 vols.

Sappho: One Hundred Lyrics. With an Introduction by Charles G. D. Roberts (Boston, Page, 1904) 130p.

. . . *Songs from a Northern Garden* (Boston, Page, 1904) 121p.

. . . *Songs of the Sea Children* (Boston, Page, 1904) 182p.

. . . *From the Book of Valentines* (Boston, Page, 1905) 103p.

Pipes of Pan. Containing "From the Book of Myths," "From the Green Book of the Bards," "Songs of the Sea Children," "Songs from a Northern Garden," "From the Book of Valentines" (Boston, Page, 1902-1905) 5 vols. in 1 [first Canadian edition: Toronto, Ryerson, 1942]

The Poetry of Life (Boston, Page, 1905) 258p.

The Princess of the Tower, The Wise Men from the East, and To the Winged Victory (New York, Village Press, 1906) 18p.

The Gate of Peace. A Poem (New York, Village Press, 1907) 14p.

The Making of Personality [with Mary Perry King] (Boston, Page, 1908) 375p.

The Path to Sankoty ([Siasconset, Mass.], The Gift Shop, 1908) 4p.

The Rough Rider, and Other Poems (New York, Kennerley, 1909) 78p.

Address to the Graduating Class 1911 of the Unitrinian School of Personal Harmonizing . . . (New York, Tabord Press, 1911) 27p.

A Painter's Holiday, and Other Poems (New York, F. F. Sherman, 1911) 43p.

Songs from Vagabondia, More Songs from Vagabondia, Last Songs from Vagabondia, by Bliss Carman and Richard Hovey (Boston, Small Maynard [1911]) 3 vols. in 1

Echoes from Vagabondia (Boston, Small Maynard, 1912) 65p.

Daughters of Dawn. A Lyrical Pageant . . ., by Bliss Carman and Mary Perry King (New York, Kennerley, 1913) 118p.

Earth Dieties, and Other Rhythmic Masques, by Bliss Carman and Mary Perry King (New York, Kennerley, 1914) 85p.

April Airs. A Book of New England Lyrics. (Boston, Small Maynard, 1916) 77p.

Four Sonnets (Boston, Small Maynard, 1916) 4p.

James Whitcomb Riley. An Essay by Bliss Carman and Some Letters to him from James Whitcomb Riley . . . (New York, Smith, [1917]) 86p.

The Man of the Marne, and Other Poems, by B. C. and M. P. K. [pseuds.] (New Canaan,

Conn., Ponus Press, 1918) 26p.

"An Open Letter" from Bliss Carman (Boston, Small Maynard, [1920]) 17p.

Later Poems. With an Appreciation by R. H. Hathaway (Toronto, McClelland, [1921]) 203p.

Ballads and Lyrics (Toronto, McClelland, 1923) 293p. [a different selection from the one published under same title in 1902]

Far Horizons (Boston, Small Maynard, [1925]) 85p.

Our Canadian Literature. Representative Verse, English. Chosen by Bliss Carman and Lorne Pierce (Toronto, Ryerson, 1925) 361p.

Talks on Poetry and Life . . . Five Lectures Delivered before the University of Toronto, December, 1925 (Toronto, Ryerson, 1926) 58p.

Sanctuary. Sunshine House Sonnets (New York, Dodd Mead, 1929) 55p.

Wild Garden (New York, Dodd Mead, [1929]) 76p.

Bliss Carman's Poems (Toronto, McClelland, 1931) 546p.

Bliss Carman's Scrap Book. A Table of Contents. Edited with a Postscript by Lorne Pierce (Toronto, Ryerson, [1931]) 18p. [an index of a scrap book kept by Carman of his fugitive writings, 1883-1919]

The Music of Earth. With Foreword and Notes by Lorne Pierce (Toronto, Ryerson, 1931) 45p.

Youth in the Air. A Poem (Palo Alto, Calif., Yerba Buena Press, 1932) 4p.

To A Chickadee . . . (Palo Alto, Calif., Yerba Buena Press, 1933) 7p.

The Selected Poems of Bliss Carman, edited with an Introduction by Lorne Pierce (Toronto, McClelland, 1954) 122p. [Second edition, 1961]

Collections of Carman manuscripts, letters, fugitive pieces, first editions, etc., are to be found in the William Inglis Morse Collection at Harvard University and the Lorne Pierce Collection at Queen's University. See Bliss Carman: *Bibliography, Letters, Fugitive Verses* . . . , by William Inglis Morse (Windham, Conn., Hawthorn House, 1941) 86p. and *A Catalogue of Canadian Manuscripts Collected by Lorne Pierce and Presented to Queen's University,* compiled by Dorothy Harlowe (Toronto, Ryerson, 1946) 164p.

Selected criticism:

Roberts, Charles G. D., "Mr. Bliss Carman's Poems," *Chap-Book* 1: 53-57 (June 15, 1894)

Brown, Harry W., "Bliss Carman's Latest Book of Poems," *Canadian Magazine* 6: 477-481 (March 1896)

Carman, Bliss, [A Letter about Himself to the Editor], *Critic,* new series 26: 164-165 (September 12, 1896)

Archer, William, "Bliss Carman," in *Poets of the Younger Generation* (London, Lane, 1902) pp. 66-82

Marshall, J., "Pipes of Pan," *Queen's Quarterly* 11: 203-208 (October 1903)

Rittenhouse, Jessie B., in *Younger American Poets* (Boston, Little Brown, 1904) pp. 46-74

Stringer, Arthur, "Canadians in New York — America's Foremost Lyricist: Bliss Carman," *National Monthly* 4: 3-5 (January 1904)

MacFarland, Kenneth, "The Poetry of Bliss Carman," *Literary Miscellany* 2: 35-39 (Summer 1909)

Lee, H. D. C., *Bliss Carman.* A Study in Canadian Poetry (Buxton, England, Herald Printing Co., 1912) 254p.

Muddiman, Bernard, "A Vignette in Canadian Literature," *Canadian Magazine* 40: 451-458 (March 1913)

Munday, Don, "The Faith of Bliss Carman," *Westminster Hall* 6: 9-12 (September 1914)

Sherman, F. F., *A Check List of First Editions* . . . (New York, the Author, 1915) 15p.

Hathaway, R. H., "Bliss Carman: Poet of the Sea," *The Sailor* 2: 19-20 (July 1920)

——, "Bliss Carman: an Appreciation," *Canadian Magazine* 56: 521-536 (April 1921)

Douglas, R. W., "Canada's Poet Laureate — Bliss Carman," *British Columbia Monthly* 19: 5-6 (July 1922), 3-4, 14-16 (August 1922)

Hind, C. Lewis, "Bliss Carman," in his *More Authors and I* (New York, Dodd Mead, 1922) pp. 65-70

Shepard, Odell, *Bliss Carman* (Toronto, McClelland, 1923) 184p.

Hathaway, R. H., "The Poetry of Bliss Carman," *Sewanee Review* 33: 467-483 (October 1925)

Van Patten, Nathan, "Bliss Carman and the Bibliophile," *Queen's Quarterly* 33: 202-205 (November 1925)

Stevenson, O. J., "The Dawning's Troubador," in his *A People's Best* (Toronto, Musson, 1927) pp. 53-62

Hathaway, R. H., "Vale! Bliss Carman," *Canadian Bookman* 11: 155-159 (July 1929)

Cappon, James, "Bliss Carman's Beginnings," *Queen's Quarterly* 36: 637-665 (October 1929)

——, *Bliss Carman and the Literary Currents and Influences of his Time* (Toronto, Ryerson, [1930]) 340p.

Roberts, Charles G. D., "Bliss Carman," *Dalhousie Review* 9: 409-417 (January 1930)

——, "Carman and his own Country," *Acadie* 1: 2-4 (April 1930)

——, "More Reminiscences of Bliss Carman," *Dalhousie Review* 10: 1-9 (April 15, 1930)

Wade, H. G., "Bliss Carman's Shrine," *Western Home Monthly* 32: 28ff (February 1931)

Ross, M. M., "A Symbolic Approach to Carman," *Canadian Bookman* 14: 140-144 (December 1932)

MacKay, L. A., "Bliss Carman," *Canadian Forum* 13: 182-183 (February 1933) [also in *Masks of Poetry*, edited by A. J. M. Smith (Toronto, McClelland, 1962) pp. 55-59]

Miller, Muriel, *A Mental Biography of Bliss Carman in a Creative Interpretation of his Poetry* (Thesis, University of Toronto, 1933)

Pierce, Lorne, "Bliss Carman," in his *Three Fredericton Poets* . . . (Toronto, Ryerson, 1933) pp. 18-24

Roberts, T. G., "The Writing of 'The Red Wolf,' " *Canadian Bookman* 15: 103-104 (August 1933)

Miller, Muriel, *Bliss Carman, A Portrait* (Toronto, Ryerson, 1935) 136p.

McCracken, M. S., *Bliss Carman: His Status in the Annals of Canadian Literature* (Thesis, Ottawa University, 1936)

Roberts, Lloyd, "Bliss Carman: A Memory," *Canadian Bookman* 21: 42-46 (April 1939)

Roberts, Charles G. D., "Some Reminiscences of Bliss Carman in New York," *Canadian Poetry Magazine* 5: 5-10 (December 1940)

Edgar, Pelham, "Bliss Carman," *Educational Record* (Quebec) 57: 140-143 (May 1941) [also in *Leading Canadian Poets*, edited by W. P. Percival (Toronto, Ryerson, 1948) pp. 45-50]

Morse, William Inglis, *Bliss Carman: Bibliography, Letters, Fugitive Verses, and Other Data* (Windham, Conn., Hawthorn House, 1941) 86p.

Stringer, Arthur, "Wild Poets I've Known: Bliss Carman," *Saturday Night* 56: 29, 36 (March 1, 1941)

Massey, Vincent, "Roberts, Carman, Sherman: Canadian Poets," *Canadian Author and Bookman* 23: 29-32 (Fall 1947)

Ross, M. M., "Carman by the Sea," *Dalhousie Review* 27: 294-298 (October 1947)

McPherson, Hugo, *The Literary Reputation of Bliss Carman. A Study in the Development of Canadian Taste in Poetry* (Thesis, University of Western Ontario, 1950)

Pacey, Desmond, "Bliss Carman: A Reappraisal," *Northern Review* 3: 2-10 (February-March 1950)

Pierce, Lorne, Introduction to *The Selected Poems of Bliss Carman* (Toronto, McClelland, 1954) pp. 17-30

Stephens, D. G., *The Influence of English Poets Upon the Poetry of Bliss Carman* (Thesis, University of New Brunswick, 1955)

Macdonald, Allan H., *Richard Hovey: Man and Craftsman* (Durham, N. C., Duke University Press, 1957) *passim*

Martin, Mary C., *The Early Development of Bliss Carman* (Thesis, University of New Brunswick, 1957)

Pacey, Desmond, "Bliss Carman," in his *Ten Canadian Poets* (Toronto, Ryerson, 1958) pp. 59-113

——, "Garland for Bliss Carman," *Atlantic Advocate* 51: 17, 19-20 (April 1961)

Gundy, H. P., "The Bliss Carman Centenary," *Douglas Library Notes* 10: 1-16 (Summer 1961) [Author's note, and letters and extracts from Carman's correspondence]

Stephens, D. G., "A Maritime Myth," *Canadian Literature* No. 9: 38-48 (Summer 1961)

——, *Bliss Carman* (New York, Twayne, 1966) 144p.

Rogers, A. R., "American Recognation of Bliss Carman and Sir Charles G. D. Roberts," *Humanities Association Bulletin* 22: 19-25 (Spring 1971)

Sorfleet, John Robert, *Bliss Carman's Major Years: A Chronological Study of his Work* in *Relation to his Thought* (Thesis, University of Manitoba, 1971)

Gundy, H. Pearson, "Bliss Carman's Comic Muse," *Douglas Library Notes* 20: 8-18 (Winter 1972)

EMILY CARR (1871-1945)

Klee Wyck (Toronto, Oxford University Press, 1941) 155p.

The Book of Small (Toronto, Oxford University Press, 1942) 245p.

The House of All Sorts (Toronto, Oxford University Press, 1944) 222p.

Emily Carr: Her Paintings and Sketches (Toronto, Oxford University Press, 1945) 64p.

Growing Pains. The Autobiography of Emily Carr (Toronto, Oxford University Press, 1946) 381p.

The Heart of a Peacock, edited by Ira Dilworth (Toronto, Oxford University Press, 1953) 234p.

Pause. A Sketch Book (Toronto, Clarke Irwin, 1953) 148p.

An Address by Emily Carr. With an Introduction by Ira Dilworth (Toronto, Oxford University Press, 1955) ix + 15p.

Hundreds and Thousands. The Journals of Emily Carr (Toronto, Clarke Irwin, 1966) 332p.

Fresh Seeing. Two Addresses (Toronto, Clarke Irwin, 1973) 38p.

Selected criticism:

Harris, Lawren, "Emily Carr and her Work," *Canadian Forum* 21: 277-278 (December 1941)

National Gallery of Canada, *Emily Carr: Her Paintings and Sketches* (Toronto, Oxford University Press, 1945)

Colman, M. E., "Emily and her Sisters," *Dalhousie Review* 27: 29-32 (April 1947)

Henry, Lorne J., "Emily Carr (1871-1945)," in his *Canadians: A Book of Biographies* (Toronto, Longmans, 1950) pp.83-90

Stacton, David D., "The Art of Emily Carr," *Queen's Quarterly* 57: 499-509 (Winter 1950)

Dilworth, Ira, Foreword to *Klee Wyck*

(Toronto, Clarke Irwin, 1951) pp. v-xvi [Canadian Classics edition]

Nesbitt, J. K., "The Genius We Laughed At," *Maclean's* 64: 12-13, 29-30 (January 7, 1951)

Pearson, Carol, *Emily Carr as I Knew Her* (Toronto, Clarke Irwin, 1954) 162p.

Humphrey, Ruth, "Emily Carr — an Appreciation," *Queen's Quarterly* 65: 270-276 (Summer 1958)

Sanders, Byrne Hope, "Emily Carr," in her *Canadian Portraits — Famous Women* (Toronto, Clarke Irwin, 1958) pp. 3-43.

McDonald, J. A., "Emily Carr: Painter as Writer," *British Columbia Library Quarterly* 22: 17-23 (April 1959)

Fry, J. "Emily Carr's Forgotten Guardian Eagles," *Maclean's* 74: 42 (February 25, 1961)

Daniells, Roy, "Emily Carr," in *Our Living Tradition*, Fourth series, edited by Robert L. McDougall (Toronto, University of Toronto Press, 1962) pp. 119-134.

Turpin, M., *The Life and Work of Emily Carr (1871-1945)*. A Selected Bibliography (Vancouver, School of Librarianship, University of British Columbia, 1965)

Burns, F. H., "Emily Carr," in *The Clear Spirit*, edited by Mary Q. Innis (Toronto, University of Toronto Press, 1966)

Schleicher, Edythe H., *M. E.: A Portrayal of Emily Carr* (Toronto, Clarke Irwin, 1969) 123p.

Shadbolt, Doris, "Emily Carr: Legend and Reality," *Arts/Canada* 28: 17-21 (June/July 1971)

Humphrey, Ruth (ed.), "Letters from Emily Carr," *University of Toronto Quarterly* 41: 93-150 (Winter 1972)

Posner, Michael, "Emily Carr, Major Canadian Artist," *Canada & the World* 38: 22 (December 1972)

FREDERICK WILLIAM COGSWELL (1917-   )

The Stunted Strong (Fredericton, University of New Brunswick, 1954) 16p.

The Haloed Tree (Toronto, Ryerson, 1956) 16p.

The Testament of Cresseid, by Robert Henryson [1430?-1506?]. Translated by Fred Cogswell (Toronto, Ryerson, 1957) 24p.

Descent from Eden (Toronto, Ryerson, 1959) 38p.

Lost Dimension (Dulwich [England], Outposts Publications, 1960) 12p.

Five New Brunswick Poets: Elizabeth Brewster, Fred Cogswell, Robert Gibbs, Alden Nowlan, Kay Smith (Fredericton, The Fiddlehead, 1962) 64p.

Star-People (Fredericton, Fiddlehead Books, 1968) 48p.

Immortal Plowman (Fredericton, Fiddlehead Poetry Books, 1969) 38p.

In Praise of Chastity (Fredericton, University of New Brunswick, 1970) 30p.

One Hundred Poems of Modern Quebec. edited by —— (Fredericton, Fiddlehead Poetry Books, 1970)

The Chains of Liliput [sic] (Fredericton, Fiddlehead Poetry Books, 1971) 32p.

A Second Hundred Poems of Modern Quebec, edited by —— (Fredericton, Fiddlehead Poetry Books, 1971)

The House Without a Door (Fredericton, Fiddlehead Poetry Books, 1973) 32p.

Selected criticism:

Gustafson, Ralph, Review of *The Stunted Strong,* in *Fiddlehead* Nos. 23-24: 21-22 (February 1955)

MacLure, Millar, Review of *The Haloed Tree,* in *Fiddlehead No. 28: 31, 33 (*May 1956)

Frye, Northrop, Review of *Descent from Eden,* in *University of Toronto Quarterly* 29: 449-450 (July 1960)

Lucas, Alec, Review of *Lost Dimension,* in *Fiddlehead* No. 47: 53-54 (Winter 1961)

Livesay, Dorothy, "Fred and *The Fiddlehead,*" *Atlantic Advocate* 57: 26-28 (May 1967)

LEONARD COHEN (1934-   )

Let Us Compare Mythologies (Toronto, Contact Press, 1956) 79p. [Reprinted: Toronto, McClelland, 1966]

The Spice-Box of Earth (Toronto, McClelland, 1961) 99p.

The Favourite Game [a novel] (London, Secker & Warburg, 1963) 223p.

Flowers for Hitler (Toronto, McClelland, 1964) 128p.

Beautiful Losers (Toronto, McClelland, 1966) 243p.

Parasites of Heaven (Toronto, McClelland, 1966) 80p.

Selected Poems, 1956-1968 (Toronto, McClelland, 1968) 245p.

Songs of Leonard Cohen [with musical scores] (New York, Collier-Macmillan, 1969) 96p.

The Energy of Slaves (Toronto, McClelland, 1972) 127p.

Selected criticism:

Pacey, Desmond, Review of *Let Us Compare Mythologies,* in *Queen's Quarterly* 63: 438-439 (Autumn 1956)

Wilson, Milton, Review of *Let Us Compare Mythologies,* in *Canadian Forum* 36: 282-284 (March 1957)

Mandel, Eli, Review of *The Spice-Box of Earth,* in *Canadian Forum* 41: 140-141 (September 1961)

Wilson, Milton, Review of *The Spice-Box of Earth,* in *University of Toronto Quarterly* 31: 432-437 (July 1962)

Purdy, A. W., "Leonard Cohen: A Personal Look," *Canadian Literature* No. 23: 7-16 (Winter 1965)

Duffy, Dennis "Beautiful Beginners," *Tamarack Review* No. 40: 75-79 (Fall 1966)

Gose, E. B., "Of Beauty and Unmeaning," *Canadian Literature* No. 29: 61-63 (Summer 1966)

Ruddy, Jon, "Is the World (or Anybody) Ready for Leonard Cohen?" *Maclean's* 79: 18-19, 33-34 (October 1, 1966)

Djwa, Sandra, "Leonard Cohen: Black Romantic," *Canadian Literature* No. 34: 32-42 (Autumn 1967)

Pacey, Desmond, "The Phenomenon of Leonard Cohen," *Canadian Literature* No. 34: 5-23 (Autumn 1967)

Batten, Jack, Michael Harris, and Don Owen, "Leonard Cohen: The Poet as Hero," *Saturday Night* 84, No. 6: 23-32 (June 1969)

Knelsen, Richard J., *Flesh and Spirit in the Writings of Leonard Cohen* (Thesis, University of Manitoba, 1969)

Davey, Frank, "Leonard Cohen and Bob Dylan: Poetry and the Popular Song," *Alphabet* No. 17: 12-29 (December 1970)

Ondaatje, Michael, *Leonard Cohen* (Toronto, McClelland, 1970) 64p. [Canadian Writers Series No. 5]

Scobie, Stephen, "Magic, not Magicians:

'Beautiful Losers' and 'Story of O,' "
Canadian Literature No. 45: 56-60 (Summer
1970)
Smith, Rowland J., Introduction to *The
Favourite Game* (Toronto, McClelland, 1970)
pp. iii-x [New Canadian Library No. 73]
Buitenhuis, Peter, "Two Solitudes Revisited:
Hugh MacLennan and Leonard Cohen,"
"The Literary Half-Yearly (University of
Mysore, India) 13: 19-32 (July 1972)
Jantzen, Dorothy H., *The Poetry of Leonard
Cohen: "His Perfect Body"* (Thesis, York
University, 1972)
Morley, Patricia A., *The Immoral Moralists:
Hugh MacLennan and Leonard Cohen*
(Toronto, Clarke Irwin, 1972) 144p.
——, "The Knowledge of Strangerhood: 'The
Monuments were Made of Worms,' " *Journal
of Canadian Fiction* 1: 56-60 (Summer 1972)
Rockett, W. H., "Leonard Cohen and the Killer
Instinct," *Saturday Night* 87: 52, 54, 56
(December 1972)
Wilson, Paula M., *In Search of Magic: A
Study of the Creative Process in the Novels of
Leonard Cohen* (Thesis, Queen's University,
1972)
Macri, F. M., *"Beautiful Losers* and the
Canadian Experience," *Journal of
Commonwealth Literature* 0: 89-96 (June
1973)

Isabella Valancy Crawford (1850-1887)

*Old Spookses' Pass, Malcolm's Katie, and
Other Poems* (Toronto, James Bain, 1884)
224p. [reissued in 1886 and 1898]
*The Collected Poems of Isabella Valancy
Crawford*, edited by J. W. Garvin, with
Introduction by Ethelwyn Wetherald
(Toronto, Briggs, 1905) 309p. [Reprinted
with an Introduction by James Reaney
(Toronto, University of Toronto Press,
1972) xl + 310p.]

Various uncollected writings and unpublished
manuscripts — including prose fiction — are
listed in *A Catalogue of Canadian Manuscripts
Collected by Lorne Pierce and Presented to
Queen's University*, compiled by Dorothy Harlowe (Toronto, Ryerson, 1946) pp. 100-104.

Selected criticism:

"Seranus" [Mrs. J. W. F. Harrison],
"Isabella Valancy Crawford," *The Week* 4:
202-203 (February 24, 1887)
Hathaway, E. J., "Isabella Valancy Crawford,"
Canadian Magazine 5: 569-572 (October 1895)
Burpee, L. J., "Isabella Valancy Crawford . . .,"
Poet Lore 13: 575-586 (October 1901) [also
in *A Little Book of Canadian Essays*
(Toronto, Musson, 1909) pp. 1-16]
Wetherald, Ethelwyn, Introduction to *The
Collected Poems of Isabella Valancy
Crawford*, edited by J. W. Garvin (Toronto,
Briggs, 1905) pp. 15-29
Hale, Katherine, *Isabella Valancy Crawford*
(Toronto, Ryerson, [1923]) 125p.
Garvin, John W., "Who's Who in Canadian
Literature: Isabella Valancy Crawford,"
Canadian Bookman 9: 131-133 (May 1927)
Hale, Katherine, "Isabella Valancy Crawford,"
Educational Record (Quebec) 59: 83-88
(April-June 1943) [also in *Leading Canadian
Poets,* edited by W. P. Percival (Toronto,
Ryerson, 1948) pp. 63-70]
Pomeroy, E. M., "Isabella Valancy Crawford,"
Canadian Poetry Magazine 7: 36-38 (June
1944)
Reaney, James, "Isabella Valancy Crawford,"
in *Our Living Tradition.* Second and Third
Series, edited by Robert L. McDougall
(Toronto, University of Toronto Press,
1959) pp. 268-286
MacGillivray, Richard, *Theme and Imagery in
the Poetry of Isabella Valancy Crawford*
(Thesis, University of New Brunswick, 1963)
Ower, John B., "Isabella Valancy Crawford:
The Canoe," Canadian Literature No. 34:
54-62 (Autumn 1967)
Bessai, Frank, "The Ambivalence of Love in
the Poetry of Isabella Valancy Crawford,"
Queen's Quarterly 77: 404-418 (Winter 1970)
Livesay, Dorothy, "The Native People in our
Canadian Literature," *English Quarterly* 4:
21-32 (Spring 1971)
Yeoman, Ann, "Towards a Native Mythology:
The Poetry of Isabella Valancy Crawford,"
Canadian Literature No. 52: 39-47 (Spring
1972)
Martin, Mary F., "The Short Life of Isabella
Valancy Crawford," *Dalhousie Review* 52:
391-400 (Autumn 1972)

Reaney, James, Introduction to *Collected Poems of Isabella Crawford* (Toronto, University of Toronto Press, 1972) pp. vii-xxxiv

Livesay, Dorothy, "The Hunters Twain," *Canadian Literature* No. 55: 75-98 (Winter 1973)

ROY DANIELLS (1902-   )

Thomas Traherne, A Serious and Pathetic Contemplation of Mercies of God . . . edited by Roy Daniells (Toronto, University of Toronto Press, 1941) 127p.

Deeper Into the Forest (Toronto, McClelland, 1948) 67p.

The Chequered Shade. Poems (Toronto, McClelland, 1963) 91p.

Milton, Mannerism and Baroque (Toronto, University of Toronto Press, 1963) 229p.

Alexander Mackenzie and the Northwest (London, Faber, 1969) 219p.

Selected criticism:

Anon., Biographical Note, *Canadian Author and Bookman* 34: 5 (September 1958)

McPherson, Hugo, "Roy Daniells: Humanist," *British Columbia Library Quarterly* 24: 29-35 (July 1960)

Dudek, Louis, "Ironic Pilgrimage," *Canadian Literature* No. 16: 67-69 (Spring 1963)

Rajan, B., "Milton Seen Anew," *Canadian Literature* No. 21: 55-58 (Summer 1964)

ROBERTSON DAVIES (1913-   )

Shakespeare's Boy Actors (London, Dent, 1939) 208p.

Shakespeare for Young Players (Toronto, Clarke Irwin, 1942) 255p.

The Diary of Samuel Marchbanks (Toronto, Clarke Irwin, 1947) 204p.

Overlaid. A Comedy (Toronto, French, 1948) 24p.

Eros at Breakfast and Other Plays (Toronto, Clarke Irwin, 1949) 129p.

Fortune, My Foe (Toronto, Clarke Irwin, 1949) 99p.

The Table Talk of Samuel Marchbanks (Toronto, Clarke Irwin, 1949) 248p.

At My Heart's Core (Toronto, Clarke Irwin, 1950) 91p.

Tempest-Tost (Toronto, Clarke Irwin, 1951) 376p.

A Masque of Aesop (Toronto, Clarke Irwin, 1952) 47p.

Renown at Stratford. A Record of the Shakespeare Festival in Canada 1953 [with Tyrone Guthrie and Grant Macdonald] (Toronto, Clarke Irwin, 1953) 127p.

A Jig for the Gypsy (Toronto, Clarke Irwin, 1954) 98p.

Leaven of Malice (Toronto, Clarke Irwin, 1954) 312p.

Twice Have the Trumpets Sounded. A Record of the Stratford Shakespearean Festival in Canada 1954 [with Tyrone Guthrie and Grant Macdonald] (Toronto, Clarke Irwin, 1954) 192p.

Thrice the Brinded Cat Hath Mew'd. A Record of the Stratford Shakespearean Festival in Canada 1955 (Toronto, Clarke Irwin, 1955) 178p.

A Mixture of Frailties (Toronto, Macmillan, 1958) 379p.

A Voice from the Attic (Toronto, McClelland, 1960) 360p. [published in England under the title: *The Personal Art.* Reading to Good Purpose (London, Secker, 1961) 268p.]

A Masque of Mr. Punch (Toronto, Oxford, 1963) 58p.

Marchbank's Almanack (Toronto, McClelland, 1967) 205p. [New Canadian Library No. 61]

Four Favourite Plays (Toronto, Clarke Irwin 1968) 157p. [First pub. 1949. Clarke Irwin Canadian Paperback No. 30]

A Feast of Stephen. A Leacock Anthology. Edited by —— (Toronto, McClelland, 1970) 160p.

Fifth Business (Toronto, Macmillan, 1970) 314p.

Hunting Stuart and Other Plays (Toronto, New Press, 1972) 274p.

The Manticore (Toronto, Macmillan, 1972) 288p.

Selected criticism:

McInnes, Graham, "An Editor from Skunk's Misery is Winning Fame for Peterboro," *Saturday Night* 62: 14-15 (April 26, 1947)

Kirkwood, Hilda, "Robertson Davies," *Canadian Forum* 30: 59-60 (June 1950)

Callwood, June, "The Beard," *Maclean's* 65:

16-17, 30-33 (March 15, 1952)

Marchbanks, Samuel [pseud.], "The Double Life of Robertson Davies," *Liberty* pp. 18-19, 53-58 (April 1954) [also in second edition of *Canadian Anthology*, edited by C. F. Klinck and R. E. Waters (Toronto, Gage, 1966) pp. 393-400]

Owen, Ivan, "The Salterton Novels," *Tamarack Review* No. 9: 56-63 (Autumn 1958)

Turner, James Ogden Freeman, *Robertson Davies: Critic and Author* (Thesis, University of Manitoba, 1958)

McPherson, Hugo, "The Mask of Satire: Character and Symbolic Pattern in Robertson Davies' Fiction," *Canadian Literature* No. 4: 18-30 (Spring 1960) [also in *Masks of Fiction*, edited by A. J. M. Smith (Toronto, McClelland, 1961) pp. 162-175]

Read, S. E., "A Call to the Clerisy," *Canadian Literature* No. 7: 65-68 (Winter 1961)

Steinberg, M. W., "Don Quixote and the Puppets: Theme and Structure in Robertson Davies' Drama," *Canadian Literature* No. 7: 45-53 (Winter 1961)

Fisher, Elspeth, *Robertson Davies as Satirist* (Thesis, University of New Brunswick, 1965)

Murphy, Sharon M., *Self-Discovery: The Search for Values in the Work of Robertson Davies* (Thesis, Carleton University, 1968)

Lawrence, Robert G., "A Survey of the Three Novels of Robertson Davies," *B. C. Library Quarterly* 32: 3-9 (April 1969).

Wing, Ted, *Puritan Ethic and Social Response in Novels of Sinclair Ross, Robertson Davies, and Hugh MacLennan* (Thesis, University of Alberta, 1969)

Buitenhuis, Elspeth, *Robertson Davies* (Toronto, Forum House, 1972) 80p. [Canadian Writers and Their Works Series]

Moore, Mavor, "Robertson Davies," *English Quarterly* 5: 15-20 (Fall 1972)

Newman, Peter C., "The Master's Voice: The Table Talk of Robertson Davies," *Maclean's* 85: 42-43 (September 1972)

Roper, Gordon, "Robertson Davies' *Fifth Business*, and 'That Old Fantastical Duke of Dark Corners, C. G. Jung,' " *Journal of Canadian Fiction*, 1: 33-39 (Winter 1972)

Cameron, Donald, "Robertson Davies: The Bizarre and Passionate Life of the Canadian People," *Conversations with Canadian Novelists*, Part 1 (Toronto, Macmillan, 1973) pp. 30-48

EDWARD HARTLEY DEWART (1828-1903)

Selections from Canadian Poets. With Occasional Critical and Biographical Notes, edited by E. H. Dewart (Montreal, Lovell, 1864) 304p.

The Canadian Speaker and Elocutionary Reader. Comprising a Choice Selection of Orations, Dialogues and Poetry . . ., edited and compiled by E. H. Dewart (Toronto, Miller, 1868) 326p.

Broken Reeds; or, the Heresies of the Plymouth Brethren, Shown to be Contrary to Scripture and Reason (Toronto, Wesleyan, 1869) 34p.

Songs of Life. A Collection of Poems (Toronto, Dudley & Burns, 1869) 256p.

High Church Pretensions Disproved; or, Methodism and the Church of England (Toronto, Methodist Book Room, 1877) 59p.

Living Epistles; or, Christ's Witnesses in the World, &c. &c. (Toronto, Christian Guardian, 1878) 288p.

Jesus the Messiah in Prophecy and Fulfilment. A Review and Refutation of the Negative Theory of Messianic Prophecy (Toronto, Briggs, 1890) 256p.

Essays for the Times. Studies of Eminent Men and Important Living Questions (Toronto, Briggs, 1898) 198p.

The Bible Under Higher Criticism. A Review of Current Evolutionary Theories about the Old Testament (Toronto, Briggs, 1900) 214p.

LOUIS DUDEK (1918-   )

Unit of Five. Poems by Louis Dudek, Ronald Hambleton, P. K. Page, Raymond Souster, James Wreford, edited by Ronald Hambleton (Toronto, Ryerson, 1944) pp. 3-18

East of the City (Toronto, Ryerson, 1946) 51p.

Canadian Poems 1850-1952, edited by Louis Dudek and Irving Layton. Second edition (Toronto, Contact Press, [ca. 1952]) 127p.

Cerberus. Poems by Louis Dudek, Irving Layton, Raymond Souster (Toronto, Contact Press, [ca. 1952]) 98p.

The Searching Image (Toronto, Ryerson, [1952]) 12p.

Twenty-Four Poems (Toronto, Contact Press, 1952) 24p.

Europe (Toronto, Laocoön [Contact] Press, 1954) 139p.

The Transparent Sea (Toronto, Contact Press, 1956) 114p.

En México (Toronto, Contact Press, 1958) 78p.

Laughing Stalks (Toronto, Contact Press, 1958) 113p.

Literature and the Press. A History of Printing, Printed Media, and Their Relation to Literature (Toronto, Ryerson, 1960) 238p.

Atlantis (Montreal, Delta Canada, 1967) 151p.

The First Person in Literature (Toronto, CBC, 1967) 69p.

The Making of Modern Poetry in Canada, edited by Louis Dudek and Michael Gnarowski (Toronto, Ryerson, 1967) 303p.

Collected Poetry (Montreal, Delta Canada, 1971) viii + 327p.

Selected criticism:

Anon., "Three New Poets," *First Statement* Vol. 1, No. 12: 1-4 [undated]

Smith, A. J. M., "Turning New Leaves," *Canadian Forum* 27: 42-43 (May 1947)

W., M., Review of *Twenty-Four Poems*, in *Canadian Forum* 33: 161, 163 (October 1953)

Wilson, Milton, Review of *Europe*, in *Canadian Forum* 35: 162-163 (October 1955)

——, *et al*, "Correspondence [concerning Dudek's *Europe*]," *Canadian Forum* 35: 182-184 (November 1955)

Anon., Biographical Note, *Canadian Author and Bookman* 34: 7 (Spring 1958)

Frye, Northrop, Review of *En México* and *Laughing Stalks*, in *University of Toronto Quarterly* 28: 354-356 (July 1959)

Layton, Irving, "An Open Letter to Louis Dudek," *Cataract* Vol. 1, No. 2 (Winter 1962)

Francis, Wynne, "A Critic of Life: Dudek as Man of Letters," *Canadian Literature* No. 22: 5-23 (Autumn 1964)

Livesay, Dorothy, "The Sculpture of Poetry," *Canadian Literature* No. 30: 26-35 (Autumn 1966)

Barbour, Douglas, "Poet as Philosopher," *Canadian Literature* No. 53: 18-29 (Summer 1972)

Dagg, Mel, Review of *Collected Poetry*, *Fiddlehead* No. 94: 111-116 (Summer 1972)

Watt, F. W., Review of Dudek's *Collected Poetry, Canadian Forum* 51: 82-83 (January/February 1972)

SARA JEANNETTE DUNCAN (1861-1922)

A Social Departure: How Orthodocia and I Went Around the World by Ourselves (London, Chatto and Windus, 1890) 417p.

An American Girl in London (London, Chatto and Windus, 1891) 321p.

The Simple Adventures of a Memsahib (New York, Appleton, 1893) 311p.

A Daughter of To-Day (New York, Appleton, 1894) 392p.

The Story of Sonny Sahib (London, Macmillan, 1894) 114p.

Vernon's Aunt, Being the Oriental Experiences of Miss Lavinia Moffat (London, Chatto and Windus, 1894) 200p.

His Honour and a Lady (Toronto, Rose, 1896) 321p.

Hilda, a Story of Calcutta (New York, Stokes, 1898) 317p.

A Voyage of Consolation, Being . . . a Sequel to . . . "An American Girl in London" (London, Methuen, 1898) 318p.

The Path of a Star (London, Methuen, 1899) 311p.

On the Other Side of the Latch (London, Methuen, 1901) 266p. [also published under the title *The Crow's Nest* (New York, Dodd Mead, 1901) 248p.]

Those Delightful Americans (New York, Appleton, 1902) 352p.

The Pool in the Desert [short stories] (New York, Appleton, 1903) 318p.

The Imperialist (Toronto, Copp Clark, 1904) 472p.

Set in Authority (London, Constable, 1906) 344p.

Cousin Cinderella, A Canadian Girl in London (Toronto, Macmillan, 1908) 365p.

The Burnt Offering (London, Methuen, 1909) 324p.

The Consort (London, Stanley Paul, 1912) 344p.

His Royal Happiness (New York, Appleton, 1914) 377p.

Title Clear. A Novel (London, Hutchinson, 1922) 288p.

The Gold Cure. A Novel (London, Hutchinson, 1924) 286p.

Selected criticism:

Donaldson, F., "Mrs. Everard Cotes," *Bookman* (London) 14: 65-67 (June 1898)

Anon., [Women Writers], *Canadian Magazine* 25: 583, 585 (October 1905)

MacMurchy, M., "Mrs. Everard Cotes," *Bookman* (London) 48: 39-40 (May 1915)

MacCallum, H. R., "Sara Jeannette Duncan," in *A Standard Dictionary of Canadian Biography: The Canadian Who Was Who*, edited by C. G. D. Roberts and A. L. Tunnell (Toronto, Trans-Canada Press, 1934) 1: 168-170

Bissell, Claude T., Introduction to *The Imperialist* by Sara Jeannette Duncan (Toronto, McClelland, 1961) pp. v-ix [New Canadian Library No. 20]

Burness, Jean F., "Sara Jeannette Duncan — A Neglected Canadian Author," *Ontario Library Review* 45: 205-206 (August 1961)

Goodwin, Rae, *The Early Journalism of Sara Jeannette Duncan, with a Chapter of Biography* (Thesis, University of Toronto, 1964)

R., M. E., "Sara Jeannette Duncan: Personal Glimpses," *Canadian Literature* No. 27: 15-19 (Winter 1966)

HUGH GARNER (1913-)

Storm Below (Toronto, Collins, 1949) 227p.

Cabbagetown (Toronto, Collins, 1950) 160p. [Revised edition: (Toronto, Ryerson, 1968) 415p.]

Present Reckoning (Toronto, Collins, 1951) 158p.

Waste No Tears by Jarvis Warwick [pseud.] (New Toronto, Export Publishing Enterprises, 1951)

The Yellow Sweater and Other Stories (Toronto, Collins, 1952) 238p.

The Silence on the Shore (Toronto, McClelland, 1962) 332p.

Hugh Garner's Best Stories (Toronto, Ryerson, 1963) 254p.

Author, Author! (Toronto, Ryerson, 1964) 157p.

Men and Women. Stories (Toronto, Ryerson, 1966) 172p.

A Nice Place to Visit (Toronto, Ryerson, 1970) 255p.

The Sin Sniper (Toronto, Pocket Books, 1970) 279p.

Violation of the Virgins [short stories] (Toronto, McGraw-Hill, 1971) 259p.

One Damn Thing after Another [Autobiography] (Toronto, McGraw-Hill Ryerson, 1973)

Selected criticism:

Fulford, Robert, "On Hugh Garner: Everyone Loses Everything. Nobody Knows Anybody," *Maclean's* 76: 73-74 (November 2, 1963)

Hall, William, "Without Camouflage," *Canadian Literature* No. 19: 55-57 (Winter 1964)

Arthur, Constance J., *A Comparative Study of the Short Stories of Morley Callaghan and Hugh Garner* (Thesis, University of New Brunswick, 1967)

Weaver, Robert, "Garner Restored," *Saturday Night* 83: 36, 41-42 (November 1968)

Anderson, Allan, "An Interview with Hugh Garner," *Tamarack Review* No. 52: 5-18 (1969)

Hall, W. F., "New Interest in Reality," *Canadian Literature* No. 40: 66-68 (Spring 1969)

Waddington, Miriam, "Garner's Good Ear," *Canadian Literature* No. 50: 72-75 (Autumn 1971) [Review of *A Nice Place to Visit*]

Fetherling. Doug, *Hugh Garner* (Toronto, Forum House, 1972) 80p. [Canadian Writers & their Works Series]

Moss, John G., "A Conversation with Hugh Garner," *Journal of Canadian Fiction* 1: 50-55 (Spring 1972)

Fetherling, Doug, "The Old Pro in Action: An Encounter with Hugh Garner . . . ," *Saturday Night* 88: 25-27 (May 1973)

Garner, Hugh, "When I Was Very Young: Early Pages from an Autobiography," *Saturday Night* 88: 24-29 (August 1973)

DAVE GODFREY (1938-)

Death Goes Better with Coca-Cola (Toronto, Anansi, 1967) 115p.

Man Deserves Man. CUSO in Developing Countries, edited by —— and William McWhinney (Toronto, McGraw-Hill, 1968) xxii + 461p.

New Canadian Writing 1968 (Toronto, Clarke

Irwin, 1968) [With David Lewis Stein and Clark Blaise]

Gordon to Watkins to You. A Documentary: The Battle for Control of our Economy (Toronto, New Press, 1970) 261p. [With Mel Watkins]

The New Ancestors (Toronto, New Press, 1970) 392p.

Read Canadian. A Book about Canadian Books (Toronto, James Lewis & Samuel, 1972) 275p. [Co-edited with Robert Fulford and Abraham Rotstein]

Selected criticism:

Laurence, Margaret, "Ancestral Voices Prophesying . . . ," *The Mysterious East,* Fall Book Supplement, 1970, pp. 6-10 [Review of *The New Ancestors*]

Thomas A., "The Smell of Recognition," *Canadian Literature* No. 49: 78-80 (Summer 1971) [Review of *The New Ancestors*]

Cameron, Donald, "The Three People Inside Dave Godfrey," *Saturday Night* 86: 20-22 (September, 1971)

——, "Dave Godfrey: Myths and Gardens," *Conversations with Canadian Novelists,* Part II (Toronto, Macmillan, 1973) pp. 34-47

Gibson, Graeme, "Dave Godfrey," *Eleven Canadian Novelists* (Toronto, Anansi, 1973) pp. 151-179

OLIVER GOLDSMITH (1794-1861)

The Rising Village. A Poem (London, Sharpe, 1825) 48p.

The Rising Village, with Other Poems (Saint John, M'Millan, 1834) 144p.

The Autobiography of Oliver Goldsmith. Published for the First Time from the Original Manuscript of the Author of "The Rising Village," with Introduction and Notes by . . . Wilfrid E. Myatt . . . (Toronto, Ryerson, 1943) 76p.

The Manuscript Book of Oliver Goldsmith, Author of "The Rising Village," with Description and Comment by E. Cockburn Kyte (Toronto, Bibliographical Society of Canada, 1950) 13p.

The Rising Village, edited by Michael Gnarowski (Montreal, Delta, 1968) 47p.

Selected criticism:

Gammon, Donald B., *The Concept of Nature in Nineteenth Century Canadian Poetry, with Special Reference to Goldsmith, Sangster and Roberts* (Thesis, University of New Brunswick, 1948)

Pacey, Desmond, "The Goldsmiths and their Villages," *University of Toronto Quarterly* 21: 27-38 (October 1951)

Lande, Lawrence M., "Oliver Goldsmith," in his *Old Lamps Aglow* (Montreal, the Author, 1957) pp. 67-74

FREDERICK PHILIP GROVE (1879-1948)

Over Prairie Trails (Toronto, McClelland, 1922) 231p.

The Turn of the Year (Toronto, McClelland, 1923) 237p.

Settlers of the Marsh (New York, Doran, 1925) 341p.

A Search for America (Ottawa, Graphic, 1927) 448p.

Our Daily Bread. A Novel (New York, Macmillan, 1928) 390p.

It Needs To Be Said . . . (Toronto, Macmillan, 1929) 163p.

The Yoke of Life (New York, Smith, 1930) 355p.

Fruits of the Earth (Toronto, Dent, 1933) 335p.

Two Generations. A Story of Present Day Ontario (Toronto, Ryerson, 1939) 261p.

The Master of the Mill (Toronto, Macmillan, 1944) 393p.

In Search of Myself (Toronto, Macmillan, 1946) 457p.

Consider Her Ways (Toronto, Macmillan, 1947) 298p.

Tales from the Margin. The Selected Short Stories of ——. Edited with Introduction and Notes by Desmond Pacey (Toronto, Ryerson, 1971) x + 319p.

Selected criticism:

Perry, A. A., "Who's Who in Canadian Literature: Frederick Philip Grove," *Canadian Bookman* 12: 51-53 (March 1930)

Grove, F. P., "Apologia pro Vita et Opere Sua," *Canadian Forum* 11: 420-422 (August 1931)

Ayre, Robert, "Canadian Writers of Today—Frederick Philip Grove," *Canadian Forum* 12: 255-257 (April 1932)

Grove, F. P., "The Plight of Canadian Fiction: A Reply," *University of Toronto Quarterly* 7: 451-467 (July 1938)

Skelton, Isobel, "Frederick Philip Grove," *Dalhousie Review* 19: 147-163 (July 1939)

Eaton, Charles Ernest, *The Life and Works of Frederick Philip Grove* (Thesis, Acadia University, 1940)

Grove, F. P., "In search of myself," *University of Toronto Quarterly* 10: 60-67 (October 1940) [also in *Masks of Fiction*, edited by A. J. M. Smith (Toronto, McClelland, 1961) pp. 14-22]

——, "A Postscript to *A Search for America*," *Queen's Quarterly* 49:197-213 (Autumn 1942)

Pacey, Desmond, "Frederick Philip Grove," *Manitoba Arts Review* 3:28-41 (Spring 1943)

——, *Frederick Philip Grove* (Toronto, Ryerson, 1945) 150p.

Stanley, C., "Voices in the Wilderness," *Dalhousie Review* 25: 173-181 (July 1945)

Sandwell, B. K., "Frederick Philip Grove and the Culture of Canada," *Saturday Night* 61: 10 (November 24, 1945)

Clarke, G. H. "A Canadian Novelist and His Critic," *Queen's Quarterly* 53: 362-368 (August 1946)

Collin, W. E., "La Tragique Ironie de Frederick Philip Grove," *Gants du Ciel* 4: 15-40 (Winter 1946)

Grant, Gwendolen Margaret, *Frederick Philip Grove: Birth of the Canadian Novel* (Thesis, Dalhousie University, 1946)

Stanley, C. W., "Frederick Philip Grove," *Dalhousie Review* 25: 433-441 (January 1946)

Ferguson, Mildred (Mrs. G. M. Davies), *A Study of the Tragic Element in the Novels of Frederick Philip Grove* (Thesis, University of Manitoba, 1947)

Anon., "Canadian Dreiser," *Canadian Forum* 28: 46-47 (September 1948)

Pierce, Lorne, "Frederick Philip Grove (1871-1948)" in *Transactions of the Royal Society of Canada*, Third Series, Vol. 43: 113-119 (1948)

McCourt, E. A., "Spokesman of a Race?" in his *The Canadian West in Fiction* (Toronto, Ryerson, 1949) pp. 55-70

Phelps, Arthur L., "Frederick Philip Grove," in his *Canadian Writers* (Toronto, McClelland, 1951) pp. 36-42

Eggleston, Wilfrid, "Frederick Philip Grove," in *Our Living Tradition*, edited by Claude T. Bissell (Toronto, University of Toronto Press, 1957) pp. 105-127

Ross, Malcolm, Introduction to *Over Prairie Trails* by Frederick Philip Grove (Toronto, McClelland, 1957) pp. v-x [New Canadian Library No. 1]

Holliday, W. B., "Frederick Philip Grove: An Impression," *Canadian Literature* No. 3: 17-22 (Winter 1960)

Watters, R. E., Introduction to *The Master of the Mill* by Frederick Philip Grove (Toronto, McClelland, 1961) pp. vii-xii [New Canadian Library No. 19]

Pacey, Desmond, "Frederick Philip Grove: A Group of Letters," *Canadian Literature* No. 11: 28-38 (Winter 1962)

Wilson, Jennie M., *A Comparative Study of the Novels of Frederick Philip Grove and Theodore Dreiser* (Thesis, University of New Brunswick, 1962)

Nesbitt, Bruce H., "*The Seasons:* Grove's Unfinished Novel," *Canadian Literature* No. 18: 47-51 (Autumn 1963)

Saunders, Doris B., "The Grove Collection in the University of Manitoba: A Tentative Evaluation," in *Papers of the Bibliographical Society of Canada* (Toronto, the Society, 1963) pp. 7-20

Saunders, Thomas, "The Grove Papers," *Queen's Quarterly* 70: 22-29 (Spring 1963)

——, "A Novelist as Poet: Frederick Philip Grove," *Dalhousie Review* 43: 235-241 (Summer 1963)

Myles, Mrs. E., *The Self as Theme in Grove's Novels* (Thesis, University of Alberta, 1965)

Parks, M. G., Introduction to *Fruits of the Earth* by Frederick Philip Grove (Toronto, McClelland, 1965) pp. vii-xiii [New Canadian Library No. 49]

Saunders, Thomas, Introduction to *Settlers of The Marsh* by Frederick Philip Grove (Toronto, McClelland, 1966) pp. vii-xiii [New Canadian Library No. 50]

McLeod, Gordon D., *The Primeval Element in the Prairie Novels of Frederick Philip Grove* (Thesis, University of Manitoba, 1967)

McMullin, Stanley E., *The Promised Land*

Motif in the Works of Frederick Philip Grove
(Thesis, Carleton University, 1968)

Dunphy, John W., *The Technique of Fiction in
the Novels of F. P. Grove* (Thesis, University
of Alberta, 1969)

Rideout, E. Christopher, *The Women in the
Novels of Frederick Philip Grove* (Thesis,
University of Alberta, 1969)

Spettigue, Douglas, *Frederick Philip Grove*
(Toronto, Copp Clark, 1969) 175p.

Sutherland, Ronald, *Frederick Philip Grove*
(Toronto, McClelland, 1969) 64p.

Thompson, Joyce L., *Structural Technique in
the Fiction of Frederick Philip Grove* (Thesis,
University of Manitoba, 1969)

Birbalsingh, Frank, "Grove and Existentialism,"
Canadian Literature No. 43: 67-76 (Winter
1970)

Pacey, Desmond (ed.), *Frederick Philip Grove*
(Toronto, Ryerson, 1970) 202p.
[Critical Views on Canadian Writers]

Spettigue, Douglas, "Frederick Philip Grove in
Manitoba," *Mosaic* 3: 19-33 (Spring 1970)

McMullin, Stanley E., "Grove and the
Promised Land," *Canadian Literature*
No. 49: 10-19 (Summer 1971)

——Introduction to *A Search for America* ...by
Frederick Philip Grove (Toronto, McClelland,
1971) pp. ix-xv [New Canadian Library No. 76]

Pesando, Frank Joseph, *The Women in the
Prairie Novels of Frederick Philip Grove*
(Thesis, York University, 1971) 77p.

Sirois, A. "Grove et Rinquet: témoins d'une
époque," *Canadian Literature* No. 49: 20-27
(Summer 1971)

Spettigue, Douglas, " 'Frederick Philip
Grove': A Report from Europe," *Queen's
Quarterly* 78: 614-615 (Winter 1971)

Keith, W. J., "Grove's *Over Prairie Trails:* A
Re-Examination," *The Literary Half-Yearly*
13: 76-85 (July 1972)

Offenburger, Linda, *"In Search of Myself"* as
Bildungsroman (Thesis, University of
Alberta, 1972)

Pacey, Desmond, "In Search of Grove in
Sweden: A Progress Report," *Journal of
Canadian Fiction* 1: 69-73 (Winter 1972)

Spettigue, Douglas, "The Grove Enigma
Resolved," *Queen's Quarterly* 79: 1-2
(Spring 1972)

Dewar, K. C., "Technology and the Pastoral
Ideal in Frederick Philip Grove," *Journal of
Canadian Studies* 8: 19-28 (February 1973)

Keith, W. J., "F. P. Grove's 'Difficult' Novel:
The Master of the Mill," *Ariel, A Review of
International English Literature* 4: 34-48
(April 1973)

Spettigue, D. O., *FPG: The European Years*
(Ottawa, Oberon Press, 1973) 254p.

RALPH BARKER GUSTAFSON (1909-   )

The Golden Chalice (London, Nicholson &
Watson, 1935) 105p.

Alfred the Great (London, Joseph, 1937) 119p.

Epithalamium in Time of War (New York, the
Author, 1941) 11p.

Anthology of Canadian Poetry (English),
compiled by Ralph Gustafson
(Harmondsworth [England], Penguin Books,
1942) 123p.

Lyrics Unromantic (New York, the Author,
1942) 19p.

A Little Anthology of Canadian Poets, edited by
Ralph Gustafson (Norfolk, Conn., New
Directions, 1943) 26p.

Canadian Accent. A Collection of Stories and
Poems, edited by Ralph Gustafson
(Harmondsworth [England], Penguin Books,
1944) 144p.

Poetry and Canada. A Guide to Reading
(Ottawa, Canadian Legion Educational
Services, 1945) 16p.

Flight Into Darkness (New York, Pantheon,
1946) 96p.

The Penguin Book of Canadian Verse, edited,
with an Introduction and Notes, by Ralph
Gustafson (Harmondsworth [England],
Penguin Books, 1958) 225p.

Rivers Among Rocks (Toronto, McClelland,
1960) [68p.]

Rocky Mountain Poems (Vancouver, Klanak
Press, 1960) 36p.

Sift in an Hour Glass (Toronto, McClelland,
1966) 96p.

Ixion's Wheel (Toronto, McClelland, 1969) 128p.

Selected Poems (Toronto, McClelland, 1972)
128p.

Theme and Variations for Sounding Brass
(Sherbrooke, Quebec, Progressive Publications, 1972) 24p.

Selected criticism:

Scott, D. C., "Letter . . . to Ralph Gustafson [17 July 1945—about Lampman]," *Fiddlehead* No. 41: 12-14 (Summer 1959)

Dudek, Louis, "Two Canadian Poets: Ralph Gustafson and Eli Mandel," *Culture* 22: 145-151 (June 1961)

Wilson, Milton, Review of *Rocky Mountain Poems* and *Rivers Among Rocks*, in *University of Toronto Quarterly* 30: 390-393 (July 1961)

Mullins, S. G., "Ralph Gustafson's Poetry," *Culture* 22: 417-422 (December 1961)

Fetherling, Doug, "A Rare Sense of the Continuity of Things," *Saturday Night* 87: 56-57 (December 1972)

Lane, Travis, "The Fundamental Question About Poetry," *Fiddlehead* No. 96: 106-114 (Winter 1973)

THOMAS CHANDLER HALIBURTON (1796-1865)

A General Description of Nova Scotia (Halifax, Royal Canadian School, 1823) 200p.

An Historical and Statistical Account of Nova Scotia (Halifax, Joseph Howe, 1829) 2 vols.

The Clockmaker; or, The Sayings and Doings of Samuel Slick, of Slickville. First Series (Halifax, Joseph Howe, 1836), Second Series (London, Bentley, 1838); Third Series (London, Bentley, 1840)

The Bubbles of Canada (London, Bentley, 1839) 332p.

A Reply to the Report of The Earl of Durham. By a Colonist [pseud.] (London, Bentley, 1839) 91p.

The Letter-Bag of the Great Western; or, Life in a Steamer (London, Bentley, 1840) 323p.

The Attaché; or, Sam Slick in England. First Series (London, Bentley, 1843) 2 vols.; Second Series (London, Bentley, 1844) 2 vols.

The Old Judge; or, Life in a Colony (London, Colburn, 1849) 2 vols.

Rule and Misrule of the English in America (London, Colburn, 1851) 2 vols.

Traits of American Humor, By Native Authors, edited and adapted by the Author of "Sam Slick" (London, Colburn, 1852) 3 vols.

Sam Slick's Wise Saws and Modern Instances; or, What He Said, Did, or Invented (London, Hurst & Blackett, 1853) 2 vols.

The Americans at Home; or, Byeways,

Backwoods, and Prairies (London, Hurst & Blackett, 1854) 3 vols.

Nature and Human Nature (London, Hurst & Blackett, 1855) 2 vols.

An Address on the Present Condition, Resources, and Prospects of British North America . . . (London, Hurst & Blackett, 1857) 44p.

The Season Ticket (London, Bentley, 1860) 376p.

Fragments from Sam Slick, selected and arranged by Lawrence J. Burpee (Toronto, Musson, 1909) 91p.

Sam Slick, edited with a Critical Estimate and a Bibliography by Ray Palmer Baker (Toronto, McClelland, 1923) 420p.

Selections from Sam Slick (Judge Haliburton), edited by Paul A. W. Wallace (Toronto, Ryerson, 1923) 150p.

Jeffreys, Charles W., *Slick in Politics . . . ,* edited with an introduction by Lorne Pierce (Toronto, Ryerson, 1956) pp. xx + 204

The Old Judge, or Life in a Colony. A Selection of Sketches. Edited and Introduced by R. E. Watters (Toronto, Clarke Irwin, 1968) xxix + 247p.

The Sam Slick Anthology. Selected and Introduced by R. E. Watters; Text Edited for Modern Readers by W. S. Avis (Toronto, Clarke Irwin, 1969) xxix + 263p.

Selected criticism:

Montégut, Emile, "Un Humoriste Anglo-Américaine," *Revue des Deux Mondes* 5: 731-748 (February 1850)

Chasles, Philarète, "Samuel Slick," *Anglo-American Literature and Manners* (New York, 1852) pp. 222-248 [published originally in *Revue des Deux Mondes* 26: 306-326 (April 15, 1841)]

Crofton, F. Blake, *Haliburton, The Man and the Thinker* (Winslow, N. S., Anslow, 1889) 73p.

——, "Thomas Chandler Haliburton," *Atlantic Monthly* 69: 355-363 (March 1892)

Fenety, G. E., *Life and Times of the Hon. Joseph Howe* (Saint John, N.B., 1896) pp. 39-46

Calnek, W. A. and Savary, A. W., "Thomas Chandler Haliburton," in *History of the County of Annapolis* (Toronto, 1897) pp. 418-426

Chisholm, M. P. F., "Sam Slick and Catholic

Disabilities in Nova Scotia," *Catholic World* 64: 459-465 (January 1897)

Haliburton Club, *Haliburton, A Centenary Chaplet* (Toronto, 1897) 116p.

Baker, E. A., Introduction to *Sam Slick the Clockmaker* (London, Routledge, 1904) pp. xi-xvi

O'Brien, A. H., "Thomas Chandler Haliburton, 1796-1865: a Sketch and a Bibliography," *Transactions of the Royal Society of Canada,* Third Series, Vol. 3, Sec. 2: 43-66 (1909)

Mahon, A. Wylie, "Sam Slick Letters," *Canadian Magazine* 44: 75-79 (November 1914)

Wood, Ruth K., "The Creator of the First Yankee in Literature," *Bookman* (New York) 41: 152-160 (April 1915)

Howells, William Dean, "Editor's Easy Chair," *Harper's* 134: 442-445 (February 1917)

Baker, Ray Palmer, *A History of English-Canadian Literature to the Confederation* (Cambridge, Mass., Harvard University Press, 1920) pp. 68-97

Logan, J. D., *Scott and Haliburton* (Halifax, T. C. Allen, 1921) 22p.

——, "Why Haliburton Has No Successor," *Canadian Magazine* 57: 362-368 (September 1921)

Trent, W. P., "A Retrospect of American Humor," *Century,* New Series 41: 45-64 (November 1921)

Ross, Effie May, "Thomas Chandler Haliburton: Sam Slick, The Founder of American Humor," *Americana* 16: 62-70 (January 1922)

Baker, Ray Palmer (ed.), *Sam Slick* [A Selection . . .] (New York, Doran, 1923), Introduction, pp. 13-28

Chittick, V. L. O., *Thomas Chandler Haliburton* (New York, Columbia University Press, 1924) 695p.

Reid, R. L., "Sam Slick and his Creator," *British Columbia Monthly* 22: 3-6, 12-13 (January 1924)

Macdonald, Adrian, "Thomas Chandler Haliburton," in his *Canadian Portraits* (Toronto, Ryerson, 1925) pp. 52-63

Logan, J. D., *Thomas Chandler Haliburton* (Toronto, Ryerson, [192-?]) 176p.

Marquis, T. G., Biographical Sketch in *Sam Slick the Clockmaker* (Toronto, Musson, n.d.) "Centenary Edition" [1936?] pp. ix-xxii

Harvey, D. C., "The Centenary of Sam Slick," *Dalhousie Review* 16: 429-440 (January 1937)

Martell, J. S., "Creator of Sam Slick," *Journal of Education for Nova Scotia,* Series 4, Vol. 8: 63-67 (January 1937)

Anon., "Testi Americana: II, T. C. Haliburton (1855)," *Anglica* 1: 20-23 (April-June 1946)

Fullerton, A., "Funny Old Go-Getter," *Canadian Business* 19: 66-67, 90, 92 (April 1946)

Bond, W. H. (ed.), "The Correspondence of Thomas Chandler Haliburton and Richard Bentley," in *The Canadian Collection at Harvard University,* edited by W. I. Morse, Bulletin IV (1947) pp. 48-105

Avis, W. S., *The Speech of Sam Slick* (Thesis, Queen's University, 1950)

Chittick, V. L. O., "Persuasiveness of Sam Slick," *Dalhousie Review* 33: 88-101 (Summer 1953)

Seeley, S., "Clifton," *Canadian Geographic Journal* 48: 40-44 (January 1954)

MacDonald, D., "Sam Slick Slept Here," *Maclean's* 67: 22-23, 30, 35-36 (July 1, 1954)

Bengtsson, Elna, *The Language and Vocabulary of Sam Slick* (Upsala, Lundequistoka Bokhandeln, 1956)

Chittick, V. L. O., "Haliburton Postscript I: Ring-Tailed Yankee," *Dalhousie Review* 37: 19-36 (Spring 1957)

——, "Haliburton on Men and Things," *Dalhousie Review* 38: 55-65 (Spring 1958)

——, "Books and Music in Haliburton," *Dalhousie Review* 38: 207-221 (Summer 1958)

——, "Haliburton's 'Wise Saws' and Homely Imagery," *Dalhousie Review* 38: 348-363 (Autumn 1958)

McDougall, Robert L., Introduction to *The Clockmaker* (Toronto, McClelland, 1958) pp. ix-xvi [New Canadian Library No. 6]

——, "Thomas Chandler Haliburton," in *Our Living Tradition,* Second Series, edited by Robert L. McDougall (Toronto, University of Toronto Press, 1959) pp. 3-30

Chittick, V. L. O., "Many-Sided Haliburton," *Dalhousie Review* 41: 194-207 (Summer 1961)

——, "The Hybrid Comic: Origins of Sam Slick," *Canadian Literature* No. 14: 35-42 (Autumn 1962)

Frye, Northrop, "Haliburton: Mask and Ego," *Alphabet* No. 5: 58-63 (December 1962)

Chittick, V. L. O., "Haliburton as Member of Parliament," *University of Toronto Quarterly* 33: 78-88 (October 1963)

Harding, L. A. A., "Folk Language in Haliburton's Humour," *Canadian Literature* No. 24: 37-46 (Spring 1965)

Stuart-Stubbs, Basil, "On the Authorship of 'A General Description of Nova Scotia, 1823,' " *Papers of the Bibliographical Society of Canada* 4: 14-18 (1965)

Thompson, David Glen, *Thomas Chandler Haliburton and the Failure of Canadian Humour* (Thesis, St. John's College, University of Manitoba, 1965)

Van Tongerloo, R. R. *Thomas Chandler Haliburton: Satirical Humourist* (Thesis, St. John's College, University of Manitoba, 1966)

Wesley, Gordon, "Sam Slick's House," *Atlantic Advocate* 56: 40-45 (January 1966)

Belanger, Reynald, *Canadian Humorists: Leacock, Haliburton, Earle Birney, W. O. Mitchell* (Thesis, Université Laval, 1968)

Watters, R. E., Introduction to *The Old Judge; or Life in a Colony* by T. C. Haliburton (Toronto, Clarke Irwin, 1968) pp. vii-xxvi

Bissell, Claude T., "Haliburton, Leacock and the American Humourous Tradition," *Canadian Literature* No. 39: 5-19 (Winter 1969)

Rimmington, Gerald T., "The Geography of Haliburton's Nova Scotia," *Dalhousie Review* 48: 488-499 (Winter 1968/69)

Harding, L. A. A., "Compassionate Humour in Haliburton," *Dalhousie Review* 49: 223-228 (Summer 1969)

——"A Yankee at the Court of Judge Haliburton," *Canadian Literature* No. 39: 62-73 (Winter 1969)

Watters, R. E., Introduction to *The Sam Slick Anthology* by T. C. Haliburton. Text edited for modern readers by W. S. Avis (Toronto, Clarke Irwin, 1969) pp. vii-xviii. [Clarke Irwin Paperback No 37]

Liljegren, Sten Bodar, *Canadian History and Thomas Chandler Haliburton. Some Notes on Sam Slick* (Upsala, Lundequistska, 1969-70) 3 vol. [Upsala Canadian Studies 8, 9, & 10]

Fredericks, Carrie M., *The Development of Sam Slick: Twenty Years of Change in a Character, 1835-1855* (Thesis, Dalhousie University, 1970)

Harding, L. A. A., "Commodore of the Mackerel Fleet, or the Brine in Haliburton " *Dalhousie Review* 50: 517-527 (Winter 1970/71)

CHARLES HEAVYSEGE (1816-1876)

The Revolt of Tartarus. A Poem [anon.] (Liverpool, Hamilton, 1852) [also: Montreal, 1853)]

Sonnets. By the Author of "The Revolt of Tartarus" [pseud.] (Montreal, Rose, 1855)

Saul. A Drama, in Three Parts [anon.] (Montreal, Rose, 1857) 315p. [Second edition, revised: (Montreal, 1859) 328p. Also published under title: *Saul: A Drama in Three Parts*, by Charles Heavysege, new and revised edition (Boston, Fields Osgood, 1869) 436p.]

Count Filippo; or, The Unequal Marriage. A Drama in Five Acts, by the Author of *Saul* [pseud.] (Montreal, the Author, 1860) 153p.

The Dark Huntsman. A Dream [anon.] (Montreal, 1864) 8p.

The Owl [anon.] (Montreal, 1864) 4p.

The Advocate. A Novel (Montreal, Worthington, 1865) 125p.

Jephthah's Daughter [and Twenty Sonnets] (Montreal, Dawson, 1865) 74 + 20p.

Jezebel. A Poem in Three Cantos (Montreal, Golden Dog, 1972) 31p. [First published in *New Dominion Monthly* 1: 224-231 (January 1868)]

Selected criticism:

Anon., "The Modern British Drama," *North British Review* (August 1858) [an article attributed to Coventry Patmore. Partly reproduced in the Third Edition of *Saul* (1869)]

Anon., "Notice: The Life and Poems of Charles Heavysege," *New Dominion Monthly*, pp. 281-286 (September 1876)

Clark, Daniel, "The Poetry of Charles Heavysege, 1817-1876," *Canadian Monthly and National Review* 10: 127-134 (August 1876)

Anon., "Charles Heavysege," *Dominion Illustrated* 2: 263, 266 (April 27, 1889)

Burpee, Lawrence J., "Charles Heavysege," *Transactions of the Royal Society of Canada,*

Second Series, 7: 19-60 (1901)

Greenshields, E. B., "A Forgotten Poet,"
University Magazine (Montreal) 7: 343-359
(October 1908)

Baker, Ray Palmer, "Charles Heavysege," in
his *A History of English-Canadian Literature
to the Confederation* (Cambridge, Mass.,
Harvard University Press, 1920)
pp. 168-176

Montgomery, M. J., "Charles Heavysege,"
Canadian Poetry Magazine 5: 5-12
(September 1940)

Dale, T. R., *The Life and Works of Charles
Heavysege, 1817-1876* (Thesis, University
of Chicago, 1951)

——, "The Revolt of Charles Heavysege,"
University of Toronto Quarterly 22: 35-42
(October 1952)

——, "Our Greatest Poet—a Century Ago,"
Canadian Forum 37: 245-246 (February 1958)

Tait, Michael, "Playwrights in a Vacuum:
English-Canadian Drama in the Nineteenth
Century," *Canadian Literature* No. 16:
3-18 (Spring 1963)

Newton, Norman, "Classical Canadian Poetry
and the Public Muse," *Canadian Literature*
No. 51: 39-54 (Winter 1972)

DAVID HELWIG (1938-   )

Figures in a Landscape (Ottawa, Oberon, 1967)
217p.

The Sign of the Gunman (Ottawa, Oberon,
1969) 151p.

The Streets of Summer (Ottawa, Oberon, 1969)
188p.

The Day Before Tomorrow (Ottawa, Oberon,
1971) 183p.

Fourteen Stories High, edited by David
Helwig and Tom Marshall (Ottawa, Oberon,
1971) 172p.

The Best Name of Silence (Ottawa, Oberon,
1972) 140p.

72: New Canadian Studies, edited by David
Helwig and Joan Harcourt (Ottawa, Oberon,
1972) 135p.

Selected criticism:

Armand, Louis, Review of *Figures in a
Landscape, Fiddlehead* No. 78: 100-103
(January/February 1969)

Colombo, John R., *Rhymes and Reasons:
Nine Canadian Poets Discuss Their Work*
(Toronto, Holt Rinehart, 1971) 117p.

Wolfe, Morris, "The Spy Who Lived for the
Future," *Saturday Night* 86: 38-41 (December
1971) [Review of *The Day Before Tomorrow*]

Paget, Patricia, Review of *The Day Before
Tomorrow, Fiddlehead* No. 93: 103-107
(Spring 1972)

PAUL HIEBERT (1892-   )

Sarah Binks (Toronto, Oxford University Press,
1947) 182p.

Tower in Siloam (Toronto, McClelland, 1966)
213p.

Willows Revisited (Toronto, McClelland, 1967)
176p.

Selected criticism:

Fowke, Edith, Review of *Sarah Binks,
Canadian Forum* 27: 284 (March 1948)

Lamberton, C. L., Review of *Sarah Binks,
Dalhousie Review* 28: 195-196 (July 1948)

Wheeler, A. Lloyd, Introduction to *Sarah
Binks* by Paul Hiebert (Toronto, McClelland,
1964) pp. vii-xiii [New Canadian Library
No. 44]

Hiebert, Paul, "The Comic Spirit at Forty
Below Zero," *Mosaic* 3: 58-68 (Spring 1970)

HUGH HOOD (1928-   )

Flying a Red Kite (Toronto, Ryerson, 1962) 240p.

White Figure, White Ground (Toronto,
1964) 251p.

Around the Mountain. Scenes from Montreal
Life (Toronto, Peter Martin, 1967) 175p.

The Camera Always Lies (New York, Harcourt,
1967) 246p.

A Game of Touch (Toronto, Longmans, 1970)
192p.

Strength Down Centre. The Jean Béliveau
Story (Scarborough, Prentice-Hall, 1970)
192p.

The Fruit Man, the Meat Man & the Manager.
Stories (Ottawa, Oberon Press, 1971) 207p.

You Can't Get There from Here (Ottawa,
Oberon, 1972) 202p.

The Governor's Bridge is Closed (Ottawa Oberon, 1973) 144p.

Selected criticism:

Godfrey, Dave, "Line and Form," *Tamarack Review* No. 35: 96-101 (Spring 1965) [Review of *White Figure, White Ground*]

Warren, Michael, "Artist's Passion," *Canadian Literature* No. 25: 76-77 (Summer 1965) [Review of *White Figure, White Ground*]

Morgan, John, "Hugh Hood," *Montrealer* 41: 28, 32 (September 1967)

Duffy, Dennis, "Grace: the Novels of Hugh Hood," *Canadian Literature* No. 47: 10-25 (Winter 1971)

Grosskurth, Phyllis, "There's No Doubt He Loves the Place," *Saturday Night* 86: 42-43 (December 1971) [Review of *The Fruit Man, the Meat Man & the Manager*]

Hood, Hugh, "Sober Colouring: The Ontology of Super-Realism," *Canadian Literature* 49: 28-34 (Summer 1971) [An extract from this essay can be found in this edition of *Canadian Anthology*, pages 511-512]

Hale, Victoria G., "An Interview with Hugh Hood," *WLWE* [World Literature Written in English] 11: 35-41 (April 1972)

Thompson, Kent, Review of *The Fruit Man, the Meat Man & the Manager, Fiddlehead* No. 92: 116-123 (Winter 1972)

Cloutier, Pierre, "An Interview with Hugh Hood," *Journal of Canadian Fiction* 2: 49-52 (Winter 1973)

JOSEPH HOWE (1804-1873)

Address Delivered before the Halifax Mechanics' Institute, on the 5th of Nov. 1834 (Halifax, 1834) 23p.

May-Flowers of Nova Scotia (Halifax, June 8, 1840)

A Poem on the Same Subject [Sable Island] . (Bound with *Sable Island, its Past History, Present Appearance, Natural History, etc.* [Halifax, Wesleyan Conference, 1858] 34p.)

Confederation Considered in Relation to the Interests of the Empire (London, Stanford, 1866) 37p.

Address Delivered ... at the Howe Festival, Framingham, Mass., August 31, 1871

(Boston, Rockwell & Churchill, 1871) 21p. [reprinted in his *Poems and Essays* (1874) *q.v.*]

Address Delivered ... before the Young Men's Christian Association, Ottawa, Feb. 27, 1872 (Ottawa, Taylor, 1872) [reprinted in his *Poems and Essays* (1874) *q.v.*]

Poems and Essays (Montreal, Lovell, 1874) 341p.

The Speeches and Public Letters of the Hon. Joseph Howe, edited by William Annand, revised and augmented by J. A. Chisholm (Halifax, Chronicle Pub. Co., 1909) 2 vols.

The Heart of Howe: Selections from the Letters and Speeches ... , edited by D. C. Harvey (Toronto, Oxford, 1939) 197p.

Western and Eastern Rambles. Travel Sketches of Nova Scotia. Edited by M. G. Parks (Toronto, University of Toronto Press, 1973) 220p.

Selected criticism:

Taylor, F., "Hon. Joseph Howe," in *Portraits of British Americans,* edited by W. Notman (Montreal, Notman, 1865) pp. 291-308

Fenety, G. E., *Life and Times of the Hon. Joseph Howe* (Saint John, N.B., Carter, 1896) 376p.

Longley, J. W., *Joseph Howe* (Toronto, Morang, 1904) 307p.

Weaver, Emily P., "Homes and Haunts of Joseph Howe," *Canadian Magazine* 25. 195-202 (July 1905)

Grant, George M., *Joseph Howe,* Second Edition (Halifax, MacKinley, 1906) 110p.

Weaver, Emily P., "Recollections of Joseph Howe and His Family," *Canadian Magazine* 28: 278-281 (January 1907)

Chisholm, J. A., *Joseph Howe. A Sketch, with a Chronology* (Halifax, Chronicle Print., 1909) 44p.

Saunders, Edward Manning, *Three Premiers of Nova Scotia:* The Hon. J. W. Johnstone, The Hon. Joseph Howe, The Hon. Charles Tupper (Toronto, Briggs, 1909) 628p.

Carman, Francis A., "The Howe Papers," *Canadian Magazine* 45: 365-369 (September 1915)

Grant, William L., *The Tribune of Nova Scotia.* A Chronicle of Joseph Howe (Toronto, Glasgow Brook, 1915) 163p.

Burpee, L. J., "Joseph Howe and the Anti-

Confederation League," *Transactions of the Royal Society of Canada*, Third Series, Vol. 10, Sec. 2: 409-473 (1916)

Hassard, A. R., "Great Canadian Orators. II: Joseph Howe," *Canadian Magazine* 53: 423-430 (September 1919)

Baker, Ray P., "Joseph Howe and the 'Nova Scotian,'" in *A History of English-Canadian Literature to the Confederation* (Cambridge, Harvard University Press, 1920) pp. 57-67

Harvey, Daniel C., *Joseph Howe and Local Patriotism* (Winnipeg, 1921) 28p.

Logan, J. D., "Joseph Howe," *Canadian Magazine* 62: 19-25 (November 1923)

Macdonald, Adrian, "Joseph Howe," in his *Canadian Portraits* (Toronto, Ryerson, 1925) pp. 64-81

Rhodenizer, V. B., "Who's Who in Canadian Literature: Joseph Howe (1804-1873)," *Canadian Bookman* 8: 139-141 (May 1926)

Meagher, Sir Nicholas H., *The Religious Warfare in Nova Scotia, 1855-1860 . . .* Joseph Howe's Part in It and the Attitude of Catholics (Halifax, the Author, [1927?]) 193p.

Henderson, John, "Joseph Howe," in his *Great Men of Canada* (Toronto, Southam, 1928) pp. 131-153

Patterson, Hon. Judge, "Joseph Howe and the Anti-Confederation League," *Dalhousie Review* 10: 397-402 (October 1930)

Chisholm, J. A., "Hitherto Unpublished Letters of Joseph Howe," *Dalhousie Review* 12: 309-314 (October 1932)

———, "More Letters of Joseph Howe," *Dalhousie Review* 12: 481-496 (January 1933)

Roy, J. A., *Joseph Howe: A Study in Achievement and Frustration* (Toronto, Macmillan, 1935) 347p.

Munroe, David, "Joseph Howe as Man of Letters," *Dalhousie Review* 20: 451-457 (January 1941)

Raddall, T. H., "Joe Howe: Maritimes Gadfly," *Saturday Night* 67: 13, 49 (December 8, 1951)

Macdonald, D., "Nova Scotia's Strangest Son," *Maclean's* 66: 22, 30ff (April 1, 1953)

Thomas, W. K., "Canadian Political Oratory in the Nineteenth Century," *Dalhousie Review* 39: 377-389 (Autumn 1959)

Beck, J. M., "Joseph Howe: Opportunist or Empire-Builder," *Canadian Historical Review* 41: 185-202 (September 1960)

Lysyshyn, J., "Joseph Howe, Tribune of Nova Scotia," *Atlantic Advocate* 51: 65-68 (April 1961)

Beck, J. M., "Joseph Howe," in *Our Living Tradition,* Fourth Series, edited by Robert L. McDougall (Toronto, University of Toronto Press, 1962) pp. 3-30

Lumsden, Susan, *Joseph Howe: Editor of the "Novascotian"* (Thesis, Carleton University, 1966)

Bruce, Harry, "Making a Tourist Buck from Joe Howe's Bones," *Saturday Night* 88: 11-13 (July 1973)

GEORGE JOHNSTON (1913-   )

The Cruising Auk (Toronto, Oxford University Press, 1959) 72p.

Home Free (Toronto, Oxford University Press, 1966) 64p.

Happy Enough. Poems, 1935-1972 (Toronto, Oxford University Press, 1972) 154p.

Selected criticism:

Dobbs, Kildare, Review of *The Cruising Auk,* in *Tamarack Review* No. 12: 99-101 (Summer 1959)

Nicol, Eric, Review of *The Cruising Auk,* in *Canadian Literature* No. 1: 83-84 (Summer 1959)

Frye, Northrop, Review of *The Cruising Auk,* in *University of Toronto Quarterly* 29: 440-441 (July 1960)

Whalley, George, "George Johnston" [A review article] *Canadian Literature* No. 35: 85-90 (Winter 1968)

Jones, L. W., "The Cruising Auk and the World Below," *Canadian Literature* No. 48: 28-36 (Spring 1971)

D. G. JONES (1929-   )

Frost on the Sun (Toronto, Contact Press, 1957) 46p.

The Sun is Axeman (Toronto, University of Toronto Press, 1961) 70p.

Phrases from Orpheus (Toronto, Oxford University Press, 1967) 88p.

Butterfly on Rock. A Study of Themes and
Images in Canadian Literature (Toronto,
University of Toronto Press, 1970) 197p.

Selected criticism:

Reaney, James, Review of *Frost on the Sun,*
in *Canadian Forum* 38: 95 (July 1958)
Webb, Phyllis, Review of *The Sun is Axeman,*
in *Canadian Literature* No. 12: 58-59
(Spring 1962)
Wilson, Milton, Review of *The Sun is Axeman,*
in *University of Toronto Quarterly* 31:
437-439 (July 1962)
Barbour, Douglas, Review of *Butterfly on Rock,*
Dalhousie Review 50: 417-419 (Autumn 1971)
New, W. H., Review of *Butterfly on Rock,*
Canadian Literature No. 47: 94-97 (Winter
1971)

LEO KENNEDY (1907-   )

The Shrouding. Poems (Toronto, Macmillan,
1933) 59p.
New Provinces. Poems of Several Authors
[edited by F. R. Scott] (Toronto, Macmillan,
1936) pp. 15-25

Selected criticism:

Collin, W. E., "Leo Kennedy," *Canadian
Forum* 14: 24-27 (October 1933)
Pratt, E. J., "New Notes in Canadian Poetry,"
Canadian Comment 3: 26-27 (February 1934)
Collin, W. E., "The Man of April," in his
The White Savannahs (Toronto, Macmillan,
1936) pp. 267-284
Schultz Gregory Peter, *The Periodical Poetry
of A. J. M. Smith, F. R. Scott, Leo
Kennedy, A. M. Klein, and Dorothy Livesay,
1925-1950* (Thesis, University of Western
Ontario, 1957)
Ross, G. Arthur, *Three Minor Canadian Poets:
Louis A. Mackay, Leo Kennedy, and Raymond
Knister* (Thesis, University of Alberta, 1969)
Stevens, Peter (ed.), *On the McGill Movement:
A. J. M. Smith, F. R. Scott, and Leo
Kennedy* (Toronto, Ryerson, 1969) pp. 21-50
McMullen, Lorraine, "Leo Kennedy,"
Le Chien d'or/The Golden Dog No. 1,
unpaged [16 pages]

A. M. KLEIN (1909-1972)

New Provinces. Poems of Several Authors
[edited by F. R. Scott] (Toronto, Macmillan,
1936) pp. 29-48
Hath Not a Jew (New York, Behrman's
Jewish Book House, 1940) 116p.
The Hitleriad (New York, New Directions,
1944) 30p.
Poems (Philadelphia, Jewish Publishing Society,
1944) 82p.
Seven Poems (Montreal, the Author, 1947) 8p.
Huit poèmes canadiens (en anglais)
(Montreal, the Author, 1948) 16p.
The Rocking Chair and Other Poems
(Toronto, Ryerson, 1948) 56p.
The Second Scroll (New York, Knopf, 1951)
198p.

Selected criticism:

Edel, Leon, "Abraham M. Klein," *Canadian
Forum* 12: 300-302 (May 1932)
Collin, W. E., "The Spirit's Palestine," in
his *The White Savannahs* (Toronto,
Macmillan, 1936) pp. 207-231
Lewisohn, Ludwig, Foreword to *Hath Not a
Jew . . . by A. M. Klein* (New York,
Behrman's Jewish Book House, 1940)
pp. v-viii
Edel, Leon, "Poetry and the Jewish Tradition,"
Poetry (Chicago) 30. 51 53 (April 1941)
Smith, A. J. M., "Abraham Moses Klein,"
Gants du Ciel 11: 67-81 (Printemps 1946)
Sutherland, John, "The Poetry of
A. M. Klein," *Index* Vol. 1, No. 6: 8-12
(August 1946)
Régimbal, A., "Artistes israélites au Canada
français," *Relations* 8: 184-185 (June 1948)
Crawley, Alan, "Notes on A. M. Klein,"
Contemporary Verse 28: 20 (Summer 1949)
Sutherland, John, "Canadian Comment,"
Northern Review 2: 30-34 (August-
September 1949)
Dudek, Louis, "A. M. Klein," *Canadian
Forum* 30: 10-12 (April 1950)
Spurgeon, D. C., "Whither Green-Haired
Poet?" *Saturday Night* 65: 12, 46
(May 23, 1950)
Schultz, Gregory Peter, *The Periodical Poetry
of A. J. M. Smith, F. R. Scott, Leo
Kennedy, A. M. Klein, and Dorothy Livesay,*

1925-1950 (Thesis, University of Western Ontario, 1957)

Pacey, Desmond, "A. M. Klein," in his *Ten Canadian Poets* (Toronto, Ryerson, 1958) pp. 254-292

Steinberg, M. W., "A Twentieth Century Pentateuch," *Canadian Literature* No. 2: 37-46 (Autumn 1959)

Wilson, Milton, "Klein's Drowned Poet," *Canadian Literature* No. 6: 5-17 (Autumn 1960)

Gotlieb, Phyllis, "Klein's Sources," *Canadian Literature* No. 26: 82-84 (Autumn 1965)

Livesay, Dorothy, "The Polished Lens: Poetic Techniques of Pratt and Klein," *Canadian Literature* No. 25: 33-42 (Summer 1965)

Marshall, T. A., "Theorems Made Flesh: Klein's Poetic Universe" *Canadian Literature* No. 25: 43-52 (Summer 1965)

Matthews, John, "Abraham Klein and the Problem of Synthesis, *Journal of Commonwealth Literature* 1: 149-163 (September 1965)

Steinberg, M. W., "Poet of a Living Past," *Canadian Literature* No. 25: 5-20 (Summer 1965)

Waddington, Miriam, "Signs on a White Field: Klein's *Second Scroll*," *Canadian Literature* No. 25: 21-32 (Summer 1965)

——"The Cloudless Days: the Radical Poems of A. M. Klein," *Tamarack Review* No. 45: 65-92 (Autumn 1967)

Fischer, G. K., "A. M. Klein's Forgotten Play," *Canadian Literature* No. 43: 42-53 (Winter 1970)

Marshall, Tom (ed.), *On A. M. Klein* (Toronto, Ryerson, 1970) xxv + 192p. [Critical Views on Canadian Writers]

Waddington, Miriam, *A. M. Klein* (Toronto, Copp Clark, 1970) 145p. [Studies in Canadian Literature]

Barrie, Brian Douglas, *The Structure and Genre of A. M. Klein's "The Second Scroll"* (Thesis, University of New Brunswick, 1972)

Fischer, Gretl K., *A. M. Klein: Religious Philosophy and Ethics in his Writings* (Thesis, McGill University, 1972)

Marshall, Tom, "Portrait of a People: Some Afterthoughts about the Landscape of A.M. Klein," *Jewish Dialog*, Rosh Hashanah, 1972, pp. 32-33

Nadel, Ira, "The Absent Prophet in Canadian Jewish Fiction," *English Quarterly* 5: 83-92 (Spring 1972)

Spiro, Solomon, *A. M. Klein, "The Second Scroll"* (Thesis, Sir George Williams University, 1972).

Staskevicius, Aronas, *Quest for Identity in Jewish-Canadian Literature: Klein and Richler* (Thesis, McMaster University, 1972)

Waddington, Miriam, "On A. M. Klein," *Canadian Forum* 52: 4-5 (October/November 1972)

ARCHIBALD LAMPMAN (1861-1899)

Among the Millet and Other Poems (Ottawa, Durie, 1888) 151p.

Lyrics of Earth (Boston, Copeland & Day, 1895) 56p.

Two Poems. By Archibald Lampman and Duncan Campbell Scott . . . . Issued to Their Friends at Christmastide, 1896 [N.p., the Authors, 1896] 3p.

These Poems. By Archibald Lampman and Duncan Campbell Scott . . . (N.p., the Authors, 1897) 6p.

Alcyone (Ottawa, Ogilvy, 1899) 110p.

The Poems of Archibald Lampman, edited with a Memoir by Duncan Campbell Scott (Toronto, Morang, 1900) 473p.

Little Book, Thy Pages Stir. An Autograph Poem [facsim.] (Toronto, Ryerson, 1923) 3p.

Happiness: a Preachment . . . Carrying to You the Best Wishes of the Ryerson Press, Christmas, 1925 (Toronto, Ryerson, 1925) 15p.

Lyrics of Earth: Sonnets and Ballads, with an Introduction by Duncan Campbell Scott (Toronto, Musson, 1925) 276p.

At the Long Sault and Other New Poems, with Foreword by Duncan Campbell Scott, Introduction by E. K. Brown (Toronto, Ryerson, 1943) 45p.

Selected Poems of Archibald Lampman, chosen and with a Memoir by Duncan Campbell Scott (Toronto, Ryerson, 1947) 176p.

Archibald Lampman's Letters to Edward William Thomson (1890-1898), edited with an Introduction, Annotations, a Bibliography with Notes, and [Lampman's] "Essay on Happiness," by Arthur S. Bourinot (Ottawa, Bourinot, 1956) 74p.

At the Mermaid Inn, Conducted by A. Lampman, W. W. Campbell, Duncan C. Scott. Being Selections from Essays . . . which Appeared in the Toronto *Globe*, 1892-1893, edited by Arthur S. Bourinot (Ottawa, Bourinot, 1958) 96p.

Some Letters of Duncan Campbell Scott, Archibald Lampman, and Others, edited by Arthur S. Bourinot (Ottawa, Bourinot, 1959) 63p.

Selected criticism:

"Fidelis" [pseud.] (Agnes Maule Machar), "Among the Millet," *The Week* 6: 251-252 (March 22, 1889)

Howells, W. D., "Editor's Study," *Harper's* 78: 821-823 (April 1889)

Barry, L. E. F., "Prominent Canadians: Archibald Lampman," *The Week* 8: 298-300 (April 10, 1891)

Stringer, Arthur, "A Glance at Lampman," *Canadian Magazine* 2: 545-548 (April 1894)

Crawford, A. W., "Archibald Lampman," *Acta Victoriana* 17: 77-81 (December 1895)

Scott, Duncan Campbell, Memoir, in *The Poems of Archibald Lampman* (Toronto, Morang, 1900) pp. xi-xxv

Wendell, W. L., "Sketch," *Bookman* (N.Y.) 11: 515-526 (August 1900)

Marshall, John, "Archibald Lampman," *Queen's Quarterly* 9: 63-79 (July 1901)

Burpee, L. J., "Archibald Lampman" in his *A Little Book of Canadian Essays* (Toronto, Musson, 1909) pp. 30-42

Untermeyer, L., "Archibald Lampman and the Sonnet," *Poet Lore* 20: 432-437 (November 1909)

Logan, J. D., "Literary Group of '61," *Canadian Magazine* 37: 555-563 (October 1911)

Munday, Don, "Soul-Standards of Archibald Lampman," *Westminster Hall* 4: 15-17 (October 1914)

Muddiman, Bernard, "Archibald Lampman," *Queen's Quarterly* 22: 233-243 (January 1915)

Unwin, G. H., "The Poetry of Lampman," *University Magazine* 16: 55-73 (February 1917)

Macdonald, E. R., "A Little Talk about Lampman," *Canadian Magazine* 52: 1012-1016 (April 1919)

Voorhis, Ernest, "The Ancestry of Archibald Lampman, Poet," *Transactions of the Royal Society of Canada*, Third Series, Vol. 15, Sec. 2: 103-121 (1921)

Macdonald, Adrian, "Archibald Lampman," in his *Canadian Portraits* (Toronto, Ryerson, 1925) pp. 220-230

Scott, Duncan Campbell, Introduction to *Lyrics of Earth* by Archibald Lampman (Toronto, Musson, 1925) pp. 3-47

Guthrie, Norman G., *The Poetry of Archibald Lampman* (Toronto, Musson, 1927) 58p.

Knister, Raymond, "The Poetry of Archibald Lampman," *Dalhousie Review* 7: 348-361 (October 1927)

Stevenson, O. J., "The Song of the Spirit," in his *A People's Best* (Toronto, Musson, 1927) pp. 127-134

Swift, S. C., "Lampman and Lecomte de Lisle," *Canadian Bookman* 9: 261-264 (September 1927)

Burton, Jean, "Archibald Lampman's Poetry of Release," *Willison's Monthly* 3: 425-427 (April 1928)

Connor, Carl Y., *Archibald Lampman, Canadian Poet of Nature* (Montreal, Carrier, 1929) 210p.

Brennan, M. W., *The Prosody of Archibald Lampman* (Thesis, Queen's University, 1931)

Kennedy, Leo, "Archibald Lampman," *Canadian Forum* 13: 301, 303 (May 1933)

Collin, W. E., "Natural Landscape," in his *The White Savannahs* (Toronto, Macmillan, 1936) pp. 3-40 [also, greatly abridged, in *Masks of Poetry*, edited by A. J. M. Smith (Toronto, McClelland, 1962) pp. 60-64]

Stringer, Arthur, "Wild Poets I've Known: Archibald Lampman," *Saturday Night* 56: 29 (May 24, 1941)

Brown, E. K., Foreword to *At the Long Sault and Other New Poems* by Archibald Lampman (Toronto, Ryerson, 1943) pp. vii-xxix

Scott, Duncan Campbell, "Archibald Lampman," *Educational Record* (Quebec) 59: 221-225 (October-December 1943)

Brown, E. K., "Archibald Lampman," in his *On Canadian Poetry*, revised edition (Toronto, Ryerson, 1944) pp. 88-118

Gustafson, Ralph, "Among the Millet,"

Northern Review 1: 26-34 (February-March 1947)

Scott, Duncan Campbell, Memoir, in *Selected Poems of Archibald Lampman* (Toronto, Ryerson, 1947) pp. xiii-xxvii

Bourinot, Arthur S., "Archibald Lampman and What Some Writers Have Said of Him," *Canadian Author and Bookman* 26: 20-22 (1950) [also in his *Five Canadian Poets* (Montreal, Quality Press, 1956) pp. 4-7]

Sutherland, John, "Edgar Allan Poe in Canada," *Northern Review* 4: 22-37 (February-March 1951)

Pacey, Desmond, "A Reading of Lampman's 'Heat,' " *Culture* 14: 292-297 (September 1953)

Beattie, Munro, "Archibald Lampman," in *Our Living Tradition*, edited by Claude T. Bissell (Toronto, University of Toronto Press, 1957) pp. 63-88

Bourinot, Arthur S., *The Letters of Edward William Thomson to Archibald Lampman (1891-1897)*, edited with Notes, a Bibliography, and Other Material on Thomson and Lampman (Ottawa, Bourinot, 1957) 49p.

Dudek, Louis, "Significance of Lampman," *Culture* 18: 277-290 (September 1957)

Pacey, Desmond, "Archibald Lampman," in his *Ten Canadian Poets* (Toronto, Ryerson, 1958) pp. 114-140

Watt, Frank W., "The Masks of Archibald Lampman," *University of Toronto Quarterly* 27: 169-184 (January 1958)

Scott, Duncan Campbell, "Copy of a Letter by Duncan Campbell Scott to Ralph Gustafson, 17 July, '45 [about Lampman]," *Fiddlehead* No. 41: 12-14 (Summer 1959)

Nesbitt, Bruce, "Matthew Arnold in Canada: A Dialogue Begun?" *Culture* 28: 53-54 (mars 1967)

Gnarowski, Michael (ed.), *On Archibald Lampman* (Toronto, Ryerson, 1969) xxvii + 224p. [Critical Views on Canadian Writers Series]

Davies, Barry, *The Alien Mind: A Study of the Poetry of Archibald Lampman* (Thesis, University of New Brunswick, 1970)

Miller, Judith, *Towards a Canadian Aesthetic: Descriptive Colour in the Landscape Poetry of Duncan Campbell Scott, Archibald Lampman, and William Wilfred Campbell* (Thesis, University of Waterloo, 1970)

Campbell, Brian R., *Motion in the Poems of Archibald Lampman* (Thesis, University of Alberta, 1971)

Davies, Barry, "Lampman, Radical Poet of Nature," *English Quarterly* 4: 33-43 (Spring 1971)

Haines, V. Y., "Archibald Lampman: This or That," *Revue de l'Université d'Ottawa* 41: 455-471 (July-September 1971)

Jobin, M., *Archibald Lampman* (Thesis, McGill University, 1971)

Nesbitt, Bruce, "A Gift of Love: Lampman and Life," *Canadian Literature* No. 50: 35-40 (Autumn 1971)

Ower, J., "Portraits of the Landscape as Poet: Canadian Nature as Aesthetic Symbol in Three Confederation Writers," [Lampman, Campbell, Roberts] *Journal of Canadian Studies* 6: 27-32 (February 1971)

Davies, Barry, "A Lampman Manuscript," *Journal of Canadian Fiction* 1: 55-58 (Spring 1972)

——, "Answering Harmonies," *Humanities Association Bulletin* 23: 57-68 (Spring 1972)

—— "Lampman and Religion," *Canadian Literature* No. 56: 40-60 (Spring 1973)

Djwa, Sandra, "Lampman's Fleeting Vision," *Canadian Literature* No. 56: 22-39 (Spring 1973)

MARGARET LAURENCE (1926-   )

A Tree for Poverty. Somali Poetry and Prose (British Protectorate of Somaliland, 1954) [Reprinted: Hamilton, Ont., McMaster University Library Press, 1971, 146p.]

This Side Jordan (Toronto, McClelland, 1960) xi + 281p.

The Prophet's Camel Bell (Toronto, McClelland, 1963) 241p. [Published in the United States as *New Wind in a Dry Land* (New York, Knopf, 1964)]

The Tomorrow-Tamer (Toronto, McClelland, 1963) 244p.

The Stone Angel (Toronto, McClelland, 1964) 308p.

A Jest of God (Toronto, McClelland, 1966) 202p. [Also as: *Rachel, Rachel* (New York, Popular Library, 1966) 175p.]

Long Drums and Cannons (Toronto, Macmillan, 1968) 209p. [On Nigerian fiction and drama]

Now I Lay Me Down (London, Panther Books, 1968) 188p.

The Fire-Dwellers (Toronto, McClelland, 1969) 308p.

A Bird in the House (Toronto, McClelland, 1970) 207p.

Jason's Quest (Toronto, McClelland, 1970) 224p. [Juvenile]

Selected criticism:

Kreisel, Henry, "The African Stories of Margaret Laurence," *Canadian Forum* 41: 8-10 (April 1961)

Robertson, George, "An Artist's Progress," *Canadian Literature* No. 21: 53-55 (Summer 1964)

Read, S. E., "Margaret Laurence, The Stone Angel," *British Columbia Library Quarterly* 28: 41-44 (July-October 1964)

Callaghan, Barry, "The Writing of Margaret Laurence," *Tamarack Review* No. 36: 45-51 (Summer 1965)

Anonymous, "Laurence of Manitoba," *Canadian Author and Bookman* 41: 4-6 (Winter 1966)

Read, S. E., "The Maze of Life, the Work of Margaret Laurence," *Canadian Literature* No. 27: 5-14 (Winter 1966)

Boyd, Bonita, *Patterns and Parallels in the Fiction of Margaret Laurence* (Thesis, Acadia University, 1968)

New, William H., Introduction to *The Stone Angel* by Margaret Laurence, (Toronto, McClelland, 1968) pp. iii-x [New Canadian Library No. 59]

Gotlieb, Phyllis, "On Margaret Laurence," *Tamarack Review* No. 52: 76-80 (Fall 1969)

Laurence, Margaret, "Ten Years' Sentences," *Canadian Literature* No. 41: 10-16 (Summer 1969)

Thomas, Clara, *Margaret Laurence* (Toronto, McClelland, 1969) 64p.

Kreisel, Henry, "Familiar Landscape," *Tamarack Review* No. 55: 91-92, 94 (1970)

Laurence, Margaret, "Sources," *Mosaic* 3: 80-84 (Spring 1970)

Swayze, Walter, "The Odyssey of Margaret Laurence," *English Quarterly* 3: 7-17 (Fall 1970)

Thomas, Clara, Introduction to *The Tomorrow-Tamer* by Margaret Laurence (Toronto, McClelland, 1970) pp. xi-xvii [New Canadian Library No. 70]

Thompson, Kent, Review of *A Bird in the House, Fiddlehead* No. 84: 108-111 (March/April 1970)

Bowering, George, "That Fool of a Fear: Notes on *A Jest of God*," *Canadian Literature* No. 50: 41-56 (Autumn 1971)

Darby, Clare Alexander, *The Novels and Short Stories of Margaret Laurence* (Thesis, University of New Brunswick, 1971)

Gom, Leona, *The Manawaka Fiction of Margaret Laurence* (Thesis, University of Alberta, 1971)

McLay, C. M., "Every Man Is an Island: Isolation in *A Jest of God*," *Canadian Literature* No. 50: 57-68 (Autumn 1971)

Thomas, Clara, "Proud Lineage: Willa Cather and Margaret Laurence," *Canadian Review of American Studies* 2: 1-12 (Spring 1971)

Wigmore, D., "Margaret Laurence: The Woman Behind the Writing," *Chatelaine* 44: 28-29, 52, 54 (February 1971)

Djwa, Sandra, "False Gods and the True Covenant: Thematic Continuity between Margaret Laurence and Sinclair Ross," *Journal of Canadian Fiction* 1: 43-50 (Fall 1972)

Forman, Denyse and Una Parameswaran, "Echoes and Refrains in the Canadian Novels of Margaret Laurence," *Centennial Review* 16: 233-253 (1972)

Froese, Edna, *The Guilty Heroes in the Novels of Hugh MacLennan and Margaret Laurence* (Thesis, University of Saskatchewan, 1972)

Pell, Barbara, *Margaret Laurence's Treatment of the Heroine* (Thesis, University of Windsor, 1972)

Sokolowski, Thelma K., *Exile and Return in the Fiction of Margaret Laurence* (Thesis University of Alberta, 1972)

Thomas, Clara, "A Conversation about Literature: An Interview with Margaret Laurence and Irving Layton," *Journal of Canadian Fiction* 1: 65-69 (Winter 1972)

——, "The Short Stories of Margaret Laurence," *WLWE* [World Literature Written in English] 11: 25-33 (April 1972)

Bevan, Allan, Introduction to *The Fire-Dwellers* by Margaret Laurence (Toronto, McClelland, 1973) pp. v-xiv [New Canadian Library No. 87]

Cameron, Donald, "Margaret Laurence: The Black Celt Speaks of Freedom," *Conversations with Canadian Novelists* Part I (Toronto, Macmillan, 1973) pp. 96-115

Gibson, Graeme, "Margaret Laurence," *Eleven Canadian Novelists* (Toronto, Anansi, 1973) pp. 151-179

Pesando, Frank, "In the Nameless Land — The Use of Apocalyptic Mythology in the Writings of Margaret Laurence," *Journal of Canadian Fiction* 2: 53-58 (Winter 1973)

IRVING LAYTON (1912-   )

Here and Now (Montreal, First Statement Press, 1945) 44 p.

Now Is the Place. Stories and Poems (Montreal, First Statement Press, 1948) 57p.

The Black Huntsmen (Toronto, Contact Press, 1952) 56p.

Cerberus. Poems by Louis Dudek, Irving Layton, Raymond Souster (Toronto, Contact Press, 1952) 98p.

Canadian Poems 1850-1952, edited by Louis Dudek and Irving Layton, revised second edition (Toronto, Contact Press, 1953) 160p.

Love the Conqueror Worm (Toronto, Contact Press, 1953) 49p.

In the Midst of My Fever ([Palma de Mallorca, Spain], Divers Press, 1954) 39p.

The Long Pea-Shooter (Montreal, Laocoön Press, 1954) 68p.

The Blue Propeller (Montreal, Contact Press, 1955) 50p.

The Cold Green Element (Toronto, Contact Press, 1955) 56p.

The Bull Calf and Other Poems (Toronto, Contact Press, 1956) 49p.

The Improved Binoculars. Selected Poems, with an Introduction by William Carlos Williams (Highlands, [N.C.], J. Williams, 1956) 106p. [second edition, with thirty additional poems, 1957]

Music on a Kazoo (Toronto, Contact Press, 1956) 59p.

A Laughter in the Mind (Highlands, [N.C.], J. Williams, 1958) 54p. [second printing, with twenty additional poems (Montreal, Editions d'Orphée, 1959) 97p.]

A Red Carpet for the Sun (Toronto, McClelland, 1959) 240p.

Poems for 27 Cents. Edited by Irving Layton (Montreal, priv. print., 1961) 32p.

The Swinging Flesh [Stories and Poems] (Toronto, McClelland, 1961) 189p.

Love Where the Nights are Long. Canadian Love Poems, edited by Irving Layton (Toronto, McClelland, 1962) 78p.

Balls for a One-Armed Juggler (Toronto, McClelland, 1963) xxii + 121p.

The Laughing Rooster (Toronto, McClelland, 1964) 112p.

Collected Poems (Toronto, McClelland, 1965) xxii + 353p.

Periods of the Moon. Poems (Toronto, McClelland, 1967) 127p.

The Shattered Plinth (Toronto, McClelland, 1968) 95p.

Selected Poems, edited by Wynne Francis (Toronto, McClelland, 1969) 139p.

The Whole Bloody Bird. Obs, aphs and Pomes (Toronto, McClelland, 1969) 155p.

The Collected Poems of Irving Layton [Special Edition] (Toronto, McClelland, 1971) 589p. [Limited edition, with a Harold Town lithograph portrait of the poet.]

Nail Polish (Toronto, McClelland, 1971) 87p.

Engagements: The Prose of Irving Layton, edited by Seymour Mayne (Toronto, McClelland, 1972) xvi + 336p.

Lovers and Lesser Men (Toronto, McClelland, 1973) 109p.

Selected criticism:

Smith, A. J. M., "The Recent Poetry of Irving Layton"—Reply by Louis Dudek, "Layton Now and Then," *Queen's Quarterly* 62: 587-591 (Winter 1956); 63: 291-293 (Summer 1956)

Williams, William Carlos, "A Note on Layton," in *The Improved Binoculars* by Irving Layton (Highland, [N.C.], J. Williams, 1956) pp. 9-10

Dudek, Louis, "Layton on the Carpet," *Delta* No. 9: 17-19 (October-December 1959)

Layton, Irving, Foreword, in his *A Red Carpet for the Sun* (Toronto, McClelland, 1959) pp. v-viii [also in *Masks of Poetry,* edited by A. J. M. Smith (Toronto, McClelland, 1962) pp. 139-142]

Mandel, Eli, Review of Layton's *A Red Carpet for the Sun,* in *Tamarack Review* No. 13: 124-126 (Autumn 1959)

Marcotte, Gilles, "Le Poète Irving Layton,

vu d'ici," *Le Devoir,* samedi, 17 octobre, 1959, p. 11

Wilson, Milton, "Turning New Leaves (1)," *Canadian Forum* 39: 231-232 (January 1960)

Hale, Barrie, "Baggy-Pants Rhetoric" [review of *The Swinging Flesh* by Irving Layton], *Canadian Literature* No. 9: 66-67 (Summer 1961)

Ellenbogen, George, "An Open Letter to Irving Layton," *Cataract* Vol. 1, No. 3 (July 1962)

Layton, Irving, "Correspondence," *Canadian Forum* 41: 281-282 (March 1962); 42: 41-42 (May 1962)

——, "An Open Letter to Louis Dudek," *Cataract* Vol. 1, No. 2 (Winter 1962)

Mathews, Robin, "Correspondence," *Canadian Forum* 42: 58 (June 1962)

Layton, Irving, Foreword, in his *Balls for a One-Armed Juggler* (Toronto, McClelland, 1963) pp. xviii-xxii

Taaffe, Gerald, "Diary of a Montreal Newspaper Reader," *Tamarack Review* No. 27: 49-62 (Spring 1963)

Carruth, Hayden, "That Heaven-Sent Lively Rope-Walker, Irving Layton," *Tamarack Review* No. 39: 68-73 (Spring 1966)

Woodcock, George, "A Grab at Proteus: Notes on Irving Layton," *Canadian Literature* No. 28: 5-21 (Spring 1966)

Francis, Wynne, "Irving Layton," *Journal of Commonwealth Literature* 3: 34-48 (July 1967)

Lund, K. A., "Satyric Layton," *Canadian Author and Bookman* 42: 8 (Spring 1967)

Reif, Eric A., *Irving Layton: The Role of the Poet* (Thesis, University of Toronto, 1967)

Mandel, Eli, *Irving Layton* (Toronto, Forum House, 1969) 82p.

Adams, Richard, *The Poetic Theories of Irving Layton. A Study in Polarities* (Thesis, University of New Brunswick, 1971)

Smith, Patricia K., "Irving Layton and the Theme of Death," *Canadian Literature* No. 48: 6-15 (Spring 1971)

Waterston, Elizabeth, "Haloing Snake," *Alphabet* Nos. 18-19: 24-29 (June 1971)

——, "Irving Layton: Apocalypse in Montreal," *Canadian Literature* No. 48: 16-24 (Spring 1971)

Doyle, Mike, "The Occasions of Irving Layton," *Canadian Literature* No. 54: 70-83 (Autumn 1972)

Smith, Patricia K., *The Theme of Death in the Poetry of Irving Layton* (Thesis, Sir George Williams University, 1972)

Thomas, Clara, "A Conversation about Literature: An Interview with Margaret Laurence and Irving Layton," *Journal of Canadian Fiction* 1: 65-69 (Winter 1972)

Reznitsky, Lawrence J., "Interview with Irving Layton," *Le Chien d'Or/The Golden Dog* No. 1, unpaged [15pp.]

STEPHEN LEACOCK (1869-1944)

Elements of Political Science (London, Constable, 1906) 417p.

... Baldwin, Lafontaine, Hincks; Responsible Government (Toronto, Morang, 1907) 371p. [later revised and expanded under title: *Mackenzie, Baldwin, Lafontaine, Hincks* (Toronto, Oxford, 1926) 395p.]

Greater Canada, An Appeal. Let Us No Longer Be a Colony (Montreal, Montreal News, 1907) 10p.

Literary Lapses. A Book of Sketches (Montreal, Gazette Printing Co., 1910) 125p.

Nonsense Novels (London, Lane, 1911) 230p.

Sunshine Sketches of a Little Town (London, Lane, 1912) 264p.

Behind the Beyond, and Other Contributions to Human Knowledge (London, Lane, 1913) 195p.

Adventurers of the Far North. A Chronicle of the Frozen Seas (Toronto, Glasgow Brook, 1914) 152p.

Arcadian Adventures With the Idle Rich (London, Lane, 1914) 310p.

The Dawn of Canadian History. A Chronicle of Aboriginal Canada and the Coming of the White Man (Toronto, Glasgow Brook, 1914) 112p.

The Mariner of St. Malo. A Chronicle of the Voyages of Jacques Cartier (Toronto, Glasgow Brook, 1914) 125p.

The Methods of Mr. Sellyer. A Book Store Study (New York, Lane, 1914) 37p.

The Marionette's Calendar. Rhymes by Stephen Leacock, Drawings by A. H. Fish (London, Lane, 1915) 14p.

Moonbeams from the Larger Lunacy (New York, Lane, 1915) 282p.

"Q." A Farce in One Act [collaboration with B. M. Hastings] (New York, French, 1915) 23p.

Essays and Literary Studies (New York, Lane, 1916) 310p.

Further Foolishness. Sketches and Satires on the Follies of the Day (New York, Lane, 1916) 312p.

The Greatest Pages of American Humor. Selected and Discussed . . . (New York, Doubleday, 1916) 293p.

Frenzied Fiction (New York, Lane, 1918) 240p.

The Hohenzollerns in America; With the Bolsheviks in Berlin and Other Impossibilities (New York, Lane, 1919) 269p.

The Unsolved Riddle of Social Justice (New York, Lane, 1920) 152p.

Winsome Winnie, and Other New Nonsense Novels (New York Lane, 1920) 243p.

My Discovery of England (London, Lane, 1922) 219p.

College Days (New York, Dodd Mead, 1923) 169p.

Over the Footlights, and Other Fancies (London, Lane, 1923) 278p.

The Garden of Folly (Toronto, Gundy, 1924) 282p.

The Proper Limitations of State Interference (Toronto, 1924) 14p.

Winnowed Wisdom. A New Book of Humour (New York, Dodd Mead, 1926) 288p.

Short Circuits (Toronto, Macmillan, 1928) 336p.

The Iron Man and the Tin Woman, With Other Such Futurities . . . (New York, Dodd Mead, 1929) 309p.

Economic Prosperity in the British Empire Toronto, Macmillan, 1930) 246p.

Laugh with Leacock (New York, Dodd Mead, 1930) 339p. [Reprinted 1961. Canadian edition: (Toronto, McClelland, 1968)]

The Leacock Book. Selections . . . Arranged with an Introduction by Ben Travers (London, Lane, 1930) 248p.

Wet Wit and Dry Humour, Distilled from the Pages of Stephen Leacock (New York, Dodd Mead, 1931) 260p.

Afternoons in Utopia. Tales of the New Time (Toronto, Macmillan, 1932) 240p.

Back to Prosperity: The Great Opportunity of the British Conference (Toronto, Macmillan, 1932) 103p.

The Dry Pickwick and Other Incongruities (London, Lane, 1932) 271p.

Lahontan's Voyages, edited with Introduction and Notes . . . (Ottawa, Graphic, 1932) 348p.

Mark Twain (London, Davies, 1932) 167p.

Winsome Winnie, A Romantic Drama, by V. C. Clinton-Baddeley and S. B. Leacock (London, Gowans, 1932) 31p.

Charles Dickens, His Life and Work (London, Davies, 1933) 275p.

Stephen Leacock's Plan to Relieve the Depression in 6 Days, To Remove It in 6 Months, To Eradicate It in 6 Years (Toronto, Macmillan, 1933) 18p.

The Greatest Pages of Charles Dickens. A Biographical Reader and a Chronological Selection . . . With a Commentary. (New York, Doubleday, 1934) 233p.

Lincoln Frees the Slaves (New York, Putnam, 1934) 178p.

The Perfect Salesman, edited by E. V. Knox (New York, McBride, 1934) 151p.

The Pursuit of Knowledge. A Discussion of Freedom and Compulsion in Education (New York, Liveright, 1934) 48p.

Humor, Its Theory and Technique, with Examples and Samples. (New York, Dodd Mead, 1935) 268p.

Funny Pieces. A Book of Random Sketches (New York, Dodd Mead, 1936) 292p.

Hellements of Hickonomics, in Hiccoughs of Verse Done in Our Social Planning Mill (New Yord, Dodd Mead, 1936) 84p.

Here are My Lectures and Stories (New York, Dodd Mead, 1937) 251p.

Humour and Humanity. An Introduction to the Study of Humour (London, Butterworth, 1937) 254p. [Home University Library No. 184]

My Discovery of the West. A Discussion of East and West in Canada (Toronto, Allen, 1937) 272p.

Model Memoirs and Other Sketches from Simple to Serious (New York, Dodd Mead, 1938) 316p.

All Right, Mr. Roosevelt (Canada and the United States) (Toronto, Oxford, 1939) 40p.

Too Much College; or, Education Eating Up Life, with Kindred Essays in Education and Humour (New York, Dodd Mead, 1939) 255p.

Laugh Parade. A New Collection of the Wit and Humor of Stephen Leacock (New York, Dodd Mead, 1940) 326p.

Canada: the Foundations of Its Future
(Montreal, Distillers Corp. Ltd., 1941) 257p.

Montreal: Seaport and City (New York,
Doubleday, 1942) 340p.

My Remarkable Uncle, and Other Sketches
(New York, Dodd Mead, 1942) 313p.

*Our Heritage of Liberty, Its Origin, Its
Achievement, Its Crisis*. A Book for War
Time (New York, Dodd Mead, 1942) 86p.

Happy Stories, Just to Laugh At (New York,
Dodd Mead, 1943) 240p.

How to Write (New York, Dodd Mead, 1943)
261p.

"My Old College" 1843-1943 ([Montreal], the
Author, 1943) 16p.

Canada and the Sea (Montreal, A. M. Beatty,
1944) 63p.

Last Leaves (Toronto, McClelland, 1945) 213p.

*While There is Time: the Case Against Social
Catastrophe* (Toronto, McClelland, 1945)
136p.

The Boy I Left Behind Me (New York,
Doubleday, 1946) 184p.

The Leacock Roundabout. A Treasury of the
Best Works of Stephen Leacock (New
York, Dodd Mead, 1946) 422p.

The Bodley Head Leacock, edited with
Introduction by J. B. Priestley (London,
Bodley Head, 1957) 464p. [published in
Canada as *The Best of Leacock* (Toronto,
McClelland, 1957) 464p.]

Perfect Lover's Guide and Other Stories.
Second edition (Moscow [Russia], Foreign
Languages Publishing House, 1960) 350p.
[Introduction and Notes in Russian]

The Unicorn Leacock, edited by James Reeves
(London, Hutchinson, 1960) 191p.

A Feast of Stephen. A Leacock Anthology,
edited by Robertson Davies (Toronto,
McClelland, 1970) 160p.

Selected criticism:

Leacock, Stephen, *My Memories and Miseries
as a Schoolmaster* (Toronto, Upper Canada
College Endowment Fund, n.d.) 15p.

Macphail, Andrew, "Stephen Leacock," in
*The Yearbook of Canadian Art, 1913-   *,
compiled by the Arts and Letters Club of
Toronto (Toronto, Dent, n.d.) pp. 1-7

Leacock, Stephen, "Humor As I See It,"
Maclean's Magazine 29: 11-13, 111, 113 (May
1916)

Collins, J. P., "Professor Leacock, Ph.D.:
Savant and Humorist," *Bookman* (London)
51: 39-44 (November 1916) [also in *Living
Age* 291: 800 ff. (December 30, 1916)]

Caldwell, W., "A Visit to a Canadian Author,"
Canadian Magazine 59: 55-60 (May 1922)

Hind, C. Lewis, "Stephen Leacock," in his
More Authors and I (New York, Dodd Mead,
1922) pp. 180-185

McArthur, Peter, *Stephen Leacock* (Toronto,
Ryerson, 1923) 176p.

Braybrooke, Patrick, [on Leacock's *My
Discovery of England*], in his *Peeps at the
Mighty* (London, Drane, 1927) pp. 130-146

Murphy, Bruce, "Stephen Leacock—the
Greatest Living Humorist," *Ontario Library
Review* 12: 67-69 (February 1928)

Masson, T. L., "Stephen Leacock," in his
Our American Humorists (New York, 1931)
pp. 209-229

L., R. T. [Charles A. M. Vining], "Mr.
Leacock," *Maclean's* 47: 10 (August 1, 1934)

McGill University Library School, *A
Bibliography of Stephen Butler Leacock*
(Montreal, McGill, 1935) 36p.

Wheelwright, J., "Poet as Funny Man,"
Poetry 50: 210-215 (July 1937)

Feibleman, James Kerr, "Criticism of Modern
Theories of Comedy," in his *In Praise of
Comedy*. A Study in Its Theory and
Practice (London, Allen & Unwin, 1939)
pp. 123-167

Anon., "Stephen Butler Leacock, Select
Bibliography . . . Contributions to the
Social Sciences," *Canadian Journal of
Economics* 10: 228-230 (May 1944)

Day, J. P., "Professor Leacock at McGill,"
Canadian Journal of Economics 10: 226-228
(May 1944)

Innis, Harold, "Stephen Butler Leacock
(1869-1944)," *Canadian Journal of Economics*
10: 216-226 (May 1944)

Clements, C., "An Evening with Stephen
Leacock," *Catholic World* 159: 236-241
(June 1944)

Nimmo, Barbara, "Stephen Leacock
(December 30, 1869-March 28, 1944),"
in *Last Leaves* by Stephen Leacock (Toronto,
McClelland, 1945) pp. vii-xx

Sedgewick, G. G., "Stephen Leacock as a
Man of Letters," *University of Toronto
Quarterly* 15: 17-26 (October 1945)

Edgar, Pelham, "Stephen Leacock," *Queen's Quarterly* 53: 173-184 (Summer 1946)

Leacock, Stephen, *The Boy I Left Behind Me* (New York, Doubleday, 1946) 184p.

Ross, David W., *Stephen Leacock, Scholar and Humorist* (Thesis, Columbia University, 1947)

Sandwell, B. K., "He Made Humour Almost Respectable," *Canadian Author and Bookman* 23: 15-16 (Fall 1947)

Lower, Arthur, "The Mariposa Belle," *Queen's Quarterly* 58: 220-226 (Summer 1951)

Pacey, Desmond, "Leacock as a Satirist," *Queen's Quarterly* 58: 208-219 (Summer 1951)

Phelps, Arthur L., "Stephen Leacock," in his *Canadian Writers* (Toronto, McClelland, 1951) pp. 70-76

Sandwell, B. K., "Leacock Recalled: How the 'Sketches' Started," *Saturday Night* 67: 7 (August 23, 1952)

Frayne, T. G., "Erudite Jester of McGill," *Maclean's* 66: 18-19, 37-39 (January 1, 1953)

Lomer, Gerhard R., *Stephen Leacock: A Check-List and Index of His Writings* (Ottawa, National Library, 1954) 153p.

Mikes, George, "Stephen Leacock," in his *Eight Humorists* (London, Wingate, 1954) pp. 41-65

Milford, Barney, "There's Still a Lot of Leacock in Orillia," *Maclean's* 68: 18-19, 80-82 (February 15, 1955)

Curry, Ralph L., "Leacock and Benchley: An Acknowledged Literary Debt," *American Book Collector* 7: 11-15 (March 1957)

Davies, Robertson, Introduction to *Literary Lapses* by Stephen Leacock (Toronto, McClelland, 1957) pp. vii-ix [New Canadian Library No. 3]

——, "Stephen Leacock," in *Our Living Tradition*, edited by Claude T. Bissell (Toronto, University of Toronto Press, 1957) pp. 128-149

Gilliss, K. E., *Stephen Leacock as a Satirist* (Thesis, University of New Brunswick, 1957)

Priestley, J. B., Introduction to *The Bodley Head Leacock* (London, Bodley Head, 1957) pp. 9-13 [published in Canada under title: *The Best of Leacock* (Toronto, McClelland, 1957)]

Curry, Ralph L., "Stephen Butler Leacock, A Check List," *Bulletin of Bibliography* 22: 106-109 (January-April 1958) [supplements Lomer's *Check-List*]

——, Introduction to *Arcadian Adventures With the Idle Rich* by Stephen Leacock (Toronto, McClelland, 1959) pp. vii-xi [New Canadian Library No. 10]

——, *Stephen Leacock: Humorist and Humanist* (Garden City, N.Y., Doubleday, 1959) 383p.

——, "Unknown Years of Stephen Leacock," *Maclean's* 72: 20-21, 45-47 (July 4, 1959); 72: 26-27, 34 (July 18, 1959)

Miller, Margaret J., "Stephen Leacock," in her *Seven Men of Wit* (London, Hutchinson, 1960)

Ross, Malcolm, Introduction to *Sunshine Sketches of a Little Town* by Stephen Leacock (Toronto, McClelland, 1960) pp. ix-xvi [New Canadian Library No. 15]

Watt, Frank W., "Critic or Entertainer: Leacock and the Growth of Materialism," *Canadian Literature* No. 5: 33-42 (Summer 1960)

Watters, R. E., "A Special Tang: Stephen Leacock's Canadian Humour," *Canadian Literature* No. 5: 21-32 (Summer 1960) [reprinted above, pages 608-615]

O'Hagan, Howard, "Stephie," *Queen's Quarterly* 68: 135-146 (Spring 1961)

Whalley, George, Introduction to *My Discovery of England* by Stephen Leacock (Toronto, McClelland, 1961) pp. vii-xiv [New Canadian Library No. 28]

Walsh, Joan, *Stephen Leacock as an American Humorist* (Thesis, University of Toronto, 1962)

Beharriell, S. Ross, Introduction to *Nonsense Novels* by Stephen Leacock (Toronto, McClelland, 1963) pp. vii-xii [New Canadian Library No. 35]

Cameron, D. A., "The Enchanted Houses: Leacock's Irony," *Canadian Literature* No. 23: 31-44 (Winter 1965)

Dooley, D. J., Introduction to *Frenzied Fiction* by Stephen Leacock (Toronto, McClelland, 1965) pp. vii-xiii [New Canadian Library No. 48]

Stevens, John, Introduction to *My Remarkable Uncle* (Toronto, McClelland, 1965) pp. vii-xii [New Canadian Library No. 53]

Cameron, Donald A., "Stephen Leacock: the Novelist Who Never Was," *Dalhousie*

Review 46: 15-28 (Spring 1966)

Graham C. R., "Common Sense Economics: The Unbranded Economist," *Industrial Canada* 66: 17-21 (January 1966)

Cameron, Donald A., *Faces of Leacock*. An Appreciation (Toronto, Ryerson, 1967) 176p.

——, "Stephen Leacock: the Boy Behind the Arras," *Journal of Commonwealth Literature* 3: 3-18 (July 1967)

Dooley, D. J., Introduction to *Short Circuits* by Stephen Leacock (Toronto, McClelland, 1967) pp. ix-xiv [New Canadian Library No. 57]

Belanger, Reynald, *Canadian Humorists: Leacock, Haliburton, Earle Birney, W. O. Mitchell* (Thesis, Université Laval, 1968)

Cole, D. W., Introduction to *Further Foolishness* by Stephen Leacock (Toronto, McClelland, 1968) pp. v-xii [New Canadian Library No. 60]

Bissell, Claude T., "Haliburton, Leacock and the American Humourous Tradition," *Canadian Literature* No. 39: 5-19 (Winter 1969)

Cameron, Donald, Introduction to *Behind the Beyond . . .* by Stephen Leacock (Toronto, McClelland, 1969) [New Canadian Library No. 67]

Crooks, Grace, "A Taste for Humour," *Canadian Library Journal* 26: 222-228 (May/June 1969)

Magee, W. H., "Stephen Leacock, Local Colourist," *Canadian Literature* No. 39: 34-42 (Winter 1969)

Davies, Robertson, *Stephen Leacock* (Toronto, McClelland, 1970) 63p. [Canadian Writers Series]

Kimball, Elizabeth, *The Man in the Panama Hat*. Reminiscences of My Uncle . . . (Toronto, McClelland, 1970) 174p.

Legate, David M., *Stephen Leacock* (Toronto, Doubleday, 1970) 296p.

Robinson, J. M., Introduction to *Last Leaves* by Stephen Leacock (Toronto, McClelland, 1970) pp. vi-xii [New Canadian Library No. 69]

Sharman, Vincent, "The Satire of Stephen Leacock's *Sunshine Sketches*," *Queen's Quarterly* 78: 261-267 (Summer 1971)

Savage, David, "Leacock on Survival: *Sunshine Sketches* Sixty Years After," *Journal of Canadian Fiction* 1: 64-67 (Fall 1972)

Spettigue, Douglas, "A Partisan Reading of Leacock," *The Literary Half-Yearly* 13: 171-180 (July 1972)

Berger, Carl, "The Other Mr. Leacock," *Canadian Literature* No. 55: 23-40 (Winter 1973)

DOUGLAS LE PAN (1914-   )

The Wounded Prince and Other Poems (London, Chatto, 1948) 39p.

The Net and the Sword (London, Chatto, 1953) 56p.

The Deserter [A Novel] (Toronto, McClelland, 1964) 298p.

Selected criticism:

Brown, E. K., Review of *The Wounded Prince*, in *University of Toronto Quarterly* 18: 257-258 (April 1949)

Anon., "Poet at Work," *Time* (Canadian Edition) 56: 17 (September 11, 1950)

Galloway, David, Review of *The Net and the Sword*, in *Fiddlehead* 20: 13-14 (February 1954)

Frye, Northrop, Review of *The Net and the Sword*, in *University of Toronto Quarterly* 23: 256-258 (April 1954)

Davies, Marilyn, "The Bird of Heavenly Airs: Thematic Strains in Douglas Le Pan's Poetry," *Canadian Literature* No. 15: 27-39 (Winter 1963)

Le Pan, Douglas, "The Dilemma of the Canadian Author," *Atlantic Monthly* 214: 160-164 (November 1964)

Lougheed, W. C., "The Defeat of Egoism: A Critique of *The Deserter*," *Queen's Quarterly* 72: 552-562 (Autumn 1965)

Hamilton, S. C., "European Emblem and Canadian Image: A Study of Douglas LePan's Poetry," *Mosaic* 3: 62-73 (Winter 1970)

DOROTHY LIVESAY (1909-   )

Green Pitcher (Toronto, Macmillan, 1928) 16p.

Signpost (Toronto, Macmillan, 1932) 61p.

Day and Night. Poems (Toronto, Ryerson, 1944) 48p.

Poems for People (Toronto, Ryerson, 1947) 40p.

Raymond Knister: Collected Poems, with a Memoir by Dorothy Livesay (Toronto, Ryerson, 1949) 45p.

Call My People Home (Toronto, Ryerson, 1950) 24p.

New Poems (Toronto, Emblem Books, 1955) 15p.

Selected Poems 1926-1956, with an Introduction by Desmond Pacey (Toronto, Ryerson, 1957) xxii + 82p.

The Colour of God's Face [Vancouver, the Author, 1965?] [11p.]

The Unquiet Bed (Toronto, Ryerson, 1967) 65p.

The Documentaries (Toronto, Ryerson, 1968) 56p.

Disasters of the Sun (Burnaby, B.C., Blackfish, 1971) 8p.

Plainsongs (Fredericton, Fiddlehead, 1969) 32p. [Extended and revised ed., 1971. 48p.]

Collected Poems: The Two Seasons (Toronto, McGraw-Hill, 1972) 368p.

A Winnipeg Childhood (Winnipeg, Peguis Publishers, 1973)

Selected criticism:

Collin, W. E., "My New Found Land," in his *The White Savannahs* (Toronto, Macmillan, 1936) pp. 147-173

Stephan, Ruth, "A Canadian Poet," *Poetry* (Chicago) 65: 220-222 (January 1945)

Pratt, E. J., "Dorothy Livesay," *Gants du Ciel* 11: 61-65 (Printemps 1946)

Crawley, Alan, "Dorothy Livesay," in *Leading Canadian Poets,* edited by W. P. Percival (Toronto, Ryerson, 1948) pp. 117-124

Weaver, Robert, "The Poetry of Dorothy Livesay," *Contemporary Verse* 26: 18-22 (Fall 1948)

Pacey, Desmond, Introduction to *Selected Poems of Dorothy Livesay 1926-1956* (Toronto, Ryerson, 1957) pp. xi-xix

Schultz, Gregory Peter, *The Periodical Poetry of A. J. M. Smith, F. R. Scott, Leo Kennedy, A. M. Klein, and Dorothy Livesay, 1925-1959* (Thesis, University of Western Ontario, 1957)

O'Donnell, Kathleen, *Dorothy Livesay* (Thesis, University of Montreal, 1959)

Steinberg, M. W., "Dorothy Livesay: Poet of Affirmation," *British Columbia Library*

Quarterly 24: 9-13 (October 1960)

Livesay, Dorothy, "Song and Dance," *Canadian Literature* No. 41: 40-48 (Summer 1969)

Gibbs, Jean, "Dorothy Livesay and the Transcendentalist Tradition," *Humanities Research Bulletin* 21: 24-39 (Spring 1970)

Livesay, Dorothy, "A Prairie Sampler," *Mosaic* 3: 85-92 (Spring 1970)

——, "The Documentary Poem: A Canadian Genre," in *Contexts of Canadian Criticism,* edited by Eli Mandel (Chicago, University of Chicago Press, 1971) pp. 267-281

Stevens, Peter, "Dorothy Livesay: The Love of Poetry," *Canadian Literature* No. 47: 26-43 (Winter 1971)

——, "Out of the Silence and Across The Distance," *Queen's Quarterly* 78: 579-591 (Winter 1971)

O'Donnell, Kathleen, "Dorothy Livesay and Simone Routier: A Parallel Study," *Humanities Association Bulletin* 23: 28-37 (Fall 1972)

MALCOLM LOWRY (1909-1957)

Ultramarine (London, Cape, 1933) 276p. [new and revised edition, with an Introductory Note by Margerie Lowry (London, Cape, 1962) 203p.]

Under the Volcano (New York, Reynal, 1947) 375p.

[Poems], in *The Book of Canadian Poetry,* revised edition, edited by A. J. M. Smith (Toronto, Gage, 1948) pp. 371-375

Hear Us O Lord from Heaven Thy Dwelling Place (Philadelphia, Lippincott, 1961) 283p.

Selected Poems, edited by Earle Birney with the assistance of Margerie Lowry (San Francisco, City Lights Books, 1962) 79p.

"Lunar Caustic" [novella], in *Paris Review* No. 29:15-72 (Winter/Spring 1963)

Selected Letters, edited by Harvey Breit and Margerie Bonner Lowry (New York, Lippincott, 1965) xix+459p.

Dark as the Grave Wherein My Friend is Laid, edited by Douglas Day and Margerie Lowry (Toronto, General Publishing Ltd., 1968) xxiii + 255p.

Lunar Caustic, edited by Earle Birney and

Margerie Lowry (London, Cape, 1968) 76p.

October Ferry to Gabriola, edited by Margerie Lowry (Toronto, Macmillan, 1970) 338p.

Selected criticism:

Woodburn, John, Review of *Under the Volcano,* in *Saturday Review of Literature* 30: 9-10 (February 22, 1947)

Mayberry, George, Review of *Under the Volcano,* in *New Republic* 116: 35-36 (February 24, 1947)

Clark, Eleanor, Review of *Under the Volcano,* in *Nation* (N.Y.) 164: 335-336 (March 22, 1947)

Flint, R. W., Review of *Under the Volcano,* in *Kenyon Review* 9: 474-477 (Summer 1947)

Heilman, Robert B., Review of *Under the Volcano,* in *Sewanee Review* 55: 483-492 (Summer 1947)

Woodcock, George, "Malcolm Lowry's 'Under the Volcano,'" *Modern Fiction Studies* 4: 151-156 (Summer 1948)

——, "On the Day of the Dead," *Northern Review* 6: 15-21 (December-January 1953/54)

Françillon, Clarisse, "Souvenirs sur Malcolm Lowry," *Les Lettres Nouvelles* 5: 588-603 (novembre 1957)

Bonnefoi, Geneviève, "Souvenir de Quauhnahuac," *Les Lettres Nouvelles* new series 5: 94-108 (juillet-août 1960)

Carroy, Jean-Roger, "Obscur Présent, le feu...," *Les Lettres Nouvelles* new series 5: 83-88 (juillet-août 1960)

Fouchet, Max-Pol., "Non se puede...,"*Les Lettres Nouvelles* new series 5: 21-25 (juillet-août 1960) [reprinted in *Canadian Literature* No. 8:25-28 (Spring 1961)]

Françillon, Clarisse, "Malcolm, mon ami," *Les Lettres Nouvelles* new series 5: 8-19 (juillet-août 1960)

Spriel, Stephen, "Le Cryptogramme Lowry," *Les Lettres Nouvelles* new series 5: 67-81 (juillet-août 1960)

McConnell, William, "Recollections of Malcolm Lowry," *Canadian Literature* No. 6: 24-31 (Autumn 1960)

Birney, Earle, "Glimpses into the Life of Malcolm Lowry," *Tamarack Review* No. 19: 35-41 (Spring 1961)

——, "The Unknown Poetry of Malcolm Lowry," *British Columbia Library Quarterly* 24: 33-40 (April 1961);

Birney, Earle and Margerie Lowry, "Bibliography of Malcolm Lowry: Part I: Works by Malcolm Lowry," *Canadian Literature* No. 8: 81-88 (Spring 1961); "Part II: Works about Malcolm Lowry," *Canadian Literature* No. 9: 80-84 (Summer 1961)

Heilman, Robert B., "The Possessed Artist and the Ailing Soul," *Canadian Literature* No. 8: 7-16 (Spring 1961)

Kirk, Downie, "More than Music: Glimpses of Malcolm Lowry," *Canadian Literature* No. 8: 31-38 (Spring 1961)

Lowry, Malcolm, "Letters from Malcolm Lowry," *Canadian Literature* No. 8: 39-46 (Spring 1961)

——, "Preface to a Novel," *Canadian Literature* No. 9: 23-29 (Summer 1961) [Translation of the preface to *Au-dessous du Volcan* (Paris, Club Français du Livre, 1949; reprint: Paris, Correa, 1960). The preface was prepared in French by Clarisse Françillon from Lowry's English notes (since lost) while she was working on the French translation of the novel. This preface is here translated back into English by George Woodcock.]

Woodcock, George, "Malcolm Lowry as Novelist," *British Columbia Library Quarterly* 24: 25-32 (April 1961)

——, "Under Seymour Mountain," *Canadian Literature* No. 8: 3-6 (Spring 1961)

Birney, Earle, "First Supplement to Malcolm Lowry Bibliography," *Canadian Literature* No. 11: 90-95 (Winter 1962)

Lowry, Malcolm, "Letter from Lowry," *Canadian Forum* 42: 62-63 (June 1962)

Birney, Earle,"Against the Spell of Death," *Prairie Schooner* 37: 328-333 (Winter 1963/64)

Day, David, "Of Tragic Joy," *Prairie Schooner* 37: 354-362 (Winter 1963/64)

Edelstein, J. M., "On Re-Reading *Under the Volcano,*" *Prairie Schooner* 37:336-339 (Winter 1963/64)

Hirschman, Jack, "Kabbala/Lowry, etc.," *Prairie Schooner* 37: 347-353 (Winter 1963/64)

Knickerbocker, Conrad, "The Voyages of Malcolm Lowry," *Prairie Schooner* 37: 301-314 (Winter 1963/64)

Lowry, Malcolm, "Three Unpublished Letters," *Prairie Schooner* 37: 321-327 (Winter 1963/64)

Markson, David, "Myth in *Under the Volcano*," *Prairie Schooner* 37: 339-346 (Winter 1963/64)

Noxon, Gerald, "Malcolm Lowry: 1930," *Prairie Schooner* 37: 315-320 (Winter 1963/64)

Birney, Earle, "Second Supplement to Malcolm Lowry Bibliography," *Canadian Literature* No. 19: 83-89 (Winter 1964)

Chittick, V. L. O., "*Ushant's* Malcolm Lowry," *Queen's Quarterly* 71: 67-75 (Spring 1964)

Kilgallin, Anthony R., "Eliot, Joyce and Lowry," *Canadian Author and Bookman* 41: 3-4, 6 (Winter 1965)

——, "Faust and *Under the Volcano*," *Canadian Literature* No. 26: 43-54 (Autumn 1965)

Magee, A. Peter, "The Quest for Love," *Emeritus* 1: 24-29 (Spring 1965)

Thomas, Hilda L., *Malcolm Lowry's "Under the Volcano": An Interpretation* (Thesis, University of British Columbia, 1965)

Jewison, D. J. P., *Grand Circle Sailing: A Study of the Imagery of Malcolm Lowry* (Thesis, St. John's College, University of Manitoba, 1966)

Lloyd, Rodney O., *Mexico and "Under the Volcano"* (Thesis, University of Western Ontario, 1966)

Robertson, Anthony, *Aspects of the Quest in the Minor Fiction of Malcolm Lowry* (Thesis, University of British Columbia, 1966)

Spender, Stephen, Introduction to *Under the Volcano* by Malcolm Lowry (Toronto, New American Library, 1966) pp. vii-xxvi [Signet Library; also: London, Cape, 1967.]

Thomas, Hilda, "Lowry's Letters," *Canadian Literature* No. 29: 56-58 (Summer 1966)

Buston, Barry C., *Structural Organization in "Under the Volcano"* (Thesis, University of Western Ontario, 1967)

Costa, Richard H., "*Ulysses*, Lowry's *Volcano*, and *The Voyage Between*: a Study of an Unacknowledged Literary Kinship," *University of Toronto Quarterly* 36: 335-352 (July 1967)

Edmonds, Dale, "The Short Fiction of Malcolm Lowry," *Tulane Studies in English* 15: 59-80 (1967)

Nyland, Agnes Cecilia (Sister Mary Rosalinda), *The Luminous Wheel: A Study of Malcolm Lowry* (Thesis, University of Ottawa, 1967)

Barnes, J., "The Myth of Sisyphus in *Under the Volcano*," *Prairie Schooner* 42: 341-348 (Winter 1968/69)

Edmonds, Dale, "*Under the Volcano*: A Reading of the 'Immediate Level,'" *Tulane Studies in English* 16: 63-105 (1968)

Leech, C., "The Shaping of Time: *Nostromo* and *Under the Volcano*," *Imagined Worlds*, edited by M. Mack and I. Gregor (London, Methuen, 1968) pp. 323-241

Tiessen, Paul, "*Under the Volcano*": *Lowry and the Cinema* (Thesis, University of Alberta, 1968)

Wild, Bernadette, "Malcolm Lowry: A study of the Sea Metaphor in *Under the Volcano*," *University of Windsor Review* 4: 46-60 (Fall 1968)

Woolmer, J. Howard, *A Malcolm Lowry Catalogue*. With Essays by Perle Epstein and Richard H. Costa (New York, York, (1968/1969) 64p. [Focus series No. 2]

Atkins, Elizabeth, *Aspects of the Absurd in Modern Fiction, with Special Reference to* Under the Volcano *and* Catch 22 (Thesis, University of British Columbia, 1969)

Benham, David, *A Liverpool of Self: A Study of Lowry's Fiction Other than* Under the Volcano (Thesis, University of British Columbia, 1969)

Doyen, V., "Elements Towards a Spatial Reading of Malcolm Lowry's *Under the Volcano*," *English Studies* 50, No. 1: 65-71 (1969) [Swets and Zeitlinger, Amsterdam, Holland]

Epstein, Perle, *The Private Labyrinth of Malcolm Lowry: "Under the Volcano" and the "Cabbala"* (New York, Holt Rinehart, 1969) 241p.

Johnsonn, Caroll, *The Making of "Under the Volcano": An Examination of Lyrical Structure, with Reference to Textual Revisions* (Thesis, University of British Columbia, 1969)

Ramsey, Robin, *The Impact of Time and Memory in Malcolm Lowry's Fiction* (Thesis, University of British Columbia, 1969)

Riddell, John A., *Malcolm Lowry: The Voyage that Never Ends* (Thesis, University of British Columbia, 1969)

Benham, David, "Lowry's Purgatory; Versions of 'Lunar Caustic'," *Canadian Literature*

No. 44: 28-37 (Spring 1970)

Costa, Ricard Hauer, "Malcolm Lowry and
the Addictions of an Era," *University of
Windsor Review* 5: 1-10 (Spring 1970)

Dodson, Daniel B., *Malcolm Lowry* (New York,
Columbia University Press, 1970) 48p.

Durrant, Geoffrey, "Death in Life: Neo-
Platonic Elements in 'Through the Panama,' "
Canadian Literature No. 44: 13-27
(Spring 1970)

Epstein, Perle, "Swinging the Maelstrom:
Malcolm Lowry and Jazz," *Canadian
Literature* No. 44: 57-66 (Spring 1970)

Lowry, Malcolm, "Two Letters," *Canadian
Literature* No. 44: 50-56 (Spring 1970)

New, W. H., "Lowry's Reading: An
Introductory Essay," *Canadian Literature*
No. 44: 4-12 (Spring 1970)

Tiessen, Paul C., "Malcolm Lowry and the
Cinema," *Canadian Literature* No. 44: 38-47
(Spring 1970)

Wright, T., "*Under the Volcano:* The Static
Art of Malcolm Lowry," *Ariel, A Review
of International English Literature* 1: 67-76
(October 1970)

Corrigan, M., "Lowry's Last Novel,"
Canadian Literature No. 48: 74-80 (Spring
1971). [Review of *October Ferry to Gabriola*]

New, W. H., *Malcolm Lowry* (Toronto,
McClelland, 1971) 64p. [Canadian Writers
Series No. 11]

Woodcock, George (ed.), *Malcolm Lowry.
The Man and his Work* (Vancouver, U.B.C.
Publications, 1971) ix + 174p.

Costa, Richard H., *Malcolm Lowry* (New York,
Twayne, 1972) 208p.

McMullen, Lorraine, "Malcolm Lowry's 'The
Forest Path to the Spring,' " *Canadian
Fiction Magazine* No. 5: 71-77 (Winter 1972)

New, W. H., "Gabriola: Malcolm Lowry's
Floating Island," in his *Articulating West*
(Toronto, New Press, 1972) pp. 196-206

Grace, Sherrill E., "*Under the Volcano:*
Narrative Mode and Technique," *Journal of
Canadian Fiction* 2: 57-61 (Spring 1973)

JOHN MCCRAE (1872-1918)

In Flanders Fields and Other Poems, with an
Essay in Character by Sir Andrew Macphail
(Toronto, Briggs, 1919) 141p.

Selected criticism:

MacNaughton, John, "In Memoriam Lieut.-
Col. John McCrae," *University Magazine*
17: 235-246 (April 1918)

Gordon, W., "On English Poetry of the War,"
Queen's Quarterly 27: 62-84 (July-
September 1919)

MacBeth, R. G., "The McCraes of Guelph,"
British Columbia Monthly 15: 13 (January
1920)

Rhodenizer, V. B., "In Flanders Fields: Poet
Psychology," *Canadian Bookman* 5: 263
(October 1923)

Wharton, Lewis and Lorne Pierce, "Who's
Who in Canadian Literature: John
McCrae," *Canadian Bookman* 6: 237-240
(August 1926)

Stevenson, O. J., "When We Save We Lose,"
in his *A People's Best* (Toronto, Musson,
1927) pp. 13-20

Byerly, Alpheus E., *The McCraes of Guelph*
(Elora, Ont., "Express," 1932) 13p.

Brodie, A. H., "John McCrae—A Centenary
Re-assessment," *Humanities Association
Bulletin* 23: 12-22 (Winter 1972)

THOMAS MCCULLOCH (1776-1843)

*Popery Condemned by Scripture and the
Fathers* . . . (Edinburgh, Pillans, 1808)
385p. [also as *Popery Again Condemned* . . .
(Edinburgh, Neill, 1810) 429p.]

Words of Peace: Being an Address delivered
to the Congregation of Halifax . . . (Halifax,
Ward, 1817) 16p.

*The Nature and Uses of a Liberal Education
Illustrated:* Being a Lecture delivered at
the Opening of the Pictou Academical
Institution (Halifax, Holland, 1819) 24p.

Colonial Gleanings . . . *William* and *Melville*
. . . [two novellas] (Edinburgh, Oliphant,
1826) 144p.

*Memorial from the Committee of Missions of
the Presbyterian Church of Nova Scotia to
the Glasgow Society for Promoting the
Religious Interests of the Scottish Settlers in
British North America* . . . (Edinburgh,
Oliver & Boyd, 1826) 75p.

*A Review of the Supplement to the First Annual
Report of the Society for Promoting the
Religious Interests of Scottish Settlers in*

British North America. In a Series of
Letters . . . (Glasgow, Young, 1828) 50p.

Calvinism, the Doctrine of the Scriptures
(Glasgow, Collins [1849]) 270p.

Letters of Mephibosheth Stepsure [pseud.]
(Halifax, Blackader, 1860) 143p. [reprinted
under title: *The Stepsure Letters* (Toronto,
McClelland, 1960), New Canadian Library
No. 16]

*The Prosperity of the Church in Troublous
Times*. A Sermon preached . . . Feb. 25,
1814 (New Glasgow, Mackenzie, 1882) 18p.

Selected criticism:

McCulloch, William, *The Life of Thomas
McCulloch* . . . (Truro, N. S., The Albion,
1920) 218p.

MacIntosh, F. C., "Some Nova Scotian
Scientists," *Dalhousie Review* 10: 199-213
(July 1930)

Harvey, D. C., "Thomas McCulloch," in
Canadian Portraits, edited by R. G. Riddell
(Toronto, Oxford, 1940) pp. 22-28

Frye, Northrop, Introduction to *The Stepsure
Letters* by Thomas McCulloch (Toronto,
McClelland, 1960) pp. iii-ix [New Canadian
Library No. 16]

Irving, John A., "The Achievement of
Thomas McCulloch," in *The Stepsure
Letters* by Thomas McCulloch (Toronto,
McClelland, 1960) pp. 150-156 [New
Canadian Library No. 16]

Lochhead, Douglas G., "A Bibliographical
Note," in *The Stepsure Letters* by Thomas
McCulloch (Toronto, McClelland, 1960)
pp. 156-159 [New Canadian Library
No. 16]

Baird, Frank, "Missionary Educator: Dr.
Thos. McCulloch, edited by Hamilton
Baird," *Dalhousie Review* 52: 611-617
(Winter 1972/73)

Sharman, Vincent, "Thomas McCulloch's
Stepsure: The Relentless Presbyterian,"
Dalhousie Review 52: 618-625 (Winter
1972/1973)

GWENDOLYN MACEWEN (1941-   )

The Drunken Clock (Toronto, Aleph Press,
1961) 15p.

Selah (Toronto, Aleph Press, 1961) 12p.

Julian, the Magician. A Novel (Toronto,
Macmillan, 1963) 151p.

The Rising Fire (Toronto, Contact Press,
1963) 82p.

A Breakfast for Barbarians (Toronto,
Ryerson, 1966) 53p.

The Shadow-Maker (Toronto, Macmillan,
1969) 93p.

King of Egypt, King of Dreams. A Novel
(Toronto, Macmillan, 1971) 287p.

The Armies of the Moon (Toronto, Macmillan,
1972) 75p.

Noman (Ottawa, Oberon, 1972) 121p.

Selected criticism:

MacEwen, Gwendolyn, "Genesis," *Teangadoir*,
Series ii, 1: 56-63 (November 1961)

Bowering, George, "A Complex Music,"
Canadian Literature No. 21: 70-71
(Summer 1964)

Gose, E. B., "They Shall Have Arcana,"
Canadian Literature No. 21: 36-45
(Summer 1964)

Wilson, Milton, Review of *The Rising Fire*, in
University of Toronto Quarterly 33: 386-388
(July 1964)

Atwood, Margaret, "MacEwen's Muse,"
Canadian Literature No. 45: 23-32
(Summer 1970) [*Cf.* next entry]

——, "La Muse de MacEwen," *Ellipse*
7: 83-93 (Spring 1971)

Colombo, John R., *Rhymes and Reasons:
Nine Canadian Poets Discuss their work* . . .
(Toronto, Holt Rinehart, 1971) 117p.

Dragland, Stan, Review of *The Armies of the
Moon, Quarry* 21: 57-62 (Autumn 1972)

THOMAS D'ARCY MCGEE (1825-1868)

*Historical Sketches of O'Connell and his
Friends* . . . With a Glance at the Future
Destiny of Ireland. Third edition (Boston,
Donahue & Rohan, 1845) 208p.

Gallery of Irish Writers. The Irish Writers
of the Seventeenth Century (Dublin, 1846)

*A Memoir of the Life and Conquest of Art
MacMurrogh, King of Leinster from A.D.
1377 to A.D. 1417* (Dublin, 1847) [later
edition: (Dublin, Duffy, 1886) 200p.]

*A History of the Irish Settlers in North
America, From the Earliest Period to the*

Census of 1850 (Boston, "American Celt," 1851) 180p.

The Political Causes and Consequences of the Protestant "Reformation." A Lecture (New York, Sadleir, 1853) 27p.

A Life of the Rt. Rev. Edward Maginn, Coadjutor Bishop of Derry: With Selections from his Correspondence (New York, O'Shea, 1857) 306p.

Canadian Ballads, and Occasional Verses (Montreal, Lovell, 1858) 124p.

Sebastian; or, The Roman Martyr. A Drama (New York, 1861) 52p.

Emigration and Colonization in Canada. A Speech delivered in the House of Assembly, Quebec, 25th April, 1862 (Quebec, Hunter, 1862) 25p.

The Crown and the Confederation. Three Letters . . . by a Backwoodsman [pseud.] (Montreal, Lovell, 1864) 36p.

Speeches and Addresses Chiefly on the Subject of British American Union (London, Chapman & Hall, 1865) 308p.

Two Speeches on the Union of the Provinces (Quebec, Hunter Rose, 1865) 34p.

The Irish Position in British and in Republican North America. A Letter to the Editors of The Irish Press . . . (Montreal, Longmoore, 1866) 36p.

The Poems of Thomas D'Arcy McGee. With Copious Notes . . . and Biographical Sketch by Mrs. J. Sadleir (New York, Sadleir, 1869) 612p.

1825—D'Arcy McGee—1925. A Collection of Speeches and Addresses, selected . . . by the Hon. Charles Murphy (Toronto, Macmillan, 1937) 366p.

Selected criticism:

Taylor, Fennings, "Hon. D'Arcy McGee," in *Portraits of British North Americans,* edited by W. Notman (Montreal, Notman, 1865) Vol. 2, pp. 1-28

Clarke, Henry J., *A Short Sketch of the Life of the Hon. D'Arcy McGee* (Montreal, Lovell, 1868) 80p.

Connolly, Rev. T. L., *Funeral Oration on the late Hon. Thomas D'Arcy McGee . . .* (Halifax, Compton, 1868) 24p.

French, H. J. O., *The Life of the Hon. D'Arcy McGee* (Montreal, 1868) [pamphlet]

Spaight, George, *Trial of Patrick J. Whelan for the Murder of the Hon. D'Arcy McGee . . .* (Ottawa, Desbarats, 1868) 88p.

Taylor, Fennings, *The Hon. D'Arcy McGee.* A Sketch of his Life and Death. New edition, revised and enlarged (Montreal, Lovell, 1868) 60p.

Sadleir, Mary Anne, Biographical Sketch and Introduction to *The Poems of Thomas D'Arcy McGee* (New York, Sadleir, 1869) pp. 15-58

Cross, Ethelbert F. H., "An Exile from Erin," in his *Fire and Frost* (Toronto, Bryant, 1898) pp. 78-88

Markey, John, "Thomas D'Arcy McGee: Poet and Patriot," *Canadian Magazine* 46: 67-72 (November 1915)

Hassard, A. R., "Great Canadian Orators: I: D'Arcy McGee," *Canadian Magazine* 53: 263-269 (August 1919)

Harvey, Daniel Cobb, *Thomas D'Arcy McGee, The Prophet of Canadian Nationality.* A Popular Lecture . . . (Winnipeg, University of Manitoba, 1923) 30p.

Brady, Alexander, *Thomas D'Arcy McGee* (Toronto, Macmillan, 1925) 182p.

Harvey, Daniel Cobb, "The Centenary of D'Arcy McGee," *Dalhousie Review* 5: 1-10 (April 1925)

O'Leary, M. Grattan, "Observing the First Centenary of D'Arcy McGee," *Maclean's* 30. 21, 50, 56 (April 1, 1925)

Skelton, Isabel, *The Life of Thomas D'Arcy McGee* (Gardenvale, P.Q., Garden City Press, 1925) 554p.

Henderson, John, "Thomas D'Arcy McGee," in his *Great Men of Canada* (Toronto, Southam, 1928) pp. 205-218

O'Neill, K., "Thomas D'Arcy McGee, Statesman, Journalist, Poet," *Catholic World* 130: 681-686 (March 1930)

Keep, G. R. C., "D'Arcy McGee and Montreal," *Culture* 12: 16-28 (March 1951)

Phelan, Josephine, *The Ardent Exile.* The Life and Times of Thos. D'Arcy McGee (Toronto, Macmillan, 1951) 317p.

O'Donnell, Kathleen, *Thomas D'Arcy McGee's Irish and Canadian Ballads* (Thesis, University of Western Ontario, 1956)

Sister Mary Louise, *Thomas D'Arcy McGee as a Man of Letters* (Thesis, University of New Brunswick, 1960)

Burns, R. B., "D'Arcy McGee and the Economic Aspects of New Nationality," *Canadian Historical Association Report* (1967) pp. 95-104

Senior, Hereward, "Quebec and the Fenians," *Canadian Historical Review* 48: 26-44 (March 1967)

O'Donnell, Kathleen, "D'Arcy McGee's *Canadian Ballads*," *Revue de l'Université d'Ottawa* 41: 314-321 (avril-juin 1971)

ALEXANDER MCLACHLAN (1818-1896)

The Spirit of Love, and Other Poems (Toronto, Cleland, 1846) 36p.

Poems [Chiefly in the Scottish Dialect] (Toronto, Geikie, 1856) 192p.

Lyrics (Toronto, Armour, 1858) 151p.

The Emigrant, and Other Poems (Toronto, Rollo & Adam, 1861) 236p.

Poems and Songs (Toronto, Hunter Rose, 1874) 223p.

The Poetical Works of Alexander McLachlan . . . (Toronto, Briggs, 1900) 424p.

Selected criticism:

Begg, W. P., "Alexander McLachlan's Poems and Ballads," *Canadian Monthly* 12: 355-362 (October 1877)

McCaig, D., "Alexander McLachlan," *Canadian Magazine* 8: 520-523 (November 1897)

Dewart, Edward H., "Introductory Essay," in *The Poetical Works of Alexander McLachlan* (Toronto, Briggs, 1900) pp. 9-15

Duff, James, "Alexander McLachlan," *Queen's Quarterly* 8: 132-144 (October 1900)

[Hamilton, Alex], "Biographical Sketch," in *The Poetical Works of Alexander McLachlan* (Toronto, Briggs, 1900) pp. 17-28

Burton, Jean, "Alexander McLachlan—the Burns of Canada," *Willison's Monthly* 3: 268-269 (December 1927)

HUGH MACLENNAN (1907-)

Oxyrhynchus, An Economic and Social Study (Princeton, University Press, 1935) 93p.

Barometer Rising (Toronto, Collins, 1941) 326p.

Canadian Unity and Quebec, by Emile Vaillancourt, J. P. Humphrey, and Hugh MacLennan (Montreal, 1942) 16p.

Two Solitudes (Toronto, Collins, 1945) 370p.

The Precipice (Toronto, Collins, 1948) 372p.

Cross Country (Toronto, Collins, 1949) 172p. [reprinted with a new Introduction by the Author: Edmonton, Hurtig, 1972) xxiii + 172p.]

Each Man's Son (Toronto, Macmillan, 1951) 244p.

The Present World as Seen in its Literature (Fredericton, University of New Brunswick, 1952) 12p.

Thirty and Three, edited by Dorothy Duncan (Toronto, Macmillan, 1954) 261p.

The Future of the Novel as an Art Form (Toronto, University of Toronto Press, [1959?]) 11p.

The Watch That Ends the Night (Toronto, Macmillan, 1959) 373p.

Scotchman's Return, and Other Essays (Toronto, Macmillan, 1960) 279p.

Seven Rivers of Canada (Toronto, Macmillan, 1961) 170p.

An Orange from Portugal (Thornhill, Ont., Village Press, 1964) 13p. [not for sale]

The Colour of Canada (Toronto, McClelland, 1967) 126p. [revised edition, 1972]

Return of the Sphinx (Toronto, Macmillan, 1967) 303p.

Selected criticism:

Duncan, Dorothy, "My Author Husband," *Maclean's* 58: 7, 36, 38, 40 (August 15, 1945)

Ballantyne, M. G., "Theology and the Man on the Street: A Catholic Commentary on *Cross Country*," *Culture* 10: 392-396 (December 1949)

Woodcock, George, "Hugh MacLennan," *Northern Review* 3: 2-10 (April-May 1950)

Phelps, Arthur L., "Hugh MacLennan," in his *Canadian Writers* (Toronto, McClelland, 1951) pp. 77-84

Smith, Harrison, "Fate, the Prime Mover," *Saturday Review of Literature* 34: 11 (June 9, 1951)

MacLennan, Hugh, "My First Book," *Canadian Author* 28: 3-4 (Summer 1952)

McPherson, Hugo, "Novels of Hugh

MacLennan," *Queen's Quarterly* 60: 186-198 (Summer 1953)

Watters, R. E., "Hugh MacLennan and the Canadian Character," in *As a Man Thinks . . .*, edited by E. Morrison and W. Robbins (Toronto, Gage, 1953) pp. 228-243

McPherson, Hugo, Introduction to *Barometer Rising* by Hugh MacLennan (Toronto, McClelland, 1958) pp. ix-xv [New Canadian Library No. 8]

Davies, Robertson, "MacLennan's Rising Sun," *Saturday Night* 74: 29-31 (March 28, 1959)

Vallerand, Jean, "Hugh MacLennan ou la tendresse dans la littérature canadienne," *Le Devoir*, samedi, 28 novembre, 1959, p. 11

Goetsch, Paul, *Hugh MacLennan's Novels* (Thesis, University of Marburg, 1960)

MacLennan, Hugh, "The Story of a Novel," *Canadian Literature* No. 3: 35-39 (Winter 1960) [also in *Masks of Fiction*, edited by A. J. M. Smith (Toronto, McClelland, 1961) pp. 33-38]

Goetsch, Paul, "Too Long to the Courtly Muses: Hugh MacLennan as a Contemporary Writer," *Canadian Literature* No. 10: 19-31 (Autumn 1961)

——, *Das Romanwerk Hugh MacLennans: eine Studie zum Literarischen Nationalismus in Kanada* (Hamburg, Gruyter, 1961) 140p.

Woodcock, George, "A Nation's Odyssey: The Novels of Hugh MacLennan," *Canadian Literature* No. 10: 7-18 (Autumn 1961) [also in *Masks of Fiction*, edited by A. J. M. Smith (Toronto, McClelland, 1961) pp. 128-140]

Lucas, Alec, Introduction to *Each Man's Son* by Hugh MacLennan (Toronto, McClelland, 1962) pp. 7-13 [New Canadian Library No. 30]

George, Gerald A., *Theme and Symbol in the Novels of Hugh MacLennan* (Thesis, Laval University, 1966)

New, W. H., "The Apprenticeship of Discovery," *Canadian Literature* No. 29: 18-33 (Summer 1966)

Chambers, Robert D., "The Novels of Hugh MacLennan," *Journal of Canadian Studies* 2: 3-11 (August 1967)

Gilley, Robert K., *Myth and Meaning in Three*

Novels of Hugh MacLennan (Thesis, University of British Columbia, 1967)

Morley, Patricia A., *Puritanism in the Novels of Hugh MacLennan* (Thesis, Carleton University, 1967)

New, W. H., "The Storm and After: Imagery and Symbolism in Hugh MacLennan's *Barometer Rising*," *Queen's Quarterly* 74: 302-313 (Summer 1967)

Hirano, Keiichi, "Jerome Martell and Norman Bethune: A Note on Hugh MacLennan's *The Watch that Ends the Night*," *Studies in English Literature* (English Literary Society of Japan) English Number, pp. 37-59 (1968)

Marshall, Tom, "Some Working Notes on *The Watch that Ends the Night*," *Quarry* 17, No. 2: 13-16 (Winter 1968)

New, W. H., "Winter and the Night-People," *Canadian Literature* No. 36: 26-33 (Spring 1968)

O'Donnell, Kathleen, "The Wanderer in *Barometer Rising*," *University of Windsor Review* 3: 12-18 (Spring 1968)

Buitenhuis, Peter, *Hugh MacLennan* (Toronto, Forum House, 1969) 83p.

Farmiloe, Dorothy, "Hugh MacLennan and the Canadian Myth," *Mosaic* 2: 1-9 (Spring 1969)

MacLennan, Hugh, "Reflections on Two Decades," *Canadian Literature* No. 41: 20-39 (Summer 1969)

Wing, Ted, *Puritan Ethic and Social Response in Novels of Sinclair Ross, Robertson Davies, and Hugh MacLennan* (Thesis, University of Alberta, 1969)

Woodcock, George, *Hugh MacLennan* (Toronto, Copp Clark, 1969) 121p. [Studies in Canadian Literature No. 5]

Cockburn, Robert H., *The Novels of Hugh MacLennan* (Montreal, Harvest House, 1970) 165p.

Lucas, Alec, *Hugh MacLennan* (Toronto, McClelland, 1970) 61p. [Canadian Writers Series No. 8]

Sutherland, Ronald, "The Fourth Separatism," *Canadian Literature* No. 45: 7-23 (Summer 1970)

Arnason, David, "Canadian Nationalism in Search of a Form: Hugh MacLennan's *Barometer Rising*," *Journal of Canadian Fiction* 1: 68-71 (Fall 1972)

Buitenhuis, Peter, "Two Solitudes Revisited: Hugh MacLennan and Leonard Cohen," *The Literary Half-Yearly* (University of Mysore, India) 13: 19-32 (July 1972)

Cameron, Donald, "Hugh MacLennan: The Tennis Racket is an Antelope Bone," *Journal of Canadian Fiction,* 1: 40-47 (Winter 1972)

Froese, Edna, *The Guilty Heroes in the Novels of Hugh MacLennan and Margaret Laurence* (Thesis, University of Saskatchewan, 1972)

Hyman, Roger L., *A Study of the Shaping Themes of Hugh MacLennan's Novels* (Thesis, University of Toronto, 1972)

Morley, Patricia A., *The Immoral Moralists: Hugh MacLennan and Leonard Cohen* (Toronto, Clarke Irwin, 1972) 144p.

Zezulka, Joseph, *Historical, Philosophical, and Scientific Perspectives in the Work of Hugh MacLennan* (Thesis, Queen's University, 1972)

JAY MACPHERSON (1931-   )

Nineteen Poems ([Deya, Mallorca, Spain, Robert Graves, The Seizin Press], 1952) 9p.

O Earth Return (Toronto, Emblem Books, 1954) 9p.

The Boatman (Toronto, Oxford, 1957) 70p.

A Dry Light & The Dark Air (Toronto, Hawkshead Press, 1959) 4p.

The Four Ages of Man. The Classical Myths (Toronto, Macmillan, 1962) 188p.

The Boatman and Other Poems (Toronto, Oxford, 1968) 86p.

Selected criticism:

Dobbs, Kildare, Review of *The Boatman,* in *Canadian Forum* 37: 88 (July 1957)

Endicott, Norman, Review of *The Boatman,* in *Tamarack Review* No. 4: 83-85 (Summer 1957)

Wilson, Milton, Review of *The Boatman,* in *Fiddlehead* No. 34: 39, 41, 43 (Fall 1957)

Frye, Northrop, Review of *The Boatman,* in *University of Toronto Quarterly* 27: 434-439 (July 1958)

Reaney, James, "The Third Eye: Jay Macpherson's *The Boatman,*" *Canadian Literature* No. 3: 23-34 (Winter 1960)

CHARLES MAIR (1838-1927)

Dreamland and Other Poems (Montreal, Dawson, 1868) 151p.

Tecumseh. A Drama (Toronto, Hunter Rose, 1886) 205p.

Tecumseh, A Drama (Second edition) *and Canadian Poems* (Toronto, Briggs, 1901) 276p.

Through the Mackenzie Basin. A Narrative of the Athabasca and Peace River Treaty Expedition of 1899 (Toronto, Briggs, 1908) 494p.

Tecumseh, A Drama, and Canadian Poems; Dreamland and Other Poems; The American Bison, Memoirs and Reminiscences, with an Introduction by Robert Norwood (Toronto, Radisson Society, 1926) 72 + 470p.

Selected criticism:

Denison, George Taylor, *The Struggle for Imperial Unity, Recollections and Experiences* (London, Macmillan, 1909) *passim*

Mackay, I. E., "Charles Mair, Poet and Patriot," *Canadian Magazine* 59: 162-165 (June 1922)

Copp, E. A., *Canada First Party (Charles Mair)* (Thesis, Queen's University, 1926)

Garvin, J. W., "Who's Who in Canadian Literature: Charles Mair," *Canadian Bookman* 8: 335-337 (November 1926)

Charlesworth, Hector, "Patriots and Poets of the West," in his *More Candid Chronicles* (Toronto, Macmillan, 1928) pp. 18-36

Fraser, A. E., "A Poet Pioneer of Canada," *Queen's Quarterly* 35: 440-450 (May 1928)

Wheeler, Christine G., "The Bard of Bathurst," *Canadian Bookman* 18: 10-11 (January 25, 1936)

Norwood, Robert, "Charles Mair," in *Leading Canadian Poets,* edited by W. P. Percival (Toronto, Ryerson, 1948) pp. 152-157

Dooley, D. J. and F. N. Shrive, "Voice of the Burdash," *Canadian Forum* 37: 80-82 (July 1957)

Shrive, Frank Norman, *Charles Mair: A Study of Canadian Literary Nationalism* (Thesis, Queen's University, 1961)

Tait, Michael, "Playwrights in a Vacuum: English-Canadian Drama in the Nineteenth Century," *Canadian Literature* No. 16: 3-18 (Spring 1963)

Shrive, Norman, "Poet and Politics: Charles Mair at Red River," *Canadian Literature* No. 17: 6-21 (Summer 1963)
——, "Poets and Patriotism: Charles Mair and Tecumseh," *Canadian Literature* No. 20: 15-26 (Spring 1964)
Matthews, John, "Charles Mair," in *Our Living Tradition*, Fifth Series, edited by Robert L. McDougall (Toronto University of Toronto Press, 1965) pp. 78-101
Shrive, Norman, *Charles Mair, Literary Nationalist* (Toronto, University of Toronto Press, 1965) 309p.

ELI MANDEL (1922-   )

Trio: First Poems by Gael Turnbull, Phyllis Webb, Eli Mandel (Toronto, Contact Press, 1954) 89p.
Fuseli Poems (Toronto, Contact Press, 1960) 66p.
Poetry 62, edited by Eli Mandel and Jean-Guy Pilon (Toronto, Ryerson, 1961) 116p.
Black and Secret Man (Toronto, Ryerson, 1964) 33p.
Criticism: The Silent-Speaking Words (Toronto, Canadian Broadcasting Corporation, 1966) 73p.
An Idiot Joy (Edmonton, Hurtig, 1967) 85p.
Irving Layton (Toronto, Forum House, 1969) 82p.
Five Modern Canadian Poets, edited by— (Toronto, Holt Rinehart, 1970) 88p.
Contexts of Canadian Criticism, edited by— (Toronto, University of Toronto Press, 1971) 304p.
Eight More Canadian Poets, edited by— (Toronto, Holt Rinehart, 1972) 88p.
Poets of Contemporary Canada, 1960-70, edited and with an Introduction by— (Toronto, McClelland, 1972) xvi + 141p.
Crusoe: Poems Selected and New (Toronto, Anansi, 1973) 108p.
Stony Plain (Erin, Ont., Press Porcépic, 1973) 96p.

Selected criticism:

McMaster, R. D., "The Unexplained Interior: A Study of E. W. Mandel's *Fuseli Poems*," *Dalhousie Review* 40: 392-396 (Fall 1960)
Dudek, Louis, "Two Canadian Poets: Ralph Gustafson and Eli Mandel," *Culture* 22: 145-151 (juin 1961)
Wilson, Milton, Review of *Fuseli Poems*, in *University of Toronto Quarterly* 30: 383-387 (July 1961)
Ower, John, "Black and Secret Poet: Notes on Eli Mandel," *Canadian Literature* No. 42: 14-25 (Autumn 1969)
Fetherling, Doug, "A Poet for All Traditions," *Saturday Night* 88: 40 (July 1973)

SUSANNA MOODIE (1803-1885)

Enthusiasm and Other Poems (London, Smith & Elder, 1831) 214p
Roughing It In the Bush; or Life in Canada (London, Bentley, 1852) 2 vols.
Life in the Clearings Versus the Bush (London, Bentley, 1853) 384p.
Mark Hurdlestone, the Gold Worshipper (London, Bentley, 1853) 2 vols.
Flora Lyndsay; or, Passages in an Eventful Life (London, Bentley, 1854) 2 vols.
Matrimonial Speculations (London, Bentley, 1854) 352p.
Geoffrey Moncton; or, The Faithless Guardian (New York, DeWitt, 1855) 362p.
The World Before Them. A Novel (London, Bentley, 1868) 3 vols.
Life in the Backwoods, a Sequel to Roughing It In the Bush (New York, Lovell, 1887) 224p.
[possibly the same work as *Life in the Clearings*]

In addition to various writings that appeared only in periodicals, Mrs. Moodie was also the reputed author of a number of works, mostly for juveniles, some published anonymously, some pseudonymously. The following are books of this class which have been attributed to Mrs. Moodie and about which some bibliographical details have been found:

Spartacus. A Roman Story (London, Newman, 1822) 131p.
The Little Prisoner; or, Passion and Patience (London, Newman, 1829)
The History of Mary Prince, a West Indian Slave [Anonymous] (London, Maunder, 1831)
Negro Slavery Described by a Negro. Being the Narrative of Ashton Warner, a Native of

St. Vincents . . . [Anonymous] (London, Maunder, 1831)

Profession and Principle. Tales (London, Dean, 1833)

Rowland Massingham, the Boy That Would Be His Own Master (London, Dean, 1837)

The Little Black Pony, and Other Stories (Philadelphia, Collins, 1850)

The Soldier's Orphan; or, Hugh Latimer (London, Dean, 1853)

Something More About the Soldier's Orphan (London, Dean, 1853)

George Leatrim; or, the Mother's Test (Edinburgh, Hamilton, 1875)

The Victoria Magazine 1847-1848, edited by Susanna and J. W. D. Moodie. Reprinted with an Introduction by William H. New (Vancouver, University of British Columbia Library, 1968) 294p.

Two other titles are sometimes attributed to Mrs. Moodie, but apparently in error: *Hugh Latimer; or, the Schoolboy's Friendship* (London Newman, 1828) 160p. and *Adventurers of Little Downy, the Field Mouse* . . . New edition (London, Dean, 1844) 78p. The first of these is attributed to Jane Margaret Strickland in the British Museum Catalogue. The second title is specifically assigned by Agnes Fitzgibbon to another of Mrs. Moodie's sisters, Catharine Parr (Strickland) Traill—see the biographical sketch of Mrs. Traill prefaced to her *Pearls and Pebbles; or, Notes of an Old Naturalist* (London, Sampson Low, [1894]) pp. iii-xxxvi.

Selected criticism:

Anonymous, *"Enthusiasm and Other Poems, by Susanna Strickland—now, Mrs. Moodie," Canadian Literary Magazine* 1: 107-110 (May 1833)

Weaver, Emily, "Mrs. Traill and Mrs. Moodie, Pioneers in Literature," *Canadian Magazine* 48: 473-476 (March 1917)

Hume, Blanche, "Grandmothers of Canadian Literature," *Willison's Monthly* 3: 474-477 (May 1928)

——, *The Strickland Sisters* (Toronto, Ryerson, 1928) 32p.

McCourt, E. A., "Roughing It With the Moodies," *Queen's Quarterly* 52: 77-89 (February 1945)

Needler, G. H., "The Otonabee Trio of Women Naturalists—Mrs. Stewart, Mrs. Traill, Mrs. Moodie," *Canadian Field Naturalist* 60: 97-101 (September-October 1946)

Markham, Mary, *An Index to "The Literary Garland," 1838-1851, with Three Essays on Colonial Fiction* (Thesis, University of Western Ontario, 1949)

Davies, Robertson, *At My Heart's Core* (Toronto, Clarke Irwin, 1950) 91p. [a dramatized character study of Mrs. Moodie]

Needler, G. H., *Otonabee Pioneers: The Story of the Stewarts, the Stricklands, the Traills and the Moodies* (Toronto, Burns & MacEachern, 1953) 172p. [reprinted 1957]

Partridge, F. G., "Stewarts and the Stricklands, the Moodies and the Traills," *Ontario Library Review* 40: 179-181 (August 1956)

Klinck, Carl F., "A Gentlewoman of Upper Canada," *Canadian Literature* No. 1: 75-77 (Summer 1959)

McDougall, Robert L., Introduction to *Life in the Clearings* . . . by Susanna Moodie (Toronto, Macmillan, 1959) pp. vii-xxiii

Scott, L. M., "The English Gentlefolk in the Backwoods of Canada," *Dalhousie Review* 39: 56-69 (Spring 1959)

Klinck, Carl F., Introduction to *Roughing It In the Bush* by Susanna Moodie [abridged edition] (Toronto, McClelland, 1962) pp. ix-xiv [New Canadian Library No. 31]

Ballstadt, Carl, *The Literary History of the Strickland Family* (Thesis, University of London, 1965)

Park, Sheila S., *Susanna Moodie and the "Literary Garland"* (Thesis, Carleton University, 1966)

Thomas, Clara, "The Strickland Sisters," in *The Clear Spirit*, edited by Mary Q. Innis (Toronto, University of Toronto Press, 1966)

Morris, Audrey, *Gentle Pioneers*. Five Nineteenth-Century Canadians (Toronto and London, Hodder & Stoughton, 1968) 253p.

Guttenberg, A. C. de, "Susanna Moodie," in his *Early Canadian Art and Literature* (Vaduz, Liechtenstein, Europe Print. [1969])

Ballstadt, Carl, "Susanna Moodie and the English Sketch," *Canadian Literature* No. 51: 32-38 (Winter 1972)

Gairdner, William D., "Traill and Moodie: Two Realities," *Journal of Canadian Fiction* 1: 35-42 (Spring 1972) [See also his

"Letter to the Editor," *Ibid.*, 1: 86 (Fall 1972)]

MacDonald, R. D., "Design and Purpose," *Canadian Literature* No. 51: 20-31 (Winter 1972)

Thomas, Clara, "Journeys to Freedom," *Canadian Literature* No. 51: 11-19 (Winter 1972)

See also entries under Catharine Parr Traill in present book, pages 722-723, for possible mention of Mrs. Moodie.

ALICE MUNRO (1931-   )

Dance of the Happy Shades Stories (Toronto, Ryerson, 1968) 224p.
Lives of Girls & Women. A Novel (Toronto, McGraw-Hill Ryerson, 1971) 254p.

Selected criticism:

Spettigue, D. O., "Alice Laidlaw Munro: A Portrait of the Artist," *Alumni Gazette,* University of Western Ontario 45: 5 (July 1969)

Stainsby, Mari, "Alice Munro Talks with Mari Stainsby," *British Columbia Library Quarterly* 35: 27-31 (July 1971)

Dahlie, Hallvard, "Unconsummated Relationships: Isolation and Rejection in Alice Munro's Stories," *WLWE* [World Literature Written in English] 11: 43-48 (April 1972)

Metcalf, John, "A Converstion with Alice Munro," *Journal of Canadian Fiction* 1: 54-62 (Fall 1972)

Tanaszi, Margaret, *Emancipation of Consciousness in Alice Munro's "Lives of Girls & Women"* (Thesis, Queen's University, 1972)

Gibson, Graeme, "Alice Munro," *Eleven Canadian Novelists* (Toronto, Anansi, 1973) pp. 237-264

JOHN NEWLOVE (1938-   )

Grave Sirs (Vancouver, Reid and Tanabe, 1962) [unpaged]
Elephants, Mothers, and Others (Vancouver, Periwinkle Press, 1963) 31p.
Moving In Alone (Toronto, Contact Press, 1965) 83p.

Notebook Pages (Toronto, Pachter, 1966) [A portfolio of lithographs; limited edition of 15 copies]
What They Say (Kitchener, Weed/flower Press, 1967) 23p.
Black Night Window (Toronto, McClelland, 1968) 112p.
The Cave (Toronto, McClelland, 1970) 85p.
7 Disasters, 3 Theses, and Welcome Home, Chick ([Vancouver ?], Very Stone Press, 1971) [16p. ?]
Lies (Toronto, McClelland, 1972) 96p.

Selected criticism:

Hunt, Russell A., Review of *The Cave,* *Fiddlehead* No. 85: 98-101 (May/June/July 1970)

Pacey, Desmond, Review of *The Cave,* *Canadian Forum* 50: 309-310 (November/December 1970)

Colombo, John R., *Rhymes and Reasons:* Nine Contemporary Poets Discuss their Work . . . (Toronto, Holt Rinehart, 1971) 117p.

Purdy, A. W., "Calm Surfaces Destroyed," *Canadian Literature* No. 48: 91-92 (Spring 1971) [Review of *The Cave*]

ALDEN NOWLAN (1933-   )

The Rose and the Puritan (Fredericton, University of New Brunswick, 1958) 16p.
A Darkness in the Earth (Eureka, Calif., Hearse Press, [1959 ?]) 16p.
Under the Ice (Toronto, Ryerson, 1960) 44p.
Wind in a Rocky Country (Toronto, Emblem Books, 1960) 16p.
Five New Brunswick Poets: Brewster, Cogswell, Nowlan *et al* (Fredericton, Fiddlehead, 1962) 64p.
The Things Which Are (Toronto, Contact Press, 1962) 71p.
Bread, Wine and Salt (Toronto, Clarke Irwin, 1967) 74p.
A Black Plastic Button and a Yellow Yo-Yo (Toronto, Pachter, 1968), 14p. [Limited edition of 20 copies]
Miracle at Indian River (Toronto, Clarke Irwin, 1968) 132p.
The Mysterious Naked Man (Toronto, Clarke Irwin, 1969) 93p.

Playing the Jesus Game. Selected Poems
   (Trumansburg, N. Y., New/Books, 1970)
   105p.
Between Tears and Laughter. Poems (Toronto,
   Clarke Irwin, 1971) 119p.
Various Persons Named Kevin O'Brien. A
   Fictional Memoir (Toronto, Clarke Irwin,
   1973) 143p.

Selected criticism:

Wilson, Milton, Review of *The Rose and the
   Puritan,* in *Canadian Forum* 39: 66-67
   (June 1959)
Waddington, Miriam, Review of *Under the Ice,*
   in *Canadian Literature* No. 9: 71-72
   (Summer 1961)
Wilson, Milton, Review of *Under the Ice* and
   Wind in a Rocky Country, in *University of
   Toronto Quarterly* 31: 442-444 (July 1962)
Lucas, Alec, Review of *Under the Ice,* in
   Fiddlehead No. 51: 59-62 (Winter 1962)
Buckler, Ernest *et al,* "Alden Nowlan
   Special Issue" [ten articles and tributes]
   Fiddlehead No. 81: [various pagings]
   (August/September/October 1969)
Bly, Robert, "For Alden Nowlan with
   Admiration," *Tamarack Review* No. 54:
   32-38 (1970)
Fraser, Keath, "Notes on Alden Nowlan,"
   Canadian Literature No. 45: 41-51
   (Summer 1970)
Colombo, John R., *Rhymes and Reasons:
   Nine Canadian Poets Discuss their Work* . . .
   (Toronto, Holt Rinehart, 1971) 117p.
Cameron, Donald, "The Poet from Desolation
   Creek: Alden Nowlan, an 18th Century
   Tory in 20th Century Fredericton, is an
   Expatriate who Never left Home," *Saturday
   Night* 88: 28-32 (May 1973)

JONATHAN ODELL (1737-1818)

The American Times. A Satire in Three Parts
   . . . by Camillo Querno [pseud.], Poet-
   Laureate to the Congress (London,
   Richardson, 1780) 40p.
The Loyalist Poetry of the Revolution, edited
   by Winthrop Sargent (Philadelphia, Collins,
   1857) 218p.
*The Loyal Verses of Joseph Stansbury and
   Doctor Jonathan Odell* . . ., edited by

Winthrop Sargent (Albany, N. Y. Munsell,
   1860) 199p.
A Collection of the Poems of Jonathan Odell,
   with a Biographical and Critical Introduction
   by Joan Johnston Anderson (Thesis,
   University of British Columbia, 1961)

Selected criticism:

Hills, G. M., *History of the Church in
   Burlington, New Jersey* (Trenton, N. Y.,
   Sharp, 1876) [Second edition, enlarged and
   illustrated, 1885]
Tyler, Moses Coit, "Jonathan Odell . . .
   Satirist," in his *The Literary History of the
   American Revolution* (New York, Putnam,
   1897) Vol. 2, pp. 98-129 [reprinted: (New
   York, Ungar Publishing Co., 1957)]
Lee, F. B., *New Jersey as a Colony and as a
   State* . . . (New York, Publishing Society of
   New Jersey, 1902) pp. 299-305
Lawrence, J. W., *The Judges of New Brunswick
   and Their Times* (Saint John, Jack, 1907)
   532p.
Parrington, Vernon Louis, "The Tory
   Satirists. I: Jonathan Odell," in his *Main
   Currents in American Thought* (New York,
   Harcourt Brace, 1927) Vol. 1, pp. 255-259
Rede, Kenneth, "A Note on the Author of
   The Times," *American Literature* 2: 79-82
   (March 1930)
Leary, Lewis, "Francis Hopkinson, Jonathan
   Odell, and 'The Temple of Cloacina,' "
   American Literature 15: 183-191 (May
   1943)
Anderson, Joan Johnston, Biographical and
   Critical Introduction to *A Collection of the
   Poems of Jonathan Odell* (Thesis, University
   of British Columbia, 1961)

STANDISH O'GRADY (*fl.* 1793-1841)

The Emigrant. A Poem in Four Cantos
   (Montreal, Lovell, 1841) 204p.

Selected criticism:

Smith, A. J. M., "Standish O'Grady," in his
   The Book of Canadian Poetry. Third edition,
   revised and enlarged [Toronto, Gage, 1957)
   p. 71

1vi + 445p. [Revised edition, 1968]

Masks of Fiction: Canadian Critics on Canadian Prose, edited with an Introduction by A. J. M. Smith (Toronto, McClelland, 1961) 176p.

Collected Poems (Toronto, Oxford University Press, 1962) 124p.

Masks of Poetry: Canadian Critics on Canadian Verse, edited with an Introduction by A. J. M. Smith (Toronto, McClelland, 1962) 144p.

The Book of Canadian Prose, Vol. 1: Early Beginnings to Confederation, edited with an Introduction by—— (Toronto, Gage 1965) 261p.

The Canadian Century: English-Canadian Writing Since Confederation, edited with an Introduction by—— (Toronto, Gage 1973) xx + 652p. [vol. 2 of preceding entry]

Modern Canadian Verse in English and French, edited by——(Toronto, Oxford University Press, 1967) 426p.

Poems, New and Collected (Toronto, Oxford University Press, 1967) 160p.

Towards a View of Canadian Letters. Selected Critical Essays, 1928-1971, of A. J. M. Smith (Vancouver, University of British Columbia Press, 1973)

Selected criticism:

Collin, W. E., "Difficult Lonely Music," in his *The White Savannahs* (Toronto, Macmillan, 1936) pp. 235-263

Smith, A. J. M., "Canadian Poetry—a Minority Report," *University of Toronto Quarterly* 8: 125-138 (January 1939)

——, "Canadian Anthologies, New and Old," *University of Toronto Quarterly* 11: 457-474 (July 1942)

Klein, A. M., "Poetry of A. J. M. Smith," *Canadian Forum* 23: 257-258 (February 1944)

Brown, E. K., "A. J. M. Smith and the Poetry of Pride," *Manitoba Arts Review* 4: 30-32 (Spring 1944)

Smith, A. J. M., "Nationalism and Canadian Poetry," *Northern Review* 1: 33-42 (December-January 1945/46)

Collin, W. E., "Arthur Smith," *Gants du Ciel* 11: 47-60 (Printemps 1946)

Sutherland, John, "Mr. Smith and 'The Tradition,' " in his *Other Canadians* (Montreal, First Statement Press, 1947) pp. 5-12

Scott, F. R., "A. J. M. Smith," *Educational Record* (Quebec) 64: 24-29 (January-March 1948)

Schultz, Gregory Peter, *The Periodical Poetry of A. J. M. Smith, F. R. Scott, Leo Kennedy, A. M. Klein, and Dorothy Livesay, 1925-1950* (Thesis, University of Western Ontario, 1957)

Pacey, Desmond, "A. J. M. Smith," in his *Ten Canadian Poets* (Toronto, Ryerson, 1958) pp. 194-222

Birney, Earle, "A. J. M. S.," *Canadian Literature* No. 15: 4-6 (Winter 1963)

Dudek, Louis, Review of *Collected Poems,* in *Delta* No. 20: 27-28 (February 1963)

Fuller, Roy, "A Poet of the Century," *Canadian Literature* No. 15: 7-10 (Winter 1963)

Smith, A. J. M., "A Self-Review," *Canadian Literature* No. 15: 20-26 (Winter 1963)

Wilson, Milton, "Second and Third Thoughts About Smith," *Canadian Literature* No. 15: 11-17 (Winter 1963)

Hughes, Peter, Review of *Collected Poems,* in *Alphabet* No. 6: 63-64 (June 1963)

Mathews, Robin, Review of *Collected Poems,* in *Queen's Quarterly* 70: 282-283 (Summer 1963)

Wilson, Milton, Review of *Collected Poems,* in *University of Toronto Quarterly* 32: 371-373 (July 1963)

Guy, E. F., Review of *Collected Poems,* in *Dalhousie Review* 43: 437, 439-441 (Autumn 1963)

Skelton, Robin, Review of *Collected Poems,* in *Tamarack Review* No. 29: 75-76 (Autumn 1963)

O Broin, Padraig, "After Strange Gods (A. J. M. Smith and the Concept of Nationalism)," *Canadian Author and Bookman* 39: 6-8 (Summer 1964)

Smith, A. J. M., "A Rejected Preface," *Canadian Literature* No. 24: 6-9 (Spring 1965) [Reprinted above, pages 585-588]

Stevens, Peter (ed.), *On the McGill Movement: A. J. M. Smith, F. R. Scott, and Leo Kennedy* (Toronto, Ryerson, 1969) pp. 95-143 [Critical Views on Canadian Writers Series]

McCallum, Maureen F., *A. J. M. Smith*
(Thesis, Queen's University, 1970)

RAYMOND SOUSTER (1921-   )

Unit of Five. Poems by Louis Dudek, Ronald
Hambleton, P. K. Page, Raymond Souster,
James Wreford, edited by Ronald Hambleton
(Toronto, Ryerson, 1944) pp. 55-67

When We Are Young (Montreal, First
Statement Press, 1946) 28p.

Go To Sleep, World (Toronto, Ryerson, 1947)
59p.

The Winter of Time, by Raymond Holmes
[pseud.] (New Toronto, Export Publishing
Enterprises, 1949) 160p. [A novel]

City Hall Street (Toronto, Ryerson, 1951) 8p.

Cerberus. Poems by Louis Dudek, Irving
Layton, Raymond Souster (Toronto,
Contact Press, [*ca.* 1952]) 98p.

Shake Hands with the Hangman. Poems
1940-1952 (Toronto, Contact Press, 1953)
24p.

Walking Death. Poems (Toronto, Contact
Press, 1954) 24p.

A Dream That is Dying. Poems (Toronto,
Contact Press, 1955) 27p.

For What Time Slays. Poems (Toronto, the
Author, 1955) 24p. [mimeographed]

Selected Poems, chosen by Louis Dudek
(Toronto, Contact Press, 1956) 135p.

Crepe-Hangers Carnival. Selected Poems,
1955-1958 (Toronto, Contact Press, 1958) 65p.

A Local Pride. Poems (Toronto, Contact Press,
1962) 131p.

Place of Meeting. Poems 1958-60 (Toronto,
Gallery Editions, 1962) 67p.

At Split Rock Falls (Vermont, American
Letters Press, 1963) 2p.

The Colour of the Times. The Collected Poems
. . . (Toronto, Ryerson, 1964) 121p.

12 New Poems [Lanham, Md., Goosetree
Press, 1964] 5p.

Ten Elephants on Yonge Street: Poems (Toronto,
Ryerson, 1965) 84p.

New Wave Canada: The New Explosion in
Canadian Poetry . . . with an Introduction
and Working Magazine Bibliography, edited
by —— (Toronto, Contact Press, 1966)
167p.

As Is (Toronto, Oxford University Press, 1967)
102p.

Lost and Found. Uncollected Poems, 1945-65
(Toronto, Clarke Irwin, 1968) 113p.

So Far So Good. Poems 1938-1968 (Ottawa,
Oberon Press, 1969) 100p.

Made in Canada. New Poems of the Seventies,
edited by Douglas Lochhead and ——
(Ottawa, Oberon Press, 1970) 192p.

The Years. Poems (Ottawa, Oberon Press,
1971) 164p.

Selected Poems (Ottawa, Oberon Press, 1972)
127p.

On Target, by John Holmes [pseud.] (Toronto,
Village Book Store Press, 1973) 248p.

100 Canadian Poems from the 19th Century,
edited by Douglas Lochhead and ——
(Toronto, New Press, 1973) 160p.

Selected criticism:

Livesay, Dorothy, Review of *When We Are
Young*, in *Canadian Forum* 26: 142
(September 1946)

G., M. R., Review of *Go To Sleep, World*, in
Canadian Forum 27: 119-120 (August 1947)

Wilson, Milton, Review of *Selected Poems*, in
Canadian Forum 36: 164-165 (October
1956)

Howith, Harry, Review of *A Local Pride*, in
Canadian Author and Bookman 38: 8
(Winter 1962)

Bowering, George, Review of *Place of Meeting*,
in *Canadian Forum* 42: 44 (May 1962)

Cogswell, Fred, "Poet Alive," *Canadian
Literature* No. 13: 70-71 (Summer 1962)

Mullins, S. G., Review of *A Local Pride*, in
Culture 23: 428-429 (December 1962)

Dudek, Louis, Review of *A Local Pride* and
Place of Meeting, in *Delta* No. 20: 30-31
(February 1963)

Jones, B. W., Review of *A Local Pride*, in
Queen's Quarterly 69: 646-647 (Winter 1963)

Mandel, Eli, "Internal Resonances," *Canadian
Literature* No. 17: 62-65 (Summer 1963)

Wilson, Milton, Review of *Place of Meeting*
and *A Local Pride*, in *University of Toronto
Quarterly* 32: 374-377 (July 1963)

Dudek, Louis, "Groundhog Among the Stars:
The Poetry of Raymond Souster," *Canadian
Literature* No. 22: 34-49 (Autumn 1964)

Fulford, Robert, "On Raymond Souster: A
Good Toronto Poet Toronto Never
Discovered," *Maclean's* 77: 59 (April 18,
1964)

Carruth, Hayden, "To Souster from Vermont," *Tamarack Review* No. 34: 81-95 (Winter 1965)

Geddes, Gary, "A Cursed and Singular Blessing," *Canadian Literature* No. 54: 27-36 (Autumn 1972)

Tee, Patrick, *The Vision and Poetry of Raymond Souster* (Thesis, Sir George Williams University, 1972)

Wood, Karen, *Raymond Souster: A Stylistic Analysis and a Chronology of Poems* (Thesis, Sir George Williams University, 1972)

JOSEPH STANSBURY (1740-1809)

The Loyal Verses of Joseph Stansbury and Doctor Jonathan Odell, edited by Winthrop Sargent (Albany, N.Y., Munsell, 1860) 199p.

Selected criticism:

Sargent, Winthrop, *The Loyalist Poetry of the Revolution* ... (Philadelphia, Collins, 1857)

Sabine, Lorenzo, *Biographical Sketches of Loyalists of the American Revolution, with an Historical Essay* (Boston, Little Brown, 1864) Vol. 2, pp. 325-326

Tyler, Moses Coit, "Joseph Stansbury, Tory Song-Writer and Satirist," in his *The Literary History of the American Revolution* (New York, Putnam, 1897) Vol. 2, pp. 79-96

[Ghent, W. J.], "Joseph Stansbury," *Dictionary of American Biography* Vol. 17, pp. 516-517

CATHARINE PARR TRAILL (1802-1899)

Reformation; or, The Cousin (London, 1819)

The Backwoods of Canada. Being Letters from the Wife of an Emigrant Officer ... (London, Knight, 1836) 352p.

Adventures of Little Downy, the Field Mouse; and *The Little Princess; or, Passion and Patience.* New edition (London, Dean, 1844) 78p.

The Canadian Crusoes. A Tale of the Rice Lake Plains (London, Hall, 1852) 368p. [also published as *Lost in the Backwoods* (London, Nelson, 1882)]

The Female Emigrant's Guide (Toronto, Maclear, 1854) 218 + 40p. [also published in later editions as *The Canadian Settler's Guide* (1855) and *The Canadian Emigrant Housekeeper's Guide* (1862)]

Lady Mary and Her Nurse (London, Hall, 1856) 204p. [also published under other titles: *Little Mary and Her Nurse, Stories of the Canadian Forest, Afar in the Forest* ..., *In the Forest* ... (various publishers and dates)]

Canadian Wild Flowers (Montreal, Lovell, 1869) 86p.

Studies of Plant Life in Canada (Ottawa, Woodburn, 1885) 288p.

Pearls and Pebbles; or, Notes of an Old Naturalist (Toronto, Briggs, 1894) 241p.

Cot and Cradle Stories, edited by Mary Agnes Fitzgibbon (Toronto, Briggs, 1895) 239p.

The Canadian Settler's Guide, with an Introduction by Clara Thomas (Toronto, McClelland, 1969) xix + 251p.

Selected criticism:

Strickland, Jane Margaret, *Life of Agnes Strickland* (Edinburgh, Blackwood, 1887) *passim*

Burnham, Hampden, "Mrs. Traill," *Canadian Magazine* 4: 388-389 (February 1895)

Fitzgibbon, Mary Agnes, "Biographical Sketch [of Mrs. Traill]," in *Pearls and Pebbles* by Catharine Parr Traill (Toronto, Briggs, 1895) pp. iii-xxxvi

Burpee, Lawrence J., "Catharine Parr Traill (1802-1899)," in his *A Little Book of Canadian Essays* (Toronto, Musson, 1909) pp. 56-64

——, "Last of the Stricklands: Mrs. Catharine Parr Traill," *Sewanee Review* 8: 207-217 (April 1909)

Weaver, Emily, "Mrs. Traill and Mrs. Moodie, Pioneers in Literature," *Canadian Magazine* 84: 473-476 (March 1917)

Hume, Blanche, "Grandmothers of Canadian Literature," *Willison's Monthly* No. 3: 474-477 (May 1928)

——, *The Strickland Sisters* (Toronto, Ryerson, 1928) 32p.

Pope-Hennessy, Una, *Agnes Strickland, Biographer of the Queens of England 1796-1874* (London, Chatto and Windus, 1940) *passim*

Needler, G. H., "The Otonabee Trio of Women Naturalists — Mrs. Stewart, Mrs. Traill, Mrs. Moodie," *Canadian Field Naturalist* 60: 97-101 (September-October 1946)

McNeil, J. L., *Mrs. Traill in Canada* (Thesis, Queen's University, 1948)

Needler, G. H., *Otonabee Pioneers: The Story of the Stewarts, The Stricklands, The Traills and the Moodies* (Toronto, Burns and MacEachern, 1953) 172p.

Partridge, F. G., "Stewarts and the Stricklands, the Moodies and the Traills," *Ontario Library Review* 40: 179-181 (August 1956)

Scott, Lloyd M., "The English Gentlefolk in the Backwoods of Canada," *Dalhousie Review* 39: 56-69 (Spring 1959)

Ballstadt, Carl, *The Literary History of the Strickland Family* (Thesis, University of London, 1965)

Thomas, Clara, "The Strickland Sisters," in *The Clear Spirit,* edited by Mary Q. Innis (Toronto, University of Toronto Press, 1966)

Morris, Audrey, *Gentle Pioneers.* Five Nineteenth-Century Canadians. (Toronto and London, Hodder & Stoughton, 1968) 253p. [Includes Mrs. Traill]

Eaton, Sara, *Lady of the Backwoods* (Toronto, McClelland, 1969) 175p.

Gairdner, William D., "Traill and Moodie: Two Realities," *Journal of Canadian Fiction* 1: 35-42 (Spring 1972)

Thomas, Clara, "Journeys to Freedom," *Canadian Literature* No. 51: 11-19 (Winter 1972)

MIRIAM WADDINGTON (1917-   )

Green World (Montreal, First Statement Press, 1945) 30p.

The Second Silence (Toronto, Ryerson, 1955) 57p.

The Season's Lovers (Toronto, Ryerson, 1958) 56p.

The Glass Trumpet (Toronto, Oxford University Press, 1966) 96p.

Call Them Canadians (Ottawa, National Film Board, 1968)

Say Yes (Don Mills, Oxford University Press, 1969) 96p.

A. M. Klein (Toronto, Copp Clark, 1970) 145p. [Studies in Canadian Literature No. 10]

Driving Home. Poems New and Selected (Toronto, Oxford University Press, 1972) 176p.

The Dream Telescope (London, Anvil-Routledge Kegan Paul, 1973)

John Sutherland: Essays, Controversies, Poems, edited with an Introduction by —— (Toronto, McClelland, 1973) 206p.

Selected criticism:

Frye, Northrop, Review of *Green World,* in *Canadian Forum* 26: 141-142 (September 1946)

Colombo, J. R., Review of *The Season's Lovers,* in *Tamarack Review* No. 11: 91-93 (Spring 1959)

Pacey, Desmond, Review of *The Season's Lovers,* in *Fiddlehead* No. 40: 56-59 (Spring 1959)

Sowton, Ian, "The Lyric Craft of Miriam Waddington," *Dalhousie Review* 39: 237-242 (Summer 1959)

Wayman, Tom, "Miriam Waddington's New Talent," *Canadian Literature* No. 56: 85-89 (Spring 1973)

ANNE WILKINSON (1910-1961)

Counterpoint to Sleep (Montreal, First Statement Press, 1951) 36p.

The Hangman Ties the Holly (Toronto, Macmillan, 1955) 57p.

Lions in the Way: A Discursive History of the Oslers (Toronto, Macmillan, 1956) 274p.

Swann and Daphne (Toronto, Oxford University Press, 1960) 48p.

The Collected Poems of Anne Wilkinson and a Prose Memoir, edited with an Introduction by A. J. M. Smith (Toronto, Macmillan, 1968) 212p.

Selected criticism:

Livesay, Dorothy, Review of *Counterpoint to Sleep,* in *Contemporary Verse* 37: 23-26 (Winter-Spring 1951/52)

Macdonald, Goodridge, Review of *Counterpoint to Sleep,* in *Canadian Poetry Magazine* 15: 31-32 (Winter 1951)

Pacey, Desmond, "A Group of Seven," *Queen's Quarterly* 63: 437-438 (Autumn 1956)

Smith, A. J. M., "A Reading of Anne Wilkinson," *Canadian Literature* No. 10: 32-39 (Autumn 1961)

ETHEL WILSON (1888-   )

Hetty Dorval (Toronto, Macmillan, 1947) 116p.

The Innocent Traveller (Toronto, Macmillan, 1949) 276p.

The Equations of Love: Tuesday and Wednesday and *Lilly's Story* (Toronto, Macmillan, 1952) 280p.

Lilly's Story (New York, Harper, 1953) 208p. [first published as one of the two stories in *The Equations of Love*]

Swamp Angel (Toronto, Macmillan, 1954) 215p.

Love and Salt Water (Toronto, Macmillan, 1956) 202p.

Mrs. Golightly and Other Stories (Toronto, Macmillan, 1961) 209p.

Selected criticism:

Livesay, Dorothy, "Ethel Wilson: West Coast Novelist," *Saturday Night* 67: 20, 36 (July 26, 1952)

Keate, Stuart, Review of *The Equations of Love*, in *New York Times*, May 3, 1953, p. 5

Stallings, Sylvia, Review of *The Equations of Love*, in *New York Herald-Tribune Book Review*, May 3, 1953, p. 4

Pacey, Desmond, "The Innocent Eye," *Queen's Quarterly* 61: 42-52 (Spring 1954)

Bissell, Claude T., Review of *Love and Salt Water*, in *University of Toronto Quarterly* 26: 316-317 (April 1957)

Waddington, Miriam, Review of *Love and Salt Water*, in *Queen's Quarterly* 64: 143-144 (Spring 1957)

Watters, R. E., "Ethel Wilson, The Experienced Traveller," *British Columbia Library Quarterly* 21: 21-27 (April 1958)

Wilson, Ethel, "A Cat Among the Falcons," *Canadian Literature* No. 2: 10-19 (Autumn 1959)

——, "The Bridge or the Stokehold? Views of the Novelist's Art," *Canadian Literature* No. 5: 43-47 (Summer 1960)

Kirkwood, Hilda, "Realist with a Difference," *Saturday Night* 76: 41-42 (October 28, 1961)

Pacey, Desmond, Introduction to *Swamp Angel* by Ethel Wilson (Toronto, McClelland, 1962) pp. 5-10 [New Canadian Library No. 29]

Smith, Marion B., "Sipped and Savoured," *Canadian Literature* No. 11: 67-68 (Winter 1962)

Watt, Frank W., Review of *Mrs. Golightly and Other Stories*, in *University of Toronto Quarterly* 31: 471-472 (July 1962)

Clarke, Mrs. Rita, *Appearance and Reality in the Fiction of Ethel Wilson* (Thesis, University of British Columbia, 1964)

Sontoff, H. W., "The Novels of Ethel Wilson," *Canadian Literature* No. 26: 33-42 (Autumn 1965)

Pacey, Desmond, "Ethel Wilson's First Novel," *Canadian Literature* No. 29: 43-55 (Summer 1966)

Campbell, Barbara, *The Fiction of Ethel Wilson: A Study of Theme and Technique* (Thesis, University of Toronto, 1967)

Campbell, Robert L., *Imagery and Symbolism in the Fiction of Ethel Wilson* (Thesis, University of New Brunswick, 1967)

Pacey, Desmond, *Ethel Wilson* (New York, Twayne, 1967) 194p. [Twayne World Authors Series: Canada]

New, William H., "The 'Genius' of Place and Time: the Fiction of Ethel Wilson," *Journal of Canadian Studies* 3: 39-48 (November 1968)

——, "The Irony of Order: Ethel Wilson's *The Innocent Traveller*," *Critique: Studies in Modern Fiction* 10, No. 3: 22-30 (1968)

Birbalsingh, Frank, "Ethel Wilson: Innocent Traveller," *Canadian Literature* No. 49: 35-46 (Summer 1971)

McLay, C. M., "The Initiation of Mrs. Golightly," *Journal of Canadian Fiction* 1: 52-55 (Summer 1972)

Urbas, Jeannette, "Equations and Flutes," *Journal of Canadian Fiction* 1: 69-73 (Spring 1972)

Hinchcliffe, P. M., " 'To Keep the Memory of So Worthy a Friend': Ethel Wilson as an Elegist," *Journal of Canadian Fiction* 2: 62-67 (Spring 1973)

Acknowledgments

It is a pleasure to acknowledge our indebtedness for assistance of various kinds: to Wynne Frances, F. R. Scott, A. J. M. Smith, D. O. Spettigue, and others with whom we have spoken or corresponded; to the librarians at our universities and to their staffs — especially the corps of reference librarians; and to the Royal Military College and to the University of Western Ontario for providing valuable steno-graphic help. We are particularly grateful to the many scholars and teachers of Canadian literature who have made suggestions relating to this edition of Canadian Anthology. We also wish to thank a host of authors and publishers for permission to reprint copyrighted material. A detailed list follows:

Milton Acorn: "I've Tasted my Blood," "Detail of a Cityscape," and "Nature," by courtesy of the author.

Anonymous ballads and folk songs: "Come All You Bold Canadians" from *Shantymen and Shanty-boys: Songs of the Sailor and Lumberman,* © 1951 by William M. Doerflinger, reprinted by permission of The Macmillan Company of Canada Limited; "The Alberta Homesteaders," "The Battle of Queenston Heights," and "The Poor Little Girls of Ontario" from *Canada's Story in Song,* reprinted by permission of Edith Fowke; "Ye Maidens of Ontario" from *Ballads and Songs of The Shanty-Boy,* © 1926 by Harvard University Press, © 1954 by Lillian Rickaby Dykstra, reprinted by permission of Harvard University Press; "A Noble Fleet of Sealers" from *Old-Time Songs of Newfoundland,* by permission of Mrs. Gerald S. Doyle.

Margaret Atwood: "Journey to the Interior" and "This Is a Photograph of Me" from *The Circle Game,* © 1966, "You Have Made your Escape" from *Power Politics,* © 1971, by House of Anansi Press Ltd.; "The Landlady," © 1968, "For Archeologists" and "Woman Skating" from *Procedures for Underground,* © 1970, by Oxford University Press (Canadian Branch) reprinted by permission of Oxford University Press, and Little, Brown and Company; "The Immigrants," "Dream 1: The Bush Garden," and "The Planters" from *The Journals of Susanna Moodie,* by permission of Oxford University Press.

Margaret Avison: "The Apex Animal," "New Year's Poem," and "Butterfly Bones" from *Winter Sun,* by permission of University of Toronto Press and of Routledge and Kegan Paul Ltd.; "The World Still Needs" and "Perspective," by permission of the author; excerpt from "The Earth that Falls Away," © 1966 by the author, reprinted by permission of W. W. Norton & Company Ltd.; "We the Poor who Are Always with Us," by permission of the author and Talonbooks.

Earle Birney: "David," "Vancouver Lights," "Anglosaxon Street," "The Road to Nijmegen," "World Conference," "From The Hazel Bough," "The Ebb Begins from Dream," "Mappe-mounde," "Man is a Snow," and excerpt from *The Creative Writer,* by permission of the author; "Ellesmereland," "Wind-Chimes in a Temple Ruin," "El Greco: *Espolio*," and "The Bear on the Delhi Road" from *Ice Cod Bell or Stone,* "For George Lamming" from *Near False Creek Mouth,* "Buildings 2" from *Rag and Bone Shop,* and "Ellesmereland II" from *Selected Poems,* by permission of the author and The Canadian Publishers, McClelland and Stewart Limited, Toronto.

George Bowering: "Grandfather," "For WCW," "Cadence," and "News," by permission of the author.

Elizabeth Brewster: "The Idiot" and "Coach Class" from *Passage of Summer,* by permission of McGraw-Hill Ryerson Ltd.

Ernest Buckler: "David Comes Home," © 1944, and "Penny in the Dust," © 1948, by the author, reprinted by permission of Collins-Knowlton-Wing, Inc.

Morley Callaghan: "An Escapade," © 1956, "Two Fishermen," © 1961, "Why He Selected 'Two Fishermen,' " © 1942, 1970, and "The Shining Red Apple," © 1962, © by the author, reprinted by permission of Harold Matson Company, Inc.

Donald Cameron: "The Bizarre and the Freaky in Recent Canadian Fiction," by permission of the author.

Bliss Carman: "A Northern Vigil," "The Eaves-dropper," "Low Tide on Grand Pré," "Spring Song," "A Vagabond Song," "The Gravedigger," "Overlord," "Lord of My Heart's Elation," "The Ships of Yule," "The World Voice," "Vestigia," and "Subconscious Art," reprinted by special permission of the Bliss Carman Trust (University of New Brunswick); three odes from *Sappho,* by permission of Chatto and Windus Ltd.

Emily Carr: "Juice" and "The Stare" from *Klee Wyck,* © 1941 by Clarke, Irwin and Company Limited. Reprinted by permission.

Leonard Cohen: "I Have Not Lingered in European Monasteries," "The Sleeping Beauty," "You Have the Lovers," and "Song" from *The Spice-Box of Earth,* © 1961, by McClelland and Stewart, Limited, reprinted by permission of The Canadian Publishers, McClelland and Stewart Limited, Toronto, and The Viking Press, Inc.; "I Believe You Heard Your Master Sing," "Suzanne Takes You Down," and five lyrics from *The Energy of Slaves,* by permission of Machat and Kronfeld.

Fred Cogswell: "A Ballad of Loving," "Ode to Fredericton," "A Sunbeam Rolled the Stone Away," "The Widower," "The Senses," and "But Sometimes Rising," by permission of the author.

Roy Daniells: "So They Went Deeper into the Forest . . ." from *Deeper Into the Forest* and "Three Lecture Hours per Week" from *The Chequered Shade,* by permission of The Canadian Publishers, McClelland and Stewart Limited, Toronto.

Robertson Davies: excerpt from *Leaven of Malice,* © 1954 by Clarke, Irwin and Company Limited, reprinted by permission.

Louis Dudek: "Night Train" from *East of the City,* by permission of The Ryerson Press; "Puerto Rican Side Street," "Danger," "Poem for Spring," "A Child Blowing Bubbles," "City and Field," and "Coming Suddenly to the Sea," by permission of the author.

Northrop Frye: "The Narrative Tradition in English-Canadian Poetry," by permission of the author; "Preface to an Uncollected Anthology" from *Studia Varia,* by permission of University of Toronto Press.

Hugh Garner: "Another Time, Another Place, Another Me" from *Violation of the Virgins,* by permission of McGraw-Hill Ryerson Ltd.

Dave Godfrey: "Night Tripper," by permission of the author.

Frederick Philip Grove: "The Sower" from *The Turn of the Year,* by permission of The Ryerson Press; "The Midwife" from *Tales from the Margin,* by permission of McGraw-Hill Ryerson Ltd.

Ralph Gustafson: "Quebec Winterscene" from *Rivers Among Rocks,* "My Love Eats an Apple" from *Sift in an Hourglass,* and "The Grandeur Was When" and "Of Tigers and Pebbles" from *Fire on Stone,* by permission of The Canadian Publishers, McClelland and Stewart Limited, Toronto.

David Helwig: "Songs for Papageno," "On a Train," and "The Bugbear" from *Figures in a Landscape,* and "Deerslayer" from *The Streets of Summer,* by permission of Oberon Press.

Paul Hiebert: Introduction to *Sarah Binks,* by permission of Oxford University Press.

Hugh Hood: "Whos Paying for this Call" from *The Fruit Man, The Meat Man & The Manager,* by permission of Oberon Press; "The Hole" and an excerpt from "Sober Colouring," by permission of the author.

George Johnston: "Elaine in a Bikini," "Night Noises," and "Art and Life" from *The Cruising Auk,* "Us Together," "An Affluent Grace," and "Bliss," by permission of Oxford University Press (Canadian Branch); "O Earth, Turn " by permission of the author and, © 1955, The New Yorker Magazine Inc.

D. G. Jones: "Beautiful Creatures Brief As These" and "Like One of Botticelli's Daughters" from *The Sun is Axeman,* by permission of University of Toronto Press; "To Eve in Bitterness" and "Summer Is a Poem by Ovid" from *Phrases From Orpheus,* by permission of Oxford University Press (Canadian Branch).

Leo Kennedy: "Epithalamium" and "Words for a Resurrection" from *The Glass of Form,* by permission of the author and The Macmillan Company of Canada Limited.

A. M. Klein: "Sonnets Semitic I, IV, V," "Greeting on this Day," "Reb Levi Yitschok Talks to God," "Upon the Heavenly Scarp," and "A Psalm Touching Genealogy," by permission of Behrman House Inc.; "For the Sisters of the Hotel Dieu," "Pastoral of the City Streets," "Political Meeting," "Indian Reservation: Caughnawaga," "Monsieur Gaston," "Lone Bather," and "Portrait of the Poet as Landscape," by permission of The Ryerson Press; "Autobiographical," © 1951, by the author, by permission of Alfred A. Knopf, Inc.

Henry Kreisel: "The Prairie: A State of Mind" from the *Transactions of the Royal Society of Canada* Series IV, 6 (June 1968), by permission of the author.

Margaret Laurence: "The Mask of the Bear" from *A Bird in the House,* © 1965 by the author, reprinted by permission of The Canadian Publishers, McClelland and Stewart Limited, Toronto, John Cushman Associates, Inc., and Alfred A. Knopf, Inc.

Irving Layton: "Newsboy," "The Black Huntsman," "The Birth of Tragedy," "Misunderstanding," "The Cold Green Element," "Song For Naomi," "The Bull Calf," "Cat Dying in Autumn," "Berry Picking," "Keine Lazarovitch, 1870–1959," and "A Tall Man Executes a Jig"; "Butterfly on Rock" from *Balls for a One-Armed Juggler,*

"Cemeteries" from *Nail Polish,* and "Whatever Else Poetry is Freedom" and Foreword from *A Red Carpet for the Sun.* Reprinted by permission of The Canadian Publishers, McClelland and Stewart Limited, Toronto.

Stephen Leacock: "The Devil and the Deep Sea" and an excerpt from "American Humour" from *Essays and Literary Studies,* "The Retroactive Existence of Mr. Juggins" from *Behind the Beyond,* "Reflections on Riding," "My Financial Career," and "The Awful Fate of Melpomenus Jones" from *Literary Lapses,* and "The Rival Churches of St. Asaph and St. Osoph" from *The Bodley Head Leacock,* by permission of The Canadian Publishers, McClelland and Stewart Limited, Toronto, Dodd Mead and Co., Inc., and The Bodley Head Ltd.

Douglas Le Pan: "Canoe-Trip," "A Country Without a Mythology," "Finale," "Image of Silenus," "No Music is Abroad," "The Net and the Sword," and "Elegy in the Romagna" from *The Net and the Sword,* © 1953 by Clarke, Irwin and Company Limited, reprinted by permission; "The Green Man," by permission of the author.

Dorothy Livesay: "The Difference," "Night's Soft Armor . . . ," "The Child Looks Out . . . ," "Generation," "Bartok and the Geranium," and "Lament" from *Day and Night,* "Of Mourners" from *Poems for People,* and "For Abe Klein: Poet," "The Unquiet Bed," "The Incendiary," and "Eve" from *Collected Poems: The Two Seasons,* by permission of The Ryerson Press.

Malcolm Lowry: "Strange Comfort Afforded by the Profession," © 1947, and "Under the Volcano," by permission of Harold Matson Co., Inc.

Gwendolyn MacEwen: "Exploration and Discovery" and "Skulls and Drums" from *The Rising Sun,* by permission of the author; "The House," "Poems in Braille," "Arcanum One," and "Poem Improvised Around a First Line" from *A Breakfast for Barbarians,* by permission of The Ryerson Press; "The Shadow-Maker" and "The Discovery" from *The Shadow-Maker* and "Sea Things" from *The Armies of the Moon,* by permission of The Macmillan Company of Canada Limited; "Snow" from *Noman* by permission of Oberon Press.

Hugh MacLennan: "The Rivers that Made a Nation" from *Seven Rivers of Canada,* by permission of The Macmillan Company of Canada Limited.

Jay Macpherson: "True North" from *Nineteen Poems,* "The Beauty of Job's Daughters" from *The Boatman and Other Poems,* and eight poems from *The Boatman,* by permission of Oxford University Press (Canadian Branch); "The Caverned Woman" from *New Voices,* by permission of J. M. Dent & Sons (Canada) Ltd.

Charles Mair: lines from "Summer" (1868) from *Dreamland and Other Poems* and lines from "Summer" (1901) from *Tecumseh and Other Canadian Poems,* reprinted by permission of The Ryerson Press.

Eli Mandel: "The Minotaur Poems" from *Two,* "Children of the Sun" from *Fuseli Poems,* and "Marina," "Houdini," and "The Speaking Earth" from *An Idiot Joy,* by permission of the author.

Marshall McLuhan: "Culture Without Literacy," by permission of the author.

Alice Munro: "The Shining Houses" from *Dance of the Happy Shades,* by permission of McGraw-Hill Ryerson Ltd.

John Newlove: "The Pride" from *Black Night Window,* by permission of The Canadian Publishers, McClelland and Stewart Limited, Toronto.